Taste of Home

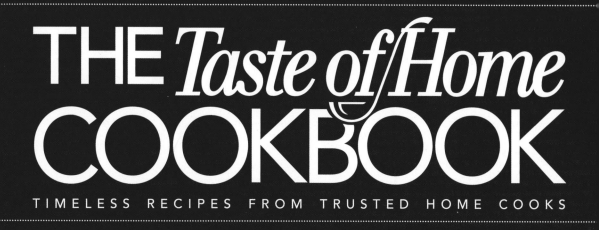

THE *Taste of Home* COOKBOOK

TIMELESS RECIPES FROM TRUSTED HOME COOKS

Taste of Home
B O O K S

REIMAN MEDIA GROUP, INC. • GREENDALE, WISCONSIN

Taste of Home

TASTE OF HOME BOOKS

© 2007 REIMAN MEDIA GROUP, INC.
5400 SOUTH 60TH STREET
GREENDALE WI 53129
All rights reserved.

TASTE OF HOME IS A REGISTERED TRADEMARK OF THE
READER'S DIGEST ASSOCIATION, INC.

EDITORS: **JANET BRIGGS, BETH WITTLINGER**
ART DIRECTOR: **NATHAN CHOW**

LAYOUT DESIGNERS:
**EMMA ACEVEDO, KATHY CRAWFORD,
CATHERINE FLETCHER, JOE STANGARONE, JULIE WAGNER**

COVER DESIGN: **SANDRA PLOY**

PROOFREADERS:
**LINNE BRUSKEWITZ, JULIE SCHNITTKA,
JEAN STEINER**
EDITORIAL ASSISTANT: **BARB CZYSZ**

FOOD EDITOR: **JANAAN CUNNINGHAM**
SENIOR RECIPE EDITOR: **SUE A. JURACK**
RECIPE TESTING: **TASTE OF HOME TEST KITCHEN**

FOOD PHOTOGRAPHY: **REIMAN PHOTO STUDIO**

PREPRESS/MANAGER:
REIMAN PREPRESS DEPARTMENT/SCOTT BERGER

SENIOR EDITOR, RETAIL BOOKS: **JENNIFER OLSKI**
VICE PRESIDENT/EXECUTIVE EDITOR, BOOKS: **HEIDI REUTER LLOYD**
CREATIVE DIRECTOR: **ARDYTH COPE**
SENIOR VICE PRESIDENT/EDITOR IN CHIEF: **CATHERINE CASSIDY**
PRESIDENT: **BARBARA NEWTON**
FOUNDER: **ROY REIMAN**

International Standard Book Number: (10): 0-89821-586-2
International Standard Book Number: (13): 978-0-89821-586-1
Library of Congress Control Number: 2007921833

FOR MORE *TASTE OF HOME* BOOKS
AND PRODUCTS, VISIT:
WWW.TASTEOFHOME.COM

FOR MORE READER'S DIGEST PRODUCTS
AND INFORMATION, VISIT:
WWW.RD.COM (IN THE UNITED STATES)
WWW.RD.CA (IN CANADA)

PRINTED IN CHINA
3 5 7 9 10 8 6 4 2

TASTE OF HOME GUIDELINES

■ The Nutrition Facts provided in *The Taste of Home Cookbook* are calculated using products that include the normal amount of fat, sugars and sodium (for example, whole milk or chicken broth rather than fat-free milk or reduced-sodium chicken broth) unless otherwise noted. Nutrition Facts reflect only the amount of marinade absorbed during preparation.

Nutrition Facts are calculated with the first measurement of an ingredient in a range (for example, 2 to 3 tablespoons), the first ingredient listed (for example, 1/4 cup half-and-half cream or heavy whipping cream) and the second serving size (for example, 12 to 14 servings).

Optional ingredients or garnishes without a specific amount are not included in the Nutrition Facts. Other ingredients will be noted if they are not included (for example, assorted crackers).

■ Recipes have been tested in a 1,100-watt microwave.

■ Temperatures provided are in degrees Fahrenheit (°F).

CONTENTS

OUR BIGGEST & BEST COOKBOOK EVER!

Welcome to *The Taste of Home Cookbook*! Millions of people turn to *Taste of Home* magazine, the No. 1 cooking publication in the world, for the best recipes from great home cooks. Now, we share the very best of those family-pleasing dishes in the most comprehensive cookbook we've ever published!

Each page of *The Taste of Home Cookbook* is packed with tips, techniques and recipes to make your cooking experience a breeze and every dish simply delicious.

Whether you need to whip up something quick during the week, plan a special Sunday supper, supply a casserole for the family reunion or bring cookies for the church bake sale, *The Taste of Home Cookbook* has hundreds and hundreds of delicious family favorites to choose from...and more! Inside you'll find:

• **1,125 timeless recipes and variations,** all made from easy-to-find everyday ingredients, all from trusted home cooks just like you. PLUS 107 "Light & Tasty" recipes—dishes that have 300 calories or less, 10 grams of fat or less *and* 500 milligrams of sodium or less. That's over 1,200 recipes total!

• **Nutrition Facts for every recipe,** so you can find the recipes that meet your family's dietary needs.

• **More than 1,000 full-color photos,** many of which showcase our recipes so you'll know how the finished dish will look on your own table.

• **Hundreds of tips, techniques and how-to's** from the experts on our Test Kitchen staff to answer all your questions and help you enjoy delicious results from any recipe.

• **Easy-to-follow references and indexes.** Each recipe chapter has a quick-reference alphabetical listing—so you can see at a glance all the recipes included in the chapter. In addition, you can turn to the reference and indexes section that organize all recipes and variations alphabetically and by Major Ingredient, Preparation Method and Food Category. There's also an index of all References & Tips.

• **Our guarantee that absolutely every recipe will work!** *Taste of Home* Test Kitchen home economists have tested each recipe so that every one will turn out perfectly in your own kitchen—every time!

Best of all, with this book you get the everyday, home-style goodness for which *Taste of Home* is trusted and loved. Whether you're a new friend or a longtime fan, you'll be sure to find a delicious dish for every occasion in *The Taste of Home Cookbook*.

Share your recipes on-line for a chance to have your recipe published in a Taste of Home cookbook! Visit us at www.tasteofhome.com/cookbookrecipes

CHAPTER 1
KITCHEN BASICS

5

KITCHEN BASICS

Measuring Tools and Techniques

To ensure delicious and consistent cooking results, it's important to know how to accurately and correctly measure ingredients. Not all measuring cups are the same, and not all ingredients are measured in the same manner. There are specific measuring cups designed for measuring liquid and dry ingredients, and they are not interchangeable.

A liquid measuring cup is either clear glass or transparent plastic with a handle and a pour spout. They are available in 1-cup, 2-cup, 4-cup and 8-cup sizes. Liquid measures are used for milk, honey, molasses, corn syrup, water and oil.

A dry measuring cup is made from metal or plastic and has a handle. The food to be measured should be even with the rim of the cup. Dry measuring cups usually come in a set with 1/4-cup, 1/3-cup, 1/2-cup and 1-cup sizes. Some sets may have additional sizes such as 1/8 cup or 2/3 cup.

Dry measures are used for flour and sugar. They also are used to measure shortening, sour cream, yogurt and applesauce. While these ingredients are not "dry," they can mound when measured. The dry measure allows you to level the ingredient at the top of the cup for an accurate measurement.

Standard measuring spoons are used to measure both liquid and dry ingredients. Sets often include a 1/4 teaspoon, 1/2 teaspoon, 1 teaspoon and 1 tablespoon. Some sets are available with a 1/8 teaspoon.

Weight and Measure Equivalents

TEASPOON AND TABLESPOON MEASURES

Dash or pinch	=	less than 1/8 teaspoon
1-1/2 teaspoons	=	1/2 tablespoon
3 teaspoons	=	1 tablespoon; 1/2 fluid ounce
4-1/2 teaspoons	=	1-1/2 tablespoons
2 tablespoons	=	1/8 cup; 1 fluid ounce
4 tablespoons	=	1/4 cup; 2 fluid ounces
8 tablespoons	=	1/2 cup; 4 fluid ounces
12 tablespoons	=	3/4 cup; 6 fluid ounces
16 tablespoons	=	1 cup; 8 fluid ounces; 1/2 pint

CUP MEASURES

1/8 cup	=	2 tablespoons; 1 fluid ounce
1/4 cup	=	4 tablespoons; 2 fluid ounces
1/3 cup	=	5-1/3 tablespoons
1/2 cup	=	8 tablespoons; 4 fluid ounces
2/3 cup	=	10-2/3 tablespoons
3/4 cup	=	12 tablespoons; 6 fluid ounces
7/8 cup	=	3/4 cup plus 2 tablespoons
1 cup	=	16 tablespoons; 8 fluid ounces; 1/2 pint
2 cups	=	1 pint; 16 fluid ounces
4 cups	=	2 pints; 1 quart; 32 fluid ounces

PINTS, QUARTS, GALLONS AND POUNDS

1/2 pint	=	1 cup; 8 fluid ounces
1 pint	=	2 cups; 16 fluid ounces
1 quart	=	4 cups; 32 fluid ounces
1 gallon	=	4 quarts; 16 cups
1/4 pound	=	4 ounces
1/2 pound	=	8 ounces
3/4 pound	=	12 ounces
1 pound	=	16 ounces

Proper Measuring Techniques

Measuring Liquid

Place a liquid measuring cup on a level surface. For a traditional liquid measuring cup, view the amount at eye level to be sure of an accurate measure. Do not lift cup to check the level. Some newer liquid measuring cups are designed so that they can be accurately read from above.

For sticky liquids such as molasses, corn syrup or honey, spray the measuring cup with nonstick cooking spray before adding the liquid. This will make it easier to pour out the liquid and clean the cup.

Measuring Sour Cream and Yogurt

Spoon sour cream and yogurt into a dry measuring cup, then level top by sweeping a metal spatula or flat side of a knife across the top of the cup.

Measuring Brown Sugar

Since brown sugar has a unique moist texture, it needs to be packed into a dry measuring cup. Firmly press or "pack" brown sugar into the cup with your fingers or the back of a spoon. Level with the rim of the cup. Brown sugar should hold the shape of the cup when it is turned out.

Using Measuring Spoons

For dry ingredients such as flour, sugar or spices, heap the ingredient into the spoon over a canister or waxed paper. With a metal spatula or flat side of a knife, level with the rim of the spoon.

For shortening or butter, spread into spoon and level off. For liquids, pour into measuring spoon over a bowl or custard cup.

Measuring Dry Ingredients

For dry ingredients such as flour, sugar or cornmeal, spoon ingredients into a dry measuring cup over a canister or waxed paper. Fill cup to overflowing, then level by sweeping a metal spatula or flat side of a knife across the top.

Measuring Bulk Dry Ingredients

Spoon bulk dry ingredients such as cranberries, raisins or chocolate chips into the measuring cup. If necessary, level the top with a spatula or flat side of a knife.

Measuring Shortening

Press shortening into a dry measuring cup with a spatula to make sure it is solidly packed without air pockets. With a metal spatula or flat side of a knife, level with the rim. Some shortenings come in sticks and may be measured like butter.

Measuring Butter

The wrappers for sticks of butter come with markings for tablespoons, 1/4 cup, 1/3 cup and 1/2 cup. Use a knife to cut off the desired amount.

> **MEASURING TIP**
>
> Never measure over the batter because some may spill, adding too much to the batter.

Kitchen Cutlery

A basic set of knives is essential to any well-equipped kitchen. There are a variety of knives made from many materials. The best knives, made from high-carbon steel, are resistant to corrosion (unlike carbon steel) and remain sharper longer than stainless steel.

A. Steel

This long, thin rod with a handle is used to smooth out small rough spots on the edge of the blade and to reset the edge of the blade. You can also use a whetstone or electric knife sharpener to sharpen knives.

B. Chef's Knife

This 8-in. to 10-in. multipurpose knife is used for mincing, chopping and dicing.

C. Santoku

This is a Japanese variation of a chef's knife. The 6-1/2-in. to 7-in. multipurpose knife is used for mincing, chopping, dicing and slicing. The blade's dimple design helps reduce drag during slicing.

D. Carving Knife

This 8-in. to 10-in. knife is perfect for slicing roasts and turkey.

E. Serrated or Bread Knife

This knife's serrated blade is used for slicing breads, cakes and delicate foods. An 8-in. knife is most versatile, but a range of lengths is available.

F. Utility Knife

This 6-in. knife is the right size to slice small foods.

G. Boning Knife

This knife's 5-in. or 6-in. tapered blade is designed to remove the meat from poultry, beef, pork or fish bones.

H. Paring Knife

This 3-in. to 4-in. knife is used for peeling, mincing and slicing small foods.

I. Kitchen Shears

This versatile tool is used to snip fresh herbs, disjoint chicken, trim pastry, etc.

Caring for Knives

To keep knives sharp, cut foods on a soft plastic or wooden cutting board. Ceramic, granite, metal and other hard surfaces will dull the blade.

Always wash and dry knives by hand immediately after use. Never let them soak in water or wash in the dishwasher. Store knives in a slotted wooden block or hang them on a magnetic rack especially designed for knives. Proper storage will protect knife edges, keep blades sharper longer and guard against injury.

A

B

C

D

E

F

G

H

I

USING A STEEL

Rest the tip of the steel on the work surface. Hold your knife at a 20° angle to the steel. Start with the heel of the blade against the steel and draw the blade up across the steel until you reach the tip of the knife. Repeat five times on both sides of knife blade. Repeat as needed.

Common Cutting and Chopping Techniques

Mincing and Chopping

Holding the handle of a chef's knife with one hand, rest the fingers of your other hand on the top of the blade near the tip. Using the handle to guide and apply pressure, move knife in an arc across the food with a rocking motion until pieces of food are the desired size. Mincing results in pieces no larger than 1/8 in., and chopping can produce 1/4-in. to 1/2-in. pieces.

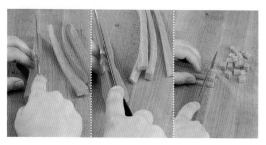

Dicing and Cubing Vegetables

1) Using a utility knife, trim each side of the vegetable, squaring it off. Cut lengthwise into evenly spaced strips. The narrower the strips, the smaller the pieces will be. Dicing results in 1/8-in. to 1/4-in. uniform pieces, and cubing yields 1/2-in. to 1-in. uniform pieces.

2) Stack the strips and cut lengthwise into uniform-sized strips.

3) Arrange the square-shaped strips into a pile and cut widthwise into cubes.

Making Bias/Diagonal Cuts

Holding a chef's knife at an angle to the length of the food, slice as thick or thin as desired. This technique is often used in stir-fry recipes.

Making Julienne Strips

1) Using a utility knife, cut a thin strip from one side of carrot. Turn so flat side is down.

2) Cut widthwise into 2-in. lengths, then cut each piece lengthwise into thin strips.

3) Stack the strips and cut lengthwise into thinner strips.

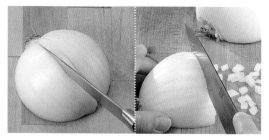

Chopping an Onion

1) To quickly chop an onion, peel and cut in half from the root to the top. Leaving root attached, place flat side down on work surface. Cut vertically through the onion, leaving the root end uncut.

2) Cut across the onion, discarding root end. The closer the cuts, the finer the onion will be chopped. This method can also be used for shallots.

Peeling and Mincing Fresh Garlic

Using the blade of a chef's knife, crush garlic clove. Peel away skin. Mince as directed at top left.

Slicing or Chopping a Sweet Pepper

1) To slice or chop, cut each side from pepper by cutting close to the stem and down. Discard top and scrape out seeds.

2) Cut away any ribs.

3) Place cut side down on work surface and flatten slightly with your hand. Cut lengthwise into strip, then widthwise into pieces if desired.

Peeling

Placing your thumbs on the fruit or vegetable, move the blade of a paring or utility knife toward you.

Snipping Fresh Herbs

Hold herbs over a small bowl and make 1/8-in. to 1/4-in. cuts with a kitchen shears.

FREEZING HERBS

You can freeze chopped herbs in freezer containers or bags and just use the amount you need directly from the freezer.

COMMON COOKING TECHNIQUES

TO FRY
Place food, such as chicken, in 1/2 to 1 in. of hot oil in a skillet. Fry, uncovered, until food is browned and cooked through.

TO SAUTE
Place food, such as fresh vegetables, in a small amount of hot oil in a skillet or saute pan. Cook quickly and stir frequently.

TO STEAM
Place food, such as beans, in a perforated basket (steamer insert) set just above, but not touching, the boiling water in a saucepan. Cover pan and allow food to cook in the steam given off by the boiling water.

TO BRAISE
In a Dutch oven, brown meat, such as pork ribs, in a little oil, then add a small amount of liquid. Cover and simmer until cooked.

Cookware

Using the right cookware can help simplify meal preparation. It's best to start with a basic selection for everyday cooking, then add to it as needed.

Most kitchens should have a large (5 qt. or larger) Dutch oven, 1-qt. and 2-qt. saucepans with lids, a 10-in. to 12-in. skillet with lid, an 8-in. or 9-in. saute/omelet pan and a shallow roaster. A stockpot, double boiler, steamer insert basket, griddle and additional saucepans and skillets are also useful.

Selecting Cookware

Good cookware should do two things: conduct heat quickly and then evenly distribute that heat over the pan's surface to cook food evenly. These qualities are determined by the type of material the pan is made from and its thickness. There are pros and cons to the different materials used in cookware.

Of all the metals used, **copper** conducts heat the best but is expensive, requires polishing and reacts with acidic ingredients. That is why copper pans are lined with tin or stainless steel. **Aluminum** is less expensive and is also a good heat conductor, but aluminum also reacts with acidic ingredients. **Anodized aluminum** cookware has a surface that is electrochemical-treated. This treatment produces a cookware that does not react to acidic foods. It is also easier to clean and is resistant to food sticking and scratches. **Cast iron** also conducts heat well but is heavy and must be seasoned periodically. **Stainless steel** is a poor heat conductor but is durable and remains looking like new for years. Manufacturers combine stainless steel with an aluminum or copper core or bottom for durable, even-cooking pans.

Thicker-gauge cookware offers more even heating so it is less likely to burn foods or have hot spots. Generally, the heavier a pan feels when picked up, the thicker the gauge is.

Pans with nonstick surfaces are nice because they make cleanup a breeze. This feature is handy for skillets and saute pans but usually not necessary for saucepans, Dutch ovens and large pots.

The handles should feel comfortable in your hand, stay cool while cooking and be oven-safe. Pots with two handles are easier to pick up when full. Lids should fit tightly.

SEASONING CAST IRON

Cast-iron pans should be seasoned before using to protect the surface and prevent food from sticking. One way to season a cast-iron skillet is to brush the inside with vegetable oil or coat with shortening. Bake at 300° for 1 hour. When cool, wipe it dry with paper towels. Repeat one or two times.

8-IN. SAUTE/OMELET PAN

12-IN. SKILLET WITH LID

10-IN. SKILLET

3-1/2-QT. SAUCEPAN

1-QT. SAUCEPAN

ROASTER

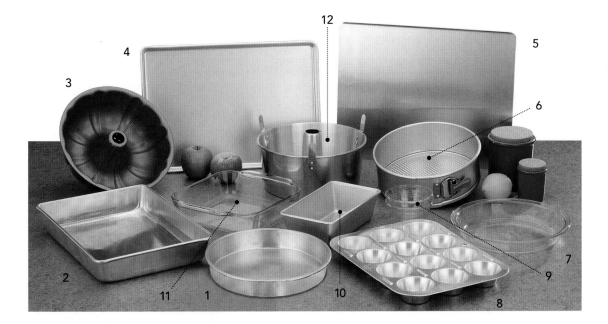

Choosing Bakeware

The recipes in this book call for standard-size baking pans and baking dishes. For best results, use the pan size called for in the recipe. However, there are some practical substitutions (see Bakeware Substitution chart on page 14).

Baking pans are made of metal. Aluminum pans with dull finishes give the best overall baking results. Pans with dark finishes often cook and brown foods more quickly. If you use pans with dark finishes, you may need to adjust the baking time and cover tops of baked goods with foil to prevent overbrowning. Insulated pans generally take longer to bake and brown foods.

Baking dishes are made of ovenproof glass or ceramic. They are often used for casseroles, egg dishes and saucy meat dishes. Always use glass or ceramic baking dishes when marinating foods or making dishes with tomato sauce. If you substitute a glass baking dish in a recipe calling for a metal baking pan, reduce the oven temperature by 25° to avoid overbaking and overbrowning.

MEASURING BAKEWARE

To measure your bakeware's diameter, length or width, use a ruler and measure from one inside top edge to the opposite inside top edge. To measure the height, place a ruler on the outside of the dish and measure from the bottom to a top edge. For volume, fill the pan or dish to the rim with water.

Basic Bakeware

A well-stocked kitchen should have the following items:

1) 9-in. x 1-1/2-in. round baking pan (two to three)
2) 13-in. x 9-in. x 2-in. baking pan and/or dish (3 qt.)
3) 10-in. fluted tube pan
4) 15-in. x 10-in. x 1-in. baking pan (jelly-roll pan)
5) Baking sheets (without sides) in assorted sizes
6) 9-in. springform pan
7) 9-in. pie plate
8) 12-cup muffin pan (standard size)
9) 6-oz. custard cups (set of six)
10) 9-in. x 5-in. x 3-in. loaf pan (two) and 8-in. x 4-in. x 2-in. loaf pan (two)
11) 9-in. x 9-in. x 2-in. and 8-in. x 8-in. x 2-in. square baking dishes and/or pans
12) 10-in. tube pan

These other items are also nice to have on hand:
- 11-in. x 7-in. x 2-in. baking pan and/or dish (2 qt.)
- 9-in. deep-dish pie plate
- 9-in. fluted tart pan with removable bottom
- 10-in. springform pan
- 5-3/4-in. x 3-in. x 2-in. loaf pan (three to four)
- Miniature muffin pans
- 10-oz. custard cups (set of six)
- 8-in. fluted tube pan

Bakeware Substitution

If you don't have the right pan for a recipe, here are a few substitutions.
(Remember that using smaller pans will require less baking time.)

IF YOU DON'T HAVE THIS PAN(S):	USE THIS PAN(S) INSTEAD:
One 9-in. x 5-in. x 3-in. loaf pan	Three 5-3/4-in. x 3-in. x 2-in. loaf pans
One 8-in. x 4-in. x 2-in. loaf pan	Two 5-3/4-in. x 3-in. x 2-in. loaf pans
One 9-in. round baking pan	One 8-in. square baking dish
Two 9-in. round baking pans	One 13-in. x 9-in. x 2-in. baking pan
One 10-in. fluted tube pan	One 10-in. tube pan *or* two 9-in. x 5-in. x 3-in. loaf pans
One 13-in. x 9-in. x 2-in. baking pan	Two 9-in. round baking pans *or* two 8-in. square baking dishes

Kitchen Tools and Gadgets

When equipping a new kitchen, there are so many tools and gadgets to consider.
Start with the basics listed below before expanding to the specialty ones.

Apple corer
Blender *and/or* food processor
Can and bottle opener
Canisters
Citrus juicer
Colander
Cookie cutters
Corkscrew
Cutting boards, wood and plastic
Dough cutter/scraper
Egg separator
Egg slicer
Garlic press
Hand grater/shredder
Ladles, large and small
Measuring cups (dry and liquid)
Measuring spoons
Meat fork
Meat mallet/tenderizer

Metal skewers
Metal strainer *or* sieve
Mixers, stand *and/or* hand
Mixing bowls
Pancake turners
Pastry bag and tips
Pastry blender
Pastry brush
Pastry wheel
Pepper mill *or* shaker
Pie server
Pizza cutter
Plastic spoons
Plastic storage and freezer containers
Potato masher
Rolling pin
Slotted spoons, large and small
Salad spinner
Salt shaker

Spatulas, rubber and metal
Thermometers, instant-read, candy/deep-fat, meat, oven, refrigerator/freezer
Timer
Tongs
Vegetable peeler
Wire whisks in assorted sizes
Wire racks
Wooden spoons

Kitchen Textiles:
Dishcloth
Dish towels
Hand towels
Hot pads/mitts
Kitchen string
Pastry cloth
Rolling pin cover

Food Safety

To ensure the foods you serve are safe to eat, follow these basic, but important, food safety rules.

Keep it clean. Before handling any food, thoroughly wash your hands in hot soapy water. Make sure all work surfaces, cutting boards, knives and any other utensils have been cleaned in hot soapy water. And, after handling raw food, clean hands and utensils in hot soapy water.

Cutting boards can be sanitized with a mixture of 1 teaspoon chlorine bleach in 1 quart of water. Allow the bleach water to stand on the cutting board for several minutes before rinsing. Let the board air dry or dry with clean paper towels.

Keep it separate. Don't cross-contaminate foods, which means allowing the juices of raw meats, poultry and fish to come in contact with other foods. Reusing a cutting board, countertop, sink, plate, knife or other utensil that came in contact with raw meat without first thoroughly washing it in hot, soapy water can cause cross-contamination. Never reuse the package material, such as foam meat trays or plastic wrap, from meat, poultry or fish.

It is not recommended that you wash raw poultry, beef, veal, pork, lamb or seafood before cooking. Any bacteria that may be present on the surface of these foods will be destroyed by properly cooking the food. Washing these items will contaminate the sink, which can cause cross-contamination if not cleaned right away.

Keep it at the right temperature. Keep hot foods hot and cold foods cold. Cooked foods and uncooked foods that require refrigeration should only be left at room temperature for up to 2 hours and only 1 hour if it is a hot day. Use warming trays, slow cookers and chafing dishes to keep hot foods to at least 140°. Use ice bowls (see page 35) or ice to keep foods cold.

Always cook foods to the proper temperatures.

140° for fully cooked ham.

145° for medium-rare beef, lamb and veal.

160° for medium beef, lamb and veal; pork, fresh ham or partially cooked ham and egg dishes.

165° for ground chicken and turkey, stuffing, casseroles and leftovers.

170° for well-done beef, well-done lamb, chicken and turkey breasts.

180° for whole chicken and turkey, thighs and wings, duck, goose and pheasant.

FOOD SAFETY TIP

Purchase several different colored plastic cutting boards. Use a different color for different items, such as green for fruits and vegetables, yellow for poultry, red for meat.

INFORMAL DINNER OR LUNCHEON
Simply start with a basic setting and add to it.

1) If a salad is to be served, the salad fork is placed to the left of the dinner fork. Eliminate the salad fork if no salad is served or place it to the right of the dinner fork to use as a dessert fork if appropriate. (The dessert fork can also be brought to the table when dessert is served.)

2) If soup is served, set the bowl on the plate and a soup spoon to the right of the beverage spoon.

3) Salad or bread and butter plates go to the left of the forks. Position butter plates above the forks with the butter spreader placed across the plate.

4) Cup and saucer go above the spoons with the handle toward the right. Wine or water glasses can be positioned to the left of the coffee cup.

Basic Table Setting

Setting the table is often a hurried task that leaves family members wondering about the correct placement of the flatware, plates, napkins and glassware. You don't have to add stress to your dinner plans, just start with a basic table setting to dress up your dinner table and set the mood for your dinner party or gathering.

BASIC SETTING
This is appropriate for most occasions, and you just add to the basic pieces as needed.

1) The dinner plate is positioned in the center of the place setting and everything else is placed around it.

2) The flatware is arranged around the plate in the order in which it will be used:

   - To the left of the plate is the fork.

   - To the right of the plate is the knife and spoon. The knife is placed to the right of the plate with the sharp edge toward the plate. To the right of the knife is the spoon.

3) A water glass goes above the knife.

4) Napkins can be placed under the forks or on the plate for an informal setting.

FORMAL DINNER
Begin with the setting for an informal dinner or luncheon and add to it.

1) White and red wine glasses (if necessary) along with the water glasses are positioned to the left of the coffee cup.

2) The beverage, soup and/or dessert spoons are to the right of the knife or can be brought to the table when soup or dessert is served.

3) To dress it up more, place a charger under the dinner plate.

Menu-Planning Pointers

Meals should be planned using foods that contain a variety of foods, flavors, colors and textures. Begin your menu planning with the main dish. Next choose the side dishes and desserts that complement the main dish. For example, if you are planning to serve a beef roast, consider serving a colorful vegetable to add eye appeal to the plate. Serve only one strong-flavored food per meal.

Select recipes that can be prepared and served together in the allotted time frame. Two dishes that are baked at the same temperature can be cooked in the same oven without any adjustments to the baking time. Make a cooking schedule, listing the recipes that can be prepared in advance, recipes that need to be started first because they require more cooking or chilling time and recipes that need to be prepared at the last minute. Once your planning is complete, make a shopping list according to the layout of your grocery store to reduce shopping time.

Serve hot foods hot and cold foods cold. Don't let any food remain at room temperature for more than 2 hours (1 hour in hot weather).

Menu Ideas for Special Occasions

CHRISTMAS DINNER	PAGE
French Onion Soup	60
Tenderloin with Creamy Garlic Sauce	83
Wilted Lettuce Salad	402
Roasted Green Beans	311
Stuffed Baked Potatoes	341
Blue-Ribbon Herb Rolls	459
Frosted Spice Cake	509
Gingerbread Cookies	568
Cream Cheese Finger Cookies	559
Two-Tiered Fudge	580
Mulled Cider	52
Holiday Eggnog	47
THANKSGIVING DINNER	
Classic Stuffed Turkey	175
Layered Lettuce Salad	398
Broccoli Corn Casserole	315
Yukon Mashed Potatoes	342
Pan Gravy	156
Autumn Pear Bread	431
Pumpkin Cheesecake Dessert	528
German Apple Pie	485
EASTER DINNER	
Dijon Leg of Lamb	232
Baked Ham with Orange Glaze	133
Duchess Potatoes	342
Crunchy Asparagus Medley	309
Braided Egg Bread	454
Cherry Brie Tossed Salad	398
Festive Fruit Tart	489
HOLIDAY BRUNCH	
Overnight Caramel French Toast	262
Cheese Sausage Strata	258
Burst o' Lemon Muffins	437
Quick and Easy Strawberry Jam	423
Sour Cream Coffee Cake	434
Layered Fruit Salad	373
SUPER BOWL PARTY	
Boston Subs	75
Three-Meat Stromboli	74

	PAGE
Spiced Chili	68
Spicy Snack Mix	44
Pretzel Mustard Dip	28
BACKYARD BARBECUE	
Raspberry Iced Tea	52
Springtime Lime Slushy	49
The Perfect Hamburger	224
Grilled Sweet Corn	243
True-Blue Potato Salad	404
Ice Cream Sandwich Dessert	542
OPEN-HOUSE	
Citrus Punch	45
Baked Spinach Dip Loaf	27
Marinated Mozzarella Cubes	43
Marinated Shrimp	35
Deviled Eggs	254
Veggie Party Pizza	36
Raspberry Linzer Cookies	568
Dipped Strawberries	584
BRIDAL SHOWER	
Champagne Party Punch	46
Iced Coffee	50
Orange-Ginger Fruit Dip	30
Chicken Salad Croissants	74
Egg Salad Cucumber Sandwiches	254
Creamy Pastel Mints	583
ITALIAN FEAST	
Italian Spaghetti and Meatballs	291
Garlic Parmesan Breadsticks	463
Curly Endive Salad	399
Strawberry Tiramisu Trifle	548
MEXICAN NIGHT OR CINCO DE MAYO	
Fresh Lime Margaritas	46
Tangy Texas Salsa	369
Simple Guacamole	28
Steak Fajitas	96
Baked Chimichangas	174
Mexican Wedding Cakes	559

Glossary

While you use this book, there will be common cooking terms in each chapter that are defined here. Within some chapters, you may find that the more specific terms for that chapter will be defined within it.

A

AL DENTE: An Italian term meaning "to the tooth" used to describe pasta that is cooked but still firm.

AU JUS: Natural, unthickened juices that collect while roasting meats.

B

BAKE: To cook in an oven surrounded by dry heat. When baking, preheat the oven before placing the food in it.

BASTE: To moisten foods while cooking by brushing with pan juices, butter, margarine, oil or a reserved marinade.

BATTER: A mixture made of flour and a liquid such as milk. It may also include other ingredients such as sugar, butter, shortening or oil, eggs, leaveners and flavorings. The consistency of batters ranges from thin to thick. Thin batters are pourable, such as pancakes or cakes. Thick batters can be dropped from a spoon, such as quick breads.

BEAT: To rapidly mix with a spoon, fork, wire whisk or electric mixer.

BETTY: A baked fruit dessert that alternates layers of sweetened fruit with cake, cookies or bread crumbs.

BIAS CUT: To cut foods diagonally into slices. Most often used in stir-fries.

BLANCH: To cook for a few minutes in boiling water. This technique is used to help remove peels, to partially cook foods as a preparation step in a recipe or to prepare foods for freezing.

BLEND: To combine several ingredients with a spoon, electric mixer, blender or food processor.

BOIL: To heat liquids until bubbles form that cannot be stirred down. In the case of water, the temperature will reach 212° at sea level.

BONE: To remove raw or cooked meat from bones. (See Boning Chicken Breasts on page 170.)

BRAISE: To cook slowly in a small amount of liquid in a covered pan on the stovetop or in the oven. Generally used for less tender cuts of meat.

BREADING: A coating of fine bread crumbs or crackers used on meat, fish or vegetables.

BROIL: To cook foods about 4 to 6 inches from a heat source.

BROWN: To cook foods in a small amount of fat over medium to high heat until the food becomes brown, sealing in the juices and developing rich pan drippings.

BROWN BITS: Little flecks of browned food that is left in the bottom of a pan after browning or cooking meat or poultry.

BUCKLE: A baked, cake-like fruit dessert made with berries. Named because the cake sometimes buckles under the weight of the topping.

BUTTERFLY: To split foods, such as chicken breast, boneless meat or shrimp, lengthwise in half, leaving the meat attached along one side.

C

CARAMELIZE: To heat sugar in a skillet or saucepan over low heat until melted and golden brown. Also refers to cooking onions in butter until soft, caramel-colored and rich in flavor.

CHILL: To cool foods to below room temperature (40° or less) by placing in the refrigerator, freezer or an ice bath.

CHOP: To cut foods into 1/4-inch to 1/2-inch pieces.

CLARIFY: To remove sediment and suspended particles from a liquid. Clarified butter has the milk solids removed, which allows the clarified butter to be heated to a higher temperature without smoking.

COAT: To dip or roll foods in flour, sugar or a sauce until covered.

"COATS SPOON": To leave a thin, even, smooth film on the back of a metal spoon. This is a doneness test for stirred custards.

COBBLER: A fruit dessert with a biscuit topping. The topping can be either in a single layer or dropped over the fruit to give a cobblestone effect.

COMBINE: To place several ingredients in a single bowl or container and thoroughly mix.

COOKING IN LIQUID: To simmer meat covered with liquid for a long time. Generally used for less tender cuts of meat to tenderize the meat.

COOL: To bring foods to room temperature (about 70°).

CORE: To remove the seed area of an apple or pear using a coring tool or a small knife.

CREAM: To beat softened butter, margarine or shortening alone or with sugar using a spoon or mixer until light and fluffy.

CRIMP: To seal the edge of a double-crusted pie by pinching or pressing the crusts together with your fingers, fork or other utensil.

CRISP: A baked fruit dessert that has a crumb topping over fruit. The topping generally has flour, sugar and butter and may or may not have oats, nuts and spices. The topping gets crisp while baking.

CRISP-TENDER: A stage of vegetable cooking where the vegetables are cooked until they are crunchy yet tender enough to be pierced with a fork.

CRUSH: To reduce foods to crumbs, paste or powder. Herbs can be crushed in a mortar and pestle. Garlic cloves and fresh gingerroot can be crushed with the side of a knife.

CUBE: To cut foods into 1/2-inch to 1-inch square pieces.

CUT IN: To break down and distribute cold butter, margarine or shortening into a flour mixture using a pastry blender or two knives.

D

DASH: A measurement less than 1/8 teaspoon that is used for herbs, spices or hot pepper sauce. This is not an accurate measurement.

DEEP-FAT FRY: To cook foods in enough hot oil so that the food floats in the oil.

DEGLAZE: To add water, broth or wine to a pan in which food, usually meat, has been cooked to remove the browned drippings to make a rich gravy.

DICE: To cut foods into small cubes (1/8-inch to 1/4-inch cubes).

DIRECT HEAT: To cook foods on an outdoor grill directly over coals or heat source.

DISSOLVE: To stir a solid food with a liquid until none of the solid remains, such as yeast with warm water or gelatin in boiling water.

DOLLOP: A small mound of soft food such as whipped cream or whipped topping.

DOT: To break up butter into small pieces and distribute over the top of a pie or dough.

DOUGH: A thick mixture made of flour and a liquid that is not pourable. It may include ingredients such as sugar, butter, shortening or oil, eggs, leaveners and flavorings. It may be stiff enough to be worked with by hand (kneading bread dough, for example).

DREDGE: To lightly coat foods with flour or bread crumbs.

DRESS: To toss salads with salad dressing. Also, to remove the internal organs of fish, poultry or game.

DRIPPINGS: The juices and melted fat that collect in the bottom of the pan as meat is cooked. The juices and some of the fat from the drippings can be used in gravies and sauces.

DRIZZLE: To slowly spoon or pour a thin stream of an icing, melted butter or other liquid over food.

DUST: To lightly sprinkle with confectioners' sugar, baking cocoa or flour.

DUTCH OVEN: A multipurpose cooking pot that can range in size from 5 to 8 quarts and is used to roast meats, cook soups and stews, boil pasta or steam vegetables.

E

EGG WASH: A mixture of beaten egg, egg yolk or egg white and water that is brushed over breads, rolls, pastries or pie crusts before baking. Egg washes give the final baked product a shiny brown finish.

EMULSIFY: To combine through a whisking action two liquids that traditionally separate, such as oil and vinegar, into a uniform mixture.

EXTRACTS: The distilled essential oils from plant materials, which are then dissolved in alcohol. Common examples are vanilla and almond.

F

FILET: A boneless cut of meat.

FILLET: A boneless piece of fish.

FLAKE: To separate foods into small pieces. The term is frequently used when describing the doneness of fish.

FLAVORINGS: Chemical compounds that replicate the flavor of a particular food or plant and do not originate from the plant material. Common examples are maple, banana and coconut.

FLUTE: To make a V-shape or scalloped edge on pie crust with thumb and fingers.

FOLD: A method of mixing to combine light or delicate ingredients such as whipped cream or egg whites with other ingredients without beating. A rubber spatula is used to gently cut down through the ingredients, move across the bottom of the bowl and bring up part of the mixture.

FOOD COLORING: Used to tint foods and is available in liquids, gels or pastes.

FULL ROLLING BOIL: To boil a liquid in which the bubbles created by the boil cannot be stirred down.

FREEZE: To store foods in the freezer.

FROST: To cover a cake, cupcake or cookie with a spreadable frosting.

FRY: To cook foods in a small amount of fat over medium to high heat.

G

GARNISH: A decorative and edible accompaniment to give a dish more eye appeal and sometimes a flavor boost.

GLAZE: To coat the exterior of sweet or savory foods with a thin, glossy mixture.

GRATE: To rub ingredients such as citrus peel, spices and chocolate over a grater to produce very fine particles.

GREASE: To rub the inside of a baking dish or pan with shortening, butter or oil, or to coat with nonstick cooking spray to keep the contents from sticking.

GREASE AND FLOUR: To rub the inside of a baking dish or pan with a thin layer of shortening, butter or oil, or coat with nonstick cooking spray and then dust with flour. The excess flour is shaken out of the pan. Cakes baked in round baking pans or fluted tube pans generally require the pan to be greased and floured.

GRILL: To cook foods outside on a grid over hot charcoals or a gas flame. Also refers to an indoor countertop electrical appliance.

GRIND: To transform a solid piece of food into smaller pieces using a food processor, blender or mortar and pestle.

H

HEADSPACE: An area left unfilled between the top of the food in a home canning jar or freezer container and the bottom of the lid. (See Boiling-Water-Bath Basics on page 422.)

HULL: To remove the green stem and leaves of strawberries.

HUSK: To remove the outer leaves from an ear of corn.

I

ICE: To spread a thin frosting over cakes or cookies.

INDIRECT HEAT: To cook foods on an outdoor grill over a drip pan with the coals banked (or other heat source) on one or both sides of the drip pan. Indirect heat is used for cooking larger cuts of meat or less tender cuts of meat.

J

JELLY ROLL: A dessert made by spreading a filling, jelly or whipped cream over a sponge cake baked in a 15-inch x 10-inch x 1-inch pan and rolling into a log. Jelly-roll style is used when any food is filled and rolled into a log shape.

JULIENNE: To cut foods into long, thin matchstick shapes about 2 inches long and 1/2 inch thick. (See Making Julienne Strips on page 10.)

K

KNEAD: To work dough by using a pressing and folding action to make it smooth and elastic.

L

LINE: To cover a baking sheet with a piece of parchment paper, waxed paper or foil to prevent sticking.

M

MARBLE: To swirl light and dark batters in a cake, bar cookie, pie or cheesecake. The batters should not be combined into one color; there should still be two distinct batters after marbling.

MARINATE: To tenderize and/or flavor foods, usually meat or raw vegetables, by placing in a liquid mixture of oil, vinegar, wine, lime or lemon juice, herbs and spices.

MINCE: To cut foods into very fine pieces no larger than 1/8 inch.

MIX: To stir or beat two or more ingredients together with a spoon or a fork until well combined.

MOISTEN: To add enough liquid to dry ingredients while stirring gently to make a wet, but not runny, mixture. Often used in the preparation of muffins.

P

PAN-BROIL: To cook tender cuts of meat, uncovered, in a skillet on the stovetop without the addition of any fat or liquid.

PAN-DRESSED: Fish or small game with the internal organs and head removed, making it ready for cooking.

PAN-FRY: To cook tender cuts of meat, uncovered, in a skillet on the stovetop with the addition of fat but no liquid.

PARBOIL: To boil foods, usually vegetables, until partially cooked. Most often used when vegetables are finished using another cooking method or chilled for marinated salads or appetizer dips.

PARTIALLY SET: The consistency of chilled gelatin (resembles unbeaten egg whites) before fruits, vegetables and nuts can be added without floating.

PEEL: To remove the skin from fruits and vegetables. To remove the peel, use a small sharp knife, a grater, a vegetable peeler or zester. Also, the outer portion of a citrus fruit is known as the peel.

PINCH: A measurement less than 1/8 teaspoon of a seasoning or spice that is easily held between the thumb and index finger. This is not an accurate measurement.

PIPE: To force a soft mixture such as whipped cream, frosting or meringue through a pastry bag for a fancy shape.

PIT: To remove the seed from fruit. Also refers to the seed in cherries, peaches, nectarines and avocados.

PLUMP: To soak dried fruit such as raisins and cherries in liquid until softened.

POACH: To cook meat, fish, eggs or fruits in simmering liquid. The liquid can be flavored with salt, bay leaves, onion, celery and white wine if desired.

PREHEAT: To bring an oven up to the baking temperature before baking.

PRESS: Often called a cookie press. Used to extract cookie dough in decorative shapes.

PRICK: To pierce food or pastry with the tines of a fork to prevent them from bursting or rising during baking. Also used when roasting ducks and geese to remove excess fat under the skin.

PROCESS: To combine, blend, chop or puree foods in a food processor or blender.

PROOF: To check the quality of yeast before using. To proof yeast, dissolve yeast and a little sugar in warm water (110° to 115°) and let stand for 5 minutes. If the yeast is alive, there will be a thick foam on the surface. To proof also refers to letting yeast dough rise after it's been shaped and before baking.

PULSE: To process foods in a food processor or in a blender using short bursts of power. This is accomplished by quickly turning the machine on and off.

PUNCH DOWN: To use a fist to deflate risen yeast dough after the first rising.

PUREE: To mash solid foods into a smooth mixture using a food processor, food mill, blender or sieve.

R..........

REDUCE: To thicken sauces and gravy by boiling down and evaporating a portion of the liquid in an uncovered pan.

REFRIGERATE: To place in the refrigerator to chill.

ROAST: To cook meat or vegetables with a dry heat as in cooking in an oven without the addition of liquid. Also refers to large cuts of meat that are intended to be roasted.

ROUNDED TEASPOON OR TABLESPOON: To mound dough slightly in measuring spoon.

ROUX: A French term for a mixture of flour and fat that is cooked together until golden brown and used to thicken gumbo soups and sauces.

S..........

SAUTE: To cook or lightly brown foods in butter, margarine or oil until tender.

SCALD: To heat milk or cream over low heat until just before it boils. Look for small bubbles around the edge of the liquid.

SCORE: To make thin slashes on the surface of breads to decorate and allow steam to escape during baking.

SEED: To remove seeds from fruits and vegetables.

SEIZE: To become thick and lumpy. Seizing refers to when a small amount of liquid comes in contact with melted chocolate.

SEPARATE: To remove the egg white from the egg yolk.

SHRED: To cut or tear foods into long, thin strips, such as cooked chicken. In the case of soft cheese, carrots or potatoes, a metal shredder is used.

SHUCK: To remove the meat of oysters, clams, etc. from their shells. Also refers to removing the husk from an ear of corn.

SIFT: To pass dry ingredients such as flour or confectioners' sugar through a fine-mesh strainer or sifter to remove lumps, add air and combine several dry ingredients.

SIMMER: To cook liquids alone or a combination of ingredients with liquid just under the boiling point (180° to 200°). The surface of the liquid will have some movement and there may be small bubbles around the side of pan.

SKIM: To remove with a spoon a layer of fat or foam that rises from the top of cooking liquids. (See Making Pan Gravy on page 156.)

SNIP: To cut herbs into small pieces using a kitchen shears.

SOFT PEAKS: The stage of beating egg whites or heavy whipping cream when the beater is lifted from the mixture and the points of the peaks curl over.

SOFTEN: To bring butter, margarine or cream cheese to a soft consistency by holding at room temperature for a short time.

SPICE BAG: A container made out of cheesecloth to hold whole spices and/or herbs. The bag makes it easy to remove and discard the spices or herbs before serving. (See Making a Spice Bag on page 52.)

STEAM: To cook foods covered on a rack or in a steamer basket over a small amount of boiling water. Most often used for vegetables.

STEEP: To place dry foods, such as tea leaves, in hot water to extract flavor and/or color.

STEW: To cover food with liquid and slowly cook over low heat in a tightly covered pot. This cooking method tenderizes tough cuts of meat and allows flavors to blend.

STIFF PEAKS: The stage of beating egg whites or heavy whipping cream when the beater is lifted from the mixture and points of peaks stand straight up.

STIR: To blend a combination of ingredients by hand using a spoon in a circular motion.

STIR-FRY: To quickly saute meats and vegetables while stirring constantly in a wok or skillet.

STOCK: A long-simmered broth made from meat, poultry, fish and/or vegetables with herbs and spices.

STRAIN: To separate solids from liquid by pouring through a sieve or colander.

STUD: To insert seasonings like whole cloves into the surface of food, such as a ham.

STUFF: To fill a cavity in fish, poultry or pork chops with a bread or rice, vegetable, fruit or nut mixture. (See Stuffing, Roasting and Carving a Whole Turkey on page 178.)

T

TEAR: To use your hands to pull food apart into unevenly sized pieces, such as when tearing salad greens.

THREAD: To place pieces of meat and vegetables onto skewers as when making kabobs.

TOSS: To quickly and gently mix ingredients with a spoon or fork. Often done with flour and candied fruit in baked goods.

TRUSS: To tie the legs and wings of poultry close to the body before roasting. If poultry is stuffed, the openings are closed with skewers that are tied or closed with string.

W

WARM: To hold foods at a low temperature, usually around 200°, without further cooking.

WATER BATH: To place a baking dish containing food, such as a custard or souffle, in a large dish. The larger dish is filled with hot or boiling water. The food is then baked in the water bath to promote even cooking.

WEAVE: To thread food on a skewer using a back and forth motion. The term is also used to describe the action when making a lattice top for a pie.

WHIP: To beat rapidly by hand or with an electric mixer to add air and increase volume.

WHISK: A multi-looped, wire mixing utensil with a handle used to whip sauces, eggs, cream, etc. to a smooth, airy consistency. Also means to whip ingredients together.

Z

ZEST: *See Peel.*

CHAPTER 2
APPETIZERS & BEVERAGES

APPETIZERS & BEVERAGES

Appetizers not only stimulate the appetite before the main course but also can be served in place of a meal. But don't overdo it. Instead, prepare a few good choices or make one spectacular item and fill in with other easy but delicious foods.

You can choose from hot, cold and room temperature foods. When selecting your appetizers, choose recipes that will give a variety of colors, textures (soft and crunchy) and flavors (sour, salty, savory, sweet, spicy or subtle). Look for appetizers that make a nice presentation and require no last-minute fussing.

How Much to Serve

The amount per person varies on the length of the party and the focus of the appetizers.

- For a social hour before dinner, plan on serving 3 or 4 different appetizers and allow 4 to 5 bites per person.

- For an open-house affair, plan on serving 4 to 5 different appetizers and allow 4 to 6 bites per person per hour.

- For an appetizer buffet that is served in place of a meal, plan on serving 6 to 8 different appetizers and allow 10 to 14 bites per person.

Tips for Tasty Appetizers

Allow cheese balls, dips and spreads that contain cream cheese to stand at room temperature for 15 minutes before serving for easier spreading and more flavor.

Place dips in colorful, edible bowls such as red or green cabbage shells or cored sweet red, yellow or green peppers. Fruit dips can be spooned into melon,

orange or grapefruit shells.

Tenderize firm vegetable dippers such as broccoli, green beans and cauliflower by blanching (see page 304) them in boiling water for a minute or two to cook partially. They should still remain crisp. After blanching, immediately plunge the vegetables in ice water to stop the cooking. Drain well before serving.

Add splashes of color by garnishing appetizer platters with sprigs of freshly picked herbs, lemon wedges, grape clusters, fresh berries or small hot peppers. For a lighter feel, decorate with citrus peel curls, fresh chives or edible flowers.

For plates, puddle the dipping sauce for a savory item or ice cream topping for a sweet food on the plate and top with the food. Or dust the plate with cocoa powder or confectioners' sugar.

Try radishes, sweet red pepper strips, sugar snap peas and cherry tomatoes in addition to your usual vegetable dippers.

Prepare appetizers ahead of serving time but store them in the refrigerator; wrap them tightly with foil or plastic wrap.

Keep cold appetizers on ice when your gathering takes you out-of-doors in the warm months (see How to Make an Ice Bowl on page 35). And keep hot appetizers hot to keep them safe from spoilage.

CHEESE TIP

Select sharp cheddar when using packaged shredded cheese for recipes that you'd like to have a bolder flavor. If you will be shredding cheese at home from bulk cheddar, you can choose from mild, medium, sharp and extra sharp.

FIESTA CHEESE BALL

Fiesta Cheese Ball
Virginia Horst, Mesa, Washington

For a change of pace, shape individual servings of this cheese spread into smaller balls, then roll in paprika or chopped nuts.

- 1 package (8 ounces) cream cheese, softened
- 1/4 cup shredded Colby-Monterey Jack cheese
- 3 to 4 tablespoons minced fresh cilantro
- 2 to 3 tablespoons grated onion
- 1 tablespoon chili powder
- 1 teaspoon dried minced garlic
- 1/2 teaspoon garlic salt
- 1/4 teaspoon dried oregano
- 1/4 teaspoon crushed red pepper flakes
- 1/8 teaspoon ground cumin
- 1/8 to 1/4 teaspoon hot pepper sauce
- 1/4 cup minced fresh parsley
- Assorted crackers

1) In a small mixing bowl, beat cream cheese. Add the cheese, cilantro, onion, chili powder, garlic, garlic salt, oregano, red pepper flakes, cumin and hot pepper sauce.

2) Cover and refrigerate for at least 1 hour. Shape into a ball. Roll in parsley. Cover and refrigerate for 8 hours or overnight. Serve with crackers.

Yield: 1 cheese ball.

NUTRITION FACTS: 2 tablespoons cheese ball (calculated without crackers) equals 79 calories, 7 g fat (5 g saturated fat), 23 mg cholesterol, 153 mg sodium, 1 g carbohydrate, trace fiber, 2 g protein.

Savory Swiss Cheesecake
Marjorie Turner, Poquoson, Virginia

Big on Swiss cheese flavor, this creamy spread is irresistible at a festive buffet table. It's terrific when entertaining because it is made ahead.

- 1 cup finely crushed thin wheat crackers
- 3 tablespoons butter, melted
- 12 ounces reduced-fat cream cheese
- 2 cartons (8 ounces *each*) reduced-fat plain yogurt
- 1 egg
- 1 egg yolk
- 1/4 teaspoon dried basil
- 1/8 teaspoon dried rosemary, crushed
- 2 cups (8 ounces) shredded reduced-fat Swiss cheese
- Assorted crackers

1) In a small bowl, combine cracker crumbs and butter. Press onto the bottom of a 9-in. springform pan; set aside.

2) In a large mixing bowl, beat cream cheese until smooth. Add the yogurt, egg, egg yolk, basil and rosemary; beat on low speed just until blended. Stir in Swiss cheese.

3) Pour into prepared crust. Place pan on a baking sheet. Bake at 350° for 40-50 minutes or until center is almost set. Cool on a wire rack for 10 minutes. Carefully run a knife around edge of pan to loosen; cool 1 hour longer.

4) Refrigerate overnight. Remove sides of pan. Cut into wedges; serve with crackers. Refrigerate leftovers.

Yield: 16 servings.

NUTRITION FACTS: 1 piece (calculated without crackers) equals 169 calories, 11 g fat (7 g saturated fat), 57 mg cholesterol, 170 mg sodium, 7 g carbohydrate, trace fiber, 9 g protein.

SHAPING A CHEESE BALL

Keep hands and countertop clean by spooning the cheese mixture onto a piece of plastic wrap. Working from the underside of the wrap, pat the mixture into a ball. Complete recipe as directed.

shell. Cube removed bread and set aside. Fill the shell with spinach dip; replace top. Wrap in heavy-duty foil; place on a baking sheet.

3) Bake at 375° for 1-1/4 to 1-1/2 hours or until dip is heated through. Open foil carefully. Serve warm with bread cubes and vegetables.

Yield: 4-1/2 cups.

NUTRITION FACTS: 1/4 cup dip (calculated without bread cubes or vegetables) equals 105 calories, 7 g fat (4 g saturated fat), 20 mg cholesterol, 303 mg sodium, 6 g carbohydrate, 1 g fiber, 6 g protein.

Party Crab Dip
Kimberly McGuire, Dunlap, Illinois

Nothing shaves time from party preparations like a no-fuss appetizer, and this flavorful seafood spread is a perfect example. Serve it with crackers or toasted bread rounds.

- 1 teaspoon cornstarch
- 1/2 cup white wine *or* chicken broth
- 1 package (8 ounces) cream cheese, cubed
- 2 cans (6 ounces *each*) crabmeat, drained, flaked and cartilage removed
- 2 tablespoons half-and-half cream
- 2 tablespoons minced fresh parsley
- 1 tablespoon Worcestershire sauce
- 1 cup (4 ounces) shredded cheddar cheese

Seafood seasoning *or* paprika, optional
Crackers *and/or* raw vegetables

1) In a large microwave-safe bowl, combine the cornstarch and the wine or broth until smooth. Add cream cheese.

2) Cover and microwave on high for 45 seconds; stir. Microwave 45-75 seconds longer or until smooth and slightly thickened.

3) Stir in the crab, cream, parsley and Worcestershire sauce. Cover and microwave on high for 45 seconds; stir. Add cheddar cheese; heat 45-60 seconds longer. Stir until the cheese is melted. Sprinkle with seafood seasoning if desired. Serve with crackers and vegetables.

Yield: about 3 cups.

Nutrition Facts: 2 tablespoons dip (calculated without crackers or vegetables) equals 71 calories, 5 g fat (3 g saturated fat), 29 mg cholesterol, 114 mg sodium, 1 g carbohydrate, trace fiber, 5 g protein.

Baked Spinach Dip Loaf
Frieda Meding, Trochu, Alberta

This baked version of spinach dip is a twist on the traditional cold variety. To save time, make and chill the dip overnight. Spoon the dip into the bread bowl and bake before guests arrive.

- 2 packages (8 ounces *each*) cream cheese, softened
- 1 cup mayonnaise
- 1 package (10 ounces) frozen chopped spinach, thawed and squeezed dry
- 1 cup (4 ounces) shredded cheddar cheese
- 1 can (8 ounces) water chestnuts, drained and chopped
- 5 bacon strips, cooked and crumbled
- 1 green onion, chopped
- 2 teaspoons dill weed
- 1 garlic clove, minced
- 1/2 teaspoon seasoned salt
- 1/8 teaspoon pepper
- 1 unsliced round loaf (1 pound) sourdough bread

Raw vegetables

1) In a large mixing bowl, beat cream cheese and mayonnaise. Stir in the spinach, cheese, water chestnuts, bacon, onion and seasonings.

2) Cut a 1-1/2-in. slice off top of the bread; set aside. Carefully hollow out bottom, leaving a 1/2-in.

Artichoke Dip

Mrs. William Garner, Austin, Texas

Give this golden dip some color after baking by sprinkling the top with sliced fresh tomatoes and chives or minced green onions.

- 1 can (14 ounces) water-packed artichoke hearts, rinsed and drained
- 1 cup mayonnaise
- 1/3 to 1/2 cup grated Parmesan cheese
- 1 garlic clove, minced

Dash hot pepper sauce

Paprika, optional

Assorted crackers

1) In a large bowl, combine the artichoke hearts, mayonnaise, Parmesan cheese, garlic and hot pepper sauce. Transfer to a greased 1-qt. baking dish. Sprinkle with paprika if desired.

2) Bake, uncovered, at 350° for 20-25 minutes or until top is lightly browned. Serve warm with crackers.

Yield: 2 cups.

NUTRITION FACTS: 2 tablespoons dip (calculated without crackers) equals 117 calories, 12 g fat (2 g saturated fat), 6 mg cholesterol, 168 mg sodium, 2 g carbohydrate, 0 fiber, 1 g protein.

- **ZIPPY ARTICHOKE DIP:** Add 1 can (4 ounces) drained chopped green chilies to the mayonnaise mixture. Bake as directed.

- **CHEESY ARTICHOKE DIP:** Add 1 cup (4 ounces) shredded mozzarella cheese, 1 tablespoon chopped onion, 1 tablespoon minced fresh parsley and 1/4 teaspoon garlic salt to the mayonnaise mixture. Bake as directed.

Pretzel Mustard Dip

Bonnie Capper-Eckstein
Brooklyn Park, Minnesota

Perfect for just a little snack, this recipe makes about 1/2 cup. It's also tasty spread on a sandwich.

- 1/4 cup mayonnaise
- 1/4 cup prepared yellow *or* Dijon mustard
- 2 tablespoons finely chopped onion
- 1 tablespoon ranch salad dressing mix
- 2-1/4 teaspoons prepared horseradish

Pretzels

1) In a small bowl, combine the mayonnaise, mustard, chopped onion, salad dressing mix and horseradish.

2) Cover and refrigerate for at least 30 minutes. Serve with pretzels.

Yield: about 1/2 cup.

NUTRITION FACTS: 2 tablespoons dip (calculated without pretzels) equals 125 calories, 11 g fat (2 g saturated fat), 5 mg cholesterol, 547 mg sodium, 4 g carbohydrate, 1 g fiber, 1 g protein.

Simple Guacamole

Heidi Main, Anchorage, Alaska

Because avocados can brown quickly, it's best to make this guacamole just before serving. If you have to make it a little in advance, place the avocado pit in the guacamole until serving.

- 2 medium ripe avocados
- 1 tablespoon lemon juice
- 1/4 cup chunky salsa
- 1/8 to 1/4 teaspoon salt

1) Peel and chop avocados; place in a small bowl. Sprinkle with lemon juice.

2) Add salsa and salt; mash coarsely with a fork. Refrigerate until serving.

Yield: 1-1/2 cups.

NUTRITION FACTS: 2 tablespoons guacamole equals 53 calories, 5 g fat (1 g saturated fat), 0 cholesterol, 51 mg sodium, 3 g carbohydrate, 2 g fiber, 1 g protein.

Eggplant Dip

Linda Roberson, Cordova, Tennessee

Pleasantly surprise party guests by offering this one-of-a-kind dip. For a little Mediterranean flair, serve it with wedges of pita bread.

- 3 cups cubed eggplant
- 1 medium onion, chopped

1/3 cup finely chopped sweet red pepper

1 jar (4-1/2 ounces) sliced mushrooms, drained

4 garlic cloves, minced

1/3 cup olive oil

1 jar (6 ounces) stuffed olives, drained and chopped

1 can (6 ounces) tomato paste

2 tablespoons red wine vinegar

1-1/2 teaspoons sugar

1 teaspoon salt

1/2 teaspoon dried oregano

Hot pepper sauce to taste

Pita bread wedges *or* tortilla *or* corn chips

1) In a large skillet, combine eggplant, onion, red pepper, mushrooms, garlic and oil. Cover and cook over medium heat for 10 minutes or until tender.

2) Stir in olives, tomato paste, vinegar, sugar, salt, oregano and hot pepper sauce; bring to a boil. Reduce the heat; cover and simmer for 20-30 minutes or until flavors are blended.

3) Serve warm or at room temperature with pita wedges or chips.

Yield: 3 cups.

NUTRITION FACTS: 2 tablespoons dip (calculated without pita bread or chips) equals 53 calories, 4 g fat (trace saturated fat), 0 cholesterol, 247 mg sodium, 4 g carbohydrate, 1 g fiber, 1 g protein.

Six-Layer Dip

Etta Gillespie, San Angelo, Texas

Tortilla chips make great scoopers for this dip. Serve in a glass bowl to show off the pretty layers.

2 medium ripe avocados, peeled and sliced

2 tablespoons lemon juice

1/2 tablespoon garlic salt

1/8 teaspoon hot pepper sauce

1 cup (8 ounces) sour cream

1 can (2-1/4 ounces) chopped ripe olives, drained

1 jar (16 ounces) thick and chunky salsa, drained

2 medium tomatoes, seeded and chopped

1 cup (8 ounces) shredded cheddar cheese

Tortilla chips

1) In a large bowl, mash the avocados with lemon juice, garlic salt and hot pepper sauce. Spoon into a deep-dish 10-in. pie plate or serving bowl.

2) Layer with the sour cream, olives, salsa, tomatoes and cheese. Cover and refrigerate for at least 1 hour. Serve with chips.

Yield: 2-1/2 cups.

NUTRITION FACTS: 2 tablespoons dip (calculated without chips) equals 88 calories, 7 g fat (3 g saturated fat), 14 mg cholesterol, 313 mg sodium, 5 g carbohydrate, 3 g fiber, 4 g protein.

TEXAS CAVIAR

Texas Caviar

Kathy Faris, Lytle, Texas

Be prepared to hand out the recipe for this tangy salsa when you take it to get-togethers. Black-eyed peas are a delicious ingredient.

1 can (15-1/2 ounces) black-eyed peas, rinsed and drained

3/4 cup chopped sweet red pepper

3/4 cup chopped green pepper

1 medium onion, chopped

3 green onions, chopped

1/4 cup minced fresh parsley

1 jar (2 ounces) diced pimientos, drained

1 garlic clove, minced

1 bottle (8 ounces) fat-free Italian salad dressing

Baked tortilla chips

1) In a large bowl, combine the peas, peppers, onions, parsley, pimientos and garlic. Pour salad dressing over pea mixture; stir gently to coat.

2) Cover and refrigerate for 24 hours. Serve with tortilla chips.

Yield: 4 cups.

NUTRITION FACTS: 1/2 cup (calculated without chips) equals 148 calories, 1 g fat (trace saturated fat), 1 mg cholesterol, 661 mg sodium, 30 g carbohydrate, 5 g fiber, 5 g protein.

FIVE-FRUIT SALSA

1) In a large bowl, combine the cantaloupe, onions, kiwi, orange, peppers and pineapple. Cover and refrigerate for 8 hours or overnight.

2) For chips, brush tortillas with butter; cut into eight wedges. Combine sugar and cinnamon; sprinkle over the tortillas. Place on ungreased baking sheets. Bake at 350° for 10-14 minutes or just until crisp.

3) Just before serving, drain salsa if desired. Stir in strawberries. Serve the fruit salsa with cinnamon tortilla chips.

Yield: 8 cups.

Editor's Note: When cutting or seeding hot peppers, use rubber or plastic gloves to protect your hands. Avoid touching your face.

NUTRITION FACTS: 1/2 cup salsa with 5 chips equals 150 calories, 5 g fat (2 g saturated fat), 8 mg cholesterol, 189 mg sodium, 29 g carbohydrate, 2 g fiber, 4 g protein.

Five-Fruit Salsa
Catherine Dawe, Kent, Ohio

You'll find it hard to stop eating this fresh, fruity salsa and homemade cinnamon tortilla chips! For extra zest, toss in some of the jalapeno seeds instead of discarding them.

- 2 cups chopped fresh cantaloupe
- 6 green onions, chopped
- 3 kiwifruit, peeled and finely chopped
- 1 medium navel orange, peeled and finely chopped
- 1 medium sweet yellow pepper, chopped
- 1 medium sweet red pepper, chopped
- 2 jalapeno peppers, seeded and chopped
- 1 can (8 ounces) crushed unsweetened pineapple, drained

CINNAMON TORTILLA CHIPS:
- 10 flour tortillas (8 inches)
- 1/4 cup butter, melted
- 1/3 cup sugar
- 2 teaspoons ground cinnamon
- 1 cup finely chopped fresh strawberries

Orange-Ginger Fruit Dip
Trisha Faulk, Athens, Michigan

With just four ingredients, this dip is great for last-minute entertaining. It can also be served with gingersnaps or graham crackers.

- 1 package (8 ounces) cream cheese, softened
- 1 jar (7 ounces) marshmallow creme
- 1 tablespoon grated orange peel
- 1/8 teaspoon ground ginger
Assorted fresh fruit

1) In a small mixing bowl, beat cream cheese until smooth. Beat in the marshmallow creme, orange peel and ginger.

2) Cover and refrigerate until serving. Serve with fruit.

Yield: 2-1/2 cups.

NUTRITION FACTS: 2 tablespoons dip (calculated without fruit) equals 73 calories, 4 g fat (2 g saturated fat), 12 mg cholesterol, 42 mg sodium, 9 g carbohydrate, trace fiber, 1 g protein.

Double Sausage Stromboli
Connie Atchley, Westport, Indiana

Every bite of this yummy stromboli is packed with pepperoni, sausage and cheese. For a hearty lunch, cut it into 6 or 8 slices.

- 1 pound bulk pork sausage
- 28 pepperoni slices, chopped
- 3/4 cup shredded mozzarella *or* cheddar cheese
- 1 package (16 ounces) hot roll mix

1 cup warm water (120° to 130°)
2 tablespoons butter, softened
1 egg, beaten
1 tablespoon dried oregano
1-1/2 teaspoons vegetable oil

1) In a large skillet, cook sausage over medium heat until no longer pink; add pepperoni. Drain well and pat dry with paper towels; stir in cheese and set aside.

2) In a large bowl, combine contents of hot roll mix, water, butter and egg until dough pulls away from side of bowl and holds together. Turn onto a lightly floured surface; knead until smooth and elastic, about 5 minutes. Cover and let rest for 5 minutes.

3) Pat dough into a greased 15-in. x 10-in. x 1-in. baking pan. Spread sausage mixture lengthwise down the center third of dough; sprinkle with oregano. Fold sides over filling; press edges lightly to seal. Cover and let rise until doubled, about 30 minutes.

4) Brush with oil. Bake at 375° for 20-25 minutes or until golden brown. Let stand for 5 minutes before cutting.

Yield: 12-14 servings.

NUTRITION FACTS: 1 piece equals 245 calories, 13 g fat (5 g saturated fat), 39 mg cholesterol, 466 mg sodium, 24 g carbohydrate, 1 g fiber, 8 g protein.

Cranberry Appetizer Meatballs
Jim Ulberg, Elk Rapids, Michigan

These tangy meatballs can be made ahead and frozen. When ready to use, thaw in the refrigerator and heat with sauce in a slow cooker.

2 eggs, beaten
1 cup dry bread crumbs
1/3 cup minced fresh parsley
1/3 cup ketchup
2 tablespoons finely chopped onion
2 tablespoons soy sauce
2 garlic cloves, minced
1/2 teaspoon salt
1/4 teaspoon pepper
2 pounds ground beef

CRANBERRY SAUCE:
1 can (16 ounces) whole-berry cranberry sauce
1 bottle (12 ounces) chili sauce
1 tablespoon brown sugar

1 tablespoon prepared mustard
1 tablespoon lemon juice
2 garlic cloves, minced

1) In a large bowl, combine the eggs, bread crumbs, parsley, ketchup, onion, soy sauce, garlic, salt and pepper. Crumble beef over mixture and mix well. Shape into 1-in. balls.

2) Place meatballs on a rack in a shallow baking pan. Bake, uncovered, at 400° for 15 minutes or until no longer pink. Transfer with a slotted spoon to a slow cooker or chafing dish.

3) Combine sauce ingredients in a saucepan; simmer for 10 minutes, stirring occasionally. Pour over meatballs. Serve warm.

Yield: about 7 dozen.

NUTRITION FACTS: 3 meatballs equals 125 calories, 5 g fat (2 g saturated fat), 37 mg cholesterol, 369 mg sodium, 13 g carbohydrate, trace fiber, 8 g protein.

■ *SWEET AND SOY APPETIZER MEATBALLS:* Omit the Cranberry Sauce from recipe above. In a small saucepan, combine 3 tablespoons plus 2 teaspoons cornstarch with 1/3 cup reduced-sodium soy sauce and 3 tablespoons lemon juice until smooth. Stir in 1-1/2 cups orange marmalade and 3 minced garlic cloves. Bring to a boil; cook and stir for 2 minutes or until thickened. Pour over meatballs and serve warm.

■ *BARBECUE APPETIZER MEATBALLS:* Omit the Cranberry Sauce from recipe above. In a large saucepan, combine 1/2 cup *each* packed brown sugar, water, cider vinegar and ketchup, 1/4 cup Dijon-mayonnaise blend and 2 cans (8 ounces *each*) drained pineapple. Bring to a boil over medium heat. Reduce the heat; simmer, uncovered, for 5 minutes. Pour over meatballs and serve warm.

Sausage Cheese Bites
Nancy Reichert, Thomasville, Georgia

These baked bites can be frozen, then reheated in a 375° oven for 6 to 8 minutes. If your family prefers foods with more spice, substitute hot pork sausage and pepper Jack cheese.

1 pound mild pork sausage
4 cups buttermilk biscuit mix
2 cups (8 ounces) shredded cheddar cheese
1 cup water

1) Crumble sausage into a skillet; cook over medium heat until no longer pink. Drain.

2) In a large bowl, combine biscuit mix and cheese. Add sausage and stir until well blended. Stir in water just until mixed. Shape into 1-1/2-in. balls.

3) Place on greased baking sheets. Bake at 375° for about 15 minutes or until golden.

Yield: 16 servings.

NUTRITION FACTS: 3 pieces equals 230 calories, 14 g fat (6 g saturated fat), 25 mg cholesterol, 579 mg sodium, 19 g carbohydrate, 1 g fiber, 7 g protein.

BACON SWISS BREAD

Bacon Swiss Bread
Shirley Mills, Tulsa, Oklahoma

I'm a busy mom, so I'm always looking for fast and easy recipes. These savory slices of jazzed-up French bread are great with soup and salad. My daughter and her friends like to snack on them.

1 loaf (1 pound) French bread (20 inches)
2/3 cup butter, softened
1/3 cup chopped green onions
4 teaspoons prepared mustard
5 slices process Swiss cheese
5 bacon strips

1) Cut bread into 1-in.-thick slices, leaving slices attached at bottom. In a bowl, combine the butter, onions and mustard; spread on both sides of each slice of bread.

2) Cut each cheese slice diagonally into four triangles; place between the slices of bread. Cut bacon in half widthwise and then lengthwise; drape a piece over each slice.

3) Place the loaf on a double thickness of heavy-duty foil. Bake at 400° for 20-25 minutes or until bacon is crisp.

Yield: 10 servings.

NUTRITION FACTS: 1 piece equals 332 calories, 23 g fat (12 g saturated fat), 49 mg cholesterol, 651 mg sodium, 24 g carbohydrate, 2 g fiber, 8 g protein.

Coconut Chicken Bites
Linda Schwarz, Bertrand, Nebraska

These tender nuggets are great for nibbling thanks to the coconut, cumin, celery salt and garlic powder that season them. Serve them alone or with sweet-sour sauce.

2 cups flaked coconut
1 egg
2 tablespoons milk
3/4 pound boneless skinless chicken breasts, cut into 3/4-inch pieces
1/2 cup all-purpose flour
Oil for deep-fat frying
1 teaspoon celery salt
1/2 teaspoon garlic powder
1/2 teaspoon ground cumin

1) In a blender or food processor, process coconut until finely chopped. Transfer to a bowl and set aside. In another bowl, combine egg and milk.

2) Toss chicken with flour; dip in egg mixture, then in coconut. Place in a single layer on a baking sheet. Refrigerate for 30 minutes.

3) In an electric skillet or deep-fat fryer, heat 2 in. of oil to 375°. Fry chicken, a few pieces at time, for 1-1/2 minutes on each side or until golden brown.

4) Drain on paper towels; place in a bowl. Sprinkle with celery salt, garlic powder and cumin; toss to coat. Serve warm.

Yield: 3 dozen.

NUTRITION FACTS: 3 pieces equals 166 calories, 10 g fat (6 g saturated fat), 34 mg cholesterol, 185 mg sodium, 12 g carbohydrate, 1 g fiber, 7 g protein.

Spicy Hot Wings
Anna Free, Loudonville, Ohio

Friends and family go wild when I serve these tongue-tingling, baked chicken wings. The creamy dipping sauce is a mild accompaniment.

- 10 chicken wings (about 2 pounds)
- 1/2 cup butter, melted
- 2 to 5 teaspoons hot pepper sauce
- 3/4 teaspoon garlic salt
- 1/4 teaspoon paprika

DIPPING SAUCE:
- 3/4 cup sour cream
- 1 tablespoon dried minced onion
- 1 tablespoon milk
- 1/2 cup crumbled blue cheese
- 1/4 teaspoon garlic salt
- 1/8 teaspoon ground mustard
- Paprika, optional
- Celery sticks, optional

1) Cut chicken wings into three sections; discard wing tips. Place wings in a greased 15-in. x 10-in. x 1-in. baking pan. Combine the butter, hot pepper sauce, garlic salt and paprika; pour over wings.

2) Bake at 375° for 30 minutes. Turn; bake 20-25 minutes longer or until chicken juices run clear.

3) Meanwhile, for sauce, combine the sour cream, onion, milk, cheese, garlic salt and mustard in a blender. Cover and process until smooth. Pour into a bowl; sprinkle with paprika if desired. Cover and refrigerate until serving.

4) Drain wings. Serve with sauce and celery if desired.

Yield: 8 servings.

NUTRITION FACTS: 4 pieces (calculated without additional paprika and celery sticks) equals 305 calories, 26 g fat (14 g saturated fat), 89 mg cholesterol, 515 mg sodium, 2 g carbohydrate, trace fiber, 15 g protein.

Raspberry Barbecue Wings
Sandra Fisher, Missoula, Montana

These out-of-the-ordinary wings are baked with onion and garlic, then broiled and basted with a mixture of raspberry jam, barbecue sauce and jalapeno peppers. The sauce is also great for dipping.

- 2/3 cup barbecue sauce
- 2/3 cup seedless raspberry jam
- 3 tablespoons finely chopped onion
- 1 to 2 jalapeno peppers, seeded and finely chopped
- 2 teaspoons minced garlic, *divided*
- 2 teaspoons Liquid Smoke, optional, *divided*
- 1/4 teaspoon salt
- 15 chicken wings (about 3 pounds)
- 1 small onion, sliced
- 1 cup water

1) In a small bowl, combine the barbecue sauce, jam, chopped onion, peppers, 1 teaspoon garlic, 1 teaspoon Liquid Smoke if desired and salt; mix well. Cover and refrigerate for at least 2 hours.

2) Cut chicken wings into three sections; discard wing tip section. Place the chicken wings in a greased 15-in. x 10-in. x 1-in. baking pan. Top with sliced onion and remaining garlic.

3) Combine the water and remaining Liquid Smoke if desired; pour over wings. Cover and bake at 350° for 30 minutes or until juices run clear.

4) Transfer wings to a greased broiler pan; brush with sauce. Broil 4-6 in. from the heat for 20-25 minutes, turning and basting every 5 minutes or until wings are well coated.

Yield: 2-1/2 dozen.

Editor's Note: When cutting or seeding hot peppers, use rubber or plastic gloves to protect your hands. Avoid touching your face. Three pounds of chicken wing sections (wingettes) may be substituted for the whole chicken wings. Omit the first line of step 2.

NUTRITION FACTS: 3 pieces equals 197 calories, 9 g fat (2 g saturated fat), 37 mg cholesterol, 231 mg sodium, 17 g carbohydrate, trace fiber, 12 g protein.

DISJOINTING CHICKEN WINGS

1) Place chicken wing on a cutting board. With a sharp knife, cut between the joint at the top of the tip end. Discard tips or use for preparing chicken broth.

2) Take remaining wing and cut between the joints. Proceed with recipe as directed.

Chicken-Pesto Pan Pizza

Juanita Fleck, Bullhead City, Arizona

A packaged pesto mix is the tasty replacement for traditional tomato sauce in this tempting pizza.

- 1 tube (13.8 ounces) refrigerated pizza crust
- 1/2 cup water
- 3 tablespoons olive oil
- 1 envelope pesto sauce mix
- 1 package (10 ounces) frozen chopped spinach, thawed and squeezed dry
- 1/2 cup ricotta cheese
- 1/4 cup chopped onion
- 2 cups shredded cooked chicken
- 1 jar (4-1/2 ounces) sliced mushrooms, drained
- 4 plum tomatoes, sliced
- 1 cup (4 ounces) shredded Swiss cheese
- 1/4 cup grated Romano cheese

1) Unroll pizza crust into an ungreased 15-in. x 10-in. x 1-in. baking pan; flatten dough and build up edges slightly. Prick dough several items with a fork. Bake at 425° for 7 minutes or until lightly browned.

2) Meanwhile, combine the water, oil and pesto sauce mix in a saucepan. Cook until heated through (do not boil). Add the spinach, ricotta and onion; mix well. Spread over crust.

3) Top with the chicken, mushrooms, tomatoes and Swiss and Romano cheeses. Bake at 425° for 7 minutes or until crust is golden and cheese is melted.

Yield: 8 servings.

NUTRITION FACTS: 1 slice equals 368 calories, 16 g fat (6 g saturated fat), 54 mg cholesterol, 866 mg sodium, 32 g carbohydrate, 3 g fiber, 24 g protein.

Empanditas

Mary Ann Kosmas, Minneapolis, Minnesota

Empanditas can be frozen after sealing. When ready to use, place frozen empanditas on a greased baking sheet, brush with milk and bake at 375° for 30-35 minutes.

- 1/2 pound boneless skinless chicken breast halves, thinly sliced
- 1 tablespoon vegetable oil
- 1/8 teaspoon ground cumin
- 1 can (4 ounces) chopped green chilies, drained

- 1/2 cup shredded pepper Jack cheese or Monterey Jack cheese
- 2 tablespoons all-purpose flour
- Pastry for 2 double-crust pies
- 1/4 cup milk

1) In a large skillet, saute chicken in oil for 7-8 minutes or until juices run clear. Sprinkle with cumin. Chop into very small pieces and place in a bowl. Add chilies and cheese. Sprinkle with flour; toss to coat.

2) Turn pastry dough onto a floured surface; roll to 1/8-in. thickness. Cut with a 2-in. round cutter. Fill each circle with about 1 tablespoon of filling. Wet edges of circle with water.

3) Fold half of pastry over filling; seal with fingers, then press with the tines of a fork. Repeat until all filling is used.

4) Place on a greased baking sheet. Brush lightly with milk. Bake at 375° for 20-25 minutes or until golden brown. Serve warm.

Yield: 3 dozen.

NUTRITION FACTS: 3 empanditas equals 757 calories, 44 g fat (18 g saturated fat), 59 mg cholesterol, 688 mg sodium, 73 g carbohydrate, trace fiber, 16 g protein.

Savory Rye Snacks

Connie Simon, Reed City, Michigan

I make the flavorful spread in advance and refrigerate it. Then all I need to do to have a quick snack is put it on the rye bread and bake.

- 1 cup sliced green onions
- 1 cup (4 ounces) shredded Monterey Jack cheese
- 1 cup (4 ounces) shredded cheddar cheese
- 1 cup mayonnaise
- 1 can (4 ounces) mushroom stems and pieces, drained
- 1/2 cup chopped ripe olives
- 1/2 cup chopped stuffed olives
- 1 loaf (1 pound) snack rye bread

1) In a bowl, combine onions, cheeses, mayonnaise, mushrooms and olives.

2) Spread on bread slices and place on ungreased baking sheets. Bake at 350° for 8-10 minutes or until bubbly.

Yield: 4 dozen.

NUTRITION FACTS: 3 pieces equals 242 calories, 17 g fat (5 g saturated fat), 19 mg cholesterol, 496 mg sodium, 15 g carbohydrate, 2 g fiber, 6 g protein.

MARINATED SHRIMP

Marinated Shrimp
Margaret DeLong, Gainesville, Florida

To keep the shrimp cold on a buffet table, serve them in a pretty ice bowl.

- 2 pounds cooked medium shrimp, peeled and deveined
- 1 medium red onion, cut into rings
- 2 medium lemons, cut into slices
- 1 cup pitted ripe olives, drained
- 1/2 cup olive oil
- 1/3 cup minced fresh parsley
- 3 tablespoons lemon juice
- 3 tablespoons red wine vinegar
- 1 garlic clove, minced
- 1 bay leaf
- 1 tablespoon minced fresh basil *or* 1 teaspoon dried basil
- 1 teaspoon salt
- 1 teaspoon ground mustard
- 1/4 teaspoon pepper

1) In a 3-qt. glass serving bowl, combine the shrimp, onion, lemons and olives.

2) In a jar with a tight-fitting lid, combine the remaining ingredients; shake well. Pour over shrimp mixture and stir gently to coat.

3) Cover and refrigerate for 24 hours, stirring occasionally. Discard bay leaf before serving.

Yield: 14 servings.

NUTRITION FACTS: 3 shrimp with 1 olive equals 157 calories, 10 g fat (1 g saturated fat), 99 mg cholesterol, 350 mg sodium, 3 g carbohydrate, 1 g fiber, 13 g protein.

HOW TO MAKE AN ICE BOWL

1) Place ice cubes over the bottom of a 2-1/2- or 3-qt. bowl. Center a 1-1/2- or 1-qt. bowl on top of the ice cubes. Weigh the smaller bowl down with ice cubes or a can of frozen juice. Place freezer tape across both bowls to hold them in place.

2) Use a wooden skewer to tuck fresh herbs, citrus slices or edible flowers between the ice cubes.

3) Pour cold water between the bowls until the water is about 2 in. from the bottom. Freeze. Add another inch of water and freeze. If desired, add or reposition herbs, citrus slices or flowers. Repeat until water is about 1/2 in. below bowl rim.

4) Remove tape from sides of bowls and ice cubes or juice can from smaller bowl. Fill smaller bowl with warm, not hot, water and let stand for 1-2 minutes. Carefully lift out of large bowl. Dip large bowl in warm, not hot, water. Remove from ice bowl. Use bowl immediately for shrimp, dips or fresh fruits.

Mini Shrimp Rolls
Jennifer Jones, Pine City, New York

These tasty tidbits are better for you than traditional egg rolls because they're baked.

- 1 pound cooked medium shrimp, peeled and deveined
- 6 ounces reduced-fat cream cheese
- 1 cup (4 ounces) shredded part-skim mozzarella cheese
- 1-1/2 cups finely chopped cabbage
- 3 green onions, finely chopped
- 1/2 cup shredded carrot
- 1 tablespoon reduced-sodium soy sauce
- 2 garlic cloves, minced
- 48 wonton wrappers
- 2 tablespoons all-purpose flour
- 3 tablespoons water

1) Chop shrimp; set aside. In a mixing bowl, beat cream cheese until smooth. Add mozzarella cheese; mix well. Stir in the cabbage, onions, carrot, soy sauce, garlic and shrimp.

2) For each shrimp roll, place 1 tablespoon of shrimp mixture across the bottom third of a wonton wrapper to within 1/4 in. of bottom and side edges. Combine flour and water until smooth; brush a 1/4-in.-wide strip on side edges and fold side edges over 1/4 in.

3) Brush the side edges and top edge with water mixture. Fold bottom third of wonton wrapper over filling, then bring top over and pinch edges to seal completely.

4) Lightly spray rolls with nonstick cooking spray. Place on a baking sheet coated with nonstick cooking spray. Bake at 400° for 15-18 minutes or until golden brown, turning once. Serve warm.

Yield: 4 dozen.

NUTRITION FACTS: 3 shrimp rolls equals 153 calories, 4 g fat (2 g saturated fat), 70 mg cholesterol, 317 mg sodium, 16 g carbohydrate, 1 g fiber, 11 g protein.

Cheesy Sausage Nachos
Jane Sodergren, Red Wing, Minnesota

Set a platter of these nachos on the table and stand back as guests dive in! This dish can be used as an appetizer as well as an entree.

- 3/4 pound bulk pork sausage
- 1/4 cup chopped onion
- 3 cups diced fresh tomatoes, *divided*
- 3/4 cup picante sauce
- 4 cups tortilla chips
- 3 cups (12 ounces) shredded Monterey Jack cheese, *divided*
- 1 medium ripe avocado, diced

1) Crumble sausage into a large skillet; add onion. Cook over medium heat until meat is no longer pink; drain well.

2) Add 2 cups tomatoes and picante sauce. Bring to a boil. Reduce heat; simmer, uncovered, for 20 minutes or until most of the liquid has evaporated.

3) Sprinkle tortilla chips over a 12-in. pizza pan. Top with 2 cups cheese and the sausage mixture; sprinkle with remaining cheese.

4) Bake at 350° for 8-10 minutes or until cheese is melted. Sprinkle with avocado and remaining tomatoes.

Yield: 8-10 servings.

NUTRITION FACTS: 1/2 cup nachos equals 290 calories, 22 g fat (10 g saturated fat), 42 mg cholesterol, 442 mg sodium, 12 g carbohydrate, 2 g fiber, 12 g protein.

■ *CHEESY TURKEY NACHOS:* Substitute 3/4 pound ground turkey for the bulk pork sausage.

Veggie Party Pizza
Laura Kadlec, Maiden Rock, Wisconsin

A classic appetizer such as this never goes out of style. Feel free to replace the suggested vegetables with your family's favorites.

- 2 cups all-purpose flour
- 2 teaspoons baking powder
- 1 teaspoon salt
- 2/3 cup fat-free milk

1/4 cup plus 1 tablespoon canola oil,
divided

TOPPING:

3 cups 2% cottage cheese

1 envelope ranch salad dressing
mix

1/2 cup fat-free mayonnaise

1/4 cup fat-free milk

1-1/2 cups chopped fresh broccoli

1-1/2 cups chopped fresh cauliflower

1/2 cup chopped celery

1/3 cup shredded carrot

1/4 cup chopped onion

2 cups (8 ounces) shredded
part-skim mozzarella cheese

Sliced ripe olives, drained, optional

1) For crust, combine the flour, baking powder and
salt. Add milk and 1/4 cup oil; mix well. Shape
into a ball; knead 10 times.

2) Press onto the bottom and up the sides of an
ungreased 15-in. x 10-in. x 1-in. baking pan. Prick
with fork; brush with remaining oil. Bake at 425°
for 12-14 minutes or until edges are lightly
browned. Cool.

3) In a mixing bowl, combine the cottage cheese,
ranch dressing mix, mayonnaise and milk; spread
over crust. Sprinkle with vegetables and cheese.
Garnish with olives if desired. Refrigerate until
serving.

Yield: 14 servings.

NUTRITION FACTS: 1 slice equals 234 calories, 11 g fat (3 g saturated
fat), 15 mg cholesterol, 592 mg sodium, 21 g carbohydrate, 1 g fiber,
14 g protein.

BLUE CHEESE APPETIZER PIZZA

Blue Cheese Appetizer Pizza
Kathy Stanaway, DeWitt, Michigan

Hot, savory pizza is a nice change of pace on an
appetizer buffet. Frozen bread dough speeds up
this recipe's prep time.

1 loaf (1 pound) frozen bread
dough, thawed

3 tablespoons olive oil

2 teaspoons dried basil

2 teaspoons dried oregano

1 teaspoon garlic powder

1 small red onion, thinly sliced and
separated into rings

2 plum tomatoes, chopped

1 cup (4 ounces) shredded
part-skim mozzarella cheese,
divided

3 ounces crumbled blue cheese

2 tablespoons grated Parmesan
cheese

1) Divide bread dough in half. Press each portion
onto the bottom of a 12-in. pizza pan coated with
nonstick cooking spray; build up edges slightly.
Prick dough several times with a fork. Cover and
let rise in a warm place for 30 minutes.

2) Brush dough with oil. Combine the basil, oregano
and garlic powder; sprinkle over dough.

3) Bake at 425° for 10 minutes. Arrange onion and
tomatoes over crust; sprinkle with cheeses. Bake
8-10 minutes longer or until golden brown.

Yield: 2 pizzas (10 slices each).

NUTRITION FACTS: 1 slice equals 118 calories, 5 g fat (2 g saturated
fat), 7 mg cholesterol, 228 mg sodium, 13 g carbohydrate, 1 g fiber,
5 g protein.

Caramelized Onion Tartlets

Jerri Hansen, Council Bluffs, Iowa

Cooking onions in sugar mellows their strong flavor, so even folks who don't care for onions will find these elegant tartlets irresistible.

- 2 tablespoons plus 1/2 cup butter, *divided*
- 2 large sweet onions, chopped
- 1/4 cup sugar
- 3/4 cup hot water
- 1 tablespoon beef bouillon granules
- 1 cup (4 ounces) shredded Swiss cheese
- 8 sheets phyllo dough (14 inches x 9 inches)

1) In a large skillet, melt 2 tablespoons butter over medium heat. Add onions and sugar. Cook for 15-20 minutes or until the onions are golden brown, stirring frequently.

2) Stir in water and bouillon. Bring to a boil. Reduce heat; simmer, uncovered, for 5-7 minutes or until liquid has evaporated. Remove from the heat; stir in cheese.

3) Melt remaining butter. Place one sheet of phyllo dough on a work surface; brush with butter (brush to distribute evenly). Repeat with a second sheet; brush with butter. Cut into 12 squares. (Keep remaining phyllo covered with plastic wrap and a damp towel to prevent drying.) Repeat three times, making 48 squares.

4) Press one square into a greased miniature muffin cup. Top with another square of phyllo, placing corners off center. Spoon about 1 tablespoon onion mixture into cup. Repeat with remaining phyllo squares and onion mixture. Bake at 375° for 10-15 minutes or until golden brown. Serve warm.

Yield: 2 dozen.

NUTRITION FACTS: 3 pieces equals 247 calories, 18 g fat (11 g saturated fat), 51 mg cholesterol, 521 mg sodium, 17 g carbohydrate, 1 g fiber, 6 g protein.

Holiday Appetizer Puffs

Kathy Fielder, Dallas, Texas

These are so versatile. Instead of crab, you can also use your favorite chicken or tuna salad.

- 1 cup water
- 1/2 cup butter
- 1/2 teaspoon salt
- 1 cup all-purpose flour
- 4 eggs

FILLING:

- 1 package (8 ounces) cream cheese, softened
- 1/4 cup mayonnaise
- 1 can (6 ounces) crabmeat, drained and cartilage removed

1/2 cup shredded Swiss cheese
1 tablespoon snipped chives
1 teaspoon garlic salt
1 teaspoon Worcestershire sauce
1/4 teaspoon pepper

1) In a small saucepan, bring water, butter and salt to a boil. Add flour all at once and stir until a smooth ball forms. Remove from the heat; let stand for 5 minutes.

2) Add eggs, one at a time, beating well after each addition. Continue beating until the mixture is smooth and shiny.

3) Drop by rounded teaspoonfuls 2 in. apart onto greased baking sheets. Bake at 400° for 25-30 minutes or until golden. Remove to wire racks. Immediately slit puffs to allow steam to escape.

4) When cool, split puffs open; remove tops and set aside. Discard soft dough from inside.

5) In a small mixing bowl, beat cream cheese and mayonnaise until smooth. Stir in remaining filling ingredients. Just before serving, spoon filling into puffs; replace tops.

Yield: 4 dozen.

NUTRITION FACTS: 3 puffs equals 195 calories, 16 g fat (8 g saturated fat), 98 mg cholesterol, 369 mg sodium, 7 g carbohydrate, trace fiber, 7 g protein.

Black Bean Quesadillas

Jane Epping, Iowa City, Iowa

Topped with salsa and sour cream, these crisp wedges are always a hit. You can also add chopped onion, black olives and green chilies.

2 cans (15 ounces *each*) black beans, rinsed and drained
1-2/3 cups salsa, *divided*
10 flour tortillas (8 inches)
2 cups (8 ounces) shredded Colby-Monterey Jack cheese
1/3 cup sour cream

1) In a bowl, mash the beans; add 1 cup salsa. Place five tortillas on ungreased baking sheets; spread with bean mixture. Sprinkle with cheese; top with the remaining tortillas.

2) Bake at 350° for 15-18 minutes or until crisp and heated through. Cut into wedges. Serve with sour cream and remaining salsa.

Yield: 5 servings.

NUTRITION FACTS: 1 quesadilla equals 645 calories, 22 g fat (12 g saturated fat), 51 mg cholesterol, 1,473 mg sodium, 85 g carbohydrate, 12 g fiber, 32 g protein.

CORN SALSA TOSTADAS

Corn Salsa Tostadas

Laurie Todd, Columbus, Mississippi

These south-of-the-border treats are sure to satisfy cravings for something a little spicy. The bite-size morsels are tasty, attractive and fun.

3 flour tortillas (8 inches)
3/4 cup fat-free sour cream
3 teaspoons minced fresh cilantro, *divided*
2 green onions, finely chopped
1/4 teaspoon garlic powder
3/4 cup fresh *or* frozen corn, thawed
1 plum tomato, diced
1 tablespoon chopped jalapeno pepper
2 tablespoons orange juice
1 teaspoon canola oil
1/2 teaspoon salt

1) Using a 2-in. round cookie cutter, cut 12 circles from each tortilla. Coat both sides of circles with nonstick cooking spray. Place in a single layer on a baking sheet. Bake at 400° for 4-5 minutes or until crisp. Cool.

2) In a small bowl, combine the sour cream, 1 teaspoon cilantro, onions and garlic powder; cover and refrigerate. In another bowl, combine the corn, tomato, jalapeno, orange juice, oil, salt and remaining cilantro; cover and refrigerate.

3) Just before serving, spread 1 teaspoon sour cream mixture over each tostada. Using a slotted spoon, top each with a teaspoonful of corn salsa.

Yield: 3 dozen.

Editor's Note: When cutting or seeding hot peppers, use rubber or plastic gloves to protect your hands. Avoid touching your face.

NUTRITION FACTS: 6 tostadas equals 141 calories, 3 g fat (trace saturated fat), 3 mg cholesterol, 347 mg sodium, 25 g carbohydrate, 1 g fiber, 5 g protein.

ITALIAN STUFFED MUSHROOMS

Italian Stuffed Mushrooms
Virginia Slater, West Sunbury, Pennsylvania

Every year during the holidays, I use this delicious recipe that I got from my brother. These appealing appetizers get hearty flavor from the ham, bacon and cheese. They look lovely and really curb the hunger of guests waiting for a meal.

4	bacon strips, diced
24	to 30 large fresh mushrooms
1/4	pound ground fully cooked ham
2	tablespoons minced fresh parsley
1/4	cup grated Parmesan cheese
1	cup onion and garlic salad croutons, crushed
1	cup (4 ounces) shredded mozzarella cheese
1	medium tomato, finely chopped
1-1/2	teaspoons minced fresh oregano *or* 1/2 teaspoon dried oregano

1) In a large skillet, cook the bacon over medium heat until crisp. Using a slotted spoon, remove to paper towels; drain, reserving 1 tablespoon drippings.

2) Remove mushroom stems from caps; set caps aside. Mince half the stems and discard the rest. Add minced stems to drippings; saute for 2-3 minutes. Remove from the heat and stir in remaining ingredients and reserved bacon.

3) Firmly stuff into mushroom caps. Place in a greased 15-in. x 10-in. x 1-in. baking pan. Bake at 425° for 12-15 minutes or until the mushrooms are tender.

Yield: 15 servings.

NUTRITION FACTS: 2 stuffed mushrooms equals 88 calories, 6 g fat (3 g saturated fat), 14 mg cholesterol, 217 mg sodium, 4 g carbohydrate, 1 g fiber, 5 g protein.

Nutty Stuffed Mushrooms
Mildred Eldred, Union City, Michigan

Basil, cheese and mushrooms star in these delicious treats while buttery pecans give a surprising crunch. You can also use pepperoni.

18	to 20 large fresh mushrooms
1	small onion, chopped
3	tablespoons butter
1/4	cup dry bread crumbs
1/4	cup finely chopped pecans
3	tablespoons grated Parmesan cheese
1/4	teaspoon salt
1/4	teaspoon dried basil

Dash cayenne pepper

1) Remove mushroom stems from caps; set caps aside. Finely chop stems; place in a paper towel and squeeze to remove any liquid. In a skillet, saute chopped stems and onion in butter for 5 minutes or until tender. Remove from the heat; set aside.

2) In a small bowl, combine the bread crumbs, pecans, Parmesan cheese, salt, basil and cayenne; add the stem mixture. Stuff firmly into mushroom caps. Place in a greased 15-in. x 10-in. x 1-in. baking pan.

3) Bake, uncovered, at 400° for 15-18 minutes or until tender. Serve warm.

Yield: 18-20 servings.

NUTRITION FACTS: 1 stuffed mushroom equals 41 calories, 3 g fat (1 g saturated fat), 5 mg cholesterol, 73 mg sodium, 2 g carbohydrate, trace fiber, 1 g protein.

PREPARING MUSHROOMS FOR STUFFING

1) Hold the mushroom cap in one hand and grab the stem with the other hand. Twist to snap off the stem; place caps on a greased baking sheet. Mince or finely chop stems.

2) Spoon chopped stems onto paper towel and proceed with recipe as directed.

■ *PEPPERONI STUFFED MUSHROOMS:* Prepare mushroom caps as directed. Omit pecans, salt, basil and pepper. Add 1 minced garlic clove to chopped stems and onion when sauteing. Stir into mushroom mixture bread crumbs, Parmesan cheese, 3 ounces finely chopped pepperoni, 1 tablespoon minced parsley and 1/8 teaspoon pepper. Bake at 375° for 15-20 minutes or until tender. Serve warm.

CANADIAN BACON POTATO SKINS

Canadian Bacon Potato Skins
Mary Plummer, De Soto, Kansas

Need a fun appetizer or a tasty side dish? These potato skins are sure to fill the bill! Potato shells are topped with Canadian bacon, chopped tomato and reduced-fat cheese.

>   6   large baking potatoes
>   (12 ounces *each*)
>   2   teaspoons canola oil
> 1/8   teaspoon hot pepper sauce
>   1   teaspoon chili powder
>   1   medium tomato, seeded and
>   finely chopped
> 2/3   cup chopped Canadian bacon
>   2   tablespoons finely chopped
>   green onion
>   1   cup (4 ounces) shredded
>   reduced-fat cheddar cheese
> 1/2   cup reduced-fat sour cream

1) Place potatoes on a microwave-safe plate; prick with a fork. Microwave, uncovered, on high for

14-17 minutes or until tender but firm, turning once. Let stand for 5 minutes. Cut each potato in half lengthwise. Scoop out pulp, leaving a 1/4-in. shell (discard pulp or save for another use).

2) Combine oil and hot pepper sauce; brush over potato shells. Sprinkle with chili powder. Cut each potato shell in half lengthwise. Place on baking sheets coated with nonstick cooking spray. Sprinkle with the tomato, bacon, onion and cheese.

3) Bake at 450° for 12-14 minutes or until heated through and cheese is melted. Serve with sour cream.

   Yield: 8 servings.

   NUTRITION FACTS: 3 potato skins equals 211 calories, 7 g fat (4 g saturated fat), 21 mg cholesterol, 309 mg sodium, 29 g carbohydrate, 5 g fiber, 11 g protein.

Ham 'n' Cheese Quiches
Virginia Abraham, Vicksburg, Mississippi

When I need festive finger food, I reach for the recipe for these quiches featuring cheese in both the crust and the filling.

> 1/2   cup cold butter
>   1   jar (5 ounces) process sharp
>   cheese spread
>   1   cup all-purpose flour
>   2   tablespoons water

FILLING:

>   1   egg
> 1/2   cup milk
> 1/4   teaspoon salt
> 1/2   cup finely chopped fully cooked
>   ham
> 1/2   cup shredded Monterey Jack
>   cheese

1) In a small bowl, cut butter and cheese spread into flour until well blended. Add water and toss with a fork until a ball forms. Refrigerate for 1 hour.

2) Press tablespoonfuls onto the bottom and up the sides of greased miniature muffin cups. In a bowl, beat egg, milk and salt. Stir in ham and cheese. Spoon a rounded teaspoonful into each shell.

3) Bake at 350° for 30 minutes or until golden brown. Let stand for 5 minutes before serving.

   Yield: 2 dozen.

   NUTRITION FACTS: 3 quiches equals 265 calories, 19 g fat (12 g saturated fat), 81 mg cholesterol, 645 mg sodium, 15 g carbohydrate, trace fiber, 8 g protein.

Feta Bruschetta

Stacey Rinehart, Eugene, Oregon

You won't believe the compliments you'll receive when you greet guests with these wonderful appetizers. Each crispy bite offers the savory tastes of feta cheese, tomatoes, basil and garlic.

- 1/4 cup butter, melted
- 1/4 cup olive oil
- 10 slices French bread (1 inch thick)
- 1 package (4 ounces) crumbled feta cheese
- 2 to 3 garlic cloves, minced
- 1 tablespoon minced fresh basil *or* 1 teaspoon dried basil
- 1 large tomato, seeded and chopped

1) In a small bowl, combine butter and oil; brush onto both sides of bread. Place on a baking sheet. Bake at 350° for 8-10 minutes or until lightly browned on top.

2) Combine the feta cheese, garlic and basil; sprinkle over toast. Top with tomato. Bake 8-10 minutes longer or until heated through. Serve warm.

Yield: 10 appetizers.

NUTRITION FACTS: 1 piece equals 296 calories, 14 g fat (5 g saturated fat), 18 mg cholesterol, 547 mg sodium, 35 g carbohydrate, 3 g fiber, 8 g protein.

PEPPER POPPERS

Pepper Poppers

Lisa Byington, Port Crane, New York

The creamy filling in these popular treats helps mellow the zippy jalapenos. My husband is always hinting that I should prepare a batch.

- 1 package (8 ounces) cream cheese, softened
- 1 cup (4 ounces) shredded sharp cheddar cheese
- 1 cup (4 ounces) shredded Monterey Jack cheese

- 6 bacon strips, cooked and crumbled
- 1/4 teaspoon salt
- 1/4 teaspoon garlic powder
- 1/4 teaspoon chili powder
- 1 pound fresh jalapenos, halved lengthwise and seeded
- 1/2 cup dry bread crumbs

Sour cream, onion dip *or* ranch salad dressing

1) In a large mixing bowl, combine the cheeses, bacon and seasonings; mix well. Spoon about 2 tablespoonfuls into each pepper half. Roll in bread crumbs.

2) Place in a greased 15-in. x 10-in. x 1-in. baking pan. Bake, uncovered, at 300° for 20 minutes for spicy flavor, 30 minutes for medium and 40 minutes for mild. Serve with sour cream, dip or dressing.

Yield: about 2 dozen.

Editor's Note: When cutting or seeding hot peppers, use rubber or plastic gloves to protect your hands. Avoid touching your face.

NUTRITION FACTS: 3 poppers (calculated without sour cream, onion dip or ranch salad dressing) equals 273 calories, 21 g fat (13 g saturated fat), 63 mg cholesterol, 454 mg sodium, 10 g carbohydrate, 2 g fiber, 12 g protein.

Marinated Olives

Marguerite Shaeffer, Sewell, New Jersey

These olives are nice to have for get-togethers because they're simple to make and add a little zest to the buffet table offerings.

- 2 cups large stuffed olives, drained
- 1 cup pitted kalamata olives, drained
- 1 cup pitted medium ripe olives, drained
- 1/4 cup olive oil
- 2 tablespoons lemon juice
- 1 tablespoon minced fresh thyme *or* 1 teaspoon dried thyme
- 2 teaspoons minced fresh rosemary *or* 1/2 teaspoon dried rosemary, crushed
- 2 teaspoons grated lemon peel
- 4 garlic cloves, slivered

Pepper to taste

1) Place olives in a bowl. Combine the remaining ingredients; pour over olives and stir.

2) Cover and refrigerate for 1-2 days before serving, stirring several times each day. Olives may be refrigerated for 2 weeks. Serve with a slotted spoon.

Yield: 4 cups.

NUTRITION FACTS: 1/4 cup equals 98 calories, 10 g fat (1 g saturated fat), 0 cholesterol, 572 mg sodium, 3 g carbohydrate, trace fiber, trace protein.

MARINATED MOZZARELLA CUBES

Marinated Mozzarella Cubes
Arline Roggenbuck, Shawano, Wisconsin

Jars of these marinated cheese cubes make wonderful gifts any time of the year...if you can bear to part with them!

- 1 **pound mozzarella cheese, cut into 1-inch cubes**
- 1 **jar (7 ounces) roasted red peppers, drained and cut into bite-size pieces**
- 6 **fresh thyme sprigs**
- 2 **garlic cloves, minced**
- 1-1/4 **cups olive oil**
- 2 **tablespoons minced fresh rosemary**
- 2 **teaspoons Italian seasoning**
- 1/4 **teaspoon crushed red pepper flakes**

Bread *or* crackers

1) In a quart jar with a tight-fitting lid, layer a third of the cheese, peppers, thyme and garlic. Repeat layers twice.

2) In a small bowl, combine the oil, rosemary, Italian seasoning and pepper flakes; mix well. Pour into jar; seal and turn upside down.

3) Refrigerate overnight, turning several times. Serve with bread or crackers.

Yield: 12-16 servings.

NUTRITION FACTS: 1 serving (calculated without bread or crackers) equals 235 calories, 23 g fat (6 g saturated fat), 22 mg cholesterol, 151 mg sodium, 2 g carbohydrate, trace fiber, 6 g protein.

Turkey Tortilla Roll-Ups
Darlene Brenden, Salem, Oregon

You won't have to take a long time to make these tasty, hearty snacks. Cooked chicken or cold cuts also work well.

- 3/4 **cup sour cream**
- 6 **flour tortillas (8 inches)**
- 1-1/2 **cups diced cooked turkey**
- 1 **cup (4 ounces) finely shredded cheddar cheese**
- 1 **cup shredded lettuce**
- 1/2 **cup chopped ripe olives**
- 1/2 **cup chunky salsa**

1) Spread 2 tablespoons sour cream over each tortilla. Top with the turkey, cheese, lettuce, olives and salsa.

2) Roll up each tortilla tightly; wrap in plastic wrap. Refrigerate until serving. Unwrap and cut each roll-up into 6 pieces.

Yield: 12 servings.

NUTRITION FACTS: 3 pieces equals 177 calories, 8 g fat (4 g saturated fat), 33 mg cholesterol, 297 mg sodium, 15 g carbohydrate, 1 g fiber, 11 g protein.

Cayenne Pretzels
Gayle Zebo, Warren, Pennsylvania

These easy-to-coat, well-seasoned pretzels were a huge hit at my daughter's graduation party. The longer they sit, the spicier they get!

- 1 **cup vegetable oil**
- 1 **envelope ranch salad dressing mix**
- 1 **teaspoon garlic salt**
- 1 **teaspoon cayenne pepper**
- 2 **packages (10 ounces *each*) pretzel sticks**

1) In a small bowl, combine the oil, dressing mix, garlic salt and cayenne. Divide pretzels between two ungreased 15-in. x 10-in. x 1-in. baking pans. Pour oil mixture over pretzels; stir to coat.

2) Bake at 200° for 1-1/4 to 1-1/2 hours or until golden brown, stirring occasionally. Cool completely. Store in an airtight container.

Yield: 3-1/2 quarts.

NUTRITION FACTS: 2 ounces equals 424 calories, 24 g fat (3 g saturated fat), 0 cholesterol, 1,254 mg sodium, 48 g carbohydrate, 2 g fiber, 6 g protein.

Spiced Pecans

Miriam Herschberger, Holmesville, Ohio

Toasting nuts intensifies their flavor, and the sweet, sugar-cinnamon coating on these pecans is irresistible.

  1   egg white
  1   teaspoon cold water
  4   cups (about 1 pound) pecan halves
1/2   cup sugar
1/2   teaspoon ground cinnamon
1/4   teaspoon salt

1) In a small mixing bowl, beat egg white lightly. Add water; beat until frothy but not stiff. Add pecans; stir until well coated.

2) Combine the sugar, cinnamon and salt. Sprinkle over pecans; toss to mix. Spread in a greased 15-in. x 10-in. x 1-in. baking pan. Bake at 250° for 1 hour, stirring occasionally.

Yield: 12 servings.

NUTRITION FACTS: 1/3 cup equals 283 calories, 26 g fat (2 g saturated fat), 0 cholesterol, 54 mg sodium, 13 g carbohydrate, 4 g fiber, 4 g protein.

PIZZA POPCORN

Pizza Popcorn

Sheri Warner, Louisville, Nebraska

Looking for something different for a bake sale? Whip up this fun popcorn snack. It's lightly spiced with pizza seasonings and very munchable.

2-1/2   quarts popped popcorn
  1/3   cup butter
  1/4   cup grated Parmesan cheese
  1/2   teaspoon garlic salt
  1/2   teaspoon dried oregano
  1/2   teaspoon dried basil

1/4   teaspoon onion powder
1/4   teaspoon salt

1) Place popcorn in an ungreased 13-in. x 9-in. x 2-in. baking pan. Melt butter in a small saucepan; add remaining ingredients.

2) Pour over the popcorn and mix well. Bake, uncovered, at 350° for 15 minutes.

Yield: 2-1/2 quarts.

NUTRITION FACTS: 1 cup equals 118 calories, 10 g fat (5 g saturated fat), 18 mg cholesterol, 346 mg sodium, 7 g carbohydrate, 1 g fiber, 2 g protein.

ZIPPIER MICROWAVE POPCORN

You can spice up regular microwave popcorn by sprinkling in a bit of cayenne pepper. Then refold the bag and shake well to distribute the flavor.

Spicy Snack Mix

Betty Sitzman, Wary, Colorado

This is a tasty snack mix that you can make more or less spicy to suit your tastes by adjusting the amount of hot pepper sauce.

1/2   cup butter
  1   tablespoon seasoned salt
  1   tablespoon Worcestershire sauce
1/2   to 1 teaspoon garlic powder
1/2   to 1 teaspoon hot pepper sauce
  5   cups Wheat Chex cereal
  7   cups Rice Chex cereal
  6   cups Cheerios cereal
  1   can (12 ounces) mixed nuts

1) In a small saucepan, melt the butter. Add the seasoned salt, Worcestershire sauce, garlic powder and hot pepper sauce; set aside.

2) In a large mixing bowl, combine cereal and nuts; mix well. Stir in butter mixture; stir until well blended.

3) Spread into two greased 15-in. x 10-in. x 1-in. baking pans. Bake at 250° for 1 hour, stirring every 15 minutes.

Yield: 22 cups.

NUTRITION FACTS: 1/2 cup equals 117 calories, 7 g fat (2 g saturated fat), 6 mg cholesterol, 314 mg sodium, 12 g carbohydrate, 2 g fiber, 3 g protein.

Garnishes for Beverages

Part of the enjoyment of drinking a cool, refreshing beverage is its presentation. Add a simple garnish, and a delicious drink becomes a festive drink. Here are no-fuss suggestions to give beverages a little pizzazz.

Place fresh berries, such as raspberries or strawberries, and a fresh mint leaf in ice cube trays and fill partway with water. Freeze and use as ice cubes.

For a more delicate look, use flowers, such as pansies, rose petals or dianthus, for ice cubes. If using flowers, make sure to properly identify flowers before picking. Double-check that they're edible and have not been treated with chemicals.

Skewer various fruits with a bamboo or reusable picks. Some suggestions are:

- Place a slice of star fruit on the end of a skewer and place in the drink.

- Cut 3/4-inch-thick slices of seedless watermelon, cantaloupe and honeydew, then cut out the melon with a small, heart-shaped cookie or appetizer cutter. Thread several pieces of melon or one of each melon on a skewer.

- Take a slice of a citrus fruit, orange, lemon or lime and make a cut from the center to one end. Twist the slice and thread onto a skewer. If desired, thread strawberries or small pieces of fruit between each turn of the citrus fruit slice.

- Using a vegetable peeler, peel wide strips of citrus fruit peel. With a sharp knife, trim the long edges so they are smooth. Weave peel accordion-style onto skewers. If desired, add a piece of fruit or mint to one end.

Other Simple Garnishes

To Decorate a Rim of a Glass

Use a wedge of pineapple or citrus fruit slice, a slice of strawberry or a whole strawberry, a curl of citrus peel.

To Make a Citrus Curl

Use a citrus stripper to remove a long continuous strip of peel. Tightly wind the strip around a straw and secure ends with waterproof tape; let stand for 20 minutes. The longer it stands, the longer the strip will hold its shape. To use, remove tape and slip off straw or unwind from the straw.

For a Sugar- or Salt-Coated Rim

Dip rim of glass in water, then dip in coarse sugar or salt. Or use colored sugar to match your party theme.

For a Cold Shake or Ice Coffee

Melt semisweet chocolate chips and place in a small resealable plastic bag. Cut off a small piece of the corner of the bag and pipe a design on waxed paper (the design should not be too thin). Let stand until set and gently peel off the paper. Top your shake or coffee with whipped cream and insert the chocolate garnish. Or hang the garnish off the side of the glass.

For a Frosted Glass

Place in the freezer 15-30 minutes before using. Fill with ice and a cold beverage.

Citrus Punch

Dianne Conway, London, Ontario

Zesty, fruity flavors combine in this refreshing punch that's easy to double for larger groups.

  2 **cups pineapple juice**
  2 **cups orange juice**
  1 **cup grapefruit juice**
  1 **cup lemonade**
  2 **cups ginger ale, chilled**

1) In a large pitcher, combine the fruit juices and lemonade. Refrigerate until chilled.

2) Just before serving, pour into a punch bowl. Slowly add ginger ale.

Yield: 12-16 servings (2 quarts).

NUTRITION FACTS: 1 cup equals 109 calories, trace fat (trace saturated fat), 0 cholesterol, 7 mg sodium, 27 g carbohydrate, trace fiber, 1 g protein.

CHAMPAGNE PARTY PUNCH, SANGRIA, FRESH LIME MARGARITA

- *FROZEN LIME MARGARITAS:* Reduce lemon and lime juices to 2 tablespoons *each.* Increase the superfine sugar to 1/4 cup and the crushed ice to 4 cups. Add 3/4 cup limeade concentrate. Prepare glasses as directed. In a blender, combine the tequila, Triple Sec, lime juice, lemon juice, limeade concentrate, superfine sugar and ice; cover and process until smooth.

- *FROZEN STRAWBERRY MARGARITAS:* Follow directions for Frozen Lime Margaritas, except reduce ice to 2 cups and add 2 cups frozen unsweetened strawberries.

Sangria
Taste of Home Test Kitchen

This is a great make-ahead beverage because it allows time for the flavors to blend together.

- 1   **bottle (750 ml) Zinfandel *or* other fruity red wine**
- 3/4 **cup orange juice**
- 1/3 **cup unsweetened pineapple juice**
- 1/4 **cup superfine sugar**
- 1   **medium orange, sliced**
- 1   **medium lemon, sliced**
- 1   **medium lime, cut into wedges**

1) In a pitcher, combine the wine, orange juice, pineapple juice and sugar; stir until sugar is dissolved.

2) Add fruit; press lightly with a wooden spoon.

3) Refrigerate for 2-4 hours. Serve over ice.

Yield: 5 servings.

NUTRITION FACTS: 3/4 cup equals 186 calories, trace fat (trace saturated fat), 0 cholesterol, 8 mg sodium, 23 g carbohydrate, 1 g fiber, 1 g protein.

NO-FUSS ICE BOWL

Fill a large glass or plastic serving bowl with ice cubes or crushed ice. Fill a smaller bowl with dip and set on top of the ice. Replace the ice as it melts.

Champagne Party Punch
Taste of Home Test Kitchen

To make this punch even more festive, float an ice ring in the punch.

- 1 **cup sugar**
- 1 **cup water**
- 2 **cups unsweetened apple juice**
- 2 **cups unsweetened pineapple juice**

Fresh Lime Margaritas
Taste of Home Test Kitchen

This basic margarita recipe is easy to modify to your tastes. Try it frozen or with strawberries!

- 4 **lime wedges**
- 1 **tablespoon kosher salt**
- 1/2 **cup gold tequila**
- 1/4 **cup Triple Sec**
- 1/4 **cup lime juice**
- 1/4 **cup lemon juice**
- 2 **tablespoons superfine sugar**
- 1-1/3 **cups crushed ice**

1) Using lime wedges, moisten rim of four glasses. Holding each glass upside down, dip rim into salt; set aside.

2) In a pitcher, combine the tequila, Triple Sec, lime juice, lemon juice and sugar; stir until sugar is dissolved. Serve in prepared glasses over ice.

Yield: 4 servings.

NUTRITION FACTS: 1/3 cup equals 149 calories, trace fat (trace saturated fat), 0 cholesterol, 1,413 mg sodium, 16 g carbohydrate, trace fiber, trace protein.

- 1/2 cup lemon juice
- 1/3 cup frozen orange juice concentrate, thawed
- 1/4 cup lime juice
- 2 cups ice cubes
- 1 quart ginger ale, chilled
- 1 bottle (750 ml) champagne, chilled

1) In a large pitcher, combine the sugar and water; stir until sugar is dissolved. Add the apple juice, pineapple juice, lemon juice, orange juice concentrate and lime juice. Refrigerate until serving.

2) Just before serving, pour into a punch bowl and add ice cubes. Slowly add the ginger ale and champagne.

Yield: 16-18 servings (3-1/2 quarts).

NUTRITION FACTS: 3/4 cup equals 129 calories, trace fat (trace saturated fat), 0 cholesterol, 8 mg sodium, 26 g carbohydrate, trace fiber, trace protein.

MAKING AN ICE RING

1) Fill a ring mold halfway with water. Freeze until solid. Top with your choice of fruit. Add lemon leaves if desired. Add enough water to almost cover fruit. Freeze until solid.

2) Unmold by wrapping the bottom of the mold with a hot, damp dishcloth. Turn out onto a baking sheet; place in punch bowl fruit side up.

Holiday Eggnog
Taste of Home Test Kitchen

For a nice, rich and creamy treat, try this eggnog recipe. You can serve it plain or add rum for adult holiday guests.

- 6 eggs
- 3/4 cup sugar
- 1/4 teaspoon salt
- 4 cups milk, *divided*
- 1 tablespoon vanilla extract

- 1/2 teaspoon ground nutmeg
- 1 cup heavy whipping cream

Additional whipped cream and ground nutmeg, optional

1) In a large heavy saucepan, whisk together the eggs, sugar and salt. Gradually add 2 cups milk. Cook over low heat, stirring constantly, until a thermometer reads 160°, about 25 minutes.

2) Pour into a large bowl; stir in the vanilla, nutmeg and remaining milk. Place the bowl in an ice-water bath; stir frequently until mixture is cool. If mixture separates, process in a blender until smooth. Cover and refrigerate for at least 3 hours.

3) When ready to serve, in a small mixing bowl, beat cream on high speed until soft peaks form; whisk gently into cooled mixture. Pour into a chilled punch bowl. If desired, top with dollops of whipped cream and sprinkle with nutmeg.

Yield: 6 servings (about 4 cups).

NUTRITION FACTS: 3/4 cup equals 413 calories, 25 g fat (14 g saturated fat), 289 mg cholesterol, 256 mg sodium, 34 g carbohydrate, 0 fiber, 12 g protein.

■ *SPIKED HOLIDAY EGGNOG:* Reduce milk to 3-1/4 cups. Heat 2 cups milk with eggs, sugar and salt. Add 1-1/4 cups milk with vanilla and nutmeg. After mixture has cooled in ice bath, stir in 3/4 cup rum, brandy or bourbon. Proceed as recipe directs.

Old-Fashioned Chocolate Malted Milk
Taste of Home Test Kitchen

With a few ingredients, you can make this old-fashioned favorite just like the old malt shops used to have!

- 2 cups vanilla ice cream
- 2/3 cup cold milk
- 2 tablespoons malted milk powder
- 2 tablespoons chocolate syrup
- 2 to 4 tablespoons whipped cream

1) In a blender, combine the ice cream, milk, malted milk powder and chocolate syrup; cover and process until smooth.

2) Pour into chilled glasses. Top with a dollop of whipped cream; serve immediately.

Yield: 2 servings.

NUTRITION FACTS: 1-1/3 cup equals 430 calories, 19 g fat (12 g saturated fat), 75 mg cholesterol, 217 mg sodium, 59 g carbohydrate, 1 g fiber, 9 g protein.

Strawberry Cooler

Judy Robertson, Russell Springs, Kentucky

This refreshing beverage is easy to double. Just make two batches ahead of time and add ginger ale and ice when you're ready for more!

3 cups water
5 cups sliced fresh strawberries
3/4 to 1 cup sugar
1/4 cup lemon juice
2 teaspoons grated lemon peel
1 cup ginger ale
Crushed ice
Whole strawberries, optional

1) In a blender, process the water, strawberries, sugar, lemon juice and peel in batches until smooth. Strain the berry seeds if desired.

2) Pour into a pitcher; stir in the ginger ale. Serve over ice. Garnish with whole berries if desired.

Yield: 8 servings.

NUTRITION FACTS: 1 cup equals 116 calories, trace fat (trace saturated fat), 0 cholesterol, 3 mg sodium, 29 g carbohydrate, 2 g fiber, 1 g protein.

SPICY TOMATO JUICE

Spicy Tomato Juice

Susan Zambito, New Orleans, Louisiana

A few ingredients make this spicy beverage ideal for a brunch.

1 can (11-1/2 ounces) V8 juice *or* tomato juice, chilled
1/4 cup beef broth
1/4 teaspoon pepper
1/8 teaspoon celery salt
1/8 teaspoon Worcestershire sauce
Dash hot pepper sauce, optional
Celery sticks, optional

1) In a small pitcher, combine first six ingredients. Serve over ice with celery sticks if desired.

Yield: 2 servings.

NUTRITION FACTS: 1 cup equals 40 calories, trace fat (trace saturated fat), 0 cholesterol, 644 mg sodium, 8 g carbohydrate, 1 g fiber, 1 g protein.

■ *SPIKED SPICY TOMATO JUICE:* Add 1/4 cup vodka to the juice mixture.

Raspberry Refresher

Doreen Patterson
Qualicum Beach, British Columbia

This recipe explodes with raspberry flavor! It's a wonderful summertime treat.

8 cups fresh *or* frozen raspberries, thawed
1-1/2 cups sugar
2/3 cup cider vinegar
2-1/2 cups cold water, *divided*
2 liters ginger ale, chilled

1) In a large saucepan, crush the berries. Stir in sugar, vinegar and 1/2 cup water. Bring to a boil; reduce heat. Simmer, uncovered, for 20 minutes. Strain to remove seeds; refrigerate.

2) Just before serving, stir in ginger ale and remaining water. Serve over ice.

Yield: 14 servings (about 3-1/2 quarts).

NUTRITION FACTS: 1 cup equals 169 calories, trace fat (trace saturated fat), 0 cholesterol, 11 mg sodium, 43 g carbohydrate, 5 g fiber, 1 g protein.

Apricot Peach Smoothies

DeAnn Alleva, Hudson, Wisconsin

The mellow mingling of peach, banana and apricot flavors makes this refreshing smoothie so soothing. A spark of lemon adds a little tang but honey keeps it on the lightly sweet side.

1 can (5-1/2 ounces) apricot nectar
1 medium ripe banana, frozen and cut into chunks
1 cup (8 ounces) fat-free vanilla yogurt
2 cups sliced fresh *or* frozen unsweetened peaches
1 tablespoon lemon juice
1 tablespoon honey
1 teaspoon grated lemon peel
6 ice cubes

1) In a blender or food processor, combine all of the ingredients. Cover and process until smooth. Pour into glasses; serve immediately.

Yield: 4 servings.

NUTRITION FACTS: 1 cup equals 160 calories, trace fat (0 saturated fat), 2 mg cholesterol, 35 mg sodium, 37 g carbohydrate, 3 g fiber, 4 g protein.

■ *RASPBERRY CREAM SMOOTHIES:* In a blender or food processor, combine 1 cup orange juice, 1 cup raspberry yogurt, 1 cup frozen vanilla yogurt, 1/2 cup frozen banana chunks, 1-1/2 cups frozen raspberries and 1 teaspoon vanilla extract. Cover and process until smooth.

■ *STRAWBERRY SMOOTHIES:* In a blender or food processor, combine 1 cup milk, 1 cup strawberry yogurt, 1 pint vanilla ice cream, 1 quartered medium banana, 1/2 cup frozen unsweetened strawberries and 1 tablespoon honey. Cover and process until smooth.

Springtime Lime Slushy
Joyce Minge-Johns, Jacksonville, Florida

For more fun variations, try using your favorite gelatin and sherbet flavors.

  2   packages (3 ounces *each*) lime gelatin
  2   cups boiling water
  2   cups cold water
  2   quarts lime sherbet
  3   cups ginger ale, chilled

1) In a freezer container, dissolve gelatin in boiling water. Stir in the cold water and sherbet until combined. Freeze for 4 hours or until set.

2) Remove from the freezer 45 minutes before serving. For each serving, place 1 cup of slush mixture in a glass; add about 1/3 cup ginger ale.

Yield: 8 servings.

NUTRITION FACTS: 1 cup equals 313 calories, 3 g fat (2 g saturated fat), 9 mg cholesterol, 123 mg sodium, 71 g carbohydrate, 0 fiber, 4 g protein.

Old-Fashioned Strawberry Soda
Ginger Hubbard, Anderson, Missouri

Strawberries and ice cream blend together in this creamy favorite. Adding ginger ale gives it a fun, bubbly twist.

  1   cup milk
  1/2   cup fresh *or* frozen strawberries
  1/2   cup vanilla ice cream, softened
  2   tablespoons sugar
  2   to 3 drops red food coloring, optional
  1   cup ginger ale, chilled

1) In a blender container, combine the milk, strawberries, ice cream, sugar and food coloring if desired; cover and process until smooth.

2) Pour into two tall glasses. Add ginger ale and serve immediately.

Yield: 2 servings.

NUTRITION FACTS: 1 cup equals 242 calories, 8 g fat (5 g saturated fat), 31 mg cholesterol, 95 mg sodium, 39 g carbohydrate, 1 g fiber, 5 g protein.

Homemade Lemonade
Becky Baird, Salt Lake City, Utah

This old-fashioned thirst quencher gets a little fizz from club soda, creating a refreshing, sweet-tart beverage.

  3   cups sugar
  2   cups water
  1   cup lemon peel strips (about 6 lemons)
  3   cups lemon juice (about 14 lemons)
  1   bottle (1 liter) club soda, chilled

1) In a large saucepan, heat sugar and water over medium heat until sugar is dissolved, stirring frequently. Stir in lemon strips. Bring to a boil. Reduce heat; simmer, uncovered, for 5 minutes.

2) Remove from the heat. Cool slightly. Stir in lemon juice; cover and refrigerate until chilled. Discard lemon strips. Pour mixture into a pitcher and gradually stir in club soda.

Yield: 10 cups.

NUTRITION FACTS: 1 cup equals 251 calories, 0 fat (0 saturated fat), 0 cholesterol, 22 mg sodium, 66 g carbohydrate, trace fiber, trace protein.

■ *ORANGE LEMONADE:* Heat 1-3/4 cups sugar with 2-1/2 cups water as directed. Cool sugar syrup. Add 1-1/2 cups *each* lemon and orange juices, and 2 tablespoons *each* grated lemon and orange peels. Strain lemonade mixture and refrigerate until chilled. For each serving, fill a glass with 1/2 cup of lemonade mixture and 1/2 cup of chilled water or club soda. Add ice and serve.

LIQUEFYING ICE IN A BLENDER

Chill and thicken beverages with ice by placing all ingredients except ice in blender. Cover and process on high until blended. With the motor running, remove feeder cap in the center of cover and drop in one ice cube at a time. Continue until all the ice is liquefied or until the beverage is as thick as desired.

SPICE COFFEE

Coffee

A good cup of coffee starts with a clean pot, fresh cold water and fresh coffee. Coffee manufacturers will generally recommend between 1 to 2 tablespoons ground coffee per 3/4 cup (6 ounces) of water; check the package for the recommendation of the brand you are using. If you are grinding the beans, only grind enough for what you are planning to use.

When serving coffee at a party, use insulated carafes to keep the coffee warm for up to 2 hours. Offer guests both decaf and regular. Choose a quality basic coffee and allow your guests the option to flavor their own mugs with orange twist, flavored liqueurs or syrups such as hazelnut.

Store unopened containers of ground, instant and freeze-dried coffee at room temperature for up to a year. Once the package is open, it loses its flavor quickly. Store opened packages in the refrigerator for up to 3 weeks. If there is more ground coffee than you would use in 3 weeks, divide the remaining ground coffee into weekly portions and store in the freezer in airtight, freezerproof containers.

Coffee beans should be used within 3 weeks. Store beans in the freezer in airtight, freezerproof containers for up to 1 year. Thaw beans before grinding.

Spice Coffee
Joanne Holt, Bowling Green, Ohio

Even those who usually don't drink coffee will find this special blend with a hint of chocolate appealing. I keep a big batch simmering at a brunch or open house.

- 8 cups brewed coffee
- 1/3 cup sugar
- 1/4 cup chocolate syrup
- 1/2 teaspoon anise extract
- 4 cinnamon sticks (3 inches)

1-1/2 teaspoons whole cloves
Additional cinnamon sticks, optional

1) In a 3-qt. slow cooker, combine the coffee, sugar, chocolate syrup and anise extract.

2) Place cinnamon sticks and cloves in a double thickness of cheesecloth; bring up corners of cloth and tie with string to form a bag. Add to slow cooker. Cover and cook on low for 2-3 hours.

3) Discard spice bag. Ladle coffee into mugs; garnish each with a cinnamon stick if desired.

Yield: 8 cups.

NUTRITION FACTS: 1 cup equals 64 calories, trace fat (trace saturated fat), 0 cholesterol, 10 mg sodium, 15 g carbohydrate, trace fiber, trace protein.

Hot Ginger Coffee
Audrey Thibodeau, Mesa, Arizona

This is wonderful after skiing or sledding. Try the crystallized ginger in baked goods or over ice cream.

- 6 tablespoons ground coffee (not instant)
- 1 tablespoon grated orange peel
- 1 tablespoon chopped crystallized *or* candied ginger
- 1/2 teaspoon ground cinnamon
- 6 cups cold water

Whipped cream, cinnamon sticks *and/or* additional orange peel, optional

1) Combine the coffee, orange peel, ginger and cinnamon; pour mixture into a coffee filter. Brew according to manufacturer's directions using the 6 cups cold water.

2) Pour into mugs; garnish with whipped cream, cinnamon sticks and orange peel if desired.

Yield: 6 servings.

Editor's Note: Look for crystallized or candied ginger in the spice or baking section of your grocery store.

NUTRITION FACTS: 1 cup equals 22 calories, trace fat (trace saturated fat), 0 cholesterol, 3 mg sodium, 5 g carbohydrate, trace fiber, 1 g protein.

Iced Coffee
Jenny Reece, Lowry, Minnesota

When I first tried iced coffee, I didn't think I'd like it. But I created this fast-to-fix version, and it's a refreshing alternative to hot coffee.

- 4 teaspoons instant coffee granules
- 1 cup boiling water

Artificial sweetener equivalent to 4
teaspoons sugar, optional
- 1 cup fat-free milk
- 4 teaspoons chocolate syrup
- 1/8 teaspoon vanilla extract

Ice cubes

1) In a small bowl, dissolve coffee in water. Add sweetener if desired.

2) Stir in the milk, chocolate syrup and vanilla; mix well. Serve over ice.

Yield: 2 servings.

NUTRITION FACTS: 1 cup equals 79 calories, 1 g fat (0 saturated fat), 2 mg cholesterol, 76 mg sodium, 15 g carbohydrate, 0 fiber, 5 g protein.

Tea

Tea is available in loose leaves or tea bags and in a variety of types—black, green and oolong—and blends. A good cup of tea starts with fresh cold water and your favorite tea blend.

For tea bags, bring water to a rolling boil and pour over the tea bag in a cup or small pot and let steep (stand) for 3 to 5 minutes depending on the blend of tea. Remove and discard the tea bag after steeping so the tea does not become bitter.

For loose leaf tea, warm the tea pot with warm water; add round 1 teaspoon of tea leaves per each 6-ounce cup. Pour boiling water over tea leaves and steep. Again, it is best if leaves are removed and discarded or the tea is strained and poured into another pot.

If stored properly, tea will stay fresh from 1-1/2 to 2 years. Moisture, temperature, light and odors will affect the quality of the tea. So, it is best to store tea in an airtight container that keeps light out. Keep the container in a cool dry place. And, store different types of teas separately to prevent them from mingling their flavors.

Chai

Terese Block, Waukesha, Wisconsin

Chai (rhymes with "pie") is a spiced milk tea that's becoming more popular. This recipe is just as tasty as any coffeehouse chai I've tried.

- 2 cups water
- 2 individual tea bags
- 1 cinnamon stick
- 6 cardamom seeds, crushed
- 1 whole clove
- 1/4 teaspoon ground ginger
- 2-1/2 cups milk
- 1/3 cup sugar

Sweetened whipped cream, ground cinnamon and cinnamon sticks, optional

1) In a small saucepan, combine the first six ingredients. Bring to a boil. Reduce heat; cover and simmer for 5 minutes.

2) Stir in milk. Return to a boil; boil for 1 minute, then strain. Stir in sugar until dissolved. Top with whipped cream and garnish with a cinnamon stick if desired.

Yield: 4 servings.

NUTRITION FACTS: 1 cup equals 159 calories, 5 g fat (3 g saturated fat), 21 mg cholesterol, 75 mg sodium, 24 g carbohydrate, trace fiber, 5 g protein.

Summertime Fruit Tea

Rosalee Dixon, Sardis, Mississippi

Pineapple-orange juice gives ordinary iced tea a refreshing citrus flavor.

- 12 cups water, *divided*
- 1-1/2 cups sugar
- 9 individual tea bags
- 1 can (12 ounces) frozen lemonade concentrate, thawed
- 1 can (12 ounces) frozen pineapple-orange juice concentrate, thawed

1) In a Dutch oven, bring 4 cups water to a boil. Stir in sugar until dissolved. Remove from the heat; add tea bags.

2) Steep for 5-8 minutes. Discard tea bags. Stir in juice concentrates and remaining water. Serve over ice.

Yield: 3-1/2 quarts.

NUTRITION FACTS: 1 cup equals 173 calories, trace fat (trace saturated fat), 0 cholesterol, 15 mg sodium, 44 g carbohydrate, trace fiber, trace protein.

Raspberry Iced Tea

Lois McGrady, Hillsville, Virginia

I like to serve this beverage on hot summer days over raspberry ice cubes.

  4   quarts water
1-1/2 cups sugar
  1   package (12 ounces) frozen
       unsweetened raspberries
 10   individual tea bags
 1/4   cup lemon juice

1) In a Dutch oven, bring water and sugar to a boil. Remove from the heat; stir until sugar is dissolved. Add the raspberries, tea bags and lemon juice. Cover and steep for 3 minutes.

2) Strain; discard berries and tea bags. Refrigerate until chilled. Serve over ice.

Yield: 16 servings (4 quarts).

Editor's Note: To make fruited ice cubes, see Garnishes for Beverages on page 45.

NUTRITION FACTS: 1 cup equals 83 calories, trace fat (0 saturated fat), 0 cholesterol, 1 mg sodium, 21 g carbohydrate, 1 g fiber, trace protein.

■ *TOUCH-OF-MINT ICED TEA:* Bring 2 quarts of water to a boil. Steep 5 individual tea bags for 5 minutes and discard; cool for 15 minutes. Add 1-1/3 cups packed fresh mint and steep for 5 minutes. Strain tea and stir in 1 cup lemonade concentrate. Refrigerate until chilled. Serve over ice. Makes about 2 quarts.

Mulled Cider

Taste of Home Test Kitchen

This is a classic warmer-upper that you can serve on chilly winter days. Pass the brandy separately for those who want it.

  3   cinnamon sticks (3 inches)
  3   whole cloves
  2   whole allspice
  1   bay leaf
  3   quarts apple cider *or* apple juice
 1/4   cup orange juice
 1/4   cup lemon juice
  1   tablespoon grated orange peel
  2   tablespoons brown sugar
Dash salt
  1   to 1-1/2 cups brandy, optional

1) Place the cinnamon stick, cloves, allspice and bay leaf on a double thickness of cheesecloth; bring up corners of cloth and tie with kitchen string to form a bag.

2) In a large saucepan, combine the apple cider, juices, orange peel, brown sugar, salt and spice bag. Bring to a boil. Reduce heat to medium-low; simmer, uncovered, for 30 minutes to blend flavors.

3) Discard spice bag. Strain cider mixture and stir in brandy if desired. Serve immediately.

Yield: 13 servings (about 3 quarts).

NUTRITION FACTS: 1 cup (calculated without brandy) equals 122 calories, 0 fat (0 saturated fat), 0 cholesterol, 35 mg sodium, 31 g carbohydrate, trace fiber, trace protein.

MAKING A SPICE BAG

Keep spices together so they can be removed from a saucepan or Dutch oven by placing them on several layers of cotton cheesecloth that has been cut into 3-in. squares. Bring up corners of cloth and tie with kitchen string to form a bag.

Cozy Hot Chocolate

Marie Hattrup, The Dalles, Oregon

This mixes up a perfect mugful for two. If maple is your favorite flavor, try that as well.

  2   tablespoons baking cocoa
  2   tablespoons sugar
 1/4   cup water
  2   cups milk
 1/2   teaspoon vanilla extract
 1/4   cup whipped cream
Ground cinnamon, optional

1) In a small saucepan, mix the cocoa and sugar; add water and stir until smooth. Bring to a boil, stirring constantly. Boil for 1 minute. Reduce heat; stir in milk and heat through.

2) Remove from the heat and stir in vanilla. Pour into 2 cups; top with whipped cream and sprinkle with cinnamon if desired.

Yield: 2 servings.

NUTRITION FACTS: 1 cup equals 235 calories, 10 g fat (6 g saturated fat), 39 mg cholesterol, 129 mg sodium, 28 g carbohydrate, 1 g fiber, 9 g protein.

■ *MAPLE HOT CHOCOLATE:* Omit whipped cream and cinnamon. Add 1 tablespoon butter to cocoa mixture before bringing it to a boil. Add 3 large marshmallows with the milk and heat until marshmallows are melted. Add 1/2 teaspoon maple flavoring with the vanilla. Pour into mugs and top with additional marshmallows.

CHAPTER 3
SOUPS &
SANDWICHES

SOUPS & SANDWICHES

Soups are versatile and can satisfy many menu-planning needs. Use a light broth or a cream-based soup as a first course. A full-bodied bean or a loaded chicken vegetable soup just needs a crisp salad or a hearty bread to complete the meal. Or just a cupful is a perfect accompaniment to a sandwich or salad.

Useful Definitions

The following terms are specific to this chapter. You can also refer to the Glossary (pages 18-22).

BISQUE: A thick, rich pureed soup often made with seafood but may be made with poultry or vegetables.

BROTH: Made from simmering meats, poultry, fish or vegetables, broths have less body than stocks. Broths and stocks may be used interchangeably for the recipes in this book.

CHILI: A hearty dish usually made with tomatoes and chili powder, but some chili dishes are white. The variations on chili seem endless. A chili can be mild or hot, have ground beef, stew meat, sausage, poultry or be meatless. It may have macaroni or spaghetti or no pasta at all.

CHOWDER: A chunky, thick, rich soup frequently made with seafood or vegetables, such as corn, but it can be made with other meat. Chowders have a milk or cream base and may be thickened with flour.

CONSOMME: A completely degreased, clarified stock. It has a rich flavor, and due to its high gelatin content, will set up when chilled.

CREAMED SOUPS: Pureed soups with a smooth, silky texture. The main flavor is frequently a single vegetable, such as asparagus or carrot. They may be thickened with flour or potatoes and can be made without cream.

GAZPACHO: An uncooked cold soup. The most common version uses tomatoes, cucumbers, sweet peppers, onion and garlic.

GUMBO: A hearty stew-like soup usually served with white rice that starts with a dark roux (see page 58) of flour and oil or butter. It may contain shellfish, chicken, sausage, ham, tomatoes, onions, garlic, sweet peppers and celery. In addition to the roux, okra is used as a thickening agent.

STOCKS: Usually made with meaty bones (possibly roasted), meat and vegetables. Stock should be clear, be free of grease and have a subtle flavor.

Making Stocks, Broths & Soups

Start making a stock with cold water. Just cover the bones, meat and/or vegetables with water. Add seasonings but do not salt (add salt, if necessary, after cooking). Bring slowly to a boil over low heat. Using a ladle, skim foam from the top of liquid. If water evaporates, add enough additional water to cover the bones, meat and/or vegetables. Skim fat or remove solidified fat after chilling. Strain stock; divide among several containers. Place containers in an ice bath to cool quickly. When chilled, refrigerate or freeze.

Add little or no salt, as well as other flavors, when making stock since it concentrates as it simmers and the liquid evaporates. Taste the soup when it is just about ready to be served and add enough salt to suit your family's preferences.

Add a pinch of turmeric or simmer an unpeeled whole yellow onion in the cooking liquid for golden homemade chicken and turkey broths.

Store soups in the refrigerator for up to 3 days. If there is rice or pasta in the soup, you may want to cook and store them separately, since they may continue to absorb the liquid.

Many broth-based soups freeze well for up to 3 months. Thaw in the refrigerator before reheating. It's best not to freeze soups prepared with potatoes, fruit, cheese, sour cream, yogurt, eggs, milk or cream.

1) Remove the excess fat from the cut up chicken. In a kettle or Dutch oven, combine chicken, vegetables, cold water and seasonings.

2) Bring to a boil over low heat. Skim foam as it rises to the top of the water. Reduce heat; cover and simmer until the chicken is tender, about 1 hour.

3) Remove chicken; let stand until cool enough to handle. Remove chicken from bones; discard skin and bones. Dice chicken; use immediately or cover and refrigerate. Chill broth several hours or overnight; lift fat from surface of broth and discard.

4) Bring soup to a boil; add noodles. Cook until tender. Stir in reserved chicken; heat through.

STRAINING STOCK OR BROTH

Remove meat and bones from stock. Line a colander with a double thickness of cheesecloth; place in a large heat-resistant bowl. Pour stock into colander. Discard vegetables, seasonings and cheesecloth. For a clear stock or broth, do not press liquid from vegetables and seasonings in the colander.

Chicken Broth
Nila Grahl, Gurnee, Illinois

Whether you're making a chicken soup or just a broth to use in other dishes, this recipe makes a tasty base for most anything.

1	broiler/fryer chicken (3 to 4 pounds), cut up
10	cups water
1	large carrot, sliced
1	large onion, sliced
1	celery rib, sliced
1	garlic clove, minced
1	bay leaf
1	teaspoon dried thyme
1	teaspoon salt
1/4	teaspoon pepper

1) In a large soup kettle or Dutch oven, combine all the ingredients. Slowly bring to a boil over low heat. Cover and simmer for 45-60 minutes or until the meat is tender, skimming the surface as foam rises.

2) Remove chicken and set aside until cool enough to handle. Remove and discard skin and bones. Chop chicken; set aside for soup or save for another use.

3) Strain broth through a cheesecloth-lined colander, discarding vegetables and bay leaf. If using immediately, skim fat or refrigerate for 8 hours or overnight, then remove fat from surface. Broth can be covered and refrigerated for up to 3 days or frozen for 4 to 6 months.

Yield: about 2 quarts.

NUTRITION FACTS: 1 cup equals 105 calories, 5 g fat (1 g saturated fat), 33 mg cholesterol, 331 mg sodium, 3 g carbohydrate, 1 g fiber, 11 g protein.

■ *CHICKEN NOODLE SOUP:* Place broth in a large saucepan or Dutch oven. Add 2 sliced large carrots, 2 sliced celery ribs and 1 chopped onion. Bring to a boil. Reduce heat; cover and simmer for 10 minutes or until the vegetables are tender. Add 2 cups uncooked fine egg noodles and reserved chicken. Bring to a boil. Reduce heat; cover and simmer for 6 minutes. Stir in 1 cup frozen peas and 1/2 cup frozen cut beans; cook for 2-4 minutes or until beans and noodles are tender.

■ *CHICKEN SOUP WITH SPAETZLE:* Prepare Chicken Noodle Soup as directed, omitting the noodles, peas and beans. With the carrots, add 1 minced garlic clove. With the chicken, add

2 cups sliced fresh mushrooms. For spaetzle, combine 1-1/4 cups all-purpose flour, and 1/8 teaspoon *each* baking powder and salt. Stir in 1 beaten egg and 1/4 cup *each* water and milk until blended. Drop batter by 1/2 teaspoonfuls onto boiling soup. Cook, uncovered, 10 minutes or until spaetzle float.

Vegetable Broth
Taste of Home Test Kitchen

The flavors of celery and mushrooms come through in this homemade vegetable broth. You can use it in place of chicken or beef broth.

>   2   tablespoons olive oil
>   2   medium onions, cut into wedges
>   2   celery ribs, cut into 1-inch pieces
>   1   whole garlic bulb, separated into
>   cloves and peeled
>   3   medium leeks, white and light
>   green parts only, cleaned and cut
>   into 1-inch pieces
>   3   medium carrots, cut into 1-inch
>   pieces
>   8   cups water
>   1/2   pound fresh mushrooms,
>   quartered
>   1   cup packed fresh parsley sprigs
>   4   sprigs fresh thyme
>   1   teaspoon salt
>   1/2   teaspoon whole peppercorns
>   1   bay leaf

1) Heat oil in a stockpot over medium heat until hot. Add the onions, celery and garlic. Cook and stir for 5 minutes or until tender. Add leeks and carrots; cook and stir 5 minutes longer. Add the water, mushrooms, parsley, thyme, salt, peppercorns and bay leaf; bring to a boil. Reduce heat; simmer, uncovered, for 1 hour.

2) Remove from the heat. Strain through a cheesecloth-lined colander; discard vegetables. If using immediately, skim fat or refrigerate for 8 hours or overnight, then remove fat from surface. Broth can be covered and refrigerated for up to 3 days or frozen for up to 4 to 6 months.

Yield: 5-1/2 cups.

NUTRITION FACTS: 1 cup equals 148 calories, 6 g fat (1 g saturated fat), 0 cholesterol, 521 mg sodium, 22 g carbohydrate, 5 g fiber, 4 g protein.

Homemade Beef Broth
Taste of Home Test Kitchen

Roasting the soup bones brings out delicious beefy flavors for this soup base. It refrigerates and freezes well to use as needed.

>   4   pounds meaty beef soup bones
>   (beef shanks *or* short ribs)
>   3   medium carrots, cut into chunks
>   3   celery ribs, cut into chunks
>   2   medium onions, quartered
>   1/2   cup warm water
>   3   bay leaves
>   3   garlic cloves
>   8   to 10 whole peppercorns
>   3   to 4 sprigs fresh parsley
>   1   teaspoon *each* dried thyme,
>   marjoram and oregano
>   3   quarts cold water

1) Place soup bones in a large roasting pan. Bake, uncovered, at 450° for 30 minutes. Add the carrots, celery and onions. Bake 30 minutes longer; drain fat.

2) Using a slotted spoon, transfer bones and vegetables to a large Dutch oven. Add warm water to the roasting pan; stir to loosen browned bits from pan. Transfer pan juices to kettle. Add seasonings and enough cold water just to cover.

3) Slowly bring to a boil, about 30 minutes. Reduce heat; simmer, uncovered, for 4-5 hours, skimming the surface as foam rises. If necessary, add hot water during the first 2 hours to keep ingredients covered.

4) Remove beef bones and set aside until cool enough to handle. If desired, remove meat from bones; discard bones and save meat for another use. Strain broth through a cheesecloth-lined colander, discarding vegetables and seasonings.

5) If using immediately, skim fat or refrigerate for 8 hours or overnight, then remove fat from surface. Broth can be covered and refrigerated for up to 3 days or frozen for 4 to 6 months.

Yield: about 2-1/2 quarts.

NUTRITION FACTS: 1 cup equals 209 calories, 10 g fat (4 g saturated fat), 56 mg cholesterol, 61 mg sodium, 6 g carbohydrate, 2 g fiber, 22 g protein.

LOUISIANA GUMBO

Louisiana Gumbo
Wilton and Gloria Mason, Springhill, Louisiana

Gumbo is a stew-like dish made with meat or seafood, tomatoes, peppers and okra. I also serve it with the hot pepper sauce on the side.

1	broiler/fryer chicken (3 to 3-1/2 pounds), cut up
2	quarts water
3/4	cup all-purpose flour
1/2	cup vegetable oil
1/2	cup sliced green onions
1/2	cup chopped onion
1/2	cup chopped green pepper
1/2	cup chopped sweet red pepper
1/2	cup chopped celery
2	garlic cloves, minced
1/2	pound fully cooked smoked sausage, cut into 1-inch cubes
1/2	pound fully cooked ham, cut into 3/4-inch cubes
1/2	pound uncooked medium fresh *or* frozen shrimp, thawed, peeled and deveined
1	cup cut fresh *or* frozen okra (3/4-inch pieces)
1	can (16 ounces) kidney beans, rinsed and drained
1/2	teaspoon salt
1/4	teaspoon pepper
1/4	teaspoon hot pepper sauce
6	cups hot cooked rice

1) Place the chicken and water in a Dutch oven. Slowly bring to a boil. Reduce heat; cover and simmer 45-60 minutes or until chicken is tender, skimming the surface as foam rises.

2) Remove chicken and set aside until cool enough to handle. Remove and discard skin and bones. Cut chicken into bite-size pieces.

3) Strain the broth through a cheesecloth-lined colander; skim fat. Reserve 6 cups broth. Any remaining broth can be covered and refrigerated for up to 3 days or frozen for 4 to 6 months.

4) In a Dutch oven, combine flour and oil until smooth; cook and stir over medium-low heat for 2-3 minutes or until browned. Stir in the onions, peppers, celery and garlic; cook for 5 minutes or until vegetables are tender.

5) Stir in the sausage, ham and reserved broth and chicken. Bring to a boil. Reduce heat; cover and simmer for 45 minutes.

6) Add the shrimp, okra, beans, salt, pepper and hot pepper sauce; cover and simmer 10 minutes longer or until shrimp is cooked. Spoon 1 cup gumbo into bowl and top with 1/2 cup rice.

Yield: 12 servings.

NUTRITION FACTS: 1 cup equals 473 calories, 22 g fat (6 g saturated fat), 94 mg cholesterol, 646 mg sodium, 38 g carbohydrate, 3 g fiber, 29 g protein.

BROWNING A ROUX

Thicken gravy and soup using a roux, which is a mixture of fat and flour. In a traditional gumbo, flour is added to the fat and heated until it reaches a reddish-brown color. It is important to stir while the mixture is browning.

Italian Wedding Soup
Nancy Ducharme, Deltona, Florida

This soup always satisfies! I add cooked pasta at the end of the cooking time to keep it from getting mushy.

1	egg
3/4	cup grated Parmesan *or* Romano cheese
1/2	cup dry bread crumbs
1	small onion, chopped
3/4	teaspoon salt, *divided*
1-1/4	teaspoons pepper, *divided*

1-1/4   teaspoons garlic powder, *divided*
   2   pounds ground beef
   2   quarts chicken broth
 1/3   cup chopped fresh spinach
   1   teaspoon onion powder
   1   teaspoon dried parsley flakes
1-1/4   cups cooked medium pasta shells

1) In a large bowl, combine the egg, cheese, bread crumbs, onion, 1/4 teaspoon salt, 1/4 teaspoon pepper and 1/4 teaspoon garlic powder. Crumble beef over mixture; mix well. Shape into 1-in. balls.

2) In a Dutch oven, brown meatballs in small batches; drain. Add the broth, spinach, onion powder, parsley and remaining salt, pepper and garlic powder; bring to a boil. Reduce heat; simmer, uncovered, for 5 minutes. Stir in pasta; heat through.

Yield: 12 servings (3 quarts).

NUTRITION FACTS: 1 cup equals 226 calories, 12 g fat (5 g saturated fat), 72 mg cholesterol, 942 mg sodium, 9 g carbohydrate, trace fiber, 20 g protein.

White Bean Fennel Soup
Donna Quinn, Salem, Wisconsin

This filling soup is often requested for company dinners. A hint of fennel accents the flavor of this quick-to-fix bean soup.

   1   large onion, chopped
   1   small fennel bulb, thinly sliced
   1   tablespoon olive oil
   5   cups reduced-sodium chicken broth *or* vegetable broth
   1   can (15 ounces) white kidney *or* cannellini beans, rinsed and drained
   1   can (14-1/2 ounces) diced tomatoes, undrained
   1   teaspoon dried thyme
 1/4   teaspoon pepper
   1   bay leaf
   3   cups shredded fresh spinach

1) In a large saucepan, saute onion and fennel in oil until tender. Add the broth, beans, tomatoes, thyme, pepper and bay leaf; bring to a boil.

2) Reduce heat; cover and simmer for 30 minutes or until fennel is tender. Discard bay leaf. Add spinach; cook 3-4 minutes longer or until spinach is wilted.

Yield: 5 servings.

NUTRITION FACTS: 1-1/2 cups equals 152 calories, 3 g fat (trace saturated fat), 0 cholesterol, 976 mg sodium, 23 g carbohydrate, 7 g fiber, 8 g protein.

Old-Fashioned Turkey Soup
Linda Sand, Winsted, Connecticut

For added convenience, freeze some of the soup in individual serving-size portions.

   1   leftover turkey carcass (from a 12-pound turkey)
   5   quarts water

SOUP:

   3   cups cubed cooked turkey
   1   can (28 ounces) stewed tomatoes
   1   large onion, chopped
   2   large carrots, shredded
   1   cup chopped celery
   1   package (10 ounces) frozen chopped spinach, thawed
 3/4   cup fresh *or* frozen peas
 3/4   cup uncooked long grain rice
   4   chicken bouillon cubes
   2   teaspoons salt
 3/4   teaspoon pepper
 1/2   teaspoon dried marjoram
 1/2   teaspoon dried thyme

1) Place the turkey carcass and water in a Dutch oven or soup kettle; slowly bring to a boil over low heat. Cover and simmer for 1-1/2 hours.

2) Remove carcass and discard. Strain the broth through a cheesecloth-lined colander. If using immediately, skim fat or refrigerate for 8 hours or overnight, then remove fat from surface. Stock may be refrigerated for up to 3 days or frozen for 4 to 6 months.

3) For soup, return strained broth to pan. Add the turkey, vegetables, rice, bouillon and seasonings; bring to a boil. Reduce heat; cover and simmer for 30 minutes or until rice and vegetables are tender.

Yield: 22 servings (5-1/2 quarts).

NUTRITION FACTS: 1 cup equals 96 calories, 2 g fat (1 g saturated fat), 23 mg cholesterol, 522 mg sodium, 11 g carbohydrate, 2 g fiber, 9 g protein.

■ *TURKEY BARLEY SOUP:* Prepare stock as directed in steps 1 and 2 above. For soup, omit stewed tomatoes and rice. Bring stock to a boil; add 1 cup uncooked medium pearl barley. Reduce heat; cover and simmer for 30 minutes. Add remaining ingredients. Cook, uncovered, for 20-25 minutes or until barley and vegetables are tender.

Black Bean Soup

Audrey Thibodeau, Mesa, Arizona

This soup is so hearty because of the black beans, you don't miss the meat. Beans are a good source of protein, and this soup is a tasty way to get in a serving.

1	pound dried black beans
6	cups chicken broth
4	cups water
1-1/2	cups chopped onions
1	cup thinly sliced celery
1	large carrot, chopped
1/2	cup *each* chopped green, sweet red and yellow peppers
2	garlic cloves, minced
3	tablespoons olive oil
1/4	cup tomato paste
3	tablespoons minced fresh parsley
3	bay leaves
1	tablespoon minced fresh thyme *or* 1 teaspoon dried thyme
1-1/2	teaspoons ground cumin
1	teaspoon pepper
3/4	teaspoon salt, optional

Chopped tomato, optional

1) Place beans in a Dutch oven or soup kettle; add water to cover by 2 in. Bring to a boil; boil for 2 minutes. Remove from the heat; cover and let stand for 1 to 4 hours or until beans are softened. Drain and rinse beans, discarding liquid.

2) Return beans to pan; add broth and water. Bring to a boil. Reduce heat; cover and simmer for 1 hour or until the beans are almost tender.

3) Meanwhile, in a large skillet, saute the onions, celery, carrot, peppers and garlic in oil until tender. Add the tomato paste, herbs and seasonings to the bean mixture. Add the sauteed vegetables; bring to a boil.

4) Reduce heat; cover and simmer for 1 hour or until beans are tender. Discard bay leaves. Garnish with chopped tomato if desired.

Yield: 12 servings (3 quarts).

NUTRITION FACTS: 1 cup equals 191 calories, 4 g fat (1 g saturated fat), 0 cholesterol, 484 mg sodium, 30 g carbohydrate, 7 g fiber, 10 g protein.

CUTTING DOWN ON FAT

If you are using canned broth that is not fat-free, just chill in the refrigerator. After it's cold, remove the top of the can and lift off the solidified fat.

PREPARING DRIED BEANS FOR COOKING

Soak dried beans such as navy, great northern, pinto and kidney beans before cooking. There are two methods for soaking beans—the quick soaking method, which takes a little over an hour and the overnight method. See instructions for both methods in the Beans & Grains chapter on page 269.

FRENCH ONION SOUP

French Onion Soup

Lise Thomson, Magrath, Alberta

My version of onion soup has a slightly sweet flavor that makes it unique.

6	cups thinly sliced onions
1	tablespoon sugar
1/2	teaspoon pepper
1/3	cup vegetable oil
6	cups beef broth
8	slices French bread (3/4 inch thick), toasted
1/2	cup shredded Parmesan *or* Swiss cheese

1) In a Dutch oven, cook the onions, sugar and pepper in oil over medium-low heat for 20 minutes or until onions are caramelized, stirring frequently. Add the broth; bring to a boil. Reduce heat; cover and simmer for 30 minutes.

2) Ladle soup into ovenproof bowls. Top each with a slice of French bread; sprinkle with cheese. Broil 4-6 in. from heat until cheese is melted. Serve immediately.

Yield: 8 servings.

NUTRITION FACTS: 1 cup equals 330 calories, 13 g fat (3 g saturated fat), 4 mg cholesterol, 1,092 mg sodium, 43 g carbohydrate, 4 g fiber, 10 g protein.

Lentil Soup
Joyce Pyra, North Battleford, Saskatchewan

This is a great soup because it can be easily doubled. Try it topped with shredded cheddar cheese.

    1   cup dried lentils, rinsed
    6   cups chicken broth
    2   cups chopped onion
    1   garlic clove, minced
    1   tablespoon vegetable oil
2-1/2   cups chopped fresh tomatoes
    1   cup sliced carrots
  1/2   teaspoon dried thyme
  1/4   teaspoon dried marjoram

1) In a large saucepan, bring lentils and chicken broth to a boil. Reduce heat; simmer for 30 minutes.

2) Meanwhile, in a large skillet, saute onion and garlic in oil; add to saucepan. Add the tomatoes, carrots, thyme and marjoram. Cook 30 minutes longer or until lentils and vegetables are tender.

Yield: about 8 servings (2 quarts).

NUTRITION FACTS: 1 cup equals 142 calories, 3 g fat (trace saturated fat), 0 cholesterol, 712 mg sodium, 22 g carbohydrate, 9 g fiber, 9 g protein.

RAVIOLI SOUP

Ravioli Soup
Shelley Way, Douglas, Wyoming

So fast and easy to make, this soup always hits the spot.

    1   pound ground beef
    2   cups water
    1   can (28 ounces) crushed tomatoes, undrained
    1   can (14-1/2 ounces) crushed tomatoes, undrained
    1   can (6 ounces) tomato paste

1-1/2   cups chopped onion
  1/4   cup minced fresh parsley
    2   garlic cloves, minced
  3/4   teaspoon dried basil
  1/2   teaspoon dried oregano
  1/2   teaspoon onion salt
  1/2   teaspoon sugar
  1/2   teaspoon salt
  1/4   teaspoon pepper
  1/4   teaspoon dried thyme
    1   package (9 ounces) refrigerated cheese ravioli
  1/4   cup grated Parmesan cheese

1) In a Dutch oven, cook beef over medium heat until no longer pink; drain. Add the water, tomatoes, tomato paste, onion, parsley, garlic and seasonings; bring to a boil. Reduce heat; cover and simmer for 30 minutes.

2) Meanwhile, cook ravioli according to package directions; drain. Add to soup and heat through. Stir in the Parmesan cheese. Serve immediately.

Yield: 10 servings (2-1/2 quarts).

NUTRITION FACTS: 1 cup equals 235 calories, 8 g fat (4 g saturated fat), 42 mg cholesterol, 542 mg sodium, 25 g carbohydrate, 4 g fiber, 17 g protein.

Spicy Fish Soup
Linda Murry, Allenstown, New Hampshire

Salsa packs a punch in this soup recipe, which we like to serve with warm homemade bread slices.

    2   cans (14-1/2 ounces *each*) chicken broth
2-1/2   cups water
  2/3   cup uncooked instant rice
1-1/2   cups salsa
    1   package (10 ounces) frozen corn
    1   pound frozen cod, thawed and cut into 2-inch pieces
Fresh lime wedges, optional

1) In a large saucepan, bring the broth, water and rice to a boil. Reduce heat; cover and simmer for 5 minutes. Add the salsa and corn; return to a boil. Add fish.

2) Reduce heat; cover and simmer for 5 minutes or until fish flakes easily with a fork. Serve with lime if desired.

Yield: 8 servings (about 2-1/4 quarts).

NUTRITION FACTS: 1 cup (calculated without lime) equals 124 calories, 1 g fat (trace saturated fat), 22 mg cholesterol, 663 mg sodium, 19 g carbohydrate, 4 g fiber, 15 g protein.

MINESTRONE

1 cup uncooked ditalini *or* 4
ounces spaghetti, broken
into 3-inch pieces
1 cup grated Parmesan cheese

1) In an 8-qt. soup kettle, saute the onions, celery,
parsley and garlic in oil until tender. Stir in the
broth, tomatoes, tomato sauce, cabbage, carrots,
basil, salt and pepper. Bring to a boil. Reduce
heat; cover and simmer for 1 hour.

2) In a large skillet, cook beef over medium heat until
no longer pink; drain and set aside. Stir into soup
along with the zucchini, beans and pasta. Cover
and simmer for 15 to 20 minutes or until the
vegetables and pasta are tender. Top each serving
with Parmesan cheese.

Yield: 20 servings (5 quarts).

NUTRITION FACTS: 1 cup equals 209 calories, 9 g fat (3 g saturated
fat), 26 mg cholesterol, 538 mg sodium, 19 g carbohydrate, 4 g fiber,
14 g protein.

Minestrone
Virginia Bauer, Botkins, Ohio

Vegetables and herbs fresh from my garden make
this one of our favorite soups. This recipe makes
a lot, so it's perfect for large gatherings or to
freeze in smaller containers for fast meals.

2 cups coarsely chopped onions
1 cup sliced celery
1/4 cup minced fresh parsley
2 garlic cloves, minced
1/4 cup vegetable oil
5 cups beef broth
2 cups chopped tomatoes *or* 1 can
(14-1/2 ounces) diced tomatoes,
drained
1 can (15 ounces) tomato sauce
2 cups coarsely chopped cabbage
1 cup sliced fresh carrots
2 teaspoons dried basil *or* Italian
seasoning
1/2 teaspoon salt
1/4 teaspoon pepper
1-1/2 pounds ground beef
1-1/2 cups sliced zucchini
1 cup cut fresh green beans
1 can (16 ounces) kidney beans,
rinsed and drained
1 can (15 ounces) garbanzo beans
or chickpeas, rinsed and drained

Southern Garden Soup
Leslie Owens, Poplar Bluff, Missouri

Filled with garden-fresh flavors of cauliflower,
asparagus and spinach, this soup is my favorite
way to use up summer's produce.

12-1/4 cups water, *divided*
1/2 cup pearl onions
5 chicken bouillon cubes
2 cups cauliflowerets
2 pounds fresh asparagus, cut
into 1/2-inch pieces
1 can (8 ounces) sliced water
chestnuts, drained
1 cup chopped fresh spinach
1/2 cup chopped chives
1/2 teaspoon dried marjoram
1/2 teaspoon salt
1/8 to 1/4 teaspoon pepper
1/8 teaspoon ground nutmeg
3 tablespoons cornstarch

1) In a Dutch oven, bring 6 cups water to a boil. Add
pearl onions; boil for 3 minutes. Drain and rinse
in cold water; peel and set aside.

2) In a 3-qt. saucepan, bring 6 cups water and
bouillon to a boil. Add cauliflower and onions;
cover and cook for 5 minutes. Add the asparagus,
water chestnuts, spinach and seasonings; cover
and cook for 5 minutes or until asparagus is
tender.

3) Combine cornstarch and remaining water until

smooth; stir into soup. Bring to a boil; cook and stir for 2 minutes or until thickened. Serve immediately.

Yield: 9 servings (2-1/4 quarts).

NUTRITION FACTS: 1 cup equals 58 calories, 1 g fat (trace saturated fat), trace cholesterol, 770 mg sodium, 11 g carbohydrate, 2 g fiber, 3 g protein.

GAZPACHO

Gazpacho
Robynn Shannon, Alexandria, Virginia

Nothing equals the taste of an ice-cold bowl of gazpacho on a hot summer day. This soup is a wonderful way to use up homegrown tomatoes.

- 3   cups chopped seeded peeled fresh tomatoes
- 2   celery ribs, finely chopped
- 1   medium green pepper, finely chopped
- 1   medium cucumber, peeled, seeded and finely chopped
- 1/4   cup minced fresh parsley
- 1   tablespoon minced chives
- 1   green onion, thinly sliced
- 1   garlic clove, minced
- 1   can (46 ounces) tomato juice
- 1/3   cup red wine vinegar
- 1/4   cup olive oil
- 1   teaspoon salt
- 1/2   teaspoon Worcestershire sauce
- 1/2   teaspoon pepper

Seasoned croutons

1) In a large bowl, combine the tomatoes, celery, green pepper, cucumber, parsley, chives, onion, garlic, tomato juice, vinegar, oil, salt, Worcestershire sauce and pepper.

2) Cover and refrigerate for several hours or overnight. Garnish each serving with croutons.

Yield: 10 servings (2-1/2 quarts).

NUTRITION FACTS: 1 cup (calculated without croutons) equals 94 calories, 6 g fat (1 g saturated fat), 0 cholesterol, 757 mg sodium, 11 g carbohydrate, 2 g fiber, 2 g protein.

Chilled Strawberry Soup
Sara Laker, Loda, Illinois

Guests at my garden theme party loved the flavor of this beautiful fruit soup, calling it elegant, surprising and a real treat! Strawberry yogurt, pureed berries and a spicy syrup are blended to produce a fancy first course.

- 1   cup apple juice
- 1   cup water, *divided*
- 2/3   cup sugar
- 1/2   teaspoon ground cinnamon
- 1/8   teaspoon ground cloves
- 2   cups fresh strawberries
- 2   cartons (8 ounces *each*) strawberry yogurt
- 2   drops red food coloring, optional

Additional strawberry halves, optional

1) In a saucepan, combine the apple juice, 3/4 cup water, sugar, cinnamon and cloves; bring to a boil over medium heat. Remove from the heat; cool.

2) Place strawberries and remaining water in a blender or food processor; cover and process until smooth. Pour into a large bowl.

3) Add the apple juice mixture, yogurt and food coloring if desired. Cover and refrigerate until well chilled. Garnish with additional strawberries if desired.

Yield: 6 servings.

NUTRITION FACTS: 1 cup (calculated without additional berries) equals 195 calories, 1 g fat (1 g saturated fat), 4 mg cholesterol, 42 mg sodium, 45 g carbohydrate, 1 g fiber, 3 g protein.

GARNISHES FOR SOUPS

Dress up a soup with a sprinkle of nuts, chopped fresh herbs, sliced green onions, slivers of fresh vegetables, croutons, shredded cheese or crumbled bacon.

Manhattan Clam Chowder
Joan Hopewell, Pennington, New Jersey

This chowder also cooks up wonderfully in a slow cooker. Just add all the ingredients in the morning and come home to the aroma of dinner.

  1 cup chopped onion
 2/3 cup chopped celery
  2 teaspoons minced green pepper
  1 garlic clove, minced
  2 tablespoons butter
  2 cups hot water
  1 cup cubed peeled potatoes
  1 can (28 ounces) diced tomatoes, undrained
  2 cans (6-1/2 ounces *each*) minced clams, undrained
  1 teaspoon salt
 1/2 teaspoon dried thyme
 1/4 teaspoon pepper
Dash cayenne pepper
  2 teaspoons minced fresh parsley

1) In a 3-qt. saucepan, cook the onion, celery, green pepper and garlic in butter over low heat for 20 minutes, stirring frequently.

2) Add water and potatoes; bring to a boil. Reduce heat; cover and simmer for 15 minutes or until potatoes are tender.

3) Add the tomatoes, clams, salt, thyme, pepper and cayenne; heat through. Stir in parsley. Serve immediately.

Yield: 6-8 servings (about 2 quarts).

NUTRITION FACTS: 1 cup equals 91 calories, 3 g fat (2 g saturated fat), 15 mg cholesterol, 652 mg sodium, 13 g carbohydrate, 3 g fiber, 5 g protein.

Cream of Carrot Soup
Ruth Andrewson, Leavenworth, Washington

This rich, yummy soup is versatile, too. You can substitute most any vegetable with excellent results. For a quick garnish, top with some shredded fresh carrot. For a flavor twist, add 1/2 cup sauteed onion along with the broth mixture.

  4 cups chicken broth
  4 large carrots, cut into chunks
 1/2 cup heavy whipping cream
  1 teaspoon sugar

1) In a large saucepan, bring broth and carrots to a boil. Reduce heat; simmer, uncovered, for 15

minutes or until carrots are tender. Cool for 10 minutes.

2) In a blender, cover and process soup in small batches until smooth; return to the pan. Stir in cream and sugar; heat through.

Yield: 5 servings.

NUTRITION FACTS: 1 cup equals 122 calories, 9 g fat (5 g saturated fat), 33 mg cholesterol, 773 mg sodium, 8 g carbohydrate, 2 g fiber, 3 g protein.

■ *CREAM OF ASPARAGUS SOUP:* Substitute 1-1/2 pounds fresh asparagus for the carrots. Cut asparagus into 1-in. pieces. Simmer for 5-7 minutes or until tender.

■ *CREAM OF BROCCOLI SOUP:* Substitute 3 cups chopped fresh broccoli for the carrots. Simmer 7-10 minutes or until tender.

■ *CREAM OF CAULIFLOWER SOUP:* Substitute 3 cups cauliflower florets for the carrots. Simmer for 7-10 minutes or until tender.

SOUTHWESTERN CORN CHOWDER

Southwestern Corn Chowder
Nancy Winters, Moorpark, California

This chowder gets a little spice from picante sauce. It travels well, and leftovers are good the next day.

  4 boneless skinless chicken breast halves, cut into 3/4-inch cubes
  1 medium onion, cut into thin wedges
  1 tablespoon vegetable oil
  2 teaspoons ground cumin
  2 cans (14-1/2 ounces *each*) chicken broth

1 package (10 ounces) frozen corn
3/4 cup picante sauce
1/2 cup chopped sweet red pepper
1/2 cup chopped green pepper
2 tablespoons minced fresh cilantro
2 tablespoons cornstarch
2 tablespoons water
Shredded Monterey Jack cheese, optional

1) In a 3-qt. saucepan, cook chicken and onion in oil until chicken juices run clear. Stir in cumin. Add broth, corn and picante sauce; bring to a boil. Reduce heat; cover and simmer for 15 minutes. Stir in peppers and cilantro.

2) Combine cornstarch and water until smooth; stir into soup. Bring to a boil; cook and stir for 2 minutes or until slightly thickened. Spoon into bowls; top with cheese if desired.

Yield: 7 servings (about 2 quarts).

NUTRITION FACTS: 1 cup (calculated without cheese) equals 164 calories, 4 g fat (1 g saturated fat), 36 mg cholesterol, 611 mg sodium, 16 g carbohydrate, 2 g fiber, 16 g protein.

New England Fish Chowder
Dorothy Noonan, Quincy, Massachusetts

Adjust the flavor by adding a bay leaf or dried thyme along with the potatoes (discard bay leaf before serving). Or garnish each serving with chopped fresh parsley or crumbled cooked bacon.

1-1/2 cups sliced onions
4 tablespoons butter, *divided*
1-1/2 cups water
3 medium potatoes, peeled and diced
1-1/4 teaspoons salt
1/2 teaspoon pepper
2 tablespoons all-purpose flour
1-1/4 cups milk
1 can (12 ounces) evaporated milk
1 pound fresh *or* frozen haddock fillets, cut into large chunks

1) In a large saucepan, saute onions in 2 tablespoons butter. Add the water, potatoes, salt and pepper. Bring to a boil. Reduce heat; cover and simmer for 25 minutes or until potatoes are tender.

2) Combine the flour and milk until smooth. Stir into potato mixture along with evaporated milk. Add fish and the remaining butter; bring to a boil.

Reduce heat; cook 5-10 minutes longer or until fish is opaque.

Yield: 8 servings (2 quarts).

NUTRITION FACTS: 1 cup equals 262 calories, 11 g fat (7 g saturated fat), 68 mg cholesterol, 534 mg sodium, 24 g carbohydrate, 2 g fiber, 17 g protein.

■ *NEW ENGLAND SALMON CHOWDER:* Omit haddock and add 1 pound fresh *or* frozen salmon cut into chunks. To use 1 pound canned salmon, remove the skin and bones; add to the soup along with milk.

■ *NEW ENGLAND CLAM CHOWDER:* Omit the haddock and add two cans (6-1/2 ounces *each*) drained chopped clams along with the milk. For a stronger clam flavor, substitute 1 bottle (8 ounces) clam juice for 1 cup of the water.

Corn Chowder
Kristy Knight, Bayside, New York

Chowder is a classic comfort food here in the Northeast, especially during cooler weather. Whenever I make a trip home to Pittsburgh, Mom has this simmering on the stove for me.

1 large onion, chopped
1/2 cup butter
2-1/2 cups water
2 cans (14-3/4 ounces *each*) cream-style corn
4 medium potatoes, peeled and cut into 1/2-inch cubes
2 cups milk
1-1/2 teaspoons salt
3/4 teaspoon pepper
Minced fresh parsley

1) In a Dutch oven, saute onion in butter until tender. Add the water, corn and potatoes; bring to a boil. Reduce heat; cover and simmer for 16-20 minutes or until potatoes are tender. Reduce heat to low.

2) Stir in the milk, salt and pepper. Cook for 5-10 minutes or until heated through, stirring occasionally. Sprinkle with parsley.

Yield: 8 servings (about 2 quarts).

Editor's Note: You may substitute 2-1/2 cups chicken broth for the water. Omit salt.

NUTRITION FACTS: 1 cup (calculated without parsley) equals 271 calories, 14 g fat (8 g saturated fat), 39 mg cholesterol, 889 mg sodium, 35 g carbohydrate, 3 g fiber, 5 g protein.

TUSCAN SOUP

Tuscan Soup

Rosemary Goetz, Hudson, New York

This meatless soup can be prepared in a flash. It's perfect after working full time outside the home.

    1 small onion, chopped
    1 small carrot, sliced
    1 tablespoon olive oil
    2 cans (14-1/2 ounces *each*)
       chicken broth
    1 cup water
  3/4 teaspoon salt
  1/4 teaspoon pepper
    1 can (15 to 16 ounces) white
       kidney *or* great northern beans,
       rinsed and drained
  2/3 cup uncooked small spiral pasta
    3 cups thinly sliced fresh escarole
       or spinach

1) In a 2-qt. saucepan, saute onion and carrot in oil until onion is tender. Add the broth, water, salt and pepper; bring to a boil. Stir in beans and pasta; return to a boil.

2) Reduce heat; cover and simmer for 15 minutes or until pasta and vegetables are tender, stirring occasionally. Add escarole; heat through.

Yield: 4 servings.

NUTRITION FACTS: 1 cup equals 196 calories, 5 g fat (1 g saturated fat), 0 cholesterol, 1,432 mg sodium, 30 g carbohydrate, 6 g fiber, 9 g protein.

Monterey Jack Cheese Soup

Susan Salenski, Copemish, Michigan

Main-meal soups are something I'm always on the lookout for. Since I love cheese and our kids like anything with Mexican flavor, I knew this one would be popular at our house. I've served it with tacos, nachos or a loaf of bread.

      1 cup chicken broth
      1 large tomato, peeled, seeded
         and diced
    1/2 cup finely chopped onion
      2 tablespoons chopped green
         chilies
      1 garlic clove, minced
      2 tablespoons butter
      2 tablespoons all-purpose flour
  Salt and pepper to taste
      3 cups milk, *divided*
  1-1/2 cups (6 ounces) shredded
         Monterey Jack cheese

1) In a 3-qt. saucepan, combine the broth, tomato, onion, chilies and garlic; bring to a boil. Reduce heat; cover and simmer for 10 minutes or until vegetables are tender. Remove from the heat and set aside.

2) In another saucepan, melt butter. Stir in the flour, salt and pepper until smooth; gradually stir in 1-1/2 cups milk. Bring to a boil; cook and stir for 1 minute or until thickened.

3) Slowly stir into vegetable mixture. Reduce heat; add cheese and remaining milk. Cook and stir over low heat until cheese is melted. Serve immediately.

Yield: 5 servings.

NUTRITION FACTS: 1 cup (calculated without salt and pepper) equals 286 calories, 20 g fat (12 g saturated fat), 62 mg cholesterol, 503 mg sodium, 13 g carbohydrate, 1 g fiber, 14 g protein.

Split Pea Soup

Holly Dow, Chapman, Maine

The split peas are rinsed to clear out any shriveled peas or bits of dirt before they are added to the soup. This recipe is the only way I like to make split pea soup.

      1 small onion, diced
      1 tablespoon vegetable oil
      4 cups water
      1 can (14-1/2 ounces)
         chicken broth
  1-1/2 cups dried split peas, rinsed
      1 cup cubed fully cooked ham

3 bay leaves

1-1/2 teaspoons salt

1/2 teaspoon dried rosemary, crushed

1/4 teaspoon dried thyme

1/4 teaspoon pepper

1) In a large saucepan, saute onion in oil until tender. Add the remaining ingredients. Bring to a boil; reduce heat.

2) Cover and simmer for 1 hour or until peas are tender. Discard bay leaves.

Yield: 6 servings.

NUTRITION FACTS: 1 cup equals 236 calories, 5 g fat (1 g saturated fat), 12 mg cholesterol, 1,177 mg sodium, 32 g carbohydrate, 13 g fiber, 17 g protein.

CREAMY WHITE CHILI

Wild Rice Soup
Elienore Myhre, Balaton, Minnesota

Wild rice has an intense, nutty flavor. It's delicious in this soup, and a small amount goes a long way in satisfying a hungry diner.

1/3 cup uncooked wild rice

1 tablespoon vegetable oil

1 quart water

1 medium onion, chopped

1 celery rib, finely chopped

1 medium carrot, finely chopped

1/2 cup butter

1/2 cup all-purpose flour

3 cups chicken broth

2 cups half-and-half cream

1/2 teaspoon dried rosemary, crushed

1 teaspoon salt

1) In a medium saucepan, combine the rice, oil and water; bring to a boil. Reduce heat; cover and simmer for 30 minutes.

2) Meanwhile, in a Dutch oven, cook the onion, celery and carrot in butter until vegetables are almost tender. Stir in flour until blended; cook and stir for 2 minutes. Slowly stir in broth and undrained rice. Bring to a boil; cook and stir for 2 minutes or until slightly thickened.

3) Reduce heat; stir in the cream, rosemary and salt. Simmer, uncovered, for about 20 minutes or until rice is tender.

Yield: 8 servings (about 2 quarts).

NUTRITION FACTS: 1 cup equals 270 calories, 19 g fat (11 g saturated fat), 61 mg cholesterol, 797 mg sodium, 17 g carbohydrate, 1 g fiber, 5 g protein.

Creamy White Chili
Laura Brewer, Lafayette, Indiana

I got this wonderful recipe from my sister-in-law, who made a big batch and served a crowd one night. It was a hit. Plus, it's easy and quick.

1 pound boneless skinless chicken breasts, cut into 1/2-inch cubes

1 medium onion, chopped

1-1/2 teaspoons garlic powder

1 tablespoon vegetable oil

2 cans (15-1/2 ounces *each*) great northern beans, rinsed and drained

1 can (14-1/2 ounces) chicken broth

2 cans (4 ounces *each*) chopped green chilies

1 teaspoon salt

1 teaspoon ground cumin

1 teaspoon dried oregano

1/2 teaspoon pepper

1/4 teaspoon cayenne pepper

1 cup (8 ounces) sour cream

1/2 cup heavy whipping cream

1) In a large saucepan, saute chicken, onion and garlic powder in oil until chicken is no longer pink. Add the beans, broth, chilies and seasonings. Bring to a boil.

2) Reduce heat; simmer, uncovered, for 30 minutes. Remove from the heat; stir in sour cream and cream. Serve immediately.

Yield: 7 servings.

NUTRITION FACTS: 1 cup equals 334 calories, 16 g fat (8 g saturated fat), 81 mg cholesterol, 1,045 mg sodium, 24 g carbohydrate, 7 g fiber, 22 g protein.

SPICED CHILI

Spiced Chili

Julie Brendt, Antelope, California

Using a slow cooker makes it easy to prepare this chili. But it also tastes great made on the stovetop.

- 1-1/2 **pounds ground beef**
- 1/2 **cup chopped onion**
- 4 **garlic cloves, minced**
- 2 **cans (16 ounces** *each***) kidney beans, rinsed and drained**
- 2 **cans (15 ounces** *each***) tomato sauce**
- 2 **cans (14-1/2 ounces** *each***) stewed tomatoes, cut up**
- 1 **cup water**
- 2 **bay leaves**
- 1/4 **cup chili powder**
- 1 **tablespoon salt**
- 1 **tablespoon brown sugar**
- 1 **tablespoon dried basil**
- 1 **tablespoon Italian seasoning**
- 1 **tablespoon dried thyme**
- 1 **tablespoon pepper**
- 1 **teaspoon dried oregano**
- 1 **teaspoon dried marjoram**

Bread bowls, shredded cheddar cheese and additional chopped onions, optional

1) In a large skillet, cook the beef, onion and garlic over medium heat until meat is no longer pink; drain.

2) Transfer to a 5-qt. slow cooker. Stir in the beans, tomato sauce, tomatoes, water and seasonings.

3) Cover and cook on low for 4-5 hours. Discard bay leaves. If desired, serve in bread bowl and garnish with cheese and onions.

Yield: 12 servings (about 3 quarts).

■ *STOVETOP SPICED CHILI:* If you like to make the chili on the stovetop, use a Dutch oven instead of a skillet to cook the beef, onion and garlic. Add the ingredients to the Dutch oven instead of the slow cooker. Bring to boil. Reduce heat; cover and simmer for 45 minutes. Discard bay leaves.

NUTRITION FACTS: 1 cup equals 236 calories, 7 g fat (3 g saturated fat), 38 mg cholesterol, 1,240 mg sodium, 25 g carbohydrate, 6 g fiber, 18 g protein.

Roasted Veggie Chili

C.J. Counts, Murphy, North Carolina

You're sure to get a kick out of this good-for-you chili that uses a bounty of veggies.

- 2 cups fresh *or* frozen corn
- 2 cups *each* cubed zucchini, yellow summer squash and eggplant
- 2 *each* medium green peppers and sweet red peppers, cut into 1-inch pieces
- 2 large onions, chopped
- 1/2 cup garlic cloves, peeled
- 1/4 cup olive oil
- 4 quarts chicken broth
- 2 cans (14-1/2 ounces *each*) stewed tomatoes
- 2 cans (14-1/2 ounces *each*) tomato puree
- 1/4 cup lime juice
- 4 teaspoon chili powder
- 1-1/4 teaspoon cayenne pepper
- 1 teaspoon ground cumin
- 1/2 cup butter
- 1/2 cup all-purpose flour
- 3 cans (15 ounces *each*) white kidney beans *or* cannellini beans, rinsed and drained
- 1/2 cup minced fresh cilantro

1) Place the vegetables and garlic in a roasting pan. Drizzle with oil; toss to coat. Cover and bake at 400° for 20-30 minutes or until vegetables are tender; cool slightly. Remove and chop garlic.

2) In a Dutch oven or soup kettle, combine the broth, tomatoes, tomato puree, lime juice, chili powder, cayenne and cumin. Bring to a boil. Reduce heat; simmer, uncovered, for 25-35 minutes or until mixture is reduced by a quarter.

3) In a large saucepan or Dutch oven, melt butter; stir in flour until smooth. Cook and stir until bubbly and starting to brown. Slowly whisk into tomato mixture. Add roasted vegetables, garlic, beans and cilantro; mix well.

4) Simmer, uncovered, until chili reaches desired thickness.

Yield: 24 servings (6 quarts).

NUTRITION FACTS: 1 cup equals 168 calories, 7 g fat (3 g saturated fat), 10 mg cholesterol, 802 mg sodium, 22 g carbohydrate, 4 g fiber, 6 g protein.

Cincinnati Chili

Edith Joyce, Parkman, Ohio

Cinnamon and cocoa give a rich brown color to this hearty chili. One heaping dish will warm you up on a cold day.

- 1 pound ground beef
- 1 pound ground pork
- 4 medium onions, chopped
- 6 garlic cloves, minced
- 2 cans (16 ounces *each*) kidney beans, rinsed and drained
- 1 can (28 ounces) crushed tomatoes
- 1/4 cup white vinegar
- 1/4 cup baking cocoa
- 2 tablespoons chili powder
- 2 tablespoons Worcestershire sauce
- 4 teaspoons ground cinnamon
- 3 teaspoons dried oregano
- 2 teaspoons ground cumin
- 2 teaspoons ground allspice
- 2 teaspoons hot pepper sauce
- 3 bay leaves
- 1 teaspoon sugar

Salt and pepper to taste

Hot cooked spaghetti

Shredded cheddar cheese, sour cream, chopped tomatoes and green onions

1) In a Dutch oven or soup kettle, cook beef, pork, onions and garlic over medium heat until meat is no longer pink; drain.

2) Add the beans, tomatoes, vinegar, cocoa and seasonings; bring to a boil. Reduce heat; cover and simmer for 1-1/2 hours or until heated through.

3) Discard bay leaves. Serve over spaghetti. Garnish with cheese, sour cream, tomatoes and onions.

Yield: 8 servings.

NUTRITION FACTS: 1 cup (calculated without spaghetti, cheese, sour cream, tomatoes and green onions) equals 421 calories, 16 g fat (6 g saturated fat), 75 mg cholesterol, 443 mg sodium, 38 g carbohydrate, 11 g fiber, 32 g protein.

CALIFORNIA CLUBS

Sandwiches

Sandwiches are often defined as a portable meal between two pieces of bread or on a roll, perfect for taking to picnics, school or work.

Sandwiches come in a variety of sizes and shapes. Many are handheld, while some need to be eaten with a knife and fork. Sandwiches can be served hot or cold, presented open-faced, stacked high or enclosed in a tortilla.

Sandwich Pizzazz

Take the humdrum out of a deli sandwich by replacing butter or mayonnaise with one of these quick-to-make spreads. Just slather or drizzle over bread or rolls.

■ *HORSERADISH MAYONNAISE:* Mix 1/4 cup mayonnaise with 1-1/2 teaspoons *each* chopped green onions and prepared horseradish.

■ *ITALIAN-STYLE MAYONNAISE:* Mix 1/4 cup mayonnaise with 3/4 teaspoon tomato paste and 1/8 teaspoon dried basil.

■ *TAPENADE MAYONNAISE:* Mix 2 tablespoons *each* mayonnaise and finely chopped ripe *or* Greek olives, 1/8 teaspoon minced garlic and a dash *each* dried thyme and pepper.

■ *AVOCADO SANDWICH SPREAD:* Mash 1/2 a large avocado and mix in 1 tablespoon minced green onion, 1 teaspoon white balsamic vinegar and 1/8 teaspoon *each* salt and pepper.

■ *CHIMICHURRI SANDWICH SPREAD:* Whisk together 2 tablespoons olive oil, 1 tablespoon *each* red wine vinegar, minced onion and minced fresh cilantro, 1 minced garlic clove, 1/4 teaspoon dried oregano and 1/8 teaspoon *each* salt and cayenne pepper.

■ *OIL AND VINEGAR DRIZZLE:* Whisk together 2 tablespoons *each* olive oil and white wine vinegar, 1 tablespoon grated Parmesan cheese, 1 teaspoon sugar, 1/4 teaspoon *each* dried oregano and paprika and 1/8 teaspoon *each* garlic powder and ground mustard.

■ *SUN-DRIED TOMATO SPREAD:* Mix 2 tablespoons *each* mayonnaise and finely chopped oil-packed sun-dried tomatoes and 2 teaspoons minced red onion.

■ *ARTICHOKE PEPPERONCINI SANDWICH SPREAD:* Process 1/3 cup rinsed and drained water-packed artichoke hearts with 2 whole pepperoncini peppers in a food processor until spreadable but not smooth.

California Clubs
Diane Cigel, Stevens Point, Wisconsin

Ranch dressing and Dijon mustard create a tasty sauce to top this sandwich. Pairing tomato and avocado with the chicken and bacon is just the right combination on sourdough bread.

1/2   cup ranch salad dressing
1/4   cup Dijon mustard
8   slices sourdough bread, toasted
4   boneless skinless chicken breast halves, cooked and sliced
1   large tomato, sliced
1   medium ripe avocado, peeled and sliced
12   bacon strips, cooked and drained

1) In a small bowl, combine salad dressing and mustard; spread on each slice of bread.

2) On four slices of bread, layer the chicken, tomato, avocado and bacon. Top with remaining bread.

Yield: 4 servings.

NUTRITION FACTS: 1 sandwich equals 837 calories, 41 g fat (9 g saturated fat), 84 mg cholesterol, 1,765 mg sodium, 74 g carbohydrate, 7 g fiber, 42 g protein.

TASTY SANDWICH TOPPER

Out of mayo? Try spreading your bread or roll with ranch or a creamy Caesar salad dressing.

Shredded French Dip
Carla Kimball, Callaway, Nebraska

A chuck roast slow-simmered in a beefy broth is delicious when shredded and spooned onto rolls. I like to serve the cooking juices in individual cups for dipping.

  1 boneless beef chuck roast
     (3 pounds), trimmed
  1 can (10-1/2 ounces) condensed
     French onion soup, undiluted
  1 can (10-1/2 ounces) condensed
     beef consomme, undiluted
  1 can (10-1/2 ounces) condensed
     beef broth, undiluted
  1 teaspoon beef bouillon granules
  8 to 10 French *or* Italian rolls, split

1) Halve roast and place in a 3-qt. slow cooker. Combine the soup, consomme, broth and bouillon; pour over roast. Cover and cook on low for 6-8 hours or until meat is tender.

2) Remove meat and shred with two forks. Serve on rolls. Skim fat from cooking juices and serve as a dipping sauce.

Yield: 10 servings.

NUTRITION FACTS: 1 serving equals 399 calories, 15 g fat (5 g saturated fat), 91 mg cholesterol, 1,104 mg sodium, 30 g carbohydrate, 2 g fiber, 33 g protein.

SHREDDING MEAT FOR SANDWICHES

Remove meat from broth and place in a shallow pan. With two forks, pull meat into thin shreds.

Pork BBQ Sandwiches
Julie Fella, Skaneateles, New York

When having a crowd over, you can also serve this barbecue on mini rolls for a great-tasting appetizer.

   1 bone-in pork shoulder roast
      (about 4 pounds)
   1 cup water
   1 teaspoon salt
   2 cups finely chopped celery
 1/3 cup steak sauce
 1/4 cup packed brown sugar
 1/4 cup cider vinegar
   2 teaspoons lemon juice
   2 teaspoons chili sauce
   1 teaspoon ketchup
   2 medium onions, sliced
   2 teaspoons sugar
   1 tablespoon olive oil
   1 tablespoon butter
  16 hoagie buns, split

1) In a Dutch oven, bring the pork roast, water and salt to a boil. Reduce heat; cover and simmer for 3-1/2 to 4 hours or until the meat is very tender.

2) Remove meat and let stand until cool enough to handle. Discard bone; shred meat with two forks. Skim fat from pan juices.

3) Stir in the celery, steak sauce, brown sugar, vinegar, lemon juice, chili sauce, ketchup and shredded pork. Bring to a boil. Reduce heat; cover and simmer for 1 hour.

4) In a large skillet, cook onions and sugar in oil and butter over low heat for 20-30 minutes or until golden brown and tender, stirring occasionally. Serve pork and onions on buns.

Yield: 16 servings.

NUTRITION FACTS: 1 sandwich equals 422 calories, 16 g fat (6 g saturated fat), 59 mg cholesterol, 660 mg sodium, 43 g carbohydrate, 2 g fiber, 26 g protein.

TASTY SANDWICHES

If you enjoy grilled sandwiches, you may want to invest in an electric or stovetop griddle, which will allow you to grill four to six sandwiches at a time.

When assembling sandwiches ahead, spread them with butter or margarine to seal the bread and keep the meat's moisture from being absorbed into the bread.

Enhance a sandwich with toppings such as guacamole, salsa, cheese spreads, mayonnaise, Swiss cheese, blue cheese, sauteed mushrooms or strips of crisp bacon.

ITALIAN BEEF SANDWICHES

Italian Beef Sandwiches
Kristin Swihart, Perrysburg, Ohio

You can enjoy this beef mixture right away, but it also freezes well. Store individual portions in the freezer and take them out for a quick lunch or dinner.

- 1 jar (11-1/2 ounces) pepperoncinis
- 1 boneless beef chuck roast (3-1/2 to 4 pounds)
- 1/4 cup water
- 1-3/4 teaspoons dried basil
- 1-1/2 teaspoons garlic powder
- 1-1/2 teaspoons dried oregano
- 1-1/4 teaspoons salt
- 1/4 teaspoon pepper
- 1 large onion, sliced and quartered
- 10 to 12 hard rolls, split

1) Drain pepperoncinis, reserving liquid. Remove and discard stems of peppers; set peppers aside. Cut roast into large chunks; place a third of the meat in a 5-qt. slow cooker. Add water.

2) In a small bowl, combine the seasonings; sprinkle half over beef. Layer with half of the remaining meat, then onion, reserved peppers and liquid. Top with remaining meat and herb mixture.

3) Cover and cook on low for 8-9 hours or until meat is tender. Shred beef with two forks. Using a slotted spoon, serve beef and peppers on rolls.

Yield: 10-12 servings.

Editor's Note: Look for pepperoncinis (pickled peppers) in the pickle and olive section of your grocery store.

NUTRITION FACTS: 1 sandwich equals 376 calories, 15 g fat (5 g saturated fat), 86 mg cholesterol, 1,132 mg sodium, 27 g carbohydrate, 2 g fiber, 31 g protein.

Pizza Sandwich Loaf
Eleanor Dunbar, Peoria, Illinois

Served with a green salad, slices of this sandwich make a terrific lunch or dinner.

- 2 loaves (8 ounces *each*) unsliced Italian bread
- 6 tablespoons olive oil, *divided*
- 1 can (14-1/2 ounces) Italian diced tomatoes, drained
- 1 can (6 ounces) tomato paste
- 1 package (6 ounces) Canadian bacon, chopped
- 1 package (3-1/2 ounces) sliced pepperoni
- 1 garlic clove, minced
- 1/2 teaspoon dried basil
- 1/2 teaspoon dried oregano
- 1/8 teaspoon pepper
- 1 cup (4 ounces) shredded mozzarella cheese
- 1/2 cup grated Parmesan *or* Romano cheese

1) Cut about 1/2 in. from the top of each loaf of bread; set aside. Hollow out bottom portion, leaving a 1/2-in. shell (discard removed bread or save for another use). Brush insides of shells and crust with 4 tablespoons oil. Place on a baking sheet. Bake at 350° for 5-10 minutes or until toasted.

2) In a 3-qt. saucepan, combine the tomatoes, tomato paste, bacon, pepperoni, garlic, basil, oregano and pepper. Bring to a boil over medium heat. Reduce heat; simmer, uncovered, for 10 minutes. Remove from heat and stir in cheeses.

3) Spoon into bread shells; replace tops and brush with remaining oil. Bake 15 minutes longer or until heated through.

Yield: 10-12 servings.

NUTRITION FACTS: 1 slice equals 286 calories, 16 g fat (5 g saturated fat), 22 mg cholesterol, 751 mg sodium, 25 g carbohydrate, 2 g fiber, 11 g protein.

Cheese Steak Subs
Taste of Home Test Kitchen

Thin slices of roast beef are topped with peppers, onions and cheese to create this satisfying stacked sandwich. Accompany it with deli potato salad and peanut butter brownies, or serve frozen French fries and store-bought sugar cookies.

- 1/2 cup julienned sweet red pepper
- 1/2 cup julienned green pepper

- 1/2 cup sliced onion
- 1/2 teaspoon vegetable oil
- 2 slices mozzarella cheese
- 4 ounces thinly sliced deli roast beef
- 2 submarine sandwich buns, split

1) In a small skillet, saute the peppers and onion in oil until tender. Cut cheese slices in half. Place beef and cheese on the bottom of each bun.

2) Broil 4 in. from the heat for 1-2 minutes or until cheese is melted. Top with pepper mixture and bun tops.

Yield: 2 servings.

NUTRITION FACTS: 1 sandwich equals 599 calories, 16 g fat (6 g saturated fat), 45 mg cholesterol, 1,679 mg sodium, 77 g carbohydrate, 5 g fiber, 34 g protein.

GREEK PITAS

Greek Pitas

Lisa Hockersmith, Bakersfield, California

These taste like gyros but can be made right at home! Plus, you can prepare the meat and sauce ahead of time for added convenience.

- 1 cup (8 ounces) plain yogurt
- 1 cup diced peeled cucumber
- 1 teaspoon dill weed
- 1/4 teaspoon seasoned salt
- 1/4 cup olive oil
- 1/4 cup lemon juice
- 2 tablespoons Dijon mustard
- 2 garlic cloves, minced
- 1-1/2 teaspoon dried oregano
- 1 teaspoon dried thyme
- 1-1/4 pounds lean boneless pork, thinly sliced
- 6 pita breads (6 inches), halved and warmed

- 1 medium tomato, chopped
- 2 tablespoons chopped onion

1) In a small bowl, combine the yogurt, cucumber, dill and seasoned salt; cover and refrigerate for 6 hours or overnight.

2) In a large resealable plastic bag, combine the oil, lemon juice, mustard, garlic, oregano and thyme; add pork. Seal bag and turn to coat; refrigerate for 6 hours or overnight, turning occasionally.

3) Drain and discard marinade. In a skillet, stir-fry pork for about 4 minutes or until no longer pink. Stuff into pita halves; top with cucumber sauce, tomato and onion.

Yield: 6 servings.

NUTRITION FACTS: 2 filled pita halves equals 375 calories, 12 g fat (4 g saturated fat), 60 mg cholesterol, 509 mg sodium, 38 g carbohydrate, 2 g fiber, 27 g protein.

Quesadilla

Amber Waddell, Grand Rapids, Michigan

This single-serving quesadilla is a snap to make. It is equally as delicious made with cooked chicken, turkey, pork or beef.

- 1 to 2 teaspoons vegetable oil
- 2 flour tortillas (6 inches)
- 1/2 cup shredded cheddar cheese, *divided*
- 1/2 cup cubed cooked chicken, turkey, pork *or* beef
- 1/4 cup sliced fresh mushrooms
- 1/2 cup shredded Monterey Jack cheese, *divided*
  Sour cream and salsa, optional

1) Heat oil in a nonstick skillet; add one tortilla. Layer with half the cheddar cheese, all of the chicken and mushrooms and half the Monterey Jack cheese. Top with the second tortilla.

2) Cover and heat until cheese melts and bottom tortilla is crisp and golden brown. Turn over; sprinkle remaining cheese on top.

3) Cook until bottom tortilla is crisp and golden brown and cheese is melted. Cut into wedges; serve with sour cream and salsa if desired.

Yield: 1 serving.

NUTRITION FACTS: 1 quesadilla equals 768 calories, 49 g fat (25 g saturated fat), 173 mg cholesterol, 1,152 mg sodium, 29 g carbohydrate, trace fiber, 53 g protein.

Chicken Salad Croissants

Laura Koziarski, Battle Creek, Michigan

This tempting chicken salad gets its special taste from Swiss cheese and pickle relish. It's a favorite of my brother, who insists I make it when he visits.

  2 **cups cubed cooked chicken**
  1 **cup cubed Swiss cheese**
1/2 **cup dill pickle relish**
2/3 **cup mayonnaise**
  1 **tablespoon minced fresh parsley**
  1 **teaspoon lemon juice**
1/2 **teaspoon seasoned salt**
1/8 **teaspoon pepper**
Lettuce leaves
  6 **croissants, split**

1) In a large bowl, combine the chicken, cheese and pickle relish. Combine the mayonnaise, parsley, lemon juice, seasoned salt and pepper; add to chicken mixture and mix well.

2) Place a lettuce leaf on each croissant; top with about 1/2 cup of the chicken mixture.

Yield: 6 servings.

NUTRITION FACTS: 1 serving (calculated without lettuce) equals 607 calories, 41 g fat (14 g saturated fat), 109 mg cholesterol, 1,001 mg sodium, 34 g carbohydrate, 2 g fiber, 25 g protein.

THREE-MEAT STROMBOLI

Three-Meat Stromboli

Lorelei Hull, Luling, Louisiana

This hearty sandwich features three different meats. But you can easily vary the stromboli filling to your liking and have delicious results.

  2 **loaves (1 pound *each*) frozen bread dough, thawed**
  2 **tablespoons Dijon mustard**
1/2 **cup grated Parmesan cheese, *divided***
1/4 **pound pastrami, finely chopped**
1/4 **pound pepperoni, finely chopped**

1/4 **pound hard salami, finely chopped**
  1 **cup (4 ounces) shredded Swiss cheese**
  1 **egg, beaten**

1) Roll each loaf of bread into a 12-in. x 7-in. rectangle. Spread mustard to within 1 in. of edges. Sprinkle each with 2 tablespoons of Parmesan cheese.

2) Combine the pastrami, pepperoni, salami and Swiss cheese; sprinkle over dough. Top with the remaining Parmesan. Brush edges of dough with egg. Roll up jelly-roll style, beginning with a long side. Seal edge and ends.

3) Place seam side down on a greased baking sheet; cut three slits in the top of each loaf. Bake at 350° for 35-40 minutes. Slice; serve warm.

Yield: 2 loaves (12-16 servings each).

NUTRITION FACTS: 1 slice equals 135 calories, 6 g fat (2 g saturated fat), 18 mg cholesterol, 377 mg sodium, 15 g carbohydrate, 1 g fiber, 7 g protein.

■ *THREE-CHEESE MEAT STROMBOLI:* Substitute a 1/4 pound chopped fully cooked ham for the pastrami and omit the pepperoni. Use 3/4 cup *each* shredded mozzarella and cheddar cheeses for the Swiss cheese. Add 1/4 cup chopped roasted red pepper to the meat-cheese mixture. Proceed as recipe directs.

Ham and Swiss Stromboli

Pat Raport, Gainesville, Florida

This pretty swirled sandwich loaf is fast, easy and versatile. Fill it with anything your family likes. Try sliced pepperoni and provolone cheese, or anchovies and ripe olives if you're feeling adventurous.

    1 **tube (11 ounces) refrigerated crusty French loaf**
    6 **ounces thinly sliced deli ham**
    6 **green onions, sliced**
    8 **bacon strips, cooked and crumbled**
1-1/2 **cups (6 ounces) shredded Swiss cheese**

1) Unroll dough on a greased baking sheet. Place ham over dough to within 1/2 in. of edges; sprinkle evenly with onions, bacon and cheese.

2) Roll up jelly-roll style, starting with a long side. Pinch seams to seal and tuck ends under. Place seam side down on baking sheet. With a sharp knife, cut several 1/4-in.-deep slits on top of loaf.

3) Bake at 350° for 26-30 minutes or until golden brown. Cool slightly before slicing. Serve warm.

Yield: 8 servings.

NUTRITION FACTS: 1 piece equals 289 calories, 15 g fat (8 g saturated fat), 46 mg cholesterol, 725 mg sodium, 19 g carbohydrate, 1 g fiber, 18 g protein.

BLUE CHEESE HAM WRAPS

Blue Cheese Ham Wraps
Marie Yockel, Smyrna, Tennessee

Bottled blue cheese salad dressing gives these wraps a burst of flavor. After topping the deli ham with Swiss cheese, I like to melt the cheese in the microwave and then assemble the rest of the wrap.

- 4 flour tortillas (6 inches)
- 12 thin slices deli ham
- 4 thin slices Swiss cheese
- 1-1/2 cups shredded lettuce
- 1 medium tomato, diced
- 2 hard-cooked eggs, chopped
- 4 teaspoons blue cheese salad dressing

1) On each tortilla, layer a fourth of the ham, Swiss cheese, lettuce, tomato and eggs.

2) Drizzle each with 1 teaspoon dressing; fold in sides.

Yield: 4 servings.

NUTRITION FACTS: 1 serving equals 603 calories, 35 g fat (13 g saturated fat), 249 mg cholesterol, 3,298 mg sodium, 18 g carbohydrate, 1 g fiber, 52 g protein.

Boston Subs
Sue Erdos, Meriden, Connecticut

My mother has made these sandwiches ever since she left her hometown of Boston many years ago. They're quick to prepare and travel well. The recipe is great for parties if you use a loaf of French or Italian bread instead of the individual rolls.

- 1/2 cup mayonnaise
- 12 submarine sandwich buns, split

- 1/2 cup Italian salad dressing, *divided*
- 1/4 pound *each* thinly sliced bologna, deli ham, hard salami, pepperoni and olive loaf
- 1/4 pound thinly sliced provolone cheese
- 1 medium onion, diced
- 1 medium tomato, diced
- 1/2 cup diced dill pickles
- 1 cup shredded lettuce
- 1 teaspoon dried oregano

1) Spread mayonnaise on inside of buns. Brush with half of the salad dressing. Layer deli meats and cheese on bun bottoms.

2) Top with onion, tomato, pickles and lettuce. Sprinkle with oregano and drizzle with remaining dressing. Replace bun tops.

Yield: 12 servings.

NUTRITION FACTS: 1 sandwich equals 682 calories, 33 g fat (9 g saturated fat), 45 mg cholesterol, 1,863 mg sodium, 72 g carbohydrate, 4 g fiber, 22 g protein.

Mozzarella Tuna Melts
Jo Maasberg, Farson, Wyoming

While soup simmers for my lunch, I assemble these tasty melts. Using a mini food processor to chop the celery and onion for the filling helps shave preparation time. Then just pop the sandwiches in the oven.

- 1 can (6 ounces) water-packed tuna, drained and flaked
- 1/4 cup finely chopped celery
- 1/4 cup finely chopped onion
- 1/4 cup mayonnaise
- 4 hamburger buns, split
- 4 mozzarella cheese slices
- 4 tomato slices
- 4 lettuce leaves

1) In a small bowl, combine the tuna, celery, onion and mayonnaise. Spread on bottom of buns; set bun tops aside. Top tuna mixture with a slice of cheese and tomato.

2) Place on an ungreased baking sheet. Bake, uncovered, at 350° for 12-15 minutes or until heated through and cheese is melted. Top each with a lettuce leaf; replace bun tops.

Yield: 4 servings.

NUTRITION FACTS: 1 sandwich equals 363 calories, 20 g fat (6 g saturated fat), 40 mg cholesterol, 575 mg sodium, 25 g carbohydrate, 2 g fiber, 20 g protein.

Toasted Reubens
Patty Kile, Greentown, Pennsylvania

When New Yorkers taste my Reuben, they say it's like those served by delis in "The Big Apple." For a little less kick, omit the horseradish from the mayonnaise mixture.

- 1/2 cup mayonnaise
- 3 tablespoons ketchup
- 2 tablespoons sweet pickle relish
- 1 tablespoon prepared horseradish
- 4 teaspoons prepared mustard
- 8 slices rye bread
- 1 pound thinly sliced deli corned beef
- 4 slices Swiss cheese
- 1 can (8 ounces) sauerkraut, rinsed and well drained
- 2 tablespoons butter

1) In a small bowl, combine the mayonnaise, ketchup, pickle relish and horseradish; set aside. Spread mustard on one side of four slices of bread, then layer with the corned beef, cheese, sauerkraut and mayonnaise mixture; top with remaining bread.

2) In a large skillet, melt butter over medium heat. Add sandwiches; cover and cook on both sides until bread is lightly toasted and cheese is melted.

Yield: 4 servings.

NUTRITION FACTS: 1 sandwich equals 705 calories, 45 g fat (15 g saturated fat), 124 mg cholesterol, 2,830 mg sodium, 41 g carbohydrate, 6 g fiber, 34 g protein.

Roasted Veggie Sandwiches
Taste of Home Test Kitchen

Looking for a delicious way to use a variety of veggies? Tuck your garden harvest into this hearty sandwich. The pleasant flavor of eggplant, red pepper, onion, zucchini and yellow summer squash is enhanced by a basil yogurt spread.

- 3 tablespoons balsamic vinegar
- 2 teaspoons olive oil
- 1/4 cup minced fresh basil *or* 1 tablespoon dried basil
- 1 small eggplant, peeled and sliced lengthwise
- 1 medium sweet red pepper, sliced
- 1 small red onion, sliced and separated into rings
- 1 small zucchini, thinly sliced
- 1 small yellow summer squash, thinly sliced

BASIL YOGURT SPREAD:

- 1/4 cup fat-free plain yogurt
- 2 tablespoons reduced-fat mayonnaise
- 1 tablespoon minced fresh basil *or* 1 teaspoon dried basil
- 1 teaspoon lemon juice
- 4 French rolls, split and warmed

1) In a large bowl, combine the vinegar, oil and basil. Add the eggplant, red pepper, onion, zucchini and yellow squash; toss to coat. Place vegetables in a single layer in a large roasting pan.

2) Roast, uncovered, at 450° for 20-30 minutes or until tender, stirring occasionally.

3) Meanwhile, in a small bowl, combine the yogurt, mayonnaise, basil and lemon juice. Hollow out rolls if necessary. Serve roasted vegetables on rolls with yogurt spread.

Yield: 4 servings.

NUTRITION FACTS: 1 sandwich equals 275 calories, 7 g fat (1 g saturated fat), 3 mg cholesterol, 421 mg sodium, 47 g carbohydrate, 8 g fiber, 9 g protein.

Taco Avocado Wraps
Renee Rutherford, Andover, Minnesota

I came up with this one summer when we wanted a light supper and didn't want to turn on the oven. We also serve it for lunch or a snack.

- 1 package (8 ounces) cream cheese, softened
- 1/2 cup sour cream
- 1 can (4 ounces) chopped green chilies, drained
- 1 tablespoon taco seasoning
- 4 flour tortillas (10 inches), warmed
- 2 medium ripe avocados, peeled and sliced
- 2 plum tomatoes, thinly sliced
- 5 green onions, sliced
- 1 can (4 ounces) sliced ripe olives, drained

1) In a small bowl, combine the cream cheese, sour cream, chilies and taco seasoning.

2) Spread about 1/2 cup over each tortilla. Top with the avocados, tomatoes, onions and olives; roll up.

Yield: 4 servings.

NUTRITION FACTS: 1 serving equals 683 calories, 47 g fat (20 g saturated fat), 82 mg cholesterol, 1,158 mg sodium, 47 g carbohydrate, 12 g fiber, 14 g protein.

CHAPTER 4
BEEF & VEAL

BEEF & VEAL

Beef and ground beef are staples in many kitchens and lend themselves to many cooking methods. When purchasing beef and ground beef, you'll want to select beef with a bright, cherry-red color and without any gray or brown patches. Select veal that has a fine-grained texture and is creamy pink in color.

Make sure the package is cold and free of holes or tears. Also make sure the package does not have excessive liquid, as this might indicate that the meat was subjected to improper temperatures.

Purchase before the "sell by" date on the packaging for best quality.

Determine the amount of beef or veal you need to buy based on the cut and amount of bone:

- 1 pound of bone-in roasts yields 2-1/2 servings.
- 1 pound of bone-in steaks yields 2 servings.
- 1 pound of boneless cuts that will be trimmed of fat yields 2-1/2 to 3-1/2 servings.
- 1 pound of lean boneless cuts without waste —such as eye of round, flank and tenderloin— yields 3 to 4 servings.

Marinate less tender cuts of beef to tenderize and add flavor. A tenderizing marinade contains an acidic ingredient such as lemon juice, vinegar, yogurt or wine. Marinades without an acid can be used to flavor tender cuts.

Marinate meat in the refrigerator, turning or stirring several times to evenly coat. Always marinate meat in the refrigerator unless you are marinating it for 30 minutes or less.

Allow 6 to 24 hours to tenderize less tender cuts of large steaks or roasts. Marinating longer than 24 hours will result in a mushy surface texture. Smaller cuts, such as cubes for kabobs or thin steaks, can be marinated in a few hours.

Set aside a portion of marinade before adding the beef if the marinade is to be used later for basting or as a serving sauce. Allow 1/4 cup of marinade for each pound of beef.

Apply a "rub" or blend of seasonings, such as fresh or dried herbs and spices, to the surface of uncooked cuts, such as roasts or steaks. Rubs add a burst of flavor to the meat but do not tenderize.

Choose an appropriate cooking method for the cut you select. Tender cuts can be cooked quickly using dry-heat methods (broiling, grilling, pan-broiling, pan-frying, roasting and stir-frying); less tender cuts need to be cooked slowly using moist-heat methods (braising and cooking in liquid).

Cooking Methods for Beef

COOKING METHOD	CUT OF BEEF
BRAISING	Chuck Roasts, Bottom Round Roast, Bottom Round Steak, Short Ribs
BROILING	Sirloin, T-Bones, Porterhouse Steaks, Rib and Rib Eye Steaks, Top Loin Steak, Skirt Steak, Flank Steak, Top Round, Ground Beef Patties
COOKING IN LIQUID	Beef Stew Meat, Brisket, Beef Shanks
GRILLING	Sirloin, T-Bones, Porterhouse Steaks, Rib and Rib Eye Steaks, Top Loin Steak, Skirt Steak, Flank Steak, Top Round Steak, Ground Beef Patties
PAN-BROILING	Steaks, Tenderloin, Ground Beef Patties
PAN-FRYING	Steaks, Liver, Cube Steaks
ROASTING	Rib Roasts, Rib Eye Roasts, Sirloin Tip Roast, Tri-Tip Roast, Whole Tenderloin, Back Ribs

Defrosting Guidelines

The thicker the package, the longer it will take to defrost. Here are some guidelines for defrosting beef or veal in the refrigerator:

- For 1/2- to 3/4-in.-thick ground beef or veal patties, allow at least 12 hours.

- For 1- to 1-1/2-in.-thick meat pieces or packages of ground beef or veal, allow at least 24 hours.

- For steaks, allow 12 to 24 hours.

- For a large roast or a thick pot roast, allow about 6 hours per pound.

SLICING BONELESS ROASTS

1) To slice boneless roasts, slice the meat vertically across the grain into 1/4-in. to 1/2-in. slices. If the roast is tied, remove the string as you carve to help hold the roast together.

CARVING CHUCK ROASTS

1) To carve arm or blade chuck roasts, first separate the individual muscles by cutting around each muscle and bone.

2) Carve each muscle across the grain of the meat to desired thickness.

Roasting Beef and Veal

Place meat on a rack in a shallow roasting pan with the fat side up. Insert an oven-safe meat thermometer in the thickest portion of the muscle without touching bone or fat. Or use an instant-read thermometer toward the end of the roasting time. If the roast needs to cook longer, remove the instant-read thermometer before you return the roast to the oven.

Roast without liquid, uncovered, according to the temperature and time given in the chart below or provided in the recipe. Because roasts will continue to cook after being removed from the oven, remove the meat when the meat thermometer reads 5-10° below desired doneness. Cover with foil and let stand for 10-15 minutes before carving.

CUT	WEIGHT	COOKING TIME (MINUTES PER POUND)			OVEN TEMP.
		MEDIUM-RARE 145°	MEDIUM 160°	WELL-DONE 170°	
BEEF RIB EYE ROAST (small end)	3 to 4 lbs.	25 to 30	30 to 35	35 to 38	350°
	4 to 6 lbs.	20 to 25	25 to 30	30 to 35	350°
BEEF RIB ROAST	4 to 6 lbs. (2 ribs)	22 to 25	25 to 30	30 to 35	350°
	6 to 8 lbs. (2 to 4 ribs)	19 to 22	22 to 28	28 to 33	350°
BEEF ROUND TIP ROAST	3 to 4 lbs.	30 to 35	33 to 38	38 to 42	325°
	4 to 6 lbs.	25 to 30	30 to 35	35 to 40	325°
BEEF TRI-TIP ROAST	1-1/2 to 2 lbs.	30 to 60 (minutes total)	40 to 45 (minutes total)		425°
BEEF BONELESS ROLLED RUMP ROAST	4 to 6 lbs.		22 to 27	30	325°
BEEF EYE OF ROUND ROAST	2 to 3 lbs.	35 to 45			325°
BEEF TENDERLOIN	4 to 5 lbs.	50 to 60 (minutes total)	60 to 70 (minutes total)	70 to 80 (minutes total)	425°
VEAL LOIN ROAST	3 to 4 lbs.		34 to 36	38 to 40	325°
VEAL BONELESS LEG ROAST	2 to 3 lbs.		18 to 20	22 to 24	325°
VEAL RIB ROAST	4 to 5 lbs.		25 to 27	29 to 31	325°
VEAL BONELESS SHOULDER ROAST	2-1/2 to 3 lbs.		31 to 34	34 to 37	325°

CARVING STANDING RIB ROASTS

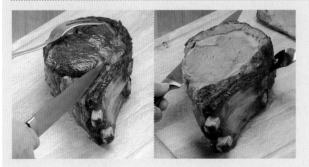

1) To carve a standing rib roast, place meat on a cutting board with large side down and rib bones to one side. Make about a 1- to 2-in. cut along the curve of the bone to separate meat from bone.

2) Slice meat horizontally into 1/4-in. to 1/2-in. slices from the top edge to the bones. Repeat slicing, loosening meat from bone as necessary.

Seasoned Rib Roast
Evelyn Gebhardt, Kasilof, Alaska

Gravy made from the drippings of this boneless beef rib roast is exceptional. You can also use a rib eye roast with excellent results.

1-1/2   teaspoons lemon-pepper seasoning

1-1/2   teaspoons paprika

  3/4   teaspoon garlic salt

  1/2   teaspoon dried rosemary, crushed

  1/4   teaspoon cayenne pepper

    1   boneless beef rib roast (3 to 4 pounds)

1)   In a small bowl, combine the seasonings; rub over roast. Place roast fat side up on a rack in a shallow roasting pan.

2)   Bake, uncovered, at 350° for 1-3/4 to 2-1/2 hours or until meat reaches desired doneness (for medium-rare, a meat thermometer should read 145°; medium, 160°; well-done, 170°).

3)   Remove to a warm serving platter. Let stand for 10-15 minutes before carving.

Yield: 6-8 servings.

NUTRITION FACTS: 5 ounces cooked beef equals 434 calories, 34 g fat (14 g saturated fat), 110 mg cholesterol, 342 mg sodium, trace carbohydrate, trace fiber, 30 g protein.

Herbed Roast Beef
Kerry Sullivan, Maitland, Florida

This is a great recipe to serve guests, and it can be easily doubled for a larger group.

    1   bone-in beef rib roast (4 to 6 pounds)

    1   teaspoon fennel seed, crushed

    1   teaspoon dried rosemary, crushed

    1   teaspoon *each* dried basil, marjoram, savory and thyme

    1   teaspoon rubbed sage

    1   medium onion, sliced

    3   fresh rosemary sprigs

HORSERADISH SAUCE:

  3/4   cup sour cream

    2   tablespoons prepared horseradish

    1   tablespoon snipped chives

4-1/2   teaspoons lemon juice

1)   Trim and tie roast if desired. In a small bowl, combine the fennel seed, crushed rosemary, basil, marjoram, savory, thyme and sage; rub over roast.

2)   Place fat side up in a roasting pan. Top with onion and rosemary sprigs. Bake, uncovered, at 350° for 2 to 3 hours or until meat reaches desired doneness (for medium-rare, a meat thermometer should read 145°; medium, 160°; well-done, 170°).

3)   Discard onion and rosemary. Let roast stand for 10-15 minutes before slicing. Meanwhile, in a small bowl, combine the sauce ingredients. Serve with beef.

Yield: 8 servings.

NUTRITION FACTS: 5 ounces cooked beef equals 544 calories, 42 g fat (18 g saturated fat), 138 mg cholesterol, 120 mg sodium, 4 g carbohydrate, 1 g fiber, 35 g protein.

Roast Prime Rib
Wendell Obermeier, Charles City, Iowa

This roast is perfect for when you want an easy yet elegant entree. It turns out moist and tender every time.

    1   tablespoon ground mustard

1-1/2   teaspoons salt

  1/2   teaspoon paprika

  1/4   teaspoon ground allspice

  1/4   teaspoon pepper

    1   boneless beef rib roast (4 to 5 pounds), rolled and tied

    1   small onion, cut into thin slivers

    2   garlic cloves, cut into slivers

Fresh parsley sprigs

1)   In a small bowl, combine the mustard, salt, paprika, allspice and pepper. Using a sharp knife,

cut long deep slits in the top of the roast, approximately 1 in. apart.

2) Stuff each slit with onion, garlic, parsley and a small amount of spice mixture. Rub remaining spice mixture on the outside of the roast.

3) Place on a rack in a shallow roasting pan. Bake, uncovered, at 325° for 2 to 2-1/2 hours or until meat reaches desired doneness (for medium-rare, a meat thermometer should read 145°; medium, 160°; well-done, 170°).

Yield: 10 servings.

NUTRITION FACTS: 8 ounces (calculated without parsley) equals 470 calories, 36 g fat (14 g saturated fat), 117 mg cholesterol, 445 mg sodium, 1 g carbohydrate, trace fiber, 33 g protein.

Spinach-Stuffed Beef Tenderloin

Taste of Home Test Kitchen

Make this entree the centerpiece of Christmas dinner...and you're sure to be serving up seconds.

1/2 pound fresh mushrooms, chopped

4 green onions, sliced

2 tablespoons olive oil, *divided*

2 garlic cloves, minced, *divided*

2 packages (10 ounces *each*) fresh spinach leaves

1 teaspoon salt, *divided*

1/8 to 1/4 teaspoon cayenne pepper

1 whole beef tenderloin (about 3-1/2 pounds), trimmed

1/4 teaspoon onion powder

1/4 teaspoon coarsely ground pepper

1) In a large nonstick skillet, saute mushrooms and onions in 1 tablespoon oil for 2 minutes. Add half of the garlic; cook until mushrooms are tender. Add spinach, 1/2 teaspoon salt and cayenne. Cook until the spinach is wilted. Remove from the heat; set aside.

2) Cut a lengthwise slit down the center of tenderloin to within 3/4 in. of bottom. Open so meat lies flat. Spread with spinach stuffing. Fold one side of meat over stuffing; tie several times with kitchen string. Rub remaining oil over beef.

3) Combine the onion powder, pepper and remaining garlic and salt; rub over beef. Place on a rack in a shallow roasting pan.

4) Bake, uncovered, at 425° for 40-55 minutes or until meat reaches desired doneness (for medium-rare, a meat thermometer should read 145°;

medium, 160°; well-done, 170°). Let stand for 10-15 minutes. Remove string before slicing.

Yield: 12 servings.

NUTRITION FACTS: 1 serving equals 241 calories, 12 g fat (4 g saturated fat), 83 mg cholesterol, 298 mg sodium, 3 g carbohydrate, 2 g fiber, 30 g protein.

Tenderloin with Creamy Garlic Sauce

Beth Taylor, Chapin, South Carolina

I like to serve this main course with green beans, garlic mashed potatoes and seven-layer salad for a special holiday dinner. The garlic sauce is also good with pork or poultry.

1 jar (8 ounces) Dijon mustard, *divided*

10 garlic cloves, peeled, *divided*

2 tablespoons whole black peppercorns, coarsely crushed, *divided*

3 tablespoons vegetable oil, *divided*

1 beef tenderloin (4 to 5 pounds), halved

2 cups heavy whipping cream

1 cup (8 ounces) sour cream

1) In a blender, combine half of the mustard, eight garlic cloves and 1 tablespoon peppercorns; cover and process for 1 minute, scraping the sides occasionally. Add 1 tablespoon oil; process until a paste forms. Spread over beef.

2) In a large skillet, heat the remaining oil over medium-high heat. Brown beef, one piece at a time, on all sides. Place in a shallow roasting pan coated with nonstick cooking spray.

3) Bake, uncovered, at 400° for 25-45 minutes or until meat reaches desired doneness (for medium-rare, a meat thermometer should read 145°; medium, 160°; well done, 170°). Remove to a warm serving platter. Let stand for 10-15 minutes.

4) Meanwhile, mince the remaining garlic. In a saucepan, combine garlic, whipping cream, sour cream and remaining mustard and peppercorns. Cook and stir over low heat until heated through. Slice beef; serve with the sauce.

Yield: 12 servings.

NUTRITION FACTS: 4 ounces with 1/4 cup sauce equals 499 calories, 38 g fat (18 g saturated fat), 163 mg cholesterol, 553 mg sodium, 5 g carbohydrate, trace fiber, 33 g protein.

YANKEE-DOODLE SIRLOIN ROAST

Brisket with Chunky Tomato Sauce
Linda Blaska, Atlanta, Georgia

Treat dinner guests to this impressive brisket, and they'll agree it's the best beef they've ever tasted. A savory tomato sauce adds the finishing touch.

- 1 fresh beef brisket (4-1/2 pounds)
- 1 teaspoon salt
- 1/4 to 1/2 teaspoon pepper
- 1 tablespoon olive oil
- 3 large onions, chopped
- 2 garlic cloves, minced
- 1 cup dry red wine *or* beef broth
- 1 can (14-1/2 ounces) diced tomatoes, undrained
- 2 celery ribs with leaves, chopped
- 1/2 teaspoon dried thyme
- 1/2 teaspoon dried rosemary, crushed
- 1 bay leaf
- 1 pound carrots, cut into 1/2-inch slices

1) Season brisket with salt and pepper. In a Dutch oven, brown brisket in oil over medium-high heat. Remove and keep warm.

2) In the same pan, saute onions and garlic until tender. Place brisket over onions. Add the wine or broth, tomatoes, celery, thyme, rosemary and bay leaf.

3) Cover and bake at 325° for 2 hours, basting occasionally. Add carrots; bake 1 hour longer or until meat is tender. Discard bay leaf. Cool for 1 hour; cover and refrigerate overnight.

4) Trim visible fat from brisket and skim fat from tomato mixture. Thinly slice beef across the grain.

5) In a saucepan, warm tomato mixture; transfer to a shallow roasting pan. Top with sliced beef. Cover and bake at 325° for 30 minutes or until heated through. Serve sauce over beef.

Yield: 12 servings.

Editor's Note: This is a fresh beef brisket, not corned beef. The meat comes from the first cut of the brisket.

NUTRITION FACTS: 1 serving equals 316 calories, 12 g fat (4 g saturated fat), 100 mg cholesterol, 394 mg sodium, 10 g carbohydrate, 2 g fiber, 38 g protein.

Yankee-Doodle Sirloin Roast
Laurie Neverman, Green Bay, Wisconsin

In the spirit of July Fourth, we planned a theme menu for our families including this wonderful beef roast. Marinating the meat overnight really boosts the flavor.

- 1/2 cup beef broth
- 1/2 cup teriyaki *or* soy sauce
- 1/4 cup vegetable oil
- 2 tablespoons brown sugar
- 2 tablespoons finely chopped onion
- 3 garlic cloves, minced
- 1 teaspoon Worcestershire sauce
- 1/2 teaspoon hot pepper sauce
- 1 boneless beef sirloin tip roast (about 4 pounds)

1) In a large resealable plastic bag, combine the first eight ingredients; add roast. Seal bag and turn to coat; refrigerate overnight.

2) Drain and discard marinade. Place roast on a rack in a shallow roasting pan.

3) Bake, uncovered, at 350° for 1-1/2 to 2-1/4 hours or until meat reaches desired doneness (for medium-rare, a meat thermometer should read 145°; medium, 160°; well-done, 170°). Let stand for 10-15 minutes before slicing.

Yield: 12-14 servings.

Editor's Note: To grill the roast, grill, covered, over indirect medium heat for 1-1/2 to 2-1/4 hours or until meat reaches desired doneness.

NUTRITION FACTS: 3 ounces cooked beef equals 183 calories, 8 g fat (2 g saturated fat), 69 mg cholesterol, 247 mg sodium, 2 g carbohydrate, trace fiber, 25 g protein.

BRISKET FOR A BUNCH

Brisket for a Bunch
Dawn Fagerstrom, Warren, Minnesota

This makes tender slices of beef in a delicious au jus. To easily get very thin slices, chill the brisket before slicing and reheat in the juices.

- 1   fresh beef brisket (2-1/2 pounds), cut in half
- 1   tablespoon vegetable oil
- 1/2   cup chopped celery
- 1/2   cup chopped onion
- 3/4   cup beef broth
- 1/2   cup tomato sauce
- 1/4   cup water
- 1/4   cup sugar
- 2   tablespoons onion soup mix
- 1   tablespoon cider vinegar
- 12   hamburger buns, split

1) In a large skillet, brown the brisket on each side in oil; transfer to a slow cooker. In the same skillet, saute celery and onion for 1 minute. Gradually add the broth, tomato sauce and water; stir to loosen the browned bits from pan. Add sugar, soup mix and vinegar; bring to a boil. Pour over brisket.

2) Cover and cook on low for 7-8 hours or until meat is tender. Let stand for 5 minutes before slicing. Skim fat from cooking juices. Serve meat in buns with cooking juices.

Yield: 10 servings.

Editor's Note: This is a fresh beef brisket, not corned beef. The meat comes from the first cut of the brisket.

NUTRITION FACTS: 3 ounces equals 404 calories, 18 g fat (6 g saturated fat), 68 mg cholesterol, 583 mg sodium, 33 g carbohydrate, 2 g fiber, 25 g protein.

Corned Beef Dinner
Michelle Rhodes, Cleveland, Ohio

This flavorful meal is a must for St. Patrick's Day but great any time of the year. A slow cooker makes it easy to serve four with enough leftover meat for Reuben sandwiches or other dishes.

- 4   to 5 medium red potatoes, quartered
- 2   cups fresh baby carrots, halved lengthwise
- 3   cups chopped cabbage
- 1   corned beef brisket (3-1/2 pounds) with spice packet
- 3   cups water
- 1   tablespoon caraway seeds

1) Place the potatoes, carrots and cabbage in a 5-qt. slow cooker. Cut brisket in half; place over vegetables. Add the water, caraway seeds and contents of spice packet.

2) Cover and cook on low for 9-10 hours or until the meat and vegetables are tender.

Yield: 8 servings.

NUTRITION FACTS: 1 serving equals 457 calories, 30 g fat (9 g saturated fat), 107 mg cholesterol, 2,452 mg sodium, 14 g carbohydrate, 3 g fiber, 31 g protein.

SLICING CORNED BEEF

For melt-in-your-mouth corned beef, thinly slice the meat across the grain.

Slow-Cooked Coffee Beef Roast

Charles Trahan, San Dimas, California

Day-old coffee is the key to this flavorful beef roast that simmers in the slow cooker until it's fall-apart tender. Try it once and I'm sure you'll cook it again.

1	boneless beef sirloin tip roast (2-1/2 pounds), cut in half
2	teaspoons canola oil
1-1/2	cups sliced fresh mushrooms
1/3	cup sliced green onions
2	garlic cloves, minced
1-1/2	cups brewed coffee
1	teaspoon Liquid Smoke, optional
1/2	teaspoon salt
1/2	teaspoon chili powder
1/4	teaspoon pepper
1/4	cup cornstarch
1/3	cup cold water

1) In a large nonstick skillet, brown roast on all sides in oil over medium-high heat. Place in a 5-qt. slow cooker.

2) In the same skillet, saute mushrooms, onions and garlic until tender; stir in the coffee, Liquid Smoke if desired, salt, chili powder and pepper. Pour over roast.

3) Cover and cook on low for 8-10 hours or until meat is tender. Remove roast and keep warm.

Pour cooking juices into a 2-cup measuring cup; skim fat.

4) In a saucepan, combine cornstarch and water until smooth. Gradually stir in 2 cups cooking juices. Bring to a boil; cook and stir for 2 minutes or until thickened. Serve with sliced beef.

Yield: 6 servings.

NUTRITION FACTS: 1 serving (3 ounces cooked beef with 1/3 cup gravy) equals 209 calories, 7 g fat (2 g saturated fat), 82 mg cholesterol, 244 mg sodium, 6 g carbohydrate, trace fiber, 28 g protein.

SLOW COOKER TIPS

Choose the correct size slow cooker for your recipe. A slow cooker should be from half to three-quarters full.

Cut roasts over 3 pounds in half to ensure proper and even cooking.

Trim as much fat from meat before placing in the slow cooker to avoid greasy gravy.

Add more flavor to gravy by first browning the meat in a skillet. Then scrape all of the browned bits from the bottom of the skillet and add to the slow cooker along with the meat.

Do not remove the lid during cooking unless the recipe specifically says to stir or add an ingredient. Removing the lid allows a significant amount of heat to be lost and will increase the cooking time.

POT ROAST
DONENESS TEST

Pot roasts are done when a long-handled fork can be inserted into the thickest part of the roast easily. If the pot roast is cooked until it falls apart, the meat is actually overcooked and will be stringy, tough and dry.

Saucy Italian Roast
Jan Roat, Red Lodge, Montana

This tender roast is one of my favorite fix-and-forget meals. I thicken the juices with a little flour and add ketchup, then serve the sauce and beef slices over pasta.

- 1 boneless rump roast
  (3 to 3-1/2 pounds)
- 1/2 to 1 teaspoon salt
- 1/2 teaspoon garlic powder
- 1/4 teaspoon pepper
- 1 jar (4-1/2 ounces) sliced mushrooms, drained
- 1 medium onion, diced
- 1 jar (14 ounces) spaghetti sauce
- 1/4 to 1/2 cup red wine *or* beef broth

Hot cooked pasta

1) Cut the roast in half. Combine the salt, garlic powder and pepper; rub over roast. Place in a 5-qt. slow cooker. Top with mushrooms and onion. Combine the spaghetti sauce and wine or broth; pour over meat and vegetables.

2) Cover and cook on low for 8-9 hours or until meat is tender. Slice roast; serve over pasta with pan juices.

Yield: 10 servings.

NUTRITION FACTS: 1/3 pound (calculated without pasta) equals 218 calories, 8 g fat (3 g saturated fat), 82 mg cholesterol, 415 mg sodium, 6 g carbohydrate, 1 g fiber, 28 g protein.

REDUCING PAN JUICES FOR GRAVY

To thicken pan juices without flour, remove the meat to a warm serving platter. Transfer pan juices along with browned bit to a saucepan. Bring to a boil; cook, uncovered, until the liquid evaporates enough that it thickens to a gravy consistency.

BEEF BARBECUE

Beef Barbecue
Karen Walker, Sterling, Virginia

We like to keep our freezer stocked with plenty of beef roasts. When we're not in the mood for pot roast, I fix these satisfying sandwiches instead. The meat cooks in a tasty sauce while I'm at work. Then I just slice it thinly and serve it on rolls.

- 1 boneless chuck roast (3 pounds)
- 1 cup barbecue sauce
- 1/2 cup apricot preserves
- 1/3 cup chopped green *or* sweet red pepper
- 1 small onion, chopped
- 1 tablespoon Dijon mustard
- 2 teaspoons brown sugar
- 12 sandwich rolls, split

1) Cut the roast into quarters; place in a greased 5-qt. slow cooker. In a bowl, combine barbecue sauce, preserves, green pepper, onion, mustard and brown sugar; pour over roast. Cover and cook on low for 6-8 hours or until meat is tender.

2) Remove roast and thinly slice; return meat to slow cooker and stir gently. Cover and cook 20-30 minutes longer. Skim fat from sauce. Serve beef and sauce on rolls.

Yield: 12 servings.

NUTRITION FACTS: 3 ounces cooked beef equals 414 calories, 14 g fat (5 g saturated fat), 74 mg cholesterol, 564 mg sodium, 43 g carbohydrate, 2 g fiber, 28 g protein.

BRAISED BEEF WITH BARLEY

Braised Beef with Barley

June Formanek, Belle Plaine, Iowa

Braising works well for less tender cuts of meat, and brings out the flavor of the chuck roast in this recipe. Barley, mushrooms and peas are a wonderful addition to the meal.

1	boneless chuck roast (2 to 2-1/2 pounds)
1	tablespoon vegetable oil
1	medium onion, chopped
1/2	pound fresh mushrooms, sliced
3	garlic cloves, minced
1	can (14-1/2 ounces) beef broth
1	bay leaf
1-1/2	teaspoons salt
1/4	teaspoon pepper
1/2	cup medium pearl barley
1	cup frozen peas
1/3	cup sour cream, optional

1) In a Dutch oven, brown meat in oil on all sides over medium-high heat. Remove roast and set aside. Drain, reserving 1 tablespoon of drippings. Saute the onion, mushrooms and garlic in drippings until tender.

2) Return roast to the pan. Add the broth, bay leaf, salt and pepper; bring to a boil. Reduce heat; cover and simmer for 1-1/2 hours. Add barley. Cover and simmer for 45 minutes or until meat and barley are tender. Add peas; cover and

simmer for 5 minutes or until peas are tender. Discard bay leaf.

3) Set the roast and barley aside; keep warm. Skim fat from pan juices. If desired, add sour cream to the pan juices; stir until heated through over low heat (do not boil). Slice roast; serve with barley and gravy.

Yield: 6 servings.

NUTRITION FACTS: 1 serving equals 380 calories, 17 g fat (6 g saturated fat), 98 mg cholesterol, 922 mg sodium, 21 g carbohydrate, 5 g fiber, 35 g protein.

BRAISING BEEF

1) Heat oil in a Dutch oven over medium-high. Brown roast on all sides, turning with a sturdy meat fork.

2) Combine liquid ingredients and seasonings; pour over roast. Cover and simmer for 1 to 2 hours or bake at 325° for 2 to 3 hours or until tender. Proceed with recipe.

THICKENING PAN JUICES FROM BRAISED BEEF

Remove meat to a warm serving platter; skim fat from pan juices. (See Step 1 of Making Pan Gravy on page 156.) Measure juices and transfer to a saucepan. For each cup of juices, combine 3 tablespoons all-purpose flour and 1/3 cup cold water until smooth. Stir flour mixture into pan; bring to a boil, stirring constantly. Cook and stir for 2 minutes or until thickened, adding additional water if necessary. Season to taste with salt and pepper.

Down-Home Pot Roast

Lenore Rein, Kelliher, Saskatchewan

The aroma of my mom's pot roast made our mouths water. I've tried different variations, but this one is my favorite.

- 1 boneless beef sirloin tip roast (3 pounds)
- 1 tablespoon canola oil
- 1 can (14-1/2 ounces) reduced-sodium beef broth
- 3 tablespoons cider vinegar
- 2 garlic cloves, minced
- 1/2 teaspoon dried basil
- 1/4 teaspoon dried thyme
- 1 small head cabbage, cut into wedges
- 4 medium potatoes, quartered
- 2 medium onions, cut into chunks
- 3 medium carrots, cut into chunks
- 1 medium sweet red pepper, cut into 1-inch pieces
- 1/2 teaspoon salt
- 1/2 teaspoon pepper
- 1/4 cup all-purpose flour
- 1/4 cup cold water

1) In a Dutch oven, brown roast on all sides in oil over medium-high heat; drain. Add broth. Pour vinegar over roast. Sprinkle with garlic, basil and thyme. Bring to a boil. Reduce heat; cover and simmer for 2 hours, turning roast occasionally. Add water if needed. Skim off fat.

2) Add vegetables to pan. Sprinkle with salt and pepper. Cover and simmer for 35-45 minutes or until vegetables and meat are tender. Remove meat and vegetables to a serving platter and keep warm.

3) For gravy, pour drippings and loosened browned bits into a measuring cup. Skim fat, reserving 2 cups drippings. Return drippings to pan.

4) Combine flour and cold water until smooth; gradually stir into drippings. Bring to a boil; cook and stir for 2 minutes or until thickened. Serve with meat and vegetables.

Yield: 12 servings.

NUTRITION FACTS: 3 ounces cooked beef with 2 tablespoons sauce equals 258 calories, 7 g fat (2 g saturated fat), 61 mg cholesterol, 235 mg sodium, 25 g carbohydrate, 4 g fiber, 25 g protein.

German Sauerbraten

Cathy Eland, Highstown, New Jersey

Our family loves it when Mom prepares this wonderful old-world dish. The tender beef has a bold blend of mouth-watering seasonings. It smells so good in the oven and tastes even better!

- 2 teaspoons salt
- 1 teaspoon ground ginger
- 1 beef top round roast (about 4 pounds)
- 2-1/2 cups water
- 2 cups cider vinegar
- 2 medium onions, sliced
- 1/3 cup sugar
- 2 tablespoons mixed pickling spices
- 1 teaspoon whole peppercorns
- 8 whole cloves
- 2 bay leaves
- 2 tablespoons vegetable oil
- 14 to 16 gingersnaps, crushed

1) Combine salt and ginger; rub over roast. Place in a deep glass bowl. In a saucepan, combine water, vinegar, onions, sugar, pickling spices, peppercorns, cloves and bay leaves; bring to a boil.

2) Pour over roast; turn to coat. Cover and refrigerate for 2 days, turning twice a day.

3) Remove roast, reserving marinade; pat roast dry. In a large kettle or Dutch oven, brown roast on all sides in oil over medium-high heat.

4) Strain marinade, reserving half of the onions and seasonings. Pour 1 cup of marinade and reserved onions and seasonings over roast (cover and refrigerate remaining marinade). Bring to a boil. Reduce heat; cover and simmer for 3 hours or until meat is tender.

5) Strain cooking liquid, discarding the onions and seasonings. Measure liquid; if necessary, add enough reserved marinade to equal 3 cups. Pour into a saucepan and bring to a full rolling boil; boil for 1 minute. Add gingersnaps. Reduce heat; simmer, uncovered, until gravy is thickened. Slice roast and serve with gravy.

Yield: 14 servings.

NUTRITION FACTS: 3-1/2 ounces cooked beef with about 3 tablespoons gravy equals 241 calories, 7 g fat (2 g saturated fat), 73 mg cholesterol, 420 mg sodium, 15 g carbohydrate, 1 g fiber, 30 g protein.

Beef Stew with Potato Dumplings

Shawn Asiala, Boca Raton, Florida

You could call me a "recipe tinkerer." It's fun for me to take a recipe, substitute ingredients, add seasonings to spice it up and make the final result my own!

- 1/4 cup all-purpose flour
- 3/4 teaspoon salt
- 1/2 teaspoon pepper
- 2 pounds beef stew meat
- 2 medium onions, chopped
- 2 tablespoons vegetable oil
- 2 cans (10-1/2 ounces *each*) condensed beef broth, undiluted
- 3/4 cup water
- 1 tablespoon red wine vinegar
- 6 medium carrots, cut into 2-inch chunks
- 2 bay leaves
- 1 teaspoon dried thyme
- 1/4 teaspoon garlic powder

DUMPLINGS:

- 1 egg
- 3/4 cup seasoned dry bread crumbs
- 1 tablespoon all-purpose flour
- 1 tablespoon minced fresh parsley
- 1 tablespoon minced onion
- 1/2 teaspoon dried thyme
- 1/2 teaspoon salt
- 1/2 teaspoon pepper
- 2-1/2 cups finely shredded raw potatoes
  Additional all-purpose flour

1) In a plastic bag, combine the flour, salt and pepper. Add meat; toss to coat. In a Dutch oven, cook meat along with onions in oil until the meat is browned on all sides and onions are tender.

2) Stir in the broth, water, vinegar, carrots and seasonings; bring to a boil. Reduce heat; cover and simmer for 1-1/2 hours or until meat is almost tender. Discard bay leaves.

3) In a large bowl, beat egg; add the crumbs, flour, parsley, onion and seasonings. Stir in potatoes; mix well. With floured hands, shape into 1-1/2-in. balls. Dust with flour.

4) Bring stew to a boil; drop dumplings onto stew. Cover and simmer for 30 minutes (do not lift cover while simmering). Serve immediately.

Yield: 6 servings.

NUTRITION FACTS: 1 serving (calculated without additional all-purpose flour) equals 487 calories, 18 g fat (5 g saturated fat), 130 mg cholesterol, 1,486 mg sodium, 42 g carbohydrate, 5 g fiber, 38 g protein.

BEEF BARLEY STEW

Beef Barley Stew

June Formanek, Belle Plaine, Iowa

I like barley, and this recipe makes a filling dish that's lower in fat.

- 1-1/2 pounds lean beef stew meat, cut into 1/2-inch cubes
- 1 medium onion, chopped
- 1 tablespoon vegetable oil
- 3 cans (14-1/2 ounces *each*) beef broth
- 1 cup medium pearl barley
- 1 teaspoon dried thyme
- 1/2 teaspoon dried marjoram
- 1/4 teaspoon dried rosemary, crushed
- 1/4 teaspoon pepper
- 4 medium carrots, sliced
- 2 tablespoons chopped fresh parsley

1) In a large saucepan or Dutch oven, brown meat on all sides and onion in oil over medium-high heat. Add the broth, barley and seasonings; bring to a boil. Reduce the heat; cover and simmer for 1 hour.

2) Add carrots; bring to a boil. Reduce heat; cover and simmer 30-40 minutes or until meat and carrots are tender. Add parsley just before serving.

Yield: 8 servings.

NUTRITION FACTS: 1 cup equals 266 calories, 8 g fat (0 saturated fat), 40 mg cholesterol, 618 mg sodium, 24 g carbohydrate, 0 fiber, 23 g protein.

1) In a Dutch oven, brown beef on all sides in oil over medium-high heat; drain. Add the cider, vinegar, salt if desired, thyme and pepper; bring to a boil. Reduce heat; cover and simmer for 1-1/4 hours.

2) Add the potatoes, carrots, celery and onions; return to a boil. Reduce heat; cover and simmer for 30-35 minutes or until beef and vegetables are tender.

3) Combine flour and water until smooth; stir into stew. Bring to a boil; cook and stir for 2 minutes or until slightly thickened.

Yield: 8 servings.

NUTRITION FACTS: 1 cup equals 315 calories, 12 g fat (0 saturated fat), 70 mg cholesterol, 238 mg sodium, 29 g carbohydrate, 0 fiber, 24 g protein.

Hungarian Goulash
Joan Rose, Langley, British Columbia

With tender beef and a rich flavorful sauce, this entree is an old favorite with my family.

- 1 pound beef stew meat, cut into 1-inch cubes
- 1 pound lean boneless pork, cut into 1-inch cubes
- 2 large onions, thinly sliced
- 2 tablespoons vegetable oil
- 2 cups water
- 2 tablespoons paprika
- 1/2 teaspoon salt
- 1/2 teaspoon dried marjoram
- 1 tablespoon all-purpose flour
- 1 cup (8 ounces) sour cream

Hot cooked noodles

1) In a large skillet, brown beef, pork and onions in oil over medium heat; drain. Add the water, paprika, salt and marjoram; bring to a boil. Reduce heat; cover and simmer for 1-1/2 hours or until meat is tender.

2) Just before serving, combine flour and sour cream until smooth; stir into meat mixture. Bring to a boil over medium heat; cook and stir for 1-2 minutes or until thickened and bubbly. Serve over noodles.

Yield: 6-8 servings.

Editor's Note: You can use additional beef stew meat for the pork in this recipe.

NUTRITION FACTS: 1 cup goulash (calculated without noodles) equals 273 calories, 16 g fat (7 g saturated fat), 89 mg cholesterol, 212 mg sodium, 6 g carbohydrate, 1 g fiber, 24 g protein.

CIDER BEEF STEW

Cider Beef Stew
Joyce Glaesemann, Lincoln, Nebraska

It's especially nice to use this recipe in fall, when the weather gets crisp and Nebraska's apple orchards start selling fresh apple cider. This entree's subtle sweetness is a welcome change from other savory stews. We enjoy it with biscuits and slices of apple and cheddar cheese.

- 2 pounds beef stew meat, cut into 1-inch cubes
- 2 tablespoons vegetable oil
- 3 cups apple cider *or* juice
- 2 tablespoons cider vinegar
- 2 teaspoons salt, optional
- 1/4 to 1/2 teaspoon dried thyme
- 1/4 teaspoon pepper
- 3 medium potatoes, peeled and cubed
- 4 medium carrots, cut into 3/4-inch pieces
- 3 celery ribs, cut into 3/4-inch pieces
- 2 medium onions, cut into wedges
- 1/4 cup all-purpose flour
- 1/4 cup water

Surf 'n' Turf Tenderloin
Colleen Gonring, Brookfield, Wisconsin

The twist on this recipe is the steaks are stuffed with shrimp. This main-course pleaser only looks tricky, but it's really a cinch to prepare.

  1 tablespoon finely chopped onion
  1 garlic clove, minced
  2 tablespoons olive oil, *divided*
  2 tablespoons butter, *divided*
1/4 cup beef broth
 16 uncooked medium shrimp (about 1/2 pound), peeled and deveined
  1 tablespoon minced fresh parsley
  4 beef tenderloin steaks (1-1/2 to 2 inches thick and 6 ounces *each*)

1) In a small skillet, saute onion and garlic in 1 tablespoon oil and 1 tablespoon butter until tender. Add broth; cook and stir for 1 minute. Add the shrimp; cook and stir until shrimp turn pink, about 3-5 minutes. Add parsley.

2) Meanwhile, make a horizontal cut three-fourths of the way through each steak. Place three shrimp in each pocket. Cover remaining shrimp and sauce for garnish; set aside and keep warm.

3) In a large skillet, heat remaining oil and butter over medium-high heat. Add steaks; cook until meat reaches desired doneness (about 10-13 minutes for medium, 160°), turning once. Top with remaining shrimp and sauce.

Yield: 4 servings.

NUTRITION FACTS: 1 serving equals 453 calories, 30 g fat (11 g saturated fat), 205 mg cholesterol, 282 mg sodium, 1 g carbohydrate, trace fiber, 43 g protein.

Beef Tenderloin Stroganoff
Elizabeth Deguit, Richmond Hill, Georgia

This entree is easy to prepare, and it's a great dish to serve company. Using tenderloin makes it special.

   2 tablespoons all-purpose flour
1-1/2 pound beef tenderloin, cut into thin strips
   2 tablespoons olive oil
   2 tablespoons butter
1-1/2 cups beef broth
 1/4 cup sour cream
   2 tablespoons tomato paste
 1/2 teaspoon paprika
  Salt to taste
  Hot cooked noodles

1) Place flour in resealable plastic bag; add beef, a few pieces at a time, and shake to coat. In a large skillet, brown beef in oil and butter over medium heat.

2) Gradually stir in broth; bring to a boil. Reduce heat to low. In a small bowl, combine the sour cream, tomato paste, paprika and salt; slowly stir in sour cream mixture (do not boil).

3) Cook, uncovered, over low heat for 15-20 minutes, stirring frequently. Serve over noodles.

Yield: 4-6 servings.

NUTRITION FACTS: 1 serving (calculated without salt and noodles) equals 312 calories, 21 g fat (9 g saturated fat), 89 mg cholesterol, 305 mg sodium, 4 g carbohydrate, trace fiber, 24 g protein.

Marinated Beef Fondue
DeEtta Rasmussen, Fort Madison, Iowa

Guests will enjoy cooking this boldly seasoned meat, then dipping it in either zippy sauce.

- 3/4 **cup soy sauce**
- 1/4 **cup Worcestershire sauce**
- 2 **garlic cloves, minced**
- 2-1/2 **pounds beef tenderloin, cut into 1-inch cubes**
- 2-1/2 **pounds pork tenderloin, cut into 1-inch cubes**

HORSERADISH SAUCE:

- 1 **cup (8 ounces) sour cream**
- 3 **tablespoons prepared horseradish**
- 1 **tablespoon chopped onion**
- 1 **teaspoon white vinegar**
- 1/2 **teaspoon salt**
- 1/4 **teaspoon pepper**

BARBECUE SAUCE:

- 1 **can (8 ounces) tomato sauce**
- 1/3 **cup steak sauce**
- 2 **tablespoons brown sugar**
- 6 **to 9 cups peanut *or* vegetable oil**

1) In a large resealable plastic bag, combine the soy sauce, Worcestershire sauce and garlic; add meat. Seal bag and turn to coat; refrigerate for 4 hours, turning occasionally.

2) Meanwhile, in a small bowl, combine horseradish sauce ingredients; cover and refrigerate.

3) In another bowl, combine the tomato sauce, steak sauce and brown sugar; cover and refrigerate. Drain and discard marinade. Pat meat dry with paper towels.

4) Using one fondue pot for every six people, heat 2-3 cups oil in each pot to 375°. Use fondue forks to cook meat in oil until it reaches desired doneness. Serve with the horseradish and barbecue sauces.

Yield: 12-16 servings.

Editor's Note: You can use additional beef tenderloin for the pork tenderloin.

NUTRITION FACTS: 1 serving equals 272 calories, 13 g fat (5 g saturated fat), 94 mg cholesterol, 680 mg sodium, 5 g carbohydrate, trace fiber, 30 g protein.

Mongolian Fondue
Marion Lowery, Medford, Oregon

Mealtime is so much fun and filled with laughter and conversation when fondue is on the menu. I created this recipe after tasting something similar in a restaurant. Family and friends request it often.

- 1/2 **cup soy sauce**
- 1/4 **cup water**
- 1 **teaspoon white wine vinegar**
- 1-1/2 **teaspoons minced garlic, *divided***
- 1 **cup sliced carrots (1/4 inch thick)**
- 2 **cans (14-1/2 ounces *each*) beef broth**
- 1 **teaspoon minced fresh gingerroot**
- 2 **pounds boneless beef sirloin steak, cut into 2-1/2-inch x 1/4-inch strips**
- 1 **pound turkey breast, cut into 2-1/2-inch x 1/4-inch strips**
- 1 **pound uncooked large shrimp, peeled and deveined**
- 3 **small zucchini, cut into 1/2-inch slices**
- 1 ***each* medium sweet red, yellow and green pepper, cut into 1-inch chunks**
- 1 **to 2 cups whole fresh mushrooms**
- 1 **cup cubed red onion (1-inch pieces)**
- 1 **jar (7 ounces) hoisin sauce**
- 1 **jar (4 ounces) Chinese hot mustard**

1) In a saucepan, combine the soy sauce, water, vinegar and 1/2 teaspoon garlic; bring to a boil. Remove from the heat. Cover and refrigerate for at least 1 hour.

2) In a small saucepan, cook carrots in a small amount of water for 3 minutes or until crisp-tender; drain and pat dry. In a large saucepan, bring broth, ginger and remaining garlic to a boil.

3) Transfer to a fondue pot and keep warm. Pat meat and shrimp dry with paper towels.

4) Use fondue forks to cook beef to desired doneness. Cook turkey until juices run clear. Cook shrimp until pink. Cook vegetables until they reach desired doneness. Serve with hoisin sauce, mustard sauce and reserved garlic-soy sauce.

Yield: 8 servings.

NUTRITION FACTS: 1 serving equals 364 calories, 8 g fat (2 g saturated fat), 184 mg cholesterol, 1,826 mg sodium, 21 g carbohydrate, 3 g fiber, 50 g protein.

Santa Fe Strip Steaks
Joan Hallford, North Richland Hills, Texas

If you love Southwestern flavor, this recipe certainly provides it.

- 1/2 **cup chopped onion**
- 1 **tablespoon olive oil**
- 2 **cans (4 ounces *each*) chopped green chilies**
- 1/2 **cup fresh cilantro leaves**
- 1 **jalapeno pepper, seeded**
- 2 **teaspoons red currant jelly**
- 1 **teaspoon chicken bouillon granules**
- 1 **teaspoon Worcestershire sauce**
- 1 **garlic clove, peeled**
- 1/2 **teaspoon seasoned salt**
- 1/4 **teaspoon dried oregano**

Salt and pepper to taste
- 1/2 **cup shredded Monterey Jack cheese, optional**
- 4 **New York strip steaks (about 1 inch and 7 ounces *each*)**

1) In a small saucepan, saute onion in oil until tender. Transfer to a blender or food processor. Add the green chilies, cilantro, jalapeno, jelly, bouillon, Worcestershire sauce, garlic, seasoned salt and oregano; cover and process until smooth.

2) Return mixture to saucepan. Bring to a boil. Reduce heat; simmer, uncovered, for 10 minutes. Set aside and keep warm.

3) Sprinkle steaks with salt and pepper. Broil 4-6 in. from heat for 4-8 minutes on each side or until meat reaches desired doneness (for medium-rare, a meat thermometer should read 145°; medium, 160°; well-done, 170°).

4) Serve steaks with green chili sauce and sprinkle with cheese if desired.

Yield: 4 servings.

Editor's Note: Steak may be known as strip steak, Kansas City steak, New York Strip steak, Ambassador Steak or boneless Club Steak in your region. Steaks may also be grilled, uncovered, over medium heat. When cutting or seeding hot peppers, use rubber or plastic gloves to protect your hands. Avoid touching your face.

NUTRITION FACTS: 1 serving (calculated without salt and pepper) equals 457 calories, 31 g fat (11 g saturated fat), 109 mg cholesterol, 727 mg sodium, 8 g carbohydrate, 2 g fiber, 36 g protein.

Peppercorn Steaks
Taste of Home Test Kitchen

These tender peppered steaks get plenty of zip from a quick-to-fix sauce flavored with mustard and Worcestershire.

- 1 **tablespoon whole black peppercorns, crushed**
- 2 **New York strip steaks (8 ounces *each*)**
- 2 **to 3 tablespoons butter, melted**
- 1 **to 2 garlic cloves, minced**
- 1 **tablespoon Worcestershire sauce**
- 1/2 **cup red wine *or* beef broth**
- 1 **teaspoon ground mustard**
- 1/2 **teaspoon sugar**
- 2 **teaspoons cornstarch**
- 1 **tablespoon water**

1) Rub pepper over both sides of steaks. Refrigerate for 15 minutes. In an ungreased skillet, brown steaks on both sides over medium-high heat.

2) Reduce heat to medium; add butter and garlic; cook for 4-6 minutes, turning steaks once. Add Worcestershire sauce; cook 4-6 minutes longer, turning once, or until meat reaches desired doneness (for medium-rare, a meat thermometer should read 145°; medium, 160°; well-done, 170°). Remove steaks and keep warm.

3) Combine wine or broth, mustard and sugar; add to the pan. Stir to loosen browned bits. Combine cornstarch and water until smooth; add to pan. Bring to a boil; cook and stir for 2 minutes or until thickened. Serve with the steaks.

Yield: 2 servings.

Editor's Note: Steak may be known as strip steak, Kansas City steak, New York Strip steak, Ambassador Steak or boneless Club Steak in your region.

NUTRITION FACTS: 1 serving equals 626 calories, 43 g fat (19 g saturated fat), 155 mg cholesterol, 301 mg sodium, 8 g carbohydrate, trace fiber, 41 g protein.

Spinach Beef Stir-Fry

LaVerne Heath, Fountain, North Carolina

With tender strips of steak and fresh colorful vegetables, this mouth-watering stir-fry sizzles with flavor! My versatile entree can also be made with chicken breasts instead of beef. If you like zucchini or squash, toss some in. A bag of frozen vegetables can also be used.

1/4 cup reduced-sodium soy sauce

1 boneless beef sirloin steak
(1 pound), cut into thin strips

2 teaspoons cornstarch

1/2 teaspoon beef bouillon granules

1/2 teaspoon Chinese five-spice
powder

1/2 cup water

2 tablespoons canola oil, *divided*

1 cup sliced fresh carrots

1 medium green pepper, julienned

1 cup sliced celery

1 cup sliced fresh mushrooms

1 can (8 ounces) sliced water
chestnuts, drained

1/2 cup sliced green onions

6 cups torn fresh spinach

Hot cooked rice, optional

1) Place soy sauce in a large resealable plastic bag; add steak. Seal bag and turn to coat; refrigerate for up to 2 hours. Drain and discard soy sauce.

2) In a bowl, combine the cornstarch, bouillon, five-spice powder and water until smooth; set aside. In a large nonstick skillet or wok, sir-fry beef in batches in 1 tablespoon hot oil until beef is no longer pink. Remove from skillet and set aside.

3) Stir-fry carrots in remaining oil for 2 minutes. Add the green pepper, celery and mushrooms; stir-fry for 3 minutes. Add the water chestnuts and onions; stir-fry for 2 minutes or until the vegetables are crisp-tender.

4) Stir cornstarch mixture and add to the pan. Bring to a boil; cook and stir for 2 minutes. Add spinach and beef; cook and stir until spinach is wilted and beef is heated through. Serve over rice if desired.

Yield: 4 servings.

NUTRITION FACTS: 1-1/4 cups equals 280 calories, 13 g fat (3 g saturated fat), 63 mg cholesterol, 597 mg sodium, 16 g carbohydrate, 6 g fiber, 25 g protein.

Broiled Sirloin

Sue Ross, Casa Grande, Arizona

A mild marinade prepared with lemon juice, thyme and oregano seasons this steak. It feeds a family of four with lots left over to enjoy in satisfying second-day dishes later in the week.

3 pounds sirloin *or* round steak
(about 1 inch thick)

1 medium onion, chopped

1/2 cup lemon juice

1/4 cup vegetable oil

1 teaspoon garlic salt

1 teaspoon dried thyme

1 teaspoon dried oregano

1/2 teaspoon celery salt

1/2 teaspoon pepper

2 tablespoons butter, melted

1) With a meat fork, pierce holes in both sides of steak. Place in a large resealable plastic bag. Combine the onion, lemon juice, oil, garlic salt, thyme, oregano, celery salt and pepper; pour over meat. Seal bag and turn to coat; refrigerate for 6 hours or overnight.

2) Drain and discard marinade. Broil steak 6 in. from the heat for 8 minutes. Brush with butter and turn. Broil 6 minutes longer or until meat reaches desired doneness (for medium-rare, a meat thermometer should read 145°; medium, 160°; well-done, 170°).

Yield: 10 servings.

NUTRITION FACTS: 1 piece equals 250 calories, 15 g fat (5 g saturated fat), 82 mg cholesterol, 335 mg sodium, 3 g carbohydrate, 1 g fiber, 26 g protein.

STEAK FAJITAS

Steak Fajitas
Shirley Hilger, Lincoln, Nebraska

Tender strips of sirloin pick up plenty of spicy flavor from a marinade seasoned with cayenne pepper and cumin. These colorful sandwiches are speedy and satisfying.

1/4 cup orange juice

1/4 cup white vinegar

4 garlic cloves, minced

1 teaspoon seasoned salt

1 teaspoon dried oregano

1 teaspoon ground cumin

1/4 teaspoon cayenne pepper

1 pound boneless beef sirloin steak, cut into 1/4-inch strips

1 medium onion, thinly sliced

1 medium green pepper, thinly sliced

1 medium sweet red pepper, thinly sliced

2 tablespoons vegetable oil, *divided*

4 to 6 flour tortillas (10 inches), warmed

Shredded cheddar cheese, picante sauce and sour cream, optional

1) In a large resealable plastic bag, combine the orange juice, vinegar, garlic and seasonings; add the beef. Seal bag and turn to coat; set aside. In a skillet, saute onion and peppers in 1 tablespoon oil until crisp-tender; remove and set aside.

2) Drain and discard marinade. In the same skillet, cook beef in remaining oil for 2-4 minutes or until it reaches desired doneness. Return vegetables to pan; heat through.

3) Spoon meat and vegetables onto tortillas. If desired, top with cheese and serve with picante sauce and sour cream.

Yield: 4-6 servings.

NUTRITION FACTS: 1 fajita equals 305 calories, 11 g fat (3 g saturated fat), 42 mg cholesterol, 422 mg sodium, 27 g carbohydrate, 5 g fiber, 19 g protein.

Beef Burgundy over Noodles
Margaret Welder, Madrid, Iowa

I got this delightful recipe from my sister-in-law many years ago. Whenever I serve it to guests, they always request the recipe. The tender beef, mushrooms and flavorful sauce are delicious over noodles.

1/2 pound boneless sirloin steak, cut into 1/4-inch strips

2 tablespoons diced onion

2 teaspoons butter

1-1/2 cups quartered fresh mushrooms

3/4 cup dry red wine *or* beef broth

1/4 cup plus 2 tablespoons water, *divided*

3 tablespoons minced fresh parsley, *divided*

1 bay leaf

1 whole clove

1/4 teaspoon salt

1/8 teaspoon pepper

1 tablespoon all-purpose flour

1/2 teaspoon browning sauce, optional

1-1/2 cups hot cooked egg noodles

1) In a Dutch oven or nonstick skillet, brown beef and onion in butter over medium heat. Add the mushrooms, wine or broth, 1/4 cup water, 2 tablespoons parsley, bay leaf, clove, salt and pepper. Bring to a boil. Reduce heat; cover and simmer for 1 hour or until beef is tender.

2) Combine flour and remaining water until smooth; stir into beef mixture. Bring to a boil; cook and stir for 2 minutes or until thickened. Discard bay leaf and clove. Stir in browning sauce if desired. Serve over noodles. Sprinkle with remaining parsley.

Yield: 2 servings.

NUTRITION FACTS: 1-1/2 cups steak mixture equals 410 calories, 12 g fat (5 g saturated fat), 125 mg cholesterol, 403 mg sodium, 37 g carbohydrate, 2 g fiber, 33 g protein.

Gingered Pepper Steak
Susan Adair, Muncie, Indiana

This wonderfully tender steak is a treat even for folks not watching their diet. When my mother-in-law shared the recipe, she said it cooks up in no time...and she was right.

- 2 teaspoons sugar
- 2 teaspoons cornstarch
- 1/4 teaspoon ground ginger
- 1/4 cup reduced-sodium soy sauce
- 1 tablespoon white wine vinegar
- 1 pound beef flank steak, thinly sliced
- 2 medium green peppers, julienned
- 1 teaspoon vegetable oil

Hot cooked rice, optional

1) In a large bowl, combine the sugar, cornstarch, ginger, soy sauce and vinegar until smooth. Add beef and toss to coat; set aside.

2) In a large skillet or wok, stir-fry green peppers in oil until crisp-tender, about 3 minutes. Remove with a slotted spoon and keep warm.

3) Add beef with marinade to pan; stir-fry for 3 minutes or until meat reaches desired doneness. Return peppers to pan; heat through. Serve over rice if desired.

Yield: 4 servings.

NUTRITION FACTS: 1 cup equals 218 calories, 9 g fat (4 g saturated fat), 54 mg cholesterol, 674 mg sodium, 8 g carbohydrate, 1 g fiber, 23 g protein.

TIPS FOR STIR-FRYING

To make it easier to slice the meat into thin strips, partially freeze it before slicing. It takes about 30 minutes in the freezer to partially freeze thin cuts of meat.

Cut and prepare all the ingredients before you begin to stir-fry, including any sauces that are added at the end of cooking.

Select a wok or skillet large enough to accommodate the volume of food you'll be stir-frying. If the food is crowded in the pan, it will steam. If necessary, stir-fry the food in batches.

Don't place the stir-fried food on the same plate that held the uncooked meat when cooking in batches. Use a clean plate or bowl.

Add oil, when called for, to the pan and heat until hot before adding the food.

Stir any sauce that has a thickener, such as cornstarch, before adding to the pan.

Snow Peas and Beef Salad
Janeen Kilpatrick, Fairbury, Illinois

In this delicious main-dish salad, savory strips of broiled streak are lightly dressed along with water chestnuts, mushrooms and onions, then tossed with crisp snow peas. Ketchup and ginger add a bit of zip to the sweet dressing.

- 1 beef flank steak (1 pound)
- 1/4 cup ketchup
- 2 tablespoons canola oil
- 2 tablespoons lemon juice
- 1 tablespoon brown sugar
- 1/4 teaspoon *each* garlic powder, garlic salt, ground ginger and pepper
- 1/2 pound fresh mushrooms, sliced
- 1 can (8 ounces) sliced water chestnuts, drained
- 1 medium onion, sliced and separated into rings
- 1 cup fresh *or* frozen snow peas, thawed
- 12 lettuce leaves
- 2 medium tomatoes, cut into wedges

1) Broil steak 4-6 in. from the heat for 8-10 minutes on each side or until a meat thermometer reads 170°. Cool completely. Thinly slice meat across the grain; place in a large resealable plastic bag.

2) In a jar with tight-fitting lid, combine the ketchup, oil, lemon juice, brown sugar and seasonings; shake well. Pour over meat; seal bag and turn to coat. Add the mushrooms, water chestnuts and onion.

3) Refrigerate for 8 hours or overnight, turning occasionally. Just before serving, add snow peas. Serve on lettuce; garnish with tomatoes.

Yield: 6 servings.

NUTRITION FACTS: 1 serving (about 1 cup salad with 2 lettuce leaves and 1/3 of a tomato) equals 304 calories, 15 g fat (5 g saturated fat), 54 mg cholesterol, 263 mg sodium, 19 g carbohydrate, 4 g fiber, 25 g protein.

Seasoned Swiss Steak

Edna Hoffman, Hebron, Indiana

Tender beef and vegetables are combined in this recipe with a gravy that melds tomato, brown sugar and mustard.

- 1/4 cup all-purpose flour
- 1 tablespoon ground mustard
- 1 teaspoon salt, *divided*
- 1/4 teaspoon pepper, *divided*
- 1-1/2 pounds boneless beef top round steak (about 1 inch thick), cut into serving-size pieces
- 2 tablespoon vegetable oil
- 1 cup diced carrots
- 1/2 cup chopped onion
- 1/2 cup chopped green pepper
- 1 tablespoon brown sugar
- 1 tablespoon Worcestershire sauce
- 1 can (14-1/2 ounces) diced tomatoes, undrained
- 1/4 cup cold water

1) Combine the flour, mustard, 1/2 teaspoon salt and 1/8 teaspoon pepper; set aside 2 tablespoons for gravy. Rub remaining flour mixture over steak. Pound with a meat mallet to tenderize.

2) In a large skillet, brown steak in oil over medium-high heat. Transfer to a greased 2-1/2-qt. baking dish. Top with carrots, onion, green pepper, brown sugar and Worcestershire sauce. Pour tomatoes over all.

3) Cover and bake at 350° for 1-1/2 to 2 hours or until meat and vegetables are tender. Transfer meat and vegetables to a serving dish; keep warm. Strain pan juices into a measuring cup; add water to measure 1 cup.

4) In a saucepan, combine reserved flour mixture with cold water until smooth. Whisk in pan juices. Bring to a boil; cook and stir for 2 minutes or until thickened. Add remaining salt and pepper. Serve over steak.

Yield: 6 servings.

NUTRITION FACTS: 1 serving equals 249 calories, 9 g fat (2 g saturated fat), 64 mg cholesterol, 549 mg sodium, 14 g carbohydrate, 3 g fiber, 28 g protein.

PINEAPPLE BEEF STIR-FRY

Pineapple Beef Stir-Fry

Helen Vail, Glenside, Pennsylvania

A zippy marinade sparks the flavor of this change-of-pace steak specialty. Chock-full of veggies, seasonings and pineapple chunks, this stir-fry makes a colorful presentation when I serve it to relatives and friends.

- 1 can (20 ounces) pineapple chunks
- 1/2 cup minced fresh cilantro
- 1/4 cup soy sauce
- 1 tablespoon ground ginger
- 1 pound boneless beef round steak, thinly sliced
- 1 teaspoon cornstarch
- 2 teaspoons vegetable oil
- 1 medium sweet red pepper, thinly sliced
- 1/2 cup cut fresh green beans
- 1 tablespoon chopped green chilies
- 2 garlic cloves, minced
- 2 green onions, sliced
- Hot cooked rice

1) Drain the pineapple, reserving 1 cup pineapple and 3/4 cup juice. (Cover and refrigerate the remaining pineapple for another use.)

2) In a small bowl, combine the cilantro, soy sauce, ginger and reserved pineapple juice; mix well. Remove 3/4 cup; cover and refrigerate.

3) In a large resealable plastic bag, combine the beef and remaining marinade. Seal bag and turn to coat; refrigerate for 30 minutes. Drain and discard marinade. Combine cornstarch and reserved juice mixture until smooth.

4) In a skillet, stir-fry beef in oil for 5-6 minutes. Remove beef with a slotted spoon and keep warm. Add the red pepper, beans, chilies and garlic to skillet; stir-fry for 5 minutes. Stir juice mixture; stir into skillet.

5) Bring to a boil; cook and stir for 1 minute or until slightly thickened. Add onions, beef and the reserved pineapple; heat through. Serve over rice.

Yield: 4 servings.

NUTRITION FACTS: 1 cup stir-fry mixture (calculated without rice) equals 257 calories, 6 g fat (2 g saturated fat), 64 mg cholesterol, 782 mg sodium, 22 g carbohydrate, 2 g fiber, 29 g protein.

ROAST BEEF PASTA SALAD

Roast Beef Pasta Salad
Sandy Shields, Mead, Washington

I made this salad one hot summer day. The cool dish was a refreshing selection that was very well received. It's great to serve all year long.

- 1 package (16 ounces) spiral pasta
- 2 cups julienned cooked roast beef
- 1 cup chopped green pepper
- 1 cup sliced celery
- 3/4 cup chopped red onion
- 1/2 cup chopped sweet red pepper
- 1/3 cup chopped dill pickle
- 2 to 3 green onions, sliced

DRESSING:
- 2 tablespoons beef bouillon granules
- 1/4 cup boiling water
- 1/2 cup milk
- 2 cups mayonnaise
- 1 cup (8 ounces) sour cream
- 1 teaspoon dill weed
- Dash pepper

1) Cook the pasta according to package directions; drain and rinse in cold water. Place in a large bowl; add the beef, green pepper, celery, onion, red pepper, pickle and green onions.

2) For dressing, dissolve bouillon in water. Add the milk, mayonnaise, sour cream, dill and pepper; mix well. Toss with pasta mixture. Cover and refrigerate until serving.

Yield: 16 servings.

NUTRITION FACTS: 1/2 cup equals 405 calories, 29 g fat (6 g saturated fat), 39 mg cholesterol, 515 mg sodium, 24 g carbohydrate, 1 g fiber, 10 g protein.

Tarragon Beef Salad
Phyllis Townsend, Vienna, Virginia

This hearty main-dish salad features grilled steak with an oil-and-vinegar dressing flavored with tarragon.

- 2 pounds beef round steak (1 inch thick)
- 1 cup olive oil
- 1/3 cup red wine vinegar
- 3 tablespoons minced fresh tarragon *or* 1 tablespoon dried tarragon
- 1 teaspoon salt
- 3/4 teaspoon sugar
- 1/2 teaspoon ground mustard
- 1/2 teaspoon pepper
- 1/4 teaspoon garlic powder
- 1 large red onion, sliced and separated into rings
- 1/2 pound fresh mushrooms, sliced
- 1 large bunch romaine
- 1/2 cup minced fresh parsley

1) Broil steak 6 in. from the heat for 7 minutes on each side or until meat reaches desired doneness (for medium-rare, a meat thermometer should read 145° medium, 160° well-done, 170°). Cool slightly. Cut steak into very thin strips.

2) In a large bowl, combine the oil, vinegar, tarragon, salt, sugar, mustard, pepper and garlic powder. Add the steak, onion and mushrooms; toss to coat. Cover and refrigerate for at least 4 hours.

3) Just before serving, place romaine on plates. Using a slotted spoon, arrange beef mixture over romaine. Garnish with parsley.

Yield: 8 servings.

NUTRITION FACTS: 1/2 cup equals 409 calories, 31 g fat (5 g saturated fat), 64 mg cholesterol, 335 mg sodium, 6 g carbohydrate, 2 g fiber, 28 g protein.

SLOW-COOKED SHORT RIBS

Slow-Cooked Short Ribs
Pam Halfhill, Medina, Ohio

Smothered in a mouth-watering barbecue sauce, these meaty ribs are a popular entree wherever I serve them. The recipe is great for a busy cook—after everything is combined, the slow cooker does all the work!

- 2/3 cup all-purpose flour
- 2 teaspoons salt
- 1/2 teaspoon pepper
- 4 to 4-1/2 pounds boneless beef short ribs
- 1/4 to 1/3 cup butter
- 1 large onion, chopped
- 1-1/2 cups beef broth
- 3/4 cup red wine vinegar
- 3/4 cup packed brown sugar
- 1/2 cup chili sauce
- 1/3 cup ketchup
- 1/3 cup Worcestershire sauce
- 5 garlic cloves, minced
- 1-1/2 teaspoons chili powder

1) In a large resealable plastic bag, combine the flour, salt and pepper. Add ribs in batches and shake to coat. In a large skillet, brown ribs in butter.

2) Transfer to a 6-qt. slow cooker. In the same skillet, combine the remaining ingredients. Cook and stir until mixture comes to a boil; pour over ribs. Cover and cook on low for 9-10 hours or until meat is tender.

Yield: 12 servings.

NUTRITION FACTS: 4 ounces equals 631 calories, 47 g fat (21 g saturated fat), 107 mg cholesterol, 901 mg sodium, 27 g carbohydrate, 1 g fiber, 24 g protein.

Sticky Bones
Berta Joy, Gering, Nebraska

I never had a recipe for short ribs that impressed me...until this one!

- 1 cup white vinegar
- 1/2 cup ketchup
- 1/2 cup honey
- 2 tablespoons Worcestershire sauce
- 1 teaspoon salt
- 1 teaspoon ground mustard
- 1 teaspoon paprika
- 1 garlic clove, minced
- 1/4 teaspoon pepper
- 4 pounds bone-in beef short ribs

1) In a small saucepan, combine the vinegar, ketchup, honey, Worcestershire sauce, salt, mustard, paprika, garlic and pepper. Bring to a boil. Reduce heat; cover and simmer for 15 minutes. Set aside 1 cup for basting.

2) Cool remaining marinade. Pour the remaining marinade in a large resealable plastic bag; add ribs. Seal bag and turn to coat; refrigerate for at least 2 hours.

3) Drain and discard marinade. Bake ribs, uncovered, at 325° for 1 hour or until meat is tender, basting frequently with reserved marinade.

Yield: 4 servings.

NUTRITION FACTS: 1 serving equals 449 calories, 21 g fat (9 g saturated fat), 109 mg cholesterol, 685 mg sodium, 27 g carbohydrate, trace fiber, 37 g protein.

Liver with Peppers and Onions
Naomi Giddis, Grawn, Michigan

A simple breading of flour, salt and pepper keeps the liver tender. The sauce of beef broth and soy sauce adds wonderful flavor.

- 1/2 cup all-purpose flour
- 1 teaspoon salt
- 1/4 teaspoon pepper
- 1 pound liver, cut into bite-size pieces
- 1 large onion, thinly sliced into rings
- 1 medium green pepper, cut into 1-inch pieces
- 1 sweet red pepper, cut into 1-inch pieces
- 4 tablespoons vegetable oil, *divided*
- 1 tablespoon cornstarch

1 **cup beef broth**

2 **tablespoons soy sauce**

Cooked rice *or* **noodles**

1) In a large bowl or resealable plastic bag, combine the flour, salt and pepper. Add liver; toss to coat.

2) In a large skillet, cook onion and peppers in 2 tablespoons oil until crisp-tender. Remove from pan; set aside. In same skillet, cook and stir liver in remaining oil for 5 to 7 minutes or until no pink remains.

3) In a small bowl, combine cornstarch, broth and soy sauce until smooth; stir into liver. Bring to a boil; cook and stir for 2 minutes or until thickened. Return vegetables to the skillet; heat through. Serve over rice or noodles.

Yield: 4-6 servings.

NUTRITION FACTS: 1 serving (calculated without rice or noodles) equals 245 calories, 12 g fat (2 g saturated fat), 332 mg cholesterol, 898 mg sodium, 17 g carbohydrate, 2 g fiber, 16 g protein.

DOUBLE-DECKER BURGERS

Buying and Cooking Ground Beef

Ground beef is often labeled using the cut of meat that it is ground from, such as ground chuck or ground round. (Ground beef comes from a combination of beef cuts.) Ground beef can also be labeled according to the fat content of the ground mixture or the percentage of lean meat to fat, such as 85% or 90% lean. The higher the percentage, the leaner the meat.

Select ground beef that is bright red in color and is in a tightly sealed package. Purchase all ground beef before the "sell by" date.

Purchase the amount you need: 1 pound of ground beef serves 3 to 4.

Handle the mixture as little as possible when shaping hamburgers, meat loaves or meatballs to keep the final product light in texture.

Cook ground beef until it is well-done and no longer pink. For patties and loaves, where it is difficult to judge color, make sure a meat thermometer reads 160° before serving.

Double-Decker Burgers
Marcy Schewe, Danube, Minnesota

These man-sized sandwiches feature a variety of flavors in a special cheese spread.

2 **eggs, lightly beaten**

1/4 **cup finely chopped onion**

2 **teaspoons Worcestershire sauce**

1 **teaspoon salt**

1/4 **teaspoon pepper**

2 **pounds ground beef**

1-1/2 **cups (6 ounces) shredded cheddar cheese**

3 **tablespoons mayonnaise**

4 **teaspoons prepared mustard**

4 **teaspoons dill pickle relish**

6 **hamburger buns, split**

Shredded lettuce

6 **onion slices**

6 **tomato slices**

1) In a large bowl, combine the eggs, onion, Worcestershire sauce, salt and pepper. Crumble beef over mixture and mix well. Shape into 12 thin patties. Broil 4 in. from the heat for 7-8 minutes on each side or until no longer pink.

2) In a small bowl, combine the cheese, mayonnaise, mustard and relish; mix well. Spoon 2 tablespoons on each burger. Return to the broiler just until cheese softens. Serve on buns with lettuce, onion and tomato.

Yield: 6 servings.

NUTRITION FACTS: 1 burger equals 615 calories, 36 g fat (15 g saturated fat), 204 mg cholesterol, 1,030 mg sodium, 28 g carbohydrate, 2 g fiber, 42 g protein.

TEST FOR DONENESS

Cook beef, pork and lamb burgers to 160°; cook chicken or turkey burgers to 165°. To test for doneness, use tongs to hold burger while inserting instant-read thermometer horizontally from a side. Make sure thermometer is far enough in to read temperature in center.

MAKING MEATBALLS OF EQUAL SIZE

1) Lightly pat meat mixture into a 1-in.-thick rectangle. Cut the rectangle into the same number of squares as meatballs in the recipe.

2) Gently roll each square into a ball.

Meatballs with Cream Sauce
Michelle Thompson, Smithfield, Utah

I get raves from my husband and even our three fussy children when I serve these satisfying meatballs with mashed potatoes. The savory cream sauce gives a tasty new twist to meatballs.

   1   egg, lightly beaten
1/4 cup milk
   2   tablespoons ketchup
   1   teaspoon Worcestershire sauce
3/4 cup quick-cooking oats
1/4 cup finely chopped onion
1/4 cup minced fresh parsley
   1   teaspoon salt
1/4 teaspoon pepper
1-1/2 pounds lean ground beef
   3   tablespoons all-purpose flour

CREAM SAUCE:
   2   tablespoons butter
   2   tablespoons all-purpose flour
1/4 teaspoon dried thyme
Salt and pepper to taste
   1   can (14 ounces) chicken broth
2/3 cup heavy whipping cream
   2   tablespoons minced fresh parsley

1) In a large bowl, combine the first nine ingredients. Crumble beef over mixture and mix well. Shape into 1-1/2-in. balls. Roll in flour, shaking off excess. Place 1 in. apart on greased 15-in. x 10-in. x 1-in. baking pans.

2) Bake, uncovered, at 400° for 10 minutes. Turn meatballs; bake 12-15 minutes longer or until meat is no longer pink.

3) Meanwhile, for sauce, melt butter in a saucepan over medium heat. Stir in the flour, thyme, salt and pepper until smooth. Gradually add broth and cream. Bring to a boil; cook and stir for 2 minutes or until thickened.

4) Drain meatballs on paper towels; transfer to a serving dish. Top with sauce; sprinkle with parsley.

Yield: 6 servings.

NUTRITION FACTS: 1 serving (calculated without the salt and pepper in cream sauce) equals 389 calories, 24 g fat (12 g saturated fat), 139 mg cholesterol, 874 mg sodium, 16 g carbohydrate, 1 g fiber, 27 g protein.

BAKING MEATBALLS & MEAT LOAVES

Place shaped meatballs on a rack in a shallow baking pan. Bake at 400° until no longer pink, about 20 minutes for 1-1/2-in. meatballs.

Insert an instant-read thermometer in the center of the meat loaf near the end of the baking time. When it reads 160°, the meat loaf is done. After baking, drain any fat. Let the meat loaf stand for 5-10 minutes before slicing.

Teriyaki Meatballs
Evette Nowicki, Oak Harbor, Washington

This Asian-inspired recipe gets its sweetness from pineapple as well as yellow and red peppers. It makes a delicious main dish over rice or a nice appetizer, too.

   2   cans (8 ounces *each*) pineapple chunks
   1   medium onion, finely chopped
1/4 cup finely chopped sweet yellow pepper
1/4 cup finely chopped sweet red pepper
1/2 cup dry bread crumbs
1/2 teaspoon ground ginger
1/4 teaspoon salt
   1   pound lean ground beef

SAUCE:
1/4 cup vegetable oil
1/4 cup soy sauce
   3   tablespoons honey

2 tablespoons vinegar

3/4 teaspoon garlic powder

1/2 teaspoon ground ginger

1) Drain pineapple, reserving 1/4 cup juice; set pineapple aside. In a bowl, combine the onion, peppers, bread crumbs, ginger, salt and reserved pineapple juice. Crumble beef over mixture and mix well. Shape into 1-in. balls.

2) Place the sauce ingredients in a blender; cover and process for 1 minute. Place 2 tablespoons of sauce in a greased 13-in. x 9-in. x 2-in. baking dish. Add meatballs. Pour remaining sauce over meatballs.

3) Bake, uncovered, at 400° for 20 minutes or until meat is no longer pink. Gently stir pineapple into sauce or place one pineapple chunk on each meatball; secure with a toothpick.

Yield: 42 meatballs.

Editor's Note: To serve these meatballs as an appetizer, place the cooked meatballs in a chafing dish.

NUTRITION FACTS: 8 meatballs equals 394 calories, 18 g fat (4 g saturated fat), 44 mg cholesterol, 1,009 mg sodium, 37 g carbohydrate, 2 g fiber, 21 g protein.

Salisbury Steak with Onion Gravy

Kim Kidd, Freedom, Pennsylvania

Moist meat patties get special treatment simmered in a tasty sauce and served over egg noodles.

1 egg

1 can (10-1/2 ounces) condensed French onion soup, undiluted, *divided*

1/2 cup dry bread crumbs

1/4 teaspoon salt

Dash pepper

1-1/2 pounds ground beef

1/4 cup water

1/4 cup ketchup

1 teaspoon Worcestershire sauce

1/2 teaspoon prepared mustard

1 tablespoon all-purpose flour

2 tablespoons cold water

6 cups hot cooked egg noodles

Chopped fresh parsley, optional

1) In a large bowl, beat egg. Stir in 1/3 cup of soup, bread crumbs, salt and pepper. Crumble beef over mixture; mix gently. Shape into six oval patties.

2) In a skillet, brown patties over medium heat for 3-4 minutes on each side. Remove and set aside; drain. Add the water, ketchup, Worcestershire sauce, mustard and remaining soup to skillet. Bring to a boil.

3) Return patties to skillet. Reduce heat; cover and simmer for 15 minutes or until meat is no longer pink. Remove patties.

4) Combine flour and cold water until smooth. Stir into pan. Bring to a boil; cook and stir for 2 minutes or until thickened. Serve patties and gravy over noodles. Garnish with parsley if desired.

Yield: 6 servings.

NUTRITION FACTS: 1 serving equals 458 calories, 18 g fat (6 g saturated fat), 149 mg cholesterol, 767 mg sodium, 42 g carbohydrate, 2 g fiber, 31 g protein.

Stuffed Green Peppers

Marlene Karnemaat, Fremont, Michigan

This classic recipe is a great way to enjoy fresh green peppers.

- 6 medium green peppers
- 1-1/2 pounds uncooked lean ground beef
- 1 cup cooked long grain rice
- 1/2 cup chopped onion
- 1/2 cup chopped celery
- 1 small tomato, seeded and chopped
- 1 garlic clove, minced
- 1 teaspoon salt
- 1/4 teaspoon pepper
- 1 can (10-3/4 ounces) condensed tomato soup, undiluted
- 1/2 teaspoon dried basil
- 1/2 cup shredded sharp cheddar cheese

1) Cut tops off peppers and remove seeds. In a large kettle, cook peppers in boiling water for 3 minutes. Drain and immediately place in ice water; invert onto paper towels.

2) In a large bowl, combine the beef, rice, onion, celery, tomato, garlic, salt and pepper. Spoon into peppers. Place in a greased 13-in. x 9-in. x 2-in. baking dish. Combine soup and basil; spoon over peppers.

3) Cover and bake at 350° for 55-60 minutes or until the beef is no longer pink. Sprinkle with cheese; bake 5 minutes longer or until the cheese is melted.

Yield: 6 servings.

NUTRITION FACTS: 1 stuffed pepper equals 312 calories, 11 g fat (5 g saturated fat), 66 mg cholesterol, 836 mg sodium, 25 g carbohydrate, 4 g fiber, 27 g protein.

PARBOILING PEPPERS

Bring water to a boil in a Dutch oven or soup kettle. Cook seeded whole peppers until crisp-tender, about 2-3 minutes depending on the size of the pepper. Remove from the water with tongs and invert onto paper towels to drain before stuffing.

OLD-FASHIONED CABBAGE ROLLS

Old-Fashioned Cabbage Rolls

Florence Krantz, Bismarck, North Dakota

Once the cabbage leaves are boiled and the vein removed, they make the perfect envelope for a filling of meat, rice and seasonings.

- 1 medium head cabbage (3 pounds)
- 1/2 pound ground beef
- 1/2 pound ground pork
- 1 can (15 ounces) tomato sauce, *divided*
- 1 small onion, chopped
- 1/2 cup uncooked long grain rice
- 1 tablespoon dried parsley flakes
- 1/2 teaspoon salt
- 1/2 teaspoon dill weed
- 1/8 teaspoon cayenne pepper
- 1 can (14-1/2 ounces) diced tomatoes, undrained
- 1/2 teaspoon sugar

1) In a Dutch oven, cook cabbage in boiling water for 2-3 minutes just until leaves fall off head. Set aside 12 large leaves for rolls. Cut out the thick vein from the bottom of each reserved leaf, making a V-shaped cut. Set aside remaining cabbage.

2) In a small bowl, combine the beef, pork, 1/2 cup tomato sauce, onion, rice, parsley, salt, dill and cayenne; mix well. Place about 1/4 cup meat mixture on each cabbage leaf; overlap cut ends of leaf. Fold in sides, beginning from the cut end. Roll up completely to enclose filling.

3) Slice the remaining cabbage; place in Dutch oven. Arrange the cabbage rolls seam side down over sliced cabbage. Combine the tomatoes, sugar and remaining tomato sauce; pour over the rolls.

Cover and bake at 350° for 1-1/2 hours or until tender and meat thermometer reads 160°.

Yield: 6 servings.

NUTRITION FACTS: 2 cabbage rolls equals 260 calories, 10 g fat (4 g saturated fat), 50 mg cholesterol, 694 mg sodium, 23 g carbohydrate, 3 g fiber, 18 g protein.

SHAPING CABBAGE ROLLS

1) Place head of cabbage in boiling water just until outer leaves begin to loosen. Remove cabbage from water and remove leaves that come off easily. Place cabbage back in water if more leaves are needed. For easier rolling, cut out thick vein from each leaf, making a V-shaped cut.

2) Place 2-3 tablespoons of ground beef mixture on each cabbage leaf; fold up sides, beginning from cut end. Roll up to completely enclose meat mixture in leaf. Fasten with a toothpick if necessary.

Spanish Noodles 'n' Ground Beef
Kelli Jones, Peris, California

Bacon adds flavor to this comforting supper my mom often made when we were growing up. Now I prepare it for my family, and it disappears quickly.

- 1 pound ground beef
- 1 small green pepper, chopped
- 1/3 cup chopped onion
- 3-1/4 cups uncooked medium egg noodles
- 1 can (14-1/2 ounces) diced tomatoes, undrained
- 1 cup water
- 1/4 cup chili sauce
- 1 teaspoon salt
- 1/8 teaspoon pepper
- 4 bacon strips, cooked and crumbled

1) In a large skillet, cook the beef, green pepper and onion over medium heat until meat is no longer pink; drain. Stir in the noodles, tomatoes, water, chili sauce, salt and pepper.

2) Cover and cook over low heat for 15-20 minutes or until the noodles are tender, stirring frequently. Top with bacon.

Yield: 5 servings.

NUTRITION FACTS: 1-1/4 cups equals 337 calories, 15 g fat (5 g saturated fat), 88 mg cholesterol, 890 mg sodium, 27 g carbohydrate, 2 g fiber, 24 g protein.

Shepherd's Pie
Carolyn Wolbers, Loveland, Ohio

For a real meat-and-potatoes meal, try this satisfying layered casserole. It's easy to assemble with lean ground beef and fresh or leftover mashed potatoes.

- 6 medium potatoes
- 1 pound carrots, cut into 1/4-inch slices
- 1-1/2 pounds lean ground beef
- 1 large onion, chopped
- 1 jar (12 ounces) fat-free beef gravy
- 1 teaspoon salt, *divided*
- 1/2 teaspoon rubbed sage
- 1/2 teaspoon dried thyme
- 1/4 teaspoon dried rosemary, crushed
- 1/4 teaspoon pepper
- 1/3 cup fat-free milk
- 1 tablespoon butter
- 2 tablespoons shredded Parmesan cheese

1) Peel and cube the potatoes; place in a large saucepan and cover with water. Bring to a boil over medium-high heat; cover and cook for 20 minutes or until tender. Add 1 in. of water to another saucepan; add carrots. Bring to a boil. Reduce heat; cover and simmer until crisp-tender, about 7-9 minutes. Drain.

2) In a large nonstick skillet, cook beef and onion over medium heat until meat is no longer pink; drain. Stir in the carrots, gravy, 1/2 teaspoon salt, sage, thyme, rosemary and pepper. Transfer to a shallow 3-qt. baking dish coated with nonstick cooking spray.

3) Drain the potatoes; mash with milk, butter and remaining salt. Spread over meat mixture. Sprinkle with Parmesan cheese. Bake, uncovered, at 375° for 40-45 minutes or until heated through.

Yield: 6 servings.

NUTRITION FACTS: 1 cup equals 390 calories, 13 g fat (6 g saturated fat), 53 mg cholesterol, 859 mg sodium, 43 g carbohydrate, 6 g fiber, 30 g protein.

SOUTH DAKOTA MEAT LOAF

South Dakota Meat Loaf
Lauree Buus, Rapid City, South Dakota

This filling meat loaf is big on flavor and very satisfying.

 1   egg, lightly beaten
1/3 cup evaporated milk
3/4 cup quick-cooking oats
1/4 cup chopped onion
 2   tablespoons Worcestershire sauce
 1   teaspoon salt
1/2 teaspoon rubbed sage
1/8 teaspoon pepper
1-1/2 pounds ground beef
1/4 cup ketchup

1) In a large bowl, combine the egg, milk, oats, onion, Worcestershire sauce and seasonings. Crumble beef over mixture and mix well.

2) Press into an ungreased 8-in. x 4-in. x 2-in. loaf pan. Bake, uncovered, at 350° for 1-1/4 hours; drain.

3) Drizzle with ketchup; bake 10 minutes longer or until meat is no longer pink and a meat thermometer reads 160°. Let stand for 5-10 minutes before slicing.

Yield: 6 servings.

NUTRITION FACTS: 1 piece equals 308 calories, 16 g fat (7 g saturated fat), 115 mg cholesterol, 646 mg sodium, 12 g carbohydrate, 1 g fiber, 26 g protein.

MAKING MEAT LOAF AND MEATBALLS

In a large bowl, combine all ingredients except the ground beef. Crumble the meat over the mixture. With a sturdy spoon or by hand, gently combine ingredients. Shape into a loaf or place in a pan. For meatballs, see Making Meatballs of Equal Size (page 102).

Greek Pasta and Beef
Dorothy Bateman, Carver, Massachusetts

This casserole gives everyday macaroni and cheese an international flavor. A co-worker who's a pro at Greek cooking shared the recipe.

 1   package (16 ounces) elbow macaroni
 1   pound ground beef
 1   large onion, chopped
 1   garlic clove, minced
 1   can (8 ounces) tomato sauce
1/2 cup water
 1   teaspoon salt
1/2 teaspoon ground cinnamon
1/4 teaspoon ground nutmeg
1/4 teaspoon pepper
 1   egg, lightly beaten
1/2 cup grated Parmesan cheese

SAUCE:
 1   cup butter
1/4 cup all-purpose flour
1/4 teaspoon ground cinnamon
 3   cups milk
 2   eggs, lightly beaten
1/3 cup grated Parmesan cheese

1) Cook macaroni according to package directions. In a large skillet, cook beef, onion and garlic over medium heat until meat is no longer pink; drain. Stir in the tomato sauce, water and seasonings. Cover and simmer for 10 minutes, stirring occasionally. Drain macaroni.

2) In a large bowl, combine the macaroni, egg and Parmesan cheese; set aside. In a large saucepan, melt butter; stir in flour and cinnamon until smooth. Gradually add milk. Bring to a boil over medium heat; cook and stir for 2 minutes or until slightly thickened.

3) Remove from the heat. Stir a small amount of hot mixture into eggs; return all to pan, stirring constantly. Stir in cheese.

4) In a greased 3-qt. baking dish, spread half of the macaroni mixture. Top with beef mixture and remaining macaroni mixture. Pour sauce over the top. Bake, uncovered, at 350° for 45-50 minutes or until bubbly and heated through. Let stand for 5 minutes before serving.

Yield: 12 servings.

NUTRITION FACTS: 1 serving equals 445 calories, 26 g fat (14 g saturated fat), 132 mg cholesterol, 607 mg sodium, 35 g carbohydrate, 2 g fiber, 19 g protein.

Garlic Beef Enchiladas

Jennifer Standridge, Dallas, Georgia

Enchiladas are typically prepared with corn tortillas, but my husband and I prefer flour tortillas. I use them in this saucy casserole that has home-cooked flavor and a subtle kick.

1 pound ground beef
1 medium onion, chopped
2 tablespoons all-purpose flour
1 tablespoon chili powder
1 teaspoon salt
1 teaspoon garlic powder
1/2 teaspoon ground cumin
1/4 teaspoon rubbed sage
1 can (14-1/2 ounces) stewed tomatoes

SAUCE:

4 to 6 garlic cloves, minced
1/3 cup butter
1/2 cup all-purpose flour
1 can (14-1/2 ounces) beef broth
1 can (15 ounces) tomato sauce
1 to 2 tablespoons chili powder
1 to 2 teaspoons ground cumin
1 to 2 teaspoons rubbed sage
1/2 teaspoon salt
10 flour tortillas (7 inches)
2 cups (8 ounces) shredded Colby-Monterey Jack cheese

1) In a saucepan, cook beef and onion over medium heat until meat is no longer pink; drain. Stir in the flour and seasonings until blended. Stir in tomatoes; bring to a boil. Reduce heat; cover and simmer for 15 minutes.

2) Meanwhile, in another saucepan, saute garlic in butter until tender. Stir in flour until blended. Gradually stir in broth; bring to a boil. Cook and stir for 2 minutes or until thickened. Stir in tomato sauce and seasonings; heat through.

3) Pour about 1-1/2 cups sauce into an ungreased 13-in. x 9-in. x 2-in. baking dish. Spread about 1/4 cup beef mixture down the center of each tortilla; top with 1-2 tablespoons cheese. Roll up tightly; place seam side down over sauce. Top with the remaining sauce.

4) Cover and bake at 350° for 30-35 minutes. Sprinkle with remaining cheese. Bake, uncovered, 10-15 minutes longer or until the cheese is melted.

Yield: 4-6 servings.

NUTRITION FACTS: 1-1/2 enchiladas equals 637 calories, 36 g fat (18 g saturated fat), 111 mg cholesterol, 2,070 mg sodium, 47 g carbohydrate, 3 g fiber, 33 g protein.

SLOPPY JOE SANDWICHES

Sloppy Joe Sandwiches

Laurie Hauser, Rochester, New York

This is one of those recipes that cooks love because it's quick, easy and inexpensive. Brown sugar adds a touch of sweetness. In addition to rolls, the beef mixture is tasty over rice, biscuits or baked potatoes.

1 pound ground beef
1 cup ketchup
1/4 cup water
2 tablespoons brown sugar
2 teaspoons Worcestershire sauce
2 teaspoons prepared mustard
1/2 teaspoon garlic powder
1/2 teaspoon onion powder
1/2 teaspoon salt
4 hamburger buns, split

1) In a large saucepan, cook beef over medium heat until no longer pink; drain. Stir in the ketchup, water, brown sugar, Worcestershire sauce, mustard, garlic powder, onion powder and salt.

2) Bring to a boil. Reduce heat; cover and simmer for 30-40 minutes. Serve on buns.

Yield: 4 servings.

NUTRITION FACTS: 1 sandwich equals 439 calories, 16 g fat (6 g saturated fat), 75 mg cholesterol, 1,360 mg sodium, 46 g carbohydrate, 2 g fiber, 27 g protein.

French Veal Chops

Betty Biehl, Mertztown, Pennsylvania

Perfectly portioned for two, this easy entree can easily be doubled to serve 4.

  2 veal chops (1 inch thick)
1/2 teaspoon salt
Dash pepper
  1 tablespoon vegetable oil
1/2 cup chopped onion
  2 tablespoons butter, *divided*
1/4 cup chicken broth
1/3 cup dry bread crumbs
  2 tablespoons grated Parmesan cheese

1) Sprinkle veal chops with salt and pepper. In a skillet, brown chops on both sides in oil. Sprinkle onion into a greased shallow baking dish; dot with 1 tablespoon butter. Top with chops; drizzle with broth.

2) Melt remaining butter; toss with bread crumbs and Parmesan cheese. Sprinkle over top.

3) Bake, uncovered, at 350° for 30-35 minutes or until the meat is no longer pink and a meat thermometer reads 160°.

Yield: 2 servings.

NUTRITION FACTS: 1 serving equals 469 calories, 31 g fat (13 g saturated fat), 144 mg cholesterol, 1,146 mg sodium, 17 g carbohydrate, 1 g fiber, 31 g protein.

Asparagus Veal Cordon Bleu

Jeanne Molloy, Feeding Hills, Massachusetts

I try to make varied meals for two that are both appetizing and interesting. I sometimes double this recipe so we can have the leftovers for lunch the next day. It reheats well in the microwave.

  8 fresh asparagus spears, trimmed
  2 tablespoons water
  2 veal cutlets (6 ounces *each*)
1/4 teaspoon salt
1/8 teaspoon pepper
  2 garlic cloves, minced
  1 tablespoon olive oil
  4 large fresh mushrooms, sliced
  2 thin slices prosciutto *or* deli ham
1/2 cup shredded Italian cheese blend

1) Place asparagus and water in an 11-in. x 7-in. x 2-in. microwave-safe dish. Cover and microwave on high for 2-3 minutes or until crisp-tender; drain and set aside.

2) If necessary, flatten veal to 1/4-in. thickness; sprinkle with salt and pepper. In a small skillet, saute garlic in oil. Add veal; brown for 2-3 minutes on each side.

3) Transfer to an ungreased 11-in. x 7-in. x 2-in. baking dish. In the pan drippings, saute the mushrooms until tender; spoon over veal. Top each with four asparagus spears and a slice of prosciutto. Sprinkle with cheese.

4) Bake, uncovered, at 350° for 5-10 minutes or until cheese is melted.

Yield: 2 servings.

NUTRITION FACTS: 1 serving equals 492 calories, 33 g fat (12 g saturated fat), 155 mg cholesterol, 1,106 mg sodium, 6 g carbohydrate, 2 g fiber, 44 g protein.

Veal Scallopini

Karen Bridges, Downers Grove, Illinois

My husband and I prepare this veal dish for birthdays and other special occasions.

  2 tablespoons all-purpose flour
1/8 teaspoon salt
1/8 teaspoon pepper
  1 egg
1/2 to 3/4 pound veal cutlets
  2 tablespoons olive oil
  4 ounces fresh mushrooms, halved
  1 cup chicken broth
  2 tablespoons Marsala wine
Hot cooked spaghetti

1) In a shallow bowl, combine the flour, salt, and pepper. In another shallow bowl, lightly beat the egg.

2) Pound veal to 1/4-in. thickness. Dip in egg, then coat with flour mixture. In a large skillet, brown veal in oil on both sides.

3) Stir in the mushrooms, broth and wine. Bring to a boil. Reduce heat; simmer, uncovered, for 5-10 minutes or until mushrooms are tender. Serve over spaghetti.

Yield: 2 servings.

NUTRITION FACTS: 1 serving (calculated without spaghetti) equals 395 calories, 27 g fat (7 g saturated fat), 180 mg cholesterol, 697 mg sodium, 10 g carbohydrate, 1 g fiber, 25 g protein.

CHAPTER 5
PORK

PORK

Today's pork is easier than ever to cook because it's lean and tender. Follow the techniques and guidelines below for cooking your favorite cuts of pork, and you'll have perfect results every time!

Purchase before the "sell by" date on the packaging for best quality. Make sure the package is cold and has no holes or tears.

Due to breeding and feeding changes over the last 20 years, the fat content of pork has been reduced to make it a leaner product.

Some of the leanest cuts of pork are boneless loin roasts or chops, boneless sirloin roasts or chops and bone-in pork loin chops. Ounce for ounce, pork tenderloin is almost as lean as boneless skinless chicken breast.

Determine the amount of pork you need to buy based on the cut and amount of bone. Follow these guidelines:

- 1 pound of bone-in roasts, chops or ham yields 2-1/2 to 3 servings.
- 1 pound of boneless roasts, chops or ham yields 3 to 4 servings.
- 1 pound of spareribs yields 1-1/4 servings.

Cooking Pork

Don't overcook lean, fresh pork; it cooks quickly and becomes dry and tough. Pork is done at 160°. Cook large roasts to 155°, then tent with foil and allow to stand for 10-15 minutes. The internal temperature will rise to 160°. At 160°, the internal color of boneless roasts may be faint pink, and bone-in roasts may be slightly pink near the bone. The juices may have a hint of pink or be clear.

Use dry-heat cooking methods (broiling, grilling, pan-broiling, roasting and stir-frying) when a firm texture is desired for cuts of pork because, unlike beef, pork cuts vary little in tenderness. The moist-heat method of braising is used when a fork-tender texture is desired.

Cooking Methods for Pork and Ham

COOKING METHOD	CUT OF PORK/HAM
BRAISING	Blade Chops, Boston Butt Roast, Pork Cubes
BROILING	Chops, Steaks, Ham Slices, Ground Pork Patties, Tenderloin
GRILLING	Chops, Steaks, Ground Pork Patties, Pork Cubes, Ham Slices, Tenderloin
PAN-BROILING	Small Cuts—Chops, Steaks, Ham Slices, Medallions, Ground Pork Patties
ROASTING	Loin Roasts, Rib Roasts, Fresh Ham or Pork Leg, Whole or Half Ham, Crown Roast, Tenderloin, Ribs

Defrosting Guidelines

Plan more time for thicker packages because they take longer to defrost. Here are some guidelines for thawing pork in the refrigerator:

- For a 1- to 1-1/2-in.-thick package of ground pork, allow at least 24 hours.
- For 1-in.-thick chops, allow 12 to 14 hours.
- For a small roast, allow 3 to 5 hours per pound.
- For a large roast, allow 4 to 7 hours per pound.

Roasting Fresh Pork and Ham

Place meat on a rack in a shallow roasting pan with the fat side up. Insert an oven-safe meat thermometer in the thickest portion of the muscle without touching bone or fat. Or use an instant-read thermometer toward the end of the roasting time. If the roast needs to cook longer, make sure to remove the instant-read thermometer before you return the roast to the oven.

Roast without liquid, uncovered, according to the temperature and time given in the chart below or recipe. Roasts continue to cook after being removed from the oven, so remove the meat when the meat thermometer reads 5-10° below desired doneness. Cover with foil and let stand for 10-15 minutes before carving.

CUT	WEIGHT	COOKING TIME (MINUTES PER POUND)	OVEN TEMP.	DONENESS
PORK LOIN ROAST, BONE-IN	3 to 5 lbs.	20 to 30	350°	160°
PORK LOIN ROAST, BONELESS	2 to 4 lbs.	18 to 20	350°	160°
PORK CROWN ROAST	6 to 8 lbs.	20 to 25	350°	160°
SHOULDER ROAST OR BOSTON BUTT	3 to 6 lbs.	30 to 40	350°	160°
LEG-HALF (FRESH HAM OR PICNIC)	3-1/2 lbs.	35 to 40	350°	160°
PORK TENDERLOIN	1/2 to 1 lb.	20 to 30 (minutes total)	425° or 450°	160°
SPARERIBS	1 to 1-1/2 lbs.	1-1/2 to 2 (hours total)	350°	tender
WHOLE HAM, FULLY COOKED, BONE-IN	10 to 14 lbs.	15 to 18	325°	140°
HALF HAM, FULLY COOKED, BONE-IN	5 to 7 lbs.	18 to 25	325°	140°
HAM, FULLY COOKED, BONELESS	4 to 6 lbs.	18 to 20	325°	140°

CARVING A RIB ROAST

1) Place roast with rib bones to one side of a cutting board to serve the roast with the rib bone attached. Hold the meat steady with a meat fork. Using a carving knife, cut between the bones, following along the curve of the bone.

2) Hold the roast upright by using paper towels to hold the rib bones with one hand to serve the roast as boneless slices. With a carving knife, cut between the meat and the rib bones. If the chine bone (backbone) is attached, cut between the meat and chine bone to remove.

3) Place the meat cut side down on a cutting board. Cut into slices.

Meat labels give you a variety of information. The label states the type of meat (beef, pork, veal or lamb), the wholesale cut (loin, rib, shoulder, leg, etc.) and the retail cut (steak, chops, roast, etc.). The label also states the sell by date, the weight of the meat, cost per pound and total price.

The wholesale cut is an indication of tenderness; for example, a loin or rib chop will be more tender than a shoulder or leg chop. Tenderness helps determine an appropriate cooking method. Tender cuts are best cooked with dry-heat methods (grilling, broiling, roasting, pan-frying, pan-broiling and stir-frying). Less-tender cuts are better cooked by moist-heat methods (braising or cooking in liquid).

Herbed Pork Rib Roast
Joyce Kramer, Donalsonville, Georgia

My husband created this, and it's a specialty of the house. The simple seasoning also works well on pork chops, beef roast and chicken.

> 1 tablespoon garlic powder
> 1 tablespoon onion powder
> 1 tablespoon dried marjoram
> 1 tablespoon dried parsley flakes
> 1 to 2 teaspoons cayenne pepper
> 1 bone-in pork rib roast (about 4 pounds)

1) In a small bowl, combine the garlic powder, onion powder, marjoram, parsley and cayenne. Rub over roast. Cover and refrigerate overnight.

2) Place roast bone side down in a shallow roasting pan. Bake, uncovered, at 350° 1-1/2 to 1-3/4 hours or until a meat thermometer reads 160°. Let stand for 10-15 minutes before carving.

Yield: 8 servings.

NUTRITION FACTS: 4-1/2 ounces equals 356 calories, 24 g fat (9 g saturated fat), 111 mg cholesterol, 88 mg sodium, 2 g carbohydrate, trace fiber, 30 g protein.

Corn-Stuffed Crown Roast
Dorothy Swanson, St. Louis, Missouri

My mother always made this elegant entree for company dinners and special family celebrations. There's a "wow!" effect when it's on the table.

> 1 pork crown roast (about 7 pounds and 12 ribs)
> 1/2 teaspoon pepper, *divided*
> 1 cup chopped celery
> 1 cup chopped onion
> 1 cup butter
> 6 cups corn bread stuffing
> 2 cups frozen corn, thawed
> 2 jars (4-1/2 ounces *each*) sliced mushrooms, undrained
> 1 teaspoon salt
> 1 teaspoon poultry seasoning

1) Place roast on a rack in a large roasting pan. Sprinkle with 1/4 teaspoon pepper. Cover rib ends with small pieces of foil. Bake, uncovered, at 350° for 2 hours.

2) In a Dutch oven, saute celery and onion in butter until tender. Stir in stuffing, corn, mushrooms, salt, poultry seasoning and remaining pepper. Loosely spoon 1-3 cups into center of roast. Place remaining stuffing in a greased 2-qt. baking dish.

3) Bake the roast for 30-60 minutes or until a meat thermometer reads 160° and juices run clear. Cover and bake extra stuffing for 30-40 minutes. Transfer roast to serving platter. Let stand for 10 minutes. Remove foil; cut between ribs to serve.

Yield: 12 servings.

NUTRITION FACTS: 1 serving equals 545 calories, 30 g fat (15 g saturated fat), 124 mg cholesterol, 826 mg sodium, 30 g carbohydrate, 3 g fiber, 38 g protein.

CORN-STUFFED CROWN ROAST

SPINACH-STUFFED PORK TENDERLOIN

Spinach-Stuffed Pork Tenderloin
Taste of Home Test Kitchen

This roast recipe comes complete with an easy lesson on how to butterfly and stuff the meat with mouth-watering filling. Just follow the directions (plus we added helpful how-to photos).

  1   pork tenderloin (about 1 pound)
1/2   teaspoon celery salt, *divided*
1/2   teaspoon garlic powder, *divided*
1/2   teaspoon pepper, *divided*
  4   slices provolone cheese
  2   cups fresh spinach
  2   thin slices deli ham
        (1/2 ounce *each*)

1) Cut a lengthwise slit down the center of the tenderloin to within 1/2 in. of bottom. Open tenderloin so it lies flat. On each half, make another lengthwise slit down the center to within 1/2 in. of bottom; cover with plastic wrap.

2) Flatten to 1/4-in. thickness. Remove plastic wrap; sprinkle pork with 1/4 teaspoon celery salt, 1/4 teaspoon garlic powder and 1/4 teaspoon pepper. Layer with the cheese, spinach and ham. Press down gently.

3) Roll up jelly-roll style, starting with a long side. Tie the roast at 1-1/2-in. to 2-in. intervals with kitchen string. Sprinkle with remaining celery salt, garlic powder and pepper. Place on a rack in a shallow baking pan.

4) Bake, uncovered, at 425° for 25-30 minutes or until a meat thermometer reads 160°. Transfer to a serving platter. Let stand for 10 minutes before slicing.

Yield: 4 servings.

NUTRITION FACTS: 1 serving equals 248 calories, 12 g fat (6 g saturated fat), 87 mg cholesterol, 588 mg sodium, 2 g carbohydrate, 1 g fiber, 32 g protein.

STUFFING A TENDERLOIN

1) Cut a lengthwise slit down the center of the tenderloin to within 1/2 in. of bottom.

2) Open tenderloin so it lies flat. On each half, make another lengthwise slit down the center to within 1/2 in. of bottom.

3) Cover with plastic wrap. Flatten to 1/4-in. thickness.

4) Remove plastic wrap. Layer or stuff as recipe directs.

5) Roll up jelly-roll style, starting with a long side. Tie roast at 1-1/2-in. to 2-in. intervals with kitchen string.

TENDERLOIN TIPS

Keep pork tenderloin in the freezer for last-minute meals since it thaws and cooks quickly. Thaw tenderloin using the "defrost" cycle of your microwave according to the manufacturer's directions.

Cut a tenderloin into 3-oz. portions, pound into patties and pan-fry for 2 to 3 minutes on each side or until juices run clear for quick, hearty sandwiches served on rolls.

Cut pork tenderloin while partially frozen into thin, even slices and cut slices into strips. Use in place of beef or chicken in your favorite stir-fry or fajita recipes.

PEPPER-CRUSTED PORK TENDERLOIN

Pepper-Crusted Pork Tenderloin
Taste of Home Test Kitchen

Guests will be impressed by this elegant entree and its golden crumb coating with peppery pizzazz. The meat slices up so moist and tender, you can serve it without sauce and still have a succulent, taste-tempting main dish.

- 2 **pork tenderloins (3/4 pound *each*)**
- 3 **tablespoons Dijon mustard**
- 1 **tablespoon 1% buttermilk**
- 2 **teaspoons minced fresh thyme**
- 1 **to 2 teaspoons coarsely ground pepper**
- 1/4 **teaspoon salt**
- 2/3 **cup soft bread crumbs**

1) Place tenderloins side by side and tie together with kitchen string. In a small bowl, combine the mustard, buttermilk, thyme, pepper and salt; spread over surface of meat. Press crumbs onto meat.

2) Place on a rack in a shallow roasting pan. Cover and bake at 425° for 15 minutes. Uncover; bake 35-40 minutes longer or until a meat thermometer reads 160°. Let stand for 10 minutes. Remove string before slicing.

Yield: 6 servings.

Roast Pork with Raspberry Sauce
Carolyn Zimmerman, Fairbury, Illinois

Want to treat your guests to a spectacular meal? Plan this pork as the centerpiece of your menu. The fruity sauce enhances the meat's flavor and looks so pretty! I decorate the platter with red spiced apples and fresh parsley.

- 1 **teaspoon salt**
- 1 **teaspoon rubbed sage**
- 1 **teaspoon pepper**
- 1 **boneless rolled pork loin roast (3-1/2 to 4 pounds)**

SAUCE:

- 1 **package (10 ounces) frozen sweetened raspberries, thawed**
- 1-1/2 **cups sugar**
- 1/4 **cup white vinegar**
- 1/4 **teaspoon *each* ground ginger, nutmeg and cloves**
- 1/4 **cup cornstarch**
- 1 **tablespoon butter, melted**
- 1 **tablespoon lemon juice**
- 3 **to 4 drops red food coloring, optional**

1) Combine the salt, sage and pepper; rub over entire roast. Place roast fat side up on a rack in a shallow roasting pan. Bake, uncovered, at 350° for 70-80 minutes or until a meat thermometer reads 160°.

2) For the sauce, drain raspberries, reserving liquid. Set berries aside. Add enough water to juice to measure 3/4 cup. In a saucepan, combine the sugar, vinegar, spices and 1/2 cup raspberry juice. Bring to a boil. Reduce heat; simmer, uncovered, for 10 minutes.

3) Combine cornstarch and remaining raspberry juice until smooth; stir into the saucepan. Bring to a boil; cook and stir for 2 minutes or until thickened. Remove from the heat. Stir in the butter, lemon juice, food coloring if desired and reserved raspberries.

4) Let roast stand for 10-15 minutes before slicing. Serve with raspberry sauce.

Yield: 10 servings.

Tuscan Pork Roast

Elinor Stabile, Canmore, Alberta

Everyone's eager to eat after the wonderful aroma of this roast tempts us all afternoon. This is a great Sunday dinner with little fuss.

- 5 to 8 garlic cloves, peeled
- 1 tablespoon dried rosemary
- 1 tablespoon olive oil
- 1/2 teaspoon salt
- 1 boneless whole pork loin roast (3 to 4 pounds)

1) In a food processor, combine garlic, rosemary, olive oil and salt; cover and process until mixture becomes a paste. Rub over the roast; cover and let stand for 30 minutes.

2) Place roast fat side up on a greased baking rack in a shallow roasting pan. Bake, uncovered, at 350° for 1 to 1-1/4 hours or until a meat thermometer reads 160°. Let stand for 10-15 minutes before slicing.

Yield: 10 servings.

NUTRITION FACTS: 3-1/2 ounces cooked pork equals 184 calories, 8 g fat (2 g saturated fat), 68 mg cholesterol, 157 mg sodium, 1 g carbohydrate, trace fiber, 26 g protein.

USING AN HERB RUB

Crush any large herbs; combine all herbs. Sprinkle mixture over entire roast and rub into the surface of the meat. Roast as directed.

Pennsylvania Pot Roast

Donna Wilkinson, Clarksburg, Maryland

This heartwarming one-dish meal is adapted from a Pennsylvania Dutch recipe. I start the pot roast cooking before I leave for church, add vegetables when I get home and then just sit back and relax until it's done.

- 1 boneless pork shoulder roast (2-1/2 to 3 pounds), halved
- 1-1/2 cups beef broth
- 1/2 cup sliced green onions
- 1 teaspoon dried basil
- 1 teaspoon dried marjoram
- 1/2 teaspoon salt
- 1/2 teaspoon pepper
- 1 bay leaf
- 6 medium red potatoes, cut into 2-inch chunks
- 4 medium carrots, cut into 2-inch chunks
- 7 to 8 fresh mushrooms, quartered
- 1/4 cup all-purpose flour
- 1/2 cup cold water
  Browning sauce, optional

1) Place roast in a 5-qt. slow cooker; add the broth, onions and seasonings. Cover and cook on high for 2 hours. Add the potatoes, carrots and mushrooms.

2) Cover and cook on low for 6 hours or until vegetables are tender. Remove the meat and vegetables; keep warm. Discard bay leaf.

3) In a saucepan, combine flour and cold water until smooth; stir in 1-1/2 cups cooking juices. Bring to a boil; cook and stir for 2 minutes or until thickened. Add browning sauce if desired. Serve with roast and vegetables.

Yield: 6 servings.

NUTRITION FACTS: 1 serving equals 331 calories, 12 g fat (4 g saturated fat), 78 mg cholesterol, 490 mg sodium, 28 g carbohydrate, 4 g fiber, 26 g protein.

Pork 'n' Pepper Tortillas

Rita Hahnbaum, Muscatine, Iowa

First I season a pork roast with onions, garlic and spices, and then I cook it slowly until tender. Shred the flavorful meat and wrap it along with peppers in warm tortillas for a wonderful main dish.

- 1 boneless pork shoulder roast (2-1/2 to 3 pounds), halved
- 1 cup boiling water
- 2 teaspoons beef bouillon granules
- 3 garlic cloves, minced
- 1 tablespoon dried basil
- 1 tablespoon dried oregano
- 1 teaspoon ground cumin
- 1 teaspoon pepper
- 1 teaspoon dried tarragon
- 1 teaspoon white pepper
- 2 medium onions, sliced
- 1 *each* large green, sweet red and yellow pepper, sliced
- 1 tablespoon butter
- 12 flour tortillas (8 inches), warmed
  Shredded lettuce, chopped ripe olives, sliced jalapeno peppers and sour cream, optional

1) Place roast in a 5-qt. slow cooker. Combine the water, bouillon, garlic and seasonings; pour over

roast. Top with onions. Cover and cook on high for 1 hour. Reduce heat to low. Cook for 7-8 hours or until pork is very tender.

2) When cool enough to handle, remove meat from bone. Shred meat and return to slow cooker; heat through. Meanwhile, in a skillet, saute peppers in butter until tender.

3) Using a slotted spoon, place about 1/2 cup pork and onion mixture down the center of each tortilla; top with peppers.

4) Add the lettuce, olives, jalapenos and sour cream if desired. Fold sides of tortilla over filling; serve immediately.

Yield: 12 servings.

NUTRITION FACTS: 1 tortilla equals 417 calories, 16 g fat (5 g saturated fat), 110 mg cholesterol, 489 mg sodium, 31 g carbohydrate, 2 g fiber, 36 g protein.

COUNTRY-STYLE RIBS

Tips for Great Ribs

Start ribs ahead if time does not permit tenderizing and cooking ribs on the same day. Cook the ribs until they are tender, about 1 hour, then refrigerate. The next day, brush the ribs with sauce and bake until heated through, basting with sauce as desired.

Hold ribs until serving time or transport hot cooked ribs to a party by placing ribs in heavy-duty foil and then in a brown paper bag. The ribs can stand this way for up to 1 hour.

Useful Definitions

For additional terms, refer to the Glossary on pages 18-22.

BABY BACK RIBS: Ribs that come from the blade and center section of the pork loin. They are called baby back ribs because they are smaller than spareribs.

COUNTRY-STYLE RIBS: Meaty ribs from the rib end of the pork loin. They are sold both in slabs and individually with and without bones.

SPARERIBS: Curved ribs from the pork belly. While they are the least meaty of the ribs, they have a meaty pork flavor.

ST. LOUIS-STYLE RIBS: Spareribs with the breast-bone removed.

Country-Style Ribs
Annette McCullough, Pahrump, Nevada

Whenever I need a surefire company pleaser, I cook up these scrumptious ribs. Usually, I double or triple the recipe, since the ribs freeze well.

1/3 cup all-purpose flour
2 teaspoons salt
1/4 teaspoon pepper
4 to 4-1/2 pounds bone-in country-style pork ribs
3 tablespoons vegetable oil
1 medium onion, sliced and separated into rings
1 can (14-1/2 ounces) beef broth
1/4 cup ketchup
3 tablespoons Worcestershire sauce
2 tablespoons cider vinegar
3 whole cloves
3 whole allspice
1 garlic clove, minced
1 bay leaf
1/2 teaspoon celery salt
1/8 teaspoon cayenne pepper

1) In a large resealable plastic bag, combine the flour, salt and pepper. Add ribs, a few pieces at a time, and shake to coat.

2) In a large skillet, brown ribs in oil; transfer to a greased 13-in. x 9-in. x 2-in. baking dish. Sprinkle with onion. Combine the remaining ingredients; pour over ribs.

3) Cover and bake at 350° for 1-1/4 hours or until meat is tender. Remove ribs to a serving platter; keep warm. Strain liquid, discarding bay leaf; skim fat. Serve sauce with ribs.

Yield: 6 servings.

NUTRITION FACTS: 6 ounces cooked ribs equals 433 calories, 25 g fat (8 g saturated fat), 115 mg cholesterol, 1,445 mg sodium, 13 g carbohydrate, 1 g fiber, 37 g protein.

HONEY-GARLIC PORK RIBS

Honey-Garlic Pork Ribs
Patsy Saulnier, South Ohio, Nova Scotia

I discovered this recipe a number of years ago, and I make it often because my family really enjoys it. I hope you do, too!

- 4 pounds pork spareribs *or* pork loin back ribs
- 1 cup honey
- 1 cup packed brown sugar
- 1/3 cup soy sauce
- 1/2 teaspoon garlic powder
- 1/2 teaspoon ground ginger
- 1 teaspoon ground mustard

1) Cut ribs into serving-size pieces; place in a large resealable plastic bag. Combine the remaining ingredients; pour half the marinade over ribs.

2) Seal bag and turn to coat; refrigerate for several hours or overnight, turning bag occasionally. Cover and refrigerate remaining marinade. Drain and discard marinade from ribs.

3) Place ribs on a rack in a greased shallow baking pan. Cover and bake at 350° for 1 hour. Drain. Pour the reserved marinade over ribs. Bake, uncovered, for 30-45 minutes or until meat is tender, brushing occasionally with pan juices.

Yield: 4 servings.

NUTRITION FACTS: 1 serving equals 799 calories, 43 g fat (16 g saturated fat), 170 mg cholesterol, 603 mg sodium, 62 g carbohydrate, trace fiber, 42 g protein.

TENDERIZING RIBS

Tenderize ribs so the meat pulls easily from the bones. First, place serving-size portions on a rack in a shallow baking pan. Cover tightly with foil and bake at 350° for 1 hour; drain. Then finish cooking as recipe directs.

Maple Barbecued Ribs
Linda Russell, Exeter, Ontario

Maple syrup adds great flavor to these ribs. But you can also try variations on the recipes with equally delicious results.

- 3 pounds pork spareribs
- 1 cup maple syrup
- 1 small onion, chopped
- 1 tablespoon sesame seeds
- 1 tablespoon white vinegar
- 1 tablespoon Worcestershire sauce
- 1 tablespoon chili sauce
- 2 garlic cloves, minced
- 1/2 teaspoon salt
- 1/2 teaspoon ground ginger
- 1/4 teaspoon ground mustard
- 1/8 teaspoon pepper

1) Cut ribs into serving-size pieces. Place ribs bone side down on a rack in a shallow roasting pan. Bake at 350° for 1 hour; drain.

2) Meanwhile, in a small saucepan, combine the remaining ingredients; cook and stir over medium heat until mixture comes to a boil.

3) Pour sauce over ribs. Bake, uncovered, at 350° for 30-45 minutes longer or until tender, basting occasionally.

Yield: 6 servings.

NUTRITION FACTS: 1 serving equals 576 calories, 33 g fat (12 g saturated fat), 128 mg cholesterol, 367 mg sodium, 39 g carbohydrate, trace fiber, 31 g protein.

■ *HONEY BARBECUED RIBS:* Bake ribs for 1 hour as directed above. In a bowl, combine 3 tablespoons lemon juice, 2 tablespoons *each* vegetable oil and honey, 1 tablespoon *each* dried minced onion and soy sauce, 1 teaspoon *each* salt and paprika, 1/2 teaspoon dried oregano and 1/8 teaspoon garlic powder. Brush some of glaze on ribs. Bake 30-45 minutes longer, brushing occasionally with remaining glaze.

- *PLUM GLAZED RIBS:* Bake ribs for 1 hour as directed in recipe. In a bowl, combine 6 tablespoons *each* soy sauce, plum jam and honey, and 2 minced garlic cloves. Brush some of glaze on ribs. Bake 30-45 minutes longer, brushing occasionally with remaining glaze.

APPLE-STUFFED PORK CHOPS

Apple-Stuffed Pork Chops
Paula Disterhaupt, Glenwood, Iowa

Usually pork chops are paired with applesauce. This delicious entree has been on my menu for many years and piles apples into the pork chops instead.

1	tablespoon chopped onion
1/4	cup butter
3	cups soft bread cubes
2	cups finely chopped apples
1/4	cup finely chopped celery
2	teaspoons minced fresh parsley
3/4	teaspoon salt, *divided*
6	bone-in pork loin chops (1-1/2 inches thick and 7 ounces *each*)
1/8	teaspoon pepper
1	tablespoon vegetable oil

1) In a small skillet, saute onion in butter until tender. Remove from heat; add the bread cubes, apples, celery, parsley and 1/4 teaspoon salt.

2) Cut a pocket in each chop by making a horizontal cut through the meat almost to the bone. Sprinkle inside and outside with pepper and remaining salt. Spoon stuffing loosely into pockets.

3) In a large skillet, brown the chops on both sides in oil. Place in an ungreased large baking pan.

4) Cover and bake at 350° for 30 minutes. Uncover; bake for 30 minutes longer or until a meat thermometer reads 160° when inserted into the meat and juices run clear.

Yield: 6 servings.

NUTRITION FACTS: 1 pork chop equals 364 calories, 19 g fat (8 g saturated fat), 107 mg cholesterol, 534 mg sodium, 15 g carbohydrate, 2 g fiber, 32 g protein.

Pork Chops with Herbed Cream Sauce
Edith Ruth Muldoon, Baldwin, New York

This recipe is perfect for a spur-of-the-moment lunch or no-fuss dinner. The meat cooks up moist and tender, and the bouillon lends instant flavor to the gravy.

4	pork rib chops (7 ounces *each*), 1/2 inch thick
2	tablespoons vegetable oil
1	tablespoon all-purpose flour
1/2	teaspoon beef bouillon granules
1	tablespoon minced fresh parsley
1/2	teaspoon dried basil, thyme *or* tarragon
2/3	cup milk *or* half-and-half cream
2	tablespoons water
1/8	to 1/4 teaspoon pepper

1) In a large skillet, cook pork chops in oil until the juices run clear. Remove and keep warm; drain.

2) Stir the flour, bouillon, parsley and basil into the skillet. Gradually stir in the milk, water and pepper until smooth. Bring to a boil; cook and stir for 2 minutes or until thickened. Spoon over chops.

Yield: 4 servings.

NUTRITION FACTS: 1 pork chop with 2 tablespoons sauce equals 278 calories, 17 g fat (5 g saturated fat), 69 mg cholesterol, 156 mg sodium, 4 g carbohydrate, trace fiber, 27 g protein.

MAKING A POCKET IN A PORK CHOP

Use a sharp knife to cut a pocket in a pork chop. Make a horizontal slit in the middle of the chop by slicing from the edge almost to the bone.

BREADED DIJON PORK CHOPS

Breaded Dijon Pork Chops
Shannon Gerardi, Dayton, Ohio

The breading that coats these tender chops is moist and subtly seasoned with Dijon mustard. I sometimes make it with pork tenderloin instead.

- 3/4 cup crushed saltines (about 20 crackers)
- 1/2 teaspoon dried thyme
- 1/4 teaspoon pepper
- 1/8 to 1/4 teaspoon rubbed sage
- 3 tablespoons Dijon mustard
- 4 pork rib chops (7 ounces each), 1/2 inch thick
- 1/4 cup vegetable oil

1) In a small bowl, combine the cracker crumbs, thyme, pepper and sage. Spread mustard on both sides of pork chops; coat with crumb mixture.

2) In a large skillet, cook pork chops in oil over medium-high heat for 4-5 minutes on each side or until golden brown and juices run clear.

Yield: 4 servings.

NUTRITION FACTS: 1 pork chop equals 366 calories, 24 g fat (5 g saturated fat), 63 mg cholesterol, 466 mg sodium, 10 g carbohydrate, 1 g fiber, 27 g protein.

Braised Pork Chops
Marilyn Larsen, Port Orange, Florida

An easy herb rub gives sensational taste to these boneless pork loin chops that can be cooked on the stovetop in minutes.

- 1 teaspoon rubbed sage
- 1 teaspoon dried rosemary, crushed
- 1 garlic clove, minced
- 1/2 teaspoon salt
- 1/8 teaspoon pepper
- 4 boneless pork loin chops (1/2 inch thick and 4 ounces *each*)
- 1 tablespoon butter
- 1 tablespoon olive oil
- 3/4 cup dry white wine *or* apple juice, *divided*
- 1 tablespoon minced fresh parsley

1) Combine the sage, rosemary, garlic, salt and pepper; rub over both sides of pork chops. In a large nonstick skillet, brown chops on both sides in butter and oil. Remove.

2) Add 1/2 cup wine or juice to the skillet; bring to a boil. Return chops to pan. Reduce heat; cover and simmer for 8-10 minutes or until meat juices run clear, basting occasionally. Remove chops to a serving platter and keep warm.

3) Add remaining wine or juice to the skillet. Bring to a boil, loosening any browned bits from pan. Cook, uncovered, until liquid is reduced to 1/2 cup. Pour over pork chops; sprinkle with parsley.

Yield: 4 servings.

NUTRITION FACTS: 1 pork chop equals 232 calories, 11 g fat (4 g saturated fat), 79 mg cholesterol, 383 mg sodium, 1 g carbohydrate, trace fiber, 24 g protein.

Pork Tenderloin Diane
Patsy Faye Steenbock, Riverton, Wyoming

Sliced tenderloins are seasoned with lemon-pepper, cooked and then served with a wonderful sauce. It's a delightful dish that my family enjoys.

- 1 pork tenderloin (1 pound), cut into 8 slices
- 2 teaspoons lemon-pepper seasoning
- 2 tablespoons butter
- 6 teaspoons lemon juice
- 1 tablespoon Worcestershire sauce
- 1 teaspoon Dijon-style mustard
- 1 tablespoon fresh minced parsley

1) Lightly pound each tenderloin slice to 1/2-in. thickness; sprinkle surfaces with lemon-pepper. In a large skillet, cook pork in butter for 3-4 minutes on each side or until juices run clear. Remove and keep warm.

2) In the same skillet, stir in the lemon juice, Worcestershire sauce and mustard; cook until heated through, scraping up any browned bits. Pour sauce over meat; sprinkle with parsley.

Yield: 4 servings.

NUTRITION FACTS: 2 cooked pork slices with 1 tablespoon sauce equals 189 calories, 10 g fat (5 g saturated fat), 78 mg cholesterol, 407 mg sodium, 2 g carbohydrate, trace fiber, 23 g protein.

Pork Schnitzel
Joyce Folker, Paraowan, Utah

I often like to serve this German dish with mashed potatoes and cinnamon applesauce. It's one of my husband's favorite meals.

- 6 boneless pork cutlets (1/2 inch thick)
- 1/2 cup all-purpose flour
- 2 teaspoons seasoned salt
- 1/2 teaspoon pepper
- 2 eggs
- 1/4 cup milk
- 1-1/2 cups dry bread crumbs
- 2 teaspoons paprika
- 6 tablespoons vegetable oil

DILL SAUCE:
- 1-1/2 cups chicken broth, *divided*
- 2 tablespoons all-purpose flour
- 1/2 teaspoon dill weed
- 1 cup (8 ounces) sour cream

1) Flatten pork cutlets to 1/4-in. thickness. In a shallow bowl, combine the flour, seasoned salt and pepper. In another bowl, beat eggs and milk. In another bowl, combine bread crumbs and paprika. Dip cutlets into flour mixture, then into egg mixture and coat with crumb mixture.

2) In a large skillet, cook pork in oil, a few pieces at a time, for 3-4 minutes per side or until meat is no longer pink. Remove to a platter; keep warm.

3) For sauce, pour 1 cup broth into skillet, scraping bottom of pan to loosen browned bits. Combine flour and remaining broth until smooth; stir into skillet. Bring to a boil. Cook; stir for 2 minutes or until thickened. Reduce heat. Stir in dill and sour cream; heat through (do not boil). Pour over pork.

Yield: 6 servings.

NUTRITION FACTS: 1 serving equals 412 calories, 25 g fat (8 g saturated fat), 107 mg cholesterol, 1,025 mg sodium, 32 g carbohydrate, 1 g fiber, 11 g protein.

Caramelized Pork Slices
Elisa Lochridge, Aloha, Oregon

This easy treatment for pork caught my eye when I saw the word "caramelized." I like to serve this over noodles or rice...or with mashed potatoes.

- 1 pork tenderloin (1 pound), cut into 1-inch slices
- 2 teaspoons canola oil
- 2 garlic cloves, minced
- 2 tablespoons brown sugar
- 1 tablespoon orange juice
- 1 tablespoon molasses
- 1/2 teaspoon salt
- 1/4 teaspoon pepper

1) Flatten pork slices to 1/2-in. thickness. In a nonstick skillet, brown pork in oil over medium-high heat. Remove and keep warm.

2) In the same skillet, saute garlic for 1 minute; stir in the brown sugar, orange juice, molasses, salt and pepper. Return pork to pan; cook, uncovered, for 3-4 minutes or until pork is no longer pink.

Yield: 4 servings.

NUTRITION FACTS: 3 ounces cooked pork equals 200 calories, 6 g fat (2 g saturated fat), 74 mg cholesterol, 355 mg sodium, 11 g carbohydrate, 1 g fiber, 24 g protein.

New England Boiled Dinner
Natalie Cook, Scarborough, Maine

This is an old favorite. We even took the recipe with us when we moved to California for a while.

- 1 smoked boneless pork shoulder butt roast (2 to 2-1/2 pounds)
- 1 pound fresh carrots, sliced lengthwise and halved
- 8 medium red potatoes, peeled and halved
- 2 medium onions, cut into quarters
- 1 large head cabbage, cut into quarters
- 1 large turnip, peeled and cut into quarters
- 1 large rutabaga, peeled, halved and sliced

1) Place pork roast in a large Dutch oven; cover with water. Bring to a boil. Reduce heat; cover and simmer for 1 hour.

2) Add the remaining ingredients; return to a boil. Reduce heat. Cover and simmer for 1 hour or until the vegetables are tender; drain.

Yield: 8-10 servings.

NUTRITION FACTS: 1 serving equals 350 calories, 17 g fat (6 g saturated fat), 52 mg cholesterol, 1,120 mg sodium, 36 g carbohydrate, 9 g fiber, 17 g protein.

WARM FAJITA SALAD

3) Drain pork, discarding marinade. Heat reserved marinade in a large skillet over medium-high heat. Add the pork, onion and peppers; stir-fry for 3-4 minutes or until pork is no longer pink. Drizzle with lemon juice. Remove from the heat.

4) Arrange lettuce on four individual plates; top with meat mixture and tomatoes.

Yield: 4 servings.

NUTRITION FACTS: 1 cup equals 278 calories, 11 g fat (3 g saturated fat), 67 mg cholesterol, 1,044 mg sodium, 19 g carbohydrate, 4 g fiber, 29 g protein.

Warm Fajita Salad
Bobbie Jo Yokley, Franklin, Kentucky

When I didn't have tortillas in the house to wrap up the meat in this recipe, I made it into a hearty salad instead. It was delicious!

- 1 cup lime juice
- 1/4 cup chicken broth
- 1/4 cup soy sauce
- 2 garlic cloves, minced
- 1 tablespoon vegetable oil
- 1 teaspoon sugar
- 1 teaspoon Liquid Smoke, optional
- 3/4 teaspoon ground cumin
- 1/2 teaspoon dried oregano
- 1/4 teaspoon ground ginger
- 1/4 teaspoon hot pepper sauce
- 1 pound boneless pork loin, trimmed and cut into thin strips
- 1 large onion, sliced
- 1 medium green pepper, cut into strips
- 1 medium sweet yellow pepper, cut into strips
- 1 tablespoon lemon juice
- 6 cups torn romaine
- 12 cherry tomatoes, quartered

1) In a large resealable plastic bag, combine the lime juice, broth, soy sauce, garlic, oil, sugar and seasonings. Reserve 2 tablespoons; cover and refrigerate.

2) Add pork to remaining marinade. Seal bag and turn to coat; refrigerate for 30 minutes to 3 hours, turning occasionally.

Spicy Pork 'n' Peanuts
Pam Beil, Bradford, Rhode Island

I add a sprinkling of peanuts to this nicely spiced stir-fry that showcases savory pork tenderloin. If your family prefers less heat, simply decrease the amount of red pepper flakes.

- 1 pound pork tenderloin, cubed
- 1/3 cup reduced-sodium soy sauce, *divided*
- 3 tablespoons sugar
- 4 teaspoons cornstarch
- 1/2 cup chicken broth
- 3 tablespoons lemon juice
- 1/4 to 1/2 teaspoon crushed red pepper flakes
- 1 small onion, julienned
- 2 garlic cloves, minced
- 1 tablespoon olive oil
- 2 small sweet red peppers, julienned
- 2 small sweet yellow peppers, julienned
- 1/4 cup unsalted dry roasted peanuts
- 6 cups hot cooked rice

1) Place pork in a bowl; drizzle with 2 tablespoons soy sauce. Set aside. In another bowl, combine sugar and cornstarch. Stir in the broth, lemon juice, red pepper flakes and remaining soy sauce until blended; set aside.

2) In a nonstick skillet or wok, stir-fry pork, onion and garlic in oil for 4 minutes. Add peppers; stir-fry for 4-5 minutes.

3) Stir cornstarch mixture and add to pan. Bring to a boil; cook and stir for 1 minute or until thickened. Stir in peanuts. Serve over rice.

Yield: 6 servings.

NUTRITION FACTS: 1-1/3 cups meat mixture with 1 cup rice equals 432 calories, 9 g fat (2 g saturated fat), 49 mg cholesterol, 713 mg sodium, 63 g carbohydrate, 3 g fiber, 25 g protein.

PORK CHOW MEIN

Pork Chow Mein

Helen Carpenter, Marble Falls, Texas

I give all the credit for my love of cooking and baking to my mother, grandmother and mother-in-law. That trio inspired delicious dishes like this hearty skillet dinner.

- 1 pound boneless pork loin
- 2 garlic cloves, minced
- 4 tablespoons soy sauce, *divided*
- 2 tablespoons cornstarch
- 1/2 to 1 teaspoon ground ginger
- 1 cup chicken broth
- 1 tablespoon vegetable oil
- 1 cup thinly sliced carrots
- 1 cup thinly sliced celery
- 1 cup chopped onion
- 1 cup coarsely chopped cabbage
- 1 cup coarsely chopped fresh spinach

Hot cooked rice

1) Cut pork into 4-in. x 1/4-in. strips; place in a bowl. Add garlic and 2 tablespoons soy sauce. Cover and refrigerate for 2-4 hours.

2) Meanwhile, combine the cornstarch, ginger, broth and remaining soy sauce until smooth; set aside. Heat oil in a large skillet or wok on high; stir-fry pork until no longer pink. Remove; keep warm.

3) Add carrots and celery; stir-fry for 3-4 minutes. Add the onion, cabbage and spinach; stir-fry for 2-3 minutes. Stir broth mixture; stir into skillet along with pork. Bring to a boil; cook and stir for 3-4 minutes or until thickened. Serve immediately over rice if desired.

Yield: 6 servings.

NUTRITION FACTS: 1 cup (calculated without rice) equals 162 calories, 6 g fat (2 g saturated fat), 38 mg cholesterol, 561 mg sodium, 10 g carbohydrate, 2 g fiber, 17 g protein.

Sweet-and-Sour Pork

Gloria Kobiak, Loveland, Colorado

You couldn't ask for a better blend of sweet-and-sour flavors! This recipe has it.

- 1/4 cup cornstarch
- 1 egg, beaten
- 1-1/2 pounds boneless pork, cut into 1/2-inch cubes
- 3 tablespoons vegetable oil, *divided*
- 2 medium carrots, sliced
- 1 medium onion, chopped
- 1 garlic clove, minced
- 1 medium green pepper, cut into 1-inch pieces
- 2 tablespoons water
- 1 can (8 ounces) unsweetened pineapple chunks

SAUCE:
- 1 tablespoon cornstarch
- 1/3 cup packed brown sugar
- 1/4 cup chicken broth
- 1/4 cup white wine vinegar
- 1 tablespoon soy sauce
- 1/2 teaspoon minced fresh gingerroot

Hot cooked rice

1) In a large bowl, combine cornstarch and egg until smooth. Add pork; toss to coat. In a skillet or wok, stir-fry half of the pork in 1 tablespoon oil until no longer pink; remove. Repeat with remaining pork and 1 tablespoon oil; set pork aside and keep warm.

2) Stir-fry the carrots, onion and garlic in the remaining oil for 3 minutes. Add green pepper and water; stir-fry for 2 minutes. Drain pineapple, reserving 1/4 cup juice. Add pineapple and pork to pan.

3) Combine cornstarch and brown sugar. Stir in chicken broth, vinegar and soy sauce until smooth. Add ginger and reserved pineapple juice; add to pan. Bring to a boil; cook and stir for 2 minutes or until thickened. Serve over rice.

Yield: 6 servings.

NUTRITION FACTS: 1 serving (calculated without rice) equals 351 calories, 14 g fat (4 g saturated fat), 102 mg cholesterol, 268 mg sodium, 29 g carbohydrate, 2 g fiber, 26 g protein.

PORK 'N' PEA POD STIR-FRY

Pork 'n' Pea Pod Stir-Fry
Jane Shapton, Tustin, California

A spicy citrus sauce coats tender strips of pork
and crisp snow peas in this speedy stir-fry. We
like this dish extra spicy, so I use a tablespoon of
red pepper flakes.

       2   tablespoons reduced-sodium
           soy sauce
       2   tablespoons honey
   1-1/2   teaspoons minced fresh
           gingerroot
     1/2   to 1 teaspoon crushed red pepper
           flakes
     3/4   pound pork tenderloin, cut
           into 2-inch strips
       2   teaspoons canola oil
       1   tablespoon cornstarch
     1/3   cup orange juice
       2   tablespoons cider vinegar
       1   pound fresh snow peas
       2   teaspoons minced garlic
       1   teaspoon grated orange peel

1) In a small bowl, combine the soy sauce, honey,
   ginger and pepper flakes. Place 3 tablespoons in
   a large resealable plastic bag; add the pork. Seal
   bag and turn to coat; refrigerate for 1 hour. Cover
   and refrigerate remaining marinade.

2) Combine the cornstarch, orange juice, vinegar
   and reserved marinade; stir until blended. Set
   aside. Drain and discard marinade from pork. In
   a large nonstick skillet or wok, stir-fry pork in oil
   for 4-5 minutes or until no longer pink. Remove
   pork and keep warm.

3) In the same pan, stir-fry snow peas for 2-3
   minutes or until crisp-tender. Stir in garlic and
   orange peel.

4) Stir cornstarch mixture and stir into pan. Bring to
   a boil; cook and stir for 1-2 minutes or until
   thickened. Return pork to the pan; heat through.

Yield: 3 servings.

NUTRITION FACTS: 1-1/3 cups equals 286 calories, 7 g fat (2 g
saturated fat), 63 mg cholesterol, 354 mg sodium, 26 g carbohydrate,
4 g fiber, 28 g protein.

Country Skillet Supper
Arlene Snyder, Ephrata, Pennsylvania

This is a super-quick way to use leftover pork.
With hearty potatoes and bright green peas, it's
creamy, comforting and so tasty.

       1   small onion, chopped
       1   tablespoon vegetable oil
       1   can (10-3/4 ounces) condensed
           cream of celery soup, undiluted
     1/2   cup milk
       1   teaspoon Worcestershire sauce

1/4   teaspoon salt
1/8   teaspoon pepper
  1   cup cubed cooked pork
  1   cup cubed cooked potatoes
  1   cup frozen peas, thawed
      Biscuits, optional

1) In a large skillet, saute onion in oil until tender.
    Stir in the soup, milk, Worcestershire, salt and
    pepper; mix well.

2) Add the pork, potatoes and peas; heat through.
    Serve with biscuits if desired.

Yield: 2-3 servings.

NUTRITION FACTS: 1 serving equals 326 calories, 15 g fat (5 g saturated fat), 52 mg cholesterol, 1,058 mg sodium, 30 g carbohydrate, 4 g fiber, 20 g protein.

Pork Fried Rice for Two
Laura Kittleson, Casselberry, Florida

My husband and I often make a meal of this nicely seasoned and appealing stir-fry.

1/8   teaspoon Chinese five-spice
      powder
  6   ounces boneless pork loin, cut
      into 1/4-inch cubes
1/2   teaspoon fennel seed, crushed
1-1/2 teaspoons canola oil, *divided*
  2   cups broccoli florets
  1   celery rib with leaves, sliced
1/2   cup shredded carrot
1/4   cup chopped green onions
1-1/2 cups cold cooked brown rice
  1   tablespoon reduced-sodium
      soy sauce
1/8   teaspoon pepper

1) Sprinkle five-spice powder over pork and toss to
    coat. In a large nonstick skillet or wok coated with
    nonstick cooking spray, stir-fry pork for 3 minutes
    or until brown. Remove and keep warm.

2) Stir-fry fennel seed in 3/4 teaspoon oil for 30
    seconds. Add the broccoli, celery, carrot and
    onions; stir-fry for 3 minutes or until crisp-tender.
    Remove and keep warm.

3) Stir-fry rice in remaining oil for 2 minutes. Stir in
    soy sauce and pepper. Return pork and vegetables
    to pan; cook and stir until heated through.

Yield: 2 servings.

NUTRITION FACTS: 1-3/4 cups equals 367 calories, 10 g fat (2 g saturated fat), 50 mg cholesterol, 417 mg sodium, 44 g carbohydrate, 5 g fiber, 26 g protein.

Spiced Pork Potpie
Kay Krause, Sioux Falls, South Dakota

Filled with cranberries, apple, sweet potatoes, cinnamon and cloves, this scrumptious meat pie smells just like autumn as it bakes! The original recipe called for a pastry crust, but I prefer the fuss-free batter crust on top.

1-1/2 pounds cubed pork shoulder
      roast
1/2   cup butter, *divided*
  2   cups apple cider *or* juice
  1   cup water
  1   cup chopped peeled tart apple
1/2   cup dried cranberries
1/2   cup dried pitted prunes, chopped
  2   teaspoons ground cinnamon
1-1/2 teaspoons ground ginger
  2   whole cloves
  6   tablespoons all-purpose flour
  1   can (15 ounces) sweet potatoes,
      drained and cubed

CRUST:
  1   cup all-purpose flour
1-1/2 teaspoons baking powder
1/2   teaspoon salt
3/4   cup milk
1/2   cup butter, melted

1) In a Dutch oven, cook pork in 2 tablespoons
    butter until no longer pink. Add the cider and
    water; bring to a boil. Reduce heat; simmer,
    uncovered, for 10 minutes. Stir in the fruit and
    seasoning; simmer 10 minutes longer.

2) Melt remaining butter; stir in flour until smooth.
    Slowly add to meat mixture. Bring to a boil; cook
    for 1-2 minutes or until thickened. Discard cloves.
    Stir in sweet potatoes. Pour into a greased 3-qt.
    baking dish.

3) For crust, combine the flour, baking powder and
    salt in a bowl. Combine the milk and butter; stir
    into dry ingredients until smooth. Spread over
    filling. Bake at 400° for 28-32 minutes or until
    crust is browned.

Yield: 6 servings.

NUTRITION FACTS: 1 cup equals 857 calories, 46 g fat (24 g saturated fat), 215 mg cholesterol, 777 mg sodium, 70 g carbohydrate, 5 g fiber, 42 g protein.

Lumberjack Stew
Bonnie Tetzlaff, Scandinavia, Wisconsin

This one-dish stew is very satisfying on a cold day. Since it simmers on the stovetop for an hour, I'm free to get other things done around the house.

- 2 pounds boneless pork, trimmed and cut into 1-inch cubes
- 1 teaspoon salt
- 1 teaspoon sugar
- 1/2 teaspoon pepper
- 1/2 teaspoon paprika
- 2 tablespoons vegetable oil
- 1 cup sliced onion
- 1 garlic clove, minced
- 3 cups water
- 1 tablespoon lemon juice
- 1 teaspoon Worcestershire sauce
- 2 chicken bouillon cubes
- 2 bay leaves
- 6 medium carrots, cut into 1-inch pieces
- 1 package (10 ounces) pearl onions, peeled
- 3 cups frozen cut green beans
- 3 tablespoons cornstarch
- 1/2 cup cold water

1) Toss pork with the salt, sugar, pepper and paprika. In a Dutch oven, brown in oil on all sides. Add sliced onion and garlic; cook over medium heat for 5 minutes.

2) Add the water, lemon juice, Worcestershire sauce, bouillon and bay leaves; cover and simmer for 1 hour.

3) Add the carrots and pearl onions; cover and simmer for 40 minutes. Add beans; cover and simmer for 10 minutes.

4) Combine cornstarch and cold water until smooth; stir into stew. Bring to a boil; cook and stir for 2 minutes or until thickened. Discard bay leaves.

Yield: 6 servings.

NUTRITION FACTS: 1 cup equals 350 calories, 14 g fat (4 g saturated fat), 89 mg cholesterol, 935 mg sodium, 22 g carbohydrate, 4 g fiber, 34 g protein.

PUEBLO GREEN CHILI STEW

Pueblo Green Chili Stew
Helen LaBrake, Rindge, New Hampshire

Green chilies add a little spice to this flavorful pork stew featuring corn, potatoes and tomatoes.

- 2 pounds lean boneless pork, cut into 1-1/2-inch cubes
- 1 tablespoon vegetable oil
- 3 cans (11 ounces *each*) whole kernel corn, drained
- 2 celery ribs, chopped
- 2 medium potatoes, peeled and chopped
- 2 medium tomatoes, coarsely chopped
- 3 cans (4 ounces *each*) chopped green chilies
- 4 cups chicken broth
- 2 teaspoons ground cumin
- 1 teaspoon dried oregano
- 1 teaspoon salt, optional

1) In a large Dutch oven, brown pork in batches in oil over medium-high heat. Add remaining ingredients.

2) Bring to a boil. Reduce heat; cover and simmer for 1 hour or until pork is tender.

Yield: 8 servings (about 2-1/2 quarts).

NUTRITION FACTS: 1-1/4 cups equals 333 calories, 10 g fat (3 g saturated fat), 67 mg cholesterol, 1,017 mg sodium, 29 g carbohydrate, 4 g fiber, 28 g protein.

Dublin Dumpling Stew

Annette Fisher, Marion, Ohio

I've become a better cook over the years...thanks to recipes, like this one, from my sister.

- 1 pound boneless pork, trimmed and cut into 1-inch cubes
- 2 tablespoons butter
- 1/2 cup chopped onion
- 1/2 cup chopped celery
- 1 garlic clove, minced
- 5 medium carrots
- 3 cups water
- 1 tablespoon beef bouillon granules
- 1 teaspoon salt
- 1/4 cup all-purpose flour
- 1/2 cup cold water
- 1 package (10 ounces) frozen mixed vegetables

DUMPLINGS:

- 1-1/2 cups all-purpose flour
- 1 tablespoon sugar
- 2 teaspoons baking powder
- 1 teaspoon caraway seed
- 1/2 teaspoon salt
- 1/4 teaspoon ground mustard
- 1 egg
- 2/3 cup milk
- 2 tablespoons vegetable oil

1) In a Dutch oven, brown pork in butter over medium heat. Add onion, celery and garlic; cook until vegetables are tender. Quarter carrots lengthwise, then cut into 2-in. pieces; add to pork mixture. Add water, bouillon and salt. Bring to a boil. Reduce heat; cover and simmer 45 minutes or until meat and vegetables are tender.

2) Combine flour and cold water until smooth; stir into stew. Bring to a boil. Cook; stir 2 minutes or until thickened. Add vegetables; reduce heat to low.

3) For dumplings, in a small bowl, combine the flour, sugar, baking powder, salt and mustard. Beat the egg, milk and oil; add to dry ingredients all at once. Stir just until moistened. Drop by tablespoonfuls over stew. Cover and simmer for 25 minutes or until a toothpick inserted into a dumpling comes out clean.

Yield: 6 servings (2-1/2 quarts).

NUTRITION FACTS: 1-2/3 cup equals 411 calories, 15 g fat (5 g saturated fat), 94 mg cholesterol, 1,256 mg sodium, 45 g carbohydrate, 5 g fiber, 24 g protein.

BISCUITS AND SAUSAGE GRAVY

Biscuits and Sausage Gravy

Sue Baker, Jonesboro, Arkansas

I adapted an old Southern recipe to make it more my own, and now my family prefers it.

- 1/4 pound bulk pork sausage
- 2 tablespoons butter
- 2 to 3 tablespoons all-purpose flour
- 1/4 teaspoon salt
- 1/8 teaspoon pepper
- 1-1/4 to 1-1/3 cups milk
- Warm biscuits

1) In a skillet, cook sausage over medium heat until no longer pink; drain. Add butter and heat until melted. Add the flour, salt and pepper; cook and stir until blended.

2) Gradually add the milk, stirring constantly. Bring to a boil; cook and stir for 2 minutes or until thickened. Serve over biscuits.

Yield: 2 servings.

NUTRITION FACTS: 3/4 cup (calculated without biscuits) equals 337 calories, 27 g fat (14 g saturated fat), 72 mg cholesterol, 718 mg sodium, 14 g carbohydrate, trace fiber, 10 g protein.

SAUSAGE TIPS

Drain, rinse and pat cooked pork sausage dry with paper towels before using in a recipe to cut calories and fat.

Combine equal amounts of ground pork and ground beef for flavorful and juicy burgers. Cook the burgers until a meat thermometer reads 160°.

BREAKFAST PATTIES

Breakfast Patties
Jeannine Stallings, East Helena, Montana

This homemade sausage is terrific because it's lean, holds together well and shrinks very little when cooked. It's incredibly easy to mix up a batch and make any breakfast special.

  1/4 cup water
    2 teaspoons salt
    2 teaspoons rubbed sage
    1 teaspoon pepper
  1/2 teaspoon ground nutmeg
  1/4 teaspoon crushed red pepper flakes
  1/8 teaspoon ground ginger
    2 pounds ground pork

1) In a large bowl, combine water and seasonings. Add pork and mix well. Shape into eight 4-in. patties.

2) In a large skillet, cook patties over medium heat for 5-6 minutes on each side or until no longer pink in the center and a meat thermometer reads 160°.

Yield: 8 patties.

NUTRITION FACTS: 1 patty equals 241 calories, 17 g fat (6 g saturated fat), 76 mg cholesterol, 649 mg sodium, trace carbohydrate, trace fiber, 21 g protein.

Zippy Praline Bacon
Myrt Pflannkuche, Pell City, Alabama

Three simple ingredients give bacon an entirely new taste. It's a real treat at any breakfast table.

    1 pound sliced bacon
    3 tablespoons brown sugar
  1-1/2 teaspoons chili powder
  1/4 cup finely chopped pecans

1) Line two 15-in. x 10-in. x 1-in. baking pans with foil. Arrange bacon in a single layer in pans. Bake at 425° for 10 minutes; drain.

2) Combine the brown sugar and chili powder; sprinkle over bacon. Sprinkle with pecans. Bake 5-10 minutes longer or until bacon is crisp. Drain on paper towels.

Yield: 10 servings.

NUTRITION FACTS: 2 slices equals 124 calories, 10 g fat (3 g saturated fat), 13 mg cholesterol, 244 mg sodium, 5 g carbohydrate, trace fiber, 5 g protein.

Canadian Bacon with Apples
Paula Marchesi, Lenhartsville, Pennsylvania

When the holidays roll around, I'd rather spend time with family and friends than be stuck in the kitchen. So I've come to rely on easy-to-fix recipes like this. No one can resist Canadian bacon and apples coated with a delicious brown sugar glaze.

  1/2 cup packed brown sugar
    1 tablespoon lemon juice
  1/8 teaspoon pepper
    1 large unpeeled red apple
    1 large unpeeled green apple
    1 pound sliced Canadian bacon

1) In a large skillet, combine the brown sugar, lemon juice and pepper. Cook and stir over medium heat until sugar is dissolved.

2) Cut each apple into 16 wedges; add to brown sugar mixture. Cook over medium heat for 5-7 minutes until tender, stirring occasionally. Remove apples to a serving platter with a slotted spoon; keep warm.

3) Add Canadian bacon to the skillet; cook over medium heat for 3 minutes or until heated through, turning once. Transfer to platter. Pour remaining brown sugar mixture over apples and bacon. Serve immediately.

Yield: 6 servings.

NUTRITION FACTS: 1 serving equals 199 calories, 4 g fat (1 g saturated fat), 28 mg cholesterol, 744 mg sodium, 30 g carbohydrate, 2 g fiber, 12 g protein.

Brats with Onions
Gunnard Stark, Englewood, Florida

After years of eating plain old brats, I came up with this great-tasting version slathered in zippy onions. Enjoy juicy bratwurst for dinner with plenty left over for meals later in the week.

    3 cans (12 ounces *each*) beer
       or 4-1/2 cups chicken broth

3 large onions, thinly sliced and
  separated into rings
6 garlic cloves, minced
1 tablespoon hot pepper sauce
2 to 3 teaspoons celery salt
2 to 3 teaspoons pepper
1 teaspoon chili powder
15 fresh bratwurst links
  (3-1/2 to 4 pounds)
15 hot dog buns *or* brat buns, split

1) In a Dutch oven, combine the beer or broth,
onion, garlic, pepper sauce, celery salt, pepper
and chili powder.

2) Bring to a boil. Add bratwurst. Reduce heat;
simmer, uncovered, for 20-25 minutes or until
bratwurst is firm and cooked. Drain, reserving
onions.

3) Broil brats 4 in. from heat or grill over medium
heat for 4-5 minutes or until browned, turning
once. Serve on buns with reserved onions.

Yield: 15 brats.

NUTRITION FACTS: 1 brat equals 512 calories, 25 g fat (9 g saturated
fat), 51 mg cholesterol, 1,341 mg sodium, 40 g carbohydrate, 3 g
fiber, 18 g protein.

Bratwurst Stew
Deborah Elliott, Ridge Spring, South Carolina

Using leftover brats hurries along the preparation
of this satisfying stew. When time is short, this
flavorful combination is so good and so easy, I
usually have all the ingredients handy.

2 cans (14-1/2 ounces *each*)
  chicken broth
4 medium carrots, cut
  into 3/4-inch chunks
2 celery ribs, cut into 3/4-inch
  chunks
1 medium onion, chopped
1/2 to 1 teaspoon dried thyme
1/2 teaspoon dried basil
1/2 teaspoon salt
1/4 to 1/2 teaspoon garlic powder
3 cups chopped cabbage
2 cans (15-1/2 ounces *each*) great
  northern beans, rinsed and
  drained
5 fully cooked bratwurst links, cut
  into 3/4-inch slices

1) In a large saucepan, combine the broth, carrots,
celery, onion and seasonings. Bring to a boil.

2) Reduce heat; cover and simmer for 15 minutes.
Add the cabbage; cover and cook for 10 minutes.
Stir in beans and bratwurst; heat through.

Yield: 10 servings.

NUTRITION FACTS: 1 serving equals 229 calories, 12 g fat (4 g
saturated fat), 26 mg cholesterol, 917 mg sodium, 20 g carbohydrate,
6 g fiber, 12 g protein.

POLISH KRAUT AND APPLES

Polish Kraut and Apples
Caren Markee, Cary, Illinois

My family loves this hearty, heartwarming meal on
cold winter nights. The tender apples, brown sugar
and smoked sausage give this dish fantastic flavor.
I like making it because the prep time is very
short.

1 can (14 ounces) sauerkraut,
  rinsed and well drained
1 package (16 ounces) smoked
  Polish sausage *or* kielbasa
3 medium tart apples, peeled and
  cut into eighths
1/2 cup packed brown sugar
1/2 teaspoon caraway seeds, optional
1/8 teaspoon pepper
3/4 cup apple juice

1) Place half of the sauerkraut in an ungreased 3-qt.
slow cooker. Top with sausage, apples, brown
sugar, caraway seeds if desired and pepper. Top
with remaining sauerkraut.

2) Pour apple juice over all. Cover and cook on low
for 4-5 hours or until apples are tender.

Yield: 4 servings.

NUTRITION FACTS: 1 cup equals 546 calories, 31 g fat (12 g
saturated fat), 81 mg cholesterol, 1,630 mg sodium, 52 g
carbohydrate, 4 g fiber, 15 g protein.

Smoked Sausage Stew
Ella Jay Tubbs, Fort Worth, Texas

Condensed bean and bacon soup adds fast flavor to this stew. It simmers together in about an hour, which is perfect after a long day.

- 2 cans (11-1/2 ounces *each*) condensed bean and bacon soup
- 1 can (14-1/2 ounces) diced tomatoes, undrained
- 2 cups water
- 2 medium potatoes, diced
- 1 cup sliced carrots
- 1 cup sliced celery
- 1 teaspoon chili powder
- 12 ounces fully cooked smoked sausage, thinly sliced

1) In a saucepan, combine the soup, tomatoes and water. Add the potatoes, carrots, celery, and chili powder. Bring to a boil.

2) Reduce heat; cover and simmer for 20 minutes. Add sausage; cover and simmer 40 minutes longer.

Yield: 8 servings (2 quarts).

NUTRITION FACTS: 1 cup equals 310 calories, 15 g fat (6 g saturated fat), 32 mg cholesterol, 1,138 mg sodium, 31 g carbohydrate, 7 g fiber, 13 g protein.

SPICY CAJUN STEW

Spicy Cajun Stew
Elizabeth Freise, Kansas City, Missouri

Packed with flavor, this dish is surprisingly quick and easy since it has just five ingredients.

- 1 package (16 ounces) fully cooked Polish sausage *or* kielbasa, cut into 1/4-inch slices

- 2 cans (10 ounces *each*) diced tomatoes and green chilies, undrained
- 1 can (14-1/2 ounces) chicken broth
- 1 package (10 ounces) frozen chopped spinach, thawed and drained
- 1/2 to 3/4 cup uncooked instant rice

1) In a large skillet, saute sausage until lightly browned; drain. Add tomatoes and broth. Bring to a boil. Stir in spinach.

2) Return to a boil; cook for 2 minutes. Stir in the rice. Cover and remove from the heat. Let stand for 5 minutes. Stir with a fork.

Yield: 5 servings.

NUTRITION FACTS: 1 serving equals 356 calories, 25 g fat (10 g saturated fat), 64 mg cholesterol, 1,604 mg sodium, 17 g carbohydrate, 3 g fiber, 15 g protein.

Pork Noodle Casserole
Bernice Morris, Marshfield, Missouri

Less expensive cuts of pork become tender and tasty in this creamy, meal-in-one casserole.

- 2 cups uncooked egg noodles
- 2 pounds boneless pork, cut into 3/4-inch cubes
- 2 medium onions, chopped
- 2 cans (15-1/4 ounces *each*) whole kernel corn, drained
- 2 cans (10-3/4 ounces *each*) condensed cream of mushroom soup, undiluted
- 1/2 teaspoon salt
- 1/2 teaspoon pepper

1) Cook noodles according to package directions. In a large skillet, cook pork and onions over medium heat until meat is no longer pink. Drain noodles. Stir the noodles, corn, soup, salt and pepper into pork mixture.

2) Transfer to a greased 3-qt. baking dish. Cover and bake at 350° for 30 minutes. Uncover; bake 15 minutes longer.

Yield: 8 servings.

NUTRITION FACTS: 1 serving equals 355 calories, 12 g fat (4 g saturated fat), 79 mg cholesterol, 1,078 mg sodium, 29 g carbohydrate, 3 g fiber, 28 g protein.

SAUSAGE CALZONES

Sausage Calzones
Janine Colasurdo, Chesapeake, Virginia

My husband and I both enjoy cooking Italian food. We took the filling we usually use for ravioli and wrapped it in a dough to make these excellent calzones. The Italian sausage blends so beautifully with the cheeses and spinach.

       1   package (1/4 ounce) active dry
           yeast
     1/2   cup warm water (110° to 115°)
     3/4   cup warm milk (110° to 115°)
       2   tablespoons olive oil plus 2
           teaspoons olive oil, *divided*
   1-1/2   teaspoons salt
       1   teaspoon sugar
       3   to 3-1/4 cups all-purpose flour
       1   pound bulk Italian sausage
       1   package (10 ounces) frozen
           chopped spinach, thawed and
           squeezed dry
       1   carton (15 ounces) ricotta cheese
     1/2   cup grated Parmesan cheese
       1   tablespoon minced fresh parsley
     1/8   teaspoon pepper
       2   tablespoons cornmeal
     1/2   teaspoon garlic salt
   1-1/2   cups pizza sauce, warmed

1) In a large mixing bowl, dissolve yeast in water. Add the milk, 2 tablespoons oil, salt, sugar and 2 cups flour; beat until smooth. Stir in enough remaining flour to form a soft dough.

2) Turn onto a floured surface; knead until smooth and elastic, 6-8 minutes. Place in a greased bowl;

turn once to grease top. Cover and let rise in a warm place until doubled, about 1 hour.

3) Meanwhile, in a large skillet, cook sausage over medium heat until no longer pink; drain. Add the spinach, cheeses, parsley and pepper; mix well.

4) Punch dough down; divide into six pieces. On a floured surface, roll each piece into an 8-in. circle. Top each with 2/3 cup filling. Fold dough over filling; pinch to seal.

5) Place on greased baking sheets sprinkled with cornmeal. Brush tops lightly with remaining oil; sprinkle with garlic salt.

6) Bake at 400° for 20-25 minutes or until golden brown. Serve with pizza sauce.

Yield: 6 servings.

NUTRITION FACTS: 1 calzone equals 616 calories, 28 g fat (11 g saturated fat), 68 mg cholesterol, 1,619 mg sodium, 63 g carbohydrate, 5 g fiber, 29 g protein.

Italian Sloppy Joes
Kimberly Speakman, McKinney, Texas

My mother used to make these for us when we were kids. When I left home, I was sure to take the recipe with me, and now it's one of my husband's favorite dinners.

       1   pound bulk Italian sausage
       1   pound bulk hot Italian sausage
       4   garlic cloves, minced
       1   cup chopped green pepper
     1/2   cup chopped onion
       1   can (15 ounces) tomato sauce
       2   tablespoons minced fresh parsley
       1   teaspoon dried oregano
     1/2   teaspoon chili powder
     1/4   teaspoon fennel seed
       8   to 10 French or submarine rolls,
           split
     3/4   cup shredded mozzarella cheese

1) In a large saucepan or Dutch oven, cook sausage, garlic, green pepper and onion over medium heat until the sausage is no longer pink; drain.

2) Add the tomato sauce and seasonings; bring to a boil. Reduce heat; cover and simmer for 30 minutes. Spoon about 1/2 cup onto each roll; sprinkle with cheese.

Yield: 8-10 servings.

NUTRITION FACTS: 1 serving equals 344 calories, 18 g fat (6 g saturated fat), 41 mg cholesterol, 877 mg sodium, 30 g carbohydrate, 2 g fiber, 15 g protein.

Polenta with Italian Sausage
Peggy Ratliff, North Tazewell, Virginia

My mom brought this recipe over from Europe. Polenta is a coarse-textured cornmeal that makes the hearty base to this main dish.

- 4 cups water, *divided*
- 1 cup cornmeal
- 1 teaspoon salt
- 1 pound Italian sausage links
- 2 garlic cloves, minced
- 1 can (14-1/2 ounces) Italian stewed tomatoes
- 1 can (6 ounces) tomato paste
- 2 tablespoons minced fresh parsley
- 1/4 cup shredded Parmesan cheese

1) In a small bowl, combine 1 cup water and cornmeal. In a saucepan, bring salt and remaining water to a boil. Slowly stir in cornmeal mixture. Reduce heat; cook for 15 minutes, stirring frequently.

2) Meanwhile, in a large skillet, cook the sausage and garlic over medium heat until sausage is no longer pink; drain. Cool slightly. Cut sausage into 1-in. pieces; return to skillet. Add the tomatoes, tomato paste and parsley; bring to a boil. Remove from the heat.

3) Spread half of the cornmeal mixture in a serving dish; top with half of the sausage mixture. Repeat layers. Sprinkle with Parmesan cheese. Serve immediately.

Yield: 6 servings.

NUTRITION FACTS: 1 piece equals 267 calories, 11 g fat (4 g saturated fat), 32 mg cholesterol, 1,057 mg sodium, 29 g carbohydrate, 5 g fiber, 12 g protein.

Chicago-Style Pan Pizza
Nikki MacDonald, Sheboygan, Wisconsin

I developed a love for Chicago's deep-dish pizzas while attending college in the Windy City. This simple recipe relies on frozen bread dough, so I can indulge in the mouth-watering sensation without leaving home.

- 1 loaf (1 pound) frozen bread dough, thawed
- 1 pound bulk Italian sausage
- 2 cups (8 ounces) shredded mozzarella cheese
- 1/2 pound sliced fresh mushrooms
- 1 small onion, chopped
- 2 teaspoons olive oil

- 1 can (28 ounces) diced tomatoes, drained
- 3/4 teaspoon dried oregano
- 1/2 teaspoon salt
- 1/2 teaspoon fennel seed, crushed
- 1/4 teaspoon garlic powder
- 1/2 cup grated Parmesan cheese

1) Press dough onto the bottom and up the sides of a greased 13-in. x 9-in. x 2-in. baking dish. In a large skillet, cook sausage over medium heat until no longer pink; drain. Sprinkle over dough. Top with mozzarella cheese.

2) In a skillet, saute mushrooms and onion in oil until onion is tender. Stir in the tomatoes, oregano, salt, fennel seed and garlic powder. Spoon over mozzarella cheese.

3) Sprinkle with Parmesan cheese. Bake at 350° for 25-35 minutes or until crust is golden brown.

Yield: 8 slices.

NUTRITION FACTS: 2 pieces equals 786 calories, 38 g fat (15 g saturated fat), 97 mg cholesterol, 2,110 mg sodium, 75 g carbohydrate, 8 g fiber, 42 g protein.

BAKED HAM WITH ORANGE GLAZE

About Ham

You can choose from several kinds of fully cooked hams. A bone-in ham can be purchased whole or cut in half. Rump (butt) portions are more expensive because they have more meat and less bone than the shank cuts. Boneless hams are also available.

Buy ham with a rosy pink color. The meat should be firm to the touch when pressed. Calorie-conscious cooks should look for extra-lean ham. Note that most hams in grocery stores have been cured, smoked and fully cooked. So they can be served warm (internal temperature 140°) or cold. On the other hand, country hams have been salt-cured, smoked and aged. They're usually labeled "cook before eating," so you'll want to follow the cooking directions on the package.

Useful Definitions

Refer to the Glossary on pages 18-22 for more terms.

BUTT END: The round end of a ham.

COUNTRY-STYLE HAM: Also known as old-fashioned or Southern-style ham. This type of ham has been dry-cured with salt, sugar and spices and may be smoked. No water has been added to the ham. These hams can be salty and should be prepared according to package directions.

CURED HAM: Infused with a solution of sugar, salt and nitrite to enhance flavor and shelf life. A cured ham can also be smoked.

FRESH HAM: From the hind leg and has not been smoked or cured.

FULLY COOKED HAM: Cooked and smoked and/or cured. It can be eaten without heating but is generally heated to 140° for optimal flavor.

PICNIC HAM: Not considered a true ham because it is from the foreleg not the hind leg. It also has a portion of the shoulder.

PROSCIUTTO: Thinly sliced Italian-style ham that is salt-cured and air-dried for 10 months to 2 years. It is not smoked.

SHANK END: The narrow end of a ham.

SMITHFIELD HAM: Processed in the Smithfield area of Virginia. This seasoned hickory-smoked ham is usually aged for 6 to 12 months. The ham is dark in color, lean and salty. Prepare according to package directions.

SMOKED HAM: Processed by being exposed to smoke or by having Liquid Smoke applied to the surface. A smoked ham can also be cured.

Baked Ham with Orange Glaze
Taste of Home Test Kitchen

This ham has a wonderful orange glaze that makes it special for any family supper or holiday gathering.

1/2   **bone-in fully cooked lean ham (6 to 7 pounds)**
2   **cups apple cider *or* apple juice**
2   **cups orange juice**
1/3   **cup orange marmalade**
1/4   **cup packed brown sugar**
1/4   **cup Dijon mustard**
1/4   **teaspoon ground ginger**

1) Place ham on a rack in a shallow roasting pan. Trim fat; score surface of ham, making diamond shapes 1/4 in. deep. Add cider and orange juice to pan. Loosely cover ham with foil; bake at 325° for 1 hour.

2) Combine remaining ingredients; brush some over ham. Bake, uncovered, 50-60 minutes longer or until a meat thermometer reads 140° and ham is heated through, brushing occasionally with glaze.

3) Let stand for 15 minutes before slicing. Serve with remaining glaze.

Yield: 12 servings.

Editor's Note: After scoring, you can insert whole cloves in the points of each diamond shape on the ham for an added touch.

NUTRITION FACTS: 4 ounces cooked ham equals 440 calories, 13 g fat (4 g saturated fat), 125 mg cholesterol, 3,147 mg sodium, 20 g carbohydrate, trace fiber, 57 g protein.

CARVING A HALF HAM WITH BONE

1) Place ham fat side up on a carving board. Using a meat fork to anchor the ham, make a horizontal cut with a carving knife from the one side of the ham to the bone. Position the cut in about middle of the ham along the natural break between the muscles. Make a second cut from the top of the ham to the first cut. Remove the large meaty area of the ham from the bone. Remove the two remaining large meaty sections in the same matter. The meat left on the ham bone may be used for soup or picked off and used in salads or casseroles.

2) Place the meaty piece of meat cut side down on a cutting board. Cut into slices.

Ham with Cherry Sauce

Carol Lee Jones, Taylors, South Carolina

I often fix this delicious ham topped with a thick cherry sauce. It's such a favorite that I've served it at Easter dinners, church breakfasts and a friend's wedding brunch.

- 1 boneless fully cooked ham (3 to 4 pounds)
- 1/2 cup apple jelly
- 2 teaspoons prepared mustard
- 2/3 cup ginger ale, *divided*
- 1 can (21 ounces) cherry pie filling
- 2 tablespoons cornstarch

1) Score surface of ham, making diamond shapes 1/2 in. deep. In a small bowl, combine the jelly, mustard and 1 tablespoon ginger ale; rub over scored surface of ham.

2) Cut ham in half; place in a 5-qt. slow cooker. Cover and cook on low for 4-5 hours or until a meat thermometer reads 140° and ham is heated through. Baste with cooking juices toward end of cooking time.

3) For the sauce, place pie filling in a saucepan. Combine cornstarch and remaining ginger ale; stir into pie filling until blended. Bring to a boil; cook and stir for 2 minutes or until thickened. Serve over ham.

Yield: 10-12 servings.

NUTRITION FACTS: 4 ounces equals 284 calories, 10 g fat (3 g saturated fat), 60 mg cholesterol, 1,469 mg sodium, 28 g carbohydrate, trace fiber, 21 g protein.

Horseradish Honey Ham

Beverly Loomis, Ithaca, Michigan

When my husband and I first tasted this delicious ham, we were surprised to learn that the sauce included horseradish. That secret ingredient definitely is the key to its tangy taste.

- 1 boneless fully cooked ham (5 to 7 pounds)
- 1/4 cup honey, warmed
- 1/8 teaspoon ground cloves
- 1 cup packed brown sugar
- 1/2 cup prepared horseradish
- 1/4 cup lemon juice

1) Cut ham into 1/4-in. slices; tie with kitchen string. Place ham on a rack in a shallow roasting pan. Combine honey and cloves; drizzle over ham.

2) Bake, uncovered, at 325° for 1-1/2 to 2 hours or until a meat thermometer reads 140° and ham is heated through, basting often with drippings.

3) Meanwhile, combine brown sugar, horseradish and lemon juice. Increase oven temperature to 400°. Baste ham with brown sugar sauce, allowing sauce to drip down between the slices. Bake, uncovered, for 15-20 minutes.

Yield: 16 servings.

NUTRITION FACTS: 4 ounces cooked ham equals 223 calories, 5 g fat (2 g saturated fat), 72 mg cholesterol, 1,500 mg sodium, 19 g carbohydrate, trace fiber, 26 g protein.

Ham with Peach Chutney

Taste of Home Test Kitchen

For a special-occasion supper or a weekday meal, this fruity ham is sure to please.

- 1 fully cooked boneless ham (about 4 pounds)
- 1 can (16 ounces) sliced peaches in natural juices, drained and coarsely chopped
- 1/2 cup cider vinegar
- 1/2 cup packed brown sugar
- 1/4 cup minced onion
- 1 apple, peeled and coarsely chopped
- 2 tablespoons lemon juice
- 1 teaspoon pickling spice

1) Place ham in a shallow pan. Bake at 325° for 1-1/2 hours or until meat thermometer reads 140° and ham is heated through.

2) Meanwhile, combine all remaining ingredients in a saucepan and bring to a boil. Reduce heat and simmer 25-30 minutes or until thickened. Cool. Serve with sliced ham.

Yield: 16 servings.

NUTRITION FACTS: 3 ounces ham equals 163 calories, 4 g fat (1 g saturated fat), 58 mg cholesterol, 1,182 mg sodium, 11 g carbohydrate, trace fiber, 21 g protein.

SCORING AND STUDDING HAM

With a sharp knife, make diagonal cuts in a diamond pattern about 1/2 in. deep in the surface of the ham. Push a whole clove into the point of each diamond.

HAM WITH MAPLE GRAVY

water until smooth; add to saucepan. Bring to a boil; cook and stir for 1 minute or until thickened.

4) Meanwhile, in a skillet, melt butter over medium heat. Add apples and remaining maple syrup. Cover and cook for 10-15 minutes, stirring occasionally. Slice ham; serve with the apples and gravy.

Yield: 14 servings.

NUTRITION FACTS: 4 ounces ham equals 328 calories, 9 g fat (3 g saturated fat), 103 mg cholesterol, 2,036 mg sodium, 27 g carbohydrate, 2 g fiber, 36 g protein.

Apple Ham Steak
Mildred Sherrer, Fort Worth, Texas

For an easy one-dish meal, you can't beat this ham steak recipe.

1-1/2	cups instant rice
1	medium onion, chopped
2	celery ribs, chopped
6	tablespoons butter, *divided*
2-1/2	cups apple juice, *divided*
1	teaspoon salt
1	pound boneless fully cooked ham steak, cut into fourths
2	medium tart apple, peeled and sliced
2	tablespoons brown sugar
1/4	teaspoon ground cinnamon
2	tablespoons raisins
1	tablespoon cornstarch

1) In a saucepan, saute rice, onion and celery in 2 tablespoons butter until tender. Add 1-1/2 cups apple juice and salt. Bring to a boil. Cover and remove from the heat; let stand for 5 minutes.

2) Meanwhile, in a skillet, cook ham in remaining butter until lightly browned. Remove and keep warm. In the same skillet, cook and stir apples, brown sugar and cinnamon over medium heat until apples are almost tender, about 5 minutes. Stir in raisins.

3) In a bowl, combine cornstarch and remaining apple just until smooth; add to the skillet. Bring to a boil; cook and stir for 2 minutes or until thickened. Return ham to skillet and heat through. Serve over rice.

Yield: 4 servings.

NUTRITION FACTS: 1 serving equals 649 calories, 27 g fat (14 g saturated fat), 106 mg cholesterol, 2,242 mg sodium, 77 g carbohydrate, 4 g fiber, 25 g protein.

Ham with Maple Gravy
Sue Ward, Thunder Bay, Ontario

Watch out when you make this hearty dish because the delicious aroma coming from the kitchen is sure to create some big appetites!

1	fully cooked boneless ham (6 pounds)
30	whole cloves
3/4	cup maple syrup, *divided*
4	teaspoons ground mustard
2	cups apple juice
3	tablespoons cornstarch
3	tablespoons water
2	tablespoons butter
6	medium tart apples, cored and cut into 1/2-inch slices

1) Place ham on a rack in a shallow roasting pan. Score the surface of the ham, making diamond shapes 1/2 in. deep; insert a clove in each diamond.

2) Combine 1/2 cup maple syrup and mustard; pour over ham. Pour apple juice into the roasting pan. Bake at 325° for 1-1/2 to 2 hours or until a meat thermometer reads 140°, basting frequently.

3) Remove ham and keep warm. Transfer the pan juices to a saucepan. Combine cornstarch and

SPICED HAM STEAK

One-Pot Ham Dinner
Jody Cohen, Mackeyville, Pennsylvania

Looking for a speedy skillet supper? Simply add potatoes and green beans to ham steak and top off the down-home dinner with a comforting mushroom sauce.

- 1 fully cooked ham slice (1 to 1-1/2 pounds)
- 4 medium potatoes, peeled and sliced
- 1/4 to 1/2 teaspoon salt
- 1/4 teaspoon pepper
- 2 cups frozen cut green beans
- 1 medium onion, thinly sliced
- 1 can (10-3/4 ounces) condensed cream of mushroom soup, undiluted
- 1/2 cup water

1) In a large skillet over medium heat, brown the ham slice. Arrange potatoes over ham; sprinkle with salt and pepper. Top with beans and onion.

2) Combine soup and water; pour over all. Cook for 2 minutes. Reduce heat; cover and simmer for 45-50 minutes or until potatoes are tender.

Yield: 4 servings.

NUTRITION FACTS: 1 serving equals 381 calories, 13 g fat (4 g saturated fat), 63 mg cholesterol, 2,209 mg sodium, 40 g carbohydrate, 5 g fiber, 25 g protein.

Spiced Ham Steak
Connie Moore, Medway, Ohio

I turn orange marmalade, mustard and a hint of ginger into a fast-to-fix glaze for my ham. The mouth-watering entree may be short on time, but it's definitely long on flavor. I like to serve it along-side cooked spaghetti.

- 1 bone-in fully cooked ham steak (about 1 pound)
- 1/4 cup orange marmalade
- 2 tablespoons water
- 1 tablespoon butter
- 1 tablespoon prepared mustard
- 1 teaspoon corn syrup
- 1/8 to 1/4 teaspoon ground ginger

1) In a large skillet coated with nonstick cooking spray, cook ham for 4 minutes on each side or until lightly browned; drain.

2) Meanwhile, combine the remaining ingredients in a saucepan; bring to a boil. Spoon over ham. Cover and cook for 1-2 minutes or until heated through.

Yield: 4 servings.

NUTRITION FACTS: 4 ounces cooked ham equals 305 calories, 17 g fat (7 g saturated fat), 67 mg cholesterol, 1,609 mg sodium, 15 g carbohydrate, trace fiber, 22 g protein.

Sweet-Sour Ham Balls
Dorothy Pritchett, Wills Point, Texas

Pineapple, brown sugar and mustard combine to create a tangy sauce for these savory ham and pork balls. I like to keep a batch on hand for card parties and other occasions.

- 4 eggs, lightly beaten
- 1/4 cup chopped onion
- 1-1/2 cups soft bread crumbs
- 2 pounds ground ham
- 1 pound ground pork
- 2 cans (8 ounces *each*) crushed pineapple, undrained
- 1 cup packed brown sugar
- 1/4 cup prepared mustard
- 2 tablespoons cider vinegar

1) In a bowl, combine the eggs, onion and bread crumbs. Crumble meat over mixture and mix well. Shape into 1-1/2-in. balls. Place in two greased 13-in. x 9-in. x 2-in. baking dishes.

2) In a blender, combine the pineapple, brown sugar, mustard and vinegar; cover and process until smooth. Pour over ham balls.

3) Bake, uncovered, at 350° for 45-50 minutes or until a meat thermometer reads 160°, basting occasionally with sauce.

Yield: 5 dozen.

Editor's Note: Ham balls may be frozen. Prepare as directed and pour sauce over ham balls. Do not bake at this point. Freeze in dinner-sized portions. Thaw completely in the refrigerator. Bake as directed in recipe.

NUTRITION FACTS: 3 ham balls equals 482 calories, 26 g fat (9 g saturated fat), 166 mg cholesterol, 1,326 mg sodium, 33 g carbohydrate, 1 g fiber, 29 g protein.

MOTHER'S HAM CASSEROLE

Mother's Ham Casserole
Linda Childers, Murfreesboro, Tennessee

One of my mother's favorite dishes, this recipe always brings back fond memories of her when I prepare it. It's a terrific use of leftover ham from a holiday dinner.

- 2   cups cubed peeled potatoes
- 1   large carrot, sliced
- 2   celery ribs, chopped
- 3   cups water
- 2   cups cubed fully cooked ham
- 2   tablespoons chopped green pepper
- 2   teaspoons finely chopped onion
- 7   tablespoons butter, *divided*
- 3   tablespoons all-purpose flour
- 1-1/2   cups milk
- 3/4   teaspoon salt

1/8   teaspoon pepper
1   cup (4 ounces) shredded cheddar cheese
1/2   cup soft bread crumbs

1) In a saucepan, bring the potatoes, carrot, celery and water to a boil. Reduce heat; cover and cook about 15 minute or until tender. Drain.

2) In a large skillet, saute the ham, green pepper and onion in 3 tablespoons butter until tender. Add to the potato mixture. Transfer to a greased 1-1/2-qt. baking dish.

3) In a saucepan, melt the remaining butter; stir in flour until smooth. Gradually add milk, salt and pepper. Bring to a boil; cook and stir for 2 minutes or until thickened. Reduce heat; add cheese and stir until melted.

4) Pour over the ham mixture. Sprinkle with bread crumbs. Bake, uncovered, at 375° for 25-30 minutes or until heated through.

Yield: 4-6 servings.

NUTRITION FACTS: 1 cup equals 374 calories, 25 g fat (15 g saturated fat), 89 mg cholesterol, 1,208 mg sodium, 22 g carbohydrate, 2 g fiber, 17 g protein.

Quick Golden Stew
Merry McNally, Ionia, Michigan

This complete meal can be prepared in a hurry. Yet it has a rich goodness that tastes like you fussed.

- 4   carrots, cut into 1-inch pieces
- 1-1/2   cups peeled and diced potatoes
- 2   medium onions, cut into chunks

Water
- 1   package (10 ounces) frozen peas, defrosted
- 2   cups cubed fully cooked ham
- 1   can (10-3/4 ounces) cream of celery soup, undiluted
- 1   jar (8 ounces) process cheese spread

1) In a large saucepan or Dutch oven, combine the carrots, potatoes, onions and just enough water to cover. Bring to a boil. Reduce heat; cover and cook for 10 minutes or until vegetables are tender.

2) Add peas and ham; cover and cook 5 minutes longer. Drain water. Stir in soup and cheese; heat through.

Yield: 4 servings.

NUTRITION FACTS: 1 cup equals 323 calories, 14 g fat (8 g saturated fat), 50 mg cholesterol, 1,654 mg sodium, 32 g carbohydrate, 6 g fiber, 18 g protein.

2) Dissolve bouillon in water. Gradually add milk and bouillon to the saucepan. Bring to a boil; cook and stir for 2 minutes or until thickened.

3) Reduce heat; add the cheese, Worcestershire sauce and mustard; stir until the cheese is melted. Add the ham, peas if desired, olives, pimientos and parsley; heat through. Serve in pastry shells.

Yield: 6 servings.

NUTRITION FACTS: 1 filled pastry shell equals 487 calories, 31 g fat (12 g saturated fat), 60 mg cholesterol, 1,232 mg sodium, 35 g carbohydrate, 3 g fiber, 17 g protein.

Kentucky Stuffed Peppers
Lucille Terry, Frankfort, Kentucky

This colorful and delicious dish is my own variation on stuffed peppers, which usually feature ground beef. The ham and mushrooms are a nice change from the ordinary.

- 4 large sweet red *and/or* yellow peppers
- 1 can (14-1/2 ounces) diced tomatoes
- 1 large onion, chopped
- 2 tablespoons butter
- 2 cups cooked rice
- 1 jar (4-1/2 ounces) sliced mushrooms, drained
- 1 cup diced fully cooked ham
- 1 teaspoon sugar
- Dash hot pepper sauce
- 3/4 cup shredded cheddar cheese

1) Cut tops off peppers and remove seeds. In a Dutch oven, cook peppers in boiling water for 3-5 minutes. Drain and rinse in cold water. Place peppers upside down on paper towels; set aside.

2) Drain tomatoes, reserving the juice; set tomatoes and juice aside. In a large skillet, saute onion in butter until tender. Add the rice, mushrooms, ham, sugar, hot pepper sauce and reserved tomatoes; mix well. Loosely spoon into peppers.

3) Place in an ungreased 2-qt. baking dish. Pour reserved tomato juice over peppers.

4) Cover and bake at 350° for 35-40 minutes; sprinkle with cheese. Bake 5 minutes longer or until the cheese is melted.

Yield: 4 servings.

NUTRITION FACTS: 1 stuffed pepper equals 375 calories, 15 g fat (9 g saturated fat), 56 mg cholesterol, 904 mg sodium, 45 g carbohydrate, 7 g fiber, 16 g protein.

HAM A LA KING

Ham a la King
Jean Grubb, Austin, Texas

My mom and I used to have a catering business, and this recipe was a popular choice from our menu. It looks elegant on the plate and always gets rave reviews. Being able to make the sauce a day ahead is a big plus.

- 1 package (10 ounces) frozen puff pastry shells
- 1/4 cup butter
- 1/4 cup all-purpose flour
- 1 teaspoon chicken bouillon granules
- 1/2 cup hot water
- 1-1/2 cups milk
- 3 slices process American cheese
- 1 teaspoon Worcestershire sauce
- 1 teaspoon prepared mustard
- 2 cups cubed fully cooked ham
- 1/2 cup frozen peas, thawed, optional
- 1 can (2-1/4 ounces) sliced ripe olives, drained
- 2 tablespoons diced pimientos
- 2 tablespoons minced fresh parsley

1) Bake the pastry shells according to package directions. Meanwhile, in a saucepan, melt butter; stir in flour until smooth.

139

LAMB

Lamb is a wonderfully tender and moist meat that lends itself to a variety of cooking styles and an assortment of flavor possibilities.

Purchase before the "sell by" date on the packaging for best quality. Look for lamb that is pinkish red. Make sure the package is cold and has no holes or tears.

Determine the amount of lamb you need to buy based on the cut and amount of bone:

- 1 pound of bone-in roasts yields 2-1/2 servings.
- 1 pound of bone-in steaks yields 2 servings.
- 1 pound of bone-in rib or loin chops yields 2 servings.
- 1 pound of rack of lamb yields 2 servings.

Don't be afraid to use generous amounts of fresh garlic and herbs when cooking lamb. These bold flavors will enhance any cut.

Use a meat thermometer when roasting lamb to ensure the meat is cooked just the way you like it. For best flavor and tenderness, serve roasted lamb medium-rare to medium-well (see page 142).

Serve lamb piping hot for best flavor. Warming the platter and dinner plates in the oven just before serving will keep your entree hot during the meal. Make sure your dishes are oven-safe, and use hot pads when handling warm plates.

Useful Definitions

For additional terms, refer to the Glossary on pages 18-22.

FELL: A thin membrane that covers the fat. To remove, use a sharp knife to loosen the fell and peel off.

FRENCHING: Refers to when about 1-1/2 in. of the meat is removed from the bones. This treatment is frequently done with rack of lamb.

LAMB: Meat from a sheep that is less than 1 year old.

MUTTON: Meat from a sheep that is over 1 year old.

Cooking Methods for Lamb

COOKING METHOD	CUT OF LAMB
BRAISING	Shoulder or Blade Chops, Breast, Shanks, Stew Cubes
BROILING	Loin or Rib Chops, Sirloin or Leg Steaks, Ground Lamb Patties
GRILLING	Loin or Rib Chops, Sirloin or Leg Steaks, Ground Lamb Patties
PAN-BROILING	Chops, Steaks, Ground Lamb Patties
PAN-FRYING	Thin Chops, Steaks, Ground Lamb Patties
ROASTING	Leg of Lamb, Sirloin Roast, Crown Roast, Rack of Lamb

Defrosting Guidelines

The thicker the package, the longer it will take to thaw. Here are some guidelines for defrosting lamb in the refrigerator.

- For 1- to 1-1/2-in.-thick packages of ground lamb or meat pieces, allow at least 24 hours.
- For 1-in.-thick chops, allow 12 to 14 hours.
- For a small roast, allow 3 to 5 hours per pound.
- For a large roast, allow 4 to 7 hours per pound.

Roasting Lamb

Place meat fat side up on a rack in a shallow roasting pan. Insert an oven-safe meat thermometer in the thickest portion of the muscle without touching bone or fat. Or use an instant-read thermometer toward the end of the roasting time. If the meat needs to cook longer, remove the instant-read thermometer before you return the meat to the oven.

Roast without liquid, uncovered, according to the temperature and time given in the chart below or recipe. Because roasts will continue to cook after being removed from the oven, remove it when the meat thermometer reads 5-10° below desired doneness. Cover with foil and let stand for 10-15 minutes before carving.

CUT	WEIGHT	COOKING TIME (MINUTES PER POUND)			OVEN TEMP.
		MEDIUM-RARE 145°	MEDIUM 160°	WELL-DONE 170°	
LEG-WHOLE, BONE-IN	5 to 7 lbs.	20 to 25	25 to 30	30 to 35	325°
LEG-SHANK HALF OR SHOULDER, BONE-IN	3 to 4 lbs.	30 to 35	40 to 45	45 to 50	325°
LEG, BONELESS	4 to 7 lbs.	25 to 30	30 to 35	35 to 40	325°
RACK OF LAMB	1-1/2 to 2-1/2 lbs.	25 to 30	30 to 35	35 to 40	375°

ITALIAN LEG OF LAMB

Italian Leg of Lamb
Mary Ann Marino, West Pittsburg, Pennsylvania

When this pleasantly seasoned roast appears on my table, no one walks away hungry. Garlic, lemon juice and seasonings make each bite of this succulent lamb irresistible.

1/2 to 2/3 cup lemon juice

1/2 cup olive oil

2 tablespoons dried oregano

2 teaspoons ground mustard

1 teaspoon garlic powder

4 garlic cloves, minced

1 boneless leg of lamb (4 to 5 pounds)

1) In a small bowl, combine the lemon juice, oil and seasonings. Pour half of the marinade into a large resealable plastic bag; add lamb. Seal bag and turn to coat; refrigerate for at least 2 hours or overnight. Cover and refrigerate the remaining marinade.

2) Drain and discard marinade from lamb. Place lamb fat side up on a rack in a shallow roasting pan. Bake, uncovered, at 325° for 2-1/4 to 3 hours or until meat reaches desired doneness (for medium, a meat thermometer should read 160°; well-done, 170°), basting occasionally with reserved marinade. Let stand for 10-15 minutes before slicing.

Yield: 11 servings.

NUTRITION FACTS: 4 ounces cooked lamb equals 254 calories, 15 g fat (4 g saturated fat), 84 mg cholesterol, 66 mg sodium, 1 g carbohydrate, trace fiber, 26 g protein.

Roast Lamb with Plum Sauce
Dorothy Pritchett, Wills Point, Texas

The sweet-and-spicy plum sauce makes a delightful glaze and sauce to pass. To avoid burning, only baste the roast during the last hour of baking.

1 bone-in leg of lamb (5 to 6 pounds)

3 garlic cloves, slivered

1/2 cup thinly sliced green onions

1/4 cup butter

1 jar (12 ounces) plum jam
1/2 cup chili sauce
1/4 cup white grape juice
1 tablespoon lemon juice
1/2 teaspoon ground allspice
1 tablespoon dried parsley flakes

1) Remove thin fat covering from the roast. Make slits in meat; insert a garlic sliver in each. Place on a rack in a large roasting pan. Bake, uncovered, at 325° for 1-1/2 hours.

2) Meanwhile, for plum sauce, in a medium saucepan, saute onions in butter until tender. Add the jam, chili sauce, grape juice, lemon juice and allspice; bring to a boil, stirring occasionally. Simmer, uncovered, for 10 minutes.

3) Baste roast with sauce. Bake 1 hour longer, basting occasionally, or until meat reaches desired doneness (for medium, a meat thermometer should read 160°; well-done, 170°), basting occasionally with plum sauce.

4) Bring the remaining sauce to a boil; stir in parsley. Let roast stand for 10-15 minutes before carving. Serve remaining sauce with roast.

Yield: 11 servings.

NUTRITION FACTS: 4 ounces cooked lamb with 1 tablespoon sauce equals 300 calories, 11 g fat (5 g saturated fat), 104 mg cholesterol, 253 mg sodium, 25 g carbohydrate, trace fiber, 26 g protein.

CARVING A LEG OF LAMB

1) Cut a few 1/4-in. slices on the thin side of the leg and remove to a platter. Turn roast over so it rests on the cut surface.

2) Hold roast steady by using paper towels around bone with one hand. With a carving knife, make a series of 1/4-in. slices along leg down to bone. Then cut along the bone to free slices.

LAMB WITH RASPBERRY SAUCE

Lamb with Raspberry Sauce
Scott Beatrice, Lakeland, Florida

Lamb chops are dressed up with a wonderful fruity sauce in this recipe. I enjoy cooking and surprising my wife, Chrissy, with creative dishes like this one.

2 cups fresh *or* frozen unsweetened raspberries
3/4 cup finely chopped seeded peeled cucumber
1/2 cup finely chopped peeled tart apple
2 tablespoons white grape juice
1 to 2 tablespoons sugar
4 garlic cloves, minced
3 tablespoons olive oil
8 lamb loin chops (6 to 7 ounces *each* and 1 to 1-1/2 inches thick)

1) Place raspberries in a blender or food processor; cover and process until pureed. Strain and discard seeds; transfer puree to a small saucepan.

2) Stir in the cucumber, apple, grape juice and sugar. Bring to a boil. Reduce heat; simmer, uncovered, for 5-7 minutes or until cucumber and apple are tender.

3) Meanwhile, in a large skillet, saute garlic in oil until tender. Add lamb chops. Cook, uncovered, for 7-10 minutes on each side or until meat reaches desired doneness (for medium-rare, a meat thermometer should read 145°; medium, 160°; well-done, 170°). Serve with raspberry sauce.

Yield: 4 servings.

NUTRITION FACTS: 1 serving equals 460 calories, 24 g fat (6 g saturated fat), 136 mg cholesterol, 122 mg sodium, 15 g carbohydrate, 5 g fiber, 44 g protein.

Lamb with Sauteed Veggies
Ruth Lee, Troy, Ontario

My parents raised sheep for more than 30 years, so I have several lamb recipes. Not only are these chops tender, but they cook quickly. I saute red pepper and zucchini while the lamb broils. People always comment on this great combination.

- 3 tablespoons olive oil, *divided*
- 2 tablespoons Dijon mustard
- 2 tablespoons balsamic vinegar
- 2 teaspoons dried thyme
- 2 garlic cloves, minced
- 1/4 teaspoon salt
- 1/4 teaspoon pepper
- 12 lamb loin chops (6 to 7 ounces *each* and 1 inch thick)
- 1 medium sweet red pepper, thinly sliced
- 2 small zucchini, thinly sliced
- 1 medium sweet onion, thinly sliced

1) In a small bowl, combine 2 tablespoons oil, mustard, vinegar, thyme, garlic, salt and pepper; set aside 1 tablespoon. Place the lamb chops on a broiler pan. Spread remaining mustard mixture over both sides of chops.

2) Broil 4-6 in. from the heat for 4-6 minutes on each side or until meat reaches desired doneness (for medium-rare, a meat thermometer should read 145°; medium, 160°; well-done, 170°).

3) Meanwhile, in a large skillet, saute the red pepper, zucchini and onion in remaining oil until crisp-tender. Stir in reserved mustard mixture; toss to coat. Serve with lamb chops.

Yield: 6 servings.

NUTRITION FACTS: 1 serving equals 402 calories, 21 g fat (6 g saturated fat), 136 mg cholesterol, 349 mg sodium, 7 g carbohydrate, 2 g fiber, 44 g protein.

Mushroom-Swiss Lamb Chops
Candy McMenamin, Lexington, South Carolina

These lamb chops make a really nice, last-minute meal for guests. I pick up the ingredients on the way home from work and usually finish off the menu with a green salad and new potatoes.

- 4 lamb loin chops (2 inches thick and 8 ounces *each*)
- 1/2 teaspoon salt
- 1/2 teaspoon pepper

- 2 cups sliced fresh mushrooms
- 2 tablespoons butter
- 1/4 cup Russian salad dressing
- 1/2 cup shredded Swiss cheese

1) Sprinkle both sides of lamb chops with salt and pepper. Broil 4-6 in. from the heat for 10-15 minutes on each side or until meat reaches desired doneness (for medium-rare, a meat thermometer should read 145°; medium, 160°; well-done, 170°).

2) Meanwhile, in a large skillet, saute mushrooms in butter for 5-6 minutes or until tender. Stir in salad dressing. Bring to a boil; cook until liquid is reduced by half.

3) Sprinkle cheese over lamb chops; broil 1-2 minutes longer or until cheese is melted. Serve with mushroom mixture.

Yield: 4 servings.

NUTRITION FACTS: 1 serving equals 381 calories, 24 g fat (10 g saturated fat), 118 mg cholesterol, 624 mg sodium, 7 g carbohydrate, trace fiber, 34 g protein.

RACK OF LAMB

Rack of Lamb
Bob Paffenroth, Brookfield, Wisconsin

I often bake this rack of lamb in the oven and always have wonderful results.

- 4 racks of lamb (1 to 1-1/2 pounds *each*), trimmed
- 2 tablespoons Dijon mustard
- 1 cup soft bread crumbs
- 1/4 cup minced fresh parsley
- 1/4 teaspoon salt
- 1/4 teaspoon pepper

1/4 cup butter, melted

1 garlic clove, minced

1) Place lamb on a rack in a greased large roasting pan; brush with mustard. In a small bowl, combine the bread crumbs, parsley, salt and pepper. Press onto the meat. Combine butter and garlic; drizzle over the meat.

2) Bake, uncovered, at 375° for 30-35 minutes or until meat reaches desired doneness (for medium-rare, a meat thermometer should read 145°; medium, 160°; well-done, 170°). Remove from the oven and cover loosely with foil. Let stand for 5-10 minutes before slicing.

Yield: 8 servings.

NUTRITION FACTS: 4-1/2 ounces cooked lamb equals 247 calories, 16 g fat (7 g saturated fat), 82 mg cholesterol, 319 mg sodium, 3 g carbohydrate, trace fiber, 21 g protein.

Stuffed Lamb Chops
Sarah Thompson, Milwaukee, Wisconsin

The mushroom stuffing nicely complements the flavor of the lamb chops in this recipe. I like to serve mint jelly on the side.

1/2 cup chopped fresh mushrooms

1/2 cup finely chopped celery

1 tablespoon finely chopped onion

2 tablespoons butter

1-1/4 cups dry bread crumbs, *divided*

1 tablespoon minced fresh parsley

3/4 teaspoon salt, *divided*

2 eggs, lightly beaten

2 tablespoons milk

Dash paprika

6 boneless lamb loin chops (1-1/2 inches thick)

Mint jelly

1) In a large skillet, saute the mushrooms, celery and onion in butter until tender. Stir in 1/2 cup bread crumbs, parsley and 1/4 teaspoon salt; set aside.

2) In a shallow bowl, combine the eggs and milk. In another shallow bowl, combine the paprika and remaining bread crumbs and salt.

3) Cut a pocket in each chop by horizontally cutting almost to the bone; stuff with mushroom mixture. Dip chops in egg mixture, then coat with crumb mixture. Let stand for 5 minutes.

4) Place in an ungreased 9-in. square baking pan.

Bake, uncovered, at 400° for 30 minutes. Turn chops over; bake 15 minutes longer or until meat reaches desired doneness (for medium-rare, a meat thermometer should read 145°; medium, 160°; well-done, 170°). Serve with mint jelly.

Yield: 3 servings.

NUTRITION FACTS: 1 serving (calculated without mint jelly) equals 363 calories, 18 g fat (8 g saturated fat), 182 mg cholesterol, 1,133 mg sodium, 35 g carbohydrate, 2 g fiber, 15 g protein.

ORANGE BLOSSOM LAMB

Orange Blossom Lamb
Felicia Johnson, Oak Ridge, Louisiana

This special main dish is easily assembled. After browning, the chops simmer in a flavorful sauce. Lamb tastes so good cooked this way, but the recipe also works well with pork chops.

8 lamb rib chops (6 to 7 ounces *each* and 1 inch thick)

2 tablespoons butter

1 can (6 ounces) orange juice concentrate, thawed

1 medium onion, sliced

1 to 2 teaspoons soy sauce

1 teaspoon salt

Dash pepper

1) In a large skillet, brown lamb chops in butter over medium heat. Add remaining ingredients and mix well.

2) Reduce heat; cover and simmer for 20-25 minutes or until the meat is tender, turning once. To serve, spoon sauce over the lamb.

Yield: 4 servings.

NUTRITION FACTS: 1 serving equals 442 calories, 20 g fat (9 g saturated fat), 151 mg cholesterol, 847 mg sodium, 20 g carbohydrate, 1 g fiber, 45 g protein.

Slow-Cooked Lamb Chops

Sandra McKenzie, Braham, Minnesota

Chops are without a doubt the cut of lamb we like best. I usually simmer them on low for hours in a slow cooker. The aroma is irresistible, and they practically melt in your mouth!

- 1 medium onion, sliced
- 1 teaspoon dried oregano
- 1/2 teaspoon dried thyme
- 1/2 teaspoon garlic powder
- 1/4 teaspoon salt
- 1/8 teaspoon pepper
- 8 lamb loin chops (about 1-3/4 pounds)
- 2 garlic cloves, minced

1) Place onion in a 3-qt. slow cooker. Combine the oregano, thyme, garlic powder, salt and pepper; rub over the lamb chops. Place chops over onion. Top with garlic.

2) Cover and cook on low for 4-6 hours or until the meat is tender.

Yield: 4 servings.

NUTRITION FACTS: 1 serving equals 201 calories, 8 g fat (3 g saturated fat), 79 mg cholesterol, 219 mg sodium, 5 g carbohydrate, 1 g fiber, 26 g protein.

Braised Lamb Shanks

Jeanne McNamara, Camillus, New York

These lamb shanks are a great part of a meal with baked potatoes, hot vegetables and fresh fruit salad. Of course, I also like to include mint jelly on the side.

- 2 lamb shanks (1 pound *each*)
- 1 cup beef broth
- 1/4 cup soy sauce
- 2 tablespoons brown sugar
- 1 garlic clove, minced
- 2 teaspoons prepared mustard

1) Place lamb in a greased 2-1/2-qt. baking dish. Combine the broth, soy sauce, brown sugar, garlic and mustard; pour over meat.

2) Cover and bake at 325° for 1-1/2 to 2 hours or until the meat is tender.

Yield: 2 servings.

NUTRITION FACTS: 1 serving equals 451 calories, 21 g fat (9 g saturated fat), 159 mg cholesterol, 2,419 mg sodium, 15 g carbohydrate, trace fiber, 48 g protein.

WYOMING LAMB STEW

Wyoming Lamb Stew

Sandra Ramsey, Elk Mountain, Wyoming

I'll often double this recipe and make a big batch because leftovers come in handy around my busy house.

- 5 bacon strips, diced
- 1/4 cup all-purpose flour
- 1 teaspoon salt
- 1/2 teaspoon pepper
- 6 lamb shanks (about 6 pounds)
- 1 can (28 ounces) diced tomatoes, undrained
- 1 can (14-1/2 ounces) beef broth
- 1 can (8 ounces) tomato sauce
- 2 cans (4 ounces *each*) mushroom stems and pieces, drained
- 2 medium onions, chopped
- 1 cup chopped celery
- 1/2 cup minced fresh parsley
- 2 tablespoons prepared horseradish
- 1 tablespoon cider vinegar
- 2 teaspoon Worcestershire sauce
- 1 garlic clove, minced

1) In a Dutch oven, cook bacon over medium heat until crisp. Using a slotted spoon, remove to paper towels to drain, reserving drippings. Set bacon aside.

2) In a large resealable plastic bag, combine the flour, salt and pepper; add lamb shanks, one at a time, and shake to coat. In bacon drippings, brown shanks on all sides; drain. Add remaining ingredients.

3) Bring to a boil. Cover and bake at 325° for 2 to 2-1/2 hours or until the meat is very tender; skim fat. Garnish with bacon.

Yield: 6 servings.

Editor's Note: If you like, make the stew a day ahead. Cool, then refrigerate. Before reheating, lift off fat from top of stew. Bring to a boil over medium-high heat. Reduce heat; cover and simmer until heated through.

NUTRITION FACTS: 1 serving equals 569 calories, 31 g fat (13 g saturated fat), 171 mg cholesterol, 1,423 mg sodium, 21 g carbohydrate, 5 g fiber, 49 g protein.

THICKER STEWS

If your stew needs just a little extra thickening, stir in a few tablespoons of fresh white, whole wheat or rye bread crumbs.

Irish Stew
Lois Gelzer, Cape Elizabeth, Maine

This satisfying stew is chock-full of potatoes, turnips, carrots and lamb. Served with Irish soda bread, it makes a hearty St. Patrick's Day meal.

1-1/2   pounds lamb stew meat

2   teaspoons olive oil

4   cups water

2   cups sliced peeled potatoes

1   medium onion, sliced

1/2   cup sliced carrot

1/2   cup cubed turnip

1   teaspoon salt

1/2   teaspoon *each* dried marjoram, thyme and rosemary, crushed

1/8   teaspoon pepper

2   tablespoons all-purpose flour

2   tablespoons fat-free milk

1/2   teaspoon browning sauce, optional

3   tablespoons minced fresh parsley

1) In a Dutch oven, brown lamb in oil over medium-high heat. Add water; bring to a boil. Reduce heat; cover and simmer for 1 hour.

2) Add the potatoes, onion, carrot, turnip and seasonings. Bring to a boil. Reduce heat; cover and simmer for 30 minutes or until the vegetables are tender.

3) In a small bowl, combine the flour, milk and browning sauce if desired until smooth; stir into stew. Add parsley. Bring to a boil; cook and stir for 2 minutes or until thickened.

Yield: 6 servings.

NUTRITION FACTS: 1-1/2 cups equals 279 calories, 9 g fat (3 g saturated fat), 92 mg cholesterol, 469 mg sodium, 17 g carbohydrate, 2 g fiber, 31 g protein.

Hungarian Lamb Stew
Joyce Snedden, Casper, Wyoming

Full-flavored Hungarian paprika comes in mild and hot forms, and hot Hungarian paprika packs a punch similar to cayenne pepper. The milder variety works well unless you like a little more kick!

3   slices bacon, cut into 1-inch pieces

2   medium onions, thinly sliced

2   pounds lamb stew meat, cut into 1-inch cubes

2   tablespoons Hungarian paprika

1   teaspoon salt

1   teaspoon caraway seeds

1   garlic clove, minced

1   medium green pepper, sliced, *divided*

1   medium sweet red pepper, sliced, *divided*

1   cup water

3   medium potatoes, peeled and cut into 3/4-inch pieces

1   large tomato, sliced

1) In a Dutch oven, cook bacon over medium heat until crisp. Using a slotted spoon, remove to paper towel. Reserve drippings. Cook onions in drippings until tender. Remove onions. Brown meat in drippings on all sides over medium-high heat.

2) Return bacon and onions to pan along with the paprika, salt, caraway, garlic and half the peppers. Add water. Bring to a boil. Reduce heat; cover and simmer for 1-1/2 hours. Add additional water if necessary.

3) Stir in potatoes and remaining peppers. Bring to a boil. Reduce heat; simmer for 20 minutes. Add tomatoes; simmer 10 minutes longer or until meat and vegetables are tender. Adjust seasoning if necessary.

Yield: 9 servings.

NUTRITION FACTS: 1 cup equals 241 calories, 10 g fat (4 g saturated fat), 71 mg cholesterol, 388 mg sodium, 15 g carbohydrate, 2 g fiber, 23 g protein.

Lamb with Apricots

Rachel Delano, Tappahannock, Virginia

This was a favorite of mine growing up. Dried apricots add a touch of sweetness to the lamb.

- 1 large onion, chopped
- 2 tablespoons olive oil
- 1 boneless lamb shoulder roast (2-1/2 to 3 pounds), cubed
- 1 teaspoon *each* ground cumin, cinnamon and coriander

Salt and pepper to taste

- 1/2 cup dried apricots, halved
- 1/4 cup orange juice
- 1 tablespoon ground almonds
- 1/2 teaspoon grated orange peel
- 1-1/4 cups chicken broth
- 1 tablespoon sesame seeds, toasted

1) In a large skillet, saute onion in oil until tender. Add the lamb and seasonings. Cook and stir for 5 minutes or until meat is browned. Add apricots, orange juice, almonds and orange peel.

2) Transfer to a 2-1/2-qt. baking dish. Stir in broth. Cover and bake at 350° for 1-1/2 hours or until meat is tender. Sprinkle with sesame seeds.

Yield: 8 servings.

NUTRITION FACTS: 1 cup (calculated without salt and pepper) equals 280 calories, 19 g fat (7 g saturated fat), 70 mg cholesterol, 199 mg sodium, 9 g carbohydrate, 2 g fiber, 19 g protein.

Curried Lamb Stir-Fry

Priscilla Root, Englewood, Colorado

Apple lends sweetness to this mildly seasoned stir-fry. Tender strips of lamb nicely contrast the crunchy snow peas and water chestnuts.

- 1 teaspoon cornstarch
- 1/4 teaspoon curry powder
- 1/4 cup chicken broth
- 1 tablespoon soy sauce
- 3/4 pound boneless lamb, cut into 1/8-inch strips
- 1 small onion, chopped
- 2 garlic cloves, minced
- 2 tablespoons vegetable oil, *divided*
- 1 small red apple, chopped
- 1/2 cup chopped green pepper
- 1/2 cup sliced celery
- 1 can (8 ounces) sliced water chestnuts, drained
- 6 ounces fresh *or* frozen snow peas
- 1/4 teaspoon ground ginger

Hot cooked rice

1) In a small bowl, combine cornstarch and curry powder. Stir in broth and soy sauce until smooth; set aside. In a large skillet or wok, saute lamb, onion and garlic in 1 tablespoon oil until meat is browned. Remove and keep warm.

2) In the same skillet, stir-fry apple, green pepper, celery, water chestnuts, peas and ginger in remaining oil until crisp-tender. Add lamb mixture.

3) Stir broth mixture and add to skillet. Bring to a boil; cook and stir for 2 minutes or until thickened. Serve over rice.

Yield: 4 servings.

NUTRITION FACTS: 1 serving (calculated without rice) equals 250 calories, 12 g fat (3 g saturated fat), 47 mg cholesterol, 345 mg sodium, 19 g carbohydrate, 4 g fiber, 18 g protein.

Lamb Fajitas

Bonnie Hiller, Powell, Wyoming

My family enjoys these fajitas, which are a popular change of pace from grilled or roasted lamb.

- 1 boneless leg of lamb *or* lamb shoulder (3 to 4 pounds)
- 1/2 cup vegetable oil
- 1/2 cup lemon juice
- 1/3 cup soy sauce
- 1/3 cup packed brown sugar
- 1/4 cup cider vinegar
- 3 tablespoons Worcestershire sauce
- 1 tablespoon ground mustard
- 1/2 teaspoon pepper
- 1 large green pepper, sliced
- 1 large sweet red pepper, sliced
- 1 large onion, sliced
- 16 flour tortillas (8 inches), warmed

Chopped tomato and cucumber, optional

1) Cut lamb into thin bite-size strips. In a large resealable plastic bag, combine oil, lemon juice, soy sauce, sugar, vinegar, Worcestershire, mustard and pepper; add lamb. Seal bag and turn to coat; refrigerate for 3 hours, turning occasionally.

2) Place the lamb and marinade in a Dutch oven or large saucepan; bring to a boil. Reduce heat; cover and simmer for 8-10 minutes or until meat is tender. Add peppers and onion; cook until vegetables are crisp-tender, about 4 minutes.

3) Using a slotted spoon, place meat and vegetables on tortillas; top with tomato and cucumber if desired. Fold in sides of tortilla and serve.

Yield: 8 servings.

NUTRITION FACTS: 1 serving equals 697 calories, 30 g fat (6 g saturated fat), 95 mg cholesterol, 1,251 mg sodium, 67 g carbohydrate, 1 g fiber, 40 g protein.

GREEK PASTA BAKE

Greek Pasta Bake
Carol Stevens, Basye, Virginia

Lemon and herbs are complemented by the subtle sweetness of cinnamon in this pasta bake.

- 1/2 pound ground beef
- 1/2 pound ground lamb
- 1 large onion, chopped
- 4 garlic cloves, minced
- 3 teaspoons dried oregano
- 1 teaspoon dried basil
- 1/2 teaspoon salt
- 1/4 teaspoon pepper
- 1/4 teaspoon dried thyme
- 1 can (15 ounces) tomato sauce
- 1 can (14-1/2 ounces) diced tomatoes, undrained
- 1 tablespoon lemon juice
- 1 teaspoon sugar
- 1/4 teaspoon ground cinnamon
- 2 cups uncooked rigatoni *or* large tube pasta
- 4 ounces feta cheese, crumbled

1) In a large skillet, cook beef and lamb over medium heat until no longer pink; drain. Stir in onion, garlic, oregano, basil, salt, pepper and thyme; mix well. Add the tomato sauce, tomatoes and lemon juice.

2) Bring to a boil. Reduce heat; simmer, uncovered, for 20 minutes, stirring occasionally. Stir in the sugar and cinnamon. Simmer, uncovered, 15 minutes longer.

3) Meanwhile, cook the pasta according to package directions; drain. Stir into meat mixture. Transfer to a greased 2-qt. baking dish. Sprinkle with cheese.

4) Cover and bake at 325° for 45 minutes. Uncover; bake 15 minutes longer or until heated through.

Yield: 6 servings.

NUTRITION FACTS: 1 serving equals 316 calories, 12 g fat (6 g saturated fat), 54 mg cholesterol, 840 mg sodium, 29 g carbohydrate, 4 g fiber, 22 g protein.

Spring Lamb Supper
Michelle Armistead, Marlboro, New Jersey

Whenever I prepare brown rice, I fix a big batch so I have extra to make this quick dish during the week. Tender lamb is tossed with summer squash, tomatoes and mushrooms.

- 1 pound boneless lamb, cut into cubes
- 2 teaspoons olive oil
- 2 cups thinly sliced yellow summer squash
- 1/2 pound fresh mushrooms, sliced
- 2 medium tomatoes, seeded and chopped
- 1/2 cup sliced green onions
- 3 cups cooked brown rice
- 1 teaspoon salt
- 1/2 teaspoon garlic powder
- 1/2 teaspoon pepper
- 1/2 teaspoon dried rosemary, crushed

1) In a large skillet, saute lamb in oil until no longer pink; remove from the skillet with a slotted spoon. In the same skillet, stir-fry squash, mushrooms, tomatoes and onions for 2-3 minutes or until tender.

2) Return lamb to the skillet. Stir in the rice and seasonings; cook and stir until heated through.

Yield: 4 servings.

NUTRITION FACTS: 1 serving equals 376 calories, 11 g fat (3 g saturated fat), 63 mg cholesterol, 659 mg sodium, 44 g carbohydrate, 6 g fiber, 27 g protein.

Lamb Ratatouille

Maxine Cenker, Weirton, West Virginia

This quick-and-easy recipe is a great way to use up leftover lamb. It's also good with beef.

- 1 package (6.8 ounces) beef-flavored rice and vermicelli mix
- 2 tablespoons butter
- 2-1/2 cups water
- 3 medium tomatoes, peeled, seeded and chopped
- 1 medium zucchini, sliced
- 1-1/2 cups sliced fresh mushrooms
- 1 small onion, chopped
- 6 green onions, sliced
- 3 garlic cloves, minced
- 2 tablespoons olive oil
- 1 pound cooked lamb *or* beef, cut into thin strips

1) Set rice seasoning packet aside. In a large skillet, saute the rice mix in butter until browned. Stir in water and contents of seasoning packet; bring to a boil. Reduce heat. Cover; simmer 15 minutes.

2) In another skillet, saute vegetables in oil until crisp-tender. Add lamb and vegetables. Cover and simmer for 5-10 minutes or until rice is tender.

Yield: 6 servings.

NUTRITION FACTS: 1 serving equals 369 calories, 16 g fat (6 g saturated fat), 76 mg cholesterol, 580 mg sodium, 31 g carbohydrate, 3 g fiber, 25 g protein.

Lamb Broccoli Strudel

Mary Bengtson-Almquist, Petersburg, Illinois

My husband had asked for seconds before I told him it had two ingredients he doesn't like.

- 1 pound ground lamb *or* pork
- 1 medium onion, chopped
- 2 cups chopped fresh broccoli, blanched
- 1 cup (4 ounces) shredded mozzarella cheese
- 1/2 cup sour cream
- 1/4 cup dry bread crumbs
- 1 garlic clove, minced
- 1 teaspoon seasoned salt
- 1/2 teaspoon pepper
- 20 sheets phyllo dough (14 inches x 9 inches)
- 1/2 cup butter, melted

1) In a skillet, cook lamb and onion over medium heat until meat is no longer pink; drain and cool. In a large bowl, combine the broccoli, cheese, sour cream, bread crumbs, garlic, seasoned salt and pepper. Mix in meat and onion.

2) Place 1 sheet of phyllo dough on a piece of waxed paper. Brush with butter; continue layering with 9 more sheets of dough, brushing each with butter. Keep remaining phyllo dough covered with plastic wrap and a damp towel. Spoon half of the meat mixture on dough. Roll up jelly-roll style, starting with the short end.

3) Place the roll seam side down on a greased baking sheet. Repeat with remaining dough and filling. Brush tops of rolls with remaining butter. Bake at 350° for 45-50 minutes or until golden brown. Cool for 10 minutes before slicing.

Yield: 6 servings.

NUTRITION FACTS: 1 slice equals 607 calories, 35 g fat (18 g saturated fat), 119 mg cholesterol, 875 mg sodium, 50 g carbohydrate, 3 g fiber, 25 g protein.

Cheesy Lamb Cups

Pat Horton, Riverton, Wyoming

These ground lamb balls are something between a meatball and meat loaf, and they bake in no time.

- 1 envelope onion soup mix
- 1/3 cup dry bread crumbs
- 1 cup evaporated milk
- 2 pounds ground lamb
- 4 ounces cheddar cheese, cut into 12 cubes
- 1 can (10-3/4 ounces) condensed cheddar cheese soup, undiluted
- 1/2 cup milk
- 1 teaspoon Worcestershire sauce

1) In a small bowl, combine first three ingredients. Crumble lamb over mixture and mix well.

2) Press half of mixture into 12 greased muffin cups, filling each half full. Press one cube of cheese into center of each cup. Cover with remaining lamb mixture; mound slightly. Bake at 375° for 20-25 minutes or until a meat thermometer reads 160°.

3) For sauce, combine soup, milk and Worcestershire sauce in a small saucepan. Heat through; stir until smooth. Serve over lamb cups.

Yield: 6 servings.

NUTRITION FACTS: 1 serving equals 507 calories, 34 g fat (16 g saturated fat), 142 mg cholesterol, 1,112 mg sodium, 17 g carbohydrate, 1 g fiber, 36 g protein.

POULTRY

Beyond chicken, poultry also includes turkey, duck, pheasant, geese and Cornish game hens. This chapter is filled with ways to roast, bake, cook and enjoy poultry in all its forms. Here are some poultry basics to help you get started.

The skin color of chicken ranges from white to deep yellow. The skin color is due to the chicken's diet and is not an indication of freshness or quality.

While duck and geese breasts are darker in color than chicken and turkey breasts, they are still considered white meat. Duck and geese breasts are darker because these birds fly and use their breast muscles more than chickens and turkeys.

Duck and geese are generally found in the freezer case of supermarkets. During the holiday season, it is easier to find them fresh.

Make sure the package of poultry is cold and has no holes or tears. Place package in a plastic bag to prevent it from leaking onto any other groceries.

Purchase before the "sell by" date on the packaging for best quality. Refrigerate or freeze poultry immediately when you return home from the grocery store. Use uncooked poultry within 1 to 2 days of purchase.

Never defrost frozen poultry at room temperature. Thaw in the refrigerator (see Defrosting Guidelines on page 154), in cold water (see Defrosting in Cold Water on page 154) or in the microwave oven (refer to manufacturer's directions).

Always wash your hands and anything that has come in contact with the uncooked poultry (knives, cutting boards, countertops) with hot, soapy water to avoid contamination with other foods.

Cook poultry breasts to an internal temperature of 170°. Cook whole poultry and dark meat to 180°. Cook ground chicken and turkey to 165°. Stuffing in whole poultry should be cooked to 165°.

Pierce poultry with a fork in several places. The juices of thoroughly cooked poultry should run clear. Cubes and strips of chicken and turkey are cooked when they are no longer pink and juices run clear.

Purchasing Poultry

The amount of poultry you need to buy depends on the variety, portion and amount of bone.

TYPE OF POULTRY	SERVINGS PER POUND
CHICKEN, WHOLE	1 to 2
CHICKEN PARTS (BONE-IN, SKIN ON)	2 to 3
CHICKEN BREASTS (BONELESS, SKINLESS)	3 to 4
TURKEY, WHOLE (12 POUNDS OR LESS)	1
TURKEY, WHOLE (12 POUNDS OR MORE)	2
TURKEY PARTS (THIGHS, BONE-IN BREASTS)	2 to 3
TURKEY BREAST (BONELESS)	3 to 4
DUCK, WHOLE	1
GOOSE, WHOLE	1
CORNISH GAME HENS	1 to 2

Cooking Methods for Poultry

COOKING METHOD	POULTRY TYPE
BROILING	Broiler/Fryer Halves, Boneless Chicken Breast Halves, Bone-In Breasts, Thighs, Drumsticks, Breast Cubes for Kabobs, Cornish Game Hen Halves, Turkey Breast Tenderloins, Cutlets, Ground Turkey Patties
FRYING	Chicken Parts
GRILLING	Whole Chicken, Broiler/Fryer Halves, Boneless Chicken Breast Halves, Bone-In Breasts, Thighs, Drumsticks, Breast Cubes for Kabobs, Cornish Game Hen Halves, Whole Turkey, Turkey Breasts (whole and half), Turkey Breast Tenderloins, Cutlets, Ground Turkey Patties
ROASTING	Whole Birds, Halves and Pieces
SAUTEING	Boneless Chicken Breasts or Turkey Breast Tenderloins (whole or cut into cubes or strips)

Defrosting Guidelines

Defrosting times for poultry depend on the weight of the package and the thickness. When defrosting poultry in the refrigerator, place a tray under the package to catch any liquid or juices and to keep the refrigerator clean. Here are some timelines for defrosting poultry in the refrigerator:

- For bone-in parts or a small whole chicken, allow at least 1 to 2 days.

- For duck or goose parts, allow at least 1 day.

- For a whole duck or goose, allow at least 2 days.

- For a whole turkey or large whole chicken, allow 24 hours for every 4 pounds.

Defrosting in Cold Water

Cold-water thawing is an option that takes less time than thawing in the refrigerator but requires more attention.

The poultry must be in a leakproof bag such as its original, tightly sealed wrapper. If its package is not leakproof, place it in a heavy-duty resealable plastic bag.

Submerge the wrapped poultry in cold tap water. Change the water every 30 minutes until the bird is thawed. For this method, allow 30 minutes for every pound.

Useful Definitions

Refer to the Glossary on pages 18-22 for more terms.

BASTED OR SELF-BASTED: The chicken or turkey has been injected or marinated with a solution of water, broth or stock that contains a fat, such as butter, spices and flavor enhancers.

BROILER/FRYER: A chicken about 7 weeks old that weighs 2-1/2 to 4-1/2 pounds.

CAPON: A castrated male chicken between 4 and 8 months old that weighs 4 to 7 pounds.

CHICKEN LEG: The attached drumstick and thigh.

CHICKEN QUARTER: A quarter of the chicken and may be the leg or breast quarter. The leg quarter contains the drumstick, thigh and portion of the back. The breast quarter contains the breast, wing and portion of the back.

CORNISH GAME HEN: A small broiler/fryer that is less than 30 days old and weighs 1-1/2 to 2 pounds.

CUT-UP CHICKEN: A broiler/fryer that has been cut into two breast halves, two thighs, two drumsticks and two wings. It may or may not have the back.

DRUMMETTE: The first section of a chicken wing.

DRUMSTICK: The lower portion of the leg.

FREE RANGE OR FREE ROAMING: The poultry was not confined to a chicken house but was allowed outside to forage for food.

FRESH POULTRY: Uncooked poultry that has never been commercially stored below 26°.

GIBLETS: The heart, liver, neck and gizzard.

HEN OR TOM TURKEY: Indicates whether the turkey was female (hen) or male (tom). Tom turkeys are usually larger than hen turkeys. A hen or tom turkey should be equally tender.

ROASTER: A chicken between 3 and 5 months old that weighs 5 to 7 pounds.

SPLIT CHICKEN: A broiler/fryer that was cut lengthwise in half.

Roasting Poultry

Remove giblets that are usually stored in a packet in the neck area of the bird. Use for preparing broth if desired. Remove and discard any large pockets of fat that may be present in the neck area.

For whole poultry, drain juices and blot cavity dry with paper towels. Currently the USDA does not advise washing poultry before cooking. If you do, wash the sink with hot, soapy water or sanitize with a mild bleach solution of 1 teaspoon chlorine bleach to 1 quart of water. This will help prevent cross-contamination from the poultry to other foods that are washed in the sink.

Rub the inside cavity and neck area with salt. Place breast side up on a rack in a shallow roasting pan.

For chicken, turkey or Cornish game hens, brush the skin with oil or melted butter. For ducklings and geese, prick the skin all over with a fork. This allows the fat from the fat layer under the skin to drip out of the bird while it roasts. With a baster, remove and discard fat from the bottom of the roaster as it accumulates. Because the drippings are very rich with fat, gravy is not usually prepared from roasted duck or goose drippings.

Insert an oven-safe meat thermometer into the thigh area of large birds, not touching bone. Or use an instant-read thermometer toward the end of roasting time. If the bird needs to cook longer, make sure to remove the instant-read thermometer before you return it to the oven. For smaller birds, test the temperature periodically by placing and holding the thermometer in the inner thigh area.

Roast, uncovered, without liquid according to the temperature and time given in the chart below or recipe. The roasting times provided in the chart below are for defrosted poultry that is refrigerator cold.

If poultry browns too quickly, tent with foil. Because roasts will continue to cook after being removed from the oven, remove them when the internal temperature is 5-10° below desired doneness. Cover with foil and let stand for 10-20 minutes before removing any stuffing and carving. (See Stuffing, Roasting and Carving a Whole Turkey on page 178.)

TYPE OF POULTRY (*UNSTUFFED)	WEIGHT	COOKING TIME (MINUTES PER POUND)	OVEN TEMP.	DONENESS
BROILER/FRYER CHICKEN	3 to 4 lbs.	23 to 25	350°	180°
ROASTING CHICKEN, WHOLE	5 to 7 lbs.	23 to 25	350°	180°
CAPON, WHOLE	4 to 8 lbs.	22 to 30	350°	180°
CORNISH GAME HENS	1-1/4 to 1-1/2 lbs.	50 to 60 (minutes total)	350°	180°
DUCKLING, WHOLE (DOMESTIC)	4 to 6 lbs.	30 to 35	350°	180°
GOOSE, WHOLE (DOMESTIC)	8 to 12 lbs.	15 to 21	350°	180°
TURKEY, WHOLE	8 to 12 lbs. 12 to 14 lbs. 14 to 18 lbs. 18 to 20 lbs. 20 to 24 lbs.	15 to 20 15 to 17 14 to 16 13 to 14 12 to 13-1/2	325°	180°
TURKEY BREAST, WHOLE	4 to 6 lbs.	22 to 30	325°	170°
TURKEY BREAST, HALF	1-3/4 to 3-1/2 lbs.	35 to 40	325°	170°
TURKEY BREAST, ROAST	1-1/4 to 1-3/4 lbs.	45 to 60	325°	170°

★ For stuffed birds, add 15 to 45 minutes to the roasting time.

MAKING PAN GRAVY

1) Pour pan drippings into a heat-resistant measuring cup along with any browned bits scraped from roasting pan. Skim fat.

2) Reserve 1/4 cup fat and place in a saucepan. Whisk in flour until smooth.

3) Add enough broth or water to reserved pan drippings to equal 2 cups. Add all at once to flour mixture. Cook and stir over medium-high heat until mixture comes to a boil; cook and stir 2 minutes longer.

Pan Gravy
Taste of Home Test Kitchen

Use this recipe to make gravy from meats and poultry roasted in an uncovered roasting pan.

Roasted meat drippings
1/4   cup all-purpose flour
Chicken broth *or* water
Salt, pepper and browning sauce, optional

1) Pour pan drippings into a measuring cup. Loosen the browned bits from the roasting pan and add to drippings. Skim fat.

2) Reserve 1/4 cup fat and transfer to a saucepan; whisk in flour until smooth. Add enough broth or water to pan drippings to measure 2 cups.

3) Gradually stir into flour mixture in saucepan. Bring to a boil; cook and stir for 2 minutes or until thickened. Season with salt, pepper and browning sauce if desired.

Yield: 2 cups.

NUTRITION FACTS: 2 tablespoons equals 40 calories, 4 g fat (2 g saturated fat), 4 mg cholesterol, 121 mg sodium, 2 g carbohydrate, trace fiber, trace protein.

CUTTING UP A WHOLE CHICKEN

1) Pull the leg and thigh away from the body. With a small sharp knife, cut through the skin to expose the joint.

2) Cut through joint, then cut skin around thigh to free leg. Repeat with other leg.

3) Separate drumstick from thigh by cutting skin at the joint. Bend drumstick to expose joint; cut through joint and skin.

4) Pull wing away from the body. Cut through skin to expose joint. Cut through joint and skin to separate wing from body. Repeat.

5) Snip along each side of the backbone between rib joints with a kitchen or poultry shears.

6) Hold chicken breast in both hands (skin side down) and bend it back to snap breastbone. Turn over. With a knife, cut in half along breastbone. Breastbone will remain attached to one of the halves.

Baking Chicken Pieces

Place pieces in a single layer in a baking pan. Bake, uncovered, for the time listed in the chart below.

TYPE OF POULTRY	WEIGHT	COOKING TIME (MINUTES PER POUND)	OVEN TEMP.	DONENESS
CHICKEN BREAST, BONE-IN	6-8 oz. *each*	30 to 40	350°	170°
CHICKEN BREAST, BONELESS	4 oz. *each*	20 to 30	350°	170°
CHICKEN LEGS	8 oz. *each*	40 to 50	350°	180°
CHICKEN THIGHS	4 oz. *each*	40 to 50	350°	180°
CHICKEN DRUMSTICKS	4 oz. *each*	35 to 45	350°	180°
CHICKEN WINGS	2 to 3 oz. *each*	30 to 40	350°	Juices run clear

ROASTED CHICKEN WITH ROSEMARY

Roasted Chicken with Rosemary
Isabel Zienkosky, Salt Lake City, Utah

This is a lot like pot roast, only it uses chicken instead of beef. Rosemary provides a sweet taste that blends well with the garlic, butter and parsley.

1/2 cup butter

4 tablespoons minced fresh rosemary *or* 2 tablespoons dried rosemary, crushed

2 tablespoons chopped fresh parsley

3 garlic cloves, minced

1 teaspoon salt

1/2 teaspoon pepper

1 roasting chicken (5 to 6 pounds)

9 small red potatoes, halved

6 medium carrots, halved lengthwise and cut into 2-inch pieces

2 medium onions, quartered

1) In a small saucepan, melt butter and stir in the seasonings. Place chicken on a rack in a roasting pan; tie drumsticks together with kitchen string.

2) Spoon half of butter mixture over chicken. Place potatoes, carrots and onions around chicken. Drizzle remaining butter mixture over vegetables.

3) Cover and bake at 350° for 1-1/2 hours, basting every 30 minutes. Uncover; bake 30-60 minutes longer or a meat thermometer reads 180° and vegetables are tender, basting occasionally.

4) Cover with foil and let stand for 10-15 minutes before carving. Serve vegetables with roast.

Yield: 9 servings.

NUTRITION FACTS: 1 serving equals 449 calories, 28 g fat (11 g saturated fat), 126 mg cholesterol, 479 mg sodium, 16 g carbohydrate, 3 g fiber, 33 g protein.

POULTRY TIPS

A 3-1/2-pound whole chicken will yield about 3 cups of diced cooked chicken.

If you don't plan to stuff a whole chicken or turkey, place 1 to 2 cups total of chopped celery, carrot and onion into the cavity. These veggies will add some flavor to the pan juices. Discard vegetables before carving.

Apple-Stuffed Chicken

Joan Wrigley, Lynden, Washington

Packaged stuffing mix helps move this holiday meal along. You can also try golden raisins in place of the regular raisins.

> 1 package (6 ounces) chicken-flavored stuffing mix
> 1 broiler/fryer chicken (3-1/2 to 4 pounds)
> 1/2 teaspoon salt
> 1/4 teaspoon pepper
> 1 tablespoon vegetable oil
> 1 cup chopped peeled apple
> 1/4 cup chopped celery
> 1/4 cup chopped walnuts
> 1/4 cup raisins
> 1/2 teaspoon grated lemon peel

GLAZE:

> 1/2 cup apple jelly
> 1 tablespoon lemon juice
> 1/2 teaspoon ground cinnamon

1) Prepare stuffing according to package directions. Meanwhile, sprinkle inside of chicken with salt and pepper; rub outside with oil.

2) In a large bowl, mix stuffing with the apple, celery, nuts, raisins and lemon peel. Lightly stuff chicken. Place chicken breast side up on a rack in a shallow roasting pan. Bake, uncovered, at 350° for 1 hour.

3) In a saucepan, combine the glaze ingredients. Bring to a simmer; heat, uncovered, for 3 minutes. Brush over chicken.

4) Bake 20-30 minutes longer or until a meat thermometer reads 180°, brushing occasionally with glaze. Cover with foil and let stand for 10-15 minutes. Remove stuffing, then carve chicken.

Yield: 6 servings.

NUTRITION FACTS: 1 serving equals 547 calories, 23 g fat (5 g saturated fat), 102 mg cholesterol, 806 mg sodium, 46 g carbohydrate, 2 g fiber, 38 g protein.

Golden Game Hens

Andy Anderson, Graham, Washington

The game hens are an appealing entree that fills the plate and usually garners many fine comments.

> 6 Cornish game hens (20 ounces each)
> 1 medium tart apple, sliced
> 1 medium onion, sliced

> 1/4 cup butter, melted
> 1/4 cup soy sauce

1) Loosely stuff hens with apple and onion. Place on a rack in a shallow baking pan. Combine butter and soy sauce; brush over hens.

2) Bake, uncovered, at 350° for 50-60 minutes or until a meat thermometer reads 180° and juices run clear, basting occasionally.

Yield: 6 servings.

NUTRITION FACTS: 1 serving equals 1,571 calories, 111 g fat (33 g saturated fat), 763 mg cholesterol, 1,054 mg sodium, 6 g carbohydrate, 1 g fiber, 128 g protein.

RICE-STUFFED CORNISH HENS

Rice-Stuffed Cornish Hens

Becky Brunette, Minneapolis, Minnesota

My mom prepares this impressive-looking entree for many "company's coming" occasions. The rice stuffing goes wonderfully with the golden hens and sweet glaze.

> 5-1/2 cups water, *divided*
> 2 teaspoons chicken bouillon granules
> 1-1/2 teaspoons salt
> 3/4 cup uncooked wild rice
> 1-1/2 cups uncooked long grain rice
> 1 pound bulk pork sausage
> 1-1/2 cups chopped celery
> 3/4 cup chopped onion
> 6 Cornish game hens (20 ounces each)
> 1 jar (12 ounces) apricot preserves

1) In a large saucepan, bring 5 cups water, bouillon and salt to a boil. Add wild rice. Reduce heat; cover and simmer for 20 minutes. Add long grain

rice; cover and simmer 25-30 minutes longer or until rice is tender and water is absorbed.

2) Meanwhile, in a large skillet, cook the sausage, celery and onion over medium heat until meat is no longer pink and vegetables are tender; drain. Stir in rice mixture. Spoon about 3/4 cup stuffing into each hen.

3) Place remaining stuffing in a greased 2-qt. baking dish; cover and set aside. Place hens breast side up on a rack in shallow baking pan; tie drumsticks together. Bake, uncovered, at 350° for 40 minutes.

4) In a small saucepan, bring the preserves and remaining water to a boil. Pour over hens. Bake 25-35 minutes longer or until a meat thermometer reads 180° for hens and 160° for stuffing, basting occasionally.

5) Place baking dish of stuffing in the oven for the last 35-40 minutes of hens' baking time.

Yield: 6 servings.

NUTRITION FACTS: 1 serving equals 2,032 calories, 118 g fat (34 g saturated fat), 770 mg cholesterol, 1,595 mg sodium, 95 g carbohydrate, 3 g fiber, 139 g protein.

George's Barbecued Chicken
George Summer, Denver, Colorado

The homemade barbecue sauce is what makes this chicken dish unique. Your family will be licking their fingers and asking for more!

2 tablespoons chopped onion
1/3 cup vegetable oil, *divided*
2 cups ketchup
1/2 cup cider vinegar
2 tablespoons lemon juice
1 tablespoon hot pepper sauce
2/3 cup Worcestershire sauce
1 broiler/fryer chicken
 (3-1/2 to 4 pounds), cut up

1) In a large saucepan, saute onion in 1 tablespoon oil until tender. Add the ketchup, vinegar, lemon juice, pepper sauce and Worcestershire sauce. Bring to a boil. Reduce heat; simmer, uncovered, for 10 minutes, stirring occasionally.

2) Brown chicken on all sides in remaining oil over medium-high heat. Drain chicken and transfer to a 13-in. x 9-in. x 2-in. baking pan.

3) Pour sauce over chicken. Bake, uncovered, at 350° for 45-60 minutes or until juices run clear.

Yield: 6 servings.

NUTRITION FACTS: 4-1/2 ounces cooked chicken equals 503 calories, 29 g fat (6 g saturated fat), 102 mg cholesterol, 1,348 mg sodium, 29 g carbohydrate, 1 g fiber, 34 g protein.

Buttermilk Fried Chicken With Gravy
Vera Reid, Laramie, Wyoming

This is an old family favorite, but you can adjust the seasonings for many taste-tempting ways to coat your chicken for dinner.

1 broiler/fryer chicken
 (3-1/2 to 4 pounds), cut up
1 cup buttermilk
1 cup all-purpose flour
1-1/2 teaspoons salt
1/2 teaspoon pepper
 Oil for frying

GRAVY:
3 tablespoons all-purpose flour
1 cup milk
1-1/2 to 2 cups water
 Salt and pepper, optional

1) Place the chicken in a large shallow dish. Pour buttermilk over; cover and refrigerate for 1 hour. Combine the flour, salt and pepper in a large resealable plastic bag. Drain chicken pieces; add to flour mixture, one at a time, and shake to coat. Shake off excess; let stand on waxed paper for 15 minutes before frying.

2) Heat 1/8 to 1/4 in. of oil in a large skillet; fry chicken until browned on all sides. Cover and simmer, turning occasionally, for 40-45 minutes, or until juices run clear and chicken is tender. Uncover and cook 5 minutes longer. Remove chicken; drain on paper towels and keep warm.

3) Drain all but 1/4 cup drippings from skillet; stir in flour until blended. Gradually add milk, then 1-1/2 cups water. Bring to a boil over medium heat; cook and stir for 2 minutes or until thickened. Add remaining water if needed. Season with salt and pepper if desired. Serve with chicken.

Yield: 6 servings.

NUTRITION FACTS: 1 serving equals 532 calories, 34 g fat (7 g saturated fat), 108 mg cholesterol, 611 mg sodium, 17 g carbohydrate, 1 g fiber, 36 g protein.

■ *COUNTRY-FRIED CHICKEN:* To the flour mixture add 1 tablespoon paprika, 1/2 teaspoon *each* garlic powder and onion powder, 1/4 teaspoon *each* rubbed sage and dried thyme and 1/8 teaspoon baking powder. Prepare as directed.

■ *HOME-STYLE FRIED CHICKEN:* To the flour mixture add 1/4 teaspoon *each* ground cumin, dried oregano and paprika. Prepare as directed.

Chicken Cacciatore

Barbara Roberts, Courtenay, British Columbia

Cacciatore refers to an American-Italian dish prepared "hunter-style" with mushrooms, onions, tomatoes, various herbs and sometimes wine. This is a favorite for my family.

- 1 broiler/fryer chicken (3-1/2 to 4 pounds), cut up
- 1/4 cup all-purpose flour

Salt and pepper to taste

- 2 tablespoons olive oil
- 2 tablespoons butter
- 1 large onion, chopped
- 2 celery ribs, sliced diagonally
- 1 large green pepper, cut into strips
- 1/2 pound fresh mushrooms, sliced
- 1 can (28 ounces) diced tomatoes, undrained
- 1 can (8 ounces) tomato sauce
- 1 can (6 ounces) tomato paste
- 1 cup dry red wine *or* water
- 1 teaspoon dried thyme
- 1 teaspoon dried rosemary, crushed
- 1 teaspoon dried oregano
- 1 teaspoon dried basil
- 3 garlic cloves, minced
- 1 tablespoon sugar

Hot cooked pasta

Grated Parmesan cheese

1) Dust chicken with flour. Season with salt and pepper. In a large skillet, brown chicken on all sides in oil and butter over medium-high. Remove chicken to platter.

2) In same skillet, cook and stir the onion, celery, pepper and mushrooms for 5 minutes. Stir in the tomatoes, tomato sauce, tomato paste, wine or water, herbs, garlic and sugar. Bring to a boil. Reduce heat; cover and simmer for 30 minutes.

3) Return chicken to skillet. Cover and simmer for 45-60 minutes or until chicken is tender. Serve over pasta and sprinkle with Parmesan cheese.

Yield: 6 servings.

NUTRITION FACTS: 4-1/2 ounces cooked chicken (calculated without salt, pepper, pasta and Parmesan cheese) equals 517 calories, 25 g fat (8 g saturated fat), 112 mg cholesterol, 790 mg sodium, 28 g carbohydrate, 6 g fiber, 39 g protein.

CHICKEN AND RICE DINNER

Chicken and Rice Dinner

Denise Baumert, Jameson, Missouri

In this easy and tasty recipe, the chicken bakes up to a beautiful golden brown while the moist rice is packed with flavor. The taste is unbeatable.

- 1 broiler/fryer chicken (3-1/2 to 4 pounds), cut up
- 1/4 to 1/3 cup all-purpose flour
- 2 tablespoons vegetable oil
- 2-1/3 cups water
- 1-1/2 cups uncooked long grain rice
- 1 cup milk
- 1 teaspoon salt
- 1 teaspoon poultry seasoning
- 1/2 teaspoon pepper

Chopped fresh parsley

1) Dredge chicken pieces in flour. In a large skillet, brown chicken on all sides in oil over medium heat.

2) In a large bowl, combine the next six ingredients. Pour into a greased 13-in. x 9-in. x 2-in. baking dish. Top with chicken.

3) Cover lightly with foil and bake at 350° for 55 minutes or until rice and chicken are tender. Sprinkle with parsley before serving.

Yield: 6 servings.

NUTRITION FACTS: 3 ounces cooked chicken without skin with 3/4 cup rice mixture equals 541 calories, 23 g fat (6 g saturated fat), 108 mg cholesterol, 504 mg sodium, 43 g carbohydrate, 1 g fiber, 38 g protein.

Chicken and Dumplings

Edna Hoffman, Hebron, Indiana

Made with homemade broth and dumplings, this dish is an old-fashioned treat. It's worth the effort to enjoy its wonderful flavors.

- 1 broiler/fryer chicken (3-1/2 to 4 pounds), cut up

2 to 2-1/4 quarts water
1/2 cup sliced celery
1/2 cup sliced carrots
2 fresh parsley sprigs
1 bay leaf
1 teaspoon salt
1/4 teaspoon pepper

DUMPLINGS:
3/4 cup all-purpose flour
1 tablespoon minced fresh parsley
1 teaspoon baking powder
1/4 teaspoon salt
Dash ground nutmeg
1/3 cup milk
1 egg, lightly beaten
1 tablespoon vegetable oil

GRAVY:
1/4 cup all-purpose flour
1/2 cup water
1/4 teaspoon salt
1/8 teaspoon pepper

1) In a large soup kettle or Dutch oven, combine first eight ingredients. Slowly bring to a boil over low heat. Cover; simmer for 45-60 minutes or until meat is tender, skimming surface as foam rises.

2) In a bowl, combine the flour, parsley, baking powder, salt and nutmeg; stir in milk, egg and oil just until moistened. Drop batter by tablespoonfuls onto simmering broth.

3) Cover and simmer for 12-15 minutes or until a toothpick inserted in a dumpling comes out clean (do not lift the cover while simmering). Remove the dumplings and chicken with a slotted spoon to a serving dish; keep warm.

4) Strain broth, discarding vegetables and bay leaf and reserving 2 cups for gravy. (Remaining broth can be covered and refrigerated for up to 3 days or frozen for 4 to 6 months.)

5) Place reserved broth in a saucepan; bring to a boil. Combine flour, water, salt and pepper until smooth; gradually stir into broth. Cook and stir over medium heat for 2 minutes or until thickened. Pour over chicken and dumplings.

Yield: 4 servings.

NUTRITION FACTS: 1 serving equals 606 calories, 30 g fat (8 g saturated fat), 209 mg cholesterol, 1,144 mg sodium, 25 g carbohydrate, 1 g fiber, 54 g protein.

BRUNSWICK STEW

Brunswick Stew
Milded Sherrer, Fort Worth, Texas

This stew is a traditional dish from the Southeast. My version, containing beans, vegetables and chicken, turns out great every time.

1 broiler/fryer chicken (3-1/2 to 4 pounds), cut up
1 cup water
4 medium potatoes, peeled and cubed
2 medium onions, sliced
1 can (15-1/4 ounces) lima beans, rinsed and drained
1 teaspoon salt
1/2 teaspoon pepper
Dash cayenne pepper
1 can (15-1/4 ounces) corn, drained
1 can (14-1/2 ounces) diced tomatoes, undrained
1/4 cup butter
1/2 cup dry bread crumbs

1) In a Dutch oven, slowly bring the chicken and water to a boil. Cover and simmer for 45-60 minutes or until chicken is tender, skimming the surface as foam rises.

2) Remove chicken and set aside until cool enough to handle. Remove and discard skin and bones. Cube chicken and return to broth.

3) Add the potatoes, onions, beans and seasonings. Bring to a boil. Reduce heat; simmer, uncovered, for 30 minutes or until potatoes are tender. Stir in remaining ingredients. Simmer, uncovered, for 10 minutes or until slightly thickened.

Yield: 6 servings.

NUTRITION FACTS: 1 serving equals 589 calories, 25 g fat (9 g saturated fat), 123 mg cholesterol, 1,147 mg sodium, 47 g carbohydrate, 7 g fiber, 40 g protein.

GARLIC LIME CHICKEN

Garlic Lime Chicken
Dorothy Smith, El Dorado, Arkansas

I love garlic, and this golden-brown chicken with its fragrant spices and citrus tang is an excellent way to showcase its flavor.

1/2 cup lime juice
1/4 cup cider vinegar
6 garlic cloves, minced
2 tablespoons minced fresh oregano *or* 2 teaspoons dried oregano
1 tablespoon dried coriander
2 teaspoons pepper
1 teaspoon salt
1 teaspoon paprika
8 bone-in chicken breast halves (8 ounces *each*)
1/4 cup vegetable oil

1) In a large resealable plastic bag, combine the lime juice, vinegar, garlic and seasonings; add chicken. Seal bag and turn to coat; refrigerate for 8 hours or overnight.

2) Discard marinade. In a skillet, brown chicken on all sides in oil. Transfer to a greased 15-in. x 10-in. x 1-in. baking pan. Bake, uncovered, at 375° for 30-35 minutes or until a meat thermometer reads 170° and juices run clear.

Yield: 8 servings.

NUTRITION FACTS: 1 chicken breast half equals 209 calories, 7 g fat (2 g saturated fat), 90 mg cholesterol, 153 mg sodium, 1 g carbohydrate, trace fiber, 33 g protein.

Spinach-Stuffed Chicken
Barbara Eitemiller, Churchville, Maryland

A mixture of spinach, spices and three kinds of cheese are tucked into these chicken breasts. They bake to a beautiful golden brown, so they look lovely on the plate, too.

2 packages (10 ounces *each*) frozen chopped spinach, thawed and squeezed dry
1 cup (4 ounces) shredded Swiss cheese
3/4 cup ricotta cheese
1/3 cup grated Parmesan cheese
3 tablespoons finely chopped onion
1 garlic clove, minced
1/4 teaspoon salt
1/4 teaspoon ground nutmeg
1/4 teaspoon pepper
6 bone-in chicken breast halves (8 ounces *each*)
2 tablespoons olive oil
1 teaspoon paprika
1/2 teaspoon dried oregano
1/2 teaspoon dried thyme
Additional paprika, optional

1) In a large bowl, combine the spinach, cheeses, onion, garlic, salt, nutmeg and pepper. Carefully loosen the skin on one side of each chicken breast to form a pocket.

2) Stuff each breast with 1/2 cup spinach mixture. Place chicken skin side up in a greased 15-in. x 10-in. x 1-in. baking pan. Combine the oil, paprika, oregano and thyme; brush over chicken. Sprinkle with additional paprika if desired.

3) Bake, uncovered, at 350° for 1 to 1-1/4 hours or until a meat thermometer inserted into the breast meat reads 170° and juices run clear.

Yield: 6 servings.

NUTRITION FACTS: 1 stuffed chicken breast half equals 461 calories, 24 g fat (10 g saturated fat), 144 mg cholesterol, 430 mg sodium, 7 g carbohydrate, 3 g fiber, 53 g protein.

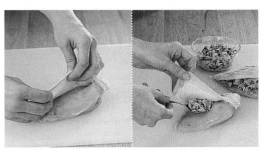

STUFFING BONE-IN CHICKEN BREASTS

1) Work fingers under the skin to loosen and form a pocket.

2) Lightly fill each pocket with the stuffing mixture. Proceed with recipe.

Chicken Cordon Bleu

Jim Wick, Orlando, Florida

The addition of bacon in this cordon bleu recipe makes it my top pick. I enjoy making this meal for friends and family.

- 4 **boneless skinless chicken breast halves (8 ounces *each*)**
- 2 **tablespoons butter, softened**
- 1 **teaspoon dried thyme**
- 4 **thin slices fully cooked ham**
- 4 **thin slices Swiss cheese**
- 8 **bacon strips**
- 2 **eggs**
- 1/2 **cup milk**
- 1/2 **cup all-purpose flour**
- 3/4 **cup dry bread crumbs**
- 1/2 **teaspoon garlic powder**
- 1 **teaspoon dried oregano**
- 1/4 **cup shredded Parmesan cheese**

1) Flatten chicken breasts to 1/8-in. thickness; spread butter on the insides. Sprinkle with thyme. Top with a slice of ham and cheese; roll up tightly. Wrap each with two slices of bacon and secure with toothpicks.

2) In a small bowl, beat eggs and milk. Place flour in another bowl. Combine the bread crumbs, garlic powder, oregano and cheese. Dip each chicken breast into egg mixture; coat with flour. Dip each again in egg mixture, then coat with crumbs.

3) Place on a greased baking sheet. Bake, uncovered, at 350° for 40-45 minutes or until chicken juices run clear. Remove toothpicks before serving.

Yield: 4 servings.

NUTRITION FACTS: 1 serving equals 883 calories, 51 g fat (23 g saturated fat), 320 mg cholesterol, 1,084 mg sodium, 30 g carbohydrate, 1 g fiber, 71 g protein.

FLATTENING CHICKEN BREASTS (OPTION 1)

Place boneless chicken breasts between two pieces of waxed paper or plastic wrap or in a resealable plastic bag. Starting in the center and working out to edges, pound lightly with the flat side of a meat mallet until the chicken is even in thickness.

CHICKEN KIEV

Chicken Kiev

Karin Erickson, Burney, California

From holiday suppers to potlucks, this is one of my most-requested meals. Folks love the mildly seasoned chicken breasts.

- 1/4 **cup butter, softened**
- 1 **tablespoon minced chives**
- 1 **garlic clove, minced**
- 6 **boneless skinless chicken breast halves (8 ounces *each*)**
- 3/4 **cup crushed cornflakes**
- 2 **tablespoons minced fresh parsley**
- 1/2 **teaspoon paprika**
- 1/3 **cup buttermilk**

Hot cooked rice, optional

1) In a small bowl, combine the butter, chives and garlic. Shape into 3-in. x 2-in. rectangle. Cover and freeze until firm, about 30 minutes.

2) Flatten each chicken breast to 1/4-in. thickness. Cut the butter mixture crosswise into six pieces; place one piece in center of each chicken breast. Fold long sides over butter; fold ends up and secure with a toothpick.

3) In a shallow dish, combine the cornflakes, parsley and paprika. Place buttermilk in another shallow dish. Dip the chicken into buttermilk, then coat evenly with cornflake mixture.

4) Place chicken seam side down in a greased 13-in. x 9-in. x 2-in. baking pan. Bake, uncovered, at 425° for 35-40 minutes or until no longer pink. Remove toothpicks before serving. Serve over rice if desired.

Yield: 6 servings.

NUTRITION FACTS: 1 serving equals 357 calories, 13 g fat (6 g saturated fat), 146 mg cholesterol, 281 mg sodium, 10 g carbohydrate, trace fiber, 47 g protein.

CRAB-STUFFED CHICKEN BREASTS

Crab-Stuffed Chicken Breasts

Therese Bechtel
Montgomery Village, Maryland

This elegant dish is often on the menu when I cook for guests. The versatile sauce is also delicious on pork chops and baked potatoes.

- 4 tablespoons butter, *divided*
- 1/4 cup all-purpose flour
- 1 cup chicken broth
- 3/4 cup milk
- 1/4 cup chopped onion
- 1 can (6 ounces) crabmeat, drained, flaked and cartilage removed
- 1 can (4 ounces) mushroom stems and pieces, drained
- 1/3 cup crushed saltines (about 10 crackers)
- 2 tablespoons minced fresh parsley
- 1/2 teaspoon salt

Dash pepper

- 4 boneless skinless chicken breast halves (6 ounces *each*)
- 1 cup (4 ounces) shredded Swiss cheese
- 1/2 teaspoon paprika

Additional minced fresh parsley, optional

Hot cooked rice, optional

1) In a small saucepan, melt 3 tablespoons butter. Stir in flour until smooth. Gradually stir in broth and milk. Bring to a boil; cook and stir for 2 minutes. Remove from the heat; set aside.

2) In a small skillet, saute onion in remaining butter until tender. Add the crab, mushrooms, cracker crumbs, parsley, salt, pepper and 2 tablespoons of the white sauce; heat through.

3) For each chicken breast, make a horizontal cut along one long side almost to the other side; leave chicken breasts attached at opposite side. Open breast so it lies flat; cover with plastic wrap and flatten chicken to 1/4-in. thickness. Remove plastic wrap.

4) Spoon about 1/2 cup of the crab mixture on each chicken breast. Fold in sides and roll up. Secure with a toothpick. Place in a greased 1-1/2-qt. baking dish. Top with remaining white sauce. Cover and bake at 350° for 30 minutes or until chicken juices run clear.

5) Sprinkle with the cheese and paprika. Bake, uncovered, 5 minutes longer or until cheese is melted. Remove toothpicks before serving. Sprinkle with parsley and serve with rice if desired.

Yield: 4 servings.

NUTRITION FACTS: 1 serving equals 520 calories, 26 g fat (14 g saturated fat), 193 mg cholesterol, 1,129 mg sodium, 15 g carbohydrate, 1 g fiber, 55 g protein.

FLATTENING CHICKEN BREASTS (OPTION 2)

1) Hold sharp knife parallel to cutting board and along one long side of breast; cut almost in half, leaving breast attached at one side.

2) Open breast so it lies flat; cover with plastic wrap. Using flat side of a meat mallet, lightly pound to 1/4-in. thickness.

3) Remove plastic wrap and stuff according to recipe.

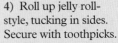

4) Roll up jelly roll-style, tucking in sides. Secure with toothpicks.

Chicken Supreme

Marlene Nutter, Thedford, Nebraska

Strips of Monterey Jack cheese tucked inside chicken make this entree extra special. Crushed croutons are a unique addition to the coating.

- 4 ounces Monterey Jack cheese
- 1/2 cup butter, softened
- 1 teaspoon minced fresh parsley
- 1 teaspoon dried oregano
- 1/2 to 1 teaspoon dried marjoram
- 8 boneless skinless chicken breast halves (6 ounces *each*)
- 1/2 teaspoon seasoned salt
- 1/2 cup all-purpose flour
- 2 eggs, beaten
- 1-3/4 cups crushed Caesar salad croutons
- 1/2 cup white wine *or* chicken broth

1) Cut cheese into eight 2-1/2-in. x 1-in. x 3/8-in. strips. In a bowl, combine the butter, parsley, oregano and marjoram; spread 1-1/2 teaspoons over each cheese strip. Cover and refrigerate cheese and remaining butter mixture at least 2 hours.

2) Flatten chicken to 1/8-in. thickness; sprinkle with seasoned salt. Place a cheese strip on each piece of chicken. Roll up and tuck in ends; secure with a toothpick. Coat chicken on all sides with flour. Dip in eggs, then coat with croutons.

3) Place seam side down in a greased 13-in. x 9-in. x 2-in. baking dish. Bake, uncovered, at 350° for 30 minutes.

4) In a saucepan, combine wine or broth and reserved butter mixture; heat until butter is melted. Pour over chicken. Bake 20-25 minutes longer or until chicken juices run clear. Remove toothpicks before serving.

Yield: 8 servings.

NUTRITION FACTS: 1 serving equals 436 calories, 23 g fat (12 g saturated fat), 193 mg cholesterol, 498 mg sodium, 12 g carbohydrate, 1 g fiber, 41 g protein.

Crispy Chicken Cutlets

Debra Smith, Brookfield, Missouri

These moist and tender cutlets feature a nutty coating and go especially well with egg noodles.

- 4 boneless skinless chicken breast halves (6 ounces *each*)
- 1 egg white
- 3/4 cup finely chopped pecans
- 3 tablespoons all-purpose flour
- 1/4 teaspoon salt
- 1/4 teaspoon pepper
- 1 tablespoon butter
- 1 tablespoon vegetable oil

1) Flatten chicken to 1/4-in. thickness. In a shallow bowl, lightly beat egg white. In another shallow bowl, combine the pecans, flour, salt and pepper. Dip chicken in egg white, then coat with pecan mixture. Let stand for 5 minutes.

2) In a large skillet, brown chicken in butter and oil over medium heat for 4-6 minutes on each side or until juices run clear.

Yield: 4 servings.

NUTRITION FACTS: 1 chicken breast half equals 418 calories, 26 g fat (5 g saturated fat), 102 mg cholesterol, 272 mg sodium, 8 g carbohydrate, 2 g fiber, 38 g protein.

■ *PECAN PARMESAN CHICKEN:* Combine 3 tablespoons ground pecans with 1/3 cup soft bread crumbs, 3 tablespoons grated Parmesan cheese, 3/4 teaspoon dried oregano, 1/4 teaspoon *each* seasoned salt and dried basil, dash pepper. Dip chicken in egg white beaten with 1 teaspoon cornstarch, then in pecan mixture. Cook as directed above.

Chicken Nuggets

Cathryn White, Newark, Delaware

With a crisp golden coating, these moist and tender bite-size pieces of chicken are greeted with enthusiasm whenever I serve them.

- 1 cup dry bread crumbs
- 1/2 cup grated Parmesan cheese
- 2 teaspoons dried basil
- 2 teaspoons dried thyme
- 2 teaspoons paprika
- 1 teaspoon salt
- 1 teaspoon pepper
- 3/4 cup butter, melted
- 2-1/2 pounds boneless skinless chicken breasts, cut into 1-inch cubes

1) In a shallow bowl, combine the bread crumbs, Parmesan cheese and seasonings. Place butter in another shallow bowl. Dip chicken in butter, then roll in bread crumb mixture.

2) Place in a greased 15-in. x 10-in. x 1-in. baking pan. Bake, uncovered, at 400° for 15-20 minutes or until juices run clear.

Yield: 8 servings.

NUTRITION FACTS: 1 serving equals 383 calories, 23 g fat (13 g saturated fat), 128 mg cholesterol, 747 mg sodium, 11 g carbohydrate, 1 g fiber, 33 g protein.

Chicken Parmigiana

Rhonda Schiel, Magnolia, Texas

A nicely seasoned breading coats the tender chicken breasts in this attractive entree. When I have extra time, I make my own herbed tomato sauce instead of using prepared spaghetti sauce.

- 1/2 cup dry bread crumbs
- 3 tablespoons grated Parmesan cheese
- 3/4 teaspoon Italian seasoning
- 1/2 teaspoon garlic powder
- 1/2 teaspoon salt
- 1/4 cup egg substitute
- 4 boneless skinless chicken breast halves (4 ounces *each*)
- 1 jar (26 ounces) meatless spaghetti sauce
- 3/4 cup shredded part-skim mozzarella cheese
- 1/4 cup shredded Parmesan cheese

1) In a shallow bowl, combine the bread crumbs, grated Parmesan cheese, Italian seasoning, garlic powder and salt. In another bowl, beat egg substitute. Dip chicken in egg substitute, then roll in crumbs.

2) Place in a 13-in. x 9-in. x 2-in. baking dish coated with nonstick cooking spray. Bake, uncovered, at 375° for 10 minutes. Turn chicken; bake for 10 minutes.

3) Pour spaghetti sauce over chicken; bake for 5 minutes. Sprinkle with cheeses; bake 10 minutes longer or until chicken juices run clear.

Yield: 4 servings.

Editor's Note: If you prefer, use 1 lightly beaten egg for the egg substitute.

NUTRITION FACTS: 1 serving equals 412 calories, 15 g fat (5 g saturated fat), 88 mg cholesterol, 1,420 mg sodium, 32 g carbohydrate, 5 g fiber, 37 g protein.

Baked Lemon Chicken

Marion Lowery, Medford, Oregon

Right out of the oven or cold the next day, this chicken is delicious. It's moist, tender and lemony with a nice crunch.

- 3 tablespoons butter, melted
- 2 tablespoons lemon juice
- 1 garlic clove, minced
- 1/2 teaspoon salt
- 1/4 teaspoon pepper
- 1/2 cup seasoned bread crumbs

- 4 boneless skinless chicken breast halves (4 ounces *each*)

1) In a shallow dish, combine the butter, lemon juice, garlic, salt and pepper. Place bread crumbs in another dish.

2) Dip chicken in butter mixture, then coat with crumbs. Place in a greased 13-in. x 9-in. x 2-in. baking dish. Drizzle with the remaining butter mixture.

3) Bake, uncovered, at 350° for 25-30 minutes or until juices run clear.

Yield: 4 servings.

NUTRITION FACTS: 1 serving equals 255 calories, 12 g fat (6 g saturated fat), 86 mg cholesterol, 652 mg sodium, 11 g carbohydrate, 1 g fiber, 25 g protein.

BRUSCHETTA CHICKEN

Bruschetta Chicken

Carolin Cattoi-Demkiw, Lethbridge, Alberta

My husband and I enjoy serving this tasty chicken to company as well as family. It looks like we fussed, but it's fast and easy to fix. I have made it often, and it usually prompts recipe requests.

- 1/2 cup all-purpose flour
- 2 eggs, lightly beaten
- 4 boneless skinless chicken breast halves (6 ounces *each*)
- 1/4 cup grated Parmesan cheese
- 1/4 cup dry bread crumbs
- 1 tablespoon butter, melted
- 2 large tomatoes, seeded and chopped

3 tablespoons minced fresh basil
2 garlic cloves, minced
1 tablespoon olive oil
1/2 teaspoon salt
1/4 teaspoon pepper

1) Place flour and eggs in separate shallow bowls. Dip chicken in flour, then in eggs. Place in a greased 13-in. x 9-in. x 2-in. baking dish. Combine the Parmesan cheese, bread crumbs and butter; sprinkle over chicken.

2) Loosely cover baking dish with foil. Bake at 375° for 20 minutes. Uncover; bake 5-10 minutes longer or until top is browned.

3) Meanwhile, in a bowl, combine the remaining ingredients. Spoon over the chicken. Return to the oven for 3-5 minutes or until tomato mixture is heated through.

Yield: 4 servings.

NUTRITION FACTS: 1 topped chicken breast equals 380 calories, 14 g fat (5 g saturated fat), 185 mg cholesterol, 589 mg sodium, 19 g carbohydrate, 2 g fiber, 42 g protein.

CREOLE SKILLET DINNER

Creole Skillet Dinner
Bonnie Brann, Pasco, Washington

This colorful dish replaced my traditional turkey at one holiday dinner. It's a recipe from my former neighbor.

    4 cups chicken broth
2-1/2 cups uncooked long grain rice
    1 cup chopped red onion
1-1/2 teaspoons minced garlic, *divided*
1-1/4 teaspoons chili powder
    1 teaspoon salt
1/2 teaspoon ground turmeric

1/4 teaspoon pepper
  1 bay leaf
  1 medium sweet red pepper, julienned
  1 medium green pepper, julienned
  2 green onions, sliced
  1 teaspoon minced fresh parsley
1/2 teaspoon dried basil
1/2 teaspoon dried thyme
1/4 teaspoon hot pepper sauce
  2 tablespoons butter
  1 cup sliced fresh mushrooms
  1 medium tomato, chopped
  1 cup frozen peas
  1 pound boneless skinless chicken breasts, thinly sliced
  2 tablespoons lemon juice
1/3 cup sliced almonds, toasted

1) In a saucepan, bring the broth, rice, onion, 1 teaspoon garlic, chili powder, salt, turmeric, pepper and bay leaf to a boil. Reduce heat; cover and simmer 20 minutes or until rice is tender. Discard bay leaf.

2) In a large skillet, cook and stir the peppers, onions, parsley, basil, thyme, hot pepper sauce and remaining garlic in butter over medium-high heat for 2 minutes. Add the mushrooms; cook until peppers are crisp-tender. Add tomato and peas; heat through. Remove from the heat. Add rice; keep warm.

3) In another skillet, cook and stir chicken in lemon juice over medium-high heat until chicken juices run clear. Add to rice mixture; toss. Sprinkle with almonds.

Yield: 6 servings.

NUTRITION FACTS: 1-1/4 cups equals 491 calories, 10 g fat (3 g saturated fat), 52 mg cholesterol, 1,131 mg sodium, 75 g carbohydrate, 5 g fiber, 26 g protein.

STORING LEFTOVERS

Any perishable food should not stand at room temperature for longer than 2 hours. So within 2 hours of roasting, the poultry meat should be removed from the carcass and put away. If desired, slice, cube or cut the meat into strips. Leftover poultry parts or pieces can be packaged without being cut up.

Meat and leftover poultry casseroles can be refrigerated for 3-4 days, stuffing for up to 3 days and gravy for 2 days. Stuffing can be frozen for 1 to 2 months, and meat and casseroles for up to 6 months. Homemade gravy does not freeze well.

CREAMY BRAISED CHICKEN

Creamy Braised Chicken
Pat Patty, Spring, Texas

A smooth, delicate cream sauce gives special taste to these tender chicken breasts. This dish is so rich tasting, you'll want to serve it to company.

- 1/2 **pound pearl onions**
- 1 **cup thinly sliced onion**
- 1/2 **cup thinly sliced carrot**
- 1/2 **cup thinly sliced celery**
- 1 **tablespoon plus 2 teaspoons butter,** *divided*
- 6 **boneless skinless chicken breast halves (4 ounces** *each***)**
- 1 **cup chardonnay** *or* **other dry white wine** *or* **reduced-sodium chicken broth**
- 1-1/3 **cups reduced-sodium chicken broth**
- 1 **tablespoon minced fresh parsley**
- 1 **teaspoon salt**
- 1 **teaspoon dried thyme**
- 1/8 **teaspoon white pepper**
- 1 **bay leaf**
- 3 **tablespoons all-purpose flour**
- 1/2 **cup fat-free evaporated milk**
- 1/2 **pound fresh mushrooms, quartered**

1) In a Dutch oven, bring 6 cups water to a boil. Add pearl onions; boil for 3 minutes. Drain and rinse in cold water; peel and set aside.

2) In the same pan, saute sliced onion, carrot and celery in 1 tablespoon butter until tender. Remove vegetables; set aside. Add chicken to pan; brown on both sides. Remove and keep warm.

3) Add wine or broth; simmer until reduced to 1/2 cup. Stir in the chicken broth and seasonings. Return chicken to pan; cover and simmer for 5 minutes or until juices run clear. Remove chicken to a serving platter; keep warm.

4) Combine flour and milk until smooth; gradually stir into pan. Bring to a boil; cook and stir for 2 minutes or until thickened. Return vegetables to pan. Remove from the heat; cover and set aside.

5) In a nonstick skillet, saute reserved pearl onions in remaining butter until tender. Remove and set aside. In the same pan, saute mushrooms until tender.

6) Add onions and mushrooms to serving platter. Discard bay leaf from sauce; spoon over chicken and vegetables.

Yield: 6 servings.

NUTRITION FACTS: 1 chicken breast half with 2/3 cup sauce equals 273 calories, 5 g fat (3 g saturated fat), 75 mg cholesterol, 748 mg sodium, 18 g carbohydrate, 2 g fiber, 31 g protein.

Chicken with Apple Cream Sauce
Victoria Casey, Coeur d'Alene, Idaho

Topping chicken with an apple cream sauce is a unique way to serve it. It's impressive, and my family and friends think the sauce is absolutely wonderful.

- 4 **boneless skinless chicken breast halves (6 ounces** *each***)**
- 1 **tablespoon vegetable oil**
- 1 **cup apple juice**
- 1 **teaspoon lemon juice**
- 1/4 **to 1/2 teaspoon dried rosemary, crushed**
- 1/2 **teaspoon salt**
- 1/8 **teaspoon pepper**
- 1 **tablespoon cornstarch**
- 1/2 **cup heavy whipping cream**
- 1 **tablespoon minced fresh parsley**
  Hot cooked rice

1) In a skillet, brown the chicken in oil over medium heat for 4 minutes on each side. Combine the apple juice, lemon juice, rosemary, salt and pepper; pour over chicken.

2) Reduce heat; cover and simmer for 10 minutes or until chicken juices run clear. Remove chicken and keep warm.

3) Combine cornstarch and cream until smooth; stir into cooking liquid in skillet. Bring to a boil; cook and stir for 2 minutes or until thickened. Add

parsley. Return chicken to skillet and heat through. Serve over rice.

Yield: 4 servings.

NUTRITION FACTS: 1 chicken breast half with 1/4 cup sauce (calculated without rice) equals 353 calories, 18 g fat (8 g saturated fat), 135 mg cholesterol, 391 mg sodium, 10 g carbohydrate, trace fiber, 35 g protein.

Szechuan Chicken Noodle Toss
Carol Roane, Sarasota, Florida

My family loves Chinese food, so I came up with this quick-and-easy, lightened-up recipe to use leftover chicken, pork or beef.

- 4 **quarts water**
- 6 **ounces uncooked thin spaghetti**
- 1 **package (16 ounces) frozen Oriental vegetables**
- 1 **tablespoon reduced-fat stick margarine**
- 1 **pound boneless skinless chicken breasts, cut into 2-inch strips**
- 2 **garlic cloves, minced**
- 1/8 **teaspoon crushed red pepper flakes**
- 1 **tablespoon canola oil**
- 1/3 **cup stir-fry sauce**
- 3 **green onions, chopped**

1) In a Dutch oven, bring water to a boil. Add spaghetti; cook for 4 minutes. Add vegetables; cook 3-4 minutes longer or until spaghetti and vegetables are tender. Drain. Toss with margarine; set aside and keep warm.

2) In a nonstick skillet, stir-fry the chicken, garlic and red pepper flakes in oil until chicken is no longer pink. Add stir-fry sauce; heat through. Add onions and spaghetti mixture; toss to coat.

Yield: 4 servings.

Editor's Note: This recipe was tested with Parkay Light stick margarine.

NUTRITION FACTS: 1-1/2 cups equals 394 calories, 7 g fat (1 g saturated fat), 66 mg cholesterol, 831 mg sodium, 44 g carbohydrate, 5 g fiber, 35 g protein.

Teriyaki Chicken
Jean Clark, Albion, Maine

I developed my own teriyaki sauce that coats the chicken before it bakes up beautifully.

- 3/4 **cup soy sauce**
- 1/4 **cup vegetable oil**
- 3 **tablespoons brown sugar**
- 2 **tablespoons sherry, optional**

- 1/2 **teaspoon ground ginger**
- 1/2 **teaspoon garlic powder**
- 12 **chicken drumsticks (4 ounces** *each***)**

1) In a large resealable plastic bag, combine the soy sauce, oil, brown sugar, sherry if desired, ginger and garlic powder; add drumsticks. Seal bag and turn to coat; cover and refrigerate 1 hour or overnight, turning occasionally.

2) Drain and discard marinade. Place chicken in a single layer on a foil-lined baking sheet. Bake, uncovered, at 375° for 35-45 minutes or until a meat thermometer reads 180° and the juices run clear.

Yield: 6 servings.

NUTRITION FACTS: 2 drumsticks equals 483 calories, 23 g fat (6 g saturated fat), 202 mg cholesterol, 1,098 mg sodium, 3 g carbohydrate, trace fiber, 62 g protein.

Chicken Piccata
Linda Carver, Cedar Rapids, Iowa

A blend of flour, garlic powder and paprika lightly coats the chicken to give it flavor and keep it moist at the same time.

- 1/2 **cup all-purpose flour**
- 1/2 **teaspoon garlic powder**
- 1/2 **teaspoon paprika**
- 2 **eggs**
- 6 **tablespoons lemon juice,** *divided*
- 4 **boneless skinless chicken breast halves (6 ounces** *each***)**
- 1/2 **cup butter**
- 2 **teaspoons chicken bouillon granules**
- 1 **cup water**

1) In a shallow bowl, combine the flour, garlic powder and paprika; set aside. In a another shallow bowl, beat eggs and 2 tablespoons lemon juice. Dip chicken in egg mixture, then coat with flour mixture.

2) In a large skillet, brown chicken on both sides in butter over medium-high heat. Combine bouillon, water and remaining lemon juice; pour over chicken. Bring to a boil. Reduce heat; cover and simmer for 20 minutes or until juices run clear.

Yield: 4 servings.

NUTRITION FACTS: 1 chicken breast half with 3 tablespoons sauce equals 488 calories, 29 g fat (16 g saturated fat), 262 mg cholesterol, 765 mg sodium, 15 g carbohydrate, 1 g fiber, 40 g protein.

Chicken Stroganoff

Lori Borrowman, Schenectady, New York

When I prepare this meal, I often tell people it's beef Stroganoff. Because of its convincing appearance and taste, they're surprised when I later confide that it's actually chicken.

- 1 pound fresh mushrooms, sliced
- 1 large onion, chopped
- 2 tablespoons butter
- 1-1/2 pounds boneless skinless chicken breasts, cut into 2-inch strips
- 1/4 cup browning sauce
- 1-1/3 cups reduced-sodium beef broth, *divided*
- 1 cup white wine *or* additional reduced-sodium beef broth
- 2 tablespoons ketchup
- 2 garlic cloves, minced
- 1 teaspoon salt
- 3 tablespoons all-purpose flour
- 1 cup (8 ounces) fat-free sour cream
- 6 cups cooked no-yolk noodles

1) In a large nonstick skillet, saute mushrooms and onion in butter until tender. Remove; set aside.

2) In the same skillet, cook chicken with browning sauce until browned. Add 1 cup broth, wine or broth, ketchup, garlic and salt. Bring to a boil. Reduce heat; cover and simmer for 15 minutes.

3) Combine flour and remaining 1/3 cup broth until smooth; stir into chicken mixture. Add reserved mushroom mixture. Bring to a boil; cook and stir for 2 minutes or until thickened. Reduce heat to low. Stir in sour cream; heat through (do not boil). Serve over noodles.

Yield: 6 servings.

NUTRITION FACTS: 1 cup cup chicken mixture with 1 cup noodles equals 535 calories, 7 g fat (3 g saturated fat), 80 mg cholesterol, 1,339 mg sodium, 66 g carbohydrate, 4 g fiber, 41 g protein.

BONING CHICKEN BREASTS

Insert a small boning or paring knife between the ribs and breast meat. Pressing knife along bones, cut to remove meat. If desired, remove skin by pulling from breast meat.

STIR-FRIED CHICKEN AND RICE NOODLES

Stir-Fried Chicken and Rice Noodles

Kim Pettipas, Oromocto, New Brunswick

This is a great dish to showcase rice noodles. Don't let the ingredients fool you; the stir-fry is very simple and features an Asian flair.

- 2-1/2 teaspoons cornstarch
- 1/3 cup reduced-sodium soy sauce
- 1/4 cup white wine *or* reduced-sodium chicken broth
- 2 teaspoons sesame oil
- 1-1/2 pounds boneless skinless chicken breasts, cut into 1-inch cubes
- 1/2 cup reduced-sodium chicken broth
- 2 tablespoons sugar
- 1 tablespoon Worcestershire sauce
- 3/4 teaspoon chili powder
- 3 ounces uncooked Asian rice noodles
- 4 teaspoons canola oil, *divided*
- 3 cups fresh broccoli florets
- 2/3 cup chopped green onions
- 3 garlic cloves, minced
- 2 teaspoons minced fresh gingerroot
- 1/4 cup unsalted dry roasted peanuts

1) In a small bowl, combine the cornstarch, soy sauce, wine or broth and sesame oil until smooth. Pour 1/4 cup marinade into a large resealable plastic bag; add the chicken. Seal bag and turn to coat; refrigerate for 20 minutes.

2) Add the broth, sugar, Worcestershire sauce and chili powder to remaining marinade; set aside.

3) Cook the rice noodles according to package directions. Meanwhile, drain and discard the marinade from chicken. In a large nonstick skillet or wok, stir-fry chicken in 2 teaspoons canola oil until juices run clear; remove and keep warm.

4) Stir-fry broccoli in remaining canola oil for 5 minutes. Add the onions, garlic and ginger; stir-fry 3-5 minutes longer or until broccoli is tender. Return chicken to the pan.

5) Stir reserved broth mixture and stir into pan. Bring to a boil; cook and stir for 2 minutes or until thickened. Drain noodles; toss with chicken mixture. Garnish with peanuts.

Yield: 6 servings.

NUTRITION FACTS: 1 cup equals 293 calories, 10 g fat (2 g saturated fat), 63 mg cholesterol, 498 mg sodium, 22 g carbohydrate, 2 g fiber, 27 g protein.

Paella
Taste of Home Test Kitchen

Paella is a Spanish dish traditionally made with rice, saffron, a variety of meat and shellfish, garlic, onions, peas, tomatoes and other vegetables. It's named for the wide, shallow pan it's cooked in, but you can cook it on the stovetop with delicious results.

      4 cups chicken broth
  2-1/2 cups uncooked long grain rice
      1 cup chopped onion
      4 garlic cloves, minced, *divided*
      1 teaspoon salt
    1/2 teaspoon ground turmeric
    1/4 teaspoon pepper
      1 bay leaf
      1 large green pepper, julienned
      3 green onions, sliced
      1 teaspoon minced fresh parsley
      1 teaspoon dried thyme
    1/4 teaspoon hot pepper sauce
      2 tablespoons olive oil
      1 cup sliced fresh mushrooms
      2 medium tomatoes, chopped
      2 cups frozen peas
    1/2 pound uncooked medium shrimp, peeled and deveined
      2 tablespoons lemon juice

     1 pound boneless skinless chicken breasts, thinly sliced

1) In a saucepan, combine the broth, rice, onion, half of the garlic, salt, turmeric, pepper and bay leaf; bring to a boil. Reduce heat; cover and simmer for 20 minutes or until rice is tender.

2) Meanwhile, in a large skillet, saute the green pepper, onions, parsley, thyme, hot pepper sauce and remaining garlic in oil for 2 minutes. Add mushrooms. Cook until green pepper is crisp-tender. Add tomatoes and peas; heat through.

3) Discard bay leaf; add rice mixture to vegetable mixture and keep warm. In a nonstick skillet, cook and stir shrimp in lemon juice for 2 minutes.

4) Add chicken; cook until chicken is no longer pink and shrimp has turned pink, about 3-5 minutes. Add to rice mixture; toss.

Yield: 10-12 servings.

NUTRITION FACTS: 1 serving equals 258 calories, 4 g fat (1 g saturated fat), 49 mg cholesterol, 591 mg sodium, 39 g carbohydrate, 3 g fiber, 16 g protein.

Hawaiian Baked Chicken
Leona Callen, Anna Maria, Florida

Here's a sweet and tangy way to dress up chicken. Pineapple and brown mustard pair perfectly for marinating the poultry.

    12 boneless skinless chicken thighs (4 ounces *each*)
     2 cans (8 ounces *each*) unsweetened crushed pineapple, undrained
   1/4 cup sherry *or* chicken broth
   1/4 cup spicy brown mustard
   1/4 cup honey
     2 tablespoons butter, melted
   1/2 teaspoon paprika

1) Arrange chicken in a shallow baking dish coated with nonstick cooking spray. In a small bowl, combine the pineapple, sherry or broth, mustard, honey and butter; mix well.

2) Spoon over chicken; sprinkle with paprika. Bake, uncovered, at 400° for 35-45 minutes or until a meat thermometer reads 180°.

Yield: 6 servings.

NUTRITION FACTS: 2 chicken thighs with about 1/4 cup sauce equals 285 calories, 10 g fat (4 g saturated fat), 118 mg cholesterol, 288 mg sodium, 22 g carbohydrate, 1 g fiber, 26 g protein.

BAKED CHICKEN AND ACORN SQUASH

Baked Chicken and Acorn Squash
Connie Svoboda, Elko, Minnesota

This main dish is ideal for harvesttime with its colorful acorn squash and sweet peaches. The fragrance of rosemary-seasoned chicken baking is heavenly.

2	small acorn squash (1-1/4 pounds)
2	to 4 garlic cloves, minced
2	tablespoons vegetable oil, *divided*
4	chicken drumsticks (4 ounces *each*)
4	chicken thighs (4 ounces *each*)
1/4	cup packed brown sugar
1	teaspoon salt
1	tablespoon minced fresh rosemary *or* 1 teaspoon dried rosemary, crushed
1	can (15-1/4 ounces) sliced peaches, undrained

1) Cut squash in half lengthwise; discard seeds. Cut each half widthwise into 1/2-in. slices; discard ends. Place slices in an ungreased 13-in. x 9-in. x 2-in. baking dish. Sprinkle with garlic and drizzle with 1 tablespoon oil.

2) In a large skillet, brown chicken in remaining oil. Arrange chicken over squash. Combine the brown sugar, salt and rosemary; sprinkle over chicken. Bake, uncovered, at 350° for 45 minutes, basting with pan juices twice.

3) Pour peaches over chicken and squash. Bake, uncovered, 15 minutes longer or until the chicken juices run clear and the peaches are heated through.

Yield: 4 servings.

NUTRITION FACTS: 1 serving equals 624 calories, 21 g fat (5 g saturated fat), 147 mg cholesterol, 740 mg sodium, 64 g carbohydrate, 5 g fiber, 45 g protein.

Poppy Seed Chicken
Ernestine Plasek, Houston, Texas

This recipe is the ideal solution when you wonder what to do with leftover cooked chicken. It's a favorite that's been in my family for years.

1	tablespoon butter
1/2	pound fresh mushrooms, sliced
5	cups cubed cooked chicken
1	can (10-3/4 ounces) condensed cream of chicken soup, undiluted
1	cup (8 ounces) sour cream
1	jar (2 ounces) diced pimientos, drained

TOPPING:

1/2	cup butter, melted
1-1/3	cups finely crushed butter-flavored crackers
2	teaspoons poppy seeds

1) In a large skillet, melt butter. Saute mushrooms until tender. Stir in the chicken, soup, sour cream and pimientos. Spoon mixture into a greased 2-qt. baking dish.

2) In a bowl, combine topping ingredients. Sprinkle over chicken. Bake at 350° for 20-25 minutes or until heated through and topping is browned.

Yield: 6 servings.

NUTRITION FACTS: 1 serving equals 619 calories, 41 g fat (19 g saturated fat), 181 mg cholesterol, 848 mg sodium, 21 g carbohydrate, 2 g fiber, 39 g protein.

Phyllo Chicken
Joyce Mummau, Mt. Airy, Maryland

I streamlined this from another recipe, and the phyllo is fun to work with. Its flakiness turns everyday ingredients into a special entree.

1/2	cup butter, melted, *divided*
12	sheets phyllo dough (14 inches x 9 inches)
3	cups diced cooked chicken
1/2	pound sliced bacon, cooked and crumbled
1	package (10 ounces) frozen chopped broccoli, thawed and drained

2 cups (8 ounces each) shredded cheddar cheese *or* Swiss cheese

6 eggs

1 cup half-and-half cream

1/2 cup milk

1 teaspoon salt

1/2 teaspoon pepper

1) Brush sides and bottom of a 13-in. x 9-in. x 2-in. baking dish with some of the melted butter. Place one sheet of phyllo in bottom of dish; lightly brush with butter; repeat with five more sheets of phyllo. Keep remaining phyllo covered with plastic wrap and a damp towel to prevent it from drying out.

2) In a bowl, combine chicken, bacon, broccoli and cheese; spread evenly over phyllo in baking dish. In another bowl, whisk together eggs, cream, milk, salt and pepper; pour over chicken mixture.

3) Cover filling with one sheet of phyllo; brush with butter. Repeat with remaining phyllo dough. Brush top with remaining butter.

4) Bake, uncovered, at 375° for 35-40 minutes or until a knife inserted near the center comes out clean. Let stand for 5-10 minutes before cutting.

Yield: 12 servings.

NUTRITION FACTS: 1 serving equals 373 calories, 24 g fat (13 g saturated fat), 195 mg cholesterol, 659 mg sodium, 16 g carbohydrate, 1 g fiber, 23 g protein.

SWEET SMOKY CHICKEN LEGS

Sweet Smoky Chicken Legs
Jane MacKinnis, Eden, Maryland

This is so easy! Just layer the ingredients in the baking dish, and a wonderful meal is ready in about an hour.

2 medium onions, sliced

3 pounds chicken legs

1-1/2 to 2 teaspoons hickory smoked salt

1/2 cup ketchup

1/2 cup maple syrup

1/4 cup vinegar

2 tablespoons prepared mustard

1) Place onions in greased 13-in. x 9-in. x 2-in. baking dish; arrange chicken in a single layer over onions. Sprinkle with salt.

2) Combine remaining ingredients and pour over all, completely coating chicken.

3) Bake, uncovered, at 350° for 1 hour or until juices run clear, basting several times.

Yield: 6 servings.

NUTRITION FACTS: 1 serving equals 345 calories, 12 g fat (3 g saturated fat), 94 mg cholesterol, 973 mg sodium, 28 g carbohydrate, 1 g fiber, 30 g protein.

Greek Chicken Salad
Donna Smith, Palisade, Colorado

Even if you or your family aren't garlic lovers, I encourage you to use the full measurement of garlic and oregano for the proper flavorings. I receive nothing but raves when I serve this salad.

3 cups cubed cooked chicken

2 medium cucumbers, peeled, seeded and chopped

1 cup crumbled feta cheese

2/3 cup sliced pitted black olives

1/4 cup minced fresh parsley

1 cup mayonnaise

3 garlic cloves, minced

1/2 cup plain yogurt

1 tablespoon dried oregano

1) In a large bowl, combine the chicken, cucumbers, cheese, olives and parsley. In a small bowl, combine remaining ingredients. Toss with chicken mixture.

2) Cover and refrigerate for several hours before serving.

Yield: 7 servings.

NUTRITION FACTS: 3/4 cup equals 426 calories, 34 g fat (7 g saturated fat), 76 mg cholesterol, 499 mg sodium, 6 g carbohydrate, 2 g fiber, 22 g protein.

Cheesy Chicken Crepes

Martha McCool, Jacksonville, Florida

While it may sound like an odd combination, the crepes make a delicious wrapping for the chicken, mushroom and cheese mixture.

- 1 cup milk
- 3 eggs
- 2/3 cup all-purpose flour
- 1/2 teaspoon salt

FILLING:

- 1/2 pound thinly sliced fresh mushrooms
- 1/3 cup sliced green onions
- 2 tablespoons butter
- 1/2 cup all-purpose flour
- 1/2 teaspoon dried rosemary, crushed
- 1/2 teaspoon salt
- 1/2 teaspoon pepper
- 1/4 teaspoon garlic powder
- 3/4 cup mayonnaise
- 2 cups milk, *divided*
- 1-1/2 cups (6 ounces) shredded cheddar cheese, *divided*
- 2 cups chopped cooked chicken

1) In a large mixing bowl, combine the milk and eggs. Add flour and salt to milk mixture and mix well. Let stand for 15 minutes.

2) Heat a lightly greased 8-in. nonstick skillet; pour 1/4 cup batter into the center of skillet. Lift and tilt pan to evenly coat bottom. Cook until top appears dry; turn and cook 15-20 seconds longer. Remove to a wire rack. Repeat with remaining batter; grease skillet as needed. When cool, stack crepes with waxed paper or paper towels in between.

3) For filling, in a large skillet, saute mushrooms and onions in butter until mushrooms are tender; set aside. In a 2-qt. saucepan, combine the flour and seasonings. Stir in mayonnaise until blended.

4) Cook over medium-low heat for 2-3 minutes. Gradually stir in 1-1/2 cups milk. Bring to a boil over medium-low heat; cook and stir for 2 minutes or until thickened. Add 1 cup cheese; stir until melted. Remove from the heat; add chicken and the mushroom mixture.

5) Spoon 1/3 cup chicken mixture down the center of each crepe. Roll up and place seam side down in a greased 13-in. x 9-in. x 2-in. baking dish.

6) In a small saucepan, heat remaining milk and cheese over medium-low heat until cheese is melted, stirring constantly. Pour over crepes. Bake, uncovered, at 350° for 15-20 minutes or until heated through.

Yield: 6 servings.

NUTRITION FACTS: 2 filled crepes equals 635 calories, 44 g fat (16 g saturated fat), 215 mg cholesterol, 886 mg sodium, 28 g carbohydrate, 1 g fiber, 30 g protein.

Baked Chimichangas

Angela Oelschlaeger, Tonganoxie, Kansas

Usually chimichangas are deep-fried, so my baked version is healthier as well as delicious. You can omit the chilies for less heat.

- 2-1/2 cups shredded cooked chicken breast
- 1 cup salsa
- 1 small onion, chopped
- 3/4 teaspoon ground cumin
- 1/2 teaspoon dried oregano
- 6 flour tortillas (10 inches), warmed
- 3/4 cup shredded reduced-fat cheddar cheese
- 1 cup reduced-sodium chicken broth
- 2 teaspoon chicken bouillon granules
- 1/8 teaspoon pepper
- 1/4 cup all-purpose flour
- 1 cup fat-free half-and-half cream
- 1 can (4 ounces) chopped green chilies

1) In a nonstick skillet, simmer first five ingredients until heated through and most of liquid evaporates. Place 1/2 cup chicken mixture down the center of each tortilla; top with 2 tablespoons cheese.

2) Fold sides and ends over filling; roll up. Place seam side down in a 13-in. x 9-in. x 2-in. baking dish coated with nonstick cooking spray. Bake, uncovered, at 425° for 15 minutes or until browned.

3) In a saucepan, heat broth, bouillon and pepper until bouillon is dissolved. Combine flour and cream until smooth; stir into the broth. Bring to a boil; cook and stir for 2 minutes or until thickened. Stir in chilies; heat through. To serve, cut chimichangas in half; spoon sauce over top.

Yield: 6 servings.

NUTRITION FACTS: 1 chimichanga with 1/3 cup sauce equals 423 calories, 9 g fat (3 g saturated fat), 57 mg cholesterol, 1,326 mg sodium, 47 g carbohydrate, 7 g fiber, 32 g protein.

CLASSIC STUFFED TURKEY

Stuffing Tips

You'll want to prepare about 3/4 cup stuffing for every 1 pound of poultry. Try using sauteed vegetables, cooked meats or egg substitute in place of fresh eggs.

Begin stuffing preparation ahead of time if desired. For example, chop and saute vegetables. Make bread cubes or measure out store-bought stuffing croutons. Combine seasonings. Store wet ingredients separate from dry, and store perishable items in the refrigerator.

Wait until just before you are ready to stuff the bird to heat the broth or water for the stuffing and combine all the ingredients.

Stuff the poultry just before you are ready to bake. Loosely spoon stuffing into the neck and body cavities to allow for expansion as the poultry roasts. See Stuffing, Roasting and Carving a Whole Turkey on page 178.

Stuffed poultry requires longer roasting time—add 15 to 45 minutes to the time unstuffed poultry takes.

The internal temperature of the stuffing must reach 165° in order to be fully cooked. If the bird is completely cooked and the stuffing has not reached 165°, remove from bird and transfer to a baking dish. Continue baking the stuffing until it reaches 165°.

Bake stuffing in a casserole dish as the poultry bakes. See specific recipes for baking directions.

Cover the whole bird and let it stand for 10-20 minutes before removing the stuffing. Remove all stuffing and store any leftovers in separate containers in the refrigerator.

Classic Stuffed Turkey
Kathi Graham, Naperville, Illinois

This moist dressing features fresh mushrooms, and its flavor nicely complements the tender and juicy slices of oven-roasted turkey.

- 2   large onions, chopped
- 2   celery ribs, chopped
- 1/2   pound fresh mushrooms, sliced
- 1/2   cup butter
- 1   can (14-1/2 ounces) chicken broth
- 1/3   cup minced fresh parsley
- 2   teaspoons rubbed sage
- 1   teaspoon salt
- 1   teaspoon poultry seasoning
- 1/2   teaspoon pepper
- 12   cups unseasoned stuffing cubes

Warm water
- 1   turkey (14 to 16 pounds)

Melted butter

1) In a large skillet, saute the onions, celery and mushrooms in butter until tender. Add broth and seasonings; mix well.

2) Place bread cubes in a large bowl; add mushroom mixture and toss to coat. Stir in enough warm water to reach desired moistness. Just before baking, loosely stuff turkey. Place any remaining stuffing in a greased baking dish; cover and refrigerate. Remove dish from refrigerator 30 minutes before baking.

3) Skewer turkey openings; tie drumsticks together with kitchen string. Place breast side up on a rack in a roasting pan. Brush with melted butter.

4) Bake turkey, uncovered, at 325° for 3-3/4 to 4-1/2 hours or until a meat thermometer reads 180° for the turkey and 165° for the stuffing, basting occasionally with pan drippings. (Cover loosely with foil if turkey browns too quickly.)

5) Bake additional stuffing, covered, for 30 minutes. Uncover; bake 10 minutes longer or until lightly browned.

6) Cover turkey with foil and let stand for 20 minutes before removing stuffing and carving. If desired, thicken pan drippings for gravy.

Yield: 12 servings (10 cups stuffing).

NUTRITION FACTS: 1 serving equals 571 calories, 26 g fat (11 g saturated fat), 153 mg cholesterol, 961 mg sodium, 42 g carbohydrate, 4 g fiber, 44 g protein.

Corn Bread Dressing

Norma Poole, Auburndale, Florida

Nothing gets the family hanging around like the aroma of this savory dressing baking alongside the turkey.

- 2-1/2 cups chopped celery
- 1-1/4 cups chopped onions
- 10 tablespoons butter
- 7-1/2 cups coarsely crumbled corn bread
- 2-1/2 cups soft bread crumbs
- 4 teaspoons rubbed sage
- 4 teaspoons poultry seasoning
- 2 eggs, lightly beaten
- 1-1/3 cups chicken broth

1) In a large skillet, saute celery and onion in butter until tender; transfer to a large bowl. Add the corn bread, bread crumbs, sage and poultry seasoning. Combine egg and broth; add to corn bread mixture, stirring gently to mix.

2) Transfer to a greased 2-qt. baking dish. Cover and bake at 325° for 30 minutes. Uncover; bake 10 minutes longer or until a thermometer reads 165° and stuffing is lightly browned.

Yield: 12 servings (9 cups stuffing).

Editor's Note: To stuff poultry, substitute 1/2 cup egg substitute for the eggs. This is suitable to stuff a 12- to 14-pound turkey.

NUTRITION FACTS: 3/4 cup equals 277 calories, 12 g fat (6 g saturated fat), 61 mg cholesterol, 683 mg sodium, 35 g carbohydrate, 3 g fiber, 6 g protein.

Apple Almond Stuffing

Laurel McLennan, Medicine Hat, Alberta

Everyone always enjoys the combination of unique ingredients in this recipe. The currants and raisins give it a nice, sweet flavor.

- 1 loaf (1 pound) sliced bread
- 3 medium onions, chopped
- 3 medium tart apples, peeled and chopped
- 1-1/2 cups diced fully cooked ham
- 1 cup sliced celery
- 1 tablespoon dried savory
- 2 teaspoons grated lemon peel
- 1-1/2 teaspoon grated orange peel
- 1 teaspoon salt
- 1/2 teaspoon pepper
- 1/2 teaspoon fennel seed, crushed
- 1/2 cup butter
- 1-1/2 cups slivered almonds, toasted
- 1/2 cup dried currants
- 1 cup chicken broth
- 1/2 cup apple juice

1) Cut bread into 1/2-in. cubes and place in a single layer on ungreased baking sheets. Bake at 225° for 30-40 minutes or until partially dried, tossing occasionally.

2) Meanwhile, in a large skillet, saute the onions, apple, ham, celery and seasonings in butter for 15 minutes or until onions and apples are tender. Transfer to a large bowl. Add the bread cubes, almonds, currants, broth and juice; toss well.

3) Place in a greased 3-qt. baking dish. Cover and bake at 325° for 1 hour. Uncover; bake for 10 minutes longer or until heated through and lightly browned.

Yield: 16 servings (12 cups stuffing).

Editor's Note: This is suitable to stuff a 14- to 16-pound turkey.

NUTRITION FACTS: 3/4 cup equals 248 calories, 13 g fat (4 g saturated fat), 23 mg cholesterol, 592 mg sodium, 27 g carbohydrate, 3 g fiber, 8 g protein.

Sausage Pecan Stuffing

Keri Scofield Lawson, Fullerton, California

Sweet, savory, crunchy and spicy ingredients make this a fabulous turkey stuffing. Leftover stuffing could be a meal in itself!

- 1 pound bulk pork sausage
- 2 large onions, chopped
- 2 packages (6 ounces *each*) herb stuffing mix
- 1 package (15 ounces) golden raisins
- 1 cup pecan halves
- 6 celery ribs, diced
- 1/4 teaspoon *each* salt, garlic powder, caraway seeds, curry powder, dried basil, dried oregano, poultry seasoning and pepper
- 2-1/2 cups chicken broth

1) In a large skillet, cook sausage and onions over medium heat until meat is no longer pink; drain. Add herb packet from the stuffing mixes. Stir in the raisins, pecans, celery and seasonings; cook for 10 minutes. Add stuffing mixes and broth; mix well. Cook and stir for about 5 minutes.

2) Transfer to a 3-qt. baking dish coated with nonstick cooking spray. Cover and bake at 325° for 1 hour. Uncover; bake 10 minutes longer or until heated through and lightly browned.

Yield: 16 servings (12 cups stuffing).

Editor's Note: This is suitable to stuff a 12- to 14-pound turkey.

NUTRITION FACTS: 3/4 cup equals 280 calories, 11 g fat (2 g saturated fat), 10 mg cholesterol, 703 mg sodium, 40 g carbohydrate, 3 g fiber, 7 g protein.

STUFFED DUCKLING

Stuffed Duckling
Joanne Callahan, Far Hills, New Jersey

I started with a basic bread stuffing and added on-hand ingredients until I came up with this pleasing recipe. The stuffing usually disappears long before the bird is gone!

1/2 cup chopped onion
1 garlic clove, minced
1 tablespoon butter
2 cups cubed day-old bread
1 cup cooked rice
1 teaspoon dried basil
1 teaspoon dried rosemary, crushed
1 teaspoon rubbed sage
1 teaspoon dried parsley flakes
1 teaspoon salt, *divided*
1/8 teaspoon pepper
1/2 cup raisins
1/2 cup chopped pecans
1/4 to 1/3 cup chicken broth
1 domestic duckling (4 to 5 pounds)

1) In a large skillet, saute onion and garlic in butter until tender; transfer to a large bowl. Add bread cubes, rice, basil, rosemary, sage, parsley flakes, 1/2 teaspoon salt and pepper. Add the raisins, pecans and enough broth to moisten; toss gently.

2) Prick skin of duckling well with a fork. Sprinkle cavity with remaining salt. Lightly stuff bread mixture into duck. Place breast side up on a rack in shallow roasting pan.

3) Bake, uncovered, at 350° for 1-3/4 to 2 hours or until a meat thermometer reads 180° for duck and 165° for stuffing. Drain fat as it accumulates during roasting. Cover and let stand 20 minutes before removing stuffing and carving.

Yield: 4 servings.

NUTRITION FACTS: 4 ounces cooked meat with skin equals 606 calories, 44 g fat (14 g saturated fat), 108 mg cholesterol, 589 mg sodium, 26 g carbohydrate, 2 g fiber, 26 g protein.

Roast Christmas Goose
Rosemarie Forcum, White Stone, Virginia

I have such fond childhood memories of my mother serving this golden-brown goose. To flavor the meat, Mom stuffed the bird with peeled and quartered fruit that's discarded after baking.

1 goose (10 to 12 pounds)
Salt and pepper
1 medium apple, peeled and quartered
1 medium navel orange, peeled and quartered
1 medium lemon, peeled and quartered
1 cup hot water

1) Sprinkle the goose cavity with salt and pepper. Place the apple, orange and lemon in the cavity. Place goose breast side up on a rack in a large shallow roasting pan. Prick skin well with a fork. Pour water into pan.

2) Bake, uncovered, at 350° for 2-1/4 to 3 hours or until a meat thermometer reads 185°. If necessary, drain fat from pan as it accumulates. Cover goose with foil and let stand for 20 minutes before carving. Discard fruit.

Yield: 8 servings.

NUTRITION FACTS: 4 ounces cooked with skin plus leftovers equals 376 calories, 26 g fat (8 g saturated fat), 108 mg cholesterol, 84 mg sodium, 4 g carbohydrate, 1 g fiber, 30 g protein.

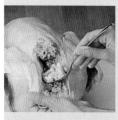

1) Combine stuffing ingredients as recipe directs. Do not stuff turkey until you're ready to place it in the oven. Spoon the stuffing loosely into neck cavity.

2) Pull neck skin over stuffing to the back of turkey and secure with a skewer. Tuck wing tips under body to avoid overbrowning while roasting.

3) Loosely spoon stuffing into the body cavity. Tie drumsticks together with kitchen string.

4) Place turkey breast side up on a rack in a shallow roasting pan. Brush with oil or melted butter if desired. Insert an oven-safe meat thermometer into thick portion of inner thigh area, not touching bone. Or use an instant-read thermometer toward end of roasting time.

5) Roast turkey as recipe directs. Baste with pan juices if desired.

6) When breast area has browned, loosely cover with foil to avoid excess browning. Continue roasting until the thermometer reads 180° and internal temperature in the center of stuffing is 165°.

7) Place bird on a carving board and remove any stuffing. Holding the end of the drumstick, pull the leg away from the body and cut between the thigh joint and body to remove the entire leg. Repeat with other leg.

8) To separate the drumstick and thigh, cut through the connecting joint.

9) Holding the drumstick by the end, slice meat into 1/4-in. slices. Cut thigh meat parallel to the bone into 1/4-in. slices.

10) Hold the bird with a meat fork and make a deep cut into the breast meat just above the wing area.

11) Slice down from the top of the breast into the cut made in Step 10. Slice meat 1/4 in. thick. Repeat Steps 10 and 11 on other side of bird.

12) To remove wings, cut through the connecting joints by the wing bones and backbone.

Duck with Cherry Sauce

Sandy Jenkins, Elkhorn, Wisconsin

My mom prepared this golden, tender roast duck often for Sunday dinner when I was growing up. It was one of my dad's favorite meals.

- 1 domestic duckling (4 to 5 pounds)
- 1 jar (12 ounces) cherry preserves
- 1 to 2 tablespoons red wine vinegar

1) Prick skin of duckling well with a fork and place breast side up on a rack in a shallow roasting pan. Tie drumsticks together.

2) Bake, uncovered, at 350° for 2 to 2-1/2 hours or until juices run clear and meat thermometer reads 180°. (Drain fat from pan as it accumulates.) Cover and let stand 20 minutes before carving.

3) For sauce, combine preserves and vinegar in a small saucepan. Cook and stir over medium heat until heated through. Serve sauce with duck.

Yield: 4-5 servings.

NUTRITION FACTS: 6 ounces cooked duck equals 664 calories, 41 g fat (14 g saturated fat), 123 mg cholesterol, 86 mg sodium, 44 g carbohydrate, 0 fiber, 28 g protein.

Pheasant with Cranberry Sauce

Sharon Shamosh, Rockville Center, New York

My Uncle Stanley, an avid hunter and fisherman, encouraged me to try game cooking, and this recipe is one of my successes. The tangy orange-cranberry sauce complements the tender meat.

- 1 pheasant (2 to 3 pounds)
- 1/4 teaspoon salt, *divided*
- 1/4 teaspoon pepper, *divided*
- 2 tablespoons butter, melted
- 1 package (12 ounces) fresh *or* frozen cranberries, thawed
- 1 cup sugar
- 1 cup orange juice
- 1/2 teaspoon ground cinnamon
- 2 tablespoons grated orange peel

1) Sprinkle cavity of pheasant with 1/8 teaspoon salt and 1/8 teaspoon pepper. Place pheasant on a rack in shallow roasting pan. Brush with butter; sprinkle with remaining salt and pepper.

2) Cover and bake at 325° for 45 minutes. Uncover; bake for 40-60 minutes longer or until a meat thermometer reads 180°; baste with pan juices frequently.

3) Meanwhile, in a large saucepan, combine the cranberries, sugar, orange juice and cinnamon.

Cook over medium heat for 10-12 minutes or until the berries begin to pop, stirring frequently. Stir in the orange peel. Simmer 5 minutes longer.

4) Cover pheasant with foil and let stand for 10 minutes before carving. Serve the sauce with pheasant.

Yield: 3 servings.

NUTRITION FACTS: 5 ounces cooked meat with skin equals 619 calories, 14 g fat (6 g saturated fat), 165 mg cholesterol, 291 mg sodium, 68 g carbohydrate, 4 g fiber, 54 g protein.

ITALIAN TURKEY SANDWICHES

Italian Turkey Sandwiches

Carol Riley, Glava, Illinois

I hope you enjoy these tasty turkey sandwiches as much as our family does. The recipe makes plenty, so it's great for potlucks. (Leftovers are just as good reheated the next day.)

- 1 bone-in turkey breast (5-1/2 pounds), skin removed
- 1/2 cup chopped green pepper
- 1 medium onion, chopped
- 1/4 cup chili sauce
- 3 tablespoons white vinegar
- 2 tablespoons dried oregano *or* Italian seasoning
- 4 teaspoons beef bouillon granules
- 11 kaiser *or* hard rolls, split

1) Cut turkey breast in half along the bone. Place the turkey breast, green pepper and onion in a 5-qt. slow cooker coated with nonstick cooking spray. Combine the chili sauce, vinegar, oregano and bouillon; pour over turkey and vegetables.

2) Cover and cook on low for 5-6 hours or until meat juices run clear and vegetables are tender.

3) Remove turkey, reserving cooking liquid. Shred the turkey with two forks; return to cooking juices. Spoon 1/2 cup onto each roll.

Yield: 11 servings.

NUTRITION FACTS: 1 sandwich equals 364 calories, 4 g fat (1 g saturated fat), 102 mg cholesterol, 576 mg sodium, 33 g carbohydrate, 1 g fiber, 46 g protein.

pan, shaping into a 8-in. x 5-in. x 2-in. mound. Cover pan; bake at 325° for 45 minutes.

3) Uncover turkey; leave stuffing covered. Bake 40-50 minutes longer or until a meat thermometer reads 170°. Cover turkey with foil and let stand for 15 minutes before slicing. Serve with stuffing.

Yield: 8 servings.

NUTRITION FACTS: 4-1/2 ounces cooked turkey (calculated without skin) with 1/2 cup stuffing equals 303 calories, 4 g fat (1 g saturated fat), 94 mg cholesterol, 181 mg sodium, 26 g carbohydrate, 2 g fiber, 38 g protein.

LEMON TURKEY WITH COUSCOUS STUFFING

Lemon Turkey with Couscous Stuffing

Kathi Graham, Naperville, Illinois

This moist tender turkey breast with its unusual dressing is perfect for a special-occasion main dish for a small family gathering. Lemon and garlic flavor the meat, while raisins and shredded carrot add sweetness and color to the couscous stuffing.

- 1 **bone-in turkey breast (4 to 4-1/2 pounds)**
- 2 **teaspoons olive oil**
- 1 **teaspoon lemon juice**
- 1 **garlic clove, minced**
- 1/2 **teaspoon grated lemon peel**
- 1/4 **teaspoon salt**
- 1/8 **teaspoon pepper**

STUFFING:

- 1-1/2 **cups boiling water**
- 1 **cup uncooked couscous**
- 1 **medium carrot, shredded**
- 1/2 **cup raisins**
- 1/3 **cup chicken broth**
- 1/4 **cup slivered almonds, toasted**
- 2 **tablespoons minced fresh parsley**

1) Carefully loosen turkey skin, leaving it attached at the back. Combine the oil, lemon juice, garlic, lemon peel, salt and pepper; spread under turkey skin. Place turkey to one side in a shallow roasting pan coated with nonstick cooking spray.

2) For stuffing, in a bowl, pour boiling water over couscous. Cover and let stand for 5 minutes or until water is absorbed. Add remaining ingredients; toss to combine. Spoon stuffing into other side of

Turkey Scallopini

Karen Adams, Seymour, Indiana

Quick-cooking turkey breast slices make it easy to prepare a satisfying meal in minutes. I've also flattened boneless skinless chicken breast halves in place of the turkey.

- 6 **turkey breast slices (about 1-1/2 pounds)**
- 1/4 **cup all-purpose flour**
- 1/8 **teaspoon salt**
- 1/8 **teaspoon pepper**
- 1 **egg**
- 2 **tablespoons water**
- 1 **cup soft bread crumbs**
- 1/2 **cup grated Parmesan cheese**
- 1/4 **cup butter**
  Minced fresh parsley

1) Pound turkey to 1/4-in. thickness. In a shallow bowl, combine the flour, salt and pepper. In another bowl, beat egg and water. On a plate, combine the bread crumbs and Parmesan cheese.

2) Dredge turkey in flour mixture, dip in egg mixture and coat with crumbs. Let stand 5 minutes.

3) Melt butter in a skillet over medium-high heat; cook turkey for 2-3 minutes on each side or until meat juices run clear and coating is golden brown. Sprinkle with parsley.

Yield: 6 servings.

NUTRITION FACTS: 1 serving equals 904 calories, 15 g fat (8 g saturated fat), 483 mg cholesterol, 635 mg sodium, 8 g carbohydrate, trace fiber, 172 g protein.

Turkey Divan

Stephanie Moon, Nampa, Idaho

I use precooked poultry, frozen broccoli and a fuss-free sauce to get this entree on the table in less than 30 minutes.

- 2 **packages (10 ounces *each*) frozen broccoli spears**

1/4   cup butter

1/4   cup all-purpose flour

2   teaspoons chicken bouillon granules

2   cups milk

3/4   pound sliced cooked turkey breast

1/4   cup grated Parmesan cheese

1) In a saucepan, cook broccoli until crisp-tender. Meanwhile, in another saucepan, melt butter; stir in flour and bouillon until smooth. Gradually add milk. Bring to a boil; cook and stir for 2 minutes or until thickened.

2) Drain broccoli and place in a greased 13-in. x 9-in. x 2-in. baking dish. Top with half of the sauce and all of the turkey. Spoon remaining sauce over the top. Sprinkle with Parmesan cheese.

3) Broil 4-6 in. from the heat for 3-4 minutes or until golden brown and edges are bubbly.

Yield: 4 servings.

NUTRITION FACTS: 1 serving equals 364 calories, 18 g fat (11 g saturated fat), 104 mg cholesterol, 764 mg sodium, 20 g carbohydrate, 4 g fiber, 32 g protein.

SAGE TURKEY THIGHS

Sage Turkey Thighs
Natalie Swanson, Catonsville, Maryland

I created this for my boys, who love dark meat. It's more convenient than cooking a whole turkey.

4   medium carrots, halved

1   medium onion, chopped

1/2   cup water

2   garlic cloves, minced

1-1/2   teaspoons rubbed sage, *divided*

2   turkey thighs *or* turkey drumsticks (2 pounds total)

1   teaspoon browning sauce, optional

1/4   teaspoon salt

1/8   teaspoon pepper

1   tablespoon cornstarch

1/4   cup cold water

1) In a 3-qt. slow cooker, combine the carrots, onion, water, garlic and 1 teaspoon sage. Top with turkey. Sprinkle with remaining sage. Cover and cook on low for 6-8 hours or until meat reaches 180°.

2) Remove turkey and keep warm. Strain broth, reserving vegetables. Skim fat from cooking juices. Place vegetables in a food processor; cover and process until smooth. Place in a saucepan; add cooking juices. Bring to a boil; cook and stir for 2 minutes or until thickened. Serve with turkey.

Yield: 4 servings.

NUTRITION FACTS: 4 ounces cooked turkey with 1/4 cup gravy equals 277 calories, 8 g fat (3 g saturated fat), 96 mg cholesterol, 280 mg sodium, 15 g carbohydrate, 3 g fiber, 34 g protein.

Marinated Turkey Thighs
Enid Karp, Carlsbad, California

The recipe originally called for lamb shanks, but I tried turkey thighs instead. The meat turns out tender, juicy and flavorful every time.

1-1/2   cups buttermilk

3   tablespoons dried minced onion

1   teaspoon salt

1/2   teaspoon pepper

1/2   teaspoon celery seed

1/2   teaspoon ground coriander

1/2   teaspoon ground ginger

2   turkey thighs (3/4 pound *each*)

1) In a resealable plastic bag, combine buttermilk, onion, salt, pepper, celery seed, coriander and ginger; add turkey. Seal bag and turn to coat; refrigerate for 8 hours or overnight. Drain and discard marinade.

2) Place turkey in greased shallow baking dish. Cover and bake at 325° for 45 minutes. Uncover; bake 30-35 minutes longer or until the turkey juices run clear and a thermometer reads 180°.

Yield: 2 servings.

NUTRITION FACTS: 1 serving equals 301 calories, 7 g fat (2 g saturated fat), 204 mg cholesterol, 595 mg sodium, 5 g carbohydrate, trace fiber, 52 g protein.

Creamed Turkey over Rice
Kathi Parker, Hendersonville, North Carolina

This is one of our favorite ways to use up leftover turkey. It's simple to prepare and tastes delicious.

1	medium onion, chopped
1/2	cup chopped celery
1/4	cup butter
1/4	cup all-purpose flour
1-1/2	cups chicken broth
2	cups cubed cooked turkey
1	cup milk
1/2	cup cubed Swiss cheese
1	tablespoon diced pimientos, drained
1/2	teaspoon salt
1/4	teaspoon pepper
1/4	teaspoon ground nutmeg

Hot cooked long grain and wild rice

1) In a large skillet, saute onion and celery in butter until tender. Stir in flour until blended. Gradually stir in broth. Bring to a boil. Cook; stir 2 minutes.

2) Reduce heat; stir in turkey, milk, cheese, pimientos, salt, pepper and nutmeg. Cook until cheese melts and mixture is heated through. Serve over rice.

Yield: 4 servings.

NUTRITION FACTS: 1 serving (calculated without rice) equals 372 calories, 22 g fat (12 g saturated fat), 107 mg cholesterol, 896 mg sodium, 14 g carbohydrate, 1 g fiber, 30 g protein.

Turkey Tetrazzini
Audrey Thibodeau, Mesa, Arizona

What a great way to use up leftover turkey! Plus, it bakes up delicious and bubbly for dinner.

1	package (1 pound) linguine
6	tablespoons butter
6	tablespoons all-purpose flour
1/2	teaspoon salt
1/4	teaspoon pepper
1/8	teaspoon cayenne pepper
3	cups chicken broth
1	cup heavy whipping cream
4	cups cubed cooked turkey
1	cup sliced fresh mushrooms
1	jar (4 ounces) diced pimientos, drained
1/4	cup chopped fresh parsley
4	to 5 drops hot pepper sauce
1/3	cup grated Parmesan cheese

1) Cook pasta according to package directions. In a saucepan, melt butter over medium heat. Stir in the flour, salt, pepper and cayenne until smooth. Gradually add broth. Bring to a boil; cook and stir for 2 minutes or until thickened. Remove from the heat; stir in cream.

2) Drain linguine; add 2 cups sauce and toss to coat. Transfer to a greased 13-in. x 9-in. x 2-in. baking dish. Make a well in center of noodles, making a space about 6 in. x 4 in.

3) To remaining sauce, add turkey, mushrooms, pimientos, parsley and hot pepper sauce; mix well. Pour into center of dish. Sprinkle with Parmesan cheese.

4) Cover and bake at 350° for 30 minutes. Uncover; bake 20-30 minutes longer or until bubbly.

Yield: 8-10 servings.

NUTRITION FACTS: 1 serving equals 340 calories, 20 g fat (11 g saturated fat), 96 mg cholesterol, 568 mg sodium, 19 g carbohydrate, 1 g fiber, 22 g protein.

Curried Turkey
Evelyn Gunn, Andrews, Texas

You'll like how the apple and curry flavors accent the meat. With a tossed salad and fresh rolls, you have a delicious and easy meal.

2	cups milk
2	chicken bouillon cubes
2	cups diced peeled apples
1	cup chopped onion
1/4	cup vegetable oil
2	tablespoons all-purpose flour
2	teaspoons curry powder
1/2	teaspoon salt
1/4	teaspoon pepper
1	tablespoon lemon juice
4	cups diced cooked turkey

Hot cooked rice

1) In a small saucepan, heat the milk and bouillon, stirring until bouillon is dissolved. Set aside.

2) In a large saucepan, saute apples and onion in oil until tender. Stir in the flour, curry powder, salt and pepper until blended.

3) Gradually add milk mixture and lemon juice. Bring to a boil; cook and stir for 2 minutes or until thickened. Add turkey; heat through. Serve over rice.

Yield: 6 servings.

NUTRITION FACTS: 1 cup (calculated without rice) equals 338 calories, 17 g fat (4 g saturated fat), 82 mg cholesterol, 675 mg sodium, 15 g carbohydrate, 2 g fiber, 31 g protein.

ALL-AMERICAN TURKEY POTPIE

All-American Turkey Potpie
Laureen Naylor, Factoryville, Pennsylvania

Ever since my sister-in-law shared this recipe with me, I haven't made any other kind of potpie. The crust is very easy to work with.

 2 cups all-purpose flour
1/2 teaspoon salt
1/2 cup finely shredded
 cheddar cheese
2/3 cup shortening
 1 tablespoon cold butter, cubed
 3 to 4 tablespoons cold water

FILLING:
 1 cup diced peeled potatoes
1/2 cup thinly sliced carrots
1/3 cup chopped celery
1/4 cup chopped onion
 1 garlic clove, minced
 1 tablespoon butter
 1 cup chicken broth
 2 tablespoons all-purpose flour
1/2 cup milk
1-1/2 cups cubed cooked turkey
1/2 cup frozen peas, thawed
1/2 cup frozen corn, thawed
1/2 teaspoon salt
1/4 teaspoon dried tarragon
1/4 teaspoon pepper

1) In a food processor, combine flour and salt; cover and pulse to blend. Add cheese; pulse until fine crumbs form. Add shortening and butter; pulse until coarse crumbs form. While processing, gradually add water until dough forms a ball.

2) Divide dough in half with one ball slightly larger than the other; wrap in plastic wrap. Refrigerate for 30 minutes.

3) For filling, in a large saucepan, saute the potatoes, carrots, celery, onion and garlic in butter for 5-6 minutes. Add broth; cover and cook for 10 minutes or until vegetables are tender.

4) In a small bowl, combine flour and milk until smooth. Gradually add to vegetable mixture. Bring to a boil; cook and stir for 2 minutes or until thickened. Add the remaining ingredients; simmer 5 minutes longer.

5) Roll out larger pastry ball to fit a 9-in. pie plate; transfer to pie plate. Trim pastry even with edge. Pour hot turkey filling into crust. Roll out remaining pastry to fit top of pie; place over filling. Trim, seal and flute edges. Cut slits in top or make decorative cutouts in pastry.

6) Bake at 350° for 35-45 minutes or until crust is light golden brown. Serve immediately.

Yield: 6 servings.

NUTRITION FACTS: 1 piece equals 551 calories, 31 g fat (11 g saturated fat), 50 mg cholesterol, 704 mg sodium, 47 g carbohydrate, 3 g fiber, 20 g protein.

Turkey Meat Loaf
Judy Prante, Portland, Oregon

I like to make just enough for two servings, but this recipe is easy to double. A friend told me it was they best turkey meat loaf she'd ever eaten!

4-1/2	teaspoons water
1-1/2	teaspoons teriyaki sauce
1	cup cubed bread
1	egg, beaten
2	tablespoons chopped onion
1	tablespoon chopped green pepper
1	tablespoon *each* shredded mozzarella and cheddar cheese
Dash garlic powder	
Dash celery seed	
1/2	pound ground turkey
1	tablespoon grated Parmesan cheese

1) In a bowl, combine the water, teriyaki sauce and bread cubes; let stand for 5 minutes. Add the egg, onion, green pepper, mozzarella and cheddar cheeses, garlic powder and celery seed. Crumble turkey over mixture and mix well.

2) Pat into an ungreased 5-3/4-in. x 3-in. x 2-in. loaf pan. Sprinkle with Parmesan cheese. Bake, uncovered, at 350° for 1 hour or until a meat thermometer reads 165°; drain.

Yield: 2 servings.

NUTRITION FACTS: 1 serving equals 355 calories, 22 g fat (8 g saturated fat), 192 mg cholesterol, 476 mg sodium, 12 g carbohydrate, 1 g fiber, 25 g protein.

Basil Turkey Burgers
Carolyn Bixenmann, Grand Island, Nebraska

These delicious sandwiches are a superb substitute for traditional beef burgers. My husband actually prefers these topped with seasoned mayonnaise.

1/4	cup fat-free mayonnaise
2	tablespoons minced fresh basil, *divided*
1/4	cup fat-free milk
2	tablespoons finely chopped onion
1	tablespoon dry bread crumbs
1/8	teaspoon salt
1/8	teaspoon pepper
3/4	pound lean ground turkey
4	hamburger buns, split
4	lettuce leaves
1	large tomato, sliced

1) In a small bowl, combine mayonnaise and 1 tablespoon basil. Cover and refrigerate until serving.

2) In a bowl, combine the milk, onion, bread crumbs, salt, pepper and remaining basil. Crumble turkey over mixture and mix well. Shape into four patties.

3) Broil 4-6 in. from heat for 5-6 minutes on each side or until meat is no longer pink and a thermometer reads 165°. Serve on buns with lettuce, tomato and basil mayonnaise.

Yield: 4 servings.

NUTRITION FACTS: 1 burger with 1 tablespoon basil mayonnaise equals 305 calories, 11 g fat (4 g saturated fat), 69 mg cholesterol, 567 mg sodium, 31 g carbohydrate, 2 g fiber, 21 g protein.

Almond Turkey Casserole
Jill Black, Troy, Ontario

A special cousin shared the recipe for this comforting casserole. The almonds and water chestnuts give it a fun crunch.

2	cans (10-3/4 ounces *each*) condensed cream of mushroom soup, undiluted
1/2	cup mayonnaise
1/2	cup sour cream
2	tablespoons chopped onion
2	tablespoons lemon juice
1	teaspoon salt
1/2	teaspoon white pepper
5	cups cubed cooked turkey
3	cups cooked rice
4	celery ribs, chopped
1	can (8 ounces) sliced water chestnuts, drained
1	cup sliced almonds

TOPPING:

1-1/2	cups crushed butter-flavored crackers (about 38 crackers)
1/3	cup butter, melted
1/4	cup sliced almonds

1) In a large bowl, combine soup, mayonnaise, sour cream, onion, lemon juice, salt and pepper. Stir in turkey, rice, celery, water chestnuts and almonds.

2) Transfer to a greased 13-in. x 9-in. x 2-in. baking dish. Combine topping ingredients; sprinkle over turkey mixture. Bake, uncovered, at 350° for 35-40 minutes or until bubbly and golden brown.

Yield: 8 servings.

NUTRITION FACTS: 1 cup equals 678 calories, 41 g fat (12 g saturated fat), 105 mg cholesterol, 1,211 mg sodium, 43 g carbohydrate, 4 g fiber, 34 g protein.

CHAPTER 8
SEAFOOD

SEAFOOD

Whether you like to use fresh or frozen fish, shellfish or canned seafood products, you'll find recipes in this chapter to make a delicious meal. Once you've selected your seafood, remember to closely follow the recipe directions to avoid overcooking.

Buy fresh fish fillets or steaks that have firm, elastic and moist-looking flesh. The skin should be shiny and bright. Whole fish should have eyes that are not sunken or cloudy and a firm body that is springy to the touch. Fresh fish should have a mild smell. Avoid fish with a strong fishy odor, bruised skin and flesh with drying edges.

Buy frozen fish in packages that are solidly frozen, tightly sealed and free of freezer burn and odor.

Follow these guidelines for how much fish to purchase per person.

- 1 pound whole fish yields 1 serving.
- 1 pound pan-dressed fish yields 2 servings.
- 1 pound steaks or fillets yields 3 to 4 servings.

Prepare fresh fish within 1 to 2 days after it is caught or purchased because it is highly perishable. Freshly caught fish should be pan-dressed, washed in cold water, blotted dry with paper towels, placed in an airtight container or heavy-duty plastic bag and refrigerated. Refrigerate freshly caught or purchased fish in the coldest area of your refrigerator.

Wrap fish in freezer paper, heavy-duty foil or heavy-duty plastic bags for long-term storage. Freeze oily fish for up to 3 months and lean fish for up to 6 months.

Not all markets carry all types of fish. The type of fish—lean, moderately oily and oily—influences the cooking method. When looking for a fish substitute, it is usually best to substitute within the same fat category.

SUBSTITUTING FISH	
LEAN	Cod, Scrod (a small cod), Flounder, Grouper, Haddock, Halibut, Mahi-Mahi, Ocean Perch, Orange Roughy, Pollock, Red Snapper, Sea Bass, Sole, Tilapia, Tilefish, Whiting
MODERATELY OILY	Bluefish, Catfish, Rainbow Trout, Striped Bass, Swordfish, Yellowfin Tuna
OILY	Bluefin Tuna, Herring, Lake Trout, Mackerel, Pompano, Salmon, Shad, Shark, Whitefish

Useful Definitions

Refer to the Glossary on pages 18-22 for more terms.

DRESSED FISH: Ready to cook; has been gutted and scaled. It still has its head and tail.

FILLETS: From the side of the fish and are boneless. They may or may not be skinless.

FLATFISH: Have both eyes on top of a flat body. Flounder, sole, turbot and halibut are flatfish. Generally flatfish are sold as fillets, but halibut is typically sold as steaks.

FRESHWATER FISH: From streams, rivers and freshwater lakes.

LEAN FISH: Has a low fat content—it can be as low as 2.5% fat. Lean fish has a delicate texture and mild flavor. Due to the low fat content it dries out easily during cooking and is best cooked with some liquid or fat. Poaching, steaming and sauteing are methods recommended for these types of fish. And if basted during cooking, they can also be baked, broiled or grilled.

MODERATELY OILY FISH: Has a fat content around 6%. They have a firmer texture than lean fish and a neutral flavor. These types of fish can be baked, broiled, grilled, pan-fried or poached.

OILY FISH: Has a fat content of more than 6% and can be as high as 50%. Due to the high fat content, these fish have a firm, meaty texture and a strong rich flavor. These fish stay moist during cooking and are suitable to be baked, broiled or grilled.

PAN-DRESSED FISH: A dressed fish with the head and tail removed.

ROUNDFISH: Have eyes on both sides of its head and a round body. Roundfish are sold dressed or pan-dressed and as steaks or fillets.

SALTWATER FISH: Fish from seas or oceans.

STEAKS: A cross-section of large roundfish and contain part of the backbone. They can be from 1/2 inch to 1 inch thick.

WHOLE FISH: Needs to be gutted and scaled before cooking.

Cooking Methods for Fish

COOKING METHOD	CUT OF FISH
BAKING	Large Whole Fish, Steaks and Fillets (Pan-Dressed Whole Fish are usually baked at 350°.)
BROILING	Fillets or Steaks
PAN-FRYING	Fillets and Pan-Dressed Fish
SAUTEING	Fish Nuggets or Chunks
POACHING	Fillets, Steaks or Pan-Dressed Fish
STEAMING	Fillets, Steaks or Pan-Dressed Fish
GRILLING	Fillets or Steaks

Defrosting Guidelines

The thicker the package, the longer it will take to defrost. When defrosting fish or shellfish in the refrigerator, place a tray under the package to catch any liquid or juices to keep the refrigerator clean. Allow 12 or more hours to thaw a 1-pound package.

Cold-water thawing is an option that takes less time than refrigeration defrosting, but requires more attention. The fish or shellfish must be in a leakproof bag such as its original tightly sealed wrapper. If its package is not leakproof, then place in a heavy-duty plastic bag. Submerge the wrapped seafood in cold tap water. Change the water every 30 minutes until the seafood is thawed. For this method, allow 1 to 2 hours for every pound.

BREADING FISH

Combine dry ingredients in a pie plate or shallow bowl. In another pie plate or bowl, whisk egg, milk and/or other liquid ingredients. Dip fish into egg mixture, then roll gently in dry ingredients. Fry or bake as directed.

Golden Catfish Fillets
Sharon Stevens, Weirton, Virginia

My grandmother always made these crisp fillets from Granddad's fresh catch from the Ohio River. We'd immediately refrigerate the cleaned, fresh fish and use them within a couple of days.

   3 eggs
3/4 cup all-purpose flour
3/4 cup cornmeal
   1 teaspoon garlic powder
1/2 teaspoon salt
1/2 teaspoon pepper
   5 catfish fillets (6 ounces *each*)
Oil for frying

1) In a shallow bowl, beat the eggs until foamy. In another shallow bowl, combine the flour, cornmeal and seasonings. Dip fillets in eggs, then coat with cornmeal mixture.

2) Heat 1/4 in. of oil in a large skillet; fry fish over medium-high heat for 3-4 minutes on each side or until fish flakes easily with a fork.

Yield: 5 servings.

NUTRITION FACTS: 1 fillet equals 377 calories, 16 g fat (4 g saturated fat), 186 mg cholesterol, 359 mg sodium, 24 g carbohydrate, 2 g fiber, 32 g protein.

FENNEL STUFFED COD

Fennel Stuffed Cod
Mary Ellen Wilcox, Scotia, New York

Moist fish, a super stuffing and a creamy sauce make for a memorable main dish. Fennel has a distinct flavor that works well in this entree.

   1 cup (8 ounces) plain yogurt
2-1/4 cups finely chopped fennel fronds, *divided*
   1 teaspoon lemon juice
   1 teaspoon snipped chives
 1/8 teaspoon salt, optional
 1/8 teaspoon pepper
   2 celery ribs, chopped
 1/4 cup chopped onion
   2 to 4 tablespoons vegetable oil
   4 cups stuffing croutons
   1 cup chicken broth
   2 eggs, beaten
   4 cod *or* flounder fillets (1-1/2 pounds)
   1 medium lemon, sliced

1) For sauce, combine the yogurt, 1/4 cup of fennel, lemon juice, chives, salt if desired and pepper in a bowl. Cover and refrigerate for 2 hours or overnight.

2) In a small skillet, saute celery and onion in oil until tender. Remove from the heat. Stir in the croutons, broth, eggs and remaining fennel. Spoon about 1 cup stuffing mixture onto each fillet; roll fish around stuffing.

3) Transfer to a greased 2-qt. baking dish. Top each with a lemon slice. Bake, uncovered, at 350° for 30-35 minutes or until fish flakes easily with a fork and a thermometer inserted into stuffing reads 160°. Serve with fennel sauce.

Yield: 4 servings.

NUTRITION FACTS: 1 serving equals 476 calories, 15 g fat (3 g saturated fat), 193 mg cholesterol, 869 mg sodium, 47 g carbohydrate, 4 g fiber, 42 g protein.

Catfish in Ginger Sauce
Mary Dixson, Decature, Alabama

Whenever I want to serve fish in a flash, I turn to this recipe. The fillets always turn out moist, tender and tasty. For even more flavor, spoon extra sauce over the fish before serving.

 1/2 cup chopped green onions
   1 tablespoon vegetable oil
 1/4 teaspoon ground ginger
   1 teaspoon cornstarch
   2 tablespoons water
   1 cup chicken broth
   1 tablespoon soy sauce
   1 tablespoon white wine vinegar
 1/8 teaspoon cayenne pepper
   4 catfish fillets (6 ounces *each*)

1) In a 2-cup microwave-safe bowl, combine the onions, oil and ginger. Microwave, uncovered, on high for 1-1/2 minutes or until onions are tender.

2) In small bowl, combine the cornstarch and water until smooth. Stir in the broth, soy sauce, vinegar and cayenne. Stir into onion mixture. Microwave, uncovered, at 70% power for 2-3 minutes, stirring after each minute, until sauce comes to a boil.

3) Place catfish in a microwave-safe 3-qt. dish; pour sauce over fish. Cover and microwave on high for 5-6 minutes or until fish flakes easily with a fork.

Yield: 4 servings.

NUTRITION FACTS: 1 serving equals 274 calories, 16 g fat (3 g saturated fat), 80 mg cholesterol, 555 mg sodium, 2 g carbohydrate, trace fiber, 28 g protein.

Spinach Catfish Skillet

Lee Bremson, Kansas City, Missouri

Nestled in a skillet with colorful, nutritious carrots and spinach, this catfish fillet comes out perfectly moist. This meal is no more trouble than heating a frozen dinner, but it tastes much better!

- 20 baby carrots
- 4 teaspoons vegetable oil
- 1/2 cup sliced onion
- 2 catfish fillets (6 ounces *each*)
- 2 packages (6 ounces *each*) fresh baby spinach
- 1/4 cup white wine vinegar
- 1/2 teaspoon sugar

1) In a large skillet, stir-fry carrots in oil for 1-2 minutes or until crisp-tender. Add onion; cook and stir for 1 minute. Add catfish; cook for 2-3 minutes on each side. Remove fish and set aside.

2) Add spinach, in batches, stir-frying until slightly wilted. Return fish to skillet. Sprinkle with vinegar and sugar.

3) Cover and cook for 5 minutes or until fish flakes easily with a fork. Remove to a warm serving dish; spoon pan juices over fillet.

Yield: 2 servings.

NUTRITION FACTS: 1 serving equals 397 calories, 23 g fat (4 g saturated fat), 80 mg cholesterol, 280 mg sodium, 17 g carbohydrate, 6 g fiber, 32 g protein.

Cilantro Lime Cod

Donna Hackman, Huddleston, Virginia

My daughter loves to cook and especially likes dishes with Mexican flair. She bakes these wonderfully seasoned fish fillets in foil to keep them moist and cut down on cleanup.

- 4 cod *or* haddock fillets (2 pounds)
- 1/4 teaspoon pepper
- 1 tablespoon dried minced onion
- 1 garlic clove, minced
- 1 tablespoon olive oil
- 1-1/2 teaspoons ground cumin
- 1/4 cup minced fresh cilantro
- 2 limes, thinly sliced
- 2 tablespoons butter, melted

1) Place each fillet on a 15-in. x 12-in. piece of heavy-duty foil. Sprinkle with pepper. In a small saucepan, saute onion and garlic in oil; stir in cumin.

2) Spoon over fillets; sprinkle with cilantro. Place lime slices over each; drizzle with butter.

3) Fold foil around fish and seal tightly. Place on a baking sheet. Bake at 375° for 35-40 minutes or until fish flakes easily with a fork.

Yield: 8 servings.

NUTRITION FACTS: 3 ounces 1 equals 131 calories, 5 g fat (2 g saturated fat), 51 mg cholesterol, 91 mg sodium, 2 g carbohydrate, 1 g fiber, 18 g protein.

HERB-COATED COD

Herb-Coated Cod

Harriet Stichter, Milford, Indiana

A simple coating bakes up nice and crisp in this fishy favorite. It's filled with buttery goodness!

- 1/4 cup butter, melted
- 2/3 cup crushed butter-flavored crackers
- 2 tablespoons grated Parmesan cheese
- 1/2 teaspoon dried oregano
- 1/2 teaspoon dried basil
- 1/4 teaspoon garlic powder
- 1 pound cod fillets

1) Place butter in a shallow bowl. In another bowl, combine the crackers, cheese and seasonings. Dip fillets in butter, then coat with crumbs.

2) Place in a greased 13-in. x 9-in. x 2-in. baking dish. Bake, uncovered, at 400° for 15-20 minutes or until fish flakes easily with a fork.

Yield: 4 servings.

NUTRITION FACTS: 4 ounces equals 274 calories, 16 g fat (8 g saturated fat), 76 mg cholesterol, 348 mg sodium, 11 g carbohydrate, trace fiber, 20 g protein.

Oven Fish 'n' Chips
Janice Mitchell, Aurora, Colorado

Enjoy moist, flavorful fish with a coating that's as crunchy and golden as the deep-fried variety. Plus you can easily bake up crisp, irresistible "chips" to serve alongside.

 2 tablespoons olive oil
1/4 teaspoon pepper
 4 medium baking potatoes
    (1 pound), peeled

FISH:

1/3 cup all-purpose flour
1/4 teaspoon pepper
 1 egg, lightly beaten
 2 tablespoons water
2/3 cup crushed cornflakes
 1 tablespoons grated Parmesan
    cheese
1/8 teaspoon cayenne pepper
 1 pound haddock fillets
 Tartar sauce, optional

1) In a medium bowl, combine oil and pepper. Cut potatoes lengthwise into 1/2-in. strips. Add to oil mixture; toss to coat.

2) Place on a 15-in. x 10-in. x 1-in. baking pan coated with nonstick cooking spray. Bake, uncovered, at 425° for 25-30 minutes or until golden brown and crisp.

3) Meanwhile, in a shallow dish, combine flour and pepper. In a second shallow dish, beat egg and water. In a third dish, combine the cornflakes, cheese and cayenne. Dredge fish in flour, then dip in egg mixture and coat with crumb mixture.

4) Place on a baking sheet coated with nonstick cooking spray. Bake at 425° for 10-15 minutes or until fish flakes easily with a fork. Serve with chips and tartar sauce if desired.

Yield: 4 servings.

NUTRITION FACTS: 1 serving equals 376 calories, 9 g fat (2 g saturated fat), 120 mg cholesterol, 228 mg sodium, 44 g carbohydrate, 2 g fiber, 28 g protein.

Mediterranean Baked Fish
Ellen De Munnik, Chesterfield, Michigan

The mouth-watering aroma of this herbed fish dish baking is sure to lure guests to your kitchen. In a pinch, you can use dried herbs and canned diced tomatoes to replace the fresh ingredients.

 1 cup thinly sliced leeks
    (white portion only)
 2 garlic cloves, minced
 2 teaspoons olive oil
12 large fresh basil leaves
1-1/2 pounds orange roughy fillets
 1 teaspoon salt
 2 plum tomatoes, sliced
 1 can (2-1/4 ounces) sliced ripe
    olives, drained
 1 medium lemon
1/8 teaspoon pepper
 4 fresh rosemary sprigs

1) In a nonstick skillet, saute leeks and garlic in oil until tender; set aside. Coat a 13-in. x 9-in. x 2-in. baking dish with nonstick cooking spray.

2) Arrange basil in a single layer in dish; top with fish fillets. Sprinkle with salt. Top with leek mixture. Arrange tomatoes and olives over fish. Thinly slice half of lemon; place over top. Squeeze juice from remaining lemon over all. Sprinkle with pepper.

3) Cover and bake at 425° for 15-20 minutes or until fish flakes easily with a fork. Garnish with rosemary.

Yield: 4 servings.

NUTRITION FACTS: 4-1/2 ounces cooked fish equals 180 calories, 5 g fat (1 g saturated fat), 34 mg cholesterol, 844 mg sodium, 7 g carbohydrate, 1 g fiber, 26 g protein.

TESTING FISH FOR DONENESS

Overcooked fish loses its flavor and becomes tough. As a general guideline, fish is cooked 10 minutes for every inch of thickness.

For fish fillets, check for doneness by inserting a fork at an angle into the thickest portion of the fish and gently parting the meat. When it is opaque and flakes into sections, it is cooked completely.

Whole fish or steaks are done when the flesh is opaque and is easily removed from the bones. The juices in cooked fish are milky white.

Tarragon Flounder

Donna Smith, Fairport, New York

I enjoy using tarragon in a number of dishes, but especially in this flounder recipe that makes just enough for two.

> 2   **flounder fillets (4 ounces** *each*)
> 1/2   **cup chicken broth**
> 2   **tablespoons butter, melted**
> 1   **tablespoon minced fresh tarragon** *or* **1 teaspoon dried tarragon**
> 1   **teaspoon ground mustard**

1) Place fillets in a greased 11-in. x 7-in. x 2-in. baking dish. Combine remaining ingredients; pour over fish.

2) Bake, uncovered, at 350° for 20-25 minutes or until fish flakes easily with a fork. Remove to a serving plate with a slotted spatula. Serve immediately.

Yield: 2 servings.

NUTRITION FACTS: 1 serving equals 200 calories, 13 g fat (7 g saturated fat), 84 mg cholesterol, 430 mg sodium, 1 g carbohydrate, trace fiber, 20 g protein.

Baked Orange Roughy With Veggies

Shannon Messmer, Oklahoma City, Oklahoma

This is a nice meal for two, but the recipe is easily doubled to serve four.

> 3/4   **teaspoon lemon-pepper seasoning**
> 1/8   **teaspoon salt**
> 2   **orange roughy, red snapper, cod** *or* **haddock fillets (6 ounces** *each*)

> 1/2   **cup sliced fresh mushrooms**
> 1/4   **cup thinly sliced green onions**
> 1/4   **cup chopped seeded tomato**
> 1/4   **cup finely chopped green pepper**
> 2   **tablespoons butter, melted**
> 1-1/2   **teaspoons orange juice**
> 1   **cup hot cooked rice**
> 4-1/2   **teaspoons grated Parmesan cheese, optional**

1) Combine lemon-pepper and salt; sprinkle over both sides of fillets. Place in a greased 11-in. x 7-in. x 2-in. baking dish.

2) Combine the mushrooms, onions, tomato and green pepper; spoon over fillets. Combine butter and orange juice; pour over fish and vegetables.

3) Cover and bake at 350° for 20-25 minutes or until fish flakes easily with a fork. Serve over rice. Sprinkle with Parmesan cheese if desired.

Yield: 2 servings.

NUTRITION FACTS: 1 serving equals 490 calories, 14 g fat (7 g saturated fat), 163 mg cholesterol, 665 mg sodium, 27 g carbohydrate, 1 g fiber, 61 g protein.

Coconut-Crusted Perch

Norma Thurber, Johnston, Rhode Island

A coconut breading lends tropical taste to tender perch served with a sweet-sour sauce for dipping. It's very good with any kind of whitefish.

> 1/2   **cup apricot preserves**
> 1/4   **cup ketchup**
> 1/4   **cup light corn syrup**
> 2   **tablespoons lemon juice**

1/4 teaspoon ground ginger

2 cups crushed butter-flavored crackers (about 50 crackers)

1 cup flaked coconut

2 eggs

2 tablespoons evaporated milk

1/2 teaspoon salt

3 pounds perch fillet

1 cup vegetable oil, *divided*

1) For sweet-sour sauce, combine the preserves, ketchup, corn syrup, lemon juice and ginger in a small saucepan. Bring to a boil. Reduce heat; simmer, uncovered, for 5 minutes or until slightly thickened. Remove from the heat and keep warm.

2) In a shallow dish, combine the cracker crumbs and coconut. In another shallow dish, whisk the eggs, milk and salt. Dip each fillet in egg mixture, then coat with crumb mixture.

3) In a large skillet, cook fish in 3 tablespoons oil in batches over medium-high heat for 1-2 minutes on each side or until fish flakes easily with a fork, adding oil as needed. Serve with sweet-sour sauce.

Yield: 8 servings.

NUTRITION FACTS: 4-1/2 ounces of cooked fish with 4 teaspoons sweet-sour sauce equals 497 calories, 20 g fat (6 g saturated fat), 201 mg cholesterol, 570 mg sodium, 42 g carbohydrate, 1 g fiber, 37 g protein.

Poached Orange Roughy with Tarragon Sauce

Taste of Home Test Kitchen

A flavorful herb-flecked sauce enhances the mild, poached-to-perfection fish fillet in this recipe.

4 cups water

1 cup dry white wine *or* vegetable broth

1/4 cup chopped celery

1/4 cup chopped carrot

2 tablespoons chopped onion

2 tablespoons lemon juice

7 whole peppercorns

1 bay leaf

2 teaspoons dried tarragon, *divided*

4 orange roughy *or* red snapper fillets (4 ounces *each*)

1/8 teaspoon *each* salt and white pepper

2 tablespoons 2% milk

1 egg yolk

1) In a large nonstick skillet, combine the water, wine or broth, vegetables, lemon juice, peppercorns, bay leaf and 1-1/2 teaspoons tarragon. Bring to a boil.

2) Reduce heat; add fillets and poach, uncovered, until fish is firm and flakes easily with a fork (about 8-10 minutes per inch of fillet thickness). Remove to a warm serving platter.

3) Strain 1 cup of the cooking liquid; place in a saucepan. Add salt and pepper. Bring to a boil; cook until liquid is reduced to about 1/3 cup. Remove from the heat.

4) In a small bowl, beat milk and egg yolk. Stir 1 tablespoon reduced liquid into egg mixture; return all to the pan, stirring constantly. Stir in remaining tarragon. Bring to a gentle boil over low heat; cook and stir for 1 minute or until thickened. Spoon over fish.

Yield: 4 servings.

NUTRITION FACTS: 1 fish fillet with 2 tablespoons sauce equals 106 calories, 2 g fat (1 g saturated fat), 76 mg cholesterol, 152 mg sodium, 1 g carbohydrate, 1 g fiber, 18 g protein.

Curried Red Snapper

Lynette Kerslake, Corbett, Oregon

My husband and daughter, who don't usually care for fish, love it prepared this way. A tasty curry sauce baked over the fish makes the delicious difference.

1-1/2 pounds fresh *or* frozen red snapper, cod, haddock *or* flounder fillets

2 medium onions, chopped

2 celery ribs, chopped

1 tablespoon butter

1 teaspoon curry powder

3/4 teaspoon salt

1/4 cup milk

1) Place the fish in a greased 13-in. x 9-in. x 2-in. baking dish. In a skillet, saute onions and celery in butter until tender. Add curry powder and salt; mix well. Remove from the heat; stir in milk.

2) Spoon over fish. Bake, uncovered, at 350° for 25 minutes or until fish flakes easily with a fork.

Yield: 6 servings.

NUTRITION FACTS: 1 serving equals 155 calories, 4 g fat (2 g saturated fat), 46 mg cholesterol, 381 mg sodium, 6 g carbohydrate, 1 g fiber, 24 g protein.

Lemon-Batter Fish

Jackie Hannahs, Muskegon, Michigan

The flour-based coating helps keep the fish moist and gives it that crispness. The hint of lemon adds just a little tang.

- 1-1/2 cups all-purpose flour, *divided*
- 1 teaspoon baking powder
- 3/4 teaspoon salt
- 1/2 teaspoon sugar
- 1 egg, beaten
- 2/3 cup water
- 2/3 cup lemon juice, *divided*
- 2 pounds perch fillets *or* walleye fillets, cut into bite-size pieces

Oil for frying

Lemon wedges, optional

1) In a shallow bowl, combine 1 cup flour, baking powder, salt and sugar; set aside. Combine the egg, water and 1/3 cup lemon juice; stir into dry ingredients until smooth.

2) In separate shallow bowls, place remaining lemon juice and remaining flour. Dip fillets in lemon juice, then flour and coat with the batter.

3) Heat 1 in. of oil in a skillet. Fry fish, a few at a time, over medium-high heat for 2-3 minutes on each side or until the fish flakes easily with a fork. Drain on paper towels. Garnish with lemon if desired.

Yield: 5 servings.

NUTRITION FACTS: 4-1/2 ounces cooked fish equals 403 calories, 14 g fat (1 g saturated fat), 206 mg cholesterol, 560 mg sodium, 27 g carbohydrate, 1 g fiber, 40 g protein.

Salmon with Ginger Pineapple Salsa

Kathleen Kelley, Days Creek, Oregon

I eat salmon at least twice a week and usually grill it, but it's just as delicious baked with this zesty, ginger pineapple salsa.

- 1 can (20 ounces) unsweetened pineapple tidbits
- 1 cup chopped seeded ripe tomatoes
- 3 green onions, sliced
- 1 jalapeno pepper, seeded and chopped
- 2 tablespoons cider vinegar
- 2 garlic cloves, minced
- 1-1/2 teaspoons sesame oil
- 1 teaspoon honey
- 1-1/2 teaspoons minced fresh gingerroot
- 1/4 teaspoon crushed red pepper flakes
- 3/4 teaspoon salt, *divided*
- 6 salmon fillets (6 ounces *each*)
- 3/4 teaspoon ground cumin
- 1/4 teaspoon pepper

1) Drain pineapple, reserving 1/4 cup juice. In a large bowl, combine the tomatoes, green onions, jalapeno, vinegar, garlic, sesame oil, honey, ginger, red pepper flakes, 1/4 teaspoon salt, pineapple and reserved juice; mix well. Cover and refrigerate until serving.

2) Pat salmon dry with paper towels. Sprinkle with cumin, pepper and remaining salt. Place skin side down in a 13-in. x 9-in. x 2-in. baking dish coated with nonstick cooking spray.

3) Bake, uncovered, at 350° for 10-15 minutes or until fish flakes easily with a fork. Serve with salsa.

Yield: 6 servings.

Editor's Note: When cutting or seeding hot peppers, use rubber or plastic gloves to protect your hands. Avoid touching your face.

NUTRITION FACTS: 1 fillet with 1/2 cup salsa equals 374 calories, 20 g fat (4 g saturated fat), 100 mg cholesterol, 405 mg sodium, 14 g carbohydrate, 1 g fiber, 34 g protein.

PECAN-CRUSTED SALMON

Pecan-Crusted Salmon

Kara Cook, Elk Ridge, Utah

These delicious salmon fillets are wonderful for company since they take only a few minutes to prepare, yet they taste like you fussed. The nutty coating is a nice complement to the fish.

- 4 salmon fillets (about 6 ounces *each*)
- 2 cups milk

1 cup finely chopped pecans
1/2 cup all-purpose flour
1/4 cup packed brown sugar
2 teaspoons seasoned salt
2 teaspoons pepper
3 tablespoons vegetable oil

1) Place salmon fillets in a large resealable plastic bag; add milk. Seal bag and turn to coat. Let stand for 10 minutes; drain.

2) Meanwhile, in a shallow bowl, combine the pecans, flour, brown sugar, seasoned salt and pepper. Coat fillets with pecan mixture, gently pressing into the fish.

3) In a large skillet, brown salmon in oil over medium-high heat. Transfer to a 15-in. x 10-in. x 1-in. baking pan coated with nonstick cooking spray. Bake at 400° for 8-10 minutes or until fish flakes easily with a fork.

Yield: 4 servings.

NUTRITION FACTS: 1 fillet equals 658 calories, 45 g fat (7 g saturated fat), 102 mg cholesterol, 778 mg sodium, 27 g carbohydrate, 3 g fiber, 38 g protein.

REMOVING SKIN FROM A FILLET

1) Use a sharp flexible knife to remove the skin from a fillet. Position the fillet with the tail end closest to you. Starting at the tail end of the fillet, make a small 45° angle cut in the meat to, but not through, the skin. Using that cut as a starting point, insert knife and angle it flat against the skin.

2) Hold the skin taut with one hand and slide the knife along the skin, separating the skin from the fillet. As you push the knife away from you, pull skin toward you.

Salmon and Shrimp with Garlic Rice
Darlene Sullivan, Wasilla, Alaska

I combined two of my favorites, salmon and shrimp, into one creamy-cheesy dish that's oh-so-good over rice.

5 tablespoons butter, *divided*
3 tablespoons all-purpose flour
1-1/2 cups half-and-half cream
1-1/2 cups (6 ounces) shredded cheddar cheese, *divided*
1 teaspoon salt
1/2 teaspoon ground mustard
1/4 teaspoon dill weed
Dash cayenne pepper
1/2 pound medium uncooked shrimp, peeled and deveined
1-1/2 pounds salmon fillets
3 garlic cloves, minced
1 cup uncooked long grain rice
2 cups chicken broth

1) In a large saucepan, melt 3 tablespoons butter. Stir in flour until smooth; gradually add cream. Bring to a boil; cook and stir for 2 minutes or until thickened.

2) Add 1 cup cheese, salt, mustard, dill and cayenne; stir until cheese is melted. Remove from the heat; stir in shrimp.

3) Pat salmon dry with paper towels; place in a greased 13-in. x 9-in. x 2-in. baking dish. Pour shrimp mixture over salmon. Top with remaining cheese.

4) Bake, uncovered, at 400° for 25-30 minutes or until the fish flakes easily with a fork and shrimp turn pink.

5) Meanwhile, in a saucepan, saute garlic in remaining butter until tender. Add rice; cook and stir for 2 minutes. Stir in broth; bring to a boil. Reduce heat; cover and cook for 15 minutes or until rice is tender. Serve with the salmon and shrimp mixture.

Yield: 6 servings.

NUTRITION FACTS: 1 serving equals 699 calories, 42 g fat (22 g saturated fat), 228 mg cholesterol, 1,241 mg sodium, 32 g carbohydrate, 1 g fiber, 44 g protein.

CRAB-TOPPED FISH FILLETS

Crab-Topped Fish Fillets
Mary Tuthill, Ft. Myers Beach, Florida

Elegant but truly no-fuss, this recipe is perfect for company. Toasting the almonds gives them a little more crunch, which is a delightful way to top the fish fillets.

- 4 sole, orange roughy *or* cod fillets (6 ounces *each*)
- 1 can (6 ounces) crabmeat, drained, flaked and cartilage removed *or* 1 cup imitation crabmeat, chopped
- 1/2 cup grated Parmesan cheese
- 1/2 cup mayonnaise
- 1 teaspoon lemon juice

Paprika, optional

- 1/3 cup slivered almonds, toasted

1) Place fillets in a greased 13-in. x 9-in. x 2-in. baking dish. Bake, uncovered, at 350° for 18-22 minutes or until fish flakes easily with a fork.

2) Meanwhile, in a bowl, combine crab, Parmesan cheese, mayonnaise and lemon juice.

3) Drain cooking juices from baking dish; spoon crab mixture over fillets. Broil 5 in. from the heat for 5 minutes or until topping is lightly browned. Sprinkle with paprika if desired and almonds.

Yield: 4 servings.

NUTRITION FACTS: 1 serving equals 457 calories, 31 g fat (5 g saturated fat), 90 mg cholesterol, 585 mg sodium, 2 g carbohydrate, 1 g fiber, 40 g protein.

Tilapia with Cucumber Relish
Mary VanHollebeke, Wyandotte, Michigan

My husband isn't big on fish, but he enjoys this mild-tasting tilapia. The relish adds garden-fresh flavor and pretty color.

- 2/3 cup chopped seeded cucumber
- 1/2 cup chopped radishes
- 1 tablespoon tarragon vinegar
- 1 teaspoon olive oil
- 1/2 teaspoon salt, *divided*
- 1/4 teaspoon pepper, *divided*
- 1/8 teaspoon sugar
- 1/8 teaspoon paprika
- 4 tilapia fillets (6 ounces *each*)
- 1 tablespoon butter

1) In a small bowl, combine cucumber and radishes. In another small bowl, whisk the vinegar, oil, 1/4 teaspoon salt, 1/8 teaspoon pepper and sugar. Pour over cucumber mixture; toss to coat evenly. Combine paprika and remaining salt and pepper; sprinkle over fillets.

2) In a large nonstick skillet coated with nonstick cooking spray, melt butter. Add fish; cook for 3-4 minutes on each side or until fish flakes easily with a fork. Serve with cucumber relish.

Yield: 4 servings.

NUTRITION FACTS: 1 fish fillet with 3 tablespoons relish equals 181 calories, 6 g fat (3 g saturated fat), 90 mg cholesterol, 388 mg sodium, 1 g carbohydrate, trace fiber, 32 g protein.

Feta Tomato-Basil Fish
Alicia Szeszol, Lindenhurst, Illinois

My husband provides the main ingredient in this dish after his summer fishing trips. Feta and Italian tomatoes give it a Mediterranean flavor.

- 1/3 cup chopped onion
- 1 garlic clove, minced
- 2 teaspoons olive oil
- 1 can (14-1/2 ounces) Italian diced tomatoes, drained
- 1-1/2 teaspoons minced fresh basil *or* 1/2 teaspoon dried basil
- 1 pound walleye, bass *or* other whitefish fillets
- 4 ounces crumbled feta cheese

1) In a saucepan, saute onion and garlic in oil until tender. Add tomatoes and basil. Bring to a boil. Reduce heat; simmer, uncovered, for 5 minutes.

2) Meanwhile, broil fish 4-6 in. from the heat for 5-6 minutes. Top each fillet with tomato mixture and cheese. Broil 5-7 minutes longer or until fish flakes easily with a fork.

Yield: 4 servings.

NUTRITION FACTS: 1 serving equals 295 calories, 10 g fat (5 g saturated fat), 172 mg cholesterol, 799 mg sodium, 11 g carbohydrate, 1 g fiber, 38 g protein.

Sunshine Halibut

Jalayne Luckett, Marion, Illinois

Seasoned with garlic, onion and citrus, these fish fillets are moist and tasty. They look especially pretty on a colorful bed of shredded carrots.

1/3	cup chopped onion
1	garlic clove, minced
2	tablespoons minced fresh parsley
1/2	teaspoon grated orange peel
4	halibut steaks (6 ounces *each*)
1/4	cup orange juice
1	tablespoon lemon juice
1/4	teaspoon salt
1/4	teaspoon lemon-pepper seasoning

1) In a nonstick skillet coated with nonstick cooking spray, saute onion and garlic until tender; remove from the heat. Stir in parsley and orange peel.

2) Place halibut in an 11-in. x 7-in. x 2-in. baking dish coated with nonstick cooking spray. Top with onion mixture. Combine orange and lemon juices; pour over fish. Sprinkle with salt and lemon-pepper.

3) Cover and bake at 400° for 15-20 minutes or until fish flakes easily with a fork.

Yield: 4 servings.

NUTRITION FACTS: 4-1/2 ounces cooked fish equals 202 calories, 4 g fat (1 g saturated fat), 54 mg cholesterol, 270 mg sodium, 4 g carbohydrate, trace fiber, 36 g protein.

Baked Halibut

Sandy Schroth, Gustavus, Alaska

Sour cream, Parmesan cheese and dill create a wonderful flavor mixture that tops flaky halibut steaks. It's a real treat when you're looking for a change from beef or chicken.

3	pounds halibut steaks (1 inch thick)
1	cup (8 ounces) sour cream
1/2	cup grated Parmesan cheese
1/4	cup butter, softened
1/2	teaspoon dill weed
1/2	teaspoon salt
1/4	teaspoon pepper
	Paprika

1) Place halibut in a greased 13-in. x 9-in. x 2-in. baking dish. Combine the sour cream, Parmesan cheese, butter, dill, salt and pepper; spoon over halibut.

2) Cover and bake at 375° for 20 minutes. Uncover; sprinkle with paprika. Bake 10-15 minutes longer or until fish flakes easily with a fork.

Yield: 6 servings.

NUTRITION FACTS: 12 ounces equals 423 calories, 21 g fat (11 g saturated fat), 123 mg cholesterol, 539 mg sodium, 2 g carbohydrate, trace fiber, 51 g protein.

SEASONED SALMON STEAKS

Seasoned Salmon Steaks

Cary Winright, Medina, Texas

A flavorful basting sauce adds spark to these special salmon steaks. The moist, firm fish broils to perfection in mere minutes.

6	salmon steaks (1 inch thick and 6 ounces *each*)
1/2	cup butter, melted
2	teaspoons seasoned salt
2	teaspoons Italian seasoning
2	teaspoons lemon juice
1/2	teaspoon garlic powder
1/2	teaspoon grated lemon peel
	Dash cayenne pepper

1) Place salmon on a greased broiler rack. Broil 4-6 in. from the heat for 8-10 minutes.

2) Meanwhile, combine the remaining ingredients. Brush some over some over salmon. Turn and broil 10 minutes longer or until fish flakes easily with a fork. Baste with remaining butter mixture.

Yield: 6 servings.

NUTRITION FACTS: 1 salmon steak equals 447 calories, 34 g fat (13 g saturated fat), 141 mg cholesterol, 761 mg sodium, 1 g carbohydrate, trace fiber, 34 g protein.

Basil-Tomato Tuna Steaks
Jan Parker, Englewood, Florida

Be prepared to reel in raves when you place this fabulous fish dish on the table. It's moist and flavorful with basil, tomato and cheese.

- 4 tuna *or* 4 salmon steaks (1 inch thick and 6 ounces *each*)
- 1 tablespoon olive oil
- 1/2 teaspoon salt
- 1/8 teaspoon pepper
- 1/3 cup loosely packed basil leaves
- 1 medium tomato, chopped
- 1/4 cup shredded part-skim mozzarella cheese

1) In a large nonstick skillet, cook tuna in oil over medium heat for 3 minutes on each side or until fish flakes easily with a fork.

2) Transfer to a broiler pan. Sprinkle fish with salt and pepper. Cover with basil leaves. Top with tomato and cheese. Broil 4-6 in. from the heat for 2 minutes or until the cheese is melted.

Yield: 4 servings.

NUTRITION FACTS: 1 serving equals 240 calories, 6 g fat (2 g saturated fat), 81 mg cholesterol, 394 mg sodium, 2 g carbohydrate, 1 g fiber, 42 g protein.

PIERSIDE SALMON PATTIES

Pierside Salmon Patties
Martha Conaway, Pataskala, Ohio

Dill adds flavor to the tasty sauce that tops the moist salmon patties. Baking them all at once makes this recipe a breeze to prepare!

- 2 eggs, beaten
- 1 cup milk
- 2 tablespoons lemon juice

- 3 cups coarsely crushed saltines (about 66 crackers)
- 2 teaspoons finely chopped onion
- 1/4 teaspoon salt
- 1/4 teaspoon pepper
- 2 cans (14-3/4 ounces *each*) salmon, drained, bones and skin removed

DILL SAUCE:
- 2 tablespoons butter
- 2 tablespoons all-purpose flour
- 1 teaspoon snipped fresh dill *or* 1/2 teaspoon dill weed
- 1/4 teaspoon salt

  Dash pepper

  Dash nutmeg
- 1-1/2 cups milk

1) In a large bowl, beat the eggs, milk, lemon juice, saltines, onion, salt and pepper. Add salmon and mix well. Shape into twelve 3-in. patties. Place in a greased 15-in. x 10-in. x 1-in. baking pan. Bake at 350° for 30-35 minutes or until lightly browned.

2) Meanwhile, melt butter in a saucepan. Stir in the flour, dill, salt, pepper and nutmeg until smooth. Gradually add milk. Bring to a boil; cook and stir for 2 minutes or until thickened. Serve with the patties.

Yield: 6 servings.

NUTRITION FACTS: 2 patties with 1/4 cup sauce equals 471 calories, 22 g fat (8 g saturated fat), 156 mg cholesterol, 1,444 mg sodium, 29 g carbohydrate, 1 g fiber, 38 g protein.

Salmon Loaf
Dorothy Bateman, Carver, Massachusetts

Topping the traditional salmon loaf recipe, an olive cream sauce makes it special and unique. You can also serve the sauce on the side.

- 1 can (14-3/4 ounces) salmon, drained, bones and skin removed
- 1 small onion, finely chopped
- 1/2 cup soft bread crumbs
- 1/4 cup butter, melted
- 3 eggs, *separated*
- 2 teaspoons lemon juice
- 1 teaspoon minced fresh parsley
- 1/2 teaspoon salt
- 1/8 teaspoon pepper

OLIVE CREAM SAUCE:
- 2 tablespoons butter

2 tablespoons all-purpose flour
1-1/2 cups milk
1/4 cup chopped stuffed olives

1) In a large bowl, combine the salmon, onion, bread crumbs and butter. Stir in the egg yolks, lemon juice, parsley, salt and pepper.

2) In a small mixing bowl, beat the egg whites on high speed until stiff peaks form. Fold into salmon mixture.

3) Pour into a greased 8-in. x 4-in. x 2-in. loaf pan. Place loaf pan in a larger baking pan. Add 1 in. of hot water to larger pan.

4) Bake at 350° for 40-45 minutes or until a knife inserted near the center comes out clean. Let stand for 10 minutes before slicing.

5) Meanwhile, in a saucepan, melt the butter. Stir in flour until smooth; gradually add milk. Bring to a boil; cook and stir for 1 minute or until thickened. Stir in olives. Serve over salmon loaf.

Yield: 4 servings (8 slices).

NUTRITION FACTS: 2 slices salmon loaf with about 1/3 cup sauce equals 476 calories, 33 g fat (15 g saturated fat), 264 mg cholesterol, 1,334 mg sodium, 13 g carbohydrate, 1 g fiber, 30 g protein.

Salmon Salad
Diane Benskin, Lewisville, Texas

This salad couldn't be easier. Just mix together, chill and serve!

2 cans (14-3/4 ounces *each*) salmon, drained and bones removed
2 celery ribs, sliced
1 large apple, peeled and chopped
5 green onions, sliced
1/2 cup mayonnaise
2 teaspoons snipped fresh dill *or* 3/4 teaspoon dill weed
3/4 teaspoon minced fresh basil *or* dash dried basil
1/4 teaspoon garlic salt
1/4 teaspoon minced fresh tarragon *or* dash dried tarragon

1) Place salmon in a large bowl and flake. Add remaining ingredients; stir gently.

2) Cover and refrigerate until serving.

Yield: 8 servings.

NUTRITION FACTS: 1 cup equals 276 calories, 19 g fat (3 g saturated fat), 51 mg cholesterol, 704 mg sodium, 4 g carbohydrate, 1 g fiber, 22 g protein.

Creole Tuna
Betty Bernat, Bethlehem, New Hampshire

This speedy recipe has been in my family for as long as I can remember. Because it relies on pantry staples, it's easy to make when you can't decide what to fix for dinner.

1/4 cup chopped green pepper
2 tablespoons butter
2 tablespoons all-purpose flour
1/2 teaspoon sugar
1/2 teaspoon salt
1/8 teaspoon pepper
1/3 cup milk
1 can (14-1/2 ounces) stewed tomatoes
1 can (6 ounces) tuna, drained and flaked
1 teaspoon Creole seasoning
Hot cooked rice, optional

1) In a saucepan, saute green pepper in butter until tender. Stir in the flour, sugar, salt and pepper until blended. Gradually add milk, stirring constantly. Stir in tomatoes.

2) Bring to a boil; cook and stir for 2 minutes. Add tuna and Creole seasoning; heat through. Serve over rice if desired.

Yield: 4 servings.

NUTRITION FACTS: 1 serving equals 160 calories, 7 g fat (4 g saturated fat), 31 mg cholesterol, 858 mg sodium, 13 g carbohydrate, 1 g fiber, 13 g protein.

■ *SUBSTITUTE FOR CREOLE SEASONING:* The following spices may be substituted for the Creole seasoning: 1/2 teaspoon *each* paprika and garlic powder, and a pinch *each* cayenne pepper, dried thyme and ground cumin.

Cheesy Tuna Noodles

Tamara Duggan, O'Fallon, Missouri

This home-style dish is quick to make using the microwave. It turns out just as good as old-fashioned, oven-baked versions.

2-1/2 cups uncooked wide egg noodles
1 medium onion, chopped
2 tablespoons butter
1 can (10-3/4 ounces) condensed cream of celery soup, undiluted
1/3 cup milk
1 can (6 ounces) tuna, drained and flaked
1 cup (4 ounces) shredded cheddar cheese
1/4 cup grated Parmesan cheese

1) Cook noodles according to package directions. Meanwhile, place onion in a greased microwave-safe 11-in. x 7-in. x 2-in. dish; dot with butter.

2) Microwave, uncovered, on high for 1 minute; stir. Microwave 1-2 minutes longer, stirring every 30 seconds.

3) In a bowl, combine soup and milk; stir in tuna and cheeses. Pour over onion. Drain noodles; add to tuna mixture and mix well. Cover and microwave on high for 3-4 minutes or until heated through and cheese is melted.

Yield: 4 servings.

NUTRITION FACTS: 1 serving equals 405 calories, 21 g fat (13 g saturated fat), 93 mg cholesterol, 1,049 mg sodium, 29 g carbohydrate, 2 g fiber, 25 g protein.

White Bean Tuna Salad

Kathleen Law, Post Falls, Idaho

I adapted this recipe with a zippy Dijon dressing that adds interest to the beans, tuna, olives and onion. It makes a filling and healthy lunch that I like to take to work.

1/4 cup red wine vinegar
3 garlic cloves, minced
2 teaspoons Dijon mustard
1 teaspoon sugar
1/2 teaspoon salt
1/4 teaspoon pepper
2 tablespoons olive oil
2 cans (15 ounces *each*) white kidney *or* cannellini beans, rinsed and drained
2 cans (6 ounces *each*) light water-packed tuna, drained and flaked
3/4 cup sliced ripe olives
1/2 cup chopped red onion

1) In a small bowl, combine vinegar, garlic, mustard, sugar, salt and pepper; gradually whisk in oil.

2) In a large bowl, combine beans, tuna, olives and onion; add dressing and toss gently. Cover and refrigerate until serving.

Yield: 6 servings.

NUTRITION FACTS: 3/4 cup equals 247 calories, 7 g fat (1 g saturated fat), 17 mg cholesterol, 754 mg sodium, 23 g carbohydrate, 6 g fiber, 20 g protein.

Tuna Burgers

Joann Brasington, Sumter, South Carolina

This tasty, change-of-pace sandwich is as quick to make as your favorite hamburger. My husband likes his topped with melted Swiss cheese and Dijon mustard. Salmon can be substituted for a more "elegant" burger.

1 can (6 ounces) tuna, drained and flaked
1 egg
1/2 cup seasoned bread crumbs
1/3 cup finely chopped onion
1/4 cup chopped celery
1/4 cup chopped sweet red pepper
1/4 cup mayonnaise
2 tablespoons chili sauce
1/2 teaspoon dill weed
1/4 teaspoon salt
1/8 teaspoon pepper
Dash hot pepper sauce
Dash Worcestershire sauce
4 hamburger buns, split
Tomato slices and lettuce leaves, optional

1) In a large bowl, combine the tuna, egg, bread crumbs, onion, celery, red pepper, mayonnaise, chili sauce and seasonings; mix well. Shape into four patties (mixture will be soft).

2) Coat a nonstick skillet with nonstick cooking spray; fry patties for 3-4 minutes on each side or until cooked through. Serve on buns with tomato and lettuce if desired.

Yield: 4 servings.

NUTRITION FACTS: 1 sandwich equals 363 calories, 16 g fat (3 g saturated fat), 71 mg cholesterol, 962 mg sodium, 36 g carbohydrate, 2 g fiber, 18 g protein.

About Shellfish

Shellfish are divided into two general categories—mollusks and crustaceans. Mollusks have soft, unsegmented bodies; many are covered by a shell. Clams, oysters, mussels and scallops are mollusks. Crustaceans have elongated bodies with jointed external shells, which are shed periodically. Crab, shrimp and lobster are crustaceans.

CLAMS-Buying and Storing

Clams are available with hard or soft shells. Hard-shell clams are classified by size—littlenecks (small), cherry stone (medium) and chowder clams, which are usually chopped. Soft-shell clams, also called longnecks, have necks that extend out of the shell.

Hard-shell calms should be tightly closed or if slightly opened, should close when tapped. Don't purchase hard-shell clams that remain opened when tapped or have cracked shells. Soft-shell clams don't tightly close their shells; they are fresh and alive if the neck moves when lightly poked.

Clams are also sold shucked. Look for clams that are plump, moist and shiny. The color depends on the variety. Buy 6 to 12 clams per person.

Store live clams, mussels and oysters in a container covered with a dampened cloth. If possible, have a bed of ice in the container. It's best to use within 24 hours of purchasing. Don't store in an airtight container or fresh water, since they will die. Store shucked clams and oysters in a leakproof covered container in the refrigerator.

CLAMS-Preparing and Cooking

Scrub hard-shell clams under cold running water with a stiff brush. Soft-shell clams or steamers may have grit in them. To remove the grit before cooking, soak them in salted cold water (about 1/3 cup salt to about a gallon of water) in the refrigerator for 2 hours. Rinse off the shells before steaming.

To steam clams, bring a cup of water to a boil in a stockpot. Add clams, cover and steam for 5 to 7 minutes or until clams open. Discard any clams that do not open. Either cut or pull clam from shell. Discard sheath that connects the clam to its shell. Shucked clam are cooked when they are plump and turn opaque.

HOW TO SHUCK A HARD-SHELL CLAM

1) Scrub under cold running water with a stiff brush. Place on a tray and refrigerate for 30 minutes. They will be easier to open.

2) Protect your hand by placing the clam in a clean kitchen towel with the hinge facing out. Insert clam knife next to the hinge.

3) Slide the knife around to loosen the shells.

4) Open the top shell and cut the muscle from the top shell. Discard the top shell.

5) Use the knife to release clam from bottom shell. If desired, pour clam juice into a strainer and reserve for your recipe.

OYSTERS-Buying and Storing

Oysters in their shell should be tightly closed; if slightly opened, they should close when tapped. Don't purchase oysters that remain opened when tapped or have cracked shells.

Shucked oysters should be plump and generally are creamy white. Their liquid should be clear not cloudy and the color of the liquid can range from milky white to light gray. Buy 6 oysters per person. For storage information, see Clams on page 201.

HOW TO SHUCK OYSTERS

1) Scrub oysters under cold running water with a stiff brush. Place oysters on a tray and refrigerate for 1 hour. They will be easier to open.

2) Protect your hands by wrapping the oyster, bigger shell down, in a clean kitchen towel with the hinge facing out. Keep oyster level to avoid loosing any juice. Insert an oyster knife next to hinge.

3) Twist the knife until you hear a snap to pry shells open.

4) Slide the knife along the top shell to cut the oyster loose. Discard the top shell.

5) Slide knife between oyster and the bottom shell to release it. If serving in the shell, discard any bits of shell particles. If cooking shucked oysters, strain juice.

OYSTERS-Preparing and Cooking

Shucked oysters can be boiled for 5 minutes or deep-fat fried at 375° for 10 minutes. Shucked oysters are cooked when they are plump, turn opaque and the edges start to curl.

MUSSELS-Buying and Storing

Mussels are cultivated or harvested wild. Most mussels sold have blue-black shells. The cultivated mussels are sold without beards—the filament that holds the mussel to rocks. Mussels should be tightly closed or if slightly opened, should close when tapped. Don't purchase mussels that remain opened when tapped or have cracked shells. Buy 3/4 to 1 pound mussels per person. For storage information, see Clams on page 201.

MUSSELS-Preparing and Cooking

Scrub mussels under cold running water with a stiff brush. If the mussels have beards, remove them from the shells by pulling the beards out with your fingers. The beards should be removed just before cooking. Farm-raised mussels may not have beards. To shuck, follow directions for Clams on page 201.

Steam mussels for 5-7 minutes or until opened. Discard any mussels that do not open. If necessary, remove from pan as they open. Shucked mussels are cooked when they are plump and turn opaque.

SCALLOPS-Buying and Storing

The three types of scallops are sea, bay and the less commonly known calico. Sea scallops are larger, about 1-1/2-in. diameter, but can be bigger. For more even cooking, cut scallops over 2-in. diameter in half or if they are very thick, cut them horizontally in half.

Bay scallops are small, about 1/2-in. diameter, and are generally found on the East Coast. They are also imported from China. They are generally available fresh in the fall and winter. Calico scallops are small scallops found deep in the waters off of Florida.

Scallops vary in color from creamy white to tan and should have a sweet, fresh odor. Buy 4 ounces scallops per serving.

Store in a leakproof covered container in the refrigerator. It's best to use scallops within 24 hours of purchasing.

SCALLOPS-Preparing and Cooking

If your scallops have a crescent-shaped muscle, cut or pull off and discard. Pat dry with paper towels if they are going to be floured. Cut large scallops in half for even cooking. Scallops are frequently sauteed or pan-fried. Depending on their size, they generally take 3-4 minutes to cook and are done when they turn opaque.

CRABS-Buying and Storing

Fresh crabs are available with hard or soft shells and as crab legs from King crab. Hard-shell varieties are blue and the large Dungeness crab. Soft-shell crabs are blue crabs that have shed their shell and have not yet hardened their new shells.

Live crabs should move when touched. Buy 1 pound whole crabs per serving. Store live crabs or lobsters in a container covered with a dampened cloth. It's best to use within 24 hours of purchasing. Don't store in an airtight container or fresh water because they will die.

CRABS-Preparing and Cooking

Hard-shell crabs should be rinsed under cold running water prior to cooking. To boil hard-shell blue crabs, in a large stockpot, bring 8 to 12 quarts of water and 2 teaspoons salt to a boil. Water can also be flavored with lemon and crab boil seasoning. Add crabs.

Reduce heat; cover and simmer for about 10 minutes or until crabs turn red and meat turns white.

With tongs, remove to a colander to drain. Serve with melted butter if desired. This is definitely a messy, hands-on eating activity. If desired, cover your table with newspaper before serving the crabs. When finished, roll up the newspaper with discarded shells and toss in the garbage.

SHRIMP-Buying and Storing

Shrimp are harvested in warm-water as well as cold-water areas. Cold-water shrimp are small and are usually sold cooked and peeled. Warm-water shrimp are larger and classified by the color of their shell—white, pink and brown. Black Tiger shrimp are farm-raised shrimp that have mostly black shells with brown stripes. Rock shrimp have sweet meat and are sold with the shells off. Prawns are freshwater crustaceans that are similar to the shrimp, which live in saltwater.

Most fresh shrimp that is sold has actually been previously frozen and thawed. Fresh shrimp should have a firm texture. Avoid shrimp that have a yellow color to their meat or black spots or rings on the shells (unless they are Tiger shrimp) or meat. Shrimp in the shell (fresh or frozen) are available in different sizes (medium, large, extra large, jumbo). See the chart of shrimp sizes below. Buy 3 to 4 ounces shelled shrimp per serving. For every pound of shelled shrimp that you want, buy 1-1/4 pounds of unshelled shrimp.

Shrimp Count

Shrimp are classified and sold by size. Shrimp count indicates the number of shrimp of a certain size that are in a pound. The more shrimp it takes to make a pound the smaller they are. The terms used to describe the count are not consistent from store to store. For example, a 16-20 count may be extra jumbo in one market and extra large in another. The count is the best indication of size.

CRACKING AND CLEANING COOKED HARD-SHELL CRAB

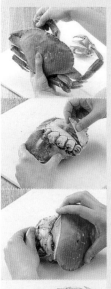

1) Twist off claws and legs. Use a nutcracker or crab mallet to crack the joints and shells and pick out meat with a seafood fork.

2) Place crab upside down on its top shell. Using your hands, pull up and off the tail flap (apron) and discard.

3) Turn over and lift off and discard top shell.

4) Turn crab back on its back; scrape off feathery gills on each side, internal organs and jaw.

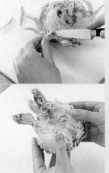

5) Break crab body in half and pick meat out with fingers or a lobster pick.

SHRIMP SIZE / NAME	COUNT
COLOSSAL	10 to 15
EXTRA JUMBO	16 to 20
JUMBO	21 to 25
EXTRA LARGE	26 to 30
LARGE	31 to 35
MEDIUM LARGE	36 to 42
MEDIUM	43 to 50
SMALL	51 to 60

SHRIMP-Preparing and Cooking

Depending on their use, shrimp can be peeled and deveined before or after cooking. To cook shrimp, in a large saucepan, bring 1 quart of water and 1 teaspoon salt to a boil. Add shrimp. Reduce heat and simmer, uncovered, for 1-3 minutes or until the shrimp turn pink and opaque. Watch closely to avoid overcooking. Drain immediately. Serve warm or chilled.

LOBSTERS-Buying and Storing

Two types of lobsters are harvested in America—the spiny or rock lobster and the American or Maine lobster. The spiny lobster is harvested around warm water—Florida and California—and has no claws and is sold as a lobster tail. American lobsters are harvested around cold water—the North Atlantic coast—and are sold whole.

Live lobsters should move when touched. When picked up, a lobster should curl its tail. Lobsters are sold by weight, and the average weigh from 1 to 2-1/2 pounds. Buy 1 to 1-1/2 pounds whole lobster or 4 ounces lobster tail meat per serving. For storage information, refer to Crabs on page 203.

CRACKING AND CLEANING COOKED WHOLE LOBSTER

1) Twist off claws. Pull off small pincer and discard. Use a nutcracker, lobster cracker or crab mallet to crack the large claws. Remove meat.

2) Twist off the legs at body and crack shells and push out meat.

3) Twist tail and body in opposite directions to separate.

4) Turn tail, belly side up. Using scissors, cut through the membrane on both sides of shell. Lift off and discard membrane. Lift out tail meat. Discard intestinal vein. Any roe or tomalley (greenish liver) may be eaten.

LOBSTERS-Preparing and Cooking

Live lobsters should be purchased the same day that you plan to cook them. Rinse them under cold, running water just before cooking.

To boil live lobsters, in a large stockpot, bring enough water to cover the lobsters to a boil along with 2 to 3 teaspoons salt. Once the water has come to a boil, plunge lobster head first into the water. Start counting the cooking time once the water has returned to a boil. Reduce heat; cover and cook until a small leg or antennae can easily be removed. Lobsters will turn red immediately in water and that is *not* an indication of doneness. Remove from water with tongs and drain in a colander. Serve when cooled enough to handle. Serve with melted butter if desired.

The cooking time depends on the size of the lobster. For a 1-pound lobster, cook 10 minutes; 1-1/4-pound lobster, cook 12 minutes; 1-1/2-pound lobster, cook 15 minutes and for a 2-pound lobster, cook 18 minutes.

Defrost frozen lobster tails before cooking. Lobster tails can be boiled, broiled, grilled and cut into pieces and sauteed. To boil lobster tails, in a large saucepan, bring 6 cups water and 1-1/2 teaspoons salt to a boil. Add lobster tails. Reduce heat; cover and simmer for 8-12 minutes or until meat is firm and opaque. Serve with melted butter if desired.

Pasta with White Clam Sauce
Kelli Soike, Tallahassee, Florida

Garlic and oregano enhance the flavor of this delicious main dish. An Italian friend of my mom's passed on the recipe to her, and I began preparing it when I was 14. For convenience, it can be made in advance...and leftovers are just as good.

12	ounces uncooked linguine
2	garlic cloves, minced
1	can (2 ounces) anchovies, undrained
1	tablespoon olive oil
1	bottle (8 ounces) clam juice
1	can (6-1/2 ounces) minced clams, undrained
1/3	cup water
2	tablespoons dried oregano
1	tablespoon minced fresh parsley
1/4	teaspoon salt
1/2	teaspoon pepper
5	tablespoons shredded Parmesan cheese

1) Cook pasta according to package directions. In a saucepan, saute garlic and anchovies in oil for 3

minutes, breaking up anchovies. Stir in the clam juice, clams, water, oregano, parsley, salt and pepper. Bring to a boil.

2) Reduce heat; simmer, uncovered, for 15 minutes or until sauce is reduced by half. Drain pasta; toss with clam sauce. Sprinkle with cheese.

Yield: 5 servings.

NUTRITION FACTS: 1 cup equals 379 calories, 13 g fat (2 g saturated fat), 19 mg cholesterol, 874 mg sodium, 50 g carbohydrate, 4 g fiber, 16 g protein.

CLASSIC CRAB CAKES

Classic Crab Cakes
Debbie Terenzini, Lusby, Maryland

This region is known for good seafood, and crab cakes are a traditional favorite. I learned to make them from a chef in a restaurant where they were a best-seller. The crabmeat's sweet and mild flavor is sparked by the blend of other ingredients.

    1   pound canned crabmeat, drained, flaked and cartilage removed
    2   to 2-1/2 cups soft bread crumbs
    1   egg, beaten
    3/4 cup mayonnaise
    1/3 cup *each* chopped celery, green pepper and onion
    1   tablespoon seafood seasoning
    1   tablespoon minced fresh parsley
    2   teaspoons lemon juice
    1   teaspoon Worcestershire sauce
    1   teaspoon prepared mustard
    1/4 teaspoon pepper
    1/8 teaspoon hot pepper sauce
    2   to 4 tablespoons vegetable oil, optional
Lemon slices, optional

1) In a large bowl, combine the crab, bread crumbs, egg, mayonnaise, vegetables and seasonings.

2) Shape into eight patties. Broil patties if desired or cook in a skillet in oil for 4 minutes on each side or until golden brown. Serve with lemon if desired.

Yield: 8 servings.

NUTRITION FACTS: 1 crab cake equals 282 calories, 22 g fat (3 g saturated fat), 85 mg cholesterol, 638 mg sodium, 7 g carbohydrate, 1 g fiber, 14 g protein.

■ *APPETIZER CRAB CAKES:* Follow recipe as directed in step 1. Shape into 16 small crab cakes; broil or fry until golden brown on each side.

Creamed Crab on Toast
Nina De Witt, Aurora, Ohio

This is a great ready-in-a-jiffy luncheon dish or Sunday supper. Marjoram and lemon juice in the sauce nicely complement the the crab.

    1   can (10-3/4 ounces) condensed cream of mushroom soup, undiluted
    1   can (6 ounces) crabmeat, rinsed, drained, and cartilage removed
    1   tablespoon lemon juice
    1/4 teaspoon dried marjoram
Dash cayenne pepper
Toast *or* biscuits

1) In a 1-qt. microwave-safe dish, combine the soup, crab, lemon juice, marjoram and cayenne.

2) Cover and microwave on high for 3-4 minutes or until heated through, stirring once. Serve on toast or biscuits.

Yield: 4 servings.

NUTRITION FACTS: 1 serving (calculated without toast or biscuits) equals 133 calories, 5 g fat (2 g saturated fat), 41 mg cholesterol, 776 mg sodium, 11 g carbohydrate, 1 g fiber, 11 g protein.

MAKING SOFT BREAD CRUMBS

Tear several slices of fresh white, French or whole wheat bread into 1-in. pieces. Place in a food processor or blender; cover and push pulse button several times to make coarse crumbs. One slice of bread yields about 1/2 cup crumbs.

Sea Shell Crab Casserole
Taste of Home Test Kitchen

This crab casserole gets color and flavor from green pepper, celery and ripe olives.

1-1/2   cups uncooked medium shell pasta
1   large onion, chopped
1   medium green pepper, chopped
3   celery ribs, chopped
3   tablespoons butter
1   can (12 ounces) evaporated milk
1/2   cup mayonnaise
1   teaspoon salt
1   teaspoon ground mustard
1   teaspoon paprika
1   teaspoon Worcestershire sauce
1   can (2-1/2 ounces) sliced ripe olives, drained
2   packages (8 ounces *each*) imitation crabmeat, flaked

1) Cook pasta according to package directions. Meanwhile, in a large skillet, saute the onion, green pepper and celery in butter until tender.

2) In a large bowl, combine milk and mayonnaise until blended. Stir in the salt, mustard, paprika and Worcestershire sauce. Drain pasta; add the pasta along with the olives, crab and vegetables to the milk mixture.

3) Transfer to a greased shallow 2-qt. baking dish. Cover and bake at 350° for 25 minutes. Uncover; bake 5-10 minutes longer or until heated through.

Yield: 6 servings.

Editor's Note: Reduced-fat or fat-free mayonnaise may not be substituted for regular mayonnaise.

NUTRITION FACTS: 1 cup equals 471 calories, 27 g fat (9 g saturated fat), 51 mg cholesterol, 1,162 mg sodium, 42 g carbohydrate, 3 g fiber, 16 g protein.

Crab Salad Supreme
Mrs. A. Mayer, Richmond, Virginia

This is a great take-along salad for potlucks and reunions. You can easily double the ingredients to make enough for a crowd.

2   cups canned crabmeat, drained, flaked and cartilage removed
1/2   cup minced green onions
1/2   cup diced celery
1/2   cup finely chopped green pepper
1   tablespoon ground mustard

1/2   teaspoon salt
1/4   teaspoon pepper
2   teaspoons celery seed

SAUCE:
1/3   cup mayonnaise
1/3   cup sour cream
1/3   cup chili sauce
2   teaspoons lemon juice
2   cups shredded lettuce
4   hard-cooked eggs, sliced
4   medium tomatoes, cut into wedges

1) In a large bowl, combine the crab, vegetables and seasonings. For sauce, combine the mayonnaise, sour cream, chili sauce and lemon juice; pour over salad and gently toss to coat.

2) Arrange the lettuce on four individual plates or a serving plate. Top with crab salad; garnish with eggs and tomatoes. Refrigerate until serving.

Yield: 4 servings.

NUTRITION FACTS: 1 serving equals 401 calories, 26 g fat (6 g saturated fat), 292 mg cholesterol, 1,031 mg sodium, 18 g carbohydrate, 4 g fiber, 24 g protein.

CRAWFISH ETOUFFEE

Crawfish Etouffee
Becky Armstrong, Canton, Georgia

Etouffee is a French word meaning to smother. This dish, featuring a tangy tomato-based sauce, is a pleasure to serve because it's attractive as well as tasty.

1/3   cup all-purpose flour
1/2   cup vegetable oil
1   large green pepper, chopped
1   large onion, chopped

1 cup chopped celery
1 can (15 ounces) tomato sauce
1 cup water
1 tablespoon Worcestershire sauce
1 teaspoon garlic powder
1 teaspoon paprika
1 teaspoon lemon juice
3/4 teaspoon Creole seasoning
2 pounds frozen cooked crawfish tails, thawed
Hot cooked rice

1) In a heavy Dutch oven, whisk the flour and oil until smooth. Cook over medium-high heat for 5 minutes, whisking constantly. Reduce heat to medium; cook and stir 10 minutes longer or until mixture is reddish-brown.

2) Add the green pepper, onion and celery; cook an stir for 5 minutes. Add tomato sauce, water, Worcestershire sauce, garlic powder, paprika, lemon juice and Creole seasoning. Bring to a boil.

3) Reduce heat; cover and simmer for 45 minutes. Add crawfish; heat through. Serve with rice.

Yield: 8 servings.

Editor's Note: The following spices may be substituted for the Creole seasoning: 1/2 teaspoon *each* paprika and garlic powder, and a pinch *each* cayenne pepper, dried thyme and ground cumin.

NUTRITION FACTS: 1 serving (calculated without rice) equals 269 calories, 15 g fat (2 g saturated fat), 155 mg cholesterol, 451 mg sodium, 11 g carbohydrate, 2 g fiber, 22 g protein.

Crab Rockefeller
Cherly Maczko, Arthurdale, West Virginia

When you're entertaining seafood lovers, you can't go wrong with this delightful main course. The spinach and golden crumb topping make the casserole so delicious.

4 tablespoons butter, *divided*
2 tablespoons all-purpose flour
1-1/3 cups milk
1/2 cup grated Parmesan cheese
1 package (10 ounces) frozen chopped spinach, thawed and squeezed dry
1 can (6 ounces) crabmeat, drained, flaked and cartilage removed
1/2 cup dry bread crumbs

1) In a large saucepan, melt 2 tablespoons butter. Stir in flour until smooth; gradually add the milk. Bring to a boil; cook and stir for 2 minutes or until

thickened. Reduce heat; add the cheese and stir until smooth. Add the spinach and crab.

2) Transfer to a greased shallow 1-qt. baking dish. Melt remaining butter; toss with bread crumbs. Sprinkle over the top. Bake, uncovered, at 375° for 15-20 minutes or until bubbly.

Yield: 3 servings.

NUTRITION FACTS: 1 serving equals 430 calories, 25 g fat (15 g saturated fat), 117 mg cholesterol, 870 mg sodium, 26 g carbohydrate, 3 g fiber, 26 g protein.

Baked Lobster Tails
Taste of Home Test Kitchen

Lobster tails are a treat in themselves, but you can serve them with steak for an extra-special dinner!

4 fresh *or* frozen lobster (8 to 10 ounces *each*), thawed
1 cup water
1 tablespoon minced fresh parsley
1/8 teaspoon salt
Dash pepper
1 tablespoon butter, melted
2 tablespoons lemon juice
Lemon wedges and additional melted butter, optional

1) Split lobster tails in half lengthwise. With cut side up and using scissors, cut along the edge of shell to loosen the cartilage covering the tail meat from the shell; remove and discard cartilage.

2) Pour water into a 13-in. x 9-in. x 2-in. baking dish; place lobster tails in dish. Combine the parsley, salt and pepper; sprinkle over lobster. Drizzle with butter and lemon juice.

3) Bake, uncovered, at 375° for 20-25 minutes or until meat is firm and opaque. Serve with lemon wedges and melted butter if desired.

Yield: 4 servings.

NUTRITION FACTS: 2 lobster tail halves equals 232 calories, 5 g fat (2 g saturated fat), 223 mg cholesterol, 775 mg sodium, 2 g carbohydrate, trace fiber, 43 g protein.

CLARIFIED BUTTER

To make clarified butter, melt butter over low heat without stirring. Skim off foam. Pour off clear liquid and discard milky residue in bottom of pan. Store clear liquid in an airtight container in the refrigerator or freeze.

LOBSTER NEWBURG

Lobster Newburg
Wendy Cornell, Hudson, Maine

We like to use fresh lobster in this time-honored recipe. It can also be made with frozen, canned or imitation lobster. No matter how you prepare it, guests will think you fussed.

- 3 cups cooked lobster meat *or* canned flaked lobster meat *or* imitation lobster chunks
- 3 tablespoons butter
- 1/4 teaspoon paprika
- 3 cups heavy whipping cream
- 1/2 teaspoon Worcestershire sauce
- 3 egg yolks, lightly beaten
- 1 tablespoon sherry, optional
- 1/4 teaspoon salt
- 1/3 cup crushed butter-flavored crackers (about 8 crackers)

1) In a large skillet, saute the lobster in butter and paprika for 3-4 minutes; set aside. In a large saucepan, bring cream and Worcestershire sauce to a gentle boil. Meanwhile, in a bowl, combine egg yolks, sherry if desired and salt.

2) Remove cream from the heat; stir a small amount into egg yolk mixture. Return all to the pan, stirring constantly. Bring to a gentle boil; cook and stir for 5-7 minutes or until slightly thickened. Stir in the lobster.

3) Divide lobster mixture between four 10-oz. baking dishes. Sprinkle with cracker crumbs. Broil 6 in. from heat 2-3 minutes or until golden brown.

Yield: 4 servings.

NUTRITION FACTS: 1 serving equals 882 calories, 81 g fat (48 g saturated fat), 505 mg cholesterol, 790 mg sodium, 12 g carbohydrate, trace fiber, 29 g protein.

Perfect Scalloped Oysters
Alice King, Nevada, Ohio

Creamy and delicious, this dish is a real treat with fresh or canned oysters.

- 2 cups crushed butter-flavored crackers (about 50)
- 1/2 cup butter, melted
- 1/2 teaspoon salt
- Dash pepper
- 1 pint shucked oysters *or* 2 cans (8 ounces each) whole oysters, drained
- 1 cup heavy whipping cream
- 1/4 teaspoon Worcestershire sauce

1) Combine cracker crumbs, butter, salt and pepper; sprinkle a third into a greased 1-1/2-qt. baking dish. Arrange half of the oysters over crumbs. Top with another third of the crumb mixture and the remaining oysters.

2) Combine cream and Worcestershire sauce; pour over oysters. Top with remaining crumb mixture. Bake, uncovered, at 350° for 30-40 minutes or until top is golden brown.

Yield: 8 servings.

NUTRITION FACTS: 1 serving equals 349 calories, 29 g fat (15 g saturated fat), 94 mg cholesterol, 508 mg sodium, 18 g carbohydrate, trace fiber, 5 g protein.

Citrus Scallops
Cheri Hawthorne, North Canton, Ohio

My husband and I like to eat seafood at least once a week. These scallops have a refreshing burst of flavor.

- 1 medium green *or* sweet red pepper, julienned
- 4 green onions, chopped
- 1 garlic clove, minced
- 2 tablespoons olive oil
- 1 pound sea scallops
- 1/2 teaspoon salt
- 1/4 teaspoon crushed red pepper flakes
- 2 tablespoons lime juice
- 1/2 teaspoon grated lime peel
- 4 medium navel oranges, peeled and sectioned
- 2 teaspoons minced fresh cilantro
- Hot cooked rice *or* pasta

1) In a large skillet, saute the pepper, onions and

garlic in oil for 1 minute. Add scallops, salt and pepper flakes; cook for 4 minutes. Add lime juice and peel; cook for 1 minute.

2) Reduce heat. Add orange sections and cilantro; cook 2 minutes longer or until scallops are opaque. Serve with rice or pasta.

Yield: 4 servings.

NUTRITION FACTS: 1/4 pound scallops (calculated without rice or pasta) equals 240 calories, 8 g fat (1 g saturated fat), 37 mg cholesterol, 482 mg sodium, 23 g carbohydrate, 4 g fiber, 21 g protein.

Stir-Fried Scallops
Stephany Gocobachi, San Rafuel, California

Scallops add interest to this mild tomato-based stovetop supper. Try serving the saucy mixture over rice or angel hair pasta...and garnish with cilantro if you like.

1	small onion, chopped
3	garlic cloves, minced
1	tablespoon olive oil
3/4	pound sea scallops, halved
2	medium plum tomatoes, chopped
2	tablespoons lemon juice
1/4	teaspoon salt
1/8	teaspoon pepper

Hot cooked pasta *or* rice, optional

1) In a nonstick skillet or wok, stir-fry onion and garlic in hot oil until tender. Add scallops; stir-fry until scallops turn opaque.

2) Add tomatoes; cook and stir 1-2 minutes longer or until heated through. Stir in lemon juice, salt and pepper. Serve over pasta or rice if desired.

Yield: 2 servings.

NUTRITION FACTS: 1 cup stir-fry mixture equals 246 calories, 8 g fat (1 g saturated fat), 56 mg cholesterol, 575 mg sodium, 13 g carbohydrate, 1 g fiber, 30 g protein.

Coconut-Fried Shrimp
Ann Atchison, O'Fallon, Missouri

These crunchy shrimp make a fun change-of-pace main dish or a tempting appetizer. The coconut coating adds a little sweetness...and the tangy orange marmalade and honey sauce is great for dipping. It's impossible to stop munching these once you start!

1-1/4	cups all-purpose flour
1-1/4	cups cornstarch
6-1/2	teaspoons baking powder
1/2	teaspoon salt
1/4	teaspoon Cajun seasoning
1-1/2	cups cold water
1/2	teaspoon vegetable oil
2-1/2	cups flaked coconut
1	pound uncooked large shrimp, peeled and deveined

Additional oil for deep-fat frying

1	cup orange marmalade
1/4	cup honey

1) In a large bowl, combine the flour, cornstarch, baking powder, salt and Cajun seasoning. Stir in water and oil until smooth.

2) Place coconut in another bowl. Dip shrimp into batter, then coat with coconut. In an electric skillet or deep-fat fryer, heat oil to 375°. Fry shrimp, a few at a time, for 3 minutes or until golden brown. Drain on paper towels.

3) In a saucepan, heat marmalade and honey; stir until blended. Serve with shrimp.

Yield: 4 servings.

NUTRITION FACTS: 1/4 of the shrimp with 5 tablespoons sauce equals 1,001 calories, 36 g fat (20 g saturated fat), 168 mg cholesterol, 1,184 mg sodium, 151 g carbohydrate, 4 g fiber, 23 g protein.

PEELING AND DEVEINING SHRIMP

1) Start on the underside by the head area to remove shell from shrimp. Pull legs and first section of shell to one side. Continue pulling shell up around the top and to the other side. Pull off shell by tail if desired.

2) Remove the black vein running down the back of shrimp by making a shallow slit with a paring knife along the back from head area to tail.

3) Rinse shrimp under cold water to remove the vein.

Shrimp Stir-Fry

Delia Kennedy, Deer Park, Washington

I've shared this recipe many times. When our children were still at home, they offered to wash the pan after dinner to encourage me to make it!

1-1/2 pounds medium uncooked shrimp, peeled and deveined
1/2 teaspoon salt
1/4 teaspoon pepper
2 tablespoons canola oil
1 cup fresh broccoli florets
1 cup julienned sweet red pepper
4 tablespoons reduced-sodium chicken broth, *divided*
1 cup sliced fresh mushrooms
1-1/2 cups fresh sugar snap peas
3/4 cup sliced green onions
3 garlic cloves, minced

1) Sprinkle shrimp with salt and pepper. In a large nonstick skillet or wok, stir-fry shrimp in hot oil until shrimp turn pink. Remove with a slotted spoon and keep warm.

2) In the same pan, stir-fry the broccoli and red pepper in 2 tablespoons broth for 5 minutes. Add mushrooms; stir-fry for 2 minutes. Add the peas, onions, garlic and remaining broth; stir-fry for 3-4 minutes or until vegetables are crisp-tender.

3) Return shrimp to the pan; stir-fry for 1-2 minutes or until heated through.

Yield: 4 servings.

NUTRITION FACTS: 1-1/2 cups equals 226 calories, 8 g fat (1 g saturated fat), 202 mg cholesterol, 581 mg sodium, 12 g carbohydrate, 4 g fiber, 25 g protein.

Spicy Shrimp Wraps

Frankie Allen Mann, Warrior, Alabama

This quick and easy recipe is deliciously big on flavor. Coated with tasty taco seasoning, the cooked shrimp are tucked inside a tortilla wrap, along with coleslaw and dressed-up bottled salsa.

1 cup salsa
1 medium ripe mango, peeled, pitted and diced
1 tablespoon ketchup
1 envelope reduced-sodium taco seasoning
1 tablespoon olive oil
1 pound uncooked medium shrimp, peeled and deveined
6 flour tortillas (10 inches), warmed
1-1/2 cups coleslaw mix
6 tablespoons reduced-fat sour cream

1) In a small bowl, combine the salsa, mango and ketchup; set aside. In a large resealable plastic bag, combine taco seasoning and oil; add shrimp. Seal bag and shake to coat.

2) In a nonstick skillet or wok, cook shrimp over medium-high heat for 2-3 minutes or shrimp turn until pink. Top tortillas with coleslaw mix, salsa mixture and shrimp.

3) Fold bottom third of tortilla up over filling; fold sides over. Serve with sour cream.

Yield: 6 servings.

NUTRITION FACTS: 1 wrap with 1 tablespoon sour cream equals 292 calories, 8 g fat (2 g saturated fat), 97 mg cholesterol, 907 mg sodium, 40 g carbohydrate, 2 g fiber, 16 g protein.

Garlic Butter Shrimp

Sheryll Hughes-Smith, Jackson, Mississippi

Garlic and lemon lend a pleasant flavor to these speedy sauteed shrimp. I like to serve them over wild rice mix from a box.

1 pound uncooked medium shrimp, peeled and deveined
2 to 3 garlic cloves, minced
1/4 cup butter
3 tablespoons lemon juice
Hot cooked rice

1) In a large skillet, saute the shrimp and garlic in butter for 5 minutes or until shrimp turn pink. Add lemon juice; heat through. Serve with rice.

Yield: 4 servings.

NUTRITION FACTS: 1/4 pound shrimp (calculated without rice) equals 191 calories, 12 g fat (7 g saturated fat), 199 mg cholesterol, 309 mg sodium, 1 g carbohydrate, trace fiber, 18 g protein.

Shrimp Dijonnaise

Wanda Penton, Franklinton, Louisiana

This easy dish for two comes together in minutes once the shrimp have marinated. It's a refreshing departure from meat.

1/2 cup lemon juice
1/4 cup butter, melted
2 tablespoons vegetable oil
2 tablespoons Dijon mustard
1 tablespoon Worcestershire sauce
3 garlic cloves, minced
3/4 pound uncooked large shrimp, peeled and deveined

1) In a large resealable bag, combine the lemon juice, butter, oil, mustard, Worcestershire sauce and garlic. Add shrimp; seal bag and turn to coat.

2) Refrigerate for 4 hours, turning occasionally. Drain and discard marinade. Broil shrimp 4 in. from the heat for 4 minutes or until pink.

Yield: 2 servings.

NUTRITION FACTS: 1 serving equals 312 calories, 20 g fat (8 g saturated fat), 283 mg cholesterol, 637 mg sodium, 5 g carbohydrate, trace fiber, 28 g protein.

CITRUS GARLIC SHRIMP

Citrus Garlic Shrimp
Diane Jackson, Las Vegas, Nevada

Garlic is paired with sunny citrus in this special shrimp and linguine combination that's pretty enough for company.

- 1 package (1 pound) linguine
- 1/2 cup olive oil
- 1/2 cup orange juice
- 1/3 cup lemon juice
- 3 to 4 garlic cloves, peeled
- 5 teaspoons grated lemon peel
- 4 teaspoons grated orange peel
- 1 teaspoon salt
- 1/4 teaspoon pepper
- 1 pound uncooked medium shrimp, peeled and deveined

Shredded Parmesan cheese and minced fresh parsley, optional

1) Cook linguine according to package directions. Meanwhile, in a blender or food processor, combine the next eight ingredients; cover and process until blended.

2) Pour into a large skillet; heat through. Add shrimp; cook for 5 minutes or until shrimp turn pink. Drain linguine; toss with shrimp mixture. Sprinkle with cheese and parsley if desired.

Yield: 6 servings.

NUTRITION FACTS: 1 cup equals 504 calories, 20 g fat (3 g saturated fat), 112 mg cholesterol, 526 mg sodium, 60 g carbohydrate, 3 g fiber, 22 g protein.

Shrimp in Cream Sauce
Jane Birch, Edison, New Jersey

This rich shrimp dish is wonderful over golden egg noodles, but you can also serve it over rice.

- 2 tablespoons butter, melted
- 1/3 cup all-purpose flour
- 1-1/2 cups chicken broth
- 4 garlic cloves, minced
- 1 cup heavy whipping cream
- 1/2 cup minced fresh parsley
- 2 teaspoons paprika

Salt and pepper to taste

- 2 pounds large uncooked shrimp, peeled and deveined

Hot cooked noodles *or* rice

1) In a small saucepan, melt butter; stir in flour until smooth. Gradually add broth and garlic. Bring to a boil; cook and stir for 2 minutes or until thickened. Remove from heat. Stir in the cream, parsley, paprika, salt and pepper.

2) Butterfly shrimp by cutting lengthwise almost in half but leaving shrimp attached at opposite side. Spread to butterfly.

3) Place cut side down in a greased 13-in. x 9-in. x 2-in. baking dish. Pour cream sauce over shrimp. Bake, uncovered, at 400° for 15-18 minutes or until shrimp turn pink. Serve over noodles.

Yield: 8 servings.

NUTRITION FACTS: 1 serving (calculated without salt, pepper and noodles or rice) equals 240 calories, 15 g fat (9 g saturated fat), 216 mg cholesterol, 410 mg sodium, 6 g carbohydrate, trace fiber, 20 g protein.

BUTTERFLYING SHRIMP

After the shrimp is deveined, cut the slit deeper into the shrimp but not all the way through, leaving shrimp attached at the bottom.

Saucy Orange Shrimp

Gloria Jarrett, Loveland, Ohio

On a trip to New Orleans, my husband picked up some fresh Gulf shrimp. The wife of the shrimp boat captain sent this recipe along with him. It's our favorite way to prepare shrimp.

- 4 pounds uncooked large shrimp in the shell
- 2 cups butter
- 2 medium navel oranges, peeled and thinly sliced
- 1 cup orange juice concentrate
- 2 tablespoons Worcestershire sauce
- 1 teaspoon *each* lemon-pepper seasoning, paprika, dried parsley flakes, garlic powder, onion powder and barbecue *or* hickory seasoning

Dash cayenne pepper

1) Place shrimp in two 13-in. x 9-in. x 2-in. baking dishes. In a saucepan, melt butter. Add orange slices; cook and stir until oranges fall apart. Stir in the remaining ingredients; heat through.

2) Pour over shrimp. Bake, uncovered, at 375° for 15-20 minutes or until shrimp turn pink.

Yield: 10 servings.

NUTRITION FACTS: 8 ounces equals 313 calories, 20 g fat (12 g saturated fat), 318 mg cholesterol, 626 mg sodium, 4 g carbohydrate, trace fiber, 29 g protein. .

Special Seafood Casserole

Angela Schwartz, Marietta, Georgia

I first sampled this casserole at a baby shower and found myself going for more. I was surprised to taste the artichokes with the seafood, but it was fantastic.

- 1/2 pound sea scallops
- 1 small onion, finely chopped
- 1 celery rib, finely chopped
- 6 tablespoons butter, cubed
- 7 tablespoons all-purpose flour
- 1-1/2 cups half-and-half cream
- 1 cup (4 ounces) shredded sharp cheddar cheese
- 6 tablespoons sherry *or* apple juice
- 3/4 teaspoon salt
- 1/4 teaspoon cayenne pepper
- 1 pound cooked medium shrimp, peeled and deveined
- 1 can (6 ounces) crabmeat, drained, flaked and cartilage removed
- 1 can (14 ounces) water-packed artichoke hearts, drained, rinsed, chopped and patted dry
- 1 can (8 ounces) sliced water chestnuts, drained
- 1/2 cup sliced almonds
- 1/4 cup grated Parmesan cheese

1) In a Dutch oven or large saucepan, saute the scallops, onion and celery in butter. Stir in the flour until blended. Add cream. Bring to a boil; cook and stir for 2 minutes or until thickened.

2) Reduce heat; add the cheddar cheese, sherry or juice, salt and cayenne, stirring until cheese is melted. Remove from the heat; set aside.

3) In a greased 11-in. x 7-in. x 2-in. baking dish, layer the shrimp, crab, artichokes and water chestnuts. Top with the sauce. Sprinkle with almonds and Parmesan cheese.

4) Bake, uncovered, at 350° for 25-30 minutes or until heated through. Let stand for 10 minutes before serving.

Yield: 6 servings.

NUTRITION FACTS: 1 serving equals 518 calories, 30 g fat (16 g saturated fat), 236 mg cholesterol, 894 mg sodium, 19 g carbohydrate, 2 g fiber, 38 g protein.

MEDITERRANEAN SEAFOOD STEW

Mediterranean Seafood Stew

Virginia Anthony, Blowing Rock, North Carolina

Mediterranean flavors make this dish special enough for company. It's loaded with orange roughy, shrimp and scallops that all bake up together easily in one baking dish.

- 1 medium onion, finely chopped
- 1-1/2 teaspoons minced garlic, *divided*
- 1 tablespoon olive oil

1/2 pound plum tomatoes, seeded and diced

1 teaspoon grated lemon peel

1/4 teaspoon crushed red pepper flakes

1 cup clam juice

1/3 cup white wine *or* additional clam juice

1 tablespoon tomato paste

1/2 teaspoon salt

1 pound orange roughy *or* red snapper fillets, cut into 1-inch cubes

1 pound uncooked large shrimp, peeled and deveined

1/2 pound sea scallops

1/3 cup minced fresh parsley

1/3 cup reduced-fat mayonnaise

1) In a Dutch oven or large saucepan, saute onion and 1/2 teaspoon garlic in oil until tender. Add the tomatoes, lemon peel and pepper flakes; cook and stir for 2 minutes.

2) Add the clam juice, wine or additional clam juice, tomato paste and salt. Bring to a boil. Reduce heat; cover and simmer for 10 minutes or until heated through.

3) Add the fish, shrimp, scallops and parsley. Cover and cook for 8-10 minutes or until fish flakes easily with a fork, the shrimp turn pink and scallops are opaque. Combine mayonnaise and remaining garlic; dollop onto each serving.

Yield: 6 servings.

NUTRITION FACTS: 1 cup stew with 2 teaspoons mayonnaise topping equals 221 calories, 8 g fat (1 g saturated fat), 123 mg cholesterol, 607 mg sodium, 7 g carbohydrate, 1 g fiber, 28 g protein.

Shrimp Patty Sandwiches
Tina Jacobs, Hurlock, Maryland

After eating at a restaurant, quite often my husband tells me I could make the dish better at home. This was the case with this shrimp patty! I added more shrimp and more flavor, and now it's one of his favorites.

4 eggs

4 cans (6 ounces *each*) shrimp, rinsed and drained *or* 2 cups medium cooked shrimp, peeled and deveined

1/2 pound haddock, cooked and flaked

1 cup plus 3 tablespoons pancake mix

2 tablespoons cornmeal

1/2 teaspoon dried parsley flakes

1/2 teaspoon celery salt

1/4 teaspoon ground mustard

1/4 teaspoon paprika

1/2 cup dry bread crumbs

3 to 4 tablespoons vegetable oil

8 hamburger buns

Lettuce leaves, tomato slices and onion slices, optional

1) In a large bowl, beat the eggs. Add the shrimp, haddock, pancake mix, cornmeal, parsley, celery salt, mustard and paprika; mix well. Shape into eight patties. Coat with bread crumbs.

2) In a large skillet, cook patties in oil over medium-high heat for 2 minutes on each side or until golden brown. Serve on buns with lettuce, tomato and onion if desired.

Yield: 8 servings.

NUTRITION FACTS: 1 sandwich equals 394 calories, 11 g fat (2 g saturated fat), 300 mg cholesterol, 1,666 mg sodium, 41 g carbohydrate, 2 g fiber, 30 g protein.

Orzo Shrimp Stew
Lisa Stinger, Hamilton, New Jersey

My husband and I really enjoy seafood, so I don't skimp on shrimp in this mildly seasoned stew. It has other satisfying ingredients, too, like broccoli, tomatoes and pasta.

2-1/2 cups reduced-sodium chicken broth

5 cups broccoli florets

1 can (14-1/2 ounces) diced tomatoes, undrained

1 cup uncooked orzo

1 pound uncooked medium shrimp, peeled and deveined

3/4 teaspoon salt

1/4 teaspoon pepper

2 teaspoons dried basil

2 tablespoons butter

1) In a large nonstick skillet or saucepan, bring broth to a boil. Add broccoli, tomatoes and orzo. Reduce heat; simmer, uncovered, for 5 minutes, stirring occasionally. Add shrimp, salt and pepper.

2) Cover; cook for 4-5 minutes or until shrimp turn pink and orzo is tender. Stir in basil and butter.

Yield: 4 servings.

NUTRITION FACTS: 1-3/4 cups equals 401 calories, 10 g fat (5 g saturated fat), 190 mg cholesterol, 919 mg sodium, 45 g carbohydrate, 4 g fiber, 35 g protein.

Creamy Seafood Enchiladas

Evelyn Gebhardt, Kasilof, Alaska

Condensed soup helps add creaminess to the sauce in this enchilada dish. I also like that it bakes up in no time.

- 1/4 cup butter
- 1/4 cup all-purpose flour
- 1 cup chicken broth
- 1 can (10-3/4 ounces) condensed cream of chicken soup, undiluted
- 1 cup (8 ounces) sour cream
- 1/2 cup salsa
- 1/8 teaspoon salt
- 1 cup (8 ounces) small-curd cottage cheese
- 1 pound small shrimp, cooked, peeled and deveined
- 1 cup cooked *or* canned crabmeat, drained, flaked and cartilage removed
- 1-1/2 cups (6 ounces) shredded Monterey Jack cheese
- 1 can (4 ounces) chopped green chilies
- 1 tablespoon dried cilantro
- 12 flour tortillas (7 inches)
- Additional salsa

1) In a saucepan over low heat, melt butter; stir in flour until smooth. Gradually stir in broth and soup until blended.

2) Bring to a boil; cook and stir for 2 minutes or until slightly thickened. Remove from the heat. Stir in sour cream, salsa and salt; set aside.

3) Place cottage cheese in a blender; cover and process until smooth. Transfer to a bowl; add the shrimp, crab, Monterey Jack cheese, chilies and cilantro.

4) Spread 3/4 cup sauce in a greased 13-in. x 9-in. x 2-in. baking dish. Place about 1/3 cup seafood mixture down the center of each tortilla. Roll up and place seam side down over sauce. Top with the remaining sauce.

5) Bake, uncovered, at 350° for 30-35 minutes or until heated through. Serve with additional salsa.

Yield: 6 servings.

NUTRITION FACTS: 2 enchiladas (calculated without additional salsa) equals 645 calories, 35 g fat (17 g saturated fat), 252 mg cholesterol, 1,812 mg sodium, 40 g carbohydrate, 2 g fiber, 42 g protein.

Dijon Tartar Sauce

Kristen Flaherty, South Portland, Maine

Fat-free mayonnaise mixed only with pickle relish seemed so tasteless, so I began experimenting and came up with my own recipe for tartar sauce. It adds lots of flavor to fish but few calories.

- 1/2 cup fat-free mayonnaise
- 3 tablespoons sweet pickle relish
- 3 tablespoons chopped onion
- 4 teaspoons Dijon mustard
- 2 teaspoons lemon juice
- 1/4 teaspoon sugar
- 1/4 teaspoon salt
- 1/8 teaspoon pepper

1) In a bowl, combine all the ingredients. Store in the refrigerator for up to 1 week.

Yield: 3/4 cup.

NUTRITION FACTS: 2 tablespoons equals 31 calories, 1 g fat (trace saturated fat), 2 mg cholesterol, 392 mg sodium, 6 g carbohydrate, 1 g fiber, trace protein.

Special Spicy Seafood Sauce

Carolyn Chapman, Snohomish, Washington

I've been serving this tangy seafood sauce for over 30 years, and I'm always asked for the recipe. Low in fat and easy to make, it's a great seafood sauce to serve with a cold shrimp as an appetizer. The recipe is easy to halve or double, too. I've found it's usually smart to make extra because it goes so fast!

- 1-1/2 cups ketchup
- 2 tablespoons finely chopped celery
- 2 tablespoons white wine vinegar
- 2 teaspoons finely chopped green onion
- 2 teaspoons water
- 2 teaspoons Worcestershire sauce
- 1 teaspoon prepared horseradish
- 1/2 teaspoon seasoned salt
- 1/2 teaspoon ground mustard
- 1/4 teaspoon cayenne pepper

1) In a small bowl, combine all ingredients. Cover and refrigerate for at least 1 hour before serving. Refrigerate leftovers.

Yield: 1-3/4 cups.

NUTRITION FACTS: 2 tablespoons equals 28 calories, trace fat (0 saturated fat), trace cholesterol, 445 mg sodium, 7 g carbohydrate, trace fiber, trace protein.

GRILLING

215

GRILLING

Grilling is a great way to prepare meals, whatever the season. Plus it leaves you with a clean kitchen and provides flavorful fare to serve your family.

Choosing a Grill

Charcoal or gas—which one to choose is a matter of preference. Both types of grills will give you delicious results. When buying a grill, consider the cost and ease of use as well as your grilling needs and frequency.

Both types of grills are available in a wide range of prices, but gas grills generally cost more than charcoal grills. Gas grills ignite immediately, take just minutes to heat up and make it easier to control the grilling temperature.

Charcoal grills take about 30 minutes for the briquettes to get hot, the coals start off hot and cool down during cooking and the ash from coals can be messy to clean up. If you don't plan to grill often or grill only small amounts, then a charcoal grill might be a good choice due to its price. A hibachi may also be the right option due to its size.

Grilling Safety and Tips

Always place your grill on a level solid surface, away from fences, shrubs, grass and overhangs. Grill in a well-ventilated area.

Store charcoal in a dry place. Damp or wet charcoal may not ignite. Never add lighter fluid to lit coals. Never use gasoline or kerosene to light briquettes. Have a water bottle handy to spray any flare-ups.

Have two pairs of long-handled tongs—one for moving the coals and one to turn food. Wear long barbecue mitts to protect your hands and arms from the hot grill.

Bring foods to a cool room temperature before grilling to ensure more even cooking results. Trim excess fat from steaks, chops and chicken. Don't crowd food on the grill. Allow some space around each piece for even cooking.

Soak wooden skewers for at least 15 minutes in cold water before using to prevent them from burning. Leave a little space between pieces of food as you thread them onto the skewer to promote thorough cooking. For items that twist around on a skewer, thread on two parallel skewers.

Always place cooked food on a clean plate—never place on a plate that held raw food.

Cooking time will vary based on the temperature of the food being cooked, the temperature of the coals and the air temperature. So use the cooking time as a guide and test meat doneness with a meat thermometer.

Opening and closing the vents in a covered charcoal grill helps regulate the coal temperature. When the vents are open, more air flows through the grill and the coals burn hotter. When the vents are closed, the coals are deprived of oxygen and will eventually extinguish themselves.

Don't discard the ashes until they are completely cold. Cover the grill, close the vents and let stand until cold.

PYRAMID STYLE

Arrange briquettes in a pyramid in the grill. Pour lighter fluid over briquettes. Recap the fluid and place away from grill. Light briquettes.

ELECTRIC STARTER

Arrange briquettes in a pyramid in the grill. Insert electric starter in the middle of coals. Plug starter into an outlet. If using an extension cord, use a heavy-duty one. It will take 8 to 10 minutes for ash to form on coals. At that point, unplug the electric starter and remove from briquettes. The starter will be very hot, so place it out of the way on a heatproof surface. Continue heating briquettes until they are covered with a light gray ash.

CHIMNEY STARTER

Crumple newspaper or waxed paper and place a chimney starter over the paper in the grill. Fill the chimney starter with briquettes. Light paper. When coals are ready, dump them out of the chimney starter and spread out.

GREASING A GRILL

Spray the food grate with nonstick cooking spray before starting the grill. Never spray directly over the fire (gas or coal) as you can cause a fire. To grease a hot grate, fold a paper towel into a small pad. Holding the pad with long-handled tongs, dip in vegetable oil and rub over the grate.

Starting a Grill

The number of briquettes needed to grill will depend on the amount of food you're grilling, the size of the grill and weather conditions. Adverse weather conditions—high winds, cold temperatures and high humidity—will require more briquettes. You need about 30 briquettes to cook 1 pound of meat.

There are three ways to start a charcoal grill: using a traditional pyramid style, an electric starter or a chimney starter. When using briquettes that just need to be lit with a match, follow package directions.

Depending on your grill, the briquettes will go on a charcoal grate or the bottom of the grill. The coals are ready when they are covered with a light gray ash—this takes about 25 to 30 minutes. Once they're ready, spread them out for direct or indirect heat. Never pour lighter fluid on coals that already have been lit.

Preparing a Grill for Direct Heat

For a charcoal grill, spread out the preheated coals in an even layer. For a gas grill, preheat the grill with all the burners on high. Place food on cooking grate, then adjust temperature according to recipe.

Direct heat is used for foods that take about 30 minutes or less to cook. The food is cooked directly over an even heat source and turned halfway through the cooking time. Grill the foods covered or uncovered according to recipe directions.

The same cuts that are recommended for broiling can be grilled over direct heat. Thin foods, such as boneless chicken breasts, 1/2-in.-thick pork chops or steaks, hot dogs or fish fillets can be grilled uncovered on a charcoal grill or covered on a gas grill. Thicker foods, such as a 1-in. steaks, hamburgers, kabobs and whole fish, should be grilled covered on both charcoal and gas grills.

Preparing a Grill for Indirect Heat

For a charcoal grill, bank half of the coals on one side of the grill and the other half on the other side. Place a foil drip pan in the center of the grill, replace the cooking grate and place the meat over the drip pan. Cover and grill according to recipe directions.

Note that for every 45 minutes of grilling, you should add more briquettes to the bank of coals. For a small grill (14 in.), add about four per side; for a large grill (26 in.), add about nine per side.

For a gas grill, preheat grill with all the burners on high. Turn center burner off and place a drip pan in the center. Place food on cooking grate over the drip pan. Adjust temperature according to recipe, then cover and grill for the recommended time. If the gas grill has only two burners, turn one burner off and place the drip pan on that side.

Indirect heat is used for foods that take longer than 30 minutes to cook, are high in fat or are usually cooked in the oven rather than on the stovetop. For example, larger cuts, such as whole chicken, bone-in chicken pieces, roasts or spareribs and those use indirect heat because they require slow, long grilling to cook through. For both charcoal and gas grills, cover the grill when cooking by indirect heat.

Foods cooked with the indirect method do not need to be turned. Some recipes call for searing the meat over direct heat for a nice brown exterior before placing over indirect heat.

Testing Grill Temperature

For a covered grill, have the cover down on the grill and open the vent slightly. Insert a grill thermometer through the vent.

For an uncovered grill, check the temperature by cautiously holding the palm of your hand 3 to 4 in. above the grate. Count the number of seconds you can hold your hand in that position before the heat forces you to pull it away. Use the chart below as a guideline.

HOT (AT LEAST 450°)	MEDIUM-HOT (400°)
2 SECONDS, COALS GLOW RED	3 SECONDS, COALS ARE GRAY WITH A RED UNDERGLOW
MEDIUM (350°)	**MEDIUM-LOW (300°)**
4 SECONDS, COALS ARE GRAY WITH A HINT OF RED	5 SECONDS, COALS ARE GRAY WITH A FAINT RED GLOW

Cleaning a Grill

Clean the food grate with a stiff wire brush after cooking.

Using Wood Chips

Wood and herbs impart wonderful flavors and richness to grilled foods. The key to remember is that a little goes a long way. Start by soaking the wood or herbs. Chunks of wood should be covered with water for at least 1 hour; chips and herbs can be soaked for 20 to 30 minutes. Shake off excess water before using.

For a charcoal grill, place wood or herbs directly on the hot coals. For a gas grill use the smoker box, if available, according to manufacturer's directions. If your grill does not have a smoker box, make a foil pouch for the chips (not chunks) and place it on the grill when preheating the grill.

Using Rubs

Rubs are a combination of herbs and spices that are rubbed onto meat, fish or poultry. They are quick to make and an easy way to add a flavor boost to a plain piece of meat without adding fat. Try one of these the next time you want to add a little zip to grilled food.

- *ZIPPY DRY RUB:* Combine 1 tablespoon salt, 1 teaspoon *each* mustard seed, chili powder, paprika and pepper, 1/2 teaspoon *each* ground cumin and dried coriander and 1/4 teaspoon garlic powder. Store in an airtight container. Rub onto meat or poultry and refrigerate for at least 4 hours before grilling.
  —*Gaynelle Fritsch, Welches, Oregon*

- *SAVORY STEAK RUB:* Combine 1 tablespoon *each* dried marjoram and basil, 2 teaspoons *each* dried thyme and rosemary, crushed and 3/4 teaspoon dried oregano. Store in an airtight container. Rub over steaks just before grilling.
  —*Donna Brockett, Kingfisher, Oklahoma*

MARINATING TIPS

When basting with marinade, reserve some for basting before adding the meat to the remaining marinade. Discard the marinade from the meat.

Brush on thick or sweet sauces during the last 10-15 minutes of cooking, basting and turning every few minutes to prevent burning.

For more marinade ideas and recipes, see Using Marinades on page 234.

WOOD:	ALDER
FLAVOR:	Delicate and sweet
USE WITH:	Fish and poultry
WOOD:	APPLE
FLAVOR:	Slightly sweet and fruity
USE WITH:	Poultry, pork and fish
WOOD:	CHERRY
FLAVOR:	Mild, slightly sweet and fruity
USE WITH:	Poultry, fish and pork
WOOD:	HICKORY
FLAVOR:	Hearty, smoky bacon-like flavor
USE WITH:	Most red meats, pork, poultry and vegetables
WOOD:	MAPLE
FLAVOR:	Mild, smoky and sweet
USE WITH:	Poultry, ham and vegetables
WOOD:	MESQUITE
FLAVOR:	Strong, sharp earthy flavor
USE WITH:	Beef, most other meats and vegetables

MAKING A FOIL POUCH

1) Place the soaked wood chips on a large piece of heavy-duty foil.

2) Bring up two edges over the center of chips and fold down twice.

3) Fold the side edges over twice.

4) Poke holes in top of packet with a knife or long handled fork and place on the grill.

Beef and Veal Grilling Chart

The cooking times shown below are for medium-rare to medium doneness. For beef, a meat thermometer should read 145° for medium-rare, 160° for medium and 170° for well-done.

Veal is done when a meat thermometer reads 160° for medium and 170° for well-done. Ground beef and veal should be 160°. For direct grilling, turn meat halfway through grilling time.

CUT	WEIGHT OR THICKNESS	HEAT	COOKING TIME (MINUTES PER POUND)
BEEF			
RIB EYE STEAK	1 in.	Medium/Direct	11 to 14
	1-1/2 in.	Medium/Direct	17 to 22
T-BONE, PORTERHOUSE OR TOP LOIN STEAK (BONELESS STRIP)	3/4 in.	Medium/Direct	10 to 12
	1 in.	Medium/Direct	15 to 18
	1-1/2 in.	Medium/Direct	19 to 23
TENDERLOIN STEAK	1 in.	Medium/Direct	13 to 15
	1-1/2 in.	Medium/Direct	14 to 16
TOP SIRLOIN STEAK (BONELESS)	1 in.	Medium/Direct	17 to 21
	1-1/2 in.	Medium/Direct	22 to 26
	2 in.	Medium/Direct	28 to 33
FLANK STEAK*	1-1/2 to 2 lbs.	Medium/Direct	12 to 15
SKIRT STEAK	1/4 to 1/2 in.	High/Direct	6 to 8
TOP ROUND STEAK*	1 in.	Medium/Direct	16 to 18
CHUCK SHOULDER STEAK*	1 in.	Medium/Direct	16 to 20
TENDERLOIN ROAST	2 to 3 lbs.	Medium-Hot/Indirect	45 to 60
	4 to 5 lbs.	Medium-Hot/Indirect	1 to 1-1/4 hours
TRI-TIP	1-3/4 to 2 lbs.	Medium/Indirect	35 to 45
GROUND BEEF OR VEAL PATTY	4 oz. and 1/2 in.	Medium/Direct	11 to 14
VEAL			
LOIN OR RIB CHOP	1 in.	Medium/Direct	12 to 14
ARM OR BLADE STEAK*	3/4 in.	Medium/Direct	16 to 18

★ These cuts of meat are best when marinated before grilling.

DONENESS TEST FOR STEAK

To test for doneness, insert an instant-read thermometer horizontally from the side, making sure to get the reading in the center of the steak.

PEPPERED T-BONE STEAKS

Herbed Beef Tenderloin
Paul Verner, Wooster, Ohio

Grilling is a hobby of mine. This flavorful dish is one of my family's favorites. Try it with baked potatoes and garden-fresh veggies.

    1   beef tenderloin (4 to 5 pounds)
  1/2   cup olive oil
    2   green onions, finely chopped
    2   garlic cloves, minced
    1   tablespoon *each* dried basil,
        thyme and rosemary, crushed
    1   tablespoon balsamic vinegar
    1   tablespoon Dijon mustard
    1   teaspoon salt
    1   teaspoon pepper

1) Place tenderloin in a large resealable heavy-duty plastic bag. In a bowl, combine the remaining ingredients; pour over meat. Seal bag and turn to coat; refrigerate overnight.

2) Prepare grill for indirect medium-hot heat, using a drip pan. Drain and discard marinade from beef. Place beef over direct heat.

3) Grill, covered, over medium-hot heat for 10-15 minutes or until beef is browned, turning frequently. Move beef to indirect side of the grill.

4) Cover and grill for 20-25 minutes longer or until meat reaches desired doneness (for medium-rare, a meat thermometer should read 145°; medium, 160°; well-done, 170°). Let stand for 10 minutes before slicing.

Yield: 12 servings.

NUTRITION FACTS: 4 ounces cooked beef equals 256 calories, 13 g fat (4 g saturated fat), 95 mg cholesterol, 129 mg sodium, 1 g carbohydrate, 1 g fiber, 32 g protein.

Peppered T-Bone Steaks
Diane Halferty, Corpus Christi, Texas

When I make these juicy steaks, I brush thin slices of potato with olive oil and grill them alongside the meat.

    3   tablespoons steak sauce
  4-1/2   teaspoons minced fresh thyme
            or 1 teaspoon dried thyme
  1/4   teaspoon coarsely ground pepper
  1/4   teaspoon cayenne pepper
    2   beef T-bone steaks (1 inch thick
            and 3/4 pound *each*)
  1/2   teaspoon salt

1) Coat grill rack with nonstick cooking spray before starting the grill. In a small bowl, combine the steak sauce, thyme, pepper and cayenne.

2) Sprinkle steaks on both sides with salt. Spoon about 2 teaspoons steak sauce mixture on one side of steaks.

3) Place on grill sauce side down. Grill, covered, over medium heat for 6 minutes. Brush with remaining sauce and turn. Grill 4-6 minutes longer or until meat reaches desired doneness (for medium-rare, a meat thermometer should read 145°; medium, 160°; well-done 170°).

Yield: 2 servings.

Editor's Note: The recipe for Grilled Vegetable Skewers as shown in the photo above is found on page 244.

NUTRITION FACTS: 1 serving equals 643 calories, 46 g fat (18 g saturated fat), 131 mg cholesterol, 1,145 mg sodium, 5 g carbohydrate, trace fiber, 47 g protein.

Barbecued Beef Brisket
Bettye Miller, Blancard, Oklahoma

A guest at the RV park and marina my husband and I used to run gave me this flavorful brisket recipe. It's become the star of countless meal gatherings, from potlucks to holiday dinners.

  1/2   cup packed brown sugar
  1/2   cup ketchup
  1/4   cup water
  1/4   cup cider vinegar
    6   tablespoons vegetable oil, *divided*
    3   tablespoons dark corn syrup
    2   tablespoons prepared mustard
    1   tablespoon prepared horseradish

1 garlic clove, minced
1 fresh beef brisket (2 to 2-1/2 pounds), trimmed

1) Prepare grill for indirect heat. In a saucepan, combine the brown sugar, ketchup, water, vinegar, 4 tablespoons oil, corn syrup, mustard, horseradish and garlic.

2) Cook and stir over medium heat for 3-4 minutes or until sugar is dissolved. Pour mixture into a disposable aluminum pan; set aside.

3) In a large skillet, brown brisket on both sides in remaining oil. Place brisket in pan; turn to coat with sauce. Cover pan tightly with foil.

4) Grill, covered, over indirect medium heat for 1 hour. Add 10 briquettes to coals. Cover and grill about 1-1/4 hours longer, adding more briquettes if needed, or until meat is fork-tender. Slice beef; serve with pan drippings.

Yield: 6 servings.

Editor's Note: This is a fresh beef brisket, not corned beef.

NUTRITION FACTS: 4 ounces cooked beef equals 529 calories, 33 g fat (9 g saturated fat), 90 mg cholesterol, 388 mg sodium, 33 g carbohydrate, 1 g fiber, 27 g protein.

T-Bones with Onions
Sheree Quate, Cave Junction, Oregon

Steak gets a dressy treatment when topped with tasty onion slices flavored with honey and mustard. I found this recipe on a bag of charcoal more than 10 years ago.

3 large onions, cut into 1/4-inch-thick slices
2 tablespoons honey
1/2 teaspoon salt
1/2 teaspoon ground mustard
1/2 teaspoon paprika
1/2 teaspoon pepper
4 beef T-bone steaks (1 inch thick and 12 ounces *each*)
Additional salt and pepper

1) Place onions in the center of a piece of heavy-duty foil (about 20 in. x 18 in.). Drizzle with honey; sprinkle with the salt, mustard, paprika and pepper.

2) Fold foil over onions and seal tightly. Season steaks with additional salt and pepper. Grill onions and steaks, covered, over medium heat. Grill onions for 10-12 minutes on each side or until tender.

3) Grill steak for 7-10 minutes on each side or until meat reaches desired doneness (for medium-rare, a meat thermometer should read 145°; medium 160°; well-done, 170°). Let steak stand for 3-5 minutes. Serve with onions.

Yield: 4 servings.

NUTRITION FACTS: 1 serving (calculated without additional salt and pepper) equals 695 calories, 46 g fat (18 g saturated fat), 131 mg cholesterol, 434 mg sodium, 19 g carbohydrate, 2 g fiber, 49 g protein.

TIPS FOR GRILLING STEAKS

Trim steaks to avoid flare-ups, leaving a thin layer of fat if desired to help maintain juiciness. Pat dry with paper towels before grilling—a dry steak will brown better than a moist one.

Avoid grilling at too high a temperature, which will char the outside of the steak before the inside reaches the desired doneness. Grill steaks to at least medium-rare, 145°, but don't overcook.

Garlic Grilled Steaks
Taste of Home Test Kitchen

For a mouth-watering change of taste at your next barbecue, take steak to new flavor heights by basting your choice of cuts with a great garlic blend that requires minutes to fix.

10 garlic cloves
1-1/2 teaspoons salt
1/2 teaspoon pepper
2 tablespoons olive oil
1 tablespoon lemon juice
2 teaspoons Worcestershire sauce
4 New York strip steak *or* 4 boneless beef rib eye steaks (1-1/4 inches thick and 8 ounces *each*)

1) With a mortar and pestle, combine the garlic, salt and pepper. Add the oil, lemon juice, Worcestershire sauce and mix to form a paste.

2) Grill steaks, covered, over medium heat for 6-8 minutes on each side or until meat reaches desired doneness (for medium-rare, a meat thermometer should read 145°; medium 160°; well-done 170°).

3) Brush with garlic mixture during the last few minutes of grilling. Let stand for 3-5 minutes before serving.

Yield: 4 servings.

NUTRITION FACTS: 1 serving equals 525 calories, 38 g fat (13 g saturated fat), 124 mg cholesterol, 1,013 mg sodium, 3 g carbohydrate, trace fiber, 41 g protein.

Oriental Beef Ribbons
Dianne Livingston, Woodland, California

A fellow nurse, who also happens to be a fabulous cook, shared this recipe with me. We like it served with steamed rice and stir-fried vegetables.

- 1-1/2 pounds beef flank steak
- 1/4 cup teriyaki sauce
- 1 tablespoon vegetable oil
- 2 garlic cloves, minced
- 2 teaspoons minced fresh gingerroot
- 1/4 teaspoon crushed red pepper flakes
- 1 teaspoon sesame seeds, toasted

1) Slice meat across the grain into 1/4-in. strips. In a resealable plastic bag, combine the teriyaki sauce, oil, garlic, ginger and red pepper flakes; add meat.

2) Seal bag and turn to coat; refrigerate for 8 hours or overnight, turning several times.

3) Coat grill rack with nonstick cooking spray before starting the grill. Drain and discard marinade. Weave meat onto metal or soaked wooden skewers.

4) Grill, covered, over medium heat for 2-4 minutes on each side or until desired doneness. Remove from grill and sprinkle with sesame seeds.

Yield: 4 servings.

NUTRITION FACTS: 4-1/2 ounces cooked beef equals 304 calories, 16 g fat (6 g saturated fat), 81 mg cholesterol, 715 mg sodium, 3 g carbohydrate, trace fiber, 34 g protein.

Pinwheel Flank Steaks
Nancy Tafoya, Fort Collins, Colorado

This yummy, elegant-looking main dish is easy to make. Plus so much prep can be done in advance.

- 1-1/2 pounds beef flank steak
- 1/4 cup olive oil
- 2 tablespoons red wine vinegar
- 2 teaspoons Worcestershire sauce
- 2 teaspoons Italian seasoning
- 1-1/2 teaspoons garlic powder
- 1-1/2 teaspoons pepper, *divided*
- 1 teaspoon seasoned salt
- 8 bacon strips, cooked and crumbled
- 2 garlic cloves, minced
- 1/4 cup minced fresh parsley
- 1/4 cup finely chopped onion
- 1/2 teaspoon salt

1) Flatten steak to 1/4-in. thickness. In a large resealable plastic bag, combine the oil, vinegar, Worcestershire sauce, Italian seasoning, garlic powder, 1 teaspoon pepper and seasoned salt; add the steak.

2) Seal bag and turn to coat; refrigerate for 8 hours or overnight. Drain and discard marinade.

3) Combine the bacon, garlic, parsley, onion, salt and remaining pepper; sprinkle over steak to within 1 in. of edges. Roll up jelly-roll style, starting with a long side; tie with kitchen string at about 1-in. intervals. Cut into 1-1/4-in. rolls.

4) Coat grill rack with nonstick cooking spray before starting the grill. Grill steak rolls, uncovered, over medium heat for 10-12 minutes on each side or until meat reaches desired doneness (for medium-rare, a meat thermometer should read 145° medium, 160° well-done, 170°). Cut and remove string before serving.

Yield: 6 servings.

NUTRITION FACTS: 1 serving equals 265 calories, 17 g fat (6 g saturated fat), 61 mg cholesterol, 663 mg sodium, 2 g carbohydrate, trace fiber, 25 g protein.

THE PERFECT HAMBURGER

The Perfect Hamburger
Shirley Kidd, New London, Minnesota

My family calls this the "perfect" burger because we think the chili sauce and horseradish add just the right amount of zip. But you can add or change the seasonings to your liking.

- 1 egg, lightly beaten

SEASONINGS:
- 2 tablespoons chili sauce

1 teaspoon dried minced onion
1 teaspoon prepared horseradish
1 teaspoon Worcestershire sauce
1/2 teaspoon salt
Dash pepper

BURGER:

1 pound lean ground beef
4 hamburger buns, split

Optional toppings: sliced tomato, onion, pickles and condiments

1) Coat grill rack with nonstick cooking spray before starting the grill. In a large bowl, combine the egg and seasonings. Crumble beef over mixture and mix well. Shape into four 3/4-in.-thick patties.

2) Grill, covered, over medium heat for 5-7 minutes on each side or until a meat thermometer reads 160° and juices run clear. Serve on buns with desired toppings.

Yield: 4 servings.

NUTRITION FACTS: 1 burger equals 321 calories, 12 g fat (4 g saturated fat), 109 mg cholesterol, 758 mg sodium, 24 g carbohydrate, 1 g fiber, 27 g protein.

■ *BACON BURGER:* Replace the seasonings with 1/2 cup shredded cheddar cheese, 1 small onion, chopped, 2 tablespoons ketchup, 1 tablespoon *each* Parmesan cheese and Worcestershire sauce, 1/2 teaspoon salt and pepper.

Shape into six patties. Wrap 1 bacon strip around each patty and secure with a toothpick. Grill as directed.

■ *HERBED BURGERS:* Omit egg. Replace seasoning mix with 5 teaspoons sour cream, 3/4 teaspoon dried parsley flakes, 1/2 teaspoon salt and 1/8 teaspoon pepper. Shape into four patties. Grill as directed.

■ *TACO BURGERS:* Replace seasoning mix with 3 tablespoons taco seasoning mix, 2 teaspoons instant minced onion and 3/4 cup finely crushed corn chips. Shape into six patties. Grill as directed.

Sirloin Caesar Salad
Carol Sinclair, St. Elmo, Illinois

A tangy sauce that combines bottled salad dressing, lemon juice and Dijon mustard flavors this filling main-dish salad. You save on cleanup time because both the steak and bread are cooked on the grill.

1 cup Caesar salad dressing
1/4 cup Dijon mustard
1/4 cup lemon juice
1 boneless top sirloin steak (3/4 inch thick and 1 pound)
6 slices French bread (1 inch thick)
12 cups torn romaine
1 medium tomato, chopped

1) In a bowl, combine the salad dressing, mustard and lemon juice; set aside 3/4 cup. Pour 3/4 cup dressing mixture in a large resealable plastic bag; add steak.

2) Seal bag and turn to coat; refrigerate for 1 hour, turning occasionally. Cover and refrigerate remaining dressing mixture.

3) Coat grill rack with nonstick cooking spray before starting the grill. Brush both sides of bread with 1/4 cup of the reserved dressing mixture.

4) Grill bread, uncovered, over medium heat for 1-2 minutes on each side or until lightly toasted. Wrap in foil and set aside.

5) Drain and discard marinade from steak. Grill, covered, over medium heat for 5-8 minutes on each side or until meat reaches desired doneness (for medium-rare, a meat thermometer should read 145°; medium, 160°; well-done, 170°).

6) Place romaine and tomato on serving platter. Slice steak diagonally; arrange over salad. Serve with the bread and remaining dressing.

Yield: 6 servings.

NUTRITION FACTS: 1 serving equals 424 calories, 18 g fat (5 g saturated fat), 57 mg cholesterol, 836 mg sodium, 39 g carbohydrate, 4 g fiber, 25 g protein.

Pork and Lamb Grilling Chart

Pork, fresh pork sausages, ground pork and ground lamb are done when the temperature reaches 160°. Cooked sausages are done when they are heated through.

Lamb chops and steaks are done when a meat thermometer reads 145° for medium-rare, 160° for medium and 170° for well-done. For direct grilling, turn meat halfway through grilling time.

CUT	WEIGHT OR THICKNESS	HEAT	COOKING TIME (MINUTES PER POUND)
PORK			
LOIN OR RIB CHOP (BONE-IN)	3/4 to 1 in. 1-1/4 to 1-1/2 in.	Medium/Direct Medium/Direct	8 to 10 12 to 18
LOIN CHOP (BONELESS)	3/4 to 1 in. 1-1/4 to 1-1/2 in.	Medium/Direct Medium/Direct	8 to 10 12 to 18
BACK RIBS OR SPARERIBS	3 to 4 lbs.	Medium/Indirect	1-1/2 to 2 hours
TENDERLOIN	3/4 to 1 lb.	Medium-Hot/Indirect	25 to 40
LOIN ROAST (BONE-IN OR BONELESS)	3 to 5 lbs.	Medium/Indirect	1-1/4 to 1-3/4 hours
KABOBS	1-in. cubes	Medium/Direct	10 to 15
SAUSAGE, COOKED		Medium/Direct	3 to 7 or until heated through
SAUSAGE, FRESH	4 oz.	Medium/Indirect	20 to 30
PORK OR LAMB PATTIES	4 oz. and 1/2 in.	Medium/Direct	8 to 10
LAMB			
RIB OR LOIN CHOPS	1 in.	Medium/Direct	10 to 18
LEG OF LAMB (BONE-IN)	5 to 7 lbs.	Medium-Low/Indirect	1-3/4 to 2-3/4 hours
LEG OF LAMB (BONELESS)	3 to 4 lbs.	Medium-Low/Indirect	1-1/2 to 2-1/2 hours
RACK OF LAMB	1 to 1-1/2 lbs.	Medium/Direct	25 to 35
KABOBS	1-in. cubes	Medium/Direct	8 to 12

Grilled Rosemary Pork Roast

Christine Wilson, Sellersville, Pennsylvania

When we're expecting guests for dinner, I often serve this flavorful grilled pork roast.

- 3 medium tart apples, peeled and chopped
- 1 cup unsweetened apple cider *or* juice
- 3 green onions, chopped
- 3 tablespoons honey
- 1 to 2 teaspoons dried rosemary, crushed
- 2 garlic cloves, minced
- 1 boneless pork loin roast (3 pounds)

1) In a small saucepan, combine the apple, cider, onions, honey, rosemary and garlic; bring to a boil. Reduce heat; simmer, uncovered, for 5 minutes. Cool to room temperature.

2) Place pork roast in a large resealable plastic bag; add half of the marinade. Seal bag and turn to

coat; refrigerate overnight, turning occasionally. Transfer the remaining marinade to a bowl; cover and refrigerate.

3) Coat grill rack with nonstick cooking spray before starting the grill. Prepare grill for indirect heat, using a drip pan. Drain and discard marinade from pork.

4) Grill roast, covered, over indirect medium heat for 1-1/4 to 1-3/4 hours or until a meat thermometer reads 160°, turning occasionally. Let stand for 10 minutes before slicing. Heat reserved marinade; serve with pork.

Yield: 8 servings.

NUTRITION FACTS: 4-1/2 ounces cooked pork with 1 tablespoon sauce equals 260 calories, 8 g fat (3 g saturated fat), 85 mg cholesterol, 52 mg sodium, 13 g carbohydrate, 1 g fiber, 33 g protein.

PORK WITH WATERMELON SALSA

Pork with Watermelon Salsa
Taste of Home Test Kitchen

A combination of watermelon, strawberries, kiwifruit and peaches makes a sweet salsa that's ideal to serve alongside grilled pork.

> 1   **cup seeded chopped watermelon**
> 1/2 **cup chopped strawberries**
> 1/2 **cup chopped kiwifruit**
> 1/4 **cup chopped peaches**
> 3   **tablespoons lime juice**
> 4   **teaspoons honey**
> 1/2 **teaspoon grated lime peel**
> 1   **to 2 mint leaves, chopped**
> 1/2 **cup peach preserves**
> 3   **pork tenderloins (3/4 pound *each*)**

1) Coat grill rack with nonstick cooking spray before starting. Prepare grill for indirect heat, using a drip pan. For salsa, in a small bowl, combine the fruit, lime juice, honey, lime peel and mint; set aside. In a saucepan or microwave, heat the preserves for 1 minute.

2) Grill pork, covered, over indirect medium-hot heat for 15 minutes. Turn; brush with some of the preserves. Grill 10-15 minutes longer or until juices run clear and a meat thermometer reads 160°, basting occasionally with preserves. Serve with salsa.

Yield: 6 servings (2 cups salsa).

NUTRITION FACTS: 4 ounces cooked pork with 1/3 cup salsa equals 304 calories, 6 g fat (2 g saturated fat), 95 mg cholesterol, 69 mg sodium, 28 g carbohydrate, 1 g fiber, 34 g protein.

Grilled Pork with Hot Mustard
Kyle Spencer, Havre, Montana

I love Chinese food, and this soy sauce-marinated tenderloin is one of my favorites. It's terrific served warm or cold, especially when dipped in the zippy mustard sauce.

> 1/4 **cup reduced-sodium soy sauce**
> 2   **tablespoons dry red wine *or* chicken broth**
> 1   **tablespoon brown sugar**
> 1   **tablespoon honey**
> 1/2 **teaspoon ground cinnamon**
> 2   **pork tenderloins (3/4 pound *each*)**

HOT MUSTARD:
> 1/4 **cup Dijon mustard**
> 1   **tablespoon honey**
> 1   **teaspoon prepared horseradish**
> 2   **teaspoons sesame seeds, toasted**

1) In a large resealable plastic bag, combine the soy sauce, wine or broth, sugar, honey and cinnamon; add pork. Seal bag and turn to coat; refrigerate for 8 hours or overnight.

2) Drain and discard marinade. Grill pork, covered, over indirect medium-hot heat for 25-40 minutes or until a meat thermometer reads 160°. Let stand for 5 minutes before slicing.

3) In a small bowl, combine the mustard, honey and horseradish. Slice pork; sprinkle with sesame seeds. Serve with hot mustard.

Yield: 6 servings.

NUTRITION FACTS: One serving equals 197 calories, 7 g fat (2 g saturated fat), 62 mg cholesterol, 408 mg sodium, 6 g carbohydrate, 1 g fiber, 26 g protein.

Dijon Pork Chops

Vivian Kelby, Crown Point, Indiana

Each of my children, grandchildren and great-grandchildren have enjoyed these simply delicious chops for years. We know you'll like them, too!

- 1/4 cup red wine vinegar
- 2 tablespoons vegetable oil
- 2 tablespoons Dijon mustard
- 2 teaspoons chopped fresh parsley
- 1/2 teaspoon chopped fresh chives
- 1/4 teaspoon dried tarragon
- 4 butterflied pork chops (4 ounces *each*), trimmed
  Additional chives, optional

1) In a small bowl, combine the vinegar, oil, mustard and herbs and set aside.

2) Grill chops, uncovered, over medium heat for 2 minutes per side for 1/2-in. chops (4 minutes per side for 1-in. chops).

3) Brush with mustard mixture and grill 2 minutes longer. Turn; baste and grill 2 minutes longer or until juices run clear. Sprinkle with chives if desired.

Yield: 4 servings.

NUTRITION FACTS: 1 serving equals 225 calories, 14 g fat (3 g saturated fat), 55 mg cholesterol, 221 mg sodium, 2 g carbohydrate, trace fiber, 22 g protein.

CORN-STUFFED PORK CHOPS

Corn-Stuffed Pork Chops

Elizabeth Jussaume, Lowell, Massachusetts

For an eye-catching entree, grill up these pork chops filled with a colorful corn, pimiento and green pepper stuffing.

- 6 bone-in center loin pork chops (1 inch thick and about 10 ounces *each*)
- 3/4 teaspoon salt, *divided*
- 1/4 teaspoon pepper, *divided*
- 1/4 cup chopped green pepper
- 1/4 cup chopped onion
- 1 tablespoon butter
- 1-1/2 cups cubed bread, toasted
- 1/2 cup frozen corn, thawed
- 1/4 cup egg substitute
- 2 tablespoons chopped pimientos
- 1/4 teaspoon ground cumin

1) Coat grill rack with nonstick cooking spray before starting the grill. Prepare grill for indirect heat, using a drip pan.

2) Cut a pocket in each chop by making a horizontal slice almost to the bone; sprinkle 1/4 teaspoon salt and 1/8 teaspoon pepper in pockets. Set aside.

3) In a nonstick skillet, saute green pepper and onion in butter until tender. Transfer to a small bowl. Add the bread cubes, corn, egg substitute, pimientos, cumin and remaining salt and pepper; mix well. Stuff into pork chops; secure with wooden toothpicks.

4) Grill chops, covered, over medium indirect heat for 15-18 minutes on each side or until a meat thermometer inserted in stuffing reads 160°.

Yield: 6 servings.

NUTRITION FACTS: 1 stuffed pork chop equals 308 calories, 12 g fat (5 g saturated fat), 102 mg cholesterol, 458 mg sodium, 10 g carbohydrate, 1 g fiber, 38 g protein.

Peanut Butter Pork with Spicy Dipping Sauce

Dennis Gilroy, Stover, Missouri

These skewers are one of my favorite things to prepare. They have a wonderfully different flavor and go great with hot cooked rice.

- 1/4 cup creamy peanut butter
- 2 tablespoons soy sauce
- 2 tablespoons ground coriander
- 1 tablespoon lemon juice
- 1 tablespoon vegetable oil
- 2 teaspoons ground cumin
- 1/2 teaspoon chili powder
- 1 garlic clove, minced
- 1 pork tenderloin (1 pound), cut into 1-inch cubes

SPICY DIPPING SAUCE:
- 1/4 cup soy sauce
- 1/4 cup white vinegar

2 tablespoons water
1 garlic clove, minced
1 tablespoon molasses
1/2 teaspoon crushed red pepper
    flakes

1) In a large resealable plastic bag, combine the peanut butter, soy sauce, coriander, lemon juice, oil, cumin, chili powder and garlic; add pork. Seal bag and turn to coat; refrigerate several hours or overnight.

2) Meanwhile, combine all of the sauce ingredients; cover and chill at least 1 hour. Coat grill rack with nonstick cooking before starting the grill. Drain and discard marinade from pork.

3) Thread meat on metal or soaked wooden skewers, leaving a small space between pieces. Grill, covered, over medium for 10-15 minutes or until meat is no longer pink, turning several times. Serve with sauce.

Yield: 4 servings.

NUTRITION FACTS: 1 serving equals 232 calories, 10 g fat (2 g saturated fat), 63 mg cholesterol, 1,237 mg sodium, 7 g carbohydrate, 2 g fiber, 27 g protein.

Honey Citrus Chops
Cheryl Stawicki, Joliet, Illinois

Three handy ingredients make a fantastic marinade for boneless pork chops. It's a grilled favorite we enjoy all summer!

2/3 cup lemon-lime soda
1/2 cup soy sauce
1/4 cup honey
  6 boneless pork loin chops (3/4 inch
    thick and 6 ounces *each*)

1) In a large resealable plastic bag, combine the soda, soy sauce and honey; add the pork. Seal bag and turn to coat; refrigerate overnight, turning occasionally.

2) Coat grill rack with nonstick cooking spray before starting the grill. Drain and discard marinade. Grill, covered, over medium heat for 4-5 minutes on each side or until juices run clear.

Yield: 6 servings.

NUTRITION FACTS: 1 serving equals 62 calories, 1 g fat (trace saturated fat), 10 mg cholesterol, 621 mg sodium, 7 g carbohydrate, trace fiber, 5 g protein.

MARINATED PORK KABOBS

Marinated Pork Kabobs
Bobbie Jo Devany, Fernly, Nevada

This recipe was originally for lamb, but I adapted it to pork and adjusted the spices. After tasting these flavorful kabobs, my husband became an instant fan of this recipe. It's always requested when the grill comes out for the season.

2 cups plain yogurt
2 tablespoons lemon juice
4 garlic cloves, minced
1/2 teaspoon ground cumin
1/4 teaspoon ground coriander
2 pounds pork tenderloin, cut
    into 1-1/2-inch cubes
8 small white onions, halved
8 cherry tomatoes
1 medium sweet red pepper, cut
    into 1-1/2-inch pieces
1 medium green pepper, cut
    into 1-1/2-inch pieces

1) In a large resealable plastic bag, combine the yogurt, lemon juice, garlic, cumin and coriander; add pork. Seal bag and turn to coat; refrigerate for 6 hours or overnight.

2) Drain and discard marinade. Alternately thread the pork, onions, tomatoes and peppers on eight metal or soaked bamboo skewers. Grill, covered, over medium heat for about 15-20 minutes or until meat juices run clear.

Yield: 8 servings.

NUTRITION FACTS: 1 serving equals 190 calories, 5 g fat (2 g saturated fat), 67 mg cholesterol, 63 mg sodium, 11 g carbohydrate, 2 g fiber, 25 g protein.

HOT 'N' SPICY SPARERIBS

Hot 'n' Spicy Spareribs
Myra Innes, Auburn, Kansas

I keep this dry rub in a shaker on my shelf so I have it ready in an instant.

2   tablespoons brown sugar
2   tablespoons paprika
2   tablespoons pepper
1   tablespoon chili powder
1-1/2   teaspoons salt
1-1/2   teaspoons crushed red pepper flakes
1   teaspoon garlic powder
6   pounds pork spareribs
6   sheets (40 inches x 18 inches) heavy-duty foil

1) In a small bowl, combine sugar and seasonings. Rub all of it onto both sides of ribs. Make two stacks of three sheets of foil. Place half of the ribs in the center of each stack.

2) Bring opposite long edges of foil together; fold down several times. Fold the short edges toward the food and crimp tightly to prevent leaks. Refrigerate overnight. Remove from refrigerator 30 minutes before grilling.

3) Place foil packets over indirect medium heat. Grill, covered, for 1-1/2 hours or until tender, turning foil packets over after 45 minutes. Remove ribs from foil; place over direct heat. Grill, uncovered, for 10-15 minutes or until crisp, turning once.

Yield: 8 servings.

NUTRITION FACTS: 1 serving equals 1,310 calories, 97 g fat (35 g saturated fat), 383 mg cholesterol, 1,204 mg sodium, 12 g carbohydrate, 2 g fiber, 93 g protein.

Spiedis
Gertrude Skinner, Binghamton, New York

Spiedis is a traditional Italian dish featuring skewered meat grilled like kabobs, then wrapped in Italian bread and eaten like a sandwich. The seasonings in this recipe work well with pork, beef, lamb, poultry and other meats.

1   cup vegetable oil
2/3   cup cider vinegar
2   tablespoons Worcestershire sauce
1/2   medium onion, finely chopped
1/2   teaspoon salt
1/2   teaspoon sugar
1/2   teaspoon dried basil
1/2   teaspoon dried marjoram
1/2   teaspoon dried rosemary, crushed
2-1/2   pounds boneless lean pork, beef, lamb, venison, chicken *or* turkey, cut into 1-1/2- to 2-inch cubes
Italian rolls *or* hot dog buns

1) In a large resealable plastic bag, combine the oil, vinegar, Worcestershire sauce, onion and seasonings; add meat. Seal bag and turn to coat; refrigerate for 24 hours, turning occasionally.

2) Coat grill rack with nonstick cooking spray before starting the grill. Drain and discard marinade. Thread meat on metal or soaked wooden skewers.

3) Grill, covered, over medium heat for 10-15 minutes or until meat reaches desired doneness. Remove meat from skewers and serve on long Italian rolls or hot dog buns.

Yield: 8 servings.

NUTRITION FACTS: 1 serving (calculated without Italian rolls) equals 323 calories, 22 g fat (5 g saturated fat), 83 mg cholesterol, 156 mg sodium, 2 g carbohydrate, trace fiber, 29 g protein.

Grilled Jalapenos
Catherine Hollie, Cleveland, Texas

When barbecuing for friends at home, I also use the grill to serve up hot appetizers. These crowd-pleasing stuffed peppers have a bit of bite.

24   fresh jalapeno peppers
3/4   pound bulk pork sausage
12   bacon strips, halved

1) Wash peppers and remove stems. Cut a slit along one side of each pepper. Remove seeds; rinse and dry peppers.

2) In a skillet, cook sausage over medium heat until

no longer pink; drain. Stuff peppers with sausage and wrap with bacon; secure with a toothpick.

3) Grill peppers, uncovered, over medium heat for about 15 minutes or until tender and bacon is crisp, turning frequently.

Yield: 2 dozen.

Editor's Note: When cutting or seeding hot peppers, use rubber or plastic gloves to protect your hands. Avoid touching your face.

NUTRITION FACTS: 2 jalapenos equals 192 calories, 18 g fat (7 g saturated fat), 25 mg cholesterol, 282 mg sodium, 2 g carbohydrate, 1 g fiber, 4 g protein.

GRILLED MANGO-GLAZED HAM

Grilled Mango-Glazed Ham
Sandy Lewis, Appleton, Wisconsin

I'm always looking for new ways to prepare ham...but many of my cookbooks have the same old tried-and-true glazes. When I tried this one, I knew I had hit the jackpot!

1-1/2 cups red wine vinegar
1/2 cup sugar
1 teaspoon finely chopped jalapeno pepper
1 teaspoon minced fresh gingerroot
1 medium ripe mango *or* 2 medium ripe peaches, peeled and cut into wedges
1 bone-in fully cooked lean ham steak (about 2 pounds)
1/8 teaspoon pepper

1) In a small saucepan, combine the vinegar, sugar, jalapeno and ginger. Bring to a boil. Reduce heat; simmer, uncovered, for 25-30 minutes or until glaze is thick and caramelized. Strain and cool.

2) Place mango in a food processor or blender; cover and process until smooth. Stir into glaze; set aside.

3) Coat grill rack with nonstick cooking spray before starting the grill. Sprinkle both sides of ham steak with pepper.

4) Grill, covered, over medium heat for 10 minutes on each side or until heated through. Brush both sides of ham with mango glaze; grill 5 minutes longer. Serve ham with remaining glaze.

Yield: 8 servings.

Editor's Note: When cutting or seeding hot peppers, use rubber or plastic gloves to protect your hands. Avoid touching your face.

NUTRITION FACTS: 4 ounces cooked ham with 2 tablespoons glaze equals 251 calories, 10 g fat (3 g saturated fat), 60 mg cholesterol, 1,454 mg sodium, 20 g carbohydrate, trace fiber, 21 g protein.

Barbecued Lamb Chops
Chris Nash, Berthoud, Colorado

At Eastertime and for other holidays, I often get requests for this lamb dish. The moist and tender chops aren't difficult to make, but they taste special. Even people who say they don't like lamb enjoy it prepared this way.

2 to 3 cups olive oil
1/4 cup chopped garlic
4 teaspoons salt
1 teaspoon minced fresh rosemary *or* 1/2 teaspoon dried rosemary, crushed
1 teaspoon salt-free garlic and herb seasoning
1 teaspoon pepper
18 lamb rib chops (1 inch thick and 4 ounces *each*)

1) In a large resealable plastic bag, combine the oil, garlic and seasonings; add lamb chops. Seal bag and turn to coat; refrigerate overnight, turning occasionally.

2) Drain and discard marinade. Grill the chops, uncovered, over medium heat for 5-9 minutes on each side or until meat reaches desired doneness (145° for medium-rare, 160° for medium-well, 170° for well-done).

Yield: 9 servings.

NUTRITION FACTS: 2 lamb chops equals 369 calories, 27 g fat (6 g saturated fat), 90 mg cholesterol, 605 mg sodium, 1 g carbohydrate, trace fiber, 29 g protein.

DIJON LEG OF LAMB

Dijon Leg of Lamb
Christy Porter, Centennial, Colorado

This special entree is always on our Easter table, and I serve it for other events all year.

 1 boneless leg of lamb
   (4 to 5 pounds)
 1 cup Dijon mustard
1/2 cup soy sauce
 2 tablespoons olive oil
 1 tablespoon chopped fresh
   rosemary *or* 1 teaspoon dried
   rosemary, crushed
 1 teaspoon ground ginger
 1 garlic cloves, minced

1) Cut leg of lamb horizontally from one long side to within 1 in. of opposite side. Open meat so it lies flat; trim and discard fat. Place lamb in a large resealable plastic bag.

2) In a small bowl, whisk the remaining ingredients. Pour 1 cup of marinade over lamb. Seal bag and turn to coat; refrigerate overnight. Cover and refrigerate remaining marinade.

3) Coat grill rack with nonstick cooking spray before starting the grill. Prepare grill for indirect heat, using a drip pan. Drain and discard marinade. Place lamb over drip pan.

4) Grill, covered, over medium-low heat for 1-1/2 to 2-1/2 hours or until meat reaches desired doneness (for medium-rare, a meat thermometer should read 145°; medium, 160°; well-done, 170°). Let stand for 10 minutes before slicing. Warm reserved mustard sauce; serve with lamb.

Yield: 9 servings.

NUTRITION FACTS: 4 ounces cooked lamb with 1 tablespoon mustard sauce equals 320 calories, 17 g fat (5 g saturated fat), 113 mg cholesterol, 1,578 mg sodium, 3 g carbohydrate, trace fiber, 38 g protein.

Grilled Rack of Lamb
Gail Cawsey, Fawnskin, California

Whenever my husband and I want to impress guests, we make this rack of lamb. The marinade keeps the meat juicy and tender.

 2 cups apple cider *or* apple juice
2/3 cup cider vinegar
2/3 cup thinly sliced green onions
1/2 cup vegetable oil
1/3 cup honey
1/4 cup steak sauce
 2 teaspoons dried tarragon
 2 teaspoons salt
1/2 teaspoon pepper
 4 racks of lamb
   (1-1/2 to 2 pounds *each*)

1) In a large saucepan, combine the cider, vinegar, onions, oil, honey, steak sauce and seasonings. Bring to a boil. Reduce heat; simmer, uncovered, for 20 minutes. Cool to room temperature. Remove 1 cup for basting; cover and refrigerate.

2) Pour remaining marinade into a large resealable plastic bag; add lamb. Seal bag and turn to coat; refrigerate for 2-3 hours or overnight, turning once or twice.

3) Coat grill rack with nonstick cooking spray before starting the grill. Drain and discard the marinade. Cover rib ends of lamb with foil.

4) Grill, covered, over medium heat for 15 minutes. Baste with reserved marinade. Grill 5-10 minutes longer or until meat reaches desired doneness (for medium-rare, a meat thermometer should read 145°; medium, 160°; well-done, 170°), basting occasionally.

Yield: 8 servings.

NUTRITION FACTS: 4-1/2 ounces cooked lamb equals 404 calories, 24 g fat (7 g saturated fat), 100 mg cholesterol, 594 mg sodium, 15 g carbohydrate, trace fiber, 30 g protein.

Rocky Mountain Grill
Rick Wertheimer, Englewood, Colorado

Rubbed sage adds wonderful seasoning to the lamb loin chops, that also get a little kick from cayenne pepper.

 2 tablespoons water
 2 tablespoons red wine vinegar
 2 tablespoons vegetable oil
1-1/2 teaspoons rubbed sage
 1 teaspoon grated onion

1/2 teaspoon lemon-pepper seasoning

1/2 teaspoon Dijon mustard

1/8 to 1/4 teaspoon cayenne pepper

4 bone-in lamb loin chops (1 inch thick and 4 ounces *each*)

1) In a small bowl, combine the water, vinegar, oil and seasonings. Pour 1/4 cup into a large resealable plastic bag; add lamb. Seal bag and turn to coat; refrigerate overnight. Cover and refrigerate remaining marinade for basting.

2) Coat grill rack with nonstick cooking spray before starting the grill. Drain and discard marinade; grill chops, covered, over medium heat for 4 minutes.

3) Turn; baste with reserved marinade. Grill for 4 minutes. Turn and grill 1-2 minutes longer or until meat reaches desired doneness (for medium-rare, a meat thermometer should read 145°; medium, 160°; well-done, 170°).

Yield: 4 servings.

NUTRITION FACTS: 1 serving equals 151 calories, 10 g fat (2 g saturated fat), 45 mg cholesterol, 95 mg sodium, 1 g carbohydrate, trace fiber, 14 g protein.

Poultry Grilling Chart

Chicken and turkey breasts and turkey tenderloins are done when they reach a temperature of 170°; whole chickens and turkeys at 180° as measured in the thigh.

Kabobs and strips are done when juices run clear. Ground chicken or turkey patties are done at 165°. For direct grilling, turn meat halfway through grilling time.

CUT	WEIGHT OR THICKNESS	HEAT	COOKING TIME (MINUTES PER POUND)
CHICKEN			
BROILER/FRYER, WHOLE	3 to 4 lbs.	Medium/Indirect	1-1/4 to 1-3/4 hours
ROASTER, WHOLE	5 to 6 lbs.	Medium/Indirect	1-3/4 to 2-1/4 hours
MEATY BONE-IN PIECES, BREAST HALVES, LEGS, QUARTERS	1-1/4 to 1-1/2 lbs.	Medium/Indirect or Medium/Direct	40 to 50 35 to 45
BONE-IN THIGHS, DRUMSTICKS, WINGS	3 to 7 oz. *each*	Medium-Low/Direct or Medium/Indirect	15 to 30 20 to 30
BREAST HALVES, BONELESS	6 oz. *each*	Medium/Direct	10 to 15
KABOBS	1-in. cubes	Medium/Direct	10 to 15
CORNISH GAME HENS	1-1/2 to 2 lbs.	Medium/Indirect	45 to 60
TURKEY			
WHOLE, UNSTUFFED	8 to 11 lbs. 12 to 16 lbs.	Medium/Indirect Medium/Indirect	2 to 3 hours 3 to 4 hours
BREAST (BONE-IN)	4 to 5 lbs.	Medium/Indirect	1-1/2 to 2 hours
BREAST (BONELESS)	1-1/4 to 1-3/4 lbs.	Medium/Indirect	1 to 1-1/4 hours
TENDERLOINS	8 oz.	Medium/Direct	15 to 20
DRUMSTICKS OR THIGHS	1/2 to 1-1/2 lbs.	Medium/Indirect	45 to 75
PATTY	4 oz. and 1/2 in.	Medium/Direct	10 to 12

Using Marinades

Marinades add flavor and can tenderize meat. However, marinades only penetrate about 1/2 in. deep, so the flavor is on the outer surface of the food. Meat and poultry need at least 1 to 4 hours to marinate; many cuts can be marinated overnight. You can make up the marinade one evening and marinate the food until the next night, or add the food in the morning and marinate until you are ready cook it that night.

Most fish and seafood only need 15 to 30 minutes and can be marinating while you prepare other items for dinner. Marinating too long may cause the meat texture to break down and become mushy.

An easy way to marinate is to use a resealable plastic bag. Pour the marinade into the bag, add the meat or vegetables and partially seal the bag. Squeeze out as much air as possible, then completely seal the bag. Place on a tray to contain any leakage. Any food marinated for more than 30 minutes must be placed in the refrigerator.

For food safety reasons, if you want to use some of the marinade for basting or for a dipping sauce, set aside some of the fresh marinade for this purpose. Any marinade that came in contact with uncooked meat, poultry or seafood should be discarded.

The following marinades would be great on chicken or pork.

- ■ *KENTUCKY MARINADE:* Combine 1/2 cup cider vinegar, 1/4 cup vegetable oil, 2-1/2 teaspoons Worcestershire sauce, 2 teaspoons hot pepper sauce and 1 teaspoon salt. Reserve 1/4 cup for basting if desired. Marinate meat in remaining marinade for up to 4 hours. (Enough to marinate about 3 pounds of meat or poultry.)
  —*Jill Evely, Wilmore, Kentucky*

- ■ *ROSEMARY ORANGE MARINADE:* Combine 1 cup orange juice, 1/4 cup olive oil, 3 minced garlic cloves and 1 tablespoon *each* dried thyme and rosemary, crushed. Reserve 1/2 cup for basting if desired. Marinate meat in remaining marinade for up to 4 hours. (Enough to marinate about 2 pounds of poultry or pork.)
  —*Marcia Morgan, Chevy Chase, Maryland*

- ■ *LEMONADE MARINADE:* Combine 1 can (12 ounces) frozen lemonade concentrate (thawed), 2 tablespoons *each* brown sugar and soy sauce, 1 teaspoon garlic powder and 1/4 teaspoon dried mint flakes. Reserve 3/4 cup for basting if desired. Marinate meat in remaining marinade for up to 4 hours. (Enough to marinate about 4 pounds of poultry, pork or fish.)
  —*Olivia Logan, Delphi, Indiana*

Golden Glazed Fryer
Peggy West, Georgetown, Delaware

This moist, grilled chicken has a savory coating that's a nice change of pace from tomato-based sauces. This recipe has been passed down in my family for generations.

1	broiler/fryer chicken (3 to 4 pounds), cut up
1/2	cup vegetable oil
1/2	cup cider vinegar
1	egg, lightly beaten
4	teaspoons salt
1-1/2	teaspoon poultry seasoning
1/4	teaspoon pepper

1) Coat grill rack with nonstick cooking spray before starting the grill. Grill chicken, covered, skin side down over medium heat for 15 minutes. Turn; cover and grill 15 minutes longer.

2) Meanwhile, combine the remaining ingredients; brush over chicken. Grill for 5 minutes. Turn and brush with glaze; grill 5 minutes longer or until meat thermometer reads 180° in the thigh and 170° in the breast. Discard unused glaze.

Yield: 6 servings.

NUTRITION FACTS: One serving equals 334 calories, 24 g fat (5 g saturated fat), 105 mg cholesterol, 867 mg sodium, 1 g carbohydrate, trace fiber, 28 g protein.

Grilled Cornish Hens
David Baruch, Weston, Florida

I like experimenting with different foods and adapting them to my own tastes. These hens are one of my specialties, an entree I concocted by combining a few different recipes. The moist meat has a pleasant grilled flavor that's accented with cloves and ginger.

1/4	cup butter, softened
2	green onions, finely chopped
2	tablespoons minced fresh parsley
2	tablespoons grated fresh gingerroot
3	garlic cloves, minced
1	teaspoon salt, *divided*
1/2	teaspoon pepper, *divided*
4	Cornish game hens (20 ounces *each*)

1) Coat grill rack with nonstick cooking spray before preparing grill for indirect heat. In a small bowl, combine butter, onions, parsley, ginger, garlic, 1/2 teaspoon of salt and 1/4 teaspoon pepper.

2) Rub mixture under the skin and over the top of each game hen. Sprinkle remaining salt and pepper inside the hen cavities.

3) Grill hens, covered, breast side up over indirect medium heat for 45-60 minutes or until a meat thermometer reads 180° and juices run clear.

Yield: 4 servings.

NUTRITION FACTS: 1 Cornish game hen equals 1,584 calories, 115 g fat (36 g saturated fat), 773 mg cholesterol, 1,071 mg sodium, 2 g carbohydrate, trace fiber, 127 g protein.

YOGURT-MARINATED CHICKEN

Yogurt-Marinated Chicken
Naheed Saleem, Stamford, Connecticut

This tender marinated chicken gets its zing from the chili powder and cumin. For variety, add a tablespoon of tomato paste to the marinade or replace the chili powder with chopped green chilies.

1/2	cup fat-free yogurt
3	garlic cloves, minced
2	tablespoons lemon juice
1	tablespoon canola oil
1	teaspoon sugar
1	teaspoon chili powder
1	tablespoon minced fresh gingerroot
1/2	teaspoon salt
1/2	teaspoon ground cumin
6	bone-in chicken breast halves (6 ounces *each*)

1) In a large resealable plastic bag, combine the yogurt, garlic, lemon juice, oil, sugar and seasonings; add the chicken. Seal bag and turn to coat; refrigerate for at least 8 hours or overnight.

2) Coat grill rack with nonstick cooking spray before starting the grill. Prepare the grill for indirect heat. Drain and discard marinade.

3) Grill chicken, covered, bone side down over indirect medium heat for 2 minutes. Turn; grill 25-35 minutes longer or until juices run clear.

Yield: 6 servings.

NUTRITION FACTS: 1 chicken breast half equals 149 calories, 4 g fat (1 g saturated fat), 68 mg cholesterol, 163 mg sodium, 2 g carbohydrate, trace fiber, 25 g protein.

Santa Fe Chicken Heroes
Bonnie Link, Goose Creek, South Carolina

My son found this recipe and shared it with me because he knows I like easy and tasty meals from the grill. The Southwestern seasonings make these sandwiches spicy and flavorful. You can adjust the crushed red pepper and chili powder to your tastes.

6	boneless skinless chicken breast halves
1	tablespoon vegetables oil
1/4 to 1/2	teaspoon pepper
1/4 to 1/2	teaspoons crushed red pepper flakes
1/4 to 1/2	teaspoon chili powder
6	slices Monterey Jack cheese
6	French *or* Italian rolls, split
2	tablespoons butter, melted

Lettuce leaves and tomato slices

Salsa *or* picante sauce, optional

1) Coat grill rack with nonstick cooking spray before starting the grill. Pound chicken breasts slightly to flatten evenly. Brush both sides with oil. Combine seasonings; sprinkle on both sides of chicken.

2) Grill, uncovered, over medium-hot heat for 6-8 minutes; turn and grill 4-6 minutes longer or until chicken is tender and no longer pink. Top with cheese; allow to melt, about 2 minutes.

3) Brush rolls with butter; grill just until toasted. Place lettuce, tomato and chicken on rolls; top with salsa or picante sauce if desired.

Yield: 6 servings.

NUTRITION FACTS: 1 sandwich (calculated without lettuce and tomato) equals 322 calories, 15 g fat (7 g saturated fat), 41 mg cholesterol, 494 mg sodium, 30 g carbohydrate, 1 g fiber, 15 g protein.

Garlic Chicken Kabobs

Sheri Jean Waked, Loveland, Ohio

Tender and moist, these grilled kabobs are extra special when served with the garlic dipping sauce. This is a lighter version of a dish my Lebanese mother-in-law taught me to make. I reduced the amount of oil and substituted yogurt for mayonnaise.

- 8 garlic cloves, minced
- 1/2 teaspoon salt
- 1/4 cup minced fresh cilantro
- 1 teaspoon ground coriander
- 1/2 cup reduced-fat plain yogurt
- 2 tablespoons lemon juice
- 1-1/2 teaspoons olive oil
- 2 pounds boneless skinless chicken breasts, cut into 1-inch cubes

GARLIC DIPPING SAUCE:
- 4 garlic cloves, minced
- 1/4 teaspoon salt
- 2 tablespoons olive oil
- 1 cup (8 ounces) reduced-fat plain yogurt

1) Place garlic and salt in a small bowl; crush with the back of a sturdy spoon. Add cilantro and coriander; crush together. Add the yogurt, lemon juice and oil; mix well.

2) Pour into a large resealable plastic bag; add the chicken. Seal bag and turn to coat; refrigerate for 2 hours.

3) For dipping sauce, place garlic and salt in a small bowl; crush with the back of a sturdy spoon. Mix in oil. Stir in yogurt. Cover and refrigerate until serving.

4) Coat grill rack with nonstick cooking spray before starting the grill. Drain and discard marinade. Thread chicken on eight metal or soaked wooden skewers.

5) Grill kabobs, covered, over medium heat for 3-4 minutes on each side or until juices run clear, turning once. Serve with dipping sauce.

Yield: 8 servings.

Editor's Note: To broil, place kabobs on a broiler pan. Broil 4 in. from the heat for 3-4 minutes on each side or until juices run clear, turning once.

NUTRITION FACTS: 1 kabob with 2 tablespoons dipping sauce equals 186 calories, 6 g fat (1 g saturated fat), 68 mg cholesterol, 246 mg sodium, 4 g carbohydrate, trace fiber, 28 g protein.

PIZZA ON THE GRILL

Pizza on the Grill

Lisa Boettcher, Columbus, Wisconsin

Pizza is such a favorite at our house I make it at least once a week. The barbecue flavor mingling with the cheese tastes delicious.

- 1 package (1/4 ounce) active dry yeast
- 1 cup warm water (110° to 115°)
- 2 tablespoons vegetable oil
- 2 teaspoons sugar
- 1 teaspoon baking soda
- 1 teaspoon salt
- 2-3/4 to 3 cups all-purpose flour

TOPPINGS:
- 2 cups cubed cooked chicken
- 1/2 to 3/4 cup barbecue sauce
- 1/2 cup julienned green pepper
- 2 cups (8 ounces) shredded Monterey Jack cheese

1) In a large mixing bowl, dissolve yeast in water. Add the oil, sugar, baking soda, salt and 2 cups flour. Stir in enough remaining flour to form a soft dough.

2) Turn onto a floured surface; knead until smooth and elastic, about 6-8 minutes. Cover and let rest for 10 minutes. On a floured surface, roll dough into a 13-in. circle. Transfer to a greased 12-in. pizza pan. Build up edges slightly.

3) Grill, covered, over medium heat for 5 minutes. Remove from the grill. Combine chicken and barbecue sauce; spread over the crust.

4) Sprinkle with green pepper and cheese. Grill, covered, 5-10 minutes longer or until crust is golden and cheese is melted.

Yield: 4 servings.

NUTRITION FACTS: 1 serving equals 757 calories, 31 g fat (13 g saturated fat), 113 mg cholesterol, 1,525 mg sodium, 73 g carbohydrate, 3 g fiber, 44 g protein.

CHICKEN FAJITAS

Chicken Fajitas

Melinda Ewbank, Fairfield, Ohio

Fresh lime juice helps you bring a taste of Mexico to your dinner table. These colorful fajitas have fresh flavors that appeal to everyone.

2	tablespoons white wine vinegar
2	tablespoons fresh lime juice
2	tablespoons vegetable oil, *divided*
1	tablespoon Worcestershire sauce
1	tablespoon chopped onion
1	garlic clove, minced
1/2	teaspoon salt, optional
1/2	teaspoon dried oregano
1/4	teaspoon ground cumin
1	pound boneless skinless chicken breasts
1	medium green pepper, halved and seeded
1	medium sweet red pepper, halved and seeded
1	medium sweet onion, sliced
6	flour tortillas (8 inches)

Salsa, guacamole, sour cream and shredded cheddar cheese, optional

1) In a large resealable plastic bag, combine the vinegar, lime juice, 1 tablespoon oil, Worcestershire sauce, onion, garlic, salt if desired, oregano and cumin; add chicken. Seal bag and turn to coat; refrigerate at least 4 hours.

2) Coat grill rack with nonstick cooking spray before starting the grill. Drain and discard marinade from chicken. Lightly brush vegetables with remaining oil.

3) Grill vegetables and chicken, covered, over medium heat for 12-15 minutes or until the vegetables begin to soften and chicken juices run clear.

4) Meanwhile, warm tortillas according to package directions. Quickly slice chicken and peppers into strips and separate onion slices into rings.

5) Spoon chicken and vegetables down the center of tortillas; fold in sides. Garnish if desired with salsa, guacamole, sour cream and cheese.

Yield: 6 servings.

NUTRITION FACTS: 1 fajita equals 282 calories, 8 g fat (1 g saturated fat), 42 mg cholesterol, 301 mg sodium, 31 g carbohydrate, 1 g fiber, 20 g protein.

■ *GRILLED BEEF FAJITAS:* Prepare as directed, using 1-1/2 pounds beef flank steak in place of the chicken. Grill over medium heat for 6 to 8 minutes on each side or until meat reaches desired doneness (for medium-rare, a meat thermometer should read 145°; medium, 160°; well-done, 170°).

Tender Turkey Burgers

Sherry Hulsman, Elkton, Florida

These juicy, tender patties on whole wheat buns make a wholesome, satisfying sandwich. We especially like to grill them, but you could also pan-fry them.

1	egg, lightly beaten
2/3	cup soft whole wheat bread crumbs
1/2	cup finely chopped celery
1/4	cup finely chopped onion
1	tablespoon minced fresh parsley
1	teaspoon Worcestershire sauce
1	teaspoon dried oregano
1/2	teaspoon salt
1/4	teaspoon pepper
1-1/4	pounds lean ground turkey
6	whole wheat hamburger buns, split

1) Coat grill rack with nonstick cooking spray before starting the grill. In a bowl, combine the first nine ingredients. Crumble turkey over mixture and mix well. Shape into six patties.

2) Grill, covered, over medium heat for 5-6 minutes on each side or until a meat thermometer reads 165° and juices run clear. Serve on buns.

Yield: 6 servings.

NUTRITION FACTS: 1 burger equals 293 calories, 11 g fat (3 g saturated fat), 110 mg cholesterol, 561 mg sodium, 27 g carbohydrate, 4 g fiber, 22 g protein.

Cider-Marinated Turkey

Wendy Stenman, Germantown, Wisconsin

Make Thanksgiving dinner memorable by serving this golden-brown turkey that's marinated in apple cider, kosher salt and spices.

8	cups apple cider *or* unsweetened apple juice
1/2	cup kosher salt
2	bay leaves
2	sprigs fresh thyme
8	whole cloves
5	garlic cloves
1	teaspoon whole allspice, crushed
2	medium navel oranges, quartered
3	quarts cold water
1	turkey (12 pounds)
1	medium onion, quartered
2	medium carrots, halved and quartered
2	sprigs fresh sage *or* 1 tablespoon rubbed sage
1	tablespoon canola oil

1) In a large kettle, combine the cider and the seasonings. Bring to a boil. Cook and stir until salt is dissolved. Stir in oranges. Remove from the heat. Add water; cool to room temperature.

2) Remove giblets from turkey; discard. Place a turkey-size oven roasting bag inside a second roasting bag; add turkey. Place in a roasting pan.

3) Carefully pour the cooled marinade into bag. Squeeze out as much air as possible; seal bag and turn to coat. Refrigerate for 12-14 hours; turn several times.

4) Coat grill rack with nonstick cooking spray. Prepare grill for indirect heat, using a drip pan. Drain and discard marinade.

5) Rinse turkey under cold water; pat dry. Place onion, carrots and sage in cavity. Rub oil over skin. Skewer turkey openings; tie drumsticks together.

6) Place turkey over drip pan; grill, covered, over indirect medium heat for 2 to 3 hours or until a meat thermometer reads 180° in the thigh, tenting turkey with foil after about 1 hour. Cover and let stand for 15 minutes.

7) If desired, thicken pan juices for gravy. Remove and discard skin and vegetables in cavity before carving turkey. Serve with gravy.

Yield: 12 servings plus leftovers.

Editor's Note: It is best not to use a prebasted turkey for this recipe. However, if you do, omit the salt in the recipe.

NUTRITION FACTS: 4 ounces light and dark cooked turkey, skin removed, calculated without gravy equals 198 calories, 6 g fat (2 g saturated fat), 86 mg cholesterol, 244 mg sodium, trace carbohydrate, 0 fiber, 33 g protein.

Citrus Grilled Turkey Breast

Taste of Home Test Kitchen

Instead of the usual outdoor barbecue, treat your guests to a sit-down dinner featuring this delicious grilled entree with a luscious herb and citrus gravy.

1	bone-in turkey breast (4 to 5 pounds)
1/4	cup fresh parsley sprigs
1/4	cup fresh basil leaves
3	tablespoons butter
4	garlic cloves, halved
1/2	teaspoon salt
1	medium lemon, thinly sliced
1	medium orange, thinly sliced
1	tablespoon cornstarch
2	tablespoons water
1	cup orange juice
1	teaspoon grated orange peel
1	teaspoon grated lemon peel
1/4	teaspoon pepper

1) Using fingers, carefully loosen the skin from both sides of turkey breast. In a food processor or blender, combine the parsley, basil, butter, garlic

and salt; cover and process until smooth.

2) Spread parsley mixture under turkey skin; arrange lemon and orange slices over herb mixture. Secure skin to underside of bread with toothpicks.

3) Coat grill rack with nonstick cooking spray before starting the grill. Prepare grill for indirect heat, using a drip pan. Place turkey over drip pan.

4) Grill, covered, over indirect medium heat for 1-1/2 to 2-1/4 hours or until a meat thermometer reads 170° and juices run clear. Cover and let stand for 10 minutes.

5) Meanwhile, pour pan drippings into a measuring cup; skim fat. In a saucepan, combine cornstarch and water until smooth. Add the orange juice, orange peel, lemon peel, pepper and pan drippings. Bring to a boil; cook and stir for 2 minutes or until thickened.

6) Discard the skin, lemon and orange slices from turkey breast. Remove herb mixture from turkey; stir into gravy. Slice turkey and serve with gravy.

Yield: 8 servings with leftovers.

NUTRITION FACTS: 4 ounces cooked turkey with 3 tablespoons gravy equals 192 calories, 2 g fat (1 g saturated fat), 101 mg cholesterol, 224 mg sodium, 5 g carbohydrate, trace fiber, 35 g protein.

Seafood Grilling Chart

Fish is done when it turns opaque in the thickest portion and flakes into sections. Scallops are done when they turn opaque. Shrimp are done when they turn pink. Watch closely to avoid overcooking. For direct grilling, turn steaks, whole fish, shrimp and scallops halfway through grilling time. Fillets generally do not need to be turned. For ease of turning, use a grill basket.

CUT	WEIGHT OR THICKNESS	HEAT	COOKING TIME (MINUTES PER POUND)
DRESSED FISH	1 lb. 2 to 2-1/2 lbs.	Medium/Direct Medium/Indirect	10 to 15 20 to 30
FILLETS OR STEAKS	1/4 to 1/2 in. 1/2 to 1 in.	High/Direct High/Direct	3 to 5 5 to 10
KABOBS	1-in. cubes	Medium/Direct	8 to 12
SCALLOPS, SEA	1 lb.	Medium/Direct	5 to 8
SHRIMP, MEDIUM	1 lb.	Medium/Direct	5 to 8

ORANGE ROUGHY BUNDLES

Orange Roughy Bundles
Margaret Wilson, Hemet, California

Cleanup is a breeze with this simple supper. Each meal-in-one packet contains zucchini, red pepper and a flaky full-flavored fish fillet. It is just as delicious with flounder or sole.

4 fresh *or* frozen orange roughy fillets (6 ounces *each*), thawed
1/4 cup grated Parmesan cheese
1/8 to 1/4 teaspoon cayenne pepper
2 medium zucchini, cut into 1/4-inch slices
1 small sweet red pepper, julienned
1/2 teaspoon salt

1) Place each fillet on a piece of heavy-duty foil (about 12-in. square). Sprinkle with cheese and cayenne. Top with zucchini, red pepper and salt.

2) Fold foil over vegetables and seal tightly. Grill, covered, over indirect heat for 8-10 minutes or until fish flakes easily with a fork.

Yield: 4 servings.

NUTRITION FACTS: 1 packet equals 159 calories, 3 g fat (1 g saturated fat), 38 mg cholesterol, 499 mg sodium, 4 g carbohydrate, 2 g fiber, 28 g protein.

Firecracker Salmon Steaks

Phyllis Schmalz, Kansas City, Kansas

Red pepper flakes and cayenne provide the fiery flavor that gives these salmon steaks their name. Basting the fish with the zippy sauce while grilling creates a glossy glaze.

- 1/4 cup balsamic vinegar
- 1/4 cup chili sauce
- 1/4 cup packed brown sugar
- 3 garlic cloves, minced
- 2 teaspoons minced fresh parsley
- 1 teaspoon minced fresh gingerroot
- 1/4 to 1/2 teaspoon cayenne pepper
- 1/4 to 1/2 teaspoon crushed red pepper flakes, optional
- 4 salmon steaks (6 ounces *each*)

1) Coat grill rack with nonstick cooking spray before starting the grill. In a small bowl, combine the vinegar, chili sauce, sugar, garlic, parsley and seasonings.

2) Grill salmon, covered, over medium heat for 4-5 minutes on each side or until fish flakes easily with a fork, brushing occasionally with sauce.

Yield: 4 servings.

Editor's Note: To broil the salmon, place on a broiler pan. Broil 4-6 in. from the heat for 4-5 minutes on each side or until fish flakes easily with a fork, brushing occasionally with sauce.

NUTRITION FACTS: 1 serving equals 373 calories, 17 g fat (4 g saturated fat), 106 mg cholesterol, 565 mg sodium, 22 g carbohydrate, trace fiber, 32 g protein.

Creole Catfish Fillets

Dave Bremstone, Plantation, Florida

I rub catfish fillets with a pleasant mixture of seasonings before cooking them quickly on the grill. The moist fish gets plenty of flavor when served with a spicy sauce and lemon wedges.

- 3 tablespoons reduced-fat plain yogurt
- 2 tablespoons finely chopped onion
- 1 tablespoon fat-free mayonnaise
- 1 tablespoon Dijon mustard
- 1 tablespoon ketchup
- 1/2 teaspoon dried thyme
- 1/4 teaspoon grated lemon peel
- 1 teaspoon paprika
- 1/2 teaspoon onion powder
- 1/4 teaspoon salt
- 1/8 teaspoon cayenne pepper
- 4 catfish fillets (4 ounces *each*)
- 4 lemon wedges

1) In a small bowl, combine the yogurt, onion, mayonnaise, mustard, ketchup, thyme and lemon peel. Cover and refrigerate until serving.

2) In another bowl, combine paprika, onion powder, salt and cayenne; rub over both sides of fillet.

3) Grill, covered, in a grill basket coated with nonstick cooking spray over medium-hot heat for 5-6 minutes on each side or until fish flakes easily with a fork. Serve with lemon wedges and yogurt sauce.

Yield: 4 servings.

NUTRITION FACTS: 1 fillet with about 1 tablespoon sauce equals 182 calories, 9 g fat (2 g saturated fat), 54 mg cholesterol, 382 mg sodium, 5 g carbohydrate, 1 g fiber, 19 g protein.

Zucchini-Wrapped Scallops

Mrs. Julie Gwinn, Hershey, Pennsylvania

This dish gets a little heat from red pepper flakes and Caribbean jerk seasoning.

- 2 tablespoons orange juice
- 1 tablespoon olive oil
- 1 teaspoon Caribbean jerk seasoning
- 1 teaspoon grated orange peel
- 1/8 teaspoon crushed red pepper flakes
- 1-1/2 pounds sea scallops (about 16)
- 2 medium zucchini

1) In a small bowl, combine the orange juice, oil, jerk seasoning, peel and pepper flakes; set aside 1 tablespoon for basting. Pour remaining marinade into a large resealable plastic bag; add the scallops. Seal bag and turn to coat; refrigerate for 30 minutes.

2) Using a vegetable peeler or metal cheese slicer, cut zucchini into very thin lengthwise strips. Drain marinade from scallops. Wrap one strip around each scallop. Secure by threading where the zucchini ends overlap onto metal or soaked wooden skewers.

3) Coat grill rack with nonstick cooking spray before starting the grill. Grill, covered, over medium heat for 3-4 minutes on each side or until scallops turn opaque, brushing with reserved marinade once.

Yield: 4 servings.

NUTRITION FACTS: 1 kabob equals 194 calories, 5 g fat (1 g saturated fat), 56 mg cholesterol, 346 mg sodium, 7 g carbohydrate, 1 g fiber, 29 g protein.

CITRUS TUNA STEAKS

Citrus Tuna Steaks
Shannon Edwards, Arlington, Texas

This grilled fish is a summertime favorite that my family requests often. I adapted it from a traditional Jamaican jerk recipe.

- 1   medium pink grapefruit
- 1/4 cup lemon juice
- 1/4 cup lime juice
- 2   tablespoons honey
- 1   tablespoon snipped fresh dill
     or 1 teaspoon dill weed
- 1   teaspoon crushed red pepper flakes
- 2   teaspoons minced fresh gingerroot
- 4   tuna steak *or* fillets
     (6 ounces *each*)

1) Peel and section grapefruit over a bowl, reserving juice. Refrigerate half of the grapefruit sections. Add remaining grapefruit to reserved grapefruit juice. Add lemon juice, lime juice, honey, dill, red pepper flakes and ginger.

2) Remove 1/4 cup for basting; cover and refrigerate. Pour remaining marinade into a large resealable plastic bag; add the tuna steaks. Seal bag and turn to coat; refrigerate for 30 minutes, turning once.

3) Coat grill rack with nonstick cooking spray before starting the grill. Drain and discard marinade from tuna. Grill tuna, uncovered, over medium heat for 6-7 minutes on each side, basting frequently with reserved marinade.

4) Top tuna steaks with reserved grapefruit sections. Cover and cook for 5 minutes or until fish flakes easily with a fork.

Yield: 4 servings.

NUTRITION FACTS: 1 serving equals 224 calories, 2 g fat (trace saturated fat), 77 mg cholesterol, 63 mg sodium, 11 g carbohydrate, 3 g fiber, 40 g protein.

Pineapple Shrimp Kabobs
Terry Hammond, Shohola, Pennsylvania

I don't remember where I found this wonderful recipe, but my husband and I just love it. It couldn't be easier and always makes an impression on dinner guests.

- 2   cans (20 ounces *each*) pineapple chunks
- 2   cups fat-free Italian salad dressing
- 2   cans (8 ounces *each*) tomato sauce
- 1/4 cup packed brown sugar
- 2   teaspoons prepared mustard
- 2   pounds uncooked medium shrimp, peeled and deveined (about 64)
- 4   large sweet red peppers, cut into chunks
- 2   large onions, cut into chunks

1) Drain the pineapple, reserving 1/2 cup juice; refrigerate pineapple. In a small bowl, combine the salad dressing, tomato sauce, brown sugar, mustard and reserved juice.

2) Pour 3 cups into a large resealable plastic bag; add the shrimp. Seal bag and turn to coat; refrigerate for 3 hours. Cover and refrigerate remaining marinade for basting.

3) Coat grill rack with nonstick cooking spray before starting the grill. Drain and discard marinade from shrimp. On 16 metal or soaked wooden skewers, alternately thread the shrimp, red peppers, onions and pineapple.

4) Grill, covered, over medium heat for 3-5 minutes on each side or until shrimp turn pink and vegetables are tender, basting occasionally with reserved marinade.

Yield: 8 servings.

NUTRITION FACTS: 2 kabobs equals 221 calories, 2 g fat (trace saturated fat), 169 mg cholesterol, 629 mg sodium, 32 g carbohydrate, 4 g fiber, 20 g protein.

Fruit and Vegetable Grilling Chart

For even grilling, cut fruit and vegetables into uniform sizes. To prevent small pieces from slipping through the grill racks, use skewers or vegetable basket.

Grill vegetables and fruits until tender. Turn halfway through grilling time.

FRUIT OR VEGETABLE	SLICE OR THICKNESS	HEAT	COOKING TIME (MINUTES PER POUND)
FRUIT			
APPLES	1/2-in. slices	Medium/Direct	4 to 6
APRICOTS, PITTED	halved	Medium/Direct	6 to 8
BANANAS	halved lengthwise	Medium/Direct	6 to 8
PEACHES, PITTED	halved	Medium/Direct	8 to 10
PEARS	halved	Medium/Direct	8 to 10
PINEAPPLE	1/2-in. rings	Medium/Direct	7 to 10
VEGETABLES			
ASPARAGUS	1/2-in. thick	Medium/Direct	6 to 8
SWEET PEPPERS	halved or quartered	Medium/Direct	8 to 10
CORN (NO HUSK)	whole	Medium/Direct	10 to 12
CORN (WITH HUSK)	whole	Medium/Direct	25 to 30
EGGPLANT	1/2-in. slices	Medium/Direct	8 to 10
FENNEL	1/4-in. slices	Medium/Direct	10 to 12
MUSHROOMS (BUTTONS)	whole	Medium/Direct	8 to 10
MUSHROOMS (PORTOBELLO)	whole	Medium/Direct	12 to 15
ONIONS	1/2-in. slices	Medium/Direct	8 to 12
POTATOES	whole	Medium/Indirect	45 to 60

Baked Apples on the Grill
Jodi Rugg, Aurora, Illinois

Sweet coconut provides the delicious difference in this fun grilled treat. Our two children enjoy helping me stuff the yummy filling into the apples. It's so easy that sometimes we don't even bother to do the measuring!

- 4 medium tart apples, cored
- 1/3 cup raisins
- 1/3 cup flaked coconut
- 1/4 cup packed brown sugar
- 1/2 teaspoon ground cinnamon

1) Place each apple on a piece of heavy-duty foil (about 12 in. square). Combine the remaining ingredients; spoon into center of apples. Fold foil over the apples and seal tightly.

2) Grill, covered, over medium heat for 20-25 minutes or until apples are tender. Open foil carefully to allow steam to escape.

Yield: 4 servings.

NUTRITION FACTS: 1 serving equals 209 calories, 3 g fat (3 g saturated fat), 0 cholesterol, 27 mg sodium, 48 g carbohydrate, 5 g fiber, 1 g protein.

GRILLED FRUIT KABOBS

Grilled Fruit Kabobs

Mrs. Travis Baker, Litchfield, Illinois

Instead of a typical fruit salad, try these grilled kabobs for your next summer gathering. They're quick and easy, and they help keep you out of the kitchen!

1/2	fresh pineapple, trimmed and cut into 1-inch chunks
3	medium nectarines, cut into 1-inch chunks
3	medium pears, cut into 1-inch chunks
3	medium fresh peaches, cut into 1-inch chunks
3 to 4	medium plums, cut into 1-inch chunks
10	apricots, halved
3	tablespoons honey *or* light corn syrup, warmed

1) Thread fruit alternately onto metal or soaked bamboo skewers. Grill, uncovered, over medium-hot heat until fruit is heated through, about 6 minutes, turning often.

2) Brush with honey or corn syrup during the last minute of grilling time.

Yield: 6 servings.

NUTRITION FACTS: 1 serving equals 201 calories, 1 g fat (trace saturated fat), 0 cholesterol, 1 mg sodium, 50 g carbohydrate, 6 g fiber, 3 g protein.

Grilled Sweet Corn

Connie Lou Hollister, Lake Odessa, Michigan

We have plenty of fresh sweet corn in our area, so we use this recipe often in summer. Seasonings perfectly accent the corn's just-picked flavor.

8	large ears sweet corn in husk
6	tablespoons butter, softened
1	tablespoon minced fresh parsley
1 to 2	teaspoons chili powder
1	teaspoon garlic salt
1/2 to 1	teaspoon ground cumin

1) Carefully peel back husks from corn to within 1 in. of bottom; remove silk. Combine remaining ingredients; spread over corn.

2) Rewrap corn in husks and secure with kitchen string. Place in a large kettle; cover with cold water. Soak for 20 minutes; drain. Grill corn, covered, over medium heat, for 25-30 minutes or until tender, turning often.

Yield: 8 servings.

NUTRITION FACTS: 1 serving equals 200 calories, 10 g fat (6 g saturated fat), 23 mg cholesterol, 338 mg sodium, 28 g carbohydrate, 4 g fiber, 5 g protein.

■ *ZESTY CORN PACKETS:* Husk corn and remove silk. Place each ear on a piece of heavy-duty foil (13 in. x 12 in.) Drizzle with a mixture of 1/3 cup melted butter, 2 tablespoons *each* prepared mustard and horseradish, 1 teaspoon Worcestershire sauce and 1/4 teaspoon lemon-pepper seasoning. Fold in edges of foil and seal tightly. Grill over medium heat for 15-20 minutes or until corn is tender. Open carefully to allow steam to escape.

Grilled Vegetable Skewers

Susan Bourque, Danielson, Connecticut

My mother and I love to eat vegetables the most flavorful way—grilled! Seasoned with fresh herbs, these colorful kabobs showcase the best of summer's bounty.

    1 medium ear fresh *or* frozen
       sweet corn, thawed and
       quartered
    1 small zucchini, quartered
 1/4 small red onion, halved
    4 cherry tomatoes
 1/4 teaspoon dried basil
 1/4 teaspoon dried rosemary,
       crushed
 1/4 teaspoon dried thyme
 1/8 teaspoon garlic powder
 1/8 teaspoon salt
 1/8 teaspoon pepper

1) Place the corn on a microwave-safe plate. Cover with waxed paper. Microwave on high for 2 minutes.

2) Coat grill rack with nonstick cooking spray before starting the grill. On two metal or soaked wooden skewers, alternately thread the corn, zucchini, onion and tomatoes.

3) Lightly coat vegetables with nonstick cooking spray. In a small bowl, combine the seasonings; sprinkle over vegetables.

4) Grill, covered, over medium heat for 3 minutes on each side or until vegetables are tender, turning three times.

Yield: 2 servings.

Editor's Note: To broil the kabobs, place on a broiler pan coated with nonstick cooking spray. Broil 4-6 in. from the heat for 3 minutes on each side or until vegetables are tender, turning three times.

NUTRITION FACTS: 1 kabob equals 69 calories, 1 g fat (trace saturated fat), 0 cholesterol, 131 mg sodium, 16 g carbohydrate, 3 g fiber, 3 g protein.

Red Potato Bundles

Kriss Erickson, Haena, Hawaii

Red potatoes just need to be scrubbed clean and quartered to start this side dish. You can grill or bake the packets with tasty results.

    6 small red potatoes, quartered
    1 small onion, thinly sliced

    6 whole garlic cloves, peeled
    2 sprigs fresh rosemary *or* 1 to 2
       teaspoons dried rosemary,
       crushed
 1/2 teaspoon salt
Dash pepper
    2 tablespoons grated Parmesan
       cheese
 1/4 cup olive oil

1) Place potatoes, onion and garlic on two pieces of heavy-duty foil (about 12 in. square); top with rosemary, salt, pepper and cheese. Drizzle with oil. Fold in edges of foil and seal tightly.

2) Grill, covered, over medium heat for 40-45 minutes or until potatoes are tender. Open foil carefully to allow steam to escape.

Yield: 2 servings.

Editor's Note: To bake the foil packets, place on a baking pan. Bake at 350° for 45 minutes or until potatoes are tender.

NUTRITION FACTS: 1 serving equals 390 calories, 29 g fat (5 g saturated fat), 4 mg cholesterol, 694 mg sodium, 29 g carbohydrate, 3 g fiber, 6 g protein.

Eggplant Mexicano

Alyce De Roos, Sarnia, Ontario

Salsa gives fun flavor to eggplant slices in this speedy dish. We had an overabundance of eggplant some years ago when this recipe caught my eye. My husband and I think it's delicious.

 1/2 cup vegetable oil
    1 teaspoon garlic powder
    1 teaspoon dried oregano
    1 medium eggplant, peeled and cut
       into 1/2-inch slices
 2/3 cup salsa, warmed
 1/2 cup shredded Monterey Jack
       cheese

1) In a bowl, combine the oil, garlic powder and oregano; brush over both sides of eggplant.

2) Grill, uncovered, over medium heat for 4 minutes on each side or until tender.

3) To serve, spoon a small amount of salsa into the center of each; sprinkle with cheese.

Yield: 6 servings.

NUTRITION FACTS: 1 serving equals 230 calories, 21 g fat (4 g saturated fat), 8 mg cholesterol, 178 mg sodium, 9 g carbohydrate, 4 g fiber, 5 g protein.

CHAPTER 10

EGGS & CHEESE

EGGS & CHEESE

No two ingredients are quite as versatile and compatible in recipes as eggs and cheese. Eggs are delicious and they are also an economical protein source. Eggs and cheese make a great combination for breakfast or a simple lunch or dinner.

Eggs also play many supporting functions in baking—they add color, flavor, texture, structure and help leaven. Egg yolks add fat and act as an emulsifier, which helps blend the shortening or oil into the liquid ingredients. Egg whites are used for their drying properties, especially for meringues.

Buying, Storing and Cooking Eggs

Brown and white eggs have the same nutritional value and they cook the same. The color of the egg is based on the breed of the chicken.

Select cartons with unbroken shells from the refrigerated case. Refrigerate them as soon as possible after purchase. Store eggs in their carton on an inside refrigerator shelf, not in a compartment on the door. The carton cushions the eggs and helps prevent moisture loss and odor adsorption.

Check the grade on the egg carton; they're either AA, A or B. The higher the grade, the higher and more nicely shaped the yolk will be. Also the higher the grade, the thicker the white and the less it spreads.

Use eggs by the expiration date printed on the carton. The expiration should be no longer than 30 days passed the date the eggs were packaged. Discard any eggs that have cracked or broken shells.

Don't use a recipe where the eggs will not be thoroughly cooked. Eggs are thoroughly cooked when they reach a temperature of 160°. Do not, for food safety reasons, leave eggs at room temperature for over 2 hours.

Pasteurized eggs have been treated with heat to destroy bacteria that may be on the shell or in the egg. These eggs are available in some markets. Due to the heat treatment, the eggs may have slightly lower amounts of heat-sensitive vitamins, such as thiamin and riboflavin.

Egg Size Equivalents

The recipes in this cookbook were tested with large eggs. The following are some guidelines for substituting other egg sizes for large eggs.

EGG SIZE	SUBSTITUTION
1 LARGE EGG	1 jumbo, 1 extra-large *or* 1 medium
2 LARGE EGGS	2 jumbo, 2 extra-large, 2 medium *or* 3 small
3 LARGE EGGS	2 jumbo, 3 extra-large, 3 medium *or* 4 small
4 LARGE EGGS	3 jumbo, 4 extra-large, 5 medium *or* 5 small
5 LARGE EGGS	4 jumbo, 4 extra-large, 6 medium *or* 7 small
6 LARGE EGGS	5 jumbo, 5 extra-large, 7 medium *or* 8 small

LIGHTLY BEATEN
Beat the egg with a fork until the yolk and white are combined.

LEMON-COLORED
Beat eggs with an electric mixer on high speed for about 5 minutes. The volume of the beaten eggs will increase, the texture will go from liquid to thick and foamy and the color will be a light yellow.

THICK AND PALE YELLOW
Beat eggs and sugar with an electric mixer on high speed for about 7-8 minutes or until mixture has thickened and turned a very pale yellow. Mixture will fall in ribbons from a spoon.

SOFT PEAKS
Beat egg whites with an electric mixer on medium speed until they are thick and white. To test for soft peaks, lift the beaters from the whites—the egg white peaks should curl down. For best results, make sure the bowl and beaters are free from oil and the egg whites contain no specks of yolk. Both will prevent the whites from reaching full volume.

STIFF PEAKS
Continue beating the egg whites after they have reached the soft-peak stage with an electric mixer on high speed until the volume increases more and they are thicker. To test for stiff peaks, lift the beaters from the whites—the egg white peaks should stand straight up and if you tilt the bowl, the whites should not slide around.

Tips for Separated Eggs

Separate the eggs while they are still cold from the refrigerator, then allow the egg whites to stand at room temperature for 30 minutes before beating to obtain maximum volume.

- To store unbroken egg yolks, place in a container and cover with water. Tightly cover the container and refrigerate for 2-4 days.

- Refrigerate egg whites in a tightly covered container for up to 4 days.

- Freeze unused egg whites in a tightly covered container for up to 1 year.

- To freeze egg yolks: for each 1/4 cup of egg yolk, beat the yolks with 1/8 teaspoon salt or 1-1/2 teaspoons corn syrup. Place in a tightly covered container for up to 1 year. Make sure you label the container, noting whether salt or corn syrup was added. Use the salt-added yolks in savory dishes and the corn syrup-added yolks in sweet (dessert) recipes.

SEPARATING EGGS
Place an egg separator over a custard cup; crack egg into the separator. As each egg is separated, place yolk in another bowl and empty egg whites into a mixing bowl. It's easier to separate eggs when they are cold.

Lightly Scrambled Eggs
Patricia Kaliska, Phillips, Wisconsin

Wake up your taste buds with this fluffy entree, enhanced with sour cream, green onions and cheese. To keep it light, I use reduced-fat and fat-free ingredients.

9	egg whites
3	eggs
1/2	cup reduced-fat sour cream
1/4	cup fat-free milk
2	green onions, thinly sliced
1/4	teaspoon salt
1/8	teaspoon pepper
6	drops yellow food coloring, optional
3/4	cup shredded reduced-fat cheddar cheese

1) In a large bowl, whisk the egg whites and eggs.

Add the sour cream, milk, onions, salt, pepper and food coloring if desired. Pour into a large nonstick skillet coated with nonstick cooking spray.

2) Cook and gently stir over medium heat until eggs are completely set. Remove from the heat. Sprinkle with cheese; cover and let stand for 5 minutes to allow cheese to melt.

Yield: 6 servings.

NUTRITION FACTS: 1/3 cup equals 135 calories, 7 g fat (4 g saturated fat), 122 mg cholesterol, 331 mg sodium, 4 g carbohydrate, 1 g fiber, 15 g protein.

FLUFFY SCRAMBLED EGGS

Fluffy Scrambled Eggs
Marjorie Carey, Freeport, Florida

I started fixing scrambled eggs years ago when we raised chickens and had fresh ingredients every morning. This recipe's hard to beat when it comes to taste and texture. Plus it's easy to add ingredients to suit your fancy.

> 8 eggs
> 1 can (5 ounces) evaporated milk
> 2 tablespoons butter
> **Salt and pepper to taste**

1) In a large bowl, whisk the eggs and milk. In a large skillet, heat butter until hot.

2) Add egg mixture; cook and stir over medium heat until eggs are completely set. Season with salt and pepper.

Yield: 4 servings.

NUTRITION FACTS: 1 serving (calculated without salt and pepper) equals 244 calories, 18 g fat (8 g saturated fat), 452 mg cholesterol, 218 mg sodium, 5 g carbohydrate, 0 fiber, 15 g protein.

■ *HEARTY SCRAMBLED EGGS*: In a large skillet, saute 1 cup *each* cubed fully cooked ham and sliced fresh mushrooms, 1/2 cup chopped sweet red pepper and 1/4 cup sliced green onions in the 2 tablespoons butter until vegetables are tender. Remove vegetables and set aside. Whisk eggs with milk as directed, add to skillet.

Cook and stir until eggs are slightly set. Add the ham mixture and continue to cook until eggs are completely set. Remove from the heat. If desired, sprinkle top with 1 cup (4 ounces) shredded cheddar cheese; cover and let stand for 1-2 minutes or until cheese is melted.

Yield: 4 servings.

SCRAMBLING EGGS

1) Pour beaten egg mixture into prepared skillet. As eggs begin to set, gently move a spatula across the bottom and sides of pan, allowing the uncooked eggs to flow underneath.

2) Continue to cook the eggs, stirring occasionally, until the eggs are set and no visible liquid remains.

Fried Eggs
Taste of Home Test Kitchen

Cook slowly over medium heat to avoid overdone eggs. If you're watching calories, fry eggs in a nonstick pan coated with nonstick cooking spray.

> 1 to 2 tablespoons butter
> 1 to 2 eggs

1) In a 7- or 8-in. skillet or omelet pan, melt butter over medium heat. Break eggs, one at a time, into a custard cup or saucer, then gently slide into the pan. Immediately reduce heat to low. Cook slowly until the whites are completely set and the yolks begin to thicken.

2) For sunny-side-up eggs, cover the pan and cook until the yolk thickens but are not hard. For basted eggs, spoon butter in pan over eggs while cooking. For over-easy eggs, carefully turn the eggs to cook both sides.

Yield: 1 serving.

NUTRITION FACTS: 1 serving equals 175 calories, 16 g fat (9 g saturated fat), 243 mg cholesterol, 179 mg sodium, 1 g carbohydrate, 0 fiber, 6 g protein.

Asparagus Crab Omelets

Mae Jean Damron, Sandy, Utah

These satisfying omelets are filled with a savory blend of crabmeat, asparagus, tomatoes and provolone cheese...and they're attractive enough to serve guests. Sometimes I top these omelets with hollandaise sauce.

> 6 fresh asparagus spears, trimmed
>
> 4 eggs
>
> Dash salt
>
> Dash pepper
>
> 1/2 cup diced plum tomatoes
>
> 2 tablespoons butter, *divided*
>
> 1 can (6 ounces) crabmeat, drained, flaked and cartilage removed
>
> 1/2 cup (2 ounces) provolone cheese, shredded

1) Place asparagus in a steamer basket. Place in a saucepan over 1 in. of water; bring to a boil. Cover and steam for 4-5 minutes or until crisp-tender; set aside. In a small bowl, whisk the eggs, salt and pepper. Stir in tomatoes.

2) Melt 1 tablespoon butter in a small skillet over medium heat; add half of the egg mixture. As eggs set, lift edges, letting uncooked portion flow underneath.

3) When the eggs are set, spoon half of the crab, asparagus and provolone cheese over one side; fold omelet over filling. Cover and let stand for 1-2 minutes or until cheese is melted. Repeat for second omelet.

Yield: 2 servings.

NUTRITION FACTS: 1 serving equals 407 calories, 27 g fat (13 g saturated fat), 541 mg cholesterol, 733 mg sodium, 6 g carbohydrate, 1 g fiber, 35 g protein.

■ *POTATO OMELET:* In a small skillet, saute 1 cubed cooked medium red potato, 1/2 cup chopped fresh broccoli, 2 tablespoon chopped onion, 1/2 teaspoon dill weed in 1 tablespoon butter. Remove and keep warm.

Whisk 4 eggs with 1 tablespoon water. Cook omelets as directed in Asparagus Crab Omelets, omitting tomatoes, crabmeat and provolone cheese. Spoon half the potato mixture over one side of each omelet; fold omelet over filling. Sprinkle each with 1/4 cup shredded cheddar or Swiss cheese. Cover and let stand 1-2 minutes or until cheese is melted.

OVEN DENVER OMELET

Oven Denver Omelet

Ellen Bower, Taneytown, Maryland

Rather than make omelets one at a time, I put all my favorite ingredients into this baked version.

> 8 eggs
>
> 1/2 cup half-and-half cream
>
> 1 cup (4 ounces) shredded cheddar cheese
>
> 1 cup finely chopped fully cooked ham

MAKING AN OMELET

1) Beat eggs, milk and any seasonings. Heat oil or butter in a 10-in. nonstick skillet over medium heat. Add eggs; cook until partially set. Lift edges, letting uncooked egg flow underneath.

2) Allow the eggs to set, and then sprinkle your favorite filling ingredients (such as ham, chopped green pepper, chopped tomato, shredded cheese or mushrooms) over half of the omelet.

3) Fold omelet in half. Proceed as recipe directs.

1/4 cup finely chopped green pepper

1/4 cup finely chopped onion

1) In a bowl, whisk the eggs and cream until light. Stir in the cheese, ham, green pepper and onion.

2) Pour into a greased 9-in. square baking dish. Bake at 400° for 25 minutes or until golden brown.

Yield: 6 servings.

NUTRITION FACTS: 1 piece equals 235 calories, 16 g fat (8 g saturated fat), 326 mg cholesterol, 506 mg sodium, 4 g carbohydrate, trace fiber, 17 g protein.

BAKED OMELET ROLL

Baked Omelet Roll
Susan Hudon, Fort Wayne, Indiana

This is an interesting way to serve an omelet, plus it bakes in the oven. So you don't have to keep an eye on it like you would on the stovetop.

6 eggs

1 cup milk

1/2 cup all-purpose flour

1/2 teaspoon salt

1/4 teaspoon pepper

1 cup (4 ounces) shredded cheddar cheese

1) Place eggs and milk in a blender. Add the flour, salt and pepper; cover and process until smooth. Pour into a greased 13-in. x 9-in. x 2-in. baking pan. Bake at 450° for 20 minutes or until eggs are set.

2) Sprinkle with cheese. Roll up omelet in pan, starting with a short side. Place with seam side down on a serving platter. Cut into 3/4-in. slices.

Yield: 6 servings.

NUTRITION FACTS: 2 slices equals 204 calories, 12 g fat (6 g saturated fat), 238 mg cholesterol, 393 mg sodium, 11 g carbohydrate, trace fiber, 13 g protein.

Asparagus Frittata
James Bates, Hermiston, Oregon

You would never guess that egg substitute takes the place of eggs in this fun variation on a traditional frittata. Chock-full of fresh asparagus, this dish is perfect for a light lunch or brunch.

1 cup water

2/3 pound fresh asparagus, trimmed and cut into 1-inch pieces

1 medium onion, chopped

2 teaspoons olive oil

2 tablespoons minced fresh parsley

1-1/2 cups egg substitute

5 tablespoons shredded Parmesan cheese, *divided*

1/4 teaspoon salt

1/8 teaspoon pepper

1/4 cup shredded reduced-fat cheddar cheese

1) In a small saucepan, bring water to a boil. Add asparagus; cover and boil for 3 minutes. Drain and immediately place asparagus in ice water; drain and pat dry. In a 10-in. ovenproof skillet, saute onion in oil until tender. Add parsley and asparagus; toss to coat.

2) In a small bowl, combine the egg substitute, 3 tablespoons Parmesan cheese, salt and pepper. Pour over asparagus mixture; cover and cook over medium heat for 8-10 minutes or until eggs are nearly set. Sprinkle with remaining Parmesan.

3) Place uncovered skillet in the broiler, 6 in. from the heat, for 2 minutes or until eggs are set. Sprinkle with cheddar cheese. Cut into quarters. Serve immediately.

Yield: 4 servings.

Editor's Note: To use whole eggs, omit the egg substitute and use 6 eggs.

NUTRITION FACTS: 1 piece equals 146 calories, 5 g fat (2 g saturated fat), 8 mg cholesterol, 533 mg sodium, 9 g carbohydrate, 2 g fiber, 16 g protein.

USING EGG SUBSTITUTE

Look in the refrigerated and frozen food section of grocery stores for egg substitutes in cartons. Egg substitutes use egg whites and contain no cholesterol and little or no fat. One-fourth cup of egg substitute is equal to one egg.

Note that baking with egg substitute may affect the quality of your baked item. Generally, it is best to use egg substitutes for only a portion of the eggs called for in a recipe. Do not use egg substitute for items such as cream puffs, popovers and sponge cakes.

Colorful Frittata

Julie Watson, Anderson, Indiana

Dijon mustard gives unique flavor and lots of zip to this pretty egg bake. It's a great way to get your family to eat their vegetables.

- 1 cup broccoli florets
- 3/4 cup sliced fresh mushrooms
- 2 green onions, finely chopped
- 1 tablespoon butter
- 1 cup cubed fully cooked ham
- 8 eggs
- 1/4 cup water
- 1/4 cup Dijon mustard
- 1/2 teaspoon Italian seasoning
- 1/4 teaspoon garlic salt
- 1-1/2 cups (6 ounces) shredded cheddar cheese
- 1/2 cup chopped tomatoes

1) In a large skillet, saute the broccoli, mushrooms and onions in butter until tender. Add ham; heat through. Remove from the heat and keep warm.

2) In a mixing bowl, beat the eggs, water, mustard, Italian seasoning and garlic salt until foamy. Stir in the cheese, tomatoes and broccoli mixture.

3) Pour into a greased shallow 1-1/2-qt. baking dish. Bake at 375° for 22-27 minutes or until a knife inserted in the center comes out clean.

Yield: 6 servings.

NUTRITION FACTS: 1 piece equals 277 calories, 20 g fat (10 g saturated fat), 331 mg cholesterol, 905 mg sodium, 6 g carbohydrate, 1 g fiber, 20 g protein.

Sunday Brunch Casserole

Patricia Throlson, Hawick, Minnesota

My husband and sons often ask if I'll make my "egg pie," using the nickname they've given this hearty casserole. It's nice for a special brunch and versatile enough for a satisfying family supper.

- 1/2 pound sliced bacon
- 1/2 cup chopped onion
- 1/2 cup chopped green pepper
- 12 eggs
- 1 cup milk
- 1 package (16 ounces) frozen hash brown potatoes, thawed
- 1 cup (4 ounces) shredded cheddar cheese
- 1 teaspoon salt
- 1/2 teaspoon pepper
- 1/4 teaspoon dill weed

1) In a large skillet, cook bacon over medium heat until crisp. Remove to paper towels; drain, reserving 2 tablespoons drippings. Crumble bacon and set aside. In same skillet, saute onion and green pepper in drippings until tender; remove with a slotted spoon.

2) In a large bowl, whisk the eggs and milk. Stir in hash browns, cheese, salt, pepper, dill, onion mixture and reserved bacon.

3) Transfer to a greased 13-in. x 9-in. x 2-in. baking dish. Bake, uncovered, at 350° for 35-45 minutes or until a knife inserted near the center comes out clean.

Yield: 8 servings.

NUTRITION FACTS: 1 piece equals 391 calories, 28 g fat (13 g saturated fat), 357 mg cholesterol, 887 mg sodium, 17 g carbohydrate, trace fiber, 18 g protein.

CAJUN CORNED BEEF HASH

Cajun Corned Beef Hash

Del Mason, Martensville, Saskatchewan

Neither the flavor nor the texture is "mushy" when you whip up a skillet of this tongue-tingling hash. This is an all-time favorite of mine. I created it after eating a similar variation in Texas.

- 6 cups frozen shredded hash brown potatoes, thawed
- 1/4 cup butter
- 1/2 cup *each* finely chopped green onions, sweet red pepper and green pepper
- 1 teaspoon seasoned salt
- 3/4 teaspoon Cajun seasoning

3/4 teaspoon chili powder

1/2 teaspoon pepper

1-1/2 cups chopped cooked corned beef

1 tablespoon white vinegar

8 eggs

Additional Cajun seasoning and hot pepper sauce, optional

1) In a large skillet, cook hash browns in butter until almost tender. Stir in onions, peppers and seasonings. Cook until hash browns are lightly browned and peppers are tender. Add corned beef; heat through.

2) Meanwhile, in a skillet with high sides, bring 2-3 in. of water and vinegar to a boil. Reduce heat; simmer gently. For each egg, break cold egg into a custard cup or saucer. Hold the cup close to the surface of the water and slip the egg into simmering water.

3) Cook 4 eggs at a time, uncovered, until whites are completely set and yolks begin to thicken, about 3-5 minutes. With a slotted spoon, remove each egg. Repeat with remaining eggs.

4) Serve over hash mixture. Sprinkle with additional Cajun seasoning and serve with hot pepper sauce if desired.

Yield: 4 servings.

Editor's Note: If poaching eggs using a metal poaching insert, increase poaching time to 6-7 minutes.

NUTRITION FACTS: 1 cup equals 569 calories, 38 g fat (16 g saturated fat), 539 mg cholesterol, 1,733 mg sodium, 25 g carbohydrate, 3 g fiber, 32 g protein.

POACHING EGGS

Break cold eggs, one at a time, into a custard cup, small measuring cup or saucer. Holding the dish close to the simmering liquid's surface, slip the eggs, one at a time, into the liquid. Cook, uncovered, until the whites are completely set and the yolks begin to thicken, about 3-5 minutes.

Double-Cheese Eggs Benedict
Megan Hakes, Wellsville, Pennsylvania

Making breakfast is my favorite part of running a bed-and-breakfast. The eggs in this recipe are served over English muffins and Canadian bacon then topped with a simple sauce.

2 tablespoons butter

2 tablespoons plus 1-1/2 teaspoons all-purpose flour

1-1/2 cups milk

1/4 cup shredded cheddar cheese

2 tablespoons shredded Parmesan cheese

1/2 teaspoon Dijon mustard

1/8 teaspoon salt

1/8 teaspoon white pepper

POACHED EGGS:

1 teaspoon white vinegar

8 cold eggs

4 English muffins, split and toasted

8 slices Canadian bacon, warmed

8 bacon strips, cooked and crumbled

1) For cheese sauce, in a saucepan, melt butter. Stir in flour until smooth; gradually add the milk. Bring to a boil; cook and stir for 2 minutes or until thickened. Reduce heat to medium-low. Add the cheese, mustard, salt and pepper, stirring until cheese is melted. Cover and keep warm.

2) In a skillet with high sides, bring 2-3 in. of water and vinegar to a boil. Reduce heat; simmer gently. For each egg, break the cold eggs into a custard cup or saucer. Hold the dish close to the water surface, slip the egg into the water.

3) Cook 4 eggs at a time, uncovered, for 3-5 minutes or until the whites are completely set and the yolks begin to thicken. With a slotted spoon, remove each egg. Repeat with remaining eggs.

4) To assemble, top each muffin half with one slice Canadian bacon, one egg, cheese sauce and bacon.

Yield: 8 servings.

Editor's Note: If poaching eggs using a metal poaching insert, increase poaching time to 6-7 minutes.

NUTRITION FACTS: 1 serving equals 301 calories, 16 g fat (7 g saturated fat), 250 mg cholesterol, 793 mg sodium, 18 g carbohydrate, 1 g fiber, 19 g protein.

Hard-Cooked Eggs

Taste of Home Test Kitchen

This basic formula for hard-cooked eggs gives you a great end result to use in salads, sandwiches and for deviled eggs.

6 eggs
Cold water

1) Place eggs in a single layer in a large saucepan; add enough cold water to cover by 1 in. Cover and quickly bring to a boil. Remove from the heat.

2) Let stand for 15 minutes for large eggs (18 minutes for extra-large eggs and 12 minutes for medium eggs).

3) Rinse eggs in cold water and place in ice water until completely cooled. Drain and refrigerate.

Yield: 6 servings.

NUTRITION FACTS: 1 egg equals 75 calories, 5 g fat (2 g saturated fat), 213 mg cholesterol, 63 mg sodium, 1 g carbohydrate, 0 fiber, 6 g protein.

DEVILED EGGS

Deviled Eggs

Margaret Sanders, Indianapolis, Indiana

For variety, you can use different ingredients. Get creative and make your own versions.

   6 hard-cooked egg
   2 tablespoons mayonnaise
   1 teaspoon sugar
   1 teaspoon white vinegar
   1 teaspoon prepared mustard
1/2 teaspoon salt
Paprika

1) Slice eggs in half lengthwise; remove yolks and set whites aside. In a small bowl, mash yolks with a fork. Add next five ingredients; mix well.

2) Stuff or pipe into egg whites. Sprinkle with paprika. Refrigerate until serving.

Yield: 6 servings.

NUTRITION FACTS: 2 egg halves equals 114 calories, 9 g fat (2 g saturated fat), 214 mg cholesterol, 293 mg sodium, 1 g carbohydrate, trace fiber, 6 g protein.

■ *PICNIC STUFFED EGGS:* To the mashed yolk, add 1/4 cup mayonnaise, 2 tablespoons drained sweet pickle relish, 1-1/2 teaspoons honey mustard, 1/2 teaspoon garlic salt, 1/4 teaspoon Worcestershire sauce and 1/8 teaspoon pepper. Stuff as directed.

■ *ALMOND DEVILED EGGS:* To the mashed egg yolk, add 1/2 cup mayonnaise, 1 teaspoon Dijon mustard, 1/4 teaspoon garlic salt and 3 tablespoons finely chopped roasted almonds. Stuffed as directed. Top each half with a whole roasted almond and sprinkle with minced fresh parsley.

■ *CRAB-STUFFED DEVILED EGGS:* Make 12 hard-cooked eggs. To the mashed yolks, add 1 can (6 ounces) crabmeat, drained, flaked and cartilage removed, 2/3 cup mayonnaise, 1/2 cup finely chopped celery, 1/2 cup slivered almonds, 2 tablespoons finely chopped green pepper and 1/2 teaspoon salt. Stuff as directed.

STUFFING EGGS USING A PASTRY BAG

Mash yolks with a fork. Add remaining filling ingredients; mix well. Spoon filling into a pastry bag fitted with a #20 decorating tip. Pipe filling into egg white halves.

Egg Salad Cucumber Sandwiches

Lucy Meyring, Walden, Colorado

This is a tasty variation of the traditional egg salad sandwich. The sliced cucumber and chopped onion add refreshing crunch.

   3 hard-cooked eggs, chopped
1/2 cup chopped green pepper
1/4 cup mayonnaise
   2 tablespoons chopped red onion
1/2 teaspoon lemon juice
1/8 teaspoon salt
1/8 teaspoon pepper
   8 slices whole wheat bread

1 small cucumber, thinly sliced
4 lettuce leaves

1) In a small bowl, combine the eggs, green pepper, mayonnaise, onion, lemon juice, salt and pepper. Spread on four slices of bread.

2) Top with the cucumber and lettuce. Top with the remaining bread.

Yield: 4 servings.

NUTRITION FACTS: 1 serving equals 310 calories, 17 g fat (3 g saturated fat), 164 mg cholesterol, 493 mg sodium, 29 g carbohydrate, 5 g fiber, 11 g protein.

OLD-FASHIONED EGG SALAD

Old-Fashioned Egg Salad
Linda Braun, Park Ridge, Illinois

You can also add a little cream cheese to the recipe for an extra-creamy sandwich-topper.

1/4 cup mayonnaise
2 teaspoons lemon juice
1 teaspoon dried minced onion
1/4 teaspoon salt
1/4 teaspoon pepper
6 hard-cooked eggs, chopped
1/2 cup finely chopped celery
Lettuce leaves *or* bread slices

1) In a large bowl, combine the mayonnaise, lemon juice, onion, salt and pepper. Stir in eggs and celery. Cover and refrigerate.

2) For each serving, spoon about 1/2 cup onto a lettuce leaf or spread on bread.

Yield: 3 servings.

NUTRITION FACTS: 1/2 cup (calculated without lettuce or bread) equals 294 calories, 25 g fat (5 g saturated fat), 431 mg cholesterol, 438 mg sodium, 3 g carbohydrate, trace fiber, 13 g protein.

■ *CREAMY EGG SALAD:* Beat 1 package (3 ounces) softened cream cheese, 1/4 cup mayonnaise, 1/2 teaspoon salt and 1/8 teaspoon pepper until smooth. Add 1/4 cup *each* finely chopped green pepper, finely chopped celery and sweet pickle relish and 2 tablespoons minced fresh parsley. Fold in 8 chopped hard-cooked eggs.

Yield: 3 cups.

GOLDENROD EGGS

Goldenrod Eggs
Richard Ramsey, Eugene, Oregon

This is a classic recipe my wife had to learn to make in her high school home economics class. I've adapted and renamed it.

2 hard-cooked eggs
2 tablespoons butter
2 tablespoons all-purpose flour
1/2 teaspoon salt
1/8 teaspoon white pepper
1 cup milk
2 slices bread, toasted and buttered

1) Cut eggs in half; remove yolks and set aside. Chop egg whites; set aside. In a small saucepan, melt butter. Stir in the flour, salt and pepper until smooth. Gradually stir in milk. Bring to a boil; cook and stir for 1-2 minutes or until thickened.

2) Stir in egg whites; heat through. Pour over toast. Force egg yolks through a sieve to break into small pieces; sprinkle over sauce.

Yield: 2 servings.

NUTRITION FACTS: 1 serving equals 382 calories, 26 g fat (14 g saturated fat), 270 mg cholesterol, 1,001 mg sodium, 25 g carbohydrate, 1 g fiber, 13 g protein.

THREE-CHEESE SOUFFLES

Three-Cheese Souffles
Jean Ference, Sherwood Park, Alberta

Make all three for today or freeze them for later.
Either way, these souffles are delicious.

1/3 cup butter
1/3 cup all-purpose flour
2 cups milk
1 teaspoon Dijon mustard
1/4 teaspoon salt
Dash hot pepper sauce
1-1/2 cups (6 ounces) shredded Swiss
    cheese
1 cup (4 ounces) shredded
    cheddar cheese
1/4 cup shredded Parmesan cheese
6 eggs, *separated*
1/2 teaspoon cream of tartar

1) Melt butter in a medium saucepan. Stir in flour
until smooth. Gradually add the milk, mustard,
salt and hot pepper sauce. Bring to a boil; cook
and stir for 2 minutes or until thickened. Reduce
heat; add cheeses, stirring until cheese is melted.
Remove from the heat and set aside.

2) In a small mixing bowl, beat egg yolks until thick
and lemon-colored, about 5 minutes. Add 1/3 cup
cheese mixture and mix well. Return all to the
saucepan, stirring constantly. Return to the heat
and cook for 1-2 minutes. Cool completely, about
30-40 minutes.

3) In another mixing bowl and with clean beaters,
beat egg whites and cream of tartar until stiff
peaks form. Fold into cheese mixture. Pour into
ungreased 1-cup souffle dishes or custard cups.

4) Place in a shallow pan; add 1 in. of hot water to

larger pan. Bake, uncovered, at 325° for 40-45
minutes or until tops are golden browned. Serve
immediately.

Yield: 8 servings.

Editor's Note: Souffles can be made ahead and
frozen. Cover each dish or cup with foil and
freeze. To bake, remove foil and place frozen
souffles in a shallow pan; add warm water to a
depth of 1 in. Bake at 325° for 60-65 minutes or
until tops are golden brown.

NUTRITION FACTS: 1 serving equals 317 calories, 24 g fat (14 g
saturated fat), 223 mg cholesterol, 424 mg sodium, 9 g carbohydrate,
trace fiber, 17 g protein.

Broccoli Souffle
Clem Hood, North Battleford, Saskatchewan

This golden-crowned souffle puffs up elegantly
into an airy treat. Guests will delight in its fluffy
texture and luscious taste. It's a great way to dress
up everyday broccoli.

1 package (10 ounces) frozen
    chopped broccoli, thawed and
    drained
2 tablespoons butter
2 tablespoons all-purpose flour
1/2 teaspoon salt
1/2 cup milk
1/4 cup grated Parmesan cheese
4 eggs, *separated*

1) In a saucepan over medium heat, cook and stir
broccoli and butter until the butter is melted. Set
2 tablespoons broccoli aside for topping. Add
flour and salt to the remaining broccoli; stir until
blended. Gradually add milk.

2) Bring to a boil; cook and stir for 2 minutes or until
thickened. Remove from the heat; add cheese,
stirring until cheese is melted.

3) In a large mixing bowl, beat egg yolks until
thickened and lemon-colored, about 5 minutes.
Add broccoli mixture and set aside. In a small
mixing bowl and with clean beaters, beat egg
whites until stiff peaks form; fold into broccoli
mixture.

4) Pour into an ungreased 1-1/2-qt. deep round
baking dish. Bake, uncovered, at 350° for 20
minutes. Sprinkle with the reserved broccoli. Bake
10 minutes longer or until a knife inserted near
the center comes out clean.

Yield: 6 servings.

NUTRITION FACTS: 1 serving equals 133 calories, 9 g fat (4 g
saturated fat), 157 mg cholesterol, 361 mg sodium, 6 g carbohydrate,
1 g fiber, 8 g protein.

Bacon Quiche Tarts
Kendra Schertz, Nappanee, Indiana

Flavored with vegetables, cheese and bacon, these tarts are an impressive addition to brunch, but they're quite easy to make.

> 2 **packages (3 ounces *each*) cream cheese, softened**
> 5 **teaspoons milk**
> 2 **eggs**
> 1/2 **cup shredded Colby cheese**
> 2 **tablespoons chopped green pepper**
> 1 **tablespoon finely chopped onion**
> 1 **tube (8 ounces) refrigerated crescent rolls**
> 5 **bacon strips, cooked and crumbled**

1) In a small mixing bowl, beat cream cheese and milk until smooth. Add the eggs, cheese, green pepper and onion; mix well.

2) Separate dough into eight triangles; press onto the bottom and up the sides of greased muffin cups. Sprinkle half of the bacon into cups. Pour egg mixture over bacon; top with remaining bacon.

3) Bake, uncovered, at 375° for 18-22 minutes or until a knife comes out clean. Serve warm.

Yield: 8 servings.

NUTRITION FACTS: 1 serving equals 258 calories, 19 g fat (9 g saturated fat), 87 mg cholesterol, 409 mg sodium, 12 g carbohydrate, trace fiber, 8 g protein.

Cheddar Cauliflower Quiche
Tracy Watson, Hobson, Montana

A dear friend shared this recipe one year when we both had an abundance of cauliflower from our gardens. My husband and I enjoy this so much that I make it for breakfast, lunch and dinner!

> 1 **cup all-purpose flour**
> 1/4 **teaspoon salt**
> 1/3 **cup shortening**
> 3 **tablespoons cold milk**
> 4 **cups chopped fresh cauliflower, cooked**
> 1/2 **cup slivered almonds, toasted**
> 2 **eggs**
> 1/2 **cup milk**
> 1/2 **cup mayonnaise**
> 1-1/2 **cups (6 ounces) shredded cheddar cheese, *divided***
> 1/8 **teaspoon ground nutmeg**
> 1/8 **teaspoon pepper**

1) In a large bowl, combine flour and salt. Cut in shortening until mixture resembles coarse crumbs. Stir in milk until mixture forms a ball. Wrap in plastic wrap; refrigerate for 30 minutes.

2) Unwrap dough. On a floured surface; roll out to fit a 9-in. pie plate. Place in pie plate; flute edges. Line unpricked pastry with a double thickness of foil. Bake at 450° for 5 minutes. Remove foil; bake 5 minutes longer.

3) Spoon cauliflower into crust; top with almonds. In a blender, combine eggs, milk, mayonnaise, 1-1/4 cups cheese, nutmeg and pepper; cover and process until smooth. Pour over almonds; sprinkle with remaining cheese.

4) Bake, uncovered, at 350° for 30-35 minutes or until a knife inserted near the center comes out clean. Let stand for 10 minutes before cutting.

Yield: 6 servings.

Editor's Note: Reduced-fat or fat-free mayonnaise may not be substituted for regular mayonnaise in this recipe.

NUTRITION FACTS: 1 piece equals 518 calories, 41 g fat (12 g saturated fat), 111 mg cholesterol, 424 mg sodium, 24 g carbohydrate, 3 g fiber, 14 g protein.

TESTING BAKED EGG DISHES FOR DONENESS

Test egg dishes containing beaten eggs—like quiche, strata or custard—for doneness by inserting a knife near the center of the dish. If the knife comes out clean, the eggs are cooked.

Easter Brunch Lasagna
Sarah Larson, La Farge, Wisconsin

Ham, broccoli and hard-cooked eggs are terrific together in this unique brunch lasagna. I came up with the recipe for a family gathering. Muffins and fresh fruit nicely round out the meal.

- 1/2 cup butter
- 1/3 cup all-purpose flour
- 1/4 teaspoon salt
- Dash white pepper
- 3 cups milk
- 1/4 cup finely chopped green onions
- 1 teaspoon lemon juice
- 1/4 teaspoon hot pepper sauce
- 9 lasagna noodles, cooked and drained
- 2 cups diced fully cooked ham
- 1 package (10 ounces) frozen chopped broccoli, thawed
- 1/2 cup grated Parmesan cheese
- 3 cups (12 ounces) shredded cheddar cheese
- 4 hard-cooked eggs, finely chopped

1) In a heavy saucepan, melt butter over medium heat. Stir in flour, salt and pepper until smooth. Gradually add milk. Bring to a boil; cook and stir for 2 minutes or until thickened. Remove from the heat; stir in the onions, lemon juice and hot pepper sauce.

2) Spread a fourth of the white sauce in a greased 13-in. x 9-in. x 2-in. baking dish. Layer with three noodles, half of the ham and broccoli, 3 tablespoons Parmesan cheese, 1 cup cheddar cheese, half of the eggs and a fourth of the white sauce. Repeat layers. Top with the remaining noodles, white sauce and cheeses.

3) Bake, uncovered, at 350° for 40-45 minutes or until bubbly. Let stand for 15 minutes before cutting.

Yield: 12 servings.

NUTRITION FACTS: 1 serving equals 371 calories, 23 g fat (14 g saturated fat), 144 mg cholesterol, 715 mg sodium, 23 g carbohydrate, 1 g fiber, 19 g protein.

CHEESE SAUSAGE STRATA

Cheese Sausage Strata
Teresa Marchese, New Berlin, Wisconsin

Sausage provides plenty of flavor in this hearty morning casserole. It's a great addition to a brunch buffet because it's assembled the night before to cut down on last-minute fuss.

- 1-1/2 pounds bulk pork sausage
- 9 eggs, lightly beaten
- 3 cups milk
- 9 slices bread, cubed
- 1-1/2 cups (6 ounces) shredded cheddar cheese
- 1/2 pound sliced bacon, cooked and crumbled
- 1-1/2 teaspoons ground mustard

1) In a large skillet, cook sausage over medium heat until no longer pink; drain. Add the eggs, milk, bread, cheese, bacon and mustard. Transfer to a greased shallow 3-qt. baking dish. Cover and refrigerate overnight.

2) Remove from the refrigerator 30 minutes before baking. Cover and bake at 350° for 60-65 minutes or until a knife inserted near the center comes out clean. Let stand for 5 minutes before serving.

Yield: 12 servings.

NUTRITION FACTS: 1 serving equals 373 calories, 25 g fat (11 g saturated fat), 217 mg cholesterol, 1,097 mg sodium, 14 g carbohydrate, trace fiber, 23 g protein.

clean. Let stand for 5 minutes before cutting.

Yield: 8 servings.

NUTRITION FACTS: 1 piece equals 246 calories, 13 g fat (6 g saturated fat), 80 mg cholesterol, 749 mg sodium, 22 g carbohydrate, 1 g fiber, 11 g protein.

Chocolate Chip Dutch Baby
Mary Thompson, Faribault, Minnesota

I modified a traditional Dutch baby recipe given to me by a friend to come up with this version my family thinks is terrific. You can try it with apples or other favorite fruit.

> 1/4 **cup miniature semisweet chocolate chips**
> 1/4 **cup packed brown sugar**

DUTCH BABY:
> 1/2 **cup all-purpose flour**
> 2 **eggs**
> 1/2 **cup half-and-half cream**
> 1/8 **teaspoon ground nutmeg**
> **Dash ground cinnamon**
> 3 **tablespoons butter**
> **Maple syrup and additional butter, optional**

1) In a small bowl, combine chocolate chips and brown sugar; set aside. In a small mixing bowl, beat the flour, eggs, cream, nutmeg and cinnamon until smooth.

2) Place butter in a 9-in. pie plate. Heat at 425° for 4-6 minutes or until melted. Pour batter into hot pie plate. Sprinkle with chocolate chip mixture.

3) Bake for 15-20 minutes or until top edges are golden brown. Serve immediately with syrup and butter if desired.

Yield: 4 servings.

NUTRITION FACTS: 1 piece equals 313 calories, 17 g fat (10 g saturated fat), 144 mg cholesterol, 140 mg sodium, 34 g carbohydrate, 1 g fiber, 6 g protein.

■ *APPLE PUFF PANCAKE:* Omit the chips, brown sugar, nutmeg, cinnamon and 3 tablespoons butter. Mix the Dutch Baby pancake as directed but add 1/8 teaspoon salt and 1 tablespoon melted butter. Pour into a greased 8-in. square baking dish. Bake at 400° for 20-25 minutes or until lightly browned.

Meanwhile, in a small saucepan, cook 1 chopped peeled medium tart apple, 1/2 cup apply jelly and 1/8 teaspoon cinnamon until jelly is melted. Cut pancake into fourths, place two pieces on each plate and top with apple mixture.

Yield: 2 servings.

CHIVE-HAM BRUNCH BAKE

Chive-Ham Brunch Bake
Edie DeSpain, Logan, Utah

Canned ham and biscuit mix get this breakfast or brunch dish ready quickly. You can also use leftover cooked ham from a holiday dinner.

> 1/2 **cup chopped onion**
> 1 **tablespoon butter**
> 1 **can (5 ounces) chunk ham, drained**
> 1 **medium tomato, chopped**
> 2 **cups biscuit/baking mix**
> 1/2 **cup water**
> 1 **cup (4 ounces) shredded Swiss *or* cheddar cheese**
> 2 **eggs**
> 1/4 **cup milk**
> 1/4 **teaspoon dill weed**
> 1/4 **teaspoon salt**
> 1/8 **teaspoon pepper**
> 3 **tablespoons minced chives**

1) In a small skillet, saute onion in butter until tender. Stir in the ham and tomato; set aside. In a small bowl, combine biscuit mix and water; mix well.

2) Press onto the bottom and 1/2 in. up the sides of a greased 13-in. x 9-in. x 2-in. baking dish. Spread ham mixture over the crust; sprinkle with cheese. In a bowl, beat the eggs, milk, dill, salt and pepper; pour over cheese. Sprinkle with chives.

3) Bake, uncovered, at 350° for 25-30 minutes or until a knife inserted near the center comes out

Basic Crepes
Taste of Home Test Kitchen

For a simple breakfast, roll up crepes and drizzle with warmed honey or jelly. Any leftover crepes may be stacked with waxed paper in between and frozen for up to 2 months. Thaw in the refrigerator before using.

> 1-1/2   **cups milk**
> 4   **eggs**
> 1   **cup all-purpose flour**
> 1-1/2   **teaspoons sugar**
> 1/8   **teaspoon salt**
> **Butter**

1) In a small mixing bowl, combine milk and eggs. Combine the flour, sugar and salt; add to milk mixture and mix well. Cover and refrigerate for 1 hour.

2) Melt 1 teaspoon butter in an 8-in. nonstick skillet; pour 2 tablespoons batter into center of skillet. Lift and tilt pan to evenly coat bottom. Cook until top appears dry; turn and cook 15-20 seconds longer. Remove to a wire rack.

3) Repeat with remaining batter, adding butter to skillet as needed. When cool, stack crepes with waxed paper or paper towels in between.

Yield: 16 crepes.

NUTRITION FACTS: 1 serving equals 79 calories, 4 g fat (2 g saturated fat), 61 mg cholesterol, 65 mg sodium, 8 g carbohydrate, trace fiber, 3 g protein.

■ *SHRIMP CREPES:* In a large skillet, cook 4-1/2 cups chopped fresh broccoli, 6 chopped green onions, 2 teaspoons minced garlic, 1/2 teaspoon salt, 1/4 teaspoon pepper and 1/4 teaspoon Worcestershire sauce in 3 tablespoons melted butter for 7-9 minutes or until broccoli is crisp-tender. Remove and set aside. In same skillet, saute 1 pound peeled deveined uncooked shrimp in 1/4 cup wine *or* broth until shrimp turns pink. Return broccoli to skillet and combine.

Spoon filling down center of crepes; roll up. Place in an ungreased 15-in. x 10-in. x 1-in. baking pan. Bake, uncovered at 350° for 15-20 minutes or until heated through. Meanwhile, prepare 1 envelope bearnaise sauce according to package directions. Serve over crepes.

Yield: 8 servings.
—Donna Barlett, Reno, Nevada

■ *CREAMY STRAWBERRY CREPES:* In a small mixing bowl, beat 1 package (8 ounces) softened cream cheese, 1-1/4 cups confectioners' sugar, 1 tablespoon lemon juice, 1 teaspoon grated lemon peel and 1/2 teaspoon vanilla extract until smooth. Fold in 2 cups sliced fresh strawberries and 2 cups whipped cream. Spoon about 1/3 cup filling down the center of 14 crepes; roll up. Garnish with additional sliced strawberries.

Yield: 7 servings.
—Kathy Kochiss, Huntington, Connecticut

■ *BANANA CREPES:* In a small skillet, bring 2/3 cup sugar, 2/3 cup orange juice, 1/2 cup butter and 4 teaspoons grated orange peel to a boil. Remove from the heat. Peel 6 medium firm bananas and cut in half lengthwise. Add to orange sauce; cook over medium heat until heated through, about 1 minute. Place 1 banana half in the center of a crepe; roll up. Place seam side down on a plate; drizzle with orange sauce.

Yield: 6 servings.
—Freda Becker, Garrettsville, Ohio

CHERRY CHEESE BLINTZES

Cherry Cheese Blintzes
Jessica Vantrease, Anderson, Alaska

These elegant blintzes can be served as an attractive dessert or a brunch entree. The bright cherry sauce gives them a delightful flavor. You can try other fruits, such as raspberries, blueberries or peaches.

> 1-1/2   **cups milk**
> 3   **eggs**
> 2   **tablespoons butter, melted**

2/3   cup all-purpose flour

1/2   teaspoon salt

FILLING:

1   cup (8 ounces) small-curd cottage cheese

1   package (3 ounces) cream cheese, softened

1/4   cup sugar

1/2   teaspoon vanilla extract

CHERRY SAUCE:

1   pound fresh *or* frozen pitted sweet cherries

2/3   cup plus 1 tablespoon water, *divided*

1/4   cup sugar

1   tablespoon cornstarch

1) In a small mixing bowl, combine the milk, eggs and butter. Combine the flour and salt; add to milk mixture and mix well. Cover and refrigerate for 2 hours.

2) Heat a lightly greased 8-in. nonstick skillet; pour 2 tablespoons batter into the center of skillet. Lift and tilt pan to evenly coat bottom. Cook until top appears dry; turn and cook 15-20 seconds longer. Remove to a wire rack.

3) Repeat with remaining batter. When cool, stack crepes with waxed paper or paper towels in between. Wrap in foil; refrigerate.

4) In a blender, process cottage cheese until smooth. Transfer to a small mixing bowl; add cream cheese. Beat until smooth. Add sugar and vanilla; mix well. Spread about 1 rounded tablespoonful onto each crepe. Fold opposite sides of crepe over filling, forming a little bundle.

5) Place seam side down in a greased 15-in. x 10-in. x 1-in. baking pan. Bake, uncovered, at 350° for 10 minutes or until heated through.

6) Meanwhile, in a saucepan, bring the cherries, 2/3 cup water and sugar to a boil over medium heat. Reduce heat; cover and simmer for 5 minutes or until cherries are heated through.

7) Combine cornstarch and remaining water until smooth; stir into cherry mixture. Bring to a boil; cook and stir for 2 minutes or until thickened. Serve over crepes.

Yield: 9 servings.

NUTRITION FACTS: 1 serving equals 247 calories, 10 g fat (6 g saturated fat), 99 mg cholesterol, 310 mg sodium, 31 g carbohydrate, 1 g fiber, 8 g protein.

FRENCH TOAST WITH ORANGE SYRUP

French Toast with Orange Syrup
Jesse & Anne Foust, Bluefield, West Virginia

The simple orange syrup turns ordinary French toast into a real treat. You can serve the syrup over the top or on the side.

3   eggs

1   cup milk

2   tablespoons sugar

1/4   teaspoon salt

1/8   teaspoon ground cinnamon

1/8   teaspoon ground nutmeg

8   slices day-old French bread (1 inch thick)

ORANGE SYRUP:

1/2   cup orange juice

1/3   cup corn syrup

1/4   cup sugar

4   teaspoons butter

1   teaspoon grated orange peel

1/2   teaspoon orange extract

1) In a bowl, beat eggs. Beat in the milk, sugar, salt, cinnamon and nutmeg. Soak the slices of bread for 30 seconds on each side. Cook on a hot greased griddle until golden brown on both sides and cooked through.

2) Meanwhile, in a saucepan, combine the orange juice, corn syrup, sugar, butter and orange peel. Bring to a boil and boil for 2 minutes, stirring constantly. Remove from the heat; stir in extract. Serve with French toast.

Yield: 4 servings.

NUTRITION FACTS: 1 serving equals 645 calories, 13 g fat (6 g saturated fat), 178 mg cholesterol, 1,076 mg sodium, 113 g carbohydrate, 4 g fiber, 18 g protein.

Overnight Caramel French Toast

Denise Goedeken, Platte Center, Nebraska

When guests are visiting or times are busy, you can prepare this ahead of time and refrigerate it overnight. The next day, it bakes up in no time.

1   **cup packed brown sugar**
1/2 **cup butter**
2   **tablespoons light corn syrup**
12 **slices white *or* whole wheat bread**
1/4 **cup sugar**
1   **teaspoon ground cinnamon, *divided***
6   **eggs**
1-1/2 **cups milk**
1   **teaspoon vanilla extract**

1) In a small saucepan, bring the brown sugar, butter and corn syrup to a boil over medium heat, stirring constantly. Remove from the heat.

2) Pour into a greased 13-in. x 9-in. x 2-in. baking dish. Top with six slices of bread. Combine sugar and 1/2 teaspoon cinnamon; sprinkle half over the bread. Place remaining bread on top. Sprinkle with remaining cinnamon-sugar; set aside.

3) In a large bowl, beat the eggs, milk, vanilla and remaining cinnamon. Pour over bread. Cover and refrigerate for 8 hours or overnight.

4) Remove from the refrigerator 30 minutes before baking. Bake, uncovered, at 350° for 30-35 minutes.

Yield: 6 servings.

NUTRITION FACTS: 1 serving equals 571 calories, 24 g fat (13 g saturated fat), 262 mg cholesterol, 539 mg sodium, 78 g carbohydrate, 1 g fiber, 13 g protein.

Macadamia French Toast

Beverly Ellis, McKenzie, Tennessee

This appetizing eye-opener is flavored with orange juice and nutmeg. The nutty French toast bake is perfect for overnight company because it's assembled a day ahead.

1   **loaf (1 pound) French bread, cut into 1-inch slices**
4   **eggs**
2/3 **cup orange juice**
1/3 **cup milk**
1/4 **cup sugar**
1/2 **teaspoon vanilla extract**
1/4 **teaspoon ground nutmeg**
1/2 **cup butter, melted**
1/2 **cup chopped macadamia nuts**

Confectioners' sugar and maple syrup, optional

1) Arrange bread slices in a greased 13-in. x 9-in. x 2-in. baking dish. In a bowl, whisk the eggs, orange juice, milk, sugar, vanilla and nutmeg until blended; pour over bread. Cover and refrigerate for 8 hours or overnight.

2) Pour butter into a 15-in. x 10-in. x 1-in. baking pan. Transfer bread slices to prepared pan; sprinkle with nuts.

3) Bake, uncovered, at 400° for 20-25 minutes or until the bread is golden brown. Dust with the confectioners' sugar and serve with syrup if desired.

Yield: 8 servings.

NUTRITION FACTS: 1 serving equals 393 calories, 22 g fat (9 g saturated fat), 138 mg cholesterol, 520 mg sodium, 40 g carbohydrate, 2 g fiber, 9 g protein.

Cheese Basics

Cheese is classified by texture from soft to hard. When buying bulk cheese, 4 ounces equals 1 cup shredded. Check sell-by or expiration date on the package before buying and make sure it is before that date.

Check the aroma, appearance and (if possible) the flavor when purchasing from a cheese store. The aroma should be characteristic of the cheese and the odor should not smell like sour milk or ammonia. The cheese should be free from interior cracks, discoloration and mold, unless it is a blue-veined cheese.

Wrap each type of cheese separately and store away from other foods with a strong aroma. Cheese tends to absorb the aroma and flavors of other foods, including other cheeses.

Store cheese in airtight containers, plastic bags or plastic wrap in the refrigerator. The humidity in the vegetable drawers can extend the life and quality of the cheese. Once opened, keep soft cheese for about 1 week and hard cheese for 3 to 4 weeks.

Discard any soft cheese that becomes moldy. For hard cheeses, if it has a small amount of mold, cut off a section about 1 in. around the mold and discard.

Freeze cheese for a longer storage time. Because the freezing process changes the cheese's texture slightly, it is best to use it in cooking or baking. Store the firmer textured cheese in the freezer for up to 6 months.

Serve fresh cheese slightly chilled. For other types of cheese to be at their flavor peak, remove from the refrigerator 30 minutes before serving.

When cooking with natural unprocessed cheese, melt at low temperatures to keep the cheese from turning tough and stringy.

Add cheese to a soup or sauce by stirring it in at the end of cooking to avoid overheating. Shredding the cheese allows it to melt faster with a minimum of heating.

Useful Definitions

Refer to the Glossary on pages 18-22 for more terms.

FRESH CHEESES: Have not been cured, such as cottage or cream cheese.

HARD CHEESES: Aged with a hard, dry texture.

SEMIFIRM CHEESE: Aged with a firm texture but are not crumbly like hard cheese.

SEMISOFT CHEESES: Have a sliceable soft texture, like Monterey Jack.

Cheddar Fondue

Norene Wright, Manilla, Indiana

This cheesy blend, sparked with mustard and Worcestershire sauce, is yummy. Serve it at a brunch or as an appetizer for a party.

- 1/4   cup butter
- 1/4   cup all-purpose flour
- 1/2   teaspoon salt, optional
- 1/4   teaspoon ground mustard
- 1/4   teaspoon pepper
- 1/4   teaspoon Worcestershire sauce
- 1-1/2   cups milk
- 2   cups (8 ounces) shredded cheddar cheese

    Bread cubes, ham cubes, bite-size sausage *and/or* broccoli florets

1) In a small saucepan, melt butter; stir in flour, salt if desired, mustard, pepper and Worcestershire sauce until smooth. Gradually add milk. Bring to a boil; cook and stir for 2 minutes or until thickened. Reduce heat. Add the cheese; cook and stir until cheese is melted.

2) Transfer to a fondue pot or slow cooker; keep warm. Serve with bread, ham, sausage and/or broccoli.

Yield: 2-1/2 cups.

NUTRITION FACTS: 2 tablespoons fondue (calculated without dippers) equals 77 calories, 6 g fat (4 g saturated fat), 21 mg cholesterol, 101 mg sodium, 2 g carbohydrate, trace fiber, 3 g protein.

SWISS CHEESE FONDUE

Swiss Cheese Fondue

Taste of Home Test Kitchen

As cold winter blows outside, warm up with this rich and creamy fondue. Don't be surprised when the pot is scraped clean!

- 1   garlic clove, halved
- 2   cups white wine, chicken broth *or* unsweetened apple juice, *divided*
- 1/4   teaspoon ground nutmeg
- 7   cups (28 ounces) shredded Swiss cheese
- 2   tablespoons cornstarch

    Cubed French bread

1) Rub garlic clove over the bottom and sides of a fondue pot; discard garlic and set fondue pot aside. In a large saucepan over medium-low heat, bring 1-3/4 cups wine and nutmeg to a simmer. Gradually add cheese, stirring after each addition until cheese is melted (cheese will separate from the wine).

2) Combine cornstarch and remaining wine until smooth; gradually stir into cheese mixture. Cook and stir until thickened and mixture is blended and smooth. Transfer to prepared fondue pot and keep warm. Serve with bread cubes.

Yield: about 4 cups.

NUTRITION FACTS: 1/2 cup fondue (calculated without bread cubes) equals 404 calories, 26 g fat (17 g saturated fat), 87 mg cholesterol, 249 mg sodium, 6 g carbohydrate, trace fiber, 27 g protein.

THREE-CHEESE GRILLED CHEESE

■ *RASPBERRY GRILLED CHEESE:* For 2 slices of bread, spread 1-1/2 teaspoons raspberry preserves on one side of each slice and 1 tablespoon softened butter on the other sides. On one slice of bread, with raspberry side up, layer with 1 tablespoon *each* chopped pecans and sliced green onion, 2 slices Muenster *or* baby Swiss cheese. Top with the other slice of bread, raspberry side down. Toast as recipe directs.

Mom's Macaroni and Cheese
Maria Costello, Monroe, North Carolina

The wonderful homemade goodness of this creamy macaroni and cheese makes it a staple side dish in my mother's kitchen and in mine as well. It has tender noodles and a crowd-pleasing golden crumb topping.

1-1/2 cups uncooked elbow macaroni
5 tablespoons butter, *divided*
3 tablespoons all-purpose flour
1/2 teaspoon salt
1/4 teaspoon pepper
1-1/2 cups milk
1 cup (4 ounces) shredded cheddar cheese
2 ounces process cheese (Velveeta), cubed
2 tablespoons dry bread crumbs

1) Cook macaroni according to package directions. Meanwhile, in a saucepan, melt 4 tablespoons butter over medium heat. Stir in flour, salt and pepper until smooth. Gradually add milk.

2) Bring to a boil; cook and stir for 2 minutes or until thickened. Reduce heat. Add the cheeses, stirring until cheese is melted. Drain macaroni.

3) Transfer macaroni to a greased 1-1/2-qt. baking dish. Pour cheese sauce over macaroni; mix well. Melt the remaining butter; add the bread crumbs. Sprinkle over top.

4) Bake, uncovered, at 375° for 30 minutes or until heated through and topping is golden brown.

Yield: 6 servings.

NUTRITION FACTS: 1 serving equals 309 calories, 20 g fat (13 g saturated fat), 60 mg cholesterol, 569 mg sodium, 22 g carbohydrate, 1 g fiber, 11 g protein.

Three-Cheese Grilled Cheese
Terri Brown, Delavan, Wisconsin

My favorite combination is Swiss and cheddar with the cream cheese. But Mexican cheese is tasty, and you can serve this along with salsa.

2 slices wheat, rye *or* sourdough bread
2 tablespoons cream cheese, softened
2 tablespoons butter, softened
2 slices white cheese (brick, Monterey Jack *or* Swiss)
2 slices yellow cheese (cheddar, pepper *or* taco)
1 red onion slice
1 tomato slice

1) For each slice of bread, spread cream cheese on one side and spread butter on the other. On one side of bread, with cream cheese side up, layer the white cheese, yellow cheese, onion and tomato. Top with the other slice of bread, cream cheese side down.

2) Toast sandwich for 2-3 minutes on each side or until bread is lightly browned. Remove from the heat; cover until cheese melts.

Yield: 1 serving.

NUTRITION FACTS: 1 sandwich equals 747 calories, 59 g fat (36 g saturated fat), 173 mg cholesterol, 1,484 mg sodium, 30 g carbohydrate, 4 g fiber, 26 g protein.

Types of Cheese

Cheese comes in many varieties, and some are more common than others. Below are some blue-veined, fresh, hard, Pasta Filata-style (cheeses that stretch or string when cooked or melted), ripened, semifirm, semisoft and soft-ripened cheeses.

ASIAGO, AGED
Hard cheese. Buttery and nutty flavor. Hard granular texture. Pale yellow color. Good with pasta, grapes, apples and pears.

BEL PAESE
Semisoft cheese. Mellow, delicate, buttery, tart flavor. Smooth, creamy, rich texture. Ivory color. Good with pasta, eggs, vegetables, fresh salads and pears.

BLUE
Blue-veined cheese. Piquant with full, earthy flavor. Firm, crumbly texture (some are creamy). Creamy ivory color with blue or green veins. Good with pears, apples, walnuts, cashews and almonds.

BRICK
Semisoft cheese. Mild, sweet flavor with a hint of nuttiness. Smooth texture. Ivory to creamy yellow color. Good with sandwiches, macaroni and cheese.

BRIE
Soft-ripened cheese. Mild to pungent flavor. Rich creamy texture. Pale ivory color. Good with melons, grapes, berries and sun-dried tomatoes.

CAMEMBERT
Soft-ripened cheese. Mild to pungent flavor. Rich creamy texture. Pale ivory color. Good with melons, grapes, berries and sun-dried tomatoes.

COLBY
Semifirm cheese. Mild, cheddar-like flavor. Firm, but softer than cheddar in texture. Golden color. Good with apples, pears, onions and tomatoes.

COTTAGE CHEESE
Soft fresh cheese. Slightly acidic but delicate flavor. Smooth tender texture. Creamy white color. Good with fresh fruit, salad, vegetables and herbs.

CHEDDAR
Semifirm cheese. Rich, nutty flavor becomes sharp when aged. Smooth, firm texture becomes granular and crumbly when aged. White or golden color. Good with apples, pears, onions and tomatoes.

CREAM CHEESE
Soft fresh cheese. Rich, nutty, slightly sweet flavor. Smooth, creamy texture. Creamy white color. Good with fresh fruits, jams and jellies, fruit and nut breads and bagels.

EDAM
Semifirm cheese. Light, buttery, nutty flavor. Smooth, firm texture. Pale yellow interior color. Good with peaches, melon, apricots and cherries.

FARMERS
Semisoft cheese. Buttery, creamy, slightly acidic flavor. Smooth texture. Ivory to buttery in color. Good with plums, grapes, seafood and poultry.

FETA
Soft fresh cheese. Tart, salty flavor. Firm, crumbly texture. Chalk white color. Good with olives, vegetables, pasta salads, mixed green salads, seafood and chicken.

FONTINA
Semisoft cheese. Slightly tart, tangy, nutty flavor. Smooth, slightly creamy texture. Pale ivory to straw yellow in color. Good with veal, crusty breads, peaches, melon and prosciutto.

GOUDA
Semisoft cheese. Light, buttery flavor. Smooth, creamy texture. Pale yellow interior color. Good with peaches, melons, apricots and cherries.

HAVARTI
Semisoft cheese. Buttery, creamy, slightly acidic flavor. Smooth, supple texture. Pale yellow color. Good with plums, grapes, poultry and seafood.

MASCARPONE
Soft fresh cheese. Rich, buttery, slightly sweet flavor. Smooth, thick, creamy texture. Creamy white color. Good with berries, shortbread and figs.

MONTEREY JACK
Semisoft cheese. Delicate, buttery flavor with a slight. tartness. Creamy texture. Creamy white color. Good with fruit, poultry, quesadillas and Mexican-style recipes.

MOZZARELLA
Mild, delicate, milky flavor. Smooth, plastic texture. Creamy white color. Good with tomatoes, cured meats, pesto, roasted red peppers and black olives.

MOZZARELLA, FRESH
Mild, delicate, milky flavor. Soft, slightly elastic texture. Creamy white color. Good with sun-dried or fresh tomatoes, cured meats, salads, sandwiches, basil and melon.

MUENSTER
Semisoft cheese. Mild to mellow flavor. Smooth and elastic texture. Creamy white interior color. Good with apples, grapes, whole-grain breads and sausages.

NEUFCHATEL
Soft fresh cheese. Nutty, slightly sweet; lower in fat than cream cheese. Creamy, but slightly firmer than cream cheese. Creamy white color. Good with fresh fruit, jam, quick breads and bagels.

PARMESAN
Hard cheese. Buttery, sweet, nutty flavor that intensifies with age. Granular texture. Pale yellow color. Good with pasta, rice, vegetable soups and tomato or cream sauces.

PROVOLONE
Full flavor, can be sharp. Firm texture. Ivory to pale beige in color. Good with cured meats, tomatoes, pears, grapes and figs.

RICOTTA
Soft fresh cheese. Mild flavor with a hint of sweetness. Creamy, but slightly grainy curd. Creamy white color. Good with pasta casseroles, stuffings, herbs and tomatoes.

ROMANO
Hard cheese. Sharp, piquant flavor. Hard, granular texture. Creamy white color. Good with apples, pears, tomatoes and olives.

SWISS
Semifirm cheese. Mellow, buttery, nutty flavor. Firm texture with eyes. Ivory color. Good with apples, pears and grapes.

CHAPTER 11
BEANS
& GRAINS

BEANS & GRAINS

Beans are a member of the legume family and add a tasty source of protein and fiber to the diet. With today's quicker preparation methods for dried beans and a variety of canned bean products, it's easy to make delicious bean recipes.

Soaking Methods for Dried Beans

Most dried beans need to be soaked before cooking. Select a soaking method below to fit your schedule. Before cooking, sort through dried beans to remove any broken beans, pebbles or grit. Rinse beans with cold water in a colander.

Soaking softens and returns moisture to the beans, which helps reduce the cooking time. Soaking also helps eliminate some of the sugar molecules, oligosaccharides, which are responsible for the gas-causing effect that beans can have. The longer the beans soak the more of the oligosaccharides are released into the water. The released sugars are discarded with the water after soaking.

Soak different kinds of beans separately. Some take longer to soak than others. Black beans can affect the color of other beans. To check to see if soaked beans have soaked long enough, slice one in half. If the center is opaque, you need to soak them longer. If you have old beans, hard water or live at higher altitudes, you may need to increase the soaking and cooking times.

Always use a large pot and plenty of water. Dried beans rehydrate to 2 to 3 times their size. After soaking, discard the soaking water and drain and rinse the beans.

Quick Hot Soak

Sort and rinse beans. Place in a soup kettle or Dutch oven; add enough water to cover beans by 2 in. Bring to a boil; boil for 2 minutes. Remove from the heat; cover and let stand for 1 to 4 hours. Drain and rinse beans; discard liquid unless recipe directs otherwise. Proceed with recipe.

Overnight Soak

Sort and rinse beans. Place in a soup kettle or Dutch oven; for every cup of beans add 3 cups of cold water. Cover and soak at room temperature for 8 hours or overnight. Drain and rinse beans; discard liquid unless recipe directs otherwise. Proceed with recipe.

Cooking Soaked Dried Beans

After soaking, beans are simmered in fresh water for about 2 hours or until tender. The time will vary on the variety and size of the bean, hardness of the water, altitude and the freshness of the dried beans.

Follow recipe or package directions for the amount of water to add to beans. To reduce foaming during cooking, add 1 tablespoon oil or butter to the pot.

Salt or acidic ingredients (like tomatoes, lemon juice, mustard, molasses, wine and vinegar) inhibit the absorption of liquid and stop the softening process. So these ingredients should not be added to the beans until they are tender.

To test beans for doneness while cooking, remove a bean from the pot and place it on a cutting board. Mash the bean with the back of a spoon. If the bean mashes easily and is soft in the center, it is thoroughly cooked. Or, if you prefer, you can bite into the bean to see if it is tender but not mushy. Allow about 1/2 cup cooked beans per serving.

Cooking Times for Beans

TYPE OF DRIED BEAN OR LEGUME	COOKING TIME
BLACK BEANS	1 to 1-1/2 hours
BLACK-EYED PEAS	1/2 to 1 hour
CRANBERRY BEANS	3/4 to 1 hour
GARBANZO BEANS	1 to 1-1/2 hours
GREAT NORTHERN BEANS	3/4 to 1 hour
KIDNEY BEANS	1-1/2 to 2 hours
LENTILS, GREEN OR BROWN	20 to 30 minutes
LENTILS, RED	15 minutes
LIMA BEANS, BABY	1 hour
LIMA BEANS, LARGE	1 to 1-1/2 hours
NAVY BEANS	1-1/2 to 2 hours
PINK BEANS	1 hour
PINTO BEANS	1-1/2 to 2 hours
RED BEANS, SMALL	1 to 1-1/2 hours
SPLIT PEAS	20 to 30 minutes

Storing Dried Beans

Store uncooked dried beans tightly covered in a cool, dry area. It is best to use dried beans within 12 months; the older the bean, the longer it takes to cook. Store cooked beans covered in the refrigerator for up to 5 days or freeze up to 6 months.

- One pound packaged dried beans (uncooked) equals 2 cups dried or about 6 cups cooked and drained.
- One cup packaged dried beans (uncooked) equals about two 15-1/2-ounce cans of drained beans.
- One cup dried split peas equals about 2 cups cooked.
- One 15-1/2-ounce can of beans equals about 1-2/3 cups drained beans.

Canned Beans

Rinse and drain canned beans before using. You will not only reduce the sodium content of the beans but also eliminate some of the gas-producing sugars.

THREE-BEAN BARLEY SALAD

Three-Bean Barley Salad
Pat Miller, North Fork, California

Three kinds of beans—kidney beans, black beans and garbanzo beans—are deliciously combined in this salad.

- 2 cups water
- 1 tablespoon chicken bouillon granules
- 1 cup quick-cooking barley
- 1 can (16 ounces) kidney beans, rinsed and drained
- 1 can (15 ounces) black beans, rinsed and drained

1 can (15 ounces) garbanzo beans *or* chickpeas, rinsed and drained

4 green onions, thinly sliced

1 cup honey Dijon salad dressing

1) In a saucepan, bring water and bouillon to a boil. Stir in barley. Reduce heat; cover and simmer for 11-13 minutes or until barley is tender and liquid is absorbed. Cool for 10 minutes.

2) Transfer barley to a serving bowl. Add the beans and onions. Pour dressing over top; gently stir to coat. Cover and refrigerate until serving.

Yield: 12 servings.

NUTRITION FACTS: 1/2 cup equals 224 calories, 8 g fat (1 g saturated fat), trace cholesterol, 526 mg sodium, 32 g carbohydrate, 7 g fiber, 7 g protein.

Meatless Hopping John
Ann Buckendahl, Benton, Kansas

I traditionally make this black-eyed pea dish for New Year's celebrations. My version has more seasonings and veggies than other recipes for the classic Southern dish.

3/4 cup uncooked long grain rice

1 cup frozen corn

3 medium carrots, thinly sliced

1/2 cup *each* chopped green, sweet red and yellow pepper

1/4 cup chopped onion

4 garlic cloves, minced

1 tablespoon canola oil

1 can (15-1/2 ounces) black-eyed peas, rinsed and drained

1 can (14-1/2 ounces) diced tomatoes, drained

2 tablespoons minced fresh parsley

1 teaspoon dried thyme

1/2 teaspoon salt

1/4 teaspoon pepper

1/4 teaspoon crushed red pepper flakes

1) Cook rice according to package directions. Meanwhile, in a large nonstick skillet, saute the corn, carrots, peppers, onion and garlic in oil for 6-8 minutes or until crisp-tender.

2) Stir in the rice, peas and tomatoes; bring to a boil. Reduce heat; cover and simmer for 5 minutes or until heated though, stirring occasionally. Add the seasonings; cook 2-3 minutes longer.

Yield: 10 servings.

NUTRITION FACTS: 3/4 cup equals 149 calories, 2 g fat (trace saturated fat), 0 cholesterol, 313 mg sodium, 29 g carbohydrate, 4 g fiber, 5 g protein.

BLACK BEAN TORTILLA CASSEROLE

Black Bean Tortilla Casserole
Sue Briski, Appleton, Wisconsin

A cousin gave me this recipe because she knows my family loves Southwestern fare. This is a delicious meatless meal that we really enjoy!

2 large onions, chopped

1-1/2 cups chopped green peppers

1 can (14-1/2 ounces) diced tomatoes, drained

3/4 cup picante sauce

2 garlic cloves, minced

2 teaspoons ground cumin

2 cans (15 ounces *each*) black beans, rinsed and drained

8 corn tortillas (6 inches)

2 cups (8 ounces) shredded reduced-fat Mexican cheese blend

TOPPINGS:

1-1/2 cups shredded lettuce

1 cup chopped fresh tomatoes

1/2 cup thinly sliced green onions

1/2 cup sliced ripe olives

1) In a large saucepan, combine the onions, peppers, tomatoes, picante sauce, garlic and cumin. Bring to a boil. Reduce heat; simmer, uncovered, for 10 minutes. Stir in the beans.

2) Spread a third of the mixture in a 13-in. x 9-in. x 2-in. baking dish coated with nonstick cooking spray. Layer with four tortillas and 2/3 cup cheese. Repeat layers; top with remaining beans.

3) Cover and bake at 350° for 30-35 minutes or until heated through. Sprinkle with remaining cheese. Let stand for 5 minutes or until cheese is melted. Serve with toppings.

Yield: 9 servings.

NUTRITION FACTS: 1 serving equals 251 calories, 7 g fat (3 g saturated fat), 18 mg cholesterol, 609 mg sodium, 36 g carbohydrate, 8 g fiber, 14 g protein.

Moroccan Stew

Rita Reinke, Wauwatosa, Wisconsin

Fragrant cinnamon, cumin and coriander give this hearty meatless medley its exotic Moroccan flavor.

- 2 cups cauliflowerets
- 3 medium carrots, cut into 2-inch julienned strips
- 1 medium onion, quartered and thinly sliced
- 2 teaspoons olive oil
- 1 cup sliced zucchini
- 1/2 cup water
- 1 teaspoon ground cumin
- 1/2 teaspoon salt
- 1/2 teaspoon ground coriander
- 1/4 teaspoon ground cinnamon
- 1/8 teaspoon cayenne pepper
- 1/8 teaspoon pepper
- 1 can (15 ounces) garbanzo beans *or* chickpeas, rinsed and drained
- 1 can (14-1/2 ounces) diced tomatoes, undrained

  Hot cooked rice, optional

1) In a large nonstick skillet, saute the cauliflower, carrots and onion in oil for 10 minutes. Add the zucchini, water, cumin, salt, coriander, cinnamon, cayenne and pepper.

2) Bring to a boil. Reduce heat; cover and simmer for 5 minutes. Stir in garbanzo beans and tomatoes; simmer 5 minutes longer. Serve over rice if desired.

Yield: 5 servings.

NUTRITION FACTS: 1 cup stew equals 138 calories, 3 g fat (trace saturated fat), 0 cholesterol, 512 mg sodium, 25 g carbohydrate, 6 g fiber, 5 g protein.

Spicy Hummus

Taste of Home Test Kitchen

Hummus is a Middle Eastern spread made from seasoned mashed chickpeas. Served with pita wedges, this is a simple and satisfying snack.

- 1/4 cup packed fresh parsley sprigs
- 2 tablespoons chopped onion
- 1 garlic clove, peeled
- 1 can (15 ounces) chickpeas *or* garbanzo beans, rinsed and drained
- 2 tablespoons sesame seeds, ground
- 2 tablespoons cider vinegar
- 2 teaspoons soy sauce
- 2 teaspoons lime juice
- 1 teaspoon honey
- 1 teaspoon Dijon mustard
- 1/4 teaspoon salt
- 1/4 teaspoon *each* ground cumin, ginger, coriander and paprika

  Pita bread, cut into wedges

1) In a food processor or blender, combine the parsley, onion and garlic; cover and process until smooth.

2) Add the chickpeas, sesame seeds, vinegar, soy sauce, lime juice, honey, mustard and seasonings; cover and process until smooth. Serve with pita bread.

Yield: 1-1/2 cups.

NUTRITION FACTS: 1/4 cup (calculated without pita bread) equals 89 calories, 3 g fat (trace saturated fat), 0 cholesterol, 316 mg sodium, 14 g carbohydrate, 3 g fiber, 4 g protein.

OLD-FASHIONED BAKED BEANS

Old-Fashioned Baked Beans

Marjorie Thompson
West Sacramento, California

The enticing aroma of these beans cooking reminds me of Grandma's cooking.

- 1 pound dried great northern beans
- 1 quart water
- 1/2 teaspoon salt
- 1 medium onion, chopped
- 2 tablespoons prepared mustard

2 tablespoons brown sugar

2 tablespoons dark molasses

1/2 pound sliced bacon, cooked and crumbled

1) Place beans in a Dutch oven or kettle; add water to cover by 2 in. Bring to a boil; boil for 2 minutes. Remove from the heat; cover and let stand for 1 to 4 hours or until beans are softened. Drain and rinse beans, discarding liquid.

2) Return beans to pan. Add water and salt; bring to a boil. Reduce heat; cover and simmer for 1 to 1-1/4 hours or until the beans are tender. Drain, reserving 2 cups cooking liquid.

3) In a greased 13-in. x 9-in. x 2-in. baking dish, combine the beans, onion, mustard, brown sugar, molasses, bacon and 1 cup of reserved cooking liquid.

4) Cover and bake at 400° for 45 minutes or until the beans have reached desired thickness, stirring occasionally (add additional reserved cooking liquid if needed).

Yield: 8 servings.

NUTRITION FACTS: 1/2 cup equals 283 calories, 5 g fat (2 g saturated fat), 8 mg cholesterol, 351 mg sodium, 44 g carbohydrate, 12 g fiber, 16 g protein.

HEARTY RED BEANS AND RICE

Hearty Red Beans and Rice
Kathy Jacques, Chesterfield, Michigan

If you want to get the beans started ahead of time, cover them with the water and let soak overnight. Drain beans and continue with the recipe as directed.

1 pound dried kidney beans

2 teaspoons garlic salt

1 teaspoon Worcestershire sauce

1/4 teaspoon hot pepper sauce

1 quart water

1/2 pound fully cooked ham, diced

1/2 pound fully cooked smoked sausage, diced

1 cup chopped onion

1/2 cup chopped celery

3 garlic cloves, minced

1 can (8 ounces) tomato sauce

2 bay leaves

1/4 cup minced fresh parsley

1/2 teaspoon salt

1/2 teaspoon pepper

Hot cooked rice

Additional parsley, optional

1) Place beans in a Dutch oven or kettle; add water to cover by 2 in. Bring to a boil; boil for 2 minutes. Remove from the heat; cover and let stand for 1 to 4 hours or until beans are softened.

2) Drain and rinse beans, discarding liquid. Return to pan. Add the garlic salt, Worcestershire sauce, hot pepper sauce and water; bring to a boil. Reduce heat; cover and simmer for 1-1/2 hours.

3) Meanwhile, in a large skillet, saute ham and sausage until lightly browned. Remove with a slotted spoon to bean mixture. Saute the onion, celery and garlic in drippings until tender; add to the bean mixture. Stir in tomato sauce and bay leaves. Cover and simmer for 30 minutes or until beans are tender.

4) Discard bay leaves. Measure 2 cups of beans; mash and return to the bean mixture. Stir in the parsley, salt and pepper. Serve over rice. Garnish with parsley if desired.

Yield: 10 servings.

NUTRITION FACTS: 1 cup (calculated without rice) equals 276 calories, 9 g fat (3 g saturated fat), 27 mg cholesterol, 1,149 mg sodium, 32 g carbohydrate, 8 g fiber, 18 g protein.

PINTO BEAN CHILI

for 1-1/2 hours or until beans are tender. Stir in the tomatoes, vinegar and salt; heat through, stirring occasionally.

4) Meanwhile, for quesadillas, spread about 1 tablespoon of chilies on half of each tortilla. Sprinkle with 1/4 cup of cheese; fold in half.

5) In a large skillet, cook tortillas in 1 teaspoon of oil over medium heat until lightly browned on each side, adding more oil as needed. Cut each in half. Serve with chili.

Yield: 8 servings.

NUTRITION FACTS: 1-1/2 cups chili with 3 quesadilla wedges equals 787 calories, 34 g fat (15 g saturated fat), 120 mg cholesterol, 1,373 mg sodium, 72 g carbohydrate, 18 g fiber, 51 g protein.

Pinto Bean Chili
Sandy Dilatush, Denver, Colorado

Cumin and chili powder season this traditional chili. Quesadillas on the side make this Southwestern soup a meal.

- 1 pound dried pinto beans
- 2 pounds ground beef
- 1 medium onion, chopped
- 3 celery ribs, chopped
- 3 tablespoons all-purpose flour
- 4 cups water
- 2 tablespoons chili powder
- 2 tablespoons ground cumin
- 1/2 teaspoon sugar
- 1 can (28 ounces) crushed tomatoes
- 2 teaspoons cider vinegar
- 1-1/2 teaspoons salt

CHILI CHEESE QUESADILLAS:

- 2 cans (4 ounces *each*) chopped green chilies
- 12 flour tortillas (6 inches)
- 3 cups (12 ounces) shredded cheddar cheese
- 3 teaspoons vegetable oil

1) Place beans in a Dutch oven or soup kettle; add water to cover by 2 in. Bring to a boil; boil for 2 minutes. Remove from the heat; cover and let stand for 1 to 4 hours or until beans are softened. Drain and rinse beans, discarding liquid.

2) In a Dutch oven, cook the beef, onion and celery over medium heat until meat is no longer pink; drain. Stir in flour until blended. Gradually stir in water.

3) Add the beans, chili powder, cumin and sugar. Bring to a boil. Reduce heat; cover and simmer

Tuscan Bean Salad
Dixie Cannafax, Oroville, California

This marinated bean salad is a favorite of mine that is especially good alongside a pork entree.

- 1 cup dried navy beans
- 4 cups cold water
- 1/2 cup diced red onion
- 1/2 cup thinly sliced celery
- 1/4 cup chopped fresh parsley
- 3 tablespoons chicken broth
- 2 tablespoons balsamic vinegar
- 1 tablespoon olive oil
- 1 teaspoon Dijon mustard
- 1/2 teaspoon minced garlic
- 1 teaspoon salt
- 1/4 teaspoon ground oregano
- 1/4 teaspoon ground thyme

1) Place beans in Dutch oven or kettle; add water to cover by 2 in. Bring to a boil; boil for 2 minutes. Remove beans from the heat; cover and let stand for 1 to 4 hours or until beans are softened.

2) Drain and rinse beans, discarding liquid. Return beans to the pan. Add cold water. Bring to a boil. Reduce the heat; cover and simmer for 50-60 minutes or until beans are tender.

3) Drain beans; place in a bowl. Add the onion, celery and parsley. In a jar with a tight-fitting lid, combine the remaining ingredients; shake well. Pour over bean mixture and stir to coat. Cover and refrigerate for at least 2 hours.

Yield: 4 servings.

NUTRITION FACTS: 3/4 cup equals 224 calories, 4 g fat (1 g saturated fat), 0 cholesterol, 682 mg sodium, 36 g carbohydrate, 14 g fiber, 12 g protein.

Lentils and Split Peas

Lentils and split peas should not be presoaked before cooking. However, just like dried beans, they should be sorted before cooking to remove any damaged lentils or peas, pebbles or grit. Rinse with cold water in a colander. Then cook according to the recipe or package directions.

Lentils are available in several colors, but the most commonly available in supermarkets is the brown lentil. Look for green and red lentils in specialty markets. Brown and green lentils hold their shape well and are good for salads. Red lentils cook faster, have a softer texture and are good for pureed dishes. Green and yellow split peas are widely available.

Tasty Lentil Tacos
Michelle Thomas, Bangor, Maine

My husband has to watch his cholesterol. This is a dish I found that's healthy for him and yummy for our five children.

      1 cup finely chopped onion
      1 garlic clove, minced
      1 teaspoon canola oil
      1 cup dried lentils, rinsed
      1 tablespoon chili powder
      2 teaspoons ground cumin
      1 teaspoon dried oregano
  2-1/2 cups chicken broth
      1 cup salsa
     12 taco shells
  1-1/2 cups shredded lettuce
      1 cup chopped fresh tomato
  1-1/2 cups (6 ounces) shredded
         reduced-fat cheddar cheese
      6 tablespoons fat-free sour cream

1) In a large nonstick skillet, saute the onion and garlic in oil until tender. Add the lentils, chili powder, cumin and oregano; cook and stir for 1 minute.

2) Add broth; bring to a boil. Reduce heat; cover and simmer for 25-30 minutes or until the lentils are tender. Uncover; cook for 6-8 minutes or until mixture is thickened. Mash lentils slightly.

3) Stir in salsa. Spoon about 1/4 cup lentil mixture into each taco shell. Top with lettuce, tomato, cheese and sour cream.

Yield: 6 servings.

NUTRITION FACTS: 2 tacos equals 364 calories, 11 g fat (4 g saturated fat), 17 mg cholesterol, 815 mg sodium, 45 g carbohydrate, 9 g fiber, 22 g protein.

East Indian Split Pea Pilaf
Marilyn Rodriquez, Fairbanks, Alaska

Yellow split peas, chicken broth and savory spices turn long grain rice into a piquant pilaf. This recipe was given to me by a friend from India. It's a great side dish to go with curry recipes.

    2/3 cup dried yellow split peas
  4-3/4 cups water, *divided*
      1 bay leaf
      3 tablespoons canola oil
      1 large onion, chopped
    1/2 to 1 teaspoon ground cinnamon
    3/4 teaspoon ground cumin
    1/2 teaspoon salt
    1/4 teaspoon ground cloves
    1/4 teaspoon ground turmeric
  1-1/2 cups uncooked long grain rice
  2-1/2 cups chicken broth

1) In a large saucepan, combine peas and 4 cups water. Bring to a boil. Reduce heat; simmer, uncovered, for 30-35 minutes or until tender. Drain and keep warm.

2) In a large nonstick skillet, cook the bay leaf in oil until golden, about 3 minutes. Add onion; saute until tender. Stir in the seasonings; saute for 30 seconds. Add the rice; cook and stir for 3 minutes. Stir in broth and remaining water.

3) Bring to a boil. Reduce heat; cover and simmer for 20-25 minutes or until rice is tender. Add peas; heat through. Discard bay leaf.

Yield: 6 servings.

NUTRITION FACTS: 1 cup equals 214 calories, 7 g fat (1 g saturated fat), 0 cholesterol, 572 mg sodium, 30 g carbohydrate, 1 g fiber, 8 g protein.

Lemon Lentil Salad
Renate Kheim, St. Louis, Missouri

At first, this sounds like an odd combination. But once you try this refreshing and hearty salad, I think you'll want to make it again.

5	tablespoons olive oil, *divided*
1	tablespoon lemon juice
2	teaspoons red wine vinegar
2	teaspoons sugar
1	teaspoon Dijon mustard
1/2	teaspoon dried thyme
1/4	teaspoon salt
1/4	teaspoon pepper
1	garlic clove, minced
3	cups water
1	cup dried lentils, rinsed
1	bay leaf
1	large tomato, diced
1/2	cup minced fresh parsley
2	to 3 green onions, sliced

1) In a small bowl, combine 4 tablespoons oil, lemon juice, vinegar, sugar, mustard, thyme, salt, pepper and garlic; set aside.

2) In a medium saucepan, bring the water, lentils, bay leaf and remaining oil to a boil. Reduce heat; simmer, uncovered, for 30 minutes. Remove from heat. Let stand 30 minutes; drain if necessary.

3) Discard bay leaf. Add the tomato, parsley, onions and dressing; mix gently. Cover and refrigerate for at least 2 hours.

Yield: 6 servings.

NUTRITION FACTS: 1 serving equals 226 calories, 12 g fat (2 g saturated fat), 0 cholesterol, 129 mg sodium, 22 g carbohydrate, 11 g fiber, 10 g protein.

Tofu

Tofu, also known as soybean curd or bean curd, is created when soy milk is mixed with calcium or magnesium salt to create curds. The process is similar to cheese making. The more whey (liquid) that is pressed out of the curd, the firmer the tofu. Tofu has a bland flavor, but it acts as a flavor sponge and will absorb the flavors it is exposed to.

The two types of tofu, regular and silken, are available in textures from soft, firm and extra-firm. The difference between regular and silken is that the silken tofu is smoother, creamier and has a more custard-like texture.

When buying tofu, select the texture according to how you plan to use it:

- For marinating, grilling or broiling, use extra-firm tofu.

- For stir-frying or sauteing, use firm or extra-firm tofu.

- For making salad dressings, smoothies or desserts, use soft silken tofu.

- For reducing calories or fat, look for lite tofu.

Check the use-by date on the package and store in the refrigerator. Store opened tofu submerged in water in a covered container for up to 1 week. Change water daily.

To use tofu, drain and discard the liquid from package. Pat tofu dry with paper towels. Cut or slice according to recipe directions.

TOFU-STUFFED PASTA SHELLS

Tofu-Stuffed Pasta Shells
Jenni Dise, Phoenix, Arizona

Your gang won't even miss the meat in this hearty pasta dish. I jazzed up tofu with cheese, spinach and garlic for unbeatable flavor. Accented with a hint of red wine, an easy tomato sauce completes the entree.

15	uncooked jumbo pasta shells
1-1/2	cups firm silken tofu
3	tablespoons grated Romano cheese, *divided*
2	garlic cloves, peeled
1	package (10 ounces) frozen chopped spinach, thawed and squeezed dry
1	can (14-1/2 ounces) Italian diced tomatoes, drained

1   can (8 ounces) tomato sauce
1/4   cup dry red wine *or* vegetable broth
1/2   cup shredded part-skim
      mozzarella cheese

1) Cook pasta shells according to package directions.
   Meanwhile, in a blender, combine the tofu, 2
   tablespoons Romano cheese and garlic; cover and
   process until smooth. (Add 1 tablespoon of water
   if mixture is too thick.) Add spinach; process until
   blended. Drain shells; stuff with tofu mixture.

2) In a small bowl, combine the tomatoes, tomato
   sauce and wine or broth. Spread about 1/2 cup
   sauce in an 11-in. x 7-in. x 2-in. baking dish
   coated with nonstick cooking spray. Arrange
   stuffed shells over sauce. Top with remaining
   sauce.

3) Cover and bake at 350° for 25 minutes. Uncover;
   sprinkle with mozzarella and remaining Romano
   cheese. Bake 8-10 minutes longer or until shells
   are heated through and cheese is melted.

Yield: 5 servings.

NUTRITION FACTS: 3 stuffed shells equals 262 calories, 5 g fat (2 g
saturated fat), 10 mg cholesterol, 754 mg sodium, 39 g carbohydrate,
4 g fiber, 14 g protein.

Broccoli Tofu Stir-Fry

Denise Lee, Louisville, Kentucky

I received this recipe from a friend when I wanted
more meatless meals. Much to my surprise, my
family doesn't mind the tofu and asks me to make
it all the time.

1   package (12.3 ounces)
    reduced-fat extra-firm tofu,
    cubed
4   green onions, chopped
1   tablespoon minced fresh
    gingerroot
1   garlic clove, minced
1/4   teaspoon crushed red pepper
      flakes
4   teaspoons olive oil, *divided*
1   package (16 ounces) broccoli
    coleslaw mix
1/3   cup reduced-fat peanut butter
1/4   cup reduced-sodium teriyaki
      sauce

1) In a nonstick skillet or wok, stir-fry the tofu,
   onions, ginger, garlic and pepper flakes in 3
   teaspoons oil until onions are tender. Remove and
   set aside. In the same pan, stir-fry the broccoli
   coleslaw mix in remaining oil for 4-5 minutes.

2) Combine the peanut butter and teriyaki sauce; stir
   into coleslaw mix. Return tofu mixture to the pan.
   Stir-fry for 1-2 minutes or until heated through.

Yield: 4 servings.

Editor's Note: Broccoli coleslaw mix may be
found in the produce section of most grocery
stores.

NUTRITION FACTS: 1 cup equals 276 calories, 15 g fat (3 g saturated
fat), 0 cholesterol, 526 mg sodium, 23 g carbohydrate, 5 g fiber,
16 g protein.

Grains

Common grains, which include rice, barley, wild rice,
oats and hominy grits, can be found in many classic
recipes. Team grains with vegetables, beans, meat or
fish for hearty, nutritious and budget-conscious side-
dish or main-dish fare.

BARLEY is a more flavorful and
chewy alternative to white rice.
You can find pearl barley and
quick-cooking barley in most
supermarkets. Some may also carry
Scotch barley. Pearl barley has had
the double outer hull and bran layer removed during
processing. Quick-cooking barley is pearl barley that
was precooked by steaming. Scotch barley has been
milled less than pearl barley and retains some of the
bran layer.

In health-food stores, you may be able to find barley
flakes, grits and hulled barley. Flakes and grits can be
used for breakfast as a cereal. Barley flakes have been
rolled and flattened. Grits have been toasted and
cracked. Hulled barley only has the hulled removed,
so it still has the bran and the nutrients that the bran
contains. Hulled barley takes about 1-3/4 hours to
cook.

Store barley in an airtight container in a cool dry
place. It may also be stored in the refrigerator or
freezer.

BULGUR is whole wheat that is
processed similar to converted rice.
The whole-wheat kernels are
cleaned, steam-cooked, dried and
cracked or ground into pieces.
Bulgur is ready to eat after soaking
in water or broth for about 30 minutes.

Bulgur is available in coarse, medium and fine grains.
The coarse grain is used for stuffing, casserole and
pilaf; medium grain for breakfast cereal, bread, stew
and soup; and fine grain for tabbouleh, breakfast
cereal and bread. Once opened, store bulgur in an
airtight container in a cool dry place for up to 1
month. In warm climates, store in the refrigerator or
freezer.

BUCKWHEAT is the seed of a plant related to rhubarb. It is not a wheat. The black, triangular seeds are sold as groats, grits, kasha or buckwheat flour. Groats are the kernels with the inedible black shells removed. Grits are finely ground, unroasted groats that are used for cereal. Kasha are roasted groats that have been cracked into coarse, medium or fine grain. Kasha has a toasty, nutty flavor. Buckwheat flour is ground groats used for pancakes, breads, muffins and noodles. Since buckwheat flour is gluten-free, it is usually used in combination with all-purpose flour.

Once opened, store buckwheat in an airtight container in a cool dry place. In warm climates, store in the refrigerator or freezer. Always store buckwheat flour in the refrigerator.

 CORNMEAL is dried corn that has been hulled and finely ground. Corn can be ground between two stones, labeled stone ground, or between steel rollers. Stone-ground cornmeal is usually a coarser grind and may have some of the hull and oil-containing germ. Therefore, stone-ground cornmeal has a shorter shelf life and should be stored in an airtight container in the refrigerator for up to 4 months. The steel-ground cornmeal should be used before the use-by date on the package.

White and yellow cornmeal is available in most supermarkets. Blue cornmeal can be found in specialty markets. White and yellow may be used interchangeably. Self-rising cornmeal has baking powder and salt mixed with the cornmeal and should not be used interchangeably with plain cornmeal.

Use cornmeal for corn bread or muffins, cornmeal mush, polenta or as a coating for fried foods.

 GRITS is dried corn that has been hulled and coarsely ground. The difference between cornmeal and grits is how finely it is ground. Grits are available as grits, quick-cooking grits and instant grits. Regular grits take the longest to cook. Quick-cooking grits are passed through a roller and crushed into smaller pieces. Quick-cooking grits take about 5-7 minutes to simmer. Instant grits are precooked, then dried. Instant grits are rehydrated by adding boiling water to them.

Grits are generally used for breakfast and a side dish. Grits should be used before the use-by date on the package.

 MILLET is generally known as bird food. It is available in health-food stores and some supermarkets. Pearl millet is hulled and sold as a hold kernel. The color can range from pale yellow to reddish orange. A 1/2 cup of millet can be simmered in 1-1/2 cups liquid for about 25 minutes.

 OATS are one of the most popular grains and are readily available in the supermarket. Oats are usually available as old-fashioned, quick-cooking, instant and oat bran. Old-fashioned oats are made from whole oat groats that still contain the bran, endosperm and germ portion that have been rolled to flatten. Quick-cooking oats are old-fashioned oats that are cut into smaller pieces so that they cook faster. Instant oats are precooked and dried and are cut even finer than quick-cooking. Oat bran is the outer bran layer, which is high in fiber.

Old-fashioned and quick-cooking oats can be used interchangeably for cookies, breads, muffins, pancakes, extenders in ground meat products. Old-fashioned oats are large and will give the product a chewier texture and more whole grain appearance. Do not substitute instant oats for old-fashioned or quick-cooking oats.

Once opened, store oats in an airtight container in a cool, dry place. In warm climates, store in the refrigerator or freezer. Use oats by the use-by date on the package.

 QUINOA is a seed from a plant related to spinach and chard. Quinoa is a more complete protein than most other grains. The flattened, oval grains of quinoa come in a variety of colors, the most common being, white, pale gold, black and red. Look for quinoa in health-food stores or large supermarkets.

Rinse quinoa under cold running water before cooking to remove any residue from its naturally bitter coating. For a roasted flavor, toast in a skillet before cooking. Quinoa is done when the grains are translucent and the germ spirals out to form a tail. Quinoa has a mild taste with a light fluffy texture. The "tail" is crunchy.

Store uncooked quinoa in an airtight container in a cool dry place. In warm climates, store in the refrigerator or freezer.

NUTTY BARLEY BAKE

Nutty Barley Bake
Renate Crump, Los Angeles, California

When I started bringing this dish to holiday dinners, a lot of people had never seen barley in anything but soup. They have dubbed me "the barley lady," and I bring it every year.

  1 medium onion, chopped
  1 cup medium pearl barley
  1/2 cup slivered almonds *or* pine nuts
  1/4 cup butter
  1/2 cup minced fresh parsley
  1/4 cup thinly sliced green onions
  1/4 teaspoon salt
  1/8 teaspoon pepper
  2 cans (14-1/2 ounces *each*) beef broth
  Additional parsley, optional

1) In a large skillet, saute the onion, barley and nuts in butter until barley is lightly browned. Stir in the parsley, green onions, salt and pepper.

2) Transfer to a greased 2-qt. baking dish. Stir in broth. Bake, uncovered, at 350° for 1-1/4 hours or until the barley is tender and the liquid is absorbed. Sprinkle with parsley if desired.

Yield: 6 servings.

NUTRITION FACTS: 1 serving equals 262 calories, 13 g fat (5 g saturated fat), 20 mg cholesterol, 678 mg sodium, 31 g carbohydrate, 7 g fiber, 7 g protein.

Apricot Barley Casserole
Diane Swink, Signal Mountain, Tennessee

It doesn't take long to put together this pretty side dish dotted with dried apricots and golden raisins. Then just pop it into the oven and enjoy.

  2/3 cup pine nuts *or* slivered almonds

  1/4 cup butter, *divided*
  2 cups medium pearl barley
  1 cup sliced green onions
  7 cups chicken broth
  2/3 cup diced dried apricots
  1/2 cup golden raisins

1) In a large skillet, saute nuts in 2 tablespoons butter until lightly browned; remove and set aside. In the same skillet, saute the barley and onions in remaining butter until onions are tender. Add broth; bring to a boil. Stir in the apricots, raisins and reserved nuts.

2) Pour into a greased 13-in. x 9-in. x 2-in. baking dish. Bake, uncovered, at 325° for 1-1/4 hours or until barley is tender.

Yield: 8-10 servings.

NUTRITION FACTS: 1 cup equals 290 calories, 10 g fat (4 g saturated fat), 12 mg cholesterol, 710 mg sodium, 45 g carbohydrate, 8 g fiber, 8 g protein.

Vegetable Barley Saute
Taste of Home Test Kitchen

This wonderful side dish can easily be turned into a hearty entree by adding cooked chicken.

  1/2 cup quick-cooking barley
  2 teaspoons cornstarch
  1/3 cup water
  3 tablespoons soy sauce
  1 garlic clove, minced
  1 tablespoon vegetable oil
  2 carrots, thinly sliced
  1 cup cut fresh green beans (2-inch pieces)
  2 green onions, sliced
  1/2 cup unsalted cashews, optional

1) Prepare barley according to package directions. In a small bowl, combine, water and soy sauce until smooth; set aside.

2) In a large skillet or wok, saute garlic in oil for 15 seconds. Add carrots and beans; stir-fry for 1 minute. Add onions; stir-fry for 2-3 minutes.

3) Stir the soy sauce mixture; stir into the skillet. Bring to a boil; cook and simmer stir for 1 minute or until thickened. Add barley; heat through. Stir in cashews if desired.

Yield: 4 servings.

NUTRITION FACTS: 2/3 cup equals 149 calories, 4 g fat (1 g saturated fat), 0 cholesterol, 707 mg sodium, 24 g carbohydrate, 6 g fiber, 5 g protein.

THREE-GRAIN PILAF

Three-Grain Pilaf
Mary Knudson, Bermuda Dunes, California

This is an old family recipe that everyone still looks forward to. The satisfying combination of brown rice, pearl barley and bulgur makes this tasty side dish special enough for company.

   1   large onion, chopped
   1   garlic clove, minced
   2   tablespoons olive oil
 2/3   cup shredded carrot
 1/3   cup uncooked brown rice
 1/3   cup uncooked medium
       pearl barley
 1/3   cup uncooked bulgur
   2   cups vegetable *or*
       reduced-sodium chicken broth
 1/4   cup sherry, optional
   1   teaspoon minced fresh oregano
       or 1/4 teaspoon dried oregano
   1   teaspoon minced fresh basil
       or 1/4 teaspoon dried basil
 1/2   teaspoon salt
 1/4   teaspoon pepper
 1/3   cup minced fresh parsley
 1/3   cup sliced almonds, toasted

1) In a large nonstick skillet, saute onion and garlic in oil for 2 minutes. Add carrot; saute for 2 minutes or until the vegetables are crisp-tender.

2) Stir in the rice, barley and bulgur; saute for 4 minutes or until grains are lightly browned. Gradually add broth and sherry if desired. Bring to a boil. Reduce heat; stir in oregano, basil, salt and pepper.

3) Cover and simmer for 40-45 minutes or until grains are tender and the liquid is absorbed. Stir in parsley and sprinkle with almonds.

Yield: 5 servings.

NUTRITION FACTS: 3/4 cup equals 238 calories, 9 g fat (1 g saturated fat), 0 cholesterol, 498 mg sodium, 33 g carbohydrate, 6 g fiber, 7 g protein.

Bulgur Barbecue
Jackie Blankenship, Sherwood, Oregon

Use this recipe to stretch ground beef into saucy and satisfying sloppy Joes. Then add bulgur for a healthy measure of fiber.

 2-3/4   cups water, *divided*
   2/3   cup bulgur
 1-1/2   pounds lean ground beef
 1-1/2   cups chopped celery
     1   large onion, chopped
     1   can (8 ounces) tomato sauce
   1/2   cup packed brown sugar
   1/2   cup ketchup
     1   tablespoon white vinegar
   1/2   teaspoon prepared mustard
   1/4   teaspoon salt
   1/4   teaspoon pepper
    12   hamburger buns, split

1) In a saucepan, bring 2 cups water to a boil. Stir in bulgur. Reduce heat; cover and simmer for 15 minutes. Remove from the heat. Drain and squeeze dry; set aside.

2) In a large nonstick skillet, cook the beef, celery and onion over medium heat until meat is no longer pink; drain. Add the tomato sauce, brown sugar, ketchup, vinegar, mustard, salt, pepper and remaining water. Stir in reserved bulgur.

3) Transfer to a 2-qt. baking dish. Cover and bake at 350° for 50-60 minutes or until heated through. Serve on buns.

Yield: 12 servings.

NUTRITION FACTS: 1 sandwich equals 289 calories, 7 g fat (2 g saturated fat), 21 mg cholesterol, 521 mg sodium, 41 g carbohydrate, 5 g fiber, 17 g protein.

BUYING BULGUR

Look for bulgur in the cereal, rice or organic food aisle of your grocery store.

BUCKWHEAT BRUNCH CREPES

Buckwheat Brunch Crepes
Sharon Dyck, Roxton Falls, Quebec

Try these delicious crepes with sweet berry sauce and cream on Saturday mornings or even at supper time with sausage and eggs. They're especially tasty with a drizzle of maple syrup.

> 5 tablespoons heavy whipping cream
> 1/2 cup sour cream
> 1/2 cup milk
> 2 eggs
> 1/3 cup all-purpose flour
> 3 tablespoons buckwheat flour *or* whole wheat flour
> 1/2 teaspoon salt

BERRY SAUCE:
> 1/2 cup sugar
> 1 tablespoon cornstarch
> Dash salt
> 1/2 cup water
> 1/3 cup fresh blueberries
> 1/3 cup fresh raspberries
> 4-1/2 teaspoons butter, *divided*
> 1 teaspoon lemon juice

1) In a small mixing bowl, beat whipping cream until stiff peaks form; fold into sour cream. Cover and refrigerate.

2) In a small mixing bowl, combine milk and eggs. Combine the flours and salt; add to milk mixture and mix well. Let stand for 30 minutes.

3) Meanwhile, in a small saucepan, combine the sugar, cornstarch and salt; stir in water until smooth. Bring to a boil; cook and stir for 1-2 minutes or until thickened.

4) Add berries; cook over medium-low heat until berries burst. Add 1-1/2 teaspoons butter and lemon juice, stirring until butter is melted. Set aside and keep warm.

5) Melt 1 teaspoon butter in an 8-in. nonstick skillet; pour 2 tablespoons batter into the center of skillet. Lift and tilt pan to evenly coat bottom. Cook until top appears dry; turn and cook 15-20 seconds longer. Remove to a wire rack. Repeat with remaining batter, adding butter to skillet as needed.

6) When cool, stack crepes with waxed paper or paper towels in between and keep warm. Serve crepes with berry sauce and cream mixture.

Yield: about 6 crepes.

NUTRITION FACTS: 1 serving equals 782 calories, 40 g fat (24 g saturated fat), 335 mg cholesterol, 965 mg sodium, 90 g carbohydrate, 4 g fiber, 15 g protein.

Grits Casserole
Georgia Johnston, Auburndale, Florida

Grits are a traditional breakfast item in the South. This quick-cooking recipe features sausage and cheese to turn it into a main dish.

> 1 pound bulk pork sausage
> 4 cups water
> 1 teaspoon salt
> 1 cup quick-cooking grits
> 4 eggs, lightly beaten
> 1-1/2 cups (6 ounces) shredded sharp cheddar cheese, *divided*
> 1/2 cup milk
> 1/4 cup butter, softened

1) Crumble sausage into a large skillet. Cook over medium heat until no longer pink; drain and set aside. In a saucepan, bring water and salt to a boil. Slowly stir in grits. Reduce heat and cook 4-5 minutes, stirring occasionally. Remove from the heat.

2) Stir a small amount of hot grits into the eggs; return all to the saucepan, stirring constantly. Add the sausage, 1 cup cheese, milk and butter, stirring until the butter is melted.

3) Pour into a greased 13-in. x 9-in. x 2-in. baking dish. Sprinkle with remaining cheese. Bake at 350° for 50-55 minutes or until the top begins to brown.

Yield: 10 servings.

NUTRITION FACTS: 1/2 cup equals 280 calories, 20 g fat (10 g saturated fat), 133 mg cholesterol, 602 mg sodium, 14 g carbohydrate, 1 g fiber, 11 g protein.

Millet-Stuffed Red Peppers
Kitty Jones, Chicago, Illinois

This vibrant alternative to tuna-filled tomatoes and stuffed green peppers has an out-of-the-ordinary filling made with millet.

- 1/2   cup uncooked millet, rinsed and drained
- 1-1/2 cups vegetable broth
- 4   medium sweet red peppers
- 3/4   cup frozen corn, thawed
- 1   medium onion, finely chopped
- 1/3   cup finely chopped celery
- 1/4   cup chopped walnuts
- 1   green onion, finely chopped
- 1   tablespoon chopped fresh mint *or* 1 teaspoon dried mint flakes
- 2   teaspoons shredded lemon peel
- 1-1/2 teaspoons fresh chopped oregano *or* 1/2 teaspoon dried oregano
- 1   garlic clove, minced
- 1/2   teaspoon salt
- 1/4   teaspoon pepper
- 2   tablespoons olive oil

1) In a saucepan, bring millet and broth to a boil. Reduce heat; simmer, covered, until millet is tender and broth is absorbed, about 30-35 minutes. Transfer to a large bowl and cool.

2) Meanwhile, cut tops off peppers and remove seeds. In a large kettle, cook peppers in boiling water for 3-5 minutes. Drain and rinse in cold water; set aside.

3) With a fork, fluff cooled millet. Add the corn, onion, celery, nuts, green onion and seasonings; blend well. Spoon into sweet peppers. Drizzle with oil.

4) Place in a 11-in. x 7-in. x 2-in. baking dish coated with nonstick cooking spray. Cover and bake at 350° for 55-60 minutes or until tender.

Yield: 4 servings.

Editor's Note: Look for millet in the grains or natural food aisle of your grocery store.

NUTRITION FACTS: 1 stuffed pepper equals 281 calories, 13 g fat (1 g saturated fat), 0 cholesterol, 684 mg sodium, 37 g carbohydrate, 6 g fiber, 8 g protein.

■ *COUSCOUS-STUFFED PEPPERS:* Use 1-1/2 cups cooked couscous for the millet and vegetable broth. Proceed with recipe as directed.

SAGE POLENTA

Sage Polenta
Taste of Home Test Kitchen

Bits of sweet red pepper peek through these pretty polenta squares that have a slightly sweet corn flavor and are generously seasoned with sage. Serve this traditional ethnic side dish with Italian or Southwestern fare.

- 1/2   cup chopped onion
- 1/2   cup chopped sweet red pepper
- 1   garlic clove, minced
- 1   teaspoon butter
- 3   cups water
- 1   cup fat-free milk
- 1   cup cornmeal
- 1/4   cup grated Parmesan cheese
- 2   tablespoons minced fresh sage
- 3/4   teaspoon salt
- 1/4   teaspoon pepper
- 2   teaspoons canola oil

1) In a large nonstick saucepan, saute the onion, red pepper and garlic in butter until tender. Stir in water and milk; bring to a boil over medium heat.

2) Gradually whisk in cornmeal, whisking constantly to prevent lumping. Reduce heat; cover and simmer for 8-10 minutes or until cornmeal is tender.

3) Stir in the Parmesan cheese, sage, salt and pepper. Spread into a 13-in. x 9-in. x 2-in. pan coated with nonstick cooking spray. Cover and refrigerate for 30-45 minutes or until firm.

4) Cut into 12 squares. In a large nonstick skillet, cook polenta in batches in oil over medium-high heat for 3-4 minutes on each side or until lightly browned. Serve warm.

Yield: 6 servings.

NUTRITION FACTS: 2 squares equals 143 calories, 4 g fat (1 g saturated fat), 5 mg cholesterol, 386 mg sodium, 22 g carbohydrate, 2 g fiber, 5 g protein.

TOASTED ALMOND GRANOLA

Toasted Almond Granola
Tracy Weakly, Aloha, Oregon

I combined several granola recipes to come up with this crunchy, cranberry-and-apricot-flavored treat. The possibilities are endless when you vary the kinds of fruits and nuts.

3	cups old-fashioned oats
2	cups crisp rice cereal
1/2	cup wheat germ, toasted
1/2	cup nonfat dry milk powder
1/3	cup slivered almonds
1/4	cup packed brown sugar
2	tablespoons sunflower kernels
1/4	teaspoon salt
1/2	cup orange juice
1/4	cup honey
2	teaspoons canola oil
2	teaspoons vanilla extract
1/2	teaspoon almond extract
1	cup golden raisins
1	cup chopped dried apricots
1/2	cup dried cranberries

Fat-free plain yogurt, optional

1) In a large bowl, combine first eight ingredients. In a saucepan, combine the orange juice, honey and oil. Heat for 3-4 minutes over medium heat until honey is dissolved. Remove from heat; stir in extracts. Pour over oat mixture; stir to coat.

2) Transfer to a 15-in. x 10-in. x 1-in. baking pan coated with nonstick cooking spray. Bake at 350° for 20-25 minutes or until crisp, stirring every 10 minutes.

3) Remove and cool completely on a wire rack. Stir in dried fruits. Store in an airtight container. Serve over yogurt if desired.

Yield: 8 cups.

NUTRITION FACTS: 1/2 cup equals 212 calories, 4 g fat (trace saturated fat), 0 cholesterol, 88 mg sodium, 41 g carbohydrate, 3 g fiber, 6 g protein.

Greens and Quinoa Pilaf
Annette Spiegler, Arlington Heights, Illinois

Quinoa is grain that was native to the Andes. High in calcium and protein, it supplies many nutrients and is a unique addition to this dish.

1	cup quinoa, rinsed
1	can (14-1/2 ounces) vegetable broth
1/4	cup water
2	medium zucchini, halved lengthwise and sliced
1	medium yellow summer squash, halved lengthwise and sliced
1	cup chopped leeks (white portion only)
2	garlic cloves, minced
1	tablespoon olive oil
1	large tomato, chopped
1	tablespoon minced fresh cilantro
1/2	teaspoon salt
1/2	teaspoon dried oregano
1/2	teaspoon ground cumin
1/2	teaspoon chili powder
1/4	teaspoon pepper
1/8	teaspoon crushed red pepper flakes
2	cups fresh baby spinach, chopped

1) In a large nonstick skillet coated with nonstick cooking spray, toast the quinoa over medium heat until lightly browned, stirring occasionally.

2) In a small saucepan, bring broth and water to a boil. Add the quinoa. Reduce the heat; simmer, uncovered, for 15 minutes or until liquid is absorbed; set aside.

3) In a large nonstick skillet, saute the zucchini, yellow squash, leeks and garlic in oil until tender. Stir in the tomato, cilantro, seasonings and quinoa; heat through. Add spinach; cook and stir until spinach is wilted.

Yield: 8 servings.

NUTRITION FACTS: 3/4 cup equals 126 calories, 3 g fat (trace saturated fat), 0 cholesterol, 377 mg sodium, 21 g carbohydrate, 3 g fiber, 5 g protein.

Storing and Cooking Rice

You can store white and wild rice in an airtight container indefinitely. Brown rice can only be stored for up to 6 months at room temperature; refrigerate or freeze to extend its storage life.

Arborio rice is a medium grain rice used for making risottos. In risottos, this rice has a creamy texture with a chewy center.

Aromatic rice, also known as fragrant rice, is rice with natural ingredients that are responsible for their aroma and fragrant taste. Each type of aromatic rice has its own cooking characteristic. Basmati, Black Japonica, Jasmine, Texmati are types of aromatic rice. The fragrance of the type of rice can vary from one growing year to the next.

Always rinse wild rice before cooking to remove any debris. It is not necessary to rinse other grains. Wild rice may become tender without absorbing all the cooking liquid. If necessary, drain before serving or combining with other recipe ingredients.

For fluffier rice, remove the saucepan from the heat after the cooking time is complete and let stand for 5 to 10 minutes. Fluff with a fork and serve.

Cooking Rice or Grains

Follow these guidelines or use the chart below to cook grains to serve as a simple side dish or to use as an ingredient in a recipe. Allow 1/2 to 3/4 cup cooked rice or wild rice for each side-dish serving.

Bring water, 1/4 teaspoon salt if desired and 1 tablespoon butter if desired to a boil in a 2-qt. saucepan. Stir in grain; return to a boil. Cover and reduce heat to simmer. Cook for the specified time or until tender.

RICE OR GRAIN	WATER	GRAIN AMOUNT	COOKING TIME (IN MINUTES)	YIELD
 RICE, WHITE (LONG GRAIN)	2 cups	1 cup	12 to 15	3 cups
 RICE, WHITE (INSTANT)	1 cup	1 cup	5	2 cups
 RICE, WHITE (CONVERTED)	2-1/4 cups	1 cup	20	4 cups
 RICE, BROWN	2 cups	1 cup	35 to 45	3 cups
 RICE, WILD	3 cups	1 cup	45 to 60	3 cups
 BARLEY, (QUICK-COOKING)	2 cups	1-1/4 cups	10 to 12	3 cups
 BARLEY, (REGULAR PEARL)	3 cups	3/4 cup	35 to 45	3 cups
 QUINOA	2 cups	1 cup	12 to 15	4 cups

Confetti Rice

Ruth Ann Stelfox, Raymond, Alberta

Bacon and rice make a tasty combination in this dish that gets color and crunch from peas.

> 1 cup uncooked long grain rice
> 1/2 pound sliced bacon, diced
> 1 cup diced carrots
> 1 cup diced celery
> 1/2 cup fresh *or* frozen peas
> Soy sauce, optional

1) Cook rice according to package directions. Meanwhile, in a large skillet, cook bacon over medium heat until crisp. Using a slotted spoon, remove to paper towels. Drain, reserving 3 tablespoon drippings.

2) In same skillet, saute carrots and celery in reserved drippings until crisp-tender. Add the rice and peas; cook and stir until heated through. Stir in bacon. Serve with soy sauce if desired.

Yield: 8 servings.

NUTRITION FACTS: 2/3 cup equals 202 calories, 10 g fat (4 g saturated fat), 13 mg cholesterol, 198 mg sodium, 22 g carbohydrate, 1 g fiber, 5 g protein.

VEGGIE BROWN RICE WRAPS

Veggie Brown Rice Wraps

Lisa Sullivan, St. Mary's, Ohio

Salsa gives a bit of zip to the brown rice and bean filling in these meatless tortilla wraps.

> 1 medium sweet red *or* green pepper, diced
> 1 cup sliced fresh mushrooms
> 2 garlic cloves, minced
> 1 tablespoon olive oil
> 2 cups cooked brown rice
> 1 can (16 ounces) kidney beans, rinsed and drained
> 1 cup frozen corn, thawed
> 1/4 cup chopped green onions
> 1/2 teaspoon ground cumin
> 1/2 teaspoon pepper
> 1/4 teaspoon salt
> 6 flour tortillas (8 inches), warmed
> 1/2 cup shredded reduced-fat cheddar cheese
> 3/4 cup salsa

1) In a large nonstick skillet, saute the red pepper, mushrooms and garlic in oil until tender. Add the next seven ingredients. Cook and stir for 4-6 minutes or until heated through.

2) Spoon 3/4 cup onto each tortilla. Sprinkle with cheese; drizzle with salsa. Fold sides of tortilla over filling; serve immediately.

Yield: 6 servings.

NUTRITION FACTS: 1 wrap equals 371 calories, 8 g fat (2 g saturated fat), 7 mg cholesterol, 816 mg sodium, 63 g carbohydrate, 5 g fiber, 14 g protein.

Broccoli Brown Rice Pilaf

Marie Condit, Brooklyn Center, Minnesota

This delicious, low-fat dish features rosemary, garlic, almonds and sunflower kernels. Add cooked cubed chicken for a complete meal.

> 1 cup uncooked brown rice
> 2-1/4 cups reduced-sodium chicken broth *or* vegetable broth
> 2 tablespoons minced fresh rosemary *or* 2 teaspoons dried rosemary, crushed
> 2 garlic cloves, minced
> 2 cups chopped fresh broccoli
> 1/4 cup slivered almonds
> 1/4 cup unsalted sunflower kernels
> 1/2 teaspoon salt
> 1/8 teaspoon pepper

1) In a large nonstick skillet coated with nonstick cooking spray, saute rice until lightly browned. Add the broth, rosemary and garlic; bring to a boil. Reduce heat; cover and simmer for 40 minutes or until rice is almost tender.

2) Stir in the broccoli, almonds, sunflower kernels, salt and pepper. Cover and cook 3-5 minutes longer or until rice is tender and broccoli is crisp-tender. Fluff with a fork.

Yield: 6 servings.

NUTRITION FACTS: 2/3 cup equals 202 calories, 6 g fat (1 g saturated fat), 0 cholesterol, 414 mg sodium, 31 g carbohydrate, 2 g fiber, 7 g protein.

Broccoli Risotto

George Morants, Cromwell, Connecticut

You want to add liquid to the risotto a little at a time, stirring constantly and make sure to cook just until it's creamy and the grains are tender.

- 1/4 cup olive oil, *divided*
- 1 garlic clove, thinly sliced
- 2 cups broccoli florets
- 2-1/3 cups chicken broth, *divided*
- 1/4 cup chopped fresh parsley, *divided*

Salt and pepper to taste

- 1/2 small onion, chopped
- 3/4 cup uncooked long-grain *or* Italian Arborio rice
- 2/3 cup dry white wine *or* chicken broth
- 1 tablespoon lemon juice
- 2 tablespoons butter
- 1/4 cup grated Parmesan cheese, *divided*

1) In a skillet, heat 2 tablespoons oil. Saute garlic and broccoli until garlic is soft, about 3 minutes. Add 1/3 cup chicken broth, 3 tablespoons parsley, and salt and pepper to taste. Simmer, uncovered, just until the broccoli is tender, about 6 minutes. Set aside.

2) Meanwhile, heat the remaining oil in a large saucepan. Cook onion until tender, about 3 minutes. Add rice and stir until rice is coated. Add wine or broth; cook until wine or broth is absorbed, stirring constantly.

3) In a small saucepan, heat remaining broth and keep warm. Stir 2/3 cup warm broth into rice mixture. Cook, uncovered, over medium-low heat until all of the liquid is absorbed, stirring constantly.

4) Add remaining broth, 1/3 cup at a time, stirring constantly. Allow the liquid to absorb between additions. Rice will be creamy and grains will be tender when done. (Total cooking time is about 25 minutes.)

5) Stir in the lemon juice, butter, 3 tablespoons Parmesan cheese and reserved broccoli. Sprinkle with remaining Parmesan cheese and parsley. Serve immediately.

Yield: 4-6 servings.

NUTRITION FACTS: 1/2 cup (calculated without salt and pepper) equals 247 calories, 14 g fat (4 g saturated fat), 13 mg cholesterol, 473 mg sodium, 22 g carbohydrate, 1 g fiber, 5 g protein.

Cranberry Rice 'n' Onions

Tommi Roylance, Charlo, Montana

Rice provides so many options to a creative cook—the stir-in ideas are endless. In this recipe, dried cranberries star.

- 2-1/2 cups chicken broth
- 1/2 cup uncooked wild rice
- 1/2 cup uncooked brown rice
- 3 medium onions, cut into wedges
- 2 teaspoons brown sugar
- 3 tablespoons butter
- 1 cup dried cranberries
- 1/2 teaspoon grated orange peel

1) In a large saucepan, bring broth to a boil. Add wild rice. Reduce heat. Cover; simmer for 10 minutes. Add brown rice. Cover; simmer for 45-50 minutes or until rice is tender and liquid is absorbed.

2) In a large skillet over medium heat, cook the onions and sugar in butter until golden, stirring frequently. Add cranberries, orange peel and rice; heat through.

Yield: 4 servings.

NUTRITION FACTS: 1 cup equals 400 calories, 10 g fat (5 g saturated fat), 23 mg cholesterol, 674 mg sodium, 74 g carbohydrate, 6 g fiber, 8 g protein.

Fried Rice

Rhonda Olivieri, East Earl, Pennsylvania

Cook together chopped onion, cooked rice, teriyaki sauce, parsley and seasonings for this fast-to-fix side dish.

- 1/3 cup chopped onion
- 1/4 cup butter
- 4 cups cold cooked rice
- 3 tablespoons teriyaki sauce
- 2 tablespoons minced fresh parsley
- 1 teaspoon garlic powder
- 1/8 teaspoon pepper
- 1 egg, lightly beaten

1) In a large skillet, saute onion in butter until tender. Stir in the rice, teriyaki sauce, parsley, garlic powder and pepper.

2) Cook over medium-low heat for 5 minutes, stirring occasionally. Add the egg; cook and stir until egg is completely set, about 3 minutes.

Yield: 4 servings.

NUTRITION FACTS: 3/4 cup equals 344 calories, 13 g fat (8 g saturated fat), 84 mg cholesterol, 592 mg sodium, 48 g carbohydrate, 1 g fiber, 7 g protein.

PASTA & PASTA SAUCE

PASTA & PASTA SAUCE

Cooking with pasta gives you so many choices! You can prepare homemade pasta with a few simple ingredients or use packaged pasta to make a tasty meal in a snap. In general, you want to select the right pasta for the sauce. A light, thin sauce should have a thin pasta, such as angel hair or vermicelli. Heavier sauces need thicker pastas, like fettuccine. For chunky or meaty sauces, choose a tubular-shaped pasta like rigatoni.

Store uncooked dry pasta in a cool dry place for up to 1 year. Store fresh pasta in the refrigerator and cook or freeze by the use-by date.

To cook pasta evenly and prevent it from sticking together, always cook pasta in plenty of boiling water. To prevent a boil-over, cook pasta in a large kettle or Dutch oven.

Allow about 2 ounces of pasta per person for a main-dish serving.

For 8 ounces of pasta, bring 3 quarts water to a full rolling boil along with 1-1/2 teaspoons salt if desired. Add pasta all at once and stir. Return to a boil and cook, uncovered, stirring occasionally.

Cooking times vary with the size and variety of pasta. Fresh pasta cooks faster than dried. Thin pasta, such as angel hair, cooks faster than thicker pasta, such as spaghetti. For packaged pasta, follow the recommended cooking directions on package.

To test for doneness, use a fork to remove a single piece of pasta from the boiling water. Rinse in cold water and taste. Pasta should be cooked until al dente, which means firm yet tender. Test often while cooking to avoid overcooking, which would cause a soft or mushy texture. If pasta will be used in a recipe that requires further cooking, such as a casserole, undercook by one-third the recommended time.

As soon as the pasta tests done, pour into a large colander to drain, minding the steam as you pour. If using the cooked pasta in a salad or at a later time, rinse it with cold water to stop cooking and remove excess starch.

Cooked pasta can be tossed with a little olive oil and refrigerated for 3 to 4 days. To reheat refrigerated pasta, place in boiling water for 1 minute, then drain and serve.

Generally, pasta should not be frozen. However, some dishes, like lasagna, stuffed shells or manicotti, can be frozen. Make the recipe as directed, then freeze before baking for up to 2 months. Thaw in the refrigerator and bake according to recipe directions until heated through.

COOKING SPAGHETTI

Carefully hold spaghetti in boiling water and ease it down into the water as it softens, pushing it around the edge of the pan. When fully immersed in the water, stir the spaghetti to separate strands.

How Much Pasta?

The yield for pasta will vary according to its size and shape. It is sometimes difficult to determine the amount of pasta to cook for a recipe, especially if the package is opened and partially used. For long-shaped pasta, such as spaghetti, linguine and fettuccine, about 1-1/2-in. diameter of the pasta is an 8-ounce portion. The chart (at right) is a guideline for uncooked, dry pasta.

Pasta Shapes

ANGEL HAIR	VERMICELLI	SPAGHETTI
LINGUINE	FETTUCCINE	LASAGNA
SHELLS (MEDIUM)	SHELLS (JUMBO)	ELBOW MACARONI
PENNE	MANICOTTI	ROTINI (SPIRAL)
BOW TIE	EGG NOODLE	ORZO

TYPE OF PASTA	UNCOOKED AMOUNT	COOKED AMOUNT
ANGEL HAIR	8 oz.	4 cups
BOW TIE	4 cups/8 oz.	4 cups
EGG NOODLE	4 cups/8 oz.	4 cups
ELBOW MACARONI	2 cups/8 oz.	4 cups
FETTUCCINE	8 oz.	3-1/4 cups
LINGUINE	8 oz.	4 cups
RIGATONI	3 cups/8 oz.	4-1/2 cups
ROTINI	3 cups/8 oz.	4-1/2 cups
SHELL, MEDIUM	3 cups/8 oz.	4 cups
SPAGHETTI	8 oz.	5 cups
THIN SPAGHETTI	8 oz.	4-1/2 cups
VERMICELLI	8 oz.	4-1/2 cups
ZITI	3 cups/8 oz.	4-1/2 cups

FRESH TOMATO PASTA TOSS

Fresh Tomato Pasta Toss
Cheryl Travagliante, Independence, Ohio

Dipping whole tomatoes into boiling water makes them easier to peel for this garden-fresh recipe. Parmesan or Romano cheese makes a great topper.

3 pounds ripe fresh tomatoes

1 package (16 ounces) uncooked medium tube pasta *or* pasta of your choice

2 garlic cloves, minced

1 tablespoon vegetable oil

1 tablespoon minced fresh parsley *or* 1 teaspoon dried parsley flakes

1 tablespoon minced fresh basil *or* 1 teaspoon dried basil

2 teaspoons minced fresh oregano
  or 3/4 teaspoon dried oregano
1 teaspoon salt
1/4 teaspoon sugar
1/8 teaspoon pepper
1/4 cup heavy whipping cream
1/4 cup shredded Parmesan *or*
  Romano cheese

1) To remove peels from tomatoes, fill a large saucepan with water and bring to a boil. Place tomatoes, one at a time, in boiling water for 30 seconds. Immediately plunge in ice water. Peel skins with a sharp paring knife and discard. Chop pulp; set aside.

2) Cook pasta according to package directions. In a large skillet, cook garlic in oil over medium heat until golden. Add the parsley, basil, oregano, salt, sugar, pepper and reserved tomato pulp; mix well. Bring to a boil; reduce heat. Add cream; heat through.

3) Drain pasta and transfer to a serving bowl. Pour tomato sauce over pasta and toss to coat. Sprinkle with cheese.

Yield: 8 servings.

NUTRITION FACTS: 1 cup equals 277 calories, 7 g fat (0 saturated fat), 13 mg cholesterol, 244 mg sodium, 46 g carbohydrate, 0 fiber, 9 g protein.

ITALIAN SPAGHETTI AND MEATBALLS

Italian Spaghetti and Meatballs
Etta Winter, Pavillion, New York

Hearty meatballs and sauce are tasty over cooked spaghetti. They also make a satisfying sandwich topped with Parmesan cheese.

2 cans (28 ounces *each*) diced tomatoes, undrained
1 can (12 ounces) tomato paste

1-1/2 cups water, *divided*
1 tablespoon sugar
3 tablespoons grated onion
1-1/2 teaspoons dried oregano
2-1/2 teaspoons salt, *divided*
1 teaspoon minced garlic, *divided*
3/4 teaspoon pepper, *divided*
1 bay leaf
6 slices day-old bread, torn into pieces
2 eggs, lightly beaten
1/2 cup grated Parmesan cheese
2 tablespoons minced fresh parsley
1 pound ground beef

Hot cooked spaghetti
Additional Parmesan cheese, optional

1) In a Dutch oven, combine the tomatoes, tomato paste, 1 cup water, sugar, grated onion, oregano, 1-1/2 teaspoons salt, 1/2 teaspoon garlic, 1/2 teaspoon pepper and bay leaf. Bring to a boil. Reduce the heat and simmer, uncovered, for 1-1/4 hours.

2) Meanwhile, soak bread in remaining water. Squeeze out excess moisture. In a large bowl, combine the bread, eggs, Parmesan cheese, parsley and remaining salt, garlic and pepper. Crumble beef over mixture and mix well. Shape into 1-1/2-in. meatballs (about 36 meatballs).

3) Place meatballs on a rack in a shallow baking pan. Bake, uncovered, at 400° for 20 minutes or until no longer pink. Transfer to spaghetti sauce. Simmer, uncovered, until heated through, stirring occasionally. Discard the bay leaf. Serve over spaghetti with additional Parmesan if desired.

Yield: 6 servings.

NUTRITION FACTS: 1-2/3 cups (calculated without spaghetti) equals 387 calories, 14 g fat (6 g saturated fat), 126 mg cholesterol, 1,679 mg sodium, 41 g carbohydrate, 9 g fiber, 26 g protein.

■ *ITALIAN MEATBALL SANDWICHES:* Instead of serving meatballs over spaghetti, spoon onto split submarine, hoagie *or* French bread rolls. Place on a baking sheet, leaving sandwich open. Sprinkle each with 1/4 to 1/3 cup shredded mozzarella cheese. Bake, uncovered, at 350° for 10-15 minutes or until cheese is melted.

Pasta with Marinara Sauce

Diane Hixon, Niceville, Florida

You don't have to settle for prepared sauce when this homemade marinara is so simple and tasty. Add Italian sausage links for more robust flavor.

2 garlic cloves, sliced

1/3 cup olive oil

1 can (28 ounces) diced tomatoes, undrained

3 tablespoons minced fresh parsley

2 tablespoons minced onion

2 bay leaves

Salt and pepper to taste

1 tablespoon chopped fresh basil

Hot cooked pasta

1) In a large saucepan, cook garlic in oil over medium heat for 3 minutes or until golden. Add the tomatoes, parsley, onion, bay leaves, salt and pepper; bring to a boil.

2) Reduce heat; cover and simmer for 15 minutes. Add basil. Remove bay leaves. Serve over pasta.

Yield: 4 servings.

NUTRITION FACTS: 3/4 cup (calculated without salt, pepper and pasta) equals 204 calories, 18 g fat (2 g saturated fat), 0 cholesterol, 254 mg sodium, 11 g carbohydrate, 3 g fiber, 2 g protein.

■ *SAUSAGE MARINARA:* In a skillet, cook 1 pound Italian sausage links over medium heat for 12-14 minutes or until browned, turning twice. Let stand until cool enough to handle. Cut into slices and set aside. With the garlic, cook 1/2 pound sliced fresh mushrooms, 1 *each* chopped large onion, green pepper and sweet red pepper. Add remaining ingredients and cook as directed. Add reserved sausage and heat through.

Pesto Sauce

Sue Jurack, Mequon, Wisconsin

I like to serve the pesto over butter gnocchi with an extra sprinkle of Parmesan cheese. Gnocchi are light little Italian potato dumplings, which are available in Italian grocery stores and cook up in mere minutes. You can also freeze the pesto to use later on.

2/3 cup packed coarsely chopped fresh basil

1/3 cup grated Parmesan cheese

1/3 cup olive oil

2 tablespoons pine nuts *or* sunflower kernels

1/2 teaspoon salt

1/8 teaspoon pepper

1 garlic clove, peeled

1) In a food processor or blender, combine all the ingredients; cover and process until blended. Cover and freeze for up to 3 months.

Yield: 1/2 cup.

Editor's Note: When freezing the pesto, leave about 3/4 in. at the top of the container, then cover the top with a thin layer of olive oil so the pesto doesn't brown during freezing.

NUTRITION FACTS: 2 tablespoons equals 217 calories, 22 g fat (4 g saturated fat), 5 mg cholesterol, 420 mg sodium, 1 g carbohydrate, 1 g fiber, 4 g protein.

FETTUCCINE ALFREDO

Fettuccine Alfredo

Jo Gray, Park City, Montana

A creamy and comforting cheese sauce, with a hint of pepper and nutmeg, coats fettuccine noodles in fine fashion. This is wonderful as is, but sometimes I like to add sliced fresh mushrooms and black olives that have been sauteed in butter and garlic.

4 ounces uncooked fettuccine

3 tablespoons butter

1 cup heavy whipping cream

1/4 cup plus 2 tablespoons grated Parmesan cheese, *divided*

1/4 cup grated Romano cheese

1 egg yolk, lightly beaten

1/8 teaspoon salt

Dash *each* pepper and ground nutmeg

1) Cook fettuccine according to package directions. Meanwhile, in a saucepan, melt butter over medium-low heat. Stir in the cream, 1/4 cup Parmesan cheese, Romano cheese, egg yolk, salt, pepper and nutmeg.

2) Cook and stir over medium-low heat until a thermometer reads 160° (do not boil). Drain fettuccine; top with Alfredo sauce and remaining Parmesan cheese.

Yield: 2 servings.

NUTRITION FACTS: 1 cup equals 915 calories, 74 g fat (45 g saturated fat), 342 mg cholesterol, 878 mg sodium, 44 g carbohydrate, 2 g fiber, 24 g protein.

Spaghetti Carbonara
Taste of Home Test Kitchen

A homemade sauce tops spaghetti in this classic recipe featuring peas and bacon.

> 8 ounces uncooked spaghetti
> 1 tablespoon cornstarch
> 4 eggs, lightly beaten
> 1 cup half-and-half cream
> 3/4 cup chopped onion
> 2 garlic cloves, minced
> 2 tablespoons olive oil
> 1 cup frozen peas
> 8 bacon strips, cooked and crumbled
> 1/2 cup grated Parmesan cheese
> 1/2 teaspoon salt
> 1/4 teaspoon white pepper
> Additional Parmesan cheese, optional

1) Cook pasta according to package directions. Meanwhile, in a large bowl, combine the cornstarch, eggs and cream until smooth; set aside.

2) In a large skillet, saute onion and garlic in oil until tender. Gradually stir onion mixture into egg mixture. Add peas to hot skillet; cook and stir for 1 minute or until heated through. Pour egg mixture into skillet all at once, stirring constantly.

3) Cook and stir over medium-low heat until mixture is just thick enough to coat a metal spoon with a thin film and a thermometer reads 160°, about 5 minutes. Remove from the heat.

4) Drain pasta; transfer to a large bowl. Pour sauce over pasta; toss to coat. Sprinkle with the bacon, cheese, salt and white pepper; toss. Serve immediately with additional Parmesan cheese if desired.

Yield: 5 servings.

NUTRITION FACTS: 1 cup equals 474 calories, 22 g fat (9 g saturated fat), 209 mg cholesterol, 658 mg sodium, 44 g carbohydrate, 3 g fiber, 21 g protein.

Pasta Primavera
Beverly Little, Marietta, Georgia

Generous servings of this pretty pasta toss are sure to fill up your family. Broccoli, peppers, squash and more provide the lively color. Add a pinch of Parmesan cheese before serving.

> 8 ounces uncooked linguine
> 1 medium carrot, thinly sliced
> 1/2 cup chopped onion
> 1/2 cup julienned sweet red pepper
> 1/2 cup julienned sweet yellow pepper
> 1 medium zucchini, thinly sliced
> 1 medium yellow summer squash, thinly sliced
> 1 cup broccoli florets
> 1 pound thin fresh asparagus, cut into 3-inch pieces
> 8 ounces fresh mushrooms, sliced
> 1/3 cup all-purpose flour
> 2 cups cold water
> 2 teaspoons chicken bouillon granules
> 1/2 cup white wine *or* chicken broth
> 1/4 teaspoon salt
> 1/4 cup minced fresh basil *or* 4 teaspoons dried basil
> 6 tablespoons grated Parmesan cheese

1) Cook pasta according to package directions. Meanwhile, in a nonstick skillet coated with nonstick cooking spray, combine the carrot, onion, peppers, zucchini, summer squash and broccoli.

2) Cover and cook over medium-low heat for 10 minutes. Add asparagus and mushrooms; cook 5 minutes longer.

3) In a saucepan, combine flour and water until smooth. Add the bouillon. Bring to a boil; cook and stir for 2 minutes or until slightly thickened. Add wine or broth and salt; stir well. Pour over vegetables.

4) Drain pasta and add to vegetable mixture. Add basil; toss to coat. Sprinkle with Parmesan cheese.

Yield: 6 servings.

NUTRITION FACTS: 1-1/2 cups equals 168 calories, 3 g fat (1 g saturated fat), 5 mg cholesterol, 614 mg sodium, 26 g carbohydrate, 4 g fiber, 9 g protein.

ENCHILADA STUFFED SHELLS

Enchilada Stuffed Shells

Rebecca Stout, Conroe, Texas

I served this entree to my husband, my sister and my brother-in-law, who is a hard-to-please eater. He even said he liked it and took leftovers for lunch the next day...I was thrilled!

- 15 uncooked jumbo pasta shells
- 1 pound lean ground turkey
- 1 can (10 ounces) enchilada sauce
- 1/2 teaspoon dried minced onion
- 1/4 teaspoon dried basil
- 1/4 teaspoon dried oregano
- 1/4 teaspoon ground cumin
- 1/2 cup fat-free refried beans
- 1 cup (4 ounces) shredded reduced-fat cheddar cheese

1) Cook pasta according to package directions; drain. In a nonstick skillet, cook turkey over medium heat until no longer pink; drain. Stir in enchilada sauce and seasonings; set aside.

2) Place a rounded teaspoonful of refried beans in each pasta shell, then fill with turkey mixture. Place in an 11-in. x 7-in. x 2-in. baking dish coated with nonstick cooking spray.

3) Cover and bake at 350° for 25 minutes. Uncover; sprinkle with cheese. Bake 5 minutes longer or until cheese is melted.

Yield: 5 servings.

NUTRITION FACTS: 3 stuffed shells equals 379 calories, 15 g fat (6 g saturated fat), 89 mg cholesterol, 591 mg sodium, 33 g carbohydrate, 2 g fiber, 28 g protein.

Bean and Sausage Rigatoni

Irene Heath, Hastings, Michigan

Cutting the fat in this casserole doesn't make it any less hearty. The smoked turkey sausage is delicious. Serve it with a fresh green salad and crusty French bread for a balanced meal.

- 8 ounces uncooked rigatoni *or* penne
- 1 can (15 ounces) great northern beans, rinsed and drained
- 1 can (14-1/2 ounces) stewed tomatoes
- 1 package (10 ounces) frozen chopped spinach, thawed and drained
- 1/2 pound reduced-fat smoked turkey kielbasa, halved and sliced
- 5 tablespoons tomato paste
- 1/4 cup chicken broth
- 1-1/2 teaspoons Italian seasoning
- 1/4 cup shredded Parmesan cheese

1) Cook pasta according to package directions; drain. In a bowl, combine the pasta, beans, tomatoes, spinach, kielbasa, tomato paste, broth and seasoning.

2) Transfer to a 2-qt. baking dish coated with nonstick cooking spray. Sprinkle with Parmesan cheese. Bake, uncovered, at 375° for 15-20 minutes or until heated through.

Yield: 8 servings.

NUTRITION FACTS: 1 cup equals 249 calories, 3 g fat (1 g saturated fat), 15 mg cholesterol, 537 mg sodium, 42 g carbohydrate, 5 g fiber, 14 g protein.

Three-Cheese Manicotti

Vikki Rebholz, West Chester, Ohio

For a weeknight meal or special occasion, family and friends will love the rich cheese filling inside tender pasta shells.

- 20 uncooked manicotti shells
- 2 cartons (15 ounces *each*) ricotta cheese
- 5 cups (20 ounces) shredded mozzarella cheese, *divided*
- 1 cup grated Parmesan cheese
- 2 eggs, beaten
- 2 teaspoons dried basil
- 2 teaspoons dried oregano
- 1 teaspoon onion powder
- 1 teaspoon garlic powder
- 1 teaspoon seasoned salt

2   jars (26 ounces *each*) spaghetti
     sauce

1) Cook manicotti according to package directions.
    Meanwhile, in a bowl, combine the ricotta cheese,
    3 cups mozzarella cheese, Parmesan cheese, eggs
    and seasonings.

2) Spread 1 cup of spaghetti sauce each into two
    ungreased 13-in. x 9-in. x 2-in. baking dishes.
    Stuff manicotti shells with cheese mixture;
    arrange over sauce. Top with remaining sauce.

3) Cover and bake at 375° for 35-40 minutes.
    Uncover; sprinkle with remaining mozzarella
    cheese. Bake 10 minutes longer or until cheese is
    melted and manicotti is heated through.

Yield: 10 servings.

NUTRITION FACTS: 1 serving equals 574 calories, 30 g fat (16 g
saturated fat), 130 mg cholesterol, 1,365 mg sodium, 45 g
carbohydrate, 4 g fiber, 33 g protein.

BAKED ZITI

Baked Ziti

Kim Neer, Mansfield, Ohio

This comforting Italian dish has a from-scratch
spaghetti sauce, ziti pasta and a generous
combination of cheeses. You can easily double the
recipe to serve a larger crowd.

1/2   pound lean ground beef
1   medium onion, chopped
2   garlic cloves, minced
1-3/4 cups spaghetti sauce
1   can (14-1/2 ounces) diced
    tomatoes, undrained

1   can (6 ounces) tomato paste
6   tablespoons water
1   tablespoon minced fresh parsley
1-1/2 teaspoons Worcestershire sauce
1   teaspoon dried basil
3/4 teaspoon dried oregano, *divided*
8   ounces uncooked rigatoni *or*
    uncooked medium tube pasta
1   carton (8 ounces) part-skim
    ricotta cheese
1   cup (4 ounces) shredded
    part-skim mozzarella cheese
1/4 cup grated Parmesan cheese,
    divided
1   egg, lightly beaten
1/4 teaspoon salt
1/4 teaspoon pepper

1) In a large saucepan, cook the beef, onion and
    garlic over medium heat until meat is no longer
    pink; drain. Stir in spaghetti sauce, tomatoes,
    tomato paste, water, parsley, Worcestershire sauce,
    basil and 1/2 teaspoon oregano.

2) Cover and simmer meat sauce for 3 hours, stirring
    occasionally. Cook pasta according to package
    directions; drain. In a bowl, combine the ricotta,
    mozzarella, 2 tablespoons Parmesan cheese, egg,
    salt and pepper.

3) In a 13-in. x 9-in. x 2-in. baking dish coated with
    nonstick cooking spray, spread 1 cup of meat
    sauce. Layer with a half of the pasta, a third
    of meat sauce and half of cheese mixture. Repeat
    layers.

4) Top with the remaining sauce. Sprinkle with
    remaining Parmesan cheese and oregano. Cover
    and bake at 350° for 1 hour or until heated
    through.

Yield: 6 servings.

NUTRITION FACTS: 1-1/3 cups equals 431 calories, 14 g fat (7 g
saturated fat), 81 mg cholesterol, 818 mg sodium, 50 g carbohydrate,
6 g fiber, 27 g protein.

Pepperoni Macaroni

Marlene Mohr, Cincinnati, Ohio

For your next potluck offering, consider this hearty pasta bake. It's handy, too, because it can be assembled ahead of time, then baked right before serving.

2-1/2	cups uncooked elbow macaroni
1	pound bulk Italian sausage
1	large onion, chopped
1	can (15 ounces) pizza sauce
1	can (8 ounces) tomato sauce
1/3	cup milk
1	package (3-1/2 ounces) sliced pepperoni, halved
1	jar (4-1/2 ounces) sliced mushrooms, drained
1	can (2-1/4 ounces) sliced ripe olives, drained
1	cup (4 ounces) shredded mozzarella cheese

1) Cook macaroni according to package directions. Meanwhile, in a large skillet, cook sausage and onion over medium heat until meat is no longer pink; drain. Drain macaroni.

2) In a large bowl, combine the pizza sauce, tomato sauce and milk. Stir in sausage mixture, macaroni, pepperoni, mushrooms and olives.

3) Transfer to a greased 13-in. x 9-in. x 2-in. baking dish. Cover and bake at 350° for 30 minutes. Uncover; sprinkle with cheese. Bake 10-15 minutes longer or until heated through and cheese is melted.

Yield: 8 servings.

NUTRITION FACTS: 1 cup equals 334 calories, 19 g fat (7 g saturated fat), 45 mg cholesterol, 1,041 mg sodium, 26 g carbohydrate, 3 g fiber, 16 g protein.

Creamy Tortellini and Sausage

Taste of Home Test Kitchen

You don't need to spend loads of time in the kitchen creating an irresistible pasta dish. Simply jazz up a jar of store-bought Alfredo sauce.

1	pound bulk Italian sausage
1	medium onion, chopped
2	garlic cloves, minced
4	quarts water
1	package (19 ounces) frozen cheese tortellini
3	cups frozen mixed vegetables
1	jar (17 ounces) Alfredo sauce

1/4	cup minced fresh basil *or* 3 teaspoons dried basil

1) In a large skillet, cook sausage, onion and garlic over medium heat until the meat is no longer pink; drain. Meanwhile, in a Dutch oven, bring water to a boil. Add pasta and vegetables. Cook for 3-5 minutes or until pasta floats and vegetables are tender; drain.

2) Add to skillet; mix well. Pour sauce over the top. Bring to a boil, stirring occasionally. Sprinkle with basil; toss to coat.

Yield: 6 servings.

NUTRITION FACTS: 1 cup equals 622 calories, 38 g fat (17 g saturated fat), 94 mg cholesterol, 1,134 mg sodium, 46 g carbohydrate, 6 g fiber, 26 g protein.

TRADITIONAL LASAGNA

Traditional Lasagna

Lorri Foockle, Granville, Illinois

My family first tasted this rich, classic lasagna at a friend's home on Christmas Eve. We were so impressed that it became our own tradition. It's requested often by my sister's Italian in-laws, which I consider the highest compliment!

1	pound ground beef
3/4	pound bulk pork sausage
3	cans (8 ounces *each*) tomato sauce
2	cans (6 ounces *each*) tomato paste
2	garlic cloves, minced
2	teaspoons sugar
1	teaspoon Italian seasoning
1	teaspoon salt
1/2	teaspoon pepper
3	eggs

3 tablespoons minced fresh parsley

3 cups (24 ounces) small-curd cottage cheese

1 carton (8 ounces) ricotta cheese

1/2 cup grated Parmesan cheese

9 lasagna noodles, cooked and drained

6 slices provolone cheese

3 cups (12 ounces) shredded mozzarella cheese, *divided*

1) In a large skillet, cook beef and sausage over medium heat until no longer pink; drain. Add the tomato sauce, tomato paste, garlic, sugar, seasoning, salt and pepper. Bring to a boil. Reduce heat; simmer, uncovered, for 1 hour, stirring occasionally.

2) In a large bowl, combine the eggs and parsley. Stir in the cottage cheese, ricotta and Parmesan. Spread 1 cup of meat sauce in an ungreased 13-in. x 9-in. x 2-in. baking dish.

3) Layer with three noodles, provolone cheese, 2 cups cottage cheese mixture, 1 cup mozzarella, three noodles, 2 cups meat sauce, remaining cottage cheese mixture and 1 cup mozzarella. Top with the remaining noodles, meat sauce and mozzarella (dish will be full).

4) Cover and bake at 375° for 50 minutes. Uncover; bake 20 minutes longer or until heated through. Let stand for 15 minutes before cutting.

Yield: 12 servings.

NUTRITION FACTS: 1 serving equals 493 calories, 27 g fat (14 g saturated fat), 143 mg cholesterol, 1,144 mg sodium, 29 g carbohydrate, 3 g fiber, 35 g protein.

Crab Lasagna Roll-Ups
Fran Rodgers, Lake Geneva, Wisconsin

A creamy, delicate filling is rolled up into lasagna noodles for a simple and satisfying main dish. Garlic bread is the perfect side!

2 eggs, lightly beaten

2 cups (16 ounces) small-curd cottage cheese

1/4 cup grated Parmesan cheese

2 tablespoons Italian seasoning

2 tablespoons minced fresh parsley

1 teaspoon dried oregano

1/2 teaspoon dried basil

1/2 teaspoon dried thyme

1/4 teaspoon garlic powder

1 package (8 ounces) imitation crabmeat, flaked

12 lasagna noodles, cooked and drained

2 cans (8 ounces *each*) tomato sauce

1) In a large bowl, combine the eggs, cheeses and seasonings. Add crab; mix well. Place about 1/3 cup on each noodle; roll up.

2) Place seam side down in a 13-in. x 9-in. x 2-in. baking dish coated with nonstick cooking spray. Top with tomato sauce. Cover and bake at 350° for 30-40 minutes or until heated through.

Yield: 6 servings.

NUTRITION FACTS: 1 serving equals 361 calories, 7 g fat (3 g saturated fat), 95 mg cholesterol, 909 mg sodium, 50 g carbohydrate, 3 g fiber, 24 g protein.

Italian Stew
Nancy Cox, Martinsville, Indiana

I spice up many autumn evenings with this zippy stew. This tastes even better the next day.

2 pounds turkey Italian sausage links, casings removed

1 cup chopped onion

3/4 cup chopped green pepper

3 garlic cloves, minced

1 can (28 ounces) diced tomatoes, undrained

1 can (15 ounces) Italian-seasoned tomato sauce

1/2 pound fresh mushrooms, sliced

1 cup water

1/2 cup beef broth

1/2 cup red wine *or* additional beef broth

1-1/2 cups cooked spiral pasta

1/2 cup reduced-fat shredded mozzarella cheese

1) In a large nonstick saucepan coated with nonstick cooking spray, cook the first four ingredients until meat is no longer pink; drain.

2) Add the tomatoes, tomato sauce, mushrooms, water, broth and wine or additional broth. Bring to a boil. Reduce heat; cover and simmer for 1 hour. Add pasta; heat through. Top each serving with 1 tablespoon mozzarella cheese.

Yield: 8 servings.

NUTRITION FACTS: 1-1/2 cups equals 300 calories, 12 g fat (4 g saturated fat), 65 mg cholesterol, 1,237 mg sodium, 22 g carbohydrate, 3 g fiber, 25 g protein.

TOMATO PEA COUSCOUS

Tomato Pea Couscous
Sondra Ostheimer, Boscobel, Wisconsin

I modified a recipe I found in a magazine, keeping good nutrition in mind. With a hint of cumin and other mellow flavors, this is a quick-to-fix that's ideal with many entrees.

- 1/2 cup chopped onion
- 2 garlic cloves, minced
- 1 tablespoon olive oil
- 1/2 cup ground cumin
- 1 cup reduced-sodium chicken broth *or* vegetable broth
- 1 cup frozen peas
- 1/2 cup coarsely chopped seeded tomato
- 3/4 cup uncooked couscous

1) In a large saucepan, saute onion and garlic in oil until tender. Stir in cumin; cook and stir for 30 seconds. Stir in the broth, peas and tomato.

2) Cook for 1-2 minutes or until peas are almost tender. Stir in couscous; cover. Remove from the heat; let stand for 5 minutes. Fluff with fork.

Yield: 4 servings.

NUTRITION FACTS: 3/4 cup equals 184 calories, 4 g fat (1 g saturated fat), 0 cholesterol, 182 mg sodium, 31 g carbohydrate, 3 g fiber, 6 g protein.

Garlic Parmesan Orzo
Stephanie Moon, Nampa, Idaho

The buttery pasta dish calls for orzo, which cooks quickly and is a nice change from ordinary pasta shapes. This recipe makes a superb side dish anytime. The garlic and Parmesan cheese really stand out.

- 2 cups uncooked orzo pasta
- 3 teaspoons minced garlic
- 1/2 cup butter, cubed
- 1/2 cup grated Parmesan cheese
- 1/4 cup milk
- 2 tablespoons minced fresh parsley
- 1 teaspoon salt
- 1/4 cup pepper

1) Cook orzo according to package directions; drain. In a large skillet, saute garlic in butter until tender.

2) Add the orzo, Parmesan cheese, milk, parsley, salt and pepper. Cook and stir until heated through.

Yield: 8 servings.

NUTRITION FACTS: 1 cup equals 321 calories, 14 g fat (8 g saturated fat), 36 mg cholesterol, 513 mg sodium, 40 g carbohydrate, 2 g fiber, 9 g protein.

Poppy Seed Noodles
Joan Smith, Ellensburg, Washington

You can pair this with just about any meaty main dish. Poppy seeds can be stored in an airtight container in the refrigerator for up to 6 months.

- 3 cups uncooked egg noodles
- 2 teaspoons butter
- 2 green onions, chopped
- 1 teaspoon poppy seeds
- 1/4 teaspoon garlic salt
- 1/4 teaspoon pepper
- 2/3 cup sour cream

1) Cook noodles according to package directions; drain and return to pan. Add the butter, green onions, poppy seeds, garlic salt and pepper; stir until butter is melted. Stir in sour cream; serve immediately.

Yield: 4 servings.

NUTRITION FACTS: 1 cup equals 194 calories, 6 g fat (4 g saturated fat), 18 mg cholesterol, 124 mg sodium, 26 g carbohydrate, 2 g fiber, 7 g protein.

Potato Gnocchi
Tina Repak, Johnstown, Pennsylvania

This is always a favorite dish at Italian restaurants. But it's actually fun and easy to make your own gnocchi at home.

- 4 medium potatoes, peeled
- 1 egg, lightly beaten
- 3 teaspoons salt, *divided*
- 1-3/4 to 2 cups all-purpose flour
- 3 quarts water

Spaghetti sauce

1) Place potatoes in a saucepan and cover with water; bring to a boil. Reduce heat; cover and

cook for 15-20 minutes or until tender. Drain. Mash potatoes.

2) Place 2 cups mashed potatoes in a bowl (discard or save any remaining mashed potatoes for another use). Stir in egg and 2 teaspoons salt. Gradually beat in flour until blended. (Dough will be firm and elastic.)

3) Turn onto a lightly floured surface; knead 15 times. Roll into 1/2-in.-wide ropes. Cut ropes into 1-in. pieces. Press down with a lightly floured fork or roll pieces over a fork.

4) In a Dutch oven, bring water and remaining salt to a boil. Cook gnocchi in small batches in boiling water for 8-10 minutes or until dumplings float to the top and are cooked through. Remove with a slotted spoon. Serve immediately with spaghetti sauce.

Yield: 6-8 servings.

NUTRITION FACTS:1 serving (calculated without spaghetti sauce) equals 159 calories, 1 g fat (trace saturated fat), 27 mg cholesterol, 674 mg sodium, 33 g carbohydrate, 2 g fiber, 5 g protein.

Homemade Noodles
Helen Heiland, Joliet, Illinois

It's hard to beat homemade noodles in soups or as a side dish with meat and gravy. You can freeze serving-size portions to use as you need them.

> 2 **to 2-1/2 cups all-purpose flour,** *divided*
>
> 1/2 **teaspoon salt**
>
> 3 **eggs, lightly beaten**

1 **tablespoon cold water**
1 **tablespoon vegetable oil**

1) Place 2 cups flour and salt on a pastry surface or in a deep mixing bowl. Make a well in a center of the flour; add eggs and water. Gradually mix with hands or a wooden spoon until well blended.

2) Gather into a ball and knead on a floured surface until smooth, about 10 minutes. If necessary, add remaining flour to keep dough from sticking to surface or hands.

3) Divide the dough into thirds. On a lightly floured surface, roll each section into a paper-thin rectangle. Dust top of dough with flour to prevent sticking while rolling. Trim the edges and flour both sides of dough.

4) Roll dough, jelly-roll style. Using a sharp knife, cut 1/4-in. slices. Unroll noodles and allow to dry on paper towels before cooking.

5) To cook, bring salted water to a rapid boil. Add 1 tablespoon oil to the water; drop noodles into water and cook until tender but not soft.

Yield: 10 servings.

Editor's Note: You may freeze uncooked noodles. Divide uncooked noodles into serving-size portions. Defrost and cook according to directions above.

NUTRITION FACTS: 1/2 cup equals 125 calories, 3 g fat (1 g saturated fat), 64 mg cholesterol, 373 mg sodium, 19 g carbohydrate, 1 g fiber, 4 g protein.

MAKING HOMEMADE NOODLES

1) Place flour and salt in a mixing bowl or on a floured surface. Make a well in the center; add eggs and water.

2) Mix until well blended; gather mixture into a ball. Turn onto a floured surface. Knead for about 10 minutes. Divide into thirds.

3) Roll out each portion of dough into a paper-thin rectangle. Lightly dust both sides with flour; roll up jelly-roll style. Cut into 1/4-in. slices.

4) Unroll noodles on paper towels to dry for at least 1 hour. Proceed with recipe as directed.

Parmesan Noodles

Elizabeth Ewan, Cleveland, Ohio

The special blend of flavors in this quick dish makes it companionable to any meal. It's a nice change of pace from regular pasta-and-cheese dishes.

> 2 packages (3 ounces *each*) cream cheese, softened
> 1/2 cup butter, softened, *divided*
> 2 tablespoons minced fresh parsley
> 1 teaspoon dried basil
> 1/2 teaspoon lemon-pepper seasoning
> 2/3 cup boiling water
> 1 garlic clove, minced
> 6 cups hot cooked thin noodles
> 2/3 cup grated Parmesan cheese, *divided*
>
> Additional parsley, optional

1) In a small bowl, combine the cream cheese, 2 tablespoons butter, parsley, basil and lemon-pepper. Stir in water; keep warm.

2) In a saucepan, saute garlic in remaining butter until golden. Place noodles in a serving bowl; top with garlic mixture. Sprinkle with half of the Parmesan cheese; toss lightly.

3) Spoon cream sauce over noodles and sprinkle with remaining Parmesan. Garnish with parsley if desired.

Yield: 8 servings.

NUTRITION FACTS: 1 cup equals 354 calories, 21 g fat (13 g saturated fat), 59 mg cholesterol, 333 mg sodium, 31 g carbohydrate, 2 g fiber, 10 g protein.

Broccoli Noodle Side Dish

Louise Saluti, Sandwich, Massachusetts

Colorful and satisfying, this side dish cooks up quickly on the stovetop so you can free up the oven for the main course.

> 6 cups (8 ounces) uncooked wide noodles
> 3 to 4 garlic cloves, minced
> 1/4 cup olive oil
> 4 cups broccoli florets (about 1 pound)
> 1/2 pound fresh mushrooms, thinly sliced
> 1/2 teaspoon dried thyme
> 1 teaspoon salt, optional
> 1/4 teaspoon pepper

1) Cook noodles according to package directions. Meanwhile, in skillet, saute garlic in oil until tender. Add broccoli; saute for 4 minutes or until crisp-tender.

2) Add the mushrooms, thyme, salt if desired and pepper; saute for 2-3 minutes. Drain noodles; add to broccoli mixture. Stir gently over low heat until heated through.

Yield: 8 servings.

NUTRITION FACTS: 3/4 cup equals 727 calories, 14 g fat (2 g saturated fat), 162 mg cholesterol, 47 mg sodium, 124 g carbohydrate, 6 g fiber, 26 g protein.

Cheesy Noodle Casserole

Shirley McKee, Varna, Illinois

This rich, cheesy side dish is such an excellent meal extender that I always keep it in mind whenever I feel my menu needs a boost. It's a quick and easy casserole to fix, and you can easily double the recipe to feed a larger crowd.

> 5 cups uncooked egg noodles
> 2 tablespoons butter
> 1 tablespoon all-purpose flour
> 1/4 teaspoon garlic salt
> 1/4 teaspoon onion salt
> 1-1/3 cups milk
> 8 ounces process cheese (Velveeta), cubed
>
> TOPPING:
> 2 tablespoons dry bread crumbs
> 1-1/2 teaspoons butter, melted

1) Cook noodles according to package directions; drain. In a small saucepan, melt butter. Stir in the flour, garlic salt and onion salt until smooth.

2) Gradually stir in milk. Bring to a boil; cook and stir for 2 minutes or until thickened. Reduce heat. Add cheese, stirring until melted. Stir in noodles.

3) Transfer to a greased shallow 1-1/2-qt. baking dish. Toss bread crumbs and butter; sprinkle over top. Bake, uncovered, at 350° for 20-25 minutes or until golden brown.

Yield: 6 servings.

NUTRITION FACTS: 1 serving equals 334 calories, 17 g fat (10 g saturated fat), 74 mg cholesterol, 701 mg sodium, 30 g carbohydrate, 1 g fiber, 14 g protein.

VEGETABLES

Large grocery stores, small markets and home gardens offer abundant varieties of vegetables. This chapter highlights the most commonly available ones. For each vegetable, you'll find information about availability, buying, storing and preparation. The cooking chart lists recommended cooking methods and times. This information is simply a guideline. If you purchase riper vegetables, storage life will be shorter. Cooking times vary depending on the size, freshness and ripeness of the vegetable you are cooking.

To cook a vegetable, simply follow the cooking method and times listed in the Vegetable Cooking Chart beginning on page 305. Then dress them up with a sprinkle of herbs, a dab of butter, a squirt of lemon or a drizzle of balsamic vinegar. For more variety, try the delicious flavor combinations found in the recipes in this chapter.

Veggie Toppers

Steamed, boiled or sauteed vegetables are delicious by themselves but can get a flavor boost or added crunch with these easy toppings:

- Toss with a little butter or spritz with refrigerated, butter-flavored spray and sprinkle with bread crumbs.

- Sprinkle with sauteed almonds or pecans, sesame seeds or sunflower kernels.

- Saute some chopped onion, celery or garlic and stir into the cooked vegetable.

- Sprinkle with Parmesan cheese.

- Add a splash of lemon juice or balsamic vinegar.

- Season stir-fried or sauteed vegetables with a little minced fresh gingerroot, soy sauce, sherry, sesame oil or chopped green onion.

- Toss buttered vegetables with fresh herbs, like dill, basil, oregano, tarragon, marjoram, chives, rosemary or mint.

Handling Produce

Handle vegetables gently—they bruise easily. A bruised spot will lead to decay. After purchasing, promptly refrigerate vegetables that need to be refrigerated. Don't place raw or cooked vegetables on the same surfaces that came in contact with raw meat.

Before preparing, make sure your countertops, cutting boards and utensils are clean. Wash your hands in hot, soapy water. Don't leave cooked or raw vegetables that require refrigeration at room temperature for more than 2 hours.

Rinse vegetables, including pre-packaged vegetables, under cool running water. Do not wash with detergent or bleach.

Some vegetables, like potatoes or carrots, should be gently scrubbed with a vegetable brush if you are going to eat the peel. Always peel vegetables with a wax coating.

Basic Cooking Methods

BLANCHING is used to partially cook vegetables, remove skins or stop enzymatic action before freezing. Partially cooked vegetables may be used for crudites, salad or to shorten cooking time when stir-frying.

How to Blanch
1) In a large saucepan or Dutch oven, bring a large amount of water to a boil. Boil vegetables for time given in Vegetable Cooking Chart or recipe.

2) Drain and immediately place vegetable in ice water. This step quickly stops the cooking process and helps retain the color and texture. Drain and pat dry.

BOILING can be done in 1 to 2 in. of water for vegetables such as broccoli, or it can be completely covered with water for root vegetables such as potatoes. After the water is brought to a boil, the chart will say boil, simmer or cook. When it says boil, there should be large bubbles breaking the surface of the water. For a simmer, the heat needs to be reduced to medium-low or low, and there should be tiny bubbles, frequently around the side of the pan that break the surface of the water. For cook, the heat needs to be reduced to medium, and the water will be between a boil and a simmer.

When cooking vegetables in boiling or simmering water, you can sprinkle a little salt into the cooking water before adding the vegetables if desired. However, if the vegetables are to be served in a sauce containing salt or salty ingredients, omit the salt in the cooking water.

Shallow Boiling
Place 1 to 2 in. of water in a saucepan or skillet and lightly salt if desired. Bring to a boil. Add the vegetables. Cook for the time given in the Vegetable Cooking Chart or recipe or until crisp-tender; drain.

Boiling Covered in Water
Place the vegetables in a saucepan and cover with water. Lightly salt if desired. Bring to a boil. Reduce heat; cover and cook for time given in the Vegetable Cooking Chart or recipe or until crisp-tender; drain.

ROASTING AND BAKING are dry-heat methods of cooking that make the flavor of vegetables richer and sweeter. Root vegetables, corn, onions, garlic, eggplants and many other vegetables can be roasted.

For best results, cut vegetables into uniform sizes so they cook more evenly. If you roast a mixture of vegetables, cut the denser vegetables into smaller pieces so they will be done at the same time as the other vegetables. Roasted vegetables are generally roasted at 400° to 450°. Vegetables are baked at lower temperatures of 350° to 375°. Finally, make sure the roasting pan is not crowded. If it's too small, the vegetables will steam and not become crisp.

How to Roast
Spread vegetables in a shallow-sided roasting pan, making sure that the vegetables are not crowded. Drizzle with oil and sprinkle with herbs or seasoning; toss gently to coat. Roast, uncovered, for the time given in the Vegetable Cooking Chart or recipe or until tender, stirring occasionally.

SAUTEING AND STIR-FRYING both quickly cook uniform pieces of food at high temperatures while stirring or moving the food around. Food cooked by these methods should be golden or browned on the outside and tender and moist on the inside.

When sauteing or stir-frying, cut vegetables into uniform sizes so that they will cook more evenly. Vegetables should be dry before cooking. Heat oil over medium-high heat until hot. If cooking a variety of vegetables, add the longer cooking vegetables first, then add the more delicate or watery vegetables, like mushrooms or zucchini. Finally, make sure the skillet or wok is not crowded. If it's too small, the vegetables will steam and not become crisp.

STEAMING uses the heat generated from the boiling water to cook the vegetables. Since the vegetables are not in the water, more of the nutrients and flavors are preserved.

How to Saute or Stir-Fry

Heat oil over medium-high heat until hot. Add vegetables and cook for time given in the Vegetable Cooking Chart or recipe or until crisp-tender, stirring constantly.

How to Steam

Place the vegetables in a steamer basket. Place in a saucepan over 1 in. of water. The water should not be touching the bottom of the steamer basket. Bring to a boil. Cover and steam for time given in the Vegetable Cooking Chart or recipe or until crisp-tender. The cooking time begins when the water starts to boil.

Vegetable Cooking Chart

VEGETABLE	COOKING METHOD AND TIME (IN MINUTES)				
	BLANCHING	STEAMING	BOILING	SAUTEING/ STIR-FRYING	ROASTING/ BAKING
ARTICHOKES Baby Full-size	5 7	10 to 12 25 to 30 steam upside down	12 30 to 45 cover with water simmer covered		350° 45 to 60 with liquid and covered
ASPARAGUS	2 to 4	3 to 5	3 to 5 1/2 in. water simmer covered	3 to 4	400° 20 to 25 uncovered
BEANS Green or wax Lima	3 1 to 3	8 to 10	3 to 5, pieces 4 to 7, whole 10 to 15 cover with water boil covered	4 to 5	
BEETS			30 to 60, whole 20 to 25, cubed cover with water boil uncovered		350° 30 to 60 covered
BOK CHOY Stalks Leaves		5 to 6 2 to 3	3 to 4 1 to 1-1/2	5	
BROCCOFLOWER Florets	1 to 2	7 to 9	5 to 10 1 in. water simmer covered	5 blanch first	425° 10 to 15
BROCCOLI Florets Spears	3 5	3 to 4 5 to 8	3 to 5 5 to 8 1 in. water cover and boil	5 to 7	
BROCCOLI RABE	5	3 to 4	1 to 2 1/2 in. water boil covered	3 to 5	
BRUSSELS SPROUTS	3 to 5	8 to 10	8 to 10 1/2 in. water simmer covered	10 to 12	

VEGETABLE	COOKING METHOD AND TIME (IN MINUTES)				
	BLANCHING	STEAMING	BOILING	SAUTEING/ STIR-FRYING	ROASTING/ BAKING
CABBAGE, GREEN OR RED Shredded Wedges	1 1-1/2	6 to 8 15	3 to 5 6 to 8 1 in. water simmer covered	7 to 10	
CABBAGE, NAPA				3 to 4	
CARROTS Slices Whole baby	3 5	7 to 10 12 to 15	5 to 8 8 to 15 1 in. water simmer covered		425° 40 to 60 uncovered
CAULIFLOWER Florets	1 to 2	5 to 12	5 to 10 1 in. water simmer covered	5 blanch first	425° 15 to 20
CELERY, SLICED		5 to 7	5 to 7 1/2 in. water simmer covered	2 to 3	325° 30 to 35 with liquid, covered
CORN On the cob Kernels	6 to 9 5 to 6	4 to 5	3 to 5 3 to 4 cover with water cook covered		450° 15 to 20 prepare as for grilling
CUCUMBERS		3 to 5	3 to 5 1/2 in. water or broth simmer covered	2 to 3	
EGGPLANTS Cubed	4	5 to 7	5 to 8 cover with water boil uncovered	6 to 8	400° 30 to 40 for whole, pierce with fork; covered
FENNEL, STRIPS		6 to 8	6 to 10 1 in. water simmer covered		425° 60 wedges, uncovered
GARLIC				1 to 2	425° 30 to 35 wrapped in foil
GREENS Tender (Swiss chard) Coarse (kale)			8 to 10 10 to 20 1/2 in. water cook covered		
KOHLRABI Cubes or strips		6	6 to 8 1 in. water; simmer covered	5	
LEEKS		13 to 15	12 to 15 cover with water boil uncovered	5	
MUSHROOMS Buttons	3 to 5	10 to 12		2 to 5	425° 20 uncovered
OKRA	3 to 5		8 to 10 1 in. water; simmer covered		
ONIONS	3 to 5	10 to 12 pearl onions	8 to 10 1 in. water cook covered	5	400° 45 to 50 whole

VEGETABLE	COOKING METHOD AND TIME (IN MINUTES)				
	BLANCHING	STEAMING	BOILING	SAUTEING/ STIR FRYING	ROASTING/ BAKING
PARSNIPS Cubes	3	8 to 10	15 cover with water boil uncovered		425° 40 to 45 cubes or pieces uncovered
PEAS, SNOW	1 to 2	1 to 2	2 to 3 1 in. water simmer covered	1 to 2	
PEAS, SUGAR SNAP	1 to 2	4	2 1 in. water simmer covered	1 blanch first	
PEAS, SWEET	1 to 2	5 to 8	5 to 8 1 in. water simmer covered		
PEPPERS Hot Sweet	2 2	6 to 7	6 to 7 1 in. water cook covered	3 to 5 3 to 5	see p. 338 see p. 338
POTATOES New, whole Medium, whole Large, whole		20 30 to 45	15 to 20 cover with water cook covered		400° 45 to 50 pierce potato with a fork
POTATOES Cubes Chunks, wedges or quarters			15 20 cover with water cook covered		425° 45 to 50 uncovered
PUMPKIN 2 in. pieces		50	25 to 30 cover with water boil uncovered		375° 60 4 to 5 in. pieces, covered
RUTABAGA Cubes	3	18 to 20	15 to 20 cover with water boil uncovered		
SPINACH	2	3 to 4	3 to 5 1/2 in. water cook covered	3 to 4	
SQUASH Summer	1 to 2	3 to 5	3 to 5 1/2 in. water cook covered	4 to 7	425° 15 to 20 uncovered
SQUASH Winter		15 to 30 quarters or rings	15 to 30 quarters or rings 1 in. water cook covered		350° 45 (1-1/2 to 2 pounds) 2 hours (3 pounds)
SWEET POTATOES Cubes or chunks Whole		20 to 25	10 to 15 15 to 35 cover with water		400° 30 to 60 uncovered
TOMATOES	30 seconds				400° 10 to 15 uncovered
TURNIPS Cubes	3	10 to 12	15 cover with water boil uncovered		

Artichokes

Artichokes, also known as globe artichokes, are fun to eat. The soft, meaty portion of the leaf is removed by drawing the leaf across your teeth. The heart of the artichoke is revealed after the leaves are removed and the choke, the fuzzy inedible portion over the heart, is removed. Baby artichokes have not developed the fuzzy choke and are completely edible after some trimming.

Buying
Artichokes are available year-round; peak season is March through May. Select artichokes that are heavy for their size and have leaves that are tightly closed. Slight brown discoloration may be due to frost and does not affect the quality of the artichoke. Avoid artichokes with spreading leaves and a lot of brown areas.

Storage
Store unwashed artichokes in the refrigerator for up to 4 days.

Yield: 1 medium artichoke (8 to 10 ounces)
= 1 serving

PREPARING ARTICHOKES

1) Rinse artichokes well. Cut off stem at base of artichoke. Cut 1 in. from the top. With scissors, snip the tip end of each leaf. Remove outer leaves. Rub cut ends of leaves with lemon juice to help prevent browning.

2) For quarters, cut each artichoke into quarters and rubs cut sides with lemon juice. With a spoon, remove and discard the center fuzzy choke.

Elegant Artichokes
Pat Stevens, Grandbury, Texas

Lemon not only helps retain the color but also adds wonderful flavor to the artichokes as well as the dipping sauce for this dish.

> 5 medium artichokes
> 2 medium lemons, sliced
> 2 garlic cloves, minced

LEMON-PEPPER DIP:
> 1 cup vegetable oil
> 1/4 cup lemon juice
> 1/4 cup red wine vinegar
> 2 tablespoons spicy brown mustard
> 3 garlic cloves, minced
> 1 teaspoon salt
> 3/4 teaspoon pepper
> 1/2 cup diced green pepper
> 2 tablespoons sliced green onion

1) Cut off stem at base of artichoke. Cut 1 in. from top. With scissors, snip tip end of each leaf. Remove outer leaves. Rub cut ends of leaves with juice.

2) In a Dutch oven or soup kettle, combine the artichokes, lemon slices and garlic; cover with water. Bring to a boil. Reduce heat. Cover; simmer for 30-45 minutes or until tender. Drain; arrange on a serving platter. Refrigerate for 1 hour.

3) For dip, in a bowl, whisk together the oil, juice, vinegar, mustard, garlic, salt and pepper. Stir in green pepper and onion. Serve with artichokes.

Yield: 5 servings (1-3/4 cups dip).

NUTRITION FACTS: 1 artichoke with 1/3 cup dip equals 472 calories, 44 g fat (6 g saturated fat), 0 cholesterol, 667 mg sodium, 20 g carbohydrate, 7 g fiber, 5 g protein.

Asparagus

Asparagus have a slender, light green stalk with a tightly closed bud at the top. White asparagus is grown underground, so it does not produce chlorophyll. Asparagus is most often served cooked as a side dish but can be enjoyed raw on vegetable platters.

Buying

Asparagus is available February through late June; peak season is April through May. Select small straight stalks with tightly closed, compact tips. Spears should be smooth and round. Green asparagus should have bright green stalks, while the tips may have a slight lavender tint. White asparagus should have straight, firm stalks.

Storage

Store unwashed asparagus in a sealed plastic bag in the refrigerator crisper drawer for up to 4 days (2 days for white asparagus). Blanch 1-1/2 to 3 minutes depending on how thick the spears are before freezing. Freeze for up to 1 year.

Yield: 1 pound asparagus = 3-1/2 cups cut

PREPARING ASPARAGUS

Rinse asparagus stalks well in cold water to clean. Snap off the stalk ends as far down as they will easily break when gently bent, or cut off the tough white portion. If stalks are large, use a vegetable peeler to gently peel the tough area of the stalk from the end to just below the tip. If tips are large, scrape off scales with a knife.

Sesame Asparagus
Taste of Home Test Kitchen

A simple addition of garlic and sesame seeds dresses up asparagus for a wonderful taste of spring!

> 1 pound fresh asparagus, cut into 1-1/2-inch pieces
> 1 garlic clove, minced
> 2 tablespoons butter
> 1/2 cup chicken broth
> 1 tablespoon sesame seeds, toasted

1) In a skillet, saute the asparagus and garlic in butter for 2 minutes. Stir in broth; bring to a boil. Reduce heat; cover and simmer for 5-6 minutes or until asparagus is crisp-tender.

2) Remove to a serving dish with a slotted spoon; sprinkle with sesame seeds. Serve immediately.

Yield: 4 servings.

NUTRITION FACTS: 1/2 cup equals 78 calories, 7 g fat (4 g saturated fat), 15 mg cholesterol, 192 mg sodium, 3 g carbohydrate, 1 g fiber, 2 g protein.

Rosemary Asparagus
Mavis Diment, Marcus, Iowa

Rosemary creates a nice alternative to plain asparagus in a simple and flavorful way.

> 1/2 cup chicken broth
> 1 to 2 tablespoons minced fresh rosemary *or* 1 to 2 teaspoons dried rosemary, crushed
> 1 garlic clove, halved
> 1 bay leaf
> 1 pound fresh asparagus, trimmed
> 1/3 cup chopped onion
> 1 tablespoon minced fresh parsley

1) In a large skillet, combine the broth, rosemary, garlic and bay leaf. Add asparagus and onion.

2) Bring to a boil. Reduce heat; cover and simmer for 3-5 minutes or until asparagus is crisp-tender. Discard bay leaf. Garnish with parsley.

Yield: 4 servings.

NUTRITION FACTS: 4 ounces equals 23 calories, trace fat (trace saturated fat), 0 cholesterol, 124 mg sodium, 4 g carbohydrate, 1 g fiber, 2 g protein.

Crunchy Asparagus Medley
Mary Gaylord, Balsam Lake, Wisconsin

Water chestnuts and toasted almonds provide crunch and texture to this refreshing side dish.

> 1-1/2 pounds fresh asparagus, cut into 2-inch pieces
> 1 cup thinly sliced celery
> 2 cans (8 ounces *each*) sliced water chestnuts, drained
> 1/4 cup slivered almonds, toasted
> 2 tablespoons soy sauce
> 2 tablespoons butter

1) In a large saucepan, cook the asparagus and celery in a 1/2 in. of water for 3-5 minutes or until crisp-tender; drain.

2) Stir in the water chestnuts, almonds, soy sauce and butter; heat through.

Yield: 8-10 servings.

NUTRITION FACTS: 1/2 cup equals 70 calories, 4 g fat (2 g saturated fat), 6 mg cholesterol, 225 mg sodium, 8 g carbohydrate, 2 g fiber, 2 g protein.

Beans

Green and wax beans, also know as string beans, and lima beans are members of the legume family. Green and wax beans may be used interchangeably in recipes and are known for their mild flavor and general appeal. The pale-green lima bean is kidney shaped with a starchy texture and a mild, buttery flavor.

Buying

Green and wax beans are available year-round; peak season is from July through October. Select brightly colored, straight, smooth pods that are unblemished. Beans should be crisp and have a firm, velvety feel. Seeds inside the bean should be small.

Fresh lima beans are available from June through September. The Fordhook lima bean variety is larger than the baby lima bean. Select pods that are full, crisp and free of blemishes.

Storage

Store unwashed green and wax beans in a sealed plastic bag or covered container in the refrigerator crisper drawer for up to 3 days.

Store unwashed, unshelled lima beans in the refrigerator crisper drawer for up to 3 days.

Preparation

Snap off the stem end of green or wax bean and the other end if desired. Leave whole or cut into 1-in. pieces.

Shell lima beans just before cooking. Snap off one end and split pod open. Remove beans; discard pod.

Yield: 1 pound green or wax beans = about 4 cups cut
1 pound unshelled lima beans = 2/3 cup beans

Saucy Green Beans
Hazel Holley, Samson, Alabama

A special cooked sauce added to fresh green beans makes this a unique and hearty side dish.

  2 **pounds fresh green beans**
1/3 **cup chopped onion**
1/4 **cup butter**
  3 **tablespoons all-purpose flour**

  1 **tablespoon sugar**
1-1/4 **cups milk**
  1 **cup (8 ounces) sour cream**
  3 **tablespoons minced fresh parsley**
  3 **tablespoons white vinegar**
Salt and pepper to taste
  6 **bacon strips, cooked and crumbled**

1) Place beans in a large saucepan and cover with water; bring to a boil. Cook, uncovered, for 8-10 minutes or until crisp-tender.

2) Meanwhile, in another saucepan, saute onion in butter. Stir in flour and sugar until blended; gradually add milk. Bring to a boil; cook and stir for 2 minutes or until thickened. Reduce heat to low; stir in the sour cream, parsley and vinegar until blended (do not boil).

3) Drain beans; place in a serving bowl. Season with salt and pepper. Top with sauce and bacon.

Yield: 10-12 servings.

NUTRITION FACTS: 3/4 cup (calculated without salt and pepper) equals 141 calories, 10 g fat (6 g saturated fat), 30 mg cholesterol, 116 mg sodium, 10 g carbohydrate, 2 g fiber, 4 g protein.

Pepper Parmesan Beans
Marian Platt, Sequim, Washington

Peppers and beans get the Italian treatment with basil and Parmesan cheese in this dish.

  1 **large sweet red pepper, diced**
  1 **small green pepper, diced**
1/4 **cup chopped onion**
  1 **garlic clove, minced**
1/4 **cup olive oil**
1-1/2 **pounds fresh green beans, cut into 2-inch pieces**
  1 **tablespoon minced fresh basil** *or* **1 teaspoon dried basil**
  1 **teaspoon salt**
1/3 **to 1/2 cup shredded Parmesan cheese**

1) In a large skillet, saute peppers, onion and garlic in oil until vegetables are tender, about 3 minutes. Add beans, basil and salt; toss to coat. Cover and cook over medium-low heat for 7-8 minutes or until beans are crisp-tender. Stir in cheese; serve immediately.

Yield: 8 servings.

NUTRITION FACTS: 3/4 cup equals 107 calories, 8 g fat (2 g saturated fat), 2 mg cholesterol, 357 mg sodium, 8 g carbohydrate, 3 g fiber, 3 g protein.

ROASTED GREEN BEANS

Roasted Green Beans
LaVonne Hegland, St. Michael, Minnesota

Red wine vinegar really perks up everyday green beans in this simply seasoned side dish. Add a sprinkling of salt and pepper to suit your family's taste.

- 3/4 **pound fresh green beans**
- 1 **small onion, thinly sliced and separated into rings**
- 2 **garlic cloves, thinly sliced**
- 1 **tablespoon red wine vinegar**
- 2 **teaspoons olive oil**

1) Place beans in a saucepan and cover with water; bring to a boil. Cook, uncovered, for 8-10 minutes or until crisp-tender. Drain.

2) Place beans in a greased 11-in. x 7-in. x 2-in. baking dish. Top with onion and garlic. Drizzle with vinegar and oil; toss to coat.

3) Bake, uncovered, at 450° for 10 minutes. Stir; bake 5 minutes longer.

Yield: 4 servings.

NUTRITION FACTS: 1 cup equals 53 calories, 2 g fat (trace saturated fat), 0 cholesterol, 5 mg sodium, 8 g carbohydrate, 3 g fiber, 2 g protein.

Garlic Green and Wax Beans
Marilou Robinson, Portland, Oregon

Even non-garlic lovers like this fresh-tasting salad.

- 1-1/2 **pounds fresh green beans**
- 1-1/2 **pounds fresh wax beans**
- 7 **garlic cloves, minced, *divided***
- 1/4 **cup reduced-fat sour cream**
- 1/4 **cup fat-free milk**
- 1 **teaspoon white wine vinegar**
- 1 **teaspoon olive oil**
- 1/2 **teaspoon salt**
- 1/8 **teaspoon pepper**
- 1 **cup shredded part-skim mozzarella cheese**

  Minced fresh parsley

1) Place beans and 6 garlic cloves in a steamer basket. Place in a large saucepan over 1 in. of water; bring to a boil. Cover and steam for 8-10 minutes or until beans are crisp-tender. Transfer to a large bowl; set aside.

2) In a small bowl, combine the sour cream, milk and vinegar; let stand for 1 minute. Whisk in the oil, salt, pepper and remaining garlic.

3) Pour over beans and toss. Cover and refrigerate for at least 2 hours. Just before serving, sprinkle with cheese and parsley.

Yield: 12 servings.

NUTRITION FACTS: 3/4 cup equals 76 calories, 2 g fat (1 g saturated fat), 7 mg cholesterol, 157 mg sodium, 9 g carbohydrate, 4 g fiber, 5 g protein.

Savory Lemon Limas
Cathy Attig, Jacobus, Pennsylvania

Lima beans get a lemony lift with this treatment. If you are a lima bean lover like I am, this recipe just makes them even more delicious. If you simply tolerate the beans, like my husband does, you still might find these quite tasty.

- 1/2 **cup water**
- 1 **package (10 ounces) frozen lima beans**
- 1 **tablespoon butter, melted**
- 1 **tablespoon lemon juice**
- 1 **teaspoon sugar**
- 1/2 **to 3/4 teaspoon ground mustard**
- 1/4 **teaspoon salt**

1) In a small saucepan, bring water to a boil. Add lima beans; return to a boil. Reduce heat; cover and simmer for 8-10 minutes or until tender. Drain.

2) Combine the butter, lemon juice, sugar, mustard and salt; pour over beans and toss to coat.

Yield: 4 servings.

NUTRITION FACTS: 1/3 cup equals 107 calories, 3 g fat (2 g saturated fat), 8 mg cholesterol, 197 mg sodium, 15 g carbohydrate, 3 g fiber, 5 g protein.

Beets

Beets are a very deep-red, bulb-shaped root vegetable with edible dark green leaves. Beets and their greens are hearty in flavor. Beet greens can be served raw in salads or cooked. Beets are always cooked before serving and can be enjoyed whole, sliced, shredded or diced.

Buying

Beets are available June through October; peak season is June through August. Select firm, deep red, round beets with unwilted green tops. The skin should be smooth, unblemished and unbroken. Small and medium-sized beets are usually the most tender (maximum size should be about 2 in.). Beet greens should have a reddish tint.

Storage

Remove greens 2 in. from beets. If you plan on using the greens, store separately in a sealed plastic bag in the refrigerator for up to 3 days. Store uncooked beets in an open plastic bag in the refrigerator crisper drawer for about 2 weeks. Freeze cooked beets for up to 1 year.

Preparation

Wash beets gently. If you haven't already done so, remove greens. Do not peel or trim beets to help them maintain their flavor and color after cooking. If you cook beets in hard water, their brilliant color fades. To prevent this, try adding a small amount of vinegar to the cooking water.

The beet color bleeds when they are cut. To protect your hands, wear plastic gloves when peeling and cutting them.

Yield: 1 pound beets = 2-1/2 cups cooked sliced or cubed

Roasted Beet Wedges

Wendy Stenman, Germantown, Wisconsin

This recipe makes ordinary beets taste delicious. They come out sweet and tender.

- 1 **pound medium fresh beets, peeled**
- 4 **teaspoons olive oil**

- 1/2 **teaspoon kosher salt**
- 3 **to 5 fresh rosemary sprigs**

1) Cut each beet into six wedges; place in a large resealable plastic bag. Add olive oil and salt; seal and shake to coat.

2) Place a piece of heavy-duty foil (about 12 in. long) in a 15-in. x 10-in. x 1-in. baking pan. Arrange beets on foil and top with rosemary. Fold foil around beet mixture and seal tightly.

3) Bake at 400° for 1-1/4 to 1-1/2 hours or until beets are tender. Discard rosemary sprigs.

Yield: 4 servings.

NUTRITION FACTS: 3 wedges equals 61 calories, 3 g fat (trace saturated fat), 0 cholesterol, 215 mg sodium, 8 g carbohydrate, 2 g fiber, 1 g protein.

BEETS IN ORANGE SAUCE

Beets in Orange Sauce

Taste of Home Test Kitchen

To ensure your family eats their veggies, our home economists suggest you top beets with an irresistible orange glaze.

- 8 **whole fresh beets**
- 1/4 **cup sugar**
- 2 **teaspoons cornstarch**
- Dash **pepper**
- 1 **cup orange juice**
- 1 **medium navel orange, sliced and halved, optional**
- 1/2 **teaspoon grated orange peel**

1) Place beets in a large saucepan; cover with water. Bring to a boil. Reduce heat; cover and cook for 25-30 minutes or until tender.

2) Drain and cool slightly. Peel and slice; place in a serving bowl and keep warm.

3) In a saucepan, combine the sugar, cornstarch and pepper; stir in orange juice until smooth. Bring to a boil; cook and stir for 2 minutes or until thickened.

4) Remove from the heat; stir in orange slices if desired and peel. Pour over beets.

Yield: 8 servings.

Editor's Note: A 15-ounce can of sliced beets may be substituted for the fresh beets. Drain the canned beets and omit the first step of the recipe.

NUTRITION FACTS: 1 cup equals 63 calories, trace fat (trace saturated fat), 0 cholesterol, 39 mg sodium, 15 g carbohydrate, 1 g fiber, 1 g protein.

Bok Choy

Bok choy is a cruciferous vegetable and is also known as Chinese white cabbage. Bok choy, with its large white stalks and large green leaves, more closely resembles a head of celery rather than a head of green cabbage. The mild-flavored white stalks are crunchy and juicy, while the leaves are tender and require less cooking time.

Buying
Bok choy is available year-round. Select heads with firm white stalks and crisp leaves. Avoid heads with brown spots on stalks.

Storage
Store unwashed bok choy in the crisper drawer in the refrigerator for up 4 days.

Preparation
Wash before using, not before storing. Cut leaves from stalks. Slice, chop or shred stalks. The leaves can be sliced or chopped. Bok choy may be used raw in salads or cooked in stir-fries or soups. Always start by cooking the crunchy stalk first, then add the tender leaves during the last few minutes of cooking.

Yield: 1 medium head (about 11 ounces)
= 5-1/2 to 7 cups shredded or sliced

Broccoflower

Broccoflower is a cross between broccoli and cauliflower. It looks like a yellow-green cauliflower and has a milder flavor.

Buying
Broccoflower is available year-round; peak season is October through February. Select firm, solid heads that are heavy for their size. Avoid those with brown spots.

Storage
Place unwashed broccoflower in an open plastic bag in the refrigerator crisper drawer for up to 4 days.

Preparation
Trim off leaves. Cut into florets or leave whole.

Yield: 1 head (1-1/4 pounds) = 4 cups florets

Broccoli Rabe

Broccoli rabe, also known as rabe and rapini, is green with small bud clusters and resembles broccoli. It has a bitter taste that mellows during cooking.

Buying
Broccoli rabe is available year-round; peak season is fall through spring. Select bunches with crisp, bright green leaves. Avoid ones that have wilted leaves, leaves with holes or yellowed flower buds. Smaller leaves are more tender with a milder flavor.

Storage
Store unwashed broccoli rabe in an open plastic bag in the refrigerator crisper drawer for up to 3 days.

Preparation
Trim about 1/4-in. off the bottom of the stems. Discard any coarse outer leaves. Rinse in cold water. Cut stems into pieces.

Yield: 1 bunch (8 ounces) = 4 cups loosely packed

Broccoli/ Broccolini

Broccoli is a member of the cauliflower family. It has pale green, thick stalks and tightly packed, dark green heads (florets) with a slight purple tint. Stalks and florets are eaten raw or cooked.

Broccolini, also known as baby broccoli, is a cross between broccoli and Chinese kale. It has slim, individual, asparagus-like stalks with broccoli-like florets. The entire stalk is edible and does not need to be peeled. Broccolini has a sweet, mild flavor with a peppery bite. It is less fibrous than broccoli or asparagus.

Buying

Broccoli is available year-round. Select firm but tender stalks of broccoli with compact, dark green or slightly purplish florets. Select firm stalks of broccolini with compact, dark green florets.

Storage

Store unwashed broccoli or broccolini in an open plastic bag in the refrigerator crisper drawer up to 4 days. Blanch 3-4 minutes before freezing. Freeze for up to 1 year.

Preparation

For broccoli, remove larger leaves and tough ends of lower stalks. Wash broccoli. If using whole spears, cut lengthwise into 1-in.-wide pieces; stalks may also be peeled for more even cooking. If using florets, cut 1/4 in. to 1/2 in. below heads; discard stalks. For broccolini, wash and use entire stalk.

Yield: 1 pound broccoli = 3-1/2 cups florets
1 bunch (6 ounces) broccolini = 4 cups loosely packed or about 12 spears

Broccoli with Ginger-Orange Butter
Taste of Home Test Kitchen

Instead of simply topping steamed broccoli with plain butter, our home economists suggest you try serving it with an easy-to-prepare flavored butter. This is also a tasty topping for sugar snap peas, green beans and carrots.

1   pound fresh broccoli, cut into spears
2   tablespoons orange marmalade
1   tablespoon butter
1/2   teaspoon cider vinegar
1/8   teaspoon ground ginger

1) In a large saucepan, bring 1 in. of water and broccoli to a boil. Reduce heat; cover and simmer for 5-8 minutes or until crisp-tender.

2) Meanwhile, in a small saucepan, combine the marmalade, butter, vinegar and ginger. Cook until marmalade and butter are melted. Drain broccoli; drizzle with butter mixture.

Yield: 6 servings.

NUTRITION FACTS: 1 serving equals 54 calories, 2 g fat (1 g saturated fat), 5 mg cholesterol, 43 mg sodium, 8 g carbohydrate, 2 g fiber, 2 g protein.

Sunflower Broccoli
Jean Artus, Aurora, Colorado

The nutty flavor and crunchy texture of sunflower kernels is a great match for crisp-tender broccoli in this special, no-fuss dish.

2   garlic cloves, minced
3   tablespoons canola oil
2-1/2 pounds fresh broccoli, cut into florets (about 10 cups)
1/4   cup chicken broth
1/2   teaspoon dried oregano
1/2   teaspoon salt
1/8   teaspoon pepper
2   tablespoons sunflower kernels

1) In a large skillet, saute garlic in oil for 1 minute. Add broccoli; cook and stir for 3 minutes.

2) Add the broth, oregano, salt and pepper; cover and cook for 4 minutes or until broccoli is crisp-tender. Sprinkle with sunflower kernels.

Yield: 10 servings.

NUTRITION FACTS: 3/4 cup equals 80 calories, 6 g fat (trace saturated fat), 0 cholesterol, 174 mg sodium, 7 g carbohydrate, 3 g fiber, 4 g protein.

STEAMED LEMON BROCCOLI

Steamed Lemon Broccoli
Michelle Hanson, Oacoma, South Dakota

I first tried this sunny side dish because it seemed to be a fresh, nutritious and easy combination. Now it's the only way my husband will eat broccoli. I love to pair it with grilled meat on hot summer days.

> 1 large bunch broccoli, cut into spears
> 1 medium onion, halved and thinly sliced
> 1 cup thinly sliced celery
> 3 garlic cloves, minced
> 3 tablespoons butter
> 2 teaspoons grated lemon peel
> 1-1/2 teaspoons lemon juice
> 1/2 teaspoon salt
> 1/4 teaspoon pepper

1) Place broccoli in a steamer basket. Place in a large saucepan over 1 in. of water; bring to a boil. Cover and steam for 5-6 minutes or until crisp-tender. Rinse in cold water; drain and set aside.

2) In a large skillet, saute the onion, celery and garlic in butter for 5 minutes or until vegetables are tender. Add the lemon peel and juice, salt, pepper and broccoli; heat through.

Yield: 4 servings.

NUTRITION FACTS: 3/4 cup equals 142 calories, 9 g fat (5 g saturated fat), 23 mg cholesterol, 451 mg sodium, 14 g carbohydrate, 6 g fiber, 6 g protein.

Lemon-Pepper Veggies
Linda Bernhagen, Plainfield, Illinois

This is a great accompaniment to chicken, and it's a breeze to make in the microwave.

> 2 cups fresh broccoli florets
> 2 cups cauliflowerets
> 1 cup sliced carrots
> 2 tablespoons water
> 4-1/2 teaspoons butter, melted
> 1 teaspoon lemon-pepper seasoning
> 1/2 teaspoon garlic powder

1) In a microwave-safe bowl, combine the broccoli, cauliflower, carrots and water. Cover and microwave on high for 3-6 minutes or until crisp-tender; drain.

2) Combine the remaining ingredients; drizzle over vegetables and toss to coat.

Yield: 4 servings.

NUTRITION FACTS: 3/4 cup equals 75 calories, 5 g fat (3 g saturated fat), 11 mg cholesterol, 194 mg sodium, 8 g carbohydrate, 3 g fiber, 2 g protein.

Broccoli Corn Casserole
Lucille Wermes, Camp, Arkansas

I had a difficult time getting my three sons to eat vegetables when they were young. So I fooled them with this casserole that looks just like stuffing when it comes out of the oven. Now that they're grown, they still ask for "broccoli stuffing" when they come to dinner.

> 1 package (10 ounces) frozen chopped broccoli, thawed
> 1 can (14-3/4 ounces) cream-style corn
> 1 egg
> 1-1/2 cups stuffing mix
> 1/2 cup butter, melted

1) In a large bowl, combine the broccoli, corn and egg. Transfer to a greased 1-qt. baking dish. Sprinkle with stuffing mix and drizzle with butter.

2) Bake, uncovered, at 350° for 30-35 minutes or until golden brown and bubbly.

Yield: 6 servings.

NUTRITION FACTS: 1/2 cup equals 269 calories, 18 g fat (10 g saturated fat), 76 mg cholesterol, 605 mg sodium, 25 g carbohydrate, 3 g fiber, 5 g protein.

Brussels Sprouts

A member of the cabbage family, this tiny green vegetable averages 1 in. diameter. The name originates from Brussels, Belgium where brussels sprouts were first grown centuries ago.

Buying

Brussels sprouts are available September through May; peak season is October through February. Select small, firm, tightly closed heads that have a bright green color.

Storage

Store unwashed brussels sprouts in an open plastic bag in the refrigerator crisper drawer for up to 3 days. Blanch 3-5 minutes before freezing. Freeze for up to 1 year.

Yield: 1 pound brussels sprouts = 22 to 28 medium sprouts or 4 cups trimmed

PREPARING BRUSSELS SPROUTS

Remove any loose or yellowed outer leaves; trim stem end. Rinse sprouts. When cooking brussels sprouts whole, cut an X in the core end with a sharp knife.

Lemon-Dilled Brussels Sprouts

Marlyn Duff, New Berlin, Wisconsin

Brussels sprouts get dressed up when lemon and dill season the buttery sauce and chopped walnuts add just the right crunch.

- 1-1/2 **pounds fresh brussels sprouts**
- 1/3 **cup butter**
- 2 **tablespoons lemon juice**
- 1 **teaspoon dill weed**
- 1/2 **teaspoon salt**
- 1/8 **teaspoon pepper**
- 2 **tablespoons finely chopped walnuts**

1) Trim brussels sprouts and cut an X in the core end of each. In a large saucepan, bring 1 in. of water and brussels sprouts to a boil. Reduce heat; cover and simmer for 10-12 minutes or until tender.

2) Meanwhile, in another saucepan, melt butter. Stir in the lemon juice, dill, salt and pepper; cook and stir for 1 minute. Drain sprouts; add to butter mixture and toss to coat. Sprinkle with walnuts.

Yield: 6-8 servings.

NUTRITION FACTS: 3/4 cup equals 117 calories, 9 g fat (5 g saturated fat), 20 mg cholesterol, 246 mg sodium, 8 g carbohydrate, 3 g fiber, 3 g protein.

BRAISED BRUSSELS SPROUTS

Braised Brussels Sprouts

Yvonne Anderson, Philadelphia, Ohio

Cutting the core of the brussels sprouts helps heat reach the center to cook it more quickly and evenly. Bacon and caraway seeds add just the right touch.

- 2 **pounds fresh brussels sprouts**
- 2 **bacon strips, diced**
- 1 **medium onion, chopped**
- 1 **cup chicken broth**
- 1 **teaspoon caraway seeds**
- 1/4 **teaspoon salt**
- 1/8 **teaspoon pepper**

1) Trim brussels sprouts and cut an X in the core of each. In a large saucepan, bring 1 in. of water and brussels sprouts to a boil. Reduce heat; cover and cook for 8-10 minutes or until crisp-tender.

2) Meanwhile, in a large skillet, cook bacon over medium heat until crisp. Using a slotted spoon, remove to paper towels to drain, reserving drippings.

3) In same skillet, saute onion in the drippings until tender. Stir in the broth, caraway seeds, salt and pepper. Bring to a boil. Reduce heat; simmer, uncovered, until liquid is almost evaporated.

4) Drain sprouts. Add sprouts and bacon to onion mixture; toss to coat.

Yield: 8 servings.

NUTRITION FACTS: 1 cup equals 91 calories, 4 g fat (1 g saturated fat), 4 mg cholesterol, 260 mg sodium, 12 g carbohydrate, 5 g fiber, 5 g protein.

Cabbage, Green or Red

Cabbage is a fleshy-leafed member of the mustard family that ranges in color from white to green to deep reddish-purple. Heads are dense and heavy. Serve raw in salads or use cooked in entrees and side dishes. Cabbage is often shredded for slaw and sliced or cut into wedges for cooking.

Buying

Cabbage is available year-round. For green cabbage, select round, compact, solid heads that are heavy for their size. Cabbage heads will vary in size, but the leaves should be tight, smooth and unblemished. Red cabbage heads are not as compact as green cabbage heads. The color should be a reddish-purple.

Storage

Store unwashed cabbage in a sealed plastic bag in the refrigerator crisper drawer for up to 2 weeks.

Preparation

Wash head. Trim center core to within 1/4 in. of leaves; remove any discolored, damaged or tough outer leaves from head. When cooking red cabbage, add a little lemon juice or vinegar to the water to help retain the red color.

Yield: 1 medium head cabbage (2-1/2 pounds) = 8 cups

REMOVING CORE FROM CABBAGE

Cut cabbage in half or quarters. Make a V-shaped cut around core and remove.

Au Gratin Cabbage
Katherine Stallwood, Kennewick, Washington

With my Russian heritage, I've always loved cabbage. My husband does when I make it this way!

2	cups shredded cabbage
1/2	cup grated carrot
1/4	cup chopped green onions
1	egg
1/2	cup milk
3	tablespoons shredded Swiss cheese
1/4	teaspoon seasoned salt
1	tablespoon minced fresh parsley
1	tablespoon shredded Parmesan cheese

1) In a large skillet coated with nonstick cooking spray, saute the cabbage, carrot and onions for 5-7 minutes or until crisp-tender. Transfer to a greased, shallow 1-qt. baking dish.

2) In a bowl, combine the egg, milk, Swiss cheese and seasoned salt. Pour over the vegetables. Sprinkle with parsley and Parmesan cheese.

3) Bake, uncovered, at 350° for 30-35 minutes or until a knife inserted near the center comes out clean.

Yield: 2 servings.

NUTRITION FACTS: 3/4 cup equals 156 calories, 8 g fat (4 g saturated fat), 126 mg cholesterol, 345 mg sodium, 11 g carbohydrate, 3 g fiber, 10 g protein.

Creamy Cabbage
Alice Lewis, Los Osos, California

This recipe, which was handed down to me from my grandmother, makes a good side dish for any meal. It's a simple way to spruce up cabbage and is happily received at potluck suppers.

4	cups shredded cabbage
4	bacon strips
1	tablespoon all-purpose flour
1/2	teaspoon salt
1/4	teaspoon paprika
1/8	teaspoon pepper
1	cup milk
1	cup soft bread crumbs

1) In a large saucepan, bring 1 in. of water and cabbage to a boil. Reduce heat; cover and simmer for 3-5 minutes or until crisp-tender; drain.

2) In a skillet, cook bacon over medium heat until crisp. Remove to paper towels; drain, reserving 1 tablespoon drippings. Stir the flour, salt, paprika and pepper into the drippings until smooth; gradually add milk. Bring to a boil; cook and stir for 1-2 minutes or until thickened.

3) Place cabbage in an ungreased 1-qt. baking dish. Top with sauce. Sprinkle bread crumbs and bacon over the top. Bake at 400° for 15 minutes or until heated through.

Yield: 4 servings.

NUTRITION FACTS: 1 serving equals 160 calories, 9 g fat (4 g saturated fat), 17 mg cholesterol, 518 mg sodium, 14 g carbohydrate, 2 g fiber, 6 g protein.

Fried Cabbage

Bernice Morris, Marshfield, Missouri

Fried cabbage is so good with potatoes, deviled eggs and corn bread, and blackberry cobbler for dessert. We grew our own cabbage and potatoes, and it was always fun to put them to use in the kitchen.

- 2 tablespoons butter
- 1 teaspoon sugar
- 1/2 teaspoon salt
- 1/4 teaspoon crushed red pepper flakes
- 1/8 teaspoon pepper
- 6 cups coarsely chopped cabbage
- 1 tablespoon water

1) In a large skillet, melt butter over medium heat. Stir in the sugar, salt, pepper flakes and pepper.

2) Add the cabbage and water. Cook for 5-6 minutes or until tender, stirring occasionally.

Yield: 6 servings.

NUTRITION FACTS: 1 cup equals 59 calories, 4 g fat (2 g saturated fat), 10 mg cholesterol, 251 mg sodium, 6 g carbohydrate, 2 g fiber, 1 g protein.

Red Cabbage with Apples

Peg Schendel, Janesville, Minnesota

Cabbage and apples are simmered together in this wonderful side dish. Bacon adds color and crunch for a perfect topper.

- 1 medium onion, chopped
- 1/4 cup butter
- 1 medium head red cabbage (2 pounds), shredded
- 2 medium tart apples, peeled and chopped
- 1 cup apple cider *or* apple juice
- 1/4 cup packed brown sugar
- 2 tablespoons cider vinegar
- 1/2 teaspoon salt
- 1/4 teaspoon pepper
- 2 bacon strips, cooked and crumbled

Minced fresh parsley, optional

1) In a large skillet, saute onion in butter until golden and tender. Add the cabbage, apples, cider, sugar, vinegar, salt and pepper. Bring to a boil.

2) Reduce heat; cover and simmer for about 1 hour or until cabbage and apples are tender and the

liquid is reduced. Sprinkle with bacon and parsley if desired.

Yield: 6 servings.

NUTRITION FACTS: 3/4 cup equals 203 calories, 9 g fat (5 g saturated fat), 22 mg cholesterol, 331 mg sodium, 31 g carbohydrate, 4 g fiber, 3 g protein.

Ruby Red Cabbage

Keri Schofield Lawson, Fullerton, California

Dried cranberries and red cabbage are a surprising sweet combination for a side dish your family and friends are sure to rave about.

- 1 cup dried cranberries
- 1 tablespoon butter
- 1 large head red cabbage (about 3 pounds), thinly sliced
- 1/4 cup red wine vinegar
- 1/4 cup apple juice
- 1/4 cup plum *or* currant jelly
- 2 tablespoons brown sugar
- 1/2 teaspoon salt
- 1/2 teaspoon pepper

1) In a Dutch oven or large saucepan, cook cranberries in butter until softened, about 3 minutes. Add the remaining ingredients. Cover and cook over medium-low heat until cabbage is wilted, about 5-7 minutes.

2) Transfer to a greased 2-qt. baking dish. Cover and bake at 350° for 1 hour or until tender. Serve with a slotted spoon.

Yield: 8-10 servings.

NUTRITION FACTS: 1 serving equals 118 calories, 1 g fat (1 g saturated fat), 3 mg cholesterol, 146 mg sodium, 27 g carbohydrate, 3 g fiber, 2 g protein.

Cabbage, Napa

Napa cabbage, also known as Chinese cabbage, has a mild flavor and crinkly pale green to white thin leaves. Two common varieties of Chinese cabbage are sold in the stores. One is more cylindrical (Michihli) and the other is rounder (napa), but they can be used interchangeably in recipes.

Buying

Napa cabbage is available year-round. Select heads that are compact with crisp, fresh-looking leaves.

Storage

Store unwashed napa cabbage in an open plastic bag in the refrigerator crisper drawer for up to 3 days. Store away from fruits such as apples or bananas.

Preparation

Napa cabbage can be used raw or cooked. Remove outer leaves or any wilted leaves. Rinse in cold water. Cut according to recipe directions.

Yield: 1 head (3 pounds) = 12 cups chopped

Carrots

Carrots are a long, slender root vegetable related to the parsnip and have a distinctive orange color. Smaller varieties, called baby carrots, are also available.

Buying

Carrots are available year-round. Select crisp, firm, smooth, well-shaped carrots with deep orange color. Smaller carrots are tender and sweet. Carrots sold in bunches with fern-like green tops are fresher than those sold in plastic bags but are not always available.

Storage

Trim tops and roots when present. Store unwashed, unpeeled carrots in a sealed plastic bag in the refrigerator crisper drawer for 1 to 2 weeks. Blanch 3-5 minutes before freezing. Freeze for up to 1 year.

Preparation

Young carrots may be used unpeeled if they are well scrubbed. Larger carrots should be thinly peeled with a vegetable peeler.

Yield: 1 pound carrots (6 to 7 medium)
= 3 to 3-1/2 cups sliced (uncooked)
2 medium carrots = 1 cup sliced or shredded

HARVEST CARROTS

Harvest Carrots

Marty Rummel, Trout Lake, Washington

I make this often, and sometimes I add cooked turkey or chicken and turn it into a main dish.

4	cups sliced carrots
2	cups water
1	medium onion, chopped
1/2	cup butter, *divided*
1	can (10-3/4 ounces) condensed cream of celery soup, undiluted
1/2	cup shredded cheddar cheese
1/8	teaspoon pepper
3	cups seasoned stuffing croutons

1) In a large saucepan, bring carrots and water to a boil. Reduce heat; cover and simmer for 5-8 minutes or until tender. Drain. In a small skillet, saute onion in 3 tablespoons butter until tender.

2) In a large bowl, combine the carrots, onion, soup, cheese and pepper. Melt remaining butter; toss with stuffing. Fold into carrot mixture.

3) Transfer to a greased 2-qt. baking dish. Cover and bake at 350° for 20 minutes. Uncover; bake 10 minutes longer or until lightly browned.

Yield: 6 servings.

NUTRITION FACTS: 3/4 cup equals 342 calories, 21 g fat (12 g saturated fat), 53 mg cholesterol, 962 mg sodium, 34 g carbohydrate, 5 g fiber, 7 g protein.

Creamed Carrots

Eva Bailey, Olive Hill, Kentucky

These carrots are always a popular dish at my table. The rich sauce coats the carrots nicely and really perks up their flavor.

- 1   pound carrots, sliced
- 1   tablespoon butter
- 1   tablespoon all-purpose flour
- 2   tablespoons finely chopped onion
- 2   teaspoons minced fresh basil *or* 1/2 teaspoon dried basil
- 1/2 teaspoon seasoned salt
- 1/8 teaspoon pepper
- 1   cup evaporated milk

1) In a large saucepan, bring 1 in. of water and carrots to a boil. Reduce heat; cover and simmer for 7-9 minutes or until crisp-tender.

2) Meanwhile, in another saucepan, melt butter. Stir in the flour, onion, basil, seasoned salt and pepper until blended; gradually stir in milk. Bring to a boil; cook and stir for 2 minutes or until thickened. Drain carrots and transfer to a serving bowl. Add sauce and stir to coat.

Yield: 4 servings.

NUTRITION FACTS: 3/4 cup equals 163 calories, 7 g fat (5 g saturated fat), 28 mg cholesterol, 319 mg sodium, 19 g carbohydrate, 4 g fiber, 5 g protein.

Maple-Glazed Carrots

Edie DeSpain, Logan, Utah

Carrots are my favorite vegetable, so I'm always searching for different ways to prepare them. This festive dish is quick to make and nicely complements turkey or chicken.

- 12 medium carrots, peeled and julienned
- 2   tablespoons cornstarch
- 2/3 cup orange juice
- 5   tablespoons maple syrup
- 5   tablespoons butter, melted
- 1   tablespoon grated orange peel
- 3/4 teaspoon ground nutmeg
- 1/2 teaspoon salt

1) In a large saucepan, bring 1 in. of water and carrots to a boil. Reduce heat; cover and simmer for 3-5 minutes or until crisp-tender.

2) Meanwhile, in another saucepan, combine the cornstarch and orange juice until smooth. Stir in the remaining ingredients. Bring to a boil; cook and stir for 2 minutes or until thickened.

3) Drain carrots; transfer to a serving bowl. Pour glaze over carrots; gently stir to coat.

Yield: 6 servings.

Editor's Note: Two 10-ounce packages of shredded carrots can be substituted for julienned carrots.

NUTRITION FACTS: 1 cup equals 205 calories, 10 g fat (6 g saturated fat), 26 mg cholesterol, 338 mg sodium, 29 g carbohydrate, 4 g fiber, 2 g protein.

PINEAPPLE-GLAZED CARROTS

Pineapple-Glazed Carrots

Leonora Wilkie, Bellbrook, Ohio

This tangy side dish is a snap to stir up and has a unique honey-pineapple coating. The rapid recipe is an ideal accompaniment to most any entree. Even kids like these carrots!

- 3   cups baby carrots *or* medium carrot, quartered
- 1/2 cup pineapple spreadable fruit
- 2   teaspoons honey
- 2   tablespoons butter

1) Place carrots and a small amount of water in a saucepan. Bring to a boil. Reduce heat; cover and simmer for 10-15 minutes or until crisp-tender.

2) Meanwhile, in another saucepan, bring the fruit, honey and butter to a boil. Drain carrots and transfer to a serving dish. Drizzle honey mixture over carrots; toss to coat.

Yield: 4 servings.

NUTRITION FACTS: 3/4 cup equals 181 calories, 6 g fat (4 g saturated fat), 15 mg cholesterol, 148 mg sodium, 32 g carbohydrate, 2 g fiber, 1 g protein.

Confetti Carrot Fritters

Peggy Camp, Twain, California

Crispy, sweet and savory, these delicate fritters are a fun twist on the traditional fruit-filled variety. They're yummy served with a mustard dipping sauce, but our kids enjoy them with a drizzle of warm maple syrup, too.

6	cups water
2-1/2	cups finely chopped carrots
1/4	cup all-purpose flour
1/4	teaspoon salt
1/4	teaspoon pepper
2	eggs, *separated*
3	tablespoons milk
2	tablespoons finely chopped onion
2	tablespoons minced fresh parsley

Vegetable oil for deep-fat frying

MUSTARD SAUCE:

1	tablespoon minced fresh parsley
1	tablespoon red wine vinegar
1	tablespoon Dijon mustard
1	teaspoon finely chopped green onion
1/4	cup olive oil

1) In a saucepan, bring water to a boil. Add the chopped carrots; cover and boil for 3 minutes. Drain and immediately place carrots in ice water. Drain and pat dry.

2) In a large bowl, combine the flour, salt and pepper. Combine egg yolks and milk; stir into the flour mixture until smooth. Stir in the onion, parsley and carrots.

3) In a mixing bowl, beat egg whites on high speed until stiff peaks form; fold into batter.

4) In an electric skillet, heat 1/4 in. of oil over medium heat. Drop batter by 1/3 cupfuls; press lightly to flatten. Fry until golden brown, about 2 minutes on each side.

5) For mustard sauce, in a small bowl, combine the parsley, vinegar, mustard and green onion. Slowly whisk in oil until blended. Serve with the fritters.

Yield: 9 servings.

NUTRITION FACTS: 1 serving (calculated without additional oil) equals 105 calories, 8 g fat (1 g saturated fat), 48 mg cholesterol, 137 mg sodium, 7 g carbohydrate, 1 g fiber, 2 g protein.

Vegetables Mornay

Jo Anne Remmele, Echo, Minnesota

These saucy vegetables are a colorful and satisfying side dish we enjoy often. Our daughter earned the Reserve Grand Champion ribbon at our local county fair with this recipe.

6	to 8 medium carrots, sliced 1/4 inch thick
1/4	cup water
1	package (10 ounces) frozen chopped broccoli
1	package (10 ounces) frozen cauliflowerets
2	jars (4-1/2 ounces *each*) whole mushrooms, drained
2	tablespoons cornstarch
1	teaspoon salt
1/4	teaspoon pepper
1-1/2	cups milk
1/2	cup butter, melted, *divided*
1	cup (4 ounces) shredded Swiss cheese
2	tablespoons Parmesan cheese
1/2	cup seasoned croutons

1) Place the carrots and water in a 3-qt. microwave-safe dish. Cover and microwave on high for 2 minutes. Add broccoli and cauliflower.

2) Cover and microwave for 6-9 minutes or until vegetables are tender; drain. Add mushrooms; cover and set aside.

3) In another microwave-safe dish, combine the cornstarch, salt and pepper. Stir in milk and 6 tablespoons butter until smooth.

4) Cover and microwave on high for 3-5 minutes or until thickened and smooth, stirring after every minute. Add Swiss cheese and Parmesan, stirring until melted.

5) Pour over the vegetables. Cover and microwave for 2-4 minutes or until heated through. Combine the croutons and remaining butter; stir into vegetables.

Yield: 8-10 servings.

NUTRITION FACTS: 1/2 cup equals 200 calories, 14 g fat (9 g saturated fat), 40 mg cholesterol, 538 mg sodium, 12 g carbohydrate, 3 g fiber, 7 g protein.

Cauliflower

This snowy-white vegetable has a flower-like appearance and a mild cabbage-like flavor. Cauliflower can be eaten raw or cooked.

Buying

Cauliflower is available year-round; peak season is October through March. Select firm, solid white or creamy-colored heads that are heavy for their size. The florets should be clean and tightly packed. The surrounding jacket leaves should be fresh and green. Orange cauliflower can be handled and prepared in the same way as white cauliflower.

Storage

Store unwashed cauliflower in an open plastic bag in the refrigerator crisper drawer for up to 5 days. Blanch 3-4 minutes before freezing. Freeze for up to 1 year.

Preparation

Trim off leaves. Remove base stem at an angle so the core comes out in a cone and the head remains intact. Separate into florets if desired.

Yield: 1-1/2 pounds of cauliflower (about 1 head) trimmed = 4 cups florets

Oriental Cauliflower

Carol Krueger, Pewaukee, Wisconsin

Every time I make this simple side dish, I get requests for the recipe. No one can believe how easy it is to make!

> 1   **medium head cauliflower, broken into florets**
> 3   **tablespoons cold water,** *divided*
> 1/2   **cup diced celery**
> 1   **small onion, finely chopped**
> 1/4   **cup minced fresh parsley**
> 1   **tablespoon butter**
> 1   **cup hot water**
> 1   **tablespoon chicken bouillon granules**
> 2   **tablespoons cornstarch**
> 1   **tablespoon soy sauce**
> **Dash pepper**

1) Place cauliflower in a microwave-safe dish. Add 1 tablespoon cold water. Cover and microwave on high for 4-1/2 to 5-1/2 minutes or until tender; drain and set aside.

2) In a 1-qt. microwave-safe bowl, combine the celery, onion, parsley and butter. Cover and microwave on high for 1 to 1-1/2 minutes or until vegetables are tender.

3) In a small bowl, combine hot water and bouillon until dissolved. Combine the cornstarch and remaining cold water until smooth. Add soy sauce, pepper and bouillon; mix well. Stir into celery mixture.

4) Microwave, uncovered, at 70% power for 2-3 minutes or until sauce comes to a boil, stirring after each minute. Pour over cauliflower.

Yield: 4-6 servings.

NUTRITION FACTS: 1 serving equals 62 calories, 2 g fat (1 g saturated fat), 5 mg cholesterol, 632 mg sodium, 9 g carbohydrate, 3 g fiber, 3 g protein.

Crumb-Topped Cauliflower

Kathy Cochill, Ocqueoc, Michigan

This easy-to-prepare and delicious dish makes just enough for two. Plus it's a tasty way to liven up cooked cauliflower.

> 1-1/2   **cups cauliflowerets**
> 1/4   **cup finely chopped walnuts** *or* **pecans**
> 3   **tablespoons dry bread crumbs**
> 3   **tablespoons butter**
> 1/4   **cup chopped green onions**
> 1-1/2   **teaspoons minced fresh parsley**
> 1   **teaspoon lemon juice**

1) In a saucepan, place 1 in. of water; add the cauliflower. Bring to a boil. Reduce heat; cover and simmer for 4-6 minutes or until crisp-tender.

2) Meanwhile, in a small skillet, cook nuts and bread crumbs in butter for 1 minute. Add onions and parsley; cook and stir until onions are tender and nuts and crumbs are lightly browned. Stir in lemon juice. Drain cauliflower; top with crumb mixture.

Yield: 2 servings.

Editor's Note: This recipe can be easily doubled to serve 4.

NUTRITION FACTS: 3/4 cup equals 309 calories, 27 g fat (11 g saturated fat), 46 mg cholesterol, 286 mg sodium, 14 g carbohydrate, 3 g fiber, 7 g protein.

FLORET CHEESE STRUDEL

Floret Cheese Strudel

Bonnie Zaparinuk, Whitehorse, Yukon

This is a unique way to serve broccoli and cauliflower, wrapped in puff pastry. It looks so pretty on the table. Without fail, I'm asked for the recipe whenever I serve it.

3-1/2 cups broccoli florets
2-1/2 cups cauliflowerets
   1 small onion, chopped
   1 garlic clove, minced
   6 tablespoons butter, *divided*
   2 tablespoons all-purpose flour
   1 cup milk
   2 tablespoons grated Parmesan cheese
   1 package (17-1/4 ounces) frozen puff pastry, thawed
   1 cup (4 ounces) shredded mozzarella cheese
 1/2 cup shredded cheddar cheese

1) In a large saucepan, bring 1 in. of water, broccoli and cauliflower to a boil. Reduce heat; cover and simmer for 5-10 minutes or until crisp-tender. Drain and set aside.

2) In a large saucepan, saute onion and garlic in 2 tablespoons butter until tender. Stir in flour until blended; gradually add milk. Bring to a boil; cook and stir for 2 minutes or until thickened. Remove from the heat. Stir in the Parmesan cheese, broccoli and cauliflower; set aside.

3) Melt remaining butter. Place one sheet of puff pastry on a piece of waxed paper; brush with butter. Spoon half of the vegetable mixture along one long side of pastry. Sprinkle with half of the mozzarella and cheddar cheeses.

4) Roll up jelly-roll style, starting from the long side topped with the vegetables; pinch seams and ends to seal. Brush top with melted butter. Carefully place seam side down on an ungreased baking sheet. Repeat with remaining dough, vegetable mixture and cheeses.

5) Bake at 400° for 20-25 minutes or until golden brown. Let stand for 5 minutes. Slice with a serrated knife.

Yield: 2 strudels (4-6 servings each).

NUTRITION FACTS: 1 slice equals 327 calories, 21 g fat (9 g saturated fat), 31 mg cholesterol, 293 mg sodium, 28 g carbohydrate, 4 g fiber, 8 g protein.

Cheese Sauce over Cauliflower

Ruby Zein, Monona, Wisconsin

The cheese sauce makes cauliflower hard to resist, even for picky eaters! I like to serve this dish at holidays and also for lunch along with pork sausage links, croissants and a green salad.

   1 large head cauliflower
1-1/2 teaspoons salt
   3 tablespoons butter
   3 tablespoons all-purpose flour
 1/2 teaspoon dried thyme
1-1/2 cups milk
1-1/2 cups (6 ounces) shredded cheddar cheese
Paprika
Minced fresh parsley

1) In a large saucepan, bring 1 in. of water, cauliflower and salt to a boil. Reduce heat; cover and cook for 5-15 minutes or until cauliflower is crisp-tender.

2) Meanwhile, in a small saucepan, melt butter; stir in flour and thyme until blended. Gradually add milk. Bring to a boil; cook and stir for 2 minutes or until thickened. Reduce heat; add cheese, stirring until melted.

3) Drain and pat cauliflower dry; place on a serving platter. Top with cheese sauce; sprinkle with paprika and parsley. Cut into wedges.

Yield: 6 servings.

NUTRITION FACTS: 1 serving equals 237 calories, 16 g fat (11 g saturated fat), 54 mg cholesterol, 890 mg sodium, 14 g carbohydrate, 4 g fiber, 11 g protein.

Celery

Generally, celery has a subtle flavor and a crisp-crunchy texture. The most common variety is Pascal. The root of the celery is sold as celeriac.

Buying

Celery is available year-round. Select firm, crisp ribs without any blemishes. The leaves should be green, not yellowed or wilted.

Storage

Store unwashed celery in a plastic bag in the refrigerator crisper drawer for up to 2 weeks.

Preparation

Wash ribs in cold water. Trim leaves and base from ribs before using. Outer ribs can be peeled with a vegetable peeler to remove some of the thicker strings. Leaves are good for soups, stews and garnishes.

Yield: 1 medium rib = about 1/2 cup chopped

Corn

Also known as sweet corn, this is available with bright yellow or white kernels or a mix of both. Corn on the cob is served cooked with silk and husks removed. Cooked kernels can be cut from the cob and used in recipes in place of canned or frozen corn.

Buying

Corn is available May through August; peak season is July through August. Select corn that has fresh green, tightly closed husks with dark brown, dry (but not brittle) silk. The stem should be moist but not chalky, yellow or discolored. Ears should have plump, tender, small kernels in tight rows up to the tip. Kernels should be firm enough to resist slight pressure. A fresh kernel will spurt "milk" if punctured.

Storage

Store unshucked ears in opened plastic bags in the refrigerator crisper drawer and use within 2 days. Blanch corn on the cob for 8-10 minutes and whole kernel corn for 5-6 minutes before freezing. Freeze for up to 1 year.

Preparation

If boiling or steaming, remove husk by pulling the husks down the ear; break off the undeveloped tip. Trim stem. Pull out silk between kernel rows or remove with a dry vegetable brush; rinse in cold water.

Yield: 1 ear of corn = 1/3 to 1/2 cup kernels

CUTTING KERNELS FROM CORNCOBS

Stand one end of the cob on a cutting board. Starting at the top, run a sharp knife down the cob, cutting deeply to remove whole kernels. One medium cob yields 1/3 to 1/2 cup kernels.

Tex-Mex Corn on the Cob
Helen Jacobs, Euless, Texas

It's a snap to add zippy flavor to fresh corn on the cob. The tender ears get a summery treatment seasoned with chili powder, cilantro and lime.

- 12 small ears fresh corn on the cob (about 6 inches)
- 3 tablespoons minced fresh cilantro
- 1-1/2 teaspoons chili powder
- 1-1/2 teaspoons grated lime peel
- 3/4 teaspoon salt
- 3/4 teaspoon ground cumin
- 1/4 teaspoon garlic powder

Refrigerated butter-flavored spray

1) Place corn in a Dutch oven or kettle; cover with water. Bring to a boil. Reduce heat; cover and cook for 3-5 minutes or until tender.

2) Meanwhile, in a small bowl, combine the cilantro, chili powder, lime peel, salt, cumin and garlic powder.

3) Drain the corn. Spritz with butter-flavored spray; brush or pat seasoning over corn.

Yield: 12 servings.

NUTRITION FACTS: 1 ear equals 85 calories, 1 g fat (trace saturated fat), 20 mg cholesterol, 164 mg sodium, 20 g carbohydrate, 2 g fiber, 3 g protein.

Corn Medley

Ruth Andrewson, Leavenworth, Washington

With a little spark of cumin, this garden-fresh medley showcases corn in a colorful blend with tomato, green pepper and onion.

- 2 cups fresh-cut sweet corn (3 to 4 ears)
- 1/4 cup chopped onion
- 1/4 cup chopped green pepper
- 2 tablespoons butter
- 1/2 teaspoon salt
- 1/4 teaspoon ground cumin
- 1 large tomato, chopped and seeded
- 2 tablespoons sugar

1) In a large saucepan, combine the corn, onion, green pepper, butter, salt and cumin. Cook and stir over medium heat until butter is melted.

2) Cover and cook over low heat for 10 minutes. Stir in tomato and sugar; cook, covered, 5 minutes longer.

Yield: 5 servings.

NUTRITION FACTS: 1/2 cup equals 126 calories, 5 g fat (3 g saturated fat), 12 mg cholesterol, 295 mg sodium, 20 g carbohydrate, 2 g fiber, 3 g protein.

Delicious Corn Pudding

Paula Marchesi, Rocky Point, Long Island, New York

This comforting dish has been part of family meals for years, and it's been shared at many gatherings.

- 4 eggs, *separated*
- 2 tablespoons butter, melted and cooled
- 1 tablespoon sugar
- 1 tablespoon brown sugar
- 1 teaspoon salt
- 1/2 teaspoon vanilla extract
- Dash *each* ground cinnamon and nutmeg
- 2 cups fresh whole kernel corn (4 medium ears)
- 1 cup half-and-half cream
- 1 cup milk

1) In a mixing bowl, beat yolks until lemon-colored, 5 to 8 minutes. Add the butter, sugars, salt, vanilla, cinnamon and nutmeg; mix well. Add corn. Stir in cream and milk.

2) In a small mixing bowl, beat egg whites on high speed until stiff; fold into yolk mixture. Pour into a greased 1-1/2-qt. baking dish. Bake, uncovered, at 350° for 35 minutes or until a knife inserted near the center comes out clean.

3) Cover loosely with foil during the last 10 minutes of baking if top browns too quickly.

Yield: 8 servings.

NUTRITION FACTS: 1 serving equals 179 calories, 10 g fat (5 g saturated fat), 133 mg cholesterol, 393 mg sodium, 16 g carbohydrate, 1 g fiber, 7 g protein.

Eggplant

Eggplants that are generally found in stores have purple skin, but a white variety may be available in specialty markets. The common or American eggplant is pear-shaped and 6 to 10 in. long. Italian eggplant is a smaller version of the common eggplant. Its skin is thinner and more delicate. Chinese and Japanese eggplant are thin and elongated. The Chinese eggplant is slightly larger and has a more delicate flavor than the Japanese variety.

Buying

Eggplant is available year-round; peak season is July through September. Select a firm, round or pear-shaped, heavy eggplant with a uniformly smooth color and glossy taut skin. The eggplant should be free from blemishes and rust spots with intact green caps and mold-free stems.

Storage

Store unwashed eggplant in an open plastic bag in the refrigerator crisper drawer for up to 3 days.

Preparation

Wash eggplant; cut off stem and peel if desired. Cut eggplant discolors quickly, so cut into slices, strips or cubes just before salting. Salt eggplant at least 30 minutes before cooking.

Yield: 1 medium eggplant (1 pound) = 5 cups cubes

3) In a large skillet, cook eggplant in 2 tablespoons oil for 2 minutes on each side or until lightly browned. Transfer to an ungreased 13-in. x 9-in. x 2-in. baking dish.

4) In the same skillet, saute the green pepper, onion and mushrooms in remaining oil for 5 minutes or until pepper and onion are crisp-tender. Sprinkle over eggplant. Top with tomatoes.

5) Bake, uncovered, at 350° for 25 minutes. Uncover; place cheese slices over the top. Bake 25-30 minutes longer or until cheese is melted.

Yield: 6 servings.

NUTRITION FACTS: 1 serving equals 318 calories, 16 g fat (6 g saturated fat), 128 mg cholesterol, 1,609 mg sodium, 32 g carbohydrate, 5 g fiber, 14 g protein.

Baked Ratatouille
Catherine Lee, San Jose, California

Ratatouille is usually a seasoned stew made of eggplant, tomatoes, green peppers, squash and sometimes meat. Bacon and cheese make my recipe delicious.

- 4 bacon strips, cut into 2-inch pieces
- 1 cup sliced onion
- 1 can (14-1/2 ounces) diced tomatoes, undrained
- 1/3 cup tomato paste
- 1/4 cup olive oil
- 1 large garlic clove, minced
- 1 teaspoon salt
- 1 teaspoon Italian seasoning
- 1 large eggplant (about 1-1/4 pounds), peeled and cubed
- 4 medium zucchini, sliced
- 1 large green pepper, cut into strips
- 8 to 12 ounces sliced Monterey Jack cheese

1) In a large skillet, cook bacon and onion over medium heat until bacon is crisp; drain. Stir in the next six ingredients.

2) Spread half into a greased 13-in. x 9-in. x 2-in. baking dish. Layer with half of the eggplant, zucchini, green pepper and cheese. Repeat layers. Bake, uncovered, at 375° for 50-55 minutes or until hot and bubbly.

Yield: 8 servings.

NUTRITION FACTS: 1/2 cup equals 250 calories, 17 g fat (7 g saturated fat), 30 mg cholesterol, 607 mg sodium, 15 g carbohydrate, 5 g fiber, 11 g protein.

SALTING EGGPLANTS

Salting an eggplant draws out some of the moisture, giving the flesh a denser texture. This means it will give off less moisture and absorb less fat during cooking. Salting may cut some of the bitterness from an eggplant.

To salt, place slices, cubes or strips of eggplant in a colander over a plate; sprinkle with about 1/2 teaspoon salt and toss. Let stand for 30 minutes. Rinse, drain well and pat dry with paper towels.

Cheesy Eggplant Bake
Frances Sayre, Cinnaminson, New Jersey

Paired with mushrooms and tomato and topped with mozzarella cheese, eggplant really stars in this tasty dish.

- 1 medium eggplant, peeled
- 2 teaspoons salt
- 3/4 cup dry bread crumbs
- 3 teaspoons garlic salt
- 1/2 teaspoon pepper
- 3 eggs
- 3 tablespoons olive oil, *divided*
- 1 large green pepper, chopped
- 1 medium onion, chopped
- 1/2 pound fresh mushrooms, sliced
- 2 cans (14-1/2 ounces *each*) stewed tomatoes
- 1 package (6 ounces) sliced mozzarella cheese

1) Cut eggplant into 1/4-in.-thick slices. Place in a colander over a plate; sprinkle with salt. Let stand for 30 minutes. Rinse under cold water and pat dry with paper towels.

2) In a shallow bowl, combine the bread crumbs, garlic salt and pepper. In another shallow bowl, beat eggs. Dip eggplant into eggs, then coat with crumb mixture.

Fennel

Fennel has a celery-like texture and a sweet, mild anise-like flavor that mellows while it cooks. The bulb, stalks and feathery fronds can all be used.

Buying
Fennel is available August through April. Select fennel with creamy white bulbs, firm straight stalks and bright green fronds. Avoid withered bulbs or those with brown spots or yellowing. Smaller bulbs are more tender.

Storage
Store unwashed fennel is the refrigerator crisper drawer for up to 4 days.

Preparation
Trim off fronds and stalks. Trim base from bulb. Remove and discard any yellowed or split outer layers. Cut in half and remove core. Cut, slice or chop the bulb and stalks. Use raw or cooked. Use the fronds as you would a minced herb or for a garnish.

Yield: 1 fennel bulb (10-1/2 ounces) = 2 cups sliced

Garlic

Garlic can add zip or mellow undertones to foods depending on how it is prepared.

Buying
Garlic is available year-round. Select garlic heads that are firm and plump. Avoid those with signs of sprouting and heads that are shriveled or soft.

Storage
Store garlic in a cool, dark, well ventilated dry place for several weeks. Do not store in the refrigerator unless it has been peeled, sliced or chopped.

Preparation
Remove individual cloves as needed from bulb. Press cloves with the flat edge of a knife to lightly crush and loosen skin, then peel. Or cut base from clove and remove skin with fingers or a knife. If the garlic has any green sprouts, remove those before using.

The more finely chopped, the more potent the garlic flavor will be in the dish. The flavor mellows upon cooking to a delightful nutty flavor. Overcooked garlic will turn bitter, so avoid letting it turn brown during cooking.

Yield: 1 garlic clove = 1/2 teaspoon minced
1 garlic bulb = 8 to 15 cloves

PREPARING GARLIC FOR ROASTING

With a sharp knife, cut off the top of each head of garlic, exposing the cloves inside. Place in a small baking dish or place bulb in heavy-duty foil.

Greens

Greens refers to a variety of leafy produce, such as kale, collards, Swiss chard, mustard greens, turnip greens, dandelion greens and broccoli rabe.

Buying
Greens are available year-round (individual varieties have their own seasons). Select fresh crisp greens with a bright color. Avoid those with withered, yellow or blemished leaves or stems.

COLLARDS
Cabbage-like, spicy flavor. Wide green, leathery leaves with white veins. Smaller leaves are more tender. Good for braising, boiling, stir-frying. Season: December through April.
Yield: 1 bunch (10 ounces) = 8 cups chopped.

DANDELION GREENS
Strong flavor with lemon undertones and a delicate texture. Saw-tooth edges on leaves. Good for sauteing, boiling. Season: spring through summer.
Yield: 1 bunch (1 pound) = 8 cups torn greens.

KALE

Mild, cabbage-bitter flavor. Curly blue-green leaves with a thick stem; some varieties have small, smooth leaves and are used in salads. Good for braising, stir-frying, steaming. Season: year-round. **Yield:** 1 bunch (12 ounces) = 10 cups coarsely chopped.

MUSTARD GREENS

Bitter green with a mustard bite. Ruffled, lime-green leaves; some varieties are deep red or maroon. Good for boiling. Season: December through March. **Yield:** 1 bunch (12 ounces) = 16 cups chopped.

SWISS CHARD

Tangy flavor with a hint of lemon. Green leaves with a white vein and stalk. The stalk is usually removed and cooked separately. Red leaf is another variety with a red stalk. Good for braising, stir-frying, steaming. Season: June through October. **Yield:** 1 bunch (12 ounces) = 9 cups chopped.

TURNIP GREENS

Sharp flavor that mellows during cooking; smaller leaves are less sharp. Firm, coarse, textured green leaves. Good for boiling, stir-frying, steaming. Season: November through March. **Yield:** 1 bunch (15 ounces) = 10 cups chopped.

Storage

Remove any ties before storing greens. Discard any yellow or bruised leaves. Store in a plastic bag in the refrigerator crisper drawer for up to 3 days.

Preparation

Wash in cool water. Greens may need one or two changes of water to remove all of the grit. They can be spun in a salad spinner to remove water or drained in a colander. Trim thick stems or ribs.

Yield: 1 pound = about 3 cups cooked

Kale with Bacon

Margaret Wagner Allen, Abingdon, Virginia

The hearty bacon flavor makes you forget that you're eating right. Seasoned with garlic, it's a great way to enjoy vitamin-rich kale.

> 2   **pounds fresh kale, trimmed and torn**
> 8   **bacon strips, diced**
> 2   **large onions, chopped**
> 4   **garlic cloves, minced**
> 1   **teaspoon salt**
> 1/2   **teaspoon pepper**

1) In a large saucepan, bring 1 in. of water to a boil. Add kale; cook for 10-15 minutes or until tender.

2) Meanwhile, in a large nonstick skillet, cook bacon over medium heat until crisp. Using a slotted spoon, remove to paper towels; drain, reserving 1 teaspoon drippings. In the drippings, saute onions and garlic until onion is tender.

3) Drain the kale; stir into onion mixture. Add the salt, pepper and reserved bacon; heat through.

Yield: 6 servings.

NUTRITION FACTS: 1/3 cup equals 161 calories, 7 g fat (2 g saturated fat), 9 mg cholesterol, 604 mg sodium, 20 g carbohydrate, 4 g fiber, 8 g protein.

Jicama

Jicama is a beige turnip- or radish-shaped tuberous root. Its juicy, crunchy-crisp texture and slightly nutty flavor is similar to a water chestnut. Jicamas range in size from 1/2 to 6 pounds.

Buying

Jicamas are available year-round. Select smaller ones as the large ones tend to be woody and fibrous. Choose firm, unblemished tubers with thin skins.

Storage

Store in the refrigerator crisper drawer for up to 2 weeks. Once cut, wrap in plastic wrap and use within 1 week.

Preparation

Wash in cold water. Peel skin then cut into desired size and shape. Jicama will not discolor after cutting. It can be used in salads or stir-fries or as crudites. Jicama stays crunchy after cooking.

Yield: 1 pound = 3-1/3 cups cubed

Kohlrabi

Kohlrabi is a pale green, bulb-shaped vegetable with white flesh and dark green leaves. Less common varieties of kohlrabi have bulbs with purple skin. Kohlrabi bulbs have a mild, turnip-like flavor. Bulbs and leaves can be enjoyed raw or cooked.

Buying
Kohlrabi is available year-round; peak season is June through July. Select small (no larger than 3 in.), firm, pale green bulbs. The bulbs should have tender skins; the leaves should appear fresh and crisp.

Storage
Trim leaves and root ends. Store unwashed kohlrabi in an open plastic bag in the refrigerator crisper drawer for up to 5 days. If using the greens, store separately in a sealed plastic bag in the refrigerator for up to 3 days.

Preparation
Cut off leaves and stems. Thinly peel bulbs. Cut into slices, strips or cubes.

Yield: 1 pound kohlrabi (without leaves)
= 3 to 4 medium bulbs

Kohlrabi with Honey Butter
Wanda Holoubek, Salina, Kansas

If you're not acquainted with kohlrabi, this recipe will serve as a pleasant introduction. Honey and lemon lend a sweet, citrusy taste to the turnip-like veggie.

1	pound kohlrabi (4 to 5 small), peeled and cut into 1/4-inch strips
1	medium carrot, cut into 1/8-inch strips
1	tablespoon minced chives
1	tablespoon lemon juice
1	tablespoon butter, melted
2	teaspoons honey
1/4	teaspoon grated lemon peel
1/8	teaspoon pepper

1) In a large skillet, bring 1 in. of water, kohlrabi and carrot to a boil. Reduce heat; cover and simmer for 6-10 minutes or until crisp-tender.

2) In a small bowl, combine the chives, lemon juice, butter, honey, lemon peel and pepper; mix well. Drain vegetables and transfer to a serving bowl. Add honey butter and toss to coat.

Yield: 4 servings.

NUTRITION FACTS: 1/2 cup equals 77 calories, 3 g fat (2 g saturated fat), 8 mg cholesterol, 62 mg sodium, 12 g carbohydrate, 5 g fiber, 2 g protein.

Leeks

Leeks are part of the onion family and are tasty additions to soups, casseroles or egg dishes.

Buying
Leeks are available year-round. Select young, straight, cylindrical stalks with moist, pliable green upper leaves. The white bulbs should extend 2 to 3 in. above the roots; diameter should not exceed 1-1/2 in.

Storage
Store unwashed, untrimmed leeks loosely wrapped in an open plastic bag in the refrigerator crisper drawer for up to 2 weeks.

Yield: 2 pounds leeks = 1 pound trimmed
= 4 cups chopped and 2 cups cooked

PREPARING LEEKS
Remove any withered outer leaves. Trim root end. Cut off and discard the green upper leaves at the point where the pale green becomes dark green. Leeks often contain sand between their many layers.

If leeks are to be sliced or chopped, cut the leek open lengthwise down one side and rinse under cold running water, separating the leaves.

If using the leek whole, cut an X about 1/4- to 1/2-in. deep in the root end. Soak for 30 minutes in water containing a splash of vinegar. Rinse under cold running water, gently opening the slit area while rinsing.

Mushrooms

Mushrooms add an earthy, nutty flavor to recipes. Mushrooms are a fungus not a vegetable, but they are treated as vegetables in cooking.

Buying

Mushrooms are available year-round (individual varieties have their own seasons). Select mushrooms with fresh, firm, smooth caps with closed gills. Avoid mushrooms with cracks, brown spots or blemishes or ones that are shriveled or moist.

BUTTON OR WHITE

Mild mushroom flavor that intensifies on cooking. Color ranges from creamy white to beige. Comes in small (button), medium and large (used for stuffing). Season: year-round.
Yield: 1 package (8 ounces) = 3 cups whole or sliced.

CHANTERELLE

Flavor can range from nutty to fruity with a chewy texture. Color ranges from yellow to reddish orange. Resembles trumpets or inside-out umbrellas. Season: summer through fall. **Yield:** 1 package (2.5 ounces) = 1 cup whole.

CREMINI OR BROWN

More intense earthy flavor than button. Color ranges from tan to rich brown. Resembles a button mushroom. Season: year-round. **Yield:** 1 package (8 ounces) = about 3 cups whole or sliced.

ENOKI

Mild flavor with a slightly crunchy texture. Color ranges from white to golden. Tiny caps on long spaghetti-like stems; trim base and separate stems before using. Season: year-round.
Yield: 1 package (3-1/2 ounces) = about 2 cups whole.

OYSTER

Delicate, mild flavor and a silky-chewy texture. Color ranges from pinkish white to beige to gray. Fluted shell-shaped caps. Season: year-round.
Yield: 1 package (3-1/2 ounces) = 1-1/2 cups whole.

PORTOBELLO

Meaty flavor with firm texture. Tan caps with dark-brown gills. Are a large cremini (as large as 6 in. diameter). Available whole, sliced or as baby portobello, which are larger than cremini. Season: year-round. **Yield:** 1 package (6 ounces, 2 large caps) = 2-1/2 cups sliced.

SHIITAKE

Woody flavor with a meaty texture. Color ranges from tan to dark brown. Has an umbrella-shaped cap; remove and discard stems before using. Season: year-round, peaks in spring and fall. **Yield:** 1 package (3-1/2 ounces) = 2 cups sliced.

Storage

Store unwashed, loose mushrooms in a brown paper bag in the refrigerator for up to 5-10 days depending on the variety. Keep packaged mushrooms wrapped in their package. Moisture speeds spoilage in mushrooms. Store mushrooms away from other vegetables with strong aromas.

Yield: 1/2 pound button mushrooms
= 2-1/2 cups sliced or 1 cup sauteed

PREPARING MUSHROOMS

Gently remove dirt by rubbing with a mushroom brush or wipe mushrooms with a damp paper towel. Or quickly rinse under cold water, drain and pat dry with paper towels. Do not peel mushrooms. Trim stems. For shiitake mushrooms, remove and discard stems. For enoki, trim base and separate stems. Mushrooms can be eaten raw, marinated, sauteed, stir-fried, baked, broiled or grilled.

MUSHROOM GREEN BEAN CASSEROLE

Mushroom Green Bean Casserole
Pat Richter, Lake Placid, Florida

Fresh mushrooms, sliced water chestnuts and slivered almonds bake together to make this side dish so delicious.

> 1   pound fresh mushrooms, sliced
> 1   large onion, chopped
> 1/2 cup butter
> 1/4 cup all-purpose flour
> 1   cup half-and-half cream
> 1   jar (16 ounces) process cheese spread
> 2   teaspoons soy sauce
> 1/2 teaspoon pepper
> 1/8 teaspoon hot pepper sauce
> 1   can (8 ounces) sliced water chestnuts, drained
> 2   packages (16 ounces *each*) frozen French-style green beans, thawed and well drained
> 2   to 3 tablespoons slivered almonds

1) In a large skillet, saute mushrooms and onion in butter. Stir in flour until blended. Gradually stir in cream. Bring to a boil; cook and stir for 2 minutes or until thickened.

2) Reduce heat; add the cheese sauce, soy sauce, pepper and hot pepper sauce, stirring until cheese is melted. Remove from the heat; stir in water chestnuts.

3) Place beans in an ungreased 3-qt. baking dish. Pour the cheese mixture over top. Sprinkle with almonds. Bake, uncovered, at 375° for 25-30 minutes or until bubbly.

Yield: 14 servings.

NUTRITION FACTS: 1/2 cup equals 223 calories, 16 g fat (10 g saturated fat), 46 mg cholesterol, 654 mg sodium, 14 g carbohydrate, 3 g fiber, 7 g protein.

Pickled Mushrooms
Linda Keiper-Quinn, Hazelton, Pennsylvania

Pennsylvania is known for its mushrooms, and they are featured in this recipe.

> 1/2   cup red wine vinegar
> 1/2   cup water
> 2   bay leaves
> 2   tablespoons sugar
> 1-1/2 teaspoons salt
> 1   garlic clove, minced
> 1   pound fresh mushrooms, quartered

1) In a saucepan over medium heat, combine the vinegar, water, bay leaves, sugar, salt and garlic. Add mushrooms. Bring to a boil and boil for 2 minutes. Cool slightly.

2) Transfer to a bowl; cover and refrigerate for 8 hours or overnight. Discard bay leaves before serving.

Yield: about 2-1/2 cups.

NUTRITION FACTS: 1/4 cup equals 25 calories, trace fat (trace saturated fat), 0 cholesterol, 356 mg sodium, 5 g carbohydrate, 1 g fiber, 1 g protein.

Sauteed Mushrooms
Hope Meece, Ambia, Indiana

I frequently fix this speedy dish for my hungry family. Spiced carrots would be a mouth-watering companion in the pan to the mushrooms.

> 1/4 cup butter
> 1   pound fresh mushrooms, sliced
> 1   tablespoon lemon juice
> 1   tablespoon soy sauce

1) In a large skillet, melt butter. Add the mushrooms, lemon juice and soy sauce.

2) Saute for 6-8 minutes or until mushrooms are tender.

Yield: 4 servings.

NUTRITION FACTS: 1 serving equals 132 calories, 12 g fat (7 g saturated fat), 31 mg cholesterol, 350 mg sodium, 5 g carbohydrate, 1 g fiber, 4 g protein.

Okra

Okra is a slender, ribbed edible pod with small, white seeds. This mild vegetable tastes a little like asparagus and is known for its thickening power when cooked in gumbo, soups or stews.

Buying

Okra is available year-round in Southern states and from April to November in the North; peak season is June through November. Select young, tender, unblemished, bright green pods less than 4 in. long. The pods may be smooth or ridged, should snap easily and should not have any hard seeds. The tips should bend under slight pressure.

Storage

Store unwashed okra in a sealed plastic bag in the refrigerator crisper drawer for up to 2 days.

Preparation

Wash and remove stem ends. Leave small pods whole; cut larger pods into 1/2-in. slices.

Yield: 1 pound okra = 3 to 4 cups sliced

Okra Medley

Nona Cheatham, McRae, Arkansas

This recipe is wonderful served with almost any main entree and hot corn bread.

- 1 **medium onion, chopped**
- 2 **tablespoons butter**
- 2 **cups sliced fresh okra**
- 3 **to 4 medium tomatoes, peeled and chopped**
- 2 **cups frozen corn**
- 1 **teaspoon sugar**
- 1 **teaspoon salt**
- 1/4 **teaspoon pepper**

1) In a large saucepan, saute onion in butter until tender. Add okra; cook and stir for 5 minutes. Stir in remaining ingredients; bring to a boil. Reduce heat; cover and simmer for 10-15 minutes or until corn is tender.

Yield: 4-6 servings.

NUTRITION FACTS: 1/2 cup equals 127 calories, 5 g fat (2 g saturated fat), 10 mg cholesterol, 444 mg sodium, 22 g carbohydrate, 4 g fiber, 4 g protein.

Onions

Onions are a member of the lily family. They can be green, white, yellow or red with flavors ranging from sharp when eaten raw to mild and sweet when cooked.

Buying

Onions are available year-round (individual varieties have their own seasons). Select firm onions that have dry, papery skins with globe-shaped necks. Avoid those with soft spots, blemishes or green sprouts.

Pearl onions are small, about 1 in. diameter, are generally white but may be yellow or red and are sold in pint containers. Red onions have a stronger flavor than yellow and are generally used raw or for grilling. Their color fades when cooked. Sweet onions are mild, sweet and juicy. They are used raw and can be cooked. Yellow onions range in size from small to large and are the common cooking onion. White onions are milder in flavor than yellow and are frequently used in Mexican cuisine.

Storage

Store onions in a dark, cool, dry, well-ventilated area for up to 3 weeks.

Preparation

Peel skin and cut, chop or slice as recipe directs.

Yield: 1 small onion = 1/3 cup chopped
1 medium onion = 1/2 to 3/4 cup chopped
1 large onion = 1 to 1-1/4 cups chopped

PEELING A PEARL ONION

1) In a Dutch oven or large kettle, bring 6 cups water to a boil. Add pearl onions; boil for 3 minutes.

2) Drain and rinse in cold water; peel and set aside.

VEGETABLE-STUFFED BAKED ONIONS

Vegetable-Stuffed Baked Onions

Ruth Andrewson, Leavenworth, Washington

Stuffed with carrots, red pepper, diced bacon and bread crumbs, these elegant baked onions will dress up any special-occasion meal. My mother often pulled out this recipe when company was coming.

8	to 10 medium onions, peeled
4	bacon strips, diced
3/4	cup finely chopped carrots
1/2	cup finely chopped sweet red pepper
1-1/2	cups soft bread crumbs
1/3	cup minced fresh parsley
3	tablespoons butter, melted
1-1/2	teaspoons salt
1/2	teaspoon pepper
3/4	cup beef broth

1) Cut 1/2 in. off the top of each onion; trim bottom so onion sits flat. Scoop out center, leaving a 1/2-in. shell. Chop removed onion; set 1/2 cup aside (discarding remaining onion or save for another use).

2) Place onion shells in a Dutch oven or large saucepan and cover with water. Bring to a boil; reduce heat and cook for 8-10 minutes.

3) Meanwhile, in a large skillet, cook bacon over medium heat until crisp. Remove to paper towels; drain, reserving 1 teaspoon drippings.

4) In same skillet, saute the chopped onion, carrots and red pepper in drippings for 8 minutes or until tender. Remove from the heat; stir in the bread crumbs, parsley, butter, salt, pepper and bacon.

5) Drain onion shells; fill each with about 1/3 cup vegetable mixture. Place in an ungreased shallow 3-qt. baking dish. Pour broth over onions. Cover and bake at 350° for 45-50 minutes or until heated through.

Yield: 8-10 servings.

NUTRITION FACTS: 1 stuffed onion equals 155 calories, 9 g fat (4 g saturated fat), 15 mg cholesterol, 561 mg sodium, 16 g carbohydrate, 3 g fiber, 3 g protein.

Creamed Pearl Onions

Barbara Caserman, Lake Havasue City, Arizona

When our children were small, we always celebrated Christmas at our house. This was one of many recipes I relied on that can be prepared a day in advance, which gave me more time to spend with guests. Everyone expected to see this vegetable dish on the table every year.

50	pearl onions
1/4	cup butter
1/4	cup all-purpose flour
1/2	teaspoon salt

Dash pepper

1	cup chicken broth
1	cup half-and-half cream
1/4	cup minced fresh parsley
3	tablespoons grated Parmesan cheese

Pimento strips, optional

1) In a Dutch oven, or large kettle, bring 6 cups water to a boil. Add pearl onions; boil for 10-12 minutes or until tender. Drain and rinse in cold water; peel and set aside.

2) In a saucepan, melt butter. Stir in the flour, salt and pepper until smooth. Gradually stir in broth and cream. Bring to a boil; cook and stir for 2 minutes or until thickened. Stir in the parsley, cheese and onions.

3) Pour into an ungreased 1-qt. baking dish. Cover and refrigerate overnight. Remove from the refrigerator 30 minutes before baking. Cover and bake at 350° for 15 minutes; stir. Top with pimientos if desired. Bake, uncovered, 10 minutes longer or until bubbly and heated through.

Yield: 6 servings.

Editor's Note: To bake immediately after preparing the onions, transfer to 1-qt. baking dish. Bake, uncovered, at 350° for 15-20 minutes or until bubbly.

NUTRITION FACTS: 3/4 cup equals 209 calories, 13 g fat (8 g saturated fat), 42 mg cholesterol, 501 mg sodium, 18 g carbohydrate, 2 g fiber, 5 g protein.

Caramelized Onions

Taste of Home Test Kitchen

The choices are endless...serve this as a topping for sandwiches or burgers, brats or hot dogs as well as steak.

- 1 to 2 tablespoons vegetable oil
- 6 cups thinly sliced onions (about 4 large)
- 1/4 teaspoon salt
- 1 tablespoon cider vinegar
- 2 tablespoons brown sugar

1) Heat oil in a large skillet over medium heat until hot. Add onions and sprinkle with salt. Cook and stir for 15 minutes or until moisture from onions has evaporated and onions are completely wilted.

2) Reduce heat to medium-low. Sprinkle vinegar over onions. Cook and stir for 20 minutes or until lightly golden. Stir in brown sugar; cook and stir for 15-20 minutes longer or until onions are a caramel brown color. If onions begin to stick to skillet, add water, 1 tablespoon at a time, until onions no longer stick to skillet.

Yield: 1-1/2 cups.

NUTRITION FACTS: 1/4 cup equals 81 calories, 2 g fat (trace saturated fat), 0 cholesterol, 104 mg sodium, 15 g carbohydrate, 2 g fiber, 1 g protein.

Savory Onions and Spinach

Sue Smith, Norwark, Connecticut

The mixture of onions and spinach draped in a rich Parmesan cream sauce looks as festive as it tastes. So it's ideal for a holiday meal.

- 2 packages (16 ounces *each*) frozen pearl onions
- 1 garlic clove, minced
- 3 tablespoons butter, *divided*
- 1 package (10 ounces) fresh spinach
- 3/4 cup grated Parmesan cheese, *divided*
- 1/4 cup heavy whipping cream
- Salt and pepper to taste
- 3 tablespoons dry bread crumbs

1) Cook onions according to package directions; drain well and set aside.

2) In a saucepan, saute garlic in 2 tablespoons butter for 1-2 minutes. Add spinach; cook and stir until spinach is wilted and liquid has evaporated, about 3 minutes. Stir in 1/2 cup Parmesan cheese and cream. Stir in salt, pepper and reserved onions.

3) Transfer to a greased shallow 2-qt. baking dish. Combine bread crumbs and remaining cheese; sprinkle over onion mixture. Dot with remaining butter. Bake, uncovered, at 400° for 20 minutes or until golden brown. Serve with a slotted spoon.

Yield: 8 servings.

NUTRITION FACTS: 1/2 cup (calculated without salt and pepper) equals 183 calories, 10 g fat (6 g saturated fat), 28 mg cholesterol, 256 mg sodium, 20 g carbohydrate, 1 g fiber, 6 g protein.

Onions, Green

Green onions, also known as scallions, are a member of the onion family. They are immature onions that were harvested before the bulb had time to develop.

Buying

Green onions are available year-round. Select green onions with bright green tops, white bulbs and short roots. Avoid ones with dry, withered or slimy greens.

Storage

Store unwashed green onions in a plastic bag in the refrigerator crisper drawer for up to 1-2 weeks.

Preparation

Trim off root end and wash in cool water. Some recipes call for just the white portion, some use the white and green portions and some use the top. If using the tops, trim off ends along with any dry, coarse or withered portions before slicing or chopping.

Yield: 1 green onion
= 2 tablespoons, sliced

Parsnips

Parsnips are root vegetables that resemble a white or pale yellow carrot. Parsnips add a sweetness and nutty flavor to recipes.

Buying

Parsnips are available year-round; peak season is fall through winter. Select firm parsnips with a uniform shape. Avoid ones that have cracks and blemishes or are shriveled. Avoid large parsnips, since they might be tough.

Storage

Store unwashed parsnips in a perforated plastic bag in the refrigerator crisper drawer for up to 2 weeks.

Preparation

Wash parsnips in cool water. Trim root ends and tops, then peel skin.

Yield: 1 pound trimmed = 3 cups cubed

CARROT PARSNIP STIR-FRY

Carrot Parsnip Stir-Fry

Lavonne Hartel, Williston, North Dakota

Orange carrot slivers and yellow parsnips make a pretty and different side dish. If parsnips aren't available, you could substitute rutabagas or turnips. Usually, I saute the vegetables until they are crisp-tender. But they're also good well-cooked, almost browned.

1-1/2	pounds parsnips, peeled and julienned
1/4	cup butter
2	pounds carrots, julienned
2	tablespoons dried minced onion

1) In a large skillet, saute parsnips in butter for 3-4 minutes. Add carrots and onion; cook and stir until vegetables are tender, about 10-15 minutes.

Yield: 8 servings.

NUTRITION FACTS: 1 cup equals 171 calories, 6 g fat (4 g saturated fat), 15 mg cholesterol, 106 mg sodium, 29 g carbohydrate, 7 g fiber, 2 g protein.

Baked Parsnips

Robert Atwood, West Wareham, Massachusetts

We enjoy parsnips here in the Northeast, and I've experimented with different ways of fixing them. This is by far my favorite.

1-1/2	pounds parsnips, peeled and julienned
1/4	cup butter
1/4	cup water
1/2	teaspoon dried oregano
1/2	teaspoon dried parsley flakes
1/4	teaspoon salt
1/8	teaspoon pepper

1) Place parsnips in an ungreased 2-qt. baking dish; dot with butter. Add water. Sprinkle with the oregano, parsley, salt and pepper. Cover and bake at 350° for 45 minutes or until tender.

Yield: 4 servings.

NUTRITION FACTS: 1 cup equals 239 calories, 12 g fat (7 g saturated fat), 31 mg cholesterol, 280 mg sodium, 33 g carbohydrate, 7 g fiber, 2 g protein.

Peas, Green

Fresh green peas, sometimes called English peas, are a member of the legume family. Fresh peas are sweet and tender.

Buying

Green peas are available year-round; peak season is May through June. Select peas in their pods for maximum freshness. Choose ones that are crisp and firm and have a bright green color. Avoid large pods or those with thick skin, which indicates they are past mature.

Storage

Keep unwashed, unshelled green peas in an open plastic bag in the refrigerator crisper drawer for up to 2 days.

Yield: 1 pound unshelled green peas
= 1-1/2 cups shelled

SHELLING PEAS

Wash pods in cool water. Snap off stem end and pull string down. Open pod by running your thumb down the length of the seam and loosening the peas. Rinse peas before cooking.

Creamed Peas
Imogene Hutton, Norton, Texas

This recipe has been in my family for years, and we often serve it for holiday meals.

- 1 package (10 ounces) **frozen peas**
- 1 tablespoon butter
- 1 tablespoon all-purpose flour
- 1/4 teaspoon salt
- 1/8 teaspoon pepper
- 1/2 cup milk
- 1 teaspoon sugar

1) Cook peas according to package directions. Meanwhile, in a small saucepan, melt the butter. Stir in the flour, salt and pepper until blended; gradually add milk and sugar.

2) Bring to a boil; cook and stir for 1-2 minutes or until thickened. Drain peas; stir into the sauce and heat through.

Yield: 3-4 servings.

NUTRITION FACTS: 1/2 cup equals 110 calories, 4 g fat (2 g saturated fat), 12 mg cholesterol, 271 mg sodium, 14 g carbohydrate, 3 g fiber, 5 g protein.

French Peas
Ann Nace, Perkasie, Pennsylvania

I like to dress up plain peas with green onions, lettuce and water chestnuts for this simple and tasty side dish.

- 1 package (10 ounces) **frozen peas**
- 2 green onions, diced
- 1 cup finely shredded lettuce
- 1 tablespoon vegetable oil
- 1 teaspoon all-purpose flour
- 1/4 cup water
- 1 can (8 ounces) sliced water chestnuts, drained

Dash pepper

1) Cook peas according to package directions. Meanwhile, in another saucepan, cook onions and lettuce in oil over low heat for 5 minutes.

2) Combine flour with water until smooth. Stir into onion mixture; cook and stir until thickened.

3) Drain peas and add to onion mixture along with the water chestnuts and pepper; heat through.

Yield: 4 servings.

NUTRITION FACTS: 2/3 cup equals 120 calories, 4 g fat (trace saturated fat), 0 cholesterol, 86 mg sodium, 18 g carbohydrate, 5 g fiber, 5 g protein.

Minty Peas and Onions
Santa D'Addario, Brooklyn, New York

With just five ingredients, you can stir up a wonderful side dish for a special dinner or any night of the week.

- 2 large onions, cut into 1/2-inch wedges
- 1/2 cup chopped sweet red pepper
- 2 tablespoons vegetable oil
- 2 packages (16 ounces *each*) **frozen peas**
- 2 tablespoons minced fresh mint *or* 2 teaspoons dried mint

1) In a large skillet, saute onions and red pepper in oil until onions just begin to soften.

2) Add peas; cook, uncovered, stirring occasionally, for 10 minutes or until heated through. Stir in mint and cook for 1 minute.

Yield: 8 servings.

Editor's Note: You can halve this recipe to make 4 servings.

NUTRITION FACTS: 1 cup equals 134 calories, 4 g fat (1 g saturated fat), 0 cholesterol, 128 mg sodium, 19 g carbohydrate, 6 g fiber, 6 g protein.

Peas, Snow and Sugar Snap

Snow peas and sugar snap peas are sweet, tender peas in an edible pod and are eaten whole. Snow peas have smaller peas and more translucent pods than sugar snap peas.

Buying
Snow peas are available year-round. Sugar snap peas are generally available in spring and fall. Select snow peas that are flat, are about 3 in. long and have a light green color with a shiny appearance. Select sugar snap peas that have crisp plump looking dark green pods. Avoid dry or moldy pods.

Storage
Keep unwashed snow or sugar snap peas in an open plastic bag in the refrigerator crisper drawer for up to 2 days.

Yield: 1 pound snow peas or sugar snap peas
= about 4 cups

PREPARING PEAS

Rinse with cold water. Remove strings if desired. Cut off stem ends. Do not shell. If using raw, blanch before using.

Gingered Snow Peas

Suzanne Karsten, Winter Garden, Florida

A hint of ginger makes these snow peas special as well as one of my favorite dishes.

1/2 **pound fresh snow peas, trimmed**
1 **tablespoon water**
1 **tablespoon butter, melted**
1/4 **teaspoon ground ginger**
1/8 **teaspoon salt**

1) Place the peas and water in a 1-qt. microwave-safe dish. Cover and microwave on high for 3-4 minutes or until crisp-tender; drain.

2) Combine the butter, ginger and salt. Drizzle over the peas; toss to coat.

Yield: 2-3 servings.

NUTRITION FACTS: 1/2 cup equals 66 calories, 4 g fat (2 g saturated fat), 10 mg cholesterol, 140 mg sodium, 5 g carbohydrate, 2 g fiber, 3 g protein.

Sunny Snow Peas

Kathleen Bailey, Chester Springs, Pennsylvania

Turn crispy snow peas into something special by tossing them with a lovely honey-orange sauce. I enjoy serving a sauce like this that adds the bright warmth of the sun.

1/2 **cup orange juice**
2 **tablespoons honey**
1 **tablespoon butter**
1 **to 2 teaspoons grated orange peel**
1/2 **teaspoon salt**
1/8 **teaspoon ground cardamom**
1 **pound fresh snow peas *or* sugar snap peas**

1) In a small saucepan, combine the first six ingredients; bring to a boil. Reduce heat; simmer, uncovered, until mixture is reduced by half, about 15 minutes.

2) Meanwhile, in another saucepan, bring 1 in. of water and peas to a boil. Reduce heat; cover and simmer for 3-4 minutes or until crisp-tender. Drain and transfer to a serving bowl. Pour sauce over peas and toss to coat.

Yield: 6 servings.

NUTRITION FACTS: 2/3 cup equals 81 calories, 2 g fat (1 g saturated fat), 5 mg cholesterol, 218 mg sodium, 14 g carbohydrate, 2 g fiber, 2 g protein.

TANGY SUGAR SNAP PEAS

Tangy Sugar Snap Peas

Taste of Home Test Kitchen

This mouth-watering side dish comes together quickly in the microwave. A sweet and tangy glaze complements the crisp peas and onion in this made-in-moments recipe.

1 **pound fresh *or* frozen sugar snap peas, thawed**
1 **small onion, halved and sliced**
3 **tablespoons water, *divided***
4 **teaspoons sugar**
1 **teaspoon cornstarch**
1/8 **teaspoon pepper**
2 **tablespoons cider vinegar**

1) In a large microwave-safe bowl, combine the peas, onion and 2 tablespoons water. Cover and cook on high for 5-7 minutes or until crisp-tender, stirring twice; drain.

2) In a small microwave-safe bowl, combine the sugar, cornstarch and pepper; stir in the vinegar and remaining water until smooth. Cook, uncovered, on high for 30-45 seconds or until thickened, stirring once. Add to pea mixture; toss to coat.

Yield: 4 servings.

NUTRITION FACTS: 3/4 cup equals 75 calories, 1 g fat (0 saturated fat), 0 cholesterol, 1 mg sodium, 16 g carbohydrate, 5 g fiber, 3 g protein.

Peppers, Chili

Chili (hot) peppers come in
a variety of sizes, shapes and
heat levels. They generally come to a tapered point
and can be either skinny or plump. Depending on the
pepper, they can be green, red or yellow. Dried chili
peppers are most often a black-red color.

Buying

Chili peppers are available year-round. Select peppers
with firm, smooth, glossy skin. Avoid those that are
shriveled or have soft spots. Heat levels range: mild-
flavored Anaheim, Banana or Cubanelle; moderately
hot ancho or pasilla; hot jalapeno; hotter serrano; and
fiery habanero.

Storage

Store unwashed, fresh chili peppers wrapped in paper
towels in the refrigerator crisper drawer for up to 2
weeks.

PREPARING CHILIES

Chili peppers contain a skin
irritant called capsaicin.
When handling chili peppers,
wear rubber or plastic gloves
and avoid touching your
eyes or face to prevent
burning your skin or eyes.
Wash hands and cutting
surface thoroughly with hot,
soapy water when finished.

The heat of the peppers is contained in the seeds and
membranes. Use them for a spicier dish. For a milder
dish, remove and discard the seeds with the tip of a
spoon or knife. Not all chili peppers are the same; the
heat level can vary among chilies even in the same
variety. So taste-test before adding chilies to a dish.
You can always add more, but you can't salvage a dish
that's too hot.

Yield: (varies by size and shape)

Peppers, Sweet

Classified as a fruit, sweet bell peppers are used as a
vegetable. They come in green, yellow, red, orange and
purple-black. They have a mild flavor, although the
green ones are slightly stronger.

Buying

Sweet peppers are available year-round; peak season
is March through October. Select firm peppers with
smooth, shiny skin and bright colors. Avoid those that
are shriveled or have soft spots.

Storage

Store unwashed bell peppers in the refrigerator crisper
drawer for up to 5 days.

Preparation

Rinse peppers under cold water. Remove stem, seeds
and membranes (ribs). Slice or chop according to
recipe directions.

Yield: 1 medium sweet pepper = 3/4 cup chopped

ROASTING PEPPERS

1) Arrange pepper halves skin
side up or whole peppers on a
broiler pan coated with
nonstick cooking spray. Broil
on the closest rack position to
the heat without the peppers
touching the heat source. Broil until skins are
blistered and blackened, about 10 minutes.
For whole peppers, with tongs, rotate peppers
a quarter turn. Broil and rotate until all sides
are blistered and blackened.

2) Immediately place peppers
in a bowl; cover with plastic
wrap and let stand for 15-20
minutes.

3) Peel off and discard
charred skin. Remove stems
and seeds from whole
peppers.

Potatoes

Potatoes are tuberous vegetables that are delicious baked, boiled, mashed, fried, shredded or used in salads.

Baking potatoes, such as russet and Idaho, have a high starch content that produces a fluffy, dry texture after baking. Waxy potatoes, such as red round potatoes, have a low to medium starch content so they hold their shape after boiling. All-purpose potatoes, such as Yukon Gold, are suitable for both baking and boiling.

Buying
Potatoes are available year-round (individual varieties have their own seasons). Select well-shaped, firm potatoes that are free from cuts, decay, blemishes or green discoloration under the skin. Avoid sprouted or shriveled potatoes.

Storage
Store potatoes in a dark, cool, dry, well-ventilated area for up to 2 months. Do not store with onions or in the refrigerator.

Yield: 1 pound russet potatoes = 3 medium
1 pound small new potatoes = 8 to 10
1 pound potatoes = 2-1/4 cups diced or sliced

PREPARING POTATOES
Scrub with a vegetable brush under cold water. Remove eyes or sprouts. When working with lots of potatoes, peel and place in cold water to prevent discoloration. Before baking a whole potato, pierce with a fork.

FINGERLINGS
Finger-shaped potato with tan skin, 2-4 in. long. Waxy, firm and flavorful. Use boiled, steamed, in salads.

NEW POTATOES
Small potatoes with tan or red tender skin. New potatoes are fresh from the garden and have never been placed in storage. Use boiled, steamed or roasted whole.

ROUND REDS
Round-shaped potatoes with smooth red skin. Waxy or low starch. Use boiled, roasted, steamed, in casseroles, salads and soups.

ROUND WHITES
Round-shaped potato with light- to medium-brown skin. Waxy or low starch. Use baked, boiled, steamed.

RUSSETS
Oblong potato with a rough, reddish-brown skin. High starch, low moisture. Use baked, mashed, roasted, as French fries.

YELLOW-FLESHED
Round potatoes with golden-colored skin and flesh that have a buttery flavor. All-purpose potato. Use baked, boiled, mashed, roasted, steamed, as French fries, in salads. Falls apart when overcooked.

Fried Potatoes
Taste of Home Test Kitchen

Who knew a simple combination of potatoes, onion, butter, salt and pepper could taste so good?

3   **cups diced cooked potatoes**
1/2 **cup diced cooked onion**
2   **tablespoons butter**
Salt and pepper to taste

1) In a large skillet, cook potatoes and onion in butter over medium heat for 10 minutes or until golden brown. Season with salt and pepper.

Yield: 3-4 servings.

NUTRITION FACTS: 3/4 cup (calculated without salt and pepper) equals 147 calories, 6 g fat (4 g saturated fat), 15 mg cholesterol, 65 mg sodium, 22 g carbohydrate, 2 g fiber, 3 g protein.

Au Gratin Potatoes

Jeannine Clayton, Byron, Minnesota

You won't believe how simple it is to make this creamy and delicious dish! All it takes is a few handy ingredients, and you've got a special addition to your dinner table.

- 12   medium red *or* white potatoes, unpeeled
- 1   teaspoon salt
- 1/2   teaspoon pepper
- 1/2   teaspoon garlic *or* onion salt
- 2   cups (8 ounces) shredded cheddar cheese
- 1   cup heavy whipping cream

1) Place potatoes in a large saucepan and cover with water. Bring to a boil. Reduce heat; cover and cook for 30-40 minutes or until tender. Drain and refrigerate several hours or overnight.

2) Peel potatoes and coarsely shred. Combine the salt, pepper and garlic salt. In a greased 13-in. x 9-in. x 2-in. baking dish, layer potatoes and salt mixture. Sprinkle with cheese; pour cream over all. Bake, uncovered, at 350° for 1 hour or until golden.

Yield: 12-15 servings.

NUTRITION FACTS: 1/2 cup equals 174 calories, 10 g fat (7 g saturated fat), 38 mg cholesterol, 320 mg sodium, 15 g carbohydrate, 2 g fiber, 5 g protein.

SCALLOPED POTATOES

Scalloped Potatoes

Eleanore Hill, Fresno, California

Once you have the potatoes sliced up, this dish comes together in no time.

- 3   tablespoons butter, *divided*
- 1   tablespoon all-purpose flour
- 1   teaspoon salt

- 1/4   teaspoon pepper
- 1-1/2   cups milk
- 4   cups thinly sliced peeled potatoes (about 2 pounds)
- 1   medium onion, finely chopped
- 1   small green pepper, finely chopped
- 1/2   cup dry bread crumbs
- 3/4   cup shredded cheddar cheese

1) In a small saucepan, melt 2 tablespoons butter; stir in flour, salt and pepper. Gradually stir in milk. Bring to a boil over medium heat; cook and stir for 2 minutes or until thickened.

2) In a greased 1-1/2-qt. baking dish, arrange half the potatoes, onion and green pepper in layers; cover with half of the sauce. Repeat layers. Cover and bake at 350° for 35 minutes.

3) Melt remaining butter; combine with bread crumbs and sprinkle over potatoes. Bake, uncovered, about 40 minutes longer or until potatoes are tender. Sprinkle with cheddar cheese. Let stand for 5 minutes before serving.

Yield: 4 servings.

NUTRITION FACTS: 3/4 cup equals 378 calories, 18 g fat (12 g saturated fat), 58 mg cholesterol, 1,513 mg sodium, 41 g carbohydrate, 5 g fiber, 12 g protein.

Delmonico Potatoes

Mrs. Arnold Sonnenberg, Brookville, Ohio

After trying this magnificent dish at a restaurant, I found a way to duplicate it at home. The results are creamy, cheesy and delicious!

- 9   medium potatoes, unpeeled
- 1   cup milk
- 1   cup heavy whipping cream
- 1-1/2   teaspoon salt
- 1   teaspoon ground mustard
- 1/4   teaspoon pepper
- 1/4   teaspoon ground nutmeg
- 1-1/2   pounds shredded sharp cheddar cheese

1) Place potatoes in a large saucepan and cover with water. Bring to a boil. Reduce heat; cover and cook for 30-40 minutes or until tender. Drain and refrigerate several hours or overnight.

2) Peel potatoes and coarsely shred. In a saucepan, heat the milk, cream, salt, mustard, pepper and nutmeg over medium heat until bubbles form around side of pan. Reduce heat; add cheese, stirring until melted.

3) Place potatoes in a greased 13-in. x 9-in. x 2-in. baking dish. Pour cheese sauce over potatoes. Bake at 325° for 50-55 minutes or until heated through.

Yield: 12-16 servings.

NUTRITION FACTS: 1/2 cup equals 282 calories, 19 g fat (14 g saturated fat), 72 mg cholesterol, 515 mg sodium, 16 g carbohydrate, 1 g fiber, 12 g protein.

STUFFED BAKED POTATOES

Stuffed Baked Potatoes
Marge Clark, West Lebanon, Indiana

These special potatoes are a hit with my whole family. I prepare them up to a week in advance, wrap them well and freeze.

- 3 large baking potatoes (1 pound *each*)
- 1-1/2 teaspoons vegetable oil, optional
- 1/2 cup sliced green onions
- 1/2 cup butter, *divided*
- 1/2 cup half-and-half cream
- 1/2 cup sour cream
- 1 teaspoon salt
- 1/2 teaspoon white pepper
- 1 cup (4 ounces) shredded cheddar cheese
- Paprika

1) Pierce potatoes with a fork; rub with oil if desired. Bake at 400° for 1 hour and 20 minutes or until tender. Let stand until cool enough to handle.

2) Cut each potato in half lengthwise. Scoop out the pulp, leaving a thin shell. Place pulp in a large bowl and mash.

3) In a small skillet, saute onions in 1/4 cup butter until tender. Stir into potato pulp along with cream, sour cream, salt and pepper. Fold in cheese.

4) Spoon into potato shells. Place on a baking sheet. Melt remaining butter; drizzle over the potatoes. Sprinkle with paprika. Bake, uncovered, at 350° for 20-30 minutes or until heated through.

Yield: 6 servings.

Editor's Note: Potatoes may be stuffed ahead of time and refrigerated or frozen. Allow additional time for reheating.

NUTRITION FACTS: 1 serving equals 416 calories, 26 g fat (17 g saturated fat), 84 mg cholesterol, 693 mg sodium, 36 g carbohydrate, 3 g fiber, 9 g protein.

■ *RANCH STUFFED BAKED POTATOES:* Stir in 1 to 2 tablespoons ranch salad dressing mix into the sour cream before adding to the mashed potato pulp. Fold in 3 crumbled cooked bacon strips along with the cheese.

■ *TEX-MEX STUFFED BAKED POTATOES:* Omit green onions, 1/4 cup butter and paprika. Stir in 1 can (4 ounces) drained chopped green chilies. Fold in 1 cup shredded pepper Jack cheese in place of the cheddar cheese. Sprinkle with chili powder if desired.

■ *HERB-STUFFED BAKED POTATOES:* Stir in 2 tablespoons *each* minced chives and parsley along with the green onions. Use 1 cup shredded mozzarella in place of cheddar cheese.

MAKING STUFFED POTATOES

Cut a lengthwise slice from the top of each potato. With a spoon, scoop potato pulp from the slice and the inside of the potato, leaving a 1/4-in. shell. Discard skin from slice. Mash the pulp and spoon into shells. Bake as directed.

THREE-CHEESE POTATO SOUFFLE

Three-Cheese Potato Souffle
Kathy Kittell, Lenexa, Kansas

Everyday mashed potatoes become more appealing in this extra-cheesy souffle. It bakes up fluffy and golden and makes a perfect side dish.

- 4 **cups mashed potatoes (without added milk and butter)**
- 1 **cup fat-free milk**
- 1 **cup (4 ounces) shredded reduced-fat cheddar cheese**
- 2/3 **cup shredded reduced-fat Swiss cheese**
- 1/3 **cup shredded Parmesan cheese**
- 1/3 **cup chopped green onions**
- 1 **small onion, chopped**
- 1-1/4 **teaspoons salt**
- 1/4 **teaspoon pepper**
- 4 **eggs, *separated***

1) In a large bowl, combine the potatoes, milk, cheeses, onions, salt and pepper. Beat egg yolks; stir into potato mixture.

2) In a small mixing bowl, beat egg whites until stiff peaks form; gently fold into potato mixture.

3) Transfer to a 2-qt. souffle dish coated with nonstick cooking spray. Bake, uncovered, at 375° for 40-45 minutes or until golden. Serve immediately.

Yield: 12 servings.

NUTRITION FACTS: 1/2 cup equals 153 calories, 5 g fat (3 g saturated fat), 83 mg cholesterol, 442 mg sodium, 16 g carbohydrate, 1 g fiber, 11 g protein.

Yukon Mashed Potatoes
Nancy Horsburgh, Everett, Ontario

I like to use half-and-half cream. If you don't have that on hand, use milk or sour cream.

- 2-3/4 **to 3 pounds Yukon Gold potatoes, peeled and quartered**
- 1/2 **cup half-and-half cream**

- 2 **tablespoons butter**
- 1/2 **to 1 teaspoon garlic salt**
- 1/8 **teaspoon pepper**

1) Place potatoes in a large saucepan or Dutch oven and cover with water. Bring to a boil. Reduce heat; cover and cook for 15-20 minutes or until tender and drain.

2) In a large bowl, mash potatoes. Add the cream, butter, garlic salt and pepper; beat until light and fluffy.

Yield: 6 servings.

NUTRITION FACTS: 1/2 cup equals 232 calories, 6 g fat (4 g saturated fat), 20 mg cholesterol, 212 mg sodium, 37 g carbohydrate, 2 g fiber, 6 g protein.

■ *GARLIC MASHED POTATOES:* Add 4-6 peeled garlic cloves along with potatoes. Cook and mash as directed.

■ *FANCY MASHED POTATOES:* Use 1 tablespoon butter. Mash with 2 ounces softened cream cheese and 3 tablespoons minced chives.

Duchess Potatoes
Taste of Home Test Kitchen

Potatoes get an elegant treatment when piped from a pastry or heavy-duty plastic bag and baked. This is a perfect side for a meal with Cornish game hens.

- 3 **medium potatoes, peeled and quartered**
- 4 **tablespoons butter, *divided***
- 1 **to 2 tablespoons milk**
- 1 **egg**
- 1 **teaspoon minced chives**

1) Place potatoes in a large saucepan and cover with water. Bring to a boil. Reduce heat; cover and cook for 15-20 minutes or until tender.

2) Transfer to a mixing bowl; add 2 tablespoons butter and milk. Beat on low just until smooth; cool slightly. Add egg and chives; beat on low until fluffy.

3) Cut a small hole in the corner of a pastry or plastic bag; insert #8b open star pastry tip. Fill the bag with potato mixture. Pipe potatoes into four rosettes on a greased baking sheet.

4) In a saucepan, melt remaining butter. Drizzle over potatoes. Bake at 350° for 20-25 minutes or until heated through.

Yield: 4 servings.

NUTRITION FACTS: 1 serving equals 197 calories, 13 g fat (8 g saturated fat), 84 mg cholesterol, 137 mg sodium, 18 g carbohydrate, 2 g fiber, 3 g protein.

CREAMY HASH BROWN CASSEROLE

Creamy Hash Brown Casserole
Teresa Stutzman, Adair, Oklahoma

This versatile side dish is perfect with grilled steaks and other meats. Its creamy cheese sauce and crunchy topping is popular with my family.

> 1 package (32 ounces) frozen Southern-style hash brown potatoes, thawed
> 1 pound process cheese (Velveeta), cubed
> 2 cups (16 ounces) sour cream
> 1 can (10-3/4 ounces) condensed cream of chicken soup, undiluted
> 3/4 cup butter, melted, *divided*
> 3 tablespoons chopped onion
> 1/4 teaspoon paprika
> 2 cups cornflakes, slightly crushed

Fresh savory, optional

1) In a large bowl, combine the hash browns, cheese, sour cream, soup, 1/2 cup butter and onion. Spread into a greased 13-in. x 9-in. x 2-in. baking dish. Sprinkle with paprika. Combine cornflakes and remaining butter; sprinkle on top.

2) Bake, uncovered, at 350° for 50-60 minutes or until heated through. Garnish with savory if desired.

Yield: 8 servings.

NUTRITION FACTS: 3/4 cup equals 663 calories, 43 g fat (27 g saturated fat), 125 mg cholesterol, 1,359 mg sodium, 49 g carbohydrate, 3 g fiber, 19 g protein.

Oven-Roasted Potato Wedges
Ellen Benninger, Stoneboro, Pennsylvania

This recipe is perfect for company and gets delicious, delicate flavor from the rosemary.

> 4 unpeeled baking potatoes (2 pounds)

> 2 tablespoons olive oil
> 1 medium onion, chopped
> 2 garlic cloves, minced
> 1 tablespoon minced fresh rosemary *or* 1 teaspoon dried rosemary, crushed
> 1/2 teaspoon salt
> 1/4 teaspoon pepper

1) Cut potatoes lengthwise into wedges; place in a greased 13-in. x 9-in. x 2-in. baking pan. Drizzle with oil. Sprinkle with onion, garlic, rosemary, salt and pepper; stir to coat.

2) Bake, uncovered, at 400° for 45-50 minutes or until tender, turning once.

Yield: 8 servings.

NUTRITION FACTS: 1 serving equals 398 calories, 4 g fat (1 g saturated fat), 0 cholesterol, 176 mg sodium, 84 g carbohydrate, 8 g fiber, 10 g protein.

Lemon Red Potatoes
Tara Branham, Cedar Park, Texas

Butter, lemon juice, parsley and chives enhance this simple side dish. They also cook up nicely in a slow cooker.

> 1-1/2 pounds medium red potatoes
> 1/4 cup butter, melted
> 1 tablespoon lemon juice
> 3 tablespoons snipped fresh parsley
> 1 tablespoon snipped fresh chives

Salt and pepper to taste

1) Cut a strip of peel from around the middle of each potato. Place potatoes in a large saucepan and cover with water. Bring to a boil. Reduce heat; cover and cook for 15-20 minutes or until tender. Drain.

2) Combine the butter, lemon juice, parsley and chives; mix well. Pour over the potatoes and toss to coat. Season with salt and pepper.

Yield: 6 servings.

Editor's Note: The potatoes may be cooked in a slow cooker. Just place the potatoes and 1/4 cup water in a covered 3-qt. slow cooker for 2-1/2 to 3 hours on high. Then proceed as recipe directs.

NUTRITION FACTS: 1 serving (calculated without salt and pepper) equals 150 calories, 8 g fat (5 g saturated fat), 20 mg cholesterol, 85 mg sodium, 18 g carbohydrate, 2 g fiber, 2 g protein.

Perfect Potato Pancakes

Mary Peters, Swift Currant, Saskatchewan

To keep the cooked potato pancakes warm, I wrap them in foil and place them in the oven.

- 4 large potatoes (about 3 pounds)
- 2 eggs, lightly beaten
- 1/2 cup all-purpose flour
- 1/2 cup finely diced onion
- 1 teaspoon salt
- 1/8 teaspoon pepper

Oil for frying

Maple syrup *or* applesauce

1) Peel and shred potatoes; place in a bowl of cold water. Line a colander with cheesecloth or paper towels. Drain potatoes into cloth and squeeze out as much moisture as possible. In a large bowl, combine the potatoes, eggs, flour, onion, salt and pepper.

2) In an electric skillet, heat 1/4 in. of oil over medium heat. Drop batter by 1/4 cupfuls into oil, about 3 in. apart. Press lightly to flatten. Fry until golden brown, about 4 minutes on each side.

3) Drain on paper towels. Repeat with remaining batter. Top with maple syrup or applesauce.

Yield: about 16 pancakes.

NUTRITION FACTS: 2 pancakes (calculated without maple syrup or applesauce) equals 251 calories, 6 g fat (1 g saturated fat), 53 mg cholesterol, 323 mg sodium, 45 g carbohydrate, 4 g fiber, 6 g protein.

KEEPING FRIED FOODS WARM

When foods need to be cooked in stages, such as potato pancakes, you'll want to keep each batch warm until the entire recipe is cooked. Drain fried foods on paper towels, then place on an oven-proof platter. Cover loosely with foil and place in a 200° oven until the entire recipe is completed.

Pumpkin

Pumpkins are a member of the gourd family and can be cooked like any winter squash. Varieties known as pie pumpkins are smaller than the "jack-o'-lantern" type and make flavorful puree for use in pies and cakes.

Buying

Pumpkins are available in the autumn months. Select pumpkins that have firm, blemish-free rinds and are bright orange in color.

Storage

Store in a cool, dry place for up to 1 month. A cut pumpkin may be stored in an open plastic bag in the refrigerator for up to 1 week.

Preparation

Cut off the top stem section. Remove seeds and scrape out stringy fibers.

Yield: 1 pie pumpkin (3 pounds) = about 2 cups cooked pureed

TOASTING PUMPKIN SEEDS

Remove fibrous strings from the seeds; place in a colander. Rinse seeds under cold water and drain. Spread out on paper towels to dry. Spread on a greased baking sheet. Bake at 250° for 1 hour. Increase heat to 400°; bake 5 minutes longer. Season with salt if desired.

Rutabaga

Rutabaga, also known as swede, is a root vegetable. It has a stronger flavor than a turnip.

Buying

Rutabaga is available year-round; peak season is fall through winter. Select a firm, solid rutabaga that feels heavy for its size. Avoid those with scars and bruises. For best flavor, select medium to small ones.

Storage

Store unwashed rutabaga in the refrigerator crisper drawer for up to 2 weeks.

Preparation

Trim top and bottom from rutabaga, then cut in half. They are coated with wax that needs to be peeled before using. Rinse with cold water after peeling.

Yield: 1 pound trimmed = 3 cups cubed

Oven-Roasted Root Vegetables

Mitzi Sentiff, Alexandria, Virginia

All kinds of root vegetables star in this colorful medley. Fresh thyme and sage season the mix of rutabaga, parsnips and butternut squash that's satisfying any time of year.

> 2 **cups cubed peeled rutabaga**
> 2 **cups cubed peeled parsnips**
> 2 **cups cubed peeled butternut squash**
> 2 **medium onions, chopped**
> 1 **tablespoon olive oil**
> 1/2 **teaspoon salt**
> 1/8 **teaspoon pepper**
> 1 **tablespoon minced fresh thyme**
> **or 1 teaspoon dried thyme**
> 1 **tablespoon minced fresh sage**
> **or 1 teaspoon rubbed sage**

1) In a large bowl, combine the rutabaga, parsnips, squash and onions. Add the oil, salt and pepper; toss to coat. Arrange in a single layer in a 15-in. x 10-in. x 1-in. baking pan coated with nonstick cooking spray.

2) Bake, uncovered, at 400° for 40-50 minutes, stirring occasionally. Sprinkle with herbs; toss to combine.

Yield: 4 servings.

NUTRITION FACTS: 3/4 cup equals 168 calories, 4 g fat (1 g saturated fat), 0 cholesterol, 319 mg sodium, 33 g carbohydrate, 9 g fiber, 3 g protein.

Triple Mashed Vegetables

Noel Heckler, Wolcott, New York

I had trouble getting my family to eat rutabaga, until this flavor-filled recipe convinced them to try it. This is a nice variation on plain mashed potatoes.

> 1 **medium rutabaga, peeled and cubed (about 3 cups)**
> 6 **medium potatoes, peeled and cubed (3-1/2 cups)**
> 6 **medium carrots, peeled and sliced (3 cups)**
> 2 **tablespoons butter**
> 3/4 **teaspoon salt**
> 1/4 **teaspoon pepper**

1) Place vegetables in a large saucepan and cover with water. Bring to a boil. Reduce heat; cover and cook for 15-20 minutes or until very tender.

2) Drain vegetables and transfer to a mixing bowl.

Mash vegetables and add the butter, salt and pepper; beat until smooth and fluffy.

Yield: 6 servings.

NUTRITION FACTS: 2/3 cup equals 162 calories, 4 g fat (2 g saturated fat), 10 mg cholesterol, 402 mg sodium, 30 g carbohydrate, 6 g fiber, 3 g protein.

Shallots

Shallots are a member of the onion family, but their appearance resembles garlic cloves.

Buying
Shallots are available year-round. Select firm, plump shallots. Avoid those with soft spots, a shriveled appearance or green sprouts.

Storage
Store in a cool, dry, well-ventilated place for up to a month.

Preparation
Shallots can have two or three cloves attached to one head. Each clove is a shallot. Trim base and remove papery outer skin. Mince or slice as recipe directs.

Yield: 1 package (3 ounces) = 1/2 cup chopped

Spinach

Dark green in color and tender in texture, spinach leaves can be eaten raw in salads or lightly cooked and used in soups, side dishes and main dishes.

Buying
Spinach is available year-round; peak season is late spring and early summer. Select crisp, dark green, tender leaves. Avoid yellowed or wilted spinach.

Storage
Keep unwashed spinach in a sealed plastic bag in the refrigerator crisper drawer for up to 5 days.

Preparation
Cut off the tough stems. Wash several times in cold water to remove sand; drain well and pat dry.

Yield: 1 to 1-1/2 pounds fresh spinach
= 1 cup cooked

SQUEEZING SPINACH DRY

Drain spinach in a colander. If spinach was cooked, allow to cool. With clean hands, squeeze the water out of the spinach.

Spinach Supreme

Clara Coulston, Washington Court House, Ohio

Showcase spinach at its best with mushrooms, onion and crunchy walnuts.

- 1 cup sliced fresh mushrooms
- 1 medium onion, chopped
- 1/4 cup reduced-sodium chicken broth
- 8 cups chopped fresh spinach
- 1/2 teaspoon garlic powder
- 1/4 teaspoon salt
- 1/8 teaspoon pepper
- 2 tablespoons chopped walnuts, toasted

1) In a large saucepan, cook mushrooms and onion in broth over medium-low heat until tender. Stir in the spinach, garlic powder, salt and pepper. Cover; cook for 2-3 minutes or until spinach is wilted. Stir in walnuts. Serve with a slotted spoon.

Yield: 2 servings.

NUTRITION FACTS: 3/4 cup equals 108 calories, 5 g fat (trace saturated fat), 0 cholesterol, 469 mg sodium, 12 g carbohydrate, 5 g fiber, 7 g protein.

Scalloped Spinach

Patricia Bassler, Ellicott, Maryland

Spinach and bacon are always a welcome combination at my dinner table.

- 6 bacon strips, diced
- 1/4 cup chopped onion
- 1 package (10 ounces) fresh spinach, chopped
- 2 cups soft bread crumbs, *divided*
- 2 cups milk
- 2 eggs, beaten
- 1/4 cup butter, melted
- 1/2 teaspoon salt
- 1/8 teaspoon pepper

1) In a small skillet, cook bacon over medium heat until crisp. Using a slotted spoon, remove to paper towels; drain, reserving 1 tablespoon drippings.

In same skillet, saute onion in drippings until tender; set aside.

2) In a large saucepan, bring 1/2 in. water and spinach to a boil. Reduce heat; cover and cook for 6-8 minutes or until tender.

3) Drain well; transfer to a large bowl. Add 1-1/2 cups bread crumbs, milk, eggs, butter, salt, pepper and reserved onion. Pour into a greased 2-qt. baking dish. Top with the reserved bacon, then remaining crumbs. Bake, uncovered, at 350° for 50-60 minutes or until a knife inserted near the center comes out clean.

Yield: 6-8 servings.

NUTRITION FACTS: 3/4 cup equals 189 calories, 14 g fat (7 g saturated fat), 83 mg cholesterol, 425 mg sodium, 10 g carbohydrate, 1 g fiber, 7 g protein.

SAUTEED SPINACH AND PEPPERS

Sauteed Spinach and Peppers

Mary Lou Moon, Beaverton, Oregon

We often steam our fresh spinach and eat it plain. But this version is a nice change.

- 1 large sweet red pepper, coarsely chopped
- 1 tablespoon olive oil
- 1 small red onion, finely chopped
- 3 garlic cloves, minced
- 8 cups packed fresh spinach
- 1/2 teaspoon salt
- 1/4 teaspoon pepper
- 1/8 teaspoon sugar

1) In a large nonstick skillet, saute red pepper in oil for 1 minute. Add onion and garlic; saute until tender, about 1-1/2 minutes longer.

2) Stir in the spinach, salt, pepper and sugar; saute for 1-2 minutes or until spinach is wilted and tender. Serve with a slotted spoon.

Yield: 4 servings.

NUTRITION FACTS: 1/2 cup equals 65 calories, 4 g fat (1 g saturated fat), 0 cholesterol, 342 mg sodium, 7 g carbohydrate, 3 g fiber, 2 g protein.

Squash, Summer

Summer squash are members of the gourd family. Their skin and seeds are completely edible. Summer squash may be used raw or cooked.

Buying

Summer squash are available year-round; peak season is late summer through early fall. Select firm, plump squash with bright, smooth skin. Baby squash are a smaller version of their counterparts and are harvested when they are young.

Zucchini is available with green and yellow skin. Yellow summer squash is available with a crookneck (one end is narrower and has a slight bend) or straight neck. Pattypan is a small, round, squat squash with a scalloped edge; generally they are pale green or white. Sunburst is a bright yellow pattypan with a green stem.

Storage

Store unwashed summer squash in the refrigerator crisper drawer for up to 4 days.

Preparation

Wash summer squash but do not peel unless squash is mature. Remove stem and blossom ends. Serve pattypan squash whole. Cut zucchini and summer squash into 1/2-in. slices.

Yield: 1 pound = 4 cups grated or 3-1/2 cups sliced

Stuffed Zucchini
Vonnie Elledge, Pinole, California

Zucchini makes a great container for a filling of the squash, bread crumbs, cheese and onion.

- 4 medium zucchini
- 1/4 teaspoon salt
- 1 small onion, minced
- 2 tablespoons vegetable oil
- 2 eggs, lightly beaten
- 1/2 cup dry bread crumbs
- 1/4 cup grated Parmesan cheese
- 2 tablespoons minced parsley
- Salt and pepper to taste

1) Cut zucchini in half lengthwise. Scoop out pulp, leaving a 3/8-in. shell. Reserve pulp.

2) In a large saucepan, bring 8 cups water and salt to a boil. Add zucchini shells; cover and boil for 2 minutes. Drain and set aside. Chop zucchini pulp.

3) In a large skillet, saute the onion and chopped zucchini in oil until tender. Remove from the heat. Stir in the eggs, bread crumbs, cheese, parsley, salt and pepper. Fill shells.

4) Place in a greased baking dish. Bake at 375° for 15 minutes or until filling reaches 160° and is heated through.

Yield: 4 servings.

NUTRITION FACTS: 2 stuffed zucchini (calculated without salt and pepper) equals 208 calories, 12 g fat (3 g saturated fat), 110 mg cholesterol, 396 mg sodium, 18 g carbohydrate, 3 g fiber, 9 g protein.

Zucchini Fries
Debbie Brunssen, Randolph, Nebraska

These flavorful fries are the first thing we make when the zucchini in our garden is ready. I fry several batches because our family of eight loves these crispy golden wedges.

- 1 medium zucchini
- 1/2 cup all-purpose flour
- 1 teaspoon onion salt
- 1 teaspoon dried oregano
- 1/2 teaspoon garlic powder
- 1 egg, lightly beaten
- 1/3 cup milk
- 1 teaspoon vegetable oil
- 4 cups Corn Chex, crushed
- Oil for deep-fat frying

1) Cut zucchini in half widthwise, then cut each half lengthwise into eight wedges; set aside. In a bowl, combine the flour, onion salt, oregano and garlic powder.

2) Combine the egg, milk and oil; stir into the dry ingredients just until blended. Dip zucchini wedges in batter, then roll in crushed cereal.

3) In an electric skillet or deep-fat fryer, heat oil to 375°. Fry zucchini wedges, a few at a time, for 3-4 minutes or until golden brown. Drain on paper towels; keep warm.

Yield: 4 servings.

NUTRITION FACTS: 4 zucchini fries equals 250 calories, 7 g fat (1 g saturated fat), 56 mg cholesterol, 769 mg sodium, 41 g carbohydrate, 2 g fiber, 7 g protein.

GARDEN SAUTE

Garden Saute
Nena Williams, Dallas, Texas

The mixture of colors and herbs in this dish make it one of my family's favorites.

- 1/4 cup chopped red onion
- 1 garlic clove, minced
- 2 teaspoons olive oil
- 1 medium yellow summer squash, sliced
- 1 medium zucchini, sliced
- 1/2 cup sliced fresh mushrooms
- 1 medium tomato, cut into wedges
- 1/4 cup chopped celery
- 1/2 teaspoon lemon juice
- 1/4 teaspoon dried rosemary, crushed
- 1/4 teaspoon dill weed
- 1/4 teaspoon Italian seasoning
- 1/8 teaspoon fennel seed
- 1/8 teaspoon pepper

1) In a large skillet coated with nonstick cooking spray, saute onion and garlic in oil until tender. Add the remaining ingredients; gently stir. Cover and cook over medium heat for 5-7 minutes or until vegetables are tender.

Yield: 6 servings.

NUTRITION FACTS: 1/2 cup equals 36 calories, 2 g fat (trace saturated fat), 0 cholesterol, 9 mg sodium, 5 g carbohydrate, 2 g fiber, 1 g protein.

Rosemary Peas 'n' Squash
Emily Chaney, Blue Hill, Maine

When you have a bounty of squash from your garden, here's a great way to use it up!

- 1 medium yellow summer or pattypan squash
- 1 medium zucchini
- 1 tablespoon butter
- 1/4 pound fresh or frozen sugar snap peas
- 1 tablespoon minced fresh rosemary or 1 teaspoon dried rosemary, crushed

Salt and pepper to taste

1) Cut squash into 1-in. chunks. In a large skillet, melt butter. Saute squash, peas and rosemary for 5 minutes or until vegetables are crisp-tender. Sprinkle with salt and pepper.

Yield: 4 servings.

NUTRITION FACTS: 1 serving (calculated without salt and pepper) equals 55 calories, 3 g fat (2 g saturated fat), 8 mg cholesterol, 33 mg sodium, 6 g carbohydrate, 2 g fiber, 2 g protein.

Steamed Vegetable Ribbons
Taste of Home Test Kitchen

These extra-thin slices of zucchini and carrot will add a pretty touch to a dinner plate.

- 4 large carrots, peeled
- 8 small zucchini
- 4 teaspoons lemon juice
- 2 teaspoons olive oil
- 1 teaspoon salt
- 1/8 to 1/4 teaspoon pepper

1) Trim ends from the carrots and zucchini. Use a vegetable peeler to make long thin strips down the length of each carrot and zucchini, making long ribbons.

2) Place carrots in a steamer basket. Place in a large saucepan over 1 in. of water; bring to a boil. Cover and steam for 2 minutes.

3) Add zucchini; cover and steam 2-3 minutes longer or until vegetables are tender. Transfer vegetables to a bowl. Add the lemon juice, oil, salt and pepper; toss to coat.

Yield: 8 servings.

NUTRITION FACTS: 1/2 cup equals 43 calories, 1 g fat (trace saturated fat), 0 cholesterol, 309 mg sodium, 7 g carbohydrate, 3 g fiber, 2 g protein.

MAKING ZUCCHINI RIBBONS

Trim ends from zucchini. Use a vegetable peeler to make long thin strips from the zucchini.

Squash, Winter

Winter squash is a member of the gourd family. They have a hard, inedible shell and fully mature seeds.

Buying

Winter squash is available year-round; peak season is October through December. Select squash that is heavy for its size. The shells should be hard with a deep color. Avoid those with cracks or soft spots.

ACORN SQUASH

Resembles an acorn. Its ridged shell can be dark green, golden/orange or cream colored. The orange flesh is mild.

BUTTERCUP SQUASH

Has a cap or turban on one end of its green shell. The orange flesh has a sweet, classic squash flavor and creamy texture.

BUTTERNUT SQUASH

Is bell-shaped with a pale tan shell. The shell can be peeled before cooking. The orange flesh is sweet and flavorful.

DELICATA SQUASH

Is cylindrical and has a yellow shell with green stripes. Its pale yellow flesh is sweet and is sometimes compared to a sweet potato.

HUBBARD SQUASH

Is a larger squash (can grow to 25 pounds) and is sometimes sold in pieces because of its size. Its hard, bumpy shell can be orange, gray-blue or green. The orange flesh is sweet and rich.

SPAGHETTI SQUASH

Is watermelon-shaped with a thin, yellow shell. Once cooked, its mild and slightly nutty-flavored flesh separates into spaghetti-like strands.

SWEET DUMPLIING

Is a small, pumpkin-shaped squash with a yellow shell that has green stripes like the Delicata squash. Its fine-textured yellow flesh is sweet and is sometimes said to have a mild corn flavor.

TURBAN SQUASH

Has a large cap or turban on one end of its shell. The hard-to-remove shell comes in green, orange or white. Its yellow, mealy flesh has a nutty flavor.

Storage

Store unwashed winter squash in a cool, dry, well-ventilated area for up to 4 weeks.

Yield: 1-3/4 pounds winter squash = 1-3/4 cups cooked mashed

PREPARING SQUASH

Wash squash, then pat dry with paper towels. Use a sharp knife to cut in half and scrape out seeds and fibrous strings. Acorn squash can be cut into decorative rings. Generally winter squash is first cooked, then the flesh is scooped out of the shell. It can be difficult to peel the shell from raw winter squash.

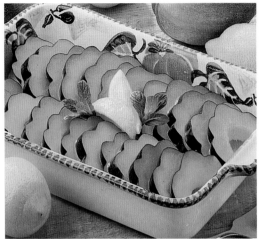

Lemony Acorn Slices
Nell Fletcher, Sedalia, Colorado

I have used this recipe often over the years. With the skins on the sliced squash and lemon sauce drizzled over it, this side dish looks as good as it tastes.

  2 **large acorn squash**
     (about 2-1/4 pounds *each***)**
  1 **cup plus 2 tablespoons water,**
     divided
1/2 **cup sugar**
  2 **tablespoons lemon juice**
  1 **tablespoon butter**
1/4 **teaspoon salt**
1/8 **teaspoon pepper**
   Lemon wedges and fresh mint, optional

1) Cut squash in half lengthwise; remove and discard the seeds and membrane. Cut each half crosswise into 1/2-in. slices; discard ends.

2) Place slices in a large skillet. Add 1 cup water; bring to a boil. Reduce heat; cover and simmer for 20 minutes or until tender.

3) Meanwhile, in a heavy saucepan, combine sugar and remaining water. Cook over medium heat until sugar melts and syrup is golden, stirring occasionally. Remove from the heat; carefully add the lemon juice, butter, salt and pepper. Cook and stir over low heat until butter melts.

4) Place squash on a serving plate; top with syrup. Garnish with lemon and mint if desired.

Yield: 6 servings.

NUTRITION FACTS: 2 slices equals 219 calories, 2 g fat (1 g saturated fat), 5 mg cholesterol, 128 mg sodium, 53 g carbohydrate, 5 g fiber, 3 g protein.

Honey-Spice Acorn Squash
Alpha Wilson, Roswell, New Mexico

Cinnamon and ginger give a nice spiced flavor to the moist tender squash halves.

  3 **tablespoons honey**
  2 **tablespoons butter, melted**
1/4 **teaspoon salt**
1/8 **teaspoon ground cinnamon**
1/8 **teaspoon ground ginger**
  2 **medium acorn squash**

1) In a small bowl, combine the honey, butter, salt, cinnamon and ginger. Cut squash in half; discard the seeds. Cut a thin slice from bottom of squash with a sharp knife to allow it to sit flat.

2) Place cavity side up in a greased 15-in. x 10-in. x 1-in. baking pan. Fill squash halves with butter mixture.

3) Cover and bake at 375° for 1 hour or until squash is tender. Uncover; bake 10 minutes longer.

Yield: 4 servings.

NUTRITION FACTS: 1 serving equals 185 calories, 6 g fat (4 g saturated fat), 15 mg cholesterol, 212 mg sodium, 36 g carbohydrate, 3 g fiber, 2 g protein.

Spaghetti Squash with Sweet Peppers
Julie Backes, Box Elder, South Dakota

For a dish with harvesttime appeal, you can't go wrong with this veggie medley I created. Served with breadsticks, it makes a satisfying main dish or a hearty side.

  1 **medium spaghetti squash**
     (2 pounds)
1/2 **medium green pepper, sliced**
1/2 **medium sweet red pepper, sliced**
  4 **medium fresh mushrooms, sliced**
  1 **small onion, chopped**
  1 **tablespoon olive oil**
  2 **medium tomatoes, quartered**
  1 **garlic clove, minced**
1/2 **cup chicken broth**
1/4 **teaspoon salt**
  3 **tablespoons shredded Parmesan**
     cheese

1) Cut squash in half lengthwise; discard seeds. Place squash cut side down in a microwave-safe dish or plate. Microwave, uncovered, on high for 10-12 minutes or until tender. Cool.

2) In a large nonstick skillet, saute the peppers, mushrooms and onion in oil until tender. Add tomatoes and garlic; saute 4-5 minutes longer. Add the broth and salt; simmer, uncovered, for 3-4 minutes.

3) When squash is cool enough to handle, use a fork to separate strands. Place squash on a serving platter or individual plates; top with the pepper mixture. Sprinkle with Parmesan cheese.

Yield: 4 servings.

NUTRITION FACTS: 1/2 cup equals 110 calories, 5 g fat (1 g saturated fat), 4 mg cholesterol, 372 mg sodium, 13 g carbohydrate, 3 g fiber, 4 g protein.

COOKING SPAGHETTI SQUASH

Cut the squash in half lengthwise and remove seeds. Place cut side down in a greased baking dish; bake at 350° for 45-60 minutes or until the shell is pierced easily with a fork. Allow to cool slightly. Use a fork to separate squash into strands, resembling spaghetti.

Sweet Potatoes

Sweet potatoes are sometimes referred to as, but are not, yams.

Buying

Sweet potatoes are available year-round; peak season is November. Select sweet potatoes with a thin, smooth skin and tapered ends that are heavy for their size. Avoid ones with shriveled skin, soft spots or bruises. Handle gently to avoid bruising.

There are two main types of sweet potatoes. The familiar, moist, orange-fleshed sweet potato and the starchier, drier, yellow-fleshed sweet potato.

Storage

Store sweet potatoes in a dark, cool, dry, well-ventilated area for up to 1 week.

Preparing Sweet Potatoes

Scrub with a vegetable brush under cold water. Depending on use, they may be peeled before or after cooking.

Yield: 1 pound = 2 cups cooked, mashed

Old-Fashioned Sweet Potato Casserole

Taste of Home Test Kitchen

This features a marshmallow topping, but you can also vary it with a crunchier texture.

4	pounds sweet potatoes (about 5 large), peeled and cubed
1	cup milk
1/2	cup packed brown sugar
6	tablespoons butter, softened
1	egg, lightly beaten
1-1/2	teaspoons ground cinnamon
1-1/2	teaspoons vanilla extract
3/4	teaspoon ground allspice
1/2	teaspoon salt
1/4	teaspoon ground nutmeg
18	large marshmallows

1) Place sweet potatoes in a large saucepan; cover with water. Bring to a boil. Reduce heat; cover and cook for 15-20 minutes or until tender; drain.

2) Transfer to a large mixing bowl and mash. Add the next nine ingredients, beat until smooth. Transfer to a greased shallow 2-1/2-qt. baking dish. Bake, uncovered, at 350° for 40-45 minutes or until heated through.

3) Top with marshmallows. Bake 5-10 minutes longer or just until marshmallows begin to puff and brown.

Yield: 10 servings.

NUTRITION FACTS: 3/4 cup equals 282 calories, 8 g fat (5 g saturated fat), 43 mg cholesterol, 227 mg sodium, 50 g carbohydrate, 4 g fiber, 4 g protein.

■ *CRUNCHY TOPPED SWEET POTATO CASSEROLE:* Omit marshmallows and reduce brown sugar in sweet potato mixture to 1/4 cup. Before baking, combine 3/4 cup all-purpose flour, 3/4 cup packed brown sugar, 3/4 cup chopped pecans and 1/2 cup melted butter in a small bowl. Sprinkle over the mashed sweet potato mixture. Bake, uncovered, at 350° for 50-55 minutes or until heated through and topping is browned.

Tomatoes

Classified as a fruit but used as a vegetable, tomatoes are smooth-skinned, round or pear-shaped. They are bright red or yellow when ripe and are eaten raw or cooked.

SWEET POTATOES WITH APPLES

Sweet Potatoes with Apples
Jean Winfree, Merrill, Wisconsin

This satisfying dish is very welcome at any meal at our house, especially on holidays. The tart apple slices taste so good baked on top of the mild sweet potatoes.

BEEFSTEAK TOMATOES
Are large, round tomatoes with a slightly flattened top. They are juicy and readily available. Use raw or cooked.

3	to 3-1/2 pounds sweet potatoes
2	tart apples, peeled, cored and cut into 1/4-inch rings
1/2	cup orange juice
1/4	cup packed brown sugar
1/4	teaspoon ground ginger
1/4	teaspoon ground cinnamon
2	tablespoons butter

CHERRY TOMATOES
May be red or yellow and are primarily used for salads or garnishes.

1) Place sweet potatoes in a large saucepan and cover with water. Bring to a boil. Reduce heat; cover and cook for 30 minutes or until just tender. Drain and cool slightly. Peel and cut into 1/4-in. slices.

GRAPE TOMATOES
Are grape-shaped, and they are sweeter and firmer than cherry tomatoes. Use for salads, crudites, garnishes or snacking.

2) In a greased 13-in. x 9-in. x 2-in. baking dish, alternately layer potatoes and apples. Pour orange juice over top. Combine the brown sugar, ginger and cinnamon; sprinkle over potatoes and apples. Dot with butter.

PLUM/ROMA TOMATOES
Are meaty tomatoes with small seeds. These short, elongated tomatoes are usually red but yellow are available. Use for cooking, sauces or salads.

3) Bake, uncovered, at 350° for 35-45 minutes or until apples and tender and heated through.

Yield: 8 servings.

NUTRITION FACTS: 1 cup equals 225 calories, 3 g fat (2 g saturated fat), 8 mg cholesterol, 106 mg sodium, 48 g carbohydrate, 5 g fiber, 2 g protein.

SUN-DRIED TOMATOES

Are dehydrated tomatoes with a leathery texture and intense flavor. They are available in cellophane package or oil-packed in jars. To rehydrate packaged sun-dried tomatoes, place in a heatproof bowl and cover with boiling water. Let stand for about 10 minutes, then drain.

PREPARING TOMATOES

1) Wash and core tomatoes. To remove peel, place tomato in boiling water for 30 seconds. Immediately plunge in ice water.

2) Remove skin with a sharp paring knife.

Buying

Tomatoes are available year-round; peak season is summer through early fall.

Storage

Keep unwashed tomatoes at room temperature until ripe. Store out of direct sunlight. Tomatoes can be kept in the refrigerator for up to 3 days.

Yield: 1 pound of tomatoes (about 2-3 medium)
= 1-1/2 to 1-3/4 cups chopped
1 pound plum tomatoes (5 medium)
= about 2-1/2 cups chopped
1 pint cherry or grape tomatoes
= 2 cups halved

Broiled Parsley Tomatoes
Howie Wiener, Spring Hill, Florida

I get loads of compliments on this recipe for my mother's tomato side dish. She loved to make great-tasting meals but preferred spending time with us rather than in the kitchen.

4 large plum tomatoes, halved lengthwise

3 tablespoons butter, melted

2 teaspoons minced fresh parsley

1/4 teaspoon salt

1/4 teaspoon pepper

1) With a knife, make deep cuts in the cut surface of each tomato. Place tomatoes cut side up on a greased baking sheet.

2) In a small bowl, combine all of the remaining ingredients; spoon over tomatoes. Broil 3-4 in. from the heat for 3-4 minutes or until tops are lightly browned.

Yield: 4 servings.

NUTRITION FACTS: 1 serving equals 89 calories, 9 g fat (5 g saturated fat), 23 mg cholesterol, 240 mg sodium, 3 g carbohydrate, 1 g fiber, 1 g protein.

SEEDING A TOMATO

To seed a tomato, cut in half. Using a teaspoon, scrape seeds.

Scalloped Tomatoes
Norma Piper, West Salem, Wisconsin

Warm and comforting, this old-fashioned side dish is a great way to use up garden bounty. I lightened the original recipe by using less butter and flour and only a bit of honey.

1/2 cup chopped onion

1/2 cup chopped celery

1 tablespoon butter

1 tablespoon all-purpose flour

1 tablespoon honey

2 teaspoons prepared mustard

1/2 teaspoon salt

1/4 teaspoon pepper

2 slices whole wheat bread, toasted and cubed

4 cups chopped fresh tomatoes

1) In a nonstick skillet, cook onion and celery in butter until tender. Stir in the flour until blended; cook 1 minute longer. Stir in the honey, mustard, salt and pepper until blended. Stir in bread cubes and tomatoes.

2) Transfer to an 8-in. square baking dish coated with nonstick cooking spray. Bake, uncovered, at 350° for 35-40 minutes or until bubbly.

Yield: 6 servings.

NUTRITION FACTS: 3/4 cup equals 88 calories, 3 g fat (1 g saturated fat), 5 mg cholesterol, 304 mg sodium, 15 g carbohydrate, 2 g fiber, 2 g protein.

Tomatillos

Tomatillos are green, tomato-like fruit with a papery outer husk. They have lemon-herb flavor and are used in Mexican and Southwestern cooking.

Buying
Tomatillos are available year-round. Select firm, dry, green tomatillos with husks that tightly surround the fruit.

Storage
Store in a paper bag in the refrigerator crisper drawer for up to 3 weeks.

Preparation
Remove and discard papery husk. Rinse under cold water and seed. Can be used raw or cooked.

Yield: 1 pound = 12 tomatillos = 3 cups sliced

Turnips

Turnips are a root vegetable and have a mild, sweet flavor.

Buying
Turnips are available year-round; peak season is fall through winter. Select turnips that are firm, unblemished and heavy for their size. Light ones may be woody. Any attached greens should be bright and fresh looking. Greens can be removed and cooked separately.

Storage
Store unwashed turnips in the refrigerator crisper drawer for up to 1 week.

Preparation
Scrub young (small) turnips under cold running water. Peel larger turnips. Trim both ends.

Yield: 1 pound trimmed = 3 cups cubed

TURNIP CASSEROLE

Turnip Casserole
Doris Hubert, East Killingly, Connecticut

Turnips are good alone or with other vegetables. Try chopping them to add texture and flavor to soups and stews.

4	medium turnips, peeled and cubed
1	cup water
1	egg, beaten
1/3	cup sugar
3	tablespoons butter
1/2	teaspoon salt
1/4	teaspoon ground cinnamon

1) Place turnips in a large saucepan and cover with water. Bring to a boil. Reduce heat; cover and cook for 15 minutes or until tender and drain.

2) Transfer turnips to a bowl and mash. Add the egg, sugar, butter and salt; mix well. Transfer to a greased 1-qt. baking dish; sprinkle with cinnamon.

3) Cover and bake at 350° for 20-25 minutes or until a thermometer reads 160° and turnip mixture is heated through.

Yield: 4 servings.

NUTRITION FACTS: 3/4 cup equals 192 calories, 10 g fat (6 g saturated fat), 76 mg cholesterol, 479 mg sodium, 25 g carbohydrate, 2 g fiber, 3 g protein.

CHAPTER 14
FRUIT

FRUIT

Fresh fruits can be eaten alone, with salads, in desserts or sauces and sometimes even as accompaniments to meats and poultry. This chapter features many delightful recipes to showcase them.

Each fruit listed has information about availability, buying and storing. If you purchase a fruit that is over-ripe, its storage life will be shorter than the times suggested here.

Handle fruits gently—they bruise easily. A bruised spot will lead to decay. After purchasing, promptly refrigerate fruits that require refrigeration.

Many types of underripe fruits such as apricots, nectarines, plums and pears can be placed in a closed paper bag and left at room temperature to ripen. Other fruits such as bananas, mangoes, melons and papayas can be placed in a bowl out of direct sunlight to ripen at room temperature.

Before preparing fruit, make sure the countertops, cutting boards and utensils are clean. Wash your hands in hot, soapy water.

Apples

Apples range in flavor from sweet to tart depending on the variety. They make great snacks but are also good for salads, sauces, pies and baking. Refer to the types of apples on page 358 for the best uses of individual varieties.

Buying

Apples are available year-round (individual varieties have their own peak seasons, see page 358). Select apples that are firm and have a smooth, unblemished skin that is free of any bruises. Handle gently to prevent bruising.

Storage

Store unwashed apples in the refrigerator away from other vegetables with strong aromas. Apples can be refrigerated for up to 6 weeks. Wash before using.

Yield: 1 pound (3 medium) = 2-3/4 cups sliced

CORING AN APPLE

Use an apple corer to core a whole apple. Push apple corer down into center of a washed apple. Twist and remove the center seeds and membranes.

Core an apple quarter by cutting out the core with a sharp knife.

Types of Apples

BRAEBURN
Sweet-tart flavor with a hint of spice. Crisp, firm apple. Good for eating, baking and using in salads and sauces. Season: October through April.

GRANNY SMITH
Tart flavor. Crisp apple; good for eating, baking and using in pies, salads and sauces. Season: year-round.

CORTLAND
Sweet with a hint of tartness. Juicy and tender apple that resists browning. Good for eating, baking and using in pies, salads and sauces. Season: September through April.

JONATHAN
Tart flavor with a hint of spice. Moderately tender apple. Good for eating, baking and using in pies, salads and sauces. Season: September through April.

EMPIRE
Sweet-tart flavor. Juicy, crisp apple. Good for eating, baking and using in pies, salads and sauces. Season: September through July.

MCINTOSH
Tart, tangy flavor. Juicy, tender apple. Good for eating and using in pies, salads and sauces. Season: September through May.

FUJI
Very sweet flavor. Juicy, crisp apple. Good for eating and using in salads and sauces. Season: October through June.

PINK LADY
Sweet-tart flavor. Crisp apple. Good for eating, baking and using in salads. Season: October through June.

GALA
Sweet flavor. Juicy, crisp apple. Good for eating and using in salads. Season: August through December.

RED DELICIOUS
Sweet flavor. Crisp apple. Good for eating and using in salads. Season: year-round.

GOLDEN DELICIOUS
Mild sweet flavor. Juicy, crisp, all-purpose apple with yellow flesh. Good for eating, baking and using in pies, salads and sauces. Season: year-round.

ROME BEAUTY
Mildly tart flavor. Firm apple. Good for baking and using in sauces and pies. Season: October through May.

Cider Apple Bake
Shelly Schierman, Louisburg, Kansas

This is a warm and wonderful way to use up apples. You can serve it as part of a brunch or top it with cream for dessert.

 6 large tart apples, peeled and sliced
 2 cups apple cider *or* apple juice
 1/3 cup packed brown sugar
 1/4 teaspoon ground cinnamon
 1 cup half-and-half *or* heavy whipping cream

1) Place apples in a greased 2-qt. baking dish. Combine cider and sugar; pour over apples.

2) Bake, uncovered, at 350° for 50-60 minutes or until apples are tender, stirring once. Sprinkle with cinnamon. Cool slightly. Serve warm with cream.

Yield: 6 servings.

NUTRITION FACTS: 1 serving equals 265 calories, 5 g fat (3 g saturated fat), 20 mg cholesterol, 33 mg sodium, 56 g carbohydrate, 6 g fiber, 2 g protein.

CINNAMON APPLES

Cinnamon Apples
Alma Dinsmore, Lebanon, Indiana

Teenagers will have fun melting the red cinnamon candies that give bright color to these tender apples. Serve this as a salad or a side dish to accompany pork.

 2 cups water
 3/4 cup red-hot candies
 1/3 cup sugar
 6 medium tart apples, peeled and quartered

1) In a large saucepan, bring the water, candies and sugar to a boil over medium heat; boil and stir until candies and sugar are dissolved. Reduce the heat and carefully add apples. Cook, uncovered, until apples are tender. Cool slightly.

2) With a slotted spoon, transfer apples to a serving dish; pour sugar syrup over apples. Cool slightly. Cover and refrigerate for at least 3 hours.

Yield: 6 servings.

NUTRITION FACTS: 3/4 cup equals 209 calories, 1 g fat (trace saturated fat), 0 cholesterol, 4 mg sodium, 51 g carbohydrate, 2 g fiber, trace protein.

Chunky Applesauce
Deborah Amrine, Grand Haven, Michigan

There's just something extra special about homemade applesauce. This simple recipe is tart and not too sweet. It makes the perfect side dish, especially with pork chops or pork roast.

 8 cups chopped peeled tart cooking apples (about 3-1/2 pounds)
 1/2 cup packed brown sugar
 2 teaspoons vanilla extract
 1 teaspoon ground cinnamon

1) In a Dutch oven, combine all the ingredients. Cover and cook over medium-low heat for 30 to 40 minutes or until apples are tender, stirring occasionally.

2) Remove from the heat; mash the apples (a potato masher works well) until sauce reaches desired consistency. Serve warm or cold.

Yield: about 3-1/2 cups.

NUTRITION FACTS: 1/2 cup equals 157 calories, trace fat (trace saturated fat), 0 cholesterol, 7 mg sodium, 40 g carbohydrate, 3 g fiber, trace protein.

Glazed Apple Rings
Mary Jane Ruther, Trenton, New Jersey

Four ingredients and a skillet are all that you'll need for these delightful apple rings. Serve them as a sweet side dish alongside pork or for dessert.

 2 tablespoons butter
 2 tablespoons sugar
 3 teaspoons lemon juice
 2 medium apples, peeled and cored

1) In a large skillet, melt butter over medium heat. Stir in sugar and lemon juice. Cut each apple into four rings; add to skillet. Reduce heat.

2) Cover and simmer for 10-15 minutes or until apple rings are tender, turning frequently. Serve warm.

Yield: 4 servings.

NUTRITION FACTS: 2 apple rings equals 107 calories, 6 g fat (4 g saturated fat), 15 mg cholesterol, 58 mg sodium, 15 g carbohydrate, 1 g fiber, trace protein.

APPLE-NUT TOSSED SALAD

Apple-Nut Tossed Salad
Maureen Reubelt, Gales Ferry, Connecticut

When you want an alternative to a plain lettuce salad, give this a try. A light dressing tops apples, walnuts and lettuce sprinkled with blue cheese.

    3   tablespoons olive oil
    1   teaspoon Dijon mustard
  3/4   teaspoon sugar
Salt and pepper to taste
  1/2   cup chopped apple
    1   tablespoon chopped green onion
    3   cups torn Bibb lettuce
    1   to 2 tablespoons chopped walnuts
    1   to 2 tablespoons crumbled blue cheese

1) In a large bowl, whisk the oil, mustard, sugar, salt and pepper. Add apple and onion; toss to coat. Add lettuce, walnuts and blue cheese; toss gently. Serve immediately.

Yield: 4 servings.

NUTRITION FACTS: 3/4 cup (calculated without salt and pepper) equals 128 calories, 12 g fat (2 g saturated fat), 2 mg cholesterol, 63 mg sodium, 5 g carbohydrate, 1 g fiber, 2 g protein.

Apple Cranberry Crumble
Teri Roberts, Hilliard, Ohio

When I first took this dessert to Thanksgiving dinner, it quickly became a tradition. We enjoy it for breakfast, lunch, dinner and snack time!

    3   cups chopped peeled apples
    2   cups fresh *or* frozen cranberries
  3/4   cup sugar
    1   cup old-fashioned *or* quick-cooking oats
  3/4   cup packed brown sugar
  1/3   cup all-purpose flour

  1/2   cup butter, melted
  1/2   cup chopped pecans, optional

1) In a greased 8-in. square baking dish, combine apples and cranberries; sprinkle with sugar. In another bowl, combine the oats, brown sugar, flour and butter; sprinkle over cranberry mixture.

2) Top with pecans if desired. Bake, uncovered, at 350° for 55-60 minutes or until browned and bubbly. Serve warm.

Yield: 6 servings.

NUTRITION FACTS: 1 cup equals 456 calories, 16 g fat (10 g saturated fat), 41 mg cholesterol, 166 mg sodium, 78 g carbohydrate, 4 g fiber, 3 g protein.

■ *PEAR AND CRANBERRY CRUMBLE:* Use 3 cups chopped peeled pears for the apples.

Hot Caramel Apples
Pat Sparks, St. Charles, Missouri

This old-time favorite goes together quickly, and it's such a treat to come home to the aroma of cinnamony baked apples just like Mom made.

    4   large tart apples, cored
  1/2   cup apple juice
  1/2   cup packed brown sugar
   12   red-hot candies
  1/4   cup butter
    8   caramels
  1/4   teaspoon ground cinnamon
Whipped cream, optional

1) Peel about 3/4 in. off the top of each apple; place in a 3-qt. slow cooker. Pour juice over apples. Fill the center of each apple with 2 tablespoons of sugar, three red-hots, 1 tablespoon butter and two caramels. Sprinkle with cinnamon.

2) Cover and cook on low for 4-6 hours or until the apples are tender. Serve immediately with whipped cream if desired.

Yield: 4 servings.

NUTRITION FACTS: 1 caramel apple equals 424 calories, 14 g fat (9 g saturated fat), 32 mg cholesterol, 177 mg sodium, 79 g carbohydrate, 6 g fiber, 1 g protein.

Cinnamon Caramel Apples
Taste of Home Test Kitchen

Cinnamon and chocolate give a tasty twist to traditional caramel apples. Rolled in nuts, coconut or colorful candies, they'll delight kids of all ages.

    2   packages (14 ounces *each*) caramels
    3   tablespoons milk chocolate chips

3 tablespoons water

1 teaspoon ground cinnamon

3/4 teaspoon vanilla extract

8 Popsicle sticks

8 large tart apples

Chocolate-covered toffee bits, finely chopped salted peanuts and cashews, flaked coconut, M&M miniature baking bits *and/or* chocolate sprinkles

1) In a microwave-safe bowl, combine the caramels, chocolate chips, water, cinnamon and vanilla. Microwave, uncovered, on high for 1-1/2 minutes; stir. Microwave 30-60 seconds longer or until caramels are melted.

2) Insert Popsicle sticks into the apples; dip into caramel mixture, turning to coat. Roll in or press on desired toppings. Place on waxed paper; let stand until set.

Yield: 8 servings.

NUTRITION FACTS: 1 serving (calculated without toffee bits, nuts, coconut, baking bits or sprinkles) equals 526 calories, 10 g fat (7 g saturated fat), 8 mg cholesterol, 246 mg sodium, 111 g carbohydrate, 7 g fiber, 5 g protein.

APPLE DUMPLINGS

Apple Dumplings

Jody Fisher, Stewartstown, Pennsylvania

The golden dumplings in this dessert are filled with apples and topped with a sweet caramel sauce. A scoop of ice cream adds the perfect touch.

2 cups all-purpose flour

1 teaspoon salt

2/3 cup shortening

4 to 5 tablespoons cold water

2 cups chopped peeled tart apples (about 5 medium)

2 cups packed brown sugar

1 cup water

1/4 cup butter, cubed

Vanilla ice cream

1) In a large bowl, combine the flour and salt; cut in shortening until crumbly. Gradually add water, tossing with a fork until dough forms a ball. On a lightly floured surface, roll out dough to a 12-in. x 18-in. rectangle. Cut into six squares.

2) Place 1/3 cup chopped apples in the center of each square. Brush edges of dough with water; fold up corners to center and pinch to seal. Place in a greased 13-in. x 9-in. x 2-in. baking dish. Bake, uncovered, at 350° for 30 minutes.

3) In a small saucepan, combine the brown sugar, water and butter; bring to a boil, stirring constantly. Remove from heat. Pour over the dumplings. Bake 25-30 minutes longer or until apples are tender. Serve warm with ice cream.

Yield: 6 servings.

NUTRITION FACTS: 1 serving (calculated without ice cream) equals 711 calories, 29 g fat (10 g saturated fat), 20 mg cholesterol, 500 mg sodium, 109 g carbohydrate, 2 g fiber, 4 g protein.

New Waldorf Salad

Marie Engwall, Willmar, Minnesota

A nice blend of colorful fruits and nuts gives this refreshing salad a great flavor and tempting texture. The citrusy topping dresses it up perfectly.

1 medium unpeeled red apple, chopped

1 medium unpeeled green apple, chopped

1 medium unpeeled pear, chopped

1/2 cup green grapes

1/4 cup raisins

1/4 cup slivered almonds, toasted

1 carton (6 ounces) reduced-fat lemon yogurt

2 teaspoons lemon juice

2 teaspoons orange juice

2 teaspoons honey

1 teaspoon grated orange peel

1) In a large bowl, combine the apples, pear, grapes, raisins and almonds. In a small bowl, combine the yogurt, lemon and orange juices, honey and orange peel. Pour over fruit mixture and stir to coat. Serve immediately.

Yield: 4 servings.

NUTRITION FACTS: 1 cup equals 193 calories, 5 g fat (1 g saturated fat), 2 mg cholesterol, 33 mg sodium, 35 g carbohydrate, 4 g fiber, 5 g protein.

Apricots

Apricots are a dense, sweet fruit with a smooth skin. Fresh apricots are used for eating and for salads and desserts.

Buying

Apricots are available May through August. Select apricots that are plump and fairly firm, not hard, and are orange-yellow to orange in color. Avoid apricots that have blemishes or soft spots or that have a pale-yellow or greenish-yellow color.

Storage

Store firm apricots at room temperature. Once the fruit yields to gentle pressure, store in the refrigerator for 2-3 days.

Yield: 1 pound (8 to 12 medium) = 2-1/2 cups sliced

SPICED HOT FRUIT

Spiced Hot Fruit

Irene Howard, Shenandoah, Iowa

This recipe takes advantage of convenient canned fruit. Assembled in a flash, the crowd-pleasing compote is sparked with cinnamon and ginger.

  2   cans (one 20 ounces, one 8 ounces) pineapple chunks
  2   cans (15-1/4 ounces *each*) apricots, drained and quartered
  1   can (29 ounces) sliced peaches, drained
  1   can (29 ounces) pear halves, drained and quartered
3/4   cup packed brown sugar
1/4   cup butter
  2   cinnamon sticks (3 inches)
1/2   teaspoon ground ginger

1) Drain pineapple, reserving juice. In an ungreased shallow 3-1/2-qt. baking dish, combine the pineapple, apricots, peaches and pears; set aside.

2) In a saucepan, combine brown sugar, butter, cinnamon, ginger and reserved pineapple juice; bring to a boil. Reduce heat; simmer for 5 minutes. Discard cinnamon sticks. Pour over fruit.

3) Bake, uncovered, at 350° for 30 minutes or until heated through. Serve warm.

Yield: 10 cups.

NUTRITION FACTS: 1/2 cup equals 131 calories, 2 g fat (0 saturated fat), 0 cholesterol, 38 mg sodium, 29 g carbohydrate, 0 fiber, 1 g protein.

Stewed Holiday Fruit

Taste of Home Test Kitchen

Dried apricots, plums and fresh bananas are drizzled with a sweet cider and marmalade sauce in this fruity concoction. Hints of cinnamon and citrus lend a festive zest to each cool spoonful. Serve a bowlful of this fun fruit for breakfast, snacktime or dessert.

   12   dried apricots
   12   dried plums
1-1/2   cups apple cider *or* unsweetened apple juice
    2   cinnamon sticks (3 inches)
    8   whole cloves
    2   whole allspice
  1/4   cup orange marmalade
    2   teaspoons lemon juice
    1   teaspoon butter
    2   medium firm bananas, sliced
    2   tablespoons sliced almonds, toasted

1) In a small saucepan, combine the apricots, plums, cider, cinnamon, cloves and allspice. Bring to a boil. Remove from the heat; refrigerate overnight.

2) Strain cider, reserving liquid; set apricots and prunes aside. Discard spices. In a small saucepan, combine the marmalade, lemon juice, butter and the reserved cider. Bring to a boil, stirring occasionally. Cool.

3) Divide apricots, prunes and bananas among serving dishes; drizzle with cooled sauce. Sprinkle with almonds.

Yield: 4 servings.

NUTRITION FACTS: 3/4 cup fruit with 1/4 cup sauce equals 259 calories, 3 g fat (1 g saturated fat), 3 mg cholesterol, 26 mg sodium, 61 g carbohydrate, 5 g fiber, 2 g protein.

Bananas

Bananas have a soft to tender texture and a sweet taste.

Buying

Bananas are available year-round. Select plump bananas that are free from bruises. The banana skin goes from green to yellow to yellow with speckles to black depending on its ripeness and how it is stored.

CAVENDISH is the most readily available banana in the supermarket.

FINGER BANANAS are a smaller version of the Cavendish and are considered to be sweeter.

RED BANANAS are short, chunky bananas and have a red skin that turns purplish-red when ripe. The pink flesh is sweet and creamy. Some say the banana has a hint of berry flavor to it.

PLANTAINS are a starchy fruit used for cooking and are served as a side dish or dessert.

Storage

Store at room temperature until ripe, then store in the refrigerator or freeze. The skin will turn black in the refrigerator. Brush cut bananas with lemon, lime, orange or pineapple juice to prevent browning.

Cooking

Use firm bananas with yellow skins and green tips for cooking. Use firm but ripe for salads, and use ripe for baking.

Yield: 1 pound (3 medium) = 1-1/3 cups mashed or 1-1/2 to 2 cups sliced

Banana Nut Salad
Sharon Mensing, Greenfield, Iowa

I combine two kid-friendly flavors in this speedy salad, and the children can help out by slicing and arranging the bananas. Then just stir up the dressing and serve in minutes.

> 2 medium ripe bananas, sliced
> Leaf lettuce
> 1/4 cup mayonnaise
> 1 tablespoon peanut butter
> 1 tablespoon honey
> 1/4 cup chopped peanuts

1) Place bananas on lettuce-lined salad plates. In a small bowl, combine the mayonnaise, peanut butter and honey. Spoon over bananas; sprinkle with peanuts.

Yield: 4 servings.

NUTRITION FACTS: 1 serving equals 242 calories, 17 g fat (3 g saturated fat), 5 mg cholesterol, 95 mg sodium, 21 g carbohydrate, 2 g fiber, 4 g protein.

Caramel Banana Dessert
Carolene Esayenko, Calgary, Alberta

This dessert leaves plenty of room for imagination. Chocolate sauce can replace the caramel. You can also substitute your favorite nut topping or create mini sundaes by serving the bananas with ice cream.

> 4 medium firm bananas, sliced
> 4 to 6 tablespoons caramel ice cream topping
> 4 to 6 tablespoons chopped pecans
> Whipped topping, optional

1) Place the bananas on individual serving dishes. Top with caramel topping and pecans. Garnish with whipped topping if desired.

Yield: 4-6 servings.

NUTRITION FACTS: 1 serving equals 141 calories, 4 g fat (trace saturated fat), trace cholesterol, 48 mg sodium, 28 g carbohydrate, 2 g fiber, 1 g protein.

Simple Bananas Foster

Janice Mitchell, Aurora, Colorado

Rather than using rum and an open flame, this recipe cooks up on the stovetop with equally delicious results.

- 1-1/2 teaspoon cornstarch
- 1/8 teaspoon apple pie spice
- 1 can (5-1/2 ounces) unsweetened apple juice
- 1/4 teaspoon rum extract
- 1/8 teaspoon maple flavoring
- 1/8 teaspoon butter flavoring *or* vanilla extract
- 2 medium firm bananas, sliced

Vanilla ice cream *or* frozen yogurt

1) In a small saucepan, combine the cornstarch and pie spice. Stir in the apple juice until smooth. Bring to a boil; cook and stir for 2 minutes or until slightly thickened.

2) Remove from the heat; stir in extracts and flavorings. Add bananas and heat through over medium heat. Serve warm over ice cream.

Yield: 4 servings.

NUTRITION FACTS: 1 serving (calculated without ice cream or yogurt) equals 79 calories, trace fat (0 saturated fat), 0 cholesterol, 2 mg sodium, 20 g carbohydrate, 0 fiber, 1 g protein.

Layered Banana Pudding

Esther Matteson, Bremen, Indiana

This old-fashioned favorite is satisfying and beats any comparison to instant pudding mixes.

- 1/2 cup all-purpose flour
- 2/3 cup packed brown sugar
- 2 cups milk
- 2 egg yolks, beaten
- 2 tablespoons butter
- 1 teaspoon vanilla extract
- 1 cup heavy whipping cream, whipped
- 4 to 6 medium firm bananas, sliced

Chopped walnuts, optional

1) In a large saucepan, combine the flour and brown sugar. Stir in milk until smooth. Cook and stir over medium-high heat until thickened and bubbly. Reduce heat; cook and stir 2 minutes longer.

2) Remove from the heat. Stir a small amount of hot filling into egg yolks; return all to pan, stirring constantly. Bring to a gentle boil; cook and stir 2 minutes longer.

3) Remove from the heat; stir in butter and vanilla. Cool to room temperature without stirring. Fold in the whipped cream.

4) Layer a third of the pudding in a 2-qt. glass bowl; top with half of the bananas. Repeat layers. Top with remaining pudding. Sprinkle with nuts if desired. Cover and refrigerate for at least 1 hour before serving.

Yield: 8 servings.

NUTRITION FACTS: 1 serving equals 333 calories, 18 g fat (10 g saturated fat), 110 mg cholesterol, 80 mg sodium, 41 g carbohydrate, 2 g fiber, 5 g protein.

Tropical Bananas

Kathleen Jones, Chicago, Illinois

Lime provides the refreshing twist to this exotic-tasting dessert that's quick, healthy and delicious. I sometimes like to serve it as a midday snack.

- 2 medium firm bananas, sliced
- 1 tablespoon lime juice
- 2 tablespoons salted peanuts
- 1 tablespoon honey
- 1 tablespoon flaked coconut
- 1-1/2 teaspoons grated lime peel

1) In a small bowl, toss bananas with lime juice. Add peanuts and honey; mix well.

2) Spoon into individual dishes. Sprinkle with coconut and lime peel. Serve immediately.

Yield: 2 servings.

NUTRITION FACTS: 1 cup equals 210 calories, 6 g fat (2 g saturated fat), 0 cholesterol, 48 mg sodium, 40 g carbohydrate, 4 g fiber, 4 g protein.

Berries

Berries come in many varieties, please refer to the individual listings for more information about each.

Buying

Individual varieties have their own peak seasons. Select berries that are plump. Avoid those that are bruised, mushy or moldy. Avoid packages with juice-stained bottoms.

Storage

Berries are fragile and very perishable. Before refrigerating, sort through and discard any crushed, mushy or moldy fruit.

Store unwashed berries in their container for 1-2 days. For longer storage, refer to the information on individual berries. To freeze, arrange in a single layer on a plastic wrap-lined baking sheet. Once frozen, transfer to a freezer container or bag. Freeze for up to 1 year. Gently wash berries before using.

Yield: 1 pint = 1-1/2 to 2 cups

BLACKBERRIES

This is a sweet and juicy, purplish-black fruit. Peak season is May through September. Boysenberries are a cross between a blackberry and a red raspberry, and they can be substituted for blackberries. Refrigerate a single layer on a paper towel-lined baking sheet covered with a paper towel for 2 days. Freeze up to 1 year.

BLUEBERRIES

This sweet-tart blue fruit has a silvery sheen. Peak season is May through October. Refrigerate blueberries in their container or tightly covered for up to 1 week. Freeze up to 1 year.

CRANBERRIES

Tart, firm, red cranberries have a peak season from October through December. Refrigerate in their bag for 1 to 2 months. Freeze in their bag for up to a year. **Yield:** 12 ounces = 3 cups whole; 2-1/2 cups finely chopped.

CURRANTS

This tart, tiny, glossy fruit grows in a cluster like grapes and comes in red, black and white varieties. Generally they are used in jams and jellies. Peak season is June through August. Refrigerate on paper towels for up to 3 days. **Yield:** 4 ounces = 1-1/4 cups.

GOOSEBERRIES

Tart, translucent gooseberries come in green, white and purple varieties. Peak season is summer. Refrigerate for up to 2 weeks. Freeze up to 1 year. Remove stem and top before using. **Yield:** 1 package (6 ounces) = 1 cup.

RASPBERRIES

Sweet and juicy raspberries come in red, black and golden colors. The black raspberry has a sweet-tart flavor. Peak seasons are from June through July and September through October. Refrigerate a single layer on a paper towel-lined baking sheet covered with a paper towel for 3 days. Freeze up to 1 year.

STRAWBERRIES

Strawberries are a sweet and juicy red fruit; pale white fruit is unripe. Strawberries do not continue to ripen after they are picked. Available year-around; peak season is April through June. Refrigerate in a paper towel-lined, moisture-proof container for 2 to 3 days. Freeze up to 1 year.

HULLING STRAWBERRIES

Use a strawberry huller or the tip of a serrated grapefruit spoon to easily remove the stem/hull. Just insert the tip of the spoon into the strawberry next to the stem and cut around the stem.

1) Place firm ripe berries with stem down on a cutting board. With a sharp knife, make cuts 1/8 in. apart through the berry to within 1/8 in. of the stem.

2) Use your fingers to gently spread apart the slices to form a fan.

3) Add further appeal with fresh mint if it's available. After carefully removing the berry leaves with the knife point, replace them with a sprig of mint.

Summer Berry Salsa
Diane Hixon, Niceville, Florida

Other fruits are often used in relishes and sauces, but I decided to make one with my favorites. I get rave reviews when I serve this fruity, distinctive salsa over chicken, pork or fish. It's also delicious atop a spinach or lettuce salad.

- 1   pint fresh blueberries
- 1   pint fresh strawberries, chopped
- 1/4 cup sugar
- 2   tablespoons finely chopped onion
- 1   tablespoon lemon juice
- 1/2 teaspoon pepper
- 2   drops hot pepper sauce
- 1/4 cup slivered *or* sliced almonds, toasted

1) In a large bowl, combine the berries, sugar, onion, lemon juice, pepper and hot pepper sauce. Cover and refrigerate for 1 hour. Just before serving, stir in almonds.

Yield: 4 cups.

NUTRITION FACTS: 1/4 cup equals 42 calories, 1 g fat (0 saturated fat), 0 cholesterol, 2 mg sodium, 8 g carbohydrate, 0 fiber, 1 g protein.

Cranberry Ice
Carolyn Butterworth, Spirit Lake, Iowa

This traditional Christmas dessert was first made in our family by my grandma. She handed the recipe down to my mother, who then shared it with me and my two sisters. The cold, tart treat is a wonderful accompaniment to a traditional turkey dinner.

- 3   cups fresh *or* frozen cranberries
- 2   cups water
- 1-1/2 cups sugar
- 1   teaspoon unflavored gelatin
- 1/2   cup cold water
- 1/2   cup lemon juice

1) In a large saucepan, bring cranberries and water to a boil. Cook over medium heat until the berries pop, about 10 minutes. Remove from the heat; cool slightly. Press mixture through a sieve or food mill, reserving juice. Discard skins and seeds.

2) In a small bowl, sprinkle gelatin over cold water; set aside. In a saucepan, combine cranberry mixture and sugar; cook and stir until sugar is dissolved and mixture just begins to boil. Remove from the heat. Stir in gelatin mixture, stirring until gelatin is dissolved. Add lemon juice.

3) Transfer to a shallow 1-qt. freezer container. Cover and freeze until ice begins to form around the edges of container, about 1 hour; stir mixture. Freeze until slushy, stirring occasionally.

Yield: 8 servings.

NUTRITION FACTS: 1 cup equals 167 calories, trace fat (trace saturated fat), 0 cholesterol, 1 mg sodium, 43 g carbohydrate, 2 g fiber, trace protein.

WASHING BERRIES

To wash berries, place berries a few at a time in a colander in the sink. Gently spray with sink sprayer. Then spread out on paper towels to pat dry.

Poppy Seed Fruit Salad
Edie DeSpain, Logan, Utah

Almonds add a nice crunch to this pretty salad that's always a hit when I serve it. It's refreshing and goes with just about anything. The dressing can be used with any combination of fruit.

- 1/4 cup honey
- 1/4 cup limeade concentrate

2 teaspoons poppy seeds
1 cup halved fresh strawberries
1 cup cubed fresh pineapple
1 cup fresh blueberries
1 cup cubed seedless watermelon
1/4 cup slivered almonds, toasted

1) In a small bowl, combine the honey, limeade concentrate and poppy seeds. In a serving bowl, combine the fruit.

2) Drizzle with dressing; toss gently to coat. Sprinkle with the almonds. Serve with a slotted spoon.

Yield: 6 servings.

NUTRITION FACTS: 3/4 cup equals 111 calories, 1 g fat (trace saturated fat), 0 cholesterol, 2 mg sodium, 29 g carbohydrate, 2 g fiber, 1 g protein.

Cherries

Cherries are available in sweet and tart varieties, which are frequently used for pies. Bing (dark red) and Royal Ann (golden) are sweet cherries and Montmorency is tart.

Buying

Sweet cherries are available May through July. Peak season for tart cherries is June through July. Select cherries that are plump and firm with a shiny skin. Avoid soft, bruised, shriveled fruit or fruit that has browned around the stem area.

Storage

Before refrigerating, sort through and discard any crushed, mushy or moldy fruit. Store unwashed cherries in a closed plastic bag in the refrigerator away from other vegetables with strong aromas for 1-2 days. To freeze, arrange in a single layer on a plastic wrap-lined baking sheet. Once frozen, transfer to a freezer container or bag. Freeze up to 1 year.

Preparation

Gently wash cherries before using, not before refrigeration. Use a cherry pitter or tip of a vegetable peeler to pit cherries.

Yield: 1 pound = 3 cups whole or 3-1/2 cups halved

Northern Cherry Puffs
Barbara Hanmer, Benzonia, Michigan

Michigan is a cherry-producing state, and that delightful fruit is highlighted in this classic recipe. Try it topped with whipped cream or ice cream.

1 cup fresh *or* frozen pitted dark sweet cherries, thawed and drained
1 tablespoon lemon juice
1-1/2 teaspoons almond extract, *divided*
1/4 teaspoon red food coloring, optional
1/3 cup shortening
2/3 cup sugar
1 egg
1 cup all-purpose flour
1/2 teaspoon baking powder
1/2 teaspoon salt
1/3 cup milk

SAUCE:
1/2 cup sugar
4-1/2 teaspoons cornstarch
1/4 cup water
2 cups fresh *or* frozen pitted dark sweet cherries
1/4 teaspoon red food coloring, optional

Whipped cream *or* vanilla ice cream

1) In a small bowl, combine cherries, lemon juice, 1/2 teaspoon extract and food coloring if desired; toss to coat. Spoon into four greased 10-oz. custard cups or ramekins.

2) In a small mixing bowl, cream shortening and sugar. Beat in egg and remaining extract. Combine flour, baking powder and salt; add to the creamed mixture alternately with milk. Spoon over cherry mixture. Bake, uncovered, at 375° for 20-25 minutes or until golden brown. Cool in cups for 10 minutes.

3) Meanwhile, in a saucepan, combine sugar and cornstarch. Stir in water until blended. Add cherries and food coloring if desired. Bring to a boil over medium heat; cook and stir for 2 minutes or until thickened. Invert puffs onto dessert plates; top with warm cherry sauce and whipped cream.

Yield: 4 servings.

NUTRITION FACTS: 1 serving equals 608 calories, 19 g fat (5 g saturated fat), 56 mg cholesterol, 372 mg sodium, 104 g carbohydrate, 3 g fiber, 7 g protein.

George Washington Cherry Cobbler

Juanita Sherwood, Charleston, Illinois

Since Dad loved fruit, my mother prepared this dessert often in different ways. You can try it with blackberries or blueberries, too.

1/2 cup sugar

2 tablespoons cornstarch

1/4 teaspoon ground cinnamon

3/4 cup water

1 package (12 ounces) frozen pitted dark sweet cherries, thawed

1 tablespoon butter

TOPPING:

1 cup all-purpose flour

4 tablespoon sugar, *divided*

2 teaspoons baking powder

1/2 teaspoon salt

3 tablespoons shortening

1/2 cup milk

Ice cream, optional

1) In a large saucepan, combine the sugar, cornstarch and cinnamon. Stir in water until smooth. Add the cherries and butter. Bring to a boil over medium heat; cook and stir for 2 minutes or until thickened. Pour into an 8-in. square baking pan; set aside.

2) In a bowl, combine the flour, 2 tablespoons sugar, baking powder and salt. Cut in shortening until mixture resembles coarse crumbs. Stir in milk just until moistened. Drop by spoonfuls over the cherries; sprinkle with remaining sugar.

3) Bake at 400° for 30-35 minutes or until golden brown. Serve warm with ice cream if desired.

Yield: 8 servings.

NUTRITION FACTS: 1 serving equals 231 calories, 7 g fat (2 g saturated fat), 6 mg cholesterol, 270 mg sodium, 40 g carbohydrate, 1 g fiber, 3 g protein.

Citrus Fruit

Citrus fruit comes in many varieties; please refer to the individual listings for more information about each.

Buying

Citrus fruit is available year-round (individual varieties have their own peak seasons). Select citrus fruit that is firm, heavy for its size and has a bright color. Avoid fruit with bruises or wrinkles. Weather conditions during the growing season can affect the thickness of the peel.

Storage

Store most citrus fruit at room temperature for about 3 days. For longer storage, store in the crisper drawer in the refrigerator for 2 to 3 weeks. Juice or grated peel may be frozen for up to 1 year.

GRAPEFRUITS have white, pink or red flesh and a refreshing, sweet-tart flavor. **Yield:** 1 medium = 3/4 cup juice or 1-1/2 cups segments.

LEMONS are a tart-tangy fruit with sunny yellow flesh. The two major varieties, Libson and Eureka, look similar. **Yield:** 1 medium = 3 tablespoons juice or 2 teaspoons grated peel.

LIMES are tart fruit with a light green flesh. Persian limes are most commonly sold and are a bright green color. They may have some small brown patches on their skin. Key limes grown in the Florida Keys have a limited season. They are smaller in size, have a yellow-green skin and are more tart. The juice is used for Key Lime Pie. **Yield:** 1 medium Persian lime = 2 tablespoons juice or 1-1/2 teaspoons grated peel.

ORANGE flavors range from sweet to sour. Oranges are divided into three groups: sweet, loose skin and bitter. Sweet oranges are the seedless navel, juicy Valencia and the red-flesh blood orange. Valencia oranges may have some green color on their skin; this is a natural occurrence and is not a sign that the orange is under ripe. Small brown patches on the skin sometimes occur and that does not affect the quality of the orange.

Loose skin oranges are very easy to peel and separate the fruit into segments. Loose skin oranges generally fall into the mandarin family. Tangerines, temple oranges, Clementines and Minneolas are examples of loose skin oranges. Bitter oranges are used for cooking or marmalade. Seville is an example of a bitter orange. **Yield:** 1 medium = 1/3 to 1/2 cup juice or 4 teaspoons grated peel.

ORANGE ROSE

1) Cut a very thin slice from bottom of orange and discard. Starting at the top of the orange, use a vegetable peeler or sharp knife to cut a continuous narrow strip of peel in a spiral fashion around the entire orange.

2) Start at the end of the strip where you started, wrap the strip around itself to form a coil. Insert one or two toothpicks horizontally into the base to secure.

LEMON WHEELS

To make lemon wheels, use a citrus stripper or large zester to make evenly spaced vertical strips around a lemon. Cut the lemon into 1/8-in. slices. Make one cut from the center of each slice through the peel to place over rim of glass.

Tangy Texas Salsa
Lois Kildahl, McAllen, Texas

This is one way to work citrus into a main dish. The combination of tangy fruit, spicy jalapeno and distinctive cilantro is perfect over any meat, poultry or fish. We also dip into it with chips.

- 1 medium grapefruit
- 1 large navel orange
- 1 *each* medium green, sweet red and yellow pepper, chopped
- 1 medium tomato, seeded and chopped
- 1 jalapeno pepper, seeded and chopped
- 3 tablespoons chopped red onion
- 1 tablespoon minced fresh oregano

- 1-1/2 teaspoons sugar
- 1/2 teaspoon salt

1) To section grapefruit and orange, cut a thin slice off the bottom and top of each. Place each fruit cut side down on a cutting board.

2) With a sharp knife, remove peel and white pith. Slice between the membrane of each section and the fruit until the knife reaches the center; remove sections. Place sections in a bowl; add remaining ingredients and mix well. Cover and refrigerate for at least 2 hours.

Yield: about 5 cups.

Editor's Note: When cutting or seeding hot peppers, use rubber or plastic gloves to protect your hands. Avoid touching your face.

NUTRITION FACTS: 1/4 cup equals 17 calories, trace fat (trace saturated fat), 0 cholesterol, 60 mg sodium, 4 g carbohydrate, 1 g fiber, trace protein.

Sweet Broiled Grapefruit
Terry Bray, Haines City, Florida

I was never a fan of grapefruit until I had it broiled at a Florida restaurant. It was so tangy and delicious! I finally got the recipe and now make it often for my husband, children and grandchildren.

- 1 large grapefruit
- 2 tablespoons butter, softened
- 2 tablespoons sugar
- 1/2 teaspoon ground cinnamon

1) Cut each grapefruit in half. With a sharp knife, cut around the membrane in the center of each half and discard. Cut around each section to loosen the fruit.

2) Place 1 tablespoon butter in the center of each half. Combine sugar and cinnamon; sprinkle over each. Place on a baking pan.

3) Broil 4 in. from heat until butter is melted and sugar is bubbly. Serve immediately.

Yield: 2 servings.

NUTRITION FACTS: 1 serving equals 203 calories, 12 g fat (7 g saturated fat), 31 mg cholesterol, 116 mg sodium, 26 g carbohydrate, 2 g fiber, 1 g protein.

GRATING CITRUS FRUIT

The peel from citrus fruit adds a burst of flavor to recipes and color to garnishes. Citrus peel, also called zest, can be grated into fine shreds with a microplane grater. For slightly thicker and longer shreds, use the zester; for long, continuous strips, use a stripper. Remove only the colored portion of the peel, not the bitter white pith.

GRAPEFRUIT ALASKA

Grapefruit Alaska
Peg Atzen, Hackensack, Minnesota

You'll easily impress guests with this dessert. It takes some time to prepare, but the rave reviews I receive make it all worth it.

      4 large grapefruit
      2 teaspoons rum extract
  1/2 cup heavy whipping cream,
         whipped
      3 egg whites
      1 teaspoon cornstarch
  1/4 teaspoon cream of tartar
  1/4 cup sugar
      8 maraschino cherries

1) Halve grapefruit and section; remove membranes. Return grapefruit sections to grapefruit halves. Drizzle 1/4 teaspoon rum extract over each.

2) Top with 1 rounded tablespoon of whipped cream; Place on an ungreased foil-lined baking sheet.

3) In a large mixing bowl, beat the egg whites, cornstarch and cream of tartar on medium speed until soft peaks form. Gradually beat in sugar, 1 tablespoon at a time, on high until stiff glossy peaks form and sugar is dissolved.

4) Mound 1/2 cup on each grapefruit half; spread meringue to edges to seal. Bake at 350° for 15 minutes or until meringue is browned. Top each with a cherry. Serve immediately.

Yield: 8 servings.

NUTRITION FACTS: 1 serving equals 152 calories, 6 g fat (3 g saturated fat), 20 mg cholesterol, 26 mg sodium, 24 g carbohydrate, 2 g fiber, 3 g protein.

Cinnamon-Honey Grapefruit
Mrs. Carson Sadler, Souris, Manitoba

Naturally delicious grapefruit gains even more great flavor with this recipe. I often like to prepare this as a light breakfast. But it also makes an appealing addition to your morning meal.

      1 medium grapefruit
      2 teaspoons honey
  Dash ground cinnamon

1) Cut each grapefruit in half. With a sharp knife, cut around each section to loosen fruit. Place cut side up in a baking pan.

2) Drizzle each half with 1 teaspoon honey; sprinkle with cinnamon. Broil 4 in. from heat for 2-3 minutes or until bubbly. Serve warm.

Yield: 2 servings.

NUTRITION FACTS: 1/2 grapefruit equals 63 calories, trace fat (trace saturated fat), 0 cholesterol, trace sodium, 16 g carbohydrate, 1 g fiber, 1 g protein.

Avocado Citrus Toss
Marie Hattrup, The Dalles, Oregon

The light dressing doesn't mask the goodness of sweet citrus sections, crisp lettuce, crunchy almonds and mellow avocados.

      6 cups torn salad greens
      2 medium grapefruit, peeled and
         sectioned
      3 navel oranges, peeled and
         sectioned
      1 ripe avocado, peeled and sliced
  1/4 cup slivered almonds, toasted

DRESSING:
  1/2 cup vegetable oil
  1/3 cup sugar
      3 tablespoons vinegar
      2 teaspoons poppy seeds
      1 teaspoon finely chopped onion
  1/2 teaspoon ground mustard
  1/2 teaspoon salt

1) In a large salad bowl, toss the greens, grapefruit, oranges, avocado and almonds.

2) In a jar with tight-fitting lid, combine the dressing ingredients; shake well. Drizzle over salad and toss to coat.

Yield: 6 servings.

NUTRITION FACTS: 1 cup equals 355 calories, 26 g fat (3 g saturated fat), 0 cholesterol, 215 mg sodium, 31 g carbohydrate, 6 g fiber, 4 g protein.

ALMOND SUNSHINE CITRUS

Almond Sunshine Citrus

Geri Barr, Calgary, Alberta

I adapted this recipe from one I found in a newspaper. The tangy combination of citrus fruits is welcome as a light dessert after a big meal or as a refreshing addition to a brunch.

3	large navel oranges
1	medium red grapefruit
1	medium white grapefruit
1	small lemon
1	small lime
1/3	cup sugar
1/8	teaspoon almond extract
2	tablespoons sliced almonds, toasted

1) Grate enough peel from the oranges, grapefruit, lemon and lime to measure 1 tablespoon of mixed citrus peel; set peel aside.

2) To section citrus fruit, cut a thin slice off the bottom and top of the oranges, grapefruit, lemon and lime. Place each fruit cut side down on a cutting board.

3) With a sharp knife, remove peel and white pith. Holding fruit over a bowl, slice between the membrane of each section and the fruit until the knife reaches the center; remove sections and place in a glass bowl. Set 1/2 cup juice aside.

4) In a small saucepan, combine the sugar and reserved peel and juice. Bring to a boil. Reduce heat; simmer, uncovered for 10 minutes.

5) Cool; stir in extract. Pour over fruit. Refrigerate overnight. Just before serving, sprinkle with almonds.

Yield: 4 servings.

NUTRITION FACTS: 3/4 cup equals 197 calories, 2 g fat (trace saturated fat), 0 cholesterol, 1 mg sodium, 47 g carbohydrate, 6 g fiber, 3 g protein.

SECTIONING A CITRUS FRUIT

1) Cut a thin slice off the bottom and top of the fruit. Rest the fruit, cut sides down, on a cutting board. With a sharp paring knife, remove peel and white pith from fruit.

2) Hold fruit over a bowl and slice between the membrane of a section and the fruit until the knife reaches the center. Turn the knife and follow the membrane so the fruit is released. Repeat until all sections are removed.

Dates

Dates have a high sugar content, which is even more concentrated when dried.

Buying
Dried dates are available year-round. Peak season for fresh dates is late summer to mid-fall. Select fresh dates that are plump with a smooth shiny skins.

Storage
Store in the refrigerator in a plastic bag for up to 2 weeks. Remove pits before using.

Yield: 1 pound dried dates
= 2-3/4 cups pitted and chopped
1 package (10 ounces) dried, pitted dates
= 1-1/4 cups chopped

Festive Stuffed Dates
Diana Debruyn, Cincinnati, Ohio

Four ingredients are all you need for these change-of-pace treats. By the way, just 1/2 cup dates contains more potassium than a medium banana.

> 3 ounces reduced-fat cream cheese
> 1/4 cup confectioners' sugar
> 2 teaspoons grated orange peel
> 30 pitted dates

1) In a small mixing bowl, beat the cream cheese, confectioners' sugar and orange peel until blended.

2) Carefully make a slit in the center of each date; fill with cream cheese mixture. Cover and refrigerate for at least 1 hour before serving.

Yield: 10 servings.

NUTRITION FACTS: 3 stuffed dates equals 102 calories, 2 g fat (1 g saturated fat), 6 mg cholesterol, 37 mg sodium, 22 g carbohydrate, 2 g fiber, 1 g protein.

Date Pudding
Opal Hamer, St. Petersburg, Florida

This pudding has been our family's favorite dessert for Thanksgiving and Christmas for years. At Christmas, I top each with a touch of green-tinted whipped cream and a red maraschino cherry.

> 3/4 cup chopped dates
> 1/2 cup chopped walnuts
> 6 tablespoons sugar
> 1 egg
> 2 tablespoons milk
> 1/2 teaspoon vanilla extract
> 2 tablespoons all-purpose flour
> 1/2 teaspoon baking powder
> Dash salt
> 1 tablespoon butter
> Whipped cream

1) In a bowl, combine the dates, walnuts and sugar. In another bowl, beat egg, milk and vanilla. Add to date mixture; mix well.

2) Combine flour, baking powder and salt; add to the date mixture. Spread into a greased 1-qt. baking dish; dot with butter.

3) Bake at 325° for 30 minutes or until a knife

inserted near the center comes out clean. Serve with whipped cream.

Yield: 2 servings.

NUTRITION FACTS: 1/2 cup (calculated without whipped cream) equals 646 calories, 27 g fat (6 g saturated fat), 124 mg cholesterol, 273 mg sodium, 97 g carbohydrate, 7 g fiber, 13 g protein.

DATE NUT BARS

Date Nut Bars
Margaret Asselin, Kimball, Michigan

Even those who aren't fond of nuts or dates enjoy these bars. They freeze well in airtight containers, so you can save some for another day.

> 2 cups sugar
> 2 cups all-purpose flour
> 2 teaspoons baking powder
> 1/4 teaspoon salt
> 2 cups chopped dates
> 2 cups chopped walnuts *or* pecans
> 4 eggs, lightly beaten
> 2 tablespoons butter, melted
> 1 teaspoon vanilla extract
> Confectioners' sugar

1) In a large bowl, combine the sugar, flour, baking powder, salt, dates and nuts. Add the eggs, butter and vanilla; stir just until dry ingredients are moistened (batter will be very stiff).

2) Spread in a greased 15-in. x 10-in. x 1-in. baking pan. Bake at 350° for 20-25 minutes or until golden brown. Cool bars on a wire rack. Dust with confectioners' sugar.

Yield: 5 dozen.

NUTRITION FACTS: 2 bars (calculated without confectioners' sugar) equals 182 calories, 6 g fat (1 g saturated fat), 30 mg cholesterol, 63 mg sodium, 30 g carbohydrate, 2 g fiber, 4 g protein.

Figs

The many varieties of figs include Black Mission, Calimyrna and Kadota. Depending on the variety, the skin may be green, brown or purplish-black; the seed-filled sweet pulp can be white, pink or purple.

Buying

Figs are available June through October. Select plump, firm fruit that is heavy for its size and gives slightly when gently pressed. Avoid bruised, soft fruit or fruit with a sour aroma. Handle carefully as figs bruise easily.

Storage

Store unwashed figs in the refrigerator and use within 2 days. Dried figs can be stored in an airtight container for up to 6 months.

Yield: 1 package (8 ounces) Black Mission Figs = 1-1/2 cups sliced

Grapes

Flavors of grapes vary from sweet to sweet-tart. They are available seedless and with seeds. Grapes are divided by their color (green or white, red and black) and their use (table, wine or commercial).

The grapes available in the store are table grapes. The most common green grapes are Thompson seedless and Perlette seedless. The most common red grapes are Flame and Ruby (both seedless) and Red Globe. Beauty or Black seedless black grapes may be available in your market.

Buying

Green grapes are available year-round (individual varieties have their own peak seasons). Select grapes that are plump, firmly attached to the stem and have good color for their variety. Avoid grapes that have bruises, soft spots or mold.

Storage

Store unwashed grapes in the refrigerator in a perforated plastic bags for about 1 week. Wash before using, not before refrigeration.

Grapes can be frozen and stored in an airtight container. Frozen grapes make a refreshing treat in the summer.

Yield: 1 pound = 3 cups

Layered Fruit Salad

Page Alexander, Baldwin City, Kansas

Fresh fruit is layered into an eye-catching salad that's a welcome side dish all summer long.

- 1/2 cup orange juice
- 1/4 cup lemon juice
- 1/4 cup packed brown sugar
- 1/2 teaspoon grated orange peel
- 1/2 teaspoon grated lemon peel
- 1 cinnamon stick (3 inches)
- 2 cups fresh *or* drained canned pineapple chunks
- 1 cup seedless red grapes
- 2 medium bananas, sliced
- 2 medium oranges, sectioned
- 1 medium grapefruit, sectioned
- 1 pint fresh strawberries, sliced
- 2 medium kiwifruit, peeled and sliced

1) In a large saucepan, combine the juices, sugar, peels and cinnamon stick; bring to a boil. Reduce heat; simmer, uncovered, for 5 minutes. Remove from the heat; cool completely.

2) Meanwhile, layer fruit in a glass serving bowl. Remove cinnamon stick from sauce; pour sauce over fruit. Cover; refrigerate for several hours.

Yield: 8 servings.

NUTRITION FACTS: 1 cup equals 137 calories, 1 g fat (trace saturated fat), 0 cholesterol, 5 mg sodium, 34 g carbohydrate, 3 g fiber, 1 g protein.

Sparkling Fruit Salad
Taste of Home Test Kitchen

Pineapple chunks, mandarin oranges, strawberries and grapes are treated to a dressing of wine and sparkling club soda in this delightful salad. Serve in dessert dishes or set the whole bowl on the table for a fetching presentation.

1   **fresh pineapple, peeled and cut into chunks**
1   **can (11 ounces) mandarin oranges, drained**
1   **cup halved fresh strawberries**
1   **cup halved green grapes**
1   **cup white wine *or* white grape juice**
1/2 **cup chilled club soda**

1) In a large serving bowl, combine the pineapple, oranges, strawberries and grapes. Combine wine or grape juice and club soda; pour over fruit.

2) Cover and refrigerate for at least 2 hours, stirring occasionally. Serve with a slotted spoon.

Yield: 8 servings.

NUTRITION FACTS: 1 cup equals 87 calories, trace fat (trace saturated fat), 0 cholesterol, 6 mg sodium, 16 g carbohydrate, 1 g fiber, 1 g protein.

Kiwifruit

Kiwifruit has a unique, sweet-tart flavor with tones of pineapple, strawberry and citrus. The two varieties of kiwifruit that are available include green and golden. The green kiwi is egg-shaped with a fuzzy brown exterior, and it has emerald green flesh with tiny black edible seeds. The golden kiwi is sweeter than the green. It has a pointed end, smooth brown skin and golden flesh with tiny black edible seeds.

Buying
Green kiwifruit is available year-round; peak season for golden kiwifruit is June through November. Select plump fruit that yields to gentle pressure. Avoid fruit with soft spots or a shriveled skin. Firm fruit will still need to ripen.

Storage
Store unripened kiwifruit at room temperature. To speed the ripening process, store in a paper bag with an apple or banana. Once ripened, store in the refrigerator for 2-3 days.

To eat, just cut in half and scoop the fruit out with a spoon. Or peel skin and cut into slices or cube.

Do not add fresh kiwifruit to gelatin salads or desserts. It contains an enzyme that prevents gelatin from setting up.

Yield: 1 medium kiwifruit (3 ounces) = 5 to 6 slices or 1/3 cup slices

PEELING A KIWIFRUIT

Cut fruit in half. Using a spoon, scoop out flesh.

Cut both ends from fruit. Using a vegetable peeler, peel off fuzzy brown skin. Cut into slices, wedges or chunks with a sharp knife.

Simply Fruit
Taste of Home Test Kitchen

Young and old alike will enjoy this fun fruit medley featuring banana, kiwifruit, oranges and grapes. A dollop of yogurt with brown sugar tops off this nourishing sweet treat.

2   **medium navel oranges, peeled and sliced**
2   **kiwifruit, peeled and cubed**
1   **medium firm banana, sliced**
1   **cup seedless red grapes**
1/2 **cup reduced-fat vanilla yogurt**
2   **tablespoons plus 2 teaspoons brown sugar**

1) In a large bowl, combine the oranges, kiwi, banana and grapes. Divide among six serving bowls.

2) Combine yogurt and brown sugar; dollop over fruit. Serve immediately.

Yield: 6 servings.

NUTRITION FACTS: 2/3 cup equals 107 calories, 1 g fat (trace saturated fat), 1 mg cholesterol, 15 mg sodium, 27 g carbohydrate, 4 g fiber, 2 g protein.

KIWI ICE

Kiwi Ice

Shirley Glaab, Hattiesburg, Mississippi

All you need is just five ingredients to blend together this tart, refreshing frozen treat. A serving is especially pretty garnished with kiwi and orange slices.

> 2 cups unsweetened apple juice
>
> 1 tablespoon lemon juice
>
> 4 medium kiwifruit, peeled and sliced
>
> Sugar substitute equivalent to 6 teaspoons sugar
>
> 1/2 teaspoon grated orange peel
>
> Sliced orange and additional kiwifruit, optional

1) In a blender, combine the juices and kiwi; cover and process just until smooth. Add the sugar substitute and orange peel. Pour mixture into an ungreased 8-in. square dish.

2) Cover and freeze for 1-1/2 to 2 hours or until partially set. Spoon into a large mixing bowl; beat on medium speed for 1-1/2 minutes. Return to pan; freeze for 2-3 hours or until firm.

3) Let stand for 10 minutes before serving. Spoon into small bowls; garnish with the orange and additional kiwi if desired.

Yield: 8 servings.

Editor's Note: This recipe was tested with Splenda No Calorie Sweetener.

NUTRITION FACTS: 1/2 cup equals 56 calories, trace fat (0 saturated fat), 0 cholesterol, 2 mg sodium, 14 g carbohydrate, 0 fiber, 1 g protein.

Kumquats

Kumquats are a member of the citrus family. This egg-shaped orange fruit has a sweet skin and tart flesh. It can be sliced and eaten, skin and all.

Buying

Kumquats are available November through March. Select fruit that is completely orange with firm and glossy skin. Avoid bruised, soft or shriveled fruit.

Storage

Store unwashed kumquats in the refrigerator for about 2 weeks.

Yield: 1 kumquat (1/2 ounce)
3 kumquats = scant 1/4 cup slices

Mangoes

This juicy, tropical fruit has a sweet-sour flavor.

Buying

Mangoes are available most of the year. Select plump fruit with a sweet, fruity aroma. Avoid very soft or bruised fruit. The skin of a ripe mango is green to yellow in color with a tinge of red. It should still feel firm when pressed. Green mangoes are not ripe.

Storage

Store unwashed mangoes in the refrigerator away from other vegetables with strong aromas. Keep green mangoes at room temperature out of direct sunlight until ripened.

Yield: 1 medium mango (9 ounces) = 1 cup chopped

1) Wash fruit. Lay fruit on the counter, then turn so the top and bottom are now the sides. Using a sharp knife, make a lengthwise cut as close to the long, flat seed as possible to remove each side of the fruit. Trim fruit away from the seed.

2) Score each side of the fruit lengthwise and widthwise, without cutting through the skin.

3) Using your hand, push the skin up, turning the fruit out. Cut fruit off at the skin with a knife.

MINTY MANGO SALSA

Minty Mango Salsa

Diane Thompson, Nutrioso, Arizona

My husband likes to smoke a whole turkey, and I make this colorful salsa with fresh mint to accompany it. It's always a hit with our guests, even served as an appetizer.

- 1 large ripe mango, peeled and diced
- 1 medium sweet red pepper, diced
- 1 can (4 ounces) chopped green chilies
- 1/4 cup chopped green onions
- 1 tablespoon lime juice
- 2 teaspoons minced fresh mint
- 1/4 teaspoon ground ginger

Tortilla chips

1) In a small bowl, combine the mango, pepper, chilies, onions, juice, mint and ginger. Cover and refrigerate for at least 8 hours. Serve with tortilla chips.

Yield: about 2-1/2 cups.

NUTRITION FACTS: 1/4 cup salsa (calculated without chips) equals 20 calories, trace fat (trace saturated fat), 0 cholesterol, 43 mg sodium, 5 g carbohydrate, 1 g fiber, trace protein.

Melons

Melons are in the same family as squash, cucumber and gourds. Melons have hard rinds and a hollow, seed-filled center. Muskmelons, which are also called cantaloupes and melons, have a musky fragrance and netted (webbed) rind. Winter melons lack the musky fragrance, typically lack the netted skin and are oblong in shape. (Watermelons are on page 392.)

Buying

Melons are available year-round (individual varieties have their own peak seasons). Select melons that are heavy for their size and have no cracks or dents in the skin. A ripe melon should have a fruity, pleasant aroma. Avoid melons that are bruised or have a strong aroma, which indicates they are overripe.

Storage

Store underripe melons at room temperature for 2-3 days. Store ripe melons in the refrigerator for 1 week. Store cut melon, wrapped in plastic wrap or in an airtight container in the refrigerator.

CANTALOUPE has a heavy netting over its cream-colored rind. Its orange flesh is sweet. Available year-round; peak season is June through October. **Yield:** 1 medium cantaloupe (3 pounds) = 4-1/2 cups cubed.

CRENSHAW has a smooth but ribbed rind, is a golden yellow when ripe and is pointed at one end. A ripe Crenshaw has sweet pink flesh with a spicy rich fragrance. Available June through October. Peak season is July. **Yield:** 1 Crenshaw (about 5-1/2 pounds) = 9 cups cubed.

HONEYDEW has a smooth, creamy white rind. Most honeydews have a pale green flesh and mild pleasant flavor. Available year-round; peak season is May through October. **Yield:** 1 medium honeydew (4-5 pounds) = 4 cups cubed.

PERSIAN resembles a cantaloupe, but the netting on the rind is more delicate. It's also slightly larger. The skin turns to a lighter green when ripe. The salmon-colored flesh is sweet. Peak season is June through November. **Yield:** 1 medium Persian (about 4 pounds) = 8 cups cubed.

MELON WITH RASPBERRY SAUCE

Melon with Raspberry Sauce
Taste of Home Test Kitchen

Refreshing melon slices fanned out in a pretty pool of raspberry sauce create a light but elegant ending to any special-occasion meal.

2-2/3   **cups unsweetened raspberries**
3   **tablespoons honey**
1   **teaspoon lemon juice**
1/2   **teaspoon minced fresh gingerroot**
1/2   **large cantaloupe**
1/2   **medium honeydew**

1) Set aside a few raspberries for garnish. Place the remaining berries in a blender or food processor; cover and process until pureed. Add the honey, lemon juice and ginger; cover and process. Strain and discard seeds; set sauce aside.

2) Cut the cantaloupe and honeydew into three wedges; cut each wedge widthwise in half. Remove seeds and rind. With a knife, slice each piece of melon lengthwise toward narrow end without cutting completely to the end. Open into a fan shape.

3) On each dessert plate, place 2 tablespoons of raspberry sauce and a cantaloupe fan and honeydew fan. Garnish with reserved raspberries.

Yield: 6 servings.

NUTRITION FACTS: 1 serving equals 130 calories, 1 g fat (1 g saturated fat), 0 cholesterol, 19 mg sodium, 33 g carbohydrate, 5 g fiber, 2 g protein.

Melon Ambrosia
Edie DeSpain, Logan, Utah

Each time I serve this light and refreshing dessert, it gets rave reviews. With three kinds of melon, it's lovely and colorful but so simple to prepare.

- 1 cup watermelon balls *or* cubes
- 1 cup cantaloupe balls *or* cubes
- 1 cup honeydew balls *or* cubes
- 1/3 cup lime juice
- 2 tablespoons sugar
- 2 tablespoons honey
- 1/4 cup flaked coconut, toasted

Fresh mint, optional

1) In a small bowl, combine the melon balls. In another bowl, combine the lime juice, sugar and honey; pour over melon and toss to coat.

2) Cover and refrigerate for at least 1 hour. Sprinkle with coconut. Garnish with mint if desired.

Yield: 4 servings.

NUTRITION FACTS: 3/4 cup equals 137 calories, 4 g fat (3 g saturated fat), 0 cholesterol, 12 mg sodium, 29 carbohydrate, 2 g fiber, 1 g protein.

Chilly Melon Cups
Katie Koziolek, Hartland, Minnesota

This cool treat is stored in the freezer so it's always handy. It's a great way to use what's left from a fruit platter or melon boat.

- 1 cup water
- 1 cup sugar
- 1/2 cup lemonade concentrate
- 1/2 cup orange juice concentrate
- 4 cups watermelon balls *or* cubes
- 2 cups cantaloupe balls *or* cubes
- 2 cups honeydew balls *or* cubes
- 2 cups pineapple chunks
- 2 cups fresh raspberries

1) In a large bowl, combine the water, sugar and concentrates; stir until the sugar is dissolved. Add fruit and stir gently to coat. Spoon into foil-lined muffin cups or 3-oz. plastic cups. Freeze for up to 3 months.

2) Before serving, thaw overnight in the refrigerator or let stand at room temperature for 30-45 minutes until mixture is slushy.

Yield: 12-14 servings.

NUTRITION FACTS: 1 serving equals 152 calories, trace fat (trace saturated fat), 0 cholesterol, 7 mg sodium, 38 g carbohydrate, 2 g fiber, 1 g protein.

GINGERED MELON

Gingered Melon
Patricia Richardson, Verona, Ontario

When I have guests, I like to let them spoon melon from a large serving bowl and add their own toppings. You can also combine the fruit with ice cream or frozen yogurt and ginger ale to make a melon float!

- 1/2 medium honeydew, cut into 1-inch cubes
- 1/4 cup orange juice
- 1-1/2 teaspoons ground ginger
- 1/2 to 1 cup whipped cream
- 1/4 cup fresh *or* frozen unsweetened raspberries

1) In a small bowl, combine the melon, orange juice and ginger. Cover; refrigerate 5-10 minutes.

2) Spoon into tall dessert glasses or bowls. Top with whipped cream and raspberries.

Yield: 4 servings.

NUTRITION FACTS: 1 cup equals 76 calories, 2 g fat (1 g saturated fat), 6 mg cholesterol, 22 mg sodium, 15 g carbohydrate, 1 g fiber, 1 g protein.

Fresh Fruit Bowl
Marion Kirst, Troy, Michigan

The glorious colors used here make this a great summer salad. Slightly sweet and chilled, it is a nice accompaniment to a grilled entree.

- 8 to 10 cups fresh melon cubes
- 1 to 2 tablespoons white corn syrup

1 pint fresh strawberries
2 cups fresh pineapple chunks
2 oranges, sectioned
Fresh mint leaves, optional

1) In a large bowl, combine melon cubes and corn syrup. Cover and refrigerate overnight. Just before serving, stir in remaining fruit. Garnish with fresh mint leaves if desired.

Yield: 3-4 quarts.

NUTRITION FACTS: 3/4 cup equals 55 calories, trace fat (trace saturated fat), 0 cholesterol, 9 mg sodium, 13 g carbohydrate, 2 g fiber, 1 g protein.

Nectarines and Peaches

Nectarines and peaches are used interchangeably in recipes. Nectarines have a smooth, thin skin; peaches have a fuzzy skin. Peaches are classified as freestone when the pit falls away from the flesh, and clingstone when the pit clings to the flesh.

Buying

Both fruits are available May through November. Select plump fruit. Avoid fruit with bruises, soft spots or cuts. Avoid peaches with a green background as these will not ripen or be sweet. Ripe nectarines and peaches will give slightly when gently pressed and have a sweet aroma.

Storage

Store ripe fruit in the refrigerator for 3-5 days. Store firm fruit at room temperature until ripened. To ripen more quickly, place in a paper bag at room temperature. Freeze for up to 1 year.

Yield: 1 pound nectarines (3 medium) = 3 cups
sliced
1 pound peaches (4 medium) = 2-3/4 cups
sliced

1) Cut peach in half, cutting around the pit and using the indentation as a guide.

2) Twist halves in opposite directions to separate. Using a sharp knife, loosen and remove pit. Treat cut surfaces with lemon juice to avoid discoloration.

Peach Crisp Cups
Aida Von Babbel, Coquitlam, British Columbia

There may be only two servings in this comforting dessert, but they're bursting with peach flavor. The recipe easily doubles to make 4 servings.

2 **medium fresh peaches, peeled and sliced**
2 **teaspoons sugar**
2 **tablespoons quick-cooking oats**
2 **tablespoons all-purpose flour**
1 **tablespoon brown sugar**
2 **teaspoons chopped almonds**
5 **teaspoons cold butter**
1/4 **teaspoon almond extract**

1) In a bowl, combine peaches and sugar. Transfer to two greased 6-oz. baking dishes. Combine the oats, flour, brown sugar and almonds.

2) Cut in butter until mixture resembles coarse crumbs. Sprinkle with almond extract; toss. Sprinkle over peaches. Bake, uncovered, at 375° for 30 minutes or until bubbly and golden brown.

Yield: 2 servings.

NUTRITION FACTS: 1 serving equals 234 calories, 11 g fat (6 g saturated fat), 26 mg cholesterol, 99 mg sodium, 32 g carbohydrate, 3 g fiber, 3 g protein.

■ *APPLE CRISP:* Peel and slice 2 medium tart apples and use in place of the peaches. If desired, mix 1/8 teaspoon ground cinnamon with the sugar before sprinkling it over the apples.

COCONUT PEACH DESSERT

Coconut Peach Dessert
Inez Orsburn, Demotte, Indiana

If you enjoy peaches and coconut, you're sure to like this sweet fruit pizza-style treat. It is also great on an appetizer table or for a potluck.

- 1-1/3 cups flaked coconut
- 1/2 cup chopped almonds
- 1/3 cup sugar
- 2 tablespoons all-purpose flour
- 1/8 teaspoon salt
- 2 egg whites, lightly beaten
- 1/2 teaspoon almond extract

TOPPING:
- 2 cups heavy whipping cream, whipped
- 4 cups sliced fresh or frozen peaches, thawed
- 1/2 cup sugar or honey

1) In a small bowl, combine the first five ingredients. Stir in egg whites and extract. Line a baking sheet with foil; grease foil well. Spread coconut mixture into a 9-in. circle on foil.

2) Bake at 325° for 20-25 minutes or until lightly browned. Cool on a wire rack. Refrigerate overnight.

3) Place the crust on a serving plate; spread with whipped cream. Combine peaches and sugar; spoon over cream. Cut into wedges. Serve immediately.

Yield: 8 servings.

NUTRITION FACTS: 1 wedge equals 358 calories, 21 g fat (12 g saturated fat), 41 mg cholesterol, 103 mg sodium, 42 g carbohydrate, 3 g fiber, 4 g protein.

Roasted Rosemary Fruit Topping
Mildred Sherrer, Fort Worth, Texas

While it seems odd to combine roasted rosemary and fruit, I think you'll find the unique flavors are perfect toppers for ice cream or frozen yogurt.

- 1 medium fresh peach
- 1 medium fresh plum
- 2 cups pitted fresh or frozen tart cherries, thawed
- 2 tablespoons butter, melted
- 2 tablespoons sugar
- 1 tablespoon lime juice
- 1 to 2 teaspoons minced fresh rosemary
- 2 cups reduced-fat vanilla ice cream or frozen yogurt

1) Prick the skin of the peach and plum with a fork. Cut in half; remove pits. Cut each half into eight slices. Place in a greased 15-in. x 10-in. x 1-in. baking pan. Add the cherries.

2) In a small bowl, combine the butter, sugar, lime juice and rosemary. Spoon over fruit. Bake at 400° for 13-15 minutes or until fruit is tender, stirring occasionally. Serve over ice cream or frozen yogurt. Drizzle with pan juices.

Yield: 4 servings.

NUTRITION FACTS: 1/2 cup equals 227 calories, 9 g fat (5 g saturated fat), 25 mg cholesterol, 117 mg sodium, 36 g carbohydrate, 2 g fiber, 4 g protein.

MIXED FRUIT COBBLER

Mixed Fruit Cobbler
Mary Katherine Pitts, Ambia, Indiana

The corn bread topping gives this old-fashioned fruit cobbler a brand-new taste. You can use most any combination of fruits to make it. A scoop of ice cream makes it extra special.

- 4 medium ripe apricots, peeled and sliced

2   large ripe nectarines, peeled and sliced

2   large ripe peaches, peeled and sliced

2/3 cup sugar, *divided*

2   tablespoons cornstarch

1   tablespoon cold butter, cut into small pieces

1   cup all-purpose flour

1/2 cup cornmeal

2   teaspoons baking powder

1/4 teaspoon ground cinnamon

1/8 teaspoon salt

1/2 cup milk

1/4 cup vegetable oil

1) In a large bowl, combine the fruit, 1/3 cup sugar and cornstarch. Spoon into a greased 8-in. square baking dish. Dot with butter.

2) In another bowl, combine the flour, cornmeal, baking powder, cinnamon, salt and remaining sugar. Stir in milk and oil just until moistened. Spread over fruit mixture. Bake at 375° for 35-40 minutes or until bubbly and top is golden brown. Serve warm.

Yield: 9 servings.

NUTRITION FACTS: 1 serving equals 247 calories, 8 g fat (2 g saturated fat), 5 mg cholesterol, 109 mg sodium, 41 g carbohydrate, 2 g fiber, 3 g protein.

Papayas

This pear-shaped, tropical fruit has a sweet-tart flavor and smooth flesh. The variety most commonly sold in America is solo, and it weighs 1 to 2 pounds. Mexican-type papayas are larger (can be up to 20 pounds) and the flesh has a deep red tint.

Buying

Papayas are available year-round. Select papayas that have a golden yellow skin. Ripe fruit will give slightly when gently pressed and have sweet aroma. Avoid bruised, soft or shriveled fruit.

PREPARING PAPAYA

1)   Wash fruit. Slice lengthwise in half. Scoop out seeds. The peppery seeds are edible but are generally discarded.

2)   Peel papaya and slice or cube.

Storage

Store ripe fruit in the refrigerator for 3-4 days. Store fruit that has slightly green skin or firm fruit at room temperature until ripened.

Yield: 1 pound (1 medium) = 1-3/4 cups sliced or cubed

PEELING PEACHES

1) Place peaches in a large pot of boiling water for 10-20 seconds or until the skin splits.

2) Remove with a slotted spoon. Immediately place in an ice water bath to cool the peaches and stop the cooking process.

3) Use a paring knife to peel the skin, which should easily peel off. If stubborn areas of skin won't peel off, just return fruit to the boiling water for a few more seconds.

Pears

This sweet-and-juicy fruit is readily available in many varieties. Depending on the variety, the skin color can be green, yellow, red or a combination of colors.

Buying

Pears are available year-round. Peak season is July through January. Select pears that are plump. Avoid those with bruises, soft spots or cuts. For some varieties, the color of the skin will change as the pear ripens. Select firm pears for baking. For eating, select pears that give slightly when gently pressed.

ANJOU
Sweet, spicy flavor. Tender, egg-shaped pear. Good for eating, cooking and in salads. Season: October through May.

BARLETT
Sweet flavor. Tender, bell-shaped pear available with yellow and red skin. Good for eating, cooking and in salads. Season: August through January.

BOSC
Sweet, spicy flavor. Dense, bell-shaped pear with golden brown skin. Good for eating, poaching and cooking. Season: September through May.

COMICE
Sweet with a fruity aroma. Smooth texture, yellow skin when ripe. Good for eating. Season: October through February.

SECKEL
Sweet spicy flavor. Firm, grainy-textured, bell-shaped pear with olive-green skin with red blush. Good for cooking. Season: August through December.

Storage

Store unwashed ripe pears in the refrigerator away from other vegetables with strong aromas for 3-5 days. To ripen firm pears, place in a paper bag at room temperature for 2-3 days. Cut pears should be brushed with lemon, lime, orange or pineapple juice to prevent browning. Freeze for up to 1 year.

Yield: 1 pound (3 medium) = 3 cups sliced

Pear Waldorf Pitas
Roxann Parker, Dover, Delaware

Here's a guaranteed table-brightener for a shower, luncheon or party. Just stand back and watch these sandwiches vanish. For an eye-catching presentation, I tuck each one into a colorful folded napkin.

- 2   medium ripe pears, diced
- 1/2   cup thinly sliced celery
- 1/2   cup halved seedless red grapes
- 2   tablespoons finely chopped walnuts
- 2   tablespoons lemon yogurt
- 2   tablespoons mayonnaise
- 1/8   teaspoon poppy seeds
- 10   miniature pita pockets, halved
- Lettuce leaves

1) In a large bowl, combine the pears, celery, grapes and walnuts. In another bowl, combine the yogurt, mayonnaise and poppy seeds; mix well. Add to pear mixture; toss to coat. Refrigerate for 1 hour or overnight.

2) To serve, line pita halves with lettuce and add 2 tablespoons pear mixture.

Yield: 10 servings.

NUTRITION FACTS: 1 pita (calculated without lettuce) equals 136 calories, 4 g fat (trace saturated fat), 1 mg cholesterol, 172 mg sodium, 23 g carbohydrate, 2 g fiber, 3 g protein.

Pears with Raspberry Sauce
Florence Palmer, Marshall, Illinois

Pears and raspberries are two seasonal favorites showcased in this simple recipe.

- 6   medium ripe pears
- 2   tablespoons honey
- 2   tablespoons lemon juice
- 1/4   cup reduced-sugar raspberry fruit spread
- 2   tablespoons cider vinegar
- 2   cups fresh *or* frozen unsweetened raspberries

1) Core pears from bottom. Cut 1/4 in. from bottom to level if necessary. Set upright in an 8-in. square baking dish. Combine honey and lemon juice; pour over pears. Cover and bake at 350° for 1-1/2 hours or until pears are tender, basting occasionally.

2) In a saucepan, combine fruit spread and vinegar; stir in berries. Cook over medium-low heat until heated through; spoon over pears. Serve warm.

Yield: 6 servings.

NUTRITION FACTS: 1 serving equals 166 calories, 1 g fat (0 saturated fat), 0 cholesterol, 4 mg sodium, 42 g carbohydrate, 0 fiber, 1 g protein.

POACHED PEAR SURPRISE

Poached Pear Surprise
Barbara Smith, Cannon Falls, Minnesota

This dessert is elegant but easy, satisfying yet light. Plus, it's fun to watch the looks on the faces of our grandkids and great-grandkids when they discover the surprise filling inside.

4	medium ripe pears
1	cup water
1/2	cup sugar
1	teaspoon vanilla extract
1/3	cup finely chopped walnuts
2	tablespoons confectioners' sugar
1	teaspoon milk

CHOCOLATE SAUCE:

1/3	cup water
1/3	cup sugar

1/4   cup butter
1-1/3 cups semisweet chocolate chips
Fresh mint, optional

1) Core pears from bottom, leaving stems intact. Peel pears. Cut 1/4 in. from bottom to level if necessary.

2) In a saucepan, bring water and sugar to a boil. Add pears; reduce heat. Cover and simmer for 10-15 minutes or until tender. Remove from the heat; stir vanilla into sugar syrup. Spoon over pears. Cover and refrigerate until chilled.

3) Meanwhile, combine walnuts, confectioners' sugar and milk; set aside. For chocolate sauce, in a small saucepan, bring the water, sugar and butter to a boil. Remove from the heat; add chocolate chips, stirring until melted.

4) To serve, drain pears well; spoon nut mixture into cavities. Place on dessert plates; top with some of the chocolate sauce. Insert a mint leaf near stem if desired. Serve with the remaining chocolate sauce.

Yield: 4 servings.

NUTRITION FACTS: 1 serving equals 709 calories, 35 g fat (17 g saturated fat), 31 mg cholesterol, 123 mg sodium, 107 g carbohydrate, 8 g fiber, 6 g protein.

Ruby Pears
Kathy Ginn, Washington Court House, Ohio

Cranberry sauce gives a sweet-tart taste to pear halves in this spiced side dish that's perfect for fall. It's excellent with chicken or pork dishes and can be enjoyed hot or cold.

1	can (29 ounces) pear halves, drained
1	can (16 ounces) whole-berry cranberry sauce
1/4	cup sugar
2	tablespoons lemon juice
1/4	teaspoon ground cinnamon

1) Place pears cut side up in a greased 8-in. square baking dish. In a saucepan, combine cranberry sauce, sugar, lemon juice and cinnamon. Cook and stir until sugar is dissolved and mixture is heated through.

2) Spoon sauce over pears. Bake, uncovered, at 350° for 25-30 minutes or until heated through.

Yield: 5-6 servings.

NUTRITION FACTS: 1 serving equals 243 calories, trace fat (trace saturated fat), 0 cholesterol, 23 mg sodium, 63 g carbohydrate, 3 g fiber, trace protein.

Baked Stuffed Pears

Marie Labanowski, New Hampton, New York

This simple dessert is a tasty ending to our Thanksgiving meal of roast turkey or pork. Pears are a yummy change from the typical apples.

4 medium ripe pears
   (about 2 pounds)
2 tablespoons lemon juice
1/3 cup coarsely chopped walnuts
1/4 cup golden raisins
2 tablespoons maple syrup
2 teaspoons brown sugar
1 teaspoon grated lemon peel
1/8 teaspoon ground cinnamon
1 tablespoon butter
2/3 cup apple juice

1) Core pears and peel 1 in. down from the top on each. Brush peeled portion with some of the lemon juice. Place in a greased 1-qt. baking dish.

2) In a bowl, combine the walnuts, raisins, syrup, brown sugar, lemon peel, cinnamon and remaining lemon juice. Spoon into pears. Dot with butter. Pour apple juice around pears.

3) Bake, uncovered, at 350° for 30-40 minutes or until pears are tender, basting several times.

Yield: 4 servings.

NUTRITION FACTS: 1 serving equals 707 calories, 12 g fat (2 g saturated fat), 8 mg cholesterol, 33 mg sodium, 160 g carbohydrate, 23 g fiber, 6 g protein.

PEAR 'N' APPLE COBBLER

Pear 'n' Apple Cobbler

Shirley Brown, Pocatello, Idaho

Nutmeg lends a homey touch to apple pie filling and canned pears topped with tender biscuits. I've received many great comments about this dessert from my family and friends. Vanilla ice cream would make a wonderful addition to it.

2 teaspoons cornstarch
1/4 teaspoon plus 1/8 teaspoon
   ground nutmeg, *divided*
2/3 cup orange juice
1 can (21 ounces) apple pie filling
1 can (15-1/4 ounces) sliced pears,
   drained
1-1/2 cups biscuit/baking mix
2 tablespoons plus 2 teaspoons
   sugar, *divided*
1/2 cup milk
2 tablespoons butter, melted

1) In a large saucepan, combine the cornstarch, 1/4 teaspoon of nutmeg and orange juice until smooth. Gently stir in pie filling and pears. Bring to a boil; cook and stir for 1-2 minutes or until thickened. Keep warm.

2) In a medium bowl, combine the biscuit mix, 2 tablespoons sugar, milk and butter just until blended. Pour hot filling into an ungreased 11-in. x 7-in. x 2-in. baking dish.

3) Drop batter in six mounds onto fruit mixture. Combine the remaining sugar and nutmeg; sprinkle over the top.

4) Bake, uncovered, at 350° for 35-40 minutes or until fruit mixture is bubbly and a toothpick inserted in the biscuit topping comes out clean. Serve warm.

Yield: 6 servings.

NUTRITION FACTS: 1 cup equals 352 calories, 9 g fat (4 g saturated fat), 13 mg cholesterol, 476 mg sodium, 66 g carbohydrate, 2 g fiber, 4 g protein.

Caramel Pear Crumble

Karen Ann Bland, Gove, Kansas

This is the first recipe I turn to after my mother shares juicy pears from her orchard. Its crumbly topping and hint of caramel keep friends asking for more.

1-1/4 cups all-purpose flour
1 cup quick-cooking oats
1 cup packed brown sugar
1 teaspoon ground cinnamon
1/2 cup butter, melted
20 caramels
1 tablespoon milk
3 medium pears, peeled and sliced

1) In a small bowl, combine the first four ingredients. Stir in butter (mixture will be crumbly); set aside

1 cup. Press remaining mixture into an ungreased 8-in. square baking dish.

2) In a small saucepan over low heat, cook and stir caramels and milk until caramels are melted and mixture is smooth. Remove from the heat.

3) Arrange pears over crust; spoon caramel mixture over pears. Sprinkle with the reserved crumb mixture.

4) Bake at 350° for 30-35 minutes or until the pears are tender and top is golden brown. Serve warm.

Yield: 6 servings.

NUTRITION FACTS: 1 slice equals 598 calories, 19 g fat (12 g saturated fat), 44 mg cholesterol, 253 mg sodium, 103 g carbohydrate, 5 g fiber, 7 g protein.

Persimmons

The two varieties available are the Hachiya and Fuyu. The Hachiya is heart-shaped and deep orange; they must be fully ripened before eating or they become astringent. Fuyu persimmons are pale orange and look somewhat like a squashed tomato.

Buying

Persimmons are available October through February. Select plump, slightly firm fruit with smooth, glossy skin; the cap end should still be attached. Avoid fruit that is bruised or has cuts in the skin.

Storage

Store ripe fruit in the refrigerator for up to 3 days. To ripen, place in a paper bag at room temperature for 1-3 days. The pulp from the Hachiya persimmon may be frozen in an airtight container.

Hachiya is ripe when it is soft. To use, cut in half and scoop out pulp with a spoon. Discard seeds. Puree pulp if desired. Use for eating and cooking. Fuyu is still firm but not hard when it is ripe. To use, peel, core and slice. Use for eating and making salads.

Yield: 1 medium (4-3/4 ounces) Fuyu
= 2/3 cup sliced
1 large (9 ounces) Hachiya = 2/3 cup pulp

> ### MAKING PERSIMMON PULP
> To prepare persimmon pulp, puree the ripe seeded fruit (peeling is optional) in a blender or food processor, then strain through a sieve.

Glazed Persimmon Bars
Delores Leach, Penn Valley, California

Persimmons are an excellent source of vitamin A, a good source of vitamin C and rich in fiber. They star in these dessert bars.

1	cup mashed ripe persimmon pulp
1	cup sugar
1/2	cup vegetable oil
1	egg
1-1/2	teaspoons lemon juice
1-3/4	cups all-purpose flour
1	teaspoon baking soda
1	teaspoon salt
1	teaspoon ground cinnamon
1	teaspoon ground nutmeg
1/4	teaspoon ground cloves, optional
1-1/2	cups chopped dates *or* raisins
1	cup chopped nuts

GLAZE:

1	cup confectioners' sugar
2	tablespoons lemon juice

1) In a large mixing bowl, combine the persimmon pulp, sugar, oil, egg and lemon juice. Combine the flour, baking soda, salt and spices; add to sugar mixture. Stir in dates and nuts.

2) Spread into a greased 15-in. x 10-in. x 1-in. baking pan. Bake at 350° for 20-25 minutes or until a toothpick inserted near the center comes out clean. Cool in pan on a wire rack. Combine glaze ingredients; spread over bars.

Yield: about 4 dozen.

NUTRITION FACTS: 1 serving equals 99 calories, 4 g fat (trace saturated fat), 4 mg cholesterol, 77 mg sodium, 16 g carbohydrate, 1 g fiber, 1 g protein.

PERSIMMON NUT ROLL

Persimmon Nut Roll
Nancy Wilson, Van Nyes, California

For holiday gift-giving, I make a dozen or so of these rolls to share with friends and neighbors. They slice nicely straight from the freezer.

 3 eggs
 1 cup sugar
2/3 cup mashed ripe persimmon pulp
 1 teaspoon lemon juice
 1 cup self-rising flour
 2 teaspoons ground cinnamon
 1 teaspoon ground ginger
 1 teaspoon baking powder
1/2 teaspoon salt
1/2 teaspoon ground nutmeg
 1 cup finely chopped pecans

FILLING:
 1 package (8 ounces) cream cheese, softened
1/4 cup butter, softened
 1 cup confectioners' sugar
 1 teaspoon vanilla extract
Additional confectioner's sugar

1) Line a 15-in. x 10-in. x 1-in. baking pan with waxed paper and grease the paper; set aside. In a large mixing bowl, beat eggs for 5 minutes on medium speed or until lemon-colored. Gradually add the sugar, persimmon pulp and lemon juice; beat for 3 minutes.

2) Combine the flour, cinnamon, ginger, baking powder, salt and nutmeg; add to egg mixture and beat well. Spread batter evenly in prepared pan; sprinkle with pecans. Bake at 375° for 15 minutes or until lightly browned. Cool in pan for 5 minutes.

3) Turn cake onto a kitchen towel dusted with confectioners' sugar. Gently peel off waxed paper. Roll up cake in the towel jelly-roll style, starting with a short side. Cool completely on a wire rack.

4) For filling, in a small mixing bowl, beat cream cheese and butter until smooth. Beat in the sugar and vanilla. Unroll cake and spread filling evenly over cake to within 1/2 in. of edges. Roll up again.

5) Cover and refrigerate until serving. Dust with confectioners' sugar. Refrigerate or freeze leftovers.

Yield: 10 servings.

Editor's Note: As a substitute for self-rising flour, place 1-1/2 teaspoons baking powder and 1/2 teaspoon salt in a measuring cup. Add all-purpose flour to measure 1 cup.

NUTRITION FACTS: 1 slice (calculated without additional confectioners' sugar) equals 402 calories, 23 g fat (9 g saturated fat), 101 mg cholesterol, 435 mg sodium, 47 g carbohydrate, 2 g fiber, 6 g protein.

Pineapple

This sweet-tangy, juicy, fibrous fruit has a bumpy diamond-shaped pattern on its skin. It must be picked ripe as it will not get sweeter after it's been picked.

Buying

Pineapple is available year-round. Select pineapple that is plump and fresh looking, is slightly soft and has a sweet fragrance. Avoid fruit with dry or brown leaves, bruises and soft spots.

Storage

Store ripe fruit in the refrigerator for up to 4 days. Refrigerate cut fruit in an airtight container for up to 3 days.

Yield: 1 medium = 3 cups chunks

Pineapple Cobbler

Aljene Wendling, Seattle, Washington

I think of our trip to Hawaii every time I taste this favorite. It's made with juicy fresh pineapple, which is a nice change from the usual cobbler ingredients.

1 cup sugar
1/3 cup biscuit/baking mix
1 teaspoon grated lemon peel
4 cups fresh pineapple chunks

TOPPING:
3/4 cup biscuit/baking mix
2/3 cup sugar
1 egg, beaten
1/4 cup butter, melted
Vanilla ice cream, optional

1) In a large bowl, combine the sugar, biscuit mix and lemon peel; stir in pineapple. Pour into a greased 9-in. square baking dish.

2) Combine biscuit mix, sugar and egg; sprinkle over top. Drizzle with butter. Bake at 350° for 40-45 minutes or until browned. Serve warm or cold with ice cream if desired.

Yield: 9 servings.

NUTRITION FACTS: 1 piece equals 289 calories, 8 g fat (4 g saturated fat), 37 mg cholesterol, 241 mg sodium, 55 g carbohydrate, 1 g fiber, 2 g protein.

HAWAIIAN FRUIT SALAD

Hawaiian Fruit Salad

Taste of Home Test Kitchen

A simple dressing made with flavored yogurt coats this refreshing combination of fresh and canned fruit. It looks spectacular when presented in a pineapple boat and sprinkled with coconut.

1 whole fresh pineapple
1 can (15 ounces) mandarin oranges, drained
1-1/2 cups sliced fresh strawberries
1-1/2 cups green grapes, halved
1-1/4 cups pina colada-flavored *or* vanilla yogurt
1/2 cup flaked coconut, toasted, *divided*
1/4 to 1/2 teaspoon coconut *or* vanilla extract

1) Stand the pineapple upright and vertically cut a third from one side, leaving the leaves attached. Set cut piece aside.

2) Using a paring or grapefruit knife, remove strips of pineapple from large section, leaving a 1/2-in. shell; discard core. Cut the strips into bite-size chunks. Invert shell onto paper towels to drain.

3) Remove fruit from the small pineapple piece and cut into chunks; discard peel. Place shell in a serving basket or bowl.

4) In another bowl, combine the pineapple chunks, oranges, strawberries and grapes. Combine the yogurt, 1/4 cup coconut and extract; spoon over fruit and stir gently. Spoon into pineapple shell. Sprinkle with remaining coconut.

Yield: 6 servings.

NUTRITION FACTS: 1 serving equals 203 calories, 5 g fat (4 g saturated fat), 5 mg cholesterol, 55 mg sodium, 38 g carbohydrate, 3 g fiber, 4 g protein.

CUTTING UP FRESH PINEAPPLE

1) Cut off crown of the fruit. Stand pineapple upright and cut off the rind using a sharp knife. Cut off the base.

2) Follow the pattern of the eyes to cut diagonal wedge-shaped grooves in pineapple. Remove the wedges.

3) Stand pineapple upright and cut off fruit next to, but not through, the core. Cut pieces into chunks or spears.

Spiced Pineapple

Chris Nash, Berthoud, Colorado

This is a nice complement to lamb chops or ham. It's an easy, no-fuss side dish that really makes a meal stand out.

  2 cans (one 20 ounces, one 8 ounces) pineapple chunks
1-1/4 cups sugar
  1/2 cup cider vinegar
    1 cinnamon stick (3 inches)
    6 to 8 whole cloves
Dash salt

1) Drain pineapple, reserving 1 cup juice. In a saucepan, combine the sugar, vinegar, cinnamon, cloves, salt and reserved juice. Bring to a boil. Reduce heat; cover and simmer for 10 minutes.

2) Discard cinnamon and cloves. Add pineapple. Return to a boil; cook and stir for 2-3 minutes. Serve warm with a slotted spoon.

Yield: 4-6 servings.

NUTRITION FACTS: 3/4 cup equals 229 calories, 0 fat (0 saturated fat), 0 cholesterol, 36 mg sodium, 59 g carbohydrate, 1 g fiber, 0 protein.

FRUIT SALSA WITH GINGER CHIPS

Fruit Salsa with Ginger Chips

Christy Johnson, Columbus, Ohio

This combination of fruity salsa and crisp gingery chips is wonderful on a hot day. I like to serve this with pineapple iced tea, which I make by simply adding some of the drained pineapple juice from this recipe to a pitcher of tea.

    1 can (20 ounces) unsweetened crushed pineapple
    1 large mango *or* 2 medium peaches, peeled and chopped
    2 medium kiwifruit, peeled and chopped

  1/4 cup chopped macadamia nuts
4-1/2 teaspoons brown sugar
4-1/2 teaspoons flaked coconut
    8 flour tortillas (8 inches)
    1 tablespoon water
  1/4 cup sugar
    1 to 2 teaspoons ground ginger

1) Drain pineapple, reserving 3 tablespoons juice. In a large bowl, combine the pineapple, mango, kiwi, nuts, brown sugar, coconut and reserved juice. Cover and refrigerate for at least 1 hour.

2) For chips, lightly brush one side of each tortilla with water. Combine sugar and ginger; sprinkle over the moistened side of tortillas. Cut each into six wedges. Place in a single layer on ungreased baking sheets. Bake at 400° for 5-7 minutes or until golden brown and crisp. Cool on wire racks. Serve with salsa.

Yield: 12 servings.

NUTRITION FACTS: 1/4 cup salsa with 4 chips equals 190 calories, 4 g fat (1 g saturated fat), 0 cholesterol, 173 mg sodium, 35 g carbohydrate, 1 g fiber, 3 g protein.

Hot Pineapple Side Dish

Alice Blackley, Elkin, North Carolina

The first time I passed along this treasured recipe was to *Taste of Home*. It's handed down from my mother, and it's always been special to me.

    1 can (20 ounces) pineapple chunks
  1/2 cup sugar
    3 tablespoons all-purpose flour
  1/4 cup butter, melted
1-1/2 cups (6 ounces) shredded cheddar cheese, *divided*
  2/3 cup coarsely crushed saltines (14 crackers)

1) Drain the pineapple, reserving 1/4 cup juice; set aside. In a small bowl, combine sugar and flour. Add the butter and 1 cup cheese; mix well. Gently stir in pineapple.

2) Pour into a greased 1-1/2-qt. baking dish. Sprinkle crushed crackers on top; drizzle with reserved pineapple juice.

3) Bake, uncovered, at 350° for 30-35 minutes or until bubbly around edges. Remove from the oven and sprinkle with the remaining cheese.

Yield: 6 servings.

NUTRITION FACTS: 1/2 cup equals 330 calories, 16 g fat (11 g saturated fat), 50 mg cholesterol, 335 mg sodium, 40 g carbohydrate, 1 g fiber, 8 g protein.

WARM FRUIT COMPOTE

Warm Fruit Compote
Page Alexander, Baldwin City, Kansas

This sunny-colored medley smells so good while it cooks. The cream cheese topping adds a touch of elegance to individual servings of the not-too-sweet fruit.

- 1/4   cup packed brown sugar
- 1   teaspoon cornstarch
- 1/4   cup water
- 1/4   cup orange juice concentrate
- 2   tablespoons butter
- 1   can (20 ounces) pineapple chunks, drained
- 1   can (15-1/4 ounces) sliced pears, drained and halved
- 1   can (15 ounces) mandarin oranges, drained

TOPPING:
- 1   package (3 ounces) cream cheese, softened
- 1   tablespoon sugar
- 1   tablespoon orange juice concentrate

1) In a large saucepan, combine the brown sugar and cornstarch. Stir in the water and orange juice concentrate until smooth.

2) Add butter. Bring to a boil; cook and stir for 2 minutes or until thickened. Reduce heat. Add the fruit; heat through.

3) In a small mixing bowl, beat all of the topping ingredients until smooth. Dollop over fruit.

Yield: 6 servings.

NUTRITION FACTS: 1 serving equals 263 calories, 9 g fat (5 g saturated fat), 26 mg cholesterol, 94 mg sodium, 45 g carbohydrate, 1 g fiber, 3 g protein.

Plums

Plums are available in a large variety, such as Santa Rosa, Kelsey, Mirabelle or Greengage. The skin may be red, purple, yellow, green and blue. The flavor may be sweet or tart. Plums must be picked ripe as they will not get sweeter after they've been picked.

Buying

Plums are available June through November. Select plump fruit. Ripe plums will give slightly when gently pressed and have a fruity aroma. Avoid hard, bruised, soft or shriveled fruit.

Storage

Store unwashed ripe plums in the refrigerator for 3-5 days. To ripen, place in a paper bag at room temperature for 1-3 days.

Yield: 1 pound (4-5 medium) = 2 to 2-1/2 cups halved or 2-1/2 cups sliced

Spiced Dried Plums
Alcy Thorne, Los Molinos, California

We harvest 42 acres of plums on our ranch. I like to serve these plums along with meats or cottage cheese salad. It also makes a nice breakfast fruit.

- 1   pound pitted dried plums
- 2   cups water
- 1   teaspoon ground cinnamon
- 1   teaspoon ground cloves
- 1/2   teaspoon ground ginger
- 3   tablespoons lemon juice

1) In a saucepan over medium heat, combine the plums, water, cinnamon, cloves and ginger; bring to a boil.

2) Remove from the heat; cover and let stand until cool. Stir in lemon juice. Store, covered, in the refrigerator.

Yield: 8 servings.

NUTRITION FACTS: 1 serving equals 159 calories, trace fat (trace saturated fat), 0 cholesterol, 8 mg sodium, 38 g carbohydrate, 3 g fiber, 1 g protein.

PRETTY PLUM PARFAITS

Pretty Plum Parfaits
Norma Reynolds, York, Pennsylvania

This is a light and refreshing way to use garden-fresh plums. Red or purple varieties both work well.

   9   to 12 medium ripe red *or* purple
         plums (2 pounds), sliced
 1/2   cup red currant jelly
 1/2   cup packed brown sugar
   1   orange peel strip (1 to 3 inches)
   1   cinnamon stick (3 inches)
   1   cup heavy whipping cream
   1   tablespoon confectioners' sugar
 1/2   teaspoon vanilla extract
**Fancy cookies and additional whipped
cream and plum slices, optional**

1) In a large heavy saucepan, combine the plums, jelly, brown sugar, orange peel and cinnamon stick. Bring to a boil. Reduce heat; simmer, uncovered, for 10-15 minutes or until plums are tender, stirring occasionally.

2) Remove from the heat; cool slightly. Discard orange peel and cinnamon stick; coarsely mash plums. Cover and refrigerate.

3) Just before serving, in a small mixing bowl, beat cream until it begins to thicken. Add confectioners' sugar and vanilla; beat until stiff peaks form.

4) Place about 1/4 cup plum mixture into each of four chilled parfait glasses; top with 1/4 cup whipped cream. Repeat the layers. Top with remaining plum mixture. Garnish with a cookie, dollop of whipped cream and plum slice if desired.

Yield: 4 servings.

NUTRITION FACTS: 1 cup equals 499 calories, 23 g fat (14 g saturated fat), 82 mg cholesterol, 33 mg sodium, 76 g carbohydrate, 2 g fiber, 2 g protein.

Plum Bumble
Arlis Enburg, Rock Island, Illinois

I've served this recipe numerous times to family and friends. Similar to a cobbler, it is always a favorite.

   1   cup plus 5 teaspoons sugar,
         divided
 1/4   cup cornstarch
   3   cups sliced fresh plums
         (about 1-1/4 pounds)
 3/4   cup pineapple tidbits
   2   tablespoons butter, melted
 1/2   teaspoon ground cinnamon
   1   tube (7-1/2 ounces) refrigerated
         buttermilk biscuits, separated
         and quartered

1) In a large bowl, combine 1 cup sugar, cornstarch, plums and pineapple. Transfer to a greased shallow 2-qt. baking dish; dot with 1 tablespoon butter. Bake, uncovered, at 400° for 15 minutes.

2) Meanwhile, melt remaining butter. In a small bowl, combine cinnamon and remaining sugar. Place biscuit pieces over hot plum mixture; brush with butter and sprinkle with cinnamon-sugar. Bake 25-30 minutes longer or until biscuits are golden brown.

Yield: 6 servings.

NUTRITION FACTS: 1 serving 344 calories, 5 g fat (3 g saturated fat), 10 mg cholesterol, 343 mg sodium, 74 g carbohydrate, 2 g fiber, 4 g protein.

Pomegranates

Pomegranates are about the size of an apple and have a deep red to purplish-red leathery rind. The only part of the pomegranate that is edible are the sweet-tart seeds and their surrounding juice sacs (arils). The fruit can cause permanent stains. Eat the seeds as a fruit or use as a garnish for salads and desserts.

Buying
Pomegranates are available September through January. Select fruit that is heavy for its size and is fresh looking. Avoid bruised, soft or shriveled fruit.

Storage

Store at room temperature out of direct sunlight for several weeks. Refrigerate for up to 3 months. The seeds may be frozen in an airtight container.

Yield: 1 medium (8 ounces) = 3/4 cup arils

OPENING A POMEGRANATE

1) Cut off the crown of the fruit and score in quarters, taking care not to cut into the red sacs.

2) Place the sections in a bowl of water and soak for 5 minutes. Break sections open with your finger and gently push out the seed clusters with your fingers. Discard skin and white membrane. Drain water, reserving seeds. Dry seeds on paper towels.

Pomegranate Gelatin
Deidre Hobbs, Redding, California

As a former home economics teacher, I like to surprise family and friends with recipes that are a little more special. This salad combines sweet and tart tastes.

  2 packages (3 ounces *each*) raspberry gelatin
  2 cups boiling water
  1 cup cold water
1-1/2 cups pomegranate seeds (about 2 pomegranates)
  1 can (8 ounces) crushed pineapple, drained
1/2 cup sour cream
1/2 cup mayonnaise

1) In a large bowl, dissolve gelatin in boiling water. Stir in the cold water, pomegranate seeds and pineapple. Pour into an 11-in. x 7-in. x 2-in. dish. Refrigerate until firm.

2) Combine sour cream and mayonnaise; spread over gelatin. Refrigerate until serving.

Yield: 10 servings.

NUTRITION FACTS: 1 cup equals 194 calories, 11 g fat (3 g saturated fat), 12 mg cholesterol, 106 mg sodium, 22 g carbohydrate, trace fiber, 2 g protein.

Rhubarb

The stalks of rhubarb vary in color from pale pink to cherry red. Its tart flavor lends itself to sugar-enhanced pies, desserts, sauces, relishes and jams.

Buying

Rhubarb is available April through June. Select rhubarb that is firm and crisp. Avoid limp stalks.

Storage

Store unwashed rhubarb in the refrigerator for up to 1 week. Sliced rhubarb can be frozen for 9 months.

Preparation

Always trim and discard any leaves, which contain oxalic acid and are toxic. Thick stalks can be peeled with a vegetable peeler to remove the fibrous strings.

Yield: 1 pound = 3 cups chopped raw
        or 2 cups cooked

Easy Rhubarb Dessert
Deb Jesse, Storm Lake, Iowa

I start with a cake mix and add fresh rhubarb, sugar and cream to create this in a jiffy.

  1 package (18-1/2 ounces) yellow cake mix
  5 cups diced fresh *or* frozen rhubarb
  1 cup sugar
  1 cup heavy whipping cream

1) Prepare the cake batter according to package directions. Pour batter into a greased 13-in. x 9-in. x 2-in. baking pan. Spread rhubarb over batter. Sprinkle with sugar; pour cream over top. Do not mix.

2) Bake at 350° for 35-40 minutes or until a toothpick inserted into the cake comes out clean. Serve warm or cooled.

Yield: 16 servings.

NUTRITION FACTS: 1 piece with 4-1/2 teaspoons sour cream mixture equals 245 calories, 9 g fat (5 g saturated fat), 20 mg cholesterol, 213 mg sodium, 41 g carbohydrate, 1 g fiber, 2 g protein.

Star Fruit

When the five-ribbed carambola is sliced, it forms a star shape, hence its common name of star fruit. The sweet-tart flavor of this fruit seems to combine plums, grapes, apples, pineapple and citrus.

Buying
Star fruit is available from late summer to mid-winter. Select plump fruit with glossy, golden-yellow skin. Choose fruit with wider-spaced ribs, which are said to be sweeter than the narrower-spaced ribs. Avoid fruit with browned ribs.

Storage
Refrigerate unwashed ripe fruit for up to 2 weeks. Fruit with green-tipped ribs is unripe. Keep at room temperature until it's yellow and has a fruity fragrance.

Preparation
Wash before using. Cut into slices. It's good for eating, using in salads and desserts or garnishing.

Yield: 1 medium (3-3/4 ounces) = 1 cup sliced

Watermelon

Watermelon belongs to the gourd family, which also includes squash and cucumbers, but more closely resembles a cucumber since the seeds are distributed throughout the fruit. This summertime favorite is available in an oblong or round shape. The flesh may be red or yellow. The melon may have seeds or may also be a seedless variety, which means it will have some edible seeds. A large watermelon can easily weigh 20 pounds.

Buying
Watermelon is available year-round. Peak season is May through September. Select watermelons with a hard, green rind that has a dull appearance. The part that rested on the ground will be creamy yellow or white color. To test for ripeness, slap the side with the palm of your hand. A deep thump means it is ripe.

Storage
Store in the refrigerator for up to 1 week. Store cut melon, wrapped in plastic wrap or in an airtight container, in the refrigerator.

Yield: 1 pound = about 1 cup cubes

Watermelon Salsa
Pat Bremson, Kansas City, Missouri

This salsa is so good, I could just eat it with a spoon! It's wonderful over fish or chicken.

    4   cups seeded chopped
        watermelon
    2   tablespoons lime juice
    1   tablespoon finely chopped
        red onion
    1   tablespoon minced fresh cilantro
    2   teaspoons finely chopped
        jalapeno pepper
  1/8   teaspoon salt

1) In a large bowl, combine all the ingredients. Cover and refrigerate for at least 1 hour before serving. Serve with a slotted spoon.

Yield: 4 cups.

Editor's Note: When cutting or seeding hot peppers, use rubber or plastic gloves to protect your hands. Avoid touching your face.

NUTRITION FACTS: 1/2 cup equals 26 calories, 0 fat (0 saturated fat), 0 cholesterol, 39 mg sodium, 6 g carbohydrate, 0 fiber, 1 g protein.

Melon Cucumber Medley
Edie DeSpain, Logan, Utah

A light, lemony dressing complements a beautiful mixture of melons and sliced cucumbers. This delightful summer salad is especially good served at a brunch or luncheon.

  1/2   cup vegetable oil
  1/4   cup lemon juice
    1   teaspoon sugar
  1/2   teaspoon salt
  Dash pepper
    6   cups melon balls *or* cubes
        (cantaloupe, honeydew *and/or*
        watermelon)
    3   medium cucumbers, thinly sliced
  Lettuce leaves, optional

1) In a jar with a tight-fitting lid, combine the oil, lemon juice, sugar, salt and pepper; shake until sugar is dissolved.

2) In a bowl, combine melon and cucumbers; drizzle with dressing. Cover and refrigerate for at least 1 hour. Serve in a lettuce-lined bowl if desired.

Yield: 12 servings.

NUTRITION FACTS: 3/4 cup equals 119 calories, 9 g fat (1 g saturated fat), 0 cholesterol, 100 mg sodium, 9 g carbohydrate, 1 g fiber, 1 g protein.

CHAPTER 15

SALADS & SALAD DRESSINGS

393

SALADS & SALAD DRESSINGS

Salads are more than just greens topped with a dressing. They can tease the appetite, round out a meal or become the entire meal itself. There are also coleslaws, potato salads, pasta salads, vegetable salads and gelatin salads.

Select the freshest greens and make sure they are dry. Wet greens can make the salad soggy. Just before serving, tear greens into bite-size pieces or use a plastic lettuce knife. Cutting greens with a metal knife will turn the edges brown with time. Allow greens to stand at room temperature no longer than 15 minutes before serving.

Select a dressing that is appropriate for the green. A sturdy lettuce like iceberg or romaine can hold a creamy blue cheese or Thousand Island dressing, while a lighter vinaigrette would be suitable for Bibb or Boston lettuce.

Toss greens with salad dressing in a large bowl and serve immediately, or place greens in a salad bowl and pass the dressing at the table. Adding too much dressing will make a salad soggy and limp.

For the best salads, select the freshest ingredients and handle and store them for maximum quality. Select lettuce that is crisp, is free of yellowing or rust spots (browning) and is not slimy. Lettuce, such as iceberg, should feel heavy for its size.

A green salad doesn't just mean iceberg lettuce. The combination of flavors (mild, sweet lettuce with bitter greens), textures (buttery, tender, crisp and crunchy) and colors (shades of green, red and white) make a salad that appeals to the eyes as well as the palate.

Main Types of Lettuce

CRISPHEAD has a round compact head with pale green leaves. Mild-flavored, crispy iceberg lettuce is a crisphead.

BUTTERHEAD has small, loosely formed heads with tender, silky, soft leaves. Bibb lettuce has tender leaves with a sweet, subtle flavor. Boston lettuce has tender, buttery leaves with a mild sweet flavor.

LEAF OR LOOSELEAF has leaves that branch out from a stalk. Green and red leaf lettuce are flavorful with crisp, curly-edged leaves. The red leaf has red-tipped leaves.

ROMAINE OR COS has a long, cylindrical head with large, crisp, green outer leaves that are slightly bitter.

Common Salad Greens

The variety of greens suitable for salads seems almost endless. Bok choy, cabbage, collard greens, kale, mustard greens, spinach and Swiss chard are suitable for salads. You can find information about these greens in the Vegetable Chapter. The following is a brief description of some commonly available greens.

 ARUGULA is also known as rocket and is a tender, bitter green that resembles a radish leaf.

 BELGIAN ENDIVE has white leaves with pale yellow-green tips. Its bitter leaves are crunchy.

 CURLY ENDIVE, also known as chicory, has curly leaves that are tough, chewy and bitter. It's best used as an accent flavor in a salad. Its flavor mellows when cooked.

 ESCAROLE has slightly bitter, firm, lettuce-like leaves.

 FRISEE gets a feathery appearance from its delicate curly leaves. This mildly bitter green ranges in color from yellow-white to yellow-green.

 RADICCHIO has satiny, red, bitter-tasting leaves.

 SORREL has tender, green leaves with a tart, acidic flavor.

 WATERCRESS has delicate, small, deep-green leaves with a slightly bitter, peppery bite.

Washing and Storing

Remove rubber bands or ties from lettuce or greens. Remove and discard any brown, wilted or damaged outer leaves. Cut off or cut out core from lettuce. Separate leaves, except for iceberg.

Greens may be sandy or dirty, such as arugula or escarole, and should be swished in a sink or bowl of cold water. Lift greens out, allowing the sand and grit to sink to the bottom. Repeat in clean water if necessary. Rinse other greens gently in cool water.

Greens need to be dried because they do not keep well in the refrigerator if they are wet. Pat them dry with a clean towel or paper towel. A salad spinner is an easy way to remove the water (fill only half to two-thirds full). Greens can also be stored in some salad spinners.

Store in a covered container or plastic bag and refrigerate for at least 30 minutes before serving to crisp the greens. Place a piece of paper towel in the bottom of the container or bag to absorb excess moisture. Store in the refrigerator crisper drawer for about 1 week.

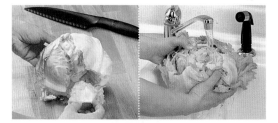

For iceberg lettuce, cut out the core with a paring knife or plastic lettuce knife. Or grasp the head in your hand and hit the core area against the countertop; lift out the core. Rinse the head under running water and drain, core side down, in a colander in the sink.

Ready-to-use salad mixes are available in the produce section. These are already washed and torn. Store in their plastic bag in the refrigerator crisper drawer. Once opened, tightly close the bag. Follow the use-by date stamped on the package.

Salad Ingredients

AVOCADOS

Most avocados have a buttery texture and a rich, slightly nutty flavor. The two most common types of avocados are the Hass and Florida.

The Hass avocado is grown in California, weighs about 1/2 pound, has a pebbly skin that goes from green to black as it ripens, and is available year-round.

The Florida avocado is grown in Florida, is larger than the Hass and has a shiny medium-green skin that doesn't change color as it ripens. They have more water and, ounce for ounce, have less fat and calories and are available early fall through winter.

Select avocados that are heavy for their size and have no blemishes. If the avocado is hard, it will need to ripen before using. If it yields to gentle pressure, it is ready to slice. If the avocado has a small dent after pressing, then it is too soft to slice but is suitable for mashing. If there is a large dent after pressing, then it is overripe and the flesh is spoiled.

To ripen avocados, place in a brown paper bag and leave at room temperature for a few days. To hasten ripening, add an apple or banana to the bag.

REMOVING AN AVOCADO PIT

1) Wash avocado. Cut in half lengthwise, cutting around the seed. Twist halves in opposite directions to separate.

2) Use a tablespoon and slip under the seed to loosen it from the fruit.

3) To remove a half an avocado from skin, loosen from skin with a large spoon and scoop out.

4) Slice peeled avocado as desired. Or, cut into unpeeled wedges and slice between the avocado and the skin.

Ripe avocados should be stored in the refrigerator for up to 3 days. Cut avocados should be brushed with lemon or lime juice to help prevent the flesh from darkening. Place in an airtight container and eat within 2 days.

CUCUMBERS

The most popular cucumber is just classified as the common cucumber. It was bred to have a thicker skin than other cucumbers to protect it during shipping. This cucumber generally has a waxed coating on the skin to increase its freshness life.

The Kirby cucumber is shorter and has bumpy skin. The Kirby was originally used for pickling but can be used in place of the common cucumber in recipes. The English cucumber, also know as Burpless or Hothouse cucumber, is narrow and about 2 feet long. This seedless cucumber is found in stores wrapped in plastic.

Select firm cucumbers with round ends. Avoid those with soft spots, bulging middles or withered ends. Store unwashed cucumbers in the refrigerator crisper drawer for up to 1 week. Avoid cold areas of the refrigerator where the cucumber might freeze. Wash before using. Peel waxed cucumbers and seed if desired.

SEEDING A CUCUMBER

Peel or score cucumber if desired. Cut lengthwise in half. Using a teaspoon, run the tip under the seeds to loosen and remove.

RADISHES

The most commonly available radish is the red radish and is round or oval. Radishes have a peppery flavor that can range from mild to fiery. White icicle radishes have a flavor similar to the red but are elongated and carrot-shaped. The Japanese daikon radishes are large, white radishes that can weigh around 2 pounds.

Select firm, well-formed radishes. Avoid those with cracks or blemishes. Store in the refrigerator crisper drawer for 1 week. Store daikon radishes only 3 days. Wash or scrub with a vegetable brush before using.

CHERRY BRIE TOSSED SALAD

Cherry Brie Tossed Salad
Toni Borden, Wellington, Florida

Draped in a light vinaigrette and sprinkled with almonds, this pretty salad is a variation of a recipe that's been passed around at school and church functions and even birthday parties. Everyone wants the recipe. You can also try different cheeses.

DRESSING:

1	cup cider vinegar
1/2	cup sugar
1/4	cup olive oil
1	teaspoon ground mustard
1-1/2	teaspoons poppy seeds

SALAD:

2	tablespoons butter
3/4	cup sliced almonds
3	tablespoons sugar
8	cups torn romaine
8	ounces Brie *or* Camembert, rind removed, cubed
1	package (6 ounces) dried cherries

1) In a jar with a tight-fitting lid, combine the dressing ingredients; shake until sugar is dissolved.

2) For salad, in a heavy skillet, melt butter over medium heat. Add almonds; cook and stir until nuts are toasted, about 4 minutes. Sprinkle with sugar; cook and stir until sugar is melted, about 3 minutes. Spread on foil to cool; break apart.

3) In a large salad bowl, combine the romaine, cheese and cherries. Shake dressing; drizzle over salad. Sprinkle with sugared almonds and toss to coat.

Yield: 10 servings.

Editor's Note: Swiss cheese can be used in place of the Brie or Camembert.

NUTRITION FACTS: 1 serving equals 309 calories, 18 g fat (6 g saturated fat), 29 mg cholesterol, 171 mg sodium, 32 g carbohydrate, 2 g fiber, 8 g protein.

Layered Lettuce Salad
Julia Burkholder, New Holland, Pennsylvania

I often make the dressing to use on other salads, especially when I have fresh basil. It's so flavorful.

1	medium head lettuce, torn
1	cup minced fresh parsley
4	hard-cooked eggs, sliced
2	large tomatoes, chopped
1	package (10 ounces) frozen peas, thawed and patted dry
6	bacon strips, cooked and crumbled
1	cup (4 ounces) shredded cheddar cheese
1	small red onion, chopped

DRESSING:

1-1/2	cups mayonnaise
1/2	cup sour cream
1	teaspoon dill weed
3/4	teaspoon dried basil
1/2	teaspoon salt
1/8	teaspoon pepper
	Fresh dill sprigs, optional

1) In a large salad bowl, layer the lettuce, parsley, eggs, tomatoes, peas, bacon, cheese and onion in the order listed.

2) In a small bowl, combine the mayonnaise, sour cream, dill, basil, salt and pepper. Carefully spread on top of salad.

3) Cover and refrigerate for several hours or overnight. Garnish with dill sprigs if desired.

Yield: 12 servings.

NUTRITION FACTS: 1 cup equals 335 calories, 30 g fat (7 g saturated fat), 101 mg cholesterol, 423 mg sodium, 7 g carbohydrate, 2 g fiber, 8 g protein.

Curly Endive Salad

Roger Burch, Staten Island, New York

My wife grows herbs in our tiny city garden. I use oregano and mint to season this refreshing unique salad I created.

- 4 cups torn curly endive, Belgian endive *and/or* escarole
- 1/4 cup chopped red onion
- 24 whole stuffed olives
- 2 tablespoons olive oil
- 1 tablespoon red wine vinegar
- 3 tablespoons minced fresh oregano *or* 3 teaspoons dried oregano
- 1 tablespoon minced fresh mint *or* 1 teaspoon dried mint flakes
- 1/4 teaspoon salt
- 1/8 teaspoon pepper
- 2 ounces crumbled feta cheese

1) In a salad bowl, toss the endive, onion and olives. In a jar with a tight-fitting lid, combine the next six ingredients. Shake well.

2) Drizzle oil mixture over salad and toss to coat. Top with cheese.

Yield: 4 servings.

NUTRITION FACTS: 1 cup equals 172 calories, 15 g fat (2 g saturated fat), 8 mg cholesterol, 956 mg sodium, 7 g carbohydrate, 2 g fiber, 3 g protein.

Artichoke Tossed Salad

Karin Graw, Hudson, Wisconsin

It's a cinch to mix together this zesty salad for a potluck. It'll feed a crowd and then some. For a lighter version, I use less oil and a sugar substitute for the dressing and toss in turkey bacon.

- 1 bunch romaine (1 pound), torn
- 1/2 pound sliced bacon, cooked and crumbled
- 1 jar (4-1/2 ounces) marinated artichoke hearts, drained and sliced
- 1/2 cup crumbled blue cheese
- 1/2 cup sliced celery
- 1/2 cup chopped sweet red pepper
- 1/2 cup chopped sweet yellow pepper
- 3 tablespoons cider vinegar
- 2 tablespoons chopped onion
- 2 teaspoons brown sugar
- 2 teaspoons spicy brown mustard
- 1/2 teaspoon salt

- 1/4 teaspoon pepper
- 2 tablespoons vegetable oil

1) In a large salad bowl, combine the romaine, bacon, artichoke hearts, cheese, celery and sweet peppers. Cover; refrigerate until serving.

2) In a blender or food processor, combine the vinegar, onion, brown sugar, mustard, salt and pepper; cover and process until smooth.

3) While processing, add oil in a steady stream; blend until thickened. Drizzle over salad; toss gently to coat. Serve immediately.

Yield: 10-12 servings.

NUTRITION FACTS: 1 cup equals 107 calories, 9 g fat (3 g saturated fat), 10 mg cholesterol, 333 mg sodium, 4 g carbohydrate, 1 g fiber, 4 g protein.

Italian Bread Salad

Kathleen Williams, St. Albans, West Virginia

For a fresh-tasting side dish, I serve this pretty blend that's a snap to prepare. For variety, add whatever veggies you like, such as green or yellow peppers, zucchini, summer squash or sliced olives.

- 4 slices Italian *or* French bread (1 inch thick)
- 2 tablespoons olive oil, *divided*
- 2 plum tomatoes, halved lengthwise and sliced
- 1 medium cucumber, seeded and chopped
- 2 to 3 green onions, sliced
- 2 tablespoons shredded Parmesan cheese

Lettuce leaves

- 3 tablespoons red wine vinegar
- 1 garlic clove, minced
- 1/4 teaspoon dried basil

1) Brush both sides of bread with 1 tablespoon of oil. Place on a baking sheet. Broil 5 in. from the heat for 1-2 minutes on each side or until lightly browned. Cut into 1/2-in. cubes.

2) In a bowl, gently toss the bread cubes, tomatoes, cucumber, onions and Parmesan cheese. Divide among four lettuce-lined salad plates.

3) In a small bowl, whisk vinegar, garlic, basil and remaining oil. Drizzle over salads. Serve immediately.

Yield: 4 servings.

NUTRITION FACTS: 1 cup (calculated without lettuce) equals 176 calories, 9 g fat (2 g saturated fat), 2 mg cholesterol, 222 mg sodium, 20 g carbohydrate, 2 g fiber, 5 g protein.

CLASSIC COBB SALAD

Classic Cobb Salad
Patty Kile, Greentown, Pennsylvania

This classic recipe is easy to modify to suit your tastes with different meats or vegetables.

- 6 cups torn lettuce
- 2 medium tomatoes, chopped
- 1 medium ripe avocado, peeled and chopped
- 3/4 cup diced fully cooked ham
- 2 hard-cooked eggs, chopped
- 3/4 cup diced cooked turkey
- 1-1/4 cups sliced fresh mushrooms
- 1/2 cup crumbled blue cheese

Red onion rings, lemon wedges and sliced ripe olives, optional

Salad dressing of your choice

1) Arrange lettuce in a large bowl. Place tomatoes across the center, dividing the bowl in half. On one half, arrange the avocado, ham and eggs in sections. On the other half, arrange the turkey, mushrooms and blue cheese.

2) Garnish with onion, lemon and olives if desired. Serve with salad dressing.

Yield: 12 servings.

NUTRITION FACTS: 3/4 cup (calculated without salad dressing) equals 98 calories, 6 g fat (2 g saturated fat), 51 mg cholesterol, 213 mg sodium, 3 g carbohydrate, 1 g fiber, 7 g protein.

Romaine Caesar Salad
Marie Hattrup, The Dalles, Oregon

After tasting this terrific salad my daughter made, I was eager to get the recipe and try it myself. The dressing is easy to mix up in the blender.

- 2 hard-cooked eggs
- 1/4 cup lemon juice
- 2 tablespoons balsamic vinegar
- 1 anchovy fillet
- 1 tablespoon Dijon mustard
- 2 garlic cloves, peeled
- 1 teaspoon Worcestershire sauce
- 1 teaspoon pepper
- 3/4 teaspoon salt
- 1/2 cup olive oil
- 1 bunch romaine, torn
- 1 cup (4 ounces) shredded Parmesan cheese
- 1 cup Caesar salad croutons

1) Slice eggs in half; remove yolks. Refrigerate whites for another use. In a blender or food processor, combine the lemon juice, vinegar, anchovy, mustard, garlic, Worcestershire sauce, pepper, salt and egg yolks; cover and process until blended. While processing, gradually add oil in a steady stream. Cover and refrigerate for 1 hour.

2) In a salad bowl, combine the romaine, Parmesan cheese and croutons. Drizzle with dressing; toss to coat. Serve immediately.

Yield: 8 servings.

NUTRITION FACTS: 1 cup equals 238 calories, 20 g fat (5 g saturated fat), 64 mg cholesterol, 617 mg sodium, 7 g carbohydrate, 1 g fiber, 9 g protein.

■ *CHICKEN CAESAR SALAD:* Grill or broil 8 chicken breast halves seasoned with salt and pepper. Cut each chicken breast half into strips. Top each individual salad with a cooked chicken breast half.

Chef's Salad
Katie Anderson, Cheney, Washington

You can quickly toss together this smaller-sized version of an all-time salad classic. Pair the fresh medley of veggies, sliced egg, deli meat and cheese with breadsticks to make a complete lunch.

- 2 cups torn salad greens
- 2 green onions, chopped
- 1/4 cup chopped celery
- 4 ounces deli ham, julienned
- 4 ounces deli turkey, julienned

4 ounces Swiss cheese, julienned
1 hard-cooked egg, sliced
4 pitted ripe olives
Salad dressing of your choice

1) On two serving plates, arrange the salad greens, onion, celery, ham, turkey, cheese, egg and olives. Serve with dressing.

Yield: 2 servings.

NUTRITION FACTS: 1 serving (calculated without salad dressing) equals 413 calories, 24 g fat (12 g saturated fat), 210 mg cholesterol, 1,783 mg sodium, 9 g carbohydrate, 2 g fiber, 41 g protein.

■ *MIX-AND-MATCH CHEF'S SALAD:* Use 4 ounces julienned deli roast beef, corned beef *or* salami for any of the meat listed above and use 4 ounces julienned cheddar, provolone, Monterey Jack, pepper Jack, muenster *or* Colby cheese for the Swiss cheese.

TWO-CABBAGE SLAW

Two-Cabbage Slaw
Carol Gaus, Itasca, Illinois

If you'd like to make a summer barbecue festive, bring out this eye-catching side dish. It's a great way to use up homegrown produce.

4 cups shredded green cabbage
1 cup shredded red cabbage
1 medium green pepper, chopped
1 medium sweet red pepper, chopped
4 green onions, finely chopped

DRESSING:

1 cup (8 ounces) reduced-fat sour cream
3 tablespoons tarragon vinegar *or* cider vinegar
1 tablespoon sugar

1 teaspoon salt
3/4 teaspoon celery seed
1/4 teaspoon white pepper

1) In a large bowl, combine the first five ingredients. In a small bowl, combine the dressing ingredients. Pour over cabbage mixture and stir to coat. Serve immediately.

Yield: 6 servings.

NUTRITION FACTS: 1 cup equals 140 calories, 4 g fat (3 g saturated fat), 13 mg cholesterol, 465 mg sodium, 21 g carbohydrate, 6 g fiber, 6 g protein.

■ *CARROT TWO-CABBAGE SLAW:* Use 3 shredded large carrots in place of the peppers.

SHREDDING CABBAGE

To shred cabbage by hand, cut cabbage into wedges. Place cut side down on a cutting board. With a large sharp knife, cut into thin slices.

Tangy Coleslaw
Pat Cole, Polebridge, Montana

The fresh flavor and crunchy texture of garden vegetables star in this tart, colorful coleslaw. Lightly dressed with vinegar and oil, it's a refreshing summer salad. My mom fixed it often when I was growing up.

6 cups shredded cabbage
4 medium carrots, shredded
4 celery ribs, chopped
1/2 cup finely chopped green pepper
1/2 cup finely chopped onion
1/2 cup cider vinegar
1/4 cup vegetable oil
1/4 cup sugar
1-1/2 teaspoons salt
1/4 teaspoon pepper
1/4 teaspoon paprika

1) In a large bowl, combine the first five ingredients. In a jar with a tight-fitting lid, combine the vinegar, oil, sugar, salt, pepper and paprika; shake well.

2) Pour over cabbage mixture and toss to coat. Cover and refrigerate until serving.

Yield: 10 servings.

NUTRITION FACTS: 1 cup equals 97 calories, 6 g fat (1 g saturated fat), 0 cholesterol, 385 mg sodium, 12 g carbohydrate, 2 g fiber, 1 g protein.

Wilted Lettuce Salad

Alberta McKay, Bartlesville, Oklahoma

This salad looks and tastes great! I've used both leaf lettuce and spinach with delicious results.

- 8 cups torn leaf lettuce *or* spinach
- 1/4 cup sliced green onions
- Pepper to taste
- 3 bacon strips, diced
- 1 tablespoon white wine vinegar
- 2 teaspoons lemon juice
- 1/2 teaspoon sugar
- 1/4 teaspoon salt
- 1 hard-cooked egg, chopped

1) In a large bowl, combine lettuce and onions. Sprinkle with pepper; set aside.

2) In a large skillet, cook bacon over medium heat until crisp. Stir the vinegar, lemon juice, sugar and salt into drippings. Pour over lettuce and toss gently until well coated. Top with hard-cooked egg. Serve immediately.

Yield: 6 servings.

NUTRITION FACTS: 1 cup equals 93 calories, 8 g fat (3 g saturated fat), 43 mg cholesterol, 199 mg sodium, 4 g carbohydrate, 2 g fiber, 3 g protein.

SOUTHWESTERN SALAD

Southwestern Salad

Jerri Moror, Rio Rancho, New Mexico

You get an explosion of Southwestern flavor in every bite of this deliciously different salad. It's a favorite for kids of all ages!

- 2-1/2 cups corn chips
- 1/2 head iceberg lettuce, torn
- 1 cup (4 ounces) shredded Mexican cheese blend
- 1 can (15 ounces) pinto beans, rinsed and drained
- 1 small tomato, seeded and diced

- 1/4 to 1/2 cup salad dressing of your choice
- 2 tablespoons sliced green onions
- 1 to 2 tablespoons chopped green chilies
- 1 small avocado, peeled and sliced

1) In a serving bowl or platter, toss together the chips, lettuce, cheese, beans, tomato, salad dressing, onions and chilies. Top with avocado. Serve immediately.

Yield: 8 servings.

NUTRITION FACTS: 1 cup equals 259 calories, 17 g fat (5 g saturated fat), 14 mg cholesterol, 291 mg sodium, 19 g carbohydrate, 4 g fiber, 7 g protein.

Spinach Salad Supreme

Gail Sykora, Menomonee Falls, Wisconsin

A tangy topping completes this fresh spinach salad, garnished with hard-cooked eggs and crumbled bacon.

- 1/2 cup vegetable oil
- 1/4 cup red wine vinegar
- 2 teaspoons sugar
- 2 teaspoons finely chopped onion
- 2 teaspoons chopped green pepper
- 2 teaspoons minced fresh parsley
- 2 teaspoons ketchup
- 1/2 teaspoon salt
- 1/2 teaspoon ground mustard
- 1/2 teaspoon paprika
- 4 cups torn fresh spinach
- 2 hard-cooked eggs, sliced
- 6 bacon strips, cooked and crumbled

1) In a jar with a tight-fitting lid, combine the oil, vinegar, sugar, onion, pepper, parsley, ketchup, salt, mustard and paprika; shake well.

2) Divide spinach between four individual plates; top with eggs and bacon. Drizzle with dressing. Serve immediately.

Yield: 4 servings.

NUTRITION FACTS: 1 serving equals 718 calories, 70 g fat (12 g saturated fat), 228 mg cholesterol, 1,063 mg sodium, 11 g carbohydrate, 2 g fiber, 14 g protein.

Jicama-Radish Spinach Salad

Taste of Home Test Kitchen

Jicama is a legume that grows underground as a tuber. Its sweet flavor and a moist but crisp texture make a nice addition to salads.

1 **package (6 ounces) fresh baby spinach**

1-1/2 **cups julienned jicama**

1/2 **cup thinly sliced red onion**

6 **radishes, sliced**

1/4 **cup orange juice**

2 **tablespoons honey**

2 **tablespoons olive oil**

1 **tablespoon Dijon mustard**

1) In a large salad bowl, combine the spinach, jicama, onion and radishes.

2) In a jar with a tight-fitting lid, combine the orange juice, honey, oil and mustard; shake well. Drizzle dressing over salad; toss gently to coat.

Yield: 6 servings.

NUTRITION FACTS: 1 cup equals 92 calories, 5 g fat (1 g saturated fat), 0 cholesterol, 88 mg sodium, 12 g carbohydrate, 3 g fiber, 1 g protein.

TANGY GERMAN POTATO SALAD

Potato Salads

Generally, potatoes with a waxy texture, such as round red potatoes and round white potatoes, or an all-purpose potato like Yukon Gold, are recommended for potato salad. Russets are mealy and may crumble when mixed with the dressing.

If cooked whole with the skin on, potatoes absorb less water but take longer to cook. So you may want to peel them when they are warm, then cube or slice. It's best to wear rubber gloves when doing this to protect your hands. If uncooked potatoes are cubed, it is a matter of preference if they're peeled or not. Unpeeled cubed potatoes give the salad a rustic or country feel.

Scrub the potatoes with a brush and remove any eyes or sprouts. Peel and cube if desired. Place potatoes in a Dutch oven or large kettle. Cover with cold water; add about 1/2 to 1 teaspoon salt for each quart of water. Bring to a boil. Cover and cook until just fork-tender yet firm. Do not overcook; the potatoes might fall apart in the salad and result in a mushy texture.

Cooking times vary greatly with size and variety—small whole potatoes may cook in 15 minutes while larger whole potatoes may need 30 minutes. Cubed potatoes may take 10-20 minutes. Drain potatoes.

Hot potatoes absorb more flavors than cold potatoes. Prepare a creamy or vinegar-based dressing in a separate bowl, then pour over the potatoes. Gently stir to coat potatoes; avoid over-mixing since the potatoes may crumble.

Dress up a classic potato salad recipe by adding diced seeded cucumber, sliced green onions, chopped radishes, chopped shallots, crumbled feta cheese, chopped fully cooked ham or cooked tiny shrimp.

Tangy German Potato Salad
Thelma Waggoner, Hopkinsville, Kentucky

This recipe has been a handed-down favorite in my family for years. It's delicious every time I make it.

7 **medium potatoes (about 1-3/4 pounds)**

8 **bacon strips**

1 **small onion, chopped**

1/2 **cup diced celery**

3 **tablespoons all-purpose flour**

3 **tablespoons sugar**

1/4 **to 1/2 teaspoon salt**

Pepper to taste

3/4 **cup water**

1/2 **to 3/4 cup vinegar**

1) Peel potatoes; place in a large saucepan and cover with water. Bring to a boil. Reduce heat; cover and cook for 30-40 minutes or until tender but firm.

2) Meanwhile, in a large skillet, cook bacon over medium heat until crisp. Remove to paper towels; drain, reserving 3 tablespoons drippings. When cool enough to handle, crumble bacon; set aside.

3) In the drippings, saute onion and celery until tender. Stir in flour, sugar, salt and pepper until blended. Add water and vinegar. Bring to a boil; cook and stir for 2 minutes or until thickened.

4) Drain potatoes; slice and place in a large bowl. Add the bacon and sauce; toss gently to coat. Serve warm or at room temperature.

Yield: 6 servings.

NUTRITION FACTS: 1/2 cup (calculated without pepper) equals 273 calories, 11 g fat (5 g saturated fat), 14 mg cholesterol, 286 mg sodium, 38 g carbohydrate, 3 g fiber, 6 g protein.

ROASTED POTATO SALAD

Roasted Potato Salad
Terri Adams, Shawnee, Kansas

Roasted garlic, potatoes and veggies bring new flavors to a classic, family-favorite salad. I pack this salad in a cooler to dish up cold at picnics or transfer it to a slow cooker to serve it warm for potlucks.

- 1/2 pound fresh green beans, cut into 1-1/2-inch pieces
- 1 large whole garlic bulb
- 2 pounds small red potatoes, quartered
- 2 medium sweet red peppers, cut into large chunks
- 2 green onions, sliced
- 1/4 cup chicken broth
- 1/4 cup balsamic vinegar
- 2 tablespoons olive oil
- 2 teaspoons sugar
- 1 teaspoon minced fresh rosemary or 1/4 teaspoon dried rosemary, crushed
- 1/2 teaspoon salt

1) In a large saucepan, bring 6 cups water to a boil. Add beans; bring to a boil. Cover and cook for 3 minutes. Drain and immediately place beans in ice water; drain and pat dry.

2) Remove papery outer skin from garlic (do not peel or separate cloves). Cut top off garlic bulb. Place cut side up in a greased 15-in. x 10-in. x 1-in. baking pan.

3) Add the potatoes, red peppers, onions and beans; drizzle with broth. Bake, uncovered, at 400° for 30-40 minutes or until garlic is softened. Remove garlic; set aside. Bake vegetables 30-35 minutes

longer or until tender. Cool for 10-15 minutes.

4) Squeeze softened garlic into a large bowl. Stir in the vinegar, oil, sugar, rosemary and salt. Add vegetables; toss to coat. Serve warm or cold.

Yield: 9 servings.

NUTRITION FACTS: 3/4 cup equals 124 calories, 3 g fat (1 g saturated fat), 0 cholesterol, 167 mg sodium, 22 g carbohydrate, 3 g fiber, 3 g protein.

True-Blue Potato Salad
Wilma Bailey, Sedona, Arizona

This is named after the blue cheese that makes it a deliciously different potato salad. It disappears quickly at family gatherings or potluck dinners.

- 2-1/2 pounds small red potatoes, cooked and cubed
- 3/4 cup chopped green onions
- 3/4 cup chopped celery
- 3/4 cup fat-free sour cream
- 1/4 cup reduced-fat mayonnaise
- 2 tablespoons minced fresh parsley
- 1 tablespoon white wine vinegar
- 1-1/2 teaspoons salt
- 1/4 teaspoon pepper
- 1/4 teaspoon celery seed
- 1/2 cup (2 ounces) crumbled blue cheese

1) In a large bowl, toss the potatoes, onions and celery. In a small bowl, combine the sour cream, mayonnaise, parsley, vinegar, salt, pepper and celery seed.

2) Pour over potato mixture; toss to coat. Sprinkle with blue cheese. Cover and refrigerate for several hours before serving.

Yield: 8 servings.

■ *TRUE-BLUE TOPPERS:* Garnish with sliced or chopped hard-cooked eggs. Use crumbled feta cheese *or* shredded cheddar cheese in place of the blue cheese.

NUTRITION FACTS: 1 cup equals 175 calories, 4 g fat (2 g saturated fat), 12 mg cholesterol, 622 mg sodium, 31 g carbohydrate, 3 g fiber, 7 g protein.

Garden State Salad
Mary Jane Ruther, Trenton, New Jersey

My state is known as the "Garden State" because it produces such a bounty of fine crops. I like this recipe since it uses so many of them!

- 1 small bunch romaine, torn
- 2 medium potatoes, cooked and cubed

- 2 large tomatoes, cut into wedges
- 1 cup diced cucumber
- 1/2 cup chopped celery
- 1/2 medium green pepper, cut into strips
- 1 small carrot, shredded
- 3 hard-cooked eggs, chopped
- 1/2 cup pitted ripe olives
- 3 radishes, sliced

DRESSING:

- 1-1/2 cups mayonnaise
- 2 tablespoons Dijon mustard
- 2 tablespoons red wine vinegar
- 1/2 teaspoon sugar
- 1/4 teaspoon salt
- 1/8 teaspoon pepper

1) In a large bowl, combine the romaine, vegetables, eggs, olives and radishes. In a small bowl, combine dressing ingredients and stir well. Serve with the salad.

Yield: 6-8 servings.

NUTRITION FACTS: 1 serving equals 394 calories, 36 g fat (5 g saturated fat), 95 mg cholesterol, 497 mg sodium, 13 g carbohydrate, 3 g fiber, 5 g protein.

ANTIPASTO PASTA SALAD

Pasta Salads

For pasta salads, choose a pasta shape that can hold up well in the salad and can compete with the shape and texture of the other foods in the salad. Elbow macaroni, shell, rotini, bow ties, wagon wheels, tortellini and radiatore are good choices for salads.

Cook pasta according to package directions until just tender and firm or al dente. Do not overcook. The pasta may fall apart in the salad.

Drain, rinse with cold water and drain again. Transfer to a bowl and, if desired, toss with a little olive oil. Cool and add other ingredients; toss to coat with dressing. Pasta salads should chill for a few hours to allow flavors to blend.

Antipasto Pasta Salad
Bernadette Nelson, Arcadia, California

This combination of beans, sausage, cheese and pasta is a hearty complement to any meal.

- 1 package (16 ounces) penne *or* medium tube pasta
- 1 green *or* sweet red pepper, julienned
- 1 can (15 ounces) garbanzo beans *or* chickpeas, rinsed and drained
- 1 bunch green onions, sliced
- 4 ounces Monterey Jack cheese, julienned
- 4 ounces mozzarella cheese, julienned
- 4 ounces brick *or* provolone cheese, julienned
- 4 ounces thinly sliced hard salami, julienned
- 3 ounces thinly sliced pepperoni
- 1 can (2-1/4 ounces) sliced ripe olives, drained
- 1 to 2 tablespoons minced fresh chives
- 2 plum tomatoes, sliced and halved

BASIL VINAIGRETTE:

- 2/3 cup vegetable oil
- 1/3 cup red wine vinegar
- 3 tablespoons minced fresh basil *or* 1 tablespoon dried basil
- 1 garlic clove, minced
- 1/4 teaspoon salt

1) Cook pasta according to package directions; rinse under cold water and drain. In a large bowl, combine the pasta, vegetables, cheeses, meats, olives, chives and tomatoes.

2) In a small bowl, whisk together the vinaigrette ingredients. Pour over salad; toss to coat. Cover and refrigerate until serving. Toss before serving.

Yield: 18 servings.

NUTRITION FACTS: 1 cup equals 248 calories, 18 g fat (5 g saturated fat), 24 mg cholesterol, 431 mg sodium, 13 g carbohydrate, 2 g fiber, 9 g protein.

VEGETABLE PASTA SALAD

Vegetable Pasta Salad
Helen Phillips, Horseheads, New York

Use up your garden's bounty and add color too, with a salad of vegetables, ham and cheese.

- 2 cups broccoli florets
- 4 cups cooked spiral pasta
- 2 medium carrots, julienned
- 1/2 cup frozen peas, thawed
- 1/2 cup cubed fully cooked ham
- 1/2 cup cubed cheddar cheese
- 1/3 cup sliced green onions

DRESSING:

- 3/4 cup mayonnaise
- 2 tablespoons cider vinegar
- 1 tablespoon Dijon mustard
- 1 garlic clove, minced
- 1 teaspoon dill weed
- 1/4 teaspoon pepper

1) Place 1 in. of water in a small saucepan; add broccoli. Bring to a boil. Reduce heat; cover and simmer for 2-3 minutes. Rinse in cold water and drain.

2) In a large bowl, combine the broccoli, pasta, carrots, peas, ham, cheese and onions. In another bowl, combine the dressing ingredients. Pour over salad and toss to coat. Cover and refrigerate for at least 1 hour.

Yield: 10 servings.

NUTRITION FACTS: 1 cup equals 252 calories, 17 g fat (3 g saturated fat), 17 mg cholesterol, 276 mg sodium, 19 g carbohydrate, 2 g fiber, 7 g protein.

Carrot Raisin Salad
Denise Baumert, Jameson, Missouri

This traditional salad is fun to eat because of its crunchy texture and slightly sweet flavor.

- 4 cups shredded carrots (about 4 to 5 large)
- 3/4 to 1-1/2 cups raisins
- 1/4 cup mayonnaise
- 2 tablespoons sugar
- 2 to 3 tablespoons milk

1) Place carrots and raisins in a large bowl. In a small bowl, whisk together the mayonnaise, sugar and enough milk to achieve the consistency of a creamy salad dressing. Pour over carrot mixture and toss to coat.

Yield: 8 servings.

NUTRITION FACTS: 1/2 cup equals 129 calories, 6 g fat (1 g saturated fat), 3 mg cholesterol, 60 mg sodium, 20 g carbohydrate, 2 g fiber, 1 g protein.

Tabbouleh
Wanda Watson, Irving, Texas

Tabbouleh is a Mediterranean dish featuring bulgur. This cool, refreshing salad is perfect to serve in warm weather. Bulgur blends deliciously with parsley, mint, tomato, onions and lemon.

- 1 cup bulgur
- 2 cups boiling water
- 3 tablespoons lemon juice
- 2 tablespoons olive oil
- 2 tablespoons sliced green onions (tops only)
- 1 tablespoon minced fresh parsley
- 1 teaspoon salt
- 1 teaspoon minced fresh mint
- 1 medium tomato, seeded and diced
- 6 romaine leaves

1) Place bulgur in a bowl; stir in water. Cover and let stand for 30 minutes or until liquid is absorbed. Drain and squeeze dry. Stir in the lemon juice, oil, onions, parsley, salt and mint.

2) Cover; refrigerate for 1 hour. Just before serving, stir in tomato. Serve in a lettuce-lined bowl.

Yield: 6 servings.

NUTRITION FACTS: 3/4 cup equals 129 calories, 5 g fat (1 g saturated fat), 0 cholesterol, 399 mg sodium, 20 g carbohydrate, 5 g fiber, 3 g protein.

Bacon Macaroni Salad

Norene Wright, Manilla, Indiana

If you like BLT, you'll like this pleasing pasta salad draped in a tangy mayonnaise and vinegar dressing.

- 2 cups uncooked elbow macaroni
- 5 green onions, finely chopped
- 1 large tomato, diced
- 1-1/4 cups diced celery
- 1-1/4 cups mayonnaise
- 5 teaspoon white vinegar
- 1/4 teaspoon salt
- 1/8 to 1/4 teaspoon pepper
- 1 pound sliced bacon, cooked and crumbled

1) Cook macaroni according to package directions; drain and rinse in cold water. In a large bowl, combine the macaroni, green onions, tomato and celery.

2) In a small bowl, combine the mayonnaise, vinegar, salt and pepper. Pour over macaroni mixture and toss to coat. Cover and refrigerate for at least 2 hours. Just before serving, add bacon.

Yield: 12 servings.

NUTRITION FACTS: 3/4 cup equals 290 calories, 25 g fat (5 g saturated fat), 19 mg cholesterol, 387 mg sodium, 11 g carbohydrate, 1 g fiber, 6 g protein.

CURRIED COUSCOUS SALAD

Curried Couscous Salad

Lynn Gamache
Campbell River, British Columbia

This delightful chilled salad can be prepared a day early and goes well with most main dishes. Add cooked shrimp or cheese cubes for a simple meal.

- 3/4 cup water
- 1/2 cup uncooked couscous
- 1 cup frozen peas, thawed
- 3/4 cup diced cucumber
- 1 large carrot, shredded
- 1/4 cup crumbled cooked bacon
- 2 green onions, chopped
- 1 teaspoon minced fresh parsley

DRESSING:
- 1/4 cup olive oil
- 1 tablespoon cider vinegar
- 1 tablespoon soy sauce
- 1 teaspoon sugar
- 1 teaspoon curry powder

1) In a small saucepan, bring water to a boil. Stir in couscous. Cover and remove from the heat; let stand for 5 minutes. Fluff with a fork.

2) In a large bowl, combine the couscous, peas, cucumber, carrot, bacon, onions and parsley. Cover and refrigerate until chilled.

3) In a jar with a tight-fitting lid, combine the dressing ingredients; shake well. Just before serving, drizzle over salad and toss to coat.

Yield: 4 servings.

NUTRITION FACTS: 3/4 cup equals 275 calories, 15 g fat (2 g saturated fat), 5 mg cholesterol, 505 mg sodium, 27 g carbohydrate, 4 g fiber, 9 g protein.

Green and White Salad

Shelia Weis, Marshfield, Wisconsin

Broccoli, cauliflower and peas combine nicely in this salad. You can also omit the peas and add chopped red onion or sweet yellow pepper.

- 1/2 cup cauliflowerets
- 1/2 cup broccoli florets
- 1/4 cup frozen peas, thawed
- 1 green onion, thinly sliced
- 1 bacon strip, cooked and crumbled

DRESSING:
- 3 tablespoons mayonnaise
- 1 tablespoon sour cream
- 3/4 teaspoon sugar
- 1/4 teaspoon white vinegar
- 1/4 teaspoon garlic salt
- Dash salt

1) In a bowl, combine the cauliflower, broccoli, peas, onion and bacon. In a small bowl, combine the dressing ingredients. Pour over vegetable mixture and toss to coat. Cover and refrigerate until serving.

Yield: 2 servings.

NUTRITION FACTS: 3/4 cup equals 217 calories, 20 g fat (4 g saturated fat), 15 mg cholesterol, 500 mg sodium, 7 g carbohydrate, 2 g fiber, 3 g protein.

Tomato Mozzarella Salad

Lynn Merendino, Duncannon, Pennsylvania

As soon as our cherry tomatoes start ripening, I pull out this recipe. It's easy to fix, so I prepare it for all our family get-togethers.

1/4 cup red wine vinegar
1 garlic clove, minced
1/2 teaspoon salt
Pepper to taste
2/3 cup olive oil
1 pint cherry tomatoes, halved
1-1/2 cups cubed mozzarella cheese
1/4 cup chopped onion
3 tablespoons minced fresh basil

1) In a small bowl, combine the vinegar, garlic, salt and pepper. Whisk in oil until well blended. Add remaining ingredients; toss to coat.

2) Cover and refrigerate for at least 1 hour, stirring occasionally. Remove with a slotted spoon to a serving dish.

Yield: 6 servings.

NUTRITION FACTS: 1 cup equals 308 calories, 30 g fat (7 g saturated fat), 22 mg cholesterol, 306 mg sodium, 4 g carbohydrate, 1 g fiber, 6 g protein.

Colorful Corn Salad

Helen Koedel, Hamilton, Ohio

Filled with corn and red and green peppers, this colorful dish makes a large serving. It's great for summer picnics and gatherings.

1 package (10 ounces) frozen corn, thawed
1 cup chopped green pepper
1 cup chopped sweet red pepper
1 cup chopped celery
1/2 cup chopped green onions
1/2 cup minced fresh parsley
1/4 cup shredded Parmesan cheese
1 teaspoon ground cumin
3/4 teaspoon salt
1/4 teaspoon pepper
1/4 teaspoon hot pepper sauce
Dash cayenne pepper
4-1/2 teaspoons olive oil
1 garlic clove, minced
3 tablespoons lime juice

1) In a large bowl, combine the vegetables, parsley, Parmesan cheese, cumin, salt, pepper, hot pepper sauce and cayenne.

2) In a microwave-safe dish, combine oil and garlic. Microwave, uncovered, on high for 1 minute. Cool. Whisk in lime juice. Pour over the corn mixture and toss to coat.

Yield: 8-9 servings.

NUTRITION FACTS: 3/4 cup equals 74 calories, 3 g fat (1 g saturated fat), 2 mg cholesterol, 252 mg sodium, 11 g carbohydrate, 2 g fiber, 2 g protein.

Brown and Wild Rice Salad

Taste of Home Test Kitchen

This side dish is twice as nice since it stars both brown and wild rice! Tangy raspberry vinegar complements the nutty flavor of the rice, while dried cranberries provide unexpected bursts of sweetness.

1 cup brown rice, cooked
1 cup wild rice, cooked
6 green onions, chopped
3/4 cup dried cranberries
1/3 cup coarsely chopped pecans, toasted
2 tablespoons chopped fresh parsley
1/4 cup olive oil
6 tablespoons raspberry vinegar
2 tablespoons honey
1-1/2 teaspoons salt
1/2 teaspoon pepper

1) In a large bowl, combine the rice, onions, cranberries, pecans and parsley. In a small bowl, whisk together the oil, vinegar, honey, salt and pepper. Pour over salad and toss to coat.

Yield: 8 servings.

NUTRITION FACTS: 1 cup equals 343 calories, 12 g fat (1 g saturated fat), 0 cholesterol, 450 mg sodium, 55 g carbohydrate, 5 g fiber, 6 g protein.

Fennel Orange Salad

Nina Hall, Spokane, Washington

You'll need just a few ingredients to fix this fresh-tasting salad. The combination of crisp fennel and juicy oranges is delightful. To reduce last-minute prep, make it the day before you plan to serve it.

- 1 fennel bulb with fronds (about 3/4 pound)
- 4 medium navel oranges, peeled and sectioned
- 1/3 cup orange juice
- 4 teaspoons olive oil
- 1 tablespoon grated orange peel
- 1/4 teaspoon salt
- 1/8 teaspoon pepper

1) Finely chop enough fennel fronds to measure 1/4 cup; set aside. Cut fennel bulb in half lengthwise; remove and discard the tough outer layer, fennel core and any green stalks. Cut widthwise into thin slices and measure 3 cups; place in a large bowl. Add orange sections.

2) In a jar with a tight-fitting lid, combine the orange juice, oil, orange peel, salt and pepper; shake well. Pour over fennel and oranges; toss gently. Sprinkle with reserved fronds.

Yield: 4 servings.

NUTRITION FACTS: 1 cup equals 143 calories, 5 g fat (1 g saturated fat), 0 cholesterol, 193 mg sodium, 25 g carbohydrate, 6 g fiber, 3 g protein.

Summer Squash Salad

Diane Hixon, Niceville, Florida

The flavors from the dressing in this salad get even better with time. My family loves this, and I love that it uses up fresh summer produce.

- 2 cups julienned zucchini
- 2 cups julienned yellow summer squash
- 1 cup sliced radish
- 1/2 cup vegetable oil
- 2 tablespoons plus 2 teaspoons cider vinegar
- 1 tablespoon Dijon mustard
- 1 tablespoon minced fresh parsley
- 3/4 teaspoon salt
- 1/2 teaspoon dill weed
- 1/4 teaspoon pepper

1) In a large bowl, toss the zucchini, squash and radishes. In a small bowl or jar with a tight-fitting

lid, combine remaining ingredients; shake well. Pour over vegetables. Cover and refrigerate for at least 2 hours.

Yield: 6-8 servings.

NUTRITION FACTS: 3/4 cup equals 137 calories, 14 g fat (2 g saturated fat), 0 cholesterol, 274 mg sodium, 3 g carbohydrate, 1 g fiber, 1 g protein.

GREEK GARDEN SALAD

Greek Garden Salad

Glenda Parsonage, Maple Creek, Saskatchewan

I like to dress up this salad by serving it in a lettuce-lined bowl. But it's gorgeous as well as tasty just served by itself.

- 2 large tomatoes, chopped
- 3/4 cup chopped cucumber
- 1/2 cup chopped green pepper
- 1/2 cup chopped sweet red pepper
- 1/2 cup crumbled feta cheese
- 1/4 cup thinly sliced green onions
- 1/4 cup sliced ripe olives
- 1/2 cup Italian salad dressing
- 1/8 teaspoon dried oregano
  Leaf lettuce, optional

1) In a bowl, combine the tomatoes, cucumber, peppers, cheese, green onions and olives. Cover and refrigerate until serving.

2) Just before serving, add salad dressing and oregano; toss to coat. Serve in a lettuce-lined bowl if desired.

Yield: 6 servings.

NUTRITION FACTS: 1 serving equals 125 calories, 10 g fat (2 g saturated fat), 5 mg cholesterol, 483 mg sodium, 7 g carbohydrate, 2 g fiber, 3 g protein.

Dilled Cucumbers

Betty Claycomb, Alverton, Pennsylvania

Simple and classic, these dilled cucumbers are a perfect side for a summer picnic or potluck. We like them alongside grilled hamburgers.

2	**medium cucumbers, peeled and thinly sliced**
1/2	**teaspoon salt**
1/2	**cup sour cream**
1	**tablespoon lemon juice**
2	**tablespoons finely chopped green onion**
1/8	**teaspoon pepper**
1/4	**teaspoon sugar**
1/2	**teaspoon dried dill weed**

1) In a small bowl, toss cucumbers with salt. Allow to stand for 10 minutes. Meanwhile, combine all of the remaining ingredients.

2) Drain cucumbers and combine with sour cream mixture. Cover; refrigerate until serving.

Yield: 6 servings.

NUTRITION FACTS: 1 cup equals 57 calories, 3 g fat (2 g saturated fat), 13 mg cholesterol, 207 mg sodium, 4 g carbohydrate, 1 g fiber, 2 g protein.

Taffy Apple Salad

Cathy LaReau, Sumava Resorts, Indiana

When you take a bite of this salad, you may think you're eating a candied apple. It's delicious!

1	**can (20 ounces) crushed pineapple**
4	**cups miniature marshmallows**
1	**egg, lightly beaten**
1/2	**cup sugar**
1/4	**cup packed brown sugar**
1	**tablespoon all-purpose flour**
4-1/2	**teaspoons cider vinegar**
1	**carton (8 ounces) frozen whipped topping, thawed**
3	**cups diced unpeeled apples**
1-1/2	**cups lightly salted peanuts, coarsely chopped**

1) Drain pineapple, reserving juice. In a large bowl, combine pineapple and marshmallows; cover and refrigerate for several hours.

2) In a saucepan, combine the egg, sugars, flour, vinegar and reserved pineapple juice; cook and stir until mixture thickens and reaches 160°. Remove from heat; cool. Cover and refrigerate.

3) Fold whipped topping into the chilled dressing. Add the apples and peanuts to the pineapple and marshmallows. Fold dressing into fruit mixture. Refrigerate leftovers.

Yield: 10-12 servings.

NUTRITION FACTS: 3/4 cup equals 315 calories, 13 g fat (5 g saturated fat), 18 mg cholesterol, 93 mg sodium, 47 g carbohydrate, 3 g fiber, 6 g protein.

APRICOT GELATIN SALAD

Better Gelatin Salads

Always use canned or cooked pineapple in gelatin salads. Fresh pineapple, kiwifruit, papaya, guava, figs or gingerroot will prevent the salad from setting.

For easy removal of gelatin salads from the mold, coat mold with nonstick cooking spray before filling. To avoid spilling when transferring the mold into the refrigerator, place mold on a baking sheet or tray in the refrigerator and then fill with the gelatin mixture.

To prevent fruits or vegetables from floating or sinking in the mold, add them when the gelatin is slightly thickened. If the gelatin is too thin, the fruit will sink; too thick, and the fruit will float.

If your gelatin mixture sets too fast and you've passed the "partially set" step, place the bowl of gelatin in a pan of warm water and stir until the gelatin has softened. Chill again until the mixture is the consistency of unbeaten raw egg whites.

For a layered mold, always start and end with gelatin mixture since the creamy layer might not be sturdy enough to support the gelatin mixture. Add creamy layer when the gelatin layer sticks to a finger when touched. If the gelatin layer is too set up, the layers may slip apart when unmolded.

Before unmolding, make sure the gelatin mixture has completely set up. The gelatin should not feel sticky and should not move when the mold is tilted. When unmolding a large salad, rinse the serving platter with cold water before turning the gelatin out. The moisture helps allow the salad to be centered on the platter.

Apricot Gelatin Salad
Neva Jane Upp, Hutchinson, Kansas

This delicious salad adds color to any table with its combination of fruity-fizzy ingredients.

> 2 **cans (16 ounces *each*) apricot halves**
>
> **Dash salt**
>
> 2 **packages (3 ounces *each*) orange gelatin**
> 1 **can (6 ounces) frozen orange juice concentrate, thawed**
> 1 **tablespoon lemon juice**
> 1 **cup lemon-lime soda**

1) Drain the apricots, reserving 1-1/2 cups juice; set apricots aside. In a small saucepan, bring apricot juice and salt to a boil over medium heat. Remove from the heat; add gelatin, stirring until gelatin is dissolved.

2) In a blender, combine orange juice concentrate, lemon juice and reserved apricots; cover and process until smooth. Add to gelatin mixture along with soda; mix well.

3) Pour into a 6-cup mold coated with nonstick cooking spray. Cover and refrigerate until firm. Unmold and transfer to a serving plate.

Yield: 10 servings.

NUTRITION FACTS: 1 piece equals 181 calories, trace fat (trace saturated fat), 0 cholesterol, 60 mg sodium, 45 g carbohydrate, 2 g fiber, 3 g protein.

UNMOLDING GELATIN SALADS

1) Loosen the gelatin from the top edge of mold by gently pulling the gelatin away from edge with a moistened finger. Then dip the mold up to its rim in a sink or large pan of warm water for a few seconds or until edges begin to release from the side of the mold.

2) Place a plate over the mold and invert. Carefully lift the mold from the salad.

Summertime Strawberry Salad
Janet England, Chillicothe, Missouri

For years, this salad has been a "must" at family dinners and special occasions. It's as pretty as it is good, so it's nice for serving at holiday feasts besides.

> 1 **package (3 ounces) strawberry gelatin**
> 1 **cup boiling water**
> 1 **cup cold water**

MIDDLE LAYER:

> 1 **envelope unflavored gelatin**
> 1/2 **cup cold water**
> 1 **cup half-and-half cream**
> 1 **package (8 ounces) cream cheese, softened**
> 1 **cup sugar**
> 1/2 **teaspoon vanilla extract**

TOP LAYER:

> 1 **package (6 ounces) strawberry gelatin**
> 1 **cup boiling water**
> 1 **cup cold water**
> 3 **to 4 cups sliced fresh strawberries**

1) In a bowl, dissolve strawberry gelatin in boiling water; stir in cold water. Pour into a 13-in. x 9-in. x 2-in. dish coated with nonstick cooking spray; refrigerate until set.

2) Meanwhile, in a small bowl, sprinkle unflavored gelatin over cold water; let stand for 1 minute. In a saucepan over medium heat, heat cream (do not boil). Add softened gelatin; stir until gelatin is dissolved. Cool to room temperature.

3) In a mixing bowl, beat the cream cheese, sugar and vanilla until smooth. Gradually add the unflavored gelatin mixture; mix well. Carefully pour over the bottom layer. Refrigerate until set, about 1 hour.

4) For top layer, dissolve the strawberry gelatin in boiling water; stir in cold water. Cool to room temperature. Stir in strawberries; carefully spoon over middle layer. Refrigerate overnight.

Yield: 12-16 servings.

NUTRITION FACTS: 1 serving equals 187 calories, 7 g fat (4 g saturated fat), 23 mg cholesterol, 87 mg sodium, 29 g carbohydrate, 1 g fiber, 4 g protein.

Ambrosia Salad
Judi Bringegar, Liberty, North Carolina

This salad is great for last-minute planning because it's easy to prepare.

- 1 can (11 ounces) mandarin oranges, drained
- 1 can (8 ounces) pineapple chunks, drained
- 1 cup miniature marshmallows
- 1 cup flaked coconut
- 1 cup (8 ounces) sour cream

1) In a large bowl, combine the oranges, pineapple, marshmallows and coconut. Add sour cream and toss to mix. Cover; refrigerate for several hours.

Yield: 4 servings.

NUTRITION FACTS: 1 cup equals 332 calories, 18 g fat (14 g saturated fat), 40 mg cholesterol, 99 mg sodium, 37 g carbohydrate, 1 g fiber, 4 g protein.

Lime Strawberry Surprise
Arline Wertz, Millington, Tennessee

Eye-catching in holiday colors, this dish looks so decorative on the table.

- 1 package (3 ounces) lime gelatin
- 1 can (8 ounces) crushed pineapple, drained
- 1 package (8 ounces) cream cheese, softened
- 1/2 cup mayonnaise
- 1/2 cup chopped pecans
- 1 package (3 ounces) cherry *or* strawberry gelatin

1) Prepare lime gelatin according to package directions. Refrigerate until partially set, about 1 hour. Stir in pineapple. Pour into an 8-cup bowl or mold coated with nonstick cooking spray. Cover and refrigerate until firm, about 3 hours.

2) In a small mixing bowl, beat cream cheese and mayonnaise until smooth; stir in pecans. Spread over lime gelatin. Refrigerate until firm, about 2 hours.

3) Prepare strawberry gelatin according to package directions; cool slightly. Carefully spoon over cream cheese layer. Refrigerate until firm, about 3 hours or overnight.

Yield: 8-10 servings.

NUTRITION FACTS: 1/2 cup equals 276 calories, 21 g fat (7 g saturated fat), 29 mg cholesterol, 166 mg sodium, 20 g carbohydrate, 1 g fiber, 4 g protein.

Homemade Salad Dressing

If you plan on serving a vinegar and oil dressing right away, you can combine all ingredients in a jar with a tight-fitting lid and shake well. The mixture will separate upon standing; simply shake before serving. To mix a vinegar and oil dressing that will stand for an hour or two without separating, see Whisking Vinegar and Oil Dressings. Also use this method for dressings with mayonnaise or prepared mustard.

Homemade salad dressings made with olive oil will thicken during refrigeration. Remove the dressing 30 minutes before using to allow the olive oil to warm up.

By experimenting with a basic vinaigrette, you can create a variety of dressings to complement different salads. Try substituting an herb-, fruit- or wine-flavored vinegar for white or cider vinegar. Use citrus juice for part or all of the vinegar. Use nut-flavored oil for vegetable oil or add a drop or two of dark sesame oil. Finally, vary the herbs to best match the flavor of foods being dressed.

Citrus Vinaigrette
Taste of Home Test Kitchen

Tart, tangy and citrusy flavors abound in this vinaigrette. Quickly whisk it together for a fancy, fuss-free salad any night of the week.

- 1/4 cup orange juice
- 3 tablespoons red wine vinegar
- 2 teaspoons honey
- 1-1/2 teaspoons Dijon mustard
- 1 tablespoon olive oil

1) In a small bowl, whisk together all the ingredients. Store in the refrigerator.

Yield: 1/2 cup.

NUTRITION FACTS: 2 tablespoons equals 53 calories, 4 g fat (trace saturated fat), 0 cholesterol, 47 mg sodium, 5 g carbohydrate, trace fiber, trace protein.

Raspberry Vinaigrette
Valerie Jordan, Kingmont, West Virginia

My family requests this light, fruity dressing all year. I especially like it in the summer as an alternative to heavier, cream-based dressings.

1/2   cup raspberry vinegar
1/3   cup sugar
3/4   cup olive oil
1/2   teaspoon Dijon mustard
1/8   teaspoon pepper

1) In a small saucepan, cook and stir vinegar and sugar over low heat until sugar is dissolved. Cool slightly. Pour into a jar with tight-fitting lid. Add remaining ingredients; cover and shake well. Refrigerate until chilled. Shake before using. Refrigerate leftovers.

Yield: 1-1/4 cups.

NUTRITION FACTS: 2 tablespoons equals 173 calories, 16 g fat (2 g saturated fat), 0 cholesterol, 6 mg sodium, 7 g carbohydrate, trace fiber, trace protein.

WHISKING VINEGAR AND OIL DRESSINGS
Combine all ingredients except oil in a small bowl. Slowly add oil while mixing vigorously with a wire whisk.

Poppy Seed Dressing
Andra Kunkle, Lenoir, North Carolina

We especially love this sweet dressing on any assortment of fresh fruit.

2   cups sugar
3/4   teaspoon salt
3/4   teaspoon onion powder
3/4   teaspoon ground mustard
3/4   cup cider vinegar
1   cup vegetable oil
3/4   teaspoon poppy seeds

1) In a small mixing bowl, combine the sugar, salt, onion powder and mustard. Add the vinegar and beat for 4 minutes.

2) Add the oil; beat for 10 minutes. Add the poppy seeds; beat for 5 minutes. Store in the refrigerator.

Yield: 2-3/4 cups.

NUTRITION FACTS: 2 tablespoons equals 159 calories, 10 g fat (1 g saturated fat), 0 cholesterol, 81 mg sodium, 18 g carbohydrate, trace fiber, trace protein.

CREAMY FRENCH DRESSING

Creamy French Dressing
Taste of Home Test Kitchen

You'll need just a few ingredients from your pantry to blend together this mild dressing. It's thick, creamy and perfect on tossed salad greens.

1   cup ketchup
1/2   cup reduced-fat mayonnaise
3   tablespoons cider vinegar
3   tablespoons honey
2   tablespoons water
1   tablespoon olive oil
1   teaspoon lemon juice
1/2   teaspoon ground mustard
1/4   teaspoon salt

1) In a blender or food processor, combine all of the ingredients; cover and process until blended. Store in the refrigerator.

Yield: 1-3/4 cups.

NUTRITION FACTS: 2 tablespoons equals 70 calories, 4 g fat (1 g saturated fat), 3 mg cholesterol, 318 mg sodium, 10 g carbohydrate, 1 g fiber, 1 g protein.

Creamy Herb Dressing

Brigitte Hinz, Des Planes, Illinois

This dressing for vegetables is so easy, I make it the night before Thanksgiving to save time. We like it over cooked asparagus, green beans or broccoli for an eye-pleasing side dish.

- 1-1/2 cups mayonnaise
- 2/3 cup whipped cream
- 1/2 cup chopped green onions
- 1/2 cup minced fresh parsley
- 1 can (2 ounces) anchovy fillets, drained, optional
- 2 tablespoons minced chives
- 2 tablespoons lemon juice

1) In a blender, combine the mayonnaise, whipped cream, onions, parsley, anchovy if desired, chives and lemon juice; cover and process until smooth. Cover and refrigerate for at least 1 hour.

Yield: 2-1/2 cups dressing.

NUTRITION FACTS: 2 tablespoons equals 133 calories, 14 g fat (2 g saturated fat), 10 mg cholesterol, 198 mg sodium, 1 g carbohydrate, trace fiber, 1 g protein.

Blue Cheese Salad Dressing

Christy Freeman, Central Point, Oregon

This distinctively flavored dressing makes a great accompaniment to a mix of fresh greens. The thick, creamy dressing does double duty at our house—I often serve it as a dip with vegetables.

- 2 cups mayonnaise
- 1 cup (8 ounces) sour cream
- 1/4 cup white wine vinegar
- 1/4 cup minced fresh parsley
- 1 garlic clove, crushed
- 1/2 teaspoon ground mustard
- 1/2 teaspoon salt
- 1/4 teaspoon pepper
- 4 ounces crumbled blue cheese

1) Place all the ingredients in a blender; cover and process until smooth. Store in the refrigerator.

Yield: 3 cups.

NUTRITION FACTS: 2 tablespoons equals 172 calories, 18 g fat (4 g saturated fat), 17 mg cholesterol, 220 mg sodium, 1 g carbohydrate, trace fiber, 1 g protein.

Tangy Bacon Salad Dressing

Barbara Birk, St. George, Utah

You can serve this over salad greens or spinach, and you can add different berries, radishes or tomatoes for color.

- 3/4 cup sugar
- 1/3 cup white vinegar
- 1/3 cup ketchup
- 1 teaspoon Worcestershire sauce
- 1/2 cup vegetable oil
- 8 bacon strips, cooked and crumbled
- 1 small onion, finely chopped

1) In a small bowl, whisk together the sugar, vinegar, ketchup and Worcestershire sauce. Gradually whisk in the oil in a steady stream. Stir in bacon and onion. Store in the refrigerator.

Yield: about 2 cups.

NUTRITION FACTS: 2 tablespoons equals 122 calories, 8 g fat (1 g saturated fat), 3 mg cholesterol, 113 mg sodium, 11 g carbohydrate, trace fiber, 1 g protein.

Seasoned Croutons

Shelley McKinney, New Castle, Indiana

You can use these croutons as a topping for salads, soups or some of your favorite side-dish casseroles.

- 2 tablespoons butter
- 1 tablespoon olive oil
- 1/4 teaspoon garlic powder
- 1/4 teaspoon onion powder
- 1/4 teaspoon dried oregano
- 1/4 teaspoon dried basil
- Pinch salt
- 6 slices day-old bread, cubed

1) In an ungreased 13-in. x 9-in. x 2-in. baking pan, combine the butter, oil and seasonings. Heat in a 300° oven until butter is melted. Remove from the oven; stir to combine.

2) Add bread cubes and toss to coat. Bake for 10-15 minutes or until lightly browned, stirring frequently. Cool. Store in the refrigerator in an airtight container.

Yield: 3 cups.

NUTRITION FACTS: 1/4 cup equals 61 calories, 3 g fat (1 g saturated fat), 5 mg cholesterol, 99 mg sodium, 6 g carbohydrate, trace fiber, 1 g protein.

■ *LIGHTER SEASONED CROUTONS:* Omit butter and oil. Spray bread cubes with butter-flavored cooking spray. Sprinkle with seasonings and bake as directed.

■ *DILLY CROUTONS:* Omit seasonings and use 1 teaspoon dill weed. Bake as directed.

SAUCES & CONDIMENTS

SAUCES & CONDIMENTS

Sauces and condiments enhance other foods with sweet or savory flavors. Sauces help dress up meat or vegetables. Condiments are served along with a meal and include everything from jams and jellies to relishes, pickled vegetables, chutneys and salsas.

White Sauces

White sauces can be used as a base for a casserole or flavored as a topping for vegetables or meats. White sauce typically starts with a roux, which is a smooth mixture of equal parts butter and flour. The amount of butter and flour per 1 cup of liquid determines the thickness of the white sauce.

- Thin sauce: 1 tablespoon *each* butter and flour.
- Medium sauce: 2 tablespoons *each* butter and flour.
- Thick sauce: 3 tablespoons *each* butter and flour.

Basic White Sauce
Lois Gelzer, Oak Bluffs, Massachusetts

For years I have used this smooth sauce to make many dishes. The recipe can easily be doubled.

> 2 tablespoons butter
> 2 tablespoons all-purpose flour
> 1/8 teaspoon salt
> Dash white pepper
> 1 cup milk

1) In a saucepan, melt butter over medium heat. Whisk in the flour, salt and pepper until smooth. Gradually whisk in the milk.

2) Bring to a boil; cook and stir for 2 minutes or until thickened. Use immediately or refrigerate.

Yield: 1 cup.

NUTRITION FACTS: 2 tablespoons equals 51 calories, 4 g fat (2 g saturated fat), 12 mg cholesterol, 81 mg sodium, 3 g carbohydrate, trace fiber, 1 g protein.

■ *CHEESE SAUCE:* Prepare Basic White Sauce as directed. Reduce the heat; stir in 1/2 to 3/4 cup shredded cheddar cheese. Continue to stir just until cheese is melted.

■ *CURRY SAUCE:* Add 1/2 teaspoon curry powder and a dash of ground ginger along with the salt and pepper. Prepare as directed.

■ *MORNAY SAUCE:* Prepare Basic White Sauce as directed. Reduce heat; stir in 1/4 cup shredded Swiss cheese, Parmesan cheese *or* a combination of both and a dash of ground nutmeg. Continue to stir just until cheese is melted.

■ *MUSTARD SAUCE:* Stir in 1 tablespoon Dijon mustard into finished Basic White Sauce.

■ *BROWN SAUCE:* Use 1 cup beef broth in place of the milk. Prepare as directed. For a richer color, add a dash of browning sauce.

■ *VELOUTE SAUCE:* Use 1 cup chicken, turkey *or* fish broth in place of the milk. Prepare as directed.

MAKING A WHITE SAUCE

1) Start a white sauce by whisking flour into melted butter over medium heat until mixture becomes smooth.

2) Gradually whisk milk into mixture until blended. Bring mixture to a boil; cook and stir 2 minutes or until thickened.

Hollandaise Sauce

Hollandaise is a lemony, butter sauce that uses egg yolks rather than flour as the thickener. Hollandaise sauce can be tricky to make, so follow these pointers:

- Heat egg yolks over low heat. If the heat is too high, it will result in scrambled eggs.

- So the sauce thickens properly, allow the yolks to absorb a little butter at a time. Gradually add the butter in small amounts and completely incorporate into the yolks.

- Beat a tablespoon of cold water into the finished sauce if it starts to separate.

HOLLANDAISE SAUCE

Hollandaise Sauce
Taste of Home Test Kitchen

This traditional sauce adds an elegant touch to fresh steamed asparagus. The rich, lemony mixture is the typical sauce for eggs Benedict and is also delicious served over broccoli.

  3 **egg yolks**
1/4 **cup water**
  2 **tablespoons lemon juice**
1/2 **cup cold butter, cut into 8 pieces**
1/8 **teaspoon salt**
1/8 **teaspoon paprika**
     Dash white pepper

1) In a small heavy saucepan or double boiler, whisk together the egg yolks, water and lemon juice. Cook and stir over low heat until mixture begins to thicken, bubbles around edges and reaches 160°, about 20 minutes.

2) Add butter to yolk mixture, one piece at a time, whisking after each addition until butter is melted.

Remove from the heat; stir in the salt, paprika and pepper. Serve immediately.

Yield: 1 cup.

Editor's Note: To make a double boiler, place a stainless-steel mixing bowl in a saucepan. The bowl should only partially fit into the saucepan. Fill the saucepan with enough water so that when the bowl rests in the saucepan the water does not touch the bottom of the bowl. Bring the water to a simmer. Add the ingredients to the bowl and place the bowl in the saucepan.

NUTRITION FACTS: 2 tablespoons equals 124 calories, 13 g fat (8 g saturated fat), 110 mg cholesterol, 155 mg sodium, trace carbohydrate, trace fiber, 1 g protein.

Bearnaise Sauce
Taste of Home Test Kitchen

This is a smooth, rich sauce that makes a tangy accompaniment to roast beef.

1/4 **cup white wine vinegar**
1/4 **cup white wine *or* chicken broth**
1/4 **cup minced shallot**
  3 **tarragon sprigs**
1/4 **teaspoon pepper**
  4 **egg yolks**
  2 **tablespoons cold water**
1/4 **teaspoon salt**
1/8 **teaspoon white pepper**
1/2 **cup butter, melted and cooled**
  2 **tablespoons minced fresh tarragon**
  1 **tablespoon minced fresh parsley**

1) In a small saucepan, combine the vinegar, wine or broth, shallot, tarragon sprigs and pepper; bring to a boil. Reduce heat; simmer for 10 minutes or until mixture is reduced by half. Strain and set liquid aside; discard solids.

2) In a small heavy saucepan whisk together the egg yolks, water, salt, white pepper and reserved vinegar liquid. Cook and stir over low heat until the mixture begins to thicken, bubbles around the edges and reaches 160°.

3) Gradually whisk in butter. Remove from the heat; stir in tarragon and parsley. Serve immediately.

Yield: 1 cup.

NUTRITION FACTS: 2 tablespoons equals 142 calories, 14 g fat (8 g saturated fat), 137 mg cholesterol, 194 mg sodium, 2 g carbohydrate, trace fiber, 2 g protein.

Jamaican Barbecue Sauce

Lee Ann Odell, Erie, Colorado

Since visiting Jamaica, I've become a big fan of jerk chicken and fish. I came up with my own version of that zesty island flavoring. It's a great sauce for ribs, whether you're grilling them or making them in the oven.

- 1 bacon strip, halved
- 1/2 cup chopped onion
- 2 tablespoons chopped green onion
- 1 tablespoon chopped jalapeno pepper
- 1 cup ketchup
- 1/2 cup chicken broth
- 1/2 cup molasses
- 2 tablespoons cider vinegar
- 2 tablespoons lemon juice
- 1 tablespoon minced fresh thyme
- 1 tablespoon soy sauce
- 1 tablespoon Worcestershire sauce
- 1 tablespoon prepared mustard
- 1 teaspoon salt
- 1/2 teaspoon pepper
- 1/4 to 1/2 teaspoon ground cinnamon
- 1/4 to 1/2 teaspoon ground nutmeg

1) In a saucepan, cook bacon over medium heat until crisp. Discard bacon or save for another use.

2) In the drippings, saute the onions and jalapeno until tender. Stir in the remaining ingredients. Bring to a boil. Remove from the heat; cool. Store in the refrigerator.

Yield: 2 cups.

Editor's Note: When cutting or seeding hot peppers, use rubber or plastic gloves to protect your hands. Avoid touching your face.

NUTRITION FACTS: 2 tablespoons equals 61 calories, 1 g fat (1 g saturated fat), 1 mg cholesterol, 450 mg sodium, 12 g carbohydrate, trace fiber, 1 g protein.

Riverboat Barbecue Sauce

Barb Loftin, Florence, Kentucky

Maple and orange are the flavors that accent this sweet and tangy sauce. I gave it this name because we live near the Ohio River and love to watch the riverboats go by. The sauce is especially good on ribs or pork chops.

- 1/2 cup maple syrup
- 1/2 cup ketchup
- 1/4 cup orange juice
- 1 tablespoon dried minced onion
- 1 tablespoon white vinegar
- 1 tablespoon steak sauce

- 1 teaspoon grated orange peel
- 1 teaspoon prepared mustard
- 1/2 teaspoon Worcestershire sauce
- 1/4 teaspoon salt
- 1/4 teaspoon pepper
- 1/4 teaspoon hot pepper sauce
- 3 whole cloves

1) In a small saucepan, combine all ingredients. Bring to a boil. Reduce heat; simmer, uncovered, for 15 minutes or until the flavors are blended.

2) Remove from the heat. Discard cloves. Cool. Store in the refrigerator.

Yield: 1-1/3 cups.

NUTRITION FACTS: 2 tablespoons equals 61 calories, trace fat (trace saturated fat), 0 cholesterol, 240 mg sodium, 15 g carbohydrate, trace fiber, trace protein.

Spicy Mustard

Joyce Lonsdale, Unionville, Pennsylvania

I like to make this using fresh horseradish from my garden and vinegar seasoned with homegrown tarragon. It's a delightful dipper for pretzel rods or as a sandwich spread.

- 1/2 cup tarragon *or* cider vinegar
- 1/2 cup water
- 1/4 cup olive oil
- 2 tablespoons prepared horseradish
- 1/2 teaspoon lemon juice
- 1 cup ground mustard
- 1/2 cup sugar
- 1/2 teaspoon salt

1) In a blender or food processor, combine all ingredients; cover and process for 1 minute. Scrape down the sides of the container and process for 30 seconds.

2) Transfer to a small saucepan and let stand for 10 minutes. Cook over low heat until bubbly, stirring constantly. Cool completely. If a thinner mustard is desired, stir in an additional 1-2 tablespoons water.

3) Pour into small containers with tight-fitting lids. Store in the refrigerator.

Yield: 1-1/2 cups.

NUTRITION FACTS: 1 tablespoon equals 67 calories, 4 g fat (trace saturated fat), 0 cholesterol, 54 mg sodium, 6 g carbohydrate, 1 g fiber, 2 g protein.

Lemon Curd
Taste of Home Test Kitchen

Lemon curd is a scrumptious spread for scones, biscuits or other baked goods. You can find it in larger grocery stores alongside jams and jellies or with baking supplies, but you may enjoy making it from scratch with this recipe.

>   3   eggs
>   1   cup sugar
>   1/2 cup lemon juice (about 2 lemons)
>   1/4 cup butter, melted
>   1   tablespoon grated lemon peel

1) In a heavy saucepan, beat eggs and sugar. Stir in the lemon juice, butter and lemon peel.

2) Cook and stir over medium-low heat for 15 minutes or until mixture is thickened and reaches 160°. Cover; store in refrigerator for up to 1 week.

Yield: 1-2/3 cups.

NUTRITION FACTS: 2 tablespoons equals 110 calories, 5 g fat (3 g saturated fat), 58 mg cholesterol, 50 mg sodium, 16 g carbohydrate, trace fiber, 2 g protein.

Hard Sauce for Cake
Deb Brass, Cedar Falls, Iowa

My grandmother used to make this sauce to dress up plain cake. It's also good over gingerbread.

>   1   cup sugar
>   2   tablespoons cornstarch
>   1/2 teaspoon salt
>   2   cups boiling water
>   1/2 teaspoon vanilla extract
>   1/4 cup butter

1) In a small saucepan, combine sugar, cornstarch and salt. Gradually stir in water until smooth.

2) Bring to a boil; cook and stir for 15 minutes until smooth, thickened and clear. Remove from heat; stir in vanilla and butter. Serve warm over cake.

Yield: 1 cup.

NUTRITION FACTS: 2 tablespoons equals 155 calories, 6 g fat (4 g saturated fat), 15 mg cholesterol, 206 mg sodium, 27 g carbohydrate, trace fiber, trace protein.

Cherry Sauce
Kathy Emberton, Cicero, Indiana

Served warm, this sauce makes a wonderful topping for sponge cake, pound cake or ice cream. Or try it as a filling for crepes or blintzes.

>   1   can (16 ounces) pitted tart red
>   cherries
>   1/4 cup sugar
>   2   tablespoons cornstarch
>   1   tablespoon butter
>   1/4 teaspoon vanilla extract
>   Few drops red food coloring, optional

1) Drain cherries, reserving juice. Set cherries aside. Add enough water to juice to equal 1-1/4 cups.

2) In a saucepan, combine sugar and cornstarch. Stir in juice. Bring to a boil; cook and stir for 2 minutes or until thickened.

3) Remove from the heat. Stir in the butter, vanilla, cherries and food coloring if desired.

Yield: 4-6 servings.

NUTRITION FACTS: 1 serving equals 116 calories, 2 g fat (1 g saturated fat), 5 mg cholesterol, 25 mg sodium, 25 g carbohydrate, 1 g fiber, 1 g protein.

Strawberry Syrup
Nancy Dunaway, Springfield, Illinois

This recipe is a spin-off of my dad's homemade syrup. Our son requests it with pancakes, waffles or ice cream whenever he and his family come to visit.

>   1   cup sugar
>   1   cup water
>   1-1/2 cups mashed unsweetened
>   strawberries

1) In a saucepan, bring sugar and water to a boil. Gradually add strawberries; return to a boil.

2) Reduce heat; simmer, uncovered, for 10 minutes, stirring occasionally.

Yield: about 2-1/2 cups.

NUTRITION FACTS: 2 tablespoons equals 57 calories, trace fat (0 saturated fat), 0 cholesterol, trace sodium, 15 g carbohydrate, trace fiber, trace protein.

CINNAMON BLUEBERRY JAM, ORANGE PEAR JAM & RASPBERRY PLUM JAM

Refrigerator & Freezer Jellies and Jams

When making jam, use firm, ripe fruit. Overripe fruit will cause the jelly or jam to be soft and watery, while underripe fruit will make it too firm and hard to spread. Make sure frozen fruit is thawed before using.

Do not reduce the sugar in recipes or use sugar substitutes. If you do, the jelly or jam will not properly set up. To make a reduced-sugar jelly or jam, look for pectin specifically designed for lower sugar recipes and follow recommended sugar amounts on the pectin box.

Do not double recipes because the spread may not properly set. If a larger yield is desired, make two separate batches.

Use containers that are no larger than 1 pint (2 cups) and are suitable for the refrigerator or freezer. Store in the refrigerator for up to 3 weeks or freeze up to 1 year. If frozen, thaw in the refrigerator and use within 3 weeks. Recipes that use gelatin do not freeze well and may become thin after thawing.

Pretty Peach Jam
Theresa Beckman, Canton, South Dakota

This has been a favorite jam in my family for as long as I can remember. It's a delicious medley of peaches, cherries, pineapple and orange.

> 8 medium peaches, cut into wedges

> 1 small unpeeled navel orange, cut into wedges

> 2 cans (8 ounces *each*) crushed pineapple, undrained

> 12 maraschino cherries

> 3 tablespoons maraschino cherry juice

> 2 packages (1-3/4 ounces *each*) powdered fruit pectin

> 10 cups sugar

1) In a blender or food processor, cover and process fruits and cherry juice in batches until smooth. Transfer to a large kettle; stir in pectin and bring to a rolling boil over high heat, stirring frequently. Add sugar and return to a rolling boil. Boil for 2 minutes, stirring constantly.

2) Remove from the heat. Pour into jars or plastic containers. Cover and let stand overnight or until set, but not longer than 24 hours. Refrigerate for up to 3 weeks or freeze for up to 1 year.

Yield: 13 cups.

NUTRITION FACTS: 2 tablespoons equals 88 calories, trace fat (trace saturated fat), 0 cholesterol, trace sodium, 22 g carbohydrate, trace fiber, trace protein.

Orange Pear Jam
Delores Ward, Decatur, Indiana

Orange gelatin brings bright citrus flavor to the pear and pineapple combination in this jam. It's great on toasted homemade bread.

> 7 cups sugar

> 5 cups chopped peeled fresh pears

> 1 cup crushed pineapple, drained

> 2 tablespoons lemon juice

> 2 packages (3 ounces *each*) orange gelatin

1) In a Dutch oven or large kettle, combine sugar, pears, pineapple and lemon juice. Bring to a full rolling boil over high heat, stirring constantly.

2) Reduce heat; simmer for 15 minutes, stirring frequently. Remove from the heat; stir in gelatin until dissolved.

3) Pour into jars or containers; cool to room temperature, about 1 hour. Cover and let stand overnight or until set, but no longer than 24 hours. Refrigerate for up to 3 weeks.

Yield: about 7 cups.

NUTRITION FACTS: 2 tablespoons equals 119 calories, trace fat (trace saturated fat), 0 cholesterol, 7 mg sodium, 31 g carbohydrate, trace fiber, trace protein.

1) Wash jars and two-piece caps in hot, soapy water; rinse thoroughly. Dry bands on a towel. Put jars in a large kettle with enough water to cover; simmer to 180°. Remove from heat. Place lids in a small saucepan and cover with water; simmer to 180°. Remove from the heat.

2) Place rack in canner. Add several inches of water; bring to a simmer. Meanwhile, prepare recipe. Ladle or pour hot mixture into hot jars, leaving the recommended amount of headspace for expansion during processing.

3) Wipe threads and rim of jar with a clean damp cloth. Place warm lids on jars with sealing compound next to the glass. Screw band onto the jars just until resistance is met.

4) Immediately after filling each jar, use a jar lifter to place the jar onto the rack in the canner, making sure the jars are not touching. Lower rack when filled. If necessary, add enough boiling water to canner to cover jar lids by 1 to 2 in. Cover canner with its lid. Adjust heat to hold a steady rolling boil. Start counting the processing time when the water returns to a boil. If the water level decreases while processing, add additional boiling water.

5) When the processing time has ended, remove jars from the canner with jar lifter. Stand upright on a towel, out of drafts, leaving 1-2 in. of space around each jar.

After 12 to 24 hours, test each of the lids to determine if they have sealed by pressing the center of the lid. If it is concave (indented), remove the band and try to lift the lid. If lid is secure, the jar is vacuum-sealed. Wipe jars to remove any food. Label and date jars.

REPROCESSING UNSEALED JARS

If a lid does not seal within 24 hours, the product must either be stored in the refrigerator and used within several days or reprocessed. To reprocess:

1) Remove and discard the lid. The band may be reused if in good condition. Don't reuse a jar with chips or cracks.

2) Reheat the product. Ladle or pour hot mixture into a hot clean jar, leaving the recommended amount of headspace. Adjust cap.

3) Process in a boiling-water bath as recipe directs.

Caramel Apple Jam
Robert Atwood, West Wareham, Massachusetts

The flavor of apples, brown sugar, cinnamon and nutmeg come together in this spreadable treat. It's a must-have at our breakfast table.

- 6 cups diced peeled apples (1/8-inch cubes)
- 1/2 cup water
- 1/2 teaspoon butter
- 1 package (1-3/4 ounces) powdered fruit pectin
- 3 cups sugar
- 2 cups packed brown sugar
- 1/2 teaspoon ground cinnamon
- 1/4 teaspoon ground nutmeg

1) In a large kettle, combine the apples, water and butter. Cook and stir over low heat until apples are soft.

2) Stir in pectin and bring to a rolling boil, stirring constantly. Add the sugars, cinnamon and nutmeg and return to a rolling boil. Boil for 1 minute, stirring constantly.

3) Remove from the heat and skim off any foam. Ladle hot jam into hot sterilized jars, leaving 1/4-in. headspace. Adjust caps. Process for 10 minutes in a boiling-water bath.

Yield: 7 half-pints.

NUTRITION FACTS: 2 tablespoons equals 83 calories, trace fat (trace saturated fat), trace cholesterol, 4 mg sodium, 21 g carbohydrate, trace fiber, trace protein.

Raspberry Plum Jam
Arlene Loker, Craigville, Indiana

Raspberries and plums are deliciously combined in this jam, which you can serve on warm bread, rolls or scones.

    4-1/2 cups chopped *or* coarsely ground
           peeled pitted fresh plums (2-1/2
           pounds)
        2 packages (10 ounces *each*) frozen
           sweetened raspberries
       10 cups sugar
      1/2 cup lemon juice
        2 pouches (3 ounces *each*) liquid
           fruit pectin

1) In a large kettle, combine the plums, raspberries, sugar and lemon juice. Bring to a full rolling boil over high heat, stirring constantly.

2) Quickly stir in pectin; return to a full rolling boil. Boil for 1 minute, stirring constantly.

3) Remove from the heat; skim off foam. Pour hot liquid into hot sterilized jars, leaving 1/4-in. headspace. Adjust caps. Process for 15 minutes in a boiling-water bath.

Yield: 6 pints.

NUTRITION FACTS: 2 tablespoons equals 91 calories, trace fat (trace saturated fat), 0 cholesterol, trace sodium, 24 g carbohydrate, trace fiber, trace protein.

SKIMMING FOAM FROM JELLIES AND JAMS
Remove kettle from the heat and skim off foam with a large spoon. Proceed with recipe.

Quick and Easy Strawberry Jam
Taste of Home Test Kitchen

This is an easy and tasty way to use up a freshly picked quarts of summer strawberries. It makes about seven half-pints, so there's enough to share.

        2 quarts strawberries, washed and
           stemmed
        1 package (1-3/4 ounces) powdered
           fruit pectin
    6-3/4 cups sugar

1) Crush strawberries and measure 4-1/2 cups berries into a large saucepan. Stir in pectin and bring to a rolling boil over high heat, stirring frequently. Add sugar and return to a rolling boil. Boil for 1 minute, stirring constantly.

2) Remove from heat and skim foam. Carefully ladle hot jam into hot sterilized jars, leaving 1/4-in. headspace. Adjust caps. Process for 10 minutes in a boiling-water bath.

Yield: about 7 half-pints.

NUTRITION FACTS: 2 tablespoons equals 104 calories, trace fat (trace saturated fat), 0 cholesterol, trace sodium, 27 g carbohydrate, trace fiber, trace protein.

Cinnamon Blueberry Jam
Barbara Burns, Phillipsburg, New Jersey

I was surprised to discover that the cinnamon-blueberry combination was so delightful.

        1 pound fresh *or* frozen blueberries
           (about 1 quart)
    3-1/2 cups sugar
        1 tablespoon lemon juice
      1/4 teaspoon ground cinnamon
      1/8 teaspoon ground cloves
        1 pouch (3 ounces) liquid fruit pectin

1) Crush blueberries; measure 2-1/2 cups and place in a large saucepan. Add the sugar, lemon juice, cinnamon and cloves; bring to a full rolling boil over high heat.

2) Quickly stir in the pectin. Return to a boil; boil for 1 minute, stirring constantly.

3) Remove from the heat. Skim off foam. Pour hot into hot sterilized jars, leaving 1/4-in headspace. Adjust caps. Process for 15 minutes in a boiling-water bath.

Yield: 4 half-pints.

NUTRITION FACTS: 2 tablespoons equals 93 calories, trace fat (trace saturated fat), 0 cholesterol, 1 mg sodium, 24 g carbohydrate, trace fiber, trace protein.

Texas Jalapeno Jelly

Lori McMullen, Victoria, Texas

A jar of this jelly is always warmly received. I like to trim the lid with a bandanna.

- 2 jalapeno peppers, seeded and chopped
- 3 medium green peppers, cut into 1-inch pieces, *divided*
- 1-1/2 cups white vinegar, *divided*
- 6-1/2 cups sugar
- 1/2 to 1 teaspoon cayenne pepper
- 2 pouches (3 ounces *each*) liquid fruit pectin

About 6 drops green food coloring, optional

Cream cheese and crackers, optional

1) In a blender or food processor, place the jalapenos, half of the green peppers and 1/2 cup vinegar; cover and process until pureed.

2) Transfer to a large Dutch oven or kettle. Repeat with remaining green peppers and another 1/2 cup vinegar. Add the sugar, cayenne and remaining vinegar to pan. Bring to a rolling boil over high heat, stirring constantly.

3) Quickly stir in pectin. Return to a rolling boil; boil for 1 minute, stirring constantly.

4) Remove from the heat. Skim off foam. Add food coloring if desired. Ladle hot liquid into hot jars, leaving 1/4-in. headspace. Adjust caps. Process for 10 minutes in a boiling-water bath. Serve over cream cheese with crackers if desired.

Yield: 7 half-pints.

Editor's Note: When cutting or seeding hot peppers, use rubber or plastic gloves to protect your hands. Avoid touching your face.

NUTRITION FACTS: 2 tablespoons equals 92 calories, trace fat (trace saturated fat), 0 cholesterol, 1 mg sodium, 24 g carbohydrate, trace fiber, trace protein.

Lime Mint Jelly

Gloria Jarrett, Loveland, Ohio

This holly-green jelly won me a "Best of Show" at the county fair. It's delicious on roasted meats.

- 4 cups sugar
- 1-3/4 cups water
- 3/4 cup lime juice
- 7 drops green food coloring, optional
- 1 pouch (3 ounces) liquid fruit pectin

- 3 tablespoons finely chopped fresh mint leaves
- 1/4 cup grated lime peel

1) In a large saucepan, combine the sugar, water and lime juice; add food coloring if desired. Bring to a rolling boil over high heat, stirring constantly.

2) Add the pectin, mint and lime peel and return to a full rolling boil. Boil for 1 minute, stirring constantly.

3) Remove from the heat; skim off foam. Carefully ladle into hot sterilized jars, leaving 1/4-in. headspace. Adjust caps. Process for 15 minutes in a boiling-water bath.

Yield: 5 half-pints.

NUTRITION FACTS: 2 tablespoons equals 79 calories, trace fat (trace saturated fat), 0 cholesterol, 1 mg sodium, 21 g carbohydrate, trace fiber, trace protein.

Easy Refrigerator Pickles

Catherine Seibold, Elma, New York

When you have an abundance of cucumbers and onions from your garden, this is a great way to use them up!

- 6 cups thinly sliced cucumbers
- 2 cups thinly sliced onions
- 1-1/2 cups sugar
- 1-1/2 cups cider vinegar
- 1/2 teaspoon salt
- 1/2 teaspoon mustard seed
- 1/2 teaspoon celery seed
- 1/2 teaspoon ground turmeric
- 1/2 teaspoon ground cloves

1) Place cucumbers and onions in a large bowl; set aside. Combine remaining ingredients in a saucepan; bring to a boil. Cook and stir just until the sugar is dissolved.

2) Pour over cucumber mixture; cool. Cover tightly and refrigerate for at least 24 hours before serving.

Yield: 6 cups.

NUTRITION FACTS: 1/4 cup equals 58 calories, trace fat (trace saturated fat), 0 cholesterol, 50 mg sodium, 15 g carbohydrate, trace fiber, trace protein.

MAKING VEGETABLE RELISHES

If you plan to prepare a lot of relish, make the chopping easier by using a food processor or a food grinder with a coarse grinding blade. Seed large zucchini or cucumbers before chopping.

Use fresh spices for maximum flavor. Spices older than 1 year begin to lose their strength.

Old-Fashioned Corn Relish
Jean Peterson, Mulliken, Michigan

This was the first recipe I received after moving away from the city—a farm wife neighbor shared it. Made with garden-fresh ingredients, you can serve it with your favorite meat.

    2   cups fresh *or* frozen corn
    2   cups chopped onions
    2   cups chopped tomatoes
    2   cups chopped seeded cucumber
    1   large green pepper, chopped
    1   cup sugar
    1   cup cider vinegar
  1-1/2 teaspoons celery seed
  1-1/2 teaspoons mustard seed
    1   teaspoon salt
    1/2 teaspoon ground turmeric

1) In a large saucepan, combine all ingredients. Bring to a boil. Reduce heat; simmer, uncovered, for 20-30 minutes or until thickened. Store in the refrigerator for up to 3 weeks.

Yield: 6-1/2 cups.

NUTRITION FACTS: 2 tablespoons equals 27 calories, trace fat (trace saturated fat), 0 cholesterol, 47 mg sodium, 6 g carbohydrate, trace fiber, trace protein.

Teapot Cranberry Relish
Carolyn Huston, Jamesport, Missouri

A Christmas party at the tearoom we operate inspired my friend and me to create this relish. It was an instant hit that turned many into cranberry lovers.

    1   package (12 ounces) fresh *or* frozen cranberries
    2   cups sugar
    1/2 cup orange juice
    1/2 cup cranberry juice
    2   cups dried cherries *or* golden raisins
    1   teaspoon grated orange peel

1) In a large saucepan, cook the cranberries, sugar and juices over medium heat until the berries pop, about 15 minutes.

2) Add the cherries and orange peel. Simmer, uncovered, for 10 minutes. Cool slightly. Transfer to a bowl; cover and refrigerate until serving.

Yield: 4 cups.

NUTRITION FACTS: 1/4 cup equals 165 calories, trace fat (trace saturated fat), 0 cholesterol, 1 mg sodium, 42 g carbohydrate, 1 g fiber, 1 g protein.

COLORFUL APRICOT CHUTNEY

Colorful Apricot Chutney
Lucile Cline, Wichita, Kansas

You can use this chutney as an appetizer on crackers or mixed with cream cheese for a spread. It's also a nice condiment with pork or poultry.

    3   large sweet red peppers, diced
   12   ounces dried apricots, diced
    1   cup raisins
    1   cup sugar
    1   large onion, finely chopped
    3/4 cup red wine vinegar
    5   garlic cloves, minced
  1-1/2 teaspoons salt
  1-1/2 teaspoons crushed red pepper flakes
    1/4 teaspoon ground ginger
    1/4 teaspoon ground cumin
    1/4 teaspoon ground mustard

1) In a large heavy saucepan, combine all the ingredients; bring to a boil. Reduce heat; simmer, uncovered, for 25-30 minutes or until thickened, stirring occasionally. Cover and refrigerate.

2) Serve as an accompaniment to pork or chicken. Chutney may be stored in the refrigerator for up to 1 month.

Yield: 4 cups.

NUTRITION FACTS: 1/4 cup equals 144 calories, trace fat (trace saturated fat), 0 cholesterol, 226 mg sodium, 37 g carbohydrate, 3 g fiber, 1 g protein.

Rhubarb Chutney

Jan Paterson, Anchorage, Alaska

This tangy-sweet chutney is a wonderfully different garnish for meat or poultry. With fine chunks of rhubarb and raisins, it has a nice consistency.

3/4   cup sugar
1/3   cup cider vinegar
1   tablespoon minced garlic
1   teaspoon ground cumin
1   tablespoon minced fresh gingerroot
1/2   teaspoon ground cinnamon
1/4 to 1/2 teaspoon ground cloves
1/4   teaspoon crushed red pepper flakes
4   cups coarsely chopped fresh *or* frozen rhubarb, thawed
1/2   cup chopped red onion
1/3   cup golden raisins
1   teaspoon red food coloring, optional

1) In a large saucepan, combine the first eight ingredients. Bring to a boil. Reduce heat; simmer, uncovered, for 2 minutes or until sugar is dissolved. Add rhubarb, onion and raisins.

2) Cook and stir over medium heat for 5-10 minutes or until rhubarb is tender and mixture is slightly thickened. Stir in food coloring if desired. Cool completely. Store in the refrigerator.

Yield: about 3 cups.

NUTRITION FACTS: 1/4 cup equals 75 calories, trace fat (trace saturated fat), 0 cholesterol, 3 mg sodium, 19 g carbohydrate, 1 g fiber, 1 g protein.

Garden Salsa

Michelle Beran, Caflin, Kansas

Ripe garden ingredients and subtle seasonings make this a real summer treat.

6   medium tomatoes, finely chopped
3/4   cup finely chopped green pepper
1/2   cup finely chopped onion
1/2   cup thinly sliced green onions
6   garlic cloves, minced
2   teaspoons cider vinegar
2   teaspoons lemon juice
2   teaspoons olive oil
1 to 2 teaspoons minced jalapeno pepper
1 to 2 teaspoons ground cumin

1/2   teaspoon salt
1/4 to 1/2 teaspoon cayenne pepper
Tortilla chips

1) In a large bowl, combine the first 12 ingredients. Cover; refrigerate until serving. Serve with chips.

Yield: 5 cups.

NUTRITION FACTS: 2 tablespoons salsa (calculated without chips) equals 17 calories, trace fat (0 saturated fat), 0 cholesterol, 62 mg sodium, 3 g carbohydrate, trace fiber, trace protein.

■ *THREE-PEPPER GARDEN SALSA:* Broil 6 Anaheim chilies 4 in. from heat until skins blister, about 2 minutes. With tongs, rotate peppers a quarter turn. Broil and rotate until all sides blister and blacken. Immediately place chilies in a bowl. Cover; let stand 15-20 minutes. Peel off and discard charred skin; remove stems and seeds. Finely chop peppers. Add with other peppers.

Peppery Black Bean Salsa

Gary Maly, West Chester, Ohio

I love foods that surprise the senses. Use this as a topping for grilled meats or serve it as a relish.

4   jalapeno peppers
2   cans (15 ounces *each*) black beans, rinsed and drained
2   cups fresh *or* frozen corn
1   medium sweet red pepper, diced
1   cup chopped seeded tomato
1   medium red onion, chopped
1/3   cup lime juice
2   tablespoons minced fresh cilantro
1   garlic clove, minced

1) Place jalapenos on a broiler pan; broil 4 in. from the heat until skins blister, about 2 minutes. With tongs, rotate jalapenos a quarter turn. Broil and rotate until all sides are blistered and blackened.

2) Immediately place peppers in a bowl; cover and let stand for 15-20 minutes. Peel off and discard charred skin. Remove stems and seeds. Finely chop peppers. In a bowl, combine remaining ingredients. Add jalapenos; mix well. Cover; refrigerate several hours.

Yield: 12 servings.

NUTRITION FACTS: 1/2 cup equals 93 calories, trace fat (trace saturated fat), 0 cholesterol, 137 mg sodium, 19 g carbohydrate, 4 g fiber, 5 g protein.

CUTTING HOT PEPPERS

When cutting or seeding hot peppers, use rubber or plastic gloves to protect your hands. Avoid touching your face.

CHAPTER 17

QUICK BREADS

QUICK BREADS

Quick breads can be sweet or savory breads and loaves, but they're also muffins, scones, biscuits, popovers, pancakes and waffles.

The convenience of quick breads comes from the fact that they're leavened with baking powder and/or baking soda, not yeast. So you can mix, bake and enjoy these baked goods in less time than traditional yeast breads.

Baking Powder and Baking Soda

Be sure your baking powder and baking soda are fresh. Always check the expiration date on the packages before using. Baking powder and baking soda are leaveners that cause baked goods to rise and have a light texture.

Baking powder is available in single-acting and double-acting varieties. Double-acting baking powder is the most readily available type and is the type used in this cookbook. Double-acting baking powder produces carbon dioxide gas in two stages: when it is mixed with liquid and when it is heated. Single-acting baking powder creates carbon dioxide gas only when it is mixed with liquid. Baking powder can lose its ability to leaven. Discard any baking powder that is past the expiration date on the package.

Baking soda is an alkaline substance used in batters that have acidic ingredients such as buttermilk, molasses and sour cream. When the baking soda is mixed with the acidic ingredient, there is an immediate release of carbon dioxide gas. Batter and dough that only use baking soda as a leavening agent should be baked immediately. Otherwise, the baked product might not rise as high and the texture won't be as light.

To test baking powder for freshness, mix 1 teaspoon baking powder and 1/3 cup hot water. For baking soda, mix 1/4 teaspoon baking soda and 2 teaspoons vinegar. If bubbling occurs, the products are still fresh. If not, they should be replaced.

Quick Bread Tips

Arrange the oven racks before preheating so that the bread will bake in the center of the oven. Preheat the oven for 10-15 minutes before baking.

Use fats such as butter, stick margarine (with at least 80% oil) or shortening. For best results, do not use whipped, tub, soft, liquid or reduced-fat products. The fat should be softened (at room temperature), meaning it is pliable when touched. Measure ingredients accurately.

Mix the liquid and dry ingredients together only until moistened. A few lumps in the batter is fine. Overmixing causes the gluten in the flour to develop and the texture to be coarse and tough.

Grease aluminum baking pans and sheets that have a dull rather than shiny or dark finish. Fill pans two-thirds full.

Bake most quick breads shortly after combining the dry ingredients and liquid ingredients because the leaveners will begin producing gas once they are moistened. If allowed to stand too long before baking, the bread may have a sunken center.

Leave at least 1 in. of space between all pans and between pans and sides of oven to allow for good air circulation while baking. Switch pan positions and rotate pans halfway through baking.

Cool in the pan for 10 minutes, unless recipe directs otherwise. Turn loaves out onto a wire rack to cool. Most quick breads should be cooled completely before slicing to prevent crumbling.

BATTERS FOR QUICK BREADS

CREAMED BATTER

When a quick bread is made with solid fat, like softened butter or shortening, the fat and sugar are creamed together just like when making a cake. Then the eggs, dry ingredients and any liquid are added. This method incorporates air bubbles into the fat, resulting in a cake-like texture. Ingredients, such as nuts, chocolate chips and dried or fresh fruit are folded in at the end.

STIRRED BATTER

When a quick bread is made with liquid fat (melted butter or oil), the fat, eggs and liquid are first combined then stirred into the dry ingredients just until moistened, leaving a few lumps. Overmixing will result in a tough baked product. Ingredients, such as nuts, chocolate chips and dried or fresh fruits are folded in at the end.

Orange Nut Bread

Helen Luksa, Las Vegas, Nevada

This bread is delicious for breakfast or with a salad. A friend shared the recipe years ago, and it has withstood the test of time.

4-1/2 cups all-purpose flour
1-3/4 cups sugar
   4 teaspoons baking powder
1-1/2 teaspoons salt
   1 teaspoon baking soda
1-1/2 cups chopped walnuts
   1 to 2 tablespoons grated orange peel
   2 eggs
   1 cup milk
   1 cup orange juice
1/4 cup butter, melted

1) In a large bowl, combine the flour, sugar, baking powder, salt and baking soda. Stir in nuts and orange peel.

2) In a small bowl, beat the eggs, milk, orange juice and butter. Stir into dry ingredients just until moistened. Pour into two greased 8-in. x 4-in. x 2-in. loaf pans.

3) Bake at 350° for 50-60 minutes or until a toothpick inserted near the center comes out clean. Cool in pans for 10 minutes before removing to a wire rack to cool completely.

Yield: 2 loaves (12 slices each).

NUTRITION FACTS: 1 slice equals 223 calories, 7 g fat (2 g saturated fat), 24 mg cholesterol, 297 mg sodium, 35 g carbohydrate, 1 g fiber, 5 g protein.

Banana Nut Bread

Susan Jones, La Grange Park, Illinois

This nutty quick bread is a family favorite, so I always seem to have ripe bananas on hand especially for this recipe.

1/4 cup butter, softened
3/4 cup sugar
   2 eggs
3/4 cup mashed ripe bananas (about 2 medium)
1/2 cup sour cream
2-1/4 cups all-purpose flour
   1 teaspoon ground cinnamon
3/4 teaspoon baking soda
1/2 teaspoon salt
1/2 cup chopped walnuts

1) In a large mixing bowl, cream the butter and sugar until light and fluffy. Add eggs, one at a time, beating well after each addition.

2) Stir in bananas and sour cream. Combine the flour, cinnamon, baking soda and salt. Stir into banana mixture just until moistened. Fold in nuts.

3) Transfer to a greased 8-in. x 4-in. x 2-in. loaf pan. Bake at 350° for 1 hour or until a toothpick inserted near the center comes out clean. Cool for 10 minutes before removing from pan to a wire rack to cool completely.

Yield: 1 loaf (12 slices).

NUTRITION FACTS: 1 slice equals 245 calories, 10 g fat (4 g saturated fat), 52 mg cholesterol, 232 mg sodium, 35 g carbohydrate, 1 g fiber, 5 g protein.

■ *BANANA CHIP BREAD:* Fold in 1 cup semisweet chocolate chips *or* vanilla *or* white chips along with the walnuts. Bake as directed.

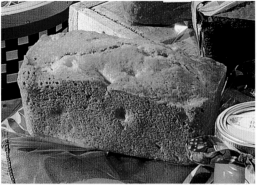

AUTUMN PEAR BREAD

Autumn Pear Bread
Mary Lynn Wilson, Linden, Texas

This recipe is easy to follow and change. A few simple substitutions, and you have another delicious, apple-nut variation to enjoy.

- 2 cups all-purpose flour
- 1 cup sugar
- 1 teaspoon baking powder
- 1/2 teaspoon baking soda
- 1/2 teaspoon salt
- 1/8 teaspoon ground nutmeg
- 1/2 cup cold butter
- 2 eggs
- 1/4 cup buttermilk
- 1 teaspoon vanilla extract
- 1 cup finely chopped peeled ripe pears

1) In a large bowl, combine the flour, sugar, baking powder, baking soda, salt and nutmeg; cut in butter until mixture resembles coarse crumbs.

2) Combine eggs, buttermilk and vanilla; stir into the flour mixture just until moistened. Fold in pears.

3) Spoon into two greased 5-3/4-in. x 3-in. x 2-in. loaf pans. Bake at 350° for 35-40 minutes or until a toothpick comes out clean. Cool for 10 minutes before removing from pans to wire racks to cool completely.

Yield: 2 mini loaves (8 slices each).

NUTRITION FACTS: 1 slice equals 173 calories, 7 g fat (4 g saturated fat), 42 mg cholesterol, 208 mg sodium, 26 g carbohydrate, 1 g fiber, 3 g protein.

■ *APPLE WALNUT BREAD:* Substitute 1 cup finely chopped unpeeled tart apples for the pears. Fold in 1/2 cup chopped walnuts along with the apples. Bake as directed or transfer to an 8-in. x 4-in. x 2-in. loaf pan. Bake at 350° for 50-65 minute or until toothpick comes out clean. Cool as directed.

Poppy Seed Cranberry Bread
Cindy Harmon, Stuarts Draft, Virginia

I make poppy seed bread about once a month. So one Christmas, I decided to make it a little more festive by stirring in some cranberries. My family loved the colorful addition.

- 2-1/2 cups all-purpose flour
- 3/4 cup sugar
- 2 tablespoons poppy seeds
- 3 teaspoons baking powder
- 1/2 teaspoon salt
- 1 egg
- 1 cup milk
- 1/3 cup butter, melted
- 2 teaspoons vanilla extract
- 2 teaspoons grated lemon peel
- 1 cup fresh *or* frozen cranberries, thawed and chopped

ICING:
- 1/2 cup confectioners' sugar
- 2 teaspoons milk

1) In a large bowl, combine the flour, sugar, poppy seeds, baking powder and salt. In a small bowl, beat the egg, milk, butter, vanilla and lemon peel.

2) Stir into dry ingredients just until moistened. Fold in cranberries. Pour into a greased 8-in. x 4-in. x 2-in. loaf pan.

3) Bake at 350° for 55-60 minutes or until a toothpick inserted near the center comes out clean. Cool for 10 minutes before removing from pan to a wire rack to cool completely. Combine icing ingredients; drizzle over cooled loaf.

Yield: 1 loaf (12 slices).

NUTRITION FACTS: 1 slice equals 239 calories, 7 g fat (4 g saturated fat), 34 mg cholesterol, 266 mg sodium, 40 g carbohydrate, 1 g fiber, 4 g protein.

TEST FOR DONENESS

Check for doneness 10-15 minutes before the end of the recommended baking time. The bread is done if a toothpick inserted near the center comes out clean. If it is not done, test again in a few more minutes. The bread may have a split in the center, which is typical of a quick bread.

DATE PECAN TEA BREAD

Date Pecan Tea Bread
Carole Resnick, Cleveland, Ohio

Packed with dates and nuts, this moist and nicely sweet bread is excellent on its own and even better topped with the chunky cream cheese spread. We enjoy it during the holiday season and for after-school and late-night snacks.

2-1/2	cups chopped dates
1-1/2	cups boiling water
1-1/2	teaspoons baking soda
1-3/4	cups all-purpose flour
1/4	teaspoon *each* ground cloves, cinnamon, ginger and nutmeg
2	tablespoons butter, softened
1-1/4	cups sugar
1	egg, lightly beaten
2	teaspoons vanilla extract
1-1/2	cups coarsely chopped pecans

SPREAD:

1	package (3 ounces) cream cheese, softened
2	tablespoons chopped dates
2	tablespoons coarsely chopped pecans
1	tablespoon milk

1) Place dates in a bowl. Combine boiling water and baking soda; pour over dates. Combine the flour, cloves, cinnamon, ginger and nutmeg in another bowl; set aside.

2) In a mixing bowl, beat butter and sugar until crumbly. Beat in egg and vanilla. Add flour mixture alternately with date mixture. Stir in pecans.

3) Pour into a greased and floured 9-in. x 5-in. x 3-in. loaf pan. Bake at 350° for 65-75 minutes or until a toothpick inserted near the center comes out clean. Cool for 10 minutes before removing from pan to wire rack to cool completely.

4) In a small bowl, combine all of the spread ingredients. Cover and refrigerate for 1 hour. Serve with the bread.

Yield: 1 loaf (16 slices with 1/2 cup spread).

NUTRITION FACTS: 1 slice with 1-1/2 teaspoons spread equals 312 calories, 13 g fat (3 g saturated fat), 23 mg cholesterol, 154 mg sodium, 50 g carbohydrate, 4 g fiber, 4 g protein.

Irish Soda Bread
Carol Fritz, Fulton, Illinois

I'm allergic to yeast, so I appreciate recipes for quick breads, biscuits and soda breads. This tender loaf that's dotted with golden raisins is great. It's one way I can enjoy toast for breakfast.

4	cups all-purpose flour
1	tablespoon sugar
1-1/2	teaspoons baking soda
1	teaspoon baking powder
1/2	teaspoon salt
1/4	cup cold butter
1	cup golden raisins
1-3/4	cups 1% buttermilk

1) In a large bowl, combine the flour, sugar, baking soda, baking powder and salt. Cut in butter until mixture resembles coarse crumbs. Add raisins. Stir in buttermilk just until moistened.

2) Turn onto a lightly floured surface; gently knead 6-8 times. Place on an ungreased baking sheet; pat into a 7-in. round loaf.

3) Using a sharp knife, cut a 1-in. cross about 1/4 in. deep on top of the loaf. Bake at 375° for 40-45 minutes or until golden brown. Cool on a wire rack.

Yield: 1 loaf (16 slices).

NUTRITION FACTS: 1 slice equals 181 calories, 3 g fat (2 g saturated fat), 9 mg cholesterol, 265 mg sodium, 33 g carbohydrate, 1 g fiber, 4 g protein.

Delicious Pumpkin Bread
Linda Burnett, Stanton, California

An enticing aroma wafts through my house when this tender, cake-like bread is in the oven. I bake extra loaves to give as holiday gifts.

5	eggs
1-1/4	cups vegetable oil

1 can (15 ounces) solid-pack pumpkin
2 cups all-purpose flour
2 cups sugar
2 packages (3 ounces *each*) cook-and-serve vanilla pudding mix
1 teaspoon baking soda
1 teaspoon ground cinnamon
1/2 teaspoon salt

1) In a large mixing bowl, beat the eggs. Add oil and pumpkin; beat until smooth. Combine all of the remaining ingredients; gradually beat into pumpkin mixture.

2) Pour batter into five greased 5-3/4-in. x 3-in. x 2-in. loaf pans. Bake at 325° for 50-55 minutes or until a toothpick inserted near the center comes out clean. Cool for 10 minutes before removing from pans to wire racks to cool completely.

Yield: 5 mini loaves (8 slices each).

NUTRITION FACTS: 1 slice equals 150 calories, 8 g fat (1 g saturated fat), 27 mg cholesterol, 96 mg sodium, 20 g carbohydrate, 1 g fiber, 2 g protein.

SWEET CORN BREAD

Sweet Corn Bread
Virginia Hanker, Essex Junction, Vermont

My basic corn bread recipe bakes up golden brown and tender. Plus, it's easy to modify into muffins or dressed-up corn breads.

1 cup all-purpose flour
1 cup cornmeal
1/4 cup sugar

1/2 teaspoon baking powder
1/2 teaspoon baking soda
1/2 teaspoon salt
1 egg, lightly beaten
1 cup (8 ounces) sour cream
1/3 cup milk
1/4 cup butter, melted

1) In a large bowl, combine the flour, cornmeal, sugar, baking powder, baking soda and salt. Combine the egg, sour cream, milk and butter; stir into dry ingredients just until moistened.

2) Pour into a greased 8-in. square baking dish. Bake at 400° for 20-25 minutes or until a toothpick comes out clean. Serve warm.

Yield: 9 servings.

NUTRITION FACTS: 1 serving equals 240 calories, 11 g fat (7 g saturated fat), 56 mg cholesterol, 300 mg sodium, 29 g carbohydrate, 2 g fiber, 5 g protein.

■ *SWEET CORN BREAD MUFFINS:* Follow recipe as directed except fill greased muffin cups two-thirds full. Bake at 400° for 15-18 minutes or until a toothpick inserted near the center comes out clean. Serve warm.

Yield: about 15 muffins.

■ *COLORFUL CORN BREAD:* Add 2 tablespoons chopped pimientos and 1 teaspoon minced dried onion to the batter. Proceed as directed in recipe.

■ *TEX-MEX CORN BREAD:* Fold in 1 cup (4 ounces) shredded Mexican cheese blend and 1 can (4 ounces) drained chopped green chilies to batter. Proceed as directed in recipe.

SERVING AND STORING QUICK BREADS

Serve quick breads (such as banana, zucchini and cranberry) a day after baking because that is when they slice and taste best. Wrap the cooled bread in foil or plastic wrap; leave at room temperature overnight. Corn breads and coffee cakes are best served warm.

Use a sawing motion to cut loaves with a thin, sharp knife. Use a serrated knife for quick breads that have fruits and/or nuts.

Store quick breads or muffins that have been wrapped in foil or plastic wrap at room temperature for up to 3 days. They should be refrigerated if made with cheese, cream cheese or other perishable foods. For longer storage, place in heavy-duty resealable plastic bags and freeze quick breads for 3 months and muffins for up to 1 month.

Hearty Brown Quick Bread

Susan Lane, Waukesha, Wisconsin

High in fiber and low in fat, this bread is also moist, rich, delicious and filling. Sweet raisins and crunchy pecans make it an instant favorite.

- 4 cups whole wheat flour
- 2 cups all-purpose flour
- 2 cups packed brown sugar
- 1/2 cup sugar
- 2 teaspoons baking soda
- 1 teaspoon salt
- 3 cups 1% buttermilk
- 2 eggs, lightly beaten
- 1 cup raisins
- 1/2 cup chopped pecans

1) In a large bowl, combine the flours, sugars, baking soda and salt. Stir in buttermilk and eggs just until moistened. Fold in raisins and nuts.

2) Pour into two 9-in. x 5-in. x 3-in. loaf pans coated with nonstick cooking spray. Bake at 350° for 50-60 minutes or until a toothpick inserted near the center comes out clean.

3) Cool for 10 minutes before removing from pans to wire racks to cool completely.

Yield: 2 loaves (16 slices each).

NUTRITION FACTS: 1 slice equals 183 calories, 2 g fat (trace saturated fat), 14 mg cholesterol, 187 mg sodium, 38 g carbohydrate, 2 g fiber, 4 g protein.

Sour Cream Coffee Cake

Doris Rice, Storm Lake, Iowa

This is a favorite for breakfast or brunch, but I've also taken to potlucks as the dessert. Tender slices feature an appealing, crunchy filling.

- 1 cup butter, softened
- 1-1/2 cups sugar
- 3 eggs
- 1 teaspoon *each* almond, lemon and vanilla extract
- 2-1/2 cups all-purpose flour
- 2 teaspoons baking powder
- 1 teaspoon baking soda
- 1 cup (8 ounces) sour cream

FILLING:
- 1/3 cup chopped pecans
- 3 tablespoons sugar
- 1 tablespoon ground cinnamon

GLAZE:
- 1 cup confectioners' sugar
- 2 tablespoons milk

1) In a large mixing bowl, cream butter and sugar. Add eggs, one at a time, beating well after each addition. Beat in extracts. Combine the flour, baking powder and baking soda; add to creamed mixture alternately with sour cream.

2) Spread half of the batter in a greased and floured 10-in. fluted tube pan. Make a well in the center of the batter. Combine filling ingredients; sprinkle into well. Carefully cover with remaining batter.

3) Bake at 350° for 45-50 minutes or until a toothpick inserted near the center comes out clean. Cool for 10 minutes before removing from pan to a wire rack. Combine glaze ingredients; drizzle over warm cake.

Yield: 16 servings.

NUTRITION FACTS: 1 piece equals 349 calories, 17 g fat (9 g saturated fat), 81 mg cholesterol, 265 mg sodium, 45 g carbohydrate, 1 g fiber, 4 g protein.

RASPBERRY CREAM CHEESE COFFEE CAKE

Raspberry Cream Cheese Coffee Cake

Susan Litwiller, Medford, Oregon

Since this recipe calls for raspberry jam and not fresh raspberries, you can make this coffee cake any time of year and bring a touch of spring to your table.

- 2-1/4 cups all-purpose flour
- 3/4 cup sugar
- 3/4 cup cold butter

1/2 teaspoon baking powder

1/2 teaspoon baking soda

1/2 teaspoon salt

3/4 cup sour cream

1 egg, beaten

1-1/2 teaspoons almond extract

FILLING:

1 package (8 ounces) cream cheese, softened

1/2 cup sugar

1 egg

1/2 cup raspberry jam

1/2 cup slivered almonds

1) In a large mixing bowl, combine flour and sugar. Cut in butter until mixture is crumbly. Remove 1 cup and set aside. To remaining crumbs, add baking powder, baking soda and salt. Add the sour cream, egg and almond extract; mix well.

2) Spread in the bottom and 2 in. up the sides of a greased 9-in. springform pan.

3) For the filling, in a small bowl, beat cream cheese, sugar and egg in a small bowl until blended. Pour over batter; spoon raspberry jam on top. Sprinkle with almonds and reserved crumbs.

4) Bake at 350° for 55-60 minutes. Let stand for 15 minutes. Carefully run a knife around the edge of pan to loosen; remove sides from pan.

Yield: 12 servings.

NUTRITION FACTS: 1 serving equals 437 calories, 24 g fat (13 g saturated fat), 97 mg cholesterol, 358 mg sodium, 49 g carbohydrate, 1 g fiber, 6 g protein.

■ *MORE BERRY COFFEE CAKES:* Vary the flavor of this coffee cake by making it with 1/2 cup blackberry *or* strawberry jam in place of the 1/2 raspberry jam.

Lemon Curd Coffee Cake
Anne Wickman, Endicott, New York

I tried this recipe for my son's birthday years ago and fell in love with the tart lemon filling, powdered sugar glaze and coconut topping.

1/2 cup all-purpose flour

1/3 cup sugar

3 tablespoons cold butter

1/2 cup flaked coconut

BATTER:

2-1/4 cups all-purpose flour

1/2 teaspoon salt

1/2 teaspoon baking powder

1/2 teaspoon baking soda

3/4 cup cold butter

2/3 cup vanilla yogurt

1 tablespoon lemon juice

2 teaspoons grated lemon peel

1 egg

1 egg yolk

1/2 cup lemon curd

GLAZE:

1/2 cup confectioners' sugar

1 teaspoon water

1 teaspoon lemon juice

1) In a small bowl, combine the flour and sugar. Cut in butter until mixture resembles coarse crumbs. Stir in coconut; set aside.

2) For batter, in a large bowl, combine the flour, salt, baking powder and baking soda. Cut in butter until mixture resembles coarse crumbs. Combine the yogurt, lemon juice, peel, egg and egg yolk; stir into crumb mixture just until moistened (batter will be stiff).

3) Spread 2 cups of the batter in a greased 9-in. springform pan; sprinkle with 3/4 cup of coconut mixture. Drop 1/2 teaspoonfuls of lemon curd over the top to within 1/2 in. of edge. Carefully spoon remaining batter over lemon curd; sprinkle with remaining coconut mixture.

4) Place pan on a baking sheet. Bake at 350° for 55-60 minutes or until a toothpick comes out clean. Cool for 10 minutes. Carefully run a knife around the edge of pan to loosen; remove sides of pan. Combine glaze ingredients; drizzle over warm cake.

Yield: 12 servings.

Editor's Note: A recipe for Lemon Curd can be found on page 420.

NUTRITION FACTS: 1 serving equals 362 calories, 18 g fat (11 g saturated fat), 85 mg cholesterol, 347 mg sodium, 46 g carbohydrate, 1 g fiber, 5 g protein.

MAKING A STREUSEL-FILLED COFFEE CAKE

Spoon about a third of the batter into greased pan. Sprinkle with a third of the streusel mixture. Repeat layers twice. Bake as directed.

Royal Rhubarb Coffee Cake

Lorraine Robinson, Stony Plain, Alberta

For another twist, you can use raspberries and blueberries in place of the rhubarb with equally delicious results.

- 1/3 cup butter, softened
- 1 cup sugar
- 1 egg
- 1 teaspoon vanilla extract
- 2 cups all-purpose flour
- 3 teaspoons baking powder
- 1/2 teaspoon salt
- 1 cup milk
- 3-1/2 cups chopped fresh *or* frozen rhubarb, thawed and drained

TOPPING:
- 3/4 cup packed brown sugar
- 1/4 cup butter, melted
- 1 teaspoon ground cinnamon

1) In a large mixing bowl, cream butter and sugar until light and fluffy. Add egg and vanilla; beat well. Combine the flour, baking powder and salt; add to creamed mixture alternately with milk.

2) Transfer to a greased 13-in. x 9-in. x 2-in. baking dish. Spoon rhubarb over top to within 1/2 in. of edges. Combine topping ingredients; sprinkle over rhubarb.

3) Bake at 350° for 45-55 minutes or until a toothpick inserted near the center comes out clean. Cool in pan on a wire rack.

Yield: 15 servings.

NUTRITION FACTS: 1 serving equals 238 calories, 8 g fat (5 g saturated fat), 35 mg cholesterol, 249 mg sodium, 39 g carbohydrate, 1 g fiber, 3 g protein.

Muffins

Standard muffin pans come in different sizes, which affect baking time. The muffin pans used by the Taste of Home Test Kitchen measure 2-1/2 in. across.

Fill greased or paper-lined muffin cups about two-thirds to three-fourths full, wiping off any spills. To quickly fill muffin cups with little mess, use an ice cream scoop with a quick release. Or pour the batter from a measuring cup. If your muffin recipe does not fill all the cups in your pan, fill the empty cups with water. The muffins will bake more evenly.

Unless directed otherwise, muffins should go into the oven as soon as the batter is mixed.

Use a kitchen timer. Check for doneness 5-7 minutes before the end of the recommended baking time to avoid overbaking.

Muffins are done when a toothpick inserted near the center comes out clean. For muffins with a filling, make sure the toothpick is inserted into the muffin and not the filling.

Cool in the pan for 5 minutes, unless the recipe directs otherwise. Muffins are best served warm, fresh from the oven.

Sour Cream Chip Muffins

Stephanie Moon, Green Bay, Wisconsin

Take one bite and you'll see why these rich, tender muffins are the best I've ever tasted. Mint chocolate chips make them a big hit with my family and friends.

- 1-1/2 cups all-purpose flour
- 2/3 cup sugar
- 3/4 teaspoon baking powder
- 3/4 teaspoon baking soda
- 1/4 teaspoon salt
- 1 egg
- 1 cup (8 ounces) sour cream
- 5 tablespoons butter, melted
- 1 teaspoon vanilla extract
- 3/4 cup mint *or* semisweet chocolate chips

1) In a large bowl, combine the flour, sugar, baking powder, baking soda and salt. Combine the egg, sour cream, butter and vanilla. Stir into dry ingredients just until moistened. Fold in chips.

2) Fill greased or paper-lined muffin cups three-fourths full. Bake at 350° for 18-20 minutes or until a toothpick comes out clean. Cool for 5 minutes before removing from pan to a wire rack.

Yield: 1 dozen.

Editor's Note: If mint chips are only available around the Christmas season, stock up and store them in a cool dry place. Or place 3/4 cup semisweet chocolate chips and 1/8 teaspoon peppermint extract in a plastic bag; seal and toss to coat. Allow chips to stand for 24-48 hours.

NUTRITION FACTS: 1 serving equals 259 calories, 13 g fat (8 g saturated fat), 44 mg cholesterol, 217 mg sodium, 33 g carbohydrate, 1 g fiber, 3 g protein.

BERRY CREAM MUFFINS

Berry Cream Muffins

Linda Gilmore, Hampstead, Maryland

Baked in greased muffin cups, these delicious treats bake up beautifully. If you like lemon or want a streusel topping, it's easy to vary this recipe to suit your fancy.

- 2 cups all-purpose flour
- 1 cup sugar
- 1/2 teaspoon baking powder
- 1/2 teaspoon baking soda
- 1/2 teaspoon salt
- 1-1/2 cups fresh *or* frozen raspberries *or* blueberries
- 2 eggs, lightly beaten
- 1 cup (8 ounces) sour cream
- 1/2 cup vegetable oil
- 1/2 teaspoon vanilla extract

1) In a large bowl, combine the flour, sugar, baking powder, baking soda and salt; add berries and toss gently. Combine the eggs, sour cream, oil and vanilla; mix well. Stir into dry ingredients just until moistened.

2) Fill greased muffin cups two-thirds full. Bake at 400° for 18-22 minutes or until a toothpick comes out clean. Cool for 5 minutes before removing from pan to a wire rack.

Yield: about 1 dozen.

Editor's Note: If using frozen berries, do not thaw before using.

NUTRITION FACTS: 1 serving equals 241 calories, 12 g fat (3 g saturated fat), 42 mg cholesterol, 162 mg sodium, 30 g carbohydrate, 1 g fiber, 3 g protein.

■ *BERRY CREAM LEMON MUFFINS:* Prepare muffin recipe as directed except substitute 1 cup lemon yogurt for the sour cream and add 2 teaspoons grated lemon peel with the vanilla.

■ *BERRY STREUSEL MUFFINS:* Prepare muffin recipe as directed. For topping, combine 3 tablespoons *each* all-purpose flour and quick-cooking oats, 2 tablespoons sugar and 1/8 teaspoon ground cinnamon. Cut in 2 tablespoons cold butter until crumbly. Sprinkle over muffins before baking.

Burst o' Lemon Muffins

Nancy Rader, Westerville, Ohio

These incredible muffins have a cake-like texture, a sweet coconut taste and mouth-watering lemon zing.

- 1-3/4 cups all-purpose flour
- 3/4 cup sugar
- 1 teaspoon baking powder
- 3/4 teaspoon baking soda
- 1/4 teaspoon salt
- 1 cup (8 ounces) lemon *or* vanilla yogurt
- 1 egg
- 1/3 cup butter, melted
- 1 to 2 tablespoons grated lemon peel
- 1 tablespoon lemon juice
- 1/2 cup flaked coconut

TOPPING:
- 1/3 cup lemon juice
- 1/4 cup sugar
- 1/4 cup flaked coconut, toasted

1) In a large bowl, combine the flour, sugar, baking powder, baking soda and salt. In a small mixing bowl, beat the yogurt, egg, butter, lemon peel and lemon juice until smooth; stir into dry ingredients just until moistened. Fold in the coconut.

2) Fill greased muffin cups two-thirds full. Bake at 400° for 18-22 minutes or until golden brown and toothpick comes out clean. Cool for 5 minutes before removing from pan to a wire rack.

3) In a saucepan, combine the lemon juice and sugar; cook and stir over medium heat until sugar is dissolved. Stir in coconut. Using a toothpick, poke 6-8 holes in each muffin. Spoon the coconut mixture over muffins. Serve warm or cool to room temperature.

Yield: 1 dozen.

NUTRITION FACTS: 1 serving equals 232 calories, 8 g fat (6 g saturated fat), 33 mg cholesterol, 246 mg sodium, 37 g carbohydrate, 1 g fiber, 4 g protein.

BROWN SUGAR OAT MUFFINS

Brown Sugar Oat Muffins
Regina Stock, Topeka, Kansas

With Kansas being one of the top wheat-producing states, it seems only fitting to share a recipe containing whole wheat flour. These are great muffins to have for breakfast.

  1 cup old-fashioned oats
  1 cup whole wheat flour
1/2 cup all-purpose flour
  2 teaspoons baking powder
1/2 teaspoon salt
  2 eggs
3/4 cup packed brown sugar
3/4 cup milk
1/4 cup vegetable oil
  1 teaspoon vanilla extract

1) In a small bowl, combine the oats, flours, baking powder and salt. In another small bowl, beat the eggs, brown sugar, milk, oil and vanilla. Stir into the dry ingredients just until moistened.

2) Fill greased or paper-lined muffin cups two-thirds full. Bake at 400° for 15-17 minutes or until a toothpick comes out clean. Cool for 5 minutes before removing from pan to a wire rack.

Yield: 1 dozen.

NUTRITION FACTS: 1 serving equals 192 calories, 7 g fat (1 g saturated fat), 37 mg cholesterol, 189 mg sodium, 30 g carbohydrate, 2 g fiber, 4 g protein.

Best Bran Muffins
Karen Hill, Willamina, Oregon

These hearty muffins were a staple with my twin sister and me all through high school. Raisins or dried cranberries can make a nice addition.

1-1/2 cups old-fashioned oats
   1 cup All-Bran
   1 cup boiling water
 1/2 cup sugar
 1/2 cup packed brown sugar
 1/2 cup butter, melted
   2 eggs, beaten
 1/4 cup toasted wheat germ
2-1/2 cups all-purpose flour
2-1/2 teaspoons baking soda
 1/2 teaspoon salt
   2 cups buttermilk

1) Place oats and cereal in a bowl; cover with boiling water. Let stand for 5 minutes. Stir in the sugars, butter, eggs and wheat germ; mix well.

2) Combine the flour, baking soda and salt; stir into oat mixture alternately with buttermilk just until moistened.

3) Fill greased muffin cups two-thirds full. Bake at 375° for 18-20 minutes or until a toothpick comes out clean. Cool for 5 minutes before removing from pans to wire racks.

Yield: 2 dozen.

NUTRITION FACTS: 1 serving equals 158 calories, 5 g fat (3 g saturated fat), 29 mg cholesterol, 254 mg sodium, 25 g carbohydrate, 2 g fiber, 4 g protein.

Baby Basil-Zucchini Muffins
Marion Lowery, Medford, Oregon

Baked up in miniature muffin pans, these tiny treasures are light and golden on top.

2-1/2 cups all-purpose flour
 1/4 cup sugar
   3 tablespoons minced fresh basil
     or 1 tablespoon dried basil
   1 teaspoon baking powder
   1 teaspoon salt
 1/2 teaspoon baking soda
   2 eggs
3/4 cup milk
2/3 cup vegetable oil
   2 cups finely shredded peeled zucchini, squeezed dry
 1/2 cup grated Parmesan cheese

1) In a large bowl, combine the flour, sugar, basil, baking powder, salt and baking soda. Beat the eggs, milk and oil; stir into dry ingredients just until moistened. Fold in zucchini.

2) Fill greased or paper-lined miniature muffin cups two-thirds full. Sprinkle with cheese. Bake at 400° for 12-15 minutes or until a toothpick inserted near the center comes out clean. Cool for 5 minutes before removing from pans to wire racks. Serve warm.

Yield: about 4-1/2 dozen.

NUTRITION FACTS: 2 muffins equals 115 calories, 7 g fat (1 g saturated fat), 18 mg cholesterol, 162 mg sodium, 11 g carbohydrate, trace fiber, 3 g protein.

Caraway Rye Muffins
Jean Tyner, Darlington, South Carolina

The distinctive taste of caraway abounds in this recipe, which also features rye flour for a change of pace.

> 1   cup rye flour
> 3/4   cup all-purpose flour
> 1/4   cup sugar
> 2-1/2   teaspoons baking powder
> 1/2   teaspoon salt
> 1/2   teaspoon caraway seeds
> 3/4   cup shredded cheddar cheese
> 1   egg, beaten
> 3/4   cup milk
> 1/3   cup vegetable oil

1) In a large bowl, combine the flours, sugar, baking powder, salt and caraway seeds. Stir in cheese. Combine the egg, milk and oil; stir into the dry ingredients just until moistened.

2) Fill greased or paper-lined muffin cups two-thirds full. Bake at 400° for 20-23 minutes or a toothpick comes out clean. Cool for 5 minutes before removing from pan to a wire rack. Serve warm.

Yield: 10 muffins.

NUTRITION FACTS: 1 serving equals 203 calories, 11 g fat (3 g saturated fat), 33 mg cholesterol, 285 mg sodium, 21 g carbohydrate, 2 g fiber, 5 g protein.

Biscuits and Scones

Use cold butter, cold stick margarine (with at least 80% oil) or shortening. Cut in butter, margarine or shortening only until mixture resembles coarse crumbs.

Biscuits and scones are done when they're golden brown on the top and bottom. The sides will always be a little light. Remove to wire racks. Biscuits are best served fresh from the oven or eaten the day they are made. Scones are best on the day they are made.

Store biscuits and scones in an airtight container at room temperature for up to 2 days. If made with cheese, cream cheese or other perishable foods, they should be stored in the refrigerator. You can freeze biscuits and scones for up to 3 months.

FLUFFY BISCUITS

Fluffy Biscuits
Nancy Horsburgh, Everett, Ontario

If you're looking for a flaky basic biscuit, this recipe is the best. These golden-brown rolls bake up tall, light and tender. Their mild flavor tastes even better spread with butter or jam.

> 2   cups all-purpose flour
> 4   teaspoons baking powder
> 3   teaspoons sugar
> 1/2   teaspoon salt
> 1/2   cup shortening
> 1   egg
> 2/3   cup milk

1) In a small bowl, combine the flour, baking powder, sugar and salt. Cut in shortening until the mixture resembles coarse crumbs. Beat egg with milk; stir into dry ingredients just until moistened.

2) Turn onto a well-floured surface; knead 20 times. Roll to 3/4-in. thickness; cut with a floured 2-1/2-in. biscuit cutter.

3) Place on a lightly greased baking sheet. Bake at 450° for 8-10 minutes or until golden brown. Serve warm.

Yield: 1 dozen.

NUTRITION FACTS: 1 serving equals 168 calories, 9 g fat (2 g saturated fat), 20 mg cholesterol, 244 mg sodium, 18 g carbohydrate, 1 g fiber, 3 g protein.

■ *ITALIAN BISCUITS:* Add 1 teaspoon of Italian seasoning with the flour.

MAKING BISCUITS AND SCONES

Stir dry ingredients together with a fork to evenly distribute the baking powder or soda. For a more tender biscuit or scone, be careful not to overmix or overknead the dough.

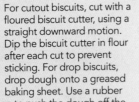

For cutout biscuits, cut with a floured biscuit cutter, using a straight downward motion. Dip the biscuit cutter in flour after each cut to prevent sticking. For drop biscuits, drop dough onto a greased baking sheet. Use a rubber spatula, knife or spoon to push the dough off the spoon.

When reworking biscuit trimmings, handle the dough as little as possible and use as little additional flour as needed. Overworking the dough or using too much flour will result in a tough, dry product.

SWISS ONION DROP BISCUITS

Swiss Onion Drop Biscuits
Edna Hoffman, Hebron, Indiana

I often bake a big batch of these tender drop biscuits made with whole wheat flour. They're yummy spread with butter alongside a bowl of soup or a luncheon salad.

- 2 cups all-purpose flour
- 3/4 cup whole wheat flour
- 1 tablespoon sugar
- 3 teaspoons baking powder
- 3/4 teaspoon onion salt
- 1/2 teaspoon baking soda
- 1/2 cup cold butter
- 1 cup (4 ounces) shredded Swiss cheese
- 1/3 cup thinly sliced green onions
- 2 eggs
- 3/4 cup plus 2 tablespoons buttermilk

1) In a large bowl, combine the flours, sugar, baking powder, onion salt and baking soda. Cut in butter until mixture resembles coarse crumbs. Stir in the cheese and onions. Combine eggs and buttermilk; stir into cheese mixture just until moistened.

2) Drop by tablespoonfuls 2 in. apart onto greased baking sheets. Bake at 425° for 12-15 minutes or until golden brown. Serve warm.

Yield: 2 dozen.

NUTRITION FACTS: 1 serving equals 113 calories, 6 g fat (3 g saturated fat), 32 mg cholesterol, 198 mg sodium, 12 g carbohydrate, 1 g fiber, 4 g protein.

■ *CHEESE PEPPER DROP BISCUITS:* Substitute 1 cup shredded cheddar, Monterey Jack *or* pepper Jack for the Swiss and 1 minced seeded jalapeno pepper for the green onions.

Cornmeal Drop Biscuits
Rhonda McKee, Greensburg, Kansas

I like to stir up a batch of these light, golden biscuits that are flecked with cheese. They taste so delicious warm and spread with butter.

- 1-1/3 cups all-purpose flour
- 1/2 cup cornmeal
- 2-1/2 teaspoons baking powder
- 1/2 teaspoon salt
- 1/2 teaspoon ground mustard
- 1/2 cup shortening
- 1/2 cup shredded cheddar cheese
- 1 cup milk

1) In a bowl, combine the flour, cornmeal, baking powder, salt and mustard; cut in shortening until crumbly.

2) Stir in cheese and milk just until moistened. Drop by 1/4 cupfuls 2 in. apart onto a greased baking sheet. Bake at 375° for 26-28 minutes or until golden brown. Serve warm.

Yield: 10 servings.

NUTRITION FACTS: 1 serving equals 210 calories, 12 g fat (4 g saturated fat), 9 mg cholesterol, 265 mg sodium, 19 g carbohydrate, 1 g fiber, 4 g protein.

CHERRY CHIP SCONES

Cherry Chip Scones
Pamela Brooks, South Berwick, Maine

Whether served for breakfast or dessert, these flaky scones dotted with dried cherries and vanilla chips are a real treat.

> 3 cups all-purpose flour
> 1/2 cup sugar
> 2-1/2 teaspoons baking powder
> 1/2 teaspoon baking soda
> 6 tablespoons cold butter
> 1 cup (8 ounces) vanilla yogurt
> 1/4 cup plus 2 tablespoons milk, *divided*
> 1-1/3 cups dried cherries
> 2/3 cup vanilla *or* white chips

1) In a large bowl, combine the flour, sugar, baking powder and baking soda. Cut in butter until the mixture resembles coarse crumbs.

2) Combine yogurt and 1/4 cup milk; stir into crumb mixture just until moistened. Knead in the cherries and chips.

3) On a greased baking sheet, pat the dough into a 9-in. circle. Cut into eight wedges; separate wedges. Brush with the remaining milk.

4) Bake at 400° for 20-25 minutes or until golden brown. Serve warm.

Yield: 8 servings.

NUTRITION FACTS: 1 serving equals 543 calories, 23 g fat (14 g saturated fat), 52 mg cholesterol, 410 mg sodium, 77 g carbohydrate, 2 g fiber, 8 g protein.

■ *CRANBERRY CHIP SCONES:* Use 1-1/3 cups dried cranberries for the dried cherries. Use vanilla *or* semisweet chips.

■ *BLUEBERRY CHIP SCONES:* Use 1-1/3 cups dried blueberries for the dried cherries.

Double Orange Scones
Margaret Frayser, Linton, Indiana

For all you orange lovers, you won't be able to resist these scones featuring citrusy flavors inside and out. The orange butter spread is absolutely delightful!

> 1 cup all-purpose flour
> 1 cup whole wheat flour
> 3 tablespoons sugar
> 2-1/2 teaspoons baking powder
> 2 teaspoons grated orange peel
> 1/4 teaspoon salt
> 1/3 cup cold butter
> 1/3 cup milk
> 1 egg
> 1/2 cup chopped mandarin oranges, well drained

Additional sugar

ORANGE BUTTER:

> 1/2 cup butter, softened
> 2 tablespoons orange marmalade

1) In a large bowl, combine the flours, sugar, baking powder, orange peel and salt. Cut in butter until mixture resembles coarse crumbs. In a bowl, whisk milk and egg. Stir into dry ingredients just until moistened. Stir in oranges.

2) Turn onto a floured surface; knead 10 times. Pat into a 6-in. circle. Sprinkle with additional sugar. Cut into eight wedges.

3) Separate wedges and place on a greased baking sheet. Bake at 400° for 15-20 minutes or until golden brown. Meanwhile, in a small mixing bowl, beat butter and marmalade until fluffy. Serve with warm scones.

Yield: 8 scones.

NUTRITION FACTS: 1 serving (calculated without additional sugar) equals 327 calories, 20 g fat (12 g saturated fat), 79 mg cholesterol, 409 mg sodium, 33 g carbohydrate, 2 g fiber, 5 g protein.

COUNTRY SCONES

Country Scones
Martha Plassmeyer, St. Elizabeth, Missouri

These tempting triangles perfectly balance a light and airy texture with a rich and moist flavor. For a savory version, try it with cheddar cheese instead of the dried currants and topping.

- 3/4 cup dried currants *or* raisins
- 2 cups all-purpose flour
- 3 tablespoons sugar
- 2 teaspoons baking powder
- 3/4 teaspoon salt
- 1/2 teaspoon baking soda
- 5 tablespoons cold butter
- 1 cup (8 ounces) sour cream
- 2 egg yolks

TOPPING:
- 1 egg white
- 1 teaspoon sugar
- 1/8 teaspoon ground cinnamon

1) Place currants in a bowl. Cover with hot water and let stand for 5 minutes. Drain well and set aside.

2) In a large bowl, combine the flour, sugar, baking powder, salt and baking soda. Cut in butter until mixture resembles coarse crumbs. Combine sour cream and egg yolks; add to crumb mixture. Stir in currants just until blended.

3) Turn onto a floured surface; knead gently 8-10 times. Divide into four portions. On ungreased baking sheets, pat dough into 4-in. circles.

4) Cut each into four wedges, but do not separate. Beat egg white; brush over dough. Combine sugar and cinnamon; sprinkle over tops. Bake at 425° for 15-18 minutes or until golden. Serve warm.

Yield: 16 scones.

NUTRITION FACTS: 1 serving equals 156 calories, 7 g fat (4 g saturated fat), 46 mg cholesterol, 249 mg sodium, 20 g carbohydrate, 1 g fiber, 3 g protein.

■ *CHEESE SCONES:* Omit dried currants and topping. Stir in 1 cup (4 ounces) shredded cheddar cheese into flour mixture. Proceed as directed.

Sage Breadsticks
Sue Wagner, West Farmington, Ohio

Sage is subtle but wonderful in these cheesy-crisp breadsticks. Try them as a snack or alongside soup or salad.

- 1 cup all-purpose flour
- 1-1/2 teaspoons baking powder
- 1 teaspoon rubbed sage
- 1/2 teaspoon salt
- 1/2 cup finely shredded cheddar cheese
- 2 tablespoons cold butter
- 1/3 cup cold water

1) In a small bowl, combine the flour, baking powder, sage and salt; stir in cheese. Cut in butter until mixture resembles coarse crumbs. Gradually add water, tossing with a fork until dough forms a ball.

2) On a lightly floured surface, roll dough into a 12-in. x 10-in. rectangle. Cut in half lengthwise; cut each half widthwise into 1-in. strips. Twist each strip two to three times.

3) Place 1 in. apart on greased baking sheets. Bake at 425° for 8-10 minutes or until golden brown. Serve warm.

Yield: 2 dozen.

NUTRITION FACTS: 2 breadsticks equals 71 calories, 3 g fat (2 g saturated fat), 10 mg cholesterol, 196 mg sodium, 8 g carbohydrate, trace fiber, 2 g protein.

Popovers and Puffs

Place oven rack in lowest position. Generously grease the muffin pan cups, custard cups or popover pan cups. Mix batter until smooth. Batter may be refrigerated for up to 1 day. Pour into cups.

Bake according to recipe directions. Don't open the oven door during baking or popovers will fall. After removing popovers from the oven, prick with the point of a sharp knife to allow steam to escape. Popovers are best served warm, fresh from the oven.

BAKED HERB PUFFS

Baked Herb Puffs
Dorothy Smith, El Dorado, Arkansas

Ground mustard, parsley and green onions make these puffs a nice addition to any meal. I often freeze them, then reheat a few minutes in the oven.

    1   cup water
    1/2 cup butter
    1   teaspoon ground mustard
    1/4 teaspoon salt
    1/8 teaspoon pepper
    1   cup all-purpose flour
    4   eggs
    1/3 cup minced fresh parsley
    1/4 cup chopped green onions

1) In a large saucepan, bring the water, butter, mustard, salt and pepper to a boil. Add flour all at once and stir until a smooth ball forms. Remove from the heat; let stand for 5 minutes.

2) Add eggs, one at a time, beating well after each addition. Continue beating until mixture is smooth and shiny. Add parsley and green onions; mix well.

3) Drop by 2 tablespoonfuls 2 in. apart onto greased baking sheets. Bake at 400° for 18-20 minutes or until golden brown. Cut a slit in each to allow steam to escape; bake 5 minutes longer. Remove to a wire rack to cool.

Yield: 1-1/2 dozen.

NUTRITION FACTS: 1 serving equals 88 calories, 6 g fat (3 g saturated fat), 61 mg cholesterol, 99 mg sodium, 6 g carbohydrate, trace fiber, 2 g protein.

Christmas Morning Popovers
Sue Jurack, Mequon, Wisconsin

Popovers are a Christmas morning tradition my father-in-law started more than 30 years ago. Now I get up early to make the popovers, then wake the family to begin opening gifts.

1-1/4   cups milk
    1   tablespoon butter, melted and cooled
    1   cup all-purpose flour
    1/4 teaspoon salt
    2   eggs

1) In a small mixing bowl, beat the milk, butter, flour and salt until blended. Add eggs, one at a time, beating well after each addition. Fill buttered popover pans or large custard cups three-fourths full. Bake at 450° for 15 minutes. Reduce heat to 350°; bake 20 minutes longer or until very firm.

2) Remove from oven; prick each popover with a sharp knife to allow steam to escape. Serve immediately.

Yield: 9 servings.

NUTRITION FACTS: 1 serving equals 99 calories, 4 g fat (2 g saturated fat), 55 mg cholesterol, 109 mg sodium, 12 g carbohydrate, trace fiber, 4 g protein.

French Breakfast Puffs
Kimberly Flora, Peru, Indiana

Rather than serve typical pastries, I like to make these light and tender treats when I have guests. Everyone enjoys the cinnamon-and-sugar coating.

    1/3 cup shortening
    1   cup sugar, *divided*
    1   egg
1-1/2   cups all-purpose flour
1-1/2   teaspoons baking powder
    1/2 teaspoon salt
    1/4 teaspoon ground nutmeg
    1/2 cup milk
    1   teaspoon ground cinnamon
    6   tablespoons butter, melted

1) In a small mixing bowl, beat shortening, 1/2 cup sugar and egg until smooth. Combine the flour, baking powder, salt and nutmeg; add to the sugar mixture alternately with milk.

2) Fill greased muffin cups two-thirds full. Bake at 350° for 20 minutes or until a toothpick inserted near the center comes out clean. Cool for 5 minutes before removing from pan.

3) Meanwhile, combine cinnamon and remaining sugar in a shallow bowl. Roll warm puffs in butter, then in cinnamon-sugar. Serve immediately.

Yield: 1 dozen.

NUTRITION FACTS: 1 serving equals 234 calories, 12 g fat (5 g saturated fat), 34 mg cholesterol, 217 mg sodium, 29 g carbohydrate, 1 g fiber, 3 g protein.

BUTTERMILK DOUGHNUTS

Buttermilk Doughnuts

Betty Rauschendorfer, Sidney, Montana

Whether you serve these at breakfast or brunch, they're sure to disappear fast.

- 4   eggs
- 2   cups sugar
- 1/3   cup butter, melted
- 1   teaspoon vanilla extract
- 5-1/2   to 6 cups all-purpose flour
- 2   teaspoons baking powder
- 2   teaspoons baking soda
- 1   teaspoon salt
- 1   teaspoon ground nutmeg
- 2   cups buttermilk

Oil for deep-fat frying

Additional sugar, cinnamon-sugar *or* confectioners' sugar, optional

1) In a large mixing bowl, beat eggs and sugar until light and lemon-colored. Add butter and vanilla; mix well. Combine flour, baking powder, baking soda, salt and nutmeg; add to egg mixture alternately with buttermilk. Cover and refrigerate for 2-3 hours.

2) On a lightly floured surface, roll dough to 1/2-in. thickness. Cut with a floured 3-in. doughnut cutter.

3) In an electric skillet or deep-fat fryer, heat oil to 375°. Fry doughnuts, a few at a time, for 1 minute on each side or until golden. Drain on paper towels. Roll in additional sugar if desired.

Yield: 4 dozen.

NUTRITION FACTS: 1 serving equals 117 calories, 3 g fat (1 g saturated fat), 22 mg cholesterol, 147 mg sodium, 20 g carbohydrate, trace fiber, 2 g protein.

Fluffy Pancakes

Eugene Presley, Council, Virginia

As the name suggests, these pancakes cook up nice and fluffy. You can also add miniature chocolate chips or maple flavoring for two other taste twists.

- 1   cup all-purpose flour
- 1   tablespoon sugar
- 2   teaspoons baking powder
- 1/2   teaspoon salt
- 1   egg
- 3/4   cup milk
- 1/4   cup shortening, melted

1) In a small bowl, combine the flour, sugar, baking powder and salt. Combine the egg, milk and shortening; stir into dry ingredients just until moistened.

2) Pour batter by 1/4 cupful onto a greased hot griddle. Turn when bubbles form on top of pancakes; cook until the second side is golden brown.

Yield: 8 pancakes.

NUTRITION FACTS: 2 pancakes equals 283 calories, 15 g fat (4 g saturated fat), 59 mg cholesterol, 534 mg sodium, 29 g carbohydrate, 1 g fiber, 6 g protein.

■ *CHOCOLATE CHIP PANCAKES:* Stir 1/2 cup miniature chocolate chips into batter. Proceed as recipe directs.

■ *MAPLE PANCAKES:* Omit sugar. Add 1 tablespoon maple syrup to milk mixture. Proceed as recipe directs.

PREPARING PANCAKES

1) Use a 1/4-cup measure to pour batter onto a hot griddle or skillet, 5-6 in. apart, making sure to leave enough room between pancakes for expansion.

2) Turn pancakes over when edges become dry and bubbles that appear on top begin to pop.

3) Pour batter by 1/4 cupful onto a greased hot griddle. Turn when bubbles form on top; cook until the second side is golden brown. Serve with blueberry topping.

Yield: about 20 pancakes (3-1/2 cups topping).

Editor's Note: If using frozen blueberries, do not thaw before adding to batter.

NUTRITION FACTS: 2 pancakes with 1/3 cup topping equals 332 calories, 13 g fat (8 g saturated fat), 79 mg cholesterol, 387 mg sodium, 48 g carbohydrate, 3 g fiber, 6 g protein.

Brown Sugar Oatmeal Pancakes
Sharon Wilson Bickett, Chester, South Carolina

My family loves these pancakes so much I make them every Saturday and Sunday. They don't believe it's the weekend unless I do! We think they're especially good topped with molasses and syrup.

1/2	cup plus 2 tablespoons quick-cooking oats
1/2	cup whole wheat flour
1/2	cup all-purpose flour
1/2	teaspoon baking soda
1/2	teaspoon salt
1/3	cup packed brown sugar
1	egg
2	tablespoons vegetable oil
1	cup buttermilk

1) In a small bowl, combine the oats, flours, baking soda, salt and sugar. In another small bowl, beat the egg, oil and buttermilk. Stir into dry ingredients just until moistened.

2) Pour batter by 1/3 cupful onto a greased hot griddle. Turn when bubbles form on top; cook until the second side is golden brown.

Yield: about 10 pancakes.

NUTRITION FACTS: 2 pancakes equals 263 calories, 8 g fat (1 g saturated fat), 44 mg cholesterol, 433 mg sodium, 42 g carbohydrate, 3 g fiber, 7 g protein.

MORE PANCAKE TOPPERS

For more recipes that make great toppings for pancakes and waffles, see Dutch Cream Waffles on page 446 or the sauces on page 420.

BLUEBERRY SOUR CREAM PANCAKES

Blueberry Sour Cream Pancakes
Paula Hadley, Forest Hill, Louisiana

When our family of 10 goes blueberry picking, we have a bounty of blueberries in no time. We especially enjoy them in these melt-in-your-mouth pancakes topped with a satisfying blueberry sauce.

1/2	cup sugar
2	tablespoons cornstarch
1	cup cold water
4	cups fresh *or* frozen blueberries

PANCAKES:

2	cups all-purpose flour
1/4	cup sugar
4	teaspoons baking powder
1/2	teaspoon salt
2	eggs
1-1/2	cups milk
1	cup (8 ounces) sour cream
1/3	cup butter, melted
1	cup fresh *or* frozen blueberries

1) In a large saucepan, combine the sugar and cornstarch. Stir in water until smooth. Add blueberries. Bring to a boil over medium heat; cook and stir for 2 minutes or until thickened. Remove from the heat; cover and keep warm.

2) For pancakes, in a large bowl, combine the flour, sugar, baking powder and salt. Combine the eggs, milk, sour cream and butter. Stir into flour mixture just until moistened. Fold in blueberries.

WAFFLES FROM SCRATCH

Waffles from Scratch
Florence Dean, Towson, Maryland

My mom always made these, and they were my favorite lunch. They're wonderful topped with fruit or maple syrup.

- 1-1/2 cups all-purpose flour
- 1 teaspoon baking powder
- 1/2 teaspoon salt
- 2 eggs, *separated*
- 1 cup milk
- 1/4 cup butter, melted

Confectioners' sugar and fresh fruit *or* maple syrup

1) In a small bowl, combine the flour, baking powder and salt. Combine egg yolks, milk and butter; stir into dry ingredients just until moistened.

2) In a small mixing bowl, beat egg whites on medium speed until soft peaks form; gently fold into batter.

3) Bake in a preheated waffle iron according to manufacturer's directions until golden brown. Top with confectioners' sugar and fruit or serve with syrup.

Yield: 4 waffles (about 6 inches).

NUTRITION FACTS: 2 waffles (calculated without confectioners' sugar, fruit or maple syrup) equals 691 calories, 33 g fat (18 g saturated fat), 290 mg cholesterol, 1,146 mg sodium, 78 g carbohydrate, 3 g fiber, 20 g protein.

Dutch Cream Waffles
Barbara Syme, Peoria, Arizona

Originally made by my grandmother on a wood-burning stove, these crispy waffles are also special to me for another reason. I served them to my husband over 50 years ago when I first cooked for him in our new home.

- 1 cup all-purpose flour
- 1/4 teaspoon salt
- 3 eggs, *separated*
- 1 cup heavy whipping cream

1) In a large mixing bowl, combine flour and salt. In a small mixing bowl, beat egg yolks on low while adding cream. Beat for 1 minute. Add to flour mixture; combine on low speed, then beat on medium-high until smooth.

2) In another small mixing bowl and with clean beaters, beat egg whites on high until stiff peaks form. Gently fold into batter.

3) Bake in a preheated waffle iron according to manufacturer's directions. Serve with warm maple syrup or fresh fruit in season.

Yield: 2-3 servings.

NUTRITION FACTS: 1 serving equals 500 calories, 35 g fat (20 g saturated fat), 321 mg cholesterol, 291 mg sodium, 35 g carbohydrate, 1 g fiber, 12 g protein.

■ *ORANGE HONEY BUTTER:* Beat together 1/2 cup softened butter with 1/3 cup honey. Beat in 2 tablespoons orange juice concentrate. Serve with pancakes or waffles.

■ *CINNAMON HONEY SYRUP:* Microwave 1 cup honey, 1/2 cup butter, cubed and 1-1/2 teaspoons ground cinnamon on high until butter is melted and syrup is hot; stir occasionally. Serve with pancakes or waffles.

FREEZING HOMEMADE WAFFLES

For fast homemade freezer waffles, bake and cool on a wire rack; freeze in a single layer on a baking sheet. When frozen, store in heavy-duty freezer bags.

When ready to use, pop into the toaster or toaster oven to defrost and reheat.

CHAPTER 18
YEAST BREADS

YEAST
BREADS

Yeast breads are divided into kneaded and batter breads. They can be savory or sweet.

Kneaded yeast breads are usually mixed, kneaded, allowed to rise, shaped, allowed to rise again and then baked. Bread machine breads are also kneaded breads.

Batter breads aren't kneaded. Rather, ingredients are beaten, allowed to rise once or twice and then baked. Batter breads have a coarser texture and rugged crust.

Baking Hints

Use butter, stick margarine (with at least 80% oil) or shortening. Do not use light or whipped butter, diet spread or tub margarine. Measure ingredients accurately. Check temperature of liquid ingredients with an instant read thermometer.

Arrange the oven racks so that the bread will bake in the center of the oven. Preheat oven for 10 to 15 minutes before baking.

When mixing dough, always start with a minimum amount of flour until dough reaches desired consistency (soft, sticky, stiff or firm). Knead dough only until it does not tear easily when stretched. Let dough rise in a warm (80° to 85°), draft-free area. Proper rising helps in the development of the bread texture.

Use aluminum pans with a dull rather than shiny or dark finish. Glass baking dishes and dark finishes will produce darker crusts. To allow for good air circulation while baking, leave at least 1 in. of space between pans and between pans and sides of oven.

Use a kitchen timer and test for doneness at the minimum recommended baking time. Bread is done when it is golden brown and sounds hollow when tapped on the bottom. Or, insert an instant-read thermometer in the thickest part of the loaf. The bread is done when the thermometer reads 200°.

Remove breads from pans and cool on wire racks. Let breads cool for at least 20 minutes before slicing. Use a serrated knife and a sawing motion when cutting.

Bread Ingredients

The ingredients used in bread making will affect the texture, density and crust. Lean breads (like French bread) are made with yeast, flour, water, salt and a minimal amount of sugar to produce a dense, chewy bread with a crisp crust. Rich or short breads (like Brioche) are made with fat such as butter or shortening, eggs and/or milk to produce a tender bread with a soft crust.

Fats and Eggs: They tenderize, add moisture, carry flavors and give a richness to the bread.

Flours: Wheat flour, the most commonly used flour, contains gluten—an elastic protein. Kneading the dough develops the gluten. During the rise time, the yeast produces carbon dioxide gas, which becomes trapped in the dough. As the gases push against the protein, the dough rises. During baking, the protein is set by the heat and gives the baked good its structure.

The terms soft and hard wheat refer to the amount of protein (gluten) in the flour—soft has less and hard has more. The amount of gluten will affect the texture of the bread.

High-gluten flours, such as all-purpose or bread flour, are used for the best yeast bread results. Whole wheat and rye flours contain less gluten, and the bread would be heavy and dense bread without the addition of all-purpose or bread flour.

Liquids: Most breads are prepared with water, milk or water reserved from cooking potatoes. Breads prepared with water will yield a crunchy crust, and milk will produce a softer crust and a tender crumb. All liquids need to be warmed to the temperature required by the yeast and mixing method.

Salt: Helps round out flavors and controls the growth of the yeast. Too much salt or too little salt will affect the final product. For best results use the amount listed in the recipe and never omit the salt.

Sugars and Other Sweeteners: Used in small amounts, sugars feed the yeast when making bread. Sugars and other sweeteners tenderize, add sweetness and flavor, promote browning and enhance the keeping quality. Depending on the recipe, you may use white or brown sugar, molasses or honey to sweeten and flavor your bread.

Yeast: This microorganism becomes activated when combined with warm water and sugar. It consumes the sugars in sweeteners and flours and produces carbon dioxide gas that helps give bread its light airy texture. There are several different types of yeast, which are all handled differently. Check the expiration date on the package before using and discard yeast if it is past the date.

Active dry yeast is available in 1/4-ounce foil packages or 4-ounce jars. With the Traditional Mixing Method for Yeast Breads at right, the active yeast is dissolved in liquid that has been warmed to 110° to 115°. If the liquid temperature is too low, the yeast will not be activated. If the liquid temperature is too high, the yeast will be killed, preventing the bread from rising.

With the Rapid Mixing Method for Yeast Breads on page 453, the active dry yeast is added directly to the flour and other dry ingredients. Then warm liquid (120° to 130°) is added.

Quick-rise yeast is available in 1/4-ounce foil packages or 4-ounce jars. Quick-rise yeast is finely granulated and should only be combined with the other ingredients using the Rapid Mixing Method for Yeast Breads on page 453. Quick-rise yeast will raise bread dough in about a third to half the traditional time.

Bread machine yeast is available in 4-ounce jars. This is an instant yeast with finer granules. The smaller granules allow the yeast to mix into the dough more evenly.

Fresh or cake yeast is most commonly available in 2-ounce cakes, which is equivalent to three 1/4-ounce packages of active dry yeast. A third of the fresh yeast cake (about 0.6 ounce) is equal to one packet of active

dry yeast. Some older bread recipes often call for a "cake" of yeast. Cake yeast is a fresh product found in your grocer's dairy case. It should be used within 10 days of purchase. To use, crumble the yeast into dry ingredients or soften in tepid water (70° to 80°).

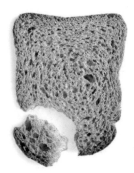

Make sure active dry yeast (not quick-rise yeast) is alive and active. You proof it by dissolving one package of yeast and 1 teaspoon sugar in 1/4 cup warm water (110° to 115°). Let stand for 5 to 10 minutes. If the mixture foams up, the yeast mixture can be used because the yeast is active. If it does not foam, the yeast should be discarded.

TRADITIONAL MIXING METHOD FOR YEAST BREADS

1) Heat liquid to 110° to 115°, using a thermometer. Measure liquid and place in a large mixing bowl. Add active dry yeast; stir until dissolved.

2) Add sugar, salt, fat, eggs (if using) and about half of the flour. Beat with an electric mixer or by hand until smooth.

3) Gradually stir in enough of the remaining flour by hand to form a dough of the consistency stated in the recipe.

1) Turn dough onto a lightly floured surface; shape into a ball. Fold top of dough toward you. With palms, push with a rolling motion away from you. Turn dough a quarter turn; repeat motion until dough is smooth and elastic. Add flour to surface only as needed.

2) Place the dough in a bowl greased with butter, oil or nonstick cooking spray. Turn dough over to grease the top. This prevents the dough from drying out while rising.

3) Cover with a clean towel or plastic wrap. Place covered dough in a warm, draft-free area (80° to 85°) until dough has doubled. (Place covered bowl on the top rack in a cold oven with a pan of steaming, hot water underneath. Or turn your oven to its lowest setting for no longer than 40 to 50 seconds. Turn off and let dough rise in the oven.)

4) Press two fingers 1/2 in. into the dough. If the dents remain, the dough is doubled in size and ready to punch down.

5) To punch dough down, make a fist and push it into the center. Gather the dough to the center and shape into a ball. Place on a floured surface.

6) Divide the dough if the recipe directs; shape into balls. Roll each ball into a 12-in. x 8-in. rectangle. You will hear air bubbles "popping" as you roll the dough.

7) Dust off any loose flour that might cling to the dough. Beginning at the short end, roll up each rectangle firmly. If it's too loose, you'll see air pockets when the bread is cut. If it's too tight, the bread will crack while baking.

8) Pinch seam and each end to seal. Place seam side down in a greased pan; cover with a towel and allow to double in size in a warm draft-free area.

9) When dough has doubled, remove towel; place pans several inches apart in the center of the preheated oven.

10) When bread is golden brown, test for doneness by carefully removing loaves from pans and tapping the bottom crusts. If it sounds hollow, the bread is done. You can also use a thermometer to check that bread reaches 200°. If the bread is browning too fast and it's not done, tent with foil and continue baking. Unless recipe directs otherwise, immediately remove breads from pans. Cool completely on a wire rack.

Baking at High Altitudes

High altitude (over 3,000 feet) affects bread baking because the lower air pressure allows the yeast to rise 25 to 50 percent faster, and the drier air makes the flour drier. If the dough over-rises, the results might be a heavy, dry loaf or misshapen or collapsed loaf. Make these adjustments when baking bread at high altitudes:

- Start checking the dough halfway through the recommended rise time to see if it has doubled. If the dough has over-risen, punch it down and allow it to rise again.

- Use about a third less yeast. If a recipe calls for one package of active dry yeast (2-1/4 teaspoons), you would need to use about 1-1/2 teaspoons.

- Add flour slowly when mixing the dough and use only enough to make the dough easy to handle. If the dough is sticky, use greased rather than floured hands for kneading.

- Oil the dough and cover with greased plastic wrap to prevent it from drying out while using.

- Check for doneness a few minutes before the minimum recommended baking time. Tent with foil if it's browning too quickly.

Dressing Up French Bread

Spread one of these flavorful toppings on French bread for a welcome treat at dinner. For each topping, cut a 1-pound loaf in half lengthwise and spread over the cut sides.

- ■ *GOLDEN GARLIC BREAD:* Combine 1/3 cup softened butter with 1/4 cup grated Parmesan cheese, 1 to 2 minced garlic cloves and 1 teaspoon dried basil. Broil 4 in. from the heat for 3-4 minutes or until golden brown.
—*Annette Self, Junction City, Ohio*

- ■ *OLIVE CHEESE BREAD:* Combine 1/2 cup melted butter, 1/2 cup mayonnaise, 1 can (2-1/4 ounces) drained sliced ripe olives, 2 chopped green onions and 1-1/2 cups shredded Monterey Jack cheese. Bake at 350° for 15-20 minutes or until cheese is melted.
—*Nancy McWhorter, Bridge City, Texas*

- ■ *RANCH GARLIC BREAD:* Combine 1 cup softened butter with 2 to 3 tablespoons ranch salad dressing mix and 2 teaspoons garlic powder. Broil 4 in. from the heat for 3-4 minutes or until golden brown.
—*John Palmer, Cottonwood, California*

HOMEMADE BREAD

Homemade Bread
Sandra Anderson, New York, New York

This basic bread bakes up golden brown. I enjoy the aroma of freshly baked bread in my kitchen.

- 1 package (1/4 ounce) active dry yeast
- 2-1/4 cups warm water (110° to 115°)
- 3 tablespoons sugar
- 1 tablespoon salt
- 2 tablespoons vegetable oil
- 6 to 6-1/4 cups all-purpose flour

1) In a large mixing bowl, dissolve yeast in warm water. Add the sugar, salt, oil and 3 cups flour. Beat until smooth. Stir in enough remaining flour to form a soft dough.

2) Turn onto a floured surface; knead until smooth and elastic, about 8-10 minutes. Place in a greased bowl, turning once to grease the top. Cover; let rise in a warm place until doubled, about 1-1/2 hours. Punch dough down. Turn onto a lightly floured surface; divide dough in half. Shape each into a loaf.

3) Place in two greased 9-in. x 5-in. x 3-in. loaf pans. Cover and let rise until doubled, about 30-45 minutes. Bake at 375° for 30-35 minutes or until golden brown and bread sounds hollow when tapped. Remove from pans to wire racks to cool.

Yield: 2 loaves (16 slices each).

NUTRITION FACTS: 1 slice equals 98 calories, 1 g fat (trace saturated fat), 0 cholesterol, 443 mg sodium, 19 g carbohydrate, 1 g fiber, 3 g protein.

Crusty French Bread
Deanna Naivar, Temple, Texas

A delicate texture makes this bread absolutely wonderful. I also use the dough to make breadsticks brushed with melted butter and garlic powder.

1 package (1/4 ounce) active
    dry yeast
1 cup warm water (110° to 115°)
2 tablespoons sugar
2 tablespoons vegetable oil
1-1/2 teaspoons salt
3 to 3-1/4 cups all-purpose flour
Cornmeal
1 egg white
1 teaspoon cold water

1) In a large mixing bowl, dissolve yeast in warm water. Add the sugar, oil, salt and 2 cups flour. Beat until blended. Stir in enough remaining flour to form a stiff dough.

2) Turn onto a floured surface; knead until smooth and elastic, about 6-8 minutes. Place in a greased bowl, turning once to grease top.

3) Cover and let rise in a warm place until doubled, about 1 hour. Punch dough down; return to bowl. Cover and let rise for 30 minutes.

4) Punch dough down. Turn onto a lightly floured surface. Shape into a loaf 16 in. long x 2-1/2 in. wide with tapered ends. Sprinkle a greased baking sheet with cornmeal and place loaf on baking sheet. Cover and let rise until doubled, about 25 minutes.

5) Beat egg white and cold water; brush over dough. With a sharp knife, make diagonal slashes 2 in. apart across top of loaf. Bake at 375° for 25-30 minutes or until golden brown. Remove from pan to a wire rack to cool.

Yield: 1 loaf (16 slices).

NUTRITION FACTS: 1 slice equals 109 calories, 2 g fat (trace saturated fat), 0 cholesterol, 225 mg sodium, 20 g carbohydrate, 1 g fiber, 3 g protein.

Traditional Wheat Bread
Kelly Jo Yaksich, St. Cloud, Minnesota

Whole wheat flour makes this bread a little more hearty and healthy. Since it makes three loaves, I put two in the freezer to use as I need them.

3-1/2 to 4 cups bread flour
2-1/2 cups whole wheat flour
2 tablespoons active dry yeast
1 tablespoon salt
1 cup water
1 cup milk
1/2 cup honey
3 tablespoons butter

1 egg
    All-purpose flour

1) In a large mixing bowl, combine 2 cups bread flour, 1 cup whole wheat flour, yeast and salt. In a small saucepan, heat the water, milk, honey and butter to 120°-130°. Add to dry ingredients; beat just until moistened. Add egg; beat until smooth. Stir in remaining whole wheat flour and enough remaining bread flour to form a stiff dough.

2) Turn onto a surface lightly dusted with all-purpose flour; knead until smooth and elastic, about 8-10 minutes. Place in a greased bowl, turning once to grease top. Cover and let rise in a warm place until doubled, about 1 hour.

3) Punch dough down; let rest for 10 minutes. Turn onto a lightly floured surface; divide into thirds. Shape each into a loaf. Place in three greased 9-in. x 5-in. x 3-in. loaf pans. Cover and let rise until doubled, about 45 minutes.

4) Bake at 350° for 35-40 minutes or until golden brown. Cover loosely with foil if tops brown too quickly. Remove from pans to wire racks to cool.

Yield: 3 loaves (16 slices each).

NUTRITION FACTS: 1 slice equals 78 calories, 1 g fat (1 g saturated fat), 7 mg cholesterol, 159 mg sodium, 15 g carbohydrate, 1 g fiber, 3 g protein.

RAPID MIXING METHOD FOR YEAST BREADS

1) In a mixing bowl, combine flour (about 2 cups), sugar, active dry or quick-rise yeast, salt and any seasonings.

2) In a saucepan, heat liquid ingredients (water, milk, honey, molasses and butter or oil) to 120°-130°. Add to dry ingredients; beat just until moistened.

3) Add any eggs; beat until smooth. Gradually stir in enough of the remaining flour to form a dough of the desired consistency.

BRAIDED EGG BREAD

Braided Egg Bread
Marlene Jeffery, Holland, Manitoba

I first made this bread a few years ago, and I already know it's one recipe I'll pass down to future generations.

3-1/4 to 3-3/4 cups all-purpose flour
1 tablespoon sugar
1 package (1/4 ounce) active dry yeast
3/4 teaspoon salt
3/4 cup water
3 tablespoons vegetable oil
2 eggs

TOPPING:
1 egg
1 teaspoon water
1/2 teaspoon poppy seeds

1) In a large mixing bowl, combine 1-1/2 cups flour, sugar, yeast and salt. In a saucepan, heat water and oil to 120°-130°. Add to the dry ingredients along with eggs. Beat on medium speed for 3 minutes. Stir in enough remaining flour to form a soft dough.

2) Turn onto a floured surface; knead until smooth and elastic, about 6-8 minutes. Place in a greased bowl, turning once to grease top. Cover and let rise in a warm place until doubled, about 1-1/2 hours.

3) Punch dough down. Turn onto a lightly floured surface. Set a third of the dough aside. Divide remaining dough into three pieces. Shape each into a 13-in. rope. Place ropes on a greased baking sheet and braid; pinch ends to seal and tuck under.

4) Divide reserved dough into three equal pieces; shape each into a 14-in. rope. Braid ropes. Center

14-in. braid on top of the shorter braid. Pinch ends to seal and tuck under. Cover and let rise until doubled, about 30 minutes.

5) Beat egg and water; brush over dough. Sprinkle with poppy seeds. Bake at 375° for 25-30 minutes or until golden brown. Cover with foil during the last 15 minutes of baking. Remove from pan to a wire rack to cool.

Yield: 1 loaf (16 slices).

NUTRITION FACTS: 1 slice equals 134 calories, 4 g fat (1 g saturated fat), 40 mg cholesterol, 123 mg sodium, 20 g carbohydrate, 1 g fiber, 4 g protein.

BRAIDING BREADS

1) Place three ropes almost touching on a baking sheet. Starting in the middle, loosely bring left rope under center rope. Bring right rope under new center rope and repeat until you reach the end.

2) Turn the pan and repeat braiding.

3) Press each end to seal; tuck ends under.

Basic Pizza Crust
Beverly Anderson, Sinclairville, New York

I like to double this recipe and keep one baked crust in the freezer for a quick snack or meal later.

1 package (1/4 ounce) active dry yeast
1 cup warm water (110° to 115°)
2 tablespoons vegetable oil

1   teaspoon sugar
1/4   teaspoon salt
2-1/2   to 2-3/4 cups all-purpose flour
Cornmeal
Pizza toppings of your choice

1) In a large mixing bowl, dissolve yeast in warm water. Add the oil, sugar, salt and 1-1/2 cups flour. Beat until smooth. Stir in enough remaining flour to form a firm dough. Turn onto a floured surface; cover and let rest for 10 minutes.

2) Roll into a 13-in. circle. Grease a 12-in. pizza pan and sprinkle with cornmeal. Transfer dough to prepared pan, building up edges slightly. Do not let rise.

3) Bake at 425° for 12-15 minutes or until browned. Add toppings; bake 10-15 minutes longer.

Yield: 1 pizza crust (6 wedges).

NUTRITION FACTS: 1 wedge (calculated without toppings) equals 236 calories, 5 g fat (1 g saturated fat), 0 cholesterol, 100 mg sodium, 41 g carbohydrate, 2 g fiber, 6 g protein.

ROSEMARY FOCACCIA

Rosemary Focaccia
Debrah Peoples, Calgary, Alberta

The savory aroma of rosemary as this classic bread bakes is irresistible. Try this bread as a side with any meal, as a snack or as a pizza crust.

2   medium onions, chopped
1/4   cup olive oil plus 3 tablespoons olive oil, *divided*

1-1/2   teaspoons active dry yeast
1-1/2   cups warm water (110° to 115°), *divided*
1/2   teaspoon sugar
1/2   teaspoon salt
3   to 4 cups all-purpose flour
2   tablespoons snipped fresh rosemary *or* 2 teaspoons dried rosemary, crushed, *divided*
Cornmeal
Coarse salt

1) In a large skillet, saute onions in 1/4 cup oil until tender; cool. In a large mixing bowl, dissolve yeast in 1/4 cup warm water. Add sugar and let stand for 5 minutes.

2) Add 2 tablespoons oil, salt and remaining water. Add 2 cups flour. Beat until smooth. Stir in enough remaining flour to form a soft dough.

3) Turn onto a floured surface; knead until smooth and elastic, about 6-8 minutes. Add onions and half of the rosemary. Knead 1 minute longer. Place in a greased bowl, turning once to grease top. Cover and let rise in a warm place until doubled, about 40 minutes.

4) Punch dough down. Turn onto a lightly floured surface; divide in half. Pat each piece flat. Let rest for 5 minutes. Grease two baking sheets and sprinkle with cornmeal. Stretch each portion of dough into a 10-in. circle on prepared pans. Cover and let rise until doubled, about 40 minutes.

5) Brush with remaining oil. Sprinkle with coarse salt and remaining rosemary. Bake at 375° for 25-30 minutes or until golden brown. Remove from pans to wire racks to cool.

Yield: 2 loaves (8 wedges each).

NUTRITION FACTS: 1 wedge (calculated without coarse salt) equals 147 calories, 6 g fat (1 g saturated fat), 0 cholesterol, 75 mg sodium, 20 g carbohydrate, 1 g fiber, 3 g protein.

■ *PARMESAN ROSEMARY FOCACCIA:* Sprinkle 1 tablespoon Parmesan cheese over each focaccia before baking.

■ *ROSEMARY OLIVE FOCACCIA:* Prepare dough as directed, omitting sauteed onions. Knead as directed, adding 1/3 cup well-drained sliced ripe olives along with half of the rosemary. Sprinkle 1 tablespoon Parmesan cheese over each focaccia before baking.

Old-World Rye Bread

Perlene Hoekema, Lynden, Washington

Rye and caraway lend to this bread's wonderful flavor, while the surprise ingredient of baking cocoa gives it a rich, dark color. I sometimes add a cup each of raisins and walnuts.

- 2 packages (1/4 ounce *each*) active dry yeast
- 1-1/2 cups warm water (110° to 115°)
- 1/2 cup molasses
- 6 tablespoons butter, softened
- 2 cups rye flour
- 1/4 cup baking cocoa
- 2 tablespoons caraway seeds
- 2 teaspoons salt
- 3-1/2 to 4 cups all-purpose flour
- Cornmeal

1) In a large mixing bowl, dissolve yeast in warm water. Beat in the molasses, butter, rye flour, cocoa, caraway seeds, salt and 2 cups all-purpose flour to form a stiff dough.

2) Turn onto a floured surface; knead until smooth and elastic, about 6-8 minutes. Place in a greased bowl, turning once to grease top. Cover and let rise in a warm place until doubled, about 1-1/2 hours.

3) Punch dough down. Turn onto a lightly floured surface; divide in half. Shape each piece into a loaf, about 10 in. long. Grease two baking sheets and sprinkle with cornmeal. Place loaves on prepared pans. Cover and let rise until doubled, about 1 hour.

4) Bake at 350° for 35-40 minutes or until bread sounds hollow when tapped. Remove from pans to wire racks to cool.

Yield: 2 loaves (12 slices each).

NUTRITION FACTS: 1 slice (calculated without cornmeal) equals 146 calories, 3 g fat (2 g saturated fat), 8 mg cholesterol, 229 mg sodium, 26 g carbohydrate, 2 g fiber, 3 g protein.

Parmesan Herb Bread

Audrey Thibodeau, Mesa, Arizona

Herbs add a savory filling to this yeast bread. It's wonderful served fresh from the oven with Italian or pasta dishes.

- 6 to 7 cups all-purpose flour
- 2 packages (1/4 ounce *each*) active dry yeast
- 2 tablespoons sugar
- 1 teaspoon salt
- 2-1/4 cups water
- 3/4 cup butter, softened, *divided*

FILLING:

- 1/2 cup grated Parmesan cheese
- 2 tablespoons dried chives
- 2 tablespoons dried parsley flakes
- 1 teaspoon garlic powder
- 1/2 teaspoon dried savory
- 1/2 teaspoon dried thyme
- Cornmeal

1) In a large mixing bowl, combine 3 cups flour, yeast, sugar and salt. In a small saucepan, heat the water and 1/4 cup butter to 120°-130°. Add to dry ingredients; beat until smooth. Stir in enough remaining flour to form a soft dough.

2) Turn onto a floured surface; knead until smooth and elastic, about 6-8 minutes. Place in a greased bowl, turning once to grease the top. Cover and let rise in a warm place until doubled, about 1 hour.

3) Punch dough down. Turn onto a lightly floured surface; divide in half. Roll each piece into an 18-in. x 15-in. rectangle. Spread remaining butter over dough to within 1/2 in. of edges.

4) In a small bowl, combine the first six filling ingredients; sprinkle over butter. Roll up jelly-roll style, starting with a long side; pinch seams to seal and tuck ends under.

5) Place seam side down on two ungreased baking sheet sprinkled with cornmeal. With a sharp knife, make four or five slashes across top of each loaf; sprinkle with cornmeal. Cover and let rise until doubled, about 1 hour.

6) Bake at 375° for 15 minutes. Reduce heat to 350°; bake 20 to 25 minutes longer or until bread sounds hollow when tapped. Remove from pans to wire racks. Serve warm or cold.

Yield: 2 loaves (16 slices each).

NUTRITION FACTS: 1 slice equals 134 calories, 5 g fat (3 g saturated fat), 12 mg cholesterol, 141 mg sodium, 19 g carbohydrate, 1 g fiber, 3 g protein.

MAKING SLASHES

Slashing or scoring the top of a bread loaf allows steam to vent, helps prevent cracking and gives bread a decorative appearance. With a sharp knife, make shallow slashes across top of loaf.

CINNAMON RAISIN BREAD

Cinnamon Raisin Bread

Joan Hutter, Warnick, Rhode Island

Two kinds of raisins are swirled into each slice of this bread. I use leftovers to make French toast.

- 2 packages (1/4 ounce *each*) active dry yeast
- 1/3 cup warm water (110° to 115°)
- 1 cup warm milk (110° to 115°)
- 1/2 cup sugar
- 6 tablespoons butter, softened
- 2 eggs, lightly beaten
- 1-1/4 teaspoons salt
- 5-1/2 to 6 cups all-purpose flour

FILLING:

- 1-1/3 cups golden raisins
- 1-1/3 cups raisins
- 1 cup water
- 1/3 cup apple juice *or* apple cider
- 1 tablespoon ground cinnamon
- 1 egg, beaten

1) In a large mixing bowl, dissolve yeast in warm water. Add milk, sugar, butter, eggs, salt and 2 cups flour. Beat on medium speed 2 minutes. Stir in enough remaining flour to form a soft dough.

2) Turn onto a floured surface; knead until smooth and elastic, about 6-8 minutes. Place in a greased bowl, turning once to grease top. Cover and let rise in a warm place until doubled, about 1 hour.

3) In a saucepan, bring first five filling ingredients to a boil. Reduce heat to medium; cook for 15-20 minutes or until almost all the liquid is absorbed, stirring occasionally. Remove from heat; set aside.

4) Punch dough down. Turn onto a lightly floured surface; knead for 1 minute. Divide in half. Roll each half into a 12-in. x 8-in. rectangle; brush with egg. Spread half of the filling over each rectangle to within 1/2 in. of edges.

5) Roll up jelly-roll style, starting with a short side;

pinch to seal. Place each loaf seam side down in a greased 9-in. x 5-in. x 3-in. loaf pan. Cover and let rise until doubled, about 1 hour.

6) Bake at 350° for 35-40 minutes or until bread sounds hollow when tapped. Cover loosely with foil if top browns too quickly. Remove from pans to cool on a wire rack.

Yield: 2 loaves (16 slices each).

NUTRITION FACTS: 1 slice equals 160 calories, 3 g fat (2 g saturated fat), 27 mg cholesterol, 126 mg sodium, 30 g carbohydrate, 1 g fiber, 4 g protein.

Hawaiian Sweet Bread

Ruthie Banks, Pryor, Oklahoma

Pineapple juice lends to the slightly sweet flavor of this delicious bread. The recipe makes three loaves, so you can keep one and give away two.

- 7 to 7-1/2 cups all-purpose flour
- 3/4 cup mashed potato flakes
- 2/3 cup sugar
- 2 packages (1/4 ounce *each*) active dry yeast
- 1 teaspoon salt
- 1/2 teaspoon ground ginger
- 1 cup milk
- 1/2 cup water
- 1/2 cup butter, softened
- 1 cup pineapple juice
- 3 eggs
- 2 teaspoons vanilla extract

1) In a large mixing bowl, combine 3 cups flour with the next five ingredients. In a small saucepan, heat milk, water, butter and juice to 120°-130°. Add to dry ingredients; beat just until moistened. Add eggs; beat until smooth. Beat in vanilla. Stir in enough remaining flour to form a soft dough.

2) Turn onto a floured surface; knead until smooth and elastic, about 6-8 minutes. Place in a greased bowl, turning once to grease the top. Cover; let rise in a warm place until doubled, about 1-1/4 hours.

3) Punch dough down. Turn onto a lightly floured surface; divide into thirds. Shape each into a ball. Place in three greased 9-in. round baking pans. Cover; let rise until doubled, about 45 minutes.

4) Bake at 375° for 20-25 minutes or until golden brown. Cover loosely with foil if top browns too quickly. Remove from pans to wire racks to cool.

Yield: 3 loaves (12 wedges each).

NUTRITION FACTS: 1 wedge equals 146 calories, 3 g fat (2 g saturated fat), 25 mg cholesterol, 103 mg sodium, 25 g carbohydrate, 1 g fiber, 4 g protein.

Batter Breads

Batter bread is beaten with an electric mixer to help develop the gluten faster and give the bread a better texture. Because these breads are not kneaded, it is important to beat them until the batter comes away from the bowl and appears to be stringy.

Stir in the remaining flour with a sturdy wooden spoon until you have a stiff batter. Since less flour is used for batter breads, it forms a batter rather than a dough and is stickier than a kneaded dough.

Most batter breads are spooned or spread into a baking pan or dish. Push batter evenly to the edge of pan or into corners with a rubber spatula. Some batter breads can be shaped.

Follow the directions given for rising in each recipe. Batter breads rise until doubled or almost doubled—they don't rise to the top of the pan. If left to rise too long, they may fall during baking. Batter breads are best served the day they are made.

CHEESE BATTER BREAD

Cheese Batter Bread
Shirley Ramsey, Wymore, Nebraska

This bread's unique flavor is sure to become a family favorite. Slices pair well with soup and chili.

- 1 package (1/4 ounce) active dry yeast
- 1 cup warm chicken broth (110° to 115°)
- 2 tablespoons sugar
- 1 tablespoon butter
- 1/2 teaspoon salt
- 1/2 teaspoon poultry seasoning
- 1 egg, beaten
- 3 cups all-purpose flour, *divided*

- 1-1/4 cups finely shredded cheddar cheese, *divided*
- Onion salt, optional

1) In a large mixing bowl, dissolve yeast in warm broth. Add the sugar, butter, salt, poultry seasoning, egg and 1 cup of flour; beat until smooth. Add 1 cup of cheese and the remaining flour; stir for 1 minute.

2) Cover and let rise in a warm place until doubled, about 30 minutes. Stir the batter about 25 strokes. Spread evenly into a greased 9-in. x 5-in. x 3-in. loaf pan. Cover and let rise until doubled, about 20 minutes.

3) Sprinkle with the remaining cheese and onion salt if desired. Bake at 375° for 25-30 minutes or until golden brown. Remove from pan to a wire rack. Serve warm. Refrigerate leftovers.

Yield: 1 loaf (16 slices).

NUTRITION FACTS: 1 slice equals 136 calories, 4 g fat (2 g saturated fat), 25 mg cholesterol, 197 mg sodium, 20 g carbohydrate, 1 g fiber, 5 g protein.

Honey Oatmeal Bread
Janice Dancer, Williamstown, Vermont

If the kneading step in making bread is what has prevented you from baking, then try this recipe. It stirs up in no time and makes two tender loaves.

- 2 cups water, *divided*
- 1 cup rolled oats
- 1/3 cup butter, softened
- 1/3 cup honey
- 1 tablespoon salt
- 2 packages (1/2 ounce *each*) active dry yeast
- 1 egg
- 4 to 5 cups all-purpose flour, *divided*
- Melted butter, optional

1) In a small saucepan, heat 1 cup water to boiling. Stir in the oats, butter, honey and salt. Let stand until mixture cools to 110°-115°, stirring occasionally. Heat remaining water to 110°-115°.

2) In a large mixing bowl, dissolve yeast in warm water. Add the egg, oat mixture and 2 cups flour. Beat until smooth. Stir in enough remaining flour to form a stiff dough.

3) Spread batter evenly into two greased 8-in. x 4-in. x 2-in. loaf pans. Smooth tops of loaves. Cover and let rise in a warm place until doubled, about 35-40 minutes.

4) Bake at 375° for 40-45 minutes. Remove from pans to wire racks to cool. Brush with melted butter if desired.

Yield: 2 loaves (12 slices each).

NUTRITION FACTS: 1 slice equals 132 calories, 3 g fat (2 g saturated fat), 16 mg cholesterol, 325 mg sodium, 22 g carbohydrate, 1 g fiber, 3 g protein.

BLUE-RIBBON HERB ROLLS

Blue-Ribbon Herb Rolls

Mary Ann Evans, Tarpon Springs, Florida

I developed these rolls using several ideas and techniques that I picked up while learning the art of bread making. They are savory and slightly sweet, and they won a blue ribbon at a county fair.

- 2 packages (1/4 ounce *each*) active dry yeast
- 2-3/4 cups warm water (110° to 115°), *divided*
- 1/3 cup vegetable oil
- 1/4 cup honey *or* molasses
- 1 tablespoon salt
- 2 teaspoons dill weed
- 2 teaspoons dried thyme
- 2 teaspoons dried basil
- 1 teaspoon onion powder
- 1 egg, beaten
- 4 cups whole wheat flour
- 4 to 4-1/2 cups all-purpose flour

1) In a large mixing bowl, dissolve yeast in 1/2 cup warm water. Add the oil, honey, salt, seasonings, egg, whole wheat flour and remaining water. Beat until smooth. Stir in enough all-purpose flour to form a soft dough.

2) Turn onto a floured surface; knead until smooth and elastic, 6-8 minutes. Place in a greased bowl, turning once to grease top. Cover and let rise in a warm place until doubled, about 1 hour.

3) Punch dough down. Turn onto a lightly floured surface; divide into six portions. Divide each into 24 pieces. Shape each into a 1-in. ball; place three balls in each greased muffin cup. Cover and let rise until doubled, 20-25 minutes. Bake at 375° for 12-15 minutes or until tops are golden brown. Remove from pans to wire racks.

Yield: 4 dozen.

NUTRITION FACTS: 1 roll equals 94 calories, 2 g fat (trace saturated fat), 4 mg cholesterol, 150 mg sodium, 17 g carbohydrate, 2 g fiber, 3 g protein.

Brioche

Wanda Kristoffersen, Owatonna, Minnesota

At 10 o'clock every morning, it's coffee time at our house. Friends, neighbors and relatives stop by just to see what's baking in my oven.

- 3-1/2 cups all-purpose flour
- 1/2 cup sugar
- 2 packages (1/4 ounce *each*) active dry yeast
- 1 teaspoon grated lemon peel
- 1/2 teaspoon salt
- 2/3 cup butter
- 1/2 cup milk
- 5 eggs

1) In a large mixing bowl, combine 1-1/2 cups flour, sugar, yeast, lemon peel and salt. In a saucepan, heat butter and milk to 120°-130°. Add to dry ingredients; beat until moistened. Add 4 eggs; beat on medium speed for 2 minutes. Add 1 cup flour.

2) Beat until smooth. Stir in the remaining flour. Do not knead. Spoon into greased bowl. Cover; let rise in a warm place until doubled, about 1 hour. Stir dough down. Cover and refrigerate overnight.

3) Punch dough down. Turn onto a lightly floured surface. Cover with a bowl; let rest for 15 minutes. Cut one-sixth from the dough; set aside. Shape remaining dough into 12 balls (about 2-1/2 in.); place in well-greased muffin cups. Divide reserved dough into 12 small balls.

4) Make an indentation in the top of each large ball; place a small ball in each indentation. Cover and let rise in a warm place until doubled, about 1 hour. Beat remaining egg; brush over rolls. Bake at 375° for 15-20 minutes or until golden brown. Remove from pan to wire racks to cool.

Yield: 1 dozen.

NUTRITION FACTS: 1 roll equals 295 calories, 13 g fat (7 g saturated fat), 117 mg cholesterol, 234 mg sodium, 37 g carbohydrate, 1 g fiber, 7 g protein.

WHOLE WHEAT DINNER ROLLS

Whole Wheat Dinner Rolls

Ruby Williams, Bogalusa, Louisiana

I love to see our gang, right down to my great-grandchildren, reach eagerly for one of my homemade rolls. These are hearty with whole wheat and rich with old-fashioned goodness. They bake up to a beautiful golden brown.

2	packages (1/4 ounce *each*) active dry yeast
2-1/4	cups warm water (110° to 115°)
1/2	cup plus 1 tablespoon sugar
1/4	cup shortening
2	teaspoons salt
2	eggs
3	cups whole wheat flour
3-1/2	to 4 cups all-purpose flour
1/4	cup butter, melted

1) In a large mixing bowl, dissolve yeast in warm water. Add the sugar, shortening, salt, eggs and whole wheat flour. Beat until smooth. Stir in enough all-purpose flour to form a soft dough.

2) Turn onto a floured surface; knead until smooth and elastic, about 6-8 minutes. Place in a greased bowl, turning once to grease top. Cover and let rise in a warm place until doubled, about 1 hour.

3) Punch dough down. Turn onto a lightly floured surface; divide into four pieces. Shape each into 12 balls. Place 1 in. apart on greased baking sheets. Cover; let rise until doubled, about 25 minutes.

4) Bake at 375° for 11-15 minutes or until browned. Remove from pans to wire racks. Brush with melted butter. Serve warm.

Yield: 4 dozen.

NUTRITION FACTS: 1 roll equals 89 calories, 2 g fat (1 g saturated fat), 11 mg cholesterol, 111 mg sodium, 15 g carbohydrate, 1 g fiber, 2 g protein.

SHAPING DINNER ROLLS

PLAIN ROLLS
Divide dough into equal pieces as recipe directs. Shape each piece into a ball, pulling edges under to smooth top. Place 1 in. to 2 in. apart on greased baking sheets. For pan rolls, place eight balls in a greased 9-in. round baking pan or 12 balls in a greased 13-in. x 9-in. x 2-in. baking pan.

CLOVERLEAF ROLLS
Divide dough into 1-1/2-in. balls. Make each ball smooth by pulling the edges under. Place three balls smooth side up in each greased muffin cup.

S-SHAPED ROLLS
Divide dough into 2-in. balls. Shape each ball into a 10-in. rope. On a greased baking sheet, coil each end in opposite directions until it touches the center and forms an S-shape.

KNOT-SHAPED ROLLS
Divide dough into 3-in. balls. Roll each ball into a 10-in. rope; tie into a knot. Tuck and pinch ends under.

Tender Potato Rolls

Lisa Owens, Brighton, Tennessee

Filled with wonderful flavors, these rolls are a delicious accompaniment to a meal. If you like, you can shape the dough into loaves.

1	medium potato, peeled and diced
2	cups water
1	package (1/4 ounce) active dry yeast
1/4	cup honey
1	tablespoon vegetable oil
1-1/2	teaspoons salt
1	egg, lightly beaten
6	to 6-1/2 cups all-purpose flour

1) Place potato in a small saucepan and cover with water. Bring to a boil. Reduce heat; cover and cook for 10-15 minutes or until tender. Drain, reserving cooking liquid.

2) Set cooking liquid aside to cool to 110°-115°. Mash potato (don't add milk or butter); set aside. In a large mixing bowl, dissolve yeast in warm cooking liquid.

3) Add the honey, oil, salt, egg, 4 cups flour and mashed potato. Beat until smooth. Stir in enough remaining flour to form a soft dough.

4) Turn onto a floured surface; knead until smooth and elastic, about 7-8 minutes. Place in a greased bowl, turning once to grease top. Cover and let rise in a warm place until doubled, about 1 hour.

5) Punch dough down. Turn onto a lightly floured surface; divide into 36 pieces. Shape each into a ball. Place in a greased 15-in. x 10-in. x 1-in. baking pan.

6) Cover and let rise until doubled, about 30 minutes. Bake at 375° for 20-25 minutes or until golden brown. Serve warm.

Yield: 3 dozen.

NUTRITION FACTS: 1 roll equals 94 calories, 1 g fat (trace saturated fat), 6 mg cholesterol, 101 mg sodium, 19 g carbohydrate, 1 g fiber, 3 g protein.

PARKER HOUSE ROLLS

Parker House Rolls
Sandra Melnychenko, Grandview, Manitoba

These tender rolls were created at Boston's Parker House Hotel in the 1870s. The folded shape makes them unique.

> 2 packages (1/4 ounce *each*) active dry yeast
> 1 teaspoon sugar plus 6 tablespoons sugar, *divided*
> 1 cup warm water (110° to 115°), *divided*
> 1 cup warm milk (110° to 115°)
> 2 teaspoons salt
> 1 egg
> 2 tablespoons plus 2 teaspoons vegetable oil
> 5-1/2 to 6 cups all-purpose flour
> 3 tablespoons butter, melted, optional

1) In a large mixing bowl, dissolve yeast and 1 teaspoon sugar in 1/2 cup water; let stand for 5 minutes. Add the milk, salt, egg, oil and remaining sugar and water.

2) Gradually add 2 cups flour; beat until smooth. Stir in enough remaining flour to make a soft dough.

3) Turn onto a floured surface; knead until smooth and elastic, about 6-8 minutes. Place in a greased bowl, turning once to grease top. Cover and let rise in a warm place until doubled, about 45 minutes.

4) Punch dough down. Turn onto a lightly floured surface; divide in half. Roll out each piece to 1/3-in. or 1/2-in. thickness. Cut with a floured 2-1/2-in. round cutter. Brush with butter if desired.

5) Using the dull edge of a table knife, make an off-center crease in each roll. Fold along crease so the large half is on top; press along folded edge. Place 2 in. apart on greased baking sheets. Cover and let rise until doubled, about 30 minutes.

6) Bake at 375° for 10-15 minutes or until golden brown. Remove from pans to wire racks to cool.

Yield: 2-1/2 dozen.

NUTRITION FACTS: 1 roll equals 113 calories, 2 g fat (trace saturated fat), 8 mg cholesterol, 164 mg sodium, 21 g carbohydrate, 1 g fiber, 3 g protein.

FORMING PARKER HOUSE ROLLS

Roll out to 1/2-in. thickness. Cut with a floured 2-1/2-in. biscuit cutter. Brush with melted butter. Using the dull edge of a table knife, make an off-center crease in each roll. Fold along crease.

Sour Cream Fan Rolls

Carrie Ormsby, West Jordan, Utah

I received this recipe from an E-mail pen pal in Canada. The dough is so easy to work with, and it makes the lightest yeast rolls. I haven't used another white bread recipe since I started making this one.

- 2 tablespoons active dry yeast
- 1 cup warm water (110° to 115°)
- 2 tablespoons plus 1/2 cup sugar, *divided*
- 2 cups warm sour cream (110° to 115°)
- 2 eggs, lightly beaten
- 6 tablespoons butter, melted
- 1-1/2 teaspoons salt
- 1/4 teaspoon baking powder
- 7 to 8 cups all-purpose flour

1) In a bowl, dissolve yeast in warm water. Add 2 tablespoons sugar; let stand for 5 minutes. In a large mixing bowl, combine the sour cream, eggs, butter, salt and remaining sugar.

2) Stir in baking powder, yeast mixture and 4 cups of flour until smooth. Stir in enough remaining flour to form a soft dough.

3) Turn onto a floured surface; knead until smooth and elastic, about 6-8 minutes. Place in a greased bowl, turning once to grease top. Cover and let rise in a warm place until doubled, about 1 hour.

4) Punch dough down. Turn onto a lightly floured surface; divide in half. Roll each portion into a 23-in. x 9-in. rectangle.

5) Cut into 1-1/2-in. strips. Stack five strips together; cut into 1-1/2-in. pieces and place cut side up in a greased muffin cup. Cover and let rise until doubled, about 20 minutes. Bake at 350° for 20-25 minutes or until golden brown. Cool on wire racks.

Yield: about 2-1/2 dozen.

NUTRITION FACTS: 1 roll equals 182 calories, 6 g fat (3 g saturated fat), 31 mg cholesterol, 158 mg sodium, 27 g carbohydrate, 1 g fiber, 4 g protein.

Sour Cream Crescents

Judie Anglen, Riverton, Wyoming

I don't mind that my family insists on having these for holiday dinners because they can be made ahead and frozen!

- 3 teaspoons active dry yeast
- 1/3 cup warm water (110° to 115°)

- 1/2 cup sugar
- 1/2 teaspoon salt
- 1 cup butter, softened
- 1 cup (8 ounces) sour cream
- 2 eggs
- 4 cups all-purpose flour

1) In a large mixing bowl, dissolve yeast in warm water. Add the sugar, salt, butter, sour cream and eggs. Beat until smooth. Add 3 cups flour; mix well. Stir in the remaining flour. Cover and refrigerate for 6 hours or overnight.

2) Punch dough down. Turn onto a floured surface; divide into four pieces. Roll each into a 10-in. circle; cut each circle into 12 wedges.

3) Roll up wedges from the wide end and place point side down 3 in. apart on greased baking sheets. Curve ends to form a crescent. Cover and let rise in a warm place until doubled, about 1-1/2 hours. Bake at 375° for 15 minutes or until golden brown. Remove from pans to wire racks.

Yield: 4 dozen.

NUTRITION FACTS: 1 roll equals 93 calories, 5 g fat (3 g saturated fat), 22 mg cholesterol, 68 mg sodium, 10 g carbohydrate, trace fiber, 2 g protein.

CRESCENT ROLLS

Roll a portion of the dough into a 10-in. to 12-in. circle. Cut into 12-in. wedges and roll up, beginning at the wide end. Place pointed side down 2 in. apart on greased baking sheets. Curve ends to form crescent shape.

Pull-Apart Garlic Buns

Carolina Hofeldt, Lloyd, Montana

My Italian neighbor has passed along many mouth-watering recipes, including this one. The soft, tender buns are easy to pull apart.

- 2-1/2 to 3 cups all-purpose flour
- 1 tablespoon sugar
- 1 package (1/4 ounce) active dry yeast
- 1 teaspoon salt
- 1/2 cup milk
- 1/2 cup water
- 2 tablespoons shortening

1 egg
1 teaspoon paprika
1/2 teaspoon garlic powder
1/4 cup butter, melted
1 tablespoon sesame seeds

1) In a large mixing bowl, combine 1-1/2 cups flour, sugar, yeast and salt. In a saucepan, heat the milk, water and shortening to 120°-130°.

2) Add to dry ingredients; beat until moistened. Add egg; beat on medium speed for 3 minutes. Stir in enough remaining flour to form a soft dough.

3) Turn onto a floured surface; knead until smooth and elastic, about 6-8 minutes. Do not let rise. Divide into 12 pieces. Shape each into a bun. Combine paprika and garlic powder. Dip each bun in melted butter, then in paprika mixture.

4) Place 6 buns in a greased 9-in. x 5-in. x 3-in. loaf pans; sprinkle with half of the sesame seeds. Top with remaining buns and sesame seeds. Cover and let rise in a warm place until doubled, about 45 minutes. Bake at 375° for 30-35 minutes or until golden brown. Remove from pan to a wire rack to cool.

Yield: 1 loaf (12 buns).

NUTRITION FACTS: 1 bun equals 169 calories, 7 g fat (3 g saturated fat), 29 mg cholesterol, 247 mg sodium, 22 g carbohydrate, 1 g fiber, 4 g protein.

SOFT ONION BREADSTICKS

Soft Onion Breadsticks
Maryellen Hays, Wolcottville, Indiana

These versatile breadsticks bake up golden and chewy. You can try many kinds of toppings in addition to sesame and poppy seeds.

3/4 cup chopped onion
1 tablespoon vegetable oil

2-1/4 teaspoons active dry yeast
1/2 cup warm water (110° to 115°)
1/2 cup warm milk (110° to 115°)
1/4 cup butter, softened
1 tablespoon sugar
1-1/2 teaspoons salt
2 eggs
3-1/2 to 4 cups all-purpose flour
2 tablespoons cold water
2 tablespoons sesame seeds
1 tablespoon poppy seeds

1) In a skillet, saute onion in oil until tender; cool. In a large mixing bowl, dissolve yeast in warm water. Add the milk, 1 egg, butter, sugar, salt, 1 egg and 1 cup flour. Beat on medium speed for 2 minutes.

2) Stir in onion and enough remaining flour to form a soft dough. Turn onto a floured surface; knead until smooth and elastic, 6-8 minutes.

3) Place in a greased bowl, turning once to grease top. Cover and let rise in a warm place until doubled, about 1 hour.

4) Punch dough down. Let stand for 10 minutes. Turn onto a lightly floured surface; divide into 32 pieces. Shape each piece into an 8-in. rope. Place 2 in. apart on greased baking sheets. Cover and let rise for 15 minutes.

5) Beat cold water and remaining egg; brush over breadsticks. Sprinkle half with sesame seeds and half with poppy seeds. Bake at 350° for 16-22 minutes or until golden brown. Remove to wire racks.

Yield: 32 breadsticks.

NUTRITION FACTS: 1 breadstick equals 81 calories, 3 g fat (1 g saturated fat), 18 mg cholesterol, 132 mg sodium, 12 g carbohydrate, 1 g fiber, 2 g protein.

■ *GARLIC PARMESAN BREADSTICKS:* Prepare the recipe as directed except omit brushing with the egg mixture and sprinkling with sesame and poppy seeds. Brush with 1/4 cup melted butter and sprinkle with garlic salt and grated Parmesan cheese. Bake as directed.

SHAPING BREADSTICKS

Divide dough as recipe directs. Shape each piece into a ball. Roll each ball back and forth with both hands until they are shaped into a rope.

RASPBERRY COFFEE CAKES

Sweet Yeast Breads

Sweet yeast breads fall into two basic categories: sweet loaves and sweet rolls. The dough can be made by hand or in a bread machine.

Sweet breads include fruit-filled breads and a variety of coffee cakes. Sweet rolls refer to fruit-filled rolls, sticky buns, cinnamon rolls, doughnuts, kolaches and individual Danishes.

After punching down the dough, let it rest for 10 minutes. This allows the dough to relax, which makes it easier to roll out.

Roll up dough firmly. If it's too loose, you'll see air pockets or large gaps when cut. If it's too tight, the bread will crack.

A simple way to slice cinnamon rolls or sticky buns is to place a piece of unflavored dental floss or heavy-duty thread under the rolled dough, 1 in. from the end. Bring the floss up around the dough and cross it over the top, cutting through the dough and filling. Repeat at 1-in. intervals.

Evenly space the cut rolls in the pan, leaving room around each to allow for the final rising.

Raspberry Coffee Cakes
Mary Bergman, Navarra, Spain

My husband and I and our three children are missionaries in northern Spain. Special treats like this flavorful swirled bread are truly a taste of home for us. With a creamy, fruity filling and sweet glaze, it's hard to eat just one slice.

- 1   tablespoon active dry yeast
- 1/3 cup warm water (110° to 115°)
- 1/2 cup warm sour cream (110° to 115°)
- 1/4 cup butter, melted
- 1/4 cup sugar
- 1   teaspoon salt
- 1   egg
- 2-1/4 to 2-1/2 cups all-purpose flour

FILLING:
- 1   package (8 ounces) cream cheese, softened
- 1   egg
- 1/2 cup sugar
- 1   teaspoon vanilla extract
- 1/8 teaspoon salt
- 1/2 cup raspberry jam

GLAZE:
- 1-1/4 cups confectioners' sugar
- 1   teaspoon vanilla extract
- 2   tablespoons milk

1) In a large bowl, dissolve yeast in warm water. Stir in sour cream, butter, sugar, salt and egg. Stir in enough flour to form a soft dough.

2) Turn onto a floured surface; knead 20 times or until smooth. Place in a greased bowl, turning once to grease top. Cover and let rise in a warm place until doubled, about 1-1/4 hours.

3) In a small mixing bowl, beat the cream cheese, egg, sugar, vanilla and salt until smooth; set aside. Punch dough down. Turn onto a lightly floured surface; divide in half.

4) Roll each piece into a 12-in. x 8-in. rectangle. Spread filling to within 1/2 in. of edges. Spoon jam lengthwise over half of the filling. Roll up jelly-roll style, starting with the long side with the jam. Pinch seams to seal; tuck ends under.

5) Place loaves seam side down on a greased baking sheet. With a sharp knife, cut shallow slashes across the top of each. Cover and let rise until doubled, about 30 minutes.

6) Bake at 375° for 15-20 minutes or until golden brown. Remove from pan to a wire rack. Combine glaze ingredients; drizzle over warm coffee cakes.

Yield: 2 loaves (10 slices each).

NUTRITION FACTS: 1 slice equals 212 calories, 8 g fat (5 g saturated fat), 44 mg cholesterol, 200 mg sodium, 32 g carbohydrate, 1 g fiber, 3 g protein.

■ *PEACH COFFEE CAKE:* Use a 1/2 cup of peach preserves for the raspberry jam.

REHEATING COFFEE CAKES

If you make a coffee cake in advance but want fresh-from-the-oven flavor when you serve it to guests, try this trick. Wrap an unfrosted coffee cake in foil. Reheat at 350° for a few minutes or until warm.

APRICOT TEA RINGS

Apricot Tea Rings

Dot Christiansen, Bettendorf, Iowa

This coffee cake is a favorite of mine. It's attractive, delicious and cuts like a dream. Sometimes I use canned pie filling when I'm pressed for time.

4-1/4   cups all-purpose flour
1/4   cup sugar
2   packages (1/4 ounce *each*) active dry yeast
1   teaspoon salt
1/4   teaspoon ground nutmeg
1   cup milk
1/4   cup water
1/4   cup butter, cubed
2   eggs

FILLING:
12   ounces dried apricots, diced
2   cups water
6   tablespoons brown sugar
4   teaspoons orange juice
1/2   cup chopped pecans

GLAZE:
1   cup confectioners' sugar
2   to 3 tablespoons milk

1) In a large mixing bowl, combine the flour, sugar, yeast, salt and nutmeg. In a saucepan, heat the milk, water and butter to 120°-130°. Add to dry ingredients; beat until moistened. Beat in eggs until smooth. Cover and refrigerate overnight.

2) In a saucepan, combine the apricots and water. Cook over medium heat for 30 minutes or until the water is absorbed and apricots are tender. Remove from the heat; stir in the brown sugar, juice and nuts. Cool.

3) Punch dough down. Turn onto a lightly floured surface; divide in half. Roll each into an 18-in. x 12-in. rectangle.

4) Spread half of the filling over each rectangle to within 1/2 in. of edges. Roll up each jelly-roll style, starting with a long side; pinch seam to seal. Place seam side down on greased baking sheets; pinch ends of each together to form a ring.

5) With scissors, cut each from outside edge two-thirds toward center of ring at 1 in. intervals. Separate strips slightly; twist so filling shows, slightly overlapping with previous piece. Cover and let rise in a warm place until doubled, about 1 hour.

6) Bake at 375° for 25-28 minutes or until golden brown. Remove from pans to wire racks to cool. Combine glaze ingredients; drizzle over warm tea rings.

Yield: 2 rings (12 slices each).

NUTRITION FACTS: 1 slice equals 205 calories, 5 g fat (2 g saturated fat), 24 mg cholesterol, 132 mg sodium, 37 g carbohydrate, 2 g fiber, 4 g protein.

SHAPING A COFFEE CAKE RING

1) Roll into a rectangle. Spread filling evenly over dough to within 1/2 in. of edges. Roll up jelly-roll style, starting with a long side; pinch seam to seal.

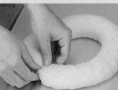
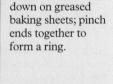

2) Place seam side down on greased baking sheets; pinch ends together to form a ring.

3) With scissors, cut from outside edge to two-thirds of the way toward center of ring at 1-in. intervals.

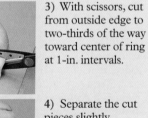

4) Separate the cut pieces slightly, twisting each individually to allow filling to show.

Orange Bubble Bread

Cyndie Wowchuk, Saskatoon, Saskatchewan

This sweet version of bubble bread is dotted with raisins and topped with an orange glaze. My great-aunt shared the recipe with me.

- 1 package (1/4 ounce) active dry yeast
- 1 teaspoon plus 1/4 cup sugar, *divided*
- 1 cup warm milk (110° to 115°)
- 3-1/2 to 4 cups all-purpose flour
- 1 teaspoon salt
- 1/2 cup cold butter
- 2 eggs, lightly beaten

ORANGE SYRUP:

- 3/4 cup orange juice
- 3/4 cup orange marmalade
- 4 to 5 tablespoons sugar
- 2 tablespoons plus 1 teaspoon butter
- 3/4 teaspoon grated orange peel
- 1 cup flaked coconut, toasted, divided
- 1/2 cup golden raisins

1) In a small bowl, dissolve yeast and 1 teaspoon sugar in warm milk; set aside. In a large bowl, combine 3-1/2 cups flour, salt and remaining sugar.

2) Cut in butter until crumbly. Stir in eggs. Stir in yeast mixture and enough remaining flour until mixture forms a firm ball (mixture will be slightly sticky).

3) Turn onto a floured surface; knead until smooth and elastic, about 6-8 minutes. Place in a greased bowl, turning once to grease top. Cover and let rise in a warm place until doubled, about 1-1/4 hours.

4) Meanwhile, for syrup, combine the orange juice, marmalade, sugar, butter and orange peel in a saucepan. Cook and stir until mixture comes to a boil. Reduce heat; simmer, uncovered, for 5 minutes. Cool to room temperature. Place 1/2 cup syrup and 1/2 cup coconut on the bottom of a greased 10-in. tube pan.

5) Punch dough down. Turn onto a lightly floured surface; divide into 32 pieces. Roll each into a 1-in. ball. Dip each into remaining orange syrup.

6) Place 16 balls in prepared pan. Sprinkle with half of the raisins and 1/4 cup coconut. Top with remaining balls, raisins and coconut. Cover and let rise until doubled, about 45 minutes.

7) Bake at 350° for 40-50 minutes or until golden brown. Cool for 5 minutes before inverting bread onto a serving plate.

Yield: 1 loaf (16 servings).

NUTRITION FACTS: 2 balls equal 294 calories, 11 g fat (7 g saturated fat), 48 mg cholesterol, 263 mg sodium, 46 g carbohydrate, 1 g fiber, 5 g protein.

Cherry Cheese Loaves

Carolyn Gregory, Hendersonville, Tennessee

This has become my "trademark" dessert. I'm asked to take it everywhere I go! Diagonal cuts in the dough give this coffee cake a pretty look without the extra work of braiding it.

- 2 packages (1/4 ounce *each*) active dry yeast
- 1/2 cup warm water (110° to 115°)
- 1 cup (8 ounces) sour cream
- 1/2 cup butter, cubed
- 1/2 cup sugar
- 2 eggs
- 4 cups all-purpose flour

FILLING:

- 2 packages (one 8 ounces, one 3 ounces) cream cheese, softened
- 1/2 cup sugar
- 1 egg
- 1 teaspoon almond extract
- 1 can (21 ounces) cherry pie filling

GLAZE:

- 2 cups confectioners' sugar
- 1/4 cup milk
- 1 teaspoon almond extract

1) In a large mixing bowl, dissolve yeast in warm water. In a saucepan, heat sour cream and butter to 110°-115°. Add to yeast mixture. Add sugar and eggs; mix well. Gradually add flour; mix well. Do not knead. Cover and refrigerate overnight.

2) For filling, in a small mixing bowl, beat the cream cheese, sugar, egg and extract until smooth; set aside. Turn dough onto a lightly floured surface; divide into four portions. Roll each into a 12-in. x 8-in. rectangle.

3) Spread a fourth of the cream cheese mixture down the center of each rectangle. Spoon a fourth

of the pie filling over the cream cheese. Fold lengthwise into thirds; pinch side seam and ends to seal. Place seam side down on greased baking sheets.

4) With a sharp scissors, make several 1-in. diagonal cuts near the center of loaves. Cover and let rise in a warm place until doubled, about 1 hour.

5) Bake at 375° for 20-25 minutes or until lightly browned. Combine glaze ingredients; drizzle over warm loaves. Cool on wire racks. Refrigerate leftovers.

Yield: 4 loaves (10 slices each).

NUTRITION FACTS: 1 slice equals 173 calories, 7 g fat (4 g saturated fat), 35 mg cholesterol, 58 mg sodium, 25 g carbohydrate, 1 g fiber, 3 g protein.

LEMON-TWIST LOAVES

Lemon-Twist Loaves
Audrey Thibodeau, Mesa, Arizona

This mouth-watering bread has a tangy twist and pretty glaze.

2 cups warm water (110° to 115°)
2 packages (1/4 ounce *each*) active dry yeast
3 cups sugar, *divided*
1 cup butter, melted and cooled, *divided*
3/4 teaspoon salt

1 egg
1 egg yolk
7 cups all-purpose flour
1 cup sliced almonds, chopped
3 tablespoons grated lemon peel

GLAZE:
3 cups confectioners' sugar
3 tablespoons grated lemon peel
1 teaspoon lemon extract
3 to 4 tablespoons milk
1 cup sliced almonds, toasted

1) In a large mixing bowl, dissolve yeast in 1/2 cup warm water. Add 1 cup sugar, 1/2 cup butter, salt, egg, egg yolk and remaining water. Beat until blended. Add 4 cups flour. Beat until smooth. Stir in enough remaining flour to form a soft dough.

2) Turn onto a floured surface; knead until smooth and elastic, 6-8 minutes. Place in a greased bowl, turning over once to grease top. Cover and refrigerate for 8 hours.

3) Punch dough down. Turn onto a lightly floured surface; divide into thirds. Roll each piece into a 16-in. x 10-in. rectangle. Spread remaining melted butter over dough.

4) Combine the chopped almonds, lemon peel and remaining sugar; sprinkle over butter. Roll up jelly-roll style, starting with a long side; pinch seams and ends to seal. Place seam side down on greased baking sheets.

5) With a knife, cut loaves in half lengthwise to within 1 in. of one end. Holding the uncut end, loosely twist strips together. Cover and let rise until doubled, about 1-1/2 hours.

6) Bake at 350° for 25-30 minutes until bread sounds hollow when tapped. Remove from pans to wire racks.

7) Combine the confectioners' sugar, lemon peel, extract and enough milk to achieve spreading consistency; spread over warm bread. Sprinkle with toasted almonds.

Yield: 3 loaves (12 slices each).

NUTRITION FACTS: 1 slice equals 274 calories, 8 g fat (4 g saturated fat), 26 mg cholesterol, 104 mg sodium, 47 g carbohydrate, 1 g fiber, 4 g protein.

APPLE LADDER LOAF

Apple Ladder Loaf
Norma Foster, Compton, Illinois

This pretty filled bread makes a nice breakfast pastry or a lovely dessert with a scoop of ice cream.

  2 **packages (1/4 ounce *each*) active dry yeast**
1/4 **cup warm water (110° to 115°)**
1/2 **cup warm milk (110° to 115°)**
1/2 **cup butter, softened**
1/3 **cup sugar**
  1 **teaspoon salt**
  4 **eggs**
4-1/2 **to 4-3/4 cups all-purpose flour**

FILLING:

1/4 **cup butter, softened**
1/3 **cup packed brown sugar**
  2 **tablespoons all-purpose flour**
1-1/4 **teaspoons ground cinnamon**
1/2 **teaspoon ground nutmeg**
1/8 **teaspoon ground allspice**
  4 **cups thinly sliced peeled tart apples**

ICING:

  1 **cup confectioners' sugar**
  1 **to 2 tablespoons orange juice**
1/4 **teaspoon vanilla extract**

1) In a large mixing bowl, dissolve yeast in water. Add the milk, butter, sugar, salt, eggs and 2 cups flour. Beat on low speed for 3 minutes. Stir in enough remaining flour to form a soft dough.

2) Turn onto a lightly floured surface; knead until smooth and elastic, about 6-8 minutes. Place in a greased bowl, turning once to grease top. Cover and refrigerate for 1-2 hours; punch dough down. Cover and refrigerate overnight.

3) Punch dough down. Turn onto a lightly floured surface; divide in half. Roll each half into a 12-in. x 9-in. rectangle. Place each on a greased baking sheet. Spread with 1/4 cup butter.

4) For filling, combine the brown sugar, flour, cinnamon, nutmeg and allspice in a large bowl; add apples and toss to coat. Spread filling down center third of each rectangle.

5) On each long side, cut 1-in.-wide strips about 3 in. into the center. Starting at one end, fold alternating strips at an angle across filling; seal ends. Cover and let rise until nearly doubled, about 45-60 minutes.

6) Bake at 350° for 30-40 minutes or until golden brown. Combine icing ingredients until smooth; drizzle over warm loaves. Serve warm or at room temperature.

Yield: 2 loaves (10 slices each).

NUTRITION FACTS: 1 slice equals 250 calories, 8 g fat (5 g saturated fat), 62 mg cholesterol, 205 mg sodium, 39 g carbohydrate, 1 g fiber, 5 g protein.

BRAIDING A FILLED BREAD

1) Spread filling down center of rectangle. On each long side, cut 1-in.-wide strips, about 1/2 in. from filling.

2) Starting at one end, fold alternating strips at an angle across filling. Seal ends.

Apricot Cheese Danish
Florence Schafer, Jackson, Minnesota

It's easy to offer your family a fresh-from-the-oven morning treat with this recipe. You mix it up at night, then just roll it out and bake the next morning.

  1 **package (1/4 ounce) active dry yeast**
1/4 **cup warm water (110° to 115°)**
  3 **tablespoons sugar**

1/2 cup butter, softened
2 eggs
1/2 cup sour cream
1/4 teaspoon salt
3 cups all-purpose flour

FILLING:
2 packages (8 ounces *each*) cream cheese, softened
1/2 cup sugar
2 egg yolks
2 teaspoons vanilla extract
1/4 cup apricot preserves
Confectioners' sugar

1) In a large mixing bowl, dissolve yeast in water. Add the sugar, butter, eggs and sour cream. Gradually add salt and 2 cups flour; beat until smooth. Stir in remaining flour (the dough will be soft and sticky). Place in a greased bowl. Cover and refrigerate overnight.

2) Punch dough down. Turn onto a lightly floured surface; knead 2-3 times. Divide in half. Roll each half into a 16-in. x 10-in. oval; place on greased baking sheets.

3) For filling, in a large mixing bowl, combine the cream cheese, sugar, egg yolks and vanilla; beat until smooth. Spread 1-1/4 cups filling over each oval to within 1 in. of edges. Fold longest side over filling; pinch edges to seal. Cover and let rise in a warm place until doubled, about 1 hour.

4) Bake at 375° for 20-22 minutes or until golden brown. Remove from pans to wire racks to cool. Spread preserves on top. Dust with confectioners' sugar. Store in the refrigerator.

Yield: 2 loaves (12 slices each).

NUTRITION FACTS: 1 slice equals 209 calories, 12 g fat (7 g saturated fat), 70 mg cholesterol, 129 mg sodium, 21 g carbohydrate, 1 g fiber, 4 g protein.

Cranberry Kuchen
Linda Bright, Wichita, Kansas

This German coffee cake has been served at family breakfasts for more than five generations. There is no recipe requested more by our large family.

2 packages (1/4 ounce *each*) active dry yeast
1/4 cup warm water (110° to 115°)
1 cup warm milk (110° to 115°)
1/4 cup butter, softened
1/4 cup sugar

1 teaspoon salt
1 egg
3-1/2 to 4 cups all-purpose flour

CRANBERRY SAUCE:
2 cups water
1-1/2 cups sugar
4 cups fresh *or* frozen cranberries

EGG MIXTURE:
8 eggs
3/4 cup evaporated milk
3/4 cup sugar

TOPPING:
2 cups all-purpose flour
2 cups sugar
1 cup cold butter

1) In a large mixing bowl, dissolve yeast in a warm water. Add the milk, butter, sugar, salt, egg and 2 cups flour. Beat until smooth.

2) Stir in enough remaining flour to form a soft dough. Do not knead. Cover and let rise in a warm place until doubled, about 1 hour.

3) For cranberry sauce, in a saucepan, bring water and sugar to a boil. Add cranberries. Reduce heat; cover and simmer for 10 minutes. Remove from the heat; set aside.

4) For egg mixture, in a bowl, combine the eggs, evaporated milk and sugar; beat well. Divide half of the egg mixture between two greased 13-in. x 9-in. x 2-in. baking pans; set remaining egg mixture aside.

5) Punch dough down. Divide in half. Pat each portion over egg mixture in pans. Spoon cranberry sauce over dough. Drizzle with remaining egg mixture.

6) For topping, combine flour and sugar in a bowl. Cut in butter until crumbly; sprinkle over the top.

7) Bake at 350° for 25-30 minutes or until lightly browned. Cool on a wire rack. Serve warm.

Yield: 2 kuchens (12 slices each).

NUTRITION FACTS: 1 slice equal 387 calories, 13 g fat (7 g saturated fat), 109 mg cholesterol, 232 mg sodium, 63 g carbohydrate, 2 g fiber, 7 g protein.

Almond Croissants

Patricia Glass, East Wenatchee, Washington

These tender croissants are a little lighter than others. The subtle flavor of almond pairs well with a cup of hot coffee or a glass of cold milk.

- 1 package (1/4 ounce) active dry yeast
- 1/4 cup warm water (110° to 115°)
- 4 cups all-purpose flour
- 1/4 cup sugar
- 1 teaspoon salt
- 1 cup cold butter
- 3/4 cup warm milk (110° to 115°)
- 3 egg yolks

FILLING:
- 1/2 cup almond paste
- 1 egg white
- 1/4 cup confectioners' sugar

EGG WASH:
- 1 egg white
- 1 tablespoon water
- 1/4 cup sliced almonds

1) In a bowl, dissolve yeast in warm water. In a large bowl, combine the flour, sugar and salt. Cut in butter until crumbly. Add milk and egg yolks to yeast mixture; mix well. Stir into flour mixture; mix well. Do not knead. Cover and refrigerate overnight.

2) In a mixing bowl, beat filling ingredients until smooth. Punch dough down. Turn dough onto a lightly floured surface; divide in half. Roll each piece into a 12-in. circle; cut each circle into eight wedges. Spread filling over wedges; roll up from wide end.

3) Place with point side down 3 in. apart on ungreased baking sheets. Curve ends to form a crescent shape. Cover and let rise in a warm place for 1 hour (dough will not double).

4) Beat egg white and water; brush over croissants. Sprinkle with almonds. Bake at 350° for 15-20 minutes. Remove from pans to wire racks to cool.

Yield: 16 rolls.

NUTRITION FACTS: 1 roll equals 296 calories, 16 g fat (8 g saturated fat), 72 mg cholesterol, 278 mg sodium, 33 g carbohydrate, 1 g fiber, 6 g protein.

CINNAMON CRISPS

Cinnamon Crisps

Sarah Bueckert, Austin, Manitoba

Are they a cookie or a bread? Either way, these crispy treats are tasty and delicious. They make a great gift for a housewarming or holiday.

- 4 cups all-purpose flour
- 1 package (1/4 ounce) active dry yeast
- 1-1/4 cups warm milk (120° to 130°)
- 1/4 cup shortening
- 1/4 cup sugar
- 1 teaspoon salt
- 1 egg

FILLING:
- 1/2 cup packed brown sugar
- 1/2 cup sugar
- 1/4 cup butter, melted
- 1 teaspoon ground cinnamon

TOPPING:
- 1 cup sugar
- 1 teaspoon ground cinnamon
- 1/2 cup chopped pecans
- 1/4 cup butter, melted

1) In a large mixing bowl, combine 2 cups flour and yeast. Combine the milk, shortening, sugar and salt; add to flour mixture and beat for 1 minute.

2) Add egg; beat on low speed for 1 minute. Beat on medium for 3 minutes. Stir in enough remaining flour to form a soft dough.

3) Turn onto a floured surface; knead until smooth and elastic, about 6-8 minutes. Place in a greased bowl, turning once to grease top. Cover and let rise in a warm place until doubled, about 1 hour.

4) Meanwhile, combine filling ingredients and set aside. For topping, combine sugar, cinnamon and pecans; set aside. Punch dough down. Turn onto a lightly floured surface; divide in half.

5) Roll each piece into a 12-in. square. Spread each with half of the filling. Roll up tightly jelly-roll style and pinch to seal.

6) Cut into 1-in. slices and place on greased baking sheets (four slices per sheet). Cover with waxed paper; flatten slices with palm of hand into 3-in. circles. Cover and let rise until doubled, about 30 minutes. Cover with waxed paper and flatten or roll to 5-in. diameter.

7) Brush with butter; sprinkle with topping. Cover with waxed paper; roll or flatten again. Discard waxed paper. Bake at 400° for 10-12 minutes or until browned.

Yield: 2 dozen.

NUTRITION FACTS: 1 crisp equals 231 calories, 8 g fat (3 g saturated fat), 21 mg cholesterol, 148 mg sodium, 36 g carbohydrate, 1 g fiber, 3 g protein.

GLAZED DOUGHNUTS

Glazed Doughnuts
Pat Siebenaler, Westminster, Colorado

The coffee-flavored glaze on these moist and tasty doughnuts makes them a perfect way to start off a morning. They're also good with a cinnamon-sugar topping.

2 packages (1/4 ounce *each*) active dry yeast
1/4 cup warm water (110° to 115°)
2 cups warm milk (110° to 115°)
1/2 cup butter

1 cup hot mashed potatoes (without added milk and butter)
3 eggs
1/2 teaspoon lemon extract, optional
1 cup sugar
1-1/2 teaspoons salt
1/2 teaspoon ground cinnamon
9-1/4 to 9-3/4 cups all-purpose flour

COFFEE GLAZE:
6 to 8 tablespoons cold milk
1 tablespoon instant coffee granules
2 teaspoons vanilla extract
3/4 cup butter, softened
6 cups confectioners' sugar
1/2 teaspoon ground cinnamon
Dash salt
Oil for deep-fat frying

1) In a large mixing bowl, dissolve yeast in warm water. Add the milk, butter, potatoes, eggs and extract if desired. Add the sugar, salt, cinnamon and 3 cups flour. Beat until smooth.

2) Stir in enough remaining flour to form a soft dough. Cover and let rise in a warm place until doubled, about 1 hour.

3) Stir down dough. On a well-floured surface, roll out to 1/2-in. thickness. Cut with a floured 2-1/2-in. doughnut cutter. Place on greased baking sheets; cover and let rise for 45 minutes.

4) Meanwhile, for glaze, combine 6 tablespoons milk, coffee and vanilla; stir to dissolve coffee. In a mixing bowl, beat the butter, sugar, cinnamon and salt. Gradually add milk mixture; beat until smooth, adding additional milk to make a dipping consistency.

5) In an electric skillet or deep-fat fryer, heat oil to 375°. Fry doughnuts, a few at a time, about 1-1/2 minutes per side or until golden. Drain on paper towels. Dip tops in glaze while warm.

Yield: about 4 dozen.

NUTRITION FACTS: 1 doughnut equals 231 calories, 7 g fat (3 g saturated fat), 28 mg cholesterol, 137 mg sodium, 39 g carbohydrate, 1 g fiber, 4 g protein.

■ *CINNAMON-SUGAR DOUGHNUTS:* Prepare recipe as directed except omit the glaze. Gently roll the warm doughnuts in a mixture of 2 cups sugar and 1 teaspoon ground cinnamon.

CARAMEL-PECAN STICKY BUNS

Caramel-Pecan Sticky Buns
Judy Powell, Star, Idaho

My mother used to make delicious cinnamon rolls when I was a child. Later, she taught my sister and me to make them. I've since added the caramel and pecans. These scrumptious buns are a huge hit wherever I take them.

- 1   package (1/4 ounce) active dry yeast
- 3/4 cup warm water (110° to 115°)
- 3/4 cup warm milk (110° to 115°)
- 1/4 cup sugar
- 3   tablespoons vegetable oil
- 2   teaspoons salt
- 3-3/4 to 4-1/4 cups all-purpose flour

FILLING:
- 1/4 cup butter, softened
- 1/4 cup sugar
- 3   teaspoons ground cinnamon
- 3/4 cup packed brown sugar
- 1/2 cup heavy whipping cream
- 1   cup coarsely chopped pecans

1) In a large mixing bowl, dissolve yeast in warm water. Add the milk, sugar, oil, salt and 1-1/4 cups flour. Beat on medium speed for 2-3 minutes or until smooth. Stir in enough remaining flour to form a soft dough.

2) Turn onto a floured surface; knead until smooth and elastic, about 6-8 minutes. Place in a greased bowl, turning once to grease top. Cover and let rise in a warm place until doubled, about 1 hour.

3) Punch dough down. Turn onto a lightly floured surface. Roll into an 18-in. x 12-in. rectangle. Spread butter to within 1/2 in. of edges. Combine sugar and cinnamon; sprinkle over butter. Roll up jelly-roll style, starting with a long side; pinch seam to seal. Cut into 12 slices.

4) Combine brown sugar and cream; pour into a greased 13-in. x 9-in. x 2-in. baking pan. Sprinkle with pecans. Place the rolls cut side down over pecans. Cover and let rise until doubled, about 1 hour.

5) Bake at 350° for 30-35 minutes or until well browned. Cool for 1 minute before inverting onto a serving platter.

Yield: 1 dozen.

NUTRITION FACTS: 1 bun equals 405 calories, 19 g fat (6 g saturated fat), 26 mg cholesterol, 450 mg sodium, 55 g carbohydrate, 2 g fiber, 6 g protein.

SHAPING CINNAMON ROLLS AND STICKY BUNS

1) Roll dough into a rectangle. Spread or brush with butter; sprinkle with filling. Roll up, starting from a long end, and pinch seam to seal.

2) Slice into rolls. Place cut side down in a greased baking pan.

3) Cover and let rise until doubled. Rolls will begin to touch each other.

4) After baking, combine glaze ingredients if desired; spoon in a thin stream over warm rolls.

Chocolate Pinwheel Bread
Dawn Onuffer, Freeport, Florida

This swirled yeast bread is chock-full of chocolate chips. The sweet slices don't need any butter. Keep one loaf for your family and share the other with a neighbor.

- 1 package (1/4 ounce) active dry yeast
- 1 cup warm milk (110° to 115°)
- 1/4 cup sugar
- 1 teaspoon salt
- 2 eggs
- 4 ounces cream cheese, softened
- 4 to 4-1/2 cups bread flour

FILLING:
- 4 ounces cream cheese, softened
- 1/2 cup confectioners' sugar
- 2 tablespoons baking cocoa
- 1 cup (6 ounces) semisweet chocolate chips
- 1 egg, beaten

1) In a large mixing bowl, dissolve yeast in warm milk. Add the sugar, salt, eggs, cream cheese and 2 cups flour; beat until smooth. Stir in enough remaining flour to form a soft dough.

2) Turn onto a floured surface; knead until smooth and elastic, about 6-8 minutes. Place in a greased bowl, turning once to grease top. Cover and let rise in a warm place until doubled, about 1 hour.

3) Punch dough down. Turn onto a floured surface; divide in half. Roll each portion into a 12-in. x 8-in. rectangle. In a small mixing bowl, beat cream cheese, confectioners' sugar and cocoa until smooth. Spread over each rectangle to within 1/2 in. of edges. Sprinkle with chocolate chips.

4) Roll up jelly-roll style, starting with a short side; pinch seam to seal. Place seam side down in two greased 9-in. x 5-in. x 3-in. loaf pans. Cover and let rise until doubled, about 45 minutes.

5) Brush tops of loaves with egg. Bake at 350° for 25 minutes. Cover loosely with foil. Bake 15-20 minutes longer or until loaves sound hollow when tapped. Remove from pans to wire racks to cool.

Yield: 2 loaves (16 slices each).

NUTRITION FACTS: 1 slice equals 127 calories, 5 g fat (3 g saturated fat), 29 mg cholesterol, 105 mg sodium, 19 g carbohydrate, 1 g fiber, 4 g protein.

Danish Kringle
Jeanne Hardaker, Quicksburg, Virginia

Everyone agrees that no store-bought kringle can top my version. The nut filling and sweet glaze give this spectacular coffee cake great flavor.

- 2 cups all-purpose flour
- 1 tablespoon sugar
- 1/2 teaspoon salt
- 1/2 cup cold butter
- 1 package (1/4 ounce) active dry yeast
- 1/4 cup warm water (110° to 115°)
- 1/2 cup warm milk (110° to 115°)
- 1 egg, beaten

FILLING:
- 1-1/2 cups finely chopped pecans
- 1 cup packed brown sugar
- 1/2 cup butter, softened

GLAZE:
- 1 cup confectioners' sugar
- 4 teaspoons water
- 1/2 teaspoon vanilla extract
- 2 tablespoons chopped pecans

1) In a large mixing bowl, combine the flour, sugar and salt; cut in butter until mixture resembles fine crumbs. Dissolve yeast in warm water; stir into flour mixture with warm milk and egg. Beat until smooth (dough will be very soft). Cover; refrigerate at least 2 hours but not more than 24 hours.

2) Punch dough down. Divide dough in half; refrigerate one half. On a well-floured surface, roll remaining half into a 15-in. x 6-in. rectangle.

3) Combine filling ingredients. Spread half of the filling down center of rectangle in a 2-in. strip. Fold sides of dough over filling; overlapping 1-1/2-in.; pinch edges to seal. Shape into an oval; pinch ends together.

4) Place seam side down on a greased 15-in. x 10-in. x 1-in. baking pan. Repeat with remaining dough and filling. Cover and let rise in a warm place for 30 minutes.

5) Bake at 375° for 20-25 minutes or until golden brown. Cool for 15 minutes. Combine the confectioners' sugar, water and vanilla; spread over the kringles. Sprinkle with nuts.

Yield: 2 kringles (10 slices each).

NUTRITION FACTS: 1 slice equals 268 calories, 17 g fat (6 g saturated fat), 36 mg cholesterol, 162 mg sodium, 29 g carbohydrate, 1 g fiber, 3 g protein.

German Stollen
Christin Dupee, Chesterfield, Virginia

I traditionally bake three of these flavorful favorites just before Thanksgiving to enjoy on Christmas and New Year's, too.

8-1/2 to 9 cups all-purpose flour
1 cup plus 2 tablespoons sugar *divided*
2 packages (1/4 ounce *each*) active dry yeast
2 teaspoons salt
2 cups milk
1-3/4 cups butter, softened, *divided*
4 eggs
1-1/2 teaspoons almond extract
1 teaspoon grated lemon peel
1 teaspoon rum extract, optional
1-1/2 cups slivered almonds
1 cup *each* red candied cherries, candied lemon peel and candied orange peel
1 cup raisins

GLAZE:
1 cup confectioners' sugar
1/4 teaspoon vanilla extract
2 to 3 tablespoons milk

1) In a large mixing bowl, combine 3 cups flour, 1 cup sugar, yeast and salt. In a saucepan, heat the milk and 1-1/2 cups butter to 120°-130°. Add to dry ingredients; beat just until moistened.

2) Beat in eggs until smooth. Stir in enough remaining flour to form a soft dough. Add the almond extract, lemon peel and rum extract if desired. Stir in the almonds, cherries, candied peels and raisins (dough will be slightly sticky).

3) Turn onto a heavily floured surface; knead until smooth and elastic, about 6-8 minutes. Place in a greased bowl, turning once to grease top. Cover and let rise in a warm place until almost doubled, about 1-1/2 hours.

4) Punch dough down; turn onto a lightly floured surface. Divide into thirds. Roll each portion into a 15-in. x 8-in. oval. Melt remaining butter. Brush each oval with 1 tablespoon butter and sprinkle with 2 teaspoons of the remaining sugar.

5) Fold a long side of oval to within 1/2 in. of the opposite side; press edges lightly to seal. Place in parchment-lined or lightly greased baking sheets.

Curve ends slightly. Cover and let rise for 30 minutes.

6) Bake at 350° for 30-35 minutes or until golden brown. Brush with remaining melted butter; remove from pans to wire racks to cool. Combine the glaze ingredients; drizzle over stollen.

Yield: 3 loaves (12 slices each).

NUTRITION FACTS: 1 slice equals 327 calories, 12 g fat (6 g saturated fat), 49 mg cholesterol, 263 mg sodium, 49 g carbohydrate, 2 g fiber, 6 g protein.

NUT-FILLED BUTTERHORNS

Nut-Filled Butterhorns
Michael Engerson, Hustisford, Wisconsin

These rich, flaky butterhorns were made on Good Friday morning or Christmas Eve morning when I was growing up. We used them to celebrate the joy of family and friends coming together. They're so special, they're worth the bit of extra effort.

3 packages (1/4 ounce *each*) active dry yeast
1/4 cup warm milk (110° to 115°)
2 tablespoons sugar
2 cups butter, softened
1 package (8 ounces) cream cheese, softened
1 cup heavy whipping cream
1 cup (8 ounces) sour cream
7 egg yolks

1/8   teaspoon salt
8   to 8-1/2 cups all-purpose flour

FILLING:
6   egg whites
1   teaspoon cream of tartar
1   cup sugar, *divided*
3   cups ground walnuts *or* pecans
2   teaspoons ground cinnamon,
     optional

ICING:
3   cups confectioners' sugar
2   tablespoons butter, softened
1/2   teaspoon almond *or* vanilla
     extract, optional
5   to 7 tablespoons milk

1) In a large mixing bowl, dissolve yeast in warm milk. Add sugar; let stand for 5 minutes. Add the butter, cream cheese, cream, sour cream, egg yolks, salt and 2-1/2 cups flour. Beat until smooth. Stir in enough remaining flour to form a soft dough.

2) Turn onto a floured surface; knead until smooth and elastic, about 6-8 minutes. Place in a greased bowl, turning once to grease top. Cover and refrigerate overnight.

3) In a mixing bowl, beat egg whites and cream of tartar on medium speed until soft peaks form. Gradually add 2 tablespoons sugar, beating until glossy stiff peaks form. Fold in nuts.

4) Turn dough onto a lightly floured surface; divide into fourths. Roll each portion into a 12-in. circle; spread a fourth of the filling over each circle. Add cinnamon if desired to remaining sugar; sprinkle over filling.

5) Cut each into 12 wedges. Roll up wedges from the wide end; place point side down 3 in. apart on greased baking sheets. Curve ends to form a crescent shape. Bake at 350° for 17-20 minutes or until golden brown. Remove from pans to wire racks to cool.

6) For the icing, in a large bowl, combine the confectioners' sugar, butter, extract if desired and enough milk to achieve drizzling consistency. Drizzle over rolls.

Yield: 4 dozen.

NUTRITION FACTS: 1 roll equals 285 calories, 17 g fat (8 g saturated fat), 68 mg cholesterol, 117 mg sodium, 30 g carbohydrate, 1 g fiber, 5 g protein.

Kolaches
Sharon Ternes, St. Peter, Minnesota

Also spelled "kolachkes," these sweet yeast buns have both Polish and Czech roots. They are usually filled with poppy seeds, nuts, jam or a mashed fruit mixture.

3   packages (1/4 ounce *each*)
     active dry yeast
1/2   cup warm water (110° to 115°)
1/2   cup sugar
1   package (3.4 ounces) instant
     vanilla pudding mix
1   cup (8 ounces) sour cream
1/2   cup vegetable oil
1   teaspoon salt
4   eggs
4-1/2   to 5 cups all-purpose flour
1   can (12 ounces) apricot, poppy
     seed *or* prune filling

1) In a large mixing bowl, dissolve yeast in water. Add the sugar, pudding mix, sour cream, oil, salt, eggs and 2 cups flour. Beat until smooth. Stir in enough of the remaining flour to form a soft dough. Cover and refrigerate dough overnight.

2) Punch dough down. Turn onto a lightly floured surface; divide into 24 pieces. Shape each into a ball. Place 2 in. apart on greased baking sheets. Cover and let rise in a warm place until doubled, about 30 minutes.

3) Using the end of a wooden spoon handle, make a large indentation in the center of each ball; fill with 2 tablespoons of filling. Bake at 350° for 14-15 minutes or until lightly browned. Remove from pans to wire racks to cool.

Yield: 2 dozen.

NUTRITION FACTS: 1 kolache equals 222 calories, 7 g fat (2 g saturated fat), 42 mg cholesterol, 181 mg sodium, 34 g carbohydrate, 1 g fiber, 4 g protein.

STORING COFFEE CAKES AND SWEET ROLLS

Cool coffee cakes and sweet rolls completely. Place in an airtight container or plastic bag; keep at room temperature for 2 to 3 days. Breads containing perishable items should be refrigerated.

For longer storage, unfrosted sweet breads can be frozen for up to 3 months. Thaw at room temperature, then frost or glaze as desired.

Hot Cross Buns

Lorri Bailey, Pulaski, Iowa

These golden buns, with a light seasoning from cinnamon and allspice, were a family Easter tradition. My mom made them only once a year using her mother's recipe.

2 packages (1/4 ounce *each*) active dry yeast
1/4 cup warm water (110° to 115°)
1 cup warm milk (110° to 115°)
1/2 cup sugar
1/4 cup shortening
2 eggs
2 teaspoons salt
1 teaspoon ground cinnamon
1/4 teaspoon ground allspice
4-1/2 to 5 cups all-purpose flour
1 cup dried currants
1 egg white, lightly beaten

ICING:

1-3/4 cups confectioners' sugar
1/2 teaspoon vanilla extract
4 to 6 teaspoons milk

1) In a large mixing bowl, dissolve yeast in warm water. Add the milk, sugar, shortening, eggs, salt, cinnamon, allspice and 3 cups flour. Beat until smooth. Stir in currants and enough remaining flour to form a soft dough.

2) Turn onto a floured surface; knead until smooth and elastic, about 6-8 minutes. Place in a greased bowl, turning once to grease top. Cover and let rise in a warm place until doubled, about 1 hour.

3) Punch dough down. Cover and let rest for 10 minutes. On a lightly floured surface, roll out to 1/2-in. thickness. Cut with a floured 2-1/2-in. biscuit cutter. Place 2 in. apart on lightly greased baking sheets. Cover and let rise until doubled, about 30 minutes.

4) Brush with egg white. Bake at 350° for 12-15 minutes or until golden brown. Remove from pans to wire racks to cool.

5) For icing, combine the confectioners' sugar, vanilla and enough milk to achieve piping consistency. Pipe a cross on top of each bun.

Yield: 2 dozen.

NUTRITION FACTS: 1 bun equals 187 calories, 3 g fat (1 g saturated fat), 19 mg cholesterol, 211 mg sodium, 36 g carbohydrate, 1 g fiber, 4 g protein.

HERBED ONION BREAD

Using Bread Machines

Before beginning, carefully read your bread machine owner's manual.

All liquid ingredients should be at room temperature (70° to 80°). This includes water, milk, yogurt, juice, cottage cheese, eggs and applesauce.

Measure ingredients accurately before adding to your machine. Then add in the order suggested by your bread machine manufacturer.

For best results, use bread flour. While either active dry yeast or bread machine yeast can be used in bread machines, bread machine yeast is a little finer, which allows for better dispersion during mixing and kneading. For 1 cup flour, it is generally recommended to use 3/4 teaspoon active dry yeast or 1/2 teaspoon bread machine yeast.

Check dough after 5 minutes of mixing. The dough should feel smooth, soft and slightly tacky. If it's moist or sticky, add 1 tablespoon flour and check again after a few more minutes of mixing. If it's dry and crumbly, add 1 tablespoon liquid, then check again.

Recipes containing eggs, milk, sour cream, cottage cheese and other dairy or perishable products should be baked immediately and not placed on a "timed-bake" cycle.

Converting Recipes

Converting a traditional yeast bread recipe for the bread machine will require some experimentation.

First, determine the size of your bread machine. Look at the recipes that came with your bread machine and note the amount of flour and liquid called for in most of those recipes.

Flour includes dry ingredients such as any type of flour, oats, cereal and cornmeal. Liquid includes milk, water, yogurt, sour cream, applesauce, eggs (1/4 cup liquid per egg), cottage cheese, etc. Sugar also includes sweeteners such as honey, molasses or brown sugar. Fat includes shortening, butter, margarine and oil.

It's best to start with a bread recipe you are familiar with and have successfully made. Once you master those familiar recipes, look for other bread recipes that use the amount of flour your bread machine needs. Or look for a recipe that makes two loaves and can be easily divided in half. Divide all the ingredients in half. Avoid recipes for sourdough, that require refrigerating the dough or that have a high ratio of fat. These types of recipes won't be successful in the bread machine.

For breads with toppings or fillings as well as ones that require special shapes or rolls—just mix, knead and proof the dough in the bread machine. Punch the dough down, fill and/or shape. Then follow the original recipe to finish the bread.

Make notes on your recipe for reference. If it wasn't quite right, make an adjustment in one ingredient and try again.

The chart below is a guideline for the ratio of ingredients for bread machines yielding 1-pound, 1-1/2-pound and 2-pound loaves.

Converting Recipes for Bread Machines

BREAD MACHINE SIZE:	1 pound	1-1/2 pounds	2 pounds
FLOUR:	2 to 2-1/2 cups	3 to 3-1/2 cups	4 to 4-1/2 cups
LIQUID:	2/3 cup	1 cup	1-1/3 cups
ACTIVE DRY YEAST:	1-1/2 teaspoons	2-1/2 teaspoons	3 teaspoons
SUGAR:	2 tablespoons	3 tablespoons	4 tablespoons
SALT:	1 teaspoon	1-1/2 teaspoons	2 teaspoons
FAT:	4 teaspoons	6 teaspoons	8 teaspoons

Herbed Onion Bread
Sue Call, Beech Grove, Indiana

I enjoy the convenience of my bread machine and use it often. This is one of my best recipes.

- 1 cup plus 1 tablespoon water (70° to 80°)
- 2 tablespoons butter, softened
- 1-1/4 teaspoons salt
- 3 cups bread flour
- 2 teaspoons dried minced onion
- 1-1/2 teaspoons dill weed
- 1 teaspoon poppy seeds
- 2 tablespoons nonfat dry milk powder
- 2 tablespoons sugar
- 1-1/2 teaspoons active dry yeast

1) In bread machine pan, place all ingredients in order suggest by manufacturer. Select basic bread setting. Choose crust color and loaf size if available. Bake according to bread machine directions (check dough after 5 minutes of mixing; add 1 to 2 tablespoons water or flour if needed).

Yield: 1 loaf (1-1/2 pounds and 16 slices).

NUTRITION FACTS: 1 slice equals 100 calories, 2 g fat (1 g saturated fat), 4 mg cholesterol, 204 mg sodium, 19 g carbohydrate, 1 g fiber, 4 g protein.

Home-Style White Bread
Yvonne Nave, Lyons, Kansas

Serve this basic white bread with butter and jam, or slice and assemble your favorite sandwiches.

- 1 cup water (70° to 80°)
- 2 tablespoons butter, softened
- 1 teaspoon salt
- 2 tablespoons sugar
- 2 tablespoons nonfat dry milk powder
- 3 cups bread flour
- 2 teaspoons active dry yeast

1) In bread machine pan, place all ingredients in order suggested by manufacturer. Select basic bread setting. Choose crust color and loaf size if available. Bake according to bread machine directions (check dough after 5 minutes of mixing; add 1 to 2 tablespoons water or flour if needed).

Yield: 1 loaf (about 1-1/2 pounds and 16 slices).

NUTRITION FACTS: 1 slice equals 98 calories, 1 g fat (1 g saturated fat), 4 mg cholesterol, 167 mg sodium, 19 g carbohydrate, 1 g fiber, 4 g protein.

Maple Oatmeal Bread
Kathy Morin, Methuen, Massachusetts

Maple syrup gives this bread its delicate flavor. Slices taste terrific when toasted.

- 3/4 cup plus 2 tablespoons water (70° to 80°)
- 1/3 cup maple syrup
- 1 tablespoon vegetable oil
- 1 teaspoon salt
- 3/4 cup quick-cooking oats
- 2-1/2 cups bread flour
- 2-1/4 teaspoons active dry yeast

1) In bread machine pan, place all ingredients in order suggested by manufacturer. Select basic bread setting. Choose crust color and loaf size if available.

2) Bake according to bread machine directions (check dough after 5 minutes of mixing; add 1 to 2 tablespoons of water or flour if needed).

Yield: 1 loaf (1-1/2 pounds and 16 slices).

NUTRITION FACTS: 1 slice equals 104 calories, 1 g fat (trace saturated fat), 0 cholesterol, 148 mg sodium, 21 g carbohydrate, 1 g fiber, 3 g protein.

Garlic Herb Bubble Loaf
Katie Crill, Priest River, Idaho

I adapted an old sour cream bread recipe for this deliciously different pull-apart loaf that has a heavenly aroma while baking.

- 1/2 cup water (70° to 80°)
- 1/2 cup sour cream
- 2 tablespoons butter, softened
- 3 tablespoons sugar
- 1-1/2 teaspoons salt
- 3 cups bread flour
- 2-1/4 teaspoons active dry yeast

GARLIC HERB BUTTER:
- 1/4 cup butter, melted
- 4 garlic cloves, minced
- 1/4 teaspoon *each* dried oregano, thyme and rosemary, crushed

1) In bread machine pan, place the first seven ingredients in order suggested by manufacturer. Select dough setting (check dough after 5 minutes of mixing; add 1 to 2 tablespoons of water or flour if needed). When cycle is completed, turn dough onto a lightly floured surface; divide dough into 36 pieces. Shape each into a ball.

2) In a bowl, combine butter, garlic and herbs. Dip each ball in mixture; place in an ungreased 9-in. x 5-in. x 3-in. loaf pan. Cover and let rise in a warm place until doubled, about 45 minutes.

3) Bake at 375° for 35-40 minutes or until golden. Remove from pan to a wire rack. Serve warm.

Yield: 1 loaf.

NUTRITION FACTS: 1 piece equals 62 calories, 2 g fat (2 g saturated fat), 7 mg cholesterol, 119 mg sodium, 9 g carbohydrate, trace fiber, 2 g protein.

Rosemary Potato Rolls
Mary Dixson, Decatur, Alabama

You can choose sesame seeds or poppy seeds to sprinkle over these golden rolls. The dough is made in the bread machine to save time.

- 1 cup plus 2 tablespoons water (70° to 80°)
- 2 tablespoons olive oil
- 1/2 cup mashed potato flakes
- 2 tablespoons nonfat dry milk powder
- 1 tablespoon sugar
- 1 teaspoon dried rosemary, crushed
- 1 to 1-1/2 teaspoons salt
- 3 cups bread flour
- 2-1/4 teaspoons active dry yeast
- 1 egg, lightly beaten

Sesame seeds *or* poppy seeds

1) In bread machine pan, place first nine ingredients in order suggested by manufacturer. Select dough setting (check dough after 5 minutes of mixing; add 1 to 2 tablespoons of water or flour if needed). When cycle is completed, turn dough onto a lightly floured surface. Punch down and let stand for 10 minutes.

2) Divide dough into 12 portions. Shape each into a 10-in. rope. Holding one end of rope, loosely form into a coil. Tuck end under; pinch to seal. Place 2 in. apart on a greased baking sheet. Cover and let rise in a warm place until doubled, about 30 minutes.

3) Brush tops with egg. Sprinkle with sesame or poppy seeds. Bake at 375° for 13-16 minutes or until golden. Remove from pan to a wire rack.

Yield: 1 dozen.

NUTRITION FACTS: 1 roll (calculated without sesame seeds or poppy seeds) equals 147 calories, 3 g fat (trace saturated fat), 18 mg cholesterol, 215 mg sodium, 26 g carbohydrate, 1 g fiber, 6 g protein.

PIES & TARTS

PIES & TARTS

While pies conjure up a homey image and tarts feel a little more elegant, they both have a sweetened filling. The main difference is that tarts are more shallow than pies (typically about 1 in. high). Tarts can be full-size, bite-size or individual tartlets.

Pie Pastry

Classic pie pastry recipes are prepared with solid shortening. Lard or butter-flavored shortening can be substituted for plain shortening if desired.

Measure all ingredients accurately. Combine flour and salt thoroughly before adding the shortening and water. Be sure to use ice-cold water. Add an ice cube to water and measure before adding to the flour mixture.

To produce a flaky crust, avoid overmixing when adding the water to the flour and shortening mixture. Overmixing develops the gluten in the flour, causing the pastry to become tough.

A floured surface is essential to prevent sticking when rolling out pastry. A pastry cloth and rolling pin cover are good investments—they keep the pastry from sticking and minimize the amount of flour used. The less flour you add while rolling, the flakier and lighter the pastry will be.

Chill pie pastry dough for 30 minutes before rolling to make it easier to handle.

Choose dull-finish aluminum or glass pie plates for crisp, golden crusts. Shiny pans can produce soggy crusts. Because of the high fat content in a pastry, do not grease the pie plate unless the recipe directs.

Never prick the bottom of a pastry crust when the filling and crust are to be baked together.

Arrange the oven racks so that the pie will bake in the center of the oven. Preheat the oven for 10-15 minutes before baking.

Finishing Touches for Pie Crusts

To top off double-crust pies before baking, use a pastry brush to lightly and evenly apply one of the following washes to the top crust, avoiding the edges.

- For a shine and light browning, brush with an egg white that was lightly beaten with 1 teaspoon of water.

- For a glossy golden appearance, brush with an egg yolk that was beaten with 1 teaspoon of water.

- For a slight shine, brush with half-and-half cream or heavy whipping cream.

- For a crisp brown crust, brush with water.

- For a little sparkle, sprinkle with sugar or decorator sugar after brushing with one of the washes.

To give a little more shine to a baked double-crust pie, warm 1 tablespoon of light corn syrup. Gently brush over the baked warm crust.

DECORATIVE PIE CRUST EDGES

RUFFLE EDGE

Used for a single- or double-crust pie. Trim pastry 1/2 in. beyond edge of pie plate (1 in. for a double-crust pie). Turn the overhanging pastry under to form the rolled edge. Position your thumb and index finger about 1 in. apart on the edge or the crust, point out. Position the index finger on your other hand between the two fingers and gently push the pastry toward the center in an upward direction. Continue around the edge.

ROPE EDGE

Used for a single- or double-crust pie. Trim pastry 1/2 in. beyond edge of pie plate (1 in. for a double-crust pie). Turn the overhanging pastry under to form the rolled edge. Make a fist with one hand and press your thumb at an angle into the pastry. Pinch some of the pastry between your thumb and index finger.

Repeat at about 1/2-in. intervals around the crust. For a looser-looking rope, position your thumb at a wider angle and repeat at 1-in. intervals.

LEAF TRIM

Used for a single-crust pie. Make enough pastry for a double crust. Line a 9-in. pie plate with the bottom pastry and trim pastry even with edge of pie plate. Roll out remaining pastry to 1/8-in. thickness.

Cut out leaf shapes, using 1-in. to 1-1/2-in. cookie cutters. With a sharp knife, score pastry to create leaf veins. Brush bottom of each leaf with water. Place one or two layers of leaves around the edge of crust; press lightly to secure. Cover with foil to protect edges from overbrowning.

You can also use this technique with other cookie cutter designs such as hearts and apples. Vary them to suit the occasion or season you are celebrating.

PROTECTING PASTRY EDGES FROM OVERBROWNING

The edges of a pie pastry often brown before the rest of the pie is thoroughly baked. To protect the edges, fold a 12-in. piece of foil in quarters. Place the folded corner toward you. Measure 3-3/4 in. up each adjacent side and cut out an arc joining the two sides. Discard the center.

Unfold the remaining foil and place it over the unbaked pie. Trim corners if necessary. Gently crimp foil around edge of crust to secure. Bake the pie for 20 to 30 minutes before removing the foil. Or add during the final 10 to 20 minutes of baking.

Pie Thickeners

Thickeners help prevent fruit pies from being too runny. All-purpose flour, cornstarch and quick-cooking tapioca are the thickeners commonly used in fruit pies. Flour gives the filling an opaque appearance, cornstarch gives a clear appearance and tapioca gives a clear to almost gel-like appearance.

One thickener can be substituted for another; however, the thickening power of each is different and you may need to make adjustments. Equal amounts of quick-cooking tapioca and cornstarch can be substituted for each other. When replacing flour in a recipe, use half the amount of cornstarch or use 2 teaspoons of quick-cooking tapioca for every 1 tablespoon of flour.

When using tapioca, mix it with the filling ingredients and allow the mixture to stand for 15 minutes before proceeding with the recipe.

Homemade Crumb Crusts

In a mixing bowl, combine the crumbs and sugar; add the melted butter and blend well. Press the mixture onto the bottom and up the sides of an ungreased 9-in. pie plate. Refrigerate for 30 minutes before filling, or bake at 375° for 8-10 minutes or until the crust is lightly browned. Cool on a wire rack before filling.

TYPE OF CRUST	CRUMBS	SUGAR	BUTTER, MELTED
GRAHAM CRACKER	1-1/2 cups (24 squares)	1/4 cup	1/3 cup
CHOCOLATE WAFER	1-1/4 cups (20 wafers)	1/4 cup	1/4 cup
VANILLA WAFER	1-1/2 cups (30 wafers)	none	1/4 cup
CREAM-FILLED CHOCOLATE	1-1/2 cups (15 cookies)	none	1/4 cup
GINGERSNAP	1-1/2 cups (24 cookies)	none	1/4 cup
MACAROON	1-1/2 cups	none	1/4 cup
PRETZEL (use a greased pie plate)	1-1/4 cups	1/4 cup	1/2 cup

Editor's Note: For desserts made in a 9-in. springform pan (such as cheesecakes), you may need to add 1/4 to 1/2 cup crumbs and 1 tablespoon butter.

Classic Pie Pastry
Taste of Home Test Kitchen

Just four ingredients are all you need to create a fabulous, flaky pie crust. The double-crust recipe should be used when making a lattice-topped pie.

INGREDIENTS FOR SINGLE-CRUST PIE:
- 1-1/4   cups all-purpose flour
- 1/2   teaspoon salt
- 1/3   cup shortening
- 4   to 5 tablespoons cold water

INGREDIENTS FOR DOUBLE-CRUST PIE:
- 2   cups all-purpose flour
- 3/4   teaspoon salt
- 2/3   cup shortening
- 6   to 7 tablespoons cold water

1) In a small bowl, combine the flour and salt; cut in the shortening until mixture is crumbly. Gradually add water, tossing with a fork until a ball forms. Cover and refrigerate for 30 minutes or until easy to handle.

2) For a single crust, roll out pastry on a lightly floured surface to fit a 9-in. or 10-in. pie plate. Transfer pastry to pie plate. Trim pastry to 1/2 in. beyond edge of pie plate; flute edges. Fill or bake shell according to recipe directions.

3) For a double crust, divide dough in half so that one ball is slightly larger than the other. Roll out larger ball on a lightly floured surface to fit a 9-in or 10-in. pie plate. Transfer pastry to pie plate. Trim pastry even with edge of plate. Add filling. Roll out remaining pastry to fit op of pie; place over filling. Trim, seal and flute edges. Cut slits in top. Bake according to recipe directions.

Yield: 1 pastry for a single- or double-crust pie (9 or 10 inches).

NUTRITION FACTS: 1/8 of single pie pastry equals 144 calories, 8 g fat (2 g saturated fat), 0 cholesterol, 148 mg sodium, 15 g carbohydrate, 1 g fiber, 2 g protein.

BAKING AND STORING PIES

A pastry shell is thoroughly baked when it is a light golden brown. Fruit pies are done when the filling bubbles and the crust is light golden brown. (The filling should be clear, not cloudy.) Meringues are properly baked when the top has set and the tips of the meringue peaks are light golden brown. Custard pies are done when a knife inserted near the center comes out clean. A small area in the center of pie should still be soft. The center will continue to cook and set up during cooling.

Cool fruit pies for at least 1 hour before serving. They can be kept at room temperature for 1 day. For longer storage, cover and refrigerate for up to 5 days. Cool meringue-topped and custard pies on a wire rack for 1 hour, then chill for at least 3 hours before serving. Store custard and cream pies in the refrigerator for up to 3 days.

1) Combine flour and salt in a bowl. With a pastry blender or two knives, cut in shortening until the mixture resembles coarse crumbs (the size of small peas).

2) Sprinkle 1 tablespoon of cold water at a time over the mixture and toss gently with a fork. Repeat until dry ingredients are moist and mixture forms a ball. Use only as much water as necessary to moisten flour.

3) Shape into a ball. (For a double-crust pie, divide pastry in half so that one ball is slightly larger than the other.) On a floured surface or floured pastry cloth, flatten the ball (the larger one, if making a double-crust pie) into a circle, pressing together any cracks or breaks.

4) Roll with a floured rolling pin from the center of the pastry to the edges, forming a circle 2 in. larger than the pie plate. The pastry should be about 1/8 in. thick.

5) To move pastry to the pie plate, roll up onto the rolling pin. Position over the edge of pie plate and unroll. Let the pastry ease into the plate. Do not stretch the pastry to fit. For a single-crust pie, trim pastry with a scissors to 1/2 in. beyond plate edge; turn under and flute as in step 8.

For a double-crust pie, trim pastry even with the edge of plate. For a lattice-crust pie, trim pastry to 1 in. beyond plate edge. Either bake the shell or fill according to recipe directions.

6) For a double-crust pie, roll out second ball into a 12-in. circle about 1/8 in. thick. Roll up pastry onto rolling pin; position over filling. With a knife, cut slits in top to allow steam to escape while baking.

7) With scissors, trim top pastry to 1 in. beyond plate edge. Fold top pastry over bottom pastry.

8) To flute the edge, position your thumb on the inside of the crust. Place the thumb and index finger of your other hand on the outside edge and pinch pastry around the thumb to form a V-shape and seal dough together. Continue around the edge.

Never-Fail Pie Crust
Ruth Gritter, Grand Rapids, Michigan

Even novice bakers can't go wrong with this recipe. It is easy to roll out and produces a tender, flaky crust every time.

INGREDIENTS FOR SINGLE-CRUST PIE:

- 1 cup all-purpose flour
- 1/4 teaspoon salt
- 1/3 cup shortening
- 1-1/2 teaspoons white vinegar
- 2 to 3 tablespoons milk

INGREDIENTS FOR DOUBLE-CRUST PIE:

- 2 cups all-purpose flour
- 1/2 teaspoon salt
- 2/3 cup shortening
- 1 tablespoon white vinegar
- 5 to 6 tablespoons milk

1) In a small bowl, combine the flour and salt; cut in shortening until mixture is crumbly. Sprinkle with vinegar. Gradually add the milk, tossing with a fork until a ball is formed. Cover and refrigerate for 30 minutes or until easy to handle.

2) For a single crust, roll out pastry on a lightly floured surface to fit a 9-in. or 10-in. pie plate. Transfer pastry to pie plate. Trim pastry 1/2 in. beyond edge of plate; flute edges. Fill or bake shell according to recipe directions.

3) For a double crust, divide pastry in half so that one ball is slightly large than the other. Roll out large ball on a lightly floured surface to fit a 9-in. or 10-in. pie plate. Transfer pastry to pie plate. Trim pastry even with edge of plate. Add filling. Roll out remaining pastry to fit top of pie; place over filling. Trim, seal and flute edges. Cut slits in top. Bake according to recipe directions.

Yield: pastry for a single- or double-crust pie (9 or 10 inches).

NUTRITION FACTS: 1/8 of single pie pastry equals 132 calories, 8 g fat (2 g saturated fat), 1 mg cholesterol, 76 mg sodium, 12 g carbohydrate, trace fiber, 2 g protein.

Apple Crumb Pie
Ardis Rollefson, Jackson Hole, Wyoming

I often brown the topping for this special-occasion pie under the broiler to give it extra eye appeal. Watch it carefully, though, because you don't want to burn Thanksgiving dessert!

Pastry for single-crust pie (9 inches)
- 6 cups chopped peeled tart apples (about 6 medium)
- 2 tablespoons butter, melted
- 2 tablespoons sour cream
- 4 teaspoons lemon juice
- 1/2 cup sugar
- 1 tablespoon all-purpose flour
- 1/2 teaspoon ground cinnamon
- 1/2 teaspoon ground nutmeg

TOPPING:
- 1/2 cup all-purpose flour
- 1/2 cup sugar
- 1/4 cup cold butter

1) Line a 9-in. pie plate with pastry; flute edges. In a large bowl, combine the apples, butter, sour cream, lemon juice, sugar, flour, cinnamon and nutmeg. Spoon into pastry shell.

2) For topping, combine flour and sugar in a bowl; cut in butter until mixture resembles coarse crumbs. Sprinkle over filling. Bake at 375° for 45-50 minutes or until the filling is bubbly and the apples are tender. Cool on a wire rack.

Yield: 8 servings.

NUTRITION FACTS: 1 piece equals 380 calories, 17 g fat (9 g saturated fat), 30 mg cholesterol, 189 mg sodium, 57 g carbohydrate, 2 g fiber, 2 g protein.

GERMAN APPLE PIE

German Apple Pie
Mrs. Woodrow Taylor, Adams Center, New York

I first tasted this apple pie many years ago when my children's baby-sitter made it. I asked for the recipe and have made it many times myself since.

- 1-1/2 cups all-purpose flour
- 1/2 teaspoon salt
- 1/2 cup shortening
- 1 teaspoon vanilla extract
- 2 to 3 tablespoons ice water

FILLING:
- 1 cup sugar
- 1/4 cup all-purpose flour
- 2 teaspoons ground cinnamon
- 6 cups sliced peeled tart apples
- 1 cup heavy whipping cream

Whipped cream, optional

1) In a small bowl, combine flour and salt; cut in the shortening until crumbly. Add vanilla. Gradually add water, tossing with a fork until dough forms a ball. Roll out pastry to fit a 9-in. pie plate. Transfer pastry to pie plate. Trim pastry to 1/2 in. beyond edge of pie plate; flute edges.

2) For filling, combine the sugar, flour and the cinnamon; sprinkle 3 tablespoons into crust. Layer with half of the apples, then sprinkle with half of the remaining sugar mixture. Repeat layers. Pour cream over all.

3) Bake at 450° for 10 minutes. Reduce heat to 350°; bake for 55-60 minutes or until apples are tender. Cool on a wire rack. Store in the refrigerator. Serve with whipped cream if desired.

Yield: 8 servings.

NUTRITION FACTS: 1 piece equals 459 calories, 24 g fat (10 g saturated fat), 41 mg cholesterol, 160 mg sodium, 59 g carbohydrate, 3 g fiber, 4 g protein.

DUTCH APRICOT PIE

Dutch Apricot Pie

Joanne Hutmacher, Lemoore, California

I freeze several bagfuls of apricots when they are in season, thinking of this pie all the while. At holiday time, there's nothing like a luscious taste of summer. The crunchy pecans in the topping make this dessert extra special.

3/4 cup sugar
2 tablespoons quick-cooking tapioca
4 cups sliced fresh apricots (about 16)
1 tablespoon lemon juice
1 pastry for single-crust pie (9 inches)

TOPPING:
2/3 cup all-purpose flour
1/2 cup sugar
1/2 cup chopped pecans, toasted
1/4 cup butter, melted

1) In a small bowl, combine sugar and tapioca; mix well. Add apricots and lemon juice; toss to coat. Let stand for 15 minutes.

2) Line a 9-in. pie plate with pastry. Trim pastry to 1/2 in. beyond edge of plate; flute edges. Pour filling into crust.

3) In a small bowl, combine the flour, sugar and pecans. Stir in butter. Sprinkle over filling. Cover edges loosely with foil. Bake at 350° for 15 minutes.

4) Remove foil; bake 25-30 minutes longer or until crust is golden brown and filling is bubbly. Cool on a wire rack. Store in the refrigerator.

Yield: 8 servings.

NUTRITION FACTS: 1 piece equals 431 calories, 18 g fat (7 g saturated fat), 20 mg cholesterol, 159 mg sodium, 65 g carbohydrate, 3 g fiber, 4 g protein.

Country Fair Cherry Pie

Taste of Home Test Kitchen

A homemade cherry filling peeks out from a star-shaped pastry top. You can try different shapes for other occasions and also add almond extract for another flavor.

1-1/4 cups sugar
2 tablespoons cornstarch
Dash salt
4 cups pitted unsweetened sour cherries
Pastry for double-crust pie (9 inches)
Star cookie cutters (1/2 inch and 2 inches)
Confectioners' sugar

1) In a large saucepan, combine sugar, cornstarch and salt; stir in cherries until blended. Let stand for 30 minutes. Bring to a boil over medium heat; cook and stir for 2 minutes or until thickened. Remove from the heat.

2) Line a 9-in. pie plate with bottom crust; trim pastry even with edge. Fill with cherry filling. Bake at 375° for 45 minutes or until crust is golden brown and filling is bubbly. Cover edges during the last 20 minutes to prevent overbrowning.

3) Meanwhile, roll out remaining pastry to 1/8-in. thickness. Cut into 12-14 large stars and 16-18 small stars; place on an ungreased baking sheet. Bake at 375° for 8-10 minutes or until golden brown. Remove to a wire rack to cool.

4) Sprinkle with confectioners' sugar. Place stars randomly over cooled pie. Sprinkle edges of pie with confectioners' sugar.

Yield: 8 servings.

NUTRITION FACTS: 1 piece (calculated without confectioners' sugar) equals 426 calories, 14 g fat (6 g saturated fat), 10 mg cholesterol, 220 mg sodium, 74 g carbohydrate, 2 g fiber, 3 g protein.

■ *CHERRY ALMOND PIE:* Once the pie filling has been removed from the heat, stir in 1/4 teaspoon almond extract.

OZARK MOUNTAIN BERRY PIE

Ozark Mountain Berry Pie
Elaine Moody, Clever, Missouri

I taste the berries or filling before adding to the pie crust to make sure it's sweet enough. Sliced berries absorb more of the flavorings.

- 1 cup sugar
- 1/4 cup cornstarch
- 1/2 teaspoon ground cinnamon, optional

Dash salt

- 1 cup blueberries
- 1 cup strawberries
- 3/4 cup blackberries
- 3/4 cup red raspberries
- 1/2 cup water
- 2 tablespoons lemon juice

Pastry for a double-crust pie (9 inches)

- 2 tablespoons butter

1) In a saucepan, combine the sugar, cornstarch, cinnamon if desired and salt. Stir in berries. Add water and lemon juice. Cook over medium heat until mixture just comes to a boil.

2) Line a 9-in. pie plate with bottom crust; trim pastry even with edge. Fill with berry filling and dot with butter. Roll out remaining pastry; make a lattice crust. Trim, seal and flute edges. Bake at 350° for about 45 minutes or until crust is golden. Cool on a wire rack. Store in the refrigerator.

Yield: 8 servings.

NUTRITION FACTS: 1 piece equals 406 calories, 17 g fat (8 g saturated fat), 18 mg cholesterol, 248 mg sodium, 62 g carbohydrate, 2 g fiber, 3 g protein.

CREATING A LATTICE-TOPPED PIE

1) Make pastry for a double-crust pie. Line a 9-in. pie plate with the bottom pastry and trim to 1 in. beyond edge of plate. Roll out remaining pastry to a 12-in. circle. With a fluted pastry wheel, pizza cutter or sharp knife, cut pastry into 1/2-in.- to 1-in.-wide strips. Lay strips in rows about 1/2 in. to 3/4 in. apart. (Use longer strips for the center of the pie and shorter strips for the sides.) Fold every other strip halfway back. Starting at the center, add strips at right angles, lifting every other strip as the cross strips are put down.

2) Continue to add strips, lifting and weaving until lattice top is completed.

3) Trim strips even with pastry edge. Fold bottom pastry up and over ends of strips and seal. Flute edges.

RUSTIC PEAR TART

Rustic Pear Tart
Taste of Home Test Kitchen

In this delightful pie, the pastry makes a "pouch" for a pleasant pear filling. For even more flavor, top with a powdered sugar glaze and toasted almonds.

1-1/3 cups all-purpose flour
   3 tablespoons sugar
  1/4 teaspoon salt
   7 tablespoons cold butter, cubed
   2 to 3 tablespoons cold water

FILLING:
  3/4 cup sugar
  1/4 cup slivered almonds, toasted
  1/4 cup all-purpose flour
1-1/2 teaspoons dried grated lemon peel
  1/2 to 3/4 teaspoon ground cinnamon
   4 medium ripe pears, peeled and sliced
   1 tablespoon butter

GLAZE (optional):
  1/4 cup confectioners' sugar
1-1/2 teaspoons milk
  1/4 teaspoon vanilla extract
  1/4 cup slivered almonds, toasted

1) In a small bowl, combine the flour, sugar and salt; cut in butter until crumbly. Gradually add water, tossing with a fork until dough forms a ball. Roll out to a 14-in. circle. Transfer pastry to a 14-in. pizza pan.

2) In a large bowl, combine the sugar, almonds, flour, lemon peel and cinnamon. Add pears; toss to coat. Spoon over the pastry to within 2 in. of edges; dot with butter. Fold edges of pastry over pears. Bake at 375° for 45-50 minutes or until golden brown.

3) For glaze, combine the confectioners' sugar, milk and vanilla. Drizzle over warm tart. Sprinkle with almonds. Cool on a wire rack. Store in refrigerator.

Yield: 10 servings.

NUTRITION FACTS: 1 piece equals 308 calories, 12 g fat (6 g saturated fat), 25 mg cholesterol, 153 mg sodium, 48 g carbohydrate, 3 g fiber, 4 g protein.

PREVENTING SOGGY TART CRUSTS
Brush tart crusts with melted jelly before layering with fruit. That will help seal the crust and keep the fruit juices from absorbing into the crust.

Golden Peach Pie
Shirley Olson, Polson, Montana

Years ago, I entered this beautiful pie in the Park County Fair in Livingston. It won a first-place blue ribbon plus a purple ribbon for "Best All Around!" My six children, 14 grandchildren and many friends all agree that it's very delicious.

Pastry for double-crust pie (9 inches)
   1 cup sugar
  1/4 cup cornstarch
  1/4 teaspoon ground nutmeg
  1/8 teaspoon salt
   2 teaspoons lemon juice
  1/2 teaspoon grated orange peel
  1/8 teaspoon almond extract
   5 cups sliced peeled fresh peaches (about 5 medium)
   2 tablespoons butter
  Milk

1) Line a 9-in. pie plate with bottom pastry; trim even with edge of plate. Set aside.

2) In a large bowl, combine the sugar, cornstarch, nutmeg and salt; stir in lemon juice, orange peel and extract. Add the peaches; toss gently. Pour into crust; dot with butter.

3) Roll out remaining pastry to fit top of pie; make decorative cutouts in pastry. Set cutouts aside. Place top crust over filling. Trim, seal and flute edges. Brush pastry and cutouts with milk; place cutouts on top of pie. Cover the edges loosely with foil.

4) Bake at 400° for 40 minutes. Remove foil; bake 10-15 minutes longer or until crust is golden brown and filling is bubbly. Cool on a wire rack. Store in the refrigerator.

Yield: 8 servings.

NUTRITION FACTS: 1 piece equals 425 calories, 17 g fat (8 g saturated fat), 18 mg cholesterol, 267 mg sodium, 67 g carbohydrate, 2 g fiber, 3 g protein.

1) In a small mixing bowl, lightly beat eggs. Combine the sugar, flour and salt; gradually add to eggs. Stir in mincemeat, nuts and butter; pour into pie shell.

2) Bake at 400° for 15 minutes. Reduce heat to 325°; bake 35-40 minutes or until a knife inserted near the center comes out clean. Cool completely. Store in the refrigerator.

Yield: 8 servings.

NUTRITION FACTS: 1 piece equals 440 calories, 18 g fat (7 g saturated fat), 73 mg cholesterol, 231 mg sodium, 65 g carbohydrate, 2 g fiber, 5 g protein.

MAKING PASTRY CUTOUTS FOR A PIE

Pastry cutouts can be used for a single- or double-crust pie. To make cutouts, roll out dough to 1/8-in. thickness. Cut out with 1-in. to 1-1/2-in. cookie cutters of desired shape. With a sharp knife, score designs (if desired) on cutouts.

For a single-crust pie, bake cutouts on an ungreased baking sheet at 400° for 6-8 minutes or until golden brown. Remove to a wire rack to cool. Arrange over cooled filling on baked pie.

For a double-crust pie, brush bottom of each unbaked cutout with water or milk and arrange over top crust of an unbaked pie. Press lightly to secure. Bake pie according to recipe.

Festive Fruit Tart
Nancy Adams, Hancock, New Hampshire

"Wow!" is what you'll hear when you serve this impressive dessert to company. The tart is not only pretty, it's also easy to make. Try it with your favorite fresh fruit.

Pastry for single-crust pie (9 inches)

- 1   **package (8 ounces) cream cheese, softened**
- 3   **tablespoons sugar**
- 1   **teaspoon vanilla extract**
- 3/4   **teaspoon almond extract, *divided***
- 1   **cup fresh blueberries**
- 1   **cup fresh raspberries**
- 1   **medium ripe peach *or* nectarines, peeled and sliced**
- 2   **tablespoons apricot preserves**

1) Press pastry onto the bottom and up the sides of an ungreased 9-in. tart pan with a removable bottom; trim edges. Generously prick the bottom with a fork. Bake at 450° for 10-12 minutes or until golden brown. Cool completely on a wire rack.

2) In a small mixing bowl, beat the cream cheese, sugar, vanilla and 1/2 teaspoon almond extract until smooth; spread over crust. Arrange fruit over cream cheese mixture.

3) In a small microwave-safe bowl, combine apricot preserves and the remaining almond extract. Microwave, uncovered, on high for 20-30 seconds or until warm; brush over fruit. Store in the refrigerator.

Yield: 12 servings.

NUTRITION FACTS: 1 piece equals 264 calories, 16 g fat (8 g saturated fat), 27 mg cholesterol, 191 mg sodium, 27 g carbohydrate, 1 g fiber, 3 g protein.

WALNUT MINCEMEAT PIE

Walnut Mincemeat Pie
Laverne Kamp, Kutztown, Pennsylvania

As a cold and tasty finishing touch, put a dip of vanilla ice cream on top of this pie.

- 2   **eggs**
- 1   **cup sugar**
- 2   **tablespoons all-purpose flour**
- 1/8   **teaspoon salt**
- 2   **cups prepared mincemeat**
- 1/2   **cup chopped walnuts**
- 1/4   **cup butter, melted**
- 1   **unbaked pastry shell (9 inches)**

White Chocolate Fruit Tart
Claire Darby, New Castle, Delaware

While it takes a little time to make, this tart is an absolutely marvelous summer dessert when fresh fruit is in abundance.

- 3/4 cup butter, softened
- 1/2 cup confectioners' sugar
- 1-1/2 cups all-purpose flour

FILLING:

- 1 package (10 to 12 ounces) vanilla *or* white chips, melted and cooled
- 1/4 cup heavy whipping cream
- 1 package (8 ounces) cream cheese, softened
- 1 can (20 ounces) pineapple chunks, undrained
- 1 pint fresh strawberries, sliced
- 1 can (11 ounces) mandarin oranges, drained
- 2 kiwifruit, peeled and sliced

GLAZE:

- 3 tablespoons sugar
- 2 teaspoons cornstarch
- 1/2 teaspoon lemon juice

1) In a small mixing bowl, cream butter and confectioners' sugar until light and fluffy. Gradually add flour; mix well. Press into an ungreased 11-in. tart pan with removable bottom or 12-in. pizza pan with sides. Bake at 300° for 25-30 minutes or until lightly browned. Cool on a wire rack.

2) For filling, in a small mixing bowl, beat melted chips and cream. Add cream cheese and beat until smooth. Spread over crust. Refrigerate for 30 minutes. Drain pineapple, reserving 1/2 cup juice; set juice aside. Arrange the pineapple, berries, oranges and kiwi over filling.

3) For glaze, in a small saucepan, combine sugar and cornstarch. Stir in lemon juice and reserved pineapple juice until smooth. Bring to a boil over medium heat; cook and stir for 2 minutes or until thickened. Cool; brush over fruit. Refrigerate for 1 hour before serving. Refrigerate leftovers.

Yield: 16 servings.

NUTRITION FACTS: 1 piece equals 342 calories, 21 g fat (13 g saturated fat), 47 mg cholesterol, 147 mg sodium, 37 g carbohydrate, 1 g fiber, 4 g protein.

Rhubarb-Strawberry Pie
Sandy Brown, Lake Worth, Florida

Strawberries and rhubarb make up the winning combination in this pie recipe. Tapioca helps thicken the filling, which features a hint of orange.

- 1/2 to 3/4 cup sugar
- 1-1/2 tablespoons instant tapioca
- 3 cups sliced fresh *or* frozen rhubarb, thawed (1/4-inch pieces)
- 3 cups sliced fresh *or* frozen unsweetened strawberries, thawed

1/3 cup fresh orange juice

1-1/2 tablespoons orange marmalade, optional

1/4 teaspoon grated orange peel

Pastry for double-crust pie (9 inches)

1) In a large bowl, combine sugar and tapioca. Add fruit; toss to coat. Gently stir in the juice, marmalade if desired and orange peel. Let stand for 15 minutes.

2) Line a deep-dish 9-in. pie plate with bottom crust; trim pastry 1 in. beyond edge. Fill with fruit filling. Roll out remaining pastry; make a lattice crust. Trim, seal and flute edges.

3) Bake at 400° for 20 minutes. Reduce heat to 375°; bake 30 minutes more or until filling is bubbly and rhubarb is tender. Cool on a wire rack. Store in the refrigerator.

Yield: 8 servings.

NUTRITION FACTS: 1 piece equals 329 calories, 14 g fat (6 g saturated fat), 10 mg cholesterol, 203 mg sodium, 48 g carbohydrate, 2 g fiber, 3 g protein.

German Plum Tart
Helga Schlape, Florham Park, New Jersey

The buttery crust of this fruit-filled treat melts in your mouth. You can substitute sliced apples or peaches for the plums with great results. I've used this crust with blueberries, too.

1/2 cup butter, softened

4 tablespoons sugar, *divided*

1 egg yolk

3/4 to 1 cup all-purpose flour

2 pounds plums, quartered (about 4 cups)

1) In a small mixing bowl, cream butter and 3 tablespoons sugar until light and fluffy. Beat in egg yolk. Gradually add flour, 1/4 cup at a time, until mixture forms a soft dough. Press onto the bottom and up the sides of a 10-in. pie plate.

2) Arrange the plums, skin side up with edges overlapping, in crust; sprinkle with remaining sugar. Bake at 350° for 35-45 minutes or until crust is golden brown and fruit is tender.

Yield: 6-8 servings.

NUTRITION FACTS: 1 piece equals 237 calories, 13 g fat (7 g saturated fat), 57 mg cholesterol, 117 mg sodium, 30 g carbohydrate, 2 g fiber, 3 g protein.

STRAWBERRY MERINGUE PIE

Strawberry Meringue Pie
Kathleen Mercier, Orrington, Maine

This recipe is simple, so don't be put off by the long directions. The meringue crust filled with chocolate and berries makes an impressive dessert.

1/3 cup finely crushed saltines (about 10 crackers), *divided*

3 egg whites

1/4 teaspoon cream of tartar

1/8 teaspoon salt

1 cup sugar

1 teaspoon vanilla extract

1/2 cup chopped pecans, toasted

1 package (4 ounces) German sweet chocolate

2 tablespoons butter

4 cups halved fresh strawberries

1 cup heavy whipping cream

2 tablespoons confectioners' sugar

1) Sprinkle 2 tablespoons cracker crumbs into a greased 9-in. pie plate. In a small mixing bowl, beat egg whites, cream of tartar and salt on medium speed until soft peaks form. Gradually beat in sugar, 1 tablespoon at a time, on high until stiff glossy peaks form and sugar is dissolved. Fold in vanilla, pecans and remaining cracker crumbs. Spread meringue onto the bottom and up the sides of prepared pan.

2) Bake at 300° for 45 minutes. Turn oven off and do not open door; let cool in the oven overnight.

3) Melt chocolate and butter; drizzle over shell. Let stand for 15 minutes or until set. Top with berries. In a small mixing bowl, beat cream until it begins to thicken. Add confectioners' sugar; beat until soft peaks form. Spoon over berries. Store in the refrigerator.

Yield: 8 servings.

NUTRITION FACTS: 1 piece equals 389 calories, 24 g fat (11 g saturated fat), 48 mg cholesterol, 131 mg sodium, 45 g carbohydrate, 3 g fiber, 4 g protein.

Creamy Banana Pie

Rita Pribyl, Indianapolis, Indiana

When friends ask me to share a recipe using bananas, I know instantly this is the best dessert to pass along. Everyone who tastes a slice enjoys its delicious old-fashioned flavor.

1	envelope unflavored gelatin
1/4	cup cold water
3/4	cup sugar
1/4	cup cornstarch
1/2	teaspoon salt
2-3/4	cups milk
4	egg yolks, beaten
2	tablespoons butter
1	tablespoon vanilla extract
4	medium firm bananas, *divided*
1	cup heavy whipping cream, whipped
1	pastry shell (10 inches), baked

Juice and grated peel of 1 lemon

1/2 cup apple jelly

1) Soften gelatin in cold water; set aside. In a saucepan, combine the sugar, cornstarch and salt. Whisk in the milk until smooth. Cook and stir over medium-high heat until thickened and bubbly. Reduce heat; cook and stir 2 minutes longer. Remove from the heat.

2) Stir a small amount of hot filling into yolks. Return all to the pan, stirring constantly. Bring to a gentle boil. Cook and stir 2 minutes longer. Remove from the heat; stir in softened gelatin until dissolved. Stir in butter and vanilla. Cover the surface of custard with plastic wrap and chill until no longer warm.

3) Slice 3 bananas; fold into custard along with whipped cream. Spoon into pie shell. Cover and refrigerate until set, about 4-5 hours.

4) Just before serving, place lemon juice in a small bowl and slice the remaining banana into it. Melt jelly in a saucepan over low heat.

5) Drain banana; pat dry and arrange over filling. Brush banana with the jelly. Sprinkle with grated lemon peel. Serve immediately. Refrigerate leftovers.

Yield: 8 servings.

NUTRITION FACTS: 1 piece equals 478 calories, 21 g fat (11 g saturated fat), 151 mg cholesterol, 330 mg sodium, 67 g carbohydrate, 1 g fiber, 7 g protein.

PREBAKING A PASTRY SHELL

1) After placing pastry in the pie plate and fluting edges, line unpricked shell with a double thickness of heavy-duty foil. If desired, fill with dried beans, uncooked rice or pie weights. The weight will keep the crust from puffing up, shrinking and slipping down the pie plate while baking.

2) Bake at 450° for 8 minutes. With oven mitts, carefully remove foil and beans, rice or weights. Bake 5-6 minutes longer or until light golden brown. Cool on a wire rack. Let beans or rice cool; store (they may be reused for pie weights but cannot be cooked and used in recipes).

COCONUT CREAM MERINGUE PIE

Coconut Cream Meringue Pie

Betty Sitzman, Wary, Colorado

We usually have a good selection of pies at our neighborhood get-togethers, but I always come home with an empty pan when I bring this classic.

2/3	cup sugar
1/4	cup cornstarch
1/4	teaspoon salt
2	cups milk
3	egg yolks, lightly beaten

1 cup flaked coconut, finely chopped
2 tablespoons butter
1/2 teaspoon vanilla extract
1 pastry shell (9 inches), baked

MERINGUE:
3 egg whites
1/4 teaspoon cream of tartar
6 tablespoons sugar
1/2 cup flaked coconut

1) In a small saucepan, combine the sugar, cornstarch and salt. Stir in milk until smooth. Cook and stir over medium-high heat until thickened and bubbly. Reduce heat; cook and stir 2 minutes longer. Remove from the heat.

2) Stir a small amount of hot filling into egg yolks; return all to pan, stirring constantly. Bring to a gentle boil; cook and stir 2 minutes longer. Remove from the heat. Gently stir in chopped coconut, butter and vanilla until butter is melted. Pour hot filling into crust.

3) For meringue, in a small mixing bowl, beat egg whites and cream of tartar on medium speed until soft peaks form. Gradually beat in the sugar, 1 tablespoon at a time, on high until stiff glossy peaks form and sugar is dissolved. Spread evenly over hot filling, sealing edges to crust.

4) Sprinkle with flaked coconut. Bake at 350° for 12-15 minutes or until the meringue is golden. Cool on a wire rack for 1 hour. Refrigerate at least 3 hours before serving. Refrigerate leftovers.

Yield: 8 servings.

NUTRITION FACTS: 1 piece equals 415 calories, 20 g fat (12 g saturated fat), 101 mg cholesterol, 302 mg sodium, 54 g carbohydrate, 1 g fiber, 6 g protein.

TOPPING A PIE WITH MERINGUE

Spread meringue over hot filling to minimize "weeping" (the watery layer between the meringue and filling) and seal to the edges of pastry. Cool the pie away from drafts on a wire rack at room temperature for 1 hour. Refrigerate for at least 3 hours before cutting and serving. Store leftovers in the refrigerator.

Very Lemony Meringue Pie
Betty Bradley, Sebring, Florida

As a winter resident of Florida, I have access to juicy tree-fresh lemons. They're at their zesty best in this mouth-watering family pie recipe.

1-1/4 cups sugar
1/3 cup cornstarch
1 cup cold water
3 egg yolks
1 cup lemon juice
3 tablespoons butter
1 pastry shell (9 inches), baked

MERINGUE:
1 tablespoon cornstarch
1/3 cup cold water
3 egg whites
1 teaspoon vanilla extract
Dash salt
6 tablespoons sugar

1) In a saucepan, combine sugar and cornstarch. Stir in water until smooth. Cook and stir over medium heat until thickened and bubbly. Reduce heat; cook and stir 2 minutes longer. Remove from heat.

2) Stir in a small amount of hot filling into egg yolks. Return all to the pan, stirring constantly. Bring to a gentle boil; cook and stir 2 minutes longer.

3) Remove from the heat. Add lemon juice and butter; stir until butter is melted and mixture is blended. Pour hot filling into pastry shell.

4) In a saucepan, combine cornstarch and water until smooth. Cook and stir over medium-low heat until mixture is thickened, about 2 minutes. Remove from the heat.

5) In a mixing bowl, beat egg whites, vanilla and salt until foamy. Gradually beat in sugar, 1 tablespoon at a time, on medium speed until soft peaks form and sugar is dissolved. Gradually beat in cornstarch mixture, 1 tablespoon at a time, on high until stiff peaks form.

6) Spread evenly over hot filling, sealing edges to crust. Bake at 325° for 18-20 minutes or until meringue is golden. Cool on a wire rack for 1 hour. Refrigerate pie for at least 3 hours before serving. Refrigerate leftovers.

Yield: 8 servings.

NUTRITION FACTS: 1 piece equals 376 calories, 13 g fat (6 g saturated fat), 96 mg cholesterol, 186 mg sodium, 62 g carbohydrate, trace fiber, 4 g protein.

PICNIC PECAN PIE

Picnic Pecan Pie
Jill Steiner, Hancock, Minnesota

Among the selection of homemade desserts at our family reunion, slices of this timeless treat disappeared fast. It's delectable topped with ice cream or whipped cream. For a milder flavor, you can use light corn syrup in place of the dark.

3 eggs
1 cup dark corn syrup
1/2 cup sugar
2 tablespoons butter, melted
1 teaspoon vanilla extract
1/8 teaspoon salt
1 cup chopped pecans
1 unbaked pastry shell (9 inches)

1) In a small bowl, lightly beat the eggs. Stir in the corn syrup, sugar, butter, vanilla and salt. Add pecans and mix well.

2) Pour into pie shell. Cover edges loosely with foil. Bake at 350° for 20 minutes. Remove foil; bake 20 minutes longer or until a knife inserted near the center comes out clean. Cool on a wire rack. Store in the refrigerator.

Yield: 8 servings.

NUTRITION FACTS: 1 piece equals 441 calories, 22 g fat (6 g saturated fat), 92 mg cholesterol, 253 mg sodium, 59 g carbohydrate, 1 g fiber, 5 g protein.

Fudgy Pecan Tartlets
Maggie Evans, Northville, Michigan

I usually bake these tiny tarts for the holidays...but they are a hit any time of year. They are easy to make, fudgy and moist. Everyone loves them!

1/4 cup butter, softened
3 tablespoons cream cheese, softened
1/2 cup all-purpose flour

FILLING:
1 egg yolk
3 tablespoons sugar
1-1/2 teaspoons butter, melted
1-1/2 teaspoons 2% milk
1/2 teaspoon vanilla extract
1/2 cup semisweet chocolate chips, melted and cooled
12 pecan halves

1) In a small mixing bowl, cream butter and cream cheese until light. Gradually add flour, beating until blended.

2) Roll into 1-in. balls. Press onto the bottom and up the sides of miniature muffin cups coated with nonstick cooking spray.

3) For filling, in a bowl, combine the egg yolk, sugar, butter, milk and vanilla; gradually stir in melted chocolate. Fill tart shells three-fourths full. Top each with a pecan half.

4) Bake at 375° for 18-22 minutes or until lightly browned and filling is set. Cool for 10 minutes before removing to a wire rack.

Yield: 1 dozen.

NUTRITION FACTS: 1 tartlet equals 134 calories, 10 g fat (5 g saturated fat), 33 mg cholesterol, 63 mg sodium, 12 g carbohydrate, 1 g fiber, 2 g protein.

Mom's Custard Pie
Barbara Hyatt, Folsom, California

Just a single bite of this traditional treat takes me back to the days when Mom would fix this pie for Dad, Grandfather and me.

1 unbaked pastry shell (9 inches)
4 eggs
1/2 cup sugar
1/4 teaspoon salt
1 teaspoon vanilla extract
2-1/2 cups milk
1/4 teaspoon ground nutmeg

1) Line unpricked pastry shell with a double thickness of heavy-duty foil. Bake at 450° for 8 minutes. Remove foil; bake 5 minutes longer. Remove from the oven and set aside.

2) Separate one egg; set the white aside. In a mixing bowl, beat the yolk and remaining eggs just until combined. Blend in the sugar, salt and vanilla. Stir in milk. Beat reserved egg white until stiff peaks form; fold into egg mixture.

3) Carefully pour into crust. Cover edges of pie with

foil. Bake at 350° for 25 minutes. Remove foil; bake 15-20 minutes longer or until a knife inserted near the center comes out clean.

4) Cool on a wire rack. Sprinkle with nutmeg. Store in the refrigerator.

Yield: 8 servings.

NUTRITION FACTS: 1 piece equals 254 calories, 12 g fat (5 g saturated fat), 122 mg cholesterol, 243 mg sodium, 29 g carbohydrate, trace fiber, 7 g protein.

Praline Pumpkin Pie

Sandra Haase, Baltimore, Maryland

I modified this from a neighbor's recipe for chocolate praline pie. The pumpkin dresses it up for the holidays and pairs well with the nuts.

1/3 cup finely chopped pecans
1/3 cup packed brown sugar
3 tablespoons butter, softened
1 unbaked pastry shell (10 inches)

FILLING:
3 eggs, lightly beaten
1/2 cup sugar
1/2 cup packed brown sugar
2 tablespoons all-purpose flour
3/4 teaspoon ground cinnamon
1/2 teaspoon salt
1/2 teaspoon ground ginger
1/4 teaspoon ground cloves
1 can (16 ounces) pumpkin
1-1/2 cups half-and-half cream
Additional chopped pecans, optional

1) Combine the pecans, sugar and butter; press into the bottom of pie shell. Prick sides of pastry with a fork. Bake at 450° for 10 minutes; cool for 5 minutes on a wire rack.

2) In a bowl, combine the first eight filling ingredients; stir in pumpkin. Gradually add cream. Pour into pie shell. If desired, sprinkle chopped pecans on top.

3) Bake at 350° for 45-50 minutes or until a knife inserted near the center comes out clean. Cool completely on a wire rack. Store in the refrigerator.

Yield: 10 servings.

NUTRITION FACTS: 1 piece equals 344 calories, 16 g fat (8 g saturated fat), 95 mg cholesterol, 279 mg sodium, 45 g carbohydrate, 2 g fiber, 5 g protein.

Raspberry Curd Tartlets

Taste of Home Test Kitchen

If you're pressed for time, use purchased lemon curd in place of the homemade raspberry curd and garnish with fresh raspberries.

1 cup butter, softened
1/2 cup confectioners' sugar
1 teaspoon vanilla extract
2 cups all-purpose flour
Dash salt
1/2 cup finely chopped almonds

RASPBERRY CURD:
1 package (10 ounces) frozen unsweetened raspberries, thawed
3 tablespoons lemon juice
1/2 cup butter
3 tablespoons sugar
4 eggs
Red liquid food coloring, optional
Whipped cream, fresh raspberries and mint

1) In a large mixing bowl, cream the butter and confectioners' sugar until light and fluffy. Add vanilla. Combine flour and salt; add to creamed mixture and beat until smooth. Stir in almonds.

2) Press into 2-1/2-in. tartlet pans; trim edges. Place pans on a baking sheet. Bake at 375° for 20-25 minutes or until golden brown. Cool on a wire rack. Remove from pans.

3) For raspberry curd, combine raspberries and lemon juice in a blender or food processor; cover and process until pureed. Press through a strainer to remove seeds.

4) In a saucepan, melt butter over medium heat. Reduce heat to low; add the raspberry puree, sugar and eggs. Cook and stir for 10-15 minutes or until mixture is smooth and thickened and reaches 160°. Remove from the heat. Add food coloring if desired. Press plastic wrap on surface of curd. Refrigerate for several hours or overnight.

5) Spoon about 3 tablespoons of curd into each tart shell; top with whipped cream, raspberries and mint. Refrigerate leftovers.

Yield: about 2 dozen.

NUTRITION FACTS: 1 tartlet equals 188 calories, 14 g fat (7 g saturated fat), 66 mg cholesterol, 133 mg sodium, 14 g carbohydrate, 1 g fiber, 3 g protein.

Strawberry Chiffon Pie

Taste of Home Test Kitchen

This scrumptious strawberry chiffon filling is so refreshing. Either a graham cracker crust or chocolate crumb crust will showcase it nicely.

2-1/2   cups sliced fresh strawberries
1   envelope unflavored gelatin
2   tablespoons lemonade concentrate
1/4   cup sugar
3   egg whites, lightly beaten
1   tablespoon orange juice
1-1/2   cups reduced-fat whipped topping
1   reduced-fat graham cracker crust (8 inches) *or* chocolate crumb crust
4   large fresh strawberries, halved

1) Place sliced strawberries in a food processor or blender; cover and process until smooth. Set aside 1-1/2 cups for filling (discard remaining puree or save for another use).

2) In a saucepan, sprinkle gelatin over lemonade concentrate; let stand for 5 minutes. Stir in sugar and reserved strawberry puree. Cook and stir over medium heat until mixture comes to a boil and gelatin is dissolved. Remove from the heat.

3) Stir a small amount of filling into egg whites; return all to the pan, stirring constantly. Cook and stir over low heat for 3 minutes or until mixture is slightly thickened and a thermometer reaches 160° (do not boil). Remove from the heat; stir in

orange juice. Cover and refrigerate for 2 hours, stirring occasionally. Fold in whipped topping; spoon into crust. Cover and refrigerate for 2 hours or until set. Just before serving, garnish with halved strawberries.

Yield: 8 servings.

NUTRITION FACTS: 1 piece equals 226 calories, 7 g fat (5 g saturated fat), 12 mg cholesterol, 145 mg sodium, 35 g carbohydrate, 2 g fiber, 4 g protein.

Chocolate Caramel Tart

Margaret Peterson, Forest City, Iowa

Look no further when you want a dessert that's gooey and good! Each piece is like a big candy bar on a plate, so a thin slice may be enough.

2   cups crushed chocolate wafers (about 35 wafers)
1/3   cup butter, melted
30   caramels
1/2   cup caramel ice cream topping
1/2   cup heavy whipping cream, *divided*
2   cups chopped pecans
3/4   cup semisweet chocolate chips

1) In a small bowl, combine the wafer crumbs and butter; press onto the bottom of a greased 9-in. springform pan. Place pan on a baking sheet. Bake at 350° for 10 minutes. Cool on a wire rack.

2) In a heavy saucepan, cook and stir caramels and caramel topping over low heat until smooth. Remove from heat; stir in 1/4 cup cream and pecans. Spread over crust. Cover; refrigerate for 1 hour.

3) In a saucepan, melt the chocolate chips with remaining cream over low heat, stirring until smooth. Drizzle over tart. Cover and refrigerate for 1 hour or until serving.

Yield: 12 servings.

NUTRITION FACTS: 1 piece equals 478 calories, 31 g fat (11 g saturated fat), 29 mg cholesterol, 274 mg sodium, 52 g carbohydrate, 4 g fiber, 5 g protein.

Lime Cheesecake Pie

Vivian Eagleson, Cumming, Georgia

This light citrus pie is the perfect treat on a hot day because you don't have to heat up the kitchen to prepare it.

1   package (8 ounces) cream cheese, softened
1   can (14 ounces) sweetened condensed milk

1/3 cup lime juice

1-1/2 teaspoons vanilla extract

1 graham cracker crust (9 inches)

1 carton (8 ounces) frozen whipped topping, thawed

Lime slices and fresh mint, optional

1) In a large mixing bowl, beat cream cheese until smooth. Add the milk, lime juice and vanilla; beat until smooth. Pour into the crust. Refrigerate for 2 hours.

2) Spread with whipped topping; refrigerate 1 hour longer. Garnish with lime and mint if desired.

Yield: 8 servings.

NUTRITION FACTS: 1 piece equals 446 calories, 24 g fat (15 g saturated fat), 48 mg cholesterol, 268 mg sodium, 49 g carbohydrate, trace fiber, 7 g protein.

CHERRY CREAM CHEESE TARTS

Cherry Cream Cheese Tarts
Cindi Mitchell, Waring, Texas

It's hard to believe that just five ingredients and a few minutes of prep can result in these delicate and scrumptious tarts.

6 ounces cream cheese, softened

1/2 cup confectioners' sugar

1/4 to 1/2 teaspoon almond *or* vanilla extract

4 individual graham cracker tart shells

1/2 cup cherry pie filling

1) In a small mixing bowl, beat the cream cheese, sugar and extract until smooth. Spoon into shells. Top with pie filling. Refrigerate until serving.

Yield: 4 servings.

NUTRITION FACTS: 1 tart equals 360 calories, 20 g fat (10 g saturated fat), 41 mg cholesterol, 275 mg sodium, 40 g carbohydrate, 1 g fiber, 4 g protein.

Chocolate Truffle Pie
Mercelle Jackson, Rochester, New York

Warm days warrant a cool dessert like this frosty and refreshing pie. The raspberry sauce combined with rich chocolate and ice cream make each slice irresistible. Try out different ice cream flavors and enjoy the results!

1 cup chocolate wafer crumbs

1/4 cup butter, melted

1 pint chocolate ice cream, softened

1 cup (6 ounces) semisweet chocolate chips

1/3 cup heavy whipping cream

1 pint vanilla ice cream, softened

2 tablespoons slivered almonds, toasted

1 package (10 ounces) frozen sweetened raspberries, thawed

1 tablespoon cornstarch

1) In a small bowl, combine wafer crumbs and butter. Press onto the bottom and up the sides of a 9-in. pie plate coated with nonstick cooking spray. Freeze for 30 minutes. Spread chocolate ice cream over crust; freeze for 1 hour or until firm.

2) Melt chocolate chips with whipping cream; stir until smooth. Cool slightly. Quickly and carefully spread over chocolate ice cream. Freeze for 30 minutes. Top with vanilla ice cream; sprinkle with almonds. Cover; freeze until firm.

3) For sauce, puree the raspberries in a blender or food processor until smooth. Strain and discard seeds. In a saucepan, combine cornstarch and raspberry juice until smooth. Bring to a boil; cook and stir for 1-2 minutes or until thickened. Cool completely.

4) Remove pie from the freezer 10 minutes before cutting. Serve over raspberry sauce.

Yield: 8 servings.

NUTRITION FACTS: 1 piece equals 435 calories, 26 g fat (15 g saturated fat), 55 mg cholesterol, 197 mg sodium, 51 g carbohydrate, 4 g fiber, 5 g protein.

■ *FAVORITE ICE CREAM PIE:* Substitute your family's favorite flavor of ice cream for either the chocolate *or* vanilla. Here are some additional combinations: chocolate and coffee, cherry and vanilla *or* caramel and coffee.

Frosty Cranberry Pie
Mildred Skrha, Oak Brook, Illinois

It's nice to have this light pie in the freezer when unexpected guests stop over.

1 package (8 ounces) cream cheese, softened
1 cup confectioners' sugar
1 can (16 ounces) whole-berry cranberry sauce
1 carton (8 ounces) frozen whipped topping, thawed
2 pastry shells (9 inches), baked
Additional whipped topping, optional
Slivered almonds, toasted, optional

1) In a mixing bowl, beat cream cheese and sugar until light. Stir in cranberry sauce. Fold in whipped topping. Spoon into crusts.

2) Cover and freeze for up to 3 months. Remove from the freezer 10-15 minutes before serving. Garnish with whipped topping and almonds if desired.

Yield: 2 pies (6-8 servings each).

NUTRITION FACTS: 1 serving equals 279 calories, 14 g fat (8 g saturated fat), 21 mg cholesterol, 148 mg sodium, 35 g carbohydrate, trace fiber, 2 g protein.

Chocolate Mint Cream Pie
Donna Christopher, Crestwood, Missouri

This pie is an ideal way to give your holiday guests a sweet treat without going through a lot of fuss.

2 cups crushed chocolate-covered mint cookies
3 to 4 tablespoons hot water
1 graham cracker crust (9 inches)
1 package (3 ounces) cream cheese, softened
1/3 cup sugar
2 tablespoons milk
1/4 teaspoon peppermint extract
1 carton (8 ounces) frozen whipped topping, thawed

1) Set aside 2 tablespoons cookie crumbs for garnish. In a small bowl, combine remaining crumbs with enough hot water to make crumbs spreadable. Spoon over the graham cracker crust; spread out evenly; set aside.

2) In a large mixing bowl, beat cream cheese until fluffy. Add the sugar, milk and extract; beat until smooth. Fold in whipped topping. Spoon into crust. Sprinkle with the reserved cookie crumbs. Cover and refrigerate for 3 hours or until firm.

Yield: 8 servings.

NUTRITION FACTS: 1 serving equals 413 calories, 22 g fat (13 g saturated fat), 13 mg cholesterol, 234 mg sodium, 50 g carbohydrate, 1 g fiber, 3 g protein.

Raspberry Ribbon Pie
Anita Ohlson, Oak Harbor, Washington

We always freeze fresh raspberries when they're in season so we can make this pie year-round.

1 cup vanilla wafer crumbs (about 29 wafers)
1/4 cup butter, melted
1 package (3 ounces) raspberry gelatin
1 cup boiling water
1/4 cup sugar
1 cup fresh raspberries
1 tablespoon lemon juice
1 package (3 ounces) cream cheese, softened
1/3 cup confectioners' sugar
1 teaspoon vanilla extract
Dash salt
1 cup heavy whipping cream

1) In a small bowl, combine the wafer crumbs and butter; press onto the bottom and up the sides of an ungreased 9-in. pie plate. Bake at 350° for 10 minutes or until golden brown.

2) In a bowl, dissolve gelatin in boiling water. Add the sugar, raspberries and lemon juice. Refrigerate until partially set, about 1-1/2 hours. In a mixing bowl, beat cream cheese and confectioners' sugar until smooth. Add vanilla and salt. In another mixing bowl, beat whipping cream until stiff peaks form. Fold into cream cheese mixture. Spread 3/4 cup over bottom of crust.

3) Spread 3/4 cup raspberry mixture over the top; repeat layers. Refrigerate for 8 hours or overnight before serving. Refrigerate leftovers.

Yield: 8 servings.

NUTRITION FACTS: 1 piece equals 345 calories, 23 g fat (13 g saturated fat), 69 mg cholesterol, 189 mg sodium, 34 g carbohydrate, 1 g fiber, 3 g protein.

■ *STRAWBERRY RIBBON PIE:* Use strawberry gelatin for the raspberry gelatin and use 1 cup sliced strawberries for the raspberries.

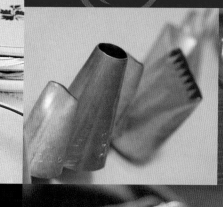

CHAPTER 20
CAKES

CAKES

Cakes add a festive air to any meal and usually make an appearance at special-occasion dinners. Cakes can be rich and moist, dense, buttery or airy and are divided into butter cakes or foam cakes.

Butter cakes get their name because the batter is made from creaming fat—such as butter or shortening—with sugar. The creaming traps air in the batter; this trapped air expands during baking and gives the cake its height. Butter cakes have a fine moist texture and a tender crumb.

Foam cakes contain a high proportion of eggs or egg whites to flour. Beaten eggs give foam cakes their light, fluffy texture. There are three kinds of foam cakes: angel food, sponge and chiffon.

Butter Cake Tips

Use butter, stick margarine (with at least 80% oil) or shortening. The fat should be softened (at room temperature), meaning it is pliable when touched. Whipped, tub, soft, liquid or reduced-fat products should not be used. Measure all ingredients accurately.

Arrange the oven racks so that the cake will bake in the center of the oven. Preheat oven for 10 to 15 minutes before baking.

Most butter cake recipes call for creaming the butter and sugar. Beat the softened butter or shortening and sugar with an electric mixer or wooden spoon to a light and fluffy consistency, about 5 minutes.

For better volume, allow eggs to stand at room temperature for 30 minutes before using. Or place eggs in their shell in a bowl of warm water while assembling the remaining ingredients.

Mix dry ingredients together to evenly distribute the leavener throughout the flour. This will ensure that it's

evenly incorporated into the batter. Stop the mixer occasionally—or between additions of ingredients—and scrape the batter down sides of bowl with a rubber or plastic spatula.

It's best to use the pan size recommended in the recipe. For substitutions, check the Bakeware Substitution chart on page 14. Baking times may need to be adjusted. For a tender, golden crust, use aluminum pans with a dull rather than shiny or dark finish. If using glass baking dishes, reduce the oven temperature 25°.

Grease and flour baking pans for butter cakes that will be removed from the pans. Cakes served from the pans should be greased but not floured. Some cake recipes call for the pan to be lined with waxed paper for easier removal of the cake from the pan. (See Lining a Baking Pan with Waxed Paper on page 508.)

Fill pans half to three-fourths full. A thin batter will rise more than a heavy batter, so allow more room for thin batters to rise. Pour thinner batters into pans, then tap pans on the countertop to remove air bubbles. Spoon firmer batters into pans, then spread gently to even out the batter.

Leave at least 1 in. of space between pans and also between pans and sides of oven for good heat circulation. If using two oven racks, stagger pans in the oven so that they are not directly over one another. Switch pan positions and rotate pans from front to back halfway through baking.

Use a kitchen timer. Check for doneness at the minimum recommended baking time, then check every 2 minutes after that. Butter cakes are done when a toothpick inserted near the center of the cake comes out clean. (See Testing Butter Cakes for Doneness on page 509.)

Cool cakes for 10 minutes in the pan, unless recipe directs otherwise. Loosen the cake by running a knife around the edge of the pan. Turn out onto a wire rack, place another rack over the cake and flip right side up. Cool completely before filling or frosting unless directed otherwise by recipe.

If a cake sticks to the pan and will not come out when inverted, return to a heated oven for 1 minute, then try again to turn it out.

Use a serrated knife or use a sawing motion when cutting. Warm the blade of the knife in hot water, then dry and make a cut. Clean and rewarm knife before each cut.

Flour Facts

All-purpose flour is the most commonly used flour and creates a good cake. Cake flour gives a more tender and delicate crumb. Self-rising flour contains the leavening agent and salt, so you only need to measure one ingredient. While you can substitute one type of flour for another, you will need to make some adjustments to the recipe.

- For 1 cup of cake flour, use 3/4 cup plus 2 tablespoons all-purpose flour.

- For 1 cup all-purpose flour, use 1 cup plus 2 tablespoons cake flour.

- For 1 cup self-rising flour, place 1-1/2 teaspoons baking powder and 1/2 teaspoon salt in a measuring cup. Add all-purpose flour to measure 1 cup.

Baking at High Altitudes

High altitude (over 3,000 feet) has less air pressure and drier air. These conditions affect baked goods. The lower air pressure allows the gases created by the leavening agents to expand more quickly and causes liquids to evaporate and boil at lower temperatures. The drier air also dries out the flour.

For cakes, this means that there might be excessive rising from the gases the leavening produced. This would cause the texture to be coarse or may even cause the cake to fall before the structure of the cake can be set by baking. Faster evaporation of the liquid, due to lower boiling point, would reduce the amount of liquid and increase the concentration of sugar. This higher sugar concentration may also weaken the structure of the cake.

Some measures to take for butter cakes are to increase the oven temperature 15° to 25°, which will allow cakes to set faster and prevent falling. Fill baking pans half full not two-thirds full, since cakes rise higher.

Reduce the leavener, reduce the sugar and increase the liquid.

For foam cakes, only beat the egg whites until soft peaks form. To strengthen the structure of the cake, decrease the amount of sugar by a tablespoon or two and increase the amount of flour or egg component of the cake a little. Increasing the oven temperature by 15° to 25° will also help set the cake structure sooner.

Here are some general guidelines for adjusting ingredients for butter cakes.

ADJUSTMENT	3000 FT.	5000 FT.	7000 FT.
For each teaspoon of baking powder, reduce by:	1/8 teaspoon	1/8 to 1/4 teaspoon	1/4 teaspoon
For each cup of sugar, reduce by:	0 to 1 tablespoon	0 to 2 tablespoons	1 to 3 tablespoons
For each cup of liquid, increase by:	1 to 2 tablespoons	2 to 4 tablespoons	3 to 4 tablespoons

White Layer Cake
Taste of Home Test Kitchen

Every recipe file should contain a standard delicious cake like this. Topped with your favorite flavor of frosting, it's great for any occasion.

1/2 cup butter, softened
1-1/2 cups sugar
4 egg whites
2 teaspoons vanilla extract
2 cups all-purpose flour
1 teaspoon baking powder
1/2 teaspoon baking soda
1/4 teaspoon salt
1-1/3 cups buttermilk
2-1/2 cups frosting of your choice

1) In a large mixing bowl, cream butter and sugar until light and fluffy. Add egg whites, one at a time, beating well after each addition. Beat in vanilla. Combine the flour, baking powder, baking soda and salt; add to creamed mixture alternately with buttermilk, beating well after each addition.

2) Spread evenly into two greased and floured 9-in. round baking pans. Bake at 350° for 30-35 minutes or until a toothpick inserted near the center comes out clean.

3) Cool for 10 minutes before removing from pans to wire racks to cool completely. Spread frosting between layers and over the top and sides of cake.

Yield: 12 servings.

NUTRITION FACTS: 1 slice equals 508 calories, 18 g fat (7 g saturated fat), 22 mg cholesterol, 376 mg sodium, 81 g carbohydrate, 1 g fiber, 4 g protein.

YELLOW LAYER CAKE

Yellow Layer Cake
Taste of Home Test Kitchen

Instead of a boxed cake mix, why not try your hand at this easy recipe for a basic yellow cake? You just can't beat the homemade goodness!

2/3	cup butter, softened
1-3/4	cups sugar
2	eggs
1-1/2	teaspoons vanilla extract
2-1/2	cups all-purpose flour
2-1/2	teaspoons baking powder
1/2	teaspoon salt
1-1/4	cups milk
2-1/2	cups frosting of your choice

1) In a large mixing bowl, cream butter and sugar until light and fluffy. Add eggs, one at a time, beating well after each addition. Stir in vanilla. Combine the flour, baking powder and salt; add to the creamed mixture alternately with milk, beating well after each addition.

2) Pour into two greased and floured 9-in. round baking pans. Bake at 350° for 25-30 minutes or until a toothpick inserted near the center comes out clean.

3) Cool for 10 minutes before removing from pans to wire racks to cool completely. Spread frosting

between layers and over the top and sides of cake.

Yield: 12 servings.

NUTRITION FACTS: 1 slice equals 576 calories, 22 g fat (10 g saturated fat), 66 mg cholesterol, 425 mg sodium, 89 g carbohydrate, 1 g fiber, 5 g protein.

Million-Dollar Pound Cake
George Dunn, Jasper, Texas

This pound cake is often on our family's table. It has a fine, rich texture that's unusually smooth.

2	cups butter, softened
3	cups sugar
6	eggs
4	cups all-purpose flour
3/4	cup milk
1	teaspoon almond extract
1	teaspoon vanilla extract

1) In a large mixing bowl, cream butter until fluffy. Gradually add sugar, beating until light and fluffy, about 5 minutes. Add eggs, one at a time, beating well after each addition.

2) Add flour to creamed mixture alternately with milk, beginning and ending with flour, just until blended. Stir in extracts. Pour batter into a greased and floured 10-in. tube pan.

3) Bake at 325° for about 1 hour and 40 minutes or until a toothpick inserted near the center comes out clean. Cool for 15 minutes before removing from pan to a wire rack to cool completely.

Yield: 16 servings.

NUTRITION FACTS: 1 slice equals 497 calories, 25 g fat (15 g saturated fat), 143 mg cholesterol, 262 mg sodium, 62 g carbohydrate, 1 g fiber, 6 g protein.

LEVELING CAKE LAYERS
Stacking layers for a layered cake is easier when the layers are level. When the cake is cool, use a long serrated knife to slice the high spot from the bottom layer of a two-layer cake or the bottom and middle layers of a three-layer cake. You can trim off the crown of the top layer or leave it for a domed effect.

PREPARING A CAKE PAN

1) Grease the sides and bottom of the pan by spreading shortening with a paper towel over the interior of the pan.

2) Sprinkle 1 to 2 tablespoons of flour into the greased pan; tilt the pan to coat bottom and sides. Turn pan over and tap to remove excess flour.

GEORGIA PECAN CAKE

Georgia Pecan Cake
Carolyn Griffin, Macon, Georgia

This recipe came from my mother and has always been a hit with our family. One taste and you'll see why!

>   1   cup butter, softened
>   2   cups sugar
>   4   eggs
>   1   teaspoon vanilla extract
>   1/2   teaspoon lemon extract
>   3   cups all-purpose flour
>   3/4   teaspoon salt
>   1/2   teaspoon baking powder
>   1/2   teaspoon baking soda
>   1   cup buttermilk
>   1   cup chopped pecans

1) In a large mixing bowl, cream butter and sugar until light and fluffy. Add the eggs, one at a time, beating well after each addition. Beat in extracts.

2) Combine the flour, salt, baking powder and baking soda; set 1/4 cup aside. Add the remaining flour mixture to the creamed mixture alternately with buttermilk. Toss pecans with the reserved flour mixture; fold into batter.

3) Pour into a greased and floured 10-in. tube pan. Bake at 325° for 60-70 minutes or until a toothpick inserted near the center comes out clean.

4) Cool for 10 minutes before removing from pan to a wire rack to cool completely.

Yield: 12-16 servings.

NUTRITION FACTS: 1 slice equals 360 calories, 18 g fat (8 g saturated fat), 84 mg cholesterol, 311 mg sodium, 45 g carbohydrate, 1 g fiber, 5 g protein.

Lemon Orange Cake
Norma Poole, Auburndale, Florida

I love to bake this lovely three-layer cake for Thanksgiving. It has that tangy Florida citrus flavor and isn't any more difficult to make than a two-layer cake.

>   1   cup butter, softened
>   1/4   cup shortening
>   2   cups sugar
>   5   eggs
>   3   cups all-purpose flour
>   1   teaspoon baking powder
>   1/2   teaspoon baking soda
>   1/2   teaspoon salt
>   1   cup buttermilk
>   1   teaspoon vanilla extract
>   1/2   teaspoon lemon extract

FROSTING:

>   1/2   cup butter, softened
>   3   tablespoons orange juice
>   3   tablespoons lemon juice
>   1   to 2 tablespoons grated orange peel
>   1   to 2 tablespoons grated lemon peel
>   1   teaspoon lemon extract
> 5-1/2   to 6 cups confectioners' sugar

1) In a mixing bowl, cream butter, shortening and sugar until light and fluffy. Add eggs, one at a time, beating well after each addition. Combine the flour, baking powder, baking soda and salt; add to the creamed mixture alternately with buttermilk, beginning and ending with dry ingredients. Beat well after each addition. Stir in extracts.

2) Pour into three greased and floured 9-in. round baking pans. Bake at 350° for 25-30 minutes or until a toothpick inserted near the center comes out clean. Cool for 10 minutes before removing from pans to wire racks to cool completely.

3) For frosting, in a mixing bowl, cream butter until light and fluffy. Add the juices, peels and extract; beat until well blended. Gradually add confectioners' sugar, beating until frosting reaches desired spreading consistency. Spread frosting between layers and over top and sides of cake.

Yield: 10-12 servings.

NUTRITION FACTS: 1 slice equals 740 calories, 29 g fat (16 g saturated fat), 151 mg cholesterol, 465 mg sodium, 114 g carbohydrate, 1 g fiber, 7 g protein.

WHITE TEXAS SHEET CAKE

White Texas Sheet Cake
Joanie Ward, Brownsburg, Indiana

This cake gets better the longer it sits, so I make it a day ahead. With its creamy frosting, no one can resist it.

1	cup butter, cubed
1	cup water
2	cups all-purpose flour
2	cups sugar
2	eggs, beaten
1/2	cup sour cream
1	teaspoon almond extract
1	teaspoon baking soda
1	teaspoon salt

FROSTING:

1/2	cup butter
1/4	cup milk
4-1/2	cups confectioners' sugar
1/2	teaspoon almond extract
1	cup chopped walnuts

1) In a large saucepan, bring butter and water just to a boil. Immediately remove from the heat; stir in

the flour, sugar, eggs, sour cream, almond extract, baking soda and salt until smooth.

2) Pour into a greased 15-in. x 10-in. x 1-in. baking pan. Bake at 375° for 20-22 minutes or until a toothpick inserted near the center comes out clean and cake is golden brown. Cool for 20 minutes.

3) For frosting, in a large saucepan, combine butter and milk. Bring to a boil. Remove from the heat; stir in sugar and extract. Stir in walnuts; spread over warm cake.

Yield: 16-20 servings.

NUTRITION FACTS: 1 slice equals 409 calories, 19 g fat (10 g saturated fat), 62 mg cholesterol, 331 mg sodium, 58 g carbohydrate, 1 g fiber, 4 g protein.

Holiday Fruitcake
Allene Spence, Delbarton, West Virginia

I came up with this recipe myself, and think it has just the right mix of nuts and fruit.

3	cups whole red and green candied cherries
3	cups diced candied pineapple
1	package (1 pound) shelled walnuts
1	package (10 ounces) golden raisins
1	cup shortening
1	cup sugar
5	eggs
4	tablespoons vanilla extract
3	cups all-purpose flour
3	teaspoons baking powder
1	teaspoon salt

1) In a large bowl, combine the cherries, pineapple, walnuts and raisins; set aside. In a large mixing bowl, cream shortening and sugar until light and fluffy. Beat in eggs and vanilla.

2) Combine the flour, baking powder and salt; add to the creamed mixture and mix well. Pour over fruit mixture and stir to coat.

3) Pour into a greased and floured 10-in. tube pan. Bake at 300° for 2 hours or until a toothpick inserted near the center comes out clean.

4) Cool for 10 minutes before removing from pan to a wire rack to cool completely. Wrap tightly and store in a cool place. Slice with a serrated knife; bring to room temperature before serving.

Yield: 16 servings.

NUTRITION FACTS: 1 slice equals 684 calories, 32 g fat (5 g saturated fat), 66 mg cholesterol, 281 mg sodium, 92 g carbohydrate, 4 g fiber, 9 g protein.

Lemon Poppy Seed Cake

Kristen Croke, Hanover, Massachusetts

Family and friends will love this buttermilk cake whether you serve tender slices with coffee at brunch or as a treat after dinner. The delicate lemon glaze adds a special touch.

  6 tablespoons butter, softened
1-1/2 cups sugar, *divided*
  1 tablespoon grated lemon peel
  2 eggs
  2 egg whites
2-1/2 cups cake flour
  2 tablespoons poppy seeds
1-1/2 teaspoons baking powder
  1/2 teaspoon baking soda
  1/2 teaspoon salt
  1/4 teaspoon ground allspice
1-1/3 cups 1% buttermilk
  1/4 cup lemon juice

1) In a large mixing bowl, beat butter and 1-1/4 cups sugar until crumbly, about 2 minutes. Add lemon peel; mix well. Add eggs and egg whites, one at a time, beating well after each addition.

2) Combine the flour, poppy seeds, baking powder, baking soda, salt and allspice. Add to the butter mixture alternately with buttermilk.

3) Transfer to a 10-in. tube pan heavily coated with nonstick cooking spray. Bake at 350° for 40-45 minutes or until a toothpick inserted near the center comes out clean.

4) Cool in pan for 10 minutes. Carefully run a knife around the edge of pan and center tube to loosen. Remove to a wire rack.

5) Meanwhile, in a small saucepan, combine the lemon juice and remaining sugar. Cook and stir until mixture comes to a boil; cook and stir 1-2 minutes longer or until sugar is dissolved.

6) Using a fork, poke holes in top of cake. Gradually pour hot syrup over cake. Cool completely.

Yield: 12 servings.

NUTRITION FACTS: 1 slice equals 266 calories, 8 g fat (4 g saturated fat), 52 mg cholesterol, 318 mg sodium, 47 g carbohydrate, 1 g fiber, 5 g protein.

SOUR CREAM CHOCOLATE CAKE

Sour Cream Chocolate Cake

Marsha Lawson, Pflugerville, Texas

Impressive to look at but easy to make, this cake is a good old-fashioned "Sunday supper" dessert that melts in your mouth.

  1 cup baking cocoa
  1 cup boiling water
  1 cup butter, softened
2-1/2 cups sugar
  4 eggs
  2 teaspoons vanilla extract
  3 cups cake flour
  2 teaspoons baking soda
  1/2 teaspoon baking powder
  1/2 teaspoon salt
  1 cup (8 ounces) sour cream

FROSTING:
  2 cups (12 ounces) semisweet chocolate chips
  1/2 cup butter
  1 cup (8 ounces) sour cream
  1 teaspoon vanilla extract
4-1/2 to 5 cups confectioners' sugar

1) Dissolve cocoa in water; let stand until cool. In a large mixing bowl, cream butter and sugar until light and fluffy. Add eggs, one at a time, beating well after each addition. Add vanilla.

2) Combine flour, baking soda, baking powder and salt; add to creamed mixture alternately with sour cream, beating well. Add cocoa mixture; beat well.

3) Pour into three greased and floured 9-in. round baking pans. Bake at 350° for 30-35 minutes or

until a toothpick inserted near the center comes out clean. Cool for 10 minutes before removing from pans to wire racks to cool completely.

4) In a heavy saucepan, melt chocolate chips and butter over low heat; stir until smooth. Remove from the heat; cool for 5 minutes. Place in a large mixing bowl. Add sour cream and vanilla; beat until blended. Add confectioners' sugar; beat until light and fluffy. Spread between layers and over top and sides of cake. Store in the refrigerator.

Yield: 16 servings.

NUTRITION FACTS: 1 slice equals 692 calories, 30 g fat (18 g saturated fat), 119 mg cholesterol, 451 mg sodium, 102 g carbohydrate, 3 g fiber, 7 g protein.

Chocolate Mocha Torte
Abby Slavings, Buchanan, Michigan

A mocha filling is spread between the layers of this decadent cake that's piled high with flavor.

- 1/2   cup unsweetened cocoa
- 1/2   cup boiling water
- 2-1/2 cups all-purpose flour
- 1-1/2 teaspoons baking soda
- 1/2   teaspoon salt
- 2/3   cup butter, softened
- 1-3/4 cups sugar
- 2   eggs
- 1   teaspoon vanilla extract
- 1   cup buttermilk

FILLING:
- 5   tablespoons all-purpose flour
- 1   cup milk
- 1   cup butter, softened
- 1   cup sugar
- 1/2   teaspoon instant coffee granules
- 2   teaspoons water
- 2   teaspoons unsweetened cocoa
- 1   teaspoon vanilla extract
- 1   cup chopped pecans

FROSTING:
- 1/2   cup shortening
- 1/4   cup butter, softened
- 2-1/2 tablespoons evaporated milk
- 1   tablespoon boiling water
- 1-1/2 teaspoons vanilla extract
- Dash salt
- 1   pound sifted confectioners' sugar, *divided*
- Pecan halves, optional

1) In a small bowl, make a paste of cocoa and water; cool and set aside. Sift together the flour, baking soda and salt; set aside.

2) In a large mixing bowl, cream butter and sugar until light and fluffy. Add eggs, one at a time, beating well after each addition. Beat in vanilla. Blend in cocoa mixture. Add flour mixture alternately with the buttermilk, beating well after each addition. Pour into two greased and floured 9-in. round baking pans.

3) Bake at 350° for 35 minutes or until a toothpick inserted near the center comes out clean. Cool for 10 minutes before removing from pans to wire racks to cool completely.

4) For filling, in a saucepan, combine flour and milk until smooth. Bring to a boil over low heat; cook and stir for 1-2 minutes or until thickened. Remove from the heat; cool.

5) Meanwhile, cream butter and sugar. Dissolve coffee in water; add to creamed mixture along with cocoa, vanilla and cooled milk mixture. Beat until fluffy, about 5 minutes. Fold in nuts.

6) Split each cake into two horizontal layers. Place bottom layer on a serving plate; top with a third of the filling. Repeat layers twice. Top with remaining cake layer.

7) For frosting, in a large mixing bowl, cream shortening and butter. Add the milk, water, vanilla, salt and half the confectioners' sugar. Beat well. Add remaining sugar and beat until smooth and fluffy. Spread over top and sides of cake. Garnish with pecan halves if desired.

Yield: 16 servings.

NUTRITION FACTS: 1 slice equals 660 calories, 35 g fat (16 g saturated fat), 89 mg cholesterol, 457 mg sodium, 84 g carbohydrate, 2 g fiber, 6 g protein.

SPLITTING CAKES INTO LAYERS
Using a ruler, mark the center of the side of the cake with a toothpick. Continue inserting toothpicks around the cake. Using the toothpicks as a guide, cut the cake horizontally in half with a long serrated knife. Carefully remove the top half. Frost or fill the bottom half as recipe instructs and replace the top cut side down.

1 teaspoon vanilla extract

1 square (1 ounce) semisweet chocolate

1/2 teaspoon shortening

1) Line three greased 9-in. round baking pans with waxed paper. Grease waxed paper and set aside. In small saucepan, melt chocolate with water over low heat; cool.

2) In a large mixing bowl, cream butter and sugar until light and fluffy. Beat in 4 egg yolks, one at a time, beating well after each addition. Blend in melted chocolate and vanilla.

3) Combine the flour, baking soda and salt; add to the creamed mixture alternately with buttermilk, beating well after each addition.

4) In a small mixing bowl and with clean beaters, beat the 4 egg whites until stiff peaks form. Fold a fourth of the egg whites into the creamed mixture; fold in remaining whites.

5) Pour batter into prepared pans. Bake at 350° for 30 minutes or until a toothpick inserted near the center comes out clean. Cool for 10 minutes before removing from pans to wire racks to cool completely.

6) For frosting, in a small saucepan, heat the sugar, milk, butter and egg yolks over medium-low heat until mixture is thickened and golden brown, stirring constantly. Remove from the heat.

7) Stir in the coconut, pecans and vanilla extract. Cool until thick enough to spread. Spread a third of the frosting over tops of each cake layer and stack the layers. Melt chocolate with shortening, stirring until smooth; drizzle down sides of cake.

Yield: 12 servings.

NUTRITION FACTS: 1 slice equals 751 calories, 42 g fat (22 g saturated fat), 193 mg cholesterol, 527 mg sodium, 89 g carbohydrate, 2 g fiber, 9 g protein.

LINING A BAKING PAN WITH WAXED PAPER

To easily remove cakes from the pan, consider lining the pan with waxed paper. Place pan on a piece of waxed paper. Trace the shape of the pan onto the waxed paper, then cut out. Grease the pan; place the waxed paper in the pan and grease it. Remove the paper as soon as the baked cake is inverted onto a wire rack to cool.

GERMAN CHOCOLATE CAKE

German Chocolate Cake

Joyce Platfood, Botkins, Ohio

This spectacular cake is not frosted. Each layer is spread with a coconut-pecan filling and drizzled with chocolate icing. To save time, the cake can be baked days before and frozen until you're ready to assemble and serve it.

1 package (4 ounces) German sweet chocolate

1/2 cup water

1 cup butter, softened

2 cups sugar

4 eggs, *separated*

1 teaspoon vanilla extract

2-1/2 cups cake flour

1 teaspoon baking soda

1/2 teaspoon salt

1 cup buttermilk

FROSTING:

1 cup sugar

1 cup evaporated milk

1/2 cup butter

3 egg yolks, beaten

1-1/3 cups flaked coconut

1 cup chopped pecans

Frosted Spice Cake
Lorraine Darocha, Mountain City, Tennessee

This moist and flavorful spice cake is easy, and you just add cinnamon to prepared vanilla frosting for the fast finishing touch.

- 3 cups all-purpose flour
- 2 cups sugar
- 2 teaspoons baking soda
- 1 teaspoon salt
- 1-1/8 teaspoons ground cinnamon, *divided*
- 1/2 teaspoon ground cloves
- 1/2 teaspoon ground nutmeg
- 2 cups water
- 2/3 cup canola oil
- 2 tablespoons white vinegar
- 2 teaspoons vanilla extract
- 1 can (12 ounces) whipped vanilla frosting

1) In a large mixing bowl, combine the flour, sugar, baking soda, salt, 1 teaspoon cinnamon, cloves and nutmeg. Combine the water, oil, vinegar and vanilla; add to dry ingredients and beat until smooth (batter will be thin).

2) Pour into a 13-in. x 9-in. x 2-in. baking pan coated with nonstick cooking spray. Bake at 350° for 25-30 minutes or until a toothpick inserted near the center comes out clean. Cool on a wire rack. Stir remaining cinnamon into frosting; spread over cake.

Yield: 20 servings.

Editor's Note: This recipe does not use eggs.

NUTRITION FACTS: 1 slice equals 283 calories, 11 g fat (2 g saturated fat), 0 cholesterol, 261 mg sodium, 45 g carbohydrate, 1 g fiber, 2 g protein.

TESTING BUTTER CAKES FOR DONENESS

Insert a toothpick in several spots near the center of the cake. If the toothpick comes out clean, the cake is done. If the toothpick comes out with crumbs, the cake needs to bake longer.

WALNUT APPLE BUNDT CAKE

Walnut Apple Bundt Cake
Donna Gonda, North Canton, Ohio

At the campground where my husband and I have a trailer, the campers hold an auction of baked goods every Fourth of July. I donated this bundt cake one year and it brought in the highest bid!

- 3 eggs
- 1 cup vegetable oil
- 1 tablespoon vanilla extract
- 2 cups shredded peeled tart apples
- 2 cups sugar
- 3 cups all-purpose flour
- 1 tablespoon ground cinnamon
- 1 teaspoon baking soda
- 1 teaspoon salt
- 3/4 teaspoon ground nutmeg
- 1/2 teaspoon baking powder
- 1 cup chopped walnuts
- 2 tablespoons confectioners' sugar
- 2 tablespoons brown sugar

1) In a large mixing bowl, beat eggs, oil and vanilla. Add apples and sugar; beat 1 minute. Combine the flour, cinnamon, baking soda, salt, nutmeg and baking powder; add to apple mixture until blended. Stir in walnuts.

2) Pour into a greased and floured 10-in. fluted tube pan. Bake at 325° for 50-60 minutes or until a toothpick inserted near the center comes out clean. Cool for 10 minutes before removing from pan to a wire rack to cool completely. Combine confectioners' sugar and brown sugar; sprinkle over cake.

Yield: 15 servings.

NUTRITION FACTS: 1 slice equals 411 calories, 21 g fat (3 g saturated fat), 43 mg cholesterol, 269 mg sodium, 52 g carbohydrate, 2 g fiber, 6 g protein.

Old-Fashioned Carrot Cake

Kim Orr, Louisville, Kentucky

A pleasingly moist cake, this treat is the one I requested that my mom make each year for my birthday. It's dotted with sweet carrots and a hint of cinnamon. The fluffy, buttery frosting is scrumptious with chopped walnuts stirred in. One piece of this cake is never enough!

4	eggs
2	cups sugar
1	cup vegetable oil
2	cups all-purpose flour
2 to 3	teaspoons ground cinnamon
3/4	teaspoon baking soda
1/2	teaspoon baking powder
1/4	teaspoon salt
1/4	teaspoon ground nutmeg
2	cups grated carrots

FROSTING:

1/2	cup butter, softened
1	package (3 ounces) cream cheese, softened
1	teaspoon vanilla extract
3-3/4	cups confectioners' sugar
2 to 3	tablespoons milk
1	cup chopped walnuts

Orange and green food coloring, optional

1) In a large mixing bowl, combine the eggs, sugar and oil. Combine the flour, cinnamon, baking soda, baking powder, salt and nutmeg; beat into egg mixture. Stir in carrots.

2) Pour into two greased and floured 9-in. round baking pans. Bake at 350° for 35-40 minutes or until a toothpick inserted near the center comes out clean. Cool for 10 minutes before removing from pans to wire racks to cool completely.

3) For frosting, in another large mixing bowl, cream butter and cream cheese. Beat in the vanilla. Gradually beat in confectioners' sugar. Add enough milk to achieve the desired spreading consistency. Reserve 1/2 cup of frosting for decorating if desired. Stir walnuts into remaining frosting.

4) Spread frosting between layers and over top and sides of cake. If decorating the cake, tint 1/4 cup reserved frosting orange and 1/4 cup green. Cut a small hole in the corner of pastry or plastic bag; insert #7 round pastry tip.

5) Fill the bag with orange frosting. Pipe twelve carrots on top of cake, so that each slice will have a carrot. Using #67 leaf pastry tip and the green frosting, pipe a leaf at the top of each carrot. Store cake in the refrigerator.

Yield: 12 servings.

NUTRITION FACTS: 1 slice equals 702 calories, 36 g fat (10 g saturated fat), 99 mg cholesterol, 273 mg sodium, 90 g carbohydrate, 2 g fiber, 8 g protein.

Triple-Layer Banana Cake

Patty Roberts, Athens, Ohio

My grandchildren can't keep their fingers out of the frosting of this cake. It tastes just like peanut butter fudge!

3/4	cup butter, softened
2	cups sugar
3	eggs
1-1/2	cups mashed bananas (about 3 medium)
1-1/2	teaspoons vanilla extract
3	cups all-purpose flour
1-1/2	teaspoons baking powder
1-1/2	teaspoons baking soda
3/4	teaspoon salt
1	cup buttermilk

FROSTING:

6	tablespoons peanut butter
3	tablespoons butter, softened

5-1/4 cups confectioners' sugar
   8 to 10 tablespoons milk
Peanut halves, optional

1) In a large mixing bowl, cream butter and sugar until light and fluffy. Add eggs, one at a time, beating well after each addition. Beat in bananas and vanilla. Combine the flour, baking powder, baking soda and salt; add to creamed mixture alternately with buttermilk.

2) Pour into three greased and floured 9-in. round baking pans. Bake at 350° for 25-30 minutes or until a toothpick inserted near the center comes out clean. Cool for 10 minutes before removing from pans to wire racks to cool completely.

3) For frosting, in another large mixing bowl, beat the peanut butter and butter until smooth. Beat in confectioners' sugar and enough milk to achieve spreading consistency. Frost between layers and over top and sides of cake. Garnish with peanuts if desired.

Yield: 14 servings.

NUTRITION FACTS: 1 slice equals 583 calories, 18 g fat (9 g saturated fat), 80 mg cholesterol, 498 mg sodium, 102 g carbohydrate, 2 g fiber, 7 g protein.

HEAVENLY SURPRISE CUPCAKES

Heavenly Surprise Cupcakes
Judie Heiderscheit, Holy Cross, Iowa

The recipe for these filled and frosted cupcakes was handed down by my mother-in-law, who taught this fledging cook what to do in the kitchen. She's no longer with us—but baking these treats reminds me of our good times together.

   2 eggs
1-1/4 cups sugar
   1 cup buttermilk
2/3 cup vegetable oil
   1 teaspoon vanilla extract

1-1/2 cups all-purpose flour
1/2 cup baking cocoa
1-1/4 teaspoons baking soda
   1 teaspoon salt

FROSTING:
2/3 cup butter-flavored shortening
2/3 cup butter, softened
   1 cup sugar
   1 can (5 ounces) evaporated milk
   1 tablespoon water
1/2 teaspoon vanilla extract
   2 cups confectioners' sugar

1) In a mixing bowl, beat the eggs, sugar, buttermilk, oil and vanilla until blended. Combine the flour, cocoa, baking soda and salt; gradually add to egg mixture. Fill paper-lined muffin cups two-thirds full.

2) Bake at 350° for 20-22 minutes or until a toothpick inserted near the center comes out clean. Cool for 10 minutes before removing from pans to wire racks to cool completely.

3) For frosting, in a large mixing bowl, cream the shortening, butter and sugar. Stir in milk, water and vanilla. Gradually beat in confectioners' sugar.

4) Cut a small hole in the corner of a pastry or resealable plastic bag; insert a small star tip. Fill bag with frosting.

5) Push tip 1 in. into center of cupcake and fill with frosting just until tip of cake begins to crack. Pipe frosting in a spiral pattern over the top, beginning near the edge of the cupcake.

Yield: 1-1/2 dozen.

Editor's Note: The texture of this frosting is typical of one made with granulated even though it's made with confectioners' sugar.

NUTRITION FACTS: 1 cupcake equals 414 calories, 23 g fat (8 g saturated fat), 45 mg cholesterol, 316 mg sodium, 49 g carbohydrate, 1 g fiber, 3 g protein.

CUPCAKE CAPERS

To make cupcakes of the same size, use a solid plastic ice cream scoop to measure out the batter and fill the muffin cups.

Batter for a two-layer 9-in. cake can be used to make 2 to 2-1/2 dozen cupcakes. Fill greased or paper-lined muffin cups two-thirds full. Bake at 350° for 20 to 30 minutes or until a toothpick comes out clean. Cool cupcakes for 10 minutes before removing from pans to wire racks to cool completely. Frost as desired.

Peanut Butter Cup Cupcakes

Heidi Harrington, Steuben, Maine

Kids love these cupcakes in school lunches or at parties. They're so easy to make because the mini peanut butter cups eliminate the need to frost them.

    1/3   cup shortening
    1/3   cup peanut butter
  1-1/4   cups packed brown sugar
      2   eggs
      1   teaspoon vanilla extract
  1-3/4   cups all-purpose flour
  1-3/4   teaspoons baking powder
      1   teaspoon salt
      1   cup milk
     16   miniature peanut butter cups

1) In a large mixing bowl, cream the shortening, peanut butter and brown sugar until light and fluffy. Add eggs, one at a time, beating well after each addition. Add vanilla. Combine the flour, baking powder and salt; add to creamed mixture alternately with milk.

2) Fill paper-lined muffin cups with 1/4 cup of batter. Press a peanut butter cup into the center of each until top edge is even with batter.

3) Bake at 350° for 22-24 minutes or until a toothpick inserted on an angle toward the center of the cupcakes comes out clean. Cool for 10 minutes before removing from pans to wire racks to cool completely.

Yield: 16 cupcakes.

NUTRITION FACTS: 1 cupcake equals 238 calories, 10 g fat (3 g saturated fat), 29 mg cholesterol, 260 mg sodium, 33 g carbohydrate, 1 g fiber, 5 g protein.

Skillet Pineapple Upside-Down Cake

Bernardine Melton, Paola, Kansas

Baking this cake in a cast-iron skillet gives it a classic, old-fashioned flavor. It's a real treat for brunch or with coffee.

    1/2   cup butter
      1   cup packed brown sugar
      1   can (20 ounces) sliced pineapple
    1/2   cup chopped pecans
      3   eggs, *separated*
      1   cup sugar
      1   teaspoon vanilla extract
      1   cup all-purpose flour

      1   teaspoon baking powder
    1/4   teaspoon salt
  Maraschino cherries

1) Melt butter in a 9- or 10-in. ovenproof skillet. Add brown sugar; mix well until sugar is melted. Drain pineapple, reserving 1/3 cup juice.

2) Arrange about 8 pineapple slices in a single layer over sugar (refrigerate remaining slices for another use). Sprinkle nuts over pineapple; set aside.

3) In a large mixing bowl, beat egg yolks until thick and lemon-colored. Gradually add sugar, beating well. Blend in vanilla and reserved pineapple juice.

4) Combine the flour, baking powder and salt; add to batter, beating well. In a small mixing bowl, beat egg whites on high speed until stiff peaks form; fold into batter. Spoon into skillet.

5) Bake at 375° for 30-35 minutes or until a toothpick inserted near the center comes out clean. Let stand for 10 minutes before inverting onto serving plate. Place cherries in center of pineapple slices.

Yield: 10 servings.

NUTRITION FACTS: 1 slice (calculated without maraschino cherries) equals 380 calories, 15 g fat (7 g saturated fat), 88 mg cholesterol, 224 mg sodium, 59 g carbohydrate, 1 g fiber, 4 g protein.

PRALINE PUMPKIN TORTE

Praline Pumpkin Torte

Esther Sinn, Princeton, Illinois

This harvest cake stays moist to the last bite. It's perfect for Thanksgiving or holiday gatherings.

    3/4   cup packed brown sugar
    1/3   cup butter

3 tablespoons heavy whipping cream

3/4 cup chopped pecans

CAKE:

4 eggs

1-2/3 cups sugar

1 cup vegetable oil

2 cups canned pumpkin

1/4 teaspoon vanilla extract

2 cups all-purpose flour

2 teaspoons baking powder

2 teaspoons pumpkin pie spice

1 teaspoon baking soda

1 teaspoon salt

TOPPING:

1-3/4 cups heavy whipping cream

1/4 cup confectioners' sugar

1/4 teaspoon vanilla extract

Additional chopped pecans

1) In a heavy saucepan, combine the brown sugar, butter and cream. Cook and stir over low heat until sugar is dissolved. Pour into two well-greased 9-in. round baking pans. Sprinkle with nuts; cool.

2) For cake, in a large mixing bowl, beat eggs, sugar and oil. Add pumpkin and vanilla. Combine the flour, baking powder, pie spice, baking soda and salt; add to pumpkin mixture and beat just until blended. Carefully spoon batter over brown sugar mixture.

3) Bake at 350° for 30-35 minutes or until a toothpick inserted near the center comes out clean. Cool for 5 minutes; remove from pans to wire racks to cool completely.

4) For topping, in a small mixing bowl, beat cream until it begins to thicken. Add confectioners' sugar and vanilla; beat until stiff peaks form.

5) Place one cake layer praline side up on a serving plate. Spread with two-thirds of the whipped cream mixture over cake.

6) Top with second cake layer and remaining whipped cream. Sprinkle with additional pecans if desired. Store in the refrigerator.

Yield: 14 servings.

NUTRITION FACTS: 1 slice (calculated without additional pecans) equals 577 calories, 38 g fat (13 g saturated fat), 118 mg cholesterol, 397 mg sodium, 56 g carbohydrate, 3 g fiber, 6 g protein.

Gingerbread with Lemon Sauce
Kristen Oak, Pocatello, Idaho

I asked my mother-in-law for this recipe once I learned it is my husband's favorite. Now I make it whenever he needs an extra-special treat.

1 cup shortening

1 cup sugar

1 cup molasses

2 eggs

3 cups all-purpose flour

1-1/2 teaspoons baking soda

1-1/2 teaspoons salt

1 teaspoon ground ginger

1 teaspoon ground cinnamon

1 cup hot water

LEMON SAUCE:

1/2 cup sugar

2 teaspoons cornstarch

Dash salt

Dash nutmeg

1 cup water

2 egg yolks, beaten

2 tablespoons butter

2 tablespoons lemon juice

1/2 teaspoon grated lemon peel

1) In a large mixing bowl, beat the shortening, sugar, molasses and eggs until well blended. Combine flour, baking soda, salt, ginger and cinnamon; add to molasses mixture alternately with hot water.

2) Pour into a greased 13-in. x 9-in. x 2-in. baking pan. Bake at 350° for 35-40 minutes or until a toothpick inserted near the center comes out clean. Cool on a wire rack.

3) Meanwhile, in a saucepan, combine the sugar, cornstarch, salt, nutmeg and water until smooth. Cook and stir over medium-high heat until thickened and bubbly. Reduce heat. Cook; stir 2 minutes longer.

4) Remove from the heat. Stir a small amount of hot filling into egg yolks; return all to pan, stirring constantly. Bring to a gentle boil; cook and stir 2 minutes longer.

5) Remove from the heat. Gently stir in butter, lemon juice and peel. Serve with warm cake. Refrigerate leftover sauce.

Yield: 20 servings.

NUTRITION FACTS: 1 slice with about 1 tablespoon sauce equals 283 calories, 12 g fat (3 g saturated fat), 46 mg cholesterol, 304 mg sodium, 41 g carbohydrate, 1 g fiber, 3 g protein.

CHOCOLATE ZUCCHINI CAKE

Chocolate Zucchini Cake
Peggy Linton, Cobourg, Ontario

The minute I can get my hands on zucchini, I start making this light and luscious cake. For years, it was an often-ordered dessert at my sister's deli. Moist and chocolaty, it's irresistible with the smooth custard sauce on top.

1-3/4   cups sugar
  1/2   cup vegetable oil
  1/4   cup butter, softened
   2   eggs
  1/2   cup buttermilk
   1   teaspoon vanilla extract
2-1/2   cups all-purpose flour
  1/4   cup baking cocoa
   1   teaspoon baking soda
  1/2   teaspoon baking powder
  1/2   teaspoon ground cinnamon
  1/4   teaspoon ground cloves
   2   cups finely shredded zucchini
  1/2   cup semisweet chocolate chips
  1/2   cup sliced almonds

CUSTARD SAUCE:
  1/2   cup sugar
   2   tablespoons all-purpose flour
   2   tablespoons cornstarch
   3   cups milk
   3   egg yolks
   3   tablespoons butter
  1/4   teaspoon almond extract

1) In a large mixing bowl, beat sugar, oil and butter. Add eggs, buttermilk and vanilla; mix well. Combine the flour, cocoa, baking soda, baking powder, cinnamon and cloves; gradually add to oil mixture. Stir in the zucchini, chocolate chips and almonds.

2) Pour into a greased and floured 10-in. tube or fluted tube pan. Bake at 325° for 55-60 minutes or until a toothpick inserted near the center comes out clean. Cool for 10 minutes before removing from pan to a wire rack.

3) For sauce, in a large saucepan, combine the sugar, flour and cornstarch. Stir in milk until smooth. Cook and stir over medium-high heat until thickened and bubbly. Reduce heat; cook and stir 2 minutes longer.

4) Remove from the heat. Stir a small amount of hot filling into egg yolks; return all to pan, stirring constantly. Bring to a gentle boil; cook and stir 2 minutes longer. Remove from the heat. Gently stir in butter and extract. Serve warm sauce with cake; store leftover sauce in the refrigerator.

Yield: 12-16 servings.

NUTRITION FACTS: 1 serving equals 392 calories, 18 g fat (7 g saturated fat), 86 mg cholesterol, 117 mg sodium, 52 g carbohydrate, 2 g fiber, 7 g protein.

Foam Cakes

When baking foam cakes in tube pans, set the oven rack in the lowest position. Preheat oven for 10 to 15 minutes before baking.

Separate eggs when they are cold. To ensure egg whites reach their maximum volume, they should stand at room temperature no more than 30 minutes before beating. Also, make sure there are no specks of egg yolk in the white.

Before beating egg whites, make sure your mixing bowl and beaters are clean by washing them thoroughly in hot, soapy water and drying with a clean kitchen towel. Use metal or glass mixing bowls. Plastic bowls, even freshly washed and dried ones, may have an oily film on them. Beat whole eggs or egg yolks until they are thick and lemon-colored.

Gently fold in the ingredients. Using a rubber spatula, gently cut down through the batter, move across the bottom of the bowl and bring up part of the mixture.

Use only the pan size recommended in the recipe. For a tender golden crust, use aluminum pans with a dull rather than a shiny or dark finish.

Do not grease or flour tube pans when baking foam cakes. To rise properly, the batter needs to cling to the sides of the pan. To avoid large air pockets in a baked cake, cut through the batter with a knife to break air bubbles.

It's important to cool foam cakes baked in a tube pan upside down in the pan, otherwise they will collapse and flatten. If using a tube pan with legs, invert the pan onto its legs. If using a tube pan without legs, invert the pan and place the neck over a funnel or narrow bottle.

Cool cakes completely in the pan before removing. To loosen from the pan, run a thin metal spatula around the edge of the pan and around the center tube using a sawing motion. Gently press the metal spatula between the pan and the cake to loosen more.

If the cake pan has a removable bottom, lift out the cake and run a knife along the bottom of the cake. If the pan is one piece, invert the pan onto a plate; tap the side of the pan with the flat side of a knife and lift the pan away from the cake. Cool the cake completely before filling or frosting.

Cut foam cakes with a serrated knife or electric knife using a sawing motion.

Lemon Angel Food Supreme
Linda Blaska, Dunwoody, Georgia

Hints of lemon abound in this homemade angel food cake. For variety, eliminate the lemon or add in raspberries.

1-1/2   cups egg whites (about 12 eggs)
1   cup cake flour
1-1/2   cups plus 2 tablespoons sugar, *divided*
1-1/2   teaspoons cream of tartar
1-1/2   teaspoons vanilla extract
1/2   teaspoon lemon extract
1/4   teaspoons salt

LEMON SAUCE:
3   eggs
1   cup sugar
1/2   cup lemon juice
1/4   cup butter, melted
1   tablespoon grated lemon peel
1/2   cup heavy whipping cream, whipped
Yellow food coloring, optional

1) Place egg whites in a large mixing bowl and let stand at room temperature for 30 minutes. Sift cake flour and 3/4 cup plus 2 tablespoons sugar together twice; set aside.

2) Beat egg whites with cream of tartar, extracts and salt on medium speed until soft peaks form. Gradually add remaining sugar, 2 tablespoons at a time, beating on high until stiff peaks form and sugar is dissolved. Gradually fold in flour mixture, a fourth at a time.

3) Gently spoon into an ungreased 10-in. tube pan. Cut through the batter with a knife to remove air pockets. Bake on the lowest rack at 375° for 30-35 minutes or until top springs back when lightly touched and cracks feel dry.

4) Immediately invert baking pan; cool completely. Run a knife around sides and center tube of pan. Invert cake onto a serving plate.

5) For sauce, beat eggs and sugar in a heavy saucepan over low heat. Stir in the juice, butter and lemon peel. Cook until the mixture thickens and reaches 160°, about 15 minutes; chill. Fold in whipped cream and food coloring if desired. Serve with cake. Store sauce in the refrigerator.

Yield: 12 servings.

NUTRITION FACTS: 1 slice with about 2 tablespoons sauce equals 318 calories, 9 g fat (5 g saturated fat), 77 mg cholesterol, 158 mg sodium, 55 g carbohydrate, trace fiber, 6 g protein.

■ *ANGEL FOOD CAKE:* Omit the lemon extract in the cake batter and omit lemon sauce.

■ *RASPBERRY ANGEL FOOD CAKE:* Use 1/2 teaspoon almond extract for the lemon extract in the cake batter. After flour has been folded in, fold in 2 cups fresh raspberries. Bake as directed. Omit lemon sauce.

FOAM CAKE TIPS

Foam cakes are done when the top springs back when touched and the cracks at the top of the cake look and feel dry.

If your tube pan has legs, invert the pan onto its legs until the cake is completely cool. If your tube pan does not have legs, place the pan over a funnel or the neck of a narrow bottle until cake is completely cool.

ICE CREAM CAKE ROLL

Ice Cream Cake Roll
Kathy Scott, Hemingford, Nebraska

This cake roll can be made and filled ahead of time, then thawed once company comes. You can use whatever ice cream flavor you have on hand.

- 4 eggs, *separated*
- 3/4 cup sugar
- 1 teaspoon vanilla extract
- 3/4 cup cake flour
- 1/4 cup baking cocoa
- 3/4 teaspoon baking powder
- 1/4 teaspoon salt
- 3 cups ice cream, softened

CHOCOLATE SAUCE:
- 2 squares (1 ounce *each*) unsweetened baking chocolate
- 1/4 cup butter
- 2/3 cup evaporated milk, heated to 160° to 170°
- 1 cup sugar

1) Let eggs stand at room temperature for 30 minutes. Line a greased 15-in. x 10-in. x 1-in. baking pan with waxed paper; grease and flour paper. Set aside.

2) In a large mixing bowl, beat egg yolks on high for 3 minutes or until lemon-colored. Gradually add sugar and vanilla, beating until thick and pale yellow. Combine the flour, cocoa and baking powder; gradually add to egg yolk mixture Beat on low until well mixed (mixture will be thick).

3) In another large mixing bowl and with clean beaters, beat egg whites and salt on high speed until soft peaks form. Fold a fourth of egg whites into the batter, then fold in remaining whites.

4) Spread batter evenly in prepared pan. Bake at 350° for 15 minutes or until cake springs back when lightly touched. Turn cake onto a kitchen towel dusted with confectioners' sugar. Gently

peel off waxed paper. Roll up cake in the towel jelly-roll style, starting with a short side. Cool completely on a wire rack.

5) Unroll cake; spread with ice cream to within 1 in. of edges. Roll up again. Cover with plastic wrap and freeze until serving.

6) In a small heavy saucepan, melt chocolate and butter over low heat, stirring until smooth. Gradually add warm milk and sugar; stir constantly for 5 minutes or until completely dissolved. Serve with cake.

Yield: 10 servings (1-1/2 cups sauce).

NUTRITION FACTS: 1 slice with about 2 tablespoons sauce equals 380 calories, 15 g fat (9 g saturated fat), 120 mg cholesterol, 210 mg sodium, 57 g carbohydrate, 1 g fiber, 7 g protein.

Sunny Sponge Cake
Candy Snyder, Salem, Oregon

This golden cake has a light texture and mild orange flavor that makes it a pleasant ending to most any meal.

- 6 egg whites
- 3 egg yolks
- 1-1/2 cups all-purpose flour
- 1-1/4 teaspoons baking powder
- 1/4 teaspoon salt
- 1 cup sugar, *divided*
- 2 teaspoons hot water
- 1/2 cup orange juice, warmed
- 1-1/4 teaspoons vanilla extract
- 3/4 teaspoon grated orange peel
- 1/4 teaspoon grated lemon peel
- 3/4 cup reduced-fat whipped topping

1) Let egg whites and egg yolks stand at room temperature for 30 minutes. Sift together the flour, baking powder and salt; set aside.

2) In a large mixing bowl, beat egg yolks until slightly thickened. Gradually add 3/4 cup sugar and hot water, beating until thick and pale yellow. Blend in the juice, vanilla and peels. Add reserved flour mixture to egg yolk mixture.

3) In another mixing bowl and with clean beaters, beat the egg whites on medium speed until soft peaks form. Gradually beat in sugar, about 1 tablespoon at a time, on high until stiff glossy peaks form and sugar is dissolved. Fold a fourth of egg whites into the batter, then fold in remaining whites.

4) Spoon batter into an ungreased 10-in. tube pan. Bake on the lowest rack at 350° for 20-25 minutes or until cake springs back when lightly touched. Immediately invert pan; cool completely. Run a knife around sides and center tube of pan. Invert cake onto a serving plate. Serve with whipped topping.

Yield: 12 servings.

NUTRITION FACTS: 1 slice with 1 tablespoon whipped topping equals 160 calories, 2 g fat (1 g saturated fat), 53 mg cholesterol, 103 mg sodium, 31 g carbohydrate, trace fiber, 4 g protein.

CHOCOLATE ANGEL CAKE

Chocolate Angel Cake

Joyce Shiffler, Manitow Springs, Colorado

When I first got married, I could barely boil water. My dear mother-in-law taught me her specialty of making the lightest angel food cakes ever. This chocolate version is an easy, impressive treat. For many years, it was our son's birthday cake.

1-1/2 cups egg whites (about 10 eggs)
1-1/2 cups confectioners' sugar
   1 cup cake flour
  1/4 cup baking cocoa
1-1/2 teaspoons cream of tartar
  1/2 teaspoon salt
   1 cup sugar

FROSTING:
1-1/2 cups heavy whipping cream
  1/2 cup sugar
  1/4 cup baking cocoa
  1/2 teaspoon salt
  1/2 teaspoon vanilla extract
  Chocolate leaves, optional

1) Place egg whites in a large mixing bowl; let stand at room temperature for 30 minutes. Combine the confectioners' sugar, flour and cocoa. Sift together three times; set aside.

2) Add cream of tartar and salt to egg whites; beat on medium speed until soft peaks form. Gradually add the sugar, about 2 tablespoons at a time, beating on high until stiff glossy peaks form. Gradually fold in cocoa mixture, about a fourth at a time.

3) Gently spoon into an ungreased 10-in. tube pan. Cut through the batter with a knife to remove air pockets. Bake on the lowest oven rack at 375° for 35-40 minutes or until the top springs back when lightly touched and cracks feel dry.

4) Immediately invert pan; cool completely, about 1 hour. Run a knife around side and center tube of pan. Remove cake to a serving plate.

5) For frosting, in a mixing bowl, combine the cream, sugar, cocoa, salt and vanilla; cover and chill for 1 hour. Beat until stiff peaks form. Spread over top and sides of cake. Store in the refrigerator. Garnish with chocolate leaves if desired.

Yield: 12-16 servings.

NUTRITION FACTS: 1 slice equals 244 calories, 9 g fat (5 g saturated fat), 31 mg cholesterol, 194 mg sodium, 39 g carbohydrate, 1 g fiber, 4 g protein.

MAKING CHOCOLATE LEAVES

1) Wash several lemon, rose or mint leaves and set aside until completely dry. Melt 1/2 cup chips—semisweet, milk, vanilla or white—and 1/4 teaspoons shortening. With a new small paintbrush, brush melted chocolate in a thin layer on the under side of each leaf. Refrigerate until set, about 10 minutes. Apply a second layer of melted chocolate; chill for at least 15 minutes or overnight.

2) Gently peel leaf from chocolate. If leaves are not to be used immediately, store in a cool dry place in a covered container until needed.

Lemon Daffodil Cake

Eunice Richardson, Shullsburg, Wisconsin

You're sure to impress dinner guests when you present this eye-catching sponge cake. A light lemon filling and frosting make it a perfect springtime dessert.

1-1/4	cups egg whites (about 10)
1	teaspoon cream of tartar
1/2	teaspoon salt
1-1/3	cups sugar
1	cup all-purpose flour
1/2	teaspoon vanilla extract
4	egg yolks
1/4	teaspoon almond extract

LEMON FILLING:

1	tablespoon unflavored gelatin
3/4	cup cold water, *divided*
1	cup sugar
3	tablespoons cornstarch
4	egg yolks, beaten
1/3	cup butter
2	tablespoons grated lemon peel
1/2	cup lemon juice
1	cup heavy whipping cream, whipped

1) Place egg whites in a large mixing bowl and let stand at room temperature for 30 minutes. Add cream of tartar and salt to egg whites; beat on medium speed until soft peaks form.

2) Gradually add sugar, 2 tablespoons at a time, beating on high until stiff glossy peaks form and sugar is dissolved. Fold in flour, 1/4 cup at a time. Divide mixture in half. Fold vanilla into one portion; set aside.

3) In another large mixing bowl, beat egg yolks on high speed until thick and lemon-colored. Stir in almond extract. Fold in the unflavored egg white batter.

4) Alternately spoon batters into an ungreased 10-in. tube pan. Gently cut through batter with a knife to swirl. Bake on the lowest rack at 325° for 50-60 minutes or until top springs back when lightly touched. Immediately invert pan; cool completely.

5) For filling, soften gelatin in 1/4 cup cold water; let stand for 1 minute. In a heavy saucepan, combine the sugar, cornstarch and remaining water until smooth. Bring to a boil over medium heat; cook and stir 2 minutes longer.

6) Remove from the heat. Gradually stir 1/2 cup hot filling into egg yolks; return all to the pan, stirring constantly. Cook and stir 2 minutes longer. Remove from the heat; stir in butter and lemon peel. Gently stir in lemon juice and softened gelatin until gelatin is dissolved.

7) Cool to room temperature without stirring. Fold in whipped cream. Refrigerate until mixture achieves spreading consistency, about 40-50 minutes.

8) Run a knife around sides and center tube of pan. Remove cake; split into two horizontal layers. Spread filling between layers and over top of cake. Store in the refrigerator.

Yield: 12 servings.

NUTRITION FACTS: 1 slice equals 334 calories, 12 g fat (7 g saturated fat), 169 mg cholesterol, 202 mg sodium, 51 g carbohydrate, trace fiber, 6 g protein.

WALNUT TORTE

Walnut Torte

Kathryn Anderson, Wallkill, New York

A hint of citrus complements the rich walnut taste of this lovely three-layer flourless cake. Toasted chopped walnuts make a great garnish atop the smooth buttercream frosting.

9	eggs, *separated*
1	cup sugar
1/2	cup water
1	tablespoon grated orange peel
2	teaspoons grated lemon peel
1	teaspoon vanilla extract
3	cups finely ground walnuts
1/2	cup dry bread crumbs

2 teaspoons baking powder
1 teaspoon ground cinnamon
1 teaspoon ground cloves
1/2 teaspoon salt
1/4 teaspoon cream of tartar

BUTTERCREAM FROSTING:
1/2 cup shortening
1/2 cup butter, softened
1 teaspoon vanilla extract
4 cups confectioners' sugar
3 tablespoons milk

Additional walnuts, chopped and toasted

1) Let eggs stand at room temperature for 30 minutes. Line three greased 9-in. round cake pans with waxed paper; grease the paper and set aside.

2) In a large mixing bowl, beat egg yolks until slightly thickened. Gradually add sugar, beating until thick and pale yellow. Beat in the water, peels and vanilla. Combine the nuts, bread crumbs, baking powder, cinnamon, cloves and salt; add to batter. Beat until smooth.

3) In another mixing bowl and with clean beaters, beat egg whites and cream of tartar on medium speed until stiff peaks form. Fold a fourth of egg whites into the batter, then fold in remaining whites.

4) Pour into prepared pans. Bake at 350° for 20-25 minutes or until a toothpick inserted near the center comes out clean. Cool for 10 minutes before removing from pans to wire racks. Carefully peel off waxed paper.

5) For frosting, in a large mixing bowl, cream shortening and butter. Beat in vanilla. Gradually beat in sugar. Add milk; beat until light and fluffy. Spread frosting between layers and over top and sides of cake. Garnish with toasted walnuts.

Yield: 15 servings.

Editor's Note: This recipe does not use flour.

NUTRITION FACTS: 1 slice (calculated without additional walnuts) equals 456 calories, 26 g fat (7 g saturated fat), 144 mg cholesterol, 265 mg sodium, 51 g carbohydrate, 1 g fiber, 7 g protein.

TOASTING NUTS AND COCONUT

To toast nuts or coconut, spread in a 15-in. x 10-in. x 1-in. baking pan. Bake at 350° for 5-10 minutes or until lightly browned, stirring occasionally. Or, spread in a dry nonstick skillet and heat over low heat until lightly browned, stirring occasionally.

Orange Chiffon Cake
Marjorie Ebert, South Dayton, New York

The delicate orange flavor of this simply delicious cake is perfect for rounding out a rich meal. The orange glaze would also be a nice way to top off slices of your favorite angel food cake.

6 eggs, *separated*
2 cups all-purpose flour
1-1/2 cups sugar
1 teaspoon salt
1/2 teaspoon baking soda
3/4 cup fresh orange juice
1/2 cup vegetable oil
2 tablespoons grated orange peel
1/2 teaspoon cream of tartar

ORANGE GLAZE:
1/2 cup butter
2 cups confectioners' sugar
2 to 4 tablespoons fresh orange juice
1/2 teaspoon grated orange peel

1) Let eggs stand at room temperature for 30 minutes. In a large mixing bowl, combine the flour, sugar, salt and baking soda. In a bowl, whisk the egg yolks, orange juice, oil and orange peel; add to dry ingredients. Beat until well blended.

2) In another large mixing bowl and with clean beaters, beat egg whites and cream of tartar on high speed until stiff peaks form. Fold into orange mixture.

3) Gently spoon batter into an ungreased 10-in. tube pan. Cut through batter with a knife to remove air pockets. Bake on lowest rack at 350° for 45-50 minutes or until top springs back when lightly touched. Immediately invert pan; cool completely. Run a knife around sides and center tube of pan. Invert cake onto a serving plate.

4) For glaze, melt butter in a small saucepan; add remaining glaze ingredients. Stir until smooth. Pour over top of cake, allowing it to drizzle down sides.

Yield: 16 servings.

NUTRITION FACTS: 1 slice equals 333 calories, 15 g fat (5 g saturated fat), 95 mg cholesterol, 269 mg sodium, 47 g carbohydrate, 1 g fiber, 4 g protein.

MARBLE CHIFFON CAKE

Marble Chiffon Cake
LuAnn Heikkila, Floodwood, Minnesota

Plain and chocolate batters are swirled together with outstanding results! Mix up a simple five-ingredient frosting for the finishing touch.

      7 eggs, *separated*
      2 squares (1 ounce *each*)
         unsweetened chocolate
1-3/4 cups sugar, *divided*
   1/4 cup hot water
      2 cups all-purpose flour
      2 teaspoons baking powder
      1 teaspoon salt
   1/4 teaspoon baking soda
   3/4 cup water
   1/2 cup vegetable oil
      2 teaspoons vanilla extract
   1/2 teaspoon cream of tartar

FROSTING:
      4 squares (1 ounce *each*)
         semisweet chocolate
      1 tablespoon butter
      7 tablespoons heavy whipping
         cream
      1 teaspoon vanilla extract
1-1/2 cups confectioners' sugar

1) Let the eggs stand at room temperature for 30 minutes. In a small saucepan, melt unsweetened chocolate over low heat. Add 1/4 cup sugar and hot water; mix well and set aside.

2) In a large mixing bowl, combine the flour, baking powder, salt, baking soda and remaining sugar. Whisk together egg yolks, water, oil and vanilla; add to flour mixture and beat until moistened. Beat for 3 minutes on medium speed; set aside.

3) In another large mixing bowl and with clean beaters, beat egg whites and cream of tartar on high speed until stiff peaks form. Fold a fourth of egg whites into the batter, then fold in remaining whites. Divide batter in half; gradually fold chocolate mixture into one portion.

4) Alternately spoon the plain and chocolate batters into an ungreased 10-in. tube pan. Swirl with a knife. Bake on the lowest rack at 325° for 60-65 minutes or until top springs back when lightly touched. Immediately invert the cake; cool completely. Run a knife around sides and center tube of pan; remove cake to serving plate.

5) For frosting, melt chocolate and butter in a small saucepan over low heat. Stir in cream and vanilla. Remove from the heat; whisk in confectioners' sugar until smooth. Immediately spoon over cake.

Yield: 16 servings.

NUTRITION FACTS: 1 slice equals 363 calories, 17 g fat (6 g saturated fat), 104 mg cholesterol, 256 mg sodium, 51 g carbohydrate, 1 g fiber, 5 g protein.

Frosting

Always sift confectioners' sugar before using it for frosting. If there are lumps in the sugar, there will be lumps in the frosting that may clog decorating tips. Frosting needs to be just the right consistency for spreading and decorating. If it's too thin, add a little confectioners' sugar. If it's too thick, add a little milk.

Tint white frosting with liquid, gel or paste food coloring. Liquid gives a pastel color; gel and paste give a deeper color. Add a little at a time, stir in and check the color. You can always add more, but it's hard to lighten the color. The color generally darkens as the frosting dries.

Vanilla Buttercream Frosting
Diana Wilson, Denver, Colorado

This basic buttery frosting has unmatchable homemade taste. With a few simple variations, you can come up with different colors and flavors.

   1/2 cup butter, softened
4-1/2 cups confectioners' sugar
1-1/2 teaspoons vanilla extract
      5 to 6 tablespoons milk

1) In a large mixing bowl, cream butter until light and fluffy. Beat in sugar and vanilla. Add enough milk to achieve desired consistency.

Yield: about 3 cups.

NUTRITION FACTS: 2 tablespoons equals 124 calories, 4 g fat (2 g saturated fat), 11 mg cholesterol, 40 mg sodium, 23 g carbohydrate, 0 fiber, trace protein.

- *ALMOND BUTTERCREAM FROSTING:* Prepare as directed, except use 1/2 to 3/4 teaspoon almond extract instead of the vanilla.

- *CHOCOLATE BUTTERCREAM FROSTING:* Prepare as directed, except use 4 cups confectioners' sugar, 1/2 cup baking cocoa and 6-7 tablespoons milk.

- *LEMON BUTTERCREAM FROSTING:* Prepare as directed, except use 5-6 tablespoons lemon juice instead of the milk and 1 teaspoon grated peel.

- *ORANGE BUTTERCREAM FROSTING:* Prepare as directed, except use 5-6 tablespoons orange juice instead of the milk and add 1 teaspoon grated orange peel.

- *PEANUT BUTTER FROSTING:* Prepare as directed, except use 1/2 cup peanut butter instead of the butter and use 6-8 tablespoons milk.

- *PEPPERMINT BUTTERCREAM FROSTING:* Prepare as directed, except use 1/2 to 3/4 teaspoon peppermint extract instead of the vanilla.

Chocolate Ganache
Taste of Home Test Kitchen

This smooth satin chocolate frosting will bring a touch of elegance to even the most basic cake. A simple garnish such as fresh fruit, mint leaves or edible flowers adds the finishing touch.

> 1   cup (6 ounces) semisweet
>   chocolate chips
> 2/3 cup heavy whipping cream

1) In a heavy saucepan, melt chocolate chips with cream over low heat. Remove from the heat. Refrigerate, stirring occasionally.

2) For a pourable ganache, cool until mixture reaches 85°-90° and is slightly thickened, about 40 minutes.

3) Pour over cake, allowing some to flow down the edges to completely coat. Spread ganache with a spatula if necessary to evenly coat, working quickly before it thickens. Chill until set.

4) For spreadable ganache, chill until mixture reaches a spreadable consistency. Spread over cake. Chill until set.

Yield: 1-1/4 cups.

NUTRITION FACTS: 2 tablespoons equals 135 calories, 11 g fat (7 g saturated fat), 22 mg cholesterol, 8 mg sodium, 11 g carbohydrate, 1 g fiber, 1 g protein.

Bakery Frosting
Barbara Jones, Pana, Illinois

This recipe captures the fabulous flavor of cakes from the best bakeries. A big batch of this sweet frosting keeps for 3 months in the refrigerator.

> 2   cups shortening
> 1/2 cup nondairy creamer
> 1   teaspoon almond extract
> 1   package (32 ounces)
>   confectioners' sugar
> 1/2 to 3/4 cup water
> Food coloring, optional

1) In a large mixing bowl, beat the shortening, creamer and extract. Gradually beat in the confectioners' sugar. Add enough water until frosting reaches desired consistency. If desired, add food coloring.

2) Store in the refrigerator for up to 3 months. Bring to room temperature before spreading.

Yield: 8 cups.

NUTRITION FACTS: 1/3 cup equals 305 calories, 17 g fat (5 g saturated fat), 0 cholesterol, trace sodium, 39 g carbohydrate, 0 fiber, 0 protein.

SIMPLE FROSTING FINISHES

PEAKS
Smooth frosting over top and sides of cake. With an icing spatula or small flat metal spatula, press a flat side of the spatula tip in frosting and pull straight up, forming a peak. Repeat over top and sides of cake.

SWIRLS
Smooth frosting over top and sides of cake. Use the back of a tablespoon or teaspoon to make a small twisting motion in one direction. Then move the spoon over a little and make another twist in the opposite directions. Repeat until entire cake is covered.

Sweetened Whipped Cream

Taste of Home Test Kitchen

Sometimes a dollop of sweetened whipped cream is all you need to top your favorite cake or other dessert. To make ahead, slightly underwhip the cream, then cover and refrigerate for several hours. Beat briefly just before using.

- 1 cup heavy whipping cream
- 3 tablespoons confectioners' sugar
- 1/2 teaspoon vanilla extract

1) In a chilled small mixing bowl and with chilled beaters, beat cream until it begins to thicken. Add confectioners' sugar and vanilla; beat until soft peaks form. Store in the refrigerator.

Yield: 2 cups.

NUTRITION FACTS: 2 tablespoons equals 57 calories, 6 g fat (3 g saturated fat), 20 mg cholesterol, 6 mg sodium, 2 g carbohydrate, 0 fiber, trace protein.

Cream Cheese Frosting

Sharon Lugdon, Costigan, Maine

This smooth, versatile frosting has a delicate vanilla flavor. Most folks agree carrot cake and pumpkin bars wouldn't be complete without it!

- 2 packages (3 ounces *each*) cream cheese, softened
- 1/2 cup butter, softened
- 2 teaspoons vanilla extract
- 1/4 teaspoon salt
- 5 to 6 cups confectioners' sugar

1) In a large mixing bowl, beat the cream cheese, butter, vanilla and salt until smooth. Gradually beat in confectioners' sugar. Store frosting in the refrigerator.

Yield: about 3 cups.

NUTRITION FACTS: 1/4 cup equals 234 calories, 9 g fat (6 g saturated fat), 27 mg cholesterol, 127 mg sodium, 38 g carbohydrate, 0 fiber, 1 g protein.

Fluffy White Frosting

Georgia Bohmann, West Allis, Wisconsin

For a heavenly light and fluffy frosting, you can't top this variation of the classic 7-minute frosting.

- 1-1/2 cups sugar
- 2 egg whites
- 1/3 cup water
- 1/4 teaspoon cream of tartar
- 1 teaspoon vanilla extract

1) In a heavy saucepan over low heat or double boiler over simmering water, combine the sugar, egg whites, water and cream of tartar.

2) With a portable mixer, beat mixture on low speed for 1 minute. Continue beating on low speed over low heat until frosting reaches 160°, about 8-10 minutes. Pour into a large mixing bowl; add vanilla. Beat on high speed until frosting forms stiff peaks, about 7 minutes.

Yield: about 5 cups.

Editor's Note: A stand mixer is recommended for beating the frosting after it reaches 160°.

NUTRITION FACTS: about 1/3 cup equals 100 calories, 0 fat (0 saturated fat), 0 cholesterol, 9 mg sodium, 25 g carbohydrate, 0 fiber, 1 g protein.

Creamy Chocolate Frosting

Jeannette Mack, Rushville, New York

Whisking up a batch of smooth-as-silk fudgy chocolate icing is a snap using this short recipe.

- 2 cups heavy whipping cream
- 2 cups semisweet chocolate chips, milk chocolate chips *or* vanilla *or* white chips
- 3 to 3-1/2 cups confectioners' sugar

1) In a medium saucepan, bring cream to a simmer, about 180°; remove from the heat. Stir in chips until melted.

2) Place pan in a bowl of ice water; stir constantly until cooled. Gradually whisk in sugar until smooth and thick. Store in the refrigerator.

Yield: 2-1/2 cups.

NUTRITION FACTS: about 3 tablespoons equals 388 calories, 23 g fat (14 g saturated fat), 54 mg cholesterol, 18 mg sodium, 49 g carbohydrate, 2 g fiber, 2 g protein.

Soft Lemon Frosting

Madge Robertson, Murfreesboro, Arkansas

This fresh-tasting citrus icing makes a pretty topping for white cake or cupcakes, especially when garnished with grated lemon peel. Plus, it's a snap to stir up in a jiffy.

- 1 can (14 ounces) sweetened condensed milk
- 3/4 cup lemonade concentrate
- 1 carton (8 ounces) frozen whipped topping, thawed

1) In a large bowl, combine milk and lemonade concentrate. Fold in whipped topping. Store in the refrigerator.

Yield: about 4 cups.

NUTRITION FACTS: 3 tablespoons equals 96 calories, 3 g fat (2 g saturated fat), 6 mg cholesterol, 21 mg sodium, 15 g carbohydrate, trace fiber, 1 g protein.

CHAPTER 21
DESSERTS

DESSERTS

As an ending to an elegant meal or as a complement to a cup of coffee or tea, a simple dessert is just the answer. This chapter is filled with ideas for tempting cheesecakes, puddings, ice cream and other tasty classics your family and friends are sure to enjoy.

Baking Cheesecakes

Before preheating the oven, arrange the oven racks so that the cheesecake will bake in the center of the oven. Preheat the oven for 10 to 15 minutes before baking.

Grease the bottom and sides of the springform pan to help prevent the filling from cracking when the cheesecake cools. It will naturally pull away from the sides.

Measure all ingredients accurately. For best results, use regular cream cheese and sour cream, unless a recipe specifically calls for reduced-fat or fat-free products.

To avoid lumps, always soften cream cheese at room temperature for about 30 minutes before mixing. To soften in the microwave, place an unwrapped 8-ounce package of cream cheese on a microwave-safe plate; microwave on 50% power for about 30 to 60 seconds or until softened. If cream cheese is not softened before mixing, it cannot be smoothed after blending.

Make sure the batter is completely smooth and free of lumps before adding eggs. Add the eggs all at once and beat on low speed just until blended. Avoid overbeating at this step. If too much air is beaten into the mixture, the cheesecake will puff during baking, then collapse and split when cooled.

Stop the mixer occasionally and scrape the batter down from the sides of the bowl with a rubber spatula.

Open the oven door as little as possible while baking the cheesecake, especially during the first 30 minutes. Drafts can cause a cheesecake to crack.

For best results, the springform pan should not be warped and should seal tightly. If in doubt about the tightness of the seal, tightly wrap heavy-duty foil around the outside of the pan to prevent butter in the crust from leaking out. Place on a baking sheet.

Use a kitchen timer. Check for doneness at the minimum recommended baking time. A cheesecake is done when the edges are slightly puffed and when the center (about 1 in. diameter) jiggles slightly when the side of the pan is tapped with a spoon. The retained heat will continue to cook the center while the cheesecake is cooling. A cheesecake cooked in a water bath will be just set across the top. The top will look dull, not shiny. Don't use a knife to test for doneness because it will cause the top to crack.

Cool the cheesecake in the pan for 10 minutes on a wire rack, then run a knife around the inside edge to loosen the cheesecake from the springform pan. Don't remove the sides of the pan yet. Cool the cheesecake on a wire rack in a draft-free location for 1 hour. Refrigerate, uncovered, for at least 3 to 4 hours. When the cheesecake is cold, cover it with a piece of foil or plastic wrap across the top of the pan and refrigerate for at least 6 hours or overnight. This allows the cheesecake to set and will make it easier to cut.

Serving Cheesecake

When ready to serve, loosen the latch of the springform and carefully lift the rim of the pan straight up. Slice the cheesecake chilled. But for maximum flavor, allow slices to stand at room temperature for 15 to 30 minutes before serving.

Use a straight-edge knife to cut a cheesecake. Warm the blade in hot water, dry and slice. Clean and rewarm the knife after each cut.

COOL LIME CHEESECAKE

Cool Lime Cheesecake
Karen Donhauser, Frazer, Pennsylvania

The mixture of tart lime and creamy cheesecake is absolutely scrumptious. At any get-together, it's a show-stopping dessert.

- 2-1/4 cups graham cracker crumbs (about 36 squares)
- 1/3 cup sugar
- 1/2 cup butter, melted

FILLING:
- 20 ounces cream cheese, softened
- 3/4 cup sugar
- 1 cup (8 ounces) sour cream
- 3 tablespoons all-purpose flour
- 3 eggs, lightly beaten
- 2/3 cup lime juice
- 1 teaspoon vanilla extract
- 1 drop green food coloring, optional

Whipped cream and lime slices

1) In a small bowl, combine crumbs and sugar; stir in butter. Press onto the bottom and 1 in. up the side of a greased 10-in. springform pan. Place pan on a baking sheet. Bake at 375° for 8 minutes. Place pan on a wire rack to cool. Reduce the heat to 325°.

2) In a large mixing bowl, beat cream cheese and sugar until smooth. Add sour cream and flour; beat well. Add eggs; beat on low speed just until combined. Stir in the lime juice, vanilla and food coloring if desired.

3) Pour into crust. Return pan to baking sheet. Bake at 325° for 50-55 minutes or until center is almost set. Cool on a wire rack for 10 minutes. Carefully run a knife around the edge of pan to loosen; cool 1 hour longer.

4) Refrigerate overnight. Remove sides of pan. Garnish with whipped cream and lime. Refrigerate leftovers.

Yield: 12-14 servings.

NUTRITION FACTS: 1 slice equals 374 calories, 26 g fat (15 g saturated fat), 118 mg cholesterol, 290 mg sodium, 30 g carbohydrate, trace fiber, 6 g protein.

DISGUISE A CRACKED CHEESECAKE

If the top of your cheesecake has a crack in it, just cover it up! Topping the cheesecake with fruit, a sour cream topping or your favorite jam will offer a delectable disguise.

Caramel Stripe Cheesecake
Brenda LaBrie, Clark, South Dakota

I love to bake cheesecakes, and this recipe is one of the best I've tried. For a nice change of pace, try it with a creamy cherry topping.

- 2 cups crushed vanilla wafers
- 1/3 cup butter, melted
- 3 packages (8 ounces *each*) cream cheese, softened
- 1 cup sugar
- 2 tablespoons all-purpose flour
- 3 eggs
- 2 tablespoons heavy whipping cream
- 1 teaspoon vanilla extract

CARAMEL TOPPING:
- 12 caramels
- 2 tablespoons heavy whipping cream

CHOCOLATE TOPPING:

> 1/2 **cup semisweet chocolate chips**
>
> 2 **teaspoons butter**
>
> 4 **teaspoons heavy whipping cream**
>
> **Whipped cream and coarsely chopped pecans, optional**

1) In a small bowl, combine wafer crumbs and butter. Press onto the bottom and 1-1/2 in. up the sides of an ungreased 9-in. springform pan. Place on a baking sheet. Bake at 400° for 10 minutes. Place pan on a wire rack to cool. Reduce the heat to 350°.

2) In a large mixing bowl, beat cream cheese until smooth. Combine the sugar and flour; add to cream cheese and mix well. Add eggs; beat on low speed just until combined. Stir in cream and vanilla. Pour into crust.

3) Return pan to a baking sheet. Bake for 40-45 minutes or until center is almost set. Cool pan on a wire rack for 10 minutes. Carefully run a knife around edge of pan to loosen; cool 1 hour longer. Refrigerate overnight.

4) In a small saucepan, melt caramels with cream over medium heat, stirring constantly. In another saucepan, melt the chocolate chips and butter with cream over low heat, stirring until smooth. Drizzle caramel and chocolate toppings over cheesecake. Refrigerate overnight.

5) Just before serving, remove sides of pan. Garnish with whipped cream and pecans if desired. Refrigerate leftovers.

Yield: 14 servings.

NUTRITION FACTS: 1 slice equals 442 calories, 30 g fat (17 g saturated fat), 122 mg cholesterol, 283 mg sodium, 40 g carbohydrate, 1 g fiber, 6 g protein.

■ *CREAMY CHERRY CHEESECAKE:* For crust, use 1-1/2 cups graham cracker crumbs and 1/4 cup sugar and 6 tablespoons melted butter for the vanilla wafer crumbs and butter if desired. Press into springform pan. Bake cheesecake as directed and let stand for 15 minutes, leaving oven on.

Combine 1 cup sour cream, 1/4 cup sugar and 1 teaspoon vanilla. Spoon topping around edge of cheesecake. Carefully spread over filling. Bake 5 minutes longer. Cool as directed. Refrigerate for about 8 hours.

For cherry topping, in a small saucepan, combine 1/2 cup sugar and 2 tablespoons cornstarch. Drain 1 can (16 ounces) of pitted tart red cherries, reserving juice. Stir juice into saucepan until smooth. Bring to a boil; cook and stir for 2 minutes or until thickened.

Remove from the heat; stir in 1 teaspoon lemon juice, a few drops of red food coloring if desired and reserved cherries. Cool for 5 minutes. Spread over top of cheesecake; refrigerate overnight.

MAKING A CHEESECAKE CRUMB CRUST

1) Place cookies or crackers in a heavy-duty resealable plastic bag. Seal bag, pushing out as much air as possible. Press a rolling pin over the bag, crushing the cookies or crackers into fine crumbs. Or, process cookies and crackers in a food processor.

2) Use a flat-bottomed measuring cup or glass to firmly press the prepared crumb mixture onto the bottom (and up the sides if recipe directs) of a springform pan.

LOOSENING THE CHEESECAKE

To prevent cracks during cooling, it's important to loosen the cheesecake from the sides of the pan after baking. First cool the cheesecake on a wire rack for 10 minutes. Then carefully run a table knife or small metal spatula between the cheesecake and the inside of the pan. Cool 1 hour longer. Refrigerate overnight before removing the sides of the pan.

Lemon Surprise Cheesecake
Karen Chesnut, Clarksburg, California

Lemon flavors sparkle throughout this cheesecake, from the crust to the filling to the topping. Build up the edges of the cheesecake to keep the lemon filling right where you want it.

1-1/2   cups lemon cream-filled sandwich cookie crumbs

   2   tablespoons sugar

 1/4   cup butter, melted

LEMON FILLING:

 2/3   cup plus 2 tablespoons sugar

   5   tablespoons cornstarch

   1   cup water

   2   egg yolks, slightly beaten

 1/3   cup lemon juice

   2   tablespoons butter

   1   teaspoon grated lemon peel

CHEESECAKE LAYER:

   1   envelope unflavored gelatin

 1/2   cup lemon juice

   3   packages (8 ounces *each*) cream cheese, softened

 3/4   cup sugar

   1   cup heavy whipping cream, whipped

   2   teaspoons grated lemon peel

1)   Combine the cookie crumbs and sugar; stir in butter. Press onto the bottom of a lightly greased 9-in. springform pan. Place on a baking sheet.

Bake at 350° for 8-10 minutes or until crust just begins to brown. Place pan on a wire rack to cool.

2)   In a saucepan, combine sugar and cornstarch. Stir in water until smooth. Cook and stir over medium-high heat until thickened and bubbly. Reduce heat; cook and stir 2 minutes longer. Remove from the heat.

3)   Stir a small amount of hot filling into egg yolks; return all to pan, stirring constantly. Bring to a gentle boil; cook and stir 2 minutes longer. Remove from the heat. Gently stir in the lemon juice, butter and peel. Cool to room temperature without stirring.

4)   In a small saucepan, sprinkle gelatin over lemon juice; let stand for 1 minute. Heat over low heat, stirring until gelatin is dissolved. Remove from the heat.

5)   In a large mixing bowl, beat cream cheese and sugar. Gradually beat in gelatin mixture until combined. Fold in the whipped cream and peel.

6)   Spoon three-fourths of cheesecake mixture into crust; build up edges slightly. Chill for 5 minutes. Spoon lemon filling over cheesecake layer to within 1/2-in. of edges. Top with the remaining cheesecake mixture. Cover and refrigerate overnight.

7)   Carefully run a knife around edge of pan; remove sides of pan. Refrigerate leftovers.

Yield: 12 servings.

NUTRITION FACTS: 1 slice equals 534 calories, 37 g fat (22 g saturated fat), 140 mg cholesterol, 308 mg sodium, 47 g carbohydrate, trace fiber, 6 g protein.

Pumpkin Cheesecake Dessert
Melissa Davies, Clermont, Florida

My family requests this dessert each Thanksgiving. For a change of pace, I sometimes use cinnamon graham crackers instead of plain ones.

 3/4   cup finely chopped walnuts

 3/4   cup graham cracker crumbs (about 12 squares)

 1/4   cup sugar

 1/4   teaspoon ground cinnamon

 1/4   teaspoon ground ginger

 1/8   teaspoon ground cloves

 1/4   cup butter, melted

FILLING:

   2   packages (8 ounces *each*) cream cheese, softened

 3/4   cup sugar

2 eggs, lightly beaten

1 cup canned pumpkin

1/2 teaspoon ground cinnamon, *divided*

2 tablespoons chopped walnuts

1) In a small bowl, combine the walnuts, cracker crumbs, sugar and spices; stir in butter. Press onto the bottom of an ungreased 10-in. tart pan with a removable bottom.

2) For filling, in a large mixing bowl, beat cream cheese and sugar until smooth. Add eggs; beat on low speed just until combined. Add pumpkin and 1/4 teaspoon cinnamon; beat on low speed just until combined.

3) Pour into crust; sprinkle with walnuts and remaining cinnamon. Place pan on a baking sheet. Bake at 350° for 35-40 minutes or until center is almost set. Cool on a wire rack for 1-1/2 hours. Store in the refrigerator.

Yield: 9-12 servings.

NUTRITION FACTS: 1 serving equals 327 calories, 24 g fat (11 g saturated fat), 87 mg cholesterol, 194 mg sodium, 25 g carbohydrate, 2 g fiber, 7 g protein.

BITTERSWEET CHOCOLATE CHEESECAKE

Bittersweet Chocolate Cheesecake

Amelia Gregory, Omemee, Ontario

My family likes the flavor of bittersweet chocolate in this cheesecake, but you can make it with semisweet baking chocolate if you like. Hazelnuts add a nice richness to the crust.

1 cup chocolate wafer crumbs

1/2 cup finely chopped toasted hazelnuts

1/3 cup butter, melted

3 packages (8 ounces *each*) cream cheese, softened

1 cup sugar

12 squares (1 ounce *each*) bittersweet baking chocolate, melted and cooled

3 eggs, lightly beaten

1 cup (8 ounces) sour cream

1-1/2 teaspoons vanilla extract

1/2 teaspoon almond extract

Dash salt

GLAZE:

4 squares (1 ounce *each*) bittersweet baking chocolate

1/4 cup heavy whipping cream

1 teaspoon vanilla extract

Whipped cream and toasted chopped hazelnuts, optional

1) In a small bowl, combine the wafer crumbs and hazelnuts; stir in butter. Press onto the bottom of an ungreased 9-in. springform pan.

2) In a large mixing bowl, beat cream cheese and sugar until smooth. Add chocolate. Add eggs; beat on low just until combined. Add sour cream, extracts and salt; beat just until blended. Pour over crust. Place pan on a baking sheet.

3) Bake at 350° for 60-65 minutes or until the center is almost set. Cool pan on a wire rack for 10 minutes. Carefully run a knife around edge of pan to loosen; cool 1 hour longer. Refrigerate for 3 hours.

4) For glaze, in a heavy saucepan or microwave, melt chocolate with cream, stirring until smooth. Remove from heat. Stir in vanilla.

5) Remove sides of pan. Spread glaze over top. Refrigerate overnight. Garnish with whipped cream and hazelnuts if desired.

Yield: 16 servings.

Editor's Note: Semisweet baking chocolate may be substituted for the bittersweet chocolate.

NUTRITION FACTS: 1 slice equals 484 calories, 39 g fat (21 g saturated fat), 112 mg cholesterol, 235 mg sodium, 34 g carbohydrate, 3 g fiber, 8 g protein.

STORING CHEESECAKES

Cover and refrigerate cheesecake for up to 3 days. To freeze, place entire cheesecake or individual slices on a baking sheet and freeze until firm. Wrap in heavy-duty plastic wrap and place in a freezer bag. Freeze for up to 2 months. Thaw in the refrigerator.

Cream Puffs and Eclairs

Cream puffs and eclairs are airy pastries made from a French dough called "pate a choux" or "choux pastry." The pastry can be formed into a variety of sizes by being dropped from a spoon or by being piped from a pastry bag. The baked puffs are used for desserts as well as appetizers. Cream puffs and eclairs get their puff from the steam that is produced from the water, eggs and fat in the batter. Follow these guidelines for foolproof cream puffs and eclairs.

When baking the dough, it's important not to crowd the baking pan. Leave about 3 in. of space around each puff or eclair. The dough needs room to expand during baking and needs air to circulate so the steam it gives off can evaporate.

Cream puffs and eclairs are done when they are golden brown and have a dry, crisp exterior.

For the best flavor, serve cream puffs and eclairs the same day they're made. If necessary, they can be prepared a day in advance. Store the unfilled pastries in a plastic bag in the refrigerator and fill just before serving.

For longer storage, arrange unfilled pastries in a single layer on a baking sheet and freeze. Once they're frozen, transfer to heavy-duty resealable plastic bags and freeze for up to 2 months. Thaw at room temperature for 15-20 minutes before using. If the thawed pastries are a little soggy, reheat them in the oven for a few minutes.

State Fair Cream Puffs
Ruth Jungbluth, Dodgeville, Wisconsin

The Wisconsin Bakers Association has been serving these treats at the Wisconsin State Fair since 1924. Now, more than 300,000 are sold annually! You can try all kinds of filling variations, too.

- 1 cup water
- 1/2 cup butter
- 1/4 teaspoon salt
- 1 cup all-purpose flour
- 4 eggs
- 2 tablespoons milk
- 1 egg yolk, lightly beaten
- 2 cups heavy whipping cream
- 1/4 cup confectioners' sugar
- 1/2 teaspoon vanilla extract
- Additional confectioners' sugar

1) In a large saucepan, bring the water, butter and salt to a boil over medium heat. Add flour all at once and stir until a smooth ball forms.

2) Remove from the heat; let stand for 5 minutes. Add eggs, one at a time, beating well after each addition. Continue beating until mixture is smooth and shiny.

3) Drop by 1/4 cupfuls 3 in. apart onto greased baking sheets. Combine milk and egg yolk; brush over puffs. Bake at 400° for 30-35 minutes or until golden brown. Remove to wire racks. Immediately cut a slit in each for the steam to escape; cool.

4) In a chilled large mixing bowl, beat cream until it begins to thicken. Add sugar and vanilla; beat until almost stiff.

5) Split cream puffs; discard soft dough from inside. Fill the cream puffs just before serving. Dust with confectioners' sugar. Refrigerate leftovers.

Yield: 10 servings.

NUTRITION FACTS: 1 filled cream puff equals 340 calories, 29 g fat (17 g saturated fat), 196 mg cholesterol, 197 mg sodium, 14 g carbohydrate, trace fiber, 5 g protein.

- *STRAWBERRY CREAM PUFFS:* Omit whipped cream filling. In a small mixing bowl, beat 2 packages (8 ounces *each*) softened cream cheese and 1 cup sugar until fluffy. Fold in 4 cups whipped cream and 3 cups coarsely chopped strawberries.

- *VANILLA CREAM PUFFS:* Omit whipped cream filling. In a bowl, whisk 1-1/2 cups milk, 1 package (5.1 ounces) instant pudding mix and 1/2 teaspoon almond extract for 2 minutes. Let stand for 2 minutes or until soft-set. Fold in 4 cups whipped cream. Fill as directed.

■ *CHOCOLATE GLAZE FOR CREAM PUFFS:* In a heavy saucepan, melt 6 tablespoons semisweet chocolate chips, 1-1/2 teaspoons shortening and 3/4 teaspoon corn syrup over low heat, stirring until smooth. Drizzle over cream puffs.

MAKING CREAM PUFFS

1) Bring water, butter and salt to a boil in a saucepan. Add the flour all at once; stir briskly until the mixture leave the sides of the pan and forms a ball.

2) Remove from heat; let stand for 5 minutes to allow mixture to cool before adding the eggs. Beat well after adding each egg. Continue beating until mixture is smooth and shiny.

3) Drop dough 3 in. apart onto a greased baking sheet. Bake as directed.

4) Remove puffs from pan to a wire rack. Immediately cut a slit in each puff to allow steam to escape; cool. Split puffs and set tops aside; remove soft dough from inside with a fork and discard. Fill as directed.

Puff Pastry

Frozen puff pastry dough is available in sheets or individual shells. It has dozens of paper-thin layers of dough separated by butter. As the pastry bakes, steam created from water in the dough makes the layers rise up and pull apart, resulting in a crisp, flaky pastry.

Thaw the pastry at room temperature for about 20 minutes before handling. Handle as little as possible to avoid stretching and tearing.

Preheat the oven as directed. Cut pastry with a sharp knife or cutter to get a clean edge.

Only brush an egg wash on the top of the dough, not the edges. If the edges are brushed, they will stick together and the pastry won't rise during baking.

Unbaked puff pastry dough may be wrapped tightly in plastic and stored in the refrigerator for 2 to 3 days or frozen for up to 1 month. Baked pastries are best enjoyed the day they are made and don't refrigerate well. Baked, unfilled pastry may be frozen in airtight containers for up to 6 weeks.

Raspberry Chocolate Puffs
Anneliese Deising, Plymouth, Michigan

This is my "show-off" dessert because it makes a spectacular presentation that my friends rave about. Although it looks like you fussed, the recipe is actually quick and easy.

1 cup vanilla *or* white chips

1 cup raspberry *or* milk chocolate chips

1 cup chopped pecans

1 package (17.3 ounces) frozen puff pastry, thawed

1 package (12 ounces) frozen unsweetened raspberries, thawed

1 cup confectioners' sugar

Fresh raspberries, additional vanilla and raspberry chips and confectioners' sugar, optional

1) In a bowl, combine the chips and pecans. On a lightly floured surface, roll each pastry sheet into a 12-in. square. Cut in half lengthwise and widthwise, making eight 6-in. squares.

2) Spoon the chip mixture in the center of each square. Pull all corners together below the tips of the corners, forming a pouch. Fold the corner tips down.

3) Place on an ungreased baking sheet. Bake at 425° for 18-20 minutes or until golden brown. Remove to a wire rack to cool.

4) In a food processor or blender, puree raspberries and confectioners' sugar. Strain and discard seeds. Spoon raspberry sauce onto dessert plates; top with pastry pouches. If desired, garnish with raspberries and chips; dust with confectioners' sugar.

Yield: 8 servings.

NUTRITION FACTS: 1 puff equals 752 calories, 42 g fat (13 g saturated fat), 6 mg cholesterol, 283 mg sodium, 88 g carbohydrate, 7 g fiber, 9 g protein.

Strawberry Napoleon

Dean Barns, Farmington, New Mexico

Flaky puff pastry is topped with a homemade custard, strawberries and whipped cream. You could also use other fresh fruits that are in season.

- 1 package (17-1/4 ounces) frozen puff pastry sheets, thawed
- 3/4 cup sugar
- 2 tablespoons cornstarch
- 1/4 teaspoon salt
- 1-1/2 cups milk
- 3 egg yolks, beaten
- 1 tablespoon butter
- 3 teaspoons vanilla extract

TOPPING:

- 2 cups heavy whipping cream
- 1/2 cup confectioners' sugar
- 1 teaspoon vanilla extract
- 3 pints fresh strawberries, sliced

Additional confectioners' sugar, optional

1) On a lightly floured surface, roll out each pastry sheet to a 9-in. square. Place on ungreased baking sheets. Bake at 350° for 30 minutes or until golden brown.

2) Meanwhile, in a saucepan, combine the sugar, cornstarch and salt. Gradually add milk until smooth. Cook and stir over medium-high heat until thickened and bubbly. Reduce heat; cook and stir 2 minutes longer.

3) Remove from the heat. Stir a small amount of hot filling into egg yolks; return all to pan, stirring constantly. Bring to a gentle boil; cook and stir 2 minutes longer. Remove from the heat. Gently stir in butter and vanilla. Pour custard into a bowl; cover surface with plastic wrap and refrigerate.

4) For topping, in a chilled large mixing bowl, beat the cream until it begins to thicken. Add confectioners' sugar and vanilla; beat until soft peaks form.

5) To serve, place one pastry square on a serving platter. Top with the custard, strawberries, sweetened whipped cream and second pastry. Dust with additional confectioners' sugar if desired. Refrigerate leftovers.

Yield: 12 servings.

NUTRITION FACTS: 1 piece equals 475 calories, 29 g fat (13 g saturated fat), 114 mg cholesterol, 226 mg sodium, 49 g carbohydrate, 5 g fiber, 6 g protein.

Phyllo Dough

Phyllo (pronounced FEE-lo) is a tissue-thin dough, generally sold in the freezer section of grocery stores. It's used for desserts, appetizers and main dishes.

Thaw phyllo according to package directions. Always have all the other ingredients assembled and ready to go before unwrapping the dough. Because phyllo is thin, fragile and tears easily, work on a smooth, dry surface. Phyllo dries out quickly. So once the dough is unwrapped and unrolled, cover it with plastic wrap and then a damp kitchen towel. Work with one sheet at a time and keep the other sheets covered.

Refrigerate unopened phyllo dough for up to 3 weeks or freeze for up to 3 months. Opened dough can be refrigerated for up to 3 days. Baked phyllo should be stored in airtight containers for up to 3 days or frozen for up to 3 months.

APPLE STRUDEL

Apple Strudel

Joanie Fuson, Indianapolis, Indiana

Old-fashioned strudel was too fattening and time-consuming, but this revised classic is just as good. It's best served warm from the oven.

- 1/3 cup raisins
- 2 tablespoons water
- 1/4 teaspoon almond extract
- 3 cups coarsely chopped peeled apples
- 1/3 cup plus 2 teaspoons sugar, *divided*
- 3 tablespoons all-purpose flour
- 1/4 teaspoon ground cinnamon
- 8 sheets phyllo dough (18 inches x 14 inches)
- 2 tablespoons butter, melted
- 2 tablespoons canola oil

1) In a microwave-safe bowl, combine the raisins, water and almond extract. Microwave, uncovered, on high for 1-1/2 minutes, let stand for 5 minutes. Drain. Add the apples, 1/3 cup sugar, flour and cinnamon; toss to coat. Set aside.

2) Place 1 sheet of phyllo dough on a work surface. Combine butter and oil; set aside 2 teaspoons. Lightly brush some of the remaining butter mixture over phyllo dough. Keep remaining phyllo dough covered with plastic wrap and a damp towel to prevent drying.

3) Layer with 7 more sheets of phyllo, brushing each layer with some of the butter mixture. Spread apple mixture over phyllo to within 2 in. of one long side. Fold the short edges over filling. Roll up jelly-roll style, starting from the long side where the apple filling is 2 in. from edge.

4) Place seam side down on a baking sheet coated with nonstick cooking spray. With a sharp knife, cut diagonal slits into top of strudel. Brush with reserved butter mixture. Sprinkle with remaining sugar. Bake at 350° for 35-40 minutes or until golden.

Yield: 8 servings.

NUTRITION FACTS: 1 piece equals 205 calories, 7 g fat (2 g saturated fat), 8 mg cholesterol, 121 mg sodium, 35 g carbohydrate, 2 g fiber, 3 g protein.

Cranberry Phyllo Triangles
Taste of Home Test Kitchen

It's hard to eat just one of these crispy cranberry-filled triangles. If you prefer, make the chocolate version instead.

1/2   cup chopped fresh *or* frozen cranberries
3   tablespoons sugar
2   tablespoons raisins
2   tablespoons chopped pecans
1   tablespoon honey
1/4   teaspoon shredded orange peel
20   sheets phyllo dough (14 inches x 9 inches)
1/2   cup butter, melted
  Confectioners' sugar

1) In a saucepan, combine the cranberries, sugar, raisins, pecans, honey and orange peel; bring to a boil. Reduce heat; simmer, uncovered, for 5 minutes, stirring occasionally. Drain and discard any juice. Cool to room temperature.

2) Lightly brush one sheet of phyllo with butter; place another sheet of phyllo on top and brush with butter. Keep remaining phyllo covered with plastic wrap and a damp towel to prevent drying.

3) Cut the two layered sheets into three 14-in. x 3-in. strips. Place a teaspoon of cranberry filling in lower corner on each strip. Fold dough over filling, forming a triangle. Fold triangle up, then fold triangle over, forming another triangle. Continue folding, like a flag, until you come to the end of the strip.

4) Brush end of dough with butter and press onto triangle to seal. Turn triangle and brush top with melted butter. Repeat with remaining strips of dough and remaining sheets of phyllo.

5) Place triangles on a greased baking sheet. Bake at 375° for 15-17 minutes or until golden brown. Cool on a wire rack. Sprinkle with confectioners' sugar.

Yield: 30 triangles.

NUTRITION FACTS: 1 triangle (calculated without confectioners' sugar) equals 78 calories, 4 g fat (2 g saturated fat), 8 mg cholesterol, 91 mg sodium, 10 g carbohydrate, trace fiber, 1 g protein.

■ *CHOCOLATE PHYLLO TRIANGLES:* Omit the first step of recipe. In a microwave or heavy saucepan, melt 8 oz. chopped semisweet chocolate. Stir in 3/4 cup toasted chopped pecans. Place a heaping teaspoonful of chocolate mixture on phyllo strip in place of the cranberry filling. Fold up and bake as directed.

MAKING PHYLLO TRIANGLES

1) Place 1 teaspoon of filling in lower corner on each strip. Fold dough over filling, forming a triangle.

2) Fold triangle up.

3) Fold triangle over, forming another triangle.

4) Continue folding like a flag, until you come to the end of the strip. Brush end of dough with melted butter and press onto triangle to seal. Turn triangle and brush top with melted butter.

Baklava

Judy Losecco, Buffalo, New York

Baklava is a traditional Middle Eastern pastry made with phyllo dough, nuts and honey. This dessert is very rich, so one pan goes a long way.

- 1-1/2 **pounds finely chopped walnuts**
- 1/2 **cup sugar**
- 1/2 **teaspoon ground cinnamon**
- 1/8 **teaspoon ground cloves**
- 2 **packages (16 ounces *each*, 18-inch x 14-inch sheet size) frozen phyllo dough, thawed**
- 1 **pound butter, melted**

SYRUP:

- 2 **cups sugar**
- 2 **cups water**
- 1 **cup honey**
- 1 **tablespoon grated lemon *or* orange peel**

1) In a small bowl, combine the walnuts, sugar, cinnamon and cloves; set aside. Brush a 15-in. x 10-in. x 1-in. baking pan with some of the butter.

2) Unroll each package of phyllo sheets; trim each stack to fit into pan. Cover dough with plastic wrap and a damp cloth to prevent drying.

3) Place one sheet of phyllo into pan; brush with butter. Repeat 14 times. Spread with 2 cups walnut mixture. Layer with five sheets of phyllo, brushing with butter between each sheet. Spread with remaining walnut mixture. Top with one sheet of phyllo; brush with butter. Repeat 14 times.

4) Cut into 2-1/2-in. squares; cut each square in half diagonally. Brush remaining butter over top. Bake at 350° for 40-45 minutes or until golden brown.

5) Meanwhile, in a saucepan, bring the syrup ingredients to a boil. Reduce the heat; simmer for 10 minutes. Strain and discard peel; cool to lukewarm. Pour syrup over warm baklava.

Yield: 4 dozen.

NUTRITION FACTS: 1 piece equals 271 calories, 16 g fat (5 g saturated fat), 21 mg cholesterol, 162 mg sodium, 30 g carbohydrate, 1 g fiber, 5 g protein.

■ *CHOCOLATE BAKLAVA:* For nut mixture, combine 1 pound finely chopped walnuts, 1 package (12 ounces) miniature semisweet chocolate chips, 3/4 cup sugar, 1-1/2 teaspoons ground cinnamon and 1 teaspoon grated lemon peel. Layer and bake as directed.

For syrup, use 1 cup plus 2 tablespoons orange juice, 3/4 cup *each* sugar, water and honey and 3 tablespoons lemon juice. Bring to a boil. Reduce heat; simmer, uncovered, for 20 minutes. Pour over warm baklava. Cool completely on a wire rack.

SWISS MERINGUE SHELLS

Meringues

Meringue is a sweetened egg white foam that can be shaped into cups to hold fruit or mousse, or made into a golden crown on Baked Alaska.

Depending on the amount of sugar beaten into the egg whites, meringue is classified as a soft meringue (as used for Baked Alaska or meringue-topped pies) or hard meringue (as used for meringue shells or cookies).

Since humidity is the most critical factor in making a successful meringue, choose a dry day. Meringues can absorb moisture on a humid day and become limp or sticky.

Separate the eggs while they are still cold from the refrigerator, then allow the egg whites to stand at room temperature for 30 minutes before beating.

For the greatest volume, place whites in a small, clean metal or glass mixing bowl. Even a drop of fat from the egg yolk or a film sometimes found on plastic bowls will prevent egg whites from foaming. For this reason, be sure to use clean beaters.

After stiff peaks form, check that the sugar is dissolved. It should feel silky smooth when rubbed between your thumb and index finger.

Swiss Meringue Shells

Linda Braun, Park Ridge, Illinois

Folks will know you fussed when you bring out these sweet, cloud-like cups topped with fresh berries (or a tart fruit filling if you like). Crisp outside, these meringues make an elegant ending to a company dinner.

    3   egg whites
    1/2 teaspoon vanilla extract
    1/4 teaspoon cream of tartar
    3/4 cup sugar
    Berries of your choice
    Whipped cream *or* vanilla ice cream,
    optional

1) Place egg whites in a small mixing bowl; let stand at room temperature for 30 minutes. Add vanilla and cream of tartar to egg whites; beat on medium speed until soft peaks form.

2) Gradually beat in sugar, 1 tablespoon at a time, on high until stiff glossy peaks form and sugar is dissolved.

3) Drop eight mounds onto parchment-lined baking sheet. Shape into 3-in. cups with the back of a spoon. Bake at 225° for 1 to 1-1/2 hours or until set and dry. Turn oven off; leave meringues in oven for 1 hour.

4) Cool on wire racks. Store in an airtight container. Fill shells with berries and whipped cream or ice cream if desired.

Yield: 8 servings.

NUTRITION FACTS: 1 meringue cup (calculated without berries, whipped cream or ice cream) equals 80 calories, 0 fat (0 saturated fat), 0 cholesterol, 21 mg sodium, 19 g carbohydrate, 0 fiber, 1 g protein.

■ *STRAWBERRY MERINGUE CUPS:* In a chilled large mixing bowl, beat 2 cups heavy whipping cream until it begins to thicken. Add 3/4 cup confectioners' sugar; beat until stiff peaks form. Just before serving, spoon into meringue shells. Top with 1 pint sliced fresh strawberries.

■ *MOCHA MERINGUE CUPS:* In a heavy saucepan, melt 2 cups milk chocolate chips, with 1 cup heavy whipping cream and 1 teaspoon instant coffee granules; stir until smooth. Remove from the heat; stir in 1 teaspoon vanilla. Transfer to a small mixing bowl; refrigerate until chilled. Beat on high speed until stiff peaks form. Pipe or spoon into meringue cups.

MAKING MERINGUE CUPS

1) In a large mixing bowl, beat the egg whites, cream of tartar, vanilla and salt on medium speed until the egg whites begin to increase in volume and soft peaks form. To test for soft peaks, lift the beaters from the whites, and the peaks of the egg white should curl down.

2) Add sugar, 1 tablespoon at a time, beating on high speed until stiff peaks form and sugar is dissolved. To test for stiff peaks, lift the beaters from the whites, and the peaks of egg white should stand straight up; if you tilt the bowl, the whites should not slide around. Sugar is dissolved when the mixture feels silky-smooth between your fingers.

3) Line a baking sheet with parchment paper. Drop meringue into mounds on the paper. Using the back of a spoon, make an indentation in the center of each mound to form a 3-in. cup.

4) Bake as recipe directs. After drying in the oven for 1 hour, remove meringues to cool completely on baking sheet. Carefully remove meringues from paper and store in an airtight container at room temperature for up to 2 days.

Brownie Baked Alaska
Carol Twardzik, Spy Hill, Saskatchewan

The name Baked Alaska originated at Delmonico's Restaurant in New York City in 1876 and was created in honor of the newly acquired territory of Alaska.

  2   squares (1 ounce *each*)
      unsweetened chocolate
1/2   cup shortening
  1   cup sugar
  1   teaspoon vanilla extract
  2   eggs
3/4   cup all-purpose flour
1/2   teaspoon baking powder
1/2   teaspoon salt
  1   cup chopped walnuts, optional
  1   quart strawberry ice cream,
      slightly softened
  1   quart vanilla ice cream, slightly
      softened

MERINGUE:

  5   egg whites
2/3   cup sugar
1/2   teaspoon cream of tartar

1) In a large saucepan, melt chocolate and shortening; remove from the heat. Stir in sugar and vanilla. Add eggs, one at a time, beating well after each addition. Combine the flour, baking powder and salt; stir into chocolate mixture. Add nuts if desired. Spread into a greased 9-in. round baking pan.

2) Bake at 350° for 20-25 minutes or until a toothpick inserted near the center comes out with moist crumbs (do not overbake). Cool for 10 minutes before removing from pan to a wire rack to cool completely.

3) Meanwhile, line an 8-in. or 9-in. round bowl (1-1/2 qts.) with foil. Quickly spread strawberry ice cream over bottom and up sides of bowl, leaving center hollow; cover and freeze for 30 minutes. Pack vanilla ice cream into center; cover and freeze.

4) To assemble, place the brownie base on a 10-in. ovenproof serving plate. Unmold ice cream onto brownie. Return to freezer while preparing meringue.

5) In a heavy saucepan or double boiler over simmering water, combine the egg whites, sugar and cream of tartar. Heat over low heat while beating egg white mixture with a portable mixer on low speed for 1 minute, scraping down sides of bowl. Continue beating until mixture reaches 160°. Remove from the heat. Beat on high speed until stiff peaks form.

6) Quickly spread over ice cream and brownie. Bake at 500° for 2-5 minutes or until meringue is lightly browned. (Or return to freezer until baking.) Transfer to a serving plate; serve immediately.

Yield: 12 servings.

NUTRITION FACTS: 1 serving equals 427 calories, 20 g fat (9 g saturated fat), 68 mg cholesterol, 211 mg sodium, 58 g carbohydrate, 1 g fiber, 7 g protein.

Strawberry Schaum Torte
Diane Krisman, Hales Corners, Wisconsin

This recipe was handed down by my German grandmother. It's wonderful with fresh berries, but frozen sliced strawberries are also nice.

  8   egg whites (about 1 cup)
  1   tablespoon white vinegar
  1   teaspoon vanilla extract

1/4 teaspoon salt

2 cups sugar

3 cups sliced fresh strawberries

1-1/2 cups whipped cream

1) Place egg whites in a large mixing bowl and let stand at room temperature for 30 minutes. Beat egg whites, vinegar, vanilla and salt on medium speed until soft peaks form.

2) Gradually beat in sugar, about 2 tablespoons at a time, on high until stiff glossy peaks form and sugar is dissolved.

3) Spread into a greased 10-in. springform pan. Bake at 300° for 65-70 minutes or until lightly browned. Remove to a wire rack to cool (meringue will fall). Serve with strawberries and whipped cream. Store leftovers in the refrigerator.

Yield: 12 servings.

Editor's Note: This recipe requires a stand mixer.

NUTRITION FACTS: 1 serving equals 173 calories, 2 g fat (1 g saturated fat), 6 mg cholesterol, 96 mg sodium, 37 g carbohydrate, 1 g fiber, 3 g protein.

Souffles

Souffles are made from an egg yolk-based custard that is lightened with beaten egg whites. This mixture bakes up into a light, airy creation that makes an impressive dessert.

Before working with egg whites, remove all fat residue from your mixing bowl and beaters by washing them thoroughly in hot, soapy water and drying with a clean kitchen towel. Use metal or glass mixing bowls. Plastic bowls, even freshly washed and dried ones, may have an oily film on them.

Separate eggs when they are cold. Make sure there are no specks of egg yolk in the white. Let the separated eggs or egg whites stand at room temperature for 30 minutes before beating. To lighten the batter, fold about a third of the beaten egg whites into the custard base. Then fold in the remaining egg whites.

Spoon or pour custard into baking dish. Souffles rise two to three times the volume of the batter. A four-egg souffle should be baked in a 1-1/2- to 2-qt. dish. Bake on the middle rack of a preheated oven according to recipe directions.

A souffle is done when the top feels firm and a knife inserted near the center comes out clean. A souffle will fall slightly once it's removed from the oven. For best results, serve the souffle immediately.

An unbaked souffle may be refrigerated up to 2 hours before baking or frozen for 3 weeks. Thaw a frozen souffle in the refrigerator before baking. A frozen souffle will not bake up as high as a freshly prepared souffle.

Baked Orange Souffle
Taste of Home Test Kitchen

This souffle with a distinctive orange flavor makes a light ending to any meal.

1 teaspoon plus 2 tablespoons butter, *divided*

2 tablespoons plus 1/2 cup sugar, *divided*

5 tablespoons all-purpose flour

1/4 teaspoon salt

1 cup milk

4 eggs, *separated*

2 tablespoons grated orange peel

1 to 1-1/4 teaspoons orange extract

1/8 teaspoon cream of tartar

1) Use 1 teaspoon butter to grease bottom and sides of a 6-cup souffle dish. Thoroughly coat inside of dish with 2 tablespoons sugar; tap out excess sugar and discard.

2) In a saucepan, combine the flour, salt and 1/4 cup sugar; gradually whisk in milk until smooth. Bring to a boil over medium heat; cook and stir for 2 minutes or until thickened. Transfer to a bowl; whisk in egg yolks, orange peel, extract and remaining butter.

3) In a mixing bowl, beat egg whites and cream of tartar on medium speed until foamy. Gradually add remaining sugar, 1 tablespoon at a time, beating until soft peaks form.

4) With a spatula, stir 1 cup of the whites into the orange batter until no white streaks remain. Fold in remaining egg whites until combined. Gently pour into prepared dish.

5) Bake at 400° for 25-30 minutes or until a knife inserted near the center comes out clean. Serve immediately.

Yield: 6-8 servings.

NUTRITION FACTS: 1 serving equals 168 calories, 7 g fat (3 g saturated fat), 119 mg cholesterol, 154 mg sodium, 21 g carbohydrate, trace fiber, 5 g protein.

CHOCOLATE SOUFFLE

Chocolate Souffle
Carol Ice, Burlingham, New York

Every bite of this creamy souffle will melt in your mouth. The sweetened cream sauce balances the richness of the chocolate.

- 2 squares (1 ounce *each*) unsweetened chocolate
- 1/4 cup butter
- 5 tablespoons all-purpose flour
- 1/3 cup plus 1 teaspoon sugar, *divided*
- 1/4 teaspoon salt
- 1 cup milk
- 3 eggs, *separated*
- 1 teaspoon vanilla extract
- 1/4 teaspoon almond extract

SAUCE:
- 1 cup heavy whipping cream
- 1/4 cup confectioners' sugar
- 1/4 teaspoon vanilla extract
  Baking cocoa *or* ground cinnamon, optional

1) In a heavy saucepan, melt chocolate and butter over low heat, stirring until smooth. In a small bowl, combine flour, 1/3 cup sugar and salt; add milk and stir until smooth. Stir into the melted chocolate. Cook and stir over medium heat until thickened and bubbly. Reduce heat; cook and stir 2 minutes longer. Remove from the heat.

2) In a small bowl, beat egg yolks. Stir a small amount of filling into yolks; return all to the pan, stirring constantly. Add extracts.

3) In a small mixing and with clean beaters, beat egg whites on medium speed until soft peaks form. Gradually beat in remaining sugar on high until stiff peaks form. With a spatula, stir a fourth of the egg whites into chocolate batter until no white streaks remain, then fold in remaining egg whites.

4) Grease the bottom of 1-1/2-qt. baking dish; add souffle batter. Place dish in a larger pan. Fill large pan with hot water to a depth of 1 in. Bake at 325° for 1 hour or until a knife inserted near the center comes out clean.

5) For topping, beat the cream in a chilled small mixing bowl until it begins to thicken. Add confectioners' sugar and vanilla; beat until soft peaks form. Serve souffle warm with a dollop of sauce. Sprinkle with cocoa or cinnamon if desired.

Yield: 6 servings.

NUTRITION FACTS: 1 serving equals 407 calories, 31 g fat (19 g saturated fat), 187 mg cholesterol, 244 mg sodium, 28 g carbohydrate, 2 g fiber, 7 g protein.

Ice Cream Bonbons
Taste of Home Test Kitchen

What a surprise to bite into a bonbon and find ice cream! Roll the ice cream in other kinds of nuts, too.

- 1 quart ice cream
- 2 cups finely chopped toasted pecans
- 2 cups (12 ounces) semisweet chocolate chips
- 1/2 cup butter
- 1 tablespoon instant coffee granules

1) Make 3/4-in. ice cream balls with a small melon-ball scoop; immediately roll in pecans. Cover and freeze until firm, at least 1 hour.

2) In a microwave or small saucepan, melt the chocolate chips and butter; stir until smooth. Stir in coffee until dissolved.

3) Remove 10 ice cream balls from freezer; push a toothpick into each. Holding toothpick and working quickly, dip balls in chocolate mixture.

4) Place on waxed paper or press toothpicks into Styrofoam block. Return to freezer. Repeat with remaining balls. Place in small paper cups or wrap with foil or plastic wrap. Store in freezer.

Yield: about 5 dozen.

NUTRITION FACTS: 2 bonbons equals 171 calories, 14 g fat (6 g saturated fat), 16 mg cholesterol, 46 mg sodium, 12 g carbohydrate, 1 g fiber, 2 g protein.

Strawberry Ice

Kim Hammond, Watsonville, California

After picking strawberries on a local farm, this is where we use up many of them. It's a refreshing, slushy mixture that kids love.

> 5 cups fresh *or* frozen unsweetened strawberries, thawed
> 2/3 cup sugar
> 2/3 cup water
> 1/4 cup lemon juice

1) Place berries in a blender or food processor; cover and process until smooth. In a saucepan, bring sugar and water to a boil. Cook and stir until sugar is dissolved, about 5 minutes; cool slightly. Add to blender. Add lemon juice; cover and process until combined.

2) Pour into a shallow freezer container; cover and freeze for 4-6 hours or until almost frozen. Just before serving, whip mixture in a blender or food processor.

Yield: 6 servings.

NUTRITION FACTS: 1 serving equals 125 calories, trace fat (trace saturated fat), 0 cholesterol, 2 mg sodium, 32 g carbohydrate, 3 g fiber, 1 g protein.

VANILLA CUSTARD ICE CREAM

Vanilla Custard Ice Cream

Margaret Gage, Roseboom, New York

This is the best homemade custard I've ever had. I like to top it with colorful sprinkles, but you can try different toppings to find your favorite!

> 2 cups milk
> 3/4 cup sugar
> 1/8 teaspoon salt
> 2 eggs, beaten
> 2 cups heavy whipping cream

> 2 tablespoons vanilla extract
> Colored sprinkles, optional

1) In a large saucepan, heat the milk to 175°; stir in the sugar and salt until dissolved. Whisk in a small amount of the hot mixture to the eggs. Return all to the pan, whisking constantly.

2) Cook and stir over low heat until mixture reaches at least 160° and coats the back of a metal spoon. Remove from the heat.

3) Cool quickly by placing pan in a bowl of ice water; stir for 2 minutes. Stir in whipping cream and vanilla. Press plastic wrap onto surface of custard. Refrigerate for several hours or overnight.

4) Fill cylinder of ice cream freezer two-thirds full; freeze according to manufacturer's directions. Refrigerate remaining mixture until ready to freeze.

5) Allow to ripen in ice cream freezer or firm up in refrigerator freezer for 2-4 hours before serving. Garnish with colored sprinkles if desired.

Yield: 1-1/2 quarts.

NUTRITION FACTS: 1/2 cup equals 227 calories, 17 g fat (10 g saturated fat), 95 mg cholesterol, 70 mg sodium, 16 g carbohydrate, 0 fiber, 3 g protein.

Tart Lemon Sorbet

Susan Garoutte, Georgetown, Texas

On hot summer days, nothing seems to satisfy like the tartness of lemons. This light, refreshing sorbet is one of my favorite ways to use that puckery fruit.

> 3 cups water
> 1-1/2 cups sugar
> 1-1/2 cups lemon juice
> 1 tablespoon grated lemon peel

1) In a saucepan, bring water and sugar to a boil. Cook and stir until sugar is dissolved, about 5 minutes. Cool. Add the lemon juice and peel.

2) Pour into the cylinder of an ice cream freezer; freeze according to manufacturer's directions. Allow to ripen in ice cream freezer or firm up in the refrigerator freezer for 2-4 hours before serving. Remove from the freezer 10 minutes before serving.

Yield: about 1 quart.

NUTRITION FACTS: 1/2 cup equals 157 calories, trace fat (0 saturated fat), 0 cholesterol, 1 mg sodium, 42 g carbohydrate, trace fiber, trace protein.

Blueberry Cheesecake Ice Cream

Melissa Symington, Neche, North Dakota

After sampling this flavor at an ice cream stand, I kept trying to duplicate it until it was just right.

- 1/2 cup sugar
- 1 tablespoon cornstarch
- 1/2 cup water
- 1-1/4 cups fresh *or* frozen blueberries
- 1 tablespoon lemon juice

GRAHAM CRACKER MIXTURE:

- 2-1/4 cups graham cracker crumbs (about 36 squares)
- 2 tablespoons sugar
- 1/2 teaspoon ground cinnamon
- 1/2 cup butter, melted

ICE CREAM:

- 1-1/2 cups sugar
- 1 package (3.4 ounces) instant cheesecake *or* vanilla pudding mix
- 1 quart heavy whipping cream
- 2 cups milk
- 2 teaspoons vanilla extract

1) In a small saucepan, combine the sugar and cornstarch. Gradually stir in water until smooth. Stir in blueberries and lemon juice. Bring to a boil. Reduce heat; simmer, uncovered, for 5 minutes or until slightly thickened, stirring occasionally. Cover and refrigerate until chilled.

2) In a large bowl, combine the cracker crumbs, sugar and cinnamon. Stir in butter. Pat into an ungreased 15-in. x 10-in. x 1-in. baking pan. Bake at 350° for 10-15 minutes or until lightly browned. Cool completely on a wire rack.

3) In a large bowl, whisk the ice cream ingredients. Fill ice cream freezer cylinder two-thirds full; freeze according to manufacturer's directions. Refrigerate remaining mixture until ready to freeze. Whisk before adding to ice cream freezer (mixture will have some lumps).

4) Crumble the graham cracker mixture. In a large container, layer the ice cream, graham cracker mixture and blueberry sauce three times; swirl. Freeze.

Yield: 2 quarts.

NUTRITION FACTS: 1/2 cup equals 459 calories, 30 g fat (18 g saturated fat), 101 mg cholesterol, 252 mg sodium, 47 g carbohydrate, 1 g fiber, 3 g protein.

GEORGIA PEACH ICE CREAM

Georgia Peach Ice Cream

Marguerite Ethridge, Americus, Georgia

This recipe makes good use of my state's peaches in this favorite that's been in my family for over 50 years.

- 1 quart milk
- 2-1/4 cups sugar, *divided*
- 1/2 teaspoon salt
- 4 eggs, lightly beaten
- 2 cans (14 ounces *each*) sweetened condensed milk
- 1-3/4 pounds fresh peaches, peeled and sliced

1) In a large heavy saucepan, heat milk to 175°; stir in 1 cup sugar and salt until dissolved. Whisk in a small amount of the hot mixture to the eggs. Return all to the pan, whisking constantly.

2) Cook and stir over low heat until mixture reaches at least 160° and coats the back of a metal spoon. Remove from the heat.

3) Cool quickly by placing pan in a bowl of ice water; stir for 2 minutes. Stir in sweetened condensed milk. Press plastic wrap onto surface of custard. Refrigerate for several hours or overnight.

4) When ready to freeze, mash peaches with remaining sugar in a small bowl; let stand for 30 minutes. Combine milk mixture and peaches in an ice cream freezer. Freeze according to manufacturer's directions.

Yield: 3-3/4 quarts.

NUTRITION FACTS: 1/2 cup equals 214 calories, 5 g fat (3 g saturated fat), 45 mg cholesterol, 109 mg sodium, 39 g carbohydrate, 1 g fiber, 5 g protein.

extracts and food coloring if desired. Press plastic wrap onto surface of custard. Refrigerate for several hours or overnight.

4) Stir in the chocolate chips. Fill ice cream freezer cylinder two-thirds full; freeze according to the manufacturer's directions. Refrigerate remaining mixture until ready to freeze.

Yield: 1-1/2 quarts.

NUTRITION FACTS: 1/2 cup equals 244 calories, 17 g fat (10 g saturated fat), 106 mg cholesterol, 59 mg sodium, 20 g carbohydrate, trace fiber, 4 g protein.

Butter Pecan Ice Cream
Jenny White, Glen, Mississippi

This rich, buttery ice cream sure beats store-bought versions. And with its pretty color and plentiful pecan crunch, it's nice enough to serve guests at a summer party.

1/2 cup chopped pecans
1 tablespoon butter
1-1/2 cups half-and-half cream
1 cup packed brown sugar
2 eggs, lightly beaten
1/2 cup heavy whipping cream
1 teaspoon vanilla extract

1) In a small skillet, toast pecans in butter for 5-6 minutes or until lightly browned. Cool.

2) In a heavy saucepan, heat half-and-half to 175°; stir in the brown sugar until dissolved. Whisk a small amount of hot cream mixture into the eggs; return all to the pan, whisking constantly. Cook and stir over low heat until mixture reaches at least 160° and coats the back of a metal spoon.

3) Remove from the heat. Cool quickly by placing pan in a bowl of ice water; stir for 2 minutes. Stir in whipping cream and vanilla. Press plastic wrap onto the surface of custard. Refrigerate for several hours or overnight. Stir in toasted pecans.

4) Fill cylinder of ice cream freezer two-thirds full; freeze according to the manufacturer's directions. Refrigerate remaining mixture until ready to freeze.

5) Allow to ripen in ice cream freezer or firm up in the refrigerator freezer for 2-4 hours before serving.

Yield: 1 quart.

NUTRITION FACTS: 1/2 cup equals 298 calories, 18 g fat (8 g saturated fat), 100 mg cholesterol, 69 mg sodium, 30 g carbohydrate, 1 g fiber, 4 g protein.

MINT CHIP ICE CREAM

Mint Chip Ice Cream
Farrah McGuire, Springdale, Washington

We have a milk cow, so homemade ice cream has become a regular treat for our family. This version is very creamy with a mild mint flavor that goes well with the mini chocolate chips. It was an instant hit with my husband and our two girls.

1-3/4 cups milk
3/4 cup sugar
Dash salt
3 eggs, lightly beaten
1-3/4 cups heavy whipping cream
1 teaspoon vanilla extract
1/4 teaspoon peppermint extract
4 drops green food coloring, optional
1/2 cup miniature semisweet chocolate chips

1) In a small saucepan, heat the milk to 175°; stir in the sugar and salt until dissolved. Whisk in a small amount of the hot mixture to the eggs. Return all to the pan, whisking constantly.

2) Cook and stir over low heat until mixture reaches at least 160° and coats the back of a metal spoon. Remove from the heat.

3) Cool quickly by placing pan in a bowl of ice water; stir for 2 minutes. Stir in whipping cream,

ICE CREAM SANDWICH DESSERT

Ice Cream Sandwich Dessert
Jody Koerber, Caledonia, Wisconsin

No one will believe this awesome dessert is just dressed-up ice cream sandwiches. For my son's birthday party, I decorated it with race cars and checkered flags because he's a big racing fan. It was a huge success!

- 19 ice cream sandwiches
- 1 carton (12 ounces) frozen whipped topping, thawed
- 1 jar (11-3/4 ounces) hot fudge ice cream topping
- 1 cup salted peanuts, *divided*

1) Cut one ice cream sandwich in half. Place one whole and one half sandwich along a short side of an ungreased 13-in. x 9-in. x 2-in. pan. Arrange eight sandwiches in opposite direction in the pan.

2) Spread with half of the whipped topping. Spoon fudge topping by teaspoonfuls onto whipped topping. Sprinkle with 1/2 cup peanuts. Repeat layers with remaining ice cream sandwiches, whipped topping and peanuts (pan will be full).

3) Cover and freeze for up to 2 months. Remove from the freezer 20 minutes before serving. Cut into squares.

Yield: 15 servings.

NUTRITION FACTS: 1 piece equals 375 calories, 17 g fat (9 g saturated fat), 25 mg cholesterol, 116 mg sodium, 48 g carbohydrate, 2 g fiber, 7 g protein.

Coffee Ice Cream Torte
Janet Hutts, Gainesville, Georgia

Not only does this make-ahead dessert go over big with company, but it calls for only four ingredients. If you can't find coffee-flavored ice cream, dissolve instant coffee granules in warm water and stir into vanilla ice cream.

- 2 packages (3 ounces *each*) ladyfingers
- 1 cup chocolate-covered English toffee bits, *divided*
- 1/2 gallon coffee ice cream, softened
- 1 carton (8 ounces) frozen whipped topping, thawed

1) Place ladyfingers around the edge of a 9-in. springform pan. Line the bottom of the pan with remaining ladyfingers. Stir 1/2 cup toffee bits into the ice cream; spoon into prepared pan.

2) Cover with plastic wrap; freeze overnight or until firm. May be frozen for up to 2 months.

3) Just before serving, remove sides of pan. Garnish with whipped topping and remaining toffee bits.

Yield: 16 servings.

NUTRITION FACTS: 1 piece equals 298 calories, 17 g fat (10 g saturated fat), 69 mg cholesterol, 136 mg sodium, 32 g carbohydrate, trace fiber, 3 g protein.

Frozen Sundae Dessert
Kimberly McKeever, Shoreview, Minnesota

In the mood for a cool, creamy dessert after a steady stream of heavy holiday sweets? Try this recipe or experiment with different ice creams or toppings to find your own combination.

- 20 chocolate sandwich cookies, crushed
- 1/4 cup butter, softened
- 1/2 gallon vanilla *or* peppermint ice cream, softened
- 1 carton (8 ounces) frozen whipped topping, thawed
- 2 to 3 tablespoons chocolate syrup
- 1/4 cup chopped pecans

1) In a large bowl, combine cookie crumbs and butter. Press into the bottom of a 13-in. x 9-in. x 2-in. pan. Carefully spread ice cream over crust. Spread whipped topping over ice cream. Drizzle chocolate syrup on top; sprinkle with nuts.

2) Freeze until firm, about 2-4 hours. Remove from the freezer 15 minutes before serving.

Yield: 16 servings.

NUTRITION FACTS: 1 piece equals 283 calories, 17 g fat (9 g saturated fat), 37 mg cholesterol, 175 mg sodium, 30 g carbohydrate, 1 g fiber, 3 g protein.

Fudge Sundae Sauce
Tammy Mckie, Seward, Nebraska

Mocha flavors are highlighted in this fudgy topping. You can make the sauce without the coffee, too. Either way, it stores well in the refrigerator to use whenever you want a little chocolaty goodness.

> 2 cups (12 ounces) semisweet chocolate chips
> 2 squares (1 ounce *each*) unsweetened chocolate
> 1 cup heavy whipping cream
> 1/4 cup cold strong brewed coffee
> Dash salt
> 1 teaspoon vanilla extract

1) In a heavy saucepan, melt the chocolate with the cream, coffee and salt over low heat, stirring constantly.

2) Remove from the heat; stir in vanilla. Cover and refrigerate. Reheat to serve over your favorite ice cream.

Yield: 2-1/2 cups.

Editor's Note: If you prefer your fudge sauce without the coffee flavor, just omit the coffee and increase the heavy whipping cream to 1-1/4 cups.

NUTRITION FACTS: 2 tablespoons equals 137 calories, 11 g fat (7 g saturated fat), 16 mg cholesterol, 14 mg sodium, 12 g carbohydrate, 1 g fiber, 1 g protein.

Praline Sauce
Pat Sturze, Campbell River, British Columbia

This is a can't-miss treat over ice cream. You can also serve it over waffles, pancakes or French toast for a fabulous breakfast.

> 1-1/2 cups dark corn syrup
> 1-1/2 cups light corn syrup
> 1 teaspoon vanilla extract
> 1/8 teaspoon ground cinnamon
> 1/8 teaspoon ground nutmeg
> 1-1/2 cups coarsely chopped pecans, toasted

1) In a large bowl, combine corn syrups, vanilla, cinnamon and nutmeg until well blended. Stir in pecans. Serve at room temperature or warm in the microwave.

2) Store any leftover sauce in an airtight container at room temperature.

Yield: 4 cups.

NUTRITION FACTS: 2 tablespoons equals 126 calories, 4 g fat (trace saturated fat), 0 cholesterol, 42 mg sodium, 24 g carbohydrate, 1 g fiber, 1 g protein.

CARAMEL ICE CREAM SAUCE

Caramel Ice Cream Sauce
Julee Wallberg, Reno, Nevada

This delightful dessert sauce stirs up on the stovetop. With its smooth texture and yummy taste from brown sugar, it's terrific drizzled over ice cream.

> 1/2 cup packed brown sugar
> 1 tablespoon cornstarch
> 1/3 cup half-and-half cream
> 2 tablespoons water
> 2 tablespoons light corn syrup
> 1 tablespoon butter
> 1/2 teaspoon vanilla extract
> Ice cream

1) In a saucepan, combine the brown sugar and cornstarch. Stir in the cream, water and corn syrup until smooth. Bring to a boil; cook and stir for 2 minutes or until thickened.

2) Remove from the heat. Stir in the butter and vanilla until butter is melted. Serve warm or cold over ice cream. Refrigerate leftovers.

Yield: about 1 cup.

NUTRITION FACTS: 2 tablespoons (calculated without ice cream) equals 96 calories, 2 g fat (2 g saturated fat), 9 mg cholesterol, 31 mg sodium, 19 g carbohydrate, trace fiber, trace protein.

Peppermint Stick Sauce

Linda Gronewaller, Hutchinson, Kansas

This pepperminty sauce is one of my favorite holiday gifts to give. I package it in a decorative jar and add a package of chopped nuts to sprinkle with it over ice cream, unfrosted brownies or chocolate cake.

- 1-1/2 cups finely crushed peppermint candies *or* candy canes
- 3/4 cup heavy whipping cream
- 1 jar (7 ounces) marshmallow creme

1) Combine all ingredients in a medium saucepan. Cook over medium-low heat, stirring occasionally, until mixture is smooth and candy is melted.

2) Pour into small airtight containers. Store in the refrigerator. Serve warm over ice cream or cake.

Yield: 3 cups.

NUTRITION FACTS: 2 tablespoons equals 76 calories, 3 g fat (2 g saturated fat), 10 mg cholesterol, 12 mg sodium, 13 g carbohydrate, 0 fiber, trace protein.

Caramel Pudding Cake

Lois Litalien, Bonners Ferry, Idaho

This recipe dates back to the 1800s. It's a quick recipe when you need dessert pronto!

- 1/2 cup butter, softened
- 1/2 cup sugar
- 1-1/2 cups all-purpose flour
- 1 teaspoon baking powder
- 1/2 teaspoon salt
- 1/2 cup milk
- 1/2 cup raisins
- 1 cup packed brown sugar
- 2 cups cold water

1) In a small mixing bowl, cream butter and sugar until light and fluffy. Combine the flour, baking powder and salt; add to creamed mixture with milk. Stir until smooth. Stir in raisins.

2) Spread in a greased 8-in. square baking pan. Combine brown sugar and cold water; pour over batter. Bake at 350° for 40 minutes or until golden brown. Serve warm.

Yield: 9 servings.

NUTRITION FACTS: 1 cup equals 332 calories, 11 g fat (7 g saturated fat), 29 mg cholesterol, 296 mg sodium, 58 g carbohydrate, 1 g fiber, 3 g protein.

RED RASPBERRY MOUSSE DSSERT

Red Raspberry Mousse Dessert

Edna Hoffman, Hebron, Indiana

When I need a light and refreshing finish to a special meal, I make this fluffy, fruity mousse. Ladyfingers add an elegant look to this pretty dessert.

- 2 packages (3 ounces *each*) raspberry gelatin
- 1-3/4 cups boiling water
- 2 packages (10 ounces *each*) frozen sweetened raspberries, thawed
- 2 cups heavy whipping cream, whipped
- 23 ladyfingers

Fresh mint, and raspberries and additional whipped cream, optional

1) In a large bowl, dissolve gelatin in boiling water. Stir in raspberries. Refrigerate until partially thickened. Fold in whipped cream.

2) Arrange the ladyfingers with rounded side out around the sides of an ungreased 9-in. springform pan. Carefully spoon raspberry mixture into pan.

3) Cover and refrigerate until firm. Garnish with mint, raspberries and whipped cream if desired.

Yield: 12 servings.

NUTRITION FACTS: 1 piece equals 314 calories, 17 g fat (10 g saturated fat), 131 mg cholesterol, 79 mg sodium, 38 g carbohydrate, 2 g fiber, 5 g protein.

Puddings and Custards

Baked custards are a sweetened mixture of milk, eggs and flavoring. They can be baked individually in custard cups or in one large baking dish.

They are usually baked in a water bath to help ensure gentle and even baking. (See Making a Water Bath on page 546.) Custards are done when a knife inserted about halfway to the center comes out clean and the top looks set.

To unmold a cooled custard, carefully run a knife around the edge of dish to loosen. If possible, lift the bottom edge of the custard with the tip of the knife blade to loosen. Place a serving dish over the top of the baking dish. Invert and remove custard dish.

Bread puddings are made with cubes or slices of bread baked in a custard mixture. They can be enriched with fruits, nuts, chocolate and spices. Bread puddings are served warm or cold and may be accompanied by a sauce. Bread puddings are done when a knife inserted near the center comes out clean.

Rice puddings are made with cooked rice, a custard mixture, flavoring and spices. They can be served warm or cold. Rice puddings are done when a knife inserted near the center comes out clean.

Store baked custards and puddings in the refrigerator for 1 to 2 days.

Old-Fashioned Rice Pudding
Laura German, North Brookfield, Massachusetts

Try a delicious classic that's a nice way to use up leftover rice. We also like to dress it up with English toffee bits, chocolate and toasted coconut.

- 2 cups cooked long grain rice
- 2 cups milk
- 3 tablespoons plus 1 teaspoon sugar
- 1/8 teaspoon salt
- 1 teaspoon vanilla extract

Whipped cream, optional

1) In a large saucepan, combine the rice, milk, sugar and salt. Cook, uncovered, over medium heat for 20 minutes or until thickened, stirring often. Remove from the heat; stir in vanilla. Spoon into serving dishes. Serve warm; top with whipped cream if desired.

Yield: 4 servings.

NUTRITION FACTS: 1 serving equals 220 calories, 4 g fat (3 g saturated fat), 17 mg cholesterol, 134 mg sodium, 38 g carbohydrate, trace fiber, 6 g protein.

■ *TOFFEE RICE PUDDING:* Combine 3 tablespoons *each* English toffee bits, miniature semisweet chocolate and toasted flaked coconut. Place half of the rice pudding in 4 individual dessert dishes and top with half the toffee mixture. Repeat layers.

ORANGE CHOCOLATE MOUSSE

Orange Chocolate Mousse
Shirley Glaab, Hattiesburg, Mississippi

Easy-to-make, this dessert looks so elegant. Its velvety texture with a hint of orange flavor is a perfect ending to any meal.

- 2 eggs, beaten
- 2 egg yolks, beaten
- 1 cup heavy whipping cream
- 1/4 cup packed brown sugar
- 3 tablespoons orange juice
- 1 to 1-1/2 teaspoons grated orange peel
- 6 squares (1 ounce *each*) semisweet chocolate, melted and cooled

Whipped cream and orange peel strips, optional

1) In a saucepan, combine the eggs, egg yolks, cream, brown sugar, juice and peel until blended. Cook and stir over medium-low heat for 15 minutes or until the mixture is thickened and reached 160°.

2) Remove from the heat; stir in melted chocolate until smooth. Pour into dessert dishes. Refrigerate for at least 2 hours or until serving.

3) Garnish with whipped cream and orange peel if desired.

Yield: 4 servings.

NUTRITION FACTS: 1 serving equals 542 calories, 41 g fat (23 g saturated fat), 294 mg cholesterol, 63 mg sodium, 41 g carbohydrate, 3 g fiber, 9 g protein.

Coconut Custard Pudding

Wilma Lincoln, Montezuma, Iowa

For a change of pace from the coconut, you can easily modify this recipe to make a delicious vanilla custard pudding.

      3   eggs
    1/3   cup sugar
  Dash salt
  2-1/4   cups milk
    1/4   teaspoon coconut extract
    1/4   teaspoon vanilla extract
  Dash ground nutmeg

1) In a small bowl, whisk the eggs, sugar and salt until the eggs are just blended. In a saucepan, heat milk just to simmering. Gradually whisk into egg mixture. Stir in extracts.

2) Pour into five 8-oz. custard cups. Sprinkle with nutmeg. Place cups in a 13-in. x 9-in. x 2-in. baking pan. Add 1 in. of hot water to the pan. Bake, uncovered, at 350° for 45-50 minutes or until a knife inserted near the center comes out clean.

3) Remove cups to a wire rack; cool for 1 hour. Store in the refrigerator.

Yield: 5 servings.

NUTRITION FACTS: 1 serving equals 165 calories, 7 g fat (3 g saturated fat), 142 mg cholesterol, 121 mg sodium, 19 g carbohydrate, trace fiber, 7 g protein.

■ *VANILLA CUSTARD PUDDING:* Omit coconut extract. Increase vanilla extract to 3/4 teaspoon. If desired use 1/3 brown sugar in place of the sugar.

: **MAKING A WATER BATH**

Place a baking dish in a larger baking pan or dish, then place on rack in oven. Using a kettle or large measuring cups, carefully pour hot or boiling water into larger pan or dish. Fill according to recipe directions, generally to a depth of 1 in. or halfway up the sides of the larger pan or dish.

Baked Lemon Pudding

Ann Berg, Chesapeake, Virginia

The tart taste of lemon brings the perfect finish to this meal. The fluffy, light cake texture is appealing.

    2   eggs, *separated*
    1   cup sugar
    3   tablespoons all-purpose flour
  3/4   cup milk
  1/4   cup lemon juice
    1   tablespoon butter, melted
    2   teaspoons grated lemon peel

1) Place egg whites in a small mixing bowl and let stand at room temperature for 30 minutes. In a large bowl, combine sugar and flour. Stir in the milk, lemon juice, butter and lemon peel. Beat egg yolks; add to the lemon mixture.

2) With clean beaters, beat egg whites until stiff peaks form. With a spatula, stir a fourth of the whites into the lemon batter until no white streaks remain. Fold in remaining egg whites until combined.

3) Pour into a greased 1-qt. baking dish. Place in a large baking pan. Fill larger pan with hot water to a depth of 1 in.

4) Bake, uncovered, at 350° for 45-50 minutes or until a knife inserted near the center comes out clean.

5) Cover loosely with foil sprayed with nonstick cooking spray during the last 10 minutes of baking if the top browns too quickly. Serve warm. Refrigerate leftovers.

Yield: 4 servings.

NUTRITION FACTS: 1 serving equals 310 calories, 7 g fat (4 g saturated fat), 120 mg cholesterol, 84 mg sodium, 58 g carbohydrate, trace fiber, 5 g protein.

Elegant Bread Pudding

Sharon Runyan, Fort Wayne, Indiana

My family looks forward to when my sister-in-law brings this best-of-the-season treat. Caramel sauce and whipped cream make it extra-special.

   10   cups cubed croissants *or* French bread
  1/2   cup raisins
    8   eggs
    2   cups half-and-half cream
    1   cup packed brown sugar
    1   teaspoon ground cinnamon
    1   teaspoon ground nutmeg

1 teaspoon grated orange peel

CARAMEL SAUCE:
1 cup packed brown sugar
1/2 cup butter
1/2 cup heavy whipping cream
1 teaspoon vanilla extract
Whipped cream, optional

1) Arrange bread cubes evenly in a greased 13-in. x 9-in. x 2-in. baking dish; sprinkle with raisins. In a large bowl, beat the eggs, half-and-half cream, sugar, cinnamon, nutmeg and orange peel; pour over bread.

2) Bake, uncovered, at 350° for 30 minutes. Cover with foil and bake 15 minutes longer or until a knife inserted near the center comes out clean.

3) For sauce, in a saucepan, combine the brown sugar, butter and whipping cream; cook and stir over low heat until smooth. Remove from the heat; stir in vanilla.

4) Serve bread pudding in bowls with caramel sauce and whipped cream if desired.

Yield: 14 servings.

NUTRITION FACTS: 1 serving equals 377 calories, 17 g fat (9 g saturated fat), 168 mg cholesterol, 270 mg sodium, 49 g carbohydrate, 1 g fiber, 7 g protein.

SUPER STRAWBERRY SHORTCAKE

Super Strawberry Shortcake
Renee Bisch, Wellesley, Ontario

"Wow!" is what people will say when you set this dessert on the table. It's fun to serve since it's bursting with flavor yet not overly sweet.

1 quart fresh strawberries, sliced
1 to 2 tablespoons sugar

SHORTCAKE:
1-3/4 cups all-purpose flour
2 tablespoons sugar
1 teaspoon baking powder
1/2 teaspoon baking soda
1/2 teaspoon salt
1/4 cup cold butter
1 egg
3/4 cup sour cream

TOPPING:
1 cup heavy whipping cream
1 to 2 tablespoons sugar
1 teaspoon vanilla extract

1) In a large bowl, combine the strawberries and sugar; set aside. For shortcake, in another large bowl, combine the flour, sugar, baking powder, baking soda and salt; cut in butter until mixture resembles coarse crumbs.

2) In a small bowl, beat egg; add sour cream. Stir into the crumb mixture just until moistened. Knead dough on a floured surface 25 times or until smooth.

3) Roll out into a 7-1/2-in. circle on a lightly greased baking sheet. Cut a 2-in. hole in center to form a ring. Bake at 425° for 12-14 minutes or until golden. Remove from baking sheet to a wire rack to cool completely.

4) For topping, in a small chilled mixing bowl, beat cream until it begins to thicken. Add sugar and vanilla; beat until stiff peaks form.

5) Just before serving, split cake into two horizontally layers. Spoon juice from berries over bottom layer. Spoon half of berries over juice. Spread with half of topping.

6) Cover with top cake layer, then spread with remaining topping and spoon remaining berries over top. Cut into wedges.

Yield: 8 servings.

NUTRITION FACTS: 1 piece equals 348 calories, 22 g fat (13 g saturated fat), 98 mg cholesterol, 366 mg sodium, 32 g carbohydrate, 2 g fiber, 5 g protein.

■ *BERRY SHORTCAKE:* Use 1 pint *each* fresh blueberries and fresh sliced strawberries for the quart of fresh strawberries.

Chocolate Fondue

Jane Shapton, Tustin, California

This creamy, delectable dip is a chocolate lover's dream. You'll want to sample it with a variety of dippers, including strawberries, banana chunks and cake cubes.

1-1/2	cups sugar
1-1/4	cups water
1/4	cup light corn syrup
1	cup baking cocoa
1/2	cup heavy whipping cream
5	squares (1 ounce *each*) semisweet chocolate, chopped

Strawberries, banana chunks, apple slices *or* angel food cake cubes

1) In a small saucepan, bring the sugar, water and corn syrup to a boil. Reduce the heat; simmer, uncovered, for 20 minutes, stirring frequently.

2) In a bowl, combine the cocoa, cream and half of the syrup mixture until smooth; return to the pan. Bring to a boil, stirring constantly. Reduce heat; simmer, uncovered, for 5 minutes. Stir in the chopped chocolate until melted.

3) Serve warm with fruit or cake for dipping. Refrigerate leftovers.

Yield: 2-1/2 cups.

NUTRITION FACTS: 2 tablespoons fondue (calculated without fruit or cake cubes) equals 138 calories, 5 g fat (3 g saturated fat), 8 mg cholesterol, 7 mg sodium, 25 g carbohydrate, 1 g fiber, 1 g protein.

Strawberry Tiramisu Trifle

Tammy Irvine, Whitby, Ontario

I love entertaining and like to make this easy trifle when I want to impress people. Berries make it different from a traditional tiramisu.

1	quart fresh strawberries
1-1/4	cups cold milk
1	package (3.4 ounces) instant vanilla pudding mix
1	package (8 ounces) cream cheese, softened
4	tablespoons strong brewed coffee, room temperature, *divided*
2	cups whipped topping
1	package (3 ounces) ladyfingers, split
6	squares (1 ounce *each*) bittersweet chocolate, grated

1) Set aside three strawberries for garnish; slice the remaining strawberries. In a bowl, whisk milk and pudding mix for 2 minutes. Let stand for 2 minutes or until soft-set.

2) In a large mixing bowl, beat cream cheese until smooth; gradually beat in 2 tablespoons coffee. Beat in pudding. Fold in whipped topping.

3) Brush remaining coffee over ladyfingers. Line the bottom of a 3-qt. trifle or glass serving bowl with half of the ladyfingers. Top with half of the sliced berries, grated chocolate and pudding mixture; repeat layers.

4) Cut reserved berries in half; place on trifle. Cover and refrigerate for 4 hours or overnight.

Yield: 12 servings.

NUTRITION FACTS: 1/2 cup equals 256 calories, 16 g fat (10 g saturated fat), 50 mg cholesterol, 193 mg sodium, 27 g carbohydrate, 2 g fiber, 4 g protein.

Mocha Mousse Brownie Trifle

Taste of Home Test Kitchen

Use some extra brownies to create this tempting time-saving trifle. It's a snap to assemble with a packaged mousse mix and whipped topping, yet it looks so special that folks will think you fussed.

5	cups prepared brownies
1	package (2.8 ounces) mocha mousse mix
1	carton (12 ounces) frozen whipped topping, thawed
1/4	cup English toffee bits *or* almond brickle chips

Grated chocolate

1) Place half of the cubed brownies in a 2-qt. serving bowl. Prepare mousse mix according to package directions.

2) Spread half over the brownies. Top with half of the whipped topping; sprinkle with toffee bits. Repeat layers of brownies, mousse and whipped topping.

3) Sprinkle with grated chocolate. Refrigerate until serving.

Yield: 10-12 servings.

NUTRITION FACTS: 1 serving equals 350 calories, 17 g fat (9 g saturated fat), 12 mg cholesterol, 212 mg sodium, 46 g carbohydrate, 1 g fiber, 3 g protein.

COOKIES & BARS

Cookies make great snacks, bake sale bundles, homemade gifts and special holiday buffet treats. They are commonly grouped into five categories: drop, shaped, refrigerator, cutout and bars.

The consistency of drop cookie dough allows it to simply be dropped from a spoon onto a baking sheet, making it the easiest kind of cookie to bake.

Shaped cookies are formed by hand into various shapes, such as balls, logs and crescents. Or they're pressed through a cookie press, such as spritz.

For refrigerator (icebox) or slice and bake cookies, the dough is shaped into logs, wrapped in plastic wrap and then refrigerated until firm enough to slice and bake.

Cutout cookies have a firmer dough. To make it easier to handle, the dough may need to be chilled before being rolled out and cut into shapes with a cookie cutter.

Bar cookies may be made with a pourable batter, spreadable dough or a crumbly crust that needs to be patted into the pan. The one thing all bar cookies have in common is that they are baked in a pan rather than on a baking sheet. After cooling, they are cut into bars, squares, fingers, triangles or diamonds.

Cookie Baking Tips

Use butter, stick margarine (with at least 80% oil) or shortening. Whipped, tub, soft, liquid or reduced-fat products contain air and water and will produce flat, tough and underbrowned cookies. Measure all ingredients accurately.

Avoid overmixing the dough. If it's handled too much, the cookies will be tough.

Use heavy-gauge dull aluminum baking sheets with one or two low sides. When a recipe calls for greased baking sheets, use shortening or nonstick cooking spray. Dark finishes may cause the cookies to become overly browned.

Preheat the oven for 10 to 15 minutes. For even baking, make cookies the same size and thickness. Unless the recipe states otherwise, place cookie dough 2 to 3 in. apart on a cool baking sheet.

Leave at least 2 in. around the baking sheet and the oven walls for good heat circulation. For best results, bake only one sheet of cookies at a time. If you need to bake two sheets at once, switch the position of the baking sheets halfway through the baking time.

Check the cookies when the minimum baking time has been reached, baking longer if needed. Follow doneness tests given in individual recipes.

Unless otherwise directed, let cookies cool for 1 minute on the baking sheet before removing to a wire rack. Cool completely before storing.

Let baking sheets cool before placing the next batch of cookie dough on it. Otherwise, the heat from the baking sheet will soften the dough and cause it to spread.

Removing Cookies from a Baking Sheet

If cookies crumble when you remove them from the baking sheet, let them cool for 1 to 2 minutes first. But if cookies cool too long, they become hard and can break when removed. If this happens, return the baking sheet to the oven to warm the cookies slightly so they'll release more easily.

Storing Cookies

Allow cookies to cool completely before storing. Store soft cookies and crisp cookies in separate airtight containers. If stored together, the moisture from the soft cookies will soften the crisp cookies, making them lose their crunch. Flavors can also blend during storage, so don't store strong-flavored cookies with delicate-flavored ones.

Layer cookies in a container, separating each layer with waxed paper. Allow icing on cookies to completely dry before storing.

Unfrosted cookies can be stored in a cool dry place in airtight containers for about 3 days. Cookies with a cream cheese frosting should be stored in the refrigerator.

For longer storage, wrap unfrosted cookies in plastic wrap, stack in an airtight container, seal and freeze for up to 3 months. Thaw wrapped cookies at room temperature before frosting and serving. If your crisp cookies became soft during storage, crisp them up by heating in a 300° oven for 5 minutes.

TOFFEE MALTED COOKIES

Drop Cookies

If your mixer begins to strain because the cookie dough is too thick, use a wooden spoon to stir in the last of the flour or ingredients such as nuts, chips or dried fruit.

For even baking, it's important that you make cookies the same size. Use a teaspoon or tablespoon from your flatware set.

Drop cookies generally melt and spread during baking. But sometimes a recipe may instruct you to flatten the cookies with the bottom of a glass dipped in sugar or with a fork, making a crisscross pattern.

Toffee Malted Cookies

Sharon Timpe, Mequon, Wisconsin

As much as I delight in sharing these goodies, my family considers them "keepers." It's a wonder I ever get them out the door to take to meetings! With their buttery melt-in-your mouth texture, they're always popular.

- 1 cup butter, softened
- 1/2 cup sugar
- 1/2 cup packed brown sugar
- 2 eggs
- 1 package (3.4 ounces) instant vanilla pudding mix
- 1 teaspoon vanilla extract
- 2-1/4 cups all-purpose flour
- 1 cup quick-cooking oats
- 1 teaspoon baking soda
- 1/2 teaspoon salt
- 1 cup malted milk balls, chopped
- 3/4 cup English toffee bits *or* almond brickle chips

1) In a large mixing bowl, cream the butter and sugars until light and fluffy. Add eggs, one at a time, beating well after each addition. Add pudding mix and vanilla.

2) Combine the flour, oats, baking soda and salt; add to creamed mixture. Fold in the malted milk balls and the toffee bits (dough will be stiff). Drop by rounded teaspoonfuls 2 in. apart onto ungreased baking sheets.

3) Bake at 350° for 12-15 minutes or until golden brown. Cool for 2 minutes before removing to wire racks.

Yield: about 6 dozen.

NUTRITION FACTS: 2 cookies equals 159 calories, 8 g fat (4 g saturated fat), 28 mg cholesterol, 194 mg sodium, 20 g carbohydrate, trace fiber, 2 g protein.

Chocolate Mint Sandwich Cookies

Bertha Bratt, Lynden, Washington

The minty filling that's sandwiched between two chocolaty cookies is a real treat.

- 6 tablespoons butter
- 1-1/2 cups packed brown sugar
- 2 tablespoons water
- 2 cups (12 ounces) semisweet chocolate chips
- 2 eggs

1 teaspoon vanilla extract

2-1/2 cups all-purpose flour

1-1/2 teaspoons baking soda

1 teaspoon salt

FILLING:

2-1/2 cups confectioners' sugar

1/4 cup butter

3 tablespoons milk

1/2 teaspoon peppermint extract

3 drops green food coloring, optional

Dash salt

1) In a saucepan, combine the butter, brown sugar, water and chocolate chips. Cook and stir over low heat until chips are melted. Cool.

2) Beat in eggs and vanilla. Combine the flour, baking soda and salt; gradually add to the chocolate mixture. Drop by rounded teaspoonfuls 2 in. apart onto ungreased baking sheets.

3) Bake at 350° for 10-12 minutes or until firm. Remove to wire racks to cool.

4) In a large mixing bowl, combine filling ingredients until smooth. Spread on the bottom of half of the cookies; top with remaining cookies.

Yield: about 15 sandwich cookies.

NUTRITION FACTS: 1 sandwich equals 424 calories, 15 g fat (9 g saturated fat), 49 mg cholesterol, 392 mg sodium, 72 g carbohydrate, 2 g fiber, 4 g protein.

MAKING DROP COOKIES

Fill a teaspoon or tablespoon with dough. Use another spoon or small rubber spatula to push the mound of dough off the spoon onto a cool baking sheet. Place dough 2 to 3 in. apart or as recipe directs.

An ice cream scoop is a perfect utensil for making uniformly sized drop cookies. (A 1 tablespoon-sized ice cream scoop will result in a standard-size 2-in. cookie.) Just scoop the dough, even off the top with a flat-edge metal spatula and release onto a baking sheet.

BROWNIE MOUNDS

Brownie Mounds
Mary Turner, Blountville, Tennessee

If you crave brownies but not the longer baking time, try these quick cookies. I usually make them for the holidays, but they're good any time of year.

1/3 cup butter, softened

3/4 cup sugar

1/3 cup light corn syrup

1 egg

3 squares (1 ounce *each*) unsweetened chocolate, melted

1 teaspoon vanilla extract

1-2/3 cups all-purpose flour

1/2 teaspoon baking powder

1/4 teaspoon salt

1/2 cup chopped walnuts

1) In a large mixing bowl, cream butter and sugar until light and fluffy. Add corn syrup and egg; beat well. Stir in chocolate and vanilla.

2) Combine the flour, baking powder and salt. Add to chocolate mixture; beat well. Stir in walnuts. Drop by tablespoonfuls 2 in. apart onto greased baking sheets.

3) Bake at 350° for 10-12 minutes or until edges are firm. Remove to wire racks to cool.

Yield: 3 dozen.

NUTRITION FACTS: 2 cookies equals 172 calories, 8 g fat (4 g saturated fat), 21 mg cholesterol, 90 mg sodium, 24 g carbohydrate, 1 g fiber, 3 g protein.

and pecans, stir in 1 cup vanilla *or* white chips and 1 cup dried cranberries. Bake as directed.

■ *WHITE CHOCOLATE CHIP COOKIES:* Omit the semisweet chocolate chips and pecans. Stir 2 cups vanilla *or* white chips and 1 cup toasted chopped hazelnuts into dough. Bake as directed.

Meringue Fudge Drops
Charlotte Elliott, Neenah, Wisconsin

Almond-flavored meringue, a fudgy filling and a sprinkling of pistachio nuts make these bite-size morsels a special addition to any dessert tray.

- 2 egg whites
- 1/4 teaspoon almond extract
- 1/8 teaspoon cream of tartar
- 1/8 teaspoon salt
- 1/2 cup sugar

FUDGE TOPPING:
- 1/2 cup semisweet chocolate chips
- 3 tablespoons butter
- 2 egg yolks, lightly beaten
- 2 tablespoons confectioners' sugar
- 2 tablespoons chopped pistachio nuts

1) Place egg whites in a small mixing bowl and let stand at room temperature for 30 minutes. Line baking sheets with parchment paper; set aside.

2) Beat egg whites with almond extract, cream of tartar and salt on medium speed until soft peaks form. Gradually add sugar, 1 tablespoon at a time, beating on high until stiff peaks form and sugar is dissolved.

3) Drop meringue mixture by teaspoonfuls onto prepared sheets. With a small spoon, make a small indentation in the center of each. Bake at 250° for 30-35 minutes or until dry to the touch.

4) For topping, combine chocolate chips and butter in a small saucepan. Cook and stir over medium-low heat until chips are melted and mixture is smooth. Combine egg yolks and confectioners' sugar. Reduce heat to low.

5) Gradually whisk into chocolate mixture. Cook and stir for 1 minute longer or until mixture reaches 160°. Cool to room temperature, whisking several times. Spoon into center of meringue. Sprinkle with pistachio.

Yield: 4-1/2 dozen.

NUTRITION FACTS: 2 cookies equals 56 calories, 3 g fat (2 g saturated fat), 35 mg cholesterol, 32 mg sodium, 6 g carbohydrate, trace fiber, 1 g protein.

Cindy's Chocolate Chip Cookies
Cindy Utter, Jacksonville, Illinois

Chocolate chip cookies are a mainstay in every cookie jar. They have mass appeal, making them perfect for gifts, bake sales or everyday snacking.

- 1 cup butter, softened
- 1 cup shortening
- 2 cups packed light brown sugar
- 1 cup sugar
- 4 eggs
- 2 teaspoons vanilla extract
- 4-1/2 cups all-purpose flour
- 2 teaspoons baking soda
- 2 teaspoons salt
- 2 cups (12 ounces) semisweet chocolate chips
- 1 cup chopped pecans

1) In a large mixing bowl, cream the butter, shortening and sugars until light and fluffy. Beat in eggs and vanilla.

2) Combine the flour, baking soda and salt; add to creamed mixture and mix well. Stir in chocolate chips and nuts (dough will be sticky). Drop by tablespoonfuls 2 in. apart onto greased baking sheets.

3) Bake at 350° for 10-12 minutes or until lightly browned. Remove to wire racks to cool.

Yield: about 11 dozen.

NUTRITION FACTS: 2 cookies equals 160 calories, 9 g fat (4 g saturated fat), 20 mg cholesterol, 145 mg sodium, 20 g carbohydrate, 1 g fiber, 2 g protein.

■ *CRANBERRY CHIP COOKIES:* Reduce semisweet chocolate chips to 1 cup. Along with the chips

SURPRISE MERINGUES

Surprise Meringues
Gloria Grant, Sterling, Illinois

These crisp, delicate cookies are light as a feather. Mini chocolate chips and chopped nuts are a delightful and yummy surprise in every bite.

    3 egg whites
    1 teaspoon vanilla extract
  1/8 teaspoon cream of tartar
  1/8 teaspoon salt
  3/4 cup sugar
    1 cup (6 ounces) miniature
       semisweet chocolate chips
  1/4 cup chopped pecans *or* walnuts

1) Place egg whites in a large mixing bowl; let stand for 30 minutes. Beat egg whites with vanilla, cream of tartar and salt on medium speed until soft peaks form. Gradually add sugar, 1 tablespoon at a time, beating on high until stiff glossy peaks form and sugar is dissolved, about 6 minutes.

2) Fold in chocolate chips and nuts. Drop by rounded teaspoonfuls 2 in. apart onto parchment paper-lined baking sheets.

3) Bake at 250° for 40-45 minutes or until firm to the touch. Turn oven off; leave meringues in oven for 1-1/2 hours. Remove to wire racks. Store in an airtight container.

Yield: 4 dozen.

NUTRITION FACTS: 2 cookies equals 70 calories, 3 g fat (1 g saturated fat), 0 cholesterol, 20 mg sodium, 11 g carbohydrate, 1 g fiber, 1 g protein.

■ *PEPPERMINT MERINGUES:* Omit vanilla extract, chocolate chips and nuts. Finely crush 2 peppermint candy canes. Drop meringue by teaspoonfuls onto parchment paper-lined baking sheets. Sprinkle with crushed candy canes. Bake as directed.

■ *MERINGUE KISSES:* Omit chocolate chips and nuts. Drop meringue by tablespoonfuls onto parchment paper-lined baking sheets. Press a chocolate kiss into the center of each cookie and cover it with meringue using a knife. Bake at 275° for 30-35 minutes or until firm to the touch. Immediately remove to a wire rack to cool.

Soft Sugar Cookies
Coleen Walter, Bancroft, Michigan

These soft cookies have been a hit in my family for four generations. I often stir up a big batch, and I sometimes add food coloring to the frosting to coordinate with the current holiday.

    1 cup butter, softened
  3/4 cup sugar
    2 eggs
    1 teaspoon vanilla extract
  1/2 teaspoon almond extract
    2 cups all-purpose flour
    1 teaspoon cream of tartar
  1/2 teaspoon baking soda
  1/4 teaspoon salt
  1/4 teaspoon ground nutmeg
FROSTING:
  1/4 cup butter, softened
    3 cups confectioners' sugar
    1 teaspoon almond extract
    2 to 4 tablespoons hot water
  Food coloring, optional

1) In a large mixing bowl, cream butter and sugar until light and fluffy. Beat in the eggs, vanilla and almond extract.

2) Combine the flour, cream of tartar, baking soda, salt and nutmeg; gradually add to creamed mixture. Drop by rounded teaspoonfuls 2 in. apart onto ungreased baking sheets.

3) Bake at 350° for 8-10 minutes or until light brown. Remove to wire racks to cool.

4) For frosting, in a large mixing bowl, combine the butter, confectioners' sugar, almond extract and enough water to achieve desired consistency. Tint with food coloring if desired. Frost the cookies.

Yield: about 6 dozen.

NUTRITION FACTS: 2 cookies equals 142 calories, 7 g fat (4 g saturated fat), 29 mg cholesterol, 102 mg sodium, 20 g carbohydrate, trace fiber, 1 g protein.

Double Orange Cookies

Pamela Kinney, Irving, Texas

Orange juice concentrate and orange peel are mixed into the cookie dough and the frosting to make these citrusy treats truly delightful.

- 1 cup butter, softened
- 1-1/2 cups sugar
- 1 cup (8 ounces) sour cream
- 2 eggs
- 1 can (6 ounces) orange juice concentrate, thawed, *divided*
- 4 cups all-purpose flour
- 1 teaspoon baking powder
- 1 teaspoon baking soda
- 1/2 teaspoon salt
- 2 tablespoons grated orange peel

FROSTING:
- 1 package (3 ounces) cream cheese, softened
- 1 tablespoon butter, softened
- 2 cups confectioners' sugar
- 1 tablespoon grated orange peel
- 1 tablespoon reserved orange juice concentrate
- 2 tablespoons milk

1) In a large mixing bowl, cream butter and sugar until light and fluffy. Add sour cream and eggs. Beat until well blended. Reserve 1 tablespoon orange juice concentrate for frosting.

2) Add the remaining concentrate with combined dry ingredients to the creamed mixture; mix well. Stir in the orange peel. Drop by rounded tablespoonfuls onto lightly greased baking sheets.

3) Bake at 350° for about 10 minutes or until edges just begin to brown. Remove to wire racks to cool completely.

4) In a small mixing bowl, combine frosting ingredients until smooth. Spread a small amount over each cookie. Store cookies in refrigerator.

Yield: about 7 dozen.

NUTRITION FACTS: 2 cookies equals 163 calories, 7 g fat (4 g saturated fat), 29 mg cholesterol, 127 mg sodium, 24 g carbohydrate, trace fiber, 2 g protein.

Honey Crunch Cookies

Germaine Stank, Pound, Wisconsin

Honey, coconut and crisp rice cereal add texture and flavor to these crunchy treats. It makes about 5 dozen, so it's a good recipe for a bake sale.

- 2 cups all-purpose flour
- 2 teaspoons baking powder
- 1/2 teaspoon salt
- 1 cup butter, softened
- 1 cup honey
- 2 eggs
- 1 cup flaked coconut
- 1 cup butterscotch chips
- 4 cups crisp rice cereal

1) Sift together the flour, baking powder and salt; set aside. In a large mixing bowl, cream butter until light and fluffy. Add honey, a little at a time, beating well after each addition.

2) Add eggs, one at a time, beating well after each addition. (Mixture will appear to separate.) Gradually add dry ingredients; mix until moistened. Fold in the coconut, chips and cereal. Drop by teaspoonfuls 2 in. apart onto greased baking sheets.

3) Bake at 350° for 12-14 minutes or until golden brown. Remove to wire racks.

Yield: about 5 dozen.

NUTRITION FACTS: 2 cookies equals 196 calories, 10 g fat (7 g saturated fat), 31 mg cholesterol, 181 mg sodium, 25 g carbohydrate, trace fiber, 2 g protein.

GOLDEN RAISIN OATMEAL COOKIES

Golden Raisin Oatmeal Cookies

Marion Lowery, Medford, Oregon

Here's a slightly different twist on a traditional favorite. These crisp, chewy oatmeal cookies feature golden raisins and have a mild orange tang. They're a staple in my picnic basket!

- 3/4 cup butter, softened
- 1 cup packed brown sugar
- 1/2 cup sugar

1 egg
2 tablespoons water
1 teaspoon vanilla extract
3 cups quick-cooking oats
2/3 cup all-purpose flour
2 tablespoons grated orange peel
1 teaspoon ground cinnamon
1/2 teaspoon baking soda
2/3 cup golden raisins

1) In a large mixing bowl, cream butter and sugars until light and fluffy. Beat in the egg, water and vanilla.

2) Combine the oats, flour, orange peel, cinnamon and baking soda; gradually add to the creamed mixture. Stir in the raisins (dough will be stiff). Drop by level tablespoonfuls 2 in. apart onto ungreased baking sheets.

3) Bake at 350° for 12-15 minutes or until the edges are lightly browned. Remove to wire racks to cool.

Yield: 4 dozen.

NUTRITION FACTS: 2 cookies equals 169 calories, 7 g fat (4 g saturated fat), 24 mg cholesterol, 91 mg sodium, 26 g carbohydrate, 1 g fiber, 2 g protein.

■ *MAPLE RAISIN OATMEAL COOKIES:* Omit the vanilla extract, orange peel and cinnamon. Add 1 teaspoon maple flavoring to creamed mixture with egg. Proceed as recipe directs.

Molasses Raisin Chews
Barbara Parker, Middlefield, Connecticut

My aunt always offered a plate of these when we visted her farm. We called them "cry baby cookies" because we thought the three raisins on each one resembled two eyes and a mouth.

1/2 cup shortening
1 cup sugar
1 cup molasses
4 cups all-purpose flour
2 teaspoons baking soda
2 teaspoons ground cinnamon
1 teaspoon ground cloves
1/4 teaspoon salt
1 cup milk
1 cup raisins

1) In a large mixing bowl, cream shortening and sugar until light and fluffy. Beat in molasses.

2) Combine the flour, baking soda, cinnamon, cloves and salt; add to the creamed mixture alternately

with milk, beating well after each addition. Drop by heaping tablespoonfuls 2 in. apart onto greased baking sheets.

3) Arrange three raisins on each cookie. Bake at 350° for 10-12 minutes or until set. Remove to wire racks to cool.

Yield: about 5-1/2 dozen.

NUTRITION FACTS: 2 cookies equals 150 calories, 3 g fat (1 g saturated fat), 1 mg cholesterol, 103 mg sodium, 28 g carbohydrate, 1 g fiber, 2 g protein.

COCONUT MACAROONS

Coconut Macaroons
Penny Ann Habeck, Shawano, Wisconsin

These cookies are my husband's favorites, so I always have to make a few batches if I make them to give away. I also like that it makes a small enough batch for the two of us to nibble on.

1-1/3 cups flaked coconut
1/3 cup sugar
2 tablespoons all-purpose flour
1/8 teaspoon salt
2 egg whites
1/2 teaspoon vanilla extract

1) In a small bowl, combine the coconut, sugar, flour and salt. Stir in egg whites and vanilla; mix well. Drop by rounded teaspoonfuls onto greased baking sheets.

2) Bake at 325° for 18-20 minutes or until golden brown. Cool on a wire rack.

Yield: about 1-1/2 dozen.

NUTRITION FACTS: 2 cookies equals 108 calories, 5 g fat (4 g saturated fat), 0 cholesterol, 81 mg sodium, 15 g carbohydrate, 1 g fiber, 1 g protein.

Sour Cream Anise Cookies

Mina Dyck, Boissevain, Manitoba

I first made these cookies when my arm was in a cast but wanted to do some baking. That should tell you how easy these are to prepare! You'll love the subtle licorice flavor from the anise.

    1   cup shortening
    1   cup packed brown sugar
    1   cup honey
    1   cup (8 ounces) sour cream
    3   eggs
3-1/2   cups all-purpose flour
    2   teaspoons baking soda
  3/4   teaspoon aniseed
  1/4   teaspoon salt

1) In a large mixing bowl, cream shortening and sugar until light and fluffy. Add the honey, sour cream and eggs; beat well.

2) Combine the flour, baking soda, aniseed and salt; add to creamed mixture and mix well. Drop by teaspoonfuls 2 in. apart onto greased baking sheets.

3) Bake at 350° for 12-15 minutes or until lightly browned. Cool on a wire rack.

Yield: about 8 dozen.

NUTRITION FACTS: 2 cookies equals 123 calories, 5 g fat (2 g saturated fat), 17 mg cholesterol, 73 mg sodium, 17 g carbohydrate, trace fiber, 2 g protein.

Toffee Cashew Treasures

Denise Sokolowski, Milwaukee, Wisconsin

After searching for a recipe that combined all my favorites, I decided to create my own cookie. The result is a lacy, crisp cookie that's sure to earn you rave reviews.

    1   cup butter, softened
    1   cup sugar
    1   cup packed brown sugar
    2   eggs
    1   teaspoon vanilla extract
    2   cups all-purpose flour
    2   cups old-fashioned oats
    1   teaspoon baking soda
  1/2   teaspoon baking powder
  1/2   teaspoon salt
    1   cup flaked coconut
    1   cup English toffee bits *or* almond brickle chips
    1   cup chopped cashews, toasted

1) In a large mixing bowl, cream butter and sugars until light and fluffy. Add the eggs, one at a time, beating well after each addition. Beat in vanilla.

2) Combine the flour, oats, baking soda, baking powder and salt; gradually add to the creamed mixture. Stir in the remaining ingredients. Drop by rounded tablespoonfuls 3 in. apart onto ungreased baking sheets.

3) Bake at 350° for 12-14 minutes or until lightly browned. Cool for 2 minutes before removing to wire racks.

Yield: about 5 dozen.

NUTRITION FACTS: 2 cookies equals 247 calories, 13 g fat (6 g saturated fat), 33 mg cholesterol, 240 mg sodium, 32 g carbohydrate, 1 g fiber, 3 g protein.

PECAN CRESCENT COOKIES

Shaped Cookies

Refrigerate the dough until it is chilled for easier handling. If there is a high butter content in the dough, the heat from your hands can soften the butter in the dough, making it harder to shape.

Dust hands lightly with flour to prevent dough from sticking while shaping it.

Pecan Crescent Cookies

Grace Yaskovic, Branchville, New Jersey

Rich, buttery and absolutely irresistible, these old-fashioned nut cookies were one of Mom's specialties. Any meal was a memorable event when she served this scrumptious treat.

    1   cup butter, softened
  1/2   cup sugar
    1   teaspoon vanilla extract
    2   cups all-purpose flour

1 cup finely chopped pecans
Confectioners' sugar

1) In a large mixing bowl, cream butter, sugar and vanilla until light and fluffy. Gradually add flour. Stir in pecans.

2) Shape rounded teaspoonfuls of dough into 2-1/2-in. logs and shape into crescents. Place 1 in. apart on ungreased baking sheets.

3) Bake at 325° for 20-22 minutes or until set and bottoms are lightly browned. Let stand for 2-3 minutes before removing to wire racks to cool. Dust with confectioners' sugar before serving.

Yield: 6 dozen.

NUTRITION FACTS: 2 cookies (calculated without confectioners' sugar) equals 104 calories, 7 g fat (3 g saturated fat), 14 mg cholesterol, 52 mg sodium, 9 g carbohydrate, 1 g fiber, 1 g protein.

■ *MEXICAN WEDDING CAKES:* Prepare as directed above except use 1/2 cup confectioner's sugar in place of sugar. Reduce vanilla extract to 1/2 teaspoon and finely chopped pecans to 1/2 cup. Shape tablespoonfuls of dough into balls. Place 2 in. apart on greased baking sheets.

Bake at 350° for 12-15 minutes or until lightly browned. Let stand for 2 minutes before removing to wire racks. Roll warm cookies in confectioners' sugar; return to wire rack to cool completely.

Yield: about 3 dozen.

Cream Cheese Finger Cookies
Jeanne Voss, Anaheim Hills, California

These melt-in-your-mouth cookies are one of my mom's creations. Made with cream cheese and butter, they're very rich...and the pecans add wonderful flavor. They're great with a hot cup of coffee or a tall glass of milk.

1/2 cup butter, softened
4 ounces cream cheese, softened
1 teaspoon vanilla extract
1-3/4 cups all-purpose flour
1 tablespoon sugar
Dash salt
1 cup finely chopped pecans
Confectioners' sugar

1) In a large mixing bowl, cream the butter and cream cheese until light and fluffy. Beat in vanilla. Combine the flour, sugar and salt; gradually add to creamed mixture.

2) Stir in pecans (dough will be crumbly). Shape tablespoonfuls into 2-in. logs. Place 2 in. apart on ungreased baking sheets.

3) Bake at 375° for 12-14 minutes or until lightly browned. Carefully roll the warm cookies in confectioners' sugar; cool on wire racks.

Yield: 2 dozen.

NUTRITION FACTS: 2 cookies (calculated without confectioners' sugar) equals 240 calories, 18 g fat (7 g saturated fat), 31 mg cholesterol, 118 mg sodium, 17 g carbohydrate, 1 g fiber, 4 g protein.

Chocolate Hazelnut Thumbprints
Ethel Garrison, Tacoma, Washington

Since we live in hazelnut country, I love making these special cookies for festive occasions. I usually bake two or three batches for parties and homemade gifts.

2/3 cup butter, softened
1/2 cup sugar
1 egg
1 egg yolk
1/2 teaspoon vanilla extract
1-1/2 cups all-purpose flour
1/4 cup baking cocoa
1/2 teaspoon salt
2/3 cup ground hazelnuts
1/2 cup raspberry preserves
Confectioners' sugar

1) In a large mixing bowl, cream butter and sugar until light and fluffy. Add the egg, yolk and vanilla; mix well. Combine the flour, cocoa and salt; add a third at a time to creamed mixture, beating well after each addition. Stir in nuts.

2) Roll dough into 1-in. balls; place 2 in. apart on ungreased baking sheets. Using the end of a wooden spoon handle, make a 1/2-in.-deep indentation in the center of each ball; fill with 1/4 teaspoon of preserves.

3) Bake at 350° for 10-12 minutes or until set. Remove to wire racks to cool. Just before serving, lightly dust with confectioners' sugar.

Yield: about 6 dozen.

NUTRITION FACTS: 2 cookies (calculated without confectioners' sugar) equals 84 calories, 5 g fat (2 g saturated fat), 21 mg cholesterol, 68 mg sodium, 10 g carbohydrate, trace fiber, 1 g protein.

REMOVING SKINS FROM HAZELNUTS

You can easily remove skins from shelled hazelnuts and then enrich their flavor by toasting. Spread the nuts in a single layer in a baking pan. Bake at 350° for 10 to 15 minutes or until the nuts are toasted and the skins begin to flake. Transfer nuts to a clean kitchen towel; rub against the towel to remove skins.

Crackle Cookies

Ruth Cain, Hartselle, Alabama

My family loves these old-fashioned favorites. Kids can roll them in sugar and place on baking sheets.

- 1 cup sugar
- 2 eggs
- 1/4 cup vegetable oil
- 2 squares (1 ounce *each*) unsweetened chocolate, melted and cooled
- 1 teaspoon vanilla extract
- 1 cup all-purpose flour
- 1 teaspoon baking powder
- 1/4 teaspoon salt
- Confectioners' sugar

1) In a large mixing bowl, combine the sugar, eggs, oil, chocolate and vanilla. Combine the flour, baking powder and salt; gradually add to sugar mixture and mix well.

2) Cover and refrigerate dough for at least 2 hours. With sugared hands, shape dough into 1-in. balls. Roll in confectioners' sugar. Place 2 in. apart on greased baking sheets. Bake at 350° for 10-12 minutes or until set. Remove to wire racks to cool.

Yield: about 3 dozen.

NUTRITION FACTS: 2 cookies (calculated without confectioners' sugar) equals 127 calories, 5 g fat (2 g saturated fat), 24 mg cholesterol, 63 mg sodium, 19 g carbohydrate, 1 g fiber, 2 g protein.

Cherry Bonbon Cookies

Pat Habiger, Spearville, Kansas

This is a very old recipe from my grandma. The sweet cherry filling makes a delightful surprise.

- 1/2 cup butter, softened
- 3/4 cup confectioners' sugar
- 2 tablespoons milk
- 1 teaspoon vanilla extract
- 1-1/2 cups all-purpose flour
- 1/8 teaspoon salt
- 24 maraschino cherries

GLAZE:

- 1 cup confectioners' sugar
- 1 tablespoon butter, melted
- 2 tablespoons maraschino cherry juice
- Additional confectioners' sugar

1) In a large mixing bowl, cream butter and sugar until light and fluffy. Add milk and vanilla.

Combine the flour and salt; gradually add to the creamed mixture. Divide dough into 24 portions; shape each portion around a cherry, forming a ball. Place on ungreased baking sheets. Bake at 350° for 18-20 minutes or until lightly browned. Cool on wire racks.

2) For glaze, combine the sugar, butter and cherry juice until smooth. Drizzle over cookies. Dust with additional sugar.

Yield: 2 dozen.

NUTRITION FACTS: 2 cookies (calculated without additional sugar) equals 225 calories, 9 g fat (5 g saturated fat), 23 mg cholesterol, 113 mg sodium, 36 g carbohydrate, trace fiber, 2 g protein.

SPLIT-SECOND COOKIES

Split-Second Cookies

Mrs. Richard Foust, Stoneboro, Pennsylvania

These easy-to-bake cookies feature raspberry jam and are a nice addition to a cookie tray.

- 3/4 cup butter, softened
- 2/3 cup sugar
- 1 egg
- 1 teaspoon vanilla extract
- 2 cups all-purpose flour
- 1/2 teaspoon baking powder
- 1/2 teaspoon salt
- 1/3 cup raspberry jam

1) In a large mixing bowl, cream butter and sugar until light and fluffy. Beat in egg and vanilla. Combine the flour, baking powder and salt; gradually add to creamed mixture and mix well.

2) Divide dough into four equal portions; shape each into a 12-in. x 3/4-in. log. Place 4 in. apart on two greased baking sheets. Make a 1/2-in. depression down center of logs; fill with jam.

3) Bake at 350° for 15-20 minutes or until lightly browned. Cool 2 minutes; cut diagonally into 3/4-in. slices. Remove to wire racks to cool completely.

Yield: about 5 dozen.

NUTRITION FACTS: 2 cookies equals 99 calories, 5 g fat (3 g saturated fat), 19 mg cholesterol, 95 mg sodium, 13 g carbohydrate, trace fiber, 1 g protein.

DIPPED GINGERSNAPS

Dipped Gingersnaps
Laura Kimball, West Jordan, Utah

Traditonal gingersnaps are one of my favorites. These chewy cookies are not only festive-looking, but they taste great, too.

>   2   cups sugar
>   1-1/2   cups vegetable oil
>   2   eggs
>   1/2   cup molasses
>   4   cups all-purpose flour
>   4   teaspoons baking soda
>   1   tablespoon ground ginger
>   2   teaspoons ground cinnamon
>   1   teaspoon salt
>   Additional sugar
>   2   packages (10 to 12 ounces *each*) vanilla *or* white chips
>   1/4   cup shortening

1) In a large mixing bowl, combine sugar and oil. Beat in eggs. Stir in molasses. Combine the flour, baking soda, ginger, cinnamon and salt; gradually add to creamed mixture and mix well.

2) Shape into 3/4-in. balls and roll in sugar. Place 2 in. apart on ungreased baking sheets. Bake at 350° for 10-12 minutes or until cookie springs back when lightly touched. Remove to wire racks to cool.

3) In a small saucepan, melt chips with shortening over low heat, stirring until smooth. Dip the cookies halfway into the melted chips; shake off excess. Place on waxed paper-lined baking sheets until set.

Yield: about 14-1/2 dozen.

NUTRITION FACTS: 2 cookies equals 128 calories, 7 g fat (2 g saturated fat), 6 mg cholesterol, 93 mg sodium, 17 g carbohydrate, trace fiber, 1 g protein.

DIPPING COOKIES IN CHOCOLATE

Melt the chocolate chips, baking chocolate or candy coating according to recipe directions. If necessary, transfer the chocolate to a narrow container.

Dip cookie partway into chocolate and scrape bottom of the cookie across the edge of the container to remove excess chocolate. Place on a baking sheet lined with waxed paper and allow to set at room temperature.

Toward the end of the process, when the chocolate is running low, it might be necessary to spoon the chocolate over the cookies. If chocolate cools too much to coat the cookies properly, rewarm before finishing dipping.

Cardamom Almond Biscotti
Verna Eberhart, Watertown, South Dakota

These crunchy slices are requested often during the holidays, particularly by my husband. He likes to dunk them in his coffee.

>   1   cup butter, softened
>   1-3/4   cups sugar
>   2   eggs
>   2   teaspoons almond extract
>   5-1/4   cups all-purpose flour
>   1   teaspoon baking soda
>   1   teaspoon salt
>   1   teaspoon ground cardamom
>   1   cup (8 ounces) sour cream
>   1   cup chopped almonds

1) In a large mixing bowl, cream butter and sugar until light and fluffy. Add eggs, one at a time, beating well after each addition. Beat in extract.

2) Combine flour, baking soda, salt and cardamom; add to the creamed mixture alternately with sour cream. Fold in almonds. Divide dough into fourths; shape each portion into a ball. On two greased baking sheets, roll each ball into a 15-in. log (two logs per pan).

3) Bake at 350° for 30 minutes or until lightly browned and firm to the touch. Transfer to a cutting board; cut at a 45° angle with a sharp knife into 1/2-in. slices. Place cut side down on greased baking sheets.

4) Bake for 5-6 minutes on each side or until lightly browned. Remove to wire racks to cool. Store in airtight containers.

Yield: about 7 dozen.

NUTRITION FACTS: 2 cookies equals 161 calories, 7 g fat (4 g saturated fat), 26 mg cholesterol, 137 mg sodium, 21 g carbohydrate, 1 g fiber, 3 g protein.

PEANUT BUTTER SANDWICH COOKIES

Peanut Butter Sandwich Cookies
Debbie Kokes, Tabor, South Dakota

When I find time to bake a treat, I like it to be special. The creamy filling in this recipe gives traditional peanut butter cookies a new twist.

- 1 cup butter-flavored shortening
- 1 cup creamy peanut butter
- 1 cup sugar
- 1 cup packed brown sugar
- 3 eggs
- 1 teaspoon vanilla extract
- 3 cups all-purpose flour
- 2 teaspoons baking soda
- 1/4 teaspoon salt

FILLING:
- 1/2 cup creamy peanut butter
- 3 cups confectioners' sugar
- 1 teaspoon vanilla extract
- 5 to 6 tablespoons milk

1) In a large mixing bowl, cream the shortening, peanut butter and sugars. Add eggs, one at a time, beating well after each addition. Add vanilla. Combine the flour, baking soda and salt; add to creamed mixture and mix well.

2) Shape into 1-in. balls and place 2 in. apart on ungreased baking sheets. Flatten to 3/8-in. thickness with fork. Bake at 375° for 7-8 minutes or until golden. Remove to wire racks to cool.

3) For filling, in a large mixing bowl, beat the peanut butter, confectioners' sugar, vanilla and enough milk to achieve spreading consistency. Spread on half of the cookies and top each with another cookie.

Yield: 2 dozen sandwich cookies.

NUTRITION FACTS: 1 sandwich cookie equals 362 calories, 17 g fat (4 g saturated fat), 27 mg cholesterol, 218 mg sodium, 47 g carbohydrate, 1 g fiber, 7 g protein.

SHAPING A PEANUT BUTTER COOKIE

Peanut butter cookie dough is generally a stiff dough and needs to be flattened before baking. Using a floured fork, press the balls of dough until 3/8 in. thick. Press again across the lines to make a crisscross pattern.

Apricot Tarts
Phyllis Hickey, Bedford, New Hampshire

These tiny tarts are an extra-special dessert for any occasion. We love the fruity, nutty flavor.

- 1/2 cup butter, softened
- 1 package (3 ounces) cream cheese, softened
- 1 cup all-purpose flour

APRICOT FILLING:
- 3/4 cup finely chopped dried apricots
- 3/4 cup water
- 1/3 cup chopped pecans
- 1/4 cup sugar
- 2 tablespoons orange marmalade
- 1/2 teaspoon ground cinnamon
- 1/8 teaspoon ground cloves

TOPPING:
- 2 tablespoons cream cheese, softened
- 1 tablespoon butter, softened
- 1/2 teaspoon vanilla extract
- 1/2 cup confectioners' sugar

1) In a large mixing bowl, beat butter, cream cheese and flour until well blended. Cover and refrigerate for 1 hour.

2) For filling, in a saucepan, bring the apricots and water to a boil. Reduce heat; simmer, uncovered, for 5 minutes. Drain and transfer to a bowl. Add the pecans, sugar, marmalade, cinnamon and cloves; set aside.

3) Shape dough into 24 balls. Press onto the bottom and up the sides of greased miniature muffins cups. Spoon apricot mixture into cups. Bake at

350° for 25-30 minutes or until browned. Cool for 10 minutes; remove from pans to a wire rack to cool completely.

4) For topping, in a small mixing bowl, combine cream cheese and butter. Stir in vanilla. Beat in confectioners' sugar. Place a dollop onto each tart just before serving.

Yield: 2 dozen.

NUTRITION FACTS: 1 tart equals 117 calories, 7 g fat (4 g saturated fat), 17 mg cholesterol, 61 mg sodium, 13 g carbohydrate, 1 g fiber, 1 g protein.

■ *CASHEW TASSIE CUPS:* Prepare cream cheese crust as directed, except omit apricot filling and topping. In a mixing bowl, beat 1/2 cup packed brown sugar, 1 egg and 1 teaspoon vanilla extract until combined. Divide 2/3 cup coarsely chopped cashews among the cups, then spoon brown sugar mixture over tops. Bake at 350° for 20-25 minutes or until filling is set and pastry is golden brown. Cool for 1 minute before removing from pans to wire racks.

Swedish Spritz Cookies
Susan Bittner, Alberta, British Columbia

A touch of almond extract gives these spritz wonderful flavor. For Christmas, you could tint the dough with red or green food coloring.

1	cup butter, softened
2/3	cup sugar
1	egg
1/2	teaspoon almond extract
1/2	teaspoon vanilla extract
2-1/4	cups all-purpose flour
1	teaspoon baking powder

1) In a large mixing bowl, cream butter and sugar until light and fluffy. Beat in egg and extracts. Combine the flour and baking powder; gradually add to the creamed mixture.

2) Using a cookie press fitted with a disk of your choice, press dough into desired shapes 1 in. apart onto ungreased baking sheets. Bake at 375° for 10-11 minutes or until edges are firm and lightly browned. Remove to wire racks to cool.

Yield: 5 dozen.

NUTRITION FACTS: 2 cookies equals 108 calories, 6 g fat (4 g saturated fat), 23 mg cholesterol, 77 mg sodium, 12 g carbohydrate, trace fiber, 1 g protein.

■ *SPICED SPRITZ COOKIES:* Omit almond extract and increase vanilla extract to 1 teaspoon. To the flour and baking powder mixture, add 1 teaspoon pumpkin pie spice. Proceed as recipe directs.

Refrigerator Cookies

To make refrigerator cookie dough easier to slice, use nuts and fruits that are finely chopped. Wrap dough tightly to prevent it from drying out in the refrigerator. Refrigerate dough until firm. Generally, the dough can be refrigerated up to 1 week or frozen up to 6 months.

To keep a nice round shape for refrigerated cookie dough, place each roll inside a tall glass and place the glass on its side in the refrigerator. The rounded glass will prevent the bottom of the roll from flattening out.

Use a thin sharp knife to slice through the dough. Cut one roll at a time, keeping additional rolls refrigerated until ready to use. After each slice, rotate the roll to avoid having one side that's flat.

Double Butterscotch Cookies
Beverly Duncan, Big Prairie, Ohio

I also like to make these with miniature chocolate chips or coconut in place of the toffee bits.

1/2	cup butter, softened
1/2	cup shortening
4	cups packed brown sugar
4	eggs
1	tablespoon vanilla extract
6	cups all-purpose flour
3	teaspoons baking soda
3	teaspoons cream of tartar
1	teaspoon salt
1	package English toffee bits (10 ounces) *or* almond brickle chips (7-1/2 ounces)
1	cup finely chopped pecans

1) In a large mixing bowl, cream the butter, shortening and brown sugar until light and fluffy. Add eggs, one at a time, beating well after each addition. Beat in vanilla. Combine the flour, baking soda, cream of tartar and salt; gradually add to the creamed mixture and mix well. Stir in toffee bits and pecans.

2) Shape into three 14-in. rolls; wrap each in plastic wrap. Refrigerate for 4 hours or until firm. Unwrap and cut into 1/2-in. slices. Place 2 in. apart on greased baking sheets. Bake at 375° for 9-11 minutes or until lightly browned. Cool for 1-2 minutes before removing from pans to wire racks to cool completely.

Yield: about 7 dozen.

NUTRITION FACTS: 2 cookies equals 248 calories, 9 g fat (3 g saturated fat), 28 mg cholesterol, 221 mg sodium, 39 g carbohydrate, 1 g fiber, 3 g protein.

Chocolate Mint Surprises
Sheila Kerr, Revelstoke, British Columbia

I came up with this recipe a few years ago and have shared it with many people. I would often snack on these treats after my baby's middle-of-the-night feeding.

- 3/4 cup butter, softened
- 1 cup sugar
- 1 egg
- 1 teaspoon vanilla extract
- 3 squares (1 ounce *each*) unsweetened chocolate, melted and cooled
- 2-1/2 cups all-purpose flour
- 1-1/2 teaspoons baking powder
- 1/2 teaspoon salt

FILLING:
- 4 cups confectioners' sugar
- 3 tablespoons butter, softened
- 1/4 cup evaporated milk
- 2 to 3 teaspoons peppermint extract
- 1/2 teaspoon vanilla extract
- 2 pounds dark chocolate candy coating, melted

1) In a large mixing bowl, cream butter and sugar until light and fluffy. Beat in egg and vanilla. Add melted chocolate.

2) Combine the flour, baking powder and salt; gradually add to chocolate mixture and mix well.

3) Shape in two 10-in. rolls; wrap each in plastic wrap. Refrigerate for 4 hours or until firm. Unwrap dough and cut into 1/4-in. slices. Place 2 in. apart on ungreased baking sheets.

4) Bake at 375° for 5-7 minutes or until edges are firm. Remove to wire racks to cool.

5) For filling, in a bowl, combine the confectioners' sugar, butter, milk and extracts until smooth. Shape into 1/2-in. balls. Place a ball in the center of each cookie; flatten.

6) Freeze for 30 minutes. Dip cookies in melted candy coating to completely cover. Place on waxed paper until set.

Yield: about 6 dozen.

NUTRITION FACTS: 1 cookie equals 148 calories, 7 g fat (5 g saturated fat), 10 mg cholesterol, 51 mg sodium, 22 g carbohydrate, 1 g fiber, 1 g protein.

COCONUT PECAN COOKIES

Coconut Pecan Cookies
Betty Matthews, South Haven, Michigan

With this recipe, making sweets has never been easier. I give cookies to friends every year, and these are a favorite. Freeze the dough in logs, then slice and bake the cookies when you need them.

- 1 cup butter, softened
- 1 cup sugar
- 1 egg
- 2-1/4 cups all-purpose flour
- 1/2 teaspoon baking soda
- 1/2 teaspoon salt
- 3 cups flaked coconut, *divided*

Pecan halves

1) In a large mixing bowl, cream butter and sugar until light and fluffy. Beat in egg. Combine the flour, baking soda and salt; add to creamed mixture and mix well. Stir in 2 cups coconut.

2) Shape into six 2-in.-diameter logs. Roll in remaining coconut. Wrap in plastic wrap. Freeze for up to 3 months.

3) Unwrap dough; cut into 1/4-in. slices. Place 3 in. apart on ungreased baking sheets. Place a pecan half in the center of each. Bake at 325° for 20-25 minutes or until lightly browned. Cool for 2-3 minutes before removing to wire racks to cool completely.

Yield: 4-1/2 dozen.

NUTRITION FACTS: 1 cookie equals 100 calories, 6 g fat (4 g saturated fat), 13 mg cholesterol, 83 mg sodium, 10 g carbohydrate, 1 g fiber, 1 g protein.

Peppernuts
Chandra Koehn, Rich Hill, Missouri

There are many pecan trees in this part of the country, so I like to make recipes with the nuts. I usually make these cookies during the holidays.

- 1 cup butter, softened
- 4 cups packed brown sugar

4 eggs
1/4 teaspoon anise extract
6 cups all-purpose flour
1 tablespoon baking soda
1 teaspoon cream of tartar
1/2 teaspoon *each* ground allspice, cinnamon, cloves and ginger
3 cups finely chopped pecans

1) In a large mixing bowl, cream butter and brown sugar until light and fluffy. Add eggs, one at a time, beating well after each addition. Add extract.

2) Combine the flour, baking soda, cream of tartar and spices; gradually add to the creamed mixture. Add pecans; mix well.

3) Shape into four 15-in. rolls; wrap each in plastic wrap. Refrigerate overnight.

4) Unwrap and cut into 1/4-in. slices. Place 1 in. apart on ungreased baking sheets. Bake at 350° for 7-8 minutes or until golden brown. Remove to wire racks to cool.

Yield: 20 dozen.

NUTRITION FACTS: 2 cookies equals 79 calories, 3 g fat (1 g saturated fat), 11 mg cholesterol, 52 mg sodium, 12 g carbohydrate, trace fiber, 1 g protein.

RASPBERRY NUT PINWHEELS

Raspberry Nut Pinwheels
Pat Habiger, Spearville, Kansas

I won first prize in a recipe contest with these yummy swirl cookies a number of years ago. The taste of raspberries and walnuts really comes through in each bite, and they're so fun to make!

1/2 cup butter, softened
1 cup sugar
1 egg
1 teaspoon vanilla extract

2 cups all-purpose flour
1 teaspoon baking powder
1/4 cup seedless raspberry jam
3/4 cup finely chopped walnuts

1) In a large mixing bowl, cream butter and sugar until light and fluffy. Beat in egg and vanilla. Combine the flour and baking powder; gradually add to creamed mixture and mix well.

2) Roll out dough between waxed paper into a 12-in. square. Remove top pieces of waxed paper. Spread dough with jam and sprinkle with nuts. Roll up tightly jelly-roll style, starting with a long side; wrap in plastic wrap. Refrigerate for 2 hours or until firm.

3) Unwrap dough and cut into 1/4-in. slices. Place 2 in. apart on ungreased baking sheets. Bake at 375° for 9-12 minutes or until edges are lightly browned. Remove to wire racks to cool.

Yield: about 3-1/2 dozen.

NUTRITION FACTS: 2 cookies equals 159 calories, 7 g fat (3 g saturated fat), 22 mg cholesterol, 66 mg sodium, 22 g carbohydrate, 1 g fiber, 3 g protein.

Cutout Cookies

For tender cookies, use a light touch when handling the dough; overhandling will cause the cookies to be tough.

For easier handling, refrigerate the dough before rolling. This is especially true if the dough was made with butter rather than shortening.

Lightly dust the rolling pin and work surface with flour to prevent sticking. Working too much extra flour into the dough will result in tough cookies.

Roll out a portion of the dough at a time and keep the remaining dough in the refrigerator. Roll out from the center to the edge, keeping a uniform thickness and checking the thickness with a ruler. If the thickness of the dough is uneven, the cookies will bake unevenly. Thinner cookies will be crisp and may burn, while thicker cookies will be chewy.

To prevent the dough from sticking to the cookie cutter, dip the cutter in flour or spray it with nonstick cooking spray.

After the dough is rolled out, position the shapes from the cookie cutters close together to avoid having too many scraps. Save all the scraps and reroll them just once to prevent tough cookies.

To keep the cutouts intact before and after baking, transfer them to and from the baking sheet with a large metal spatula or pancake turner that supports the entire cutout.

CHERRY CHEESE WINDMILLS

Cherry Cheese Windmills
Helen McGibbon, Downers Grove, Illinois

These cookies look fancy, but they are really not much work. They're perfect for any occasion.

1/3	cup butter, softened
1/3	cup shortening
3/4	cup sugar
1	egg
1	tablespoon milk
1	teaspoon vanilla extract
2	cups all-purpose flour
1-1/2	teaspoons baking powder
1/4	teaspoon salt

FILLING:

1	package (3 ounces) cream cheese, softened
1/4	cup sugar
1/4	teaspoon almond extract
1/2	cup finely chopped maraschino cherries
1/4	cup sliced almonds, toasted and chopped

1) In a large mixing bowl, cream the butter, shortening and sugar until light and fluffy. Beat in the egg, milk and vanilla. Combine the flour, baking powder and salt; gradually add to creamed mixture. Divide dough in half. Cover and refrigerate for 3 hours or until easy to handle.

2) In a small mixing bowl, beat cream cheese, sugar and extract. Fold in cherries. On a floured surface, roll each portion of dough into a 10-in. square.

3) With a sharp knife or pastry wheel, cut into 2-1/2-in. squares. Place 2 in. apart on ungreased baking sheets. Make 1-in. cuts from each corner toward the center of the dough.

4) Drop teaspoonfuls of filling in the center of each square; sprinkle with almonds. Fold alternating points to the center to form a windmill; moisten the points with water and pinch gently at center to seal. Bake at 350° for 8-10 minutes or until set. Remove to wire racks to cool.

Yield: about 2-1/2 dozen.

NUTRITION FACTS: 1 cookie equals 126 calories, 6 g fat (3 g saturated fat), 16 mg cholesterol, 73 mg sodium, 15 g carbohydrate, trace fiber, 1 g protein.

Lemon Nut Star Cookies
Taste of Home Test Kitchen

Family and friends will say "hooray!" when they see these star-spangled cookies. Make these treats throughout the year by using different cookie cutters and food coloring.

1	cup butter, softened
2	cups confectioners' sugar
2	eggs
2	tablespoons lemon juice
4	teaspoons half-and-half cream
2	teaspoons grated lemon peel
3-1/4	cups all-purpose flour
1/2	cup ground almonds
1/2	teaspoon baking soda
1/8	teaspoon salt

GLAZE:

2	cups confectioners' sugar
1/4	cup light corn syrup
2	tablespoons lemon juice
	Red and blue food coloring

1) In a large mixing bowl, cream butter and confectioners' sugar until light and fluffy. Add eggs, one at a time, beating well after each addition. Beat in the lemon juice, cream and lemon peel.

2) Combine the flour, almonds, baking soda and salt; gradually add to creamed mixture. Cover and refrigerate for 2 hours or until easy to handle.

3) On a lightly floured surface, roll out dough to 1/8-in. thickness. Cut with a floured star-shaped cookie cutter. Place 1 in. apart on ungreased baking sheets.

4) Bake at 350° for 8-10 minutes or until lightly browned. Remove to wire racks to cool.

5) For glaze, in a small bowl, combine the confectioners' sugar, corn syrup and lemon juice until smooth. Divide into three bowls. Tint one portion red and one portion blue; leave the third

portion plain. Spread over cookies; let stand overnight for glaze to set.

Yield: about 5-1/2 dozen.

NUTRITION FACTS: 2 cookies equals 171 calories, 7 g fat (4 g saturated fat), 28 mg cholesterol, 92 mg sodium, 26 g carbohydrate, 1 g fiber, 2 g protein.

SUGAR COOKIE CUTOUTS

Sugar Cookie Cutouts
Elizabeth Walters, Waterloo, Iowa
....
I must have over 100 different cookie cutters and have had fun putting them to use with this recipe over the years.

- 1   cup butter, softened
- 1   cup sugar
- 2   eggs
- 1/4 cup half-and-half cream
- 3   cups all-purpose flour
- 2   teaspoons baking powder
- 1   teaspoon baking soda
- 1/2 teaspoon salt

FROSTING:
- 1/2 cup butter, softened
- 4   cups confectioners' sugar
- 1   teaspoon vanilla extract
- 2   to 4 tablespoons half-and-half cream

Food coloring and colored sugar, optional

1) In a large mixing bowl, cream butter and sugar until light and fluffy. Add eggs, one at a time, beating well after each addition. Beat in cream.

2) Combine the flour, baking powder, baking soda and salt; gradually add to creamed mixture and mix well. Cover and refrigerate for 3 hours or until easy to handle.

3) On a lightly floured surface, roll out dough to

1/8-in. thickness. Cut with floured 2-1/2-in. cookie cutters. Place 1 in. apart on ungreased baking sheets.

4) Bake at 325° for 6-8 minutes or until edges are lightly browned. Remove to wire racks to cool.

5) In another large mixing bowl, cream butter, sugar, vanilla and enough cream to achieve spreading consistency. Add food coloring if desired. Frost cookies. Sprinkle with colored sugar if desired.

Yield: 8 dozen.

NUTRITION FACTS: 2 cookies equals 139 calories, 6 g fat (4 g saturated fat), 25 mg cholesterol, 129 mg sodium, 20 g carbohydrate, trace fiber, 1 g protein.

Holiday Shortbread
Wendy Masters, Grand Valley, Ontario
....
Five ingredients is all it takes to mix together this classic shortbread. You can also make a version with brown sugar.

- 2   cups butter, softened
- 1   cup sugar
- 1   teaspoon vanilla extract
- 4   cups all-purpose flour

Colored sugar, optional

1) In a large mixing bowl, cream butter; gradually add sugar and beat well. Add vanilla and mix well. Gradually add flour; mix until dough forms a ball.

2) On a lightly floured surface, roll dough to 1/2-in. thickness. Cut into 1-1/2-in. squares, diamonds and/or triangles. Place on ungreased baking sheets; sprinkle with colored sugar if desired.

3) Bake at 325° for 14-18 minutes or until edges are lightly browned. Cool on wire racks.

Yield: about 6-1/2 dozen.

NUTRITION FACTS: 2 shortbread equals 149 calories, 9 g fat (6 g saturated fat), 25 mg cholesterol, 95 mg sodium, 15 g carbohydrate, trace fiber, 1 g protein.

■ *BROWN SUGAR SHORTBREAD:* Omit sugar, vanilla extract and colored sugar. Cream butter with 1 cup packed brown sugar. Stir in 4 to 4-1/2 cups all-purpose flour. On a lightly floured surface, knead dough about 3 minutes or until smooth. Roll out into an 11-in. x 8-in. rectangle. Cut into 2-in. x 1-in. strips. Place 1 in. apart on baking sheets. Prick top with a fork. Bake at 300° for 25 minute or until bottoms begin to brown. Cool for 5 minutes before removing to wire racks to cool completely.

Yield: about 3-1/2 dozen.

MAKING CUTOUT COOKIES

1) For easier handling, chill dough for 1 to 2 hours before rolling out. Lightly flour the surface and rolling pin. Roll out dough as evenly as possible to the recommended thickness.

2) Dip the cutter in flour, then press the cutter into the dough. Lift each cookie with a small metal spatula or pancake turner to support the cookie as it is moved to the baking sheet.

3) Bake according to recipe directions. With a metal spatula or pancake turner, remove cookies from the baking sheet to a wire rack, being careful to support the entire cookie. Cool completely before frosting or storing.

Gingerbread Cookies

Christy Thelan, Kellogg, Iowa

Our two boys linger around the kitchen when these aromatic cookies are baking. I make them throughout the year using a variety of cutters.

>   3/4   cup butter, softened
>   1   cup packed brown sugar
>   1   egg
>   3/4   cup molasses
>   4   cups all-purpose flour
>   2   teaspoons ground ginger
>   1-1/2   teaspoons baking soda
>   1-1/2   teaspoons ground cinnamon
>   3/4   teaspoon ground cloves
>   1/4   teaspoon salt
>   Vanilla frosting of your choice, optional

1) In a large mixing bowl, cream butter and brown sugar until light and fluffy. Add egg and molasses. Combine the flour, ginger, baking soda, cinnamon, cloves and salt; gradually add to creamed mixture and mix well. Cover and refrigerate for 4 hours, overnight or until easy to handle.

2) On a lightly floured surface, roll dough to 1/8-in. thickness. Cut with floured 2-1/2-in. cookie cutters. Place 1 in. apart on ungreased baking sheets.

3) Bake at 350° for 8-10 minutes or until edges are firm. Remove to wire racks to cool. Decorate with frosting if desired.

Yield: 5 dozen.

NUTRITION FACTS: 1 cookie equals 77 calories, 2 g fat (1 g saturated fat), 10 mg cholesterol, 69 mg sodium, 13 g carbohydrate, trace fiber, 1 g protein.

Raspberry Linzer Cookies

Schelby Thompson, Winter Haven, Florida

These cookies require a bit of effort to make and assemble, but the delight of family and friends when I serve them makes it all worthwhile.

>   1   cup butter, softened
>   1-1/4   cups sugar, *divided*
>   2   eggs, *separated*
>   2-1/2   cups all-purpose flour
>   1/4   teaspoon salt
>   Confectioners' sugar
>   1/2   cup ground almonds
>   3/4   cup raspberry preserves

1) In a large mixing bowl, cream butter. Gradually add 2/3 cup sugar, beating until light and fluffy. Add egg yolks, one at a time, beating well after each addition. Combine flour and salt; gradually add to creamed mixture and mix well.

2) Shape dough into a ball; cover and refrigerate for 30-45 minutes or until firm. On a surface dusted with confectioners' sugar, roll half of the dough to 1/8-in. thickness; cut with a floured 2-1/2-in. round or heart-shaped cookie cutter. Repeat with remaining dough, using a floured 2-1/2-in. doughnut cutter or smaller heart-shaped cutter so the center is cut out of each cookie.

3) Beat egg whites until frothy. Combine almonds and remaining sugar. Brush each cookie with egg white and sprinkle with the almond mixture. Place on greased baking sheets. Bake at 350° for 6-8 minutes or until lightly browned. Remove to wire racks to cool completely.

4) Spread 2 teaspoons of raspberry preserves over the plain side of solid cookies. Place cookies with centers cut out, almond side up, on top of the preserves, making a sandwich.

Yield: 2 dozen.

NUTRITION FACTS: 1 cookie equals 200 calories, 9 g fat (5 g saturated fat), 38 mg cholesterol, 107 mg sodium, 28 g carbohydrate, 1 g fiber, 2 g protein.

Bars and Brownies

Generally, bars and brownies should cool completely on a wire rack before being cut. However, crisp bars should be cut while still slightly warm.

Cover a pan of uncut brownies and bars with foil—or put the pan in a large resealable plastic bag. If made with perishable ingredients, like cream cheese, they should be covered and refrigerated. Once the bars are cut, store them in an airtight container.

Chocolate Cream Cheese Brownies
Lisa Godfrey, Temple, Georgia

"Yummy!" That's what I hear every time I make these ooey-gooey treats!

    1 package (4 ounces) German
       sweet chocolate
    3 tablespoons butter
    2 eggs
  3/4 cup sugar
  1/2 cup all-purpose flour
  1/2 teaspoon baking powder
  1/4 teaspoon salt
    1 teaspoon vanilla extract
  1/4 teaspoon almond extract
  1/2 cup chopped nuts

FILLING:

    2 tablespoons butter, softened
    1 package (3 ounces) cream
       cheese, softened
  1/4 cup sugar
    1 egg
    1 tablespoon all-purpose flour
  1/2 teaspoon vanilla extract

1) In a saucepan, melt chocolate and butter over low heat, stirring until smooth. Remove from heat; set aside. In a small mixing bowl, beat eggs. Gradually add sugar, beating until thick and pale yellow.

2) Combine the flour, baking powder and salt; add to egg mixture and mix well. Stir in the extracts and reserved melted chocolate. Add the nuts. Pour half of the batter into a greased 8-in. square baking dish; set aside.

3) For filling, in another small mixing bowl, beat the butter, cream cheese and sugar until light and fluffy. Add the egg, flour and vanilla; mix well. Pour over batter in pan. Spoon remaining batter

over filling. With a knife, cut through batter to create a marbled effect.

4) Bake at 325° for 35-40 minutes or a toothpick inserted near the center comes out clean. Cool on a wire rack. Cut into bars. Store in the refrigerator.

Yield: about 2 dozen.

NUTRITION FACTS: 1 brownie equals 248 calories, 14 g fat (7 g saturated fat), 74 mg cholesterol, 151 mg sodium, 28 g carbohydrate, trace fiber, 5 g protein.

MARBLING BATTERS

To marble batters, spoon one batter in a random pattern over the other batter. Cut through the batter with a knife. Be careful not to overdo it, or the two batters will blend together and you'll lose the effect.

Caramel Cashew Brownies
Judy High, Berryville, Arkansas

I always have my eye out for a good recipe, like the one for these marvelous golden brownies. It's hard to eat just one!

   18 caramels
  1/3 cup butter
    2 tablespoons milk
  3/4 cup sugar
    2 eggs
  1/2 teaspoon vanilla extract
    1 cup all-purpose flour
  1/2 teaspoon baking powder
  1/4 teaspoon salt
    1 cup chopped salted cashews

1) In a saucepan, cook and stir the caramels, butter and milk over low heat until the caramels are melted and mixture is smooth. Remove from the heat; stir in sugar. Combine eggs and vanilla; stir into caramel mixture.

2) Combine flour, baking powder and salt; stir into caramel mixture until blended. Fold in cashews. Transfer to a greased 9-in. square baking pan.

3) Bake at 350° for 24-28 minutes or until a toothpick inserted near the center comes out clean. Cool on a wire rack. Cut into bars.

Yield: 25 brownies.

NUTRITION FACTS: 1 brownie equals 129 calories, 6 g fat (3 g saturated fat), 24 mg cholesterol, 115 mg sodium, 17 g carbohydrate, trace fiber, 2 g protein.

SUPER BROWNIES

Super Brownies

Bernice Muilenburg, Molalla, Oregon

Nuts in the brownies and on top make these fudgy treats a real taste-sensation. They're rich and oh-so-chocolaty!

- 1/2 cup butter
- 1-1/2 cups sugar
- 4-2/3 cups (28 ounces) semisweet chocolate chips, *divided*
- 3 tablespoons water
- 4 eggs
- 5 teaspoons vanilla extract
- 1-1/2 cups all-purpose flour
- 1/2 teaspoon baking soda
- 1/2 teaspoon salt
- 2 cups coarsely chopped macadamia nuts *or* pecans, *divided*

1) In a saucepan, melt butter and sugar over medium heat. Remove from the heat; stir in 2 cups chocolate chips until melted. Transfer to a mixing bowl; beat in water. Add eggs, one at a time, beating well after each addition. Add vanilla.

2) Combine the flour, baking soda and salt; beat into the chocolate mixture until smooth. Stir in 2 cups of chocolate chips and 1 cup of nuts. Pour into a greased 13-in. x 9-in. x 2-in. baking pan. Sprinkle with remaining chips and nuts.

3) Bake at 325° for 55 minutes or until the center is set (do not overbake). Cool on a wire rack. Cut into bars.

Yield: about 3-1/2 dozen.

NUTRITION FACTS: 1 brownie equals 206 calories, 13 g fat (6 g saturated fat), 26 mg cholesterol, 90 mg sodium, 23 g carbohydrate, 2 g fiber, 2 g protein.

Fudgy Toffee Bars

Diane Bradley, Sparta, Michigan

Sweet treats always go over well in my family, especially during the holidays. We think these rich bars—dotted with walnuts, toffee bits, chocolate chips and coconut—are better than candy! They're nice to share with a group.

- 1-3/4 cups all-purpose flour
- 3/4 cup confectioners' sugar
- 1/4 cup baking cocoa
- 3/4 cup cold butter
- 1 can (14 ounces) sweetened condensed milk
- 2 cups (12 ounces) semisweet chocolate chips, *divided*
- 1 teaspoon vanilla extract
- 1 cup coarsely chopped walnuts
- 1/2 cup flaked coconut
- 1/2 cup English toffee bits *or* almond brickle chips

1) In a bowl, combine the flour, sugar and cocoa. Cut in butter until mixture resembles coarse crumbs. Press firmly into a greased 13-in. x 9-in. x 2-in. baking pan. Bake at 350° for 10 minutes.

2) Meanwhile, in a saucepan, heat milk and 1 cup chocolate chips over medium heat until chocolate is melted, stirring until smooth. Remove from the heat. Stir in vanilla.

3) Pour filling over crust. Sprinkle with the walnuts, coconut, toffee bits and remaining chocolate chips; press down firmly. Bake for 18-20 minutes or until set. Cool on a wire rack. Cut into bars.

Yield: 3 dozen.

NUTRITION FACTS: 1 bar equals 238 calories, 14 g fat (7 g saturated fat), 15 mg cholesterol, 77 mg sodium, 28 g carbohydrate, 2 g fiber, 3 g protein.

Mixed Nut Bars

Bobbi Brown, Waupaca, Wisconsin

One pan of these bars goes a long way. They get a nice flavor from butterscotch chips.

- 1-1/2 cups all-purpose flour
- 3/4 cup packed brown sugar
- 1/4 teaspoon salt
- 1/2 cup plus 2 tablespoons cold butter, *divided*
- 1 can (11-1/2 ounces) mixed nuts
- 1 cup butterscotch chips
- 1/2 cup light corn syrup

1) In a small bowl, combine flour, sugar and salt. Cut in 1/2 cup butter until mixture resembles coarse crumbs. Press into a greased 13-in. x 9-in. x 2-in. baking pan.

2) Bake at 350° for 10 minutes. Sprinkle with nuts. In a microwave, melt butterscotch chips; stir until smooth. Add corn syrup and remaining butter; mix well. Pour over nuts.

3) Bake for 10 minutes or until set. Cool in pan on a wire rack. Cut into bars.

Yield: about 3-1/2 dozen.

NUTRITION FACTS: 1 bar equals 143 calories, 8 g fat (4 g saturated fat), 8 mg cholesterol, 104 mg sodium, 16 g carbohydrate, 1 g fiber, 2 g protein.

CHOCOLATE CHIP MERINGUE BARS

Chocolate Chip Meringue Bars
Elaine Swenson, Kindred, North Dakota

Chocolate chips and peanuts are layered in these satisfying bars. The meringue-like topping is such a special addition.

1	cup shortening
1-1/2	cups packed brown sugar, *divided*
1/2	cup sugar
3	eggs, *separated*
1	tablespoon cold water
1	tablespoon vanilla extract
2	cups all-purpose flour
1	teaspoon baking soda
1/8	teaspoon salt
1	cup (6 ounces) semisweet chocolate chips
1	cup ground salted peanuts

1) In a large mixing bowl, cream shortening, 1/2 cup of brown sugar and sugar until light and fluffy. Beat in egg yolks. Combine water and vanilla.

Combine the flour, baking soda and salt; add to creamed mixture alternately with water mixture, beating well after each addition. Spread in a greased 15-in. x 10-in. x 1-in. baking pan. Sprinkle with chocolate chips.

2) In a small mixing bowl, beat egg whites over medium speed until soft peaks form. Beat in remaining brown sugar, 2 tablespoons at a time, on high until stiff peaks form. Spread over chocolate chips. Top with peanuts.

3) Bake at 350° for 30-35 minutes or until set. Cool on a wire rack.

Yield: about 3 dozen.

NUTRITION FACTS: 1 bar equals 173 calories, 9 g fat (3 g saturated fat), 18 mg cholesterol, 69 mg sodium, 21 g carbohydrate, 1 g fiber, 2 g protein.

Ginger Bars
Deborh Haake, Minnetonka, Minnesota

We always had dessert when we visited my grandparent's farm, and this was one of our favorites. During harvesttime, my brothers and sisters and I would take this or another treat out to the field for the workers.

1	cup shortening
1	cup sugar
2	eggs
1	cup water
1/2	cup molasses
2-1/2	cups all-purpose flour
1	teaspoon baking soda
1	teaspoon ground cinnamon
1/2	teaspoon ground cloves
1/2	teaspoon ground ginger
1/2	teaspoon salt

Confectioners' sugar, optional

1) In a large mixing bowl, cream shortening and sugar until light and fluffy. Add eggs; beat well. Beat in water and molasses.

2) Combine the flour, baking soda, cinnamon, cloves, ginger and salt; add to molasses mixture and mix well. Spread into a greased 15-in. x 10-in. x 1-in. baking pan.

3) Bake at 350° for 20-22 minutes or until a toothpick inserted near the center comes out clean. Cool on a wire rack. Dust with confectioners' sugar if desired. Cut into bars.

Yield: 20 servings.

NUTRITION FACTS: 1 bar equals 213 calories, 10 g fat (3 g saturated fat), 21 mg cholesterol, 132 mg sodium, 28 g carbohydrate, 1 g fiber, 2 g protein.

Shortbread Lemon Bars

Margaret Peterson, Forest City, Iowa

These bars have a yummy crust and a refreshing flavor. I always know they will be a hit!

- 1-1/2 cups all-purpose flour
- 1/2 cup confectioners' sugar
- 1 teaspoon grated lemon peel
- 1 teaspoon grated orange peel
- 3/4 cup cold butter

FILLING:

- 4 eggs
- 2 cups sugar
- 1/3 cup lemon juice
- 1/4 cup all-purpose flour
- 2 teaspoons grated lemon peel
- 2 teaspoons grated orange peel
- 1 teaspoon baking powder

TOPPING:

- 2 cups (16 ounces) sour cream
- 1/3 cup sugar
- 1/2 teaspoon vanilla extract

1) In a food processor, combine first four ingredients. Add butter; cover and process until crumbly. Continue processing until mixture forms a ball. Pat into a greased 13-in. x 9-in. x 2-in. baking pan. Bake at 350° for 12-14 minutes or until set and the edges are lightly browned.

2) In a small mixing bowl, beat filling ingredients until blended. Pour over hot crust. Bake for 14-16 minutes or until set and lightly browned.

3) In a small bowl, combine topping ingredients. Spread over filling. Bake 7-9 minutes longer or until topping is set; cool on a wire rack. Refrigerate overnight. Cut into bars just before serving.

Yield: 3 dozen.

NUTRITION FACTS: 1 bar equals 172 calories, 9 g fat (5 g saturated fat), 51 mg cholesterol, 70 mg sodium, 20 g carbohydrate, trace fiber, 2 g protein.

Apple-Berry Streusel Bars

Jane Acree, Holcomb, Illinois

The flavor combination of apples and raspberries is fabulous in these easy-to-make bars.

- 2-1/2 cups plus 2 tablespoons all-purpose flour, *divided*
- 2 cups old-fashioned oats
- 1-1/4 cups sugar
- 2 teaspoons baking powder
- 1 teaspoon ground cinnamon
- 1 cup butter, melted
- 3 cups thinly sliced peeled tart apples
- 1 jar (12 ounces) raspberry preserves
- 1/2 cup finely chopped walnuts

1) In a large mixing bowl, combine 2-1/2 cups flour, oats, sugar, baking powder and cinnamon. Beat in butter just until moistened. Set aside 2 cups for topping. Pat remaining oat mixture into a greased 13-in. x 9-in. x 2-in. baking pan. Bake at 375° for 15 minutes.

2) Meanwhile, toss apples with remaining flour. Stir in the preserves; spread over hot crust to within 1/2 in. of edges. Combine nuts and reserved oat mixture; sprinkle over fruit mixture. Bake 30-35 minutes longer or until lightly browned. Cool completely on a wire rack before cutting into bars.

Yield: 4 dozen.

NUTRITION FACTS: 1 bar equals 121 calories, 5 g fat (2 g saturated fat), 10 mg cholesterol, 56 mg sodium, 18 g carbohydrate, 1 g fiber, 2 g protein.

Raspberry Bars

Abby Kuhn, Ellsworth, Maine

A crust is topped with raspberry jam and walnuts, and a meringue topping covers it all.

- 1/3 cup plus 1/2 cup sugar, *divided*
- 1-1/2 cups all-purpose flour
- 3/4 cup butter
- 2 eggs, *separated*
- 1 cup raspberry jam
- 1 cup broken walnuts

1) In a small bowl, combine 1/3 cup sugar, flour, butter and egg yolks. Press into a greased 13-in. x 9-in. x 2-in. baking pan. Bake at 350° for 15 minutes or until golden. Cool. Spread jam over crust; sprinkle with nuts.

2) In a small mixing bowl, beat egg whites on medium speed until soft peaks form. Gradually beat in remaining sugar, 1 tablespoon at a time, on high until stiff glossy peaks form and sugar is dissolved. Spread meringue over nuts.

3) Bake at 350° for 25 minutes or until set and lightly browned. Cool on a wire rack. To cut, use a knife dipped in hot water. Store in the refrigerator.

Yield: 3 dozen.

NUTRITION FACTS: 1 bar equals 118 calories, 6 g fat (3 g saturated fat), 22 mg cholesterol, 42 mg sodium, 15 g carbohydrate, trace fiber, 2 g protein.

CHAPTER 23
CANDIES

573

CANDIES

Homemade candies are fun to make, serve and give to friends and family. With these tips and recipes, you should have delicious, sweet treats every time.

Candy Making Tips

Always measure and assemble all ingredients for a candy recipe before beginning. Do not substitute or alter the basic ingredients. Use real butter for best results or stick margarine containing at least 80% oil.

Use heavy-gauge saucepans that are deep enough to allow candy mixtures to boil freely without boiling over. Use wooden spoons with long handles for safe stirring when preparing recipes with hot boiling sugar.

Humid weather affects results when preparing candies that are cooked to specific temperatures or that contain egg whites. For best results, make candy on days when the humidity is less than 60%.

Store homemade candies in tightly covered containers unless otherwise directed. Don't store more than one kind of candy in a single container. Individually wrap chewy candies like caramels, popcorn balls and taffy.

Using a Candy Thermometer

The best and most reliable way to check the temperature of candy is to use a candy thermometer. If none is available, use the Cold-Water Test for Candy on page 577.

Always use a thermometer designed for candy making. It must have a movable clip to secure it to the side of the pan and keep the end of the thermometer off the bottom of the pan.

Check your candy thermometer for accuracy each time you make candy. Place the thermometer in a saucepan of boiling water for several minutes before reading. If the thermometer reads 212° in boiling water, it is accurate. If it rises above or does not reach 212°, add or subtract the difference to the temperature called for in the recipe.

A candy mixture will cook very slowly when boiling until it reaches 220°, then it will cook quickly. It's important to closely watch the thermometer at this point. Some digital thermometers will beep when they reach the preset temperature. When finished using the thermometer, allow it to cool before washing to avoid breakage.

Chocolate Basics

Recipes may call for chocolate chips, baking chocolate or candy coating. Chocolate chips are available in standard, miniature and larger "chunk" sizes as well as a variety of flavors (semisweet, milk and vanilla or white). Specialty flavors such as raspberry or mint are sometimes available. Chips are designed to hold their shape during baking. They're usually used in cookies and bars but also work well in many recipes that call for melted chocolate.

Baking chocolate is available in unsweetened, semisweet, milk and German sweet chocolate as well as white. It is commonly sold in 8-ounce packages that are divided into 1- or 2-ounce squares or bars.

Baking chocolate is designed for melting. For faster melting, chop baking bars into smaller pieces. Chips can be melted in place of semisweet, milk or white baking chocolate. Simply substitute 6 ounces of the appropriate flavored chips for 6 ounces of baking chocolate.

Candy coating or almond bark is available in dark, milk or white chocolate varieties. It is commonly sold in bulk in large individual blocks, in bags of flat discs and in packages of individual 1-ounce squares. Candy coating is used as a coating for candies, cookies, fruits or nuts.

Butterscotch Hard Candy
Darlene Smithers, Elkhart, Indiana

I love making this classic butterscotch recipe. We think these irresistible bites are better than the store-bought variety. They never last long!

> 1 teaspoon plus 1 cup butter, *divided*
> 2-1/2 cups sugar
> 3/4 cup water
> 1/2 cup light corn syrup
> 1/4 cup honey
> 1/2 teaspoon salt
> 1/2 teaspoon rum extract

1) Butter a 15-in. x 10-in. x 1-in. baking pan with 1 teaspoon butter; set aside. Cube remaining butter and set aside.

2) In a heavy saucepan, combine the sugar, water and corn syrup. Cover and bring to a boil over medium heat without stirring. Cook, uncovered, until a candy thermometer reads 270° (soft-crack stage).

3) Add the honey, salt and remaining butter; stir constantly until the mixture reaches 300° (hard-crack stage). Remove from the heat. Stir in the rum extract.

4) Pour into prepared pan without scraping; do not spread. Cool for 1-2 minutes or until the candy is almost set. Score into 1-in. squares; cool completely. Break squares apart. Store in an airtight container.

Yield: 1-1/2 pounds.

NUTRITION FACTS: 1 piece equals 144 calories, 6 g fat (4 g saturated fat), 17 mg cholesterol, 109 mg sodium, 23 g carbohydrate, trace fiber, trace protein.

Hard Maple Candy
Dorothea Bohrer, Silver Springs, Maryland

During the war, the women at my grandmother's church would donate sugar rations throughout the year to make candy as a fund-raiser at Christmas. I'm lucky enough to have inherited this tried-and-true recipe.

> 1-1/2 teaspoon butter, softened
> 3-1/2 cups sugar
> 1 cup light corn syrup
> 1 cup water
> 3 tablespoons maple flavoring

1) Grease a 15-in. x 10-in. x 1-in. baking pan with butter; set aside. In a large heavy saucepan, combine the sugar, corn syrup and water. Cook over medium-high heat until a candy thermometer reads 300° (hard-crack stage), stirring occasionally.

2) Remove from the heat; stir in maple flavoring. Immediately pour into prepared pan; cool. Break into pieces. Store in airtight containers.

Yield: 1-3/4 pounds.

NUTRITION FACTS: 1/3 ounce equals 46 calories, trace fat (trace saturated fat), trace cholesterol, 5 mg sodium, 11 g carbohydrate, 0 fiber, 0 protein.

■ *ANISE HARD CANDY:* Use 2 teaspoons anise extract for the maple flavoring. Add 6-9 drops red food coloring with the extract if desired.

Terrific Toffee
Carol Gillespie, Chambersburg, Pennsylvania

This buttery toffee is one of those must-make treats my family requests for the holidays.

> 1-1/2 teaspoons plus 1 cup butter, *divided*
> 1 cup semisweet chocolate chips

1 cup milk chocolate chips
1 cup sugar
3 tablespoons water
2 cups coarsely chopped almonds, toasted, *divided*

1) Butter a large baking sheet with 1-1/2 teaspoons butter; set aside. In a small bowl, combine semisweet and milk chocolate chips; set aside.

2) In a heavy saucepan, combine the sugar, water and remaining butter. Cook and stir over medium heat until a candy thermometer reaches 290° (soft-crack stage). Remove from the heat; stir in 1 cup almonds. Immediately pour onto prepared baking sheet.

3) Sprinkle with chocolate chips; spread with a knife when melted. Sprinkle with remaining almonds. Let stand until set, about 1 hour. Break into 2-in. pieces.

Yield: about 2 pounds.

NUTRITION FACTS: 1 ounce equals 187 calories, 14 g fat (6 g saturated fat), 18 mg cholesterol, 69 mg sodium, 15 g carbohydrate, 2 g fiber, 3 g protein.

■ *ENGLISH TOFFEE:* Omit semisweet chocolate chips and almonds. Prepare toffee as directed; omit stirring in the almonds. Spread in pan and cool. Melt 1 cup milk chocolate chips in a microwave at 30% power or in a saucepan over low heat; stir until smooth. Spread over toffee and sprinkle with 1 cup chopped pecans. Let stand until set, about 1 hour.

■ *HAZELNUT TOFFEE:* Omit milk chocolate chips and almonds. Prepare toffee as directed, stirring in 1/3 cup chopped hazelnut. Spread in pan and cool. Melt 2 cups semisweet chocolate chips in a microwave at 50% power or in a saucepan over low heat; stir until smooth. Spread over toffee and sprinkle with 1/2 cup finely chopped hazelnuts. Let stand until set, about 1 hour.

SAVING TOFFEE

Sometimes when you make toffee, the ingredients separate during cooking and there is a buttery layer on top and a thicker layer underneath. To save the batch of toffee, add about 1/2 cup hot water and stir until well blended. Continue cooking as recipe directs.

COLD-WATER TEST FOR CANDY

THREAD STAGE (230°-233°). Dip a metal spoon into the hot candy mixture. Hold the spoon over the cold water. The mixture should fall off the spoon in a fine thread.

HARD-BALL STAGE (250°-266°). Drop a small amount of the hot candy mixture into the cold water. When cooled and removed from the water, the candy will form a hard yet pliable ball.

SOFT-BALL STAGE (234°-240°). Drop a small amount of the hot candy mixture into the cold water. When cooled and removed from the water, the ball will flatten immediately and run over your finger.

FIRM-BALL STAGE (244°-248°). Drop a small amount of the hot candy mixture into the cold water. When cooled and removed from the water, the ball will hold its shape and not flatten.

SOFT-CRACK STAGE (270°-290°). Drop a small amount of the hot candy mixture into the cold water. When cooled and removed from the water, the candy will separate into threads that are hard but not brittle.

HARD-CRACK STAGE (300°-310°). Drop a small amount of the hot candy mixture into the cold water. When cooled and removed from the water, the candy will separate into hard brittle threads.

MIXED NUT BRITTLE

Mixed Nut Brittle
Norma Francel, Edwardsburg, Michigan

Nut fanciers have a lot to love about this irresistible brittle. The variety of nuts is what makes it so different. It's one of the first sweet treats to appear on my Christmas candy tray...and also the first to disappear!

1-1/2   teaspoons plus 3 tablespoons butter, *divided*
1-1/2   cups sugar
1   cup water
1   cup light corn syrup
1   can (10 ounces) mixed nuts (without peanuts)
1   teaspoon vanilla extract
1-1/2   teaspoons baking soda

1) Butter a baking sheet with 1-1/2 teaspoons of butter; set aside. In a large saucepan, combine the sugar, water and corn syrup. Cook over medium heat until a candy thermometer reads 270° (soft-crack stage), stirring occasionally.

2) Add nuts; cook and stir until the mixture reaches 300° (hard-crack stage). Remove from the heat; stir in vanilla and remaining butter. Add baking soda and stir vigorously.

3) Quickly pour onto prepared baking sheet. Spread with a buttered metal spatula to 1/4-in. thickness. Cool before breaking into pieces.

Yield: about 1-3/4 pounds.

NUTRITION FACTS: 1 ounce equals 148 calories, 7 g fat (2 g saturated fat), 4 mg cholesterol, 164 mg sodium, 22 g carbohydrate, 1 g fiber, 2 g protein.

■ *PEANUT BRITTLE:* Use 2 cups peanuts for the mixed nuts.

■ *MACADAMIA ALMOND BRITTLE:* Use 1 cup *each* coarsely chopped macadamia nuts and coarsely chopped almonds for the mixed nuts.

Angel Food Candy
Carrol Holloway, Hindsville, Arkansas

Dipped in white and dark candy coating, this two-tone treat stands out on any goody tray.

1   teaspoon butter, softened
1   cup sugar
1   cup dark corn syrup
1   tablespoon white vinegar
1   tablespoon baking soda
1/2   pound white candy coating
1/2   pound dark chocolate candy coating

1) Butter a 13-in. x 9-in. x 2-in. pan with the butter; set aside. In a large heavy saucepan, combine the sugar, corn syrup and vinegar.

2) Cook and stir over medium heat until sugar is dissolved. Cook, without stirring, until a candy thermometer reads 290° (soft-crack stage). Remove from the heat; stir in baking soda. Pour into the prepared pan. Do not spread candy. Cool, then break into pieces.

3) In a small heavy saucepan or microwave, melt white candy coating, stirring until smooth. Dip the candies halfway into melted coating, shaking off excess. Place on waxed paper-lined baking sheets until set.

4) Melt dark chocolate coating; dip uncoated portion of candies in coating. Return to waxed paper until set. Store in an airtight container.

Yield: 1-1/2 pounds.

NUTRITION FACTS: 2 ounces equals 343 calories, 11 g fat (10 g saturated fat), 1 mg cholesterol, 360 mg sodium, 64 g carbohydrate, trace fiber, trace protein.

READING A CANDY THERMOMETER

For accurate temperature readings, it's important that you have the candy thermometer attached to the side of the saucepan.

Southern Pralines
Bernice Eberhart, Fort Payne, Alabama

These are a real Southern treat that I've used to fill many holiday gift tins!

3   cups packed brown sugar
1   cup heavy whipping cream
2   tablespoons light corn syrup

1/4 teaspoon salt
1/4 cup butter
2 cups chopped pecans
1-1/4 teaspoons vanilla extract

1) In a large heavy saucepan over medium heat, bring the brown sugar, cream, corn syrup and salt to a boil, stirring constantly. Cook until a candy thermometer reads 234° (soft-ball stage), stirring occasionally.

2) Remove from the heat; add butter (do not stir). Cool until candy thermometer reads 150°, about 35 minutes.

3) Stir in the pecans and vanilla. Stir with a wooden spoon until candy just begins to thicken but is still glossy, about 5-7 minutes. Quickly drop by heaping teaspoonfuls onto waxed paper; spread to form 2-in. patties. Let stand until set. Store in an airtight container.

Yield: about 3-1/2 dozen.

NUTRITION FACTS: 1 praline equals 130 calories, 7 g fat (2 g saturated fat), 11 mg cholesterol, 35 mg sodium, 17 g carbohydrate, 1 g fiber, 1 g protein.

TOASTED ALMOND CARAMELS

Toasted Almond Caramels
Mae Ondracek, Pahrump, Nevada

Preparing these caramels never fails to put me in the holiday spirit. Later, when I'm passing them around, that cheerful feeling becomes contagious.

1 teaspoon plus 1/4 cup butter, *divided*
2 cups sugar
1 cup light corn syrup
1/4 teaspoon salt
1 cup heavy whipping cream

1 teaspoon vanilla extract
1 cup chopped almonds, toasted

1) Line an 8-in. square dish with foil; butter the foil with 1 teaspoon butter. Set aside. In a heavy saucepan, combine the sugar, corn syrup, salt and remaining butter. Bring to a boil over medium heat, stirring constantly. Reduce heat to medium-low; boil gently without stirring for 4 minutes.

2) Remove from the heat; slowly stir in cream. Return to the heat; cook, without stirring, over medium-low heat until a candy thermometer reads 245° (firm-ball stage). Remove from the heat; stir in vanilla and almonds.

3) Pour into prepared pan (do not scrape sides of saucepan). Cool completely. Using foil, lift the caramel out of pan. Discard foil; cut caramel into squares. Wrap individually in waxed paper or foil; twist ends.

Yield: about 4 dozen.

NUTRITION FACTS: 1 caramel equals 94 calories, 4 g fat (2 g saturated fat), 10 mg cholesterol, 33 mg sodium, 14 g carbohydrate, trace fiber, 1 g protein.

Sugared Peanut Clusters
Gail McClantoc, Sweet Water, Iowa

Coffee and cinnamon provide the flavor in these nutty treats. Remember to work quickly to form the small clusters!

2 teaspoons butter, softened
1-1/2 cups sugar
1/2 cup brewed coffee
1 tablespoon light corn syrup
1 teaspoon ground cinnamon
1 teaspoon vanilla extract
1 jar (16 ounces) dry roasted peanuts

1) Butter two baking sheets with the 2 teaspoons butter; set aside. In a heavy saucepan, combine the sugar, coffee, corn syrup and cinnamon.

2) Bring to a boil over medium heat, stirring occasionally. Cook until a candy thermometer reads 234°-240° (soft-ball stage). Remove from the heat; stir in vanilla. Add peanuts; stir quickly.

3) Pour onto prepared baking sheets. Quickly separate into small clumps with two forks. Cool completely. Store in an airtight container.

Yield: 6 cups.

NUTRITION FACTS: 1/4 cup equals 165 calories, 10 g fat (1 g saturated fat), 1 mg cholesterol, 158 mg sodium, 17 g carbohydrate, 2 g fiber, 4 g protein.

STIRRING FUDGE

Allow the fudge to cool to 110° undisturbed. Agitating the fudge at this stage may cause it to become grainy. Once the fudge reaches 110°, beat it with a clean dry wooden spoon. As you stir the fudge, the temperature will continue to drop and the mixture will start to become thick and harder to stir.

As you continue to stir, the fudge will become thicker. It may also have lighter colored streaks in it, and it starts to loose its gloss. This step could take up to 10 minutes. Once the fudge starts to loose its sheen, immediately pour into the prepared pan.

Determining the point when the fudge is ready to pour is important to its success. If it is poured too soon it will be soft; if stirred too much, it will be grainy or will set up right in the bowl.

Two-Tiered Fudge

Christine Richburg, Brewton, Alabama

Fudge can be tricky, but this recipe proves that the results are worth it! You can also get creative and try other fudge variations.

CHOCOLATE NUT LAYER:
- 2 teaspoons plus 2 tablespoons butter, *divided*
- 2-1/4 cups sugar
- 1 cup milk
- 3 squares (1 ounce *each*) unsweetened chocolate
- 1 tablespoon light corn syrup
- 1 teaspoon vanilla extract
- 1/2 cup chopped nuts

CHERRY VANILLA LAYER:
- 1 teaspoon plus 2 tablespoons butter, *divided*
- 2-1/2 cups sugar
- 1/2 cup half-and-half cream
- 1/2 cup milk
- 1 tablespoon light corn syrup
- 1/4 teaspoon salt
- 1 teaspoon vanilla extract
- 1/3 cup chopped candied cherries

1) Line a 9-in. square pan with foil; butter the foil with 1 teaspoon butter. Set aside. For chocolate nut layer, butter the sides of a large heavy saucepan with 1 teaspoon butter; add the sugar, milk, chocolate and corn syrup.

2) Cook and stir over medium heat until sugar is dissolved. Bring mixture to a boil. Boil until mixture reaches 236° (soft-ball stage), stirring occasionally. Remove from the heat.

3) Add vanilla and remaining butter (do not stir). Cool to 110° without stirring. Stir with a clean dry wooden spoon until fudge begins to thicken; add nuts. Continue stirring until fudge becomes thick and begins to lose its gloss, about 10 minutes. Immediately spread into prepared pan; set aside.

4) For cherry vanilla layer, butter the sides of a clean large heavy saucepan with 1 teaspoon butter; add the sugar, cream, milk, corn syrup and salt. Cook and stir over medium heat until sugar is dissolved. Bring to a boil. Boil until mixture reaches 236° (soft-ball stage), stirring occasionally. Remove from the heat.

5) Add vanilla and remaining butter (do not stir). Cool to 110° without stirring. Stir with a clean dry wooden spoon until fudge begins to thicken; add cherries. Continue stirring until fudge becomes thick and begins to lose its gloss, about 8 minutes. Immediately spread over first layer.

6) Score into squares while still warm. Using foil, lift fudge out of pan. Discard foil; cut fudge into 1-in. squares. Store in an airtight container at room temperature.

Yield: about 2-1/2 pounds.

NUTRITION FACTS: 1 piece equals 70 calories, 2 g fat (1 g saturated fat), 3 mg cholesterol, 19 mg sodium, 13 g carbohydrate, trace fiber, 1 g protein.

■ *CHOCOLATE NUT FUDGE:* Line a 9-in. x 5-in. x 3-in. loaf pan with foil and butter the foil. Prepare chocolate layer as directed and pour into prepared pan. Score into squares while still warm.

■ *CHOCOLATE FUDGE:* Line a 9-in. x 5-in. x 3-in. loaf pan with foil and butter the foil. Prepare chocolate layer as directed, except omit nuts. Pour into prepared pan. Score into squares while still warm.

■ *CHERRY VANILLA FUDGE:* Line a 9-in. x 5-in. x 3-in. loaf pan with foil and butter the foil. Prepare Cherry Vanilla Layer as directed and pour into prepared pan. Score into squares while still warm.

AVOIDING FUDGE FOILS

The recipes in this cookbook often instruct you to butter the foil in your pan before pouring in the fudge mixture. That way, when the fudge is cooled, you can easily lift the foil and fudge out of the pan and cut the fudge into squares.

CASHEW CARAMEL FUDGE

Cashew Caramel Fudge
Cathy Grubelnik, Raton, New Mexico

I especially enjoy making this fudge for a holiday treat, and I've found that a pretty plate of this yummy confection makes a great present. Cashews and caramel are such a delicious combination.

- 2 teaspoons plus 1/2 cup butter, softened, *divided*
- 1 can (5 ounces) evaporated milk
- 2-1/2 cups sugar
- 2 cups (12 ounces) semisweet chocolate chips
- 1 jar (7 ounces) marshmallow creme
- 24 caramels, quartered
- 3/4 cup salted cashew halves
- 1 teaspoon vanilla extract

1) Line a 9-in. square baking pan with foil; butter the foil with 2 teaspoons butter. Set aside. In a large heavy saucepan, combine the milk, sugar and remaining butter.

2) Cook and stir over medium heat until sugar is dissolved. Bring to a rapid boil; boil for 5 minutes, stirring constantly. Remove from the heat; stir in chocolate chips and marshmallow creme until melted. Fold in the caramels, cashews and vanilla; mix well.

3) Pour into prepared pan. Cool. Using foil, lift fudge out of pan. Discard foil; cut fudge into 1-in. squares. Store at room temperature.

Yield: about 3 pounds.

NUTRITION FACTS: 1 piece equals 85 calories, 4 g fat (2 g saturated fat), 4 mg cholesterol, 33 mg sodium, 14 g carbohydrate, trace fiber, 1 g protein.

Macadamia Nut Fudge
Vicki Fioranelli, Cleveland, Mississippi

My aunt lives in Hawaii and keeps us supplied with macadamia nuts. When I run out, I also like to make this fudge with pecans.

- 2 teaspoons plus 1/2 cup butter, *divided*
- 4-1/2 cups sugar
- 1 can (12 ounces) evaporated milk
- 3 cups chopped macadamia nuts, *divided*
- 3 packages (4 ounces *each*) German sweet chocolate, chopped
- 1 package (12 ounces) semisweet chocolate chips
- 1 jar (7 ounces) marshmallow creme
- 2 teaspoons vanilla extract
- 1/2 teaspoon salt, optional

1) Line two 9-in. square pans with foil; butter the foil with the 2 teaspoons butter. Set aside. In a large heavy saucepan, combine the sugar, milk and remaining butter. Bring to a gentle boil. Cook for 5 minutes, stirring constantly.

2) Remove from the heat; Stir in 2 cups nuts, chopped chocolate, chocolate chips, marshmallow creme, vanilla and salt if desired.

3) Pour the fudge into prepared pans; sprinkle remaining nuts over top and press in lightly. Refrigerate until firm. Using foil, lift fudge out of pans. Discard foil; cut fudge into 1-in. squares.

Yield: about 5 pounds.

NUTRITION FACTS: 1 piece equals 72 calories, 4 g fat (1 g saturated fat), 2 mg cholesterol, 16 mg sodium, 10 g carbohydrate, trace fiber, 1 g protein.

■ *PECAN NUT FUDGE:* Use 3 cups chopped toasted pecans in place of the macadamia nuts.

MELTING CHOCOLATE

Break or chop large pieces of chocolate so it will melt more evenly. Melt chocolate in a dry heavy saucepan over low heat; stir until smooth. Even small amounts of water will cause the chocolate to seize (become thick and lumpy) and become unusable. If the chocolate needs to set up after melting (such as when it's used for dipping or garnishes), add 1/4 to 1/2 teaspoon of shortening for every 6 ounces of chocolate.

To melt chocolate in the microwave, place it in a microwave-safe bowl. Melt semisweet chocolate at 50% power, and milk chocolate and vanilla or white chocolate at 30% power. Stir frequently until the chocolate is melted; do not overheat.

Double Chocolate Truffles
Ruth Gordon, Lakewood, New York

Chocolate lovers of all kinds will appreciate these yummy truffles. Another nice combination is the flavor of orange extract in place of the vanilla.

- 1-1/3 cups semisweet chocolate chips
- 1/3 cup heavy whipping cream
- 3 tablespoons butter
- 1 teaspoon vanilla extract
- 1 cup vanilla *or* white chips
- 2 tablespoons shortening, *divided*
- 1 cup milk chocolate chips

1) In a microwave-safe bowl, melt the semisweet chocolate chips with whipping cream and butter at 50% power for 2-3 minutes; stir until blended. Add vanilla; cool. Refrigerate until almost solid but still workable, about 1 hour.

2) Shape into 1/2-in. balls. Microwave white chips and 1 tablespoon shortening at 30% power until melted; stir until smooth. Dip balls in white chocolate mixture to coat. Place on waxed paper; let stand until set.

3) Microwave milk chocolate chips and remaining shortening at 30% power until melted; stir until smooth. Dip balls into milk chocolate mixture to coat. Place on waxed paper; let stand until set.

Yield: 2-1/2 dozen.

NUTRITION FACTS: 1 truffle equals 122 calories, 9 g fat (5 g saturated fat), 9 mg cholesterol, 23 mg sodium, 11 g carbohydrate, 1 g fiber, 1 g protein.

■ *ORANGE TRUFFLES:* Use 3/4 teaspoon orange extract in place of the vanilla extract.

DIPPING CANDY INTO CHOCOLATE

Place candy on a table fork or a special two-tined candy fork; dip into the melted chocolate to cover entirely. Remove from the chocolate; scrape off any excess chocolate on the side of the bowl. Place on waxed paper to cool and harden.

Coconut Bonbons
Beverly Cray, Epping, New Hampshire

Family and friends always include these bonbons on their wish lists. Luckily, this recipe makes a huge batch to meet the demand.

- 1/2 cup butter, softened
- 2 pounds confectioners' sugar
- 1 can (14 ounces) sweetened condensed milk

- 4 cups chopped pecans
- 1 package (10 ounces) flaked coconut
- 1 teaspoon vanilla extract
- 2 cups (12 ounces) semisweet chocolate chips
- 1 tablespoon shortening

1) In a large mixing bowl, cream butter and sugar until light and fluffy. Add the milk, pecans, coconut and vanilla; mix well. Shape into 1-in. balls. Refrigerate for 30-45 minutes or until firm.

2) In a heavy saucepan or microwave, melt the chips and shortening; stir until smooth. Dip balls and place on waxed paper to set. Store in an airtight container.

Yield: about 21 dozen.

Editor's Note: Candies can be frozen for up to 3 months before dipping in chocolate. Thaw in refrigerator before dipping.

NUTRITION FACTS: 1 bonbon equals 48 calories, 3 g fat (1 g saturated fat), 2 mg cholesterol, 9 mg sodium, 6 g carbohydrate, trace fiber, trace protein.

Peanut Candy Popcorn Balls
Alida Jaeger, Ixonia, Wisconsin

Kids love these colorful novelties, which are made from popcorn, nuts, M&M's and marshmallows. They're also a great stocking-stuffer!

- 4 quarts popped popcorn
- 1-1/2 cups salted peanuts
- 1-1/2 cups chopped pecans
- 1 package (16 ounces) green and red milk chocolate M&M's
- 1/2 cup butter
- 1/2 cup vegetable oil
- 1 package (16 ounces) miniature marshmallows

1) In a large bowl, combine the popcorn, peanuts, pecans and M&M's; set aside. In a large saucepan, combine butter, oil and marshmallows; cook and stir until smooth. Pour over popcorn mixture; mix well.

2) When cool enough to handle, shape into popcorn balls. Let stand at room temperature until firm before wrapping in plastic wrap or stacking.

Yield: about 20 popcorn balls.

NUTRITION FACTS: 1 popcorn ball equals 440 calories, 29 g fat (8 g saturated fat), 15 mg cholesterol, 195 mg sodium, 43 g carbohydrate, 3 g fiber, 6 g protein.

Vanilla Popcorn

Carolyn Roney, Scipio Center, New York

We enjoy traveling, and this recipe makes the perfect driving snack. It's easy, too, because it can be ready in about 10 minutes.

- 3 quarts popped popcorn
- 1 cup sugar
- 1/2 cup butter
- 1/4 cup light corn syrup
- 1/4 teaspoon baking soda
- 1/2 teaspoon vanilla extract

1) Place popcorn in a large bowl; set aside. In a saucepan, combine the sugar, butter and corn syrup. Bring to a boil over medium heat; boil and stir until mixture is golden, about 2 minutes.

2) Remove from the heat; stir in baking soda and vanilla. Pour over popcorn and toss to coat. Cool slightly; break apart while warm.

Yield: 3 quarts.

NUTRITION FACTS: 1 cup equals 206 calories, 11 g fat (5 g saturated fat), 20 mg cholesterol, 209 mg sodium, 28 g carbohydrate, 1 g fiber, 1 g protein.

NUTTY CARAMEL CLUSTERS

Nutty Caramel Clusters

Charlyn Koistiner, Hayti, South Dakota

Don't be fooled by the impressive presentation of these sweet candies. They're so easy to make, even our two young sons can help.

- 25 caramels
- 1 tablespoon butter
- 1 tablespoon milk
- 1 cup sliced almonds
- 1/2 cup salted dry roasted peanuts
- 1/2 cup pecan halves
- 1/2 cup semisweet chocolate chips
- 2 teaspoons shortening

1) In a 1-qt. microwave-safe dish, combine the caramels, butter and milk. Microwave, uncovered, on high for 1-1/2 to 2 minutes or until caramels are melted, stirring once. Stir in the almonds, peanuts and pecans. Drop by tablespoonfuls onto waxed paper-lined baking sheets.

2) In a microwave-safe bowl, melt chocolate chips and shortening; stir until blended. Spoon over clusters. Refrigerate until set. Store in the refrigerator.

Yield: 1-1/2 dozen.

NUTRITION FACTS: 1 piece equals 161 calories, 10 g fat (3 g saturated fat), 3 mg cholesterol, 74 mg sodium, 16 g carbohydrate, 2 g fiber, 3 g protein.

Creamy Pastel Mints

Janice Brady, Seattle, Washington

Easy and versatile, these mints are a breeze to make and can be cut into any shape you want.

- 1 package (3 ounces) cream cheese, softened
- 3/8 teaspoon peppermint extract
- 1 drop red food coloring
- 1 drop blue food coloring
- 1 drop yellow food coloring
- 3 cups confectioners' sugar

1) Divide cream cheese equally among three small bowls. Stir in 1/8 teaspoon mint flavoring into each bowl. Using the food coloring, tint one portion red, one blue and the remaining portion yellow. Gradually stir 1/2 cup sugar into each portion.

2) Knead 1/2 cup of the remaining sugar into each color until smooth. Roll out to 1/4-in. thickness. (No sugar or flour is necessary on the rolling surface.) Use 1-in. cookie cutters to cut out various shapes. Store tightly covered in the refrigerator.

Yield: about 5 dozen.

NUTRITION FACTS: 1 piece equals 28 calories, 1 g fat (trace saturated fat), 2 mg cholesterol, 4 mg sodium, 6 g carbohydrate, 0 fiber, trace protein.

Dipped Strawberries
Marlene Wiczek, Little Falls, Minnesota

Nothing is sweeter than a ripe strawberry plucked direct from the patch. Well, almost nothing...I dip plump red berries in chocolate and vanilla chips.

   1   **quart fresh strawberries with stems**

1-2/3   **cups vanilla *or* white chips**

   2   **tablespoons shortening, *divided***

   1   **cup (6 ounces) semisweet chocolate chips**

1) Wash strawberries and gently pat until completely dry. In a heavy saucepan or microwave, melt vanilla chips and 1 tablespoon shortening; stir until smooth.

2) Dip each strawberry until two-thirds of the berry is coated, allowing the excess to drip off. Place on a waxed paper-lined baking sheet; refrigerate for 30 minutes or until set.

3) Melt chocolate chips and remaining shortening; stir until smooth. Dip each strawberry until one-third is coated. Return to baking sheet; refrigerate for 30 minutes or until set.

Yield: 2-1/2 dozen.

NUTRITION FACTS: 2 strawberries equals 182 calories, 11 g fat (6 g saturated fat), 4 mg cholesterol, 19 mg sodium, 21 g carbohydrate, 2 g fiber, 2 g protein.

Christmas Bark Candy
Taste of Home Test Kitchen

This is sure to please all ages. Create variations using different flavored chips and add-ins such as crushed candy canes, dried fruits or crunchy nuts.

   1   **package (10 to 12 ounces) vanilla *or* white chips *or* 1 package (11-1/2 ounces) milk chocolate chips**

   2   **teaspoons vegetable oil**

1-1/4   **to 1-1/2 cups M&M miniature baking bits *or* broken pretzel pieces**

1) In a heavy saucepan or microwave, melt chips with oil; stir until smooth. Cool for 5 minutes. Stir in baking bits or pretzels.

2) Spread onto a waxed paper-lined baking sheet. Refrigerate 10 minutes. Remove from refrigerator; break into pieces. Store in an airtight container.

Yield: about 1 pound.

NUTRITION FACTS: 2/3 ounce equals 127 calories, 7 g fat (4 g saturated fat), 3 mg cholesterol, 11 mg sodium, 15 g carbohydrate, 1 g fiber, 1 g protein.

Orange Jelly Candies
Leah Jackson, Washington, Utah

Making candy is my favorite thing to do. I've been collecting candy recipes for more than 40 years. These soft confections are fantastic.

   2   **teaspoons butter**

   1   **package (1-3/4 ounces) powdered fruit pectin**

1/2   **teaspoon baking soda**

3/4   **cup water**

   1   **cup sugar**

   1   **cup light corn syrup**

1/8   **teaspoon orange oil**

   5   **drops *each* red and yellow food coloring**

     Additional sugar

1) Butter a 9-in. square pan with 2 teaspoons butter; set aside. In a large saucepan, combine the pectin, baking soda and water (mixture will be foamy).

2) In another saucepan, combine sugar and corn syrup. Bring both mixtures to a boil. Cook until foam on pectin mixture thins slightly and sugar mixture comes to a full rolling boil, about 4 minutes. Gradually add pectin mixture to boiling sugar mixture, stirring constantly. Boil for 1 minute, stirring constantly.

3) Remove from heat. Stir in orange oil and food coloring. Immediately pour into prepared pan. Let stand at room temperature for 3 hours or until set.

4) Sprinkle waxed paper with additional sugar; invert pan onto sugar. With a knife dipped in warm water, cut candy into 1-in. squares; roll in additional sugar. Place on a wire rack. Let stand, uncovered, at room temperature overnight. Store in an airtight container.

Yield: 81 pieces.

NUTRITION FACTS: 3 pieces (calculated without additional sugar) equals 76 calories, trace fat (trace saturated fat), 1 mg cholesterol, 41 mg sodium, 19 g carbohydrate, 0 fiber, trace protein.

CHAPTER 24
LIGHT & TASTY

LIGHT & TASTY

Food plays a key role in many family celebrations and social and work situations. You may feel that some of those "special" recipes handed down are no longer recipes you should prepare because they are loaded with fat, sugar or sodium.

This chapter is dedicated to providing recipes that taste great yet are a bit healthier. Success in lighter cooking comes from trial and error, so don't be afraid to experiment.

The Taste of Home Test Kitchen home economists have already experimented for you and taste-tested and approved the following lighter recipes. Each recipe has 300 calories or less, 10 grams of fat or less *and* 500 milligrams of sodium or less. You can also check out the Nutrition Facts on recipes throughout this book for additional recipes that may fit into your diet.

Cutting Fat

You can use applesauce as a fat substitute as well as pureed canned pears, peaches, apricots and plums, baby food fruit purees or mashed bananas. Each of these makes a good fat substitute in baked goods. Fruit purees help tenderize baked goods and because of their naturally occurring sugar, and they also promote browning.

You can replace the desired amount of butter, margarine or other solid shortening with half as much fat substitute. For instance, if you omit 1/2 cup butter from a recipe, replace it with 1/4 cup fruit puree. If the recipe calls for oil, substitute three-fourths as much puree. Mix up the batter. If it seems too dry, add a little more fruit puree.

Try using low-gluten flours like whole wheat pastry flour and oat flour in your lighter baking. Fat generally interferes with gluten formation making the baked good more tender. If you have less fat you may want to try these low-gluten flours as a replacement for all-purpose flour.

Minimize mixing. Stirring batter excessively develops gluten and toughens baked goods. Stir only enough to mix well. Also, reduced-fat baked goods tend to bake faster than those made with fat. They can become dry. Try lowering the oven temperature 25° and check for doneness a few minutes early.

Lowering Cholesterol

Due to the high fat and cholesterol in egg yolks, you can replace at least part of the egg in your baked good recipe. Eggs perform important functions in baked goods, so they cannot be eliminated entirely. Try combining whole eggs with egg whites or fat-free egg substitute.

When reducing the eggs in a from-scratch recipe, substitute 2 egg whites or 1/4 cup fat-free egg substitute for 1 whole egg. It's best to leave at least 1 whole egg in the recipe.

Reducing Sugar

Sugar provides sweetness and flavor and aids in the browning of baked goods. Plus, sugar (white or brown) is integral to the creaming process, which incorporates air into the batter and makes the texture of the baked good lighter and more tender.

If you reduce the amount of sugar in a baked good, start by simply reducing the amount of sugar 25%. Or try reducing it 50% and add a sugar replacement to make up for the other half. The Taste of Home Test Kitchen home economists have had the best luck with the sugar substitute Splenda for replacement of part of the sugar in a baked good recipe.

WARM BROCCOLI CHEESE SPREAD

Herbed Cheese Spread

Josie Smith, Winamac, Indiana

I have a friend who runs a greenhouse and holds a spring tea showcasing herbs and recipes that use them. This cheese spread is a crowd-pleasing appetizer on crackers and breads.

- 1 package (8 ounces) fat-free cream cheese
- 1 tablespoon butter, softened
- 1 teaspoon *each* minced fresh basil, parsley and chives
- 1/2 teaspoon *each* chopped fresh oregano, dill and garlic
- 1/4 teaspoon salt

Assorted crackers *or* bread

1) In a small mixing bowl, beat cream cheese, butter, herbs and salt until smooth. Refrigerate for at least 1 hour to allow flavors to blend. Serve on crackers or bread.

Yield: 1 cup.

NUTRITION FACTS: 2 tablespoons (calculated without crackers) equals 41 calories, 2 g fat (1 g saturated fat), 6 mg cholesterol, 243 mg sodium, 2 g carbohydrate, 1 g fiber, 4 g protein.

Warm Broccoli Cheese Spread

Patricia Moore, Toledo, Ohio

I cut this recipe out of a newspaper and decided to trim it down by substituting fat-free and reduced-fat ingredients. Whenever I make this for an occasion, I end up being asked for the recipe.

- 1 package (8 ounces) fat-free cream cheese, cubed
- 1 cup (8 ounces) reduced-fat sour cream
- 1 envelope Italian salad dressing mix
- 1 package (10 ounces) frozen chopped broccoli, thawed, drained and patted dry
- 2 cups (8 ounces) shredded reduced-fat cheddar cheese, *divided*

Reduced-fat wheat snack crackers

1) In a large mixing bowl, beat the cream cheese, sour cream and salad dressing mix until blended. Fold in the broccoli and 1-1/2 cups cheese.

2) Spoon into a shallow 1-qt. baking dish coated with nonstick cooking spray. Bake, uncovered, at 350° for 20 minutes. Sprinkle with remaining cheese. Bake 5 minutes longer or until cheese is melted. Serve warm with crackers.

Yield: 3-1/2 cups.

NUTRITION FACTS: 1/4 cup equals 96 calories, 5 g fat (4 g saturated fat), 19 mg cholesterol, 287 mg sodium, 4 g carbohydrate, 1 g fiber, 8 g protein.

Sun-Dried Tomato Hummus

Kathleen Tribble, Buellton, California

I didn't like the hummus I bought in a box mix or in refrigerated tubs, so I made my own version using a pesto sauce mix. My husband and I enjoy it in sandwiches, but it's great on crackers, too. We like it so much that we eat any leftovers with a spoon!

- 1 can (15 ounces) garbanzo beans *or* chickpeas, rinsed and drained
- 1/3 cup reduced-fat mayonnaise
- 1 tablespoon sun-dried tomato pesto sauce mix
- 1 teaspoon lemon juice

Assorted crackers

1) In a food processor or blender, combine the beans, mayonnaise, sauce mix and lemon juice; cover and process until blended.

2) Transfer to a small bowl. Serve with crackers. Store in the refrigerator.

Yield: 1-1/4 cups.

Editor's Note: This recipe was tested with Knorr Sun-Dried Tomato Pesto Sauce.

NUTRITION FACTS: 1/4 cup (calculated without crackers) equals 139 calories, 7 g fat (1 g saturated fat), 6 mg cholesterol, 363 mg sodium, 16 g carbohydrate, 3 g fiber, 4 g protein.

Horseradish Mustard Dip
Shirley Glaab, Hattiesburg, Mississippi

This versatile vegetable dip is also great on ham, turkey or roast beef sandwiches. I stir a little into my potato salad, egg salad and tuna salad, too. To suit more timid tastes, cut the horseradish back to 2 teaspoons.

3/4   cup fat-free plain yogurt

3   tablespoons minced chives

2   tablespoons reduced-fat mayonnaise

1   tablespoon snipped fresh dill *or* 1 teaspoon dill weed

1   tablespoon prepared horseradish

1   tablespoon Dijon mustard

1/4   teaspoon salt

1/8   teaspoon white pepper

Assorted fresh vegetables

1)   In a small bowl, combine the yogurt, chives, mayonnaise, dill, horseradish, mustard, salt and pepper. Cover and refrigerate until serving. Serve with vegetables.

Yield: 1 cup.

NUTRITION FACTS: 1/4 cup (calculated without vegetables) equals 51 calories, 3 g fat (1 g saturated fat), 4 mg cholesterol, 338 mg sodium, 5 g carbohydrate, 1 g fiber, 2 g protein.

LIGHT GUACAMOLE

Light Guacamole
Marlene Tokarski, Mesa, Arizona

Feel guilty dipping into guacamole? This lower-fat version is a yummy alternative.

2   large ripe avocados, peeled, *divided*

1   cup (8 ounces) fat-free sour cream

1/4   cup chopped onion

3   jalapeno peppers, seeded and chopped

6   tablespoons minced fresh cilantro

4   teaspoons lemon juice

1/2   teaspoon salt

1/2   teaspoon ground cumin

1/8   teaspoon pepper

1   large tomato, seeded and chopped

Baked tortilla chips *or* fresh vegetables

1)   In a food processor, combine one avocado and the next eight ingredients; cover and process until smooth. In a bowl, mash the remaining avocado with a fork. Stir in the pureed avocado mixture. Gently fold in tomato. Serve with chips.

Yield: 3 cups.

Editor's Note: When cutting or seeding hot peppers, use rubber or plastic gloves to protect your hands. Avoid touching your face.

NUTRITION FACTS: 1/4 cup (calculated without tortilla chips or vegetables) equals 79 calories, 5 g fat (1 g saturated fat), 2 mg cholesterol, 119 mg sodium, 7 g carbohydrate, 2 g fiber, 2 g protein.

Really Good Snack Mix
Lori Genske, Waldo, Wisconsin

I grew tired of my family picking through a snack mix for their favorite items and leaving the rest. So I experimented using only their favorites and came up with this recipe. Now there's never any left!

2   cups bite-size Shredded Wheat

2   cups Corn Chex

2   cups Crispix

1-1/2   cups salted cashew halves

3   tablespoons butter, melted

1   tablespoon canola oil

4   teaspoons Worcestershire sauce

1   teaspoon seasoned salt

1/2   teaspoon garlic powder

1)   In a large bowl, combine the cereals and cashews. In a small bowl, combine remaining ingredients. Pour over cereal mixture and toss to evenly coat.

2)   Transfer to a 15-in. x 10-in. x 1-in. baking pan coated with nonstick cooking spray. Bake at 250° for 45 minutes, stirring every 15 minutes. Store in airtight containers.

Yield: 7-1/2 cups.

NUTRITION FACTS: 1/2 cup equals 158 calories, 10 g fat (3 g saturated fat), 6 mg cholesterol, 298 mg sodium, 16 g carbohydrate, 1 g fiber, 3 g protein.

SEAFOOD TRIANGLES

Seafood Triangles

Tarsia Nichols, Spirit Lake, Idaho

One chilly Easter, my creative clan was looking for an appetizer that would break family traditions and warm hearts...and we came up with these spicy bites filled with shrimp and crabmeat.

3 tablespoons chopped green onions

3 tablespoons butter, *divided*

1/2 pound uncooked shrimp, peeled, deveined and quartered

1/4 cup white wine *or* chicken broth

4 teaspoons cornstarch

1/3 cup 2% milk

1/2 cup grated Parmesan cheese

1 can (6 ounces) crabmeat, drained, flaked and cartilage removed

1 teaspoon sugar

1 teaspoon lemon juice

1/4 teaspoon cayenne pepper

1/8 teaspoon white pepper, optional

22 sheets phyllo dough (14 inch x 9 inch sheet size)

1 egg white, beaten

1) In a large nonstick skillet, saute onions in 1 tablespoon butter until tender. Add shrimp and wine or broth; cook and stir over medium-high heat for 2 minutes or until shrimp turn pink. Using a slotted spoon, remove shrimp.

2) Combine cornstarch and milk until smooth; stir into the cooking juices. Bring to a boil; cook and stir for 2 minutes or until thickened. Reduce heat to low. Stir in the Parmesan cheese, crab, sugar, lemon juice, cayenne, white pepper if desired and shrimp. Remove from the heat; cool.

3) On a dry surface, carefully remove two sheets of phyllo dough and place on top of each other (keep remaining dough covered with plastic wrap to prevent drying). Melt remaining butter. Cut sheets widthwise into six strips about 2 in. wide. Lightly brush the tops with butter.

4) Place a rounded teaspoonful of shrimp mixture near lower right corner of each strip. Fold left corner of dough over filling, forming a triangle. Fold triangle up, then fold over, forming another triangle. Continue folding like a flag for the length of the strip.

5) Place triangles on ungreased baking sheets. Brush tops with egg white. Bake at 400° for 7-10 minutes or until golden brown. Serve warm.

Yield: 5-1/2 dozen.

NUTRITION FACTS: 4 triangles equals 110 calories, 4 g fat (2 g saturated fat), 37 mg cholesterol, 218 mg sodium, 10 g carbohydrate, 1 g fiber, 7 g protein.

Roasted Garlic and Pepper Pizza

Bonnie Matherly, Buckingham, Illinois

Years ago, I found the recipe for this appealing appetizer, lightened it and added some of our favorite ingredients. It can be prepared ahead of time and put in the oven as your guests arrive. We occasionally use it as an easy Sunday evening meal, too.

1 large garlic bulb

1 teaspoon plus 2 tablespoons olive oil, *divided*

2 large sweet red peppers

1/2 cup sliced pimiento-stuffed olives

2 tablespoons red wine vinegar

1 teaspoon dried oregano

1/2 teaspoon dried basil

1/8 teaspoon white pepper

1 prebaked thin Italian bread shell crust (10 ounces)

3/4 cup sweet onion slices

3/4 cup crumbled feta cheese

1/3 cup shredded Parmesan cheese

1) Remove papery outer skin from garlic (do not peel or separate cloves). Cut top off garlic head; brush with 1 teaspoon oil. Wrap bulb in heavy-duty foil. Bake at 425° for 20-25 minutes or until softened. Cool for 10-15 minutes; squeeze softened garlic out of skins. Cut garlic into slices.

2) Cut red peppers in half; remove and discard seeds. Place cut side down on a baking sheet. Broil

4 in. from the heat until skins are blistered and blackened. Immediately place peppers in a bowl; cover and let stand for 15-20 minutes. Peel off and discard charred skin; cut peppers into julienne strips.

3) In a bowl, combine the olives, vinegar, oregano, basil, pepper and remaining oil. Place crust on a 12-in. pizza pan. Spoon oil mixture over crust. Top with garlic, peppers, onion and cheeses. Bake at 350° for 15-20 minutes or until cheese is melted.

Yield: 12 servings.

NUTRITION FACTS: 1 slice equals 138 calories, 7 g fat (2 g saturated fat), 10 mg cholesterol, 321 mg sodium, 14 g carbohydrate, 1 g fiber, 5 g protein.

Stovetop Latte
Delores Ward, Decatur, Indiana

Skip the trip to the trendy coffee shop and brew this good-for-you version of latte in the comfort of your own home. It's a great winter warm-up!

1-1/3 cups fat-free milk

Sugar substitute equivalent
  to 2 teaspoons sugar

2/3 cup hot strong brewed coffee

Ground cinnamon *or* baking cocoa,
  optional

1) In a small saucepan, combine milk and sugar substitute. Whisk over medium heat until foamy and steaming (do not boil).

2) Slowly pour into mugs. Pour coffee through the foam. Sprinkle with cinnamon or cocoa if desired.

Yield: 2 servings.

Editor's Note: This recipe was tested with Splenda No Calorie Sweetener.

NUTRITION FACTS: 1 cup equals 61 calories, 1 g fat (1 g saturated fat), 3 mg cholesterol, 86 mg sodium, 9 g carbohydrate, 0 fiber, 6 g protein.

Banana Berry Smoothies
Debbie Nelson, Sandy, Utah

My family is fond of smoothies, and we are always trying something new. This is one fruity blend they always want more of. Feel free to experiment with other juices, sherbet flavors and frozen fruits. You'll be surprised and delighted with the number of tasty combinations you can come up with.

2-1/2 cups orange juice

1 cup raspberry sherbet

1 large firm banana, sliced and
  frozen

1 cup frozen unsweetened
  strawberries

1 cup frozen blueberries

1) In a blender, combine all of the ingredients in the order listed; cover and process for 30 seconds or until smooth. Stir if necessary. Pour into chilled glasses and serve immediately.

Yield: 5 servings.

NUTRITION FACTS: 1 cup equals 148 calories, 1 g fat (1 g saturated fat), 2 mg cholesterol, 16 mg sodium, 35 g carbohydrate, 2 g fiber, 2 g protein.

PINEAPPLE COOLER

Pineapple Cooler
Ashley Braswell, Huntsville, Alabama

Five ingredients are all it takes to mix up this refreshing citrus beverage. Sparkling water gives it a little fizz, making it ideal on a summer day.

4 cups unsweetened
  pineapple juice

2 teaspoons lemon juice

1 teaspoon vanilla extract

1/2 teaspoon coconut extract

2 cups carbonated water

1) In a pitcher, combine the pineapple juice, lemon juice and extracts; chill. Just before serving, stir in carbonated water. Serve over ice.

Yield: 3 servings.

NUTRITION FACTS: 1 cup equals 120 calories, trace fat (trace saturated fat), 0 cholesterol, 5 mg sodium, 30 g carbohydrate, trace fiber, 1 g protein.

CHICKEN CORN SOUP WITH RIVELS

Chicken Corn Soup with Rivels

Elissa Armbruster, Medford, New Jersey

Traditional chicken soup gets an interesting twist from a dumpling-like broth-stretcher called rivels. This light-on-fat recipe is chock-full of chicken, vegetables and herbs.

  1   cup chopped carrots
  1   celery rib, chopped
  1   medium onion, chopped
  2   teaspoons canola oil
  2   cans (14-1/2 ounces *each*) reduced-sodium chicken broth
  2   cups fresh *or* frozen corn
  2   cups cubed cooked chicken breast
1/2   teaspoon minced fresh parsley
1/4   teaspoon salt
1/4   teaspoon dried tarragon
1/4   teaspoon pepper
3/4   cup all-purpose flour
  1   egg, beaten

1)   In a large saucepan, saute the carrots, celery and onion in oil until tender. Add the broth, corn, chicken, parsley, salt, tarragon and pepper. Bring to a boil.

2)   Meanwhile, for rivels, place the flour in a bowl; cut in egg with a fork until crumbly. Drop dough by teaspoonfuls into boiling soup, stirring constantly. Cook and stir for 1-2 minutes or until rivels are cooked through.

Yield: 7 servings.

NUTRITION FACTS: 1 cup equals 189 calories, 3 g fat (1 g saturated fat), 64 mg cholesterol, 456 mg sodium, 24 g carbohydrate, 3 g fiber, 18 g protein.

Mediterranean Seafood Chowder

Erin Nicole Morris, St. Peters, Missouri

My family is not overly fond of seafood, but they really enjoy this rich-tasting soup that combines shrimp and cod. Serve with a green salad and you have a satisfying meal.

1-1/2   cups chopped sweet yellow *or* red peppers
  1   large onion, quartered and thinly sliced
  3   garlic cloves, minced
  2   tablespoons olive oil
  1   can (28 ounces) crushed tomatoes, undrained
2-1/4   cups water
  1   can (14-1/2 ounces) chicken broth
  1   cup uncooked long grain rice
1/2   cup white wine *or* additional chicken broth
1/2   to 1 teaspoon dried thyme
1/2   to 1 teaspoon dried basil
1/2   teaspoon salt
1/8   teaspoon crushed red pepper flakes
  8   ounces uncooked medium shrimp, peeled and deveined
  8   ounces cod fillets, cut into pieces

1)   In a large saucepan or Dutch oven, saute the peppers, onion and garlic in oil until tender. Add the tomatoes, water, broth, rice, wine or additional broth and seasonings. Bring to a boil. Reduce heat; cover and simmer for 15-20 minutes or until rice is tender.

2)   Stir in the shrimp and cod; cover and simmer for 2-4 minutes or until shrimp turn pink and fish flakes easily with a fork.

Yield: 10 servings.

NUTRITION FACTS: 1 cup equals 187 calories, 4 g fat (1 g saturated fat), 44 mg cholesterol, 433 mg sodium, 25 g carbohydrate, 3 g fiber, 12 g protein.

Turkey Tenderloin Sandwiches

Kathy Thompson, Clifton, Colorado

We loved these absolutely delicious tenderloins when we visited the Iowa State Fair. We had to wait in line for more than an hour to order them, but with this recipe, we can enjoy them regularly.

  4   turkey breast tenderloins (4 ounces *each*)

1/4 cup canola oil

1/4 cup sherry *or* chicken broth

1/4 cup reduced-sodium soy sauce

2 tablespoons lemon juice

2 tablespoons dried minced onion

1/4 teaspoon ground ginger

1/8 teaspoon pepper

4 whole wheat hamburger buns, split

1 slice red onion, separated into rings

4 slices tomato

4 lettuce leaves

1) Flatten tenderloins to 3/4-in. thickness. In a large resealable plastic bag, combine the oil, sherry or broth, soy sauce, lemon juice, onion, ginger and pepper; add turkey. Seal bag and turn to coat; refrigerate at least 3 hours, turning occasionally.

2) If grilling the turkey, coat grill rack with nonstick cooking spray before starting the grill. Drain and discard marinade. Grill turkey, uncovered, over medium heat or broil 4 in. from the heat for 4-5 minutes on each side or until juices run clear. Serve on buns with onion, tomato and lettuce.

Yield: 4 servings.

NUTRITION FACTS: 1 sandwich equals 281 calories, 7 g fat (1 g saturated fat), 56 mg cholesterol, 421 mg sodium, 25 g carbohydrate, 4 g fiber, 31 g protein.

Open-Faced Crab Salad Sandwiches
Lanie Kappe, Santa Ana, California

Everyone loved the crab salad my mother-in-law contributed to a family gathering, so I reduced the fat in her recipe for this version. Serve it hot or cold or as a spread for crackers.

1/2 cup reduced-fat mayonnaise

1/8 teaspoon salt

1/8 teaspoon pepper

2 packages (8 ounces *each*) imitation crabmeat, chopped

1 cup (4 ounces) shredded mozzarella cheese

1/4 cup chopped sweet red pepper

1/4 cup chopped green onions

1/4 cup chopped celery

1 loaf (8 ounces) unsliced French bread, halved lengthwise

1) In a large bowl, combine the mayonnaise, salt and pepper. Stir in the crab, cheese, red pepper, onions and celery. Spoon over bread halves.

2) Place on a baking sheet. Broil 5 in. from the heat for 7-8 minutes or until lightly browned. Cut into 3-in. pieces.

Yield: 8 servings.

NUTRITION FACTS: 1 piece equals 236 calories, 9 g fat (3 g saturated fat), 44 mg cholesterol, 420 mg sodium, 24 g carbohydrate, 1 g fiber, 13 g protein.

Lighter Broccoli Cheese Soup
Marge Hill, Glenside, Pennsylvania

When my husband and I visit fresh-food stands, we often come home with more vegetables than we can eat. I lightened up this tarragon-flavored soup to use up the broccoli we buy. I like it with crusty bread, a salad or a sandwich.

1/2 cup chopped sweet onion

3 garlic cloves, minced

2 tablespoons all-purpose flour

1 can (14-1/2 ounces) reduced-sodium chicken broth *or* vegetable broth

4 cups fresh broccoli florets

1/4 to 1/2 teaspoon dried tarragon

1/4 teaspoon dried thyme

1/8 teaspoon pepper

1-1/2 cups 1% milk

1-1/4 cups shredded reduced-fat cheddar cheese, *divided*

1) In a large nonstick saucepan coated with nonstick cooking spray, saute onion and garlic until tender. Stir in flour until blended; cook for 1 minute. Gradually whisk in broth. Bring to a boil; cook and stir for 1-2 minutes or until slightly thickened.

2) Add the broccoli, tarragon, thyme and pepper; return to a boil. Reduce heat; cover and simmer for 10 minutes or until broccoli is tender. Add milk; cook, uncovered, 5 minutes longer. Remove from the heat; cool to room temperature.

3) In a blender, process soup in batches until smooth. Return to the pan; heat through. Reduce heat. Add 1 cup of cheese; stir just until melted. Serve immediately. Garnish with remaining cheese.

Yield: 4 servings.

NUTRITION FACTS: 1 cup equals 202 calories, 9 g fat (6 g saturated fat), 33 mg cholesterol, 340 mg sodium, 16 g carbohydrate, 3 g fiber, 17 g protein.

GREAT GRAIN BURGERS

boil. Reduce heat; cover and simmer for 30 minutes or until rice is tender. Remove from the heat; cool completely. Refrigerate.

2) In a large bowl, combine the mushrooms, oats, mozzarella cheese, cheddar cheese and onion. In a blender or food processor, process cottage cheese and egg substitute until smooth; add to the mushroom mixture. Stir in the parsley, salt, basil, celery seed and chilled rice mixture. Shape 1/2 cupfuls into patties.

3) In a large nonstick skillet, cook four patties in 1 teaspoon oil for 5 minutes on each side or until lightly browned and crisp. Repeat with remaining patties and oil. Serve on rolls with lettuce and tomato if desired.

Yield: 12 servings.

NUTRITION FACTS: 1 patty equals 126 calories, 4 g fat (2 g saturated fat), 8 mg cholesterol, 286 mg sodium, 15 g carbohydrate, 2 g fiber, 7 g protein.

Great Grain Burgers
Pat Whitaker, Lebanon, Oregon

I've experimented with many combinations of ingredients to make a good meatless burger...and this is our favorite. These patties cook up golden brown and crispy and make delicious sandwiches.

- 1/2 cup uncooked brown rice
- 1/2 cup uncooked bulgur
- 1 tablespoon salt-free seasoning blend
- 1/4 teaspoon poultry seasoning
- 2 cups water
- 2 cups finely chopped fresh mushrooms
- 3/4 cup old-fashioned oats
- 1 cup (4 ounces) shredded part-skim mozzarella cheese
- 1/4 cup shredded reduced-fat cheddar cheese
- 1/3 cup finely chopped onion
- 1/2 cup fat-free cottage cheese
- 1/4 cup egg substitute
- 2 tablespoons minced fresh parsley
- 1 teaspoon salt
- 1/2 teaspoon dried basil
- 1/8 teaspoon celery seed
- 3 teaspoons canola oil, *divided*
- 12 sandwich rolls, optional

Lettuce leaves and tomato slices, optional

1) In a saucepan, combine the rice, bulgur, seasoning blend, poultry seasoning and water; bring to a

Sweet Pepper Sandwiches
Cara Neth, Fort Collins, Colorado

My family members love this easy recipe because they can assemble the sandwiches to their liking.

- 1 *each* small green, sweet red and yellow pepper, thinly sliced
- 1 small onion, thinly sliced
- 1 garlic clove, minced
- 1 tablespoon olive oil
- 1 tablespoon balsamic vinegar
- 1 piece (2 ounces) fresh mozzarella cheese
- 1/4 cup fat-free mayonnaise
- 1/2 teaspoon prepared horseradish
- 4 hard rolls, split and toasted
- 8 fresh basil leaves
- 1 plum tomato, thinly sliced

1) In a large nonstick skillet, saute peppers, onion and garlic in oil until crisp-tender. Drizzle with vinegar; toss to coat. Cut mozzarella cheese into four slices.

2) Combine the mayonnaise and horseradish; spread over cut sides of rolls. Spoon vegetable mixture onto bottom halves; top with cheese. Broil 4-6 in. from the heat for 2-4 minutes or until cheese is melted. Top with basil leaves and tomato. Replace roll tops.

Yield: 4 servings.

NUTRITION FACTS: 1 sandwich equals 278 calories, 10 g fat (3 g saturated fat), 13 mg cholesterol, 456 mg sodium, 39 g carbohydrate, 3 g fiber, 9 g protein.

3) Remove from the heat; cool slightly. Discard bay leaf. In a blender, puree vegetable mixture in batches. Return to the pan. Stir in milk and sherry or broth; heat through (do not boil).

Yield: 8 servings.

NUTRITION FACTS: 1-1/4 cups equals 159 calories, 4 g fat (2 g saturated fat), 9 mg cholesterol, 487 mg sodium, 29 g carbohydrate, 6 g fiber, 5 g protein.

Beef Fillets with Portobello Sauce
Christel Stein, Tampa, Florida

These tasty steaks seem special, but they are fast enough for everyday dinners. We enjoy the mushroom-topped fillets with crusty French bread, mixed salad and a light lemon dessert.

- 2 beef tenderloin steaks (4 ounces *each*)
- 1/2 cup dry red wine *or* reduced-sodium beef broth
- 1 teaspoon all-purpose flour
- 1/2 cup reduced-sodium beef broth
- 1 teaspoon *each* steak sauce, Worcestershire sauce and ketchup
- 1/2 teaspoon ground mustard
- 4 ounces fresh baby portobello mushrooms, sliced
- 1/4 teaspoon pepper
- 1/8 teaspoon salt
- 1 tablespoon minced chives, optional

1) In a large nonstick skillet coated with nonstick cooking spray, brown steaks on both sides over medium-high heat. Remove and keep warm.

2) Reduce heat to medium. Add wine or broth to pan, stirring to loosen browned bits; cook for 2-3 minutes or until liquid is reduced by half. Combine flour and broth until smooth; whisk into the pan juices. Add steak sauce, Worcestershire sauce, ketchup and mustard. Bring to a boil.

3) Return steaks to the skillet; add mushrooms. Cook for 4-5 minutes on each side or until meat reaches desired doneness (for medium-rare, a meat thermometer should read 145°; medium, 160°; well-done, 170°). Sprinkle with pepper, salt and chives if desired.

Yield: 2 servings.

NUTRITION FACTS: 1 steak with 1/3 cup sauce equals 255 calories, 8 g fat (3 g saturated fat), 72 mg cholesterol, 422 mg sodium, 7 g carbohydrate, 1 g fiber, 26 g protein.

Cream of Butternut Soup
Shelly Snyder, Lafayette, Colorado

Ginger, turmeric, cinnamon and a little sherry do an incredible job of seasoning this slightly sweet soup. After I lightened up a recipe from a friend in South Africa, it quickly became a family favorite.

- 1 cup chopped onion
- 2 celery ribs, chopped
- 2 tablespoons butter
- 2 cans (14-1/2 ounces *each*) reduced-sodium chicken broth
- 1 teaspoon sugar
- 1 bay leaf
- 1/2 teaspoon salt
- 1/2 teaspoon ground ginger
- 1/2 teaspoon ground turmeric
- 1/4 teaspoon ground cinnamon
- 1 butternut squash (2-1/2 pounds), peeled and cubed
- 3 medium potatoes, peeled and cubed
- 1-1/2 cups 1% milk
- 2 tablespoons sherry *or* additional reduced-sodium chicken broth

1) In a large saucepan coated with nonstick cooking spray, cook onion and celery in butter until tender. Stir in the broth, sugar, bay leaf, salt, ginger, turmeric and cinnamon.

2) Add the squash and potatoes. Bring to a boil. Reduce the heat; cover and simmer for 15-20 minutes or until vegetables are tender.

Asparagus Beef Stir-Fry

Debby Peterson, Niagara, Wisconsin

This stir-fry is popular at our house...especially when I put a little extra bite in it with the red pepper flakes. To make sure the steak is tender, cut it into thin strips across the grain.

- 2 tablespoons reduced-sodium soy sauce, *divided*
- 2 tablespoons dry red wine *or* beef broth, *divided*
- 1/2 pound boneless beef sirloin steak, cut into thin strips
- 1 tablespoon cornstarch
- 1/2 cup water
- 4 teaspoons canola oil, *divided*
- 1 small onion, thinly sliced
- 1 pound fresh asparagus, trimmed and cut into 1-inch pieces
- 2 celery ribs, thinly sliced
- 1 garlic clove, minced
- 1/8 to 1/4 teaspoon crushed red pepper flakes

  Hot cooked rice, optional

1) In a large resealable plastic bag, combine 1 tablespoon soy sauce and 1 tablespoon wine or broth; add beef. Seal bag and turn to coat; refrigerate for 30 minutes.

2) In a small bowl, combine the cornstarch, water and remaining soy sauce and wine or broth until smooth; set aside.

3) In a large nonstick skillet or wok, stir-fry beef in 2 teaspoons oil for 3-4 minutes or until no longer pink. Remove with a slotted spoon and keep warm.

4) Stir-fry onion in remaining oil for 1 minute. Add asparagus; stir-fry for 2 minutes. Add celery, garlic and red pepper flakes; stir-fry 4-6 minutes longer or until vegetables are crisp-tender.

5) Stir cornstarch mixture and add to the pan. Bring to a boil; cook and stir for 2 minutes or until thickened. Add beef; heat through. Serve with rice if desired.

Yield: 3 servings.

NUTRITION FACTS: 1-1/3 cups stir-fry mixture equals 211 calories, 10 g fat (2 g saturated fat), 42 mg cholesterol, 461 mg sodium, 11 g carbohydrate, 3 g fiber, 18 g protein.

SIRLOIN VEGGIE KABOBS

Sirloin Veggie Kabobs

Trisha Ward, Atlanta, Georgia

Planning your Labor Day cookout menu will be no work at all when you have my classic kabob recipe to call on. Feel free to use cauliflower or other favorite vegetables.

- 2/3 cup chili sauce
- 1/2 cup dry red wine *or* beef broth
- 1/2 cup balsamic vinegar
- 2 tablespoons canola oil
- 4-1/2 teaspoons Worcestershire sauce
- 4-1/2 teaspoons dried minced onion
- 1 garlic clove, minced
- 1/2 teaspoon ground mustard
- 1/4 teaspoon salt
- 1 pound boneless beef sirloin steak, cut into 3/4-inch cubes
- 16 fresh baby portobello *or* large white mushrooms, halved
- 2 medium red onions, cut into wedges
- 1 medium sweet red pepper, cut into 3/4-inch pieces
- 1 medium sweet yellow pepper, cut into 3/4-inch pieces

1) In a small bowl, combine the first nine ingredients; mix well. Pour half into a large resealable plastic bag; add beef cubes. Seal bag and turn to coat.

2) Pour the remaining marinade into another large resealable plastic bag; add mushrooms, onions and peppers. Seal the bag and turn to coat. Refrigerate beef and vegetables for up to 4 hours.

3) If grilling the kabobs, coat grill rack with nonstick cooking spray before starting the grill. Drain and discard marinade from beef. Drain vegetables,

reserving marinade for basting. On eight metal or soaked wooden skewers, alternately thread beef and vegetables.

4) Grill, covered, over medium heat or broil 4-6 in. from the heat for 3-4 minutes on each side or until meat reaches desired doneness, turning three times and basting frequently with reserved marinade.

Yield: 4 servings.

NUTRITION FACTS: 2 kabobs equals 268 calories, 10 g fat (2 g saturated fat), 63 mg cholesterol, 480 mg sodium, 20 g carbohydrate, 2 g fiber, 24 g protein.

FLANK STEAK WITH CRANBERRY SAUCE

Flank Steak with Cranberry Sauce

Ellen De Munnik, Chesterfield, Michigan

This tasty and tender steak, served with a mild sweet-tart cranberry sauce, makes a pretty presentation for a special-occasion dinner.

2	teaspoons grated orange peel
1/2	teaspoon salt
1/2	teaspoon ground cinnamon
1	beef flank steak (1-1/2 pounds)

CRANBERRY SAUCE:

1/4	cup chopped green onions
1	garlic clove, minced
3/4	cup dried cranberries
1/2	cup reduced-sodium beef broth
1/2	cup dry red wine *or* additional reduced-sodium beef broth
1/2	cup cranberry juice
2	teaspoons cornstarch
2	tablespoons cold water
1/4	teaspoon salt
1/4	teaspoon pepper

1) Combine orange peel, salt and cinnamon; rub over flank steak. Cover and refrigerate for 1 hour.

2) In a saucepan coated with nonstick cooking spray, saute onions and garlic until tender. Add the cranberries, broth, wine or additional broth and cranberry juice. Bring to a boil. Reduce heat; simmer, uncovered, for 10 minutes.

3) Combine cornstarch and water until smooth; stir into cranberry mixture. Bring to a boil; cook and stir for 2 minutes or until thickened. Stir in salt and pepper. Reduce heat to low; keep warm.

4) Broil steak 3-4 in. from the heat for 7-9 minutes on each side or until meat reaches desired doneness (for medium-rare, a meat thermometer should read 145°; medium, 160°; well-done, 170°). Slice steak across the grain; serve with cranberry sauce.

Yield: 6 servings.

NUTRITION FACTS: 3 ounces cooked beef with 1/4 cup sauce equals 253 calories, 9 g fat (4 g saturated fat), 59 mg cholesterol, 373 mg sodium, 15 g carbohydrate, 1 g fiber, 24 g protein.

Balsamic-Seasoned Steak

Taste of Home Test Kitchen

A tasty marinade makes this sirloin so tender. You'll love its simple preparation and scrumptious Swiss-cheese topping.

2	tablespoons balsamic vinegar
2	teaspoons steak sauce
1	boneless beef sirloin steak (1 pound)
1/4	teaspoon coarsely ground pepper
2	ounces reduced-fat Swiss cheese, cut into thin strips

1) In a small bowl, combine vinegar and steak sauce; set aside. Rub steak with pepper. Place on a broiler pan. Broil 4 in. from heat for 7 minutes.

2) Turn; spoon half of the steak sauce mixture over steak. Broil 5-7 minutes longer or until meat reaches desired doneness (for medium-rare, a meat thermometer should read 145°; medium, 160°; well-done, 170°).

3) Remove steak to a cutting board; cut across the grain into 1/4-in. slices. Place on a foil-lined baking sheet; drizzle with juices from cutting board and remaining steak sauce mixture. Top with cheese. Broil for 1 minute or until cheese is melted.

Yield: 4 servings.

NUTRITION FACTS: 3 ounces cooked beef with 1/2 ounce of cheese equals 188 calories, 8 g fat (3 g saturated fat), 70 mg cholesterol, 116 mg sodium, 2 g carbohydrate, trace fiber, 26 g protein.

Flavorful Meat Loaf
Lillian Wittler, Wayne, Nebraska

Since I can't have much salt, I've come up with a recipe for meat loaf that is really tasty without it.

- 2 egg whites
- 1/2 cup 1% milk
- 3 slices whole wheat bread, torn into pieces
- 1/4 cup finely chopped onion
- 1 teaspoon Worcestershire sauce
- 1/4 teaspoon onion powder
- 1/4 teaspoon garlic powder
- 1/4 teaspoon ground mustard
- 1/4 teaspoon rubbed sage
- 1/4 teaspoon pepper
- 1 pound lean ground beef
- 3 tablespoons ketchup

1) In a large bowl, beat egg whites. Add milk and bread; let stand for 5 minutes. Stir in the onion, Worcestershire sauce and seasonings. Crumble beef over mixture and mix well.

2) Shape into a loaf in an 11-in. x 7-in. x 2-in. baking pan coated with nonstick cooking spray. Bake, uncovered, at 350° for 35 minutes; drain.

3) Spoon ketchup over loaf. Bake 10-20 minutes longer or until a meat thermometer reads 160°. Let stand for 10 minutes before slicing.

Yield: 5 servings.

NUTRITION FACTS: 1 slice equals 228 calories, 9 g fat (4 g saturated fat), 35 mg cholesterol, 307 mg sodium, 13 g carbohydrate, 1 g fiber, 23 g protein.

PORK MEDALLIONS WITH SAUTEED APPLES

Pork Medallions with Sauteed Apples
Clara Coulston, Washington Court House, Ohio

When it comes to healthy, easy and flavorful entrees, this dish is tops. The pork doesn't have much fat, and it's wonderful with the apple slices.

- 1 pork tenderloin (1 pound), cut into 1-inch slices
- 3/4 teaspoon dried thyme
- 1/2 teaspoon paprika
- 1/4 teaspoon salt
- 1/4 teaspoon pepper
- 1/4 cup sliced green onions
- 1 garlic clove, minced
- 1 tablespoon butter
- 2 medium apples, cut into wedges
- 2 teaspoons cornstarch
- 2/3 cup reduced-sodium chicken broth
- 1/4 cup unsweetened apple juice

1) Flatten pork to 1/2-in. thickness. Combine the thyme, paprika, salt and pepper; sprinkle over both sides of pork. Broil pork 3-4 in. from the heat for 3-4 minutes on each side or until juices run clear; keep warm.

2) In a nonstick skillet, saute onions and garlic in butter until tender. Add the apples; cook and stir for 2 minutes or until crisp-tender. Combine the cornstarch, broth and apple juice until smooth; stir into apple mixture. Bring to a boil; cook and stir for 1-2 minutes or until thickened. Serve with pork.

Yield: 4 servings.

NUTRITION FACTS: 3 ounces cooked pork with 1/2 cup apples equals 251 calories, 10 g fat (4 g saturated fat), 85 mg cholesterol, 335 mg sodium, 15 g carbohydrate, 3 g fiber, 25 g protein.

Herb-Stuffed Pork Loin
Michele Montgomery, Lethbridge, Alberta

I serve this pork roast often when I'm entertaining company. It's especially good with garden-fresh herbs, but dried works nicely as well.

- 1 boneless pork loin roast (3 pounds)
- 1/4 cup Dijon mustard
- 4 garlic cloves, minced
- 1/3 cup minced chives
- 1/4 cup minced fresh sage *or* 4 teaspoons rubbed sage
- 2 tablespoons minced fresh thyme *or* 2 teaspoons dried thyme
- 1 tablespoon minced fresh rosemary *or* 1 teaspoon dried rosemary, crushed
- 2-3/4 teaspoons pepper, *divided*
- 1 teaspoon salt, *divided*
- 1 tablespoon olive oil

1) Starting about a third in from one side, make a lengthwise slit down the roast to within 1/2 in. of the bottom. Turn roast over and make another lengthwise slit, starting about a third in from the opposite side. Open roast so it lies flat; cover with plastic wrap. Flatten to 3/4-in. thickness; remove plastic wrap.

2) Combine mustard and garlic; rub two-thirds of the mixture over roast. Combine the chives, sage, thyme, rosemary, 3/4 teaspoon pepper and 1/2 teaspoon salt. Sprinkle two-thirds of the herb mixture over roast.

3) Roll up jelly-roll style, starting with a long side; tie several times with kitchen string. Rub oil over roast; sprinkle with remaining salt and pepper.

4) If grilling the roast, coat grill rack with nonstick cooking spray before starting the grill. Grill roast, covered, over indirect medium heat or bake, uncovered, at 350° for 1 hour.

5) Brush remaining mustard mixture over roast; sprinkle with remaining herb mixture. Grill or bake 20-25 minutes longer or until a meat thermometer reads 160°. Let stand 10 minutes before slicing.

Yield: 12 servings.

NUTRITION FACTS: 1 serving equals 199 calories, 10 g fat (3 g saturated fat), 69 mg cholesterol, 372 mg sodium, 2 g carbohydrate, 1 g fiber, 25 g protein.

LIME-GLAZED PORK CHOPS

Lime-Glazed Pork Chops
Jacqui Correa, Landing, New Jersey

A wonderful sweet-sour citrus glaze makes my recipe for tender chops tangy and tasty. The grilled chops are perfect for picnics and barbecues.

- 1/3 cup orange marmalade
- 1 jalapeno pepper, seeded and finely chopped
- 2 tablespoons lime juice

- 1 teaspoon grated fresh gingerroot
- 4 bone-in pork loin chops (8 ounces *each*)
- 4 teaspoons minced fresh cilantro
- Lime wedges

1) For glaze, in a small saucepan, combine the marmalade, jalapeno, lime juice and ginger. Cook and stir over medium heat for 5 minutes or until marmalade melts. Remove from heat; set aside.

2) Coat grill rack with nonstick cooking spray before starting the grill. Grill pork chops, covered, over medium heat for 6-7 minutes on each side or until juices run clear, brushing with glaze during the last 5 minutes of grilling. Sprinkle with cilantro and serve with lime wedges.

Yield: 4 servings.

Editor's Note: When cutting or seeding hot peppers, use rubber or plastic gloves to protect your hands. Avoid touching your face.

NUTRITION FACTS: 1 pork chop equals 286 calories, 8 g fat (3 g saturated fat), 86 mg cholesterol, 85 mg sodium, 18 g carbohydrate, 1 g fiber, 34 g protein.

Teriyaki Pork Tenderloin
Kristen Croke, Hanover, Massachusetts

When there are just two of us for dinner, I prepare one tenderloin and marinate the other in the freezer for later use.

- 5 tablespoons reduced-sodium soy sauce
- 2 tablespoons olive oil
- 2 garlic cloves, minced
- 2 teaspoons brown sugar
- 1 teaspoon ground ginger
- 1 teaspoon coarsely ground pepper
- 2 pork tenderloins (about 1 pound *each*)

1) In a large resealable plastic bag, combine the first six ingredients; add pork. Seal bag and turn to coat; refrigerate for 8 hours or overnight.

2) Drain and discard marinade. Place tenderloins in an 11-in. x 7-in. x 2-in. baking pan coated with nonstick cooking spray. Bake, uncovered, at 425° for 25-35 minutes or until a meat thermometer reads 160°. Let stand for 5 minutes before slicing. Serve with pan drippings.

Yield: 6 servings.

NUTRITION FACTS: 4 ounces cooked pork equals 217 calories, 8 g fat (2 g saturated fat), 91 mg cholesterol, 317 mg sodium, 2 g carbohydrate, trace fiber, 33 g protein.

Lamb with Mint Salsa

Taste of Home Test Kitchen

This flavorful entree is well-seasoned with an herb rub of basil, garlic, rosemary and thyme. Tender slices of meat are served with a refreshing salsa that will have guests licking their lips.

<table>
<tr><td>5</td><td>teaspoons olive oil</td></tr>
<tr><td>2</td><td>garlic cloves, minced</td></tr>
<tr><td>1</td><td>teaspoon each dried basil, thyme and rosemary, crushed</td></tr>
<tr><td>1/2</td><td>teaspoon salt</td></tr>
<tr><td>1/4</td><td>teaspoon pepper</td></tr>
<tr><td>2</td><td>racks of lamb (8 ribs each)</td></tr>
</table>

MINT SALSA:

<table>
<tr><td>1</td><td>cup minced fresh mint</td></tr>
<tr><td>1</td><td>small cucumber, peeled, seeded and chopped</td></tr>
<tr><td>1/2</td><td>cup seeded chopped tomato</td></tr>
<tr><td>1/3</td><td>cup finely chopped onion</td></tr>
<tr><td>1/3</td><td>cup chopped sweet yellow pepper</td></tr>
<tr><td>1</td><td>jalapeno pepper, seeded and chopped</td></tr>
<tr><td>3</td><td>tablespoons lemon juice</td></tr>
<tr><td>2</td><td>tablespoons sugar</td></tr>
<tr><td>2</td><td>garlic cloves, minced</td></tr>
<tr><td>3/4</td><td>teaspoon ground ginger</td></tr>
<tr><td>1/4</td><td>teaspoon salt</td></tr>
</table>

1) In a small bowl, combine the oil, garlic and seasonings. Rub over lamb. Place in a roasting pan; cover and refrigerate for 1 hour. In a bowl, combine the salsa ingredients; cover and refrigerate until serving.

2) Bake lamb, uncovered, at 425° for 20-30 minutes or until meat reaches desired doneness (for medium-rare, a meat thermometer should read 145°; medium, 160°; well-done, 170°). Cover loosely with foil and let stand for 5-10 minutes before slicing. Serve with mint salsa.

Yield: 8 servings (2 cups salsa).

Editor's Note: When cutting or seeding hot peppers, use rubber or plastic gloves to protect your hands. Avoid touching your face.

NUTRITION FACTS: 2 ribs with 1/4 cup salsa equals 191 calories, 9 g fat (3 g saturated fat), 60 mg cholesterol, 278 mg sodium, 7 g carbohydrate, 1 g fiber, 20 g protein.

Artichoke-Lamb Sandwich Loaves

Helen Hassler, Denver, Pennsylvania

These tender sandwiches will surely become the talk of any get-together. Just fill hollowed out sourdough baguettes with cucumber, cheese and marinated lamb and artichokes. Simply delicious, the mouth-watering bites are perfect for a spring brunch.

<table>
<tr><td>1/2</td><td>cup lemon juice</td></tr>
<tr><td>1/2</td><td>cup olive oil</td></tr>
<tr><td>6</td><td>garlic cloves, minced</td></tr>
<tr><td>2</td><td>tablespoons minced fresh rosemary</td></tr>
<tr><td>1</td><td>teaspoon salt</td></tr>
<tr><td>1/4</td><td>teaspoon cayenne pepper</td></tr>
<tr><td>1</td><td>boneless leg of lamb (2-1/2 pounds)</td></tr>
<tr><td>2</td><td>cans (14 ounces each) water-packed artichoke hearts, rinsed and drained</td></tr>
<tr><td>2/3</td><td>cup plus 6 tablespoons reduced-fat balsamic vinaigrette, divided</td></tr>
<tr><td>2</td><td>sourdough baguettes (1 pound each)</td></tr>
<tr><td>1</td><td>medium cucumber, thinly sliced</td></tr>
<tr><td>2</td><td>medium tomatoes, thinly sliced</td></tr>
<tr><td>6</td><td>ounces goat cheese, sliced</td></tr>
</table>

1) In a large resealable plastic bag, combine the first six ingredients; add lamb. Seal bag and turn to coat. Refrigerate for 8 hours or overnight.

2) Drain and discard marinade. Place lamb on a rack in a shallow roasting pan. Bake, uncovered, at 325° for 80-90 minutes or until meat reaches desired doneness (for medium-rare, a meat thermometer should read 145°; medium, 160°; well-done, 170°). Cool to room temperature. Cover and refrigerate for at least 2 hours.

3) Place artichokes in a resealable plastic bag; add 2/3 cup vinaigrette. Seal bag and turn to coat; let stand for 10 minutes. Drain and discard marinade.

4) Cut lamb into thin slices. Cut each baguette in half horizontally. Carefully hollow out top and bottom, leaving a 3/4-in. shell. Brush the bottom half of each loaf with 2 tablespoons vinaigrette. Layer with the cucumber, tomatoes, lamb and artichokes; drizzle with remaining vinaigrette. Top with goat cheese.

5) Replace bread tops and press down firmly; wrap tightly in plastic wrap. Refrigerate for at least 2 hours. Cut into slices.

Yield: 24 servings.

NUTRITION FACTS: 2 slices equals 156 calories, 9 g fat (3 g saturated fat), 32 mg cholesterol, 302 mg sodium, 7 g carbohydrate, 1 g fiber, 11 g protein.

GREEK LAMB KABOBS

Greek Lamb Kabobs
Kathy Herrola, Martinez, California

We have a gas grill and use it year-round, especially to make these tender, juicy kabobs. The lamb marinates overnight, and the attractive skewers can be quickly assembled the next day.

1/2 **cup lemon juice**
  4 **teaspoons olive oil**
  2 **tablespoons dried oregano**
  6 **garlic cloves, minced**
  1 **pound boneless lean lamb, cut into 1-inch cubes**
 16 **cherry tomatoes**
  1 **large green pepper, cut into 1-inch pieces**
  1 **large onion, cut into 1-inch wedges**

1) In a small bowl, combine the lemon juice, oil, oregano and garlic. Remove 1/4 cup for basting; cover and refrigerate. Pour the remaining

marinade into a large resealable plastic bag; add the lamb. Seal bag and turn to coat; refrigerate for at least 8 hours or overnight, turning occasionally.

2) Coat grill rack with nonstick cooking spray before starting the grill. Drain and discard marinade from lamb. On eight metal or soaked wooden skewers, alternately thread lamb, tomatoes, green pepper and onion.

3) Grill kabobs, uncovered, over medium heat for 3 minutes on each side. Baste with reserved marinade. Grill 8-10 minutes longer or until meat reaches desired doneness, turning and basting frequently.

Yield: 4 servings.

NUTRITION FACTS: 2 kabobs equals 226 calories, 9 g fat (3 g saturated fat), 74 mg cholesterol, 83 mg sodium, 13 g carbohydrate, 2 g fiber, 25 g protein.

Thai-Style Chicken
Vicki Floden, Story City, Iowa

When you add the chicken to the peppery marinade a night early, there isn't much dinner preparation the following day.

1/4 **cup reduced-sodium soy sauce**
  3 **tablespoons lemon juice**
  3 **tablespoons minced fresh basil** *or* **1 tablespoon dried basil**
  2 **tablespoons fat-free plain yogurt**
  2 **teaspoons grated lemon peel**
  3 **garlic cloves, minced**
  1 **teaspoon ground ginger**
1/2 **to 1 teaspoon crushed red pepper flakes**
  4 **boneless skinless chicken breast halves (4 ounces** *each***)**

1) In a small bowl, combine the soy sauce, lemon juice, basil, yogurt, lemon peel, garlic, ginger and red pepper flakes. Remove 1/4 cup to another bowl; cover and refrigerate.

2) Pour the remaining marinade into a large resealable plastic bag; add chicken. Seal bag and turn to coat; refrigerate overnight.

3) Drain and discard marinade. Place chicken in a 13-in. x 9-in. x 2-in. baking dish coated with nonstick cooking spray. Spoon reserved marinade over chicken. Bake, uncovered, at 375° for 20 minutes or until a meat thermometer reads 170°.

Yield: 4 servings.

NUTRITION FACTS: 1 chicken breast half equals 134 calories, 3 g fat (1 g saturated fat), 63 mg cholesterol, 360 mg sodium, 2 g carbohydrate, trace fiber, 24 g protein.

Chicken with Sun-Dried Tomatoes

Heather Nandell, Johnston, Iowa

Sun-dried tomatoes provide intense flavor in this delightful chicken entree. If you have all the ingredients for this dish ready before you start to cook, the recipe comes together quickly.

- 1/2 cup plus 3 tablespoons reduced-sodium chicken broth
- 1/4 cup chopped dry-packed sun-dried tomatoes
- 1/2 cup sliced fresh mushrooms
- 1 green onion, thinly sliced
- 2 teaspoons minced garlic, *divided*
- 4 boneless skinless chicken breast halves (4 ounces *each*)
- 1 teaspoon olive oil
- 2 teaspoons cornstarch
- 1/2 teaspoon dried basil
- 1/4 teaspoon salt
- 1/4 teaspoon pepper
- 1/2 cup fat-free milk
- Hot cooked pasta, optional

1) Bring 1/2 cup broth to a boil; remove from the heat. Stir in sun-dried tomatoes; let stand for 10 minutes.

2) In a large nonstick skillet coated with nonstick cooking spray, saute the mushrooms, onion and 1 teaspoon garlic for 1 minute. Stir in the remaining broth; cook 2 minutes longer or until mushrooms are tender. Remove mushroom mixture and set aside.

3) Rub chicken with remaining garlic. In the same skillet, brown chicken in oil for 3 minutes on each side. Stir in tomato mixture; bring to a boil. Reduce heat; cover and simmer for 10-12 minutes or until chicken juices run clear. Remove chicken; slice and keep warm.

4) In a small bowl, combine the cornstarch, basil, salt and pepper. Stir in milk until smooth; add to tomato mixture. Bring to a boil; cook and stir for 1-2 minutes or until thickened. Stir in mushroom mixture. Spoon over chicken. Serve with pasta if desired.

Yield: 4 servings.

NUTRITION FACTS: 1 chicken breast half with 1/4 cup sauce equals 190 calories, 5 g fat (1 g saturated fat), 66 mg cholesterol, 416 mg sodium, 7 g carbohydrate, 1 g fiber, 29 g protein.

Chicken and Shrimp Satay

Hannah Barringer, Loudon, Tennessee

I lightened up a recipe that I found in a cookbook, and these grilled kabobs were the tasty result. The scrumptious dipping sauce is always a hit.

- 3/4 pound uncooked medium shrimp, peeled and deveined
- 3/4 pound chicken tenderloin, cut into 1-inch cubes
- 4 green onions, chopped
- 2 garlic cloves, minced
- 1 tablespoon butter
- 1 tablespoon minced fresh parsley
- 1/2 cup white wine *or* chicken broth
- 1 tablespoon lemon juice
- 1 tablespoon lime juice

SAUCE:
- 1/4 cup chopped onion
- 1 tablespoon butter
- 2/3 cup reduced-sodium chicken broth
- 1/4 cup reduced-fat chunky peanut butter
- 2-1/4 teaspoons brown sugar
- 3/4 teaspoon lemon juice
- 3/4 teaspoon lime juice
- 1/4 teaspoon salt
- 1/4 teaspoon *each* dried basil, thyme and rosemary, crushed
- 1/8 teaspoon cayenne pepper

1) Thread shrimp and chicken onto 12 metal or soaked wooden skewers. Place in a large shallow dish; set aside.

2) In a small skillet, saute the green onions and garlic in butter. Stir in the parsley, wine or broth, lemon

juice and lime juice. Remove from the heat; cool slightly. Pour over skewers and turn to coat. Cover and refrigerate for 4 hours, turning every 30 minutes.

3) In a small saucepan, saute onion in butter. Add the remaining sauce ingredients; cook and stir until blended. Remove from the heat; set aside.

4) Coat grill rack with nonstick cooking spray before starting the grill; prepare for indirect heat. Drain and discard marinade. Grill skewers, covered, over indirect medium heat for 7-8 minutes, turning often. Brush with 1/4 cup sauce during the last minute of grilling. Serve with remaining sauce.

Yield: 6 servings.

NUTRITION FACTS: 2 kabobs with 2 tablespoons sauce equals 190 calories, 7 g fat (3 g saturated fat), 126 mg cholesterol, 339 mg sodium, 7 g carbohydrate, 1 g fiber, 25 g protein.

Curry Chicken
Judie White, Florien, Louisiana

A little curry powder makes this meal-in-one a vibrant change of pace from weeknight staples. I like how the dash of red pepper flakes adds extra spice to the stir-fry.

1	tablespoon cornstarch
2	teaspoons curry powder
1/8	teaspoon crushed red pepper flakes
1	cup reduced-sodium chicken broth
1	tablespoon reduced-sodium soy sauce
1	pound boneless skinless chicken breasts, cut into cubes
2	teaspoons canola oil, *divided*
1	cup sliced fresh carrots
2	garlic cloves, minced
3	cups fresh broccoli florets
4	green onions, thinly sliced

1) In a small bowl, combine the cornstarch, curry and red pepper flakes. Stir in broth and soy sauce until smooth; set aside. In a large nonstick skillet or wok coated with nonstick cooking spray, stir-fry chicken in 1 teaspoon oil for 5-6 minutes or until no longer pink. Remove and keep warm.

2) In the same pan, stir-fry carrots and garlic in remaining oil for 1 minute. Stir in broccoli; cook 2 minutes longer. Add onions; cook 1-2 minutes longer.

3) Stir broth mixture and stir into vegetables. Bring to a boil; cook and stir for 2 minutes or until thickened. Return chicken to the pan; heat through.

Yield: 4 servings.

NUTRITION FACTS: 1 cup equals 194 calories, 5 g fat (1 g saturated fat), 63 mg cholesterol, 389 mg sodium, 10 g carbohydrate, 3 g fiber, 26 g protein.

CHICKEN SALAD WITH CRISPY WONTONS

Chicken Salad with Crispy Wontons

Kylea Rorabaugh, Kansas City, Missouri

Here's a quick easy meal. My mom made it when I was growing up, but I added veggies and lightened the sweet-and-sour dressing. I also broil the crispy wontons instead of frying them.

- 10 wonton wrappers, cut into 1/4-inch strips
- 1/4 cup cider vinegar
- 3 tablespoons canola oil
- 3/4 teaspoon sesame oil
- 2 tablespoons sugar
- 3/4 teaspoon salt
- 1/4 teaspoon pepper
- 5 cups torn romaine
- 3 cups cubed cooked chicken breast
- 1 medium sweet red pepper, cut into 1/4-inch strips
- 1 medium sweet yellow pepper, cut into 1/4-inch strips
- 1/2 cup halved grape tomatoes

1) Lightly spritz both sides of wonton strips with nonstick cooking spray; place on a baking sheet. Broil 4-6 in. from the heat for 2-3 minutes or until golden brown. Turn strips over; broil 2-3 minutes longer or until golden brown. Remove to wire racks to cool.

2) For dressing, in a small bowl, whisk the vinegar, oils, sugar, salt and pepper; set aside. In a large bowl, combine the romaine, chicken, peppers and tomatoes. Just before serving, drizzle with dressing and toss to coat. Top with wonton strips.

Yield: 10 servings.

NUTRITION FACTS: 1 cup equals 149 calories, 6 g fat (1 g saturated fat), 33 mg cholesterol, 253 mg sodium, 10 g carbohydrate, 1 g fiber, 14 g protein.

Turkey Marsala

Deborah Williams, Wildwood, Missouri

This recipe originally called for beef, but I used turkey to make it healthier. It's easy to prepare, but the rich sauce makes it seem like you spent all day in the kitchen. I serve this with a baked sweet potato and a green vegetable.

- 1 package (20 ounces) turkey breast tenderloins
- 1/4 cup all-purpose flour
- 1/2 teaspoon salt, *divided*
- 1/2 teaspoon pepper, *divided*
- 1 tablespoon olive oil
- 1/2 pound fresh mushrooms, sliced
- 1 tablespoon butter
- 1/2 cup reduced-sodium chicken broth
- 1/2 cup Marsala wine *or* 1/3 cup reduced-sodium chicken broth, 3 tablespoons white grape juice and 2 teaspoons white wine vinegar
- 1 teaspoon lemon juice

1) Cut tenderloins in half and flatten to 3/4-in. thickness. In a large resealable plastic bag, combine the flour, 1/4 teaspoon salt and 1/4 teaspoon pepper. Add turkey and shake to coat.

2) In a large nonstick skillet, cook turkey in oil over medium heat for 7-8 minutes on each side or until juices run clear. Remove and keep warm.

3) In the same skillet, saute mushrooms in butter for 4 minutes or until tender. Stir in the broth and wine or broth mixture. Cook over medium heat for 12-15 minutes or until liquid is reduced by half. Stir in lemon juice and remaining salt and pepper. Serve over turkey.

Yield: 4 servings.

NUTRITION FACTS: 4 ounces cooked turkey with 1/4 cup mushroom mixture equals 295 calories, 8 g fat (3 g saturated fat), 77 mg cholesterol, 482 mg sodium, 12 g carbohydrate, 1 g fiber, 36 g protein.

Peppery Herbed Turkey Tenderloin

Virginia Anthony, Blowing Rock, North Carolina

I won the North Carolina Turkey Cook-Off one year with these full-flavored tenderloins in rich sauce. Marinating the turkey in wine, garlic, rosemary and thyme gives it a fantastic taste.

- 3 turkey breast tenderloins (12 ounces *each*)
- 1 cup dry white wine *or* apple juice
- 3 green onions, chopped
- 3 tablespoons minced fresh parsley
- 6 teaspoons olive oil, *divided*
- 1 tablespoon finely chopped garlic
- 3/4 teaspoon dried rosemary, crushed
- 3/4 teaspoon dried thyme
- 1 teaspoon coarsely ground pepper
- 3/4 teaspoon salt, *divided*
- 4 teaspoons cornstarch
- 1 cup reduced-sodium chicken broth

1) Pat tenderloins dry; flatten to 3/4-in. thickness. In a bowl, combine the wine or juice, onions, parsley, 4 teaspoons oil, garlic, rosemary and thyme.

2) Pour 3/4 cup marinade into a large resealable plastic bag; add turkey. Seal bag and turn to coat; refrigerate for at least 4 hours, turning occasionally. Cover and refrigerate remaining marinade.

3) Drain and discard marinade from turkey. Sprinkle turkey with pepper and 1/2 teaspoon salt. In a large nonstick skillet, cook turkey in remaining oil for 5-6 minutes on each side or until no longer pink. Remove and keep warm.

4) In a small bowl, combine the cornstarch, broth, reserved marinade and remaining salt until smooth; pour into skillet. Bring to a boil; cook and stir for 1-2 minutes or until thickened. Slice turkey; serve with sauce.

Yield: 6 servings.

Editor's Note: If using the broth instead of wine, add 1 tablespoon white wine vinegar *or* cider vinegar to the marinade.

NUTRITION FACTS: 5 ounces cooked turkey equals 258 calories, 5 g fat (1 g saturated fat), 116 mg cholesterol, 476 mg sodium, 4 g carbohydrate, trace fiber, 41 g protein.

Brown Rice 'n' Apple Stuffed Turkey

Taste of Home Test Kitchen

Mouth-watering flavors of autumn permeate this lovely stuffing. Apple bits and plump raisins add fruity flavor to the brown rice.

- 1 can (14-1/2 ounces) reduced-sodium chicken broth
- 1/2 cup unsweetened apple juice, *divided*
- 1/2 teaspoon salt, *divided*
- 1 cup uncooked long grain brown rice
- 1/3 cup raisins
- 1/2 cup *each* chopped celery and onion
- 1 tablespoon butter
- 1 cup chopped tart apple
- 1 teaspoon poultry seasoning
- 1/4 teaspoon pepper
- 1 turkey (10 to 12 pounds)

1) In a saucepan, combine broth, 1/3 cup juice and 1/4 teaspoon salt. Bring to a boil. Stir in rice and raisins. Return to a boil. Reduce heat; cover and simmer for 40-50 minutes or until rice is tender.

2) Meanwhile, in a nonstick skillet, cook celery and onion in butter for 2 minutes. Add apple; cook and stir for 3 minutes or until vegetables are tender. Combine the rice mixture, apple mixture, poultry seasoning, pepper and remaining juice and salt.

3) Just before baking, loosely stuff turkey. Skewer turkey openings; tie drumsticks together. Place breast side up on a rack in a roasting pan. Bake, uncovered, at 325° for 2-3/4 to 3 hours or until a meat thermometer reads 180° for the turkey and 165° for the stuffing. (Cover loosely with foil if turkey browns too quickly.)

4) Cover turkey and let stand for 20 minutes. Remove stuffing and carve turkey, discarding skin. If desired, thicken pan drippings for gravy.

Yield: 6 servings with leftovers.

Editor's Note: Stuffing may be prepared as directed and baked separately in a 1-1/2-qt. baking dish coated with nonstick cooking spray. Cover; bake at 325° for 25 minutes. Uncover; bake 10-15 minutes longer or until heated through.

NUTRITION FACTS: 3 ounces cooked turkey with 3/4 cup stuffing (calculated without gravy) equals 286 calories, 8 g fat (3 g saturated fat), 51 mg cholesterol, 443 mg sodium, 37 g carbohydrate, 3 g fiber, 17 g protein.

Turkey Biscuit Bake
Taste of Home Test Kitchen

This lightened up recipe started with 40 grams of fat per serving. The results are a better-for-you bake that's just as satisfying.

- 1 cup baby carrots, halved lengthwise
- 1 cup julienned parsnips
- 1 tablespoon water
- 2 cups sliced fresh mushrooms
- 2 tablespoons butter
- 1/2 cup all-purpose flour
- 1/2 teaspoon salt
- 1/8 teaspoon white pepper
- 4 cups fat-free milk
- 3 cups diced cooked turkey breast
- 1/2 cup frozen peas, thawed

BISCUITS:
- 1 cup all-purpose flour
- 1/2 cup cake flour
- 3/4 teaspoon baking powder
- 1/2 teaspoon salt
- 1/8 teaspoon baking soda
- 1 egg
- 1/2 cup 1% buttermilk
- 2 tablespoons butter, melted

1) In a microwave-safe bowl, combine carrots, parsnips and water; cover and microwave on high for 4-5 minutes or until tender. Drain and set aside.

2) In a large nonstick skillet, saute mushrooms in butter until tender. Combine flour, salt, pepper and milk until smooth; stir into mushrooms. Bring to a boil; cook and stir for 1-2 minutes or until thickened. Stir in the carrots, parsnips, turkey and peas. Transfer to a 13-in. x 9-in. x 2-in. baking dish coated with nonstick cooking spray.

3) For biscuits, in a bowl, combine the flours, baking powder, salt and baking soda. Combine the egg, buttermilk and butter; stir into dry ingredients until a soft dough forms. Drop dough into nine mounds onto turkey mixture.

4) Bake at 425° for 15-18 minutes or until a toothpick inserted in biscuits comes out clean and biscuits are golden brown.

Yield: 9 servings.

NUTRITION FACTS: 2/3 cup turkey mixture with 1 biscuit equals 290 calories, 7 g fat (4 g saturated fat), 82 mg cholesterol, 494 mg sodium, 32 g carbohydrate, 2 g fiber, 24 g protein.

Salsa Fish Skillet
Taste of Home Test Kitchen

Zucchini and yellow summer squash add seasonal flair to this colorful fish dish.

- 1 pound halibut steaks *or* other firm whitefish, cut into 1-inch pieces
- 3 teaspoons canola oil, *divided*
- 1 medium yellow summer squash, julienned
- 1 medium zucchini, julienned
- 1 cup sliced fresh mushrooms
- 2 garlic cloves, minced
- 1/4 to 1/2 teaspoon ground cumin
- 1-1/2 cups chunky salsa
- 4 teaspoons minced fresh cilantro

1) In a large nonstick skillet or wok, stir-fry halibut in 2 teaspoons hot oil for 3-4 minutes or until fish flakes easily with a fork; remove and keep warm.

2) Add the yellow squash, zucchini, mushrooms, garlic, cumin and remaining oil to the pan. Stir-fry for 2-3 minutes or until vegetables are crisp-tender. Return fish to the pan. Add salsa; heat through. Sprinkle with cilantro.

Yield: 4 servings.

NUTRITION FACTS: 1 cup equals 207 calories, 6 g fat (1 g saturated fat), 36 mg cholesterol, 486 mg sodium, 11 g carbohydrate, 3 g fiber, 27 g protein.

Baked Flounder

Brenda Taylor, Benton, Kentucky

I fix this fish frequently because my husband is on a low-calorie diet, and my whole family enjoys it. The flounder is baked on a bed of mushrooms and green onions and topped with bread crumbs and reduced-fat cheese.

- 2/3 cup sliced green onions
- 1/2 cup sliced fresh mushrooms
- 2 pounds flounder *or* sole fillets
- 1 teaspoon dried marjoram
- 1/2 teaspoon salt
- 1/8 teaspoon pepper
- 2 tablespoons dry white wine *or* chicken broth
- 2 teaspoons lemon juice
- 1/4 cup shredded reduced-fat Mexican cheese blend
- 1/4 cup soft whole wheat bread crumbs
- 2 tablespoons butter, melted

1) Sprinkle the green onions and mushrooms into a 13-in. x 9-in. x 2-in. baking dish coated with nonstick cooking spray. Arrange the fish over vegetables, overlapping the thickest end of fillets over the thin end. Sprinkle with marjoram, salt and pepper.

2) Pour wine or broth and lemon juice over fish. Cover with cheese and bread crumbs; drizzle with butter. Bake, uncovered, at 400° for 10-12 minutes or until fish flakes easily with a fork.

Yield: 6 servings.

NUTRITION FACTS: 1 serving equals 212 calories, 7 g fat (4 g saturated fat), 86 mg cholesterol, 438 mg sodium, 5 g carbohydrate, 1 g fiber, 31 g protein.

Lemon-Soy Sauce Roughy

Anne Powers, Munford, Alabama

I enjoy fried fish very much, but my doctor said it's a no-no! So this is a very tasty way to prepare fish without adding lots of extra fat and calories.

- 1/4 cup lemon juice
- 1/4 cup reduced-sodium soy sauce
- 1 tablespoon sugar
- 1/2 teaspoon ground ginger
- 4 fresh *or* frozen orange roughy fillets (6 ounces *each*), thawed
- 1/2 teaspoon salt-free lemon-pepper seasoning

1) In a large resealable plastic bag, combine juice, soy sauce, sugar and ginger; add fish. Seal bag and turn to coat; refrigerate for 30 minutes.

2) Drain and discard marinade. Arrange fillets in a 15-in. x 10-in. x 1-in. baking pan coated with nonstick cooking spray; sprinkle with lemon-pepper. Bake, uncovered, at 350° for 12-15 minutes or until fish flakes easily with a fork.

Yield: 4 servings.

NUTRITION FACTS: 1 fillet equals 124 calories, 1 g fat (trace saturated fat), 34 mg cholesterol, 258 mg sodium, 1 g carbohydrate, trace fiber, 25 g protein.

FLOUNDER ZUCCHINI BUNDLES

Flounder Zucchini Bundles

Isabelle Rooney, Summerville, South Carolina

A lovely hint of lemon carries the flavors of this colorful meal-in-one. My husband is not a fish eater, but he certainly enjoys this recipe.

- 8 flounder fillets (3 ounces *each*)
- 1/4 teaspoon lemon-pepper seasoning
- 1 medium lemon, thinly sliced
- 1 medium zucchini, cut into 1/4-inch slices
- 12 cherry tomatoes, halved
- 1/4 teaspoon dill weed
- 1/4 teaspoon dried basil

1) For each bundle, place two fillets on a double thickness of heavy-duty foil (18 in. x 15 in.); sprinkle with lemon-pepper. Top with lemon slices, zucchini and tomatoes. Sprinkle with dill and basil.

2) Fold foil around fish and seal tightly. Place on a baking sheet. Bake at 425° for 15-20 minutes or until fish flakes easily with a fork.

Yield: 4 servings.

NUTRITION FACTS: 1 bundle equals 159 calories, 2 g fat (trace saturated fat), 80 mg cholesterol, 160 mg sodium, 5 g carbohydrate, 1 g fiber, 29 g protein.

FIERY SKEWERED SHRIMP

Fiery Skewered Shrimp
Kara de la Vega, Somerset, California

This easy-to-make entree gets its great taste from a simple yet spicy marinade. You can broil the kabobs or throw them on the grill outside. We like to serve the shrimp on a bed of greens.

- 1 tablespoon olive oil
- 2 garlic cloves, minced
- 1/2 to 1 teaspoon crushed red pepper flakes
- 1 teaspoon minced fresh gingerroot
- 1-1/2 pounds uncooked large shrimp, peeled and deveined
- 2 small green peppers, cut into 1-inch squares
- 1 medium lemon, sliced

1) In a shallow bowl, combine the oil, garlic, pepper flakes and ginger. Add shrimp; stir to coat evenly. Cover and refrigerate for 2 hours.

2) Thread shrimp and green peppers alternately on metal or soaked wooden skewers. Place on a broiler pan coated with nonstick cooking spray.

3) Broil 4-6 in. from the heat for 3 minutes. Turn; broil 2-3 minutes longer or until shrimp turn pink. Garnish with lemon slices.

Yield: 4 servings.

NUTRITION FACTS: 1 serving equals 173 calories, 5 g fat (1 g saturated fat), 252 mg cholesterol, 291 mg sodium, 4 g carbohydrate, 1 g fiber, 28 g protein.

Scallops and Asparagus Stir-Fry
Lisa Lancaster, Tracy, California

Savory scallops, crisp-tender asparagus and juicy cherry tomatoes blend together beautifully in this fresh-tasting stir-fry. Sesame oil and soy sauce delicately accent the colorful combo that's festive enough to serve when company comes.

- 3/4 pound fresh asparagus, trimmed and cut into 2-inch pieces
- 1 tablespoon cornstarch
- 3/4 cup chicken broth
- 1 teaspoon reduced-sodium soy sauce
- 3/4 pound sea scallops, halved
- 1 cup sliced fresh mushrooms
- 1 garlic clove, minced
- 2 teaspoons canola oil
- 1 cup halved cherry tomatoes
- 2 green onions, sliced
- 1 teaspoon sesame oil
- 1/8 teaspoon pepper
- 2 cups hot cooked rice

1) Place asparagus in a saucepan and cover with water; bring to a boil. Cook, uncovered, for 3-5 minutes or until crisp-tender; drain and set aside. In a small bowl, combine the cornstarch, broth and soy sauce until smooth; set aside.

2) In a large nonstick skillet or wok, stir-fry scallops, mushrooms and garlic in canola oil until scallops are opaque and mushrooms are tender. Stir cornstarch mixture; add to skillet. Bring to a boil; cook and stir for 1-2 minutes until sauce is thickened.

3) Add the asparagus, tomatoes, onions, sesame oil and pepper; heat through. Serve over rice.

Yield: 4 servings.

NUTRITION FACTS: 1 cup stir-fry mixture with 1/2 cup rice equals 215 calories, 5 g fat (1 g saturated fat), 14 mg cholesterol, 314 mg sodium, 30 g carbohydrate, 2 g fiber, 11 g protein.

Easy Smoked Salmon
Norma Fell, Boyne City, Michigan

A fellow *Taste of Home* reader shared this recipe years ago...and it has become my favorite way to prepare salmon.

- 1 salmon fillet (about 2 pounds)
- 2 tablespoons brown sugar
- 2 teaspoons salt
- 1/2 teaspoon pepper
- 1 to 2 tablespoons Liquid Smoke

1) Place salmon, skin side down, in an 11-in. x 7-in. x 2-in. baking pan coated with nonstick cooking spray. Sprinkle with brown sugar, salt and pepper. Drizzle with Liquid Smoke. Cover and refrigerate for 4-8 hours.

2) Drain and discard liquid. Bake, uncovered, at 350° for 35-45 minutes or until fish flakes easily with a fork. Cool to room temperature. Cover and refrigerate for 8 hours or overnight.

Yield: 16 servings.

NUTRITION FACTS: 2 ounces equals 110 calories, 6 g fat (1 g saturated fat), 33 mg cholesterol, 327 mg sodium, 2 g carbohydrate, trace fiber, 11 g protein.

SHRIMP SALAD WITH VINAIGRETTE

Shrimp Salad with Vinaigrette
Lisa Casey, Roanoke, Virginia

This is a wonderful light main dish to serve when you aren't in the mood for a heavy meal. I love the fresh seafood flavor and hint of citrus in the dressing.

- 3 tablespoons white wine vinegar
- 1 garlic clove, minced
- 1 teaspoon sugar
- 1 teaspoon grated orange peel
- 3 tablespoons olive oil
- 2 medium navel oranges, peeled
- 1 pound cooked medium shrimp, peeled and deveined
- 1 tablespoon diced pimientos
- 5 cups torn Bibb *or* Boston lettuce
- 5 cups torn leaf lettuce
- 1/4 cup sliced green onions

1) In a large bowl, combine the vinegar, garlic, sugar and orange peel. Whisk in oil; set aside. Cut oranges into 1/2-in. slices; cut slices into quarters. Add oranges, shrimp and pimientos to dressing; toss to coat.

2) Cover and chill for at least 1 hour. Just before serving, toss the shrimp mixture with lettuces and onions.

Yield: 6 servings.

NUTRITION FACTS: 2 cups equals 174 calories, 8 g fat (1 g saturated fat), 115 mg cholesterol, 130 mg sodium, 9 g carbohydrate, 2 g fiber, 17 g protein.

Grilled Tuna with Pineapple Salsa
Beveylon Concha, Chesapeake, Virginia

After spending some time in Honolulu, I came upon this tropical treatment for tuna. I prepare the pineapple salsa for everything from grilled fish to pork and poultry.

- 1/2 medium fresh pineapple, peeled and cut into 1/2-inch slices
- 1 small onion, diced
- 2 jalapeno peppers, seeded and diced
- 2 tablespoons minced fresh cilantro
- 2 tablespoons lime juice
- 4 tuna steaks (6 ounces *each*)
- 1 tablespoon olive oil
- 1/4 teaspoon salt
- 1/4 teaspoon pepper

1) Grill pineapple slices, uncovered, over medium heat for 5-7 minutes on each side. Chill for 30 minutes. Dice the pineapple; place in a bowl. Stir in the onion, jalapenos, cilantro and lime juice. Refrigerate for 1 hour or until chilled.

2) Brush tuna steaks with oil; sprinkle with salt and pepper. Grill, covered, over medium heat for 5 minutes on each side or until fish flakes easily with a fork. Serve with pineapple salsa.

Yield: 4 servings.

Editor's Note: When cutting or seeding hot peppers, use rubber or plastic gloves to protect your hands. Avoid touching your face.

NUTRITION FACTS: 1 tuna steak with 1/2 cup salsa equals 252 calories, 5 g fat (1 g saturated fat), 77 mg cholesterol, 212 mg sodium, 10 g carbohydrate, 1 g fiber, 40 g protein.

Veggie Egg Scramble

Phyllis Behringer, Defiance, Ohio

While staying with friends one weekend, we enjoyed the most wonderful eggs. I created this version to reduce the calorie and fat content. White wine turns this egg dish into a sophisticated brunch specialty.

- 6 egg whites
- 2 eggs
- 1/4 cup white wine *or* chicken broth
- 1/4 teaspoon salt
- 1/8 teaspoon pepper
- 1/8 teaspoon garlic powder
- 1/2 cup chopped green pepper
- 1/2 cup chopped onion
- 1/2 cup sliced fresh mushrooms
- 1 teaspoon butter
- 1 teaspoon olive oil
- 1/2 cup shredded reduced-fat cheddar cheese
- 2 teaspoons minced fresh basil

1) In a bowl, whisk the egg whites, eggs, wine or broth, salt, pepper and garlic powder; set aside. In a large nonstick skillet, saute the green pepper, onion and mushrooms in butter and oil for 3 minutes or until crisp-tender.

2) Reduce heat to medium. Stir in the egg mixture; cook and stir until eggs are completely set. Sprinkle with cheese and basil. Cover and remove from the heat; let stand for 5 minutes or until cheese is melted.

Yield: 3 servings.

NUTRITION FACTS: 1 cup equals 201 calories, 10 g fat (5 g saturated fat), 158 mg cholesterol, 365 mg sodium, 8 g carbohydrate, 1 g fiber, 18 g protein.

Vegetarian Jambalaya

Lynn Marie Frucci, Pullman, Washington

This make-ahead main or side dish has all the flavor and boldness of traditional jambalaya. If there's any left over, roll it up in a flour tortilla and add your favorite topping.

- 1 medium onion, finely chopped
- 1 cup chopped celery
- 1 cup chopped green pepper
- 1 cup sliced fresh mushrooms
- 2 garlic cloves, minced
- 1 teaspoon olive oil
- 3 cups chopped fresh tomatoes
- 2 cups water
- 1 cup uncooked long grain rice
- 2 tablespoons reduced-sodium soy sauce
- 1 tablespoon minced fresh parsley
- 1/4 teaspoon salt
- 1/4 teaspoon paprika
- 1/8 teaspoon cayenne pepper
- 1/8 teaspoon chili powder
- 1/8 teaspoon pepper
- 6 tablespoons reduced-fat sour cream

1) In a large nonstick skillet, saute the onion, celery, green pepper, mushrooms and garlic in oil until tender. Stir in the tomatoes, water, rice, soy sauce, parsley, salt, paprika, cayenne, chili powder and pepper.

2) Transfer to a 2-1/2-qt. baking dish coated with nonstick cooking spray. Cover and bake at 350° for 65-70 minutes or until rice is tender and liquid is absorbed. Top each serving with 1 tablespoon sour cream.

Yield: 6 servings.

NUTRITION FACTS: 1 cup equals 187 calories, 3 g fat (1 g saturated fat), 5 mg cholesterol, 339 mg sodium, 36 g carbohydrate, 3 g fiber, 5 g protein.

Pinto Bean Stew

Gina Passantino, Amherst, New York

This thick, hearty stew is chock-full of beans and vegetables and makes a wonderful supper on cold winter days. It also freezes well.

- 1 cup dried pinto beans
- 2 cups cold water
- 1/2 cup chopped carrot
- 2 garlic cloves, minced
- 3/4 teaspoon chili powder
- 1/2 teaspoon salt
- Dash cayenne pepper
- 1 package (16 ounces) frozen corn, thawed
- 1 large onion, chopped
- 1 medium green pepper, chopped
- 1 can (14-1/2 ounces) diced tomatoes, undrained
- 2 to 3 teaspoons balsamic vinegar
- 1/4 teaspoon sugar

1) Place the beans in a large saucepan; add water to cover by 2 in. Bring to a boil; boil for 2 minutes.

Remove from the heat; cover and let stand for 1-4 hours or until softened.

2) Drain and rinse beans, discarding liquid. Return beans to the pan; add cold water, carrot, garlic, chili powder, salt and cayenne. Bring to a boil. Reduce heat; cover and simmer for 45 minutes or until beans are almost tender.

3) In a nonstick skillet coated with nonstick cooking spray, saute the corn, onion and green pepper until tender. Add to the bean mixture. Cover and cook for 45 minutes.

4) Stir in the tomatoes, vinegar and sugar. Cook 5 minutes longer or until heated through.

Yield: 6 servings.

NUTRITION FACTS: 1 cup equals 214 calories, 1 g fat (trace saturated fat), 0 cholesterol, 309 mg sodium, 45 g carbohydrate, 10 g fiber, 10 g protein.

VEGETARIAN TACO SALAD

Vegetarian Taco Salad
Susan LeBrun, Sulphur, Louisiana

The cute tortilla bowls that hold this Southwestern salad are a snap to bake. We use canned beans that include hot spices to punch up the flavor.

- 4 **whole wheat tortillas (8 inches)**
- 6 **cups shredded romaine**
- 1/2 **cup canned pinto beans, rinsed and drained**
- 1 **small tomato, chopped**
- 1/4 **cup shredded reduced-fat cheddar cheese**
- 1/4 **cup chopped green onions**

- 2 **tablespoons sliced ripe olives, drained**
- **Sliced jalapeno peppers, optional**

DRESSING:
- 1/2 **cup fat-free sour cream**
- 2 **tablespoons prepared fat-free ranch salad dressing**
- 1 **teaspoon taco seasoning**
- 1/4 **teaspoon hot pepper sauce, optional**

1) Place four 10-oz. custard cups upside down in a shallow baking pan; set aside. Place the tortillas in a single layer on ungreased baking sheets. Bake at 425° for 1 minute.

2) Place a tortilla over each custard cup, pinching sides to form a bowl shape. Bake for 7-8 minutes or until crisp. Remove tortillas from cups to cool on wire racks.

3) In a large bowl, combine the romaine, beans, tomato, cheese, onions, olives and jalapenos if desired. In a small bowl, whisk the dressing ingredients; pour over salad and toss to coat. Serve in tortilla bowls.

Yield: 4 servings.

NUTRITION FACTS: 1 tortilla bowl with 1-1/4 cups salad equals 194 calories, 3 g fat (1 g saturated fat), 10 mg cholesterol, 489 mg sodium, 38 g carbohydrate, 5 g fiber, 10 g protein.

Spanish Rice
Sharon Donat, Kalispell, Montana

This rice recipe has been in our family for years. It's handy when you're in a hurry for a side dish to complement almost any main dish, not just Tex-Mex fare.

- 1 **can (14-1/2 ounces) vegetable broth**
- 1 **can (14-1/2 ounces) stewed tomatoes**
- 1 **cup uncooked long grain rice**
- 1 **teaspoon olive oil**
- 1 **teaspoon chili powder**
- 1/4 **teaspoon dried oregano**
- 1/4 **teaspoon garlic salt**

1) In a large saucepan, combine all ingredients. Bring to a boil. Reduce heat; cover and simmer for 20-25 minutes or until rice is tender and liquid is absorbed.

Yield: 6 servings.

NUTRITION FACTS: 2/3 cup equals 156 calories, 1 g fat (trace saturated fat), 0 cholesterol, 350 mg sodium, 32 g carbohydrate, 1 g fiber, 4 g protein.

VEGETABLE BARLEY BAKE

Vegetable Barley Bake
Shirley Doyle, Mt. Prospect, Illinois

Forget the potatoes or rice, and consider this change-of-pace dinner accompaniment. I rely on wholesome barley for the heart-smart dish that complements most any main course.

- 3 medium sweet red *or* green peppers, chopped
- 4 cups sliced fresh mushrooms
- 2 medium onions, chopped
- 2 tablespoons butter
- 2 cups reduced-sodium chicken broth *or* vegetable broth
- 1-1/2 cups medium pearl barley
- 1/8 teaspoon pepper

1) In a large nonstick skillet, saute the peppers, mushrooms and onions in butter for 8-10 minutes or until tender. Transfer to a 13-in. x 9-in. x 2-in. baking dish coated with nonstick cooking spray. Stir in the broth, barley and pepper.

2) Cover and bake at 350° for 50 minutes. Uncover; bake 5-10 minutes longer or until barley is tender and liquid is absorbed.

Yield: 10 servings.

NUTRITION FACTS: 3/4 cup equals 157 calories, 3 g fat (2 g saturated fat), 6 mg cholesterol, 153 mg sodium, 30 g carbohydrate, 6 g fiber, 5 g protein.

Great Grain Pilaf
Joyce Graves, Sterling Heights, Michigan

This pilaf is mild tasting and a great way to include fiber in your diet. Because I like experimenting with different grains, I buy at a bulk food store. Being able to purchase just the amount you need for a recipe is a real advantage.

- 1/2 cup chopped green onions
- 2 garlic cloves, minced
- 2 teaspoons butter
- 1 cup uncooked long grain rice
- 1/2 cup bulgur
- 1/4 cup quick-cooking barley
- 3 cups reduced-sodium chicken broth *or* vegetable broth
- 1/2 teaspoon salt
- Dash pepper
- 1/3 cup minced fresh parsley

1) In a large saucepan, saute onions and garlic in butter until tender. Add the rice, bulgur and barley; cook and stir for 5 minutes.

2) Gradually stir in the broth, salt and pepper. Bring to a boil. Reduce heat; cover and simmer for 25 minutes or until grains are tender and broth is absorbed. Stir in parsley.

Yield: 8 servings.

NUTRITION FACTS: 2/3 cup equals 154 calories, 2 g fat (1 g saturated fat), 4 mg cholesterol, 202 mg sodium, 30 g carbohydrate, 3 g fiber, 5 g protein.

Ziti Alfredo with Vegetables
Emma Magielda, Amsterdam, New York

A creamy dressing and an unexpected hint of nutmeg make this hearty pasta dish so delicious. I can't resist fixing it often.

- 1 medium onion, chopped
- 2 garlic cloves, minced
- 2 teaspoons olive oil
- 8 ounces uncooked ziti *or* small tube pasta
- 2 tablespoons butter
- 3 tablespoons all-purpose flour
- 1 cup fat-free milk
- 1-1/2 cups fat-free half-and-half
- 1 cup shredded Parmesan cheese
- 2 teaspoons Italian seasoning
- 1/4 teaspoon salt
- Dash white pepper
- Dash ground nutmeg
- 1 can (14-1/2 ounces) Italian diced tomatoes, drained
- 1 package (10 ounces) frozen chopped spinach, thawed and squeezed dry

1) In a small saucepan, saute onion and garlic in oil until tender; set aside. Cook the ziti according

to package directions. Meanwhile, in a large saucepan, melt butter; stir in flour until smooth. Reduce heat; slowly add milk.

2) Stir in half-and-half. Bring to a boil over medium-low heat; cook and stir for 2 minutes or until thickened. Reduce heat; add the Parmesan cheese, Italian seasoning, salt, pepper and nutmeg. Stir until cheese is melted.

3) Add the tomatoes, spinach and onion mixture; heat through. Drain the ziti; toss with vegetable mixture.

Yield: 8 servings.

NUTRITION FACTS: 1 cup equals 264 calories, 8 g fat (4 g saturated fat), 16 mg cholesterol, 488 mg sodium, 35 g carbohydrate, 3 g fiber, 13 g protein.

FETTUCCINE PRIMAVERA

Fettuccine Primavera
Marietta Howell, Okmulgee, Oklahoma

A mild lemon sauce seasoned with thyme lightly coats this attractive medley of tender chicken, pasta, asparagus, red pepper and peas.

- 8 ounces uncooked fettuccine
- 1 cup julienned sweet red pepper
- 1 tablespoon canola oil
- 1/2 pound boneless skinless chicken breasts, cut into 1/4-inch strips
- 6 green onions, sliced
- 1/2 pound fresh asparagus, trimmed and cut into 1-inch pieces
- 3/4 cup chicken broth
- 1-1/2 teaspoons lemon juice
- 1/2 teaspoon salt
- 1/2 teaspoon dried thyme
- 1/2 teaspoon grated lemon peel

- 2/3 cup frozen peas, thawed
- 2 teaspoons cornstarch
- 1 tablespoon water
- 2 tablespoons reduced-fat sour cream
- 1/4 cup shredded Parmesan cheese

1) Cook fettuccine according to package directions. Meanwhile, in a 12-in. nonstick skillet, saute red pepper in oil for 3 minutes or until crisp-tender.

2) Stir in the chicken, onions, asparagus, broth, lemon juice, salt, thyme and lemon peel. Cook for 1 minute or until asparagus is crisp-tender. Stir in peas; saute for 1 minute or until heated through.

3) Combine cornstarch and water until smooth; stir into chicken mixture. Bring to a boil; cook and stir for 1-2 minutes or until thickened and chicken is no longer pink.

4) Remove from heat; stir in sour cream. Transfer to a large bowl. Drain fettuccine and add to chicken mixture. Sprinkle with Parmesan cheese and toss to coat.

Yield: 6 servings.

NUTRITION FACTS: 1-1/3 cups equals 274 calories, 6 g fat (2 g saturated fat), 27 mg cholesterol, 431 mg sodium, 38 g carbohydrate, 4 g fiber, 18 g protein.

Whipped Cauliflower
Taste of Home Test Kitchen

Need a low-carb substitute for mashed potatoes? This five-ingredient dish has a mild cauliflower flavor with a smooth creamy texture.

- 1 medium head cauliflower, cut into florets
- 1/4 cup fat-free milk
- 2 tablespoons canola oil
- 1/4 teaspoon salt
- 1/8 teaspoon white pepper

1) Place cauliflower in a steamer basket; place in a saucepan over 1 in. of water. Bring to a boil; cover and steam for 8-10 minutes or until tender. Cool slightly.

2) Place milk and oil in a blender or food processor. Add the cauliflower, salt and pepper; cover and process until blended. Transfer to a bowl. Serve immediately.

Yield: 4 servings.

NUTRITION FACTS: 1/2 cup equals 105 calories, 7 g fat (1 g saturated fat), 1 mg cholesterol, 199 mg sodium, 8 g carbohydrate, 4 g fiber, 3 g protein.

Light 'n' Creamy Mashed Potatoes

Taste of Home Test Kitchen

You'd never know that these mashed potatoes are on the lighter side. Garlic and chives season them while sour cream and cream cheese add richness.

- 6 cups quartered peeled potatoes (about 3 pounds)
- 4 ounces fat-free cream cheese, cubed
- 1/2 cup reduced-fat sour cream
- 1/2 cup fat-free milk
- 3/4 teaspoon salt
- 1/4 teaspoon garlic powder
- 1/4 teaspoon pepper
- 1 tablespoon minced chives

Dash paprika

1) Place potatoes in a saucepan and cover with water. Bring to a boil. Reduce heat; cover and cook for 10-15 minutes or until tender. Drain.

2) In a large mixing bowl, mash the potatoes. Add the cream cheese, sour cream, milk, salt, garlic powder and pepper; beat until smooth. Stir in chives. Sprinkle with paprika.

Yield: 8 servings.

NUTRITION FACTS: 2/3 cup equals 140 calories, 2 g fat (1 g saturated fat), 6 mg cholesterol, 322 mg sodium, 26 g carbohydrate, 2 g fiber, 6 g protein.

MUSHROOM BROCCOLI PIZZA

Mushroom Broccoli Pizza

Kathleen Kelly, Days Creek, Oregon

I wouldn't say I'm a vegetarian, but I do like meatless entrees. Since I enjoy gardening, I often cook with homegrown veggies.

- 1 package (1/4 ounce) active dry yeast
- 3/4 cup warm water (110° to 115°)
- 1 teaspoon olive oil
- 1/2 teaspoon sugar
- 1/2 cup whole wheat flour
- 1/2 teaspoon salt
- 1-1/2 cups all-purpose flour

TOPPINGS:

- 3 cups broccoli florets
- 1 cup sliced fresh mushrooms
- 1/4 cup chopped onion
- 4 garlic cloves, minced
- 1 tablespoon olive oil
- 1/2 cup pizza sauce
- 4 plum tomatoes, sliced lengthwise
- 1/4 cup chopped fresh basil
- 1-1/2 cups (6 ounces) shredded part-skim mozzarella cheese
- 1/3 cup shredded Parmesan cheese

1) In a bowl, dissolve yeast in warm water. Add oil and sugar; mix well. Combine whole wheat flour and salt; stir into yeast mixture until smooth. Stir in enough all-purpose flour to form a soft dough.

2) Turn onto a floured surface; knead until smooth and elastic, about 6-8 minutes. Place in a bowl coated with nonstick cooking spray, turning once to coat top. Cover and let rise in a warm place until doubled, about 1-1/2 hours.

3) Punch dough down. Press onto the bottom and 1 in. up the sides of a 12-in. pizza pan coated with nonstick cooking spray. Prick dough several times with a fork. Bake at 425° for 6-8 minutes.

4) Place broccoli in a steamer basket; place in a saucepan over 1 in. of water. Bring to a boil; cover and steam for 5-6 minutes or until crisp-tender. Transfer broccoli to a colander. Rinse with cold water; drain and set aside.

5) In a nonstick skillet, saute mushrooms, onion and garlic in oil until mushrooms are tender. Spread pizza sauce over crust. Top with mushroom mixture, tomatoes, broccoli, basil and cheeses. Bake at 425° for 12-14 minutes or until crust is golden and cheese is melted.

Yield: 6 slices.

NUTRITION FACTS: 1 slice equals 283 calories, 9 g fat (4 g saturated fat), 19 mg cholesterol, 492 mg sodium, 39 g carbohydrate, 4 g fiber, 15 g protein.

THREE-PEPPER CORN PUDDING

Three-Pepper Corn Pudding
Virginia Anthony, Jacksonville, Florida

Red peppers, chili peppers and jalapeno peppers liven up this comforting side dish. I lightened it up from the original by using reduced-fat sour cream and milk, plus fewer eggs. It tastes just as good...but it's much better for us!

- 1 medium sweet red pepper, chopped
- 6 green onions, thinly sliced
- 1 tablespoon olive oil
- 1 can (4 ounces) chopped green chilies, drained
- 3 medium jalapeno peppers, seeded and chopped
- 2 packages (10 ounces *each*) frozen corn, thawed, *divided*
- 1 can (12 ounces) reduced-fat evaporated milk
- 1/3 cup reduced-fat sour cream
- 1/4 cup fat-free milk
- 3 egg whites
- 2 eggs
- 1/4 cup cornstarch
- 1 teaspoon salt
- 1 teaspoon ground cumin
- 3/4 teaspoon ground thyme

1) In a nonstick skillet, saute the red pepper and onions in oil until tender. Remove from the heat. Stir in the chilies, jalapenos and half of the corn. Transfer to a 13-in. x 9-in. x 2-in. baking dish coated with nonstick cooking spray.

2) In a blender, combine the remaining ingredients; add remaining corn. Cover and process for 3 minutes or until smooth. Pour over red pepper mixture. Bake, uncovered, at 350° for 45-50 minutes or until a knife inserted near the center comes out clean.

Yield: 12 servings.

Editor's Note: When cutting or seeding hot peppers, use rubber or plastic gloves to protect your hands. Avoid touching your face.

NUTRITION FACTS: 1 piece equals 119 calories, 3 g fat (1 g saturated fat), 39 mg cholesterol, 298 mg sodium, 18 g carbohydrate, 2 g fiber, 6 g protein.

Green Bean Corn Casserole
Dawn Harvey, Danville, Pennsylvania

This is a classic church-social casserole, which has become a family favorite, even with my extended family. I reduced fat in many of the ingredients and find that it still has a very satisfying flavor that everyone loves.

- 1 can (10-3/4 ounces) reduced-fat condensed cream of celery soup, undiluted
- 1 cup (8 ounces) reduced-fat sour cream
- 1 cup (4 ounces) shredded reduced-fat cheddar cheese
- 1/2 cup finely chopped onion
- 1 package (16 ounces) frozen French-style green beans, thawed
- 2 cups frozen corn, thawed
- 1/4 cup crushed reduced-fat cheese crackers

Refrigerated butter-flavored spray

1) In a large bowl, combine the soup, sour cream, cheese and onion. Stir in the beans and corn. Transfer to a 2-qt. baking dish coated with nonstick cooking spray. Cover and bake at 350° for 25 minutes.

2) Uncover; sprinkle cracker crumbs around the edges. Spritz several times with butter-flavored spray. Bake 10-15 minutes longer or until heated through and edges are lightly browned.

Yield: 7 servings.

Editor's Note: This recipe was tested with I Can't Believe It's Not Butter Spray.

NUTRITION FACTS: 3/4 cup equals 178 calories, 7 g fat (4 g saturated fat), 18 mg cholesterol, 454 mg sodium, 22 g carbohydrate, 3 g fiber, 8 g protein.

Molasses Baked Beans

Erin Anderson, Far Hills, New Jersey

Two types of beans with a little kick from jalapeno pepper help these beans steal the show at potlucks and other get-togethers.

- 1 cup chopped onion
- 1 medium jalapeno pepper, seeded and chopped
- 2 teaspoons olive oil
- 1/2 cup water
- 1/2 cup ketchup
- 3 tablespoons brown sugar
- 3 tablespoons molasses
- 2 tablespoons prepared mustard
- 1 tablespoon chili powder
- 1/2 teaspoon Liquid Smoke, optional
- 2 cans (15-1/2 ounces *each*) great northern beans, rinsed and drained
- 1 can (15 ounces) pinto beans, rinsed and drained

1) In a nonstick skillet, saute onion and jalapeno in oil until onion is tender. Remove from heat. In a large bowl, combine water, ketchup, brown sugar, molasses, mustard, chili powder and Liquid Smoke if desired. Stir in beans and onion mixture.

2) Transfer to a 1-1/2-qt. baking dish coated with nonstick cooking spray. Bake, uncovered, at 350° for 1 hour or until beans are bubbly and as thick as desired.

Yield: 9 servings.

Editor's Note: When cutting or seeding hot peppers, use rubber or plastic gloves to protect your hands. Avoid touching your face.

NUTRITION FACTS: 1/2 cup equals 191 calories, 2 g fat (trace saturated fat), 0 cholesterol, 422 mg sodium, 37 g carbohydrate, 7 g fiber, 7 g protein.

Supreme Potato Casserole

Joy Allen, Forsyth, Georgia

Cottage cheese and sour cream give a delicious creamy coating to the tender cubes of potatoes in this side dish. I usually double the recipe when serving it to guests. They never realize it's light.

- 3 medium potatoes (about 1-1/2 pounds)
- 1 cup (8 ounces) fat-free cottage cheese
- 1/2 cup reduced-fat sour cream
- 1 tablespoon fat-free milk
- 1 teaspoon sugar
- 1/2 teaspoon salt
- 1/8 teaspoon garlic powder
- 2 tablespoons sliced green onion
- 1/2 cup shredded reduced-fat cheddar cheese

1) Place the potatoes in a large saucepan and cover with water. Cover and bring to a boil. Reduce heat; cook for 10-15 minutes or until tender. Drain. Let stand until cool enough to handle. Peel potatoes and cut into cubes.

2) In a blender or food processor, combine the cottage cheese, sour cream, milk, sugar, salt and garlic powder; cover and process until smooth. Transfer to a large bowl; stir in the potatoes and onion. Pour into a 1-qt. baking dish coated with nonstick cooking spray.

3) Bake, uncovered, at 350° for 30 minutes. Sprinkle with cheese. Bake 15 minutes longer or until the cheese is melted.

Yield: 6 servings.

NUTRITION FACTS: 1/2 cup equals 158 calories, 3 g fat (2 g saturated fat), 15 mg cholesterol, 391 mg sodium, 24 g carbohydrate, 2 g fiber, 12 g protein.

Summer Garden Medley

Elaine Nelson, Fresno, California

This side dish brings back memories of the corn-and-tomato dish my mother often prepared. Farmers in our area supply us with eggplant, so I sometimes substitute them for the zucchini.

- 2 medium zucchini, halved lengthwise and cut into 1/4-inch slices
- 1 cup fresh *or* frozen corn, thawed
- 3/4 cup diced green pepper
- 1 medium leek (white portion only), sliced
- 1/2 teaspoon seasoned salt
- 1 tablespoon olive oil
- 2 medium tomatoes, seeded and diced

1) In a large nonstick skillet, saute the zucchini, corn, green pepper, leek and seasoned salt in oil until vegetables are tender. Stir in the tomatoes; heat through.

Yield: 4 servings.

NUTRITION FACTS: 1 cup equals 113 calories, 4 g fat (1 g saturated fat), 0 cholesterol, 202 mg sodium, 19 g carbohydrate, 3 g fiber, 3 g protein.

Lemon Carrots and Rutabaga

Bernice Larsen, Gretna, Nebraska

Ever since I found this recipe in a newspaper, it's become a staple at my house.

 4 medium carrots, cut into 3-inch julienne strips (about 2 cups)
 1 small rutabaga (10 ounces), peeled and cut into 3-inch julienne strips (about 2 cups)
 1/2 cup water
 2 tablespoons butter
 1 tablespoon brown sugar
 1 tablespoon lemon juice
 1/2 teaspoon grated lemon peel
 1/4 teaspoon dill weed

1) In a large saucepan, combine the carrots, rutabaga and water. Bring to a boil. Reduce heat to medium; cover and cook for 13-15 minutes.

2) Meanwhile, in a small saucepan, combine the remaining ingredients; cook, uncovered, over medium heat for 2-3 minutes or until butter is melted.

3) Drain vegetables; add butter mixture. Cook for 3-4 minutes or until vegetables are glazed, stirring occasionally.

Yield: 5 servings.

NUTRITION FACTS: 3/4 cup equals 93 calories, 5 g fat (3 g saturated fat), 12 mg cholesterol, 77 mg sodium, 13 g carbohydrate, 3 g fiber, 1 g protein.

GREENS WITH CREAMY HERBED SALAD DRESSING

Greens with Creamy Herbed Salad Dressing

Janet Les, Chilliwack, British Columbia

If you're looking for a way to spice up everyday greens, try this salad dressing. With its thick consistency, it also makes a delectable veggie dip.

 1/2 cup fat-free mayonnaise
 2 tablespoons plus 2 teaspoons fat-free milk
 4 teaspoons white vinegar
 1 teaspoon dried oregano
 1/2 teaspoon dried basil
 1/4 teaspoon sugar
 1/4 teaspoon salt
 1/4 garlic powder
 1/4 teaspoon pepper
 5 cups mixed salad greens

1) In a small bowl, whisk the mayonnaise, milk and vinegar until combined. Whisk in the oregano, basil, sugar, salt, garlic powder and pepper. Serve over salad greens.

Yield: 5 servings.

NUTRITION FACTS: 1 cup greens with 2 tablespoons dressing equals 33 calories, 1 g fat (trace saturated fat), 3 mg cholesterol, 328 mg sodium, 6 g carbohydrate, 2 g fiber, 1 g protein.

Asian Crunch Salad

Linda Kees, Boise, Idaho

Fresh veggies are lightly coated with a dressing of soy sauce, cider vinegar and sesame oil. You can also add carrots for more color.

 1 cup fresh broccoli florets
 1 cup fresh cauliflowerets
 1 cup cherry tomatoes
 1/2 cup fresh snow peas
 2 green onions, thinly sliced
 1/2 cup sliced water chestnuts, drained
 4-1/2 teaspoons reduced-sodium soy sauce
 1 tablespoon cider vinegar
 1 tablespoon sesame oil
 3/4 teaspoon sugar
 1/2 teaspoon sesame seeds, toasted
 1/2 teaspoon olive oil
Dash pepper

1) In a large bowl, combine the broccoli, cauliflower, tomatoes, peas and onions. Stir in water chestnuts. In a small bowl, whisk the soy sauce, vinegar, sesame oil, sugar, sesame seeds, olive oil and pepper. Pour over vegetables and stir to coat. Cover and refrigerate until chilled.

Yield: 4 servings.

NUTRITION FACTS: 1 cup equals 82 calories, 4 g fat (1 g saturated fat), 0 cholesterol, 246 mg sodium, 10 g carbohydrate, 3 g fiber, 2 g protein.

Crunchy Peanut Coleslaw

Judy Madsen, Ellis, Idaho

When entertaining my large family, I like to offer a buffet of delicious food. This salad has been enjoyed by all.

- 1 cup (8 ounces) reduced-fat sour cream
- 1/2 cup fat-free mayonnaise
- 1 tablespoon sugar
- 1 tablespoon tarragon vinegar
- 1/2 teaspoon salt
- 1/4 teaspoon white pepper
- 4 cups finely chopped cabbage
- 1 cup coarsely chopped cauliflower
- 1 cup chopped celery
- 1/4 cup finely chopped onion
- 1/4 cup chopped green pepper
- 1/4 cup finely chopped cucumber
- 1/2 cup chopped peanuts

1) For dressing, in a small bowl, combine the sour cream, mayonnaise, sugar, vinegar, salt and pepper until blended.

2) In a large bowl, combine the cabbage, cauliflower, celery, onion, green pepper and cucumber. Add dressing and toss to coat. Sprinkle with peanuts.

Yield: 8 servings.

NUTRITION FACTS: 3/4 cup equals 121 calories, 7 g fat (2 g saturated fat), 12 mg cholesterol, 323 mg sodium, 14 g carbohydrate, 3 g fiber, 4 g protein.

TANGY FOUR-BEAN SALAD

Tangy Four-Bean Salad

Sharon Cain, Revelstoke, British Columbia

Canned beans make this colorful salad easy to fix, while a no-fuss dressing lends sweet-and-sour flair. Green pepper and mushrooms help it stand out from other bean medleys.

- 1 can (16 ounces) kidney beans, rinsed and drained
- 1 can (15 ounces) garbanzo beans or chickpeas, rinsed and drained
- 1 can (14-1/2 ounces) cut green beans, drained
- 1 can (14-1/2 ounces) cut wax beans, drained
- 1 cup sliced fresh mushrooms
- 1 cup chopped green pepper
- 1 cup chopped onion

DRESSING:
- 1/2 cup cider vinegar
- 1/3 cup sugar
- 1/4 cup canola oil
- 1 teaspoon celery seed
- 1/2 teaspoon pepper
- 1/4 teaspoon salt
- 1/8 teaspoon dried basil
- 1/8 teaspoon dried oregano

1) In a large bowl, combine the beans, mushrooms, green pepper and onion. In a jar with a tight-fitting lid, combine the dressing ingredients; shake well.

2) Pour dressing over bean mixture and stir to coat. Cover and refrigerate for at least 4 hours. Serve with a slotted spoon.

Yield: 12 servings.

NUTRITION FACTS: 3/4 cup equals 162 calories, 6 g fat (trace saturated fat), 0 cholesterol, 366 mg sodium, 24 g carbohydrate, 5 g fiber, 5 g protein.

Healthy Potato Salad

Pat Potter, Calumet City, Illinois

Here's a heart-healthy version of my longtime favorite potato salad recipe. It's colorful and chock-full of good crunchy ingredients.

- 2 pounds small red potatoes, quartered
- 5 hard-cooked eggs
- 3/4 cup fat-free mayonnaise
- 2 teaspoons cider vinegar
- 1 teaspoon sugar
- 1 teaspoon ground mustard
- 1/2 teaspoon salt
- 1/4 teaspoon pepper
- 1 large sweet onion, chopped
- 2 celery ribs, chopped
- 1/2 cup chopped green onions

1/2 cup julienned sweet red pepper
1/4 cup minced fresh parsley

1) Place the potatoes in a saucepan and cover with water. Bring to a boil. Reduce heat; cover and simmer for 12-14 minutes or until tender. Drain; cool for 30 minutes.

2) Slice eggs in half (discard yolks or save for another use). Cut the whites into 1/2-in. pieces.

3) In a large bowl, combine the mayonnaise, vinegar, sugar, mustard, salt and pepper. Add the potatoes, egg whites, onion, celery, green onions, red pepper and parsley; toss to coat. Cover and refrigerate for 2 hours or until chilled.

Yield: 10 servings.

NUTRITION FACTS: 3/4 cup equals 110 calories, 1 g fat (trace saturated fat), 2 mg cholesterol, 305 mg sodium, 22 g carbohydrate, 3 g fiber, 4 g protein.

ROASTED PEAR SALAD

Roasted Pear Salad
Taste of Home Test Kitchen

Oven-roasted pears take the ho-hum out of this green salad. Toss together a good-for-you medley of mellow pear slices, crispy greens, nuts and dried cranberries. The creamy dressing carries yet more pear flavor sweetened with just a touch of honey.

2 firm ripe pears, halved and cored
4 teaspoons olive oil, *divided*
2 tablespoons cider vinegar
1 teaspoon water
1 teaspoon honey
1/4 teaspoon salt
1/8 teaspoon white pepper
1 package (10 ounces) mixed baby salad greens
1 cup watercress sprigs
1/4 cup chopped hazelnuts, toasted
1/4 cup dried cranberries

1) In a bowl, toss pears with 1 teaspoon oil. Place in a 15-in. x 10-in. x 1-in. baking pan coated with nonstick cooking spray. Bake at 400° for 10 minutes. Turn pears over; bake 5-7 minutes longer or until golden and tender.

2) When cool enough to handle, peel pears. Thinly slice two pear halves lengthwise and set aside. Place remaining pear halves in a food processor or blender. Add the vinegar, water, honey, salt and white pepper; cover and process until smooth. While processing, slowly add remaining oil.

3) In a large bowl, toss the salad greens, watercress, nuts and cranberries. Arrange pear slices on top; drizzle with dressing.

Yield: 4 servings.

NUTRITION FACTS: 1 serving equals 174 calories, 9 g fat (1 g saturated fat), 0 cholesterol, 178 mg sodium, 24 g carbohydrate, 5 g fiber, 3 g protein.

Macaroni Garden Salad
Bonnie Sturgeon, Berwick, New Brunswick

I enjoy making this delightful salad during the summer. Tomato, cucumber and sweet red pepper are tossed with macaroni and herbs, then coated in a creamy fat-free mayonnaise dressing. Serve it as a light lunch or as a side dish with your favorite meat for supper.

1 cup cooked elbow macaroni
1 medium tomato, seeded and chopped
1/2 cup chopped seeded cucumber
1/2 cup chopped sweet red pepper
2 tablespoons minced fresh basil
1 tablespoon minced fresh parsley
2 tablespoons fat-free mayonnaise
2 teaspoons olive oil
1 teaspoon balsamic vinegar
1 garlic clove, minced
1/4 teaspoon salt
1/8 teaspoon pepper

1) In a bowl, combine the macaroni, tomato, cucumber, red pepper, basil and parsley. In a small bowl, whisk the mayonnaise, oil, vinegar, garlic, salt and pepper until blended.

2) Pour over macaroni mixture and stir until coated. Cover and refrigerate for at least 2 hours.

Yield: 2 servings.

NUTRITION FACTS: 1-1/4 cups equals 181 calories, 6 g fat (1 g saturated fat), 2 mg cholesterol, 426 mg sodium, 29 g carbohydrate, 3 g fiber, 5 g protein.

Dijon Sauce for Veggies

Jan Allen, Thermopolis, Wyoming

Here's a deliciously different way to serve good-for-you vegetables to your family. The creamy trimmed-down sauce with its subtle Dijon flavor drapes nicely over cauliflower, carrots or most any vegetable. I like to blanch broccoli florets and toss them with the sauce.

- 1/2 cup finely chopped onion
- 2 garlic cloves, minced
- 1 teaspoon olive oil
- 2-1/2 cups fat-free milk
- 3 tablespoons cornstarch
- 1/4 cup vegetable broth
- 2 ounces reduced-fat cream cheese, cubed
- 2 tablespoons Dijon mustard
- 1/4 teaspoon salt
- 1/8 teaspoon pepper
- Dash ground nutmeg

1) In a small nonstick saucepan, saute the onion and garlic in oil until tender. Stir in milk. Combine cornstarch and broth until smooth; stir into the pan. Bring to a boil; cook and stir for 1 minute or until thickened.

2) Remove from the heat. Whisk in cream cheese until melted. Stir in the mustard, salt, pepper and nutmeg. Serve with vegetables.

Yield: 2-1/2 cups.

NUTRITION FACTS: 1/4 cup equals 58 calories, 2 fat (1 saturated fat), 6 mg cholesterol, 212 mg sodium, 7 g carbohydrate, trace fiber, 3 g protein.

Cinnamon Apple Syrup

Alberta McKay, Bartlesville, Oklahoma

Cinnamon and vanilla take center stage in this no-fuss syrup. Try it warm over pancakes or crepes.

- 2 tablespoons cornstarch
- 1/2 teaspoon ground cinnamon
- 1/8 teaspoon salt
- 1 cup water
- 3/4 cup unsweetened apple juice concentrate
- 1/2 teaspoon vanilla extract

1) In a small saucepan, combine the cornstarch, cinnamon and salt. Gradually stir in water and apple juice concentrate until smooth. Bring to a boil; cook and stir for 2 minutes or until thickened.

2) Remove from the heat; stir in vanilla. Serve warm. Refrigerate leftovers.

Yield: 1-1/2 cups.

NUTRITION FACTS: 2 tablespoons equals 35 calories, trace fat (trace saturated fat), 0 cholesterol, 29 mg sodium, 9 g carbohydrate, trace fiber, trace protein.

THREE-PEPPER CHUTNEY

Three-Pepper Chutney

Lisa Louw, Alachua, Florida

This sweet chutney is as tasty on pork, beef and poultry as it is on grilled hot dogs and hamburgers. We like it on sandwiches instead of high-fat mayonnaise.

- 1-1/2 cups packed brown sugar
- 1-1/2 cups cider vinegar
- 3 medium green peppers, chopped
- 3 medium sweet red peppers, chopped
- 3 jalapeno peppers, seeded and chopped
- 1 medium onion, chopped
- 1 teaspoon salt

1) In a large saucepan, combine all ingredients. Bring to a boil. Reduce heat; simmer, uncovered, for 1-1/2 to 2 hours or until thickened. Cool.

2) Pour into a serving bowl. Cover and refrigerate for 1-2 hours or until chilled.

Yield: 2 cups.

Editor's Note: When cutting or seeding hot peppers, use rubber or plastic gloves to protect your hands. Avoid touching your face.

NUTRITION FACTS: 2 tablespoons equals 97 calories, trace fat (trace saturated fat), 0 cholesterol, 157 mg sodium, 25 g carbohydrate, 1 g fiber, 1 g protein.

APRICOT COFFEE CAKE

4) Bake at 350° for 40-45 minutes or until a toothpick inserted near the center comes out clean. Cool for 15 minutes before removing from pan to a wire rack. In a microwave, warm the reserved spreadable fruit; brush over warm cake. Cool completely.

Yield: 16 servings.

Editor's Note: This recipe was tested with Splenda No Calorie Sweetener.

NUTRITION FACTS: 1 slice equals 213 calories, 8 g fat (2 g saturated fat), 32 mg cholesterol, 313 mg sodium, 32 g carbohydrate, 1 g fiber, 4 g protein.

Apricot Coffee Cake
Taste of Home Test Kitchen

Having friends over for coffee? Serve them this scrumptious cake...they'll never guess it's light!

> 1 jar (10 ounces) 100% apricot spreadable fruit, *divided*
> 3/4 cup chopped pecans
> Sugar substitute equivalent to 1/3 cup sugar
> 4 teaspoons ground cinnamon

CAKE:
> 3-1/4 cups reduced-fat biscuit/baking mix
> Sugar substitute equivalent to 3/4 cup sugar
> 1/8 teaspoon ground cardamom
> 2 eggs
> 1 cup fat-free milk
> 2/3 cup reduced-fat sour cream
> 1 tablespoon butter, melted

1) Place 3 tablespoons spreadable fruit in a small microwave-safe bowl; cover and refrigerate. In another bowl, combine the pecans, sugar substitute, cinnamon and remaining spreadable fruit; set aside.

2) For cake, in a large bowl, combine the biscuit mix, sugar substitute and cardamom. Combine the eggs, milk, sour cream and butter; stir into dry ingredients just until moistened.

3) Spread a third of the batter into a 10-in. fluted tube pan coated with nonstick cooking spray. Spread with half of the pecan mixture. Repeat layers. Top with remaining batter.

Lemon Ginger Muffins
Joyce Baker-Mabry, Hamilton, Montana

These quick muffins are tender and have a lovely aroma while they're baking. Fat-free yogurt keeps them moist. If you like lemon and ginger, you're sure to enjoy their fresh flavor.

> 1/3 cup butter, softened
> 1/2 cup sugar
> Sugar substitute equivalent to 1/2 cup sugar
> 4 egg whites
> 2 tablespoons minced fresh gingerroot
> 2 tablespoons grated lemon peel
> 2 cups all-purpose flour
> 1 teaspoon baking soda
> 1 cup (8 ounces) fat-free plain yogurt

1) In a large mixing bowl, beat butter, sugar and sugar substitute until crumbly. Add egg whites; beat well. Stir in ginger and lemon peel. Combine flour and baking soda; add to butter mixture alternately with yogurt.

2) Coat muffin cups with nonstick cooking spray; fill three-fourths full with batter. Bake at 375° for 18-20 minutes or until a toothpick comes out clean. Cool for 5 minutes before removing from pan to a wire rack. Serve warm.

Yield: 1 dozen.

Editor's Note: This recipe was tested with Splenda No Calorie Sweetener.

NUTRITION FACTS: 1 muffin equals 171 calories, 5 g fat (3 g saturated fat), 14 mg cholesterol, 186 mg sodium, 27 g carbohydrate, 1 g fiber, 4 g protein.

CHOCOLATE CHIP BANANA MUFFINS

Chocolate Chip Banana Muffins
Lauren Heyn, Oak Creek, Wisconsin

Lots of banana flavor and plenty of chocolate chips "disguise" the whole wheat taste in these moist muffins. They're perfect for breakfast or an anytime snack.

3/4	cup all-purpose flour
3/4	cup whole wheat flour
1/2	cup wheat bran
1/2	cup packed brown sugar
1	teaspoon baking powder
3/4	teaspoon baking soda
1/2	teaspoon salt
2	eggs, lightly beaten
1/4	cup fat-free milk
1-1/3	cups mashed ripe bananas (2 to 3 medium)
1/3	cup unsweetened applesauce
1	teaspoon vanilla extract
1/2	cup miniature chocolate chips
1/3	cup chopped pecans

1) In a large bowl, combine the first seven ingredients. In another bowl, combine the eggs and milk; stir in the bananas, applesauce and vanilla. Stir into dry ingredients just until moistened. Stir in chocolate chips.

2) Coat muffin cups with nonstick cooking spray or use paper liners; fill three-fourths full with batter. Sprinkle with pecans. Bake at 375° for 18-22 minutes or until a toothpick comes out clean. Cool for 5 minutes before removing from pan to a wire rack.

Yield: 1 dozen.

NUTRITION FACTS: 1 muffin equals 191 calories, 6 g fat (2 g saturated fat), 36 mg cholesterol, 236 mg sodium, 33 g carbohydrate, 4 g fiber, 4 g protein.

Sour Cream Blueberry Coffee Cake
Taste of Home Test Kitchen

Oozing with blueberry flavor, this coffee cake is tender and moist with a topping of brown sugar, cinnamon and oats.

2	cups all-purpose flour
3/4	cup sugar
1	teaspoon baking powder
1/2	teaspoon salt
1/4	teaspoon baking soda
1	egg
1	cup (8 ounces) reduced-fat sour cream
1/4	cup unsweetened applesauce
3	tablespoons canola oil
1	teaspoon vanilla extract
1-1/2	cups fresh *or* frozen blueberries

TOPPING:

1/4	cup packed brown sugar
1/4	cup quick-cooking oats
1/2	teaspoon ground cinnamon
2	tablespoons cold butter

1) In a large bowl, combine the flour, sugar, baking powder, salt and baking soda. In another bowl, combine the egg, sour cream, applesauce, oil and vanilla. Stir into dry ingredients just until moistened. Fold in berries. Pour into a 9-in. square baking pan coated with nonstick cooking spray.

2) For topping, in a bowl, combine the brown sugar, oats and cinnamon; cut in butter until mixture resembles coarse crumbs. Sprinkle over the batter. Bake at 350° for 40-45 minutes or until a toothpick inserted near the center comes out clean. Cool on a wire rack.

Yield: 12 servings.

Editor's Note: If using frozen blueberries, do not thaw before adding to batter.

NUTRITION FACTS: 1 piece equals 242 calories, 9 g fat (3 g saturated fat), 31 mg cholesterol, 201 mg sodium, 38 g carbohydrate, 1 g fiber, 4 g protein.

Cranberry Scones

Kathy Zielicke, Moore Haven, Florida

Cornmeal adds a slight crunch to these breakfast or brunch treats. For a change of pace, try them with the dried berries of your choice. They're sure to brighten your day.

- 2 cups all-purpose flour
- 3/4 cup dried cranberries
- 1/3 cup cornmeal
- 1/4 cup plus 1 tablespoon sugar, *divided*
- 2 teaspoons baking powder
- 2 teaspoons grated orange peel
- 1/2 teaspoon baking soda
- 1/4 teaspoon salt
- 1/4 teaspoon ground nutmeg
- 2 egg whites, lightly beaten
- 2/3 cup 1% buttermilk
- 1/4 cup canola oil

1) In a large bowl, combine the flour, cranberries, cornmeal, 1/4 cup sugar, baking powder, orange peel, baking soda, salt and nutmeg. In another bowl, combine the egg whites, buttermilk and oil. Add to dry ingredients and stir until a soft dough forms.

2) Turn onto a floured surface; gently knead 6-8 times. Pat dough into an 8-1/2-in. circle. Place on a baking sheet coated with nonstick cooking spray. Cut into 12 wedges; do not separate. Sprinkle with remaining sugar.

3) Bake at 400° for 15-17 minutes or until golden brown. Remove to a wire rack. Serve warm.

Yield: 1 dozen.

NUTRITION FACTS: 1 scone equals 183 calories, 5 g fat (trace saturated fat), 0 cholesterol, 216 mg sodium, 30 g carbohydrate, 1 g fiber, 4 g protein.

Cinnamon Apple Pancakes

Kim McConnell, Tulsa, Oklahoma

My family loves the apple and cinnamon flavor in these light yet hearty pancakes. And best of all, they're sweet enough to eat without syrup.

- 2 cups whole wheat flour
- 4 teaspoons baking powder
- 1 teaspoon ground cinnamon
- 1/2 teaspoon salt
- 2 eggs, lightly beaten
- 2 cups fat-free milk
- 2 tablespoons honey
- 1 tablespoon canola oil
- 1 medium apple, peeled, cored and chopped

1) In a large bowl, combine flour, baking powder, cinnamon and salt. Combine eggs, milk, honey and oil; stir into dry ingredients just until moistened. Add apple.

2) Pour batter by 1/3 cupfuls onto a hot nonstick skillet coated with nonstick cooking spray. Turn when bubbles form on top; cook until second side is golden brown.

Yield: 6 servings.

NUTRITION FACTS: 2 pancakes equals 246 calories, 5 g fat (1 g saturated fat), 73 mg cholesterol, 416 mg sodium, 43 g carbohydrate, 5 g fiber, 11 g protein.

Blueberry Waffles

Lori Daniels, Beverly, West Virginia

Waffles are my husband's favorite Sunday brunch. We like them with fresh fruit on the side.

- 1 cup all-purpose flour
- 2 tablespoons sugar
- 1 teaspoon baking powder
- 1/4 teaspoon salt
- 1 egg yolk
- 1/4 cup fat-free milk
- 1/4 cup orange juice
- 1 tablespoon butter, melted
- 1 teaspoon grated orange peel
- 1/8 teaspoon orange extract
- 4 egg whites
- 1 cup fresh blueberries
- 1 tablespoon confectioners' sugar

1) In a large bowl, combine the flour, sugar, baking powder and salt. In another bowl, whisk the egg yolk, milk, orange juice, butter, orange peel and extract; stir into dry ingredients just until combined. In a small mixing bowl, beat egg whites until stiff peaks form; fold into batter. Fold in blueberries.

2) Bake in a preheated waffle iron according to manufacturer's directions until golden brown. Sprinkle with confectioners' sugar.

Yield: 4 servings.

NUTRITION FACTS: 1 waffle equals 235 calories, 5 g fat (2 g saturated fat), 61 mg cholesterol, 301 mg sodium, 40 g carbohydrate, 1 g fiber, 8 g protein.

ROASTED GARLIC BREAD

Roasted Garlic Bread
Barb Alexander, Princeton, New Jersey

I came up with this bread recipe one very stormy morning when we lived on the beach in the Florida Panhandle. While lightning blinked over the Gulf and rain tap-tap-tapped on our balcony, the wonderful aroma of this bread baking gave me such a cozy feeling.

2	medium whole garlic bulbs
2	teaspoons olive oil
1	package (1/4 ounce) active dry yeast
1	cup warm water (110° to 115°)
1	tablespoon sugar
1	teaspoon salt
2-1/2	to 3 cups all-purpose flour
2	tablespoons minced fresh sage *or* 2 teaspoons rubbed sage
2	teaspoons minced fresh marjoram *or* 3/4 teaspoon dried marjoram
1	teaspoon minced fresh rosemary *or* 1/2 teaspoon dried rosemary, crushed
2	tablespoons grated Parmesan cheese
1	tablespoon butter, melted

1) Remove papery outer skin from garlic (do not peel or separate cloves). Cut top off garlic bulbs; brush with oil. Wrap each bulb in heavy-duty foil. Bake at 425° for 30-35 minutes or until softened. Cool for 10-15 minutes. Squeeze softened garlic into a small bowl; set aside.

2) In a large mixing bowl, dissolve yeast in warm water. Add the sugar, salt and 1 cup flour; beat until smooth. Stir in enough remaining flour to form a soft dough.

3) Turn onto a lightly floured surface; knead until smooth and elastic, about 6-8 minutes. Place in a bowl coated with nonstick cooking spray, turning once to coat top. Cover and let the dough rise in a warm place until doubled, about 45 minutes. Meanwhile, add the sage, marjoram and rosemary to the reserved roasted garlic.

4) Punch dough down. Turn onto a lightly floured surface; divide in half. Roll each portion into a 10-in. x 8-in. rectangle. Spread each with half the garlic mixture to within 1/2 in. of edges. Sprinkle each with 1 tablespoon Parmesan cheese. Roll up jelly-roll style, starting with a long side; pinch seam and ends to seal.

5) Coat a baking sheet with nonstick cooking spray. Place loaves seam side down on pan; tuck ends under. With a sharp knife, make several slashes across the top of each loaf. Cover and let rise until doubled, about 30 minutes.

6) Bake at 375° for 20-25 minutes or until golden brown. Remove to wire racks; brush with butter.

Yield: 2 loaves (10 slices each).

NUTRITION FACTS: 1 slice equals 84 calories, 1 g fat (1 g saturated fat), 2 mg cholesterol, 136 mg sodium, 15 g carbohydrate, 1 g fiber, 2 g protein.

Three-Grain Pan Rolls
Montserrat Wadsworth, Fallon, Nevada

The first time I made these rolls, I was a little worried that my husband wouldn't like them. But he loved them! The seeds on top add flavor and fun crunch.

2	cups water
1/2	cup bulgur
1	package (1/4 ounce) active dry yeast
1	cup warm milk (110° to 115°)
1/2	cup quick-cooking oats
1/3	cup honey
2	eggs
2	teaspoons salt
3/4	teaspoon pepper
1-1/2	cups whole wheat flour
2-1/2	to 3-1/2 cups all-purpose flour
2	tablespoons olive oil
2	teaspoons *each* celery seed, fennel seed and sesame seeds
1	teaspoon poppy seeds

1) In a saucepan, bring water to a boil. Stir in bulgur. Reduce heat; cover and simmer for 15 minutes or until tender. Drain.

2) In a large mixing bowl, dissolve yeast in warm milk. Add the oats, honey, eggs, salt, pepper, cooked bulgur and whole wheat flour; beat until smooth. Stir in enough all-purpose flour to form a soft dough.

3) Turn onto a lightly floured surface; knead until elastic, about 6-8 minutes (mixture will be lumpy). Place in a bowl coated with nonstick cooking spray, turning once to coat top. Cover and let rise in a warm place until doubled, about 1-1/4 hours.

4) Punch dough down. Turn onto a lightly floured surface; divide into 22 pieces. Roll each into a ball. Brush two 9-in. round baking pans with some of the oil. Arrange 11 balls in each pan; brush tops with remaining oil.

5) Combine the celery seed, fennel seed, sesame seeds and poppy seeds; sprinkle over rolls. Cover and let rise in a warm place until doubled, about 40 minutes. Bake at 375° for 18-22 minutes or until golden brown. Remove from pans to wire racks.

Yield: 22 rolls.

NUTRITION FACTS: 1 roll equals 157 calories, 3 g fat (1 g saturated fat), 21 mg cholesterol, 227 mg sodium, 29 g carbohydrate, 2 g fiber, 5 g protein.

CRAN-APPLE TEA RING

Cran-Apple Tea Ring
Nellie Grimes, Jacksonville, Texas

A comforting combination of cranberries, apples and walnuts makes this tea ring a lovely addition to brunch. Invite friends and family over to enjoy a few slices with coffee.

  1 **package (1/4 ounce) active dry yeast**
1/4 **cup warm water (110° to 115°)**
1/2 **cup warm fat-free milk (110° to 115°)**

  1 **egg**
  2 **tablespoons butter, softened**
  1 **tablespoon grated orange peel**
  1 **teaspoon salt**
  3 **tablespoons plus 1/2 cup sugar, *divided***
2-3/4 **to 3-1/4 cups all-purpose flour**
  1 **cup thinly sliced peeled apple**
  1 **cup dried cranberries**
1/2 **cup chopped walnuts, toasted**
1-1/2 **teaspoons ground cinnamon**
  1 **egg white**
  1 **tablespoon water**
1/2 **cup confectioners' sugar**
  1 **tablespoon orange juice**

1) In a large mixing bowl, dissolve yeast in warm water. Add milk, egg, butter, orange peel, salt, 3 tablespoons sugar and 1 cup flour; beat until smooth. Stir in enough remaining flour to form a soft dough.

2) Turn onto a floured surface; knead until smooth and elastic, about 6-8 minutes. Place in a bowl coated with nonstick cooking spray; turn once to coat top. Cover and let rise in a warm place for 1 hour.

3) In a bowl, toss the apple, cranberries, walnuts, cinnamon and remaining sugar; set aside. Punch dough down; turn onto a lightly floured surface. Roll into a 20-in. x 10-in. rectangle.

4) Combine egg white and water; chill 3 tablespoons. Brush remaining mixture over dough. Spoon fruit mixture to within 1 in. of edges. Roll up tightly jelly-roll style starting with a long side; seal ends.

5) Place seam side down in a 15-in. x 10-in. x 1-in. baking pan coated with nonstick cooking spray; pinch ends to form a ring. With scissors, cut from outside edge two-thirds of the way toward center of ring at 1-in. intervals. Separate strips slightly; twist so filling shows. Cover and let rise until doubled, about 40 minutes.

6) Brush with reserved egg white mixture. Bake at 375° for 20-25 minutes or until golden brown (cover with foil during the last 10 minutes). Remove to a wire rack to cool. Combine the confectioners' sugar and orange juice; drizzle over ring.

Yield: 16 servings.

NUTRITION FACTS: 1 piece equals 200 calories, 4 g fat (1 g saturated fat), 17 mg cholesterol, 174 mg sodium, 37 g carbohydrate, 2 g fiber, 4 g protein.

Orange Marmalade Sweet Rolls

Lacey Griffin, Fredonia, Pennsylvania

My husband has heart trouble, so we had to get away from all the brown sugar, honey and butter I used to bake with. My family enjoys the citrus taste of these tender low-fat rolls that I bake in muffin cups.

    1   loaf (1 pound) frozen bread
        dough, thawed
    1/3 cup 100% orange marmalade
        spreadable fruit
    2   tablespoons raisins
    1/3 cup confectioners' sugar
    1/2 teaspoon grated orange peel
    2   teaspoons orange juice

1) On a floured surface, roll dough into a 12-in. x 8-in. rectangle; brush with spreadable fruit. Sprinkle with raisins. Roll up jelly-roll style, starting with a long side; pinch seam to seal.

2) Cut into 12 slices. Place cut side down in muffin cups coated with nonstick cooking spray. Cover and let rise until doubled, about 45 minutes.

3) Bake at 350° for 15-20 minutes or until golden brown. Immediately invert onto serving plates. Combine the confectioners' sugar, orange peel and orange juice; drizzle over warm rolls.

Yield: 12 servings.

NUTRITION FACTS: 1 roll equals 140 calories, 2 g fat (trace saturated fat), 0 cholesterol, 211 mg sodium, 28 g carbohydrate, 1 g fiber, 4 g protein.

Cherry Cheesecake Pie

Sandra Lee Herr, Stevens, Pennsylvania

Cottage cheese is the secret to this creamy slimmed-down dessert. It's festively topped with sweet cherry pie filling.

    2   eggs, lightly beaten
    4   ounces reduced-fat cream
        cheese, cubed
    1/2 cup fat-free cottage cheese
    1/4 cup nonfat dry milk powder
    Sugar substitute equivalent
      to 1/4 cup sugar
    1   tablespoon lemon juice
    2   teaspoons vanilla extract
    1   reduced-fat graham cracker
        crust (8 inches)
    1   can (20 ounces) reduced-sugar
        cherry pie filling

1) In a food processor, combine the first seven ingredients; cover and process until smooth. Pour into the crust. Bake at 350° for 25-30 minutes or until the center is almost set. Cool on a wire rack for 1 hour.

2) Cover and refrigerate overnight. Cut into slices; top with cherry pie filling.

Yield: 8 servings.

Editor's Note: This recipe was tested with Splenda No Calorie Sweetener.

NUTRITION FACTS: 1 piece equals 225 calories, 6 g fat (2 g saturated fat), 59 mg cholesterol, 241 mg sodium, 35 g carbohydrate, trace fiber, 7 g protein.

APPLESAUCE LATTICE PIE

Applesauce Lattice Pie

Cherie Sweet, Evansville, Indiana

I had some apples that needed to be used up, so I combined them with a can of applesauce and turned out my best-tasting apple pie ever.

    1-1/2 cups all-purpose flour
    3   tablespoons sugar
    1/4   teaspoon plus 1/8 teaspoon
          baking powder
    1/4   teaspoon plus 1/8 teaspoon salt
    6   tablespoons cold butter
    4   to 6 tablespoons cold water
    4-1/2 teaspoons fat-free milk
    1-1/2 teaspoons cider vinegar

FILLING:

    5   cups sliced peeled tart apples

1/4   cup raisins

Sugar substitute equivalent
to 3 tablespoons sugar

    2   tablespoons all-purpose flour

    4   teaspoons brown sugar

    2   teaspoons ground cinnamon

1-1/2 cups unsweetened applesauce

    2   teaspoons butter

1) In a bowl, combine flour, sugar, baking powder and salt; cut in butter until mixture resembles coarse crumbs. Combine water, milk and vinegar; gradually add to crumb mixture, tossing with a fork until dough forms a ball.

2) Coat a 9-in. pie plate with nonstick cooking spray. Set aside a third of the dough. On a lightly floured surface, roll out remaining dough to fit pie plate. Transfer pastry to plate; trim even with edge.

3) In a large bowl, combine apples and raisins. Combine the sugar substitute, flour, brown sugar and cinnamon; add to apple mixture and toss to coat. Spoon 3 cups into the crust; cover with applesauce. Top with remaining apple mixture; dot with butter.

4) Roll out reserved portion of dough; make a lattice crust. Trim and flute edges. Bake at 375° for 40-45 minutes or until crust is golden brown and filling is bubbly. Cool on a wire rack.

Yield: 8 servings.

Editor's Note: This recipe was tested with Splenda No Calorie Sweetener.

NUTRITION FACTS: 1 piece equals 281 calories, 10 g fat (6 g saturated fat), 26 mg cholesterol, 235 mg sodium, 47 g carbohydrate, 3 fiber, 3 g protein.

Cranberry Apple Tart
Taste of Home Test Kitchen

Bursting with the colors and flavors of autumn, this eye-fetching treat is a welcomed addition to any celebration. Sweeten the crispy golden crust with honey and your guests will never suspect that the dessert is actually low in fat.

1/2   teaspoon active dry yeast

    1   tablespoon warm water
       (110° to 115°)

    2   tablespoons beaten egg

    2   tablespoons butter, softened

4-1/2 teaspoons sugar

    1   teaspoon grated orange peel

3/4   cup plus 2 tablespoons
       all-purpose flour

1/4   teaspoon salt

FILLING:

    1   package (12 ounces) fresh *or*
       frozen cranberries

1-1/2 cups chopped dried apples

1-1/2 cups unsweetened apple juice

1-1/4 cups sugar

Sugar substitute equivalent
to 1 cup sugar

1/2   cup water

1/4   teaspoon salt

1/4   cup cornstarch

1/3   cup cold water

1) In a small mixing bowl, dissolve yeast in warm water. Beat in the egg, butter, sugar and orange peel. Combine flour and salt; beat into yeast mixture on low speed just until mixture holds together.

2) Shape into a ball. Place in a small bowl coated with nonstick cooking spray, turning once to coat top. Cover and let rise in a warm place for 1-1/4 hours (dough will not double, but will leave a slight indentation when pressed).

3) Coat an 11-in. fluted tart pan with removable bottom with nonstick cooking spray; set aside. Place dough on a piece of waxed paper. Lightly flour dough and roll into a 13-in. circle. Invert into prepared pan; gently peel off waxed paper.

4) Line unpricked tart shell with a double thickness of heavy-duty foil. Bake at 375° for 8 minutes. Remove foil; bake 6 minutes longer or until golden brown. Cool on a wire rack.

5) In a large saucepan, combine the first seven filling ingredients. Cook and stir until mixture comes to a boil and cranberries pop.

6) Combine cornstarch and cold water until smooth; gradually stir into cranberry mixture. Cook 2 minutes longer or until thickened. Cool for 20 minutes. Pour into crust. Refrigerate for at least 3 hours before cutting.

Yield: 14 servings.

Editor's Note: This recipe was tested with Splenda No Calorie Sweetener.

NUTRITION FACTS: 1 piece equals 183 calories, 2 g fat (1 g saturated fat), 14 mg cholesterol, 113 mg sodium, 41 g carbohydrate, 2 g fiber, 1 g protein.

Raspberry Custard Tart
Taste of Home Test Kitchen

This pretty dessert will help you impress guests at your next gathering. With a yummy raspberry layer and nutty homemade crust, it's hard to believe that a slice isn't an invitation to stray from healthy eating goals.

3 tablespoons reduced-fat butter
1/2 cup sugar
3/4 cup all-purpose flour
1/4 cup finely chopped pecans, toasted

FILLING:

1/3 cup sugar
1/4 cup all-purpose flour
2-1/4 cups fat-free milk
1 egg yolk
1/4 teaspoon almond extract
1 jar (12 ounces) 100% seedless raspberry spreadable fruit
1-1/2 cups fresh raspberries

1) In a small mixing bowl, beat butter and sugar for 2 minutes or until crumbly. Beat in flour and nuts. Coat a 9-in. fluted tart pan with removable bottom with nonstick cooking spray.

2) Press crumb mixture onto the bottom and up the sides of pan. Bake at 425° for 8-10 minutes or until lightly browned. Cool on a wire rack.

3) In a small saucepan, combine sugar and flour. Stir in milk until smooth. Cook and stir over medium-high heat until thickened and bubbly. Reduce heat; cook and stir 2 minutes longer. Remove from the heat.

4) Stir a small amount of hot filling into egg yolk; return all to the pan, stirring constantly. Bring to a gentle boil; cook and stir 2 minutes longer. Remove from the heat; gently stir in extract. Pour over crust. Refrigerate until set. In a small bowl, whisk fruit spread until smooth; spread over filling. Garnish with raspberries.

Yield: 12 servings.

Editor's Note: This recipe was tested with Land O' Lakes light stick butter.

NUTRITION FACTS: 1 piece equals 210 calories, 4 g fat (1 g saturated fat), 24 mg cholesterol, 42 mg sodium, 41 g carbohydrate, 2 g fiber, 3 g protein.

Coconut-Banana Chocolate Cream Pie
Mary Jones, St. Louis, Missouri

What's not to like about this pie? It's easy to prepare and chock-full of delicious ingredients.

1-1/3 cups cold water
2/3 cup nonfat dry milk powder
1 package (1.4 ounces) sugar-free instant chocolate pudding mix
1 cup reduced-fat whipped topping, *divided*
1/2 teaspoon coconut extract, *divided*
2 medium ripe bananas, cut into 1/4-inch slices
1 chocolate crumb crust (9 inches)
1 tablespoon flaked coconut, toasted

1) In a bowl, stir water and milk powder until powder is dissolved. Add pudding mix; whisk for 1-2 minutes or until thickened. Fold in 1/4 cup whipped topping and 1/4 teaspoon extract. Layer banana slices in the crust; top with pudding mixture. Cover and refrigerate.

2) Combine remaining whipped topping and extract; spread over pudding. Sprinkle with coconut. Cover and refrigerate for at least 1 hour before serving.

Yield: 8 servings.

NUTRITION FACTS: 1 piece equals 172 calories, 5 g fat (2 g saturated fat), 1 mg cholesterol, 172 mg sodium, 28 g carbohydrate, 2 g fiber, 4 g protein.

Chocolate Sheet Cake
Kristi Wells, Raleigh, North Carolina

With half of the fat from the original recipe, this cake is nothing short of delicious. In fact, guests may not be able to get enough of the moist chocolate cake and rich icing.

1/2 cup butter, cubed
1 cup water

1/4   cup baking cocoa

1   cup all-purpose flour

1   cup cake flour

1   cup sugar blend for baking

1   teaspoon baking soda

1/2   teaspoon salt

2   eggs, lightly beaten

1/2   cup reduced-fat sour cream

1/2   cup unsweetened applesauce

FROSTING:

1/2   cup reduced-fat butter, softened

3   cups confectioners' sugar

1/4   cup baking cocoa

1   teaspoon vanilla extract

2   to 3 tablespoons fat-free milk

1) In a saucepan, bring the butter, water and cocoa just to a boil. Immediately remove from the heat. Combine the flours, sugar blend, baking soda and salt; stir into butter mixture. Combine the eggs, sour cream and applesauce; stir into butter mixture until blended.

2) Transfer to a 15-in. x 10-in. x 1-in. baking pan coated with nonstick cooking spray. Bake at 350° for 18-25 minutes or until a toothpick inserted near the center comes out clean. Cool on a wire rack.

3) For frosting, in a large mixing bowl, beat butter and confectioners' sugar. Add cocoa, vanilla and enough milk to achieve desired consistency. Spread over cake.

Yield: 20 servings.

Editor's Note: This recipe was tested with Land O' Lakes light stick butter and Splenda Sugar Blend for Baking.

NUTRITION FACTS: 1 piece equals 242 calories, 8 g fat (5 g saturated fat), 44 mg cholesterol, 208 mg sodium, 40 g carbohydrate, 1 g fiber, 3 g protein.

Streuseled Zucchini Bundt Cake
Regina Stock, Topeka, Kansas

After managing to lose 40 pounds, I like to keep a number of healthy recipes on hand. This cake is a favorite morning snack.

3   cups all-purpose flour

3/4   cup sugar

1-1/2   teaspoons baking powder

1   teaspoon baking soda

1/2   teaspoon salt

2   egg whites

STREUSELED ZUCCHINI BUNDT CAKE

1   egg

1-1/3   cups fat-free plain yogurt

1/3   cup canola oil

2   cups shredded zucchini, patted dry

4   teaspoons vanilla extract, *divided*

1   tablespoon dry bread crumbs

1/3   cup packed brown sugar

1/3   cup chopped walnuts

1/3   cup raisins

1   tablespoon ground cinnamon

1/2   teaspoon ground allspice

3/4   cup confectioners' sugar

2   to 3 teaspoons fat-free milk

1) In a large mixing bowl, combine the first five ingredients. In another bowl, beat the egg whites, egg, yogurt and oil until blended. Stir in zucchini and 3 teaspoons vanilla. Add to dry ingredients; mix well.

2) Coat a 10-in. fluted tube pan with nonstick cooking spray; sprinkle with bread crumbs. Pour a third of the batter into pan. Combine the brown sugar, walnuts, raisins, cinnamon and allspice; sprinkle half over batter. Top with another third of the batter. Sprinkle with remaining brown sugar mixture; top with remaining batter.

3) Bake at 350° for 55-65 minutes or until a toothpick comes out clean. Cool for 10 minutes before removing from pan to a wire rack to cool completely. In a small bowl, combine confectioners' sugar, milk and remaining vanilla; drizzle over cake.

Yield: 14 servings.

NUTRITION FACTS: 1 piece equals 279 calories, 8 g fat (1 g saturated fat), 16 mg cholesterol, 233 mg sodium, 48 g carbohydrate, 2 g fiber, 6 g protein.

Miracle Baklava
Sue Klima, Northlake, Illinois

Since I'm always asked to bring baklava to special occasions, I created this lighter version to help everyone cut back on calories and fat. The layers of phyllo dough make it very flaky. Try it...you'll like it!

- 1 package (12 ounces) vanilla wafers, crushed
- 2 tablespoons sugar
- 1 teaspoon ground cinnamon
  Refrigerated butter-flavored spray (about 4 ounces)
- 1 package frozen phyllo dough (14-inch x 9-inch sheet size), thawed

SYRUP:

- 1 cup sugar
- 1 cup water
- 1/2 cup honey
- 1 teaspoon grated lemon peel
- 1 teaspoon vanilla extract

1) In a large bowl, combine the wafer crumbs, sugar and cinnamon; set aside. Spritz a 13-in. x 9-in. x 2-in. baking pan with butter-flavored spray.

2) Unroll phyllo sheets. Place one sheet of phyllo in pan; spritz with butter-flavored spray and brush to coat evenly. Repeat seven times, spritzing and brushing each layer. Keep remaining phyllo dough covered with plastic wrap to prevent drying.

3) Sprinkle 1/4 cup crumb mixture over phyllo in pan. Layer with two sheets of phyllo, spritzing and brushing with butter-flavored spray between each. Sprinkle with 1/4 cup crumb mixture; repeat 11 times.

4) Top with one phyllo sheet; spritz and brush with butter-flavored spray. Repeat seven more times, spritzing and brushing each layer. Cut into 15 squares; cut each square in half diagonally. Bake at 350° for 40-45 minutes or until golden brown.

5) Meanwhile, in a saucepan, bring the sugar, water, honey and lemon peel to a boil. Reduce heat; simmer, uncovered, for 20 minutes. Remove from the heat; stir in vanilla. Cool to lukewarm. Pour syrup over warm baklava.

Yield: 30 servings.

Editor's Note: This recipe was tested with I Can't Believe It's Not Butter Spray.

NUTRITION FACTS: 1 piece equals 154 calories, 4 g fat (1 g saturated fat), 1 mg cholesterol, 154 mg sodium, 30 g carbohydrate, 1 g fiber, 2 g protein.

Cinnamon Peach Crisp
Leona Luecking, West Burlington, Iowa

This dessert is so good yet so easy to make. Fresh peaches and a sweet crunchy topping give it comforting flavor. I like to dish it up warm with a scoop of frozen yogurt.

- 4 cups sliced peeled fresh peaches
- 1/2 cup orange juice
- 2 tablespoons brown sugar
- 1/2 teaspoon ground cinnamon
- 1 cup all-purpose flour
- 1/3 cup sugar
- 1 teaspoon baking powder
- 1 egg, lightly beaten
- 2 tablespoons butter, melted

CINNAMON-SUGAR:

- 1-1/2 teaspoons sugar
- 1/8 teaspoon ground cinnamon

1) In a bowl, combine the peaches, orange juice, brown sugar and cinnamon. Transfer to an 8-in. square baking dish coated with nonstick cooking spray.

2) Combine the flour, sugar and baking powder. Add egg and butter; mix until crumbly. Sprinkle over peaches. Combine sugar and cinnamon; sprinkle over crumb mixture.

3) Bake at 350° for 40-45 minutes or until filling is bubbly and topping is golden brown. Serve warm.

Yield: 6 servings.

NUTRITION FACTS: 1 cup equals 245 calories, 5 g fat (3 g saturated fat), 46 mg cholesterol, 90 mg sodium, 48 g carbohydrate, 3 g fiber, 4 g protein.

Pineapple Buttermilk Sherbet

Dolores Kastello, Waukesha, Wisconsin

This icy sweet sherbet stirs up easily for freezing in a jiffy.

- 2 cups 1% buttermilk
- 1 can (20 ounces) unsweetened crushed pineapple, undrained
- 3/4 cup sugar

1) In a bowl, combine all ingredients; stir until sugar is dissolved. Pour into a 9-in. square dish. Cover and freeze for 1 to 1-1/2 hours or until mixture begins to harden.

2) Stir; freeze 3-4 hours longer or until firm, stirring occasionally. Remove from the freezer 20-25 minutes before serving.

Yield: 10 servings.

NUTRITION FACTS: 1/2 cup equals 113 calories, trace fat (trace saturated fat), 3 mg cholesterol, 57 mg sodium, 26 g carbohydrate, trace fiber, 2 g protein.

Cream Cheese Bonbons

Beverly Coyde, Gasport, New York

These pretty coconut-speckled candies are rolled in grated chocolate, but you could also coat them in finely chopped nuts, chocolate sprinkles or jimmies. For variety, substitute almond extract for the vanilla and chopped toasted almonds for the coconut.

- 1 package (8 ounces) reduced-fat cream cheese

Sugar substitute equivalent to 1/3 cup sugar

- 1 tablespoon sugar
- 1/2 teaspoon vanilla extract
- 1 cup flaked coconut
- 1 square (1 ounce) unsweetened chocolate, grated

1) In a small mixing bowl, beat the cream cheese, sugar substitute, sugar and vanilla until smooth. Stir in coconut until combined. Refrigerate for 30 minutes or until easy to handle.

2) Shape into 1-in. balls; roll in grated chocolate. Refrigerate for at least 1 hour. Store in an airtight container in the refrigerator.

Yield: 1-1/2 dozen.

Editor's Note: This recipe was tested with Splenda No Calorie Sweetener.

NUTRITION FACTS: 1 bonbon equals 73 calories, 6 g fat (4 g saturated fat), 10 mg cholesterol, 64 mg sodium, 5 g carbohydrate, trace fiber, 2 g protein.

Peachy Cinnamon Rice Pudding

Shanna Webb, Provo, Utah

This delicious variation on a classic has become a family favorite. Anyone who loves the comfort of rice pudding will love this recipe.

- 1 cup water
- 1/3 cup uncooked long grain rice
- 1 tablespoon butter
- 1/8 teaspoon salt
- 1 can (15 ounces) reduced-sugar sliced peaches
- 2 teaspoons cornstarch
- 1/2 cup fat-free milk
- 1/4 cup 100% peach *or* apricot spreadable fruit
- 1/2 teaspoon ground cinnamon

1) In a saucepan, bring the water, rice, butter and salt to a boil. Reduce heat; cover and simmer for 15-20 minutes or until rice is tender (some of the liquid will not be absorbed).

2) Drain peaches, reserving 1/3 cup juice; set peaches aside. In a small bowl, combine the cornstarch, milk and reserved juice until smooth. Gradually stir into rice mixture. Bring to a boil; cook and stir for 2 minutes or until thickened.

3) Remove from the heat; stir in spreadable fruit and cinnamon until fruit is melted. Cool to room temperature. Chop peaches; stir into rice mixture. Serve immediately.

Yield: 4 servings.

NUTRITION FACTS: 2/3 cup equals 195 calories, 3 g fat (2 g saturated fat), 8 mg cholesterol, 125 mg sodium, 41 g carbohydrate, 2 g fiber, 3 g protein.

Fudgy Peanut Butter Brownies

Martha Domeny, Overland Park, Kansas

No one believes these fudgy brownies are actually low-fat. They feature a hint of peanut butter and are so full of flavor, they'll satisfy anyone's chocolate cravings.

- 2 cups sugar
- 1-1/2 cups all-purpose flour
- 3/4 cup baking cocoa
- 1/2 teaspoon salt
- 2/3 cup unsweetened applesauce
- 3/4 cup egg substitute
- 2 teaspoons vanilla extract

FILLING:

- 3 ounces reduced-fat cream cheese, softened
- 1/3 cup reduced-fat peanut butter
- 1/4 cup sugar
- 1/4 cup egg substitute
- 1 teaspoon vanilla extract

FROSTING:

- 1 cup confectioners' sugar
- 3 tablespoons baking cocoa
- 2 tablespoons 2% milk
- 1 teaspoon vanilla extract
- 1 teaspoon water

1) In a large bowl, combine the sugar, flour, cocoa and salt. Stir in applesauce, egg substitute and vanilla; mix well. Pour about half of the batter into a 13-in. x 9-in. x 2-in. baking pan coated with nonstick cooking spray.

2) In a mixing bowl, combine the filling ingredients; beat until smooth. Drop by tablespoonfuls onto batter. Spoon remaining batter over the top; cut through batter with a knife to swirl peanut butter mixture.

3) Bake at 325° for 25-30 minutes or until edges are firm and center is almost set. Cool on a wire rack.

4) In a small bowl, combine the frosting ingredients until smooth. Spread over brownies.

Yield: 20 brownies.

NUTRITION FACTS: 1 brownie equals 201 calories, 3 g fat (1 g saturated fat), 3 mg cholesterol, 119 mg sodium, 40 g carbohydrate, 2 g fiber, 5 g protein.

Chewy Chocolate Cookies

Taste of Home Test Kitchen

With only a trace of fat, these nibbles will satisfy chocoholics who don't want to pack on extra pounds. Top the soft, bite-size cookies with a pretty white drizzle.

- 1-1/2 cups all-purpose flour
- 1/2 cup sugar
- 1/2 cup baking cocoa
- 1/2 teaspoon baking soda
- 1/2 teaspoon salt
- 3 egg whites
- 1/2 cup corn syrup
- 1 cup confectioners' sugar
- 4 teaspoons fat-free milk

1) In a large bowl, combine the flour, sugar, cocoa, baking soda and salt. Combine the egg whites and corn syrup; stir into dry ingredients just until moistened.

2) Drop by tablespoonfuls 2 in. apart onto baking sheets coated with nonstick cooking spray. Bake at 350° for 5-7 minutes or until set (do not overbake). Remove to wire racks to cool.

3) In a small bowl, combine the confectioners' sugar and milk until smooth. Drizzle over cookies. Store in an airtight container.

Yield: about 2-1/2 dozen.

NUTRITION FACTS: 1 cookie equals 72 calories, trace fat (trace saturated fat), trace cholesterol, 73 mg sodium, 17 g carbohydrate, 1 g fiber, 1 g protein.

CRANBERRY ALMOND BISCOTTI

Cranberry Almond Biscotti

Evelyn Bethards Wohlers, Columbia, Maryland

A fellow stay-at-home mom gave me this recipe so we could enjoy our latte breaks more affordably with homemade biscotti. I modified the original version by using a sugar substitute and reducing the carbohydrates and fat. Tangy dried cranberries and spices give it delicious flavor.

>   2   eggs
>   3   egg whites
>   2   tablespoons molasses
>   3/4   teaspoon almond extract
>   Sugar substitute equivalent
>   to 1 cup sugar
> 2-1/4   cups all-purpose flour
>   1   teaspoon baking powder
>   1   teaspoon ground cinnamon
>   1/2   teaspoon baking soda
>   1/2   teaspoon ground nutmeg
>   3/4   cup slivered almonds
>   1/2   cup dried cranberries
>   1/2   cup chopped white candy coating

1) In a large mixing bowl, beat the eggs, egg whites, molasses and extract. Beat in sugar substitute. Combine the flour, baking powder, cinnamon, baking soda and nutmeg; gradually add to egg mixture (dough will be sticky).

2) Turn onto a floured surface. Knead in almonds and cranberries. Divide dough in half; shape each portion into a 12-in. x 3-in. rectangle. Transfer to a baking sheet coated with nonstick cooking spray.

3) Bake at 325° for 15-20 minutes or until lightly browned. Cool for 5 minutes. Transfer to a cutting board; with a serrated knife, cut each loaf into 16 slices. Place slices cut side down on baking sheets coated with nonstick cooking spray. Bake for 25-35 minutes or until firm, turning once. Remove to wire racks to cool.

4) In a microwave or heavy saucepan, melt candy coating; stir until smooth. Drizzle over biscotti. Store in an airtight container.

Yield: 32 cookies.

Editor's Note: This recipe was tested with Splenda No Calorie Sweetener.

NUTRITION FACTS: 1 cookie equals 84 calories, 3 g fat (1 g saturated fat), 14 mg cholesterol, 39 mg sodium, 13 g carbohydrate, 1 g fiber, 2 g protein.

Almond Cookie Cutouts

Taste of Home Test Kitchen

Colored sugar and sprinkles create a festive look for these easy-to-decorate cookies. A little almond extract gives them a pleasant flavor. They're a nice lighter addition to a Christmas cookie tray.

6	tablespoons butter, softened
1/2	cup sugar
1/2	cup packed brown sugar
1	egg
3/4	teaspoon almond extract
1/2	teaspoon vanilla extract
1-1/4	cups all-purpose flour
1/4	cup cornstarch
3	tablespoons ground almonds
1/2	teaspoon baking powder
1/2	teaspoon salt

Red and green colored sugar *and/or* sprinkles, optional

1) In a small mixing bowl, cream butter and sugars. Add egg and extracts; mix well. Combine the flour, cornstarch, almonds, baking powder and salt; add to creamed mixture just until blended. Shape into two balls. Cover and refrigerate for at least 2 hours.

2) On a lightly floured surface, roll out dough to 1/4-in. thickness. Cut out with lightly floured 2-1/2-in. cookie cutters. Place on baking sheets coated with nonstick cooking spray. Sprinkle with colored sugar and/or sprinkles if desired.

3) Bake at 350° for 7-9 minutes or until set and bottoms are lightly browned. Cool for 2 minutes before removing to wire racks.

Yield: 28 cookies.

NUTRITION FACTS: 2 cookies equals 163 calories, 6 g fat (3 g saturated fat), 28 mg cholesterol, 159 mg sodium, 25 g carbohydrate, 1 g fiber, 2 g protein.

Crunchy Coconut Cookies

Taste of Home Test Kitchen

These cookies have a sweet coconut taste and a bit of crunch from cornflakes.

1/4	cup butter, softened
1/4	cup canola oil
1/2	cup packed brown sugar
1/4	cup sugar
1	egg
3	egg whites
3	teaspoons vanilla extract
2	teaspoons coconut extract
1-3/4	cups all-purpose flour
3	teaspoons baking powder
1/2	teaspoon salt
4	cups cornflakes

1) In a large mixing bowl, combine the butter, oil and sugars. Beat in egg, egg whites and extracts. Combine the flour, baking powder and salt; gradually add to egg mixture. Stir in cornflakes.

2) Drop by tablespoonfuls 2 in. apart onto baking sheets coated with nonstick cooking spray. Bake at 375° for 10-12 minutes or until lightly browned. Remove to wire racks.

Yield: 3-1/2 dozen.

NUTRITION FACTS: 1 cookie equals 69 calories, 3 g fat (1 g saturated fat), 8 mg cholesterol, 94 mg sodium, 10 g carbohydrate, trace fiber, 1 g protein.

Blondies with Chips

Kai Skupinski, Canton, Michigan

My friends and family love this pared-down version of the classic blond brownie and never suspect that I use whole wheat flour.

1/3	cup all-purpose flour
1/3	cup whole wheat flour
1/4	cup packed brown sugar
1/2	teaspoon baking powder
1/4	teaspoon salt
1	egg
1/4	cup canola oil
2	tablespoons honey
1	teaspoon vanilla extract
1/2	cup semisweet chocolate chips

1) In a small bowl, combine the first five ingredients. In another bowl, whisk the egg, oil, honey and vanilla; stir into dry ingredients until blended. Stir in chocolate chips (batter will be thick).

2) Spread into an 8-in. square baking dish coated with nonstick cooking spray. Bake at 350° for 20-22 minutes or until a toothpick inserted near the center comes out clean. Cool on a wire rack. Cut into bars.

Yield: 1 dozen.

NUTRITION FACTS: 1 bar equals 133 calories, 7 g fat (2 g saturated fat), 18 mg cholesterol, 67 mg sodium, 17 g carbohydrate, 1 g fiber, 2 g protein.

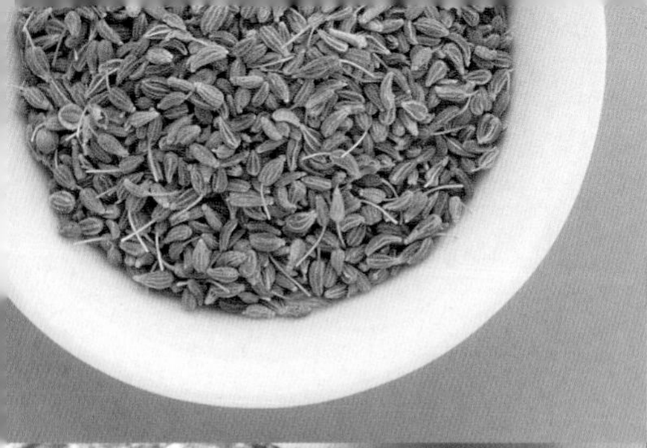

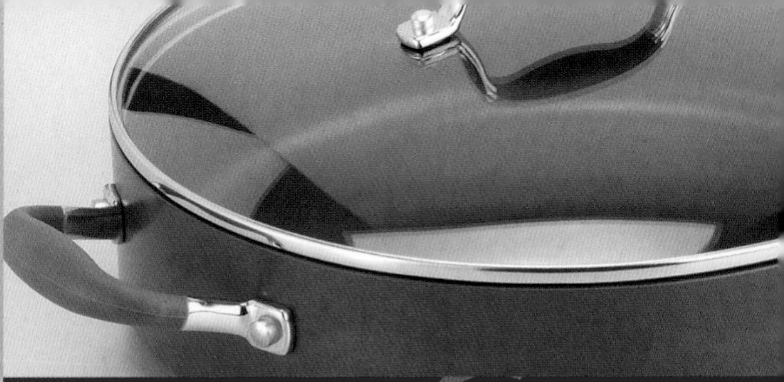

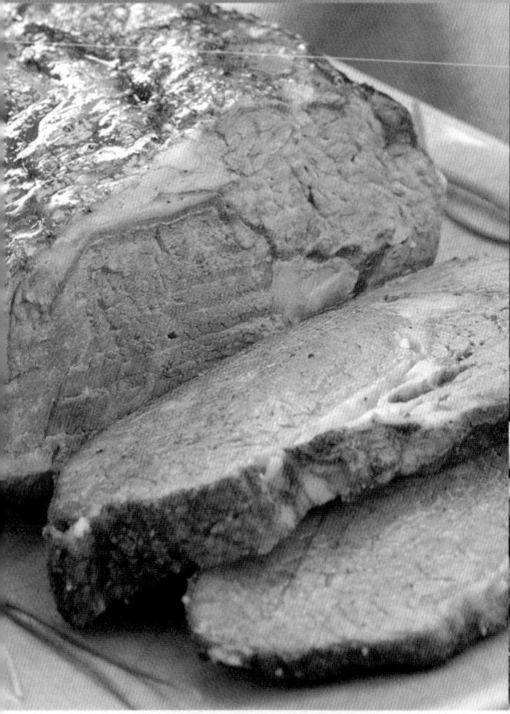

CHAPTER 25

REFERENCES & INDEXES

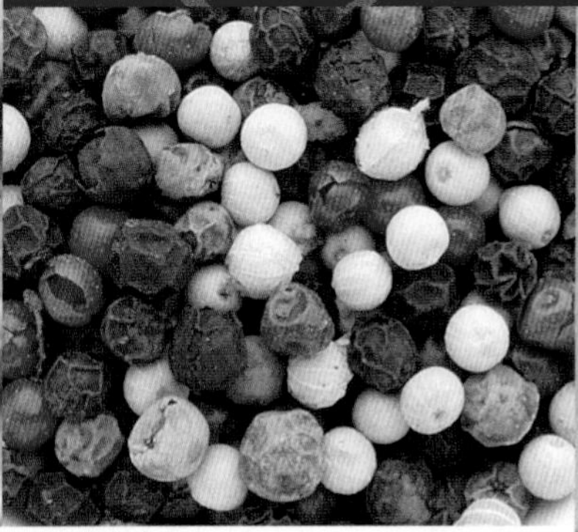

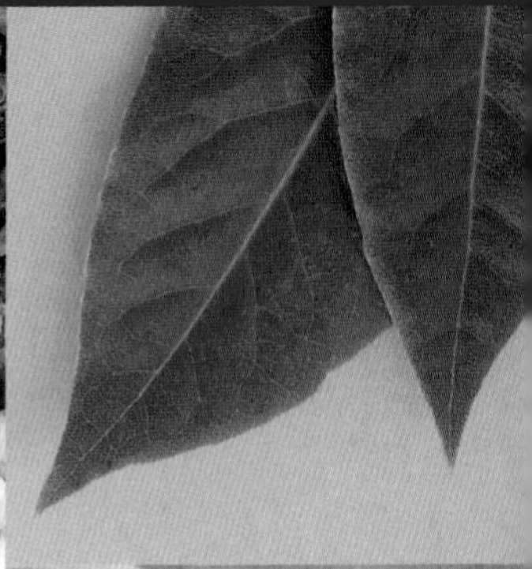

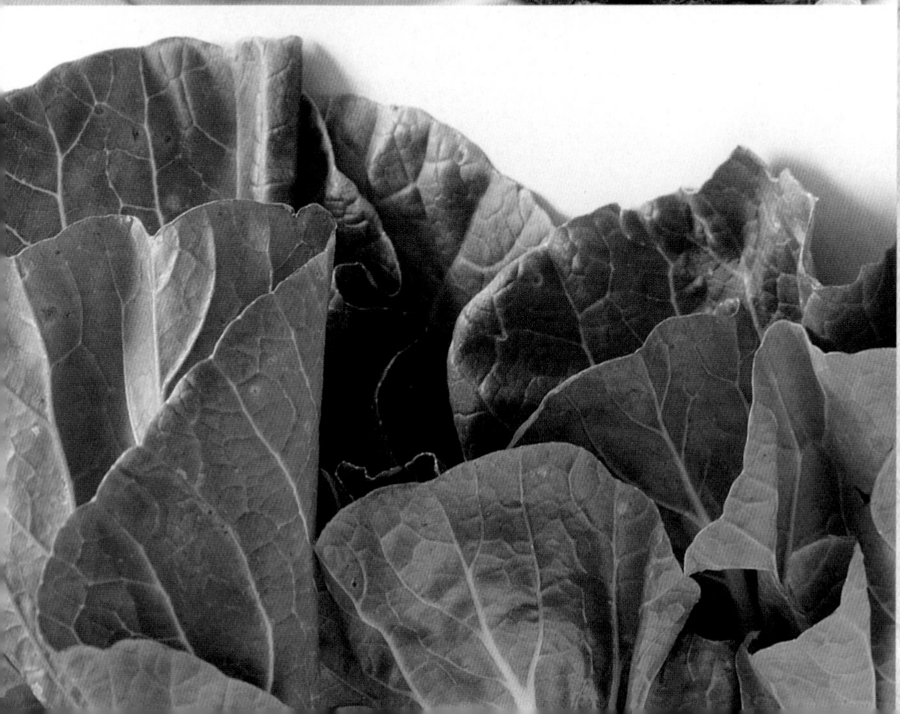

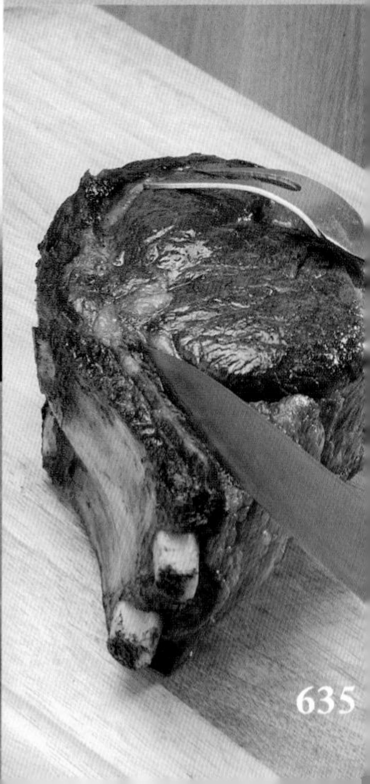

REFERENCES & INDEXES

Selecting the perfect recipe to prepare is just the beginning. This chapter gathers all the extras you'll need for success in the kitchen, including tips on storing food, using herbs and spices, reading a food label as well as identifying cuts of meat. You'll also find four indexes organized by Major Ingredient, Food Category, Preparation Method and References & Tips.

Food Storage Guidelines

Pantry Storage

Check the sell-by or use-by dates on pantry items. Discard items that are past those dates. In the pantry, store opened items tightly closed and place in a cool, dry place. Times given in the charts on pages 638-639 are for pantry storage of opened items.

Refrigerated Foods

The use-by date on refrigerated items is only for the unopened item. Use the times given in the chart for opened foods. Keep the refrigerator temperature between 34°-40°. In the refrigerator, store leftovers in covered refrigerator containers or wrap them in plastic wrap or foil. Resealable plastic bags also are great for storage.

Frozen Foods

For the best quality, foods should be frozen in a freezer that maintains 0° and is at least two-thirds full. Cool cooked food quickly before freezing. Store food in containers that are moisture-proof and vapor-proof, such as foil, freezer bags, freezer wrap and plastic freezer containers. Remove as much air as possible when packaging the food. Label and date packages before freezing. Spread out the packages for quicker freezing, and then stack them after they are solidly frozen.

Defrost foods in the refrigerator, microwave oven or cold water. Generally, small items will defrost overnight in the refrigerator. Most items take 1 or 2 days. Bulky, large items will take even longer to thaw. To defrost in a microwave oven, follow the manufacturer's directions. To defrost in cold water, place food in a watertight plastic storage bag. Place the bag in cold water. Change the water every 30 minutes until the food is thawed.

OPENED FOOD ITEM	REFRIGERATOR TEMP. 34° TO 40°	FREEZER TEMP. 0°
DAIRY		
BUTTER	1 to 3 months	6 to 9 months
CHEESE		
Brie	1 week	6 months
Cottage/Ricotta	1 week	not suitable
Cream Cheese	2 weeks	not suitable
Cheddar, Brick, Swiss, Monterey Jack	3 to 4 weeks	6 months
Mozzarella	1 week	6 months
Parmesan/Romano, Grated	2 months	6 months
CREAM		
Ultrapasteurized	1 month	not suitable
Heavy Whipping or Half-and-Half	3 days	2 to 4 months
EGGS		
Whole, In the shell	4 to 5 weeks	not suitable
Whites or Yolks, Uncooked	2 to 4 days	12 months
MILK		
Milk	7 days	3 months
Buttermilk	7 to 14 days	3 months
Evaporated or Sweetened Condensed	4 to 5 days	
MARGARINE	4 to 5 months	12 months
SOUR CREAM	7 to 21 days	not suitable
YOGURT	7 to 14 days	1 to 2 months
MEATS—BEEF, PORK, LAMB		
FRESH		
Chops	3 to 5 days	4 to 6 months
Ground or Stew Meat	1 to 2 days	3 to 4 months
Roasts	3 to 5 days	4 to 12 months
Sausage, Fresh	1 to 2 days	1 to 2 months
Steaks	3 to 5 days	6 to 12 months
Leftover Cooked Meats/Casseroles	1 to 4 days	2 to 3 months
PROCESS MEATS		
Bacon	7 days	1 month
Ham	3 to 5 days	1 to 2 months
Luncheon Meats	3 to 5 days	1 to 2 months
POULTRY		
CHICKEN/TURKEY		
Whole	1 to 2 days	1 year
Parts	1 to 2 days	9 months
Leftover, Cooked	1 to 4 days	1 to 4 months
FISH AND SEAFOOD		
LEAN FISH (Fillets/Steaks)		
Cod, Sole, Halibut, Orange Roughy, Flounder	1 to 2 days	6 months
FATTY FISH (Fillets/Steaks)		
Catfish, Perch, Salmon, Whitefish	1 to 2 days	2 to 3 months
CRAB, COOKED	1 to 2 days	3 months
SCALLOPS/SHRIMP		
Uncooked	1 to 2 days	3 to 6 months
Cooked	3 to 4 days	3 months
LEFTOVER, COOKED SEAFOOD	3 to 4 days	3 to 6 months

OPENED FOOD ITEM	PANTRY STORAGE TEMP. 70°	REFRIGERATOR TEMP. 34° TO 40°	FREEZER TEMP. 0°
STAPLES			
BAKING POWDER	18 months		
BAKING SODA	18 months		
BOUILLON CUBES	1 year		
BREAD	2 to 7 days	4 to 7 days	3 months
CANNED GOODS			
Fish and Seafood		2 days	
Fruit		1 week	
Pasta Sauces		5 days	
Vegetables		2 to 3 days	
CEREAL			
Cook before eating	6 months		
Ready to eat	2 to 3 months		
CORNMEAL	12 months		
CORNSTARCH	18 months		
FLOUR			
All-Purpose	15 months		
Whole Wheat	6 months		
FRUIT, DRIED	6 months		
HONEY	12 months		
JAM AND JELLY		12 months	
KETCHUP OR CHILI SAUCE		4 to 6 months	
MAYONNAISE		2 months	
MUSTARD		6 to 12 months	
NUTS	3 to 6 months	3 to 6 months	6 to 12 months
OILS			
Canola or Corn Oil	6 months		
Olive Oil	4 months		
PEANUT BUTTER	2 to 3 months		
PICKLES		1 to 2 months	
PIES			
Custard		2 to 3 days	not suitable
Fruit, Unbaked			8 months
Fruit, Baked		4 to 5 days	1 to 2 months
Pumpkin		4 to 5 days	2 months
RICE			
Brown	1 month	6 months	
White	2 years		
SALAD DRESSINGS		3 months	
SALSA		1 month	
SHORTENING	8 months		
SOY SAUCE		12 months	
SUGAR			
Brown	4 months		
Granulated	2 years		
WORCESTERSHIRE SAUCE	12 months		

Herbs and Spices

Store dried herbs and spices in tightly closed glass or heavy-duty plastic containers. It's best to keep them in a cool, dry place; avoid storing them in direct sunlight, over the stove or near other heat sources.

For best flavor, keep dried herbs and ground spices for up to 6 months. They can be used if they are older, but the flavors might not be as intense. Whole spices can be stored for 1 to 2 years.

Select fresh herbs that are fragrant with bright, fresh-looking leaves. Avoid those with wilted or yellowing or browning leaves. Wrap fresh herbs in a slightly damp paper towel and place in a resealable plastic bag. Press as much air as possible out of the bag and seal. Store in the refrigerator for 5 to 7 days.

To substitute dried herbs for fresh, use one-third less. For example if a recipe calls for 1 tablespoon fresh, use 1 teaspoon dried.

ALLSPICE
Available as whole, dried berries or ground. Blend of cinnamon, clove and nutmeg. Use for baked goods, jerked meats, sauces, sausage, preserves, roasts, root vegetables.

ANISEED
Available as oval, greenish-brown seeds. Licorice-like flavor similar to fennel. Use for cookies, cakes, breads, pickles, stews, seafood, beets, cauliflower, pasta sauces.

BASIL
Available as fresh green or purple leaves or dried and crushed. Sweet flavor with hints of mint, pepper and cloves. Use for tomato sauce, pestos, chicken, meat, zucchini, summer squashes.

BAY LEAF
Available as whole, fresh or dried, dull green leaves. Savory, spicy and aromatic. Use for soups, stews, casseroles, pickles, meat.

BLACK/WHITE PEPPER
Available whole, cracked, coarse or ground (black); whole or ground (white). Black has a sharp, hot piney flavor; white is milder. Use for all types of cooking; white adds pepper flavor without flecks.

CARAWAY SEEDS
Available as light to dark brown seeds. Sweet blend of dill and anise flavors. Use for breads, cakes, biscuits, pork, cheese, potatoes, sauerkraut.

CARDAMOM
Available as green pods, brownish-black seeds or ground. Sweet, spicy flavor and slightly pungent. Use for baked goods, chicken, curries, meat.

CAYENNE PEPPER
Available ground, also known as ground red pepper. Pungent, hot flavor. Use for chili, soups, sauces, beans, poultry, meat, seafood.

CELERY SEED
Available as light-brown or tan seeds. Strong and bitter flavor. Use for fish, eggs, cheese, salad dressings.

CUMIN
Available as seeds and ground. Pungent, earthy, slightly bitter flavor. Use for beans, chili, pork, chicken, stews.

CHERVIL
Available as fresh leaves or dried and crushed. Fresh has a hint of anise and dry has a hint of parsley flavor. Use for fish, eggs, poultry, salads.

DILL
Available as fresh leaves, dried and crushed or seeds. Fresh, sweet, grassy flavor. Use for pickles, fish, cucumbers, breads, tomatoes.

CHIVES
Available as fresh or freeze-dried hollow stems. Delicate and peppery, mild onion flavor. Use for potatoes, eggs, sauces, seafood, salads.

FENNEL
Available as seeds. Sweet and mildly licorice-like flavor. Use for baked goods, seafood, sausage, pork.

CILANTRO
Available as fresh leaves. When dried, it's known as coriander. Pungent, strong flavor. Use for ethnic dishes (such as Mexican or Asian), salsa, tomatoes, chicken, pork, seafood.

GINGER
Available as fresh root, crystallized or ground. Pungent, sweet, spicy, hot flavor. Use for baked goods, pumpkin, pork, chicken.

CINNAMON
Available as sticks or ground. Sweet and pungent flavor. Use for baked goods, fruit desserts, warm beverages.

MACE
Available ground. Nutmeg-like flavor. Use for baked goods, poultry, fish.

CLOVES
Available whole or ground. Pungent, medicinal, sweet flavor. Use for baked goods, fruit desserts, ham, lamb, warm beverages.

MARJORAM
Available as fresh leaves, dried and crushed. Oregano-like flavor. Use for tomato dishes, meat, poultry, seafood, vegetables.

CORIANDER
Available as dried and crushed leaves, seeds or ground seeds. Mildly sweet, spicy flavor. Use for ethnic dishes (North African, Mediterranean, Asian), stews, curries, pork, lentils.

MINT
Available as fresh leaves or dried and crushed. Fresh, strong, cool flavor. Use for lamb, salsas, vegetables, meats.

MUSTARD
Available ground or as seeds. Pungent, sharp, hot flavor. Use for meats, vinaigrettes, seafood, sauces.

NUTMEG
Available whole or ground. Sweet, spicy flavor. Use for baked goods, custards, vegetables, poultry, meat.

OREGANO
Available as fresh leaves, dried and crushed or ground. Pungent, slightly bitter flavor. Use for tomato dishes, chicken, pork, lamb, vegetables.

PAPRIKA
Available ground. Mild to hot, sweet flavor. Use for poultry, shellfish, meat, vegetables.

PARSLEY
Available as fresh leaves, curly or Italian (flat-leaf), or dried and flaked. Fresh, slightly peppery flavor. Use for poultry, seafood, tomatoes, pasta, vegetables.

POPPY SEEDS
Available as seeds. Nut-like flavor. Use for baked goods, fruits, pasta.

ROSEMARY
Available as fresh leaves on stems or dried. Pungent flavor with a hint of pine. Use for lamb, poultry, pork, vegetables.

SAFFRON
Available as threads (whole stigmas) or powder. Pungent, bitter flavor. Use for bouillabaisse, curries, fish, poultry, rice.

SAGE
Available as fresh leaves, dried and crushed or rubbed. Pungent, slightly bitter, musty mint flavor. Use for pork, poultry, stuffing.

SAVORY
Available as fresh leaves, dried and crushed or ground. Piquant blend of mint and thyme. Use for beans, lentils, lamb, poultry.

SESAME SEEDS
Available as seeds. Nut-like flavor. Use for breads, chicken, seafood, noodles, chickpeas.

TARRAGON
Available as fresh leaves or dried and crushed. Strong, spicy, anise-like flavors. Use for poultry, seafood, meats, vegetables.

THYME
Available as fresh leaves or dried and crushed. Pungent, earthy, spicy flavor. Use for meat, poultry, lentils, soups, stews.

TURMERIC
Available ground. Pungent, bitter, earthy flavor. Use for curries, lamb, chicken, meat, beans, lentils.

Understanding the Food Label

As of Jan. 1, 2006, the Food and Drug Administration (FDA) requires food manufacturers to list trans fat (trans fatty acids) on Nutrition Facts panels for the foods you purchase at the supermarket. Trans fats are found in vegetable shortenings, some margarines, crackers, cookies, snack foods and other foods made with or fried in partially hydrogenated oils.

You should be able to find trans fat listed on the Nutrition Facts panel directly under the line for saturated fat. If the information is missing, it may be because some manufacturers are still transitioning to the new label or the label value for trans fat is 0.5 g or less per serving.

Below is a sample label showing the new listing for trans fat.

Nutrition Facts

1 .... **Nutrition Facts**

2 .... Serving Size 1 cup (288g)
Servings Per Container 2

Amount Per Serving

3 .... Calories 250   Calories from Fat 110

4 .... % Daily Value*

Total Fat 12g	18%
Saturated Fat 3g	15%
Trans Fat 1.5g	
Cholesterol 30mg	10%
5 ..... **Sodium 470mg**	20%
6 ..... **Total Carbohydrate 31g**	10%
Dietary Fiber 0g	0%
7 ..... **Sugars 5g**	
Protein 5g	

Vitamin A	4%
Vitamin C	2%
Calcium	20%
Iron	4%

8 .....

* Percent Daily Values are based on a 2,000 calorie diet. Your Daily Values may be higher or lower depending on your calorie needs:

	Calories	2,000	2,500
Total Fat	Less than	65g	80g
Sat Fat	Less than	20g	25g
Cholesterol	Less than	300mg	300mg
Sodium	Less than	2,400mg	2,400mg
Total Carbohydrate		300g	375g
Dietary Fiber		25g	30g

9 .....

1) **NUTRITION FACTS:** The header that manufacturers are required to use.

2) **SERVING SIZE:** The information is based on the amount of food in one serving shown in both common household (1 cup) and metric (288 g) measures.

3) **CALORIES FROM FAT, TOTAL FAT, SATURATED FAT, CHOLESTEROL:** Limit saturated fat to less than 10% of your total calories and consume no more than 300 mg cholesterol daily.

   TRANS FAT: Trans fat, like saturated fat and dietary cholesterol, raises the LDL (or "bad") cholesterol that increases your risk for coronary heart disease.

4) **% DAILY VALUES:** This is the percent of each nutrient provided in one serving of the product, based on the daily values for 2,000 calories per day (an average caloric intake for adults per day).

5) **SODIUM:** Most healthy adults and people with mild to moderate hypertension (high blood pressure) should consume less than 1,500 mg sodium daily.

6) **TOTAL CARBOHYDRATE:** Look at the total carbohydrate, which is the amount in one serving of the food. If you are counting carbohydrate choices or exchanges, you need to know that 1 choice or exchange contains 15 grams of carbohydrate. It's equal to 1 starch, fruit, or milk serving or exchange.

7) **SUGARS:** Listed on as a subcategory of Total Carbohydrate; look at the total amount of carbohydrate.

8) **VITAMINS AND MINERALS:** The percent of the Reference Daily Intake (RDI) for vitamin A, vitamin C, calcium and iron provided in a serving of the food.

9) **DAILY VALUES:** Two calorie levels are used because an "average" woman needs around 2,000 calories per day and an "average" man needs 2,500. This is mandatory, unless the label is too small.

Other required items on labels:

- Name of food.
- Manufacturer's name and address.
- Net weight of contents in package.
- Ingredient list in descending order of quantity by weight.

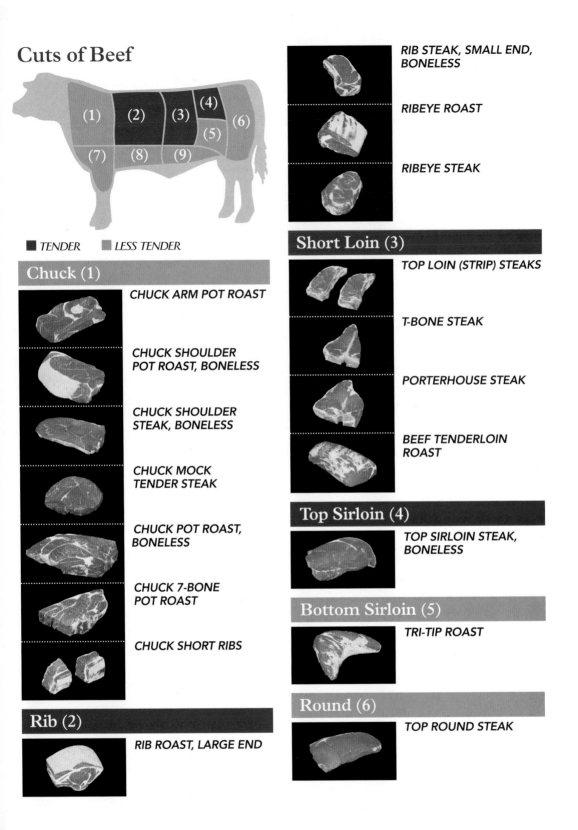

Cuts of Beef

(1) (2) (3) (4) (5) (6) (7) (8) (9)

■ *TENDER* ■ *LESS TENDER*

Chuck (1)

CHUCK ARM POT ROAST

CHUCK SHOULDER POT ROAST, BONELESS

CHUCK SHOULDER STEAK, BONELESS

CHUCK MOCK TENDER STEAK

CHUCK POT ROAST, BONELESS

CHUCK 7-BONE POT ROAST

CHUCK SHORT RIBS

Rib (2)

RIB ROAST, LARGE END

RIB STEAK, SMALL END, BONELESS

RIBEYE ROAST

RIBEYE STEAK

Short Loin (3)

TOP LOIN (STRIP) STEAKS

T-BONE STEAK

PORTERHOUSE STEAK

BEEF TENDERLOIN ROAST

Top Sirloin (4)

TOP SIRLOIN STEAK, BONELESS

Bottom Sirloin (5)

TRI-TIP ROAST

Round (6)

TOP ROUND STEAK

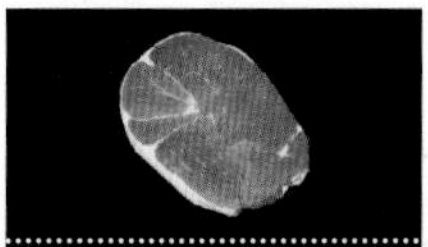

ROUND STEAK,
BONELESS

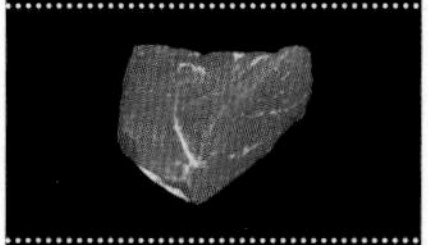

BOTTOM ROUND
RUMP ROAST

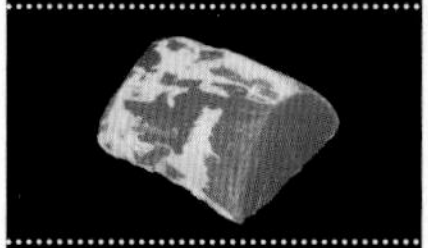

EYE ROUND ROAST

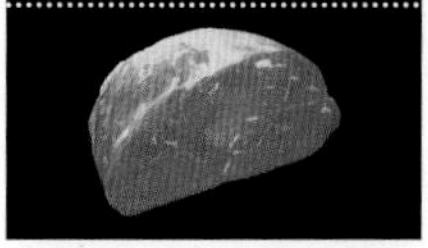

ROUND TIP ROAST,
CAP OFF

Shank & Brisket (7)

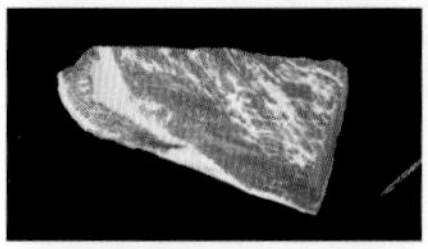

BRISKET, WHOLE,
BONELESS

Plate & Flank (8 & 9)

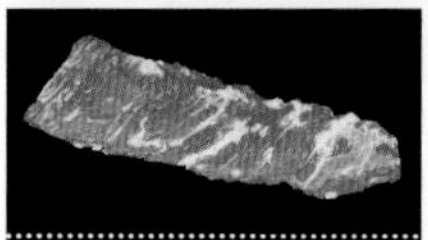

SKIRT STEAK, BONELESS

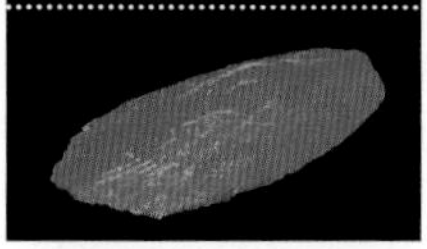

FLANK STEAK

Other Cuts

GROUND BEEF

CUBED STEAK

BEEF FOR STEW

Photos Courtesy of The Beef Checkoff.

Veal

Leg

LEG RUMP ROAST,
BONELESS

Loin

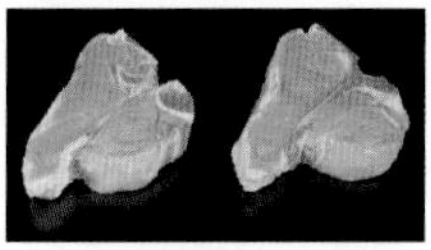

LOIN CHOPS

Rib

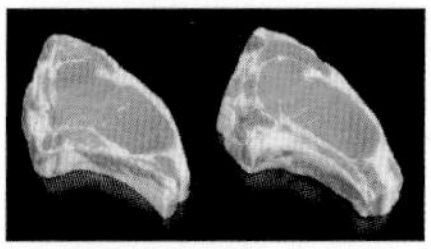

RIB CHOPS

Shoulder

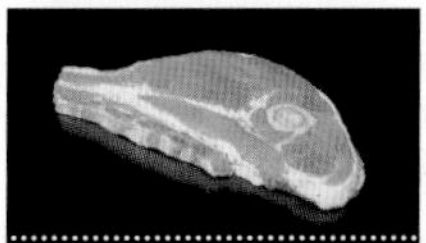

SHOULDER ARM STEAK

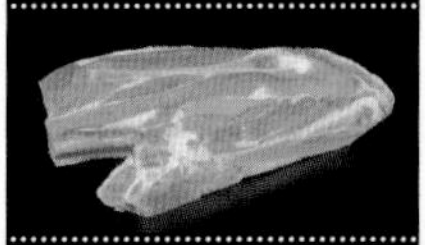

SHOULDER BLADE STEAK

SHOULDER ARM ROAST,
BONELESS

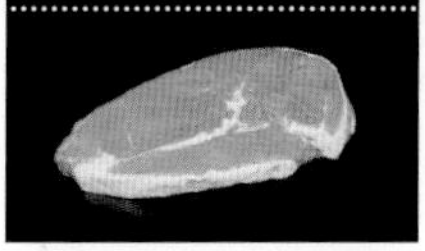

SHOULDER ARM STEAK,
BONELESS

Breast

BREAST, BONELESS

Cuts of Pork

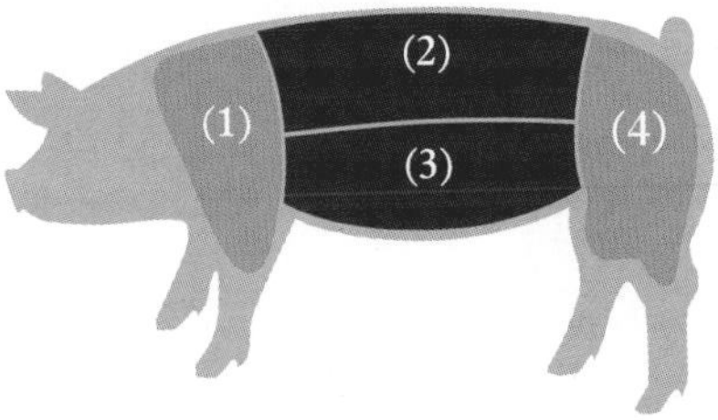

■ *TENDER* ■ *LESS TENDER*

Shoulder (1)

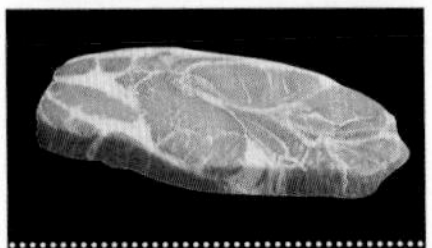

BLADE STEAK

PICNIC SHOULDER

SHOULDER CUT
BONELESS PORK BUTT

SIRLOIN CUTS
GROUND PORK,
EXTRA LEAN

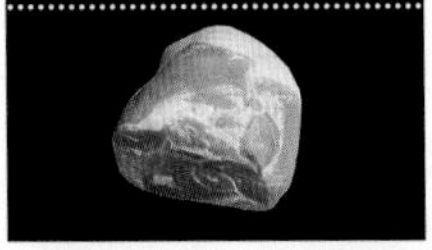

ARM PICNIC ROAST

Loin (2)

BONELESS LOIN ROAST

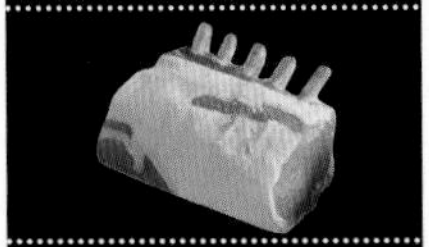

CENTER RIB ROAST

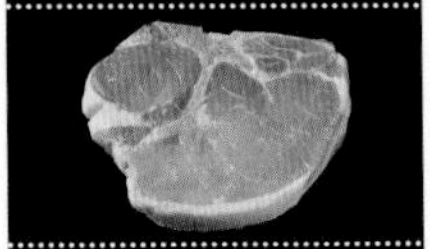

LOIN CHOP

CENTER CUT ROAST

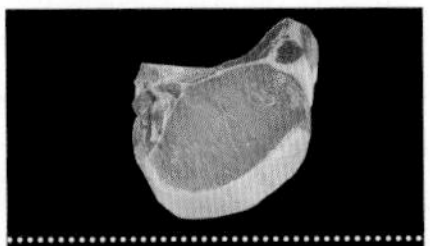

PORK RIB CHOP

PORK TENDERLOIN

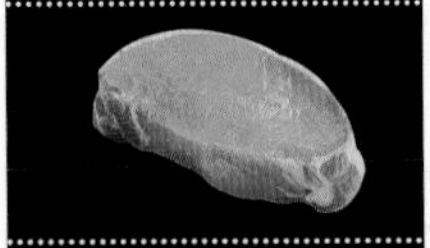

PORK TOP LOIN CHOP

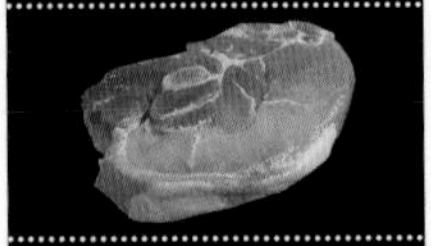

SIRLOIN CHOP

BACK RIBS

SIRLOIN STEAKS

Side (3)

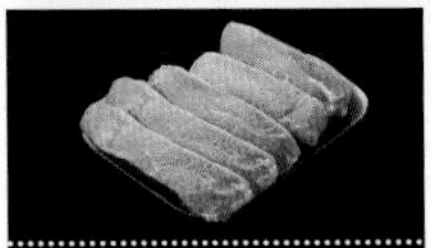

COUNTRY-STYLE
SPARE RIBS

SPARE RIBS

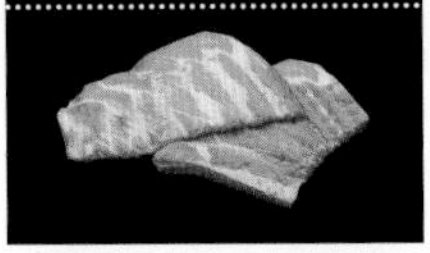

ST. LOUIS-STYLE RIBS

Leg (4)

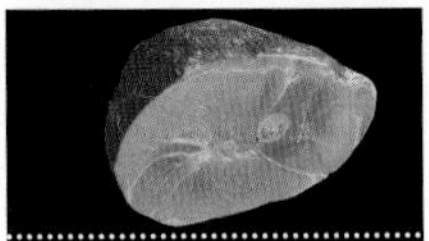

SMOKED HAM

SANDWICH STEAKS

Photos Courtesy of the National Pork Board.

C

T

Major Ingredient Index

Food Category Index

Preparation Method Index

References & Tips Index (by chapter)